Elements of Ecological Economics

Elements of Ecological Economics provides a comprehensive introduction to the field of ecological economics, an interdisciplinary project trying to give answers to the problems related to the overexploitation of the earth's resources today. These include the problems of global warming (the greenhouse effect) and the overuse of the seas (e.g. overfishing). The book also gives an exposition of the closely related problems of global welfare and justice.

The book covers topics including:

* The general policy perspective required by sustainability
* Economic growth in a historical perspective
* Sustainability conceptions and measurement within ecological economics
* Economics and ethics of climate change
* Global food security
* The state of the seas on earth and locally (the Baltic Sea).

As an introductory-level text the book will be useful to undergraduate students taking basic courses in economics and related fields, and be comprehensible to anyone interested in environmental problems. Through the separate chapters on the problems of climate change, sustainable food production, and the overuse of the seas, the reader will easily see the practical relevance to the theoretical concepts presented and used in the book.

Ralf Eriksson is a lecturer in economics at Åbo Akademi University of Turku, Finland.

Jan Otto Andersson is also currently a lecturer in economics at Åbo Akademi University of Turku, Finland. He is also a founding member of Basic Income European Network (BIEN) and the European Association for Evolutionary Political Economy (EAEPE).

Elements of Ecological Economics

Ralf Eriksson and Jan Otto Andersson

Routledge
Taylor & Francis Group

LONDON AND NEW YORK

First published 2010
by Routledge
2 Park Square, Milton Park, Abingdon, Oxon OX14 4RN

Simultaneously published in the USA and Canada
by Routledge
270 Madison Avenue, New York, NY 10016

Routledge is an imprint of the Taylor & Francis Group, an informa
business

© 2010 Ralf Eriksson and Jan Otto Andersson
Typeset in Times New Roman by Saxon Graphics Ltd, Derby
Printed and bound in Great Britain by TJ International Ltd, Padstow,
Cornwall

British Library Cataloguing in Publication Data
A catalogue record for this book is available from the British Library

Library of Congress Cataloging in Publication Data
Eriksson, Ralf
  Elements of ecological economics / Ralf Eriksson and Jan Otto
  Andersson.
    p. cm.
  Includes bibliographical references and index.
  1. Environmental economics. 2. Sustainable development. 3. Climate
  change. 4.Food supply. I. Andersson, Jan Otto. II. Title.
  HC79.E5E7474 2010
  333.7--dc22
  2009034681

ISBN10: 0-415-47380-2 (hbk)
ISBN10: 0-415-47381-0 (pbk)
ISBN10: 0-203-85704-6 (ebk)

ISBN13: 978-0-415-47380-4 (hbk)
ISBN13: 978-0-415-47381-1 (pbk)
ISBN13: 978-0-203-85704-5 (ebk)

Contents

Figures

Tables

Preface

In the emerging field of ecological economics there by now exists a body of text-books, and luckily their number seems to be growing rapidly. However, as Robert Langham kindly pointed out to us, the same cannot be said about books on elementary ecological economics. This is where we hope that our book fits in. It strives to be a comprehensive introduction to the field, without making it too vast in scope.

The book is intended for introductory courses in ecological economics in various disciplines, emphasizing the necessary elementary understanding. We also believe that the book will be self-contained in the sense that it will be readable on its own by everyone who is interested in the relation between the economy and ecology; how we perceive it and problems related to sustainable development. The book emphasizes that the environmental problems of today are not just about what you are spilling in the backyard, but truly global. The activities of humankind have reached the level where we all, individually as well as collectively, are forced to think about our share of the load on the Earth. We live in a world that is not only "full" from an ecological point of view. It is also very unequal. Some people's footstep is far heavier than others', and therefore ecological economics has to include questions not only related to sustainability and prosperity, but also to global justice.

The first chapter presents a description of the global trilemma confronting us today, which gives ecological economics its field of study. The following chapters deal with the edges of this trilemma: growth and prosperity (Chapter 2), global distributive justice (Chapter 3), and ecological sustainability (Chapter 5). Chapters 4 and 5 introduce the reader to the central concepts in environmental and ecological economics respectively. In the next three chapters we present three global problems and how they can be discussed from the point of view of ecological economics. They are: global warming (Chapter 6), world food security (Chapter 7), and the threats to our seas (Chapter 8). The final chapter links back to the global ethical trilemma: Is "degrowth" a necessary answer?

We want to dedicate this book to our grandchildren: Alec, Aron, Eemil, Ella, Ethan, Amilia and Aleena.

Ralf Eriksson, Jan Otto Andersson, Turku/Åbo, Finland, August 2009

Chapter 1

The global ethical trilemma

Ecological economics arose from the need to confront a challenge that humankind had not experienced before. We are now living in a world economy the destiny of which we all share. While producing prosperity on a scale never conceived of in earlier generations, we have been forced to admit that threats to the life-supporting ecological systems are accumulating at an unprecedented speed. The clash between the economic and the ecological systems has become an elementary fact, not only locally but globally. The need for an approach that can tackle this dilemma in a straightforward way is obvious.

Looking at the ecological problems from a global perspective we cannot abstract from the glaring inequalities between peoples. Some earn and consume much more than others; the question of how to tackle the ecological challenges therefore has to be linked to the question of how to achieve a more just distribution of the economic opportunities. Ecological economics has to place global equity on its agenda – a task that makes it even more demanding, scientifically as well as politically.

The need for integrating justice into the analysis of the interaction between economy and ecology was obvious soon after the publication of the path-breaking report *Limits to Growth* (Meadows *et al.* 1972). The message of this Club of Rome publication was that if humankind continued to expand its population and consumption as it had until then it was heading for grave ecological catastrophes in the twenty-first century. There were physical limits to growth and the only way to avoid a catastrophic future was through the reduction of population growth and the stabilization of industrial production. For many this implied not only a stop to population growth in the poor South, but also reducing industrial growth everywhere.

A group of Latin American researchers wrote a counter-report, *Catastrophe or New Society? A Latin American World Model* (Herrera *et al.* 1976), arguing that the majority of humankind already was living in a state of misery, and that for them the crisis was already here. Therefore, economic growth had to be speeded up in the South. The inequities of the world could not be maintained while trying to avoid a future catastrophe that would bring the crisis also to the North.

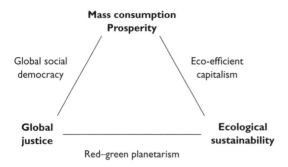

Figure 1.1 The global ethical trilemma: pick two – ignore the third

The Latin American world model – also called the Bariloche model – pointed to a global ethical trilemma. There are three goals that most of humankind subscribes to – prosperity, justice and sustainability – but to combine the three goals on the global level is a challenge that is hard to confront. Let us discuss this global ethical trilemma with the help of Figure 1.1.

The corners of the triangle correspond to the three components often included in the definitions of sustainable development: the ecological (sustainability), the economic (prosperity) and the social (justice) dimensions. The difficulty to achieve all three on a global level is an enormous challenge for all who see sustainable development as the central political goal of our age. It is this challenge that makes ecological economics so fascinating.

Let us start by looking at each corner separately. We shall then go into the three sides, each representing an important ideological stance in the world of today.

Prosperity

Let us take a step back to the "Golden Age" of the 1950s and 1960s. The mood of that time was characterized by the belief in economic growth and mass consumption. A most influential book was written by the American economist and political theorist Walt Whitman Rostow. *The Stages of Economic Growth: A Non-Communist Manifesto* (1960) became a classic text in several fields of social sciences.

According to Rostow's stage theory the mass consumption society constitutes the end goal of humanity. Through a *take off into self-sustained growth* each country can start a process of economic growth that will bring it to the final stage – that of a mature mass consumption society. They can become as prosperous, democratic and bored as the United States already had become. When Rostow wrote his book only the USA had achieved this fifth stage – "the age of high mass-consumption." Western Europe and Japan were on the verge of achieving it, and the Soviet Union was, according to Rostow, engaged in an unhappy love affair with it. This is how he described the mature mass consumption society:

The emergence of the welfare state is one manifestation of a society's moving beyond technical maturity; but it is also at this stage that resources tend increasingly to be directed to the production of consumer's durables and to the diffusion of services on a mass basis...Historically...the decisive element has been the cheap mass automobile with its revolutionary effects – social as well as economic – on the life and expectations of society.

(Rostow 1960, s.11)

According to the Rostowian worldview it is possible for all nations to achieve the stage of mature mass consumption. Like airplanes one after the other they could take off into self-sustained growth. This they could do through imports of ideas and capital and by taking part in the international division of labor. The rich countries were the natural allies – not obstacles – for the poor in their efforts to develop.

However, in line with the mood of his time, Rostow did not treat problems related to the environment or the limits to growth. For him exports of raw materials were the natural starting point for acquiring the means to develop.

The spirit of that age, which later was called "the Golden Age," "fordism," and "the age of oil, cars and mass consumption," was severely damaged during the 1970s, but still "the American way of life" is a much desired goal all over the world. By means of globalization and new technological advances all nations are striving to enhance their prosperity. Economic growth is still the standard for success globally.

Justice

The quest for justice is shared by all ethical doctrines. However, some doctrines are less inclusive than others. Today, probably for the first time in history, the concern for justice has, however, been extended to all of humankind, not only to those of the same nationality or religion. The human rights declaration adopted by the United Nations in 1948 marks the breakthrough of the quest for global justice, although it still was seen as the duty of every member state to secure these rights to all its citizens. The international community, through a myriad of international organizations, has gradually accepted the role as the defender of universal human rights and justice on a global level.

One way of trying to formulate what justice means is to use the concept of capability – to be or to do what you value – and to link it to sufficiency, universality and sustainability.

A regime will be deemed just if and to the degree that it promotes harmonization of capabilities to achieve functionings at a level that is sufficient, universally attainable and sustainable.

(DeMartino 2000, s.144)

Global justice means that the desired level can be achieved everywhere, and that it can be maintained. It therefore has both an international and an intergenerational aspect.

People's capabilities to live a worthy life depend on society as a whole – institutions, culture, and respect for others. We can even say that today our individual capabilities are formed by a global system – economically, culturally, and ecologically. There may be just societies in a world that is deeply unjust.

Since we live in a world where money can buy almost anything anywhere, the distribution of incomes is one central indicator of how just or unjust the world has become. In the last 200 years the income differences between the continents has grown outrageously. At the beginning of the nineteenth century incomes per capita were three times higher in Western Europe than in Africa. Today the gap between North America and Africa is greater than 20 to 1.

Everyone agrees that we do live in an unequal world. If we take that quintile of the world population that live in the richest countries, and compare their situation to that of the quintile living in the poorest countries, we find the following ratios (Hedenus and Azar 2005):

- Income (compared in terms of market exchange rates – MERs – among the respective currencies) is more than 70 times higher
- Income (compared in terms of purchasing power parity exchange rates) is reckoned as more than 10 times higher
- Consumption of animal food is 7 times higher
- Release of carbon dioxide is 22 times higher
- Consumption of electricity is 35 times higher
- Consumption of paper is 89 times higher.

Since the 1960s the income disparity reckoned in terms of MERs has grown like wildfire; the ratio used to be around 25:1, but is now around 75:1. The corresponding ratio in terms of estimated purchasing power – PPP – has remained more or less constant (around 15:1), but in absolute terms the PPP-gap has increased from $9,200 per capita in 1960 to $23,000 in 2000. Since MERs, rather than purchasing power parities, determine the price competitiveness of nations, they influence the international division of labor. A lot of clothing purchased in the USA is made in Bangladesh and wages in Bangladesh vary between 6 and 18 cents/h; that is you can buy the work of more than 100 Bangladeshis for the cost of one worker in a rich country (Schor 2005b).

The ratios of various kinds of resource–consumption inequalities have tended to diminish, but the absolute differences have been and still are growing. An exception to this general trend is that per capita consumption of animal food has started to decline in the richest countries, while increasing slightly in the poorest ones.

However, we should note that in today's world, it may well be misleading to reckon merely in the statistically convenient terms of rich and poor nations. Income distribution *within* many rich countries is becoming more unequal, and the number of rich people in the poorest countries has been growing slightly. The inequality among the world's individuals is staggering. At the turn of the twenty-first century, the richest 5 percent of people receive one-third of total global income, as much as the poorest 80 percent. While a few poor countries are catching up with the rich world, the differences between the richest and poorest individuals around the globe are huge and growing (Milanovic 2005).

We live in an *unequal world*.

Ecological sustainability

The term sustainability has its roots in ecology as the ability of an ecosystem to maintain ecological processes, functions, biodiversity, and productivity in the future. To be sustainable, nature's resources must only be used at a rate at which they can be replenished naturally. There is now clear evidence that humanity is living unsustainably by consuming the Earth's limited natural resources more rapidly than they are being replaced. Consequently sustainability has come to mean a call for action, for a collective human effort to keep human use of natural resources within the Earth's finite resource limits.

We will see that there are many definitions and measures of sustainability, but the aim of attaining sustainability has become a fundamental value comparable to liberty or justice.

Every second year the global conservation organization the World Wildlife Fund (WWF) publishes its *Living Planet Report*. The report contains several measures that indicate the extent to which humankind is overusing nature, threatening the wildlife and causing global inequities. The *Living Planet Index* reflects the health of the planet's ecosystems, and the *Ecological Footprint* shows the extent of human demand on these ecosystems. Both these measures have been deteriorating. The vertebrate species populations declined by nearly 30 percent between 1970 and 2005. Human demand on the biosphere more than doubled during the period 1961 to 2005. If we take into account the need to absorb CO_2 in order to reduce global warming, humanity's footprint had already exceeded the Earth's total biocapacity in the 1980s. By 2005 demand was 30 percent higher than supply.

Figure 1.2 shows how the global ecological footprint has increased since the 1960s and how it is expected to grow if humankind continues to increase its consumption of natural resources. A rapid reduction would be necessary to bring down the global footprint to a level that is consistent with Earth's limited biocapacity.

The ecological footprint measures our use of renewable resources, the amount of which is dependent on photosynthesis. If we also take into account the use of non-renewable resources, especially fossil fuels, it is rather obvious that humankind today is using up its natural capital in a way that is not sustainable. *Peak oil* is a concept that is much discussed. The estimates of when the yearly production of oil will reach its maximum vary, but most observers agree that world petroleum production will start to decline in our lifetime (en.wikipedia.org/wiki/Peak_oil).

We live in a *full world*.

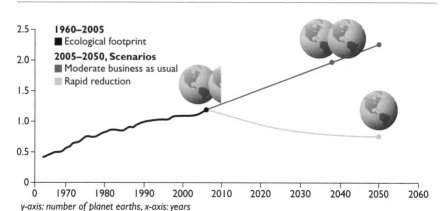

y-axis: number of planet earths, x-axis: years

Source: reproduced from the Global Footprint Network www.footprintnetwork.org/en/index.php/ GFN/page/worl footprint/(2009)

Figure 1.2 Global ecological overshoot from the 1960s to the 2050s

Pick two – ignore the third

The ethical trilemma derives from the difficulty to achieve all three goals simultaneously. It is relatively easy to pick one of the corners and to find out what would be required to achieve that specific goal. You can read books on how to promote economic growth, how to reduce inequities or how to avoid environmental degradation, but it is much harder to find works that treat all three – even just two – of the goals at the same time.

Let us mention some writings in which the authors have paid attention to two of the three aims while neglecting one of them.

The World Bank's *World Development Report 2006*, subtitled *Equity and Development*, aims to show how prosperity can be generalized globally. Previously the World Bank had stressed the importance of economic growth as a means of reducing poverty, but in this report it treats equity as an important factor enabling economic growth. In a section entitled "A glimpse of the future" the report echoes an optimistic Rostowian vision:

> The world population will stop rising and world production growth will stabilize until all countries, economically, start resembling countries like the United States, thanks to free trade and the diffusion of technology.
>
> (WDR 2006: 69)

The report does not treat any of the problems related to ecological sustainability.

The International Labor Organization (ILO) World Commission on the Social Dimension of Globalization, chaired by the Finnish and Tanzanian presidents, issued in 2004 a book entitled *A Fair Globalization: Creating Opportunities for*

All, which also stresses social justice, employment, and economic growth, while touching upon environmental problems only lightly. This report exemplifies a kind of thinking that can be dubbed "global social democracy."

Another possibility is to look at prosperity and sustainability. One can construct a vision whereby the environmental services would be priced correctly, and, where possible, user and ownership rights to natural resources would be well established. In an article entitled "Are We Consuming Too Much?", a group of renowned economists and ecologists have formulated such a prospect in the following way:

> While there may be uncertainty about whether various countries are meeting the sustainability criterion, the need for vigorous public policies to support more efficient consumption and investment choices is unambiguous. Through regulation, taxes or the establishment of clearer or more secure property rights, public policy can help prices of natural and environmental resources better approximate their social costs....Policies of this sort – especially those that deal with underpricing of natural resources or environmental amenities – will improve matters along the sustainability dimension.
>
> (Arrow *et al.* 2004: 168–69)

The authors believe that such measures will improve the prospects of future generations; but they do not address any problems of equity in our generation. Will poor people be able to pay the higher prices for water, electricity, fuels and other amenities? The message emanating from the article – and from much of the environmental economics literature – is that we should aim for an eco-efficient capitalism.

Social thinkers emphasizing equity and sustainability usually give an unambiguous answer to the question put by Arrow *et al.* They say that we already consume too much and that global justice and ecological sustainability can be achieved only if the present levels of consumption in the rich countries are reduced. Such authors echo Mahatma Gandhi's precept that the Earth provides "enough for everybody's need, but not enough for everybody's greed."[1]

Ecological economics differs in its approach from both standard and environmental economics. It puts sustainability at the center of analysis, and it focuses on distributive justice globally between present as well as future generations.

Those reports and books that treat two of the problems often only pay slight lip-service to the third. A "global social democrat" tries to find ways to achieve a "fair globalization," in which economic growth is maintained, but in such a way that the poor nations can grow faster than the rich. Those in favor of an "eco-efficient capitalism" want to create property rights and markets for as many environmental services as possible – to put the right price on the environment – but how are the already poor going to pay more for all the necessities of life – food, water, transport? The "red–green" countercurrent that strives for both justice and ecological sustainability is prone to accept a society with no further growth or even "degrowth" and to extol a simple way of life as the only way out of the trilemma.

Whereas most environmental economists are situated on the side of "eco-efficient capitalism" ecological economists tend to have a penchant towards "red–green planetarism." However, the big task for all is to find solutions that as much as possible take all three corners into account. This is a challenge especially for ecological economics, and that is one reason for us to write this textbook.

Chapter 2

Economic growth and human development

The IPAT equation

The impact an economy has on the environment depends on the number of people, what and how much each one consumes, and the natural resources required for the production of the goods and services consumed. Ecological economists use the so-called IPAT equation in order to highlight the impact as a function of these three variables, all of which have changed dramatically during the last 200 years. The IPAT equation is also called the *Commoner–Ehrlich equation* after two pioneers – Paul Ehrlich and Barry Commoner – who at the beginning of the 1970s discussed the environmental impact of different factors: What was the role of population growth, economic growth, and changes in technology? The equation is:

$I = P \times A \times T$

where:

I stands for environmental **impact**
P stands for **population**
A stands for consumption per capita or **affluence**
T stands for **throughput** – natural resources – used per unit of consumption; it is largely dependent on the **technology** used in the production of goods and services

Population is measured in numbers. Affluence is usually measured as income or consumption in monetary units per capita. Throughput is measured in physical units – e.g. tonnes, cubic feet, hectares – of natural resources that are used up in relation to income or consumption.

One way of using the equation is to look at the global impact with the following formulation:

**Global environmental impact =
World population × GDP per capita × Tonnes of natural resources/
Global GDP**

GDP – Gross Domestic Product – is the value in monetary terms of the goods and services produced in a country. It is also roughly equal to the GNI – the Gross National Income – of the country. GNI comprises the total value produced within a country (i.e. its GDP), together with its incomes received from less payments made to other countries. On a global level GDP is exactly equal to GNI.

In this chapter we are going to look at the extraordinary growth in P and A globally. How has this explosion in world population and wealth been possible? We shall also treat the factor T, but mainly leave it for Chapter 5 on ecological economics and the conditions for sustainability.

The amazing population growth

A most remarkable achievement of the modern era is the impressive increase in longevity. A long life is one of the best indicators of a good life. Therefore, life expectancy at birth is one of the central variables in the Human Development Index (HDI) calculated by the United Nations Development Programme (UNDP) and published in its yearly *Human Development Report*. The other two indicators are the level of education and income.

Before the industrial revolution the average length of life was less than 30 years. Today the average for high-income countries is close to 80 years. In middle-income countries it is about 70, and in low-income countries almost 60 years. In a short time span humans have doubled their life expectancy (Table 2.1). From a human point of view this is a fulfillment of a longstanding dream, but from an ecological point of view the consequences are definitely problematic.

Table 2.1 Life expectancy, 1000–2003 (years at birth for both sexes combined)

	World	West	Rest
1000	24	24	24
1820	26	36	24
1900	31	46	26
1950	49	66	44
2002	64	76	63

Source: Maddison 2007: 72.

Note
"West" includes Western Europe and its "offshoots" North America, Australia and New Zealand. "Rest" covers the rest of the world.

One consequence is the explosive growth of the world population (Table 2.2). When the mortality rate was high, population growth was slow even though fertility rates were high. The population explosion of the last century stems from the increase in longevity with only a moderate decrease in birth rates. Since the beginning of the industrial revolution the world population has grown more than sixfold.

And even though birth rates have been reduced in most parts of the world it still continues to grow at a rate that is abnormally high. The ongoing increase in life expectancy implies that the world population will continue to grow at least until the middle of the twenty-first century, when it is expected that birth rates will have fallen to the same level as death rates.

Table 2.2 Population (million), 1–2030

	World	West	Rest
1	226	26	200
1000	267	27	241
1500	438	60	378
1820	1,042	144	898
1913	1,791	372	1,419
1950	2,526	481	2,045
2003	6,279	741	5,537
2030*	8,175	947	7,227

Source: Maddison 2007: 70.

Note
* Prognosis.

The fabulous growth of GDP

The lengthening of our lives is only partly a consequence of medical improvements. The most important factor is the improvement in the standard of living. Before the industrial revolution the majority of the population lived in absolute poverty. Even today almost one billion people are poor in the absolute sense (that is as many as the world population 200 years ago), but a clear majority have escaped from this abject poverty, and they can look forward to a life that is longer and richer than that of their ancestors. Since the beginning of the industrial revolution income per capita has grown approximately tenfold (Table 2.3).

Table 2.3 Levels of per capita GDP (1990 international dollars)

	World	West	Rest
1	467	569	453
1000	450	426	451
1500	567	753	538
1820	667	1,202	580
1913	1,526	3,988	880
1950	2,113	6,297	1,126
2003	6,516	23,710	4,217
2030*	11,814	37,086	8,504

Source: Maddison 2007: 70.

Note
* Prognosis.

This means that the volume of goods and services we produce has increased by a multiple of 60 in just a few generations (Table 2.4). The sudden growth of people and production is the major factor behind our global ecological trials, and we must understand why it happened and also make an assessment of how strong the forces behind this unparalleled growth still are. From an ecological point of view two millennia is a rather short time span, although for us already 50 years contain dramatic social and technological changes.

Table 2.4 Levels of GDP (billion 1990 international dollars)

	World	West	Rest
I	105	15	91
1000	120	12	109
1500	248	45	203
1820	695	173	521
1913	2,733	1,485	1,248
1950	5,337	3,032	2,303
2003	40,913	17,565	23,348
2030*	96,580	35,120	61,460

Source: Maddison 2007: 70.

Note
* Prognosis.

The figures in Table 2.4 correspond to PA in our IPAT equation. If we were to assume a constant T over time the global environmental impact would have grown 340 times in 1,000 years and 8 times in the last 50 years. It is expected to double in the West and treble in the Rest in the near future. Whether T is constant, declining or increasing has been debated, but it is clear that without a substantial decrease in the throughput in relation to GDP the environmental impact has been and will be of catastrophic dimensions. In order to keep the impact at the same level in 2030 as it was in 1950 the level of T should diminish by a factor of 18. That is the amount of *"dematerialization"* or *"decoupling"* that would be needed in order to counteract the effects of economic growth.

The West and the Rest

It is striking how much faster the economy has grown in that part of the world we call the "West" or the "Rich." In the "Rest" of the world income per capita has also been growing, but it is still much lower. The West is constituted by Western Europe and the "Western offshoots" – USA, Canada, Australia and New Zealand. If we speak about the Rich we must also include Japan – the only non-Western country that managed to transform into a full-blown consumer society before the turn of the century.

Already before 1820 we observe an economic growth in the West so that its income per capita had become double that of the Rest. After the industrial revolution this divergence increased rapidly.

Despite this cleavage between the West and the Rest the twentieth century meant an extraordinary change in the lives of all. The population grew rapidly everywhere. Life expectancy more than doubled even in the poor countries and their income per capita reached the level that the West had achieved at the beginning of the century.

From an ecological point of view the tremendous increase in population is both a riddle and a cause for alarm. How has it been possible for a species to achieve such an extraordinary population growth and how sustainable can such a development be?

Basis for economic growth

Let us start from a situation of a low level of income and economic stagnation. Economists have developed theories of why such a situation is hard to break away from. Thomas Robert Malthus is famous for his book on the *Principles of Population* (1798) according to which population always tends to grow faster than the production of food, and that therefore the majority of people are doomed to poverty and life-threatening catastrophes such as famines, epidemics, and war. The only remedy he could think of was birth control, and even that did not seem easy to implement. Malthus's theory gave a plausible description of the times before his writings, but the following 200 years have proved him wrong.

Even though we are not doomed to live at subsistence level, population growth may still be a formidable obstacle to a take-off from poverty. There are different models of a *low-level income trap* showing that a rapid increase in population may not permit a sufficiently rapid rise in per capita income in order to provide for the savings necessary for capital formation. As long as the population tends to grow faster than the formation of capital there will be no increase in labor productivity and growing underemployment will tend to perpetuate poverty and stagnation. To break this low-level income trap something like a *"big push"* or a *"critical minimum effort"* is needed. Only then is a *take-off into "sustainable growth"* – that is to follow the example of the West – possible.

So what does capital formation mean? In classical economics there were three *"factors of production"* called Land, Labor and Capital. Land stood for all natural resources. Labor represented the amount of workers available. Capital was the factor that could be increased by saving, that is refraining from immediate consumption in order to invest. As a factor of production, however, only investment in *real capital* – buildings, roads, tools, machinery and the like – were to be counted. It was accumulation of real capital, not accumulation of money or financial claims such as bonds or shares, that was important for economic growth. By increasing the ratio of Capital to Land and Labor the productivity of both could be enhanced. *The higher the rate of savings and investments the faster income per capita would grow.*

Accumulation of real capital and growing incomes would lead to an extension of the markets for different products. This in turn would make possible a more advanced *division of labor*. Thus workers could specialize and improve their skills in certain tasks, increasing overall productivity. The more the division of labor developed, the more the markets could extend, and the more opportunities for innovations and capital accumulation would appear. This was the base for the optimism expressed in Adam Smith's *Wealth of Nations* (1776).

Karl Marx, using a different concept of capital, ascribed rapid economic change to a new *mode of production – capitalism*, in which "capital" had become the dominating force. Capital was *money invested to gain profit* – that is to increase the amount of money. Money was no longer only a means to simplify exchange of goods. It had become a means of accumulation and enrichment.

In a simple market economy people produce in order to get money for buying goods for ordinary consumption. A commodity is exchanged for money and that money is used for buying other commodities. Marx used the formula $C_1 - M - C_2$ to describe this kind of market activities, where C_1 and C_2 stand for different commodities and M for money.

In capitalism, however, this formula is reversed. The owner of money capital invests in different physical things – such as land, buildings, machines and unfinished products – and hires labor in order to produce something that can be sold for a profit. Marx used the formula $M - C_1 - Pr - C_2 - M'$ for this process, where M is the money invested, C_1 the means of production, including labor power, bought and used in the production (Pr) of C_2, which in turn is sold for money: M'. The rational of the process is to receive a larger sum of money than that originally invested, that is M' must be greater than M, or at least the expected M' must be greater then M. Money, land, machines, labor and other commodities all turn into different forms of capital as they become part of this process of accumulation. *Marx's capital is a socially constructed force* that, like the Hindu god Vishnu, appears in many shapes or avatars. Labor is *commodified* and subdued to the logic of capital accumulation.

In a world were capitalists have to compete against each other for the best profit opportunities there will be a continuous urge to expand and to innovate, to exploit all means to fasten the process of capital accumulation. Capitalism, therefore, is inherently linked to growth and restructuring. It becomes an engine for *creative destruction*, as Joseph Schumpeter later expressed the logic of entrepreneurial capitalism. For Marx and Schumpeter capitalism is *a necessary condition for the rapid economic development* that has transformed the world in a few hundred years. From an ecological point of view the question whether capitalism can survive a transformation into a *steady-state economy*, or whether it is doomed to an unremitting growth, becomes a question of great consequence. We will deal with this question in Chapter 9.

Six types of capital

Today ecological economists – instead of speaking of three factors of production – separate between several types of capital.

1. *Natural capital* is physical assets provided by nature; natural resources and amenities that deliver services to the economy. They are generally reproduced naturally, without human interference, but since humans nowadays are able to remake nature on a massive scale, natural capital can be degraded and destroyed, but also enhanced and created.
2. *Manufactured capital* corresponds to the "real capital" of the classical economists. It consists of man-made equipment, buildings and infrastructures that are used for productive purposes. Manufactured capital wears out and must be replaced by investments in new tools, machinery, vehicles, buildings, etc.
3. *Human capital* consists of the motivations, skills and knowledge of the workers. Investment in human capital involves upbringing, education, training, and experience.
4. *Intellectual capital* is the pool of knowledge and ideas accumulated in cultural artifacts, such as books and computer memories. Discoveries, innovations, recipes, scientific results, fiction and plays, compositions and pictures can be stored and reused. Even if the materials encoding the ideas may wear out, the ideas in fact depreciate less the more they are used. Intellectual capital is often merged with human capital, but there are good reasons to separate the two. One is that the reproduction of intellectual capital is practically delinked from the use of scarce natural resources, and therefore of great interest from an ecological point of view.
5. *Social capital* is embedded in the culture and institutions of a society. Trust, mutual understanding, and shared values are crucial for economic cooperation. Activities such as politics, legislation and governance can improve social capital. Cultural norms, customs and institutions do not wear out, but they may become obsolete and dysfunctional as times change.
6. *Financial capital*, also called fictive capital in contrast to "real capital," is funds of purchasing power necessary for facilitating transactions and investments in a capitalist economy. Since financial capital consists of symbolic assets, such as loans, currencies, stocks, futures and derivatives, astronomical amounts can be transacted cheaply and almost instantly.

Capital understood in these different material ways are not necessarily subsumed under the "capital" of Marx. They exist independently of how society is organized, and they need not be the object of private or even social capital accumulation. The growth and use of intellectual and social capital need not encroach upon the natural capital. This is also true for financial capital as long as it is not used for the expansion of production and consumption of material goods.

It is the combined growth and use of these different capitals that has enabled humanity to achieve the miracles of long life and widespread prosperity. From an ecological point of view the question remains: Has this extraordinary human development occurred at the expense of the natural capital, other living beings and future generations? And if so, can we sustain our welfare without continuing to destroy our planet's life-supporting capacity?

Energy and biomass

In a strictly physical sense all production that requires energy generates entropy. *Entropy* is a thermodynamic concept and a measure of smoothing out or disorder. Entropy increases when "useful energy" is transformed into "useless energy" that can no longer be converted into physical work. According to *the second law of thermodynamics* or *the entropy law*, changes in an isolated system tend to smooth out differences in temperature, pressure and density, which means that entropy tends to increase, and that the amount of useful energy and matter decreases. When we consume coal, oil, gas, firewood or food we do reduce the "natural capital" of the Earth.[1]

However, Earth is not an isolated system; it constantly receives useful energy from the sun. Life on our planet is sustained thanks to *photosynthesis*, a process by which energy in the form of light is converted into chemical energy. It requires carbon dioxide, water and sunlight. The end products are oxygen and carbohydrates, such as sugar and starch. Life on Earth depends on this source of energy, which is available only through plants, algae and some bacteria.

Biomass is the mass of living biological organisms in a given area or ecosystem. It includes microorganisms, plants and animals. Biomass can be measured in several ways, but in strict scientific applications it is measured as the mass of organically bound carbon. Biomass is also the most important renewable energy resource, consisting of living or recently dead biological material that can be used as fuel or as material for production of goods.

Whereas renewable energy sources are naturally replenished in a relatively short time, non-renewable energy resources are finite, and will eventually become too scarce for economic use. The *fossil fuels* – coal, oil and natural gas – originate from biomass produced long before the emergence of human beings, and they cannot be replenished in historical time. Neither can *nuclear energy* fuel, such as uranium. Modern lifestyles are heavily dependent on fossil fuels and nuclear energy and therefore the continuation of our present prosperity is threatened as these finite resources become more difficult to extract.

Since the renewable energies are constantly reproduced, thanks to the effects of solar activity on Earth, they constitute a more permanent resource. However, they also are in limited supply. The supply of biomass clearly depends on the availability of land and water that is suitable for plants and algae. How big is the area needed to produce all the ecological services that we need for maintaining our living standards? That is a question that ecological economists are trying to assess, in particular by using the concept of the *ecological footprint* (EF).

The ecological footprint is a measure of the area of land and water that is required to produce what an economy consumes, and to absorb all the wastes it generates. Since the production of biomass differs a lot between different types of land and water, the ecological footprint is measured in "*global hectares,*" i.e. the average area needed globally.[2]

Using our IPAT equation we can measure the global environmental impact in terms of ecological footprints in the following way:

Impact = Population × GDP/capita × EF/GDP

Since the ecological footprints are measured in global hectares and since we can estimate the amount of biomass producing hectares available on the Earth, it is straightforward to think that the ecological footprint must not exceed the area available. There is an unmistakable limit – the capacity of the Earth to produce renewable resources – that must not be exceeded by humankind's ecological footprint. Since we already live in a full world, any increase in population or consumption per capita should be offset by a drop of EF relative to GDP that is at least as sizeable.

Strong and weak sustainability

Standard economic growth theory often disregards the ecological aspects. The simple textbook formula for economic growth – the production function – considers only capital (K) and labor (L), and total income (Y) is divided between capital income (αY) and labor income (($1 - \alpha$)Y). The limits to growth are investments and technological improvements; ecological aspects are not included in the analysis. When standard economists are pressed to include land and other natural resources they treat natural capital in analogy with man-made capital. The depletion of resources may be treated as a loss of capital, but as capital that can be substituted by man-made capital. This approach has given rise to the concept of *genuine savings* applied by the World Bank to measure if the economic growth is sustainable or not.

When calculating the genuine savings of a country the depletion of natural resources and the losses caused by pollution are valued in money terms and deducted from investments in manufactured and human capital. Sustainability is defined as a positive genuine saving, that is a reduction in the natural capital is sustainable if it is offset by other investments in money terms. This is an example of what ecological economists call *weak sustainability* as investments in roads, buildings or education can substitute for a deterioration of the ecosystem. *Strong sustainability* requires that the capacities of the ecosystems are preserved, or that the natural capital is more or less constant.

A similar problem arises as we try to assess the economic costs of global warming. Should we tell future generations that they should be content despite the negative consequences of climate change since they probably will have more consumption possibilities than we have today? Strong sustainability would mean a more radical attitude to global warming than if we value the future in terms of a weak sustainability concept, according to which climate is just one part of our overall prosperity.

Decoupling and the rebound effect

The technology-factor T in the IPAT equation is crucial in any assessment of the environmental impacts of economic growth (PA). How much can throughput be reduced in relation to consumption by technological improvements? Is it possible to *decouple* the use of energy and other natural resources from the production of goods and services?

An optimistic position is connected to the so-called *Environmental Kuznets Curve* (EKC). According to this view pollution and T increases as industrialization gets going, but as the economy reaches a certain level of industrial maturity, more efforts will be directed towards the alleviation of environmental problems. Throughput and pollution will begin to decline relative to GDP. In certain cases we may even expect an absolute decline of pollution despite a continuing GDP-growth. Thus decoupling could allow an economy to grow in an ecologically sustainable way.

There are many important examples of a gradual decoupling, but whether the decoupling is absolute, global and permanent is hard to assess. Polluting activities may be transferred from one part of the world to another. Since many countries are on the ascending part of the EKC they may outweigh those on the declining side, and global depletion or pollution may reach catastrophic proportions before all countries become mature enough for the optimistic part of the EKC-logic to work its wonders.

A phenomenon that makes decoupling quite problematic is the so-called *rebound effect*, also called *Jevons' paradox*, after the economist William Stanley Jevons. In his 1865 book *The Coal Question,* Jevons observed that England's consumption of coal soared after James Watt introduced his coal-fired steam engine, which greatly improved the efficiency of earlier designs. Watt's innovations made coal a more cost-effective power source, leading to the increased use of the steam engine in a wide range of industries. This in turn increased total coal consumption, even as the amount of coal required for any particular application fell. Jevons argued that any further increases in efficiency in the use of coal would tend to increase the use of coal. Hence, it would tend to increase, rather than reduce, the rate at which England's deposits of coal were being depleted (Wikipedia on "Jevons paradox").

For the economy as a whole any improvement in the technology that raises the productivity of a resource tends to increase total income and consumption, and consequently inflate the demand for goods and services that – even though unrelated to the resource that is now used more efficiently – will require an increased use of other natural resources. If I can save money by using electrical equipment that requires less energy, but spend this extra money on a cheap flight, one can hardly say that I have contributed to decoupling.

Caring, happiness and sustainability

One way of looking at this problematic is to give the value *caring* a much more central role in economics, than it has had until now. Most caring work has not been included in the measurement of economic production and wellbeing, despite the fact that it constitutes a large part of all work and life. But care should be extended to include caring for all humans and living beings – both for our and for future generations. The value triad Freedom, Equality and Care should all be equally important when assessing economic wellbeing. Until now freedom (to choose, to consume, to become rich) has dominated over equality, and care has been left aside.[3]

Another important finding is that for already-rich societies, prosperity, in a broad sense of the term, is no longer linked to higher incomes and consumption. Variables such as life expectancy, child mortality, level of education and subjective life satisfaction are related to income up to levels below $15,000–20,000 per capita, but above this threshold these relationships are blurred. While happiness studies generally find that *within* countries wealthier people are, on average, happier than poor ones, studies across countries and over time find very little, if any, relationship between increases in per capita income and average happiness levels. This finding is called the *Easterlin paradox* after Richard Easterlin, who came across this fascinating phenomenon in the 1970s, and thereby laid the foundation for today's happiness economics.[4] If prosperity in the already rich countries is delinked from economic growth, as suggested by Tim Jackson in the report "Prosperity without Growth" (2009), this has appealing consequences for ecological economics and for the resolution of our global ethical trilemma.

Ecological economics is one important part of an ongoing revolution in economics that de-emphasizes traditional economic growth, and looks for an economics concerned with quality of life, care and sustainability. Other important contributions have been made by social economists, feminist economists, institutional economists, and behavioral economists.

Chapter 3

Ethics and ecological economics

Introduction

As described in the introductory chapter, a central feature of mainstream economics, at least according to official methodology, is that the economist (the scientist) is considered to be a positive value-free observer of whatever happens in the real world. This means that her/his own visions and values or wishes and feelings do not, and should not, have anything to do with the results of research. The economist, in other words, is considered to be value-free and objective. Furthermore, the economic agent (the consumer and producer) is considered to be motivated only by self-interest.[1]

Ecological economists look at this relation a bit differently. Ethics makes a difference both for the scientist him/herself as well as for the economic agent; i.e. at a minimum, it may be considered good for the economist to be aware of what kind of ethical and philosophical basis his/her own thinking rests on; this knowledge increases his/her self-understanding. And, equally important, a wider knowledge of what actually motivates the economic agent – you and me – is likely to increase the economist's understanding of the decisions that the agent makes, and so, eventually, help to shape a firmer ground for economic policy.

Furthermore, it might be argued, that if ethics is of importance in an empty world, it must be even more so in a full world. For instance, in a full world it cannot be trusted (or pretended) that inequality will be remedied by growth, simply because growth is not possible anymore without a very high and rising cost on nature; ethics has to be taken seriously in the sense that ethical questions and decisions cannot be postponed, but must be acknowledged as soon as possible.

In this chapter we shall take a brief look at some theories that may prove helpful in understanding why this is important. This overview must necessarily be brief because the area is immense and here we will discuss, in turn, the vast area of justice in relation to nature (species, ecosystems) and justice between people. Of the latter we may distinguish between justice *within* generations and justice *between* generations. Of these we will mainly postpone the treatment of justice between generations (intergenerational justice) to Chapter 5.

Why ethics?

So, more specifically, why is it of interest to have knowledge of ethics (and environmental philosophy)? Why is it not enough to think of humans as profit-maximizing creatures? At least the following three reasons seem important:

- *Goals and policy objectives*
  In real public choice situations social policy-makers must choose specific values to guide their decisions. Politicians and social planners – in fact almost anybody in political discussion – do not express themselves (officially at least) in the language of *homo economicus*, such as, for example: "We want to do this, because this is what gives us the highest profit." Rather the expressions in the political vocabulary centers on social values. "Freedom" and "equality" and lesser epithets are not just empty words but express common values (let it be that they are hard to define).[2] As such discussion is not built on the present "newspeak," but reflects tradition – which of course differs from place to place – it is of importance to have a knowledge about the basic values this rests on.
- *Institutions and social values*
  Even if people undoubtedly often act self-interestedly, and indeed sometimes must do so, all this takes place within the limiting frame of what is called institutions. In other words, this means that the market – perhaps the most central concept of economics – should be understood as an institution in itself, working within the other institutions of society.[3] There are, in fact, not many instances of human life (except in dreams, perhaps?) where institutions (broadly speaking) do not play a role. In reality, firms are also institutions, with different kinds of rules and norms and sub-institutions, which regulate, formally and informally, consciously and unconsciously, the behavior of the people working in the firm. Values are represented as for example laws and rules about rights and duties, but are by no means restricted to these. For instance, history is full of examples of laws that have appeared to be forceless, as they have not corresponded to people's conception of a just or reasonable law.
- *Motivation and individual behavior*
  What motivates humans is what they value. *Homo economicus*,[4] is far from the only single explanation of why humans act – and why they do not. People act on many different kinds of motives and values, a characteristic which economists call altruism (words like sympathy and empathy are also used in this connection). Such other-regarding behavior is important in real life and does not fit very well into the standard economic model. However, explanations of human behavior (relating to nature) seem to transcend even the other-regarding motive; also more general beliefs concerned with, say, other species or ecosystems clearly seem to influence people's behavior.

These three points are, of course, closely interrelated and in a sense represent three sides of the same thing. Institutions, in general, form motivation and individual behavior, and, the other way around. These three reasons are quite generally stated and apply to different spheres of life. Below we shall discuss these points specifically with regard to humankind's relation to nature.

Values, morals and ethics

Value, for the mainstream economist of today, is identified with *economic* value, which actually quite often boils down to the market price. Thus value is something that is objectively observable, instead of some "muddy," introspective thing. What is it that ecological economists have to offer instead of this "objective" value? To see this we have to go to the time before economics was as specialized as it is to day. We have to look at the philosophy of value.

The general and traditional classification of the philosophy of value is the one of *functional*, *aesthetic* and *moral* values, a classification which must be considered to understand environmental values.

Functional values are values that are related to the goodness of an object in fulfilling its purpose. A good knife, for instance, is good in cutting, which may be related to characteristics such as sharpness and form of the blade, the shape of the handle, and so on. This in turn, of course, is related to the purpose the knife is made for, such as whether it is made for carving wood or cutting vegetables. Functional values are thus also named *instrumental values*, i.e. their value is seen in their relation to usefulness of producing something else.

Aesthetic values are about beauty. A knife may have an aesthetic value, as a knife may be considered as a beautiful instrument. However, this is a by-product of the making of the knife as an instrument, rather than the purpose. A *pure* aesthetic value is a value in itself, an inner or *intrinsic* value of something. An aesthetic value is thus a value that needs no further justification. Thus we may look at a landscape, a human being, an animal, or a work of art, and, from this point of view, we do not need to ask why we like or value it; we value it because of its intrinsic beauty, which is not a means but an end.

Likewise, *moral values* need no further justification. Inquiry about moral values implies questions of what it means to be a good man (woman) and what it means to lead a good life. This includes questions like that of virtue, rightness of action, and justice. Consequently moral values with respect to nature and environment are values that reflect what a good human being considers to be the good or right thing to do towards nature.

The discussion about the moral virtue is probably one of the oldest questions in philosophy, as we understand the term. The relation of virtue towards nature was commented upon by Aristotle whose opinion deserves to be quoted here:

> [w]e suggested that the end of political science is the highest good; and the chief concern of this science is to endue the citizens with certain qualities, namely virtue and the readiness to do fine deeds. Naturally, therefore, we do not speak of an ox or a horse or any other animal as happy, because none of

them can take part in this sort of activity. For the same reason no child is happy either, because its age debars it as yet from such activities.

(Aristotle 1976: 81)

Plants exist for the sake of animals, and brute beasts for the sake of man – domestic animals for his use and food, wild ones (or at any rate most of them) for food and other accessories of life, such as clothing and various tools. Since nature makes nothing purposeless or in vain, it is undeniably true that she has made all animals for the sake of man.

(Aristotle, *Politics*, quoted after Singer 1976: 192)

There are at least three things here that we should pay attention to. First, Aristotle defines virtue and good deeds as the highest good. Second, he defines the ability to be happy as some kind of a quality that animals and children cannot have, that as a matter of fact can be grasped only by mature men. Third, the role of nature is very clearly defined as a *means* for man.

This is clearly an outstanding example of *anthropocentric ethics*.[5] Such thinking has since changed, at least in some camps, and many people now criticize this view from a wider perspective. It is important to understand why. It is obviously not a question about reason and intelligence, since Aristotle is seen by many as one of the foremost thinkers of all times. It is a question about the fact that through the growth of human experiences and the ethical discourse the sphere of morally considerable beings expanded, and by that values have changed in an interactive manner. So, for instance, not all human beings have always been considered (that is by "free men") morally considerable, or at least not morally reliable.

These three types of values – functional, aesthetic and moral – taken alone, or together, may take the form of environmental values and are frequently used in environmental argumentation. So, for example, opposition against cutting down Indonesian rainforest for palm oil plantations is motivated by a combination of all these three values: a rainforest is more functional than a monocultural plantation, because of loss in biodiversity compared to the latter. Thus, the rainforest should be preserved because this could be utilized as, say, medicines, in the future. Furthermore the flora and the fauna and the landscape of the rainforest may be seen as an aesthetic experience, greatly exceeding the one you can get from plantations. From the *moral* point of view it can be claimed that the endogenous people (or species) living there have a right to live there and/or it can be claimed to be morally wrong that business interests destroy the rainforest. Let us now continue by looking a bit more in detail at these arguments.

Anthropocentric arguments

The anthropocentric arguments may be split into two: human welfare arguments[6] and human virtue arguments:

Human welfare arguments

This type of argument recognizes that there is a value in conservation of nature to the extent that it helps to promote human welfare. The concept of welfare may here be interpreted on an individualistic basis, like in utilitarianism, but as far as we can understand, arguments of human welfare may well be thought of as being more collectivistic and social. We may distinguish between two general arguments here. One is the importance of nature's life-support systems on different levels. The other is the direct enjoyment of the aesthetic/recreational kind. [7]

Human virtue arguments

These types of arguments are not utilitarian as such, but rather held important as they are thought to develop human capacities (Edwards-Jones *et al.* 2000: 78). Among the classical economists John Stuart Mill gave expression to this argument. Natural experiences of wilderness, animals and so on may have several kinds of "educative" effects, which may not be received otherwise.

Biocentrism

Here the arguments of welfare are extended to encompass non-human individuals as well. Two forms of biocentrism may be distinguished, between animal welfarism and teleological biocentrism. In animal welfarism the class of morally considerable creatures is extended to all beings that are sentient, that is they have the capacity to experience pleasure and pain. Perhaps the best-known representative for this line of thought is Peter Singer (Singer 1976).

Teleological biocentrism goes further than this and says that we should take into consideration not only sentient beings, but all forms of life. Everything, that shows an *organic development path* such as a seed, for example, should be taken into moral consideration. The development path may be seen as the unconscious interest of a living being, which in principle it is wrong to hinder. Taylor (1986) has developed this idea into a "theory of respect for nature" based on biocentric egalitarianism that is developed into a set of rules concerning duties of humans towards other living things (see Edwards-Jones *et al.* 2000: 81).

Ecocentrism

Ecocentric arguments take as their point of departure the moral concern for whole species or ecosystems. Rather than taking individual life as a starting point the focus is on the interconnectedness between different forms of life and inorganic matter. In principle ecocentrism is about admitting that everything in nature has intrinsic value. Among varieties of ecocentric ideas we could mention Aldo Leopold's *land ethic, deep ecology*, and the *Gaia hypothesis*. Leopold in his land ethic, which is perhaps most well known in the USA, says "A thing is right when it tends to preserve the integrity, stability and beauty of the biotic community. It is wrong when it tends otherwise" (Leopold 1949: 262). On this view man is removed from the role of "conqueror of the earth-and-community to a plain member and citizen of it."

Although the term deep ecology applies to many ecocentric ideas (like Leopold's land ethics), the term originates from the Norwegian philosopher Arne Næss (1976). Næss (who also called his deep ecology "ecosophy T") builds on two general principles: (1) a right to development for all life (and man's "togetherness" with all life); and (2) identification and self-realization (in relation to nature). Both these principles are related. In identification we can overcome the alienation, which has arisen through "unfavorable social circumstances," and rediscover our position and place in nature. And in this position man does not have any special privileges.

The original Gaia hypothesis takes as its point of departure the remarkable stability that the Earth's temperature has shown during at least one billion years, compared to what a "purely physical" development should have implied. This stability seems to have persisted despite tremendous geological and other catastrophes. This behavior led James Lovelock[8] and his collaborators to develop the hypothesis of Gaia (Mother Earth), which says that living matter, Earth's surface, the oceans and the atmosphere are parts of a system that seems to be able to control the temperature, the composition of the oceans and the atmosphere and so on in a way that seems to provide the circumstances for life as favorably as possible.

However, it can be said that the moral interpretation of the role of human intervention within Gaia is not altogether clear. If Gaia is a self-regulating system, it can surely survive humankind even from the most disastrous event. Gaia can survive man as it survived dinosaurs (and whatever killed them). Thus, if Gaia as such is our *only* moral concern, we can destroy ourselves and obviously take some other species with us, because Gaia will survive (in one form or another). On the other hand, of course, realizing that the organic unity of life and Earth is as big a miracle as life itself, might suggest a more modest attitude towards Gaia.

Distributive justice

In this section we want to complement the previous section on environmental ethics by giving a background to *economic* (i.e. *anthropocentric*) ethical thinking that can be related to sustainability, by briefly surveying some of the most important concepts and principles of *distributive justice*.

We will not here discuss the relation between the two, the nature-centered and the human-centered ethics. Here, we will just assume that, in some way or another, the question about "nature's share of the earth" has been solved, and we now concentrate on how to divide the produce between people. The purpose with this is to equip the reader with some intellectual tools that are necessary to understand the discussions – and perhaps even one's own thoughts – about what justice is, or could be, in social circumstances.

As environmental ethics in its broadest sense is concerned with justice in our relation to nature – including the relation to other people – social justice is of course a narrower view than this. Social justice is concerned with all relationships occurring in society, from the treatment of the elderly to the relationship to domestic animals. Distributive justice is a narrower concept, how much narrower, however, seems to be in dispute. For instance Phelps (1987) equals distributive justice with *economic justice*[9] and makes a difference between three types of distributive justice: (1) terms to the working poor (e.g. what are the just rates of taxation and subsidies); (2) intergenerational justice (whether distribution between generations should be on the basis of the sum of utilities over time or according to the difference principle (see below); and (3) international trade (in relation to unequal exchange). This interpretation, to consider only the justice in the distribution of goods is characteristic for the standpoint of many economists, but it is quite a restricted one. Many philosophers and some economists take a wider view. Under the topic of "distributive justice" we may well see such themes as justice in terms of social institutions, rights, capabilities or entitlements (see e.g. Sen 1985, 1999).

Justice to whom and of what?

It may be, as Hayek[10] says, that sex and money are the things most capable of animating people's imagination. However, even if being less open to free fantasy – and requiring much more logical thinking – the principles of justice, as in the right way of behaving, and leading a good life, have been the matter of great intellectual efforts. Despite this, it seems fair to say, progress has been slow and indeed there is a bewildering range of different theories and criteria as to how to classify the theories of justice.

However interesting it would be, this is not the occasion to go into a detailed discussion of all principles of justice and the complicated relations between them.[11] Instead we shall focus (perhaps a bit unfairly) on four of the principles most discussed in the last few decennia (at least from the perspective of (economic) distributive justice): first, we will discuss equality; second, the so-called difference principle; third, utilitarianism (also called welfarism); and finally libertarian principles. These principles are developed to the degree that they can be called theories. So, for instance, the quite popular principle of capabilities developed and advanced by Amartya Sen (and Martha Nussbaum) is not considered by most writers to be a fully developed theory (see Robeyns 2008: 15–18).

Equality and need

Principles of justice concerned with equality and need usually focus on the welfare of those in society who are the least advantaged and thus this view emphasizes the satisfaction of basic human needs.

Strict egalitarianism

This principle simply holds that every person should have the same level of goods and services. Goods and services should be divided equally on for example the grounds that people are due equal respect ("people are born equal" as the United Nations Universal Declaration of Human Rights says).

The two main objections against this principle are the *index problem* and the *time-frame problem*. The index problem is about how we should measure the "same level of goods." If specified as a bundle of goods, it seems likely that some will be better off than others because of differences in taste. Economists usually propose money as a solution to this problem.

The second problem about the time frame has to do with the practical matter of anchoring the equal situation to some point (or period) in time. A natural answer to this is to say that equality requires that people start from the same line at the same time, that is that all people should hold the same wealth at some initial time-point (after which you can do what you wish with your wealth).

Perhaps the one example which comes closest to this principle is inheritance tax (i.e. the higher the tax on inherited wealth, the more equal people are).

Probably the most common popular counterargument against egalitarianism would be that it is unfair, because the resources are distributed equally to everybody disregarding the effort or work that people put in. Another critical argument comes from the productivity/incentive point of view: if you are paid for effort and work, you are more likely to put in more.

The difference principle

John Rawls's work *A Theory of Justice* (1971) implied a revitalization of the discussion of ethics within the social sciences; also within economics the theory appeared as the first alternative in a long time to the utilitarian theory.

Rawls's theory is based on a thought experiment in which people are assembled (in the so-called original position) to make a decision about what the just society should look like. They do not know what their position will be in the future society, that is whether they will be rich or poor, man or woman, black or white, and so on. In the terminology of Rawls they are "behind the veil of ignorance." Rawls's question is, starting from these premises: What principles of justice will be chosen by self-interested and rational persons?[12] Two principles, according to Rawls, would be chosen: (1) equal basic rights and liberties, and (2) social *ine-*qualities should fulfill two conditions: (a) (these unequal) social positions should be equally open to all, and (b) they should be to the benefit of the least advantaged in society. Of these principles, it is (2), commonly referred to as the *difference principle*, that has provoked most discussion.

If this should sound somewhat abstract it may be in place to look at the principle by a simple example.

In Table 3.1 we have depicted a hypothetical income distribution in three different social orders or societies, A, B and C, with respect to three social classes, the poor (who are to be seen as representing the least advantaged in this society), the middle class and the rich. The numbers should be interpreted as the utility or welfare that the classes get from the distributions.

Which society would be the choice according to Rawls's principle? Since the focus, according to this view, is on the poor, the choice must obviously be society B, since it gives the highest utility (100 compared to 90 and 50) to this group.

Which society would be chosen by the egalitarians? Since society A obviously has the most egalitarian income distribution it must be their choice. It is understandable that they would not choose society C because it has the greatest inequalities in income, but why would they not choose society B instead as in this every class is better off and so is the poor? One argument would be that even if the poorest are better off in B than in A the income differences are still unacceptable in B.

Table 3.1 Principles of justice and income

	Poor	Middle	Rich
Society A	90	100	110
Society B	100	200	500
Society C	50	300	600

Utilitarianism and welfare economics

Historically, welfare economics is the offspring of utilitarianism and the common denominator between these two is efficiency. Even people that understand this connection often want to ask how efficiency can be interpreted as a principle of *justice*? Efficiency is often, in common speech, connected with exploitation and unequal distribution of income. Utilitarianism is usually divided into two main forms.[13] Act utilitarianism says that an act is just if, and only if, it maximizes the total wellbeing in the world. Rule utilitarianism says that an act is just if, and only if, it conforms to rules that if generally followed would maximize the total wellbeing in the world. Although the stuff that is maximized is usually defined as the difference between pleasure and pain, utilitarianism can also be thought of as measured in happiness satisfaction or human flourishing.

Which of the societies in Table 3.1 above would be chosen according to utilitarianism? Since the rule is that one should choose the outcome that maximizes total utility, society C should obviously be chosen because the total utility is 950 compared to 200 and 800 for society A and B respectively.

Libertarianism

The principle of libertarianism is that an action is just if and only if this does not violate anyone's libertarian rights, meaning rights that are "derived from the exercise of initial *full self-ownership* and of a *moral power to acquire property rights* in unowned external (non-agent) things" (Vallentyne 2009: 19). This means that people own themselves as they can own inanimate objects with all that it means, such as the right to get compensation and to transfer these rights to others. If this should sound like an unnecessary enlargement of private ownership to the reader, it should be pointed out that these rights are absolute in the sense that, for example, it is wrong to enslave or torture persons without their consent, no matter how effective these persons are on achieving an equal society or any other moral goal for that matter.

The most famous of the libertarians is Robert Nozick, who in his *Anarchy, State and Utopia* (1974) outlined a persuasive example of how people can be seen as having the right to what they own, or more correctly, what they get as a result of "exchange." Nozick's thought experiment starts with an initial distribution, which everyone can choose according to his/her taste and then there is thought to be a change in the income distribution due to people's voluntary contribution to someone. If you go to Bruce Springsteen's concert and pay $100 for a ticket, this means that he will get a much higher income than most people from this concert (not to speak about what the whole tour gives). The point here is that people going to the concert voluntarily give this sum of money to Bruce Springsteen – or, in other words, they consider it a fair exchange. The question here then is how the new distribution of income could be unjust since the exchange of the *Working on a dream* concert against $100 was all voluntary?[14] Clearly, this theory is in favor for non-intervention from the state, since the allocation based on voluntary exchange is seen as just.

Nozick emphasizes that as long as a person has not acquired anything unjustly, he is entitled to what he has. That is, independently of whether he has inherited, got something by luck, or by effort, we should accept that that person's holdings are legitimate. We shall not discuss this question widely here, but it does not seem unreasonable to claim, speaking about a full world, that there are problems with this approach. To understand this, it will be helpful to remember that Nozick's master, Locke, said: "For this 'labour' being the unquestionable property of the labourer, no man can have a right to what that is once joined to, or at least where there is enough, and as good left in common for others" (Locke 2005: 80). In the language used here, it seems clear that Locke's, and thus reasonably also Nozick's, thoughts are made for an empty world, but with a proviso added. That is, when there is not enough left for others, the rights of "the labourer" do not seem unquestionable anymore (if it ever were, except amongst free, Western men). Rather, there is clearly room for new libertarian principles. This is what the so-called *left-wing libertarians* have argued for, in that they claim that natural resources should be divided equally (see Vallentyne 2009: 20).

Justice in the real world[15]

The dealing with the subject of justice or ethics so far has been about giving a brief introduction to some of the theories which may be informative as far as the subject of Global justice (in the trilemma) is concerned. What about justice in the real world? How are the Earth's resources distributed among its (human and non-human) inhabitants? This chapter will be concerned with the distribution between humans.

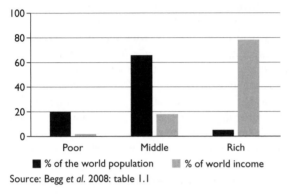

Source: Begg *et al.* 2008: table 1.1

Figure 3.1 Distribution of population and income

There exist a lot of methods and ways to describe and picture this distribution, from simple tables showing some variables to more complex measures. Also what is measured may vary from one variable, such as income, to more complex variables, such as the human development index, or even more complicated measures. Here we want to demonstrate the distribution with relatively simple methods (graphs and some figures) containing just a few variables.

As a start, if we divide the world into three strata – the poor, the middle class and the rich – and look at how the income is divided among the population we get the picture as in Figure 3.1. The poorest countries (e.g. many African countries and Bangladesh) have 21 percent of world's population but only 3 percent of the income. The middle country group (recently industrializing countries such as Brazil and China) has 70 percent of the population and 19 percent of the income. In the richest country group (North America, Western Europe, Australia, New Zealand, Japan) lives 9 percent of the world's population on 78 percent of the world's income.

Already these quite "raw" data give us a picture of the fact that the income of the world is not equally distributed. A somewhat more sophisticated way of studying income distribution is the Gini coefficent.

The Gini coefficient and the Lorenz diagram

One of the most important measures of inequality in income distribution is the Gini coefficient, which, expressed in percents, is called the Gini index. The Gini index can be expressed in a Lorenz diagram (curve).

In Figure 3.2 the horizontal axis shows the cumulated share of people from the poorest to the richest. On the vertical axis is the corresponding cumulative share of the income. If the income distribution were perfectly equal the cumulative share of, say, 10 percent of the poorest would correspond to their cumulative share of the income, that is 10 percent. And so would every cumulative percentage be the same; the 10 percent of "the richest" would get 10 percent of the total income.

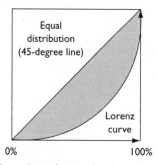

Cumulative share of people from lower income

Figure 3.2 The Lorenz curve

It does not require much thought to understand that the further away from the 45-degree line the Lorenz curve is, the more unequally will the income be distributed. For example in the Lorenz curve as drawn in Figure 3.2, we can see that, starting from the left on the horizontal axis, and focusing on the point where the curve slightly begins to divert from the axis (at about 20 percent of the poorest people) we see that this corresponds to only a few percent of their income share. In fact the Gini coefficient can be defined as the relation between the area between the 45-degree line and the Lorenz curve, that is the relation between the shaded area and the whole (lower) triangle in the figure. Thus (if counted as percentages), the lower the value of the Gini coefficient the greater the equality and vice versa (going from 0 to 100).

So how do the Gini coefficients look like around the world? Table 3.2 gives some examples. The Gini coefficient varies between 23 (Sweden) and 70.7 (Namibia), which thus means that the area between the Lorenz diagram and the 45-degree line is roughly three times higher in Namibia than in Sweden.

Table 3.2 Gini coefficients for some countries

Country	Gini coefficient (observation year)	
Albania	26.7	(2005)
Austria	26	(2007)
Bolivia	59.2	(2006)
Botswana	63	(1993)
Brazil	56.7	(2005)
China	47	(2007)
Czech Republic	26	(2005)
Denmark	24	(2005)
Finland	29.5	(2007)
Guinea	38.1	(2006)
Haiti	59.2	(2001)
Iceland	25	(2005)
India	36.8	(2004)
Israel	38.6	(2005)
Japan	38.1	(2002)
Lesotho	63.2	(1995)
Luxembourg	26	(2005)
Macedonia	39	(2003)
Malawi	39	(2004)
Malta	26	(2007)
Mauritania	39	(2000)
Namibia	70.7	(2003)
Norway	25	(2008)
Paraguay	56.8	(2008)
Portugal	38.5	(2007)
Russia	41.5	(2008)
Sierra Leone	62.9	(1989)
Slovakia	26	(2005)
South Africa	65	(2005)
Sweden	23	(2005)
United States	45	(2007)

Source: CIA *World Factbook*.

Among the countries with the lowest coefficients, we have different types, such as former communist states like Albania, the Czech Republic and Slovakia. In this class we also have the Nordic countries (Denmark, Iceland, Norway and Sweden). However, in this class we also have such diverse countries as Austria, Luxembourg and Malta. In the "winners" class besides Namibia we also have other African countries such as Botswana, Lesotho, Sierra Leone and South Africa. China, Russia and the United States have a coefficient over 40, with China, perhaps a bit surprisingly, leading with a coefficient of 47.

The 45-degree line in the Lorenz diagram is a utopia, which is hard to achieve, and which few would hold it worth to achieve, because an equal income for all would probably incur a high cost. It is also hard to say what a "reasonable" income distribution should look like in practice.[16] Nonetheless, is seems plausible to argue that in some countries the income inequalities seem so high (say, with a Gini coefficient over 60) that they are difficult to legitimate from any perspective, especially when we know that these countries suffer from serious social problems.

The Gini coefficient is concerned with income distribution *within* countries. Let us now look at the *global distribution* not of income, but of consumption, in Figure 3.3. In this the Earth's population is divided into ten deciles (on the horizontal axis), from the least consuming to the most consuming. On the vertical axis (and in the columns) we can see the percentage share of consumption. Although this is not, as the reader will observe, a Lorenz diagram, it conveys much of the same information.

Equality in consumption

In Figure 3.3 we can observe that the seven least-consuming decils (70 percent) consume 15.3 percent of the world's total consumption. From this we can conclude, and read from Figure 3.3, that the three most consuming decils consume 84.7 percent (of which the most consuming decile consumes 59 percent).

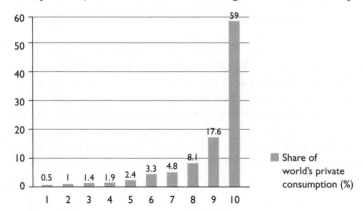

Figure 3.3 Equality in consumption, 2005

So the same pattern as in the earlier figures can be said to be repeated here, and the message is clear: the distribution of consumption (and) income is very uneven. This observation can be confirmed by the global Gini coefficient which (depending somewhat on how different countries are counted, and so on), at around 60, is clearly in the upper end of the land coefficients given in Table 3.2.[17]

Figure 3.4 is based on a comparison based on purchasing power parity (PPP), which means an assumption that the purchasing power of a dollar (or x dollars) would be the same in all countries. The idea of Figure 3.4 is to see how big a part of the world's population can be classified as poor or not, that is how many percent will be below or above some assumed poverty line, defined in dollars per day. The higher this dollar amount, the bigger part of world's population will fall under the line, of course. The poverty line in Figure 3.4 varies from $1 to $10.

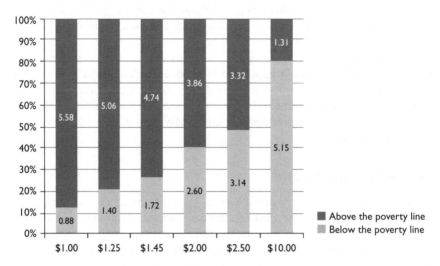

Figure 3.4 Percentage of the world's people at different poverty levels, 2005

The reader can think about her/his conception about what it would mean to be (really) poor. Can one manage with 1 dollar a day or does one need 10? Let us say that the poverty line is $2. Looking at that column we can see that 40 percent of the world's population has to manage on this sum a day. If the poverty line is thought to be $2.50 nearly 50 percent has to manage and 80 percent has to live on $10 per day.

Do these figures feel abstract and far? Let us change the perspective to something a little more personal, that is to what we consume.

Spending on luxuries and necessities

Consider Table 3.3a: here we see examples of spending on different items rising from the "modest" sum of 8 milliard dollars on cosmetics in the USA to the even more incomprehensible sums put on narcotic drugs and military spending.

Table 3.3a Spending on different goods in 1998 (milliards of dollars)

Cosmetics in the USA	8
Ice cream in Europe	11
Perfumes in Europe and USA	12
Pet foods in Europe and USA	17
Business entertainment in Japan	35
Cigarettes in Europe	50
Alcoholic drinks in Europe	105
Narcotic drugs in the world	400
Military spending in the world	780

Compare these sums with an estimate of how much additional money would be needed to get universal access to basic social services in all developing countries in Table 3.3b. One can see, for example, that the attainment of basic needs could well have been achieved with the money that people in Europe spent on cigarettes.

Table 3.3b Estimated additional costs for universal access to basic social services in all developing countries (milliards of dollars)

Basic education of all	6
Water sanitation for all	9
Reproductive health for all women	12
Basic health and nutrition	13

We could go on with these diagrams and figures, but the picture cannot get much clearer. The distribution of resources – here measured in money, but the same goes for the distribution of real resources and capabilities as well – is very unequal. The next question is, of course: How can it be like this?

Thinking back on the theories of justice discussed earlier in this chapter, we may now ponder how the figures relate to these, that is in what sense they are *just*. Even if theory is theory and practice is practice, we may perhaps still say something about this. The practice here of course is the global economic system, which functions by and large according to what will be outlined in Chapter 4. People react to this in different ways. A common (fatalist) reaction is: this is how the world works and there is not much we can do about it. A slightly more sophisticated (perhaps?) attitude is that which we could call analytical: for example the world is ruled by human greed, and this is why it looks like this. A third attitude is to relate this to justice: for example the world looks like this because people have earned (or are entitled to) what they have got.

People may have surprisingly similar ethical intuitions even if these may be motivated by different theories of justice. The reader may him/herself choose his/her favorite from the theories of justice we have discussed and think about whether the world's resource distribution corresponds to that. It would be surprising if the existing distribution goes together with your favorite ethics, because the global distribution is so twisted, in the want of a better word.

Table 3.3a/b above illustrates one case in point. The world economy is complicated, but the world is what it is (with unequally distributed resources and otherwise) at least partly because of the consumption choices we make. And the consumption choices are made where the money is.

As has been emphasized already in the beginning of this book, even if we are against inequalities per se, the restriction which the "full world" puts before us, adds a further argument against inequality. The full world requirement, or sustainability, requires us to live within the Earth's productive capacity. To do so in a global world requires us to distribute the world's resources more evenly. There are plenty of examples of the catastrophic effects of inequality, many wars being the most destructive instance. The most dramatic examples lately, clearly related to this, are the piracy in Somalian waters and the poachers of elephants and other rare animals in Africa.

Finally, we will say a few words about justice and nature in the real world. The problem is not so far from the problem of human justice as some may believe. For instance, even if unfair treatment of animals will not lead to an animals' revolution, recent experiences from many (developed) countries show that animal activists may take action against what they consider unethical treatment of animals, which may in fact be quite costly for society.

The use of natural resources are discussed in the other chapters. Suffice it to say here, the fact that humans are now estimated to be expropriating (directly and indirectly) about 60 percent of the world's photosynthesis is speaking the truth of its own, that is the maintenance of one species, *Homo sapiens*, requires more than half of the rest of the Earth. No matter what we think of this otherwise, it is hard to think of a better (worse) example of unfairness.[18] In the media it is mostly natural scientists who deal with this problem, and the upshot is commonly about the risk for human existence in the destruction of nature, that is the problem is mostly presented from an anthropocentric perspective. We suppose, though, that this is because these are arguments that bite in public discussion. However, we suspect that some of these scientists may have other views than anthropocentric ones. Facts about the unequal treatment of animals – in practice it is mostly a question of (risk of) extinction – will appear in the other chapters, such as Chapter 8, on Man and the seas.

Chapter 4

Environmental economics

Since ancient times, so the story goes, people have met on suitable places to exchange goods – for mutual benefit. Today the marketplace may be said to embrace practically the whole globe – not always for mutual benefit as we have seen. This growth is not only a question of geographical expansion. We have experienced an expansion of the market into such areas as child care, care of the elderly, nursing and so on. Market thinking (ideology) is one of the most powerful ideas in the world today. So, whether one likes it or not, it is important, if not inevitable, to understand the functioning of the market. In this chapter we will discuss the main features of the market, trying to understand both how it works and how it does not work.

How markets work

The model that economists use to describe what is going on in the economy has many names: the economic model, the market (mechanism), the price system (mechanism), among others. By and large these all are about a simplified picture of the working of the economy. The simple starting point is that there are two main actors or groups (agents) in the economy, the buyers (consumers) and the sellers (producers). The consumers want to buy the goods as cheaply as possible; the lower the price the more the consumer wants to buy, and vice versa. The producers want to sell the goods for as high a price as possible, and the higher the price the more goods they want to sell, and vice versa. The graphic model for the behavior of both consumers and producers can be drawn into one single figure: the demand and supply diagram. It might help the understanding of this image to think of some concrete market, say, the fish market in Tokyo (Tsukiji). In this, the world's biggest fish wholesale market up to 3,000 tons of seafood are exchanged every day. To come to grips with the concept of the market, let us specify the problem a bit. Let us study the market for one particular fish, the bluefin tuna, which today is one of the fish most appreciated for sushi.

Without pretending that Figure 4.1 is a very realistic picture of the real bluefin tuna market, it still should convey the essence of the market model. The downward-sloping line (Demand) describes the behavior of the fish buyers: the

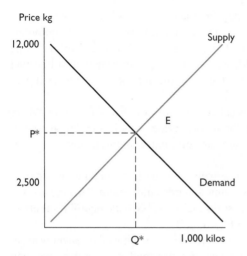

Figure 4.1 The market for bluefin tuna

higher the price, the less the buyers want to buy and conversely. The behavior of
the sellers (suppliers) is described by the supply curve line. The higher the price,
the more the sellers want to sell (the more intensively the fish is caught). Thus,
expressed in the relation between price and bought/sold fish, the wishes of the
buyers/sellers are the opposite. Only at one point, say, at the price 5,000 yen[1] and
the quantity sold 500 kilos do the sellers and buyers agree. At this *equilibrium*
price (often shortened as P*) the consumers' marginal willingness to pay corresponds to the marginal cost (the addition in cost caused by the increase of the last
entity of the goods, e.g. wages, materials, fuel, etc.) of selling.

This result, as a matter of fact, tells us more than what is apparent at first sight.
This means that the quantity Q* sold at price P* gives the best possible economic
result for the market as a whole. In other words, it is not possible to change the
allocation of goods in a way that some people would fare as well as before while
some at the same time would be better off (this is called Pareto optimum, named
after the Swiss economist Wilfredo Pareto).

The assumptions for perfect competition

However, it should be observed that this result is true only if the assumptions that
the model rests on are true. The specifications of the assumptions vary somewhat
but a common list could be the following:

a   The number of consumers and producers is large
b   The goods are homogenous (no product diversification or advertising)
c   All actors on the market have full information about all the relevant features
    of the market, such as prices
d   Free entry and exit (no costs for establishing in a market or going out from it).

One does not have to ponder for a long time about these assumptions to understand that they seldom can be realized in a real economy. When these assumptions do not hold, economists speak about *market failure*. When for instance the assumption (c) above does not hold, we are dealing with a market failure that implies that if some actors do not have the right information it is clearly not possible to make decisions that are optimal.

Such decisions may lead to what is called *externalities*, that is a situation where all the costs are not calculated into the market price. This is a common way to describe an environmental problem, such as pollution, in environmental and ecological economics.

One important and particular characteristic of the perfectly competitive market is the assumed characteristic of its striving towards equilibrium. This means that if the price, for instance, for some reason should be above the equilibrium price, this will lead to an *excess supply* (see Figure 4.2).

This means that the buyers do not want to buy as much as the sellers want to sell. It is easy to imagine what will happen on a fish market if, for example, you have to store tuna for a few days; it is certainly not suitable for sushi anymore. (Tuna stays fresh for a very short time, and also the storing time for frozen fish is limited to a few months.) You have to get the fish sold quite quickly and the best way of doing this is to lower the price. As long as the price is above the equilibrium price there will exist an excess supply.[2] Important to keep in mind here is that these equilibrating forces function only when the assumptions (a)–(d) are valid. Under other types of "market failures," such as for instance in a monopoly, the market failure that there is only one seller, the equilibrium price will not be reached but will be higher, exactly because of the market power of the monopolist, who can keep the price higher by keeping the supply smaller than under perfect competition.

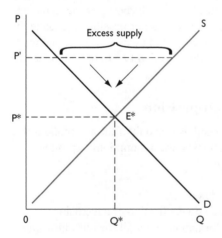

Figure 4.2 The market equilibrium

Before we continue it is necessary to further deepen our insights into the main body of (micro-) economics. The two central concepts to consider next are the concepts of *marginal cost* and *marginal revenue*. Let us start with the latter. Where does marginal revenue come from? To understand this we may look at Figure 4.3. Let us again think about a fish market, not the bluefin tuna market but the market for, say, farmed trout. The reason for this is the latter resembles more a market for *perfect competition* than the former.

Figure 4.3 illustrates one fundamental feature of the perfect competition market, which is the feature that from the point of view of a single seller (as well as buyer) price must be taken as given. Why is that? This can be intuitively understood at least from two points of view.

From one point of view of the whole market, a firm on a competitive market is only a "drop in the sea," that is its production decision has no effect whatsoever on the total supply of the market. On the other hand we might look at the situation from the point of view of the consumer: if the single consumer buys a little or big amount of the product, it disappears in the total demand. Or one could also express it like this: if a single firm raises its price, a rational consumer would not buy from that firm, because he could buy the good cheaper from other firms. If, on the other hand, the firm wanted to lower its price, in trying to undercut its competitors, it would not be able to do that for long because, in perfect competition, the firm is working at the limits of its existence, that is at zero profit. Thus there is (theoretically) one and only one viable price for a firm to choose. In perfect competition, the firm is thus called a *price-taker*. From this there is a short step to the economically important concept of *marginal revenue*. The marginal revenue is the additional revenue (income) which the firm gets from an additional sold unit of the good. If our trout farmer decides to sell his whole production of 10 tons he has to sell the whole quantity at the same price per kilo. He cannot sell the first kilo at a

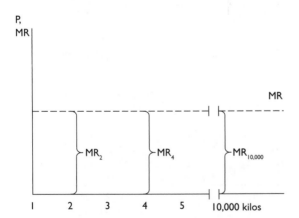

Figure 4.3 Marginal revenue on the trout market

higher price than the last 10,000th kilo. The perfectly competitive firm thus has a constant *marginal revenue*. The *total* revenue is naturally received by multiplying the amount of trout sold (kilos) with the price per kilo. Figure 4.3 shows how the marginal revenue (MR) is constant independently of whether the fish farmer sells 2, 4 or 10,000 kilos of trout.

Thus far we understand what the total income is: quantity times price. However, to be able to say something about how much to produce, we should also know something about what the costs of the production are. The total costs are usually divided into *fixed costs* (FC) and *variable costs* (VC). The fixed costs do not change with produced quantity. For example, for the fish farmer the costs for a fish cage (a big net bag where the fish are grown) is the same whether or not he is farming one or thousands of fish. Variable costs, conversely, vary with production quantity. If the fish farmer wants to produce more he must for example buy juvenile fish, more fodder and so on. In economics the analysis is often simplified by neglecting the fixed costs, that are considered as constant, and instead concentrating on the variable costs in marginal terms (change in MC when production changes one unit) (MVC). A typical MVC-curve is drawn in Figure 4.4.

To fully understand Figure 4.4 we have to consider the relation of it to the concept of *productivity*. We can see that for each additional produced unit the costs are sinking till the 10th unit. This means that up to this point productivity is rising. After this point the MVC-curve begins to rise, which means that productivity is diminishing.

Let us make a thought experiment to understand this. In terms of our fish farming this may be put as follows: we have a cage of a given size, a given amount of juvenile fish to raise, a given amount of fodder and so on. Let us now investigate what happens when the fish farmer hires more workers. In starting the

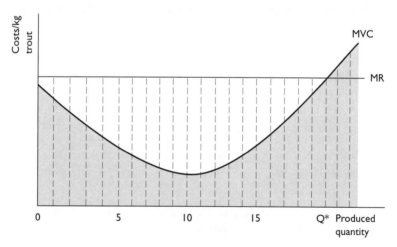

Figure 4.4 Marginal variable cost and marginal revenue

farm there is only one worker that takes care of the whole farm. The work will very much be about hurrying around in different tasks such as feeding, picking up and gutting the fish; the cages have to be serviced and so on. In such a situation the production of the farm may be, say, 100 kilos a day (on average). The hiring of a second worker may, because of the possibility of allocating and distributing the work in a more rational way, lead to an increase that is more than two times than what a single worker can produce. This means, assuming that the workers get the same wage, that the cost per kilo of fish now is lower. A third worker may contribute with an increase in production that is more than three times than what a single worker can produce. And so on. However, sooner or later, depending on the size of the farm, a point is reached where the last hired worker's contribution will be less than his wage. Intuitively: sooner or later the workers will be so many that they will literally be in each others' way.[3]

The question which now arises is how much should be produced (to get the largest profit)? Looking at Figure 4.4 one possible answer that comes to mind could be "the quantity where MVC is lowest" (the 10th unit). This answer is worth consideration, but to be able to give the complete answer we should also consider the marginal revenues. In Figure 4.4 we have also drawn the marginal revenue (MR), which is some given price per kilo trout. The MR appears as a horizontal line, the price being the same independently of whether the amount sold is 1 kilogram or 10,000 kilograms. Every column in the figure (under the MR-line) shows the price (say €1,000) for every ton of fish.

Let us now with the aid of the diagram study what happens when production is increased by comparing the columns with the portion of the column which lies under the MVC-line (the shadowed part of the column). If we produce 1 ton of trout we notice that the light part of the column is higher than the shadowed. This means simply that the revenue for the first sold ton is higher than the cost.[4] What will happen when we increase production to 2 tons? Not much, really, except that the lighter area is somewhat larger than with the production at 1 ton, which means that the addition to revenue caused by the second ton produced is bigger than the addition to the costs. And when we go towards the right in the figure, this difference between addition in revenue and addition in costs grow. And, as noted, by the production of 10 tons the marginal cost is at its lowest – and the difference between addition to revenue and addition to cost (MR–MVC) is at its highest. Is not this the quantity then, where profit (the difference between total revenue and total cost) is highest? No, because it should be noted that also after this point (quantity) the marginal revenue is still bigger than the *marginal* variable cost, so the net profit continues to grow. If this is the case, it will obviously be profitable to increase the production further. How much? The production must be increased to Q*, where the last produced (sold) item costs as much to produce as it brings in revenue (i.e. the price). If someone thinks that increasing production to more than Q* would give an even bigger profit, this can be easily refuted by looking at Figure 4.4: immediately when producing more than Q* the bar showing the increase in cost (MVC) is higher than the increase in revenue rectangle (MR).

This means that the net profit is diminished at increase in production from Q* to Q*+1 by the little shaded triangle above the MR-rectangle. Going even further to the right in the figure shows a growth in the *diminishing* of the profit. Thus it will be profitable to go back to produce Q*.

What Figure 4.4 illustrates is "The fundamental economic principle": all economic activity shall be expanded to the point that marginal cost is equal to marginal revenue. But as in many other walks of life the achievement of a *golden rule*, like the MR = MC, is an ideal that in practice is many times difficult if not impossible to achieve. As the understanding of this difference in view seems to be at the root of endless controversies and fights concerning economic policy, whether defined in more specific or in general terms, as well as also being at the root of the differences in opinion between mainstream economics and ecological economics it might well be worth giving some thought to this problem.[5]

To understand fully the power and persuasiveness of the equimarginal principle (MR=MC, as described in Figure 4.5) we must relate it to the concept of the perfectly competitive market (as briefly summed in Figure 4.1, for example). That is, not only do we have a principle which describes how to reach optimality (the best result) by equating marginal revenue and marginal cost, but furthermore, this result can be reached without any deliberate intention or consciousness by the market actors themselves. How is this possible? It is not possible because some benevolent and omniscient creature(s) have calculated this, but because there are a lot of agents (buyers and sellers) on the market who think only of their self-interest. Now, as by an "invisible hand," as the father of economics, Adam Smith, expressed this: "[i]t is not from the benevolence of the butcher, the brewer, or the baker that we expect our dinner, but from their regard to their own interest." Briefly put: business is not charity, on the contrary everyone wants to make as much money as possible, but just because every other businessman as well as every consumer is construed in this way everyone will find himself in a ruthless competition where eventually everyone is buying and selling at the lowest cost possible. Since in this case all "excess" profit has been pressed out through the process of competition, this result is the best (Pareto optimal) result, that is the best for the whole society.

One obvious question here to ask is how can the result be good if all the profit has been drained out and people are living, in a sense, on existence minimum? Behind this result, again, we have the assumption that man is rational and self-interested. Another way of expressing this is to say man is the best judge of his own satisfaction or welfare. Consequently, no one would be willing to make a contract (buy and sell) without considering it to be a betterment in his/her situation. Thus, when every agent (consumer and producer) in the economy acts in this way every possibility for profitable exchange will be exploited. In other words every agent will end up in a situation where their marginal cost is equal to their marginal revenue.[6] This situation, where no improvement is possible for anyone – without making the situation worse for somebody else – is a more exact description of the term Pareto optimality.

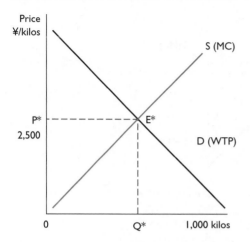

Figure 4.5 The bluefin tuna market and the producer and consumer surplus

We are now in a position to interpret the supply-demand diagram introduced earlier in the chapter in a somewhat different light.

We saw, for example, in Figure 4.2 that the equilibrium market price and quantity are P* and Q*, which is given by the intersection of the supply and demand curves (E*). This is because E* is the only point where sellers' and buyers' wants meet. Should there be, say, a higher price than P*, this would soon lead to a decrease in this price because the consumers would not wish to buy as much as the sellers would like to sell (excess supply), and the warehouses would soon fill up and sellers would be forced to sell out quite soon.

The willingness to pay and consumer surplus

Now, from this, there is but a short step to understand that the demand curve – besides showing how much consumers demand at different prices – is at the same time telling how much they are willing to pay (Willingness To Pay (WTP)) for different amounts of goods. So, for instance, at a very high price of tuna (12,000 ¥ or more) there are just a few people who desire it and/or are rich enough to by the tuna at that price. As the price goes down there are more and more people willing (and/or who can afford) to buy the tuna. In fact they would be willing to pay more than the price P*, but they get the tuna at this price, so they receive a surplus in a situation like this. This is called the *consumer surplus*.

On the other hand, on the sellers' side, we have the supply curve, which could be called the "willingness to sell" because this is exactly what it is: as the market price varies, for the individual seller, this is the price which the seller has to accept (this is in fact the marginal revenue, MR). Because the producer determines the maximal profit by looking at the quantity where the MC is equal to MR, the supply curve can be derived from the MC curve and is in fact mostly identical with that.[7]

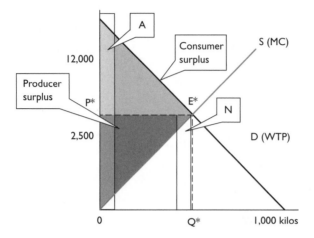

Figure 4.6 The consumer and producer surplus

Graphically, putting this together, it means that for each quantity, the (vertical) distance between what the buyer is willing to pay (WTP) and the price at which the seller is willing to sell (MC) reflects the gain which is available from buying and selling (exchange). How this gain will be distributed between seller and buyer depends on the market situation or the parts' bargaining power, but if we stick to the perfect competition framework, the consumer and producer surpluses have the following general traits, as pictured in Figure 4.6. The gains of trade may be described as follows: the first rectangle, A, shows that we have a total surplus equal to the height of the rectangle. Now, when we assume a perfectly competitive market, the price is given as the equilibrium price, P*. The buyer's willingness to pay is shown by the whole height of the rectangle, that is, he would be willing to pay, say 13,000 for the first fish, but, thanks to competition, he only pays P*, which gives the buyer a surplus (in terms of his valuation). What about the seller? The seller's "willingness to sell" is shown by S (MC), so he would in fact be willing to sell at a price shown by the price exceeding the white area under the MC curve of rectangle A. But what the seller gets, under perfect competition, is, of course, P*. Thus the seller of the "first fish," who does not have to go as far out on the sea as his fellow fishermen – who must go further and further the more scarce the tuna gets – and thus saves in costs, has a relatively low marginal cost for this. This means that he would, under other circumstances, have been willing to sell at a price corresponding to this, however, given the perfect competition he can get a relatively much higher price for the fish, thus earning a *producer surplus*.

We see that, in a situation like this, contrary to common knowledge, not only consumers gain from competition, but also producers. Now, if this is true for "the first fish," A, this will be so for all catch, up to the rectangle N, where the fished quantity is Q*. After this, as Figure 4.6 shows, the consumers' willingness to pay goes below the sellers' willingness to sell (MC), and consequently, no more exchange will take place. But up to this quantity, both sellers and buyers have reason to exchange, that is a surplus (a gain from trade) to earn.

When we add together all the surplus rectangles A–N (not all drawn in the diagram), we get the total economic surplus, which consists of consumer surplus (the top triangle) and the producer surplus (the bottom triangle). Under perfect competition this surplus is the highest possible, that is the highest possible amount of goods is sold/bought at the lowest (from the consumers' point of view)/highest (from the producers' point of view) possible price.

The message for economic policy often drawn from this is: free markets lead to the best possible result, thus there should be no political intervention with the market, because such an intervention (almost by definition) – by hindering possibilities of mutually beneficial exchange between people – would make the result worse!

If this is the case, why, then, do we observe so much political intervention in the real world? In most countries of the world over half of the GNP goes through the government budget. There are lots of reasons for this which there is not room to go into here; we shall discuss here only the most basic ones – and basically from an ecological economic perspective.

Let us start with the supply curve: the supply (marginal cost) curve reflects firms' "willingness to sell," or in somewhat more exact language the costs a firm considers in its decision to sell. But does this curve really reflect a "social optimum," that is a state which is the best one (in the sense described above)? One already classical answer is that it does not necessarily reflect the true social costs of an activity. The marginal cost is only about the costs that matter to the firm.

External costs

Let us as an example return to our trout farm again. The farm of course produces (relatively) cheap fish. However, the fish farming, besides producing fish, will also produce side effects, which will pollute the local (or even regional) environment as a result of the fish excrement and excessive feeding that may disturb local fishing, local natural fish environment, and so on. Such effects are not voluntarily included by the fish farmer in his calculations, but nonetheless, in one way or the other, have to be carried by "the society" (i.e. other people). With the aid of the tools introduced in Figure 4.1 we may now illustrate such a situation in the following way.

In the figure the private costs for the individual fish farmer are shown by the curve S_p. Included here are the costs of staff, fodder, etc., which the fish farmer includes in his bookkeeping. To show the real costs for the whole society (community) we have to add the extra (i.e. the *external* costs (X)) to the S_p-curve, caused by the farming. Through this addition we get the higher curve, S_s, showing the total costs (private costs plus social costs) of farming for the society. Now, the economic way of looking at the problem is that in a situation where there is no intervention, the fish is "too cheap" and the production "too high." This is because

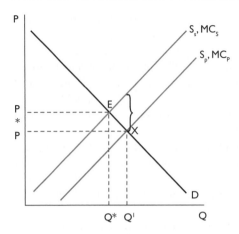

Figure 4.7 External costs

the production, besides goods, also produces "bads." The right (socially optimal situation) would be the price P* which would lead to the sold quantity of Q*. The price, given by the intersection of the two curves D and S_s is P* at which the amount of fish sold is Q*. Here the golden rule formula of MC = MR would be followed by filling in the true values of the costs. How can we reach this point, if intervention always leads to a worse situation? This is in fact not considered true always, because we can have *market failures* as obviously here, and the view can be defended that intervention is justified to repair this. This can be done by imposing a tax on fish production, a tax corresponding to the marginal damage of fish production, i.e. the difference between S_s and S_p.[8] Elegant as this may seem, there are in reality great problems with the implementation of environmental taxes, both of political and informational kind, which means that such taxes have not exactly been a policy measure success.[9] Hitherto such taxes have been imposed on energy-related products such as petroleum and cars.

Correspondingly, looking at the demand (WTP) curve the optimality result referred to above of course requires that people have the perfect information that is assumed in the model. In other words, the demand curve just reflects people's willingness to pay, but does not necessarily reflect a "social optimum," that is a state which is the best one (in the sense described above). The WTP simply and only reflects what people are willing to pay for anything, be that for organic food, preserving values, or for that matter, cigarettes or drugs (what you prefer is strictly a personal business). So if people are willing to pay for bluefin tuna, they pay. One aspect of this problem is exactly that people's willingness to pay does not reflect the correct social values, because people do not have information about all the effects of their demands, such as the threat of extinction for the bluefin tuna.

The traditional answer to this kind of criticism is that this is no problem, because when a resource gets scarce, its price will rise and the demand will fall. Thus the market (i.e. the price mechanism) will take care of the problem. Alas – and this is a viewpoint emphasized by ecological economics – the situation is not that simple. At least two points are of importance here: first, as for the absolute demand of resources, the consumption of the more wealthy in the Western world corresponds to the consumption of a king in the seventeenth century (not in every aspects of course). So if we in the seventeenth century had a few hundred emperors with a certain "luxury" consumption standard, today we have a few hundred millions with a comparable consumption standard.[10] This means that there is purchasing power enough in the world today to drive species to extinction. The market mechanism cannot be trusted to save species from extinction.[11] Another related point is that we do not have enough knowledge of how much exploitation a species can stand; there is clear evidence that a biological stock cannot be counted on a linear scale, but rather there seems to be thresholds beyond which a biological stock collapses, as the collapse of the big predator fish in the oceans shows (see Chapter 8).

Theory and practice

The most basic feature in the model for perfect competition is that it is (necessarily) a theoretical model, which rest on assumptions which focus on certain features of reality while it overlooks and abstracts from others. So whenever one hears someone proclaiming that free competition should be carried through in a certain area of human activity, such as, say, care of the elderly or public transport, one should ask oneself as to whether and to what extent this area corresponds to the assumptions of perfect competition and/or whether it is reasonable to try to put these assumptions to work in this particular area. For example, are there enough actors on the market to make competition work? Do the consumers have enough information to make rational choices?

A central point of dispute in economics almost since the dawn of the discipline has been whether competition really is a harmonious process which automatically reaches equilibrium or whether the economy is unstable and needs different kinds of corrective measure (or planning). The latter point has been emphasized by many great economists such as Marx, Keynes, Schumpeter and others; there is no guarantee that a competitive process leads to equilibrium even if the critical factors are present. "Free competition" might as well lead to less competition, such as oligopoly and monopoly, that is there is a tendency in competition to destroy itself, as we frequently may observe from the real world.

A further problem with the marginal analysis is that, by definition, the decisions in many dimensions rest on what could be called infinitesimalism, that is the assumption that all decisions (as well as in fact the decision-makers) can be divided into very small pieces (otherwise it is hard to come to the *marginalist* conclusions). In fact this assumption is seldom fulfilled except for perhaps some bulk agricultural goods. Many, if not most decisions are in reality made in "lumps." For instance you do not buy a house per square centimeter or build a bridge per meter; you either build a bridge in whole or not at all.

Ecological economics and the market model

All this, however, from the point of view of ecological economics, does not mean that the market model should be abandoned. Environmental problems are so complex and difficult that all tools should be taken into use. And, of course, the mainstream economic model contains a good deal of truth. Even if people are not *homo economicus*, that is all the time selfish and calculating, most of us react for instance on rising energy or food prices by buying less. So even an ecological economist definitely needs a thorough understanding of the market mechanism. The question is if something is lacking in this view, though. This will be the theme of the next chapter.

Appendix: measuring value when there are no markets: an example with coastal systems

Before going to the next chapter we shall in this appendix have a look at the question of how to behave if we do not have a market and thus not a price, as often is the case with natural resources. In doing this we are at the border between environmental and ecological economics. That is we are trying to mimic the methods of economics to study the problems of ecology.[12]

Figure 4.8. illustrates an attempt to combine the insights from natural and social sciences in the context of the management of the coasts of the world. The first two upper levels deal with the ecology of the coasts. The third level is the interface between the ecology and the economy and the lower half of the figure is about the economics, i.e. how to measure the value of the different products and services which the coastal system in total produces.

The first level (boundary conditions) may perhaps be said to define the coast as a physical system. As there is no technological solution in the sense that it could be carried out at zero cost we must, as with the greenhouse effect, for the first time in history, perhaps, as a species adapt to the situation of absolute limits. In other words, and contrary to the usual economic jargon, this is a zero-sum game (or a perhaps negative-sum game).

And also, contrary to the *political* jargon (of the financial crisis at the end of the first decade of the second millennia), there is "no growth track to go back to." That is, there is no *sustainable* growth track to go back to. This means, that, by and large, we have to learn to manage our (coastal) resources so as to keep human activity within the boundary conditions of nature.

This management, which is quite the opposite to the ideology of growth, is something which is still under development but something which has to be learned and applied. In fact this means only a returning – from a relatively short excursion into a world where the limits were only put by economic growth – to a world where the limits are again determined by nature. This is to be interpreted not only metaphorically but concretely. Speaking about the coastal regions, this means that we have to learn to consider and live with nature's variations, such as currents,

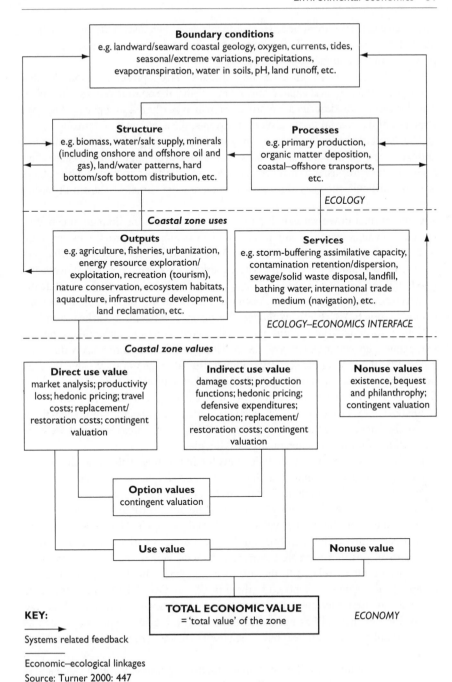

Figure 4.8 Coastal zone functions, uses and values

tides, seasonal variations, and, very probably, also increased extreme variations due to the rising sea level. This in turn means that we have to adapt our production processes to the boundary conditions.

Going further down Figure 4.8 the "structure" box represents a more detailed description of the natural capital "raw material" that the coastal system consists of. The "process" box describes the processes which partly use and partly shape the structure of the coastal system, such as currents, the ecological system and so on.

The "structure" and "processes" may then be seen as giving rise to "outputs" and "services," which are not, of course, quite easy to distinguish from each other. Some of these are easier to measure, such as fisheries and agriculture while others are more difficult, such as nature conservation or local climate, or storm-buffering capacity.

Going further downwards in Figure 4.8, we now reach the domain of economics, i.e. the valuation of the outputs and services in monetary terms. This valuation is usually divided into three classes: *direct use value, indirect use value* and *nonuse values*. Since there often exist no markets for these types of resources and goods and services, we have to rely on other indirect methods to try to evaluate the natural resource in question.[13] For instance, one commonly used method is *contingent valuation* (CV). Briefly explained, this means that people are asked to answer (carefully formulated) questions about their valuation of a resource. Thus, people may value a coastal area for, say, the possibility of fishing (direct use value), the possibility of enjoying the scenery (indirect use value) and/or may value the area because they think that it belongs to the cultural or natural heritage of the world or that it is a place of unique ecological qualities (nonuse value). In such a case (which may also be called existence value), it means that people would be willing to pay for guaranteeing the bare existence of this coastal area, even if there were no possibility for them to personally visit the place.

In other words, the direct use value plus the indirect use value plus the nonuse value together give the total value for the resource and this is what we try to estimate by using the CV-method. This means that in an ideal situation, we may, even if we do not have a functioning market, still be able to calculate a value that is much greater than the market value (which may be zero). Thus, many environmental economists think that this will help to put non-market goods in a "more competitive" position compared to marketed goods. Perhaps needless to say, there are many problems related to the use of contingent valuation. People may not comprehend the questions posed to them in CV-studies, at least not in the same sense as the questioner, they may lie to their own advantage, and so on. True, the use of the CV-method has not remained without criticism. Expressions such as "pick a number – any number" have been used to characterize the alleged ambiguousness of CV.

It is clear that this simplified system in practice is extremely complicated and is very hard to assess. However, the CV-method has been used, and it has developed into a veritable industry,[14] which might, perhaps, be seen as a sign of the fact that there is more to the CV-method than academic merit.

This may be easier to understand if we look at perhaps the most well-known application of the CV-method. This is the assessment of the damages from the oil slick of the tanker *Exxon Valdez* in Prince William Sound, Alaska. The estimated cost (by CV) of the willingness to pay to prevent a similar accident was at its lowest value $2.9 billion with the mean of $7.2 billion.

So far estimates of damages and thus legitimized demands for compensation in big environmental accidents have been based on "objective facts," such as soiled beaches, a loss in fish catches and so on. Now, the use of the CV-method implies that a monetary value should/could also be given to nonuse value, i.e. such as what value people placed on the existence of untouched nature or what rights animals living in this area were perceived to have to live undisturbed or endangered by pollution . The question asked by many – and certainly Exxon and insurance companies – was whether in such a case there would be any limit to what people could demand in compensation for damages.

An important consequence of this concern was that the National Oceanic and Atmospheric Administration (NOAA) established a committee with the purpose of answering the question "Is CV a valid method for determining the lost economic value from natural resource damages?" The panel[15] concluded "that CV studies can produce estimates reliable enough to be the starting point of a judicial process of damage assessment, including lost passive-use value." The importance of this conclusion should not be underestimated: it was thus considered possible, by this prominent panel, to scientifically measure (loss of) natural capital and even nonuse (existence) value – providing that the study meets the required standards.[16]

Chapter 5

Ecological economics: the science of sustainability

Ecological economics is sometimes described as a system of knowledge that tries to bring together the housekeeping of humans (economics) and the housekeeping of nature (ecology). As we have seen so far, this is not an easy task. Today it is no exaggeration to say that there is a large conflict between these two. For tens of thousands of years the relation between human and nature's housekeeping was unproblematic – at least from the point of view of nature's housekeeping, because the human economy was an "infinitesimally" small part of nature's economy. Somewhere along the road, something took place that disturbed nature's economy, first locally and then regionally. What happened were the rise of agriculture and the implementation of monocultures; the biodiversity of the land declined. However, as these large-scale agricultural systems were tied to one place – as opposed to hunting or a slash-and-burn systems – they had to be sustainable, working as closed systems, with quite little input from the outside – except for energy from the sun. With the cultural change that came with agriculture also the first economic science was born, that of bookkeeping – the essence of housekeeping.

There was a seed of change implanted in this monocultural system, however, in that it implied specialization (one-sidedness, compared to the hunter-gatherer economy). For this the natural remedy was – trade. As agriculture/societies grew bigger and technology developed, trade could extend even further. In, and with, this process, the innovations in transportation and weaponry flourished and empires rose and cultures spread with trade (and wars). Kingdoms rose and some rudimentary conception of an economics of a kingdom (state) began to develop. To make a long story short, this, eventually, led to the first essential school of economics, which was, however, really an extension of the king's economy (bookkeeping) to embrace the whole kingdom, and thereby keep account of the kingdom's riches. This economic system was called Mercantilism.[1] It is important to keep in mind that the economic system at this time was essentially stationary; economic growth did not exist in its modern meaning, there was growth mainly in the form of geographic expansion (of agriculture and simple manufacture and construction).[2]

Growth, in the modern sense, came about with the invention and spreading of non-animal and non-human productive resources: the industrial revolution. With the industrial revolution the pace and the scale of natural resource use reached virtually another level of efficiency. The simple, individual processes of handicraft could now be cut into pieces as already Adam Smith could observe – and so well describe in the beginning of the *Wealth of Nations* (1776). In this book the mercantile (and mental) shackles on the economy were broken, and the ruler of the economy was no more the king (as in mercantilism). Instead, the individual, free man was now placed on the overthrown throne – at this stage mainly as producer, later also as consumer. The result of this freedom was to be the market,[3] by which, like with "an invisible hand," the outcome would be the best conceivable. The impact of this idea, in terms of efficiency and economic growth, should not be underestimated (see Chapter 4). As regards the relation towards nature, the *Wealth of Nations*, as well as other works of the classical tradition of economics, or Political Economy as it was called then, held the "dismal" view of a coming stationary state, mainly on the basis of the expectation of diminishing returns of land.

The industrial revolution is generally pictured as the heroic victory of reason. However, it is clear that this victory was won only at an enormous cost in both human suffering and environmental degradation. It was not until the co-evolutive product of the assembly line and other specializing inventions that mass consumption could be realized and "scientific management" of nature could take place.[4] And now it was time to cast away the image of the dismal science from Political Economy which now became Economics. In combination with political democracy (and different political ideas) it also became the main instrument for growth.

The economics school of macroeconomics (Keynesianism), which in contrast to "the classics" saw the market's self-balancing traits to be defective (or too slow), required an active policy role for the government to stabilize the economy on the right track. Since "blood, sweat and tears" are not the way to win the people's votes in democratic elections, it is only natural that growth became – and as a matter of fact still is – the mantra of economic policy.[5]

However, many ecological economists look critically on both the "victory and the reason" of the industrial revolution. That is even if it seems that Malthus's prophesy of the catastrophe, which would follow falling productivity in agriculture in relation to population growth, failed in *agricultural production*, it might well be that the limits of the Earth will be met in other places such as with global warming (see Chapter 6). In the same vein the rationality of economic thinking might, even if it is logical in the short run, not be logical in the long run. This will be our main theme in the section on sustainability below.

The first political document where these sustainability problems received careful attention was the Brundtland report.[6] The central point of view in this report is: "development that meets the needs of the present without compromising the ability of future generations to meet their own needs." The Brundtland report may perhaps be seen mainly as a document to encourage developing countries to growth. In the two decades that has passed since the report was published the discussion about sustainability has flourished in a lot of directions. The main contribution of the Brundtland report was the introduction of the concept of sustainability to the general awareness of media and politicians and citizens. In other words it gave birth to a development concept that provided an alternative way of thinking about long-run economic policy different from that of economic growth.[7]

We will soon return to the discussion concerning different thoughts about sustainability. Before that, however, we shall look in greater detail at why the traditional view of the economy falls short of a genuine and rational economics.

To understand this, it is necessary to look at how the picture of the standard-mainstream view of the economic process differs from that of ecological economics. In its simplest form the economic view can be pictured as in Figure 5.1. This is the so-called two-sector model of the economy. The two sectors are the two main types of agents in the economy: households (consumers) and business (producers) and this is the model upon which the supply–demand diagrams in the preceding chapter are built. Households demand goods and services for which they pay (spending). On the other hand (as households are assumed to be the owners of all resources) they sell or hire these to business. The households then in turn get paid (depending on what kind of productive resources (work, capital, etc.) they sell) in the form of wages, interest and profits. This they in turn spend, and so on. In Figure 5.1 the inner arrows picture this circulation of income in the economy.

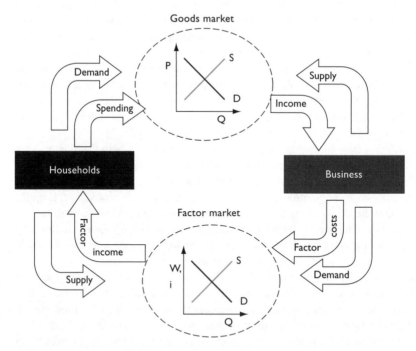

Figure 5.1 Goods–money flow from households to business or from business to households, the standard view

The outer arrows in Figure 5.1 show how supply and demand meet on the goods and factor markets respectively and thus, through the adaption of prices, the goods and factors are *allocated* between different uses. Figure 5.1 can thus be called a model of the economy as a *closed system* where resources and money circulate. How long can this circulation go on; forever perhaps?

Thinking about this for a while reveals the fundamental flaw of this model from an environmental point of view. As we all know, production and consumption require *physical* resources and produces (besides goods) also waste. For the economy to function as in Figure 5.1, it would literally be using its own waste as input, which is a physical impossibility.[8] It is possible to imagine, though, that when there is *enough of nature*, it would be possible to describe an economy as a closed system. In a hunter–gatherer economy nature is so big compared to the (human) economy that there is no need to consider physical inputs and outputs. It is easy to imagine a cowboy in nineteenth-century (North) America riding towards the sunset, shooting a buffalo, and then cutting some meat from the animal, which he grills over a fire. After drinking his coffee he pours what is left on the fire to put it out, leaves the rest of the animal at this site and continues his ride. Nature will take care of the rest. The coyotes will soon be there, and in a few days nothing will be left except perhaps for some bones, which also soon will disappear and disintegrate. Following this picture this economy is called a "cowboy economy."

The economic system today, however, is not insignificant in relation to nature. On the contrary, the economy has invaded huge parts of nature, in different dimensions, such as land, forest, seas, mining, the atmosphere and so on. This has happened to the extent that nature's economy is not only disturbed, but in many cases destroyed to the degree that we cannot know whether it can recover. We daily read in the newspapers about new catastrophes in different areas.[9] Thus, it is not a possibility anymore to rely on nature's assimilative capacity to take care of our pollution; it has to be taken care of by ourselves, with technical means. In fact this technical development has also been a prerequisite for the history of human expansion and welfare. Thus it is an impossibility that the great cities of today would exist without such everyday equipment as the water closet.[10]

Thus, the cowboy economy might be seen as a reason for the situation we are living in today. In fact one of the first ecological economists, Kenneth Boulding (1966), coined the term "spaceman economy"[11] to contrast the two ways of living. By this term he wanted to emphasize that the Earth is a closed system. The

> "spaceman" economy, in which the Earth has become a single spaceship, without unlimited reservoirs of anything, either for extraction or for pollution, and in which, therefore, man must find his place in a cyclical ecological system which is capable of continuous reproduction of material form even though it cannot escape having inputs of energy.

The contrast between these two economies can described as in Figure 5.2. The figure illustrates that, in both types of systems, the economy is an *open*

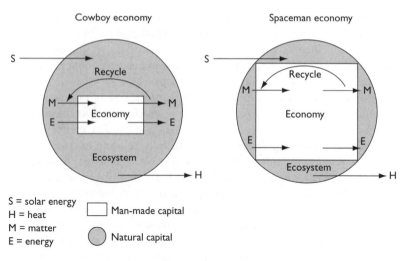

Figure 5.2 The economy as an open subsystem of the ecosystem

subsystem of the ecosystem and that the Earth as an ecosystem is closed. This means that the stuff that goes in and out is energy, while matter circulates within the system. Energy here is in the form of solar radiation (S) which goes out from the system in the form of heat radiation (H). This radiation can be seen as constant over time. As can be seen, matter and energy are inputs and outputs to the economy from the ecosystem. We combine matter and energy (e.g. metal ore, fossil fuels) to make cars and eventually this ends up as heat, metal scrap, etc. As can be seen, the difference between the two economies is that the economy part is much smaller in relation to (to the basically constant) ecosystem part.

The economy may also be called *man-made capital* and the ecosystem *natural capital*. This means that a parallel may be drawn between these two, which in turn means that both are seen as productive stocks, which produces goods (in the wide sense) or rather *services* for us. The fundamental economic question (i.e. the long-run economic question) is, then: Which form of capital produces the services most effectively?

In a moment we shall return to this question. However, it is already at this stage of importance to note the limits as to how widely this question can and should be applied: There are certain spheres of nature – life-sustaining functions – that cannot be replaced. For instance, on the most general and large scale: the atmosphere cannot be replaced by an artificial system. Indeed, on closer inspection, all ecosystems, big or small, have traits that make them (almost) impossible to substitute with something else, and at least not with man-made capital. Even if technological solutions may exist, such as, say, machines for dissolving carbon-dioxide into oxygen and carbon, they may be extremely costly compared to natural systems. In other cases destroyed local ecosystems may be replaced by other ones, but the adaption may take a very long time. In general the question of *substitutability* is of utmost importance for *sustainability*, and the ordinary tools of economics (which assume substitutability) are as such inappropriate tools for analyzing sustainability.

Now, the fundamental difference between the cowboy and the spaceman economies[12] is the relative size of the economy, that is the whole human socio-technologic system in relation to the ecosystem. The bigger the relative part of the economy, the less room there is for the ecosystem to take care of the recycling (less absorption capacity). The Earth has more and more begun to resemble a spaceship, where practically everything must be recycled. In other words, the Earth must be conceived of as a closed system for which the adequate model or picture is a spaceship – and not the Wild West.[13]

So if the standard economic model of the closed (or isolated) economy is no more valid, what does ecological economics have to offer instead? As envisaged above, the problem is not that the economic model is closed as such, but that the closure is "shortcut" in the sense that the *absolute* limits are not acknowledged.[14] What are these limits, then? These are the Earth, with its non-renewable – but mainly its renewable – resources and which sustains all life (and the economy) with that.

Interestingly, the basic principle behind sustainability that can be viewed as a common denominator for both physics and economics[15] can be found in the *second law of thermodynamics* – the *law of entropy*. Simply put, this is about explaining the phenomenon of irreversibility ("the time's arrow") in nature: in a closed system the differences (measured in, for example, temperature of molecules) tend to even out. This in turn means that if we assume that the universe is a closed system, the degree of order will decrease, that is the universe's entropy (disorder) will increase. The interpretation from the economic point of view of this is that the economic process means that the resources and goods are used up: concentrations of minerals such as ore or oil wells are used as inputs in the economic process and the output is dispersed in the environment. Some of this can, as we know, be organized so that the materials can be used again, that is recycled. However, recycling does not mean that the entropy law has been eliminated. The entropy law is still working in the sense that the energy (at least from the human point of view) is used up for ever. As all recycling requires the input of energy, the entropy law is still working however effective the process may be. Otherwise we would be dealing with a *perpetuum mobile* (eternal mover).

This idea (of how entropy works in the economic system) has often been conveyed by the entropy hourglass (see Figure 5.3). Here the ultimate resource (and unlimited from the human point of view) is the solar radiation flow which is generated by the sun. This flow downwards in the hourglass reflects time's arrow – which is not, like a real hourglass, reversible.

Some of the solar radiation has been stocked during millions of years in the ground in the form of coal and oil (organic material concentrated in energy-rich compounds by high pressure). Compared to the solar flow which is renewable, the terrestrial flow, however, is (practically) non-renewable and will be used up within a few hundred years.

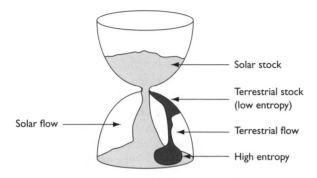

Figure 5.3 The entropy hourglass

The solar radiation becomes useful through the photosynthesis of plants and microbes, which, in turn, provides suitable food for animals such as *Homo sapiens*. The food provides minerals and energy for the animals which upon their death will again be used by for example larvae, fungi, plants and so the cycle goes on.

Thus, to understand the true meaning of sustainability, the concept of entropy is necessary, because (as pictured in the entropy hourglass view) it illustrates clearly what it means to live in a sustainable manner: it requires us to adapt our use to what flows through the slim "waistline" of the hourglass. It may be possible to use this limited radiation in a more efficient way,[16] but in any case the bottle neck comes against us sooner or later. This means that, in the long run (but the sooner the better) we have to adapt to *renewable resources*, that is organic resources. The *non-renewable* resources may seem to exist in plenty, but from a sustainability view these have only limited importance. That is from a sustainability perspective they have only importance so far as they are not used in a wasteful way, used to create renewable ways of producing energy. Many non-renewable resources can be recycled. However, as noted, all recycling requires the input of energy.

The entropy hourglass illustrates that practically all energy that we have on the Earth originates from the sun. The higher up in the hourglass, the higher is the entropy (the amount of useful energy). When we go down in the hourglass, entropy of the energy rises; it is used up, at least from the human perspective. Part of the energy (also originating from the sun) is stored as fossil energy, which also when burned goes from a higher form of organization to a lower, useless form. The entropy hourglass allegory thus illustrates how ecological economists look at the world, also like a closed system, but focusing on the physical limits, not the narrowly economic ones.

What we have done so far in this chapter is to show that the economy is dependent of and tied to the physical reality, which is actually a restoration of what the classical economists had firmly in their mind, but which was forgotten with the rise of neoclassical/marginal analysis; *absolute scarcity* gave way for *relative scarcity*: the classicists (Smith, Malthus, Ricardo) were interested in questions of growth and distribution; while the neoclassicists asked "why an egg cost more than a cup of tea".[17]

However, there is a further important link to the closed economic system that needs to be considered. This link is related to the view that the economy is embedded, as well as in the ecosystem, also in the social system or social institutions.

The insights from ecology and economics have to be applied within a social/ political environment (so to speak) – and more and more often also without the political system. Generally speaking, the social dimension deals with the points which economics, strictly speaking, does not usually deal with, that is economic policy – again, in a wide sense. With this we mean economic policy, not as calculating the optimal level of interest or some other economic variable, but economic policy when aspects of distribution and justice are also under consideration. That is, in questions for example concerning global environmental policy, there is often a lack of political infrastructure, or governance, that have to be formed if real results are going to be achieved. Unequal income distribution, different political cultures, developmental stage, history and other aspects have a role to play in the formation of these structures.

Some of these features are depicted in Figure 5.4[18] (in a somewhat simplified manner). This figure is in principle similar to Figure 5.3 except that here we have implanted the economic system into "social institutions." This represents property rights, economic power and income distribution but also stands for other types of institutions including norms, laws and so on. Other forms of capital are discussed in Chapter 2.

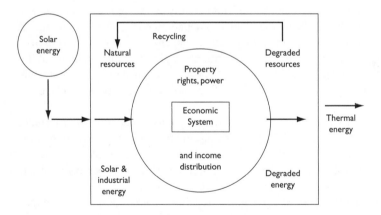

Figure 5.4 The economy embedded in social institutions and in the ecosystem

Different ways of thinking about sustainability[19]

It should be evident by now that if there is one concept that unites ecological economics, it is sustainability. With this we mean that ecological economists are very
serious about making sustainability a cornerstone of long-run economic policy.
However, the problem seems to be that sustainability also unites everyone else.
Perman *et al.* (1999) begin their review of different sustainability concepts by the
following quote by Pezzey (1997): "I see little point in expanding the collection
of fifty sustainability definitions which I made in 1989, to the five thousand definitions that one could readily find today." Today there surely exist even more
definitions of sustainability than when Pezzey wrote. There is a "scarcity of
plenty" here. This is perfectly understandable, because there are so many interests
involved. There are for example those who want to shape a concise and strict definition of sustainability and at the other end of the spectrum we have those who
want to have an all-encompassing concept which everyone could agree on.

In what follows we shall very briefly look at a few examples of sustainability
concepts, going from more narrow to wider definitions.

Sustainability as non-declining consumption (utility)

The "natural" way for economists to deal with sustainability is probably to look at
what happens to people's utility or consumption over time. As in comparisons of
consumption between nations one may take a representative individual (measured
in consumption per capita) and then measure this in consecutive generations (that
is we move from *intra-generational* to *inter-generational* comparison).

Consumption should here not be understood only as "shopping" (material consumption), but also as enjoying "environmental goods", such as hiking. A
non-declining consumption, then, means that consumption should not diminish,
but should be equal or increase over generations. A plausible interpretation of this
rule is that the generation today should not consume so much as to put future generations' consumption level at risk of diminishing compared to today's
generation.

This concept has been reached from different points of departure. For instance
Hartwick (Hartwick's rule (1977)) defines sustainability in terms of a saving rule,
which briefly states that if the net revenue from non-renewable resources is
invested in renewable capital the consumption level can be kept (under certain
conditions) constant over time.

Robert Solow (1988), again, gives the Rawls's *maximin* criterion (see Chapter
3) an intertemporal angle, and interprets this as a criterion which states that the
undiscounted (per capita) utility (consumption) (see the discussion about discounting in Chapter 6) should be constant over time.

Sustainability as maintaining production opportunities

Although, of course, considerations about the insufficiency of the resource basis were a motivating factor for specifying sustainability in this way its main emphasis is on consumption (utility) and that might be seen as a rather restricted view. A more proper focus would be on the resource basis itself. Instead of specifying some menu for future generations we should give them productive capabilities. That is we should bequeath to them capital in a wide sense and let them decide how to use it. Solow has formulated this principle (Sustainability as maintenance of production opportunities), as follows:

> [The cake-eating problem] is a damagingly narrow way to pose the question. We have no obligation to our successors to bequeath a share of this or that resource. Our obligation refers to a generalised productive capacity or, even wider, to certain standards of consumption/living possibilities over time.[20]

The present generation has very little knowledge of future technology and preferences, therefore the present generation cannot be demanded to bequeath to the next generation anything more than the potential to do as well as we have done. This definition of sustainability has much to it. It reflects a liberal, non-paternalistic attitude, emphasizing the freedom of choice. In addition it also appeals to our sense of historicity: our parents did as well as they could and left the "house and land" in at least as good shape as they got it. Can we fairly or logically be asked for more than this? On closer inspection the following problems may be noted:

1. "To do as well as we have done": that requires that we have done well, or at least that we believe that we have done so. However, today the knowledge of the state of the world is such that this is increasingly in doubt. We may have done as well as we could in some respects, but still feel that there is something wrong in this. Should we continue with this; should we pass wrongness on to future generations? This type of thinking could perhaps be called "hands off liberalism," because maybe future generations would like to inherit something *more* than a generalized productive capacity, e.g. a "specialized capacity" in which a piece of advice (in terms of a more particular rule) would be embedded?
2. The other, closely related point to this view is just to look at the problem in terms of *generalized productive capacity*. This, which in emphatic light may be seen as increasing the freedom of choice for future generations, may quickly turn to a license to use all resources freely; none is put in a prior position, man-made and natural resources are treated on an equal standing. This is clearly against the view of limited substitutability held by most ecological economists.

Sustainability as non-declining natural capital

From the point of view of ecological economics, however, to look at sustainability in terms of a generalized productive capacity is an unsound, if not absurd, point of departure. Natural capital (capital that cannot be produced) should be seen as qualitatively different from other forms of capital: man-made capital can always[21] be prepared by men – provided that there is enough natural capital – but the inverse is not true. Natural capital is a genuine and unique creation of evolution. This asymmetry also adds (more) weight to the concept of substitutability which is a central if not the central point of dispute when sustainability is concerned. If we believe that resources are perfectly *substitutable*, we think of them as if it were possible to build a house from whatever combination of bricks and wood we like: 1 percent may be bricks and 99 percent wood or something in between (perhaps we would also like to put in some windows, but that can technically be counted as bricks). We may think of bricks as man-made capital and wood as natural capital.[22] So whatever combination we choose, it is technically feasible to do so; brick and wood are perfectly substitutable. But how far is it possible to push this assumption? In some cases there is no substitutability at all: if you want to make water there is only one[23] combination of the two gases oxygen and hydrogen that will do: H_2O. If we have added more of either gas atom than the combination of two hydrogen and one oxygen, it will be superfluous.

But perhaps, if we think of some less exotic production than that of water, it might be possible to envisage more substitutability? Take town-planning: this might be a choice about whether to use much natural capital (land) and little man-made capital (buildings) or much man-made capital and little natural capital (i.e. higher buildings).

In practice, however, substitutability is rather limited, and in many cases impossible. This is true especially for life-supporting systems of the Earth, such as the seas or the atmosphere. And the fact is that we know very little about if and where the limit of collapse of such systems lays. However, we do know more and more about how parts of ecosystems hinge together, and that there may arise great problems if some chain is cut off.[24]

If one does not accept the view that nature is just another form of capital and that there is a limit to the substitutability of natural resources by man-made ones, it is reasonable to focus on natural resources (capital) as the critical resource; sustainability should be seen as development where *natural capital is not declining through time*. This view has been put forward by for example Pearce *et al.* (1989: 37): *"Each generation should inherit at least a similar natural environment"* (emphasis in the original). Besides non-substitutability (discussed above), Pearce *et al.* mention three other reasons in favor of their view: uncertainty, irreversibility and equity (discussed in Chapter 3).

Although this term is obviously considerably less general than "general productive capacity" discussed in the section above, it is still quite general. Furthermore, there is a fundamental dispute as to how substitutable different forms of natural capital are. One view could claim that all parts of the ecosystem should be conserved because they are interdependent and thus that there is no substitutability. Others can point, on the basis of geological evidence, to the many occurrences of mass-destruction of species in the Earth's history. And as we still can observe functioning ecosystems, it is hard to say what is indispensable and what is substitutable.

Of course, one great problem here is what is *natural capital* and how we should count it. For instance, if we look at the problem from the *anthropocentric* view, then natural capital is everything that produces services for humans, starting from bacteria and algae to whole ecosystems. If we take a *biocentric* or *ecocentric* point of departure then the picture is greatly complicated and we find ourselves (as humans) in a situation where, say, all species have their rights to the existing natural capital, among whom we must obviously also count ourselves as the animal *Homo sapiens*.

There are obviously no formulas on how to substitute one ton of a certain biomass with some form of other biomass. Some "biomass" may have lower entropy than others, in different senses, have more complexly organized genetics and so on.

On the basis of the difficulty of valuing natural resources the constant natural capital approach has been quite heavily criticized: "no fully satisfactory method yet exists for valuing environmental resources, and it may be that none could ever exist" (See Perman *et al.* 1999: 60). No doubt, great difficulties abound in valuating all kinds of environmental resources. However, the valuation of natural capital is not specific to the non-declining natural capital view of sustainability, but on the contrary one that all sustainability concepts have to handle somehow. If not, it may seem doubtful that the view in question takes sustainability seriously.

And lastly, to admit that there are great problems with quantitative measurement and comparison of natural resources, this does not mean that decisions of preserving natural capital on an approximately "non-declining" level could not be done. After all, seen against the background of the environmental history of humankind this species has managed to make sound decisions for almost all of the time of its existence without having any sophisticated environmental valuation tools whatsoever, except for sound common sense. And, on a positive view, if one thinks about the development of human (as well as animal) health indicators that has taken place within the past few decades, why could such a development be impossible as to ecosystem health indicators?

Sustainability as maintenance of a sustainable yield of resource services

So far we have looked at sustainability specified in terms of consumption, in terms of generalized production capacity and in terms of natural resources (capital). We now turn to a concept that is known to us from an earlier section in this chapter (from discussing the "Spaceship Earth"), *the steady state economy*. As will be remembered this is an economy from which the input and the output (matter and energy) from and to the ecosystem are equal to each other over time (i.e. that they are in equilibrium). However since it is difficult to measure matter and energy as the general concepts they are, a measure has been proposed by Daly.[25] This measure, which he calls the *Comprehensive Efficiency Identity*,[26] can be written as follows:

$$
\frac{\text{MMK services gained}}{\substack{\text{NK services}\\\text{sacrificed}}} = \frac{\text{MMK services gained}}{\text{MMK stock}} \times \frac{\text{MMK stock}}{\text{thruput}} \times \frac{\text{thruput}}{\text{NK stock}} \times \frac{\text{NK stock}}{\substack{\text{NK services}\\\text{sacrificed}}}
$$

$$
(1) \qquad\qquad (2) \qquad\qquad (3) \qquad\qquad (4)
$$

In this view, it is not production ("GDP") that should be maximized in the economy, but the services we get from the stock of capital that it rests on. On the left-hand side of the identity this is estimated by setting the services gained from man-made capital (MMK) in relation to natural capital (NK) services that must be sacrificed, since man-made capital can only be created by using natural capital.

Thus, in building for example a hydroelectric power station in a river, the service gained from this is mainly electricity (which of course cannot be enjoyed as such but in connection with other man-made capital such as bulbs, washing machines and so on). The services sacrificed when such a project is carried through are the services lost in the building of the dam and the basin created. Such service losses include the landscape and the scenery, extinction or risk of extinction of local species of aquatic animals, reduced fish movement to their spawning grounds and so on.

All creating of man-made capital, such as building a simple cottage involves a loss in natural capital services. This occurs in the form of used ground for the cottage, the trees that have to be cut down to give place to the cottage and the logs to give the material for building the cottage and so on. However, such projects are usually not of the scale to produce irreversible effects as such large-scale projects as the dam building just mentioned, which may involve loss of species or even whole ecosystems.

The identity (measure) can be refined in to smaller parts, as the ratios (1) to (4): ratio 1 is the efficiency of services which can be decomposed into design efficiency, allocative efficiency and distributive efficiency. Design efficiency is the "engineering" efficiency. When you build a cottage there are certain rules to be followed such as keeping the angles right in the corners and making a water-tight roof. Allocative efficiency can be exemplified by the decision to build the roof of copper instead of wood or tiles. An example of increased distributive efficiency would be the wood used for the cottage building had been used to provide firewood for, say, 100 sub-Saharan families for one year.[27]

Ratio 2 is the durability of the man-made capital stock. The better and more carefully the cottage is built, the longer will it give services. If I build the house of non-fertilized naturally grown wood rather than "farmed" (fertilized, efficiently grown) wood, my house will last much longer.

Ratio 3 is the relation between the yield and the stock, that is how much can be harvested without diminishing the stock. If I begin to farm trout in a pond near my cottage instead of letting it be in its natural state, this will very probably increase the amount of trout I can collect from the pond.

Ratio 4 increases by letting the stock grow or sacrificing less services. When I plant more trout into my pond it will probably increase the trout growth, but at the expense of other services received from the pond (e.g. a more diverse bio-system), and which thus have to be sacrificed.

It is of course true for this sustainability conception as well, that even if the basic idea can be presented in a neat formula (identity), the practical application might be a much more difficult (and "dirty") manual task. We will come back to Daly and Cobb's (1989) measurements later in this chapter.

Sustainability as a state which satisfies minimum conditions of ecosystem stability and resilience over time

Ecological economics is sometimes defined as combining economics and ecology. In honesty it should be admitted that there is a long way still ahead if this ambitious goal is to be reached. Most books on ecological economics contain quite little material from ecology, not to speak about reconciliation. The nearest we come to such a view here is the definition of sustainability as an *ecological system being sustainable if it is resilient.* One definition of resilience in this connection[28] is:

> "Resilience" as applied to ecosystems, or to integrated systems of people and natural resources, has three defining characteristics:

- The amount of change the system can undergo and still retain the same controls on function and structure (still be in the same state – within the same domain of attraction)
- The degree to which the system is capable of self-organization
- The ability to build and increase the capacity for learning and adaptation.

This definition differs quite a lot from the "popular" conception of resilience, that is the ability to recover from a minor shock, and involves a lot of complex relations which we do not have space to go into here. However, it should be noted that in this interpretation it is a question about integrated systems of people and natural resources, not only ecosystems with no or little interference from humans.

Of paramount focus here is of course the human ability for learning and adaptation. Man's actions have placed him in a position (the spaceship economy) where there is very little possibility to rely on resilience of "human-free systems" alone. Rather the question is to know, when and where to intervene.

As noted earlier in this discussion we have a problem with the information about how resilient an ecosystem is, and especially knowing in advance about this. Because of the great complexity of ecosystems[29] it is difficult to know that even if an ecosystem earlier has been observed to be resilient, whether this will be the case when the system is struck by a new (and perhaps somehow different) shock. It seems fair to say that the empirical research on resilience is just in its beginning. As such it is a part of a larger project of evaluating the total value of natural capital (cf. e.g. Millennium Ecosystem Assessment (MEA) 2005) including such concepts as looking at ecosystems' resilience for example as a form of insurance.[30]

Sustainability as (global) consensus

In this category we finally come to the widest view of sustainability. Although admitting the importance of the ecological limits, it most strongly emphasizes the role of the political discussion and process. The main point in this perspective is that sustainability could, and should not, be achieved by coercion. Or one could perhaps say that, to be truly sustainable, there should be a large consensus on the process. Perman *et al.* (1999) refer to de Graaf *et al.* (1996) as one example of this school of thought. De Graaf characterizes the *traditional* sustainability view as focusing on two points: (1) it recognizes that the economy is part of the ecosystem, determines the carrying capacity of the ecosystem and then needs legislation so humans do not exceed this capacity; (2) it conceptualizes environmental decline as external costs, which are then *internalized* (by taxes, for instance) with the aid of the price system.

What is wrong, then, for example with traditional ecological economics, which takes into consideration both these forms of sustainability (and in many cases goes further than this)? According to de Graaf *et al.* this would ideally be "one that searches for consensus between all the people involved in the development of a socio-environmental system as a whole" (1996: 210). This consensus, which is obviously not easy to achieve, is however necessary, because a solution "[i]f tight ecological standards cause poverty, or if pricing of natural resources causes unemployment, sustainable development will remain beyond our grasp"(1996: 209). It is easy to imagine that without consensus, the frustration about some unreached goals may lead to even more serious consequences than those already mentioned, such as outright war and terror. Such extreme action may always be seen as a collapse in sustainability, almost disregarding whatever sustainability view one subscribes to, since, besides being of resources, they will trigger a lot of multiple misallocation in the form of defensive expenditures.

The main problem, both from a traditional economic view as well as from the ecological economic view, with this sustainability concept is of course related to the negotiations costs. How much does the achieving of consensus cost in terms of time and resources and/or how large should the consensus be? Is a majority larger then 50 percent enough or should it be a perfect consensus. And as the negotiations go on: how much time do we have before we have gone over some important ecological limit?

Measuring sustainability

Against the background of this chapter so far, it must be obvious that, as there are a lot of different ways of interpreting sustainability, there must also be a corresponding variety of approaches of measuring sustainability. Furthermore, as we turn to areas farther away from the traditional economic sphere when we look at sustainability, we also have turned from the possibility of measuring utility and consumption to measuring other even more difficult aspects to quantify, such as resilience and consensus.

And as in many cases, it is perhaps easier to assess principles than to find concepts that would exactly correspond to these in practice (nature). Furthermore, and as noted earlier, there are "moral risks" involved in putting a price on everything (the economistic fallacy).[31] For instance, many would claim that natural values such as natural sceneries or life-supporting systems are "invaluable" and that extending economic principles to all walks of life is a "risky business"[32] which, in other values may be pushed away.

However, even if admitting this, there is the other side of the coin: if, for instance, the development of the gas fields in Montana requires that the millennial paths of animals are cut off (and these are thus sacrificed), if we do not try to count the value of this, are we not "sweeping the problem under the carpet"?

Another, closely related, attitude to the problems of measuring natural capital is the one that there exist no reliable prices for it – and there may never be. However, it is difficult to see what conclusions we should draw from this. Should we be confident by measuring sustainability by looking at consumption alone, because this gives us a "safe" value, resting on "sound economic principles"?

Unfortunately, the conception of non-declining consumption does give us very little advice as far as sustainability is concerned. Looking at the world's per capita consumption for the last decades the consumption as a trend at least has clearly been non-declining. The question is: Has this development been sustainable? Most people would not agree with such a view. To know what is sustainable and how sustainable the Earth's future is we must know something about the longevity of the critical resources. The critical resources in the view of a majority of ecological economists are the natural resources. Thus it would seem that any fact considering these resources is better then none. In terms of the sustainability views reviewed above, this means that as soon as we go outside the first sustainability view (defined with respect to consumption) we need information about the value of natural resources. Even the Solowian view about generalized productive capacity does need a "currency" for translating into a general standard. Thus it seems impossible to escape the measurement problem of natural resources; we have no other option.

And we should not shun qualitative data. In addition to what was just said that some data are better then none, qualitative data, even if lacking the scientific accuracy that is traditionally required in economics, may in fact affect people's way of life. To take one example: the estimates of the ecological *footprint* (see below) may vary a lot (e.g. from 1.3 to 3 earths, i.e. by how much we are over-consuming the Earth's productive capacity). However, even if there is much to be wished for in the accuracy of the figures, it is still obscure to claim that such information would be worthless. On the contrary, if the overwhelming part of the evidence

shows that we are living greatly over our resources, it is, of course, valuable information – if one is interested in sustainability. Thus it might well influence people's
way of living in a more sustainable direction.

What now follows is a brief overview of some of the methods used in measuring sustainability. The point of departure for all such measuring is that traditional
national accounting (System of National Accounts) does not give an adequate
picture of true welfare or sustainability. Why is that? It is perhaps easiest to
explain it like this: the reason is that the system was not created for this purpose.
The purpose of traditional national accounting was to give a tool for economic
policy, and its main goal was to steer the economy in such a way that there would
never again be such mass unemployment as in the crisis in the 1930s. The problem
was not scarcity but over-capacity. Thus, traditional national accounting does not
measure absolute scarcity or external costs (see Chapter 4). Neither does it
measure all contribution to welfare, such as caring and homework. In some cases
traditional national accounting would lead to such absurdities as the following:
assume a big oil slick happened somewhere (as in the case of the *Exxon Valdez*
catastrophe in Alaska); the catastrophe had an enormous long-run disastrous
effect on the flora and fauna in the region and led to a massive renovation operation. As measured in growth in GDP the effect of this was that the welfare in the
economy increased, although of course what happened was a dramatic decrease in
the environmental quality (and thus welfare) and the "growth" was in fact a result
of the expenditures put into restoration.[33]

The ecological footprint

The ecological footprint is a measure of how much pressure the human consumption exerts on the Earth. This pressure of human activity is translated in to a "footprint" that is measured in land (and water). Although the concept maybe difficult
to grasp, at least as far as the translation from different forms of consumption into
the footprint in every case, it seems to be intuitively quite easy to understand. The
reason for this is that the EF can be measured for individuals as well as for, say, the
whole Earth or a firm. Thus, anyone can calculate the ecological impact of one's
consumption (lifestyle) on a footprint calculator, for example on the Internet. Thus
one can easily see how sustainable one's lifestyle is, in that the calculator can tell
you how many earths are needed with your particular lifestyle. For instance the
lifestyle of modern North Americans or Europeans requires five earths.

The ecological footprint is defined by its creators Wackernagel and Rees as:

> the area of productive land and water ecosystems required to produce the
> resources that the population consumes and assimilate the wastes that the
> population produces, wherever on Earth the land and water is located.[34]

Despite many of the advantages mentioned above, the EF has not passed without
critique (see Fiala 2008).

A similar but more straightforward measure is the Material Input Per Service Unit (MIPS) developed by the German Wuppertal Institute.[35] The material input is simply the weight of all materials that are used in the production of a product. As an example, take the production of a book. In the Material Input (MI) we include the material needed for making the paper (felling, papermills, etc.), the material needed for printing, and the material needed for transport of the book. Let us say that this book is of the size that the MI is 100 kg. The Service unit (S) is equal to the times a book is read. If the book is read by one person the MIPS will be 100 (100/1). If the book is read by 100 people, the MIPS is 1 (100/100). Thus we may say that MIPS is a measure of the efficiency of the use of the good as the material input (measured in total weight) (cf. the Comprehensive Efficiency Identity earlier in this chapter).

Index of Sustainable Economic Welfare (ISEW)

This index was shaped by Herman Daly and John Cobb and appeared in their book *For the Common Good* (1989). The reader will recall that Daly and Cobb's conception of sustainability is based on the view that it is not production or consumption as such that counts, but the service that can be acquired from (and relative to) the stock (of natural and man-made capital). ISEW is thus an attempt to capture (to some degree at least) the service function of different forms of capital. Another special feature of ISEW is that it uses an (index of) income inequality as a weight in order to adjust the index. The following forms of services (and loss of services) are calculated: the point of departure for calculations starts from personal consumption per capita which is available from the national accounts. This sum is then weighted, i.e. multiplied by a number that is less than 1, and the more unequal the distribution of the income is in a country the smaller is the number. To this amount different services and costs are added or subtracted, depending on how they contribute to services which are not accounted for in the standard national accounting. The services added are household services (cooking, cleaning, child care), services from household capital (such as dishwashers and washing machines)[36] and infrastructure services (from roads and streets).

Next certain expenditures are subtracted as welfare diminishing. These include public expenditures for health and education of which the biggest part in ISEW is taken to be welfare diminishing, because they are thought to be purely defensive in nature, that is compensating for greater risks of urban and industrial environment.[37] Likewise, expenditures for durable capital goods as well as private education and health expenditures are classified as defensive expenditures. Costs of commuting, urbanization and vehicles are also subtracted as well as national advertising expenditures.[38]

The next point to consider for the ISEW is the more direct cost on nature, such as depletion, noise, erosion and the greenhouse effect. The final calculations for reaching the ISEW are the growth in man-made capital (which has to grow if the productivity is to keep up with the growth in population) and country's net foreign investments.

The purpose of the ISEW is to give a more correct view of the welfare that can be sustained in contrast to GDP, which measures production, without considering how much it uses natural resources.[39] This means that there are terms such as pollution which increases GDP but which is subtracted from it in the ISEW. On the other hand, household work is not counted in the GDP but is in the ISEW, as it is increasing welfare. As ISEW contains both diminishing and increasing factors relative to GDP, it might at first sight be difficult to guess whether the "ISEW-correction" will give a higher or lower value than GDP. However, a second glance at the list will probably convince you that the ISEW will be smaller than GDP, that is the GDP overestimates the effect growth has on our welfare. In fact in calculations for different countries the ISEW might be from about two-thirds to half of the GDP in a period of 40 years.

The genuine progress indicator

The genuine progress indicator actually very much resembles the ISEW, but is further developed:[40]

> The GPI is a variant of the Index of Sustainable Economic Welfare (ISEW), first proposed by Daly and Cobb (1989). Both the GPI and ISEW use the same personal consumption data as GDP but make deductions to account for income inequality and costs of crime, environmental degradation, and loss of leisure and additions to account for the services from consumer durables and public infrastructure as well as the benefits of volunteering and housework. By differentiating between economic activity that diminishes both natural and social capital and activity that enhances such capital, the GPI and its variants are designed to measure sustainable economic welfare rather than economic activity alone.

Let us illustrate with a graph of a "typical" relationship with GPI and GDP, with a calculation for the USA.

Figure 5.5 shows the aggregate of similar factors to those listed above for the ISEW and these are measured per capita to account for the increase in population.[41] Even if the years and the relation between GPI and GDP vary between countries the pattern is typical. This pattern is here illustrated by the fact that since about 1975 the GPI per capita has been practically constant around $15,000. In contrast GDP has continued to grow the whole period, being in year 2004 over two times the GPI. How should this be understood? It means that even if people are able to consume more, have more leisure and enjoy services from the household machines which they buy, this is offset by costs related to for example income inequality, depletion of natural resources, defensive expenditures and undesirable side-effects of growth.

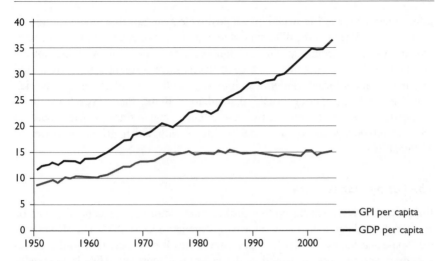

Figure 5.5 USA real GDP and GPI per capita 1950–2004 in $2000 ($ are in 1,000s)

If all this is true, it casts serious doubt on the relation between economic growth and quality of life. This would mean that each extra dollar makes less and less contribution to people's real welfare.[42] So even if economic growth were a strict economic business, that is an action that could adequately be expressed with curves and equations – with no risks for ecological catastrophes and irreversibility whatsoever – this raises the question of the prudence of growth ideology – and at least with growth as a paramount goal of economic policy. This will be discussed in Chapter 9.

If there is a limit, or threshold, in the income level after which economic growth (increased income) does not give increased satisfaction anymore, what conclusions are there to be drawn from this? Should not a simple cost–benefit analysis convince us of the futility of the growth project and make us put our personal resources in a better, that is, in this case, non-material(istic) use?

Of course, all this is stated with the proviso "after a certain income level," and few would claim that happiness has *nothing* to do with income. In greater parts of the world it is clear that this income level is far away, so this is clearly a "disease" that comes with a high living standard. The big question is whether there is a reasonable limit above which income should not rise. Some would certainly see this as an empirical question which could be decided on the basis of measures under discussion here. Others would claim that it is impossible because even if we on the aggregate could show relation with GDP and GPI this does not give any advice as to, say, a maximum personal income regulation, since we are all different, have different values. This could in principle boil down to saying that it is wrong to let income equality have a weight in the index. In any case it is clear that the conception of happiness is not an absolute figure. This means that in our way of living we give a signal about some (supposed) ideal model of life. Abandoning the unsustainable way of life would give a positive and sustainable model for how to lead a life. In other words, if happiness to a great degree is a function of the relative success in "keeping up with the Joneses" (as evidence shows) and not the absolute wealth, does not this – in face of (increasing) absolute scarcity of natural resources – add a further (un)ethical dimension to the goal of growth? If the rich would lower their luxurious/wasteful standard of living, the net result would be greater happiness, but with a lesser resource use, and – since growth would no more stand out as the prior model in life – with much greater prospect of sustainability?

The happy planet index

From this it is but a short step to a further example of how sustainability can be measured or related to happiness: the happy planet index (HPI).[43] The HPI relates the "expected happy life" (life expectancy times life satisfaction) to the corresponding resource use measured as the ecological footprint. Thus it essentially measures how effectively satisfaction is produced. This is novel in that it sets the subjectively felt satisfaction of people in relation to an "objective" measure of productive capacity, the ecological footprint. Economists are traditionally sceptical about what people say about their inner state, as people are always believed to lie to their own advantage (with free riding in view). Only recently, in some quarters at least, has it become decent to use data from "happiness studies," that is studies where people in different parts of the world are asked to position themselves on a scale (usually 0–10) concerning some claims about satisfaction (happiness) in their own life.

    Like the ecological footprint, this measure has the advantage that it can be "personalized," that is everyone can visit a site[44] and have her/his HPI calculated and also get a (decomposed) interpretation in terms of what this means in comparison with people living in other countries, for instance. The HPI gives some interesting and surprising results. For example the "happiest" region in the world is undoubtedly the Caribbean and Central America, with countries such as Colombia, Costa Rica, Dominica, Panama, Cuba, Honduras, Guatemala and El Salvador topping the list. On the end of the list we have developing countries such as Zimbabwe, Swaziland, Burundi and DRCongo (ranking 178–175), but also "transition economies": Ukraine, Estonia and Russia (174–172). The USA is 150th. Most industrialized countries are placed in the latter half of the list – together with developing countries.

What to do: responsible consumption and investment?

After reading the somewhat dismal message so far (which we also meet in the news every day), the reader could (and should) get the feeling that the issue of sustainability is not too well taken care of. The reader may wonder: Is there anything I as a single person can do, and does it make any difference?

It is perhaps something of a moral duty of authors of a book like this to answer this question in the affirmative, and point at some ways of action for the single individual when it comes to contributing to sustainability. There is no room, of course, in a book like this for detailed guides and action-lists,[45] and the (brief) discussion which follows will be kept on a rather general – and critical – level.

Even if not the whole truth, there is some point in saying that the consumer is the king (queen) of the market – at least this is one interpretation of the market model. Without consumption there would be no demand, and without demand there would be no point in production. And consumption there certainly is – in the rich parts of the world, to be sure. The problem with this consumption is that it is steadily rising, measured in quantity of goods, thus offsetting the technical progress achieved in cleaner production.

The reason for this growth is not the growth in income per se, but the fall in the prices of goods, which in turn depends on changes in global production structure. For the USA (and certainly other rich countries too) Juliet Schor (2005a: 310) pictures this as follows:

> Indeed, this recent round of consumption has been particularly significant in its environmental impact. The shift to larger size vehicles, homes, refrigerators, televisions, and other goods has increased materials and energy use. The prevalence of multiple appliances is also materials and energy intensive. Examples include cooling appliances (refrigerators and freezers), computers, televisions, and cellular telephones. Environmentally important products that are present in a growing number of households for the first time include jacuzzis, snowblowers, and large lawnmowers. The increasing globalization of the world economy has also facilitated the consumption of virgin and exotic resources on a broader scale than previously. Examples include travel to remote areas, the trade in exotic pets, and the use of rare, tropical hardwoods.

Schor points at two factors in the change in the global production structure which she calls: "global sweat shop" and the "cheap banana effect." In these processes of globalization, according to Schor, the prices are artificially lowered because the increased capital mobility has made it possible for companies to depress wages and avoid environmental costs (Schor 2005b: 309).

Schor recommends a straightforward remedy for this: to restructure the rules of the global economy so as to give labor and resources a right (or at least a higher) price. This would then transfer the purchasing power from the USA to countries with a smaller ecological footprint and thus make the world's consumption more sustainable – or rather, less unsustainable.

The increasing consciousness about the unsustainability of the modern way of living shows up in the media as expressions of bad consciousness, feelings of guilt and outright depression, visible from discussions in different public media (newspapers, blogs, etc.). People have difficulties in understanding that they have done something wrong, and wonder what they could do about the situation. Often these questions are answered with reference to a technological solution. Thus, the situation is really nothing to worry about, since the technology will take care of the problem: products become more and more energy efficient, recycling methods develop to the degree that factories begin to use each other's waste ("ecological modernization"[46]). However, much evidence shows that, as far as the rich countries are concerned, the technological savings will be offset by the increase in consumption (if a car today uses half of what it used 20 years ago, the household now has three cars instead of one). So the technological solution is really only technological, not a social one.[47]

If the solution is not technological, what about the individual consumer being a king; able to affect the structure of the global economy by making responsible choices? In essence this would mean – referring to the background given earlier in this book – that even if it is accepted that the market (competitive system, capitalism) has an indispensable role as allocator of goods in the complex world of today, the assumption of *homo economicus,* the perfectly rational and self-interested man, would not be considered correct or adequate.

Rather the assumption would be that man is also (in varying degrees, to be sure) a non-selfish, altruistic and moral being. Thus, by *consuming responsibly* the consumer gives a monetary vote for an "ethical" product and the more the consumers are doing this the more it will change the production structure in the same direction (the same goes for investment/saving decisions; see below).

Responsible behavior is thus something that we may observe in people in their role of citizens, consumers and producers. Although the role of citizen is by no means less important than the two others, we shall leave the discussion of this to the very end of the chapter, and for the moment concentrate on the role of consumers and producers.[48]

Responsible consumption stems mainly from religious roots such as the Bible's statements about man being in a stewardship position on the Earth. The Anabaptists (e.g. the Mennonites and Amish) also emphasize the consequences of one's decisions irrespective of how far they are in time and place.

Responsible consumption is of course a wider concept than ecological sustainable consumption. Thus for instance the Fair Trade[49] concept applies criteria that emphasize justice but not necessarily ecological sustainability. Also, religious ethical thought may consider the buying and selling of alcohol or gambling or pornography as unethical which may not necessarily be the case from an ecological sustainability view.

Ethical investment

The step from the responsible consumer to the responsible (ethical) investor is not large. Despite economist's jargon, the concept can be given quite a commonsense meaning: if you have some left-over money to save and do not want to keep the money in your mattress, you will probably want to put it in a bank on a savings account; you feel that your money will be taken well care of and you will even get interest on your money. However, the money will not grow by keeping it in the vault; it has to be spread out. Together with other savers' money the bank will lend it out for a price (interest) which is higher than the interest you get as a saver, of course. Now everyone who can afford to pay the price can then borrow money and do what he wants with it (within the limits of law). So your money may go to anything from a farm producing organic food to a company producing fertilizers and pesticides, from producing windmills to weapons, and so on. If you are fine with this – your only goal is to get a safe return on your money – no problem. If, on the other hand, you are interested in how your money is used, then you have to be more direct in your savings; you have to be an ethical investor. This does not mean that you have to find your own organic farmer, or what you like, but you go to the bank (or directly to an ethical investment fund) and ask to invest in an ethical fund. Of these there are different kinds, as different people have different views as to what is ethical.[50] Among these you will probably find funds in accordance with your ethical view, including those which do not invest in companies involved in alcohol, gambling, pornography or weapons.

The point of all this, like in responsible consumption, is that you "vote" with your money. You support companies which work for the same values as you. And when others also do that, the market value of your share may also rise and you benefit also economically.[51] As more and more people invest ethically, more and more companies will turn "ethical" and so the whole structure of production may change toward a more "responsible economy."

Is this too good to be true? The pessimist would say that this kind of "responsible" behavior is only something that can exist in combination with affluence, and can be practiced only by people who can reap off the value-added of the Earth and thus can only exist in a world where there is unequal distribution and exploitation of nature.

An optimist could claim that responsible investment (and consumption)[52] is an old human trait that is only coming up to the surface again. Humankind has been living for such a short period (in an evolutionary perspective) in capitalism, that people have not yet adapted to this or been able to apply the ancient moral rules to the system. And above all, what have not been realized are the moral rules for capitalism in a full world. As people conceive of these ethical rules they will behave like the good shepherd not letting the lambs graze too much (the herd grow too large) and not take too much off the heap.

It is hard to foresee what the role of responsible consumption and investment will be in a world where scarcity of natural resources is increasing. At least for the moment it is not an exaggeration to say that there is a virtual boom in this kind of behavior. As a general trend it is hard to see that responsible housekeeping would make things worse.[53] For instance, it is very probable that acting upon sustainability principles (and responsibility principles in general) in investing, will have a stabilizing effect on the investment markets as people act in the (very) long term and not only on the basis of monetary return (not to speak about speculation). And on the individual level, it is surely true that acting in accordance with one's ethical convictions gives hope for the future.

On the other hand, it seems futile, if not foolish, to hope that responsible consumption and investment as a voluntary phenomenon would mean a solution to the problem of overconsumption (or sustainability). It is absurd to think that, as the global footprint in Western Europe and North America corresponds to 5–8 earths, the people at large would voluntarily limit their consumption to what is required for sustainability, say, one-fifth of what is consumed now. The reactions to the ongoing crises (2009) shows this quite convincingly: only a one or a few percent's fall in income – or even zero growth – provokes outcries in the media which lead one to think about unbearable suffering. Thus, there have to be complementary measures to responsible economic behavior, such as a change in the rules of the global economy, as suggested for example by Schor.

Conclusion: sustainability and the ethical trilemma

In this chapter we have looked at the multifaceted character of the concept of sustainability. What often appears for example in the use of journalists and politicians to be a simple and straightforward concept appeared to be a set of largely differing assertions that do not really often seem to have much connection. Some want to look at sustainability of consumption, others want to keep natural resources intact and some want to see sustainability as a concept with different dimensions, such as economic, ecological and social. In many ways sustainability reminds us of the concept of justice. How should we, for instance, measure justice; what is the "currency" of justice? Is justice about the distribution of income, wealth, utility, rights, capabilities and so on? The same goes for sustainability: Should we measure distribution in utility, in natural resources and so on? Are we interested in the initial distribution or in the process?

On a closer inspection, this is not at all surprising, because the concepts of justice and sustainability are quite closely related. Sustainability is a wider concept, of course, but it is very difficult, if not impossible, to discuss sustainability without involving questions related to justice. But the phenomenon is more general; sustainability belongs to a class of concepts that are called *essentially contestable*. This means that most people can agree on the core of the concept, but as soon as one wants to specify what this means in practice, a bewildering difference in views arises. Other examples of essentially contestable concepts are democracy or art.

This is why we do not (and cannot) single out any specific concept of sustainability as the right one (although we have our favorites of course). And, in honesty, all conceptions have their advantages and drawbacks. This is why the reader should, hopefully inspired by this brief review, study the problem further, and decide for herself/himself what kind of sustainability would be the right one.

However, instead, this is perhaps the place (in the middle of the book) to return for a moment to our point of departure: the Global Ethical Trilemma

(GET), introduced in the first chapter: Can we look at the GET as a concept of sustainability? If so, how does this relate to the different sustainability concepts discussed above? Does the GET belong to any specific category of those mentioned?

As will be remembered, the GET describes the relation between the three alternative goals of "global policy": prosperity (mass consumption), ecological sustainability and global justice. The menu is such that only two of the three alternatives are at the list at the same time: if eco-efficient capitalism (mass consumption + ecological sustainability) is chosen, there is little room for global justice. This is because there are not enough resources on the Earth, so some people have to live in poverty (looking at the current use of resources in the mass-consuming societies (5–8 earths) it is clear that the proportion of poor must be huge. From many sustainability points of view this is not sustainable (because of the inequality involved).

On the other hand, if "global social democracy" (global justice + mass consumption) is chosen, the price of this is ecological sustainability, because this must be sacrificed to have a mass consumption living standard relatively equally distributed. Obviously, from most sustainability points of view, this is not sustainable.

However, if the third alternative, red–green planetarism (global justice + ecological sustainability) is chosen, it implies that prosperity cannot be had. This is because just distribution, fixed at sufficiently low level to guarantee ecological sustainability, does mean that this material level must be relatively low; too low to call it prosperity. (How low this is depends of course on how many people there are on Earth.) This seems to be in accordance with most conceptions of sustainability. One critical question, however, is whether this sustainability level is high enough to guarantee a standard where not all are living in misery or whether a standard that people conceive of as decent can prevail. For instance, when resources are distributed more equally (and on a lower level), the standard for a decent living may also be on a lower level.

So obviously the GET is not a conception of sustainability, because it says more than that. What it throws light on is the scarcity in the *arsenal of means in global politics*. Thus it adds a fourth dimension to the study of sustainability, besides the economic, social and ecological dimensions, namely the political one. It clarifies the fact that we cannot have all that we wish for, and at minimum forces us to think of the necessary conditions at work in this problem.

We will return to the concept in the final chapter (9) of the book.

The economics and ethics of climate change

Introduction

In a very concrete sense the *greenhouse effect* makes us see the very essence of the metaphor "Spaceship Earth": The parallel could go like this:

> The heating system of "Spaceship Earth" is not what it was. This is due to many factors, such as age, but mainly because we, the crew, have been messing around. The cover and shield of the ship has been damaged, with the consequence that the ship's life-supporting system has began malfunctioning in such a way that the crew will get living conditions that are hotter, more unstable, in some sections too dry, in some sections too moist. In some parts of the ship the conditions, mostly situated at the fore of the ship, where the officers in command are, may improve, but amidships and astern, where most of the crew is placed, the conditions will mainly deteriorate, with a great risk that the most densely populated parts of the ship will have to be abandoned due to serious water damage.

This parable could be developed further, but we shall not press it too far. However, this picture makes it clear that, even if in some sectors, like agricultural production, we have been able to push the limits to growth further, by increasing technology and energy inputs (thus seemingly discrediting Malthus's dismal vision) here the limits show up, unexpectedly and relatively firmly.[1]

In this chapter we shall give a background to the greenhouse effect, locate the hardest problems which this gives rise to, and look at the techniques and methods that have been used from an economic and an ethical point of view.

What are greenhouse gases?

In brief the greenhouse gases (GHGs) are gases that make the Earth function somewhat like a greenhouse. Instead of glass, the Earth produces gases that in different ways (different energy in incoming and outgoing radiation, see Figure 6.1.) function in such a way that solar radiation can be accumulated ("trapped") in the Earth's surface and atmosphere itself.

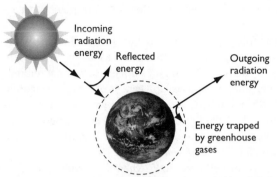

Source: http://www.agr.gc.ca/nlwis-snite/index_e.cfm?1=pubs2=ha_sa&page=8

Figure 6.1 The greenhouse effect

GHGs are a natural part of our atmosphere. Human activity, though, adds to the concentration of these gases and by this contributes to global warming. The most important GHGs are:

- water vapour
- carbon dioxide (CO_2)
- methane (CH_4)
- nitrous oxide (N_2O)
- halocarbons (e.g. CFC)

A short history of the enhanced greenhouse effect

The greenhouse effect is something that has been with the Earth at least since the Earth had some kind of atmosphere. The greenhouse effect, probably shaped by different life-forms, such as different forms of algae, is also a precondition for life as we know it; without the greenhouse effect the mean temperature would be about 30° C colder than today.

If this is so, why is the greenhouse effect considered as a problem then? The problem, as probably everyone looking at a newspaper or TV nowadays cannot have missed, is that today *human activity* is conceived of as an important factor in the greenhouse effect. In this *enhanced greenhouse effect,* the human use of energy, and more specifically, the use of fossil fuel is the most important factor. Fossil fuel was formed by organic matter during millions of years of pressure underground and when we burn it, the carbon, which all organic matter contains, is released, which again in the atmosphere combines with the oxygen and forms carbon dioxide, which is the most important GHG. This enhanced greenhouse effect is greatly contributing to the warming of the climate on Earth.

But if there exists both a natural and a man-made greenhouse effect, how do we know how important the human contribution is? And, if the human impact is very small, is there much we humans can do about it? In that case, our planned sacrifices will be in vain.

Indeed, this has been an important question on the human agenda for a while now and, from time to time, it still pops up in the media. It has taken surprisingly long to reach consensus about the human effect on the climate, somewhat reminding us of the question of whether smoking causes lung cancer. As for the scientific community, it was not until 1985, at the Villach conference,[2] when scientific consensus emerged for the first time. In 1990 the United Nations established a committee, the United Nations Framework Convention on Climate Change (UNFCCC), that started the negotiations which led to the *Kyoto protocol*.[3]

This protocol became effective in February 2005 when 55 parties ratified it, representing over 55 percent of the total carbon dioxide emissions. [4] The commitment period for the Kyoto protocol is 2008–2012, for which the protocol defines individual countries' emission targets. The goal in total is to reduce emissions of six greenhouse gases (carbon dioxide, methane, nitrous oxide, HFCs, PFCs and sulfur hexafluoride) by 5 percent from the 1990 level.

The Kyoto protocol authorizes three mechanisms that should facilitate trade with emission permits. The mechanisms are:

- *Emission trading* means that countries may trade emissions with each other according to their quotas
- *Joint implementation* means that a country can receive emission reduction credits on the basis of specific projects that reduce emissions in another country
- *Clean development mechanism* is like the above but the project can take place in a country that is not specified in the Kyoto protocol (in practice a developing country) and receive reductions in emission targets.

Emission trading is a term that is used for applying markets to pollutions as emission. Essentially it is about buying and selling rights to pollute. The idea is that some central authority (e.g. a government) sets the limits for pollution (or any resource, such as fish, see Chapter 8). After setting this "Plimsoll line,"[5] the firms are given, according to some method, like "grandfathering," which means that you are permitted to pollute according to your historical records, and then you are allowed to buy and sell these rights. If you pollute more than you are permitted to, you can buy pollution permits from firms that pollute less. This trading is thus improving the efficiency of pollution control. Essentially this is based on the fact that those firms which have the lowest cost for abating the pollution will take care (of a greater part) of it.

In fact, markets for emissions were established before the Kyoto protocol. An early example is the US acid rain program that started in 1990, and the traded emission was SO_2 (sulfur dioxide). Estimates have been made that indicate that the "cap and trade" system has reduced the costs of controlling acid rain by 80 percent compared to that of source-by-source reduction.[6] Since 2003 US corporations have been able to trade CO_2 emissions on the *Chicago Climate Exchange*.

The largest program for trading GHGs is the European Union Emission Trading Scheme. The program covers 25 of the 27 EU member countries and covers almost half of the European CO_2 emissions. The program is now in its second phase, which means that cooperation with other countries than European can take place (like in joint implementation and the clean mechanism mentioned above).

Emission trading has spurred some discussion about the morality of this system, both in a general but also more specific sense. The general view is concerned with whether emission trading as such may be seen as "letters of indulgence" or whether the "permission to pollute" destroys the social responsibility for a common resource. In a narrower sense the discussion has been concerned with how the rights or permits are allocated. A common method of allocation has been "grandfathering," with the result that many polluting economies (such as former Socialist states like Russia and Ukraine) have acquired large emission quotas, that is they have, as it were, been rewarded for pollution. The same argument has been used by the developing countries against the developed. The factor which speaks in favor of emission trading is, of course, the economic argument, which is the efficiency of trade, compared to other methods. We will come back to the question of ethics later in this chapter.

Let us now look at some figures describing emissions.

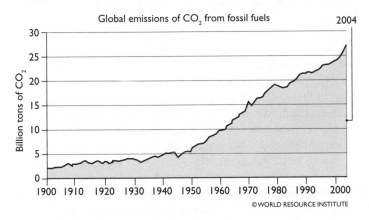

Figure 6.2 The growth of global CO_2 emissions

Figure 6.2[7] shows the emission of CO_2 from fossil fuels during the twentieth century. We can see that from 1900 the development of the curve was relatively flat, but after the Second World War, the emissions began to grow much faster. During the first five decades of the century the emissions roughly doubled, while in the second half the growth was fivefold.

The development pattern of this figure is by no means unique, and similar figures (showing exponential growth) frequently appear in the media, showing

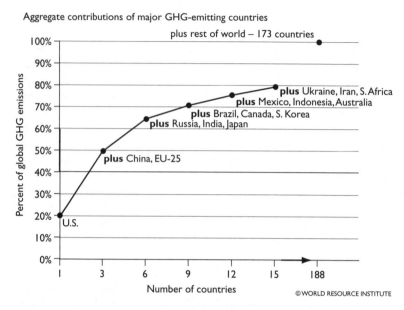

Figure 6.3 The inequality of GHG emissions

how, for example, human consumption and production have escalated. However, this figure contains even more information than this. This is because it also shows – besides the load of emissions on the atmosphere as a sink – (even if of course not with the same measures, but proportionally) the *depletion* of fossil energy, which is a non-renewable resource.

In Chapter 3 we learned about the Gini coefficent. We can see a somewhat similar construction in Figure 6.3. On the horizontal axis we have the number of countries arranged from the most emitting to the least emitting countries. Observe that the axis is cut after 15, and ends with 188 (countries). The vertical axis shows the cumulative percent of emissions. We can see that the most emitting country on Earth is the USA, which alone stands for 20 percent of the emissions. When we add to this China and the EU (which together contribute 30 percent) we get the cumulative sum of 50 percent. Then we add Russia, India and Japan and now all these nine countries (country groups) emit about 70 percent of the Earth's emissions. And so on, till we have 15 countries that emit 80 percent of total emissions. This means that the rest of the (least emitting) countries (173) together produce 20 percent of the emissions.

How about the relation between emissions and how wealthy a nation is? Are the richer countries emitting more than the poor ones or the other way around? Figure 6.4 shows the relation between income per capita and GHG emissions. We can quickly observe that there is a big group, the 115 countries (in the southeast corner), that have the lowest income also have the lowest emissions. On the other hand, there are a lot of countries with high income per capita that are quite near

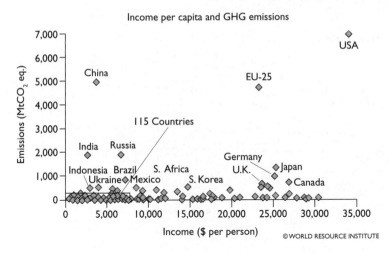

Income per capita and GHG emissions

Figure 6.4 The relation between income per capita and GHG emissions (2000)

the x-axis. Then we have the three exceptions, China, with quite low income, and the EU with a higher income and then the USA, the leading exception in both categories.

How can we be sure?

Some voices are still raised in favor of a "let's wait and see, maybe the greenhouse effect is not so dangerous after all." Such a belief is mistaken since it corresponds to applying a rowing-boat philosophy to a tanker; the rowing-boat stops in a few meters after you finish rowing at full speed, but the tanker takes many kilometers to stop if it drives at full speed. Likewise, the enhanced greenhouse effect does not stop immediately after restricting, or even stopping, the CO_2 emissions. This can be seen from Figure 6.5, which shows how fast variables that are related to CO_2 emissions reach equilibrium. If we manage to cut down CO_2 emissions enough, and quite soon, it will take a long time before the "dependent variables" react and reach a stable level. The CO_2 level itself takes 100 to 300 years to stabilize. The temperature stabilizes within a few centuries. The sea-level rise due to thermal expansion (hot water needs more room than cold) will take several centuries to millennia. The sea-level rise due to ice-melting is an even slower process: it takes millennia before a new equilibrium is stabilized (this is why it still continues to rise within the limits of the figure).

We can see from Figure 6.5, looking at only one of the factors here – sea-level rise – that the "wait and see" policy is not wise.[8] This is because when something happens because of the sea-level rise – such as a (quite probable) increase in the tendency of flooding in low coastal areas of the world – it is too late to press the brakes, because the development path may continue for centuries or more.

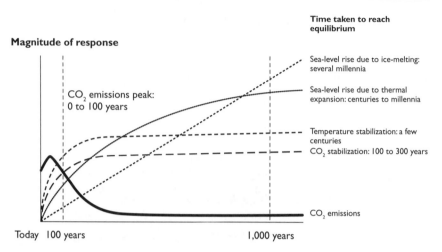

Figure 6.5 The relation between CO_2 emissions and reaction time of some variables related to these

The economics of climate warming: cost–benefit analysis

Before we discuss the actual greenhouse effect estimates it is necessary to get some primary understanding of cost–benefit analysis (CBA)[9] and the basic assumptions which it rests on. As we saw in Chapter 4 (Figure 4.6) one of the characteristics of a market is that it can give consumers a surplus, that is the consumer would be willing to pay more than she does pay. This takes place when we have an ideally functioning market. When we do not have functioning markets, such as for public goods or with many natural resources, we can still imagine that there is a consumer surplus (e.g. people are willing to pay more than they actually do for a functioning climate).

Now, what economists try to do in the absence of markets, is to get people to reveal their preferences, by mimicking markets, or in some other way (such as the contingent valuation method).[10]

Elementary welfare economics

To make a long story short, when people reveal their preferences, they are thought to give a true value of what they would be willing to pay for a good: their willingness to pay (WTP). WTP is not the only way of measuring the market value of something. WTP is a sum thought to be paid for a benefit. But what about a damage (a cost)? Economists have developed a corresponding concept for this too: the willingness to accept (WTA). A question that is supposed to figure out the WTA from a consumer could go like this: "there are plans to build a motorway one block away from your house. How much would you like in compensation to accept this?"

One of the tasks of welfare economics is, briefly, to compare the *welfare effects* of some political measure or project, like the road just mentioned. Let us give an elementary example of how this could be done.

Let us assume a society with four individuals (which could be generalized to families or groups), A, B, C and D which are affected by a project (P), say, the building of a road through these people's neighborhood. As the road is planned to be built, it will make the way shorter to central places than before for A and B. On the other hand, the new road will bring about traffic noise for C and D (since it passes near their houses). Let us say that the person's (true) estimate of the project P is as follows: A: WTP for P = €700, B: WTP for P = €600, C: WTA = €500 and D: WTAP = €400.

How can we understand these figures? Obviously A and B estimate that they will get a benefit (in terms of shorter routes). C and D will estimate a *cost* of this project (increased noise) which is why they want compensation for the project, which they give as a WTA.

Now, how should the choice be made in this "society" or neighborhood: to build or not to build? A possible rule for the social choice could be the following: "choose P if the benefits are higher than the costs." In this case the benefits are what A and B are willing to pay (WTP) and the costs will be what C and D want in compensation (WTA). As a formula the rule above can be written as:

Choose P if:

$$(\text{WTP}_A + \text{WTP}_B) - (\text{WTA}_C + \text{WTA}_D) > 0. \tag{6.1}$$

Filling in the actual numbers we get $(700 + 600) - (500 + 400) = €400$. In other words, according to the above rule, for this society as a whole, it is obviously profitable to build the road.

Compensation

But, wait a minute: what about this rule, thought of in terms of what commonly is understood by *social choice*?[11] What happens if we follow the rule above – which actually is the rule for choice in CBA – and we choose to do P, i.e. build the road? Obviously A and B will be better off, and C and D will be worse off. Does it now seem reasonable to say that the society, as a whole, is better off? This is doubtful, because two of the citizens are better off and two citizens are worse off. If there were a vote on this project two would vote for, and two against it, and many observers would probably consider it fair to decide the case by the toss of a coin.

However, there is a way to decide about this case in consensus: what if A and B would compensate C and D for their losses? Assume that A gives C €600 and B gives D €500 (i.e. they would pay them to accept the project), in compensation for their acceptance of P. We can see that in a solution like this, *everyone* is better off through realizing project P.[12] This is called a *Pareto improvement*.

So, actually, only if a compensation takes place, can we say that the rule expressed in (6.1) expresses a *fair* social choice rule. By only following the rule

(6.1) we cannot say whether for example one person will gain a mansion, while 100 others will lose their homes, as a consequence of some project or measure; in other words, it can lead to very unfair distributions.

How, and whether, compensation in the real world will actually take place is a question that has been solved in different ways, by different institutions and arrangements around the world. The brute fact, however, is that within economics the CBA is justified on the basis of an "ethic principle" which says that if CBA shows a net benefit it *is possible* for the gainers to compensate the losers (potential compensation). Since no guarantee exists that such will actually take place, the "ethic principle" collapses into the principle of efficiency.

In any case the rule in formula (6.1) is the basis for CBA. Given that (ideally) WTP stands for Benefits (B) and WTA stands for Costs (C) we can write (6.1) as follows:

$$\sum_i [Bi - Ci] > 0 \qquad\qquad (6.2)$$

Where $\sum_i$ stands for the sum of all individuals' (A, B, C, D net income or utility).

Valuation of time: discounting

In making calculations about how the choices of today affect the situation of future generations mainstream economics has traditionally relied on the method of *discounting*. Discounting is, in principle, an uncontroversial method – when used routinely in a private firm's investment decisions. An investment project in practice means that the costs and revenues are actualized at different points in time. It would be a great advantage if the costs and revenues (or utility or benefits and cost) of these could be compared and put, as it where, on the same starting line. (How) can this be done?

One way to understand this is to start with a thought experiment: if you are to choose between getting €100 today or €100 after one year, which one would you choose? Most people would surely choose to get the sum today, instead of getting it after a year. Why is that? The reasons might vary, but intuitive reasoning suggests it is because life in general is filled with uncertainty and life in itself is uncertain: *carpe diem*.

If we get the sum today we may for example invest it and get interest on the money. This human invention or characteristic, which may be seen as a sign of *impatience or myopia*, and is also called positive time preference, may actually be expressed in the form of interest (a return on the money invested). To use the same time preference (= interest) in comparing items of, say, utilities and costs at different points of time is called *discounting*.

Briefly put, the principle of discounting may be understood as the opposite to calculating interest on interest (compound interest). If you invest €100 today, how much is this sum worth in ten years if you get 10 percent interest on interest per year? The value of the investment will be 269, given by the formula of compound interest which is:

$$100(1+10)^{10} = €259$$

A bit more generally expressed: (at the interest rate r) the value now of €100 which we receive after ten years must be:

$$\frac{100}{(1+r)^{10}}$$

Still increasing the level of generality somewhat (substitute the year, ten with t) we get:

$$PV = FV\left[\frac{1}{(1+r)^t}\right] \tag{6.3}$$

Where PV is the present value, FV is the future value that we will receive. By adding all future amounts at different points in time we get the total value of our future income. Applied to CBA (i.e. equation 6.2, and dividing with the *discount factor* $(1+r)^t$ this can be expressed as:

$$\sum_i \frac{B_i - C_i}{(1+r)^i} \tag{6.4}$$

It is important to observe here what happens in the denominator: the higher the interest r and/or the longer time (t), the faster will the sum (given a constant nominator) diminish.

Example: suppose we are planning a project such as building a wind turbine. Such a project will have a large fixed (initial) cost in the building stage, but will give benefit for a long time at a negligible cost. A (relatively small) wind turbine's CBA is shown in Table 6.1.[13]

Table 6.1 Cost–benefit analysis and discounting

	Year 1	Year 2	Year 3	Year 4	Year 5
Benefit	0	15	15	20	20
Cost	60	5	0	0	0
Net benefit	-60	10	15	20	20

Assuming now that the interest rate is 5 percent, we can, according to the equation above, do the following calculation:

$$-60/1.05 + 10/(1.05)^2 + 15/(1.05)^3 + 20/(1.05)^4 + 20/(1.05)^5$$

which makes: −3. Should we build this wind turbine, or not? Obviously not in this case since the figure −3 shows that the benefits are smaller than the costs, at least if the time horizon is only five years.[14] Properly built power stations of course have considerably longer lifetimes. However, the essential thing to note here is how the sum of net benefits (65) without discounting exceeds the initial costs (60). This is now an example of how discounting lessens the value of future benefits.

However, the case may also be that discounting makes the costs smaller. A case like this can be illuminated by the following example (this is often called the "tyranny of discounting"): The problem that is usually discussed under this term[15] is the inherent problem with discounting costs, i.e. of essentially moving the costs of a project to future generations. Suppose, as this chapter is about climate change, that the costs of climate warming (e.g. sea-level rise) after 100 years can be calculated to be, say, €1 million/capita (from forced migration, building dams, etc.). When we use discounting to measure the present value of this future damage, its value can be calculated by (let us assume an interest rate of 8 percent):

$$\frac{1,000,000}{1.08^{100}} = 455$$

The damage of €1 million/capita after 100 years is today valued to €455. This sum, of course means a lot of money for poor people, in many countries it is much more than the mean income/person a year. In the industrialized countries, which are mainly responsible for the emission of GHGs, the sum can be considered negligible; you cannot even get a decent television set for that sum. In terms of CBA, the question could be put as follows: Is it worthwhile to invest in counteraction against climate warming given the cost estimated above? It is not difficult to imagine what the answer would be; surely rational people would want not to invest in measures against climate warming; i.e. if the cost is €455, it is easy to see that it must be practically impossible not to exceed this by the "savings" achieved by *not* investing in (i.e. continuing economic growth) abatement of climate change.

Thus, by using discounting one can make costs (as well as benefits) diminish in the long run. Still the value of the damage for the people living after hundred years is the €1 million (i.e. there is no reason to believe that the expected cost would differ very much from this sum), the calculated monetary value of a burden which they have to bear. This is why many (including Ramsay who first studied this in relation to optimal saving) have considered it as unethical to use a positive discount rate[16] because this puts less weight on the wellbeing of future generations.

The discount rate, that is the "social time preference" is commonly divided into two parts as illustrated by the formula:

$$r = \rho + \alpha g$$

Where r is the society's rate of discount; ρ is the pure time preference (based on the assumption that people prefer to have something today rather than tomorrow; the assumed myopia or impatience of humans). The symbol α refers to how sensitive (measured as elasticity) the wellbeing (utility) is to consumption, and g symbolizes the real growth rate in consumption.

There are some obstacles or "prejudices" related to the understanding of discounting applied and interpreted in social projects, especially long-run projects, such as climate warming:

- Students, especially those with a business background, are often confused by the use of the discounting rate in environmental, long-run discounting. The difference between calculating in business and social calculation seems to be rather difficult to grasp. It may be worthwhile to emphasize the following points: in discounting in business calculations the purpose is to compare different projects with respect to some market return rate and thus being able to choose the most profitable investment project (or invest in the general money market, i.e. deposit money in bank) – from the investor's point of view, of course.
- This view, then, is some distance away from the view of discounting in economics (mainstream, environmental or ecological). Of course, the main purpose of introducing CBA and discounting into social calculation is also to compare profitability, sort of. But profitability for an individual agent is something rather different from that of a community or a society. In social decisions the costs and benefits will often fall upon different individuals, which clearly make it an ethical problem, which it cannot be for an individual agent. The problems of distribution were already discussed to some extent in Chapter 3 and we need not dwell on these questions here.
- Sometimes discounting is conflated with the calculus of correcting for inflation. However, discounting as such has nothing to do with inflation. In other words, the calculations are done in real terms only, that is the purchasing power of the amounts calculated are thought to be in real terms.

Let us now turn closer to our main topic, and look at how CBA can be applied to study climate change.

Figure 6.6[17] shows the standard picture of the equilibrium situation. The marginal benefit of avoiding damages is thought to be positive, but steadily diminishing. The marginal control costs are thought to be rising and rising more steeply the nearer we come to 100 percent "cleaning," meaning that cleaning of the last particles of emission will be more expensive than cleaning the first. The cost may arise from cutting down emissions which is costly in itself, loss of production, or increasing the absorption by reforestation (carbon-binding). More specifically the costs can be classified into three categories:[18]

- Negative costs for correcting market failure, i.e. gains in GDP. If for instance energy efficiency is improved to reduce GHG emissions, this will lead to "secondary benefits" that increase efficiency, which should be counted as a reduction in pollution costs (and thus make the measure cheaper).
- Costs relating to moving resources from other uses, e.g. restricting the use of energy. This is the category mostly concentrated on.
- Short-term transitional costs because of e.g. unemployment caused by structural changes in the labor market. This category is not always taken into consideration.

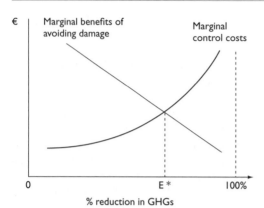

Figure 6.6 Marginal costs and benefits from reducing GHG emissions

The benefits are thought to rise with less warming, less rise of the sea level and so on, thus raising the consumer's welfare. Now, as in economic analysis in general (see Chapter 4) the idea here is that as all activity has two sides, benefits and costs, to find the optimal amount of reduction in GHGs. That is, the common intuition, that to reduce all emissions is seen as economically unsound (because emissions imply benefits and dropping emissions to the last particle would be relatively costly), as the rising marginal costs shows. The optimal amount of reduction in Figure 6.6 is where marginal control costs are equal to marginal benefits of avoiding damage, i.e. the point E*.

The cost–benefit analysis is the most common economic method in the analysis of the economy of projects of different kinds, and it is a relatively convenient tool for this. It is also a popular method in the analysis of climate warming, but it should be kept in mind that CBA rests on some assumptions that may be problematic in using it as a tool for this.

First, it should be noted that CBA was not originally created for large-scale projects covering very long lifespans, such as climatic change, but for relatively well-defined, relatively short-time projects such as waterways and harbors.[19] In the very long run the degree of uncertainty will necessarily rise, and we cannot rely on the fundamental assumption of economics – *ceteris paribus*[20]– anymore. And, what is even more important, a "serious GHG reduction programme would alter the technological base of the economy, e.g. developing alternative energy sources, new transportation systems and lifestyles" (Spash 2002: 157). In such cases there exists no independent cornerstone by which we could compare the costs and benefits.

Elegant and simple as Figure 6.6 seems, the practical problems with estimating the marginal benefits and costs of GHG control measures, *and at point E**, must be large (to make an obvious understatement), because we really do not have much possibility of estimating, say, the benefits. Furthermore, it is not always clear that the institutional independence of the CBAs made by different instances can be guaranteed. This list could be continued, but the main point we want to emphasize here is that, in light of what has been written here (and we will add some further comments in the discussion of the Stern report below), it is somewhat difficult to understand that some economists want to claim monopoly on the discussion of climate warming in the name of value-freedom and objectivity. Expressed a little differently, since this "methodology" is supposed to lead to the answer to the scientific question about what the efficient allocation is, this is seen as the final word (QED!). However, in this line of thought process, it is like putting the cart before the horse, since efficiency is only one among the goals of economic policy, such as equality.

Table 6.2 Author weighting of benefits in CBA studies of GHG control at the world level

	Nordhaus 1991 USI World %	Ayres and Walters 1991 World %	Nordhaus 1994 DICE World %	Fankhouser 1995 World %	Tol 1995 World %	Nordhaus 1998 RICE World %	Max
Losses avoided*							
Agriculture	0	0	20	15	17	7	20
Forest loss	0	0	0	1	0	0	1
Species/ecosystem loss	0	0	0	15	6	0	15
Sea-level rise	72	95	23	17	11	18	95
Energy consumption	22	0	3	9	0	0	22
Human morbidity/ mortality	0	0	0	18	52	6	52
Migration	0	5	0	2	4	0	5
Hurricanes	0	0	0	1	1	0	1
Leisure	0	0	0	0	11	0	11
Water supply	0	0	0	17	0	0	17
Urban infrastructure	0	0	0	6	0	0	6
Tropospheric ozone		0	0	0	6	0	0
Miscellaneous	0	0	53	0	0	60	60
Total	100	100	100	100	100	100	
Gains missed							
Agriculture	0	0	0	0	0	−13	
Energy consumption	−16	0	0	0	0	0	
Outdoor reaction	0	0	0	0	0	−16	
Temperature rise °C	3.0	3.0	3.0	2.5	2.5	2.5	
Meaurement basis	$1,000 m	$1,000 m	GDP	$1,000 m	$1,000 m	GDP	
Net GDP loss %	0.25	2.25	1.34	1.40	1.90	1.50	
Base year	1981	1981	1988	1988	1988	1995	

Source: Spash 2002: 195.

Note
*Figures are rounded up to the nearest whole number, so the column may not always add up to 100 exactly

Monetary valuation of GHG control

The history of the monetary valuation of climate change is about 35 years old.[21] We shall not go through history here in detail. Instead let us look at Table 6.2 which gives a summary of the main CBA studies of the GHGs. The six studies present estimates of benefits of GHG control at the world level. An interesting point is that although the temperature rise in all studies varies "only" between 2.5 and 3.0°C, the estimates of the various "losses avoided" vary quite considerably, especially when we remember that the studies classify themselves as scientific studies. To take a few examples: the benefits for agriculture from GHG control varies from 0 to 20; the diminished sea-level rise varies from 11 to 95; human morbidity (mortality) ("the value of life") varies from 0 to 52; the benefit to water supply in five studies is esti-mated at 0, while one estimates the weight at 17. Observe also that not only do the results vary between different studies, but also for the same individual.

Despite holding to epithets like "consistency and rigour," "science and objec-tivity," that is trying to separate the ethics from the "pure, derivation of benefits and costs, what does this variation in the estimates of the weights depend on, then? One important dividing line is the attitude towards discounting. Arrow *et al.* (1996, quoted in Spash 2002: 187) have expressed the mainstream economic view as follows:

> The alternative – overriding market prices on ethical grounds – opens the door to irreconcilable inconsistencies. If ethical arguments, rather than the revealed preferences of citizens, form the rationale for a low discount rate cannot ethical arguments be applied to other questions?

Another way to look at this, as we discussed above in the section on discounting, is that the market interest, which only reflects (and unstably so – as we can see in the current financial crisis), at best, an aspect of how the current generation values the future. This means, as long as we have a positive interest rate the future resources will be downvalued, that is given less weight in our calculations. To many that sounds unfair. And, again, how can it be claimed that in important political ethical discussions like this, the economic (efficiency) point of view should be given priority to other political goals?

Despite the (perhaps sincere) quest for objectivity the numbers that appear in Table 6.2 are indeed not the unambiguous result of a model, but admitted to contain "large margins of errors," which also gives room for the economists own beliefs, and is, in fact, many times guesswork.[22]

Based on an analysis of of Nordhaus (1991b), Funtowicz and Ravetz (1994) summarize some of the work on the economic analysis of the greenhouse effect as follows:

> By the time that the author has admitted the manifold oversimplifications and uncertainties in his analysis, and has shown how strong are the ad hoc

adjustments and hunches which are needed to bring his numbers back into the realm of plausibility, we might ask whether the statistical exercises are totally redundant except for rhetorical purposes.

(cited by Spash 2002: 196)

The ethics of the EGE[23]

The ethics of sustainability in general have been primarily discussed in Chapter 3, and in the section above we made some comments on the relation of the economic analysis of GHGs and the ethics. This was generally found to be on the level of announcements of objectivity and rigor. However, since all analysis within social science rests on some kind of values/ethics, be that then a declaration of "value-freedom" this must also be the case here. So, more specifically, what kind of ethics do economic analysts of climate warming adopt?

Spash (2002) identifies four ethical rules in the literature on the economic models concerning the enhanced greenhouse effect. This also means that we are talking about intergenerational ethical rules, since there is not much we can do about the greenhouse effect intragenerationally (that means within one generation):

> The *elitist rule* requires that the welfare of the best-off be improved: actions that decrease elitist welfare are wrong. The *egalitarian rule* is the exact opposite, requiring the welfare of the worst-off be increased or maximizing the minimum welfare, often termed the max-min principle. Both rules focus entirely upon the relative level of well-being, without concern about quantifying the sizes of welfare gains or losses. The *Paretian rule* reallocates resources until no generation can be made better off without making another worse-off. The neo-classical utilitarian rule reallocates resources in order to maximize total utility across all generations. The last two rules focus upon the relative size of gains and losses while ignoring absolute levels of welfare (e.g. whether the gainer is rich and the giver poor).
>
> (Spash 2002: 223, p. 223)

Of the above rules, the elitist rule is not familiar from Chapter 3, and may seem a bit strange and odd. How can this be thought of as a *moral* rule, if whatever favors the elite would be right? For example a "transfer from future generations," such as negligence to invest in diminishing of greenhouse gases, could be considered as being in accordance with this rule.

To make sense, this rule should be understood so that the elite is the best off generation that is, in practice, the generation living now. Although elitism is seldom officially proclaimed, there is something in this idea that may catch the attitude of some part or actors in today's society. Elitism may be based on hubris, that is an attitude that could be expressed for example by: "we deserve it, because without us there would be so much less for everybody."

The egalitarian rule says that welfare should be divided equally between generations. Often also Rawls's rule (maximin) is counted among the egalitarian rules. The egalitarian principle, although intuitively simple at first thought may lead to some complications. For example growth, that is more welfare to coming generations, would not be in accordance with egalitarianism, because it would make the present generation the least well off, and should thus be prohibited. Also, specifying egalitarianism, for a very long time horizon (and finite resources) would be problematic for the principle, since it would require an adjustment to a subsistence level (which would make the welfare unequal during the period of adjustment; in the earlier literature this is sometimes called the Calcutta solution).

The application of the Pareto rule (which says that welfare redistribution can be made if at least one person can be made better, while nobody is made worst off) is usually applied in this connection in the same way as in the intragenerational context: an initial endowment is given to each generation and then redistributions (between generations) are allowed if they are Pareto improvements.

As the rule is defined above, the outcome of the process is critically dependent on the initial endowment. If it is all allocated to the present generations (as it really is), the allocation to future generations is determined by the possibility to make transfers. That is, is it possible for future generations to "exchange" or give back for some transfer from the present generation to a future generation? If it is not possible, the transfer from the present generation is not in accordance with the Pareto rule, because it will make the future generation better off but the present worse off. So we might say that the Pareto rule does not seem especially fruitful in this connection.

The neoclassical utilitarian rule (maximizing total utility over generations) is concerned with the gains and losses of welfare (utility) without concern about the welfare levels. Compensation for long-time pollution is excluded if for some reason the marginal utility of the sufferer is lower than the polluter's. This argument may hold for the enhanced greenhouse effect when claiming that future generations will be better off and therefore have lower marginal utility. "An act involving the infliction of deliberate harm is then never wrong per se."[24]

As remarked earlier, these ethical theories have dominated the economic discussion concerning ethical problems. However, it is clear that by this the ideas that inform real people in their ethical choices are not drained. The teleological/utilitarian thinking of economics as referred to above certainly seems somewhat absurd, if not unethical, to many thinking non-economists. Many (if not all, of course) people would probably want to legitimate their choices in deontological terms, for example we do not want to limit the emission of GHGs because we can benefit from it, but because it is our duty (towards future generations, or our fellow creatures in nature) to do so (cf. Spash 2002: 233ff.).

Spash says that "[t]he most inadequate part of the IPCC information process has been the reporting of economics because of the desire by many of those involved to divorce the subject from ethical judgments, which they then make implicitly," and he would like to see "more open debate and a plurality of values" (Spash 2002: 244–45). Since Spash wrote his book (2002) something has changed, and we think that it is not an exaggeration to say that the most important catalyst in this has been the Stern Review, which we shall now turn to.

The Stern Review

It may be said that the Stern Review (2007) is the first report (at least from the economic camp) where the problem of global change is seen as a real threat to humankind, and not "just" an economic (cost–benefit) problem among others. The climate change is called the "biggest market failure ever."

The Stern Review is the improbable product of a government report, made by Sir Nicholas Stern (former chief economist of the World Bank) on the initiative of Gordon Brown, then the British Chancellor of the Exchequer.

Below is a list – abbreviated from the executive summary – with the most important points from the review, as well as some comments.

- It is time to act and beneficial to do so, because of the very long time-lags in the climate system due to GHGs.
- We cannot think of the climate warming only in terms of small, marginal changes, but must consider the possibility of catastrophic, irreversible changes.
- The climate change has an effect on the whole environment. Only considering the rise in the sea level makes it obvious that this must imply a serious deterioration of people's living conditions in coastal areas of the world – where most of the people live.
- Climate warming will hit the poor of the Earth much harder than the rich.
- We should not overestimate the *positive* effects of climate warming.
- New modeling indicate that the total economic impact of climate warming will be higher than earlier studies show.
- Emissions are tightly connected to growth. However, growth can, according to the Stern Review, continue even with lower emissions.
- Cutting emissions will not be free: "estimates of the annual costs of achieving stabilization between 500 and 550 ppm CO_2 are around 1 percent of global GDP by 2050.
- Energy-efficiency and low-carbon economy also means possibilities for growth.
- The carbon markets must be developed.
- Not all countries take the probable impacts of climate change seriously; adaptive measures will be necessary.
- Global institutions for dealing with climate warming must be developed.
- The situation is serious; the time is not out yet, but soon.

The review received quite a lot of criticism. The criticism from economists has mostly been about the very low discount factor (0.1 percent)

The estimates of the business-as-usual (BAU) scenario damages in the Stern Review are higher than earlier estimates because of taking into consideration people's unwillingness to take risks (risk-aversion), and the use of more recent scientific literature on the probabilities of different rises in temperature. Because these figures are higher than previously, this implies much higher damages (as they rise faster than the temperature). An additional reason is the use of a relatively low so-called pure time preference (see section on discounting above). This is because it is seen as giving an ethically more defendable way of weighting future generation's valuation of the costs. Furthermore, the Stern Review also considers the disproportional consequences for poor regions depending on the fact that poor people will be affected by reduced consumption.

The Stern analysis thus presents the stabilization of GHGs at 550 ppm (or under) as a low risk level, but not a zero-risk level. The report says that even this level is quite high, and says that it is advisable to hold the development under surveillance.

The main arguments against early and strong measures (as compared to a BAU scenario) are:

- *Some people still deny the scientific evidence of climate change.* Although it surely is a long and respected tradition within the scientific community to be critical about established truths, the fact that 97.4 percent of a poll of US climatologists answered yes to the question about whether they believed that human activity was a significant factor in changing the mean global temperature,[25] should be telling. It is scarcely possible to get a higher grade of consensus of anything within any scientific community – and this opinion is among the experts on the climate.

- *Some people accept the basic science but still think it is better to wait and see before diminishing the emissions.* This view is mainly based on two arguments: that new cheaper technology will appear and/or that future generations will have more capital, and thus it will be relatively cheaper to invest in emission-reducing measures. The problem with this view is that it does not take account of the long time lag by which the greenhouse gases disappear from the atmosphere. Thus a damage done cannot be reversed, but something that many coming generations will have to suffer from. Even if the greenhouse emissions were to drop to zero the greenhouse gases stay in the atmosphere from tens to hundreds of years. It may be useful to think about the investment in, say, on average 1 percent of the GDP, as insurance, that a reasonable country or individual should take, even if the worst scenario should not be very probable.

- *Some people choose to put a very low value on the future,* or in other words, value short-sighted consumption very high. Here it is a question of discounting which we have discussed in detail in this chapter.

Chapter 7

Global food security

World population has more than doubled in the last 50 years. At the same time the demand for food has tripled, as rising incomes have expanded the demand, not only in terms of quantities, but in terms of more valuable foods such as livestock products, fruits and stimulants. It is a remarkable fact that global agriculture has been successful in meeting this huge increase in demand. Still some 900 million people are undernourished, but the proportion of the world population starving has come down from one in three to less than one in six, and the frequency of great famines has been drastically reduced. How has this achievement been possible? Can it be sustained given the ecological limits?

World food security is the main concern of the FAO – the UN organization for food and agriculture. It regularly publishes a report *The State of Food Insecurity in the World.* In the 2008 report the optimism of the earlier reports was tempered by the extraordinary rise in food prices, which had driven millions of people into food insecurity, worsening the conditions for those who already were undernourished, and threatening long-term global food insecurity. Has the positive trend been reversed? What are the main reasons for the growing food problems?

Hunger and poverty go together. The most salient reason for undernourishment is a lack of money to buy food. Without a sufficient diet people's physical and mental capabilities are affected so that their ability to work or to study is reduced. Contributing to this vicious circle is the higher birth rate among the poor. Thus we are living in a world – with an all-embracing *world market for food* – in which a large part of the population is overfed, at the same time as many live under conditions of chronic hunger and occasional famine.

The determinants of food production

Food production growth is the combined result of growth of the *harvested area* and of *yield growth* – it is the increase in *land productivity*. Since most arable land is already in use, the increase in food production – measured in terms of tons, calories or value – has primarily come as a result of increased yields per hectare. Area expansion had ceased to be a feasible source of crop production growth by the end of the twentieth century, except for parts of Latin America and Africa, where rural population densities are still relatively low. In many poor areas there is still pressure to clear land for cultivation, and this is one important reason for *deforestation*. However, such an expansion of agricultural land cannot solve the problems of the rising demand for food. The crucial factor is the potential increase in productivity per hectare.

Yield is a function of several variables: soil quality, weather conditions, labor use, type of seed, fertilizers, herbicides and pesticides, irrigation, tractors and other machinery, as well as the abilities of the farmers. Productivity indirectly depends on how food production is linked to the rest of society through roads, markets, land ownership, prices, education, subsidies and much more.

Although the direct contribution of agriculture to GDP has dwindled during the past 50 years – and is globally no more than 4 percent – its economic, social and ecological importance is still much stronger. The different types of inputs required and the varied and extensive use of its outputs makes agriculture a central component of most national economies. One of the best indicators of the degree of development of a country is the *value produced per farmer*. At the beginning of this century the value-added per worker in agriculture, forestry and fishing was – according to World Bank figures – $24,438 in the high-income countries, $708 in the middle-income countries and $363 in low-income countries. In Burundi the value of food production per agricultural worker was only $80 per year; in France it was $39,220.

The increase in agricultural production in recent decades has been driven by productivity growth in developing countries. Two large countries – China and India – have contributed most to this positive outcome. The results of the so-called *Green Revolution* – although it started in the 1960s – seem to have matured at the end of the century. The essence of the Green Revolution was the application of *new high-yielding seeds*. These new seeds require more irrigation and more fertilizers, making it more difficult for poor peasants to compete with larger and more capital-intensive farms.

Although there are many factors influencing the possibilities to maintain and to enhance the yields, two stand out as especially important from an ecological point of view: water and fossil materials.

Water and fossil fuels

One threat to food security is the overuse of *water* in many parts of the globe. As more water is required for residential and industrial needs, and as more water becomes unavailable due to pollution, the water available for irrigation is reduced. For example in Northern China in the Yellow river basin agriculture faces serious water shortages that has led to groundwater mining that is unsustainable, and that may lead to an abrupt decline in the supply of irrigation water. Even in Southern China, in the Yangtze river basin, which is much less vulnerable, there have occurred serious droughts. One reason given for this is the massive Three Gorges Dam, which causes a reduction in the flow volume of the Yangtze. China, however, is rich enough to afford to import the required quantities of grain and soy beans. But the more China buys from abroad, the less is left for the rest of the world. The amounts required can equal the world's export supply – 200 million tons – and raise the price of food for the whole world.

In the water-scarce regions of North Africa and West Asia, growing populations and rising affluence have boosted demand much faster than farmers have been able to increase production. Due to the large imports of grain much more than half of the water footprints of consumption in Israel, Jordan, Saudi Arabia and Kuwait are external. In order to satisfy the direct and indirect water demand of the region at least another Nile would be required (Living Planet Report 2008). However, North Africa and West Asia do have another resource required for modern agriculture, fossil fuels.

Energy and food are closely linked, and the food and energy crises of 2008 were also connected. Fossil fuels are needed in modern agricultural production and distribution. Furthermore, agricultural land is also required for the production of *biofuels*. An increase in the price for oil therefore makes food production and distribution more expensive and, at the same time, increases the demand for land to produce biofuels. Since oil production is close to its peak level, and with no reduction in demand in sight, the price for oil will surely be much higher than during the second half of the twentieth century. Agriculture will therefore be affected on a world scale. The land area cultivated for food may decline, yields may be reduced, and with rising transport costs agricultural specialization between different parts of the world may be hampered.

The combined specter of growing water shortages, rising costs for fuels and fertilizers, and more land allocated to the production of biofuels, may *reverse the previous positive developments*. It may become much more difficult to achieve a balance between increased consumption of high value foods, a reduction of world undernourishment and ecologically safe agricultural production.

In a full world the efforts to achieve national food security have led to a new scramble for land, called *"the great land grab."* Countries in East Asia – China, Japan, South Korea – and in the Middle East – Saudi Arabia, Libya, the Gulf states – have bought or leased vast land areas in Africa, Latin America, Pakistan and South East Asia. The intention is to increase the productivity of the lands and to secure the food and biofuels for the investor countries. These appropriations of fertile land, where poor local populations may be evicted from the land, are politically highly sensitive, and have led to internal as well as international conflicts. The process may result in a global increase in food production, but at the same time intensify the national and global inequalities. That Jacques Diouf, general director of the FAO, has warned the world that this land grab implies a new form of neo-colonialism, shows that the phenomenon has already reached critical dimensions.

Global agribusiness and local livelihoods

Agriculture today is a global industry. *Transnational food companies* – such as Cargill, Danone, General Mills, McDonald's, Nestlé and Unilever – are established all over the world both as suppliers to consumers and as buyers of unprocessed food products. Other firms – such as Dow AgroSciences, Monsanto, Mosaic Company, Syngenta and Yara International – supply seeds, animal feed, fertilizers, pesticides and other inputs to farmers almost anywhere in the world. These companies are the most dynamic and dominating actors in what is called *agribusiness*. Agribusiness embraces all businesses involved in food production, including farming – above all contract farming, seed supply, agrichemicals, farm machinery, wholesale and distribution, processing, marketing and retail sales.

From the point of view of sustainability and equity there are constant tensions between a globally organized agribusiness that thrives on specialization and monocultures, and traditional smallholders, the livelihoods of which are made up of several crops and of nonfood rural occupations. This has also been described as a *clash between entrepreneurial and subsistence farming*. Whereas agribusiness is well suited to feed the fast growing urban agglomerations, it revolutionizes rural life in ways that have grave social and ecological consequences. Traditional smallholder societies provide poor peasants and the rural poor better opportunities to avoid the risks associated with large-scale monocultures. Therefore there is often a trade-off between higher yields and incomes on the one hand and sustainable rural livelihoods on the other, a trade-off that exemplifies the global ethical trilemma presented in the first chapter.

A new field of study – *political ecology* – has concentrated on this tension between industrial and globally oriented agriculture and traditional lifestyles and ecologies. Joan Martinez-Alier – a founder of ecological economics – has through his book *Environmentalism of the Poor. A Study of Ecological Conflicts and Valuations* (2002) linked the struggles of the poor and the preservation of sustainable ecosystems. The book gives numerous examples demonstrating that *the poor are environmentalists*, although they need not be conscious of this fact. By contrasting different views of nature, spirituality and human life Martinez-Alier exemplifies the *incommensurability of values* – and therefore the dangers of relying on economic cost–benefit analyses that require a translation of all valuations into money. The vast gaps between different lifestyles and cultures make the ecological distribution controversies both more frequent and harsh. This is the subject matter of political ecology – an area that is closely connected to ecological economics. Since the poor by definition cannot pay for the environmental services demanded by those who are moneyed, and since they seldom have the capacity to influence the political decisions, they recur to struggles and strategies that clash with the dominant views of development and prosperity.

Added to this conflict between traditional local livelihoods and global agribusiness, we find the tensions between those favoring unsubsidized *free trade in food* and those seeking to maintain a *strong national food sector*. In the WTO – the

World Trade Organization that is committed to the promotion of multilateral free trade between its members – agricultural trade has traditionally been the most controversial issue. One group of countries, the *Cairns Group*, is a coalition of agricultural exporting countries, both rich such as Australia and Canada, and developing such as Brazil, Argentina, Indonesia and the Philippines. They try to promote freer trade in agricultural products and to reduce the subsidies paid to farmers in the USA, the EU and Japan. The USA and EU protect their farmers by the use of import restrictions and heavy subsidies, which create a surplus of food that they then try to dump on to world markets. This is seen as a threat both by the members of the Cairns Group and by the poor countries (organized in the G20 in the WTO) that strive to develop their own agricultural production and exports.

On the one hand food-importing poor countries do appreciate the possibility to buy cheap grain from exporting countries, but on the other hand cheap imports tend to undermine national producers and to make the importing countries vulnerable to sudden price increases in the world food market.

The global food dilemma

We here counter a problematic that is paramount: *farmers need prices that are high* enough in order to produce food for the market, but *the poor may not be able to buy high-priced food.* Should we try to expand food production by keeping higher prices or should we try to counter undernourishment and poverty by making cheap food available through subsidies and other means that go against the logic of a free market? Since most of the world's poor live in rural areas, one solution to this dilemma could be to promote smallholders and rural occupations. This, however, may clash with the efforts to develop large-scale monocultures linked to the national or global agribusiness.

According to a World Bank report (*World Development Report 2008: Agriculture for Development*) it is necessary and possible to develop farming in poor countries in order both to increase supply and reduce poverty. For poor agricultural-based countries the most important objective is to "achieve a large-scale and sustainable smallholder-based productivity revolution."

> Large gaps between current yields and what can be economically achieved with better support services…provide optimism that the ambitious growth targets can be met. Accelerating adoption requires improved incentives, extension systems [i.e. provision of knowledge and skills to the rural population], access to financial services, "market smart" subsidies to stimulate input markets, and better mechanisms for risk management.
>
> (WDR 2008: 232)

However, the report is conscious of the political dilemmas. In the past agriculture-for-development agendas have often failed since *poor peasants prefer the food security allowed through subsistence farming.* Therefore, it asks for a major increase in foreign assistance and national budget money to agriculture to escape from the poverty trap interconnected with traditional farming (WDR 2008: 243).

Which is more sustainable from an ecological point of view: traditional agriculture, based on a combination of several crops and rural occupations, modern large-scale contract farming or modern organic production of food? We know too little to be able to answer this question in an unambiguous way. There have been efforts to make *life cycle assessments* (LCA) on some food products. LCA is used *to evaluate the environmental load of a product or activity* throughout its life cycle. It can help to find the most sustainable ways of producing a certain good or to find out which goods are more "ecological" than others. Organic production requires more land and labor than industrial farming, but the latter requires more fertilizers, pesticides and machinery. Traditional agricultural again, although ecologically quite sustainable, is unable to produce a surplus of food that is required for the feeding of the sprawling urban communities. What are the possibilities to advance *urban agriculture* using all the organic wastes that accumulate in the cities? The collapse of Soviet-style large-scale and petroleum-dependent agriculture in the 1990s left Cuba with a gigantic food security problem. Since then it has managed to organize an urban agriculture that has attracted a lot of international interest. The urban production of vegetables and condiments gives yields per square meter which are remarkably high (Koont 2008).

Climate change and food production

Climate change due to global warming will influence land yields and food security in many ways. The higher levels of atmospheric CO_2 will contribute to increased rates of net photosynthesis and reduced transpiration per unit leaf area. This will often improve water-use efficiency, and thus, by itself increased carbon emissions can increase yield and reduce water use per unit biomass.

However, higher temperatures tend to shorten the growing period. This is especially important in regions where crops are currently grown at higher temperatures. Warming at lower latitudes leads to more severe heat and water stress and greater yield decreases than at higher latitudes. In already hot areas there will be more days that are too hot for virtually all crops. The higher the speed of climate change, the more difficult adaption of agriculture to the new situation will become. The *tragedy of global warming* is that it affects food production in already poor countries negatively. These are the countries that have contributed least to CO_2 emissions and are also the countries that have the smallest resources for adapting to climate change.

Chapter 8

Man and the seas: the oceans and the Baltic Sea

In Chapter 6 we discussed the problem of climate change and discovered, among other things, that the problem is a truly global one. In this chapter we are going to discuss a topic of the same magnitude: the future of the oceans. In the second part of this chapter we will look at the Baltic Sea as a case study. In the closing part of the chapter we will discuss some general principles for a sustainable management or governance of the seas.

The oceans

Ecological importance of the oceans

It is of course not difficult to realize that oceans must have a global impact. The sheer fact that the oceans cover over 70 percent of the Earth's surface convinces us that the oceans must be important and influential in many ways. The enormous size of the oceans is part of the (perception of the) problem, as we will see below; until recently we have been living as if the seas were unlimited, that is like in a "cowboy economy" (or in this case rather a "seaman economy"): catch or throw away as much as you want – the sea will take care of it. Here we see the parallel to the same limitless thinking that has been applied to the air/atmosphere too; whatever goes up in the air – the atmosphere will take care of it.

The role of the oceans in climate

In fact, the atmosphere and the oceans interact in many complicated ways, and the role of the oceans in this process is far greater than is commonly understood. A phenomenon that has lately passed the news threshold, called *El Niño*, would not exist without this interaction. El Niño is related to the (cyclical) ocean warming on the west coast of South America. This occurs in periods of every three to seven years and alternates with a period of colder water, called El Niña. In the atmosphere this is closely related to what is called the Southern Oscillation[1] and the whole phenomenon is referred to as El Niño-Southern Oscillation (ENSO).

El Niño was first discovered by Peruvian and Ecuadorian fishermen and is related to the observed lower catch of fish during the El Niño, which again is related to the ecological changes caused by the phenomenon (because of e.g. different circulation of nutrients). El Niño probably affects the weather of the whole globe. The most well-known effects are increased rain in South and North America and the increased number and power of the hurricanes in the North Atlantic. For instance, the record-breaking season in 2005 with damaging and deadly and world famous storms and hurricanes (Wilma, Rita and Katrina) is seen as a sign of the effects induced by El Niño. Also, the connection between Indian monsoon rains and ENSO is potentially at least as severe as these catastrophes, since the effects on Indian agriculture by drought and instability may be great.[2]

These recent catastrophes (including tsunamis) – which are basically natural/ physical phenomena – have directed the attention of the media towards the rising sea level. In the media the sea-level rise – due to the greenhouse effect – is commonly associated with pictures of melting glaciers and breaking icebergs. Undoubtedly, some of the increase in global heat leads to melting of ice, thus leading to a rise in sea level. However, a great part of the rising heat goes "directly" into the sea and a large contribution to the rising sea level is the (thermal) expansion of the ocean water itself. That is as the temperature of the water rises, the volume of the water grows.

If the oceans are important in the understanding of climate, they are perhaps even more so when it comes to the creation and support of life on Earth. Life probably originates from the development of organic molecules to single cells living in water. These primitive cells, being the first life forms on Earth, were also a prerequisite for the further development of life with the development of photosynthesis, a process which, besides the characteristic of creating biological utilizable energy from light, also produced oxygen, eventually producing an atmosphere that could provide an environment in which more complex life forms could develop. Thus, looking at the Earth from this perspective, the Earth as we know it, with water, different life forms, the atmosphere, climate and so on, has developed in a co-evolution of those elements, and in that sense forms an integrated, interdependent and complex whole.[3]

Should this sound too far-fetched, it should be emphasized that the most important question that humans have to come to grips with – if sustainability is to be achieved – is related to the rules of this complexity. If there is stability, as there obviously is in this system, what are the characteristics of the maintenance of this? In the overall picture, understanding the complexity of the oceans (and coastal regions) is a central element. We will return to this in the last section of this chapter.

The economic and social importance of the seas

From what has been written so far it should be evident that the economic value of the seas cannot be overestimated (literally). Efforts have been made to estimate the economic value of the oceans. According to one study the value of the oceans and coastal systems was estimated to US$21 trillion ($10^{12}$) per year.[4]

Some people have questioned the rational in doing calculations like this, mainly because of the great uncertainties involved. Indeed, there are many problems connected to this kind of valuation, as discussed in Chapter 5, and than the researchers themselves are aware of. However it is difficult to deny the counter-argument that as "[e]cosystem services are largely outside the market and uncertain they are too often ignored or undervalued, leading to error of constructing projects whose social costs far outweigh their benefits."[5]

The social importance of the sea is comparable to (and obviously interdependent with) the economic. For millennia the sea greatly alleviated migration (as well as trade and piracy) through the relative ease of sea transportation. In many cases the sea was of course the only element for traveling from one place to another. And perhaps more important than looking just at the sea, is to focus on coastal zones, that is where the land and the sea meet and where people traditionally have learned to combine the best of both worlds and where the majority of the world's population live today.

For many millennia the human impact on the seas was very small. The size of the human population and the level of technology[6] was such that the rest of nature was not endangered. It is clear that under those circumstances the management of resources was not very institutionalized and rights where interpreted as "rights of the stronger." As population on coastal areas became more stable different types of institutions for ownership of the water also developed. These institutions (or rights) took different shape in different parts of the world. In some places the ownership of local fishing water is private, in some places the waters are commons and in some places the water is owned by the state. The remote waters were open-access (no property rights – no-one owned these) and remained so until the middle of the last century. Then, with the Cod war, Iceland unilaterally in 1972 declared an Exclusive Economic Zone (EEZ) of 200 nautical miles. Since then this policy has been applied by almost all big countries with a coastline. We will retune to this theme in the last part of this chapter.

Why is it important to study the oceans and the seas?

As has been noted several times earlier in this book the basic insight of ecological economics is that the Earth's capacity to function as a sink for human waste and as a resource for depletion is exceeded. Rather, the Earth should be conceived of as a spaceship. And like on a spaceship we cannot do without advanced technology. Although this metaphor is an exaggeration, in the sense that the Earth can never be managed by technology alone – like a spaceship – but must rely on the working of nature, it is indispensible at this stage of environmental degradation to monitor nature, and particularly one of its most important parts, the ocean. And in the preceding section we saw that even such a seemingly simple thing as determining the amount of our "daily fish" requires reliable data on how much we can harvest, that is the Total Allowable Catch (TAC). This cannot be done without a detailed knowledge of the species in question (and also all the interacting species).

But we need more general knowledge than this. On the most general level this is done in oceanography, which is the interdisciplinary study of the oceans and involves geology, biology, chemistry and physics. It is only after we have an accurate enough picture of what is going on in the oceans that we have the prerequisites to take the adequate measures to put the development on the right track. It seems fair to say that this development has not yet reached very far, but is still very much in its infancy.

However, some progress has been achieved lately. Naturally, the scientific study of the seas has progressed with the development in technology. The combined use of satellite (GPS and other) technology with video technology and hydro-acoustic tools, molecular biology and genetics makes it possible to see the complexity of sea life (almost literally) in a new light.

One example is the network of buoys operated by the US National Oceanic and Atmospheric Administration (NOAA) that is monitoring the top 500 m of the tropical Pacific Ocean, and has been established to study the behavior of ENSO.

With modern genetic techniques it is quite easy nowadays to discriminate between different populations of the same species (such as the Baltic Sea cod populations, see below section II). This information may in turn help to understand variation in different species populations.

Another example is the combination of video technologies and video-acoustic tools used to monitor the populations of Antarctic krill and related ecosystems and by this learning more about this central species of this ecosystem – in terms of biomass perhaps the most successful on Earth.[7]

Last, but not least important, modern computerization makes possible the development of complex models in different areas.[8] This means for example that real, complex ecological systems may be made much more comprehensible for the human mind.

The state of the oceans

By means of such methods, as well as of combining these with the study of historical fishing data, recent studies have shown, contrary to common belief, that the oceans are not unlimited. The studies reveal that the word "catastrophe" seems to be the adequate word to describe what has happened to the fisheries in the oceans. The population of great predatory fish, such as tuna, shark, marlin and swordfish has diminished to 10 percent of what it "originally" was. This reduction has happened within the time span of 50 years, that is, since industrial fishing fleets were introduced in the 1950s.[9]

In fact, the seriousness of the situation seems to apply to more than "just" fishing, that is more generally to the biodiversity of the oceans.[10] For instance the introduction of bottom trawls has had catastrophic effects on all life forms in the sea, since this trawling catches virtually everything living on the bottom of the sea.[11]

A picture of the state of the oceans can be acquired from Figure 8.1. It shows the decline in the stock of different species of sea animals (and two aquatic

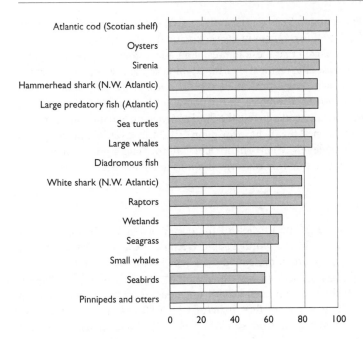

Source: Jackson 2008: 11459, table 1

Figure 8.1 Percent decline of aquatic fauna and flora

ecosystems: wetlands and seagrass), which speaks for itself; for all the species listed there is less than half of the original population, and for the most endangered, mainly those commercially important (and most important as food) there is less than 20 percent left.

What is the reason for this catastrophic decline? The single direct reason is overfishing. However, overfishing alone does not explain why the stocks have not recovered:

> For example, oysters were nearly eliminated by overfishing, but their recovery is now hampered by hypoxia due to eutrophication, by introduced species that compete for space and cause disease, and by the explosive rise of formerly uncommon predators that were previously kept in check by now overfished species.
>
> (Jackson 2008: 11460)

This means that overfishing is not only a problem of the overfishing of the species itself (e.g. oyster in this case) but a problem of the overfishing of the "top" predators checking the lower oyster predators, which in turn hinder oysters from recovering. This effect is amplified and acts together with other man-induced factors (e.g. overgrowth leading to hypoxia (lack of oxygen) due to the use of fertilizers). We will come back to this problem in the section on the Baltic Sea.

It should be emphasized that these figures, dramatic as they are, are just symptoms of the real disease: the (critical) malfunctioning of the oceanic ecosystems.

Of four major ocean ecosystems studied – (1) *coral reefs*, (2) *estuaries and coastal seas*, (3) *continental shelves* and (4) *open ocean pelagic* – the two first were found to be critically endangered, the third endangered and the fourth system was found to be threatened. In all these the main drivers are overfishing and global warming due to rising levels of carbon dioxide. A further factor present in the first three ecosystems (but not in 4) is run-offs of toxins and nutrients.

Plastics in the ocean

An additional example of the illusion of the oceans as an everlasting sink for human waste is plastic. In the North Pacific Ocean there is an area which has recently received public attention, called the Great Pacific Garbage Patch. This gigantic waste bin has been formed by the action of ocean currents in gathering and trapping rubbish. The estimated size of the area varies from 700,000 to 15 million km^2. The biggest part of this litter (of which 80 percent is estimated to come from land and 20 percent from ships) is plastic (80–90 percent). As most of this plastic is not *biodegradable* it disintegrates through solar light, called *photo-degradation*. This continues until the molecular level. As the plastic is ground into smaller and smaller pieces it also increasingly becomes part of the food chain. It is estimated that in many parts of the area there is seven times more plastic in the water than animal plankton.

At all stages of its disintegration plastic has fatal effects, and the victims of this process are popular game for natural photographers. However, the effects of plastics in different forms are still not well known, but plastics may have radical hormonal effects, which may change the sex of species, such as fish or reptiles.

This list of fatal disruptions could be continued, but these examples should give sufficient evidence of the scope of the damage that has arisen as a consequence of human activity. As was noted above, the most threatening of these are overfishing, eutrophication and global warming.

The case of the Baltic Sea

Let us now turn to the Baltic Sea. The purpose of this section is twofold. First, to present a closer and more "myopic" look at an ecosystem than a discussion of oceans can possibly present. And, as noted above, people do not, after all, to a very great extent live only on and by the oceans, but their activity is anchored at some place on land and thus can be located to a coastal system.

Second, we want to give a picture of a smaller and simpler system than the oceans both in an ecological sense as well as linked to ecological–economic–political system. As the Baltic Sea is a closed system it might be looked at as a simplified ocean. It may thus also be possible to learn something about bigger ecosystems by studying the Baltic Sea as a simpler and smaller one.

Of course we do not want to claim that what is going on/has happened in the Baltic Sea will be the fate of the oceans (after all the Baltic Sea is almost literally a drop in the sea compared to the oceans). However, since the majority of the Earth's people are living in the immediate neighborhood of the seas (estimated to be 60 percent about the year 2050), and in uncountable ways dependent on the sea (or other aquatic systems), we think that there are some lessons to be learned here.

A short description of the Baltic Sea

As a sea the Baltic is relatively young, only about 12,000 years old, and it has changed form and saltiness many times. It was formed as a basin where part of the melting water from the continental ice covering Northern Europe collected. Today it is a brackish-water sea, it drains into Kattegat through Öresund (the North Sea). Its area is about 377,000 km^2 and its volume about 21,000 km^3. The water is saltier the nearer you come to the drainage point (Öresund). Periodically (under suitable weather conditions) the Baltic Sea gets salt pulses through Öresund. These salt pulses are vital for many species in the Baltic Sea.

Figure 8.2 The Baltic Sea's drainage basin

Briefly put, this means that the plants and animals of the Baltic Sea have had only a few thousand years to adapt, while species of for example the Mediterranean have had millions of years. Thus there are only a few species that have managed to adapt better, while most species are either freshwater (perch, pike) or saltwater species (cod, herring).

The importance of the Baltic Sea is perhaps better understood if we look at the drainage area (the area from which the rivers drain into the Baltic) of the basin (see Figure 8.2). The area of the basin is about 1.6 million km² and includes more the 250 rivers covering almost all of Sweden and Finland, big parts of Poland, Estonia, Latvia, Lithuania, and parts of Russia, Belarus, Denmark, and Germany. These include the major rivers of northern Europe, such as the Oder, the Vistula, the Neman, the Daugava and the Neva. Many of these rivers are heavily polluted. Most of the rivers in the northern part of the Baltic Sea are also used for hydroelectric power.[12]

We may complete the picture by looking at Table 8.1 where the figures illustrate the relative weight of the different countries with the Baltic as a drainage basin. As will be seen below the relative weights (mainly by population) will give quite a good prognosis of the relative weight of the deposition of different substances into the Baltic Sea. The catchment area of the Baltic Sea carries the weight of a total population of 75 million people, which for a shallow and semi-closed sea is large.

Table 8.1 The Baltic Sea in figures

Country	Total surface area (km²)	Baltic Sea catchment area (km²)	% of total national area within catchment	% of total catchment area	Inhabitants within Baltic Sea catchment area in 2000	Population density in catchment area
Denmark	43094	31110	72.2	1.8	4682400	150.5
Estonia	45226	45100	99.7	2.6	1483942	32.9
Finland	337030	301300	89.4	17.5	5107790	17.0
Germany	357021	28600	8.0	1.7	3140000	109.8
Latvia	64589	64600	100.0	3.8	2529000	39.1
Lithuania	65200	65200	100.0	3.8	3717700	57.0
Poland	312685	311900	99.7	18.1	38609000	123.8
Russia	17075200	314800	1.8	18.3	7738000	24.6
Sweden	449964	440040	97.8	25.6	8374000	19.0
Total	18750009	1720170				

Source: Helsinki Commission (HELCOM) 2007: 33.

Toxins

The Baltic Sea – because of the relatively small volume of water combined with small inflow from the North Sea and the relatively big area with inflow from the drainage basin – is much more vulnerable to the occurrence of toxins, such as dioxins and heavy metals, than comparable emission would be in open sea waters.

Table 8.2 shows that compared with the North Atlantic, the Baltic Sea concentration of heavy metals is greater by a factor from 3 (lead) to 50 (zinc).

Table 8.2 Concentration of heavy metals in the North Atlantic and the Baltic Sea

Element	North Atlantic	Baltic Sea	Factor
Mercury	0.15–0.3	5–6	~ 20
Cadmium	4	12–16	~ 4
Lead	7	12–20	~ 3
Copper	75	500–700	~ 10
Zinc	10–75	600–1000	~ 10–50

Source: Helsinki Commission (HELCOM) 2007: 33

Note
Measured as dissolved metals in sea water (Ng/kg).

The pollution of the Baltic Sea may be airborne, such as sulfur (in acid rain) or water-borne. But when speaking of toxins, they mainly originate from the countries in the drainage basin, and this is shown using cadmium[13] as an example in Figure 8.3.

Although many of these toxic substances occur naturally, they chiefly originate from anthropogenic sources, that is from industrial processes that require the use of toxic substances. For instance the main contributors of the deposition of cadmium are electronics, metallurgy, paint and plastic.

Exposure to the toxins discussed here may be fatal. Not only are these toxins poisonous on the individual level, but they may be so for the whole species, especially to animals high in the food chain, such as seals, eagles and predators in general, such as humans. This is because the toxins accumulate in the fat and

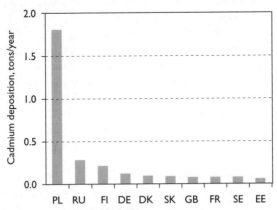

Source: Helsinki Commission (HELCOM) 2007: 33

Figure 8.3 The ten European countries with the largest contribution to the deposition of cadmium to the Baltic Sea

protein tissues of these relatively long lived animals – and the more so, the higher up in the food chain they are. As a matter of fact, this may endanger (the) whole species (as already has happened with species like the grey seal and the white-tailed-eagle[14] in the Baltic sea, as the toxins make the animals sterile). This, in turn, as will be seen below, may change the whole ecosystem, since the top predators have a key role in the maintenance of the stability of the system – as we know from the section on the oceans.

Due to the emission of toxins used by agriculture and industry the fish sold in the Baltic countries exceed regulations on contaminants. Recommendations have been released by the authorities not to eat fish (herring and salmon) more than once a week.[15]

Toxins can also be produced naturally, foremostly by green algae, the increased growth of which seems to be highly related to the eutrophication of the sea. Production of algae and toxins is furthermore very probably related to global warming.

Oil

The Baltic Sea has some of the busiest shipping routes in the world. The number of vessels at any moment on the sea is about 2,000.[16] Of the problems caused by this traffic, oil is probably the biggest one.[17] Furthermore, these problems are worsened by ice in the winter. First this makes the fairways narrower with a larger risk of collision, and second, if an oil spill happens the oil is much more difficult to collect. The traffic is steadily growing as Russia is building new oil harbors in the Finnish gulf. Half of the vessels head for Primorsk in Russia. Needless to say, even a minor accident involving a big oil tanker would have catastrophic effects on flora and fauna.[18]

But the risk for a big oil slick is not the only threat that oil transport and handling poses for the Baltic Sea. Illegal discharge of oil happens on land and on sea.[19] The distribution chain of oil and oil products is not proof, but leakages take place everywhere where oil changes media (from tank to tank, from tank to car, and so on) or form (distillation, waste oil). Of these leakages, whether mixed with rainwater, or evaporation, or some other form, many eventually end in the sea. The accumulated effect of these leakages is not well verified, but it is likely to be bigger than the more dramatic oil accidents.

Aliens[20]

Over 100 different species living in the Baltic Sea are of foreign origin and around 80 of these seem capable of reproducing there. They range from fish and crabs to microorganisms (or even mammals if we count the semiaquatic mink). Some of these have been implanted deliberately,[21] but most have come with the ballast water of ships, mainly from North America.

American comb jelly (*Mnemiopsis leidyi*)[22] is a very recent immigrant into the Baltic Sea. It was first observed in the southern Baltic Sea in 2006. It originates from ballast water from South America. At the time of writing (autumn 2008) it has invaded the northern Baltic Sea. The first examples of the damaging impact of comb jelly were found in the Black Sea. Since this species is a predator (on e.g. fish eggs and larvae) and as it managed (due to the bad state of the ecosystem?) to invade a greater part of the Black Sea in less than a year, fish stocks changed dramatically. It seems very probable that this new species can survive the Baltic Sea winter, which of course is a condition for its success. However, so far no catastrophic effects have been observed in the Baltic Sea.

Other aliens include the *Cercopagis pengoi,* which is a predatory water flea native to the Caspian Sea area. It was first observed in the Baltic Sea in 1992 after which the invasion has been fast. The problem with this species is that it soils fish nets and there may be some competition for plankton with the Baltic herring. It was observed in great numbers in the Bothnian Bay during the warm summer of 2002, but has not been observed en masse since.

It is not clear when the phytoplankton[23] *Prorocentrum minimum* arrived in the Baltic Sea or whether it arrived by ballast or through currents, but it has become well established in the Baltic during the past two decades. It has been observed blooming in the Archipelago Sea, and in coastal waters it has been observed to dominate biomass. Although potentially toxic, it has not been observed to have toxic blooming.

Marenzelleria viridis is a worm that lives inside bottom sediments. Since 1985, when it was first observed, it seems to have invaded the Baltic Sea. Owing to the relatively simple structure of the Baltic benthic (bottom) ecology there is a risk that this species may out-compete some vulnerable species and thus change the whole bottom ecosystem.

Finally, we might mention a bird species: the great (black) cormorant (*Phalacrocorax carbo*), not necessarily because it is a threat to the Baltic Sea nature, but as an example of the difference in how people perceive different species and how this can lead to quite aggressive attitudes towards certain species. Thus this also illustrates the complex relation between the social and the ecological spheres, that is how humans relate to different parts of nature.

The cormorant is not really a newcomer, but has historically shown great fluctuations in its population. But only during the last decennia has it established colonies on small islands in the Swedish and Finnish archipelago (in fact this invasion seems to have taken place all around Europe). The arguments against the cormorant are mainly two: it nests in trees and its droppings are very phosphorous and will eventually kill the trees. This has given rise to "ghost islands" where there is nothing left except the dead trees, the black cormorants and their droppings.

The second argument is that the bird eats fish and thus harms fisheries. This has given rise to a heated discussion in the press and on different chat sites on the Internet in both Sweden and Finland and the tone of the discussion has been such that it does not seem unthinkable that people "will take justice into their own hands" to reduce the number of cormorants. There is not room here to go into the details of this discussion, but it is interesting to compare this case with a corresponding one: the expansion of swans in the Finnish–Swedish archipelago. Swans, both the Whooper Swan (*Cygnus Cygnus*) and the Mute Swan (*Cygnus Olor*), have expanded as well as cormorants during the last decades and their population exceeds that of the cormorant by two to one. They nest and feed in important spawning waters of many fish species, and the swan can really behave aggressively towards people. However, depending perhaps on the fact that the swan is conceived of as a "holy bird" it is generally treated very gently.[24]

Scientists agree that the increase in the cormorant population is a result of the eutrophication of the Baltic Sea and the growth of species induced by that, especially such species as the Common Roach (*Rutilus*). Thus, a sufficient reduction of eutrophication (e.g. mainly by diminishing the use of fertilizers) would balance the cormorant population. However, there are also signs of natural controls; the white-tailed eagle (*Haliaeetus albicilla*) seems to have developed a taste for cormorant.

It is hard to say whether the Baltic Sea will suffer from catastrophes due to the immigration of alien species. Catastrophes may only be temporary and ecosystems may recover by themselves, for instance the American comb jelly disappeared from the Black Sea due to the appearance of a predator (which also probably came by ballast water).

As we shall see below, the Baltic Sea has great problems with is *original* flora and fauna. Alien species probably worsen the stress on the ecologic systems. It may also be that ecological systems that are "out of order" are more prone to the attack of invaders. In other words, it is probable that the original flora and fauna better could resist newcomers if the water was of good quality, such as, for instance, it contained less fertilizer.

Eutrophication and dead zones

The occurrence of nitrogen and phosphorus in the sea is a natural requirement for life and is not as such an environmental problem. It is only when you get too much in one place that problems arise. But as a consequence of these fertilizers, the Baltic Sea has changed quite rapidly from a quite sparsely equipped to a eutrophic ecosystem.

Algal blooming (which by no means is specific to the Baltic Sea, but rather universal) may provide some information about the relation between blooming and eutrophication, and thus about the state of the ecological system, since the Baltic Sea provides a kind of natural laboratory for studying this. Algal blooming in the Baltic Sea has increased recently due to agricultural runoff, and probably also due to climate warming. It is an example of a quite direct interconnection effect of the relation between the economy and the ecosystem. One could perhaps express it as "the ecosystem bites back." This is because many species of algae produce toxic substances with effects that are harmful for people and animals.

A recent report in *Science*[25] shows that *dead zones* (oxygen-free zones) have spread exponentially since the 1960s in the coastal oceans around the world, affecting a total area of 245,000 km^2. Dead zones are clearly concentrated in the most densely and industrialized parts of the world, such as east/northern Europe, the US east coast and coasts of China and Japan. Dead zones are present in such diverse seas as the Kattegat, Black Sea, Gulf of Mexico and East China Sea. As it happens, all these waters are densely fished areas. Dead zones are characterized as "the key stressor on marine ecosystems" and "rank with over-fishing, habitat loss, and harmful algal blooms as global environmental problems."[26] And, indeed, these problems are not separate but frequently occur together. According to this report the Baltic Sea has the largest dead zone in the world.

Fishery and the newer history of the Baltic Sea in a nutshell

We have now discussed the most important features characterizing the state of the Baltic Sea. However, we have so far not said much about how these phenomena hang together. They are connected in different ways, but perhaps the most rational way of looking at this is how it works as an ecosystem. An ecosystem can of course be described in different ways, but perhaps the best way here to try to understand it is to look at it from a perspective that is meaningful for humans. Fishing is perhaps one of the most important elements that connect the peoples around the Baltic Sea.

There are about 100 different fish species in the Baltic Sea. The commercially most important are cod, Baltic herring, sprat, salmon, and, among the fresh and brackish water fish species, whitefish, perch, pike and perchpike. Of these, cod, Baltic herring, and sprat produce over 90 percent of the Baltic Sea catch.

In the 1990s you could see big fishing vessels from around Europe in the Baltic Sea. As a matter of fact the Baltic Sea at that time provided for 20 percent of the global catch of cod, an amazing amount when you compare the sea on a world scale. Since those years the cod catch has gone down to about 20 percent of what it was then. What has happened? To get a picture of how an ecosystem like the Baltic Sea functions we may look at Figure 8.4.

The figure gives a picture of how the key species in the Baltic have fluctuated[27] during the twentieth century. The species included here are cod, clupeids (sprat and Baltic herring), Gray seal and Ringed seal.[28] We can see that great changes have occurred during the century: in the beginning of the century the population of the seal (the main predator) was high and the fish population was low. As a large seal population was seen as competing with the fishery the hunting for seal was on a high level. At about 1940 (with the Second World War and the decline in hunting after that) the seal population seems to have stabilized. However, a new decline came in the mid-1970, due to toxic pollutants. As can be seen in Figure 8.4 the decrease in the seal population led to an increase in the cod population and, as a consequence of that, a decline in clupeid population. After the stabilization of the seal stock the figure shows the curves of cods and clupeid populations roughly as mirror images. This is due to the fact that the cod as the main predator controls the clupeid population.

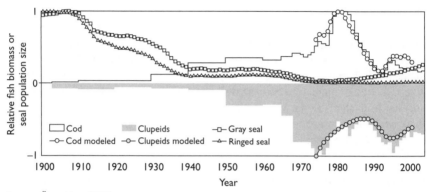

Source: Österblom 2007

Figure 8.4 The relative abundance of key species in the Baltic Sea

So during the period described in Figure 8.4, three major changes took place. After 1930 the cod took over as the main predator from the seal, mainly because of the hunting of the seal. Starting after the Second World War, the sea shifted from a "clearwater sea" to an eutrophicated sea, due to the increased use of fertilizers in agriculture all around the Baltic Sea. This in turn led to an increase in fish growth due to increased growth of food, but also created the conditions for *hypoxia* (dead zones) as the oxygen was used up. This, which meant bad conditions for cod reproduction, plus overfishing led to the shift from cod to clupeids as the dominant fish.

The picture painted above, although simplified, shows briefly how the Baltic Sea ecosystem has developed during the last decade. The change has been very abrupt. Although there certainly are natural factors involved, such as wintertime ice cover thickness, salty water pulses from the North Sea and so on, there can be no doubt that the major changes that have occurred in the Baltic Sea during the last century are anthropogenic (man-made); toxins, over-fertilization, overfishing, and most probably also the greenhouse effect, are the dominant causes of the bad state of the Baltic Sea today. The state the Baltic Sea is in right now is potentially instable, and what kind of sea and ecological system it will be in future is critically dependent upon the measures taken today as a response to the situation. There seems to be a large consensus among scientists that the most important immediate measure to take is to stop overfishing and to diminish the inflow of nutrients, mainly nitrogen and phosphorus, that largely comes through the rivers as an overflow from the use of fertilizers in agriculture.

Looking back now at part one of the chapter about the oceans, what can we say? It is true that the state of the Baltic Sea is worse than the oceans in general. The Baltic Sea is more polluted, has larger dead zones, and the whole ecological system may be on the verge of a change to quite another one – which we obviously do not even know what it will be like.

However, what we also saw was that the problems of the Baltic Sea and the oceans are surprisingly similar and, indeed, that to say that the fate of the Baltic may be the fate of the oceans, might not be such a great overstatement after all: we noted the state of the coral reefs and estuaries and coastal seas in the oceans and the greatest threats to these are overfishing, eutrophication and global warming. (Actually we knew this, the new thing here is the striking similarity between the oceans and the Baltic Sea.) So the problems we found existing for the Baltic Sea are just not some problems valid only for an exotic northern sea ecological system – the problems are global. Or, in other words, we may say that what is imaginable for a relatively small sea has taken place and/or is happening on the unimaginable scale: the oceans.

What to do with the seas

The obvious question to ask here is: with all this knowledge, how can this be happening? As we just noted one of the major environmental problems around the world is overfishing. How can we have overfishing when people can read daily in the newspapers that fishing is in crisis? The problem, of course, is very complex and implies consumer choices as well as producer choices. Let us look at the problem from the latter perspective.

Now, what has happened in the large (oceans) as well as on smaller scale (the Baltic Sea) is commonly referred to as the *tragedy of the commons*, or the *problem of open access*. These concepts refer to a situation where there is a common resource (e.g. a common parcel of land, where cows are allowed to graze). In such a situation, if the animals are privately owned, there is an incentive for a herder to increase the number of his cows grazing on this common property. The herder's profit will increase with each of his cows grazing, at a relatively small decrease in the stress on the common grazing land. However, as every herder has this incentive, the number of cows will increase with resulting overgrazing until an eventual catastrophe occurs. What is individually a rational thing to do is collectively – and in the long run – an irrational (i.e. catastrophic) thing to do.

The same metaphor can be applied to the use of the seas. From the perspective of a single fisherman, an increase of his fleet from one boat to two boats may double his catch and profit, and this at a negligible effect in the catch of other fishermen. However, when everyone has an incentive to increase his fleet, the result is eventually catastrophic for everyone.[29]

But if an Exclusive Economic Zone (EEZ)[30] has been imposed by most countries, does this not mean that the area of open access has diminished, and thus, that at least some improvement has happened in the situation, as the commons have decreased in size? Unfortunately, there is no guarantee that a mere "nationalization" of the fishing water will restore the diminished fish populations in the seas.[31] First, the diminishing of the fish stock, demands measures and management with organized international cooperation. But even disregarding this, the extension of the national fishing areas will not as such ensure a recovery (or even a status quo) of the fish stocks. The reason for this is obvious: if nothing else is specified, an extended EEZ is still *open access,* even if on a smaller, national scale. So something more obviously has to be specified concerning the *property rights* (right to use a resource).

A way (which no one other than an economist could think of) of managing property rights would be to privatize the seas, that is by some method, such as donating or selling parcels of the sea, as happened long ago with other (land) resources. Needless to say, this is more easily suggested than done because such a process would be much more difficult than on land for a variety of reasons. Most importantly, fish and sea animals migrate widely, and do not obey national or other borders. Widening the scope, different ecological and physical cycles (currents), and other ecological services can cover large areas, and may, as we have seen, be eventually globally interconnected. Besides these practical arguments against privatization, there seems to be quite a large public opinion on different levels (regionally, globally) that the aquatic commons should not be privatized.

But on the other hand, as the situation today clearly is untenable and immediate action is required, are there other alternatives available? As a matter of fact, there have been experiments going on for quite a while now on "quasi-privatization" methods of the seas. Perhaps the most popular one today is Individual Transferable Quotas (ITQ). ITQs were first introduced in New Zealand, and since then in Australia, Iceland, Canada, and the United States.

As scientists and fisheries managers begin to understand that the tragedy of the commons was a brute fact also for the oceans, it was clear that to hinder extinction an upper limit for fishing had to be set. This upper limit is, of course, the highest possible harvest which could be taken without diminishing the fish stock (sustainability). This is called the Total Allowable Catch (TAC). Briefly put, under a TAC system the upper limit is specified, but not who are allowed to fish and by what means. Because of this it led to a race for the catch, with a lot of negative effects, such as overinvestment in boats, overlooking of safety requirements because maintenance takes time from the boat on the sea, which increases the risk of (deadly) accidents. Bycatch and waste was increased as the catch was maximized. Furthermore the fishing season was shortened to a few weeks or even days, as the fishermen tried to catch as much as quickly as possible. As a result of this flooding over in the market, prices fell sharply for a short period after which the consumer had to turn to frozen fish.

As a remedy to this short-sighted behavior and the related drawbacks that this system induced the system of ITQ was proposed. These are exclusive rights to harvest a specific portion (specified in units or percentage) of the fish (-stock) for some time-period. Because ITQ guarantees a specific portion of the stock to the owner of this right, this eliminates the incentive to race, and should thus also diminish the side-effects of this.

Recent reports have indicated that ITQ has been successful, not only in reducing the risks connected to the fishing race, but also in lowering the risk for the extinction fish stocks compared to the TAC system. However, in the (relatively) few cases (about 1 percent of total fisheries) where ITQs (i.e. essentially a market for fishing rights) have been introduced it has not passed without costs. In many places the social costs have been heavy, as the small boat owners have not been able to compete with bigger fleets and thus have been forced to give up their liveli-hood, sustained for generations in small fishing communities, which are now destroyed.

Thus, the experience of the ITQs so far is too limed to draw any final conclu-sions about this introductory experiment in using the market mechanism as a tool for the governance of the seas, although the first large study shows that it might be a promising candidate. It seems quite clear though, given the great diversity and complexity of aquatic life, that ITQs can only be one (although probably impor-tant) of the many methods of managing oceans and coastal systems.

This means that there is no single solution that will do the trick and save the seas for us. The seas have to be managed and governed. So far almost nothing has been said about the political dimension of the problem. Briefly, this would mean that there is no static solution to the problems, but rather it should be depicted as a process, in which people and different groups with very different, often oppo-site, interests in the problem, from different areas and levels, must reach a solution about the general frames of the process, and then agree to stick to those frames.

For example, when humans arrived at the Baltic Sea, some 7,000 years ago, these humans were living is small tightly integrated groups, with very similar interests and their economy and social system was one integrated system. As time passed, people of different tribes learned to cooperate, the societies grew, techni-cal development took place with such phenomena as professional and occupa-tional specialization, villages became towns, and many gods were substituted for one, nation states evolved, and so on. Today we live in a society where only a small part of the population is occupied by fishing and farming, most people are living in towns, mostly looking at computer displays, quite independently of whether it is work or leisure time.

Although a unification in culture ("commercialization") has taken place largely around the world at a very rapid pace during the last decades, people's life spheres and interests are separate. Decision-makers are largely specialized and isolated from the life-world of people at the grassroots level. And we could go on with drawing upon the differences which are great at least on the technological level between us and our ancestors. However, there is one thing in common which we have with our ancestors from 7,000 years ago. Just as these people very obviously did – since we (the generation of today) are alive – we also have to learn to adapt to ultimate limits which nature puts before us. This cannot happen if we do not learn to adapt the scale of our techno-socio-economic system to a sustainable level.

If this may sound an unnecessary repetition of the central message of this book, it is still worth repeating here, because here we come to perhaps the hardest problem of all, that of solving the problem of the abyss between the political speeches and real life. As noted, in the Baltic Sea, as in many coastal regions around the world in industrialized countries, fishing is but a small part of the total economy's production, and fishermen a relatively tiny part of the work-power.

However, still fishermen seem to be disproportionally well represented when it comes to their interests. The reasons for this are manifold: fishermen represent an interest group with a concentrated and intensive interest formulation compared to other more indifferent groups. Fishermen also have a role to play in nations' interest in fish and other aquatic resources. Fishermen also represent tradition and cultural identity, and in many, if not all, coastal cultures, are seen as heroes. Everyone knows that fishing is hard work, which has been, and still is, done with the risk of your life. Fishermen fight for a disappearing tradition and lifestyle, which as much as it has changed technologically, is still pretty much the same, due to just the central element: the sea.

This is also related to the fact that fish is, and increasingly so, an important part of people's diets, directly and indirectly. Fishermen are the keepers of (the largely hidden) information about where the fish (food) can be found, which is perhaps the first and most important information humans shared with each other.

The list could be continued, but already this should illustrate one aspect of the complexity of the problem of our relation to nature in an industrial society of today. To come to grips with this type of problem traditional management has to be recast.

Coastal governance

Here we will discuss some general characteristics and principles for governance (management) of coastal systems. What do we mean with coastal governance? According to Kooiman:[32]

> *Governing* can be considered as the totality of interactions, in which public as well as private actors participate, aimed at solving societal problems or creating societal opportunities; attending to the institutions as contexts for those governing interactions; and establishing a normative foundation for all those activities. *Governance* can be seen as the totality of theoretical conceptions of governing.

Some idea of what governance could mean generally in this connection (coastal or marine governance) can be achieved from Figure 8.5. It might be instructive to illustrate this figure with what we have learned about the Baltic Sea so far, but it should be applicable to other coastal regions as well.

Governance is thus to be seen as a dynamic process where a lot of actors interact rather than merely as a static picture of "what governors do." This process involves as an ideal all stakeholders and interest groups, including scientists, business organizations, non-governmental organizations (NGOs). Of course, traditional government has an important role also in this process, but it is not decisive and "dictatoric."[33]

Starting from the left in Figure 8.5, the first column lists the most important characteristics of a coastal system. The second focuses on the main shortcomings

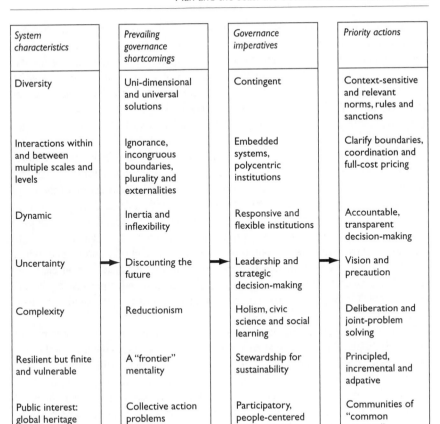

System characteristics	Prevailing governance shortcomings	Governance imperatives	Priority actions
Diversity	Uni-dimensional and universal solutions	Contingent	Context-sensitive and relevant norms, rules and sanctions
Interactions within and between multiple scales and levels	Ignorance, incongruous boundaries, plurality and externalities	Embedded systems, polycentric institutions	Clarify boundaries, coordination and full-cost pricing
Dynamic	Inertia and inflexibility	Responsive and flexible institutions	Accountable, transparent decision-making
Uncertainty	Discounting the future	Leadership and strategic decision-making	Vision and precaution
Complexity	Reductionism	Holism, civic science and social learning	Deliberation and joint-problem solving
Resilient but finite and vulnerable	A "frontier" mentality	Stewardship for sustainability	Principled, incremental and adpative
Public interest: global heritage	Collective action problems	Participatory, people-centered development	Communities of "common concern"

Source: Glavovic 2008: 333.

Figure 8.5 Marine governance characteristics and principles

of prevailing governance; what is done wrong. The third column gives the main principles according to which governance should be carried out and the fourth states main priorities for the actions carried out. As we do not have room here to discuss all the details of the figure and concepts, let us look at only one level in the columns (which is of course closely related to the others). Let us look at level 5 which starts with the concept of "complexity" in the first column. As we learned in the section "Fishery and the newer history of the Baltic Sea in a nutshell," the Baltic Sea forms a quite complex ecosystem, with complicated interactions between different species in the sea, which we are only beginning to understand now. To this we of course have to count the complexity added by human interaction with (or the role in this) ecosystem, as well as the complexity of the human socio-economic system itself that is of relevance to the Baltic Sea. The shortcoming of the prevailing governance system at this level is called "reductionism," that is it looks at isolated parts of the whole system, such as the fishing of different species, professional and leisure fishing, perhaps with the administration and management of these in separate departments and so on "with the expectation that the whole problem will be solved as each mini-solution is re-aggregated."[34] Reductionism is the traditional way of doing things, both within science and administration. Reductionism is also relatively "easy," since it usually is only concerned with one point of view of the problem and may also serve vested interests.

In contrast to reductionism the appropriate governance imperative for a complex system should be "Holism, civic science and social learning." Holism means the interaction of the part is something more than the simple aggregation of the parts. Civic science complements scientific knowledge with local and traditional (and even tacit) knowledge and does not override local values. Social learning implies that actors and groups in the system may and should learn from each other. Thus traditional knowledge may be combined with actual scientific knowledge, which could be further communicated to local schools, for instance. Actual cases for social learning could be, for example, the above-mentioned expansion of the seal or black cormorant populations, where biologists and fishermen could learn from each other.

In the priority action column we have "Deliberation and joint problem-solving." Briefly put, this could be seen as a process (or discourse) where stakeholders (among whom we count scientists and those with local and traditional knowledge) meet. By trying to solve a problem, like a decision of a fishing quota or of the preservation of a species, through a process like this it seems likely that the result is more fair and enduring, since all parties take part in it. Thus the possibility for (social) sustainability also increases. (Ecological sustainability should be ensured by the scientifically determined limits of the ecosystem.)

It is not difficult to imagine that meetings or a process construed according to such principles can easily lead to dispute and confrontation. Thus it is clear that for such discussions – given the lack of an appropriate negotiation culture – proper rules and even "training" for such gatherings would have to be established.

Compared to "traditional governance" a process like this is likely to take much more time, and is in that sense inefficient. Although efficiency is inevitable, in a full world it would seem worthwhile to sacrifice some momentary efficiency to reach sustainability. Although we have been speaking about this stage in a process, it does not mean that negotiation has to go on all the time and forever. Applying "deliberation and joint problem-solving" as a principle of governance is something that is in formation and certainly new institutional solutions will appear. And sustainability is after all about how to form the way of living in a steady-state mold, which by definition avoids the risks and eventual catastrophe which exponential growth inherently contains. This would almost logically seem to mean that (at least the fatal) questions to decide about should be smaller and fewer. We may also hope that as people become aware of the tragedy of commons it would increase their willingness to reach consensus.[35]

Chapter 9

Growth and degrowth: is another economy possible?

For the last two centuries the urge towards growth has marked humankind. The industrial revolution in Europe affected the rest of the world. The demand for raw materials, the need to extend the markets for mass-produced goods, and the establishment of huge transnational companies drew all territories into the whirlpool of global economic growth. As the two most populous countries – China and India – have been fully integrated into the capitalist world economy, not as peripheral producers of raw materials, but as fast growing workshops of the world, the connection between economic growth and ecological sustainability has been highlighted. The demand for non-renewable resources, arable land and fishing grounds increases as affluence spreads, straining our ecosystems to the limit.

Why has growth become the religion of our times? Besides the obvious and ever-present effort to eliminate abject poverty there are three interlinked mechanisms that drive us towards growth. Each mechanism constitutes a powerful growth machine, but together they form a syndrome – *growthmania* – that propels us, even though poverty could be eliminated with what we already have the capability to produce. They make our efforts to achieve ecological sustainability exceptionally difficult. The three mechanisms are capitalist profit-driven growth, the positional competition between affluent individuals, and the rivalry between collectives, especially nation-states.

In this chapter we briefly describe these three growth mechanisms and their interconnections. We shall also present some ideas for "*degrowth*" – that is curtailing the urge to grow. Which possibilities do we have to reverse the current trends and make a transition to a just and ecologically sustainable economy? We shall discuss the concept of prosperity, outline the conditions for sustainable macroeconomics and emphasize the need for a global ethic.

Profit-driven capitalism

A central question for ecological economists is the *relationship between capitalism and ecological sustainability*. Capitalism is an economic system in which employers, using privately owned capital, hire wage labor to produce commodities for the purpose of making a profit. Money is invested in assets that are supposed to give the investor/capitalist an income stream that returns that money with a profit. The system is inclined towards growth, since, in order to be preserved as profit-gaining money capital is directed towards accumulation, innovation and growth. If money could grow without being invested in real capital for the production of material commodities, this urge could be reconciled with ecological sustainability, but to earn profits money must in general be invested in real assets.

When money is not only a means of exchange and accounting, but actually the main driver, the dynamic of the economy is to a large extent determined by the financial sector. It deals in values that are expressed in symbolic money terms. Thanks to the informational revolution, astronomical amounts can be transacted cheaply and almost instantly. The participants in the financial markets try to find investments that give the highest expected return. Loans given, assets bought and shares acquired have only this purpose: to make the investor richer. In this sense the financial sector is a formidable growth machine. Money as such does not have much impact on the ecology, but money invested for gain in the commodity-producing sector certainly does.

Because of its symbolic nature the financial sector is also quite volatile. The value of stocks and other assets fluctuate in ways that often cannot be rationally explained even after they have happened. Still the fluctuations and expectations related to the financial economy determine the outcomes of the commodity producing "real" economy. Those who finance the "real" investments look for a reward that at the end must take the form of more money. "More money" translates into economic growth. "Economic growth" again can be translated into higher incomes and consumption. The pressure from the purely fictive monetary sphere, through the "real" production sphere, eventually, by extending the need for labor, energy and materials, makes its imprint on the environment.

In capitalism not only the profit motive fuels growth. Since the majority of the population is dependent on wage work for their living there is a widespread *fear of unemployment*. Employment again is closely linked to production growth. According to the so called *Okun's law* there is a fixed relationship between the rate of growth of real GDP and the change in the unemployment rate. If GDP grows less than a certain percent the rate of unemployment will increase. A 3 percent growth is often mentioned as necessary for the USA to avoid unemployment from increasing.[1] This "normal" or "natural" growth in the production of goods and services is due to growth of the labor force, capital accumulation and technological progress. The link between growth and employment makes degrowth politically unfeasible as long as job creation primarily depends on the profit motive.

Status-driven consumerism

But it is not only profit-driven accumulation that motivates the urge to grow. It works in combination with two types of rivalries that may be even more deep-rooted socially and psychologically. There is an ongoing struggle for status among individuals and on a higher level between different communities, in particular nation-states.

In his book *Social Limits to Growth* (1977) Fred Hirsch introduced the term *positional competition*. He wanted to understand why economic advance had become such a compelling goal to individuals, even though it yields disappointing fruits when most of us achieve it. Hirsch's contribution was to show that as affluence increased competition for social positions and facilities with a public character tended to become fiercer. In order to have a top career, to get an attractive spouse, or just to get the best table at the restaurant, you may have to outperform your rivals, and this can be costly. It may require a lot of work and attention and at the same time gobble up some natural resource. Since there are several strictly *positional goods* that by their nature are available only for a few, the competition for them is often fierce and resource-demanding. When you compete for status and position you get involved in a zero-sum game, where those who gain do it at the expense of those who lose.

One form of positional competition is the effort to "keep up with the Joneses." When people try to achieve at least the same standard of consumption as their fellow citizens, and if possible to show off by buying items that are likely to impress others, they enter into a game that hardly increases overall satisfaction, although the costs may be substantial both in terms of work and damage to the environment. This effort to emulate the affluent has spread to the whole globe. Thanks to the informational and communicational revolution people all over the world know of the habits in high consumption societies. Films, tourists and guest workers bring Western upper-middle-class lifestyles to every corner of the Earth.

Related to this drive to express your worth through "conspicuous consumption" – a term minted by Thorstein Veblen – is the *drive for novelty*.

> Novelty keeps us buying more stuff. Buying more stuff keeps the economy going. The end result is a society "locked in" to consumption growth by forces outside the control of individuals.
>
> Physical infrastructure and social architecture conspire against us. Lured by our evolutionary roots, bombarded with persuasion, and seduced by novelty: we are like children in the sweet shop, knowing that sugar is bad for us; unable to resist the temptation.
>
> (Jackson 2009: 95)

Standard economics sees our needs as unlimited. We can never become completely satisfied, but are constantly striving to get more, better and new. Ecological, as well as social, institutional and feminist economics, believe that there are clear limits to our basic needs. The positional rivalry between individuals, however, fits the standard assumption of unlimited needs. However, standard economics also assumes that our preferences are constant – not dependent on what others have or think of us – and therefore it does not reckon with the negative externalities of status-driven consumerism.

The drive for position and novelty can easily be exploited by profit-driven firms and by politicians who promise to promote growth. However, growth stemming from the urge to improve people's relative standing can easily become self-defeating. It is a game where the gains are not greater than before, only redistributed between the participants. However, the costs incurred by the players tend to rise as the competition gets tougher. We may invoke the "tragedy of the commons" metaphor also for this situation.

The theory of positional competition can explain the *Easterlin paradox* mentioned in Chapter 2. Happiness and life satisfaction seem to have little or no positive correlation with economic growth in the long run. In the short run, however, changes in incomes and the rate of unemployment do influence how people view their lives.

International rivalry and trade

We live in a world economy in which finance, production and consumption have become globalized. However, politically the world is divided into independent states that cooperate in many ways, but which also compete for power, status, income and resources. This international competition is analogous to the positional competition between individuals, and it also is a formidable engine for growth. When Japan in order to respond to the military and economic challenge from the West underwent the Meiji restoration its rallying call became "rich country, strong military." Japan was the only Asian country that in the nineteenth century managed to industrialize and to establish a modern military force. It became a model for other non-Western countries. Growth was not only good, it was necessary in order to cope with your rivals.

The positional competition between states is intensified by the need to get hold of scarce natural resources and by the deterioration of the environment. Only if you are rich and strong enough will it be possible to secure a steady stream of those necessities – as well as luxuries – that you want to import from other countries.

Even though violent conflicts over natural resources are serious and visible, for an ecological economist the peaceful competition between nations that occurs through trade and investments is of special interest. The possibility of "importing" land, water, energy and other resources through international trade blurs the link between production and consumption. A country can, by importing more natural resources than it exports, save the ecological capital at home, without having to reduce its consumption. There may be an *ecologically unequal exchange* that "transfers" sustainability from one nation to another. Although trade may be balanced in monetary terms, it may be nonequivalent in biophysical terms, measured in such units as tons of used up materials, exergy,[2] water or ecological footprints. Such nonequivalence may be critical if it implies a gradual deterioration of the natural capital in the exporting country.

The fact that we live in a full world implies that we should reduce our consumption of material goods. But the fact that we live in an unequal world means that many goods – commodities such as bananas and coffee, as well as finished products such as shoes and computers – can be produced at very low costs to affluent people. Even if international trade may be balanced and profitable in money terms for all producers, it may be highly *unbalanced and unsustainable in biophysical terms* (Andersson and Lindroth 2001).

In order to finance their imports or to pay their loans, some countries may be obliged to export natural resources, biomass or exergy to such an extent that their own life-support systems are weakened. The situation of such countries in the world economy can therefore deteriorate gradually. Other countries, which are able to sell high-priced products and services that require little natural resources or sinks, may be able to increase their natural capital even though their consumption measured in biophysical terms exceeds their own biocapacity.

This possibility can be labeled *ecologically unsustainable exchange*. It is not perceived in monetary terms and it is therefore unacknowledged as unequal by standard economic theory. Indeed economists may urge each low-wage country to further reduce its production costs in order to compete with other low-wage exporters. This would of course increase the troubles for the whole group of poor countries exporting similar goods.

Another possibility is that both trading parties may overshoot their biocapacity in order to improve their relative positions. This can occur if two countries engage in positional competition of the type mentioned above. The nature of the status in regard to which the countries compete is not always the same; it may be military, economic or even spiritual; but in any case the result may turn into ecological unsustainability in both countries, since they use up ecological reserves in their efforts to promote competitiveness and growth. They may also, as in the case of global warming, be destroying a global resource essential for both of them and for everybody else.

It should, however, be emphasized that trade, even if unequal in biophysical terms, normally (and in a world that is not full) increases sustainability. Thanks to international trade *a country may import and consume resources which are scarce locally but abundant in some other part of the world.* Also temporal local scarcities (due, for instance, to a bad harvest) can be compensated for by imports.

But even then *trade tends to blur the ecological consequences of production and consumption.* If production and consumption take place locally, all parties involved can register and react to the consequences. The further away and the more indirect the relations between producers and consumers are the less visible are the links of cause and effect. Today's global economy, with very distant and indirect links between producers of primary goods and final consumers, is very prone to blurring the ecological consequences of trade.

In an unequal world, rich countries can readily import bio- and sink-capacity from poor ones, and meanwhile the inhabitants of a rich country may think that their lifestyles are sustainable since the ecological capital of their own country is not eroding. They may even believe that becoming richer is the best solution to overcome ecological overshooting, and may thus blame the poor countries for not being able to sustain their own ecosystems. This *rich-country illusion* may prove fatal for the world. Poor countries strive for economic growth in order – they hope – to get out of the ecological trap, whereas rich countries wrongly maintain the belief that their current lifestyles and their further increases in consumption are sustainable.

In a full world the consequences of sharp income inequalities can become fatal. Even if we manage to avoid catastrophic world wars, the rampant commodification of the globe aggravates the inequalities between rich and poor. The environmental space for the poor deteriorates at the same time as the rich can buy temporary release from the consequences of global environmental degradation. The *long-term consequences of international trade in a full and unequal world can be quite different from the optimistic story told by orthodox economists*, who extol the advantages of free trade. In today's world, neoclassical trade theory obscures our understanding of the situation. It does not see the ecological dangers associated with growth due to the rivalry between nation-states.

The growth syndrome

The three mechanisms described above are interlinked and feed on each other. In order to get rich and strong a country needs to develop its economy in cooperation with national and international investors/capitalists. Capitalists look for states that are growth-oriented and provide the best workers and markets. Career- and consumption-oriented individuals again prefer firms and states that are economically successful.

Two factors that are crucial for success of a country are the quality of the labor force and the extent of the market. The human capital of a country is decisive for the level of income and the level of income again influences the size of the market for different goods and services. Companies that look for localities to invest in are keen to find both skilled workers and well-to-do consumers. This they can find in places imbued by the spirit of individual positional competition.

The urge to grow beyond the elimination of poverty and hardship can be seen as a syndrome involving several logics, each of which tends to strengthen the other. The syndrome has been called *growthmania* and it threatens the Earth's ecological sustainability. Until now the urge to grow has quelled the efforts to reduce throughput; that is to *decouple* production and the use of energy and materials. The efforts to invent and introduce more environmentally friendly technologies – to reduce T (throughput per unit produced) in the IPAT equation[3] – has been dwarfed by the increases in P (population) and especially in A (affluence). The *rebound effect* has been too strong in relation to the attempts to dematerialize production. The savings in natural resources that more eco-efficient technologies have made possible have also resulted in higher incomes and a more lavish consumption.

From the point of view of ecological sustainability humanity should try to free itself from this growthmania syndrome. Until now, however, the prospects for this have been bleak.

The three strong forces we have identified – profit-driven capitalism, status-driven consumerism and power-driven international competition – push humanity towards growth without consideration of the long-run ecological and social consequences. Is it possible to rein in these forces in order to launch an economy that is sustainable?

As we encountered in Chapter 5, ecological economists have discussed the conditions for a *steady-state economy* (Daly 1977/1992, 1996) – an economy in which the aggregate throughput is constant and within the limits of ecological sustainability. In a steady-state economy GDP-growth is in principle possible if changes in technology and consumption patterns allow higher incomes without any increases in the use of energy and materials. However, since there already seems to be an overshoot in terms of both non-renewable and renewable resources, the first priority should be to reduce throughput especially in the already rich economies. Therefore, some economists and social philosophers are discussing whether and how a campaign for *degrowth* should be launched.

What is degrowth?

Degrowth literally means economic contraction or downscaling. However, one should rather see the term as a red-green planetarist provocation, a radical critique of the cult of development and economic growth.[4] The aim is to liberate us from the current faith system and to create socially integrated and materially responsible societies in both the North and the South. As Serge Latouche formulates in his vision of degrowth, we should rather talk about "a-growthism," as in "a-theism."

> After all, rejecting the current economic orthodoxy means abandoning a faith system, a religion. To achieve this, we need doggedly and rigorously to deconstruct the matter of development. The term "development" has been redefined and qualified so much that it has become meaningless. Yet despite its failings, this magical concept continues to command total devotion across the political spectrum. The doctrines of "economism," in which growth is the ultimate good, die hard.
>
> (mondediplo.com/2004/11/14latouche)

In our global ethical trilemma, presented in Chapter 1, degrowth is situated at the bottom of the triangle. Increased economic prosperity is no longer perceived as a main goal. It looks for a different "prosperity" than that associated with constantly growing incomes and consumption.

Although degrowth is an important "post-materialist" and "post-developmentalist" standpoint, it still does not contain a strategy to overcome the strong forces pushing for growth. It advocates more local and regional self-reliance, a slowing down of economic activities, more participatory democracy and simpler lifestyles, all of which go against the dominant trends of globalization, consumerism, novelty and individualism. Since the drives for growth that we identified above to a large extent have socio-psychological roots, a change of social mentality is urgently needed, but *are we able to transform our societies without causing economic chaos?*

Is degrowth a possibility?

In order to become politically relevant degrowth must go beyond individual and local experimentation and be grounded in robust macroeconomic analysis. How can we achieve macroeconomic stability without being compelled to grow? A first – and very important – start to answer that question has been made by Tim Jackson in a report, "Prosperity without Growth" (2009), written for the British Sustainable Development Commission.

Conventionally prosperity has been understood as *opulence* – an increase in consumption, incomes and wealth. Another possibility is to define prosperity in terms of *subjective wellbeing* – utility or happiness. Tim Jackson, however, prefers a concept put forward by Amartya Sen. Prosperity should be defined in terms of the *capabilities* that people have to *flourish*. How well are people able to function in a given context? (Jackson 2009: 34).

Although many economists may disagree, subjective wellbeing is superior to opulence or incomes as a measure of the quality of life. As incomes and consumption increase over some threshold their relevance for a happy life rapidly diminishes. However, subjective wellbeing is often tainted by the relative position of an individual, not by her factual possibilities to achieve what she values. The term "prosperity" derives from the Latin words "pro" and "speres," which means for (what we) hope. Our capabilities to flourish – to be well nourished, healthy and secure, to take part in the life of the community, and to be free to do or to be what we value – corresponds to this original meaning. One measure that is used to assess these capabilities is the *Human Development Index* (HDI) yearly presented in the Human Development Report published by the UNDP. Another could be the *Genuine Progress Indicator* (GPI) (both are presented in Chapter 5).

Jackson, however, thinks it is necessary to bind the capabilities by the limits set by our ecological space. A society is prosperous only if people everywhere have the capability to flourish in certain basic ways.

> The point is that a fair and lasting prosperity cannot be isolated from these material conditions. Capabilities are bounded on the one hand by the scale of the global population and on the other by the finite ecology of the planet. In the presence of these ecological limits, flourishing itself becomes contingent on available resources, on the entitlements of those who share the planet with us, on the freedoms of future generations and other species.
>
> (Jackson 2009: 35)

A change of the Zeitgeist – the spirit of the time – in the direction of degrowth would affect the three growth mechanisms presented above. Since the positional competition between individuals is largely dependent on the dominating social values it would probably be directed into modes that are less damaging to the environment. The rivalry between nation-states is less sensitive to new values, but the insight that we have only one planet that we must care for together if humanity is to prosper, would certainly be more widespread and influential. Even if the establishment of a democratic world government seems to be a utopian project, a reduction of growthmania would improve the chances of a resolute international cooperation on global environmental issues.

Macroeconomics for sustainability

However, the rivalry between nation-states as well as between individuals is heavily dependent on the strength of the profit motive. Is it possible to quell capitalist accumulation without causing an economic crisis? Would not degrowth lead to more unemployment and to more severe clashes over the distribution of wealth and incomes? Macroeconomic theory has not dealt thoroughly with these questions, and only recently have there been serious attempts to construct a macroeconomics that takes the ecological limits seriously.[5]

In a strategy for degrowth three policy areas come into the forefront. They are "green" taxes, a gradual reduction of total and average working hours, and public investments in social and ecological capital.

Green taxes would discourage energy- and material-intensive economic activities, while favoring the provision of services and other labor-intensive production. Green taxes are strongly supported by environmental economic theory to internalize negative externalities such as pollution. However, green taxes could fall disproportionally on low-income households, and therefore changes in other taxes and social benefits are needed to redress this regressivity. One often proposed idea is to introduce an *unconditional minimum income,* a *basic income* or a so-called *negative income tax* that gives an automatic money transfer to those with very low incomes.

In macroeconomic textbooks the so-called Okun's law plays a key role. According to this law the rate of unemployment depends on the growth rate of real GDP. A yearly growth rate of 2–3 percent is needed just to keep unemployment from increasing. A combination of degrowth with macroeconomic stability therefore requires new policies for *sharing work* and *changing the work–life balance.* Reduced working hours can compensate for the loss of jobs due to increases in labor productivity. This is also a way of improving the work–life balance: parental leave, sabbatical breaks, better conditions for part-time work and greater individual differentiation on work conditions in general. Again an interesting step in this direction would be a *citizen's income* – a basic income given to all almost unconditionally.

Investment in social and ecological infrastructure is the task of society as a whole. The reason is that it is tricky for private investors to collect profits from this type of investment. The returns may also be realized too far into the future to be interesting for individual investors. In a socially and ecologically sustainable society savings and investments must not be reduced, but redirected into fields where the benefits are widely spread – to people with low purchasing power, future generations and other species. A larger share of the savings should be used for public investments in those forms of capital that do not directly contribute to the production of commodities.

Whether these changes imply a break with capitalism can be discussed. They would weaken the capitalist mechanisms since they would reduce the incentives for profit-driven commodity production and probably also promote a *decommodification* of the labor force. Although people could be even more active and productive than today, they would no longer be as dependent on full-time wage work. More investments and more activities would be carried out despite the lack of monetary spurs. A substantial part of the economy could, however, still be run according to capitalist principles.

Degrowth is primarily a proposition for already rich countries, with an income of at least 15,000 dollars per capita. A key motivation for degrowth is that this would make room for much-needed growth in poor countries. However, poor countries should also reconsider their development strategies in order to avoid the social and ecological pitfalls associated with a concentration on economic growth. The South needs new visions for development which are less dependent on exporting goods that require many natural resources or cheap labor. As a rough measure of success they could choose to maximize the human development index (HDI) in relation to the size of the ecological footprint (EF). The HDI/EF ratio would indicate the level of prosperity – in terms of capabilities – in relation to the national and global ecological limits.

Towards another economy

We started out by presenting a global ethical trilemma. We live in a world that is *both full and unequal*. If the world were full but equal we could try to set the limits required for a sustainable use of the natural capital of the Earth, introduce appropriate green taxes and create markets for ecological amenities. Since purchasing power would be distributed in a fair way we could opt for an "eco-efficient capitalism" drawing on the policy recommendations developed by environmental economists. It would of course be a tremendous task to find and set the proper load lines for different resources and to internalize all important environmental externalities with the help of the price mechanism. However, in a world without glaring inequalities, the task could at least be politically feasible.

If we were to live in an "empty world" – that is a world in which natural resources are bountiful – we could opt for "global social democracy" and direct our efforts towards the elimination of global inequalities. We could disregard the ecological and social limits to growth as we largely did in the "Golden Age" of the

1950s and 1960s.[6] However, since the world is not only unequal but full, the need to eliminate poverty cannot be pursued merely by economic growth. Even if growth were concentrated only to the South we risk a tragic overshooting of the ecological limits. Today the choices are harder to make than they seemed to be 50 years ago.

What about the bottom line of the trilemma – "red–green planetarism"? We suggested that this effort to reduce global injustice within the limits set by the eco-system of the Earth has become the distinctive task of ecological economics. This book has been written in the hope to clarify and elaborate this option. The discussion on growth and prosperity has tempted us to make the following adaption to the trilemma presented in Chapter 1.

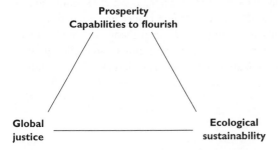

Figure 9.1 The global ethical trilemma softened: towards another economy

Figure 9.1 differs from the ethical trilemma presented in Figure1.1 in one important way. Instead of identifying prosperity with consumption and wealth, we have redefined prosperity as quality of life and, more precisely, as *capabilities to flourish*. This change of the original goal implies a radical shift in the economic priorities from "affluence" to "capabilities" and from "growth" towards "degrowth." Despite this softening of the original trilemma, it still is a daunting task to reconcile the three corners. The quest for prosperity – even when reinterpreted – is conditioned by the call for global justice and ecological sustainability. However, the choices between the three sides of the triangle are no longer as inimical as in our original version. Thanks to a growing general awareness of the situation, brought about among others by unorthodox economists, it is possible to envisage the contours of another, more just and sustainable economy.

In his book *The Bridge at the Edge of the World* James Gustave Speth (2008), a longstanding leader of the American environmental movement, quotes Paul Raskin, an initiator of the Great Transition Initiative.

> The emergence of a new suite of values is the foundation of the entire edifice of our planetary society. Consumerism, individualism, and domination of nature – the dominant values of yesteryear – have given way to a new triad: quality of life, human solidarity and ecological sensibility.
>
> (Speth 2008: 205)

We find this value-triad to be in line with the softened global ethical trilemma presented above. If we put "quality of life" at the top corner, "human solidarity" at the south-west and "ecological sensibility" at the south-east corner, the trilemma appears less threatening.

Speth outlines the contours of a "post-scarcity planetary civilization" in which fulfillment, not wealth, would become the primary measure of success and well-being. Sustainability would become a core part of the worldview. He sets a broad, almost revolutionary, agenda for the environmentalist movement.

> [T]he environmental agenda should expand to embrace a profound challenge to consumerism and commercialism and the lifestyles they offer, a healthy skepticism of growthmania and a sharp focus on what society should actually be striving to grow, a challenge to corporate dominance and a redefinition of the corporation and its goals, a commitment to deep change in both the reach and the functioning of the market, and a commitment to building what Alperovitz calls "the democratization of wealth" and Barnes calls "capitalism 3.0."
>
> (Speth 2008: 225)

Notes

I The global ethical trilemma

1   Quoted in *A Fair Globalization*, p. 5.

2 Economic growth and human development

1   Nicholas Georgescu-Roegen – considered to be a founding father of ecological economics – authored a ground-breaking book entitled *The Entropy Law and the Economic Process* (1971).
2   The ecological footprint concept and calculation method was developed by Mathis Wackernagel and William E. Rees in the 1990s. It has been widely accepted as one of the most telling measures of ecological sustainability.
3   The economics of care has been stressed by feminist economists such as Irene van Staveren (2001), Juliet Schor (1999), Julie Nelson (2003) and Nancy Folbre (2001, 2004).
4   In a recent article, "Happiness and Growth the World Over: Time Series Evidence on the Happiness-Income Paradox," Richard A. Easterlin and Laura Angelescu find that even if there is a short-run positive correlation between the growth in incomes and happiness, no such relationship can be found in the long run – 20 to 30 years. The finding is true both for already developed and developing countries. For instance, although GDP has grown in China by 10 percent a year for decades, the subjective life satisfaction has even tended to decline in the same period.

3 Ethics and ecological economics

1   The critical reader may wonder about how objective such a choice is; i.e. in what sense are real humans thought to be motivated only by self-interest? There are many motivations for such a choice (too many to be discussed here), but one sometimes told is that there exists biological evidence for *homo economicus*, with reference to the *selfish-gene argument*.
2   Of course, it may be claimed that this is just selfishness in disguise. We do not want to say that such behavior does not exist at all. However, here we want to emphasize that honest values also have their weighty role to play in human and public life.
3   This is what Adam Smith, the father of economics, had in mind when he wrote his two important works on these two different aspects of society (see Bibliography).
4   As Thorstein Veblen (1961[1919]) ridicules *homo economicus* in his classical statement: "lightning calculator of pleasures and pains who oscillates like a

homogeneous globule of desire of happiness under the impulse of stimuli that shift him about the area, but leave him intact."

5 The "anthropo" part comes from Greek "*anthropos*" which means man. Much of this thinking is still with us, also within environmental ethics, and perhaps with some reason. These things are difficult, and it is hard, for example, to put (different kinds of) animals (e.g. mammals and insects) on an equal standing in these questions.

6 For mainstream economists there exists goodness in welfare. But its special character should be noted: *welfare or utility, as located in individuals*, is the only thing that is recognized to have intrinsic value (Edwards-Jones *et al.* 2000: 77). We will return to this question below.

7 In this connection the term use value is commonly used. Thus e.g. a forest may have different use values, such as welfare (satisfaction) coming from timber cutting or hunting or photographing. (Cf. Figure 3.4.)

8 Originally published in the journal *Atmospheric Environment* (Lovelock 1972).

9 Although this may seem a fairly unambiguous description, it is in practice not clear how to define economic justice. In the literature of Distributive justice the interpretation of the term is quite wide.

10 Friedrich (von) Hayek (1899–1992), a Nobel laureate in economics and an ardent supporter of the market order.

11 The reader is referred to the Stanford encyclopedia (commonly available for free as a library service) or other sources such as e.g. the Economic justice network (http://www.progress.org/cgi/webbbs/config.pl). Wikipedia can be of help here also (http://en.wikipedia.org/wiki/Distributive_justice).

12 Observe thus that Rawls does not start from some collective or holistic view of making decisions, but has the same point of departure as standard economics.

13 See e.g.Vallentyne; Smart and Williams 1973.

14 It may be noted that despite the supposed broad support for Nozick's theory, people in experiments do not widely support the very large differences that may arise in such exchange. See Konow 2003: 1188, 1207.

15 The illustrations in this section are mostly borrowed from Shah 2009.

16 "In practice" income differences depend on institutional arrangements and social structure, e.g. the US social security system is built on private insurances, while e.g. in the Nordic countries they are financed through the taxation system.

17 See Sutcliffe 2007.

18 One may say, for instance, that this is how nature works, that there is no ethics in nature, every species would have done the same if they had had the chance. True, perhaps, but humans are supposed to have morals and have developed ethics by which it should be possible to discuss and treat these problems.

4 Environmental economics

1 It should be noted that the example here is not quite realistic but just intended to give the broad outlines. (For instance in reality, the bigger the tuna the higher the price per kilogram.) At the first tuna auction at Tsukiji in 2008 the price for tuna was 22,000 yen ($202) per kilo, which meant a price of $55,700 for 276 kilograms of fish.

2 If the price is under the equilibrium price, there would be an excess demand which would automatically have an increasing effect on the prices as many people demand the good. The increasing price will increase the supply, up to the point where demand equals supply.

3 It should be emphasized that this result is only relevant when all other resources are kept constant, except for one, in our example the amount of workers. This means that we are looking at what happens in the short run, where it is not possible to change the

scale of the whole production. This principle is called the *ceteris paribus* principle
from the Latin expression for "all other things being equal."

4   Here it should be noted that we have made the simplification that we have not
considered the fixed costs, i.e. the initial (investment) costs that exist in practice. If
these were considered we would have a *total* marginal cost curve that would be very
high at the cost–revenue-axis, but would gradually (because the constant initial cost
will be divided by the increasing quantity) approach the quantity axis. The point here
is of course that when considering the fixed costs the production will be profitable at
much higher quantities. To not consider fixed costs, however, is a simplifying
assumption often used in economics to show the main principle of marginal
calculation.

5   It should be clear that only some rudimentary points on this formidable question
– reaching from the deepest philosophical thoughts about the relation between
knowledge and reality to the questions of how to handle these questions in practice
– can be discussed here.

6   Strictly speaking in connection with the consumer's choice we speak of utility instead
of revenue but the principle is exactly the same.

7   The MC curve must be above the variable average cost curve.

8   Such a tax is called a Pigouvian tax after the Cambridge professor Arthur Pigou.

9   See Pearce and Turner 1990: 96ff.

10 What makes this comparison difficult, and, of course, what makes consumption of
today possible at all, is that Louis XIV's consumption was all based on renewable
resources, whereas the consumption today is boosted by non-renewable resources.
This of course makes the comparison even more unfavorable for our generation from
the point of view of sustainability (see Chapter 5).

11 In principle we could think of an "overfishing tax" on tuna fishing in the same way as
a pollution tax on trout. To estimate the value of such a tax would be much more
difficult than estimating a correct pollution tax, because it is very hard to estimate the
risk of extinction for a species, even in pure economic terms (the value for people,
not to speak about valuing existence value; see Chapter 3). Anyway, such a tax would
probably have a minimal effect on the consumption of bluefin tuna. This is perhaps
why such economic measures are not used to limit fishing (of e.g. tuna) but rather
physical restriction, or outright forbidding fishing for a certain time (such as in the
Mediterranean sea for many years now).

12 Thus Figure 4.8 could have been in the next chapter as well. Alternatively, it could
also have appeared in Chapter 8, since it is concerned with coastal management and
valuing of coastal zones. But since it can also be seen as a section about the
measurement of natural resources in general, we thought that the most appropriate
place for it was in the basic/background part of the book, rather than the "applied"
part, and more specifically, when passing from environmental to ecological
economics. It is recommended, though, that you look at this section when you read
Chapter 8.

13 For a brief introduction to different evaluation methods, see King and Mazzotta.

14 Although the degree of overlapping studies may be great, the figure from a search on
Google Scholar (February 5, 2009) shows 87,500 hits on "contingent valuation,"
which shows that this is true.

15 Including, among others, two Nobel Prize winners: Kenneth Arrow and Robert
Solow.

16 The panel's conclusions were followed by appendixes of caveats in the form of
instructions for CV studies (Arrow *et al.* 1993). This means, basically, that the
CV-method should not be considered as an everyman's tool, but, rather, it should be
considered as a tool that needs to be carried out by a highly qualified team of

collaborators from many fields. Also, of course, a critical attitude is necessary for the "consumers" of CV studies, be they politicians, civil servants, journalists or citizens.

5 Ecological economics: the science of sustainability

1 It was the dominant economic school from the sixteenth to the eighteenth century.
2 So, for instance, the first system of national accounting *Tableau Economique*, by Quesnay (1759), who was among other things the physician to Louis XI, describes a stationary society where all value-added (*Dépenses productives*) comes from agriculture. Quesnay belonged to a group of economic thinkers called physiocrats, who held ideas forerunning economic liberalism.
3 Markets had existed before but now it was to be the dominant form of economic business.
4 Scientific management was originally used in industry (also called Taylorism) for increasing the work-power's productivity through e.g. time-studies. However, the same logical principles where also applied in forestry and agriculture. An instance of this was for e.g. the use of biocides in agriculture, which gave rise to an early alarm, in Rachel Carson's *Silent Spring* (1962).
5 It should be noted in this connection that this mantra was by no means restricted to countries with representative democracy. Also in the former Socialist (Communist) countries this was an important feature of the so-called scientific socialism. So, even without market or democracy, the competitive spirit was present.
6 *Our Common Future* (WCED 1987).
7 Although the reception of the recession in the time of this writing (winter 2008) shows that we still have a long way to go from the one-dimensional economic growth policy. For instance, to say that the recession saves natural resources is seen in many camps as an immoral argument.
8 In the movie *Back to the Future II* Dr Brown uses banana peel to power his (time travel) car. However, this technology is something that Dr Brown got after being to the future first. So unfortunately, this possibility is as far away as time travel.
9 The day before writing this (October 11, 2008) the main news (after the financial crisis of course) was the great probability for extinction of mammals. This newsflash was built on a study by IUCN (International Union for Conservation of Nature: http://www.redlist.org/). The study shows that about 25 percent of the world's known mammals are threatened by extinction.
10 Boulding (1966).
11 Daly (Daly and Farley 2004) speaks about the empty world and the full world respectively, which conveys the same message well. Perhaps one should add to these "of people," because the empty world was really full of woods and fish whereas the full world, as we just exemplified, is rapidly emptying of other species both in amount and kind. In other words the world is getting emptier every day in terms of genetic variety.
12 Still the latter picture is very much exploited in commercials. The happy car owner always drives his SUV in wilderness or empty roads – never on crowded highways.
13 Relative, temporary scarcity is the central defining concept of standard economics, but there is nothing that cannot be overcome with time.
14 It is interesting and somewhat ironic perhaps that the remedy for this "economistic myopia" is brought into ecological economics from physics. Mainstream economics has frequently been criticized for "physics envy," meaning that the model science is taken to be physics, which is taken to be absurd from the point of view that people are teleological creatures not driven by, say, gravity like celestial bodies.
15 This application originates from Nicolas Georgescu-Roegen (1971) and his work.

Mainly because of this he is counted among the forefathers of ecological economics. See Daly 1995.

16 Robinson 1953.
17 From Martinez-Alier and Röpke 2008: xv.
18 This section owes much to Perman *et al.* (1999).
19 Solow 1988, quoted after Perman *et al.* 1999: 55. "The cake-eating problem" refers to dividing the Earth's production in time as in the first conception of sustainability.
20 Provided, of course, that man has not lost his cultural capital, i.e. science and other cultural artifacts.
21 Of course both are mixtures. Bricks require clay, sand, heat and so one as input from nature – but would not exist naturally without man's input. On the other hand wood does appear on the construction site in the form of boards, etc., although it has to be cut, transported and sawed – but it would be hard (and very expensive) to produce wood artificially.
22 Disregarding curiosities such as heavy water.
23 Horror of bacteria is a still living strong form of fear among people, which has led to many efforts of eliminating all bacteria. Today it is known that bacteria are an indispensable part of the human survival system – we are living in symbiosis with many kinds of bacteria. Fortunately, nature has been strong enough to resist our hubris-based destroying-efforts.
24 See for instance Daly and Farley 2004: 422–23.
25 This is done to distinguish this from the traditional efficiency concept of economics. See Chapter 4.
26 It should be mentioned here that most economists do not subscribe to such a concept as "distributional efficiency." Efficiency and distribution are seen as totally distinct concepts which should not be mixed together. In the language of economists, you cannot make interpersonal comparisons of utility (welfare); you cannot say whether Smith's headache is worse or easier than Jones's. Still it makes strong intuitive sense that an additional Euro means more to the beggar than to the millionaire.
27 Search the word "Resilience Defined" in the Internet Encyclopedia of Ecological Economics (http://www.ecoeco.org/education_encyclopedia.php).
28 But also where the ecosystem is relatively simple (such as the Baltic Sea; see Chapter 9).
29 Cf. Mäler 2008; Brand 2009.
30 That you know the price of everything and the value of nothing (actually Oscar Wilde on cynicism).
31 If a somewhat inappropriate expression in this connection is allowed. For a discussion of this, see Anderson 1993, 1990.
32 Such costs, called defensive expenditures, also occur under less catastrophic conditions than this. Buying bottled water because the tap water is too contaminated or installing double-glazed windows because of noise are example of such. See further the Index of Sustainable Economic Welfare in the following section.
33 The reader is invited to check her/his personal footprint at: http://www.footprintnetwork.org/en/index.php/GFN/page/personal_footprint/
34 Wackernagel and Rees (1996).
35 See the Wuppertal Institute website for more detailed information about e.g. the calculation sheets (http://www.wupperinst.org/en/projects/topicsonline/mips/index.html). Actually MIPS is built on input–output analysis, a long-used method in national accounting. See e.g. Wikipedia.
36 "If washing machines on average lasted 100 years instead of 15, fewer would be bought, and personal consumption would not rise as rapidly as it would otherwise, but welfare would not decline" (Daly and Cobb 1989, s. 421).

37 "People attend school because others are in school and the failure to attend would mean falling behind in the competition for diplomas or degrees that confer higher incomes to their recipients" (Daly and Cobb 1989: 423).

38 In contrast to local advertising which is seen as informative, national advertising is seen as creating "artificial demand."

39 Thus an oil slick may effect the GDP as much as the building of a tanker.

40 Talbert *et al.* 2007: 1.

41 Also, to account for inflation, the values are measured in the year 2000 values.

42 It could be thought that this is just a technical accounting matter. But studies in how people themselves feel about their happiness in relation to income also seem to point in the same direction. See Easterlin 1995.

43 "The (Un)happy planet" is also used as a sad joke, because although about 30 countries have an *ecological footprint* HPI of 1 or smaller, the vast majority of the countries and the population have a footprint which greatly exceeds this, going up to 9.5 (meaning that if all were living according to this standard of living, 9.5 earths would be needed).

44 http://www.happyplanetindex.org/

45 There are a lot of these on the Internet. See e.g. http://www.thementers.com/responsibleconsumption/ and http://responsibleconsumption.com/ and even YouTube got it: http://www.youtube.com/watch?v = rbnCgtsvvNg.

46 See e.g. Mol and Sonnenfeld 2000.

47 See Schor 2005a.

48 It is also clear that the distinction between these roles is somewhat unclear and artificial. See the Economic and Social Research Council (2007) where the finding from the study referred to was that: "[T]he most effective campaigns to encourage ethical consumption are those that take place at a collective level, such as the creation of Fairtrade cities, rather than those that target individual behaviour" (http://www.sciencedaily.com/releases/2007/08/070808082043.htm).

49 Fair trade (http://www.fairtrade.net/).

50 See e.g. Ethical Investment Research Services (EIRIS) directory of ethical and green funds: http://www.eiris.org/files/public%20information%20type%20publications/eirisethicalfundsdirectory.pdf

51 Studies show that the return on ethical funds may be at least as good as the average for the market.

52 Which are only two sides of the same coin, since what you do not consume you invest: a farmer who does not consume all his wheat, but saves a part for sowing next spring, is investing.

53 Many surely feel that this is a strange thing to say. However, there are some economists that are of the opinion that it is the only "moral duty" of a firm to maximize profits (Milton Friedman). Others claim that it is a mistake to act or prescribe altruistic action. The individual agent is the best knower of his needs; thus the world's affairs will be taken care of in the best possible manner by people just minding their own business.

6 The economics and ethics of climate change

1 The reactions (but not the measures) caused by the realization of this have been frequent, even among the establishment, with former USA vice president Al Gore in the forefront (earning him) the Nobel Peace prize 2007. Not everyone has been pleased with this. "The Nobel prize for a PowerPoint Presentation" was a typical comment on the discussion forums on the Internet. See e.g. www.kottke.org/remainder/07/10/14273.html

2 Named after the Austrian town where the congress was held.
3 Named after the meeting held in December 1997 in Kyoto.
4 Russia ratified the protocol later and added to the relative success of the protocol. At
   the beginning of 2009, 183 countries had ratified the protocol. At the time of this
   writing the USA has not ratified the protocol. President Obama commented on the
   protocol in Turkey in April 2009 as follows "It doesn't make sense for the United
   States to sign Kyoto because Kyoto is about to end [in 2012]."
5 The waterline depth above which a ship should not take any more cargo on board
   without risk of sinking.
6 Emissions trading: Wikipedia (retrieved July 7, 2009).
7 The following figures are from the World Research Institute.
8 See below in the section on the Stern Review.
9 In the USA the term is benefit–cost–analysis.
10 See Chapter 4.
11 Meaning what is just in society.
12 A still gets a surplus of €100 of his WTP, and C gets a compensation that is €100
   bigger than his WTA. The same net result goes for B and D.
13 Numbers are given in thousands of Euros. The example assumes that the construction
   takes one year with no benefit (income). The second year already gives an income of
   €15,000, but still involves some costs in, say, tuning the turbine. Afterwards, the
   turbines maintenance costs are negligible and after year 4 the capacity has reached its
   top.
14 The reader should as an exercise convince her/himself of the fact that taking a sixth
   year into account would make the wind turbine profitable.
15 This nickname is perhaps not quite apt, because, discounting is a tool and a method,
   which has to be used by someone. However, since the users of these tools (civil
   servants) are mostly unknown, it may be convenient to refer to the method.
16 Ramsay, who was the first to study intertemporal saving, said that it is "ethically
   indefensible and arises merely from weakness of the imagination." Harrod, who was
   a pioneer in growth theory, expressed his attitude towards discounting as "a polite
   expression for rapacity and the conquest of reason by passion." Quoted from
   Edwards-Jones *et al.* 2000: 126–27.
17 See e.g. Spash 2002: 155.
18 Boero *et al.* 1991, cited by Spash 2002: 156.
19 CBA first came to institutional use by the US Army Corps of Engineers.
20 "All other things being equal."
21 Counting from the study of d'Arge 1975.
22 "Once numbers are produced they begin to take on their own importance regardless
   of any lack of rigour or meaning; they begin to grow legs. For example the estimates
   of the cost of resettling environmental refugees produced by Cline [...] are based
   upon the $3000 per capita US local government spending on public services in 1989.
   He assumes this cost will only be incurred for 18 months as the refugees will have
   jobs and be taxpayers (i.e. 1.5 x 3,000 = 4,500). On the basis of current immigration
   figures he plucks 100,000 new immigrants from the air as the climate induced impact
   for the US. Fankhauser (1995) uses both figures, although the former is called a
   'guesstimate' and the latter unconvincing. He claims that the Cline dollar value is
   matched by that of Ayres and Walters by an alternative method which he however
   also notes to be unconvincing. In fact Ayres and Walters (1991: 245) mention
   resettlements for 1988 having cost the US $4,000 per person on the basis of a report
   in the *Economist* which would be costs in additions to those of Cline. [..] Fankhauser
   (1995: 50–51) takes $4,500 as the OECD country cost and $1,000 as that for the rest
   of the world, and using Cline's 'guesstimate' of migration now applied worldwide

gets 2.7 million refugees and produces a table of costs totaling $4,3 thousand million" (Spash 2002: 195–96).
23 This is essentially meant to be a "light version" of Spash (2002: chapter 9). However, on this difficult subject we are not quite convinced that we have succeeded. Anyway, for a more thorough treatment, see Spash 2002.
24 Ibid. 225.
25 See the postscript to the Stern Review.

8 Man and the seas: the oceans and the Baltic Sea

1 Meaning briefly that below the equator the airstreams turn down (while they turn up above the equator).
2 According to recent research, the 132-year historical record shows that whenever India experiences a severe drought, it has always been during an El Niño event (Bates *et al.* 2006). While this correlation can lead us to some conclusions about the coupling of these two processes, it must be noted that not all El Niño events are accompanied by Indian droughts. The correlation between La Niña events and the Indian drought is much stronger.
3 This insight has informed the view of Gaia (Mother Earth) in which the Earth is seen rather like an organism or self-regulating system (see Chapter 3).
4 If this number does not mean much, per capita this would be $3.5 per year. The purchasing power of this sum varies a lot around the world, but at least from an industrialized Western perspective few would claim that this estimate is an exaggeration. The economic valuation of the oceans is an ongoing project (see http://www.consvalmap.org/). In fact this measurement has been institutionalized to the degree that there now exist calculators, e.g. for the USA, where this economic value can be calculated. See National Ocean Economy Program (http://noep.mbari.org/Market/ocean/oceanEcon.asp).
5 Costanza 1999.
6 Strictly speaking this is not true, e.g. the age of the oldest fishing net extant (30 m long and 1.5 m high and a mesh size of 6 cm) is estimated to about 10,000 years. So the technology for fishing to extinction (at least in small lakes) existed but there was no use doing that because the demand for fish in these small societies was limited (as well as the technology for conservation).
7 Barange and Harris 2003.
8 Ibid.
9 Myers and Worm 2003.
10 www.sciencemag.org/cgi/content/full/314/5800/787
11 To see trawl sediment trail go to http://skytruth.mediatools.org/objects/view.acs?object_id = 11585 or download Google Earth and the file SkyTruth – Trawling_and_Other_Fishing_Impacts.kmz
12 Although hydroelectric power is usually considered to be a clean way of producing electricity as (after the construction) it practically only uses renewable resources (streaming water). However, in practice, hydroelectric power incurs environmental costs: building the dam creates artificial basins that dramatically change the ecology of the area with extinction of rare species; the dam itself also effectively blocks the fish from their spawning grounds. There has been some effort to remedy this by building "salmon ladders," i.e. passageways that allow fish to swim upstream past river-blocking dams, but such measures have not always proved successful.
13 Cadmium is of course only one of many kinds of toxins, and there is of course a variance in the countries' rankings, but the main pattern remains: the main polluters are located around the Baltic Sea.

14 A webcam of the eagles' nest in the Baltic Archipelago can be seen on http://natureit. net/site/saaksikamera.php

15 Finland and Sweden have got an exemption from contaminants regulations by the EU until 2011.

16 An overview of the ships' traffic in the Baltic Sea can be found on http://www. helcom.fi/stc/files/shipping/Overview%20of%20ships%20traffic.pdf

17 It is estimated that within a few years there will be about 100 tankers a week, half of which go to the Russian harbor of Primorsk in the northeast corner of the Finnish gulf. Some of these vessels are as big as 150,000 tons, which is vast in these shallow waters.

18 So far (May 2009) the most serious accident happened in 1979 involving MT *Antonio Gramsci* in Ventspils in Latvia, which resulted in a spillage of about 5,500 tons of crude oil. This slick drifted as far as the Åland islands and the Archipelago of Stockholm.

19 As for illegal oil discharges the trend has been diminishing, due to surveillance flights over the fairway undertaken by the countries around the Baltic.

20 This section is primarily based on the Helsinki commission homepage information (http://www.helcom.fi/) and on MERI report series, No. 62 (Olsonen 2008).

21 Of which the most well-known (and most successful, especially in fish farms) species introduced first for sport and then for food is the north American rainbow trout.

22 For descriptions of this and other species, please consult an encyclopedia, e.g. Wikipedia.

23 Phytoplankton are microorganisms who obtain energy through photosynthesis and serve as the base of all aquatic life. See e.g. Wikipedia.

24 In June 2009 it was reported that 2,000 cormorant nests had been destroyed in the Finnish archipelago.

25 Diaz and Rosenberg 2008.

26 Ibid.

27 Observe that Figure 8.4 is drawn on a *relative* scale from 1 to –1 in terms of fish biomass relative to seal population scale. So, at year 1900 both cod and clupeids are put (relatively) to zero whatever their absolute amount was.

28 There are, of course, many other species which may have or have had (even a great) role in the ecosystem, such as the porpoise, salmon, trout or the bullhead to name just a few, but the species in the figure can be considered as key actors for the explanation of the change in the ecosystem; that is except for humans, of course, whose role we will soon comment on.

29 In practice, it is not a question only of individual self-interest but also group self-interest. This may further be amplified by the insight that the resource is getting scarcer: "if we do not increase our fishing, the others (the British, the Icelanders, the Norwegians, etc.) will do it anyway."

30 See above in this chapter.

31 See Figure 8.5.

32 Cited after Glavovic 2008: 320.

33 This view of governance may perhaps also be seen as a variant of the *consensus view of sustainability* (see Chapter 6), with the corresponding strengths and weaknesses. When thinking about the amount of negotiation even simple decisions obviously demand, it is easy to fall back on traditional solutions, such as command or the market. Another way to express this is that the role of governance may be characterized as a process where the goal is to secure the resilience of the socio-ecological system as a whole.

34 Glavovic 2008: 331.

35 Some additional views on coastal governance are given in the Appendix to Chapter 4.

9 Growth and degrowth: is another economy possible?

1 Nominal GDP is the value of national production measured in current dollars or euros. Real GDP is nominal GDP adjusted for inflation, i.e. it is measured in a currency with a constant value.

A textbook definition of Okun's law is given by N. Gregory Mankiw (2003: 533): "The negative relationship between unemployment and real GDP, according to which a decrease in unemployment of 1 percentage point is associated with additional growth in real GDP of approximately 2 percent." "Additional growth" refers to growth above "normal" growth of 2–3 percent.

2 Exergy is the quality of energy in a substance, i.e. the energy which is available for mechanical work. Alf Hornborg (2001) analyzes the global inequalities in terms of an unequal exchange of exergy between different localities.

3 Introduced in Chapter 2.

4 Red–green planetarism is the ideology associated with global justice and ecological sustainability in the trilemma introduced in Chapter 1.

5 Besides Tim Jackson's work, the textbook *Macroeconomics in Context* (Goodwin *et al.* 2008) contains important insights on how to combine economic stability and ecological sustainability.

6 There were many warnings of the coming environmental crisis already by then. Rachel Carson's *Silent Spring* was published in 1962, and Kenneth Boulding's article "The Economics of the Coming Spaceship Earth" appeared in 1966.

Bibliography

Ackerman, F. *"Can We Afford the Future? The Economics of a Warming World*, London and New York, Zed Books, 2009.

Aguaron, Juan, Maria Teresa Escobar, and Jose Maria Moreno-Jimenez. "Consistency Stability Intervals for a Judgement in AHP Decision Support Systems", *European Journal of Operational Research,* vol. 145/no. 2, (2003), pp. 382–93.

Amir, Shmuel. "The Environmental Cost of Sustainable Welfare", *Ecological Economics,* vol. 13/no. 1, (1995), pp. 27–41.

Anderberg, Stefan. "Industrial Metabolism and the Linkages between Economics, Ethics and the Environment", *Ecological Economics,* vol. 24/no. 2–3, (1998), pp. 311–20.

Anderson, E. "The Ethical Limitations of the Market", *Economics and Philosophy*, vol. 6, (1990), pp. 179–205.

—. *Value in Ethics and Economics*, Cambridge, MA, Harvard University Press, 1993.

Andersson, Jan Otto, and Mattias Lindroth. "Ecologically Unsustainable Trade", *Ecological Economics,* vol. 37/no. 1, (2001), pp. 113–22.

Anon. *"Ecosystem Valuation",* <http://www.ecosystemvaluation.org/essentials.htm>.

Ariansen, Per. "Anthropocentrism with a Human Face", *Ecological Economics,* vol. 24/no. 2–3, (1998), pp. 153–62.

Aristotle. The Ethics of Aristotle (The Nicomachean Ethics), London, Penguin Books, 1976.

Arrow, K., R. Solow, P. R. Portney, *et al.* "Report of the NOAA Panel on Contingent Valuation", *Federal Register*, January 15, vol. 58/no. 10, (1993), pp. 4601–614.

Arrow, Kenneth, Partha Dasgupta, Lawrence Goulder, *et al.* "Are We Consuming Too Much?", *Journal of Economic Perspectives,* vol. 18/no. 3, (2004), pp. 147–72.

Attfield, Robin. "Existence Value and Intrinsic Value", *Ecological Economics,* vol. 24/no. 2–3, (1998), pp. 163–68.

Ayres, R.U. and J. Walters. "The Greenhouse Effect: Damages, Costs and Abatement", *Environmental and Resource Economics,* vol. 1, (1991), pp. 237–70.

Azqueta, Diego, and Gonzalo Delacámara. "Ethics, Economics and Environmental Management", *Ecological Economics,* vol. 56/no. 4, (2006), pp. 524–33.

Barange, M. and R. Harris (Eds.). "Marine Ecosystems and Global Change", International Biosphere-Geosphere Programme. Science Series, No. 5 (2003): <http://www.igbp.kva.se/page.php?pid=221http://www.igbp.kva.se/page.php?pid=221>.

Barry, John, and John Proops. "Seeking Sustainability Discourses with Q Methodology", *Ecological Economics,* vol. 28/no. 3, (1999), pp. 337–45.

Bartelmus,Peter (lead author), and Amy Richmond and Surender Kumar (topic editors). *"Green Accounting", in: Encyclopedia of Earth.* Ed. Cutler J. Cleveland (Washington, DC: Environmental Information Coalition, National Council for Science and the Environment). (First published in the *Encyclopedia of Earth*, August 9, 2006, updated September 17, 2008) <http://www.eoearth.org/article/Green_accounting>.

Bate, R. *Pick a Number. A Critique of Contingent Valuation Methodology and its Application in Public Policy*, Washington, DC, Competitive Enterprise Institute, 1994.

Bates, G., M. Cane, M. Hoerling, K. Kumar, and B. Rajagopalan. "Unraveling the Mystery of Indian Monsoon Failure During ENSO", *Science Express,* vol. 314/no. 5796, (2006), pp. 115–19.

Baumgartner, Stefan, Harald Dyckhoff, Malte Faber, *et al.* "The Concept of Joint Production and Ecological Economics", *Ecological Economics,* vol. 36/no. 3, (2001), pp. 365–72.

Begg, D. J., S. Fisher, and R. Dornbush. *Economics*, 9th edn, London, McGraw-Hill, 2008.

Berrens, Robert P., David S. Brookshire, Michael McKee, *et al.* "Implementing the Safe Minimum Standard Approach: Two Case Studies from the U.S. Endangered Species Act", *Land Economics,* vol. 74/no. 2, (1998), pp. 147–61.

Blackstock, K. L., G. J. Kelly, and B. L. Horsey. "Developing and Applying a Framework to Evaluate Participatory Research for Sustainability", *Ecological Economics,* vol. In Press, Corrected Proof.

Booth, Douglas E. "Ethics and the Limits of Environmental Economics", *Ecological Economics,* vol. 9/no. 3, (1994), pp. 241–52.

Boulding, K. E. "The Economics of the Coming Spaceship Earth", in H. Jarrett (Ed.). *Environmental Quality in a Growing Economy*, Baltimore, MD: Resources for the Future/Johns Hopkins University Press, 1966, pp. 3–14.

Brand, Fridolin. "Critical Natural Capital Revisited: Ecological Resilience and Sustainable Development", *Ecological Economics,* vol. 68, (2009), pp. 605–12.

Bromley, Daniel W. "Environmental Regulations and the Problem of Sustainability: Moving Beyond 'Market Failure'", *Ecological Economics*, vol. In Press, Corrected Proof.

—. "The Ideology of Efficiency: Searching for a Theory of Policy Analysis", *Journal of Environmental Economics and Management,* vol. 19/no. 1, (1990), pp. 86–107.

—. "Searching for Sustainability: The Poverty of Spontaneous Order", *Ecological Economics,* vol. 24/no. 2–3, (1998), pp. 231–40.

—. "Volitional Pragmatism", *Ecological Economics,* vol. 68/no. 1–2, (2008), pp. 1–13.

Brouwer, Roy. "Environmental Value Transfer: State of the Art and Future Prospects", *Ecological Economics,* vol. 32/no. 1, (2000), pp. 137–52.

Cabeza Gutés, Maite. "The Concept of Weak Sustainability", *Ecological Economics*, vol. 17/no. 3, (1996), pp. 147–56.

Cantlon, John E., and Herman E. Koenig. "Sustainable Ecological Economies", *Ecological Economics,* vol. 31/no. 1, (1999), pp. 107–21.

Carlsson, Lars, and Fikret Berkes. "Co-Management: Concepts and Methodological Implications", *Journal of Environmental Management,* vol. 75/no. 1, (2005), pp. 65–76.

Cash, D. W., W. N. Agder, F. Berkes, *et al.* "Scale and Cross-Scale Dynamics: Governance and Information in a Multi Level World", *Ecology and Society*, vol. 11/no. 2, p. 8 [online].

Chapman, Robert L. "Confessions of a Malthusian Restrictionist", *Ecological Economics,* vol. 59/no. 2, (2006), pp. 214–19.

Chee, Yung En. "An Ecological Perspective on the Valuation of Ecosystem Services", *Biological Conservation,* vol. 120/no. 4, (2004), pp. 549–65.

Chiesura, Anna, and Rudolf de Groot. "Critical Natural Capital: A Socio-Cultural Perspective", *Ecological Economics,* vol. 44/no. 2–3, (2003), pp. 219–31.

Central Intelligence Agency (CIA). *The World Factbook,* <https://www.cia.gov/library/ publications/the-world-factbook/fields/2172.html>.

Clark, Judy, Jacquelin Burgess, and Carolyn M. Harrison. "'I Struggled with this Money Business': Respondents' Perspectives on Contingent Valuation", *Ecological Economics,* vol. 33/no. 1, (2000), pp. 45–62.

Colby, Michael E. "Environmental Management in Development: The Evolution of Paradigms", *Ecological Economics,* vol. 3/no. 3, (1991), pp. 193–213.

Common, Michael, and Sigrid Stagl. *Ecological Economics. An Introduction*, first edn, Cambridge, UK, Cambridge University Press, 2005.

Comolli, Paul. "Sustainability and Growth When Manufactured Capital and Natural Capital Are Not Substitutable", *Ecological Economics*, vol. 60/no. 1, (2006), pp. 157–67.

Conservation International. <http://www.conservation.org/newsroom/pressreleases/Pages/ how_much_are_ocean_resources_worth.aspx>.

Costanza, Robert. "The Ecological, Economic, and Social Importance of the Oceans", *Ecological Economics,* vol. 31/no. 2, (1999), pp. 199–213.

Costanza, Robert, and Bernard C. Patten. "Defining and Predicting Sustainability", *Ecological Economics,* vol. 15/no. 3, (1995), pp. 193–96.

Costanza, R., R. d'Arge, R. de Groot, *et al.* "The Value of the World's Ecosystem Services and Natural Capital", *Ecological Economics*, vol. 25/no. 1, (1998), pp. 3–15.

Costanza, Robert, Francisco Andrade, Paula Antunes, *et al.* "Ecological Economics and Sustainable Governance of the Oceans", *Ecological Economics,* vol. 31/no. 2, (1999), pp. 171–87.

Curtis, Fred. "Eco-Localism and Sustainability", *Ecological Economics,* vol. 46/no. 1, (2003), pp. 83–102.

Daly, Herman E. *Steady-State Economics*, London, Earthscan, 1977/1992.

—. "On Nicholas Georgescu-Roegen's Contributions to Economics: An Obituary Essay", *Ecological Economics*, vol. 13/no. 3, (1995), pp. 149–54.

—. *Beyond Growth. The Economics of Sustainable Development*, Boston, Beacon Press, 1996.

Daly, H. E. and J. B. Cobb. *For the Common Good. Redirecting the Economy toward Community, the Environment and a Sustainable Future*, Boston, Beacon Press, 1989.

Daly, Herman E., and Joshua Farley. *Ecological Economics. Principles and Applications*, first edn, Washington, Island Press, 2004.

d'Arge, R. C. *Economic and Social Measures of Biologic and Climate Change*, Washington, DC, US Department of Transportation, Climate Impact Assessment Program, 1975.

Dasgupta, Partha. "Population, Consumption and Resources: Ethical Issues", *Ecological Economics,* vol. 24/no. 2–3, (1998), pp. 139–52.

de Graaf, H. J., C. J. M. Musters, and W. J. ter Keurs. "Sustainable Development: Looking for New Strategies", *Ecological Economics,* vol. 16/no. 3, (1996), pp. 205–16.

De Groot, Rudolf, Johan Van der Perk, Anna Chiesura, *et al.* "Importance and Threat as Determining Factors for Criticality of Natural Capital", *Ecological Economics,* vol. 44/no. 2–3, (2003), pp. 187–204.

DeMartino, G. *Global Economy, Global Justice: Theoretical Objections and Policy Alternatives to Neoliberalism*, London and New York, Routledge, 2000.

Diamond, P. A., and J. A. Hausman. "Contingent Valuation: Is Some Number Better than No Number?", *Journal of Economic Perspectives,* vol. 8/no. 4, (1994), pp. 45–64.

Diaz, Robert J. and Rutger Rosenberg. "Spreading Dead Zones and Consequences for Marine Ecosystems", *Science*, vol. 321/no. 5891, (2008), p. 926.

Dodds, Steve. "Towards a 'Science of Sustainability': Improving the Way Ecological Economics Understands Human Well-being", *Ecological Economics,* vol. 23/no. 2, (1997), pp. 95–111.

Meadows, Donella H., Dennis L. Meadows, Jørgen Randers, and William W. Behrens III. *The Limits to Growth : A Report for the Club of Rome's Project on the Predicament of Mankind*, London, Earth Island, 1972.

Doran, P. T. and M. Kendall Zimmerman. "Examining the Scientific Consensus in Climate Change", *EOS*, vol. 20, (2009), pp. 22–23.

Duxbury, Jane, and Sarah Dickinson. "Principles for Sustainable Governance of the Coastal Zone: In the Context of Coastal Disasters", *Ecological Economics,* vol. 63/no. 2–3, (2007), pp. 319–30.

Easterlin, Richard A. "Will Raising the Incomes of all Increase the Happiness of all?", *Journal of Economic Behavior & Organization*, vol. 27/no. 1, (1995), pp. 35–47.

Easterlin, Richard A., and Laura Angelescu. "Happiness and Growth the World Over: Time Series Evidence on the Happiness-Income Paradox", Discussion Paper No.4060, Bonn, Institute for the Study of Labor (IZA), 2009.

Economic and Social Research Council. "Ethical Consumption: Consumer Driven or Political Phenomenon?", *Science Daily,* August 10, (2007).

Edwards-Jones, Gareth, Ben Davies, and Salman Hussain. *Ecological Economics. An Introduction*, first edn, Oxford, Blackwell Science, 2000.

Ekins, Paul. "Identifying Critical Natural Capital: Conclusions about Critical Natural Capital", *Ecological Economics,* vol. 44/no. 2–3, (2003), pp. 277–92.

Ekins, Paul, Sandrine Simon, Lisa Deutsch, *et al.* "A Framework for the Practical Application of the Concepts of Critical Natural Capital and Strong Sustainability", *Ecological Economics,* vol. 44/no. 2–3, (2003), pp. 165–85.

Eriksson, Ralf. "On the Ethics of Environmental Economics as Seen from Textbooks", *Ecological Economics,* vol. 52/no. 4, (2005), pp. 421–35.

Faber, Malte, Thomas Petersen, and Johannes Schiller. "Homo Oeconomicus and Homo Politicus in Ecological Economics", *Ecological Economics*, vol. 40/no. 3, (2002), pp. 323–33.

Fankhauser, S. *Valuing Climate Change: The Economics of the Greenhouse*, London, Earthscan, 1995.

Farley, Joshua, Daniel Baker, David Batker, *et al.* "Opening the Policy Window for Ecological Economics: Katrina as a Focusing Event", *Ecological Economics,* vol. 63/no. 2–3, (2007), pp. 344–54.

Farmer, Michael C., and Alan Randall. "The Rationality of a Safe Minimum Standard", *Land Economics*, vol. 74/no. 3, (1998), pp. 287–302.

Fiala, Nathan. "Measuring Sustainability: Why the Ecological Footprint is Bad Economics and Bad Environmental Science", *Ecological Economics,* vol. 67/no. 4, (2008), pp. 519–25.

Fisk, George. "Criteria for a Theory of Responsible Consumption", *Journal of Marketing,* vol. 37/no. 2, (1973), pp. 24–31.

Folbre, Nancy. *The Invisible Heart: Economics and Family Values*, New York, The New Press, 2001.

—. *Family Time: The Social Organization of Care*, New York, Routledge, 2004.

Forstater, Mathew. "Visions and Scenarios: Heilbroner's Worldly Philosophy, Lowe's Political Economics, and the Methodology of Ecological Economics", *Ecological Economics,* vol. 51/no. 1–2, (2004), pp. 17–30.

Foster, J. *Valuing Nature? Ethics, Economics and the Environment*, London and New York, Routledge, 1997.

Fredericks, Sarah E. "Review of *The Death of our Planet's Species: A Challenge to Ecology and Ethics* by Martin Gorke [Translated from German by Patricia Nevers, Island Press, Washington, DC, Island Press, 2003. Original German edition J.G. Cotta'Sche Buchandlung, Stuttgart, 1999]", *Ecological Economics*, vol. 52/no. 2, (2005), pp. 255–56.

Funtowicz, Silvio O., and Jerome R. Ravetz. "The Worth of a Songbird: Ecological Economics as a Post-Normal Science", *Ecological Economics*, vol. 10/no. 3, (1994), pp. 197–207.

Gelso, Brett R., and Jeffrey M. Peterson. "The Influence of Ethical Attitudes on the Demand for Environmental Recreation: Incorporating Lexicographic Preferences", *Ecological Economics,* vol. 53/no. 1, (2005), pp. 35–45.

Georgescu-Roegen, Nicholas. *The Entropy Law and the Economic Process*, Cambridge, MA, Harvard University Press, 1971.

Glavovic, B. "Ocean and Costal Governance for Sustainability: Imperatives for Integrating Ecology and Economics", in Patterson, M. and Glavovic, B. (Eds.). *Ecological Economics of the Oceans and Coasts*, Cheltenham, Edward Elgar, 2008.

Goodland, Robert. "Environmental Sustainability in Agriculture: Diet Matters", *Ecological Economics,* vol. 23/no. 3, (1997), pp. 189–200.

Goodwin, N., J. A. Nelson, and J. Harris. *Macroeconomics in Context*, Armonk, NY, M. E. Sharpe, 2008.

Gowdy, John M. "Toward an Experimental Foundation for Benefit-Cost Analysis", *Ecological Economics,* vol. 63/no.4, (2007), pp. 649–55.

—. "The Value of Biodiversity: Markets, Society, and Ecosystems", *Land Economics,* vol. 73/no. 1, (1997), p. 25.

—. "Review of *Greenhouse Economics: Value and Ethics*, by Clive Spash [London and New York, Routledge, 2002]", *Ecological Economics,* vol. 46/no. 2, (2003), pp. 307–8.

—. "The Revolution in Welfare Economics and its Implications for Environmental Valuation and Policy", *Land Economics,* vol. 80/no. 2, (2004), pp. 239–57.

Gowdy, John M., and Richard B. Howarth. "Sustainability and Benefit–Cost Analysis: Theoretical Assessments and Policy Options", *Ecological Economics,* vol. 63, (2007), pp. 637–8.

Hamilton, Clive. "Dualism and Sustainability", *Ecological Economics,* vol. 42/no. 1–2, (2002), pp. 89–99.

Hanley, Nick, Ian Moffatt, Robin Faichney, *et al.* "Measuring Sustainability: A Time Series of Alternative Indicators for Scotland", *Ecological Economics,* vol. 28/no. 1, (1999), pp. 55–73.

Hannesson, R. "Rights Based Fishing: Use Rights Versus Property Rights to Fish", Reviews in *Fish Biology and Fisheries*, vol. 15/no. 3, (2005), pp. 231–41.

Hardin, G. "The Tragedy of the Commons", *Science,* vol. 162, (1968), pp. 1243–48.

Hartwick, J. M. "Intergenerational Equity and the Investing of Rents from Exhaustible Resources", *American Economic Review*, vol. 67, (1977), pp. 972–74.

Hattam, J. "Obama Challenged on Climate during Turkey Trip", *Treehuggers,* (2009).

Hayes, William M., and Gary D. Lynne. "Towards a Centerpiece for Ecological Economics", *Ecological Economics*, vol. 49/no. 3, (2004), pp. 287–301.

Hedenus, Fredrik, and Christian Azar. "Estimates of Trends in Global Income and Resource Inequalities", *Ecological Economics,* vol. 55/no. 3, (2005), pp. 351–64.

Helsinki Commission (HELCOM) "Heavy Metal Pollution to the Baltic Sea in 2004", *Baltic Sea Environment Proceedings*, vol. 108, (2007).

Herrera, A.O., H. D. Solnik, G. Chichilnilsky, G. G. Gallopin, J. E. Hardoy, D. Mosovich *et al. Catastrophe or New Society? A Latin American World Model*, Ottawa, Canada: International Development Research Centre, 1976.

Hirsch, F, *Social Limits to Growth*, London, Routledge & Kegan Paul, 1977.

Hornborg, A. *The Power of the Machine: Global Inequalities of Economy, Technology, and Environment*, Lanham, MD, AltaMira Press, 2001.

Howarth, Richard B. "Sustainability as Opportunity", *Land Economics,* vol. 73/no. 4, (1997), pp. 569.

—. "Price, Principle, and the Environment", *Land Economics,* vol. 81/no. 4, (2005), pp. 587–91.

—. "Towards an Operational Sustainability Criterion", *Ecological Economics,* vol. 63/no. 4, (2007), pp. 656–63.

Ikeme, Jekwu. "Equity, Environmental Justice and Sustainability: Incomplete Approaches in Climate Change Politics", *Global Environmental Change,* vol. 13/no. 3, (2003), pp. 195–206.

Jackson, Jeremy B. C. "Ecological Extinction and Evolution in the Brave New Ocean", *Proceedings of the National Academy of Sciences*, vol. 105/no. Supplement 1, (2008), pp. 11458–65.

Jackson, T. "Prosperity without Growth? The Transition to a Sustainable Economy", report, London, Sustainable Development Commission, 2009.

Jamieson, Dale. "Sustainability and Beyond", *Ecological Economics*, vol. 24/no. 2–3, (1998), pp. 183–92.

Jenkins, T. N. "Economics and the Environment: A Case of Ethical Neglect", *Ecological Economics,* vol. 26/no. 2, (1998), pp. 151–64.

Jentoft, Svein. "Institutions in Fisheries: What They Are, What They Do, and How They Change", *Marine Policy,* vol. 28/no. 2, (2004), pp. 137–49.

—. "Limits of Governability: Institutional Implications for Fisheries and Coastal Governance", *Marine Policy*, vol. 31/no. 4, (2007), pp. 360–70.

Jentoft, Svein, and Knut H. Mikalsen. "A Vicious Circle? The Dynamics of Rule-Making in Norwegian Fisheries", *Marine Policy*, vol. 28/no. 2, (2004), pp. 127–35.

Jevons, J. W. *The Coal Question*, London, Macmillan & Co, 1865).

Jochimsen, Maren, and Ulrike Knobloch. "Making the Hidden Visible: The Importance of Caring Activities and their Principles for any Economy", *Ecological Economics,* vol. 20/no. 2, (1997), pp. 107–12.

Kennedy, James J., and Niels Elers Koch. "Viewing and Managing Natural Resources as Human-Ecosystem Relationships", *Forest Policy and Economics,* vol. 6/no. 5, (2004), pp. 497–504.

Kim, Sang-Hoon. "Evaluation of Negative Environmental Impacts of Electricity Generation: Neoclassical and Institutional Approaches", *Energy Policy,* vol. In Press, Corrected Proof.

King, D. M. and M. J. Mazzotta. *"Ecosystem Valuation",* <http://www. ecosystemvaluation.org/essentials.htm> (accessed January 29, 2009).

Kitzes, Justin, Alessandro Galli, Marco Bagliani, *et al.* "A Research Agenda for Improving National Ecological Footprint Accounts", *Ecological Economics,* vol. 68/ no. 7, (2009), pp. 1991–2007.

Knetsch, Jack L. "Biased Valuations, Damage Assessments, and Policy Choices: The Choice of Measure Matters", *Ecological Economics,* vol. In Press, Corrected Proof/.

Konow, J. "Which is the Fairest of All? A Positive Analysis of Justice Theories", *Journal of Economic Literature,* vol. XLI, (2003), pp. 1188–239.

Kooiman, J., S. Jentoft, R. Pullin, and M. Bavick. *Fish for Life: Interactive Governance for Fisheries,* Amsterdam, Amsterdam University Press, 2005.

Koont, Sinan. "A Cuban Success Story: Urban Agriculture", *Review of Radical Political Economics,* vol. 40/no. 3, (2008), pp. 285–91.

Krehbiel, Timothy C., Raymond F. Gorman, O. Homer Erekson, *et al.* "Advancing Ecology and Economics through a Business-Science Synthesis", *Ecological Economics,* vol. 28/no. 2, (1999), pp. 183–96.

Krysiak, Frank C. "Entropy, Limits to Growth, and the Prospects for Weak Sustainability", *Ecological Economics,* vol. 58/no. 1, (2006), pp. 182–91.

Latouche, Serge. "Degrowth Economics", *Le Monde Diplomatique*, English Edition, November, 2004.

Leopold, A. The Sand County Almanac, New York, Oxford University Press, 1949.

Locke, J. *Two Treatises on Government and a Letter of Toleration*, in K. S. Stilwell, Digireads.com. (2005), p. 80.

Lovelock, J. E. "Gaia as Seen Through the Atmosphere", *Atmospheric Environment*, vol. 6/no. 8, (1972), pp. 579–80.

Luks, Fred. "The Rhetorics of Ecological Economics", *Ecological Economics,* vol. 26/no. 2, (1998), pp. 139–49.

Lumley, Sarah. "The Environment and the Ethics of Discounting: An Empirical Analysis", *Ecological Economics*, vol. 20/no. 1, (1997), pp. 71–82.

Maddison, Angus. *Contours of the World Economy 1–2030 AD. Essays in Macro-Economic History*, Oxford, Oxford University Press, 2007.

Mainwaring, Lynn. "Environmental Values and the Frame of Reference", *Ecological Economics,* vol. 38/no. 3, (2001), pp. 391–402.

—. "Comparing Futures: A Positional Approach to Population Ethics", *Ecological Economics,* vol. 48/no. 3, (2004), pp. 345–57.

Mäler, K-G. "Sustainable Development and Resilience in Ecosystems", *Environmental and Resource Economics*, vol. 39/no. 1, (2008), pp. 17–24

Malthus, T. R. *An Essay on the Principle of Population, as it affects the future improvement of society...*, 1798, anonymously published.

Mankiw, N. Gregory. Macroeconomics, New York, Worth Publishers, 2003.

Martínez, M. L., A. Intralawan, G. Vázquez, *et al.* "The Coasts of Our World: Ecological, Economic and Social Importance", *Ecological Economics,* vol. 63/no. 2–3, (2007), pp. 254–72.

Martinez-Alier, J. *The Environmentalism of the Poor. A Study of Ecological Conflicts and Valuation,* Cheltenham, UK, Edward Elgar, 2002.

Martinez-Alier J. and I. Röpke (Eds.). *Recent Developments in Ecological Economics,* Cheltenham, Edward Elgar, 2008.

Marx, K. *Capital, Volume I,* London, William Glaisher Ltd, 1920(1867).

Mayumi, Kozo, and Mario Giampietro. "The Epistemological Challenge of Self-Modifying Systems: Governance and Sustainability in the Post-Normal Science Era", *Ecological Economics,* vol. 57/no. 3, (2006), pp. 382–99.

Meppem, Tony. "The Discursive Community: Evolving Institutional Structures for Planning Sustainability", *Ecological Economics,* vol. 34/no. 1, (2000), pp. 47–61.

Meppem, Tony, and Simon Bourke. "Different Ways of Knowing: A Communicative Turn Toward Sustainability", *Ecological Economics,* vol. 30/no. 3, (1999), pp. 389–404.

Mikalsen, Knut H., and Svein Jentoft. "Participatory Practices in Fisheries Across Europe: Making Stakeholders More Responsible", *Marine Policy,* vol. 32/no. 2, (2008), pp. 169–77.

Milanovic, B. *Worlds Apart. Measuring International and Global Inequality,* Princeton, NJ, Princeton University Press, 2005.

Millennium Ecosystem Assessment (MEA). *Ecosystems and Human Well Being: Synthesis,* Washington, DC, Island Press, 2005.

Mol, A. P. J., and D. A. Sonnenfeld. "Ecological Modernization Around the World: An Introduction", *Environmental Politics,* vol. 9/no. 1, (2000), pp. 3–16.

Morse, Stephen. "For Better or for Worse, Till the Human Development Index Do Us Part?", *Ecological Economics,* vol. 45/no. 2, (2003), pp. 281–96.

Muller, Adrian. "A Flower in Full Blossom?: Ecological Economics at the Crossroads between Normal and Post-Normal Science", *Ecological Economics*, vol. 45/no. 1, (2003), pp. 19–27.

Munasinghe, Mohan. "Making Economic Growth More Sustainable", *Ecological Economics*, vol. 15/no. 2, (1995), pp. 121–24.

Myers, R. A. and B. Worm "Rapid Worldwide Depletion of Predatory Fish Communities", *Nature,* vol. 423, (2003), pp. 280–83.

Naeem, Shahid. "Ecology: Gini in the Bottle", *Nature,* vol. 458/no. 7238, (2009), pp. 579–80.

Naess, A. Økologi, samfunn og livsstil, Oslo, Universitetsforlaget, 1976.

Nelson, Julia A., co-edited with Marianne A. Ferber. Feminist Economics Today: Beyond Economic Man, Chicago, University of Chicago Press, 2003.

Nordhaus, W.D. "To Slow or Not to Slow: The Economics of the Greenhouse Effect", *Economic Journal,* vol. 101, (1991), pp. 920–38.

—. *Managing the Global Commons: The Economics of Climate Change,* Cambridge, MA, MIT Press, 1994.

—. *New Estimates of the Economic Impacts of Climate Change*, New Haven, CT, Yale University Press, 1998.

Norton, Bryan G. "Context and Hierarchy in Aldo Leopold's Theory of Environmental Management", *Ecological Economics,* vol. 2/no. 2, (1990), pp. 119–27.

Norton, Bryan G., and Douglas Noonan. "Ecology and Valuation: Big Changes Needed", *Ecological Economics,* vol. 63/no.4, (2007), pp. 664–75.

Norton, Bryan G., and Michael A. Toman. "Sustainability: Ecological and Economic Perspectives", *Land Economics,* vol. 73/no. 4, (1997), pp. 553.

Nozick, R. *Anarchy, State, and Utopia,* New York, Basic Books, 1974.

Nussbaum, M. C. *Women and Human Development. The Capabilities Approach,* Cambridge, Cambridge University Press, 2000.

Nussbaum, M. C. and A. Sen (Eds.). *The Quality of Life,* Oxford, Clarendon Press, 1993.

O'Connor, Martin. "Pathways for Environmental Evaluation: A Walk in the (Hanging) Gardens of Babylon", *Ecological Economics,* vol. 34/no. 2, (2000), pp. 175–93.

Office of Climate Observation. <http://www.oco.noaa.gov/index.jsp?show_page = page_roc.jsp&nav = universal>.

O'Hara, Sabine U. "Discursive Ethics in Ecosystems Valuation and Environmental Policy", *Ecological Economics,* vol. 16/no. 2, (1996), pp. 95–107.

Ojea, Elena, and Maria L. Loureiro. "Altruistic, Egoistic and Biospheric Values in Willingness to Pay (WTP) for Wildlife", *Ecological Economics,* vol. 63/no. 4, (2007), pp. 807–14.

Oliveira de Paula, Gabriela, and Rachel Negrão Cavalcanti. "Ethics: Essence for Sustainability", *Journal of Cleaner Production,* vol. 8/no. 2, (2000), pp. 109–17.

Olsonen, R. (Ed.). MERI – Report Series of the Finnish Institute of Marine Research, No. 62, 2008.

Österblom, H., S. Hansson, U. Larsson, O. Hjeme, F. Wulff *et al.* "Human-induced Trophic Cascades and Ecological Regime Shifts in the Baltic Sea", *Ecosystems,* vol. 10/no. 6, (2007), pp. 877–89.

Paavola, Jouni. "Institutions and Environmental Governance: A Reconceptualization", *Ecological Economics,* vol. In Press, Corrected Proof/.

Paavola, Jouni, and W. Neil Adger. "Institutional Ecological Economics", *Ecological Economics,* vol. 53/no. 3, (2005), pp. 353–68.

Padilla, Emilio. "Intergenerational Equity and Sustainability", *Ecological Economics,* vol. 41/no. 1, (2002), pp. 69–83.

Patterson, Murray. "Commensuration and Theories of Value in Ecological Economics", *Ecological Economics,* vol. 25/no. 1, (1998), pp. 105–26.

Patterson, M. and B. Glavovic (Eds.). *Ecological Economics of the Oceans and Coasts,* Cheltenham, Edward Elgar, 2008.

Pearce, D. W. and Turner, R. K. *Economics of Natural Resources and the Environment,* London, Harvester Wheatsheaf, 1990.

Pearce, D., A. Markandya, and E. B. Barbier. *Blueprint For A Green Economy,* London, Earthscan, 1989.

Perman, R., Yue Ma, J. McGilvray, and M. Common, *Natural Resource and Environmental Economics*, Harlow, Essex, Pearson Education, 1999.

Peterson, Garry. "Political Ecology and Ecological Resilience: An Integration of Human and Ecological Dynamics", *Ecological Economics,* vol. 35/no. 3, (2000), pp. 323–36.

Pezzey, J. "Sustainability Constraints Versus 'Optimality' Versus Intertemporal Concern, and Axioms Versus Data", *Land Economics,* vol. 73/no. 4, (1997), pp. 448–66.

Phelps, E. S. "Distributive Justice", *The New Palgrave: A Dictionary of Economics,* v. 1, (1987), pp. 886–88.

Pikitch, E. K., C. Santora, E. A. Babcock, *et al.* "ECOLOGY: Ecosystem-Based Fishery Management", *Science,* vol. 305/no. 5682, (2004), pp. 346–47.

Rapport, David J. *"Beyond the Land Ethic: More Essays in Environmental Philosophy* [edited by J. Baird Callicott, Albany, State University of New York Press, 1999]", *Ecological Economics,* vol. 37/no. 1, (2001), pp. 155–57.

Rawls, J. *A Theory of Justice,* Cambridge, MA, Harvard University Press, 1971.

—.*Political Liberalism, The John Dewey Essays in Philosophy, 4,* New York, Columbia University Press, 1993.

Reibstein, Rick. "Ethics, Equity and International Negotiations on Climate Change", *Ecological Economics,* vol. 52/no. 4, (2005), pp. 545–46.

Robeyns, I. "Sen's Capabilities Approach and Feminist Concerns", in F. Comim, M. Qizilbash, and S. Alkire (Eds.) *The Capability Approach: Concepts, Measures and Applications,* Cambridge, Cambridge University Press, 2008.

Robinson, J. *On Re-Reading Marx,* Cambridge, Cambridge University Press, 1953.

Robinson, John. "Squaring the Circle? Some Thoughts on the Idea of Sustainable Development", *Ecological Economics,* vol. 48/no. 4, (2004), pp. 369–84.

Roma, Antonio. "Energy, Money, and Pollution", *Ecological Economics,* vol. 56/no. 4, (2006), pp. 534–45.

Røpke, Inge. "Trends in the Development of Ecological Economics from the Late 1980s to the Early 2000s", *Ecological Economics,* vol. 55/no. 2, (2005), pp. 262–90.

Rosenberger, Randall S., George L. Peterson, Andrea Clarke, *et al.* "Measuring Dispositions for Lexicographic Preferences of Environmental Goods: Integrating Economics, Psychology and Ethics", *Ecological Economics,* vol. 44/no. 1, (2003), pp. 63–76.

Rostow, W. W. *The Stages of Economic Growth: A Non-Communist Manifesto,* Cambridge, Cambridge University Press, 1960.

Ruth, Matthias. *"Sustainable Development: Science, Ethics, and Public Policy* [edited by John Lemons and Donald A. Brown, Dordrecht, Kluwer Academic, 1995]", *Ecological Economics,* vol. 18/no. 3, (1996), pp. 259–60.

—. "A Quest for the Economics of Sustainability and the Sustainability of Economics", *Ecological Economics,* vol. 56/no. 3, (2006), pp. 332–42.

Saez, Carmen Almansa, and Javier Calatrava Requena. "Reconciling Sustainability and Discounting in Cost-Benefit Analysis: A Methodological Proposal", *Ecological Economics,* vol. 60/no. 4, (2007), pp. 712–25.

Schor, Juliet B. *The Overspent American: Upscaling, Downshifting and the New Consumer,* London, HarperCollins, 1999.

—. "The New Consumers: The Influence of Affluence on the Environment", *Ecological Economics,* vol. 55/no. 3, (2005a), pp. 444–45.

—. "Prices and Quantities: Unsustainable Consumption and the Global Economy", *Ecological Economics,* vol. 55/no. 3, (2005b), pp. 309–20.

Sen, A. *Commodities and Capabilities,* Oxford, Oxford University Press, 1985.

—. *Development As Freedom,* New York, Knopf, 1999.

Shah, A. *"Poverty Facts and Stats"* (updated March 22, 2009), <http://www.globalissues.org/article/26/poverty-facts-and-stats#src24>.

Shi, Tian. "Ecological Economics as a Policy Science: Rhetoric or Commitment Towards an Improved Decision-Making Process on Sustainability", *Ecological Economics,* vol. 48/no. 1, (2004), pp. 23–36.

Singer, P. "Not for Humans Only: The Place of Nonhumans in Environmental Issues", in K. E. Goodpaster and K. M. Sayre (Eds.) *Ethics and the Problems of the 21st Century,* Notre Dame, IN, University of Notre Dame Press, 1976.

Small, Bruce, and Nigel Jollands. "Technology and Ecological Economics: Promethean Technology, Pandorian Potential", *Ecological Economics,* vol. 56/no. 3, (2006), pp. 343–58.

Smart, J. J. C. and B. Williams. *Utilitarianism: For and Against,* Cambridge, Cambridge University Press, 1973.

Smith, A. *An Inquiry into the Nature and Causes of the Wealth of Nations,* London, George Routledge & Sons, 1903 (1776).

—. *The Theory of Moral Sentiments,* edited by D. D. Raphael, and A. L. MacFie, Indianapolis, IN, Liberty Press, 1976.

Sneddon, Chris, Richard B. Howarth, and Richard B. Norgaard. "Sustainable Development in a Post-Brundtland World", *Ecological Economics,* vol. 57/no. 2, (2006), pp. 253–68.

Söderbaum, Peter. "Values, Ideology and Politics in Ecological Economics", *Ecological Economics,* vol. 28/no. 2, (1999), pp. 161–70.

—. "Issues of Paradigm, Ideology and Democracy in Sustainability Assessment", *Ecological Economics,* vol. 60/no. 3, (2007), pp. 613–26.

Söderholm, Patrik, and Thomas Sundqvist. "Pricing Environmental Externalities in the Power Sector: Ethical Limits and Implications for Social Choice", *Ecological Economics,* vol. 46/no. 3, (2003), pp. 333–50.

Solow, R. M. "On the Intergenerational Allocation of Natural Resources", *Scandinavian Journal of Economics,* vol. 88/(1988), pp. 141–49.

—. "Sustainability: An Economists Perspective", in R. Dorfman and N. S. Dorfman (Eds.) *Economics of the Environment. Selected Readings,* 3rd edn, New York, W. W. Norton, 1991, pp. 162–88.

Sonntag, Viki. "Sustainability – in Light of Competitiveness", *Ecological Economics,* vol. 34/no. 1, (2000), pp. 101–13.

Spash, Clive L. "Deliberative Monetary Valuation (DMV): Issues in Combining Economic and Political Processes to Value Environmental Change", *Ecological Economics,* vol. 63/no. 4, (2007), pp. 690–9.

—. "Ecosystems, Contingent Valuation and Ethics: The Case of Wetland Re-Creation", *Ecological Economics,* vol. 34/no. 2, (2000), pp. 195–215.

—.*Greenhouse Economics. Value and Ethics,* London and New York, Routledge, 2002.

Spash, Clive L., and Nick Hanley. "Preferences, Information and Biodiversity Preservation", *Ecological Economics,* vol. 12/no. 3, (1995), pp. 191–208.

Spash, Clive L., Kevin Urama, Rob Burton, *et al.* "Motives Behind Willingness to Pay for Improving Biodiversity in a Water Ecosystem: Economics, Ethics and Social Psychology", *Ecological Economics,* vol.68/no. 4, (2009), pp. 955–64.

Spash, Clive L., and Arild Vatn. "Transferring Environmental Value Estimates: Issues and Alternatives", *Ecological Economics,* vol. 60/no. 2, (2006), pp. 379–88.

Speth, James Gustave. *The Bridge at the Edge of the World: Capitalism, the Environment, and Crossing from Crisis to Sustainability*, New Haven, CT, Yale University Press, 2008.

Stern, Nicholas. *et al.* "The Stern Review: The Economics of Climate Change", (2007): <http://www.hm-treasury.gov.uk/independent_reviews/stern_review_economics_climate_change/sternreview_index.cfm>.

Sutcliffe, B. "Postscript to the Article 'World Inequality and Globalization'", *Oxford Review of Economic Policy,* April, 2007.

Svedin, Uno. "Implicit and Explicit Ethical Norms in the Environmental Policy Arena", *Ecological Economics,* vol. 24/no. 2–3, (1998), pp. 299–309.

Tacconi, Luca. "Scientific Methodology for Ecological Economics", *Ecological Economics,* vol. 27/no. 1, (1998), pp. 91–105.

Talbert, J., C. Cobb, and N. Slattery. "The Genuine Progress Indicator 2006. A Tool for Sustainable Development", 2007, <http://www.rprogress.org/publications/2007/GPI%202006.pdf#search=>.

Taylor, P. W. *Respect for Nature. A Theory of Environmental Ethics*, Princeton, NJ, University of Princeton Press, 1986.

Tietenberg, Tom. "Ethical Influences on the Evolution of the US Tradable Permit Approach to Air Pollution Control", *Ecological Economics,* vol. 24/no. 2–3, (1998), pp. 241–57.

Tognetti, Sylvia S. "Science in a Double-Bind: Gregory Bateson and the Origins of Post-Normal Science", *Futures,* vol. 31/no. 7, (1999), pp. 689–703.

Tol, R. S. J. "The Damage Cost of Climate Change: Towards More Comprehensive Calculations", *Environmental and Resource Economics,* vol. 5, (1995), pp. 353–74.

Toman, Michael A. "Economics and 'Sustainability': Balancing Trade-Offs and Imperatives", *Land Economics,* vol. 70/no. 4, (1994), pp. 399.

Trebeth, K. E. "The Role of the Oceans in Climate," *Annual Report on the State of the Ocean Observing System for Climate*, <http://www.oco.noaa.gov.uk>.

Trosper, Ronald L. "Northwest Coast Indigenous Institutions that Supported Resilience and Sustainability", *Ecological Economics,* vol. 41/no. 2, (2002), pp. 329–44.

Turner, Nancy. "*Hunting for Sustainability in Tropical Forests* [edited by John G. Robinson and Elizabeth L. Bennett, New York, Columbia University Press, 2000]", *Ecological Economics,* vol. 39/no. 1, (2001), pp. 163–64.

Turner, R. Kerry. "Integrating Natural and Socio-Economic Science in Coastal Management", *Journal of Marine Systems,* vol. 25/no. 3–4, (2000), pp. 447–60.

Turner, R. K., D. Pearce, and I. Bateman. *Environmental Economics. An Elementary Introduction*, Baltimore, MD, Johns Hopkins University Press, 1993.

Turner, R. Kerry, Jouni Paavola, Philip Cooper, *et al.* "Valuing Nature: Lessons Learned and Future Research Directions", *Ecological Economics,* vol. 46/no. 3, (2003), pp. 493–510.

Vail, David, and Lars Hultkrantz. "Property Rights and Sustainable Nature Tourism: Adaptation and Mal-Adaptation in Dalarna (Sweden) and Maine (USA)", *Ecological Economics,* vol. 35/no. 2, (2000), pp. 223–42.

Vallentyne, Peter. *"Distributive Justice",* (2009) <http://klinechair.missouri.edu/on-line%20papers/distributive%20justice%20(handbook).doc>.

Vallentyne, P. and H. Steiner (Eds.). *The Origins of Left Libertarianism: An Anthology of Historical Writings*, in Anonymous, New York, Palgrave, 2000.

van den Bergh, Jeroen C. J. M., Ada Ferrer-i-Carbonell, and Giuseppe Munda. "Alternative Models of Individual Behaviour and Implications for Environmental Policy", *Ecological Economics,* vol. 32/no. 1, (2000), pp. 43–61.

Van Overwalle, Geertrui. "Protecting and Sharing Biodiversity and Traditional Knowledge: Holder and User Tools", *Ecological Economics,* vol. 53/no. 4, (2005), pp. 585–607.

Van Staveren, Irene. *The Values of Economics: An Aristotelian Perspective,* London, Routledge, 2001.

Vatn, Arild. "Environmental Valuation and Rationality", *Land Economics,* vol. 80/no. 1, (2004), pp. 1–18.

—. "Rationality, Institutions and Environmental Policy", *Ecological Economics,* vol. 55/no. 2, (2005), pp. 203–17.

Veblen, T. *The Theory of the Leisure Class: An Economic Study of Institutions,* London, 1925 (1899).

—. *The Place of Science in Modern Civilization and Other Essays,* New York, Russell & Russell, 1961 (1919), pp. 73–73.

Venkatachalam, L. "Environmental Economics and Ecological Economics: Where They Can Converge?", *Ecological Economics,* vol. 61/no.2, (2007), pp. 550–8.

Wackernagel, Mathis, and William E. Rees. "Perceptual and Structural Barriers to Investing in Natural Capital: Economics from an Ecological Footprint Perspective", *Ecological Economics,* vol. 20/no. 1, (1996), pp. 3–24.

Wagner, Jeffrey. "On the Economics of Sustainability", *Ecological Economics,* vol. 57/no. 4, (2006), pp. 659–64.

Walker, B. H., and L. Pearson. "A Resilience Perspective of the SEEA", *Ecological Economics,* vol. 61/no. 4, (2007), pp. 708–15.

Walter, Gerald R. "Economics, Ecology-Based Communities, and Sustainability", *Ecological Economics,* vol. 42/no. 1–2, (2002), pp. 81–87.

Welsch, Heinz. "Environment and Happiness: Valuation of Air Pollution using Life Satisfaction Data", *Ecological Economics,* vol. 58/no. 4, (2006), pp. 801–13.

Wittebolle, L., M. Marzorati, L. Clement, *et al.* "Initial Community Evenness Favours Functionality Under Selective Stress", *Nature,* (2009), pp. 623–26.

World Bank. *World Development Report 2006: Equity and Development,* Washington, DC, World Bank, 2006.

—. *World Development Report 2008: Agriculture for Development,* Washington, DC, World Bank, 2007.

World Commission on Environment and Development (WCED). *Our Common Future* [The Brundtland Report], Oxford, Oxford University Press,1987.

World Commission on the Social Dimension of Globalization. *A Fair Globalization. Creating Opportunities for All,* Geneva, ILO, 2004.

WWF. *Living Planet Report 2008,* Gland, WWF, 2008.

Index

Page numbers in *italics* represent tables; page numbers in **bold** represent figures.

6th Edition

BASIC NUTRITION
in
HEALTH and DISEASE

Including Selection and Care of Food

PHYLLIS SULLIVAN HOWE, R.D., B.S., M.E.

Nutrition Instructor, Contra Costa Community College,
San Pablo, California; Diablo Valley Community College,
Concord, California

W. B. SAUNDERS COMPANY
Philadelphia, London, Toronto

W. B. Saunders Company: West Washington Square
Philadelphia, PA 19105

1 St. Anne's Road
Eastbourne, East Sussex BN21 3UN, England

1 Goldthorne Avenue
Toronto, Ontario M8Z 5T9, Canada

Library of Congress Cataloging in Publication Data

Howe, Phyllis Sullivan.

Basic nutrition in health and disease.

First-4th ed. published under title: Nutrition for
practical nurses.

Bibliography: p.

Includes index.

1. Diet in disease.   2. Nutrition.   3. Food.   I. Title.
    [DNLM: 1. Diet therapy.   2. Nutrition. QU145 H857n]

RM216.H84 1976   613.2   75–31300

ISBN 0–7216–4788–X

Basic Nutrition in Health and Disease—6th Edition   ISBN   0-7216-4788-X

Last digit is the print number: 9   8   7   6   5

DEDICATION

This sixth edition is dedicated to four teachers who influenced me by their insistence upon academic achievement and upon exploring all facets of new subject areas: at Montana State University—Dean Gladys Branegan Chalkley and Bertha C. Clow; at Columbia Falls High School—Violet K. Johnston and Elsie E. Williams.

PREFACE

Students of nursing, students in many of the allied health fields, and the public need a simple and concise source for learning the basic principles of nutrition, diet therapy, and selection of food.

This text questions some current ideas which are based on practice rather than research. These are rapidly changing times, and what was considered good therapeutic practice last year may be considered obsolete next year. Although some material published several years ago still provides good basic information, texts, journals, and pamphlets published within the past five years should be used for reference reading when possible.

Sections in all chapters have been revised to include recent research findings. The table of contents lists the varied information in the three sections of the appendix.

In my opinion, history will refer to the decade of the seventies as the time in which there was a rapid acceleration of the consumer movement. Middle income as well as low income families are looking for ways to get more value from the dollars they spend. For this reason I have included a chapter titled "Groceries, Nutrition, and Dollars."

Reference readings and practical problems are suggested throughout the book for those students who are interested in and have opportunities for pursuing additional work. In content and style, the text attempts to fulfill a particular need; should readers have comments concerning the worth or weakness of individual chapters or sections of chapters, written statements citing these points will be appreciated, and will be most helpful in the preparation of the next revision.

I wish to express appreciation to Maralynn Osborne Guenther, R.R.A., for reading the entire manuscript, for her many helpful suggestions, and for compiling the list of prefixes and suffixes; to Lavern Owens, R.D., for reviewing the chapter on mental illness; to Alvis Joe Scull, M.D., for permission to include his tables on the normal behavior patterns of children; to Cheryl Beal LaFleur for manuscript typing; to my students and others whose comments helped guide this revision; to my husband, Warren, without whose assistance I would find it difficult to complete a manuscript; to the publishers who have generously granted me permission to reproduce various quotations, figures, tables, and other data as indicated in the text; and to the editors of the W. B. Saunders Company for their encouragement and helpful suggestions.

P. S. H.

CONTENTS

Section II

DIET THERAPY

Contents

Section III

SELECTION AND CARE OF FOOD

x   **Contents**

NORMAL NUTRITION

INTRODUCTORY STATEMENT

Most of the scientific study of food and its effects upon the body has been done in this century. Because new facts are discovered each year, it is important that only *recently published* books be used for reference reading.

There are many excellent texts, journals, and pamphlets that can be used for supplementary reading; a few of them are listed at the ends of chapters and in the bibliography.

Numbers in parentheses (5:56) refer to other books or professional journals. For example, 5:56 means page 56 of the fifth reference listed in the bibliography. Table or Figure 11–3 means the third table or figure in Chapter 11. You can quickly refer to a figure or table because at the top of each right hand page the chapter number as well as the chapter title is shown.

Many terms used in this text will be defined in the glossary in Appendix 2. In general, these are alphabetized, but related terms will be found in one group. For example, hemolytic and macrocytic anemia are listed under anemia. At the beginning of each chapter is a list of words you should be able to define before studying the chapter.

There are a few concepts and terms which you should know before you start your study of how the nutrients in your food become you.

Nutrients are the chemical compounds found in food. The chart on following page shows food sources of nutrients according to body use.

You should note that protein is used by the body in three ways, but this does not make it any more essential than the other nutrient groups.

Nutrition is the science which is concerned with food, its acceptance by individuals, and the body's uses of chemicals that the food contains. The practice of good nutrition should extend throughout the life span—

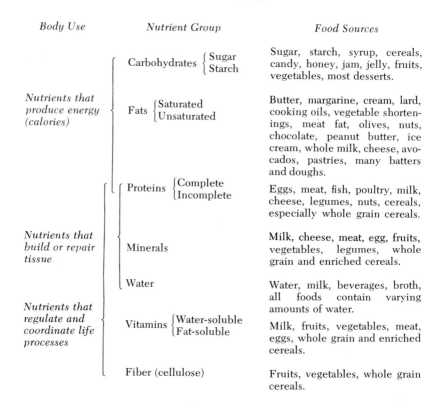

Body Use	Nutrient Group	Food Sources
Nutrients that produce energy (calories)	Carbohydrates { Sugar, Starch	Sugar, starch, syrup, cereals, candy, honey, jam, jelly, fruits, vegetables, most desserts.
	Fats { Saturated, Unsaturated	Butter, margarine, cream, lard, cooking oils, vegetable shortenings, meat fat, olives, nuts, chocolate, peanut butter, ice cream, whole milk, cheese, avocados, pastries, many batters and doughs.
Nutrients that build or repair tissue	Proteins { Complete, Incomplete	Eggs, meat, fish, poultry, milk, cheese, legumes, nuts, cereals, especially whole grain cereals.
	Minerals	Milk, cheese, meat, egg, fruits, vegetables, legumes, whole grain and enriched cereals.
	Water	Water, milk, beverages, broth, all foods contain varying amounts of water.
Nutrients that regulate and coordinate life processes	Vitamins { Water-soluble, Fat-soluble	Milk, fruits, vegetables, meat, eggs, whole grain and enriched cereals.
	Fiber (cellulose)	Fruits, vegetables, whole grain cereals.

prenatal through geriatric. Good appearance, good health, and good nutrition go together.

Diet. In this text the word diet is used to mean the food and drink consumed each day. When the lay person uses the term, he usually is thinking of a low-calorie diet to reduce his weight. The modified or therapeutic diet, sometimes called a "special diet," is the food allowance which has been changed to meet the specific requirements of the individual and may include or exclude certain foods, may increase or decrease specific nutrients, may restrict quantity, or may involve a change in texture and consistency of food. *Avoid dietary extremes. Do not make major changes in the diet without medical advice.*

Digestion and Absorption. When you swallow food you have put that food into a tube which extends through your body—mouth to anus. Digestion changes the food nutrients into the substances which will go through the *intestinal wall* into the body. Until this absorption has taken place, the body has not been nourished. Any of the nutrients which do not go through the intestinal wall into the blood stream will be excreted in the feces. Most of us digest and absorb from 90 to 98 per cent of the nutrients in food, but a few individuals have faulty digestion or faulty absorption or both. It would be possible for them to be malnourished, even though eating correctly.

Nutrient Contributions of Familiar Foods

Kind of food	Size of serving (ready-to-eat)	Protein	Calcium	Iron	Vitamin A value	B-vitamins			Vitamin C (ascorbic acid)	Food energy (in calories)
						Thiamine	Riboflavin	Niacin		
Milk............	1 cup....	★	★★★★		★	★	★★			165
Cheese, process Cheddar.	1 ounce..	★	★★★		★		★			105
Meat, poultry, fish.	2 ounces..	★★		★★	★	★	★	★★		195
Eggs............	1 large egg.	★		★	★		★			80
Dry beans and peas, nuts.	¾ cup cooked beans.	★★	★	★★★		★	★	★		170
Grain products....	2 slices bread.	★	★	★		★	★	★		120
Citrus fruits.......	½ cup...								★★★★★	50
Other fruits.......	½ cup...			★	★				★	60
Tomatoes, tomato juice.	½ cup...			★	★★★			★	★★★	25
Dark-green and deep-yellow vegetables (except sweet-potatoes).	½ cup...		★	★	★★★★★		★		★★★★	40
Sweetpotatoes.....	1 medium.		★	★	★★★★★	★	★	★	★★★	170
Light-green vegetables.¹	½ cup...		★	★	★				★★	35
Potatoes.........	1 medium.			★		★		★	★★★	90
Other vegetables..	½ cup...			★					★	40
Butter, margarine..	1 tablespoon.				★					100
Other fats........	2 tablespoons.									220
Sugar, all kinds....	2 teaspoons.									35
Molasses, sirups...	2 tablespoons.			★★						110

★★★★★ More than 50 percent of daily need.
★★★★ About 40 percent of daily need.
★★★ About 30 percent of daily need.
★★ About 20 percent of daily need.
★ About 10 percent of daily need.

¹ Includes asparagus, green snap beans, peas, green lima beans, green cabbage, brussels sprouts, green lettuce.

(From U.S.D.A.: *Nutrition—Up to Date, Up to You*, p. 11.)

Synthesis (Manufacture). One can compare the body synthesis of compounds to making words. The alphabet used in the United States has only 26 letters, but we can make thousands of words by arranging these letters differently. The body can synthesize elements into compounds and can then combine these compounds to make more complex compounds. For example, a protein is a long chain of smaller compounds called amino acids. The thousands of different proteins found in the body are different arrangements of the amino acids (see Figure 5–1).

Evaluation. To evaluate or appraise a diet is to compare it to a standard; in this text the standard used will be the basic-four food groups. The evaluation patterns may vary according to cultural patterns and foods commonly available in the community. But all should have as a desirable goal the recommended daily nutrient allowance described below.

Health. The World Health Organization defines health as "a state of complete physical, mental and social well-being and not merely the absence of disease or infirmity."

Food Composition Tables show the approximate nutrient content of food. The Department of Agriculture Handbook No. 8, *Composition of Foods*, indicates country-wide, year-round averages. For example, it lists 100 grams of raw potato as having 20 milligrams of ascorbic acid. The ascorbic acid content in different varieties of potatoes is between 19 and 33 milligrams per 100 grams of freshly dug tubers; the average for market new potatoes is 26. One month after harvest, loss due to storage is about one fourth; three months after harvest the loss is about one half; after six months, two thirds; and nine months after harvest the loss is about three fourths. The bulk of the market supply in summer contains about 25 milligrams of ascorbic acid per 100 grams of potatoes; by December the content is about 18 milligrams per 100 grams, and by late winter or early spring about 14 milligrams. Thus the year-round, country-wide average is about 20 milligrams per 100 grams of raw potato. (43)

The National Research Council (NRC) was formed by the National Academy of Sciences in 1916. Its member scientists cooperate to serve the interests of the government and research in many fields. In 1940 the Food and Nutrition Board was established to advise the council on matters concerning food and nutrition. This board composed a table of recommended daily dietary allowances based on studies made by many scientists to determine the nutrients needed daily by adults and children to obtain optimal health.

On the basis of available scientific knowledge, the NRC's *Recommended Dietary Allowances* represents a standard for the intake of a limited number of nutrients (about one third of the known essential nutrients) which should ensure the known nutritional needs of practically all healthy people. The needs of most individuals will be less than the RDA standard, but a few may require more. This variation can be due to such factors as genetic makeup, infections, continual use of pharmaceutical preparations (e.g., oral contraceptives), chronic diseases, metabolic disorders, and premature birth. An individual's food practices are not necessarily poor, nor can he be said to be suffering from malnutrition, if he does not completely meet the recommended intake. The actual nutritional status of an individual is determined by noting his nutrient intake as well as by physical, biochemical, and clinical observation. The NRC allowances are not considered adequate to meet the additional requirements of nutrient depletion resulting from disease or prior dietary inadequacies. If the RDA is provided by a varied selection of palatable and acceptable food combinations, the diet is more apt to provide for other needed nutrients; populations with limited food choices are more likely to show nutritional deficiencies. The Food and Nutrition Board states, "We are aware of no convincing evidence of unique health benefits accruing from consumption of a large excess of any one nutrient."(53:3) Harm may result from diagnostic delay while consuming large amounts of individual nutrients to try to cure the non-nutritional disease. The recommended allowance table is revised frequently to include new research findings. The 1974 table can be found inside the front cover.

The Canadian Council on Nutrition is an advisory group to the Canadian Department on National Health and Welfare. The Council has published a Canadian Dietary Standard that varies somewhat from the NRC allowances, but it, too, has recommended intakes above the minimal nutrient requirements. The 3000 calorie allowance for a young man weighing 154 pounds doing sedentary work compares with the NRC allowance of 2700 calories for the 154-pound, moderately active 23- to 50-year-old man. However, the 30 milligrams of ascorbic acid advised for the Canadian adult is one third less than the NRC allowance of 45 milligrams. Probably either the NRC or the Canadian standard could be used safely. The 1974 revision of Canadian Recommended Daily Nutrient Intakes appears inside the back cover.

The United States Food and Drug Administration has discontinued use of its minimum daily requirements. The FDA's current standard is called the *United States Recommended Daily Allowances* (USRDA). This table is derived from the Recommended Daily Allowances (RDA) and its purpose is to serve as the standard for nutritional labeling of retail foods.

Basic-Four Food Groups. The United States Department of Agriculture has translated the NRC table of recommended allowances into a daily food guide—the basic-four food groups. No food has exactly the same nutrient value as another, but there are foods which have similar nutrient value. Those of similar value have been classified into the four basic groups—milk products, fruits and vegetables, cereals, and meat. Any food within one group can be used as an alternate for any other food within the same group. By dividing the food supply into a recommended number of servings from each of these four food groups, most of the recommended nutrient intake is supplied. Serving size of the food groups is shown in Table 1–2.

Toxicity. Any substance may be harmful when ingested in excessive amounts, but individuals vary in the amount they can tolerate. Ingesting inconsequential amounts produces no harm to the body, but any amount above the individual's threshold tolerance will produce injury to the body; in this case, we say the substance is toxic to the person.

A balanced diet includes average-sized portions of the four food groups daily; these supply an adequate nutrient intake to support normal body functions. This is illustrated in Figure 1–4. Nearly every person, when asked if he eats a balanced diet, indicates that he does. How can you

Hey, Mom! Is this what you mean by a well balanced meal?

be sure he knows portion size and what foods are in the basic-four groups by merely asking him if he eats a balanced diet? There are many terms, such as balanced diet or rich food, which probably should not be used when discussing food habits. Students have listed as rich foods such varied things as fondant (sugar, corn syrup, and water), chocolate, pie crust (starch and fat), whipped cream (fat and sugar), and nuts (fat and protein). Diet instruction which states that rich foods should be omitted may cause one person to omit pastries or nuts and another chocolate milk. If you intend foods high in fat, high in sugar, or chocolate flavored to be omitted, use those terms—then there can be no misunderstanding. The only modification of an adequate diet should be that which meets the specific condition as ordered by the doctor.

EXERCISE

Use the food selection scorecard which follows to score your diet. If your score in any food group is below the maximum score, check Table 1–2 and note the nutrients which would have been furnished by that food group.

Food Selection Scorecard

Score your diet for each day using the points allowed for each food group. If your score is between 90 and 100, your food selection standard has been good; a score of 75 to 85 indicates a fair standard; a score below 75 is a low standard.

Points allowed (See basic-four food groups [Table 1–2] for serving size and substitutions.)	*Maximum points for each group*	*Columns for daily check*				
Milk (include cheese, ice cream, and milk used in cooking) Adults: 1 glass, 10 points; 1½ glasses, 15; 2 glasses, 20. Teen-agers and children 9 to 12: 1 glass, 5 points; 2 glasses, 10; 3 glasses, 15; 4 glasses, 20. Children under 9: 2 glasses, 15; 3 glasses, 20.	20					
Vegetables and fruits (serving = ½ cup) Vegetables: 1 serving, 5; 2 servings, 10. Potatoes may be included as one of these servings.	10					
Using 1 serving of dark green or deep yellow vegetable will earn you 5 extra points.	5					
Fruits: 1 serving, 5; 2 servings, 10.	10					
Using citrus fruit, raw cabbage, canned or raw tomatoes, berries, or melons gives 5 extra points.	5					
Grain products Whole grain, enriched, or restored: Bread, rice, breakfast cereals, macaroni, etc.: 2 servings, 10 points; 4 servings, 15.	15					
Meat, eggs, fish, poultry, dried peas or beans, peanut butter: 1 serving, 10; 2 servings, 15.	15					
Using 1 serving liver or other organs gives 5 extra points.	5					
Total liquids (include milk, broth, tea, coffee, other beverages) Adults: 6 glasses, 3; 8 glasses, 5. Children: 4 glasses, 3; 6 glasses, 5.	5					
Eating a breakfast which included food from the meat or milk group. Do not count cream or bacon (except Canadian bacon) in this score.	10					
Daily score	100					

(Adapted from Food Selection Score Card, Department of Agriculture, Cooperative Extension Work in Agriculture and Home Economics.)

SUMMARY SHOWING COMPARATIVE PICTURES OF GOOD AND POOR NUTRITION

Characteristics of Good Nutrition	Characteristics of Malnutrition (The presence of one or more of these characteristics indicates some failure in the nutrition of the body.)
1. Well developed body.	1. Body may be undersized or show poor development.
2. About average weight for height.	2. Usually thin but may be normal or overweight with flabby, soft fat.
3. Muscles well developed and firm.	3. Muscles small and soft.
4. Skin of healthy turgor and color.	4. Skin loose and pale, waxy or sallow.
5. Good layer of subcutaneous fat.	5. Subcutaneous fat usually lacking.
6. Mucous membranes of eyelids and mouth reddish-pink.	6. Mucous membranes pale.
7. Hair smooth and glossy.	7. Hair often rough and without luster.
8. Eyes clear and without dark circles under them.	8. Dark hollows or blue circles under eyes.
9. Facial expression alert but without strain.	9. Facial expression drawn, worried or old; or animated but strained.
10. Posture good: head erect, chest up, shoulders flat, abdomen in.	10. Fatigue posture: head thrust forward, chest narrow and flat, shoulders rounded, abdomen protruding.
11. Good-natured, full of life, buoyant.	11. Irritable, overactive, fatigued; or phlegmatic, listless, unable to concentrate; depressed.
12. Sleep, sound.	12. Sleep, restless; difficulty getting to sleep.
13. Digestion and elimination good.	13. Subject to nervous indigestion and constipation.
14. Appetite good.	14. "Finicky" about food; appetite poor.
15. General health good.	15. Susceptibility (low resistance) to infection, lack of endurance and vigor.

(From American Dietetic Association: *A Manual for Teaching Dietetics to Student Nurses*, p. 36.)

SUGGESTED READING

"Dr. Jean Mayer's Guide to Family Nutrition: How to Eat to Feel Your Best," *Family Circle,* August, 1975, p. 124.

Church, C. F., and Church, H. N.: Bowes and Church's Food Values of Portions Commonly Used, 12th Ed. Philadelphia, J. B. Lippincott, Publisher, 1975.

CHAPTER 1

You and Nutrition

TERMS TO UNDERSTAND

Anemia	Citrus	Phlegmatic
Atom	Diet	Radioisotope
Cereal	Ingest	Stamina
Enriched	Legume	Subcutaneous
Refined	Malnutrition	Therapy
Restored	Palatable	Turgor
Whole Grain		

The United States produces a great supply of food, uses food processing methods which retain the nutrients, and excels in marketing and distribution; yet there are some people in this country who are malnourished. Malnutrition, which means that the body is not supplied with a sufficient amount of each nutrient, contributes to health problems. Malnourishment can be caused by not having enough food to supply the needed nutrients (this does not occur in the United States as much as in other countries) or by not eating the combination of foods which will supply the needed nutrients (this occurs in this country and not entirely at the lower income levels). A person can be overweight because he is consuming foods containing too many calories and yet be malnourished because he is not getting the nutrients needed for optimal building or repairing of tissue and regulating of body processes. George V. Mann* states:

> There are more persons in the U.S. malnourished because of nutritional ignorance and misinformation than because of poverty. While economists, whether because more percipient or brasher, tell us that from 15 to 30 million persons in the U.S. have incomes insufficient to supply an adequate diet, no one has been interested in enumerating the persons

---

*Mann, George V.: "Nutrition Education—U.S.A.," *National Live Stock & Meat Board, Food and Nutrition News,* November, 1969.

too badly informed to select an adequate diet, even with an adequate income. It is an obvious fact, many malnourished persons make bad food choices. The prevalence of automobiles in the front yard, television in the parlor, and beer in the refrigerator ought to rank with pluckable hair, pot-bellies, and sad eyes when the nutritionists go out on their survey sallies. Perhaps this oversight occurs because poverty is a more acceptable explanation for malnutrition. If it were the cause, we would have a ready solution in this affluent society—money. But if poverty is not the main cause, neither malnutrition nor our consciences are going to be relieved by doles and food stamps. Education is not so easily accomplished.

Americans seem to be more careful about nourishing their animals than themselves. Livestock to be marketed are scientifically fed because well-nourished livestock bring top prices. Many facts of good nutrition for humans are well known—why are some of us ill-fed? Indifference; ignorance; careless habits such as skipping breakfast or lunch; omitting basic-four foods; indulging in food faddism; and setting poor dietary examples for children are important reasons why many people are poorly nourished. These undesirable habits can be changed if the individual wishes to do so, and learns how to make the changes.

Our income does determine the amount and kinds of food which we can buy, but the more we know about nutrients, their food sources, how our body uses them, and how we can cook the food so that the nutrients are not wasted, the better we can feed our families. Figure 1–1 shows the need for education of food buyers in all income groups. Note that nine per cent of the families (one of every 11) with incomes over $10,000 had poor diets in 1965.

Using a variety of foods prepared in a variety of ways provides one of the best guarantees of an adequate diet.

All homemakers should know about nutrition so that they will be able to select and prepare foods which will keep them and their families in

INCOME
AND QUALITY OF DIETS

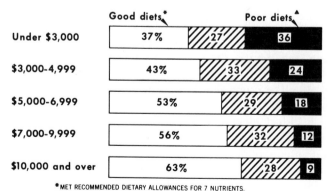

* MET RECOMMENDED DIETARY ALLOWANCES FOR 7 NUTRIENTS.
▲ HAD LESS THAN 2/3 ALLOWANCE FOR 1 TO 7 NUTRIENTS.

Figure 1–1   (From Nationwide Household Food Consumption Survey, spring 1965.)

NUTRIENT INTAKE BELOW RECOMMENDED ALLOWANCE

Average Intake of Group Below Recommended Dietary Allowance, NAS–NCR, 1968

U.S. DIETS OF MEN, WOMEN, AND CHILDREN, ONE DAY IN SPRING 1965

Sex-Age Group	Protein	Calcium	Iron	Vitamin A value	Thiamine	Riboflavin	Ascorbic acid
MALE AND FEMALE:							
Under 1 year			• • • •				
1– 2 years			• • • •				
3– 5 years			• •				
6– 8 years							
MALE:							
9–11 years		•					
12–14 years		• •	• • •		•		
15–17 years		•	•				
18–19 years							
20–34 years							
35–54 years		•					
55–64 years		• •					
65–74 years		• •					
75 years and over		• • •		•		• •	•
FEMALE:							
9–11 years		• • •	• • • •		•		
12–14 years		• • •	• • • • •	•	•		
15–17 years		• • • • •	• • • •			• •	
18–19 years		• • •	• • • • •	•	•		
20–34 years		• • •	• • • • •		•	•	
35–54 years		• • • • •	• • • •		•	• •	
55–64 years		• • • • •			•	•	
65–74 years		• • • • •	•	•	• •	• •	
75 years and over		• • • •	•	• •	• •	• • •	

BELOW BY:
1–10% •
11–20% • •
21–29% • • •
30% OR MORE • • • •

Figure 1–2   (From 1969 Agricultural Yearbook, p. 270.)

good health. A nurse has the following additional reasons for needing to know about nutrition:

1. *To teach patients.* Some patients may have questions concerning the best foods to eat each day, or if they are on a modified diet they may wonder why it is important for them to eat the foods which are served. The nurse's daily person-to-person contact makes it possible for her to influence the eating habits of her patients.

2. *To help friends.* Because she is a nurse her friends may ask what to eat to keep healthy; she should know what food combinations make an adequate diet. *She should not suggest modified diets.* For example, if her friend has a sore mouth, she should not tell him to eat foods high in vitamin C. However, if his doctor has told him to eat more foods containing vitamin C, then the nurse should be able to help him select those foods.

3. *To improve her own health and well-being.* Good nutrition is one factor in optimal health. Unless you believe in and practice good nutrition, you cannot set an example for others, nor can you be convincing when recommending an adequate diet.

4. *To increase her dependability.* The well-nourished person has more resistance to infection and is available to render service when needed.

A nurse, a homemaker, or any other successful teacher believes in and practices what he is teaching; if he does not practice the principles of good nutrition but is able to say the "right words," they will not be sincere enough to be convincing. The teacher must also listen to and understand any existing problems. A patient who believes that milk and fish in the same meal are a poisonous combination would refuse to eat New England clam chowder; an elderly person who says that he is chronically fatigued but cannot chew meat may be ingesting too little iron and, therefore, may be anemic.

Although we may seem to retain our body composition, size, and form, the use of radioisotopes in

tracer studies show that the atomic turnover in our bodies is quite rapid and quite complete. . . . Indeed, it has been shown that in a year approximately 98 per cent of the atoms in us now will be replaced by other atoms that we take in in our air, food, and drink (1:232).

Some of these atoms change quite frequently; for example, half of the sodium, hydrogen, and phosphorus atoms are replaced every week or two, and half of the carbon atoms are replaced every month or two (1:232). Each second the bone marrow replaces about 1,000,000 red blood cells. This constant rebuilding of body tissue indicates that adults as well as children need the nutrients found in a diet containing the basic-four food groups.

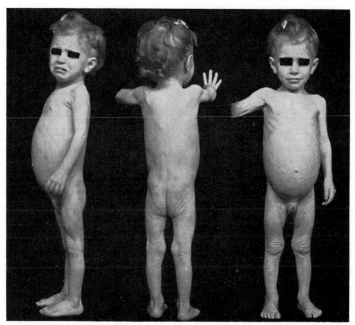

Figure 1–3   Child suffering from malnutrition. (Courtesy of Department of Pediatrics, University of Iowa Hospitals.)

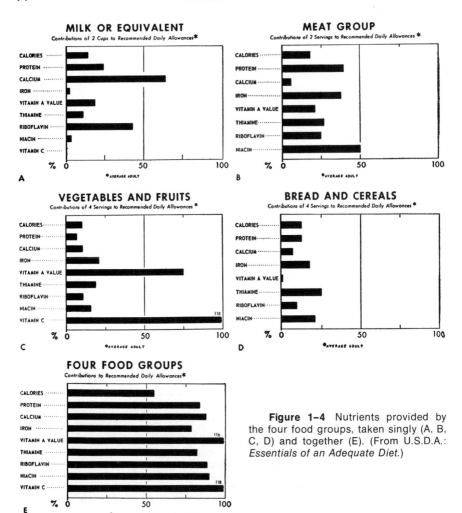

Figure 1-4 Nutrients provided by the four food groups, taken singly (A, B, C, D) and together (E). (From U.S.D.A.: *Essentials of an Adequate Diet.*)

Figure 1–4 shows the average quantity of nutrients provided by the food groups listed in the basic-four plan. To satisfy the appetite and to add palatability, butter, margarine, other fats, sugar, baked goods, desserts, and other recipe dishes probably would be added and would increase the nutrient intake.

Throughout this text the basic-four will be the pattern used. Formerly, seven food groups were used. The reclassification into four groups retains much of the previous pattern. For example, the milk group remains the same, and the fruit and vegetable groups are combined.

Because a person physically is what he eats, diet does influence the way he looks and feels. Exercise will not build muscles unless the diet provides the building materials. Food not only becomes your body, but also, if your nutrition is poor, you are seriously handicapped. You tire easily, you lack stamina, purpose, and enthusiasm. You are a drudge and a drag; you are subject to discontent, worry, and irritability. Poor nutrition is an insidious thing. Sometimes it creeps into your life, like a spy, and slyly sabotages your enjoyment. Other times it attacks outright and quickly defeats everything you try to do (42:16).

Poor health does not need to accompany aging. Evidence is accumulating that what we eat throughout our life span affects how and when we begin to age. *Some of the sickness of later years may be the delayed effects of poor nutrition.*

To omit breakfast is a poor food habit. By mid-morning those who have not eaten breakfast are less efficient, less alert (could this account for some students' poor school grades?), more tired, and perhaps are more accident prone and irritable than those who have eaten breakfast. Those who neglect breakfast perk up for a short time after lunch and then repeat the mid-morning pattern. A good breakfast contains servings from at least three of the basic-four groups. It should contain from one quarter to one third of the calories, protein, minerals, and vitamins needed daily. These nutrients give energy, build body cells, and contribute to general good health. One who has not been eating breakfast can change his habit

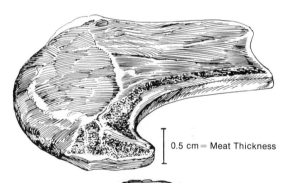

0.5 cm = Meat Thickness

Figure 1-5 Three ounces of raw meat will cook to these two-ounce sizes.

by starting with very small servings, gradually increasing the size. He will feel better throughout the entire day. He will find it much easier to incorporate the basic-four into three meals but difficult to include everything in one or two meals.

Since most of our food habits develop when we are children, that phase of nutrition will be covered in Chapter 12, Acquiring Food Acceptance.

Often repeated and very strongly worded food dislikes and preferences may be a symptom of unhappiness or neurotic problems.

Diet is influenced by the supply of available food, by economic status, by the social and cultural factors of the society in which we live, and by current ideas about food. Many young men and women do not learn the principles of good nutrition either in school or in their homes. Nutrition is a recently developed science; mothers may not know the correct principles and therefore cannot teach them. The next chapter will discuss some of the current misinformation about food.

SUGGESTED READING

American Dietetic Association: *Give Yourself A Break.*
American Medical Association:
  Can Food Make the Difference?
  Physical Fitness.
  7 Paths to Fitness.
Blue Cross of Southern California: *Food and Fitness,* 1973.
Family Health, special nutrition issue, April, 1974, and April, 1975.
Kansas Wheat Commission: *Nutrition for the Nation,* 1973.
Leverton, Ruth: *Food Becomes You.*
Metropolitan Life Insurance Company:
  What Foods Do You Choose?
  You and Your Health, 1973.
Morris: "How Does a Nurse Teach Nutrition to Patients?" *Am. J. of Nursing,* January, 1960.
National Dairy Council:
  Four Food Groups (Poster).
  How Your Body Uses Food.
  Nutrition Source Book.
U.S. Department of Agriculture:
  Eat a Good Breakfast to Start a Good Day, 1972.
  Facts About Nutrition.
  Family Fare: Food Management and Recipes, 1973.
  The Food We Eat, 1967.
  Food Is More Than Just Something to Eat, 1969.
Wheat Flour Institute: *Eat to Live,* 1969.

Table 1-1   *Canada's Food Guide*

These foods are good to eat. Eat them every day for health. Have three meals each day.

Milk.   Children (up to about 11 years)   2 1/2 cups (20 fl. oz.)
        Adolescents   4   cups (32 fl. oz.)
        Adults   1 1/2 cups (12 fl. oz.)
        Expectant and nursing mothers   4   cups (32 fl. oz.)

Fruit. Two servings of fruit or juice including a satisfactory source of vitamin C (ascorbic acid) such as oranges, tomatoes, vitaminized apple juice.

Vegetables. One serving of potatoes; two servings of other vegetables, preferably yellow or green and often raw.

Bread and Cereals. Bread (with butter or fortified margarine); one serving of whole-grain cereal.

Meat and Fish. One serving of meat, fish or poultry.
  Eat liver occasionally.
  Eggs, cheese, dried beans or peas may be used in place of meat.
  In addition, eggs and cheese each at least 3 times a week.

Vitamin D. 400 International Units for all growing persons and expectant or nursing mothers.

From *Your Food Guide,* produced by Information Directorate for Health, Protection Branch, Health and Welfare, Ottawa, Ontario, Canada.

Table 1-2   *The Basic-Four*

(Diet Pattern To Be Used Every Day In The United States And Its Nutritive Value)

Pattern	
1. Milk	Whole, skim, buttermilk, dry, evaporated (to
Children — under 9 — 2 or more cups	drink or combine with other foods), cheese,
9 to 12 — 3 or more cups	ice cream, yogurt
13 to 18 — 4 or more cups	1 eight-oz. cup of milk =
Over 18 — 2 or more cups	1½ oz. or 1½ inch cube Cheddar-type cheese
	1½ cups cottage cheese
	2 cups cream cheese
	3 or 4 tablespoons powdered milk°
	2 cups ice cream
2. Vegetable-fruit	
1 serving citrus or substitute	Orange, grapefruit, lemon, lime, tangerine, tomatoes, strawberries, melon, raw cabbage, etc.
1 serving dark green or deep yellow vegetable at least every other day	Adult serving size is ½ to ⅔ cup†
2 servings other fruits or vegetables; potatoes may count as one of these servings	
3. Meat	
2 or more servings	Meat, poultry, fish, eggs and their substitutes of legumes, nuts, lentils
	Adult serving size is†
	cooked lean meat or fish — 2 or more oz.°° or ½ cup diced
	raw lean meat or fish — 3 or more oz.
	eggs — 2 medium size
	legumes — 1 cup cooked
	peanut butter — ¼ cup (4T)
	nuts — ½ cup
4. Cereal-bread	
4 or more servings	Whole grain, enriched or restored ‡: rice, wheat, rye, barley, oats, corn
	Adult serving is†
	1 oz. (¾ cup) ready-to-eat
	1 slice bread (approximately 1 oz.)
	½ to ¾ cup cooked breakfast cereal, rice, hominy, cornmeal, Italian pasta
	1½ oz. baked goods has about 1 oz. flour

Note: Use other foods as desired to meet calorie needs and to increase palatability.
Use water or other beverages: adult — 6 to 8 cups, child — 4 to 6 cups.
°Amount used depends upon size of granule; follow label instructions.
†See p. 406 for size of children's servings.
‡See p. 380 for definitions.
°°Dividing one pound of ground meat into five equal portions would give, when cooked, five servings of approximately two ounces. This is due to shrinkage during cooking.

Table continued on opposite page.

Table 1–2   *The Basic-Four* (Continued)

Principal nutrients in the food groups

The milk group is the best source of calcium and riboflavin.

It also contains protein, phosphorus, carbohydrate, thiamine and vitamin D (if it has been added); whole milk has fat and vitamin A; vitamin A is sometimes added to non-fat milk products.

Do not substitute calcium tablets because they do not contain protein or riboflavin.

Do not substitute cream because it is the fat content of milk.

Do not substitute condensed milk because it has a very high sugar content.

All vegetables and fruits contain sugar, starch, cellulose, and varying amounts of vitamins and minerals.

Citrus fruits and tomatoes are the principal sources of vitamin C in many diets. Other good sources are cantaloup, strawberries, broccoli, Brussels sprouts, and raw, green, sweet, or red peppers.

Fair sources of vitamin C include other melons and berries, raw cabbage, asparagus, cauliflower, and the green leaves of collards, kale, mustard, turnips, or spinach.

Dark green or deep yellow vegetables are good sources of vitamin A. The leafy green vegetables contain iron.

Potatoes have thiamine, iron, and vitamin C.

Other fruits and vegetables should not be substituted for the fruits and vegetables which are listed as high in vitamins A and C.

The meat group supplies protein, iron, thiamine, niacin, fat, phosphorus, and some riboflavin.

Liver is an excellent source of vitamin A and iron.

Salt water fish contains iodine.

Eggs have protein, iron, thiamine, phosphorus, riboflavin, and the yolk has vitamin A and fat.

The protein in legumes is a lower quality than that found in meat, fish, and eggs.

Nuts yield fat, protein, iron, thiamine, riboflavin, and niacin.

All cereals contain starch and some incomplete protein.°

Whole grain cereals contain cellulose.

If whole grain, restored, or enriched, the cereal will be a good source of iron, thiamine, riboflavin, and niacin.

°See Figure 32–1.

EXERCISES

1. This menu was planned for a 16-year-old girl. Evaluate it according to the basic-four food groups. (The vegetable-fruit section has been filled in to illustrate the recommended form to use.) Serving size of fruits, vegetables, and meat is ½ cup. Cream is not a substitute for milk; bacon is considered a fat exchange, not a meat exchange.

Breakfast
  Stewed prunes
  Oatmeal (with cream and sugar)
  Scrambled egg and bacon
  Cracked wheat toast (2 slices)
  Butter—jelly
  Cocoa (made with water)

Pattern for a 16-year-old girl
  Vegetable—fruit
    1 citrus or substitute
    1 green or yellow vegetable
    2 others, including potato

Complete the basic-four pattern.

Luncheon
  Salad: Peach and ¾ cup cottage cheese
  Soda crackers—butter
  Chocolate cake
  Coca-Cola

Milk

Meat

Cereals

Dinner
  Ground round steak
  Baked potato—sour cream with chives
  Spiced beets
  Hot rolls (enriched)—margarine
  Baked apple
  Glass of milk

For a 16-year-old girl this menu does not have:
  1 citrus fruit
  1 green or yellow vegetable

Complete the evaluation for the other three food groups.

2. Evaluate according to the basic-four what you ate yesterday (or today).

Breakfast   *Basic Pattern for Your Age*

Dinner

Luncheon or Supper

Snacks

This menu lacks:

Did your diet omit any groups of foods? If so, check in Table 1–2 and note the nutrients which would have been furnished by that food group.

3. Can a nurse identify any of the characteristics of malnutrition listed in the summary showing comparative pictures of good and poor nutrition in the introductory statement to Section I? Could any of these characteristics have other causes?

Food Misinformation

Appetite
Deleterious
Etiology
Flatulence
Hunger

Quackery
Misconception
Sterilize
Supplement

As early as 1929 Walter Campbell of the Food and Drug Administration warned the American people that there is no such thing as a health food. Since that time the FDA has been combatting such misrepresentation.

The use of the word "health" implies that these products have health-giving or curative properties, when in general, they merely possess some of the nutritive qualities to be expected in any wholesome food product. The label claims on these products are such that the consumer is led to believe that your ordinary diet is sorely deficient in such vital substances as vitamins and minerals, and that these so-called "health-foods" are absolutely necessary to conserve life and health.*

Month by month there is more scientific information concerning food and nutrition, but faddism appeals to people's emotions and grows where there is a lack of knowledge. Quackery includes the purveying of misinformation about health which encompasses false claims for drugs and cosmetics, food fads and unneeded food supplements, and fake medical devices. The promoter does not protect or restore your health but does seriously deplete your pocketbook.

In the United States, dollars wasted on food fads alone have been estimated to be almost a billion dollars each year; this is nearly 2¾ million dollars daily. The chronically ill and obese seek miraculous dietary regi-

---

*Young, James: *The Medical Messiahs*, 1967, p. 336.

mens and cure-alls. Unfortunately, the elderly and poorly educated are particularly prone to spend their dollars unwisely. They eat poorly not only because they have less money but because of misconceptions and real ignorance concerning nutrition and food values; therefore they are easily exploited by food fads, faddists, and quacks. The monetary drain from health quackery includes money spent for fake diagnostic and treatment machines, "youth restorers," and "energy restorers"; arthritis, cancer, epilepsy, and diabetes cures; mail order eyeglasses or dental plates and adhesives; "health foods" or pills which "cure" high blood pressure or ulcers; trusses for ruptures; unlicensed mental health "therapists"; and reducing pills. Arthritics alone spend $400 million* for worthless products and treatments that include filtered sea water, alfalfa tablets, radioactivity, uranium mine tunnel visits, and "immune milk." This milk is supposed to come from cows injected with streptococcus and staphylococcus vaccines and sells for two or three times the cost of fluid milk.

There is no sure method of recognizing health quackery, but the following rules may help you recognize quackery:

1. Is the product or service not available from other sources or is it available at this price for a limited time?
2. Is the secret formula, machine, or remedy claimed to cure disease, pep you up, or to be the cure for a vast variety of illnesses?
3. Are testimonials and case histories used to impress you with the miracles this product or service has performed for others?
4. Does the seller claim he is battling the medical profession for recognition and medical investigation or that doctors are persecuting him and are afraid of his competition?
5. Is the remedy, drug, device, or diet being promoted by public lectures, being sold from door to door by "health advisers," or being promoted by a faith healer's group, a crusading organization of laymen, or in a sensational magazine?
6. Is it claimed that the method of treatment is better than surgery, X-rays, and drugs prescribed by a physician?

Beeuwkes† describes some of the salesmen's techniques:

1. They make exaggerated claims and promises for prevention and cure of disease or diseases which encourage self-diagnosis and self-treatment.

2. They state or imply that the food in the average grocery store cannot meet nutritional needs because American agriculture is producing "devitalized" foods.

3. They take out of context from scientific reports sentences, phrases, and technical terms to "prove" their point and to appeal to the buyer's emotions. Often the sales pitch intimates that the scientist is "stubborn" and will not recognize the advantages of the product which is for sale.

*Winter 1974 *Newsletter.* The Arthritis Foundation, Northern California Chapter.
†Beeuwkes, Adelia M.: "Characteristics of the Self-Styled Scientist," *J. Am. Dietet. A.,* 32:627–630, July, 1956.

4. They have a sales method described as follows:

Perhaps a comparison of the direct-sales technique of the faddist with the individualized, studied care of the physician would be impressive to some of our vast public who still waver on the brink of the faddist's trap. For example, does the surgeon in your community hospital set aside August as the best month for appendectomies with a special price if three members of one family participate in the plan this August? The faddist usually offers an extra bottle of pills or an extra book for a reduced price. Does your physician run a testimonial advertisement showing pictures of ten patients whose gall bladder disease was treated with medicine X? The faddist is apt to do just that. Does your physician offer a money-back guarantee if your diabetes is not cured in thirty days? Some faddists offer a money-back guarantee for the cure of arthritis, cancer, diabetes, and so on. Does your physician send you a circular suggesting that if you are tired and did not sleep well last night, you are suffering from a lack of two vitamins and twenty-eight minerals? The faddist has no qualms whatever about diagnosing across the miles. In fact, just one convincing advertisement in fifty newspapers covers a good bit of territory, and perhaps the "take" will be great enough so that the faddist can be "curing" people thousands of miles away before the thirty-day guarantee runs out.

5. They are *selling* a product. If it is a food, they "enshrine" that particular food, whereas for health, the diet as a whole should be considered, not just one or two particular products.

Many have had food experiences which they may think are applicable to everyone, but

people will have to learn sooner or later that a person, who knows nothing of the intricacies of food chemistry or of the complicated mechanism of the body with its various parts interacting to influence one another, is not qualified to draw conclusions from his experiences with food; he is probably more apt to give the wrong interpretation than the right one, and incalculable harm is done by those who thus draw unwarranted conclusions from scanty evidence, then close their minds to all further reasoning and endeavor to make converts to their pet theories about diet (18:171).

Food misinformation may cause you to spend a great portion of your income for food, yet your family may be bordering on poor nutrition or may in fact be poorly nourished. As research goes on it is probable that some of our present views will be changed, but in the light of present knowledge the following statements can be considered food misinformation:

1. *Myth.* There is danger in eating wrong food combinations, for example, milk and fish or cherries and milk.
   Right. Combinations of *uncontaminated, unspoiled* food taken in *moderate amounts* should not harm the normal, healthy individual.
2. *Myth.* Cheese is hard to digest and/or is constipating.
   Right. Cheese is a concentrated nutritious food. Normally over 90 per cent of the carbohydrate, protein, and fat consumed is digested and absorbed.
3. *Myth.* Lemons, oranges, etc., cause "acid stomach" or make the body acidic.
   Right. The presence of hydrochloric acid in the gastric juice is normal and thus acidity in the stomach is a normal condition. Most fruits have an alkaline metabolic residue (see p. 82 and Table 8–1).

4. *Myth.* Grape juice, beef juice, tomato juice, or beets make rich red blood.
   Right. Many nutrients are needed to build tissue. A variety of foods is "good insurance" for securing a variety of nutrients.
5. *Myth.* Celery and fish are brain food.
   Right. One particular food is not used to build a specialized tissue.
6. *Myth.* Prunes, bran, etc., are "sure cures" for constipation.
   Right. In atonic constipation, foods containing cellulose are helpful; in spastic constipation, "roughage" is reduced.
7. *Myth.* Milk, potato, bread, and water are "fattening."
   Right. No food in itself is fattening. Calorie intake above metabolic needs results in weight gain. Water retention in edema increases pounds, but with medical treatment the excess water is removed from the tissue and the weight of the water is no longer registered on the scales.
8. *Myth.* Vegetable juices are more nutritious than vegetables.
   Right. The juice made from a vegetable would not contain anything more than the original vegetable contained.
9. *Myth.* Diabetes is caused by eating sugar.
   Right. Insufficient secretion or non-utilization of insulin is the etiology. Treatment includes carbohydrate restriction.
10. *Myth.* Garlic, eggs, grapes, rice, and/or food cooked in aluminum cause or cure cancer, high blood pressure, hardening of the arteries, etc.
    Right. Scientists are trying to find the causes of cancer, hypertension, and arteriosclerosis. To date, the evidence as to etiology of any of these is not conclusive.
11. *Myth.* Starve a fever.
    Right. Metabolism is increased in fever and if food intake is not sufficient, the body tissue will be used for fuel.
12. *Myth.* White bread contains many calories but dark bread has few.
    Right. A 23-gram slice of white bread contains 65 calories and a 23-gram slice of whole wheat bread contains 55 calories.
13. *Myth.* Toast has fewer calories than bread.
    Right. Heat browns the starch particles on the exterior of the slice but does not change the caloric value.
14. *Myth.* Large amounts of gelatin strengthen fingernails.
    Right. Disease, environment, endocrine state, and nutritional state are among the factors influencing fingernail formation. Gelatin is an incomplete protein, so it cannot build a cell.
15. *Myths.* There are many pregnancy and lactation taboos. Included are:
    (a) A particular food taken during pregnancy "marks" the child.
    (b) Eating salmon during pregnancy makes the baby wet the bed.
    (c) Pepper eaten during pregnancy causes the baby to be born with pepper in his eyes.
    (d) Lactation is increased by drinking beer.

(e) Cravings for a particular food indicate physical need.

(f) Red and/or white clay, cornstarch, flour, and baking soda must be eaten in quantity during pregnancy.

(g) Breast milk becomes "tainted" by consumption of some particular food such as cabbage, greens, fruit juice, or chocolate. (If the mother consumes these, the breast-fed infant is supposed to have gastrointestinal disturbances.)

(h) Milk, greens, rabbit and/or fish cannot be eaten for a specified length of time (usually 1 or 2 months) post partum.

Right. Craving for a particular food does not result from a physical need. A craving is often for a well-liked food and may be indulged unless it interferes with good food habits. Scientific literature does not document the theory of "tainted" milk. Meyer states, "The day is gone when every gastric, intestinal and skin disturbance of either mother or neonate can be easily ascribed to the specific diet of the mother or to the quality of her milk"(51:52).

16. *Myth.* A particular food will combat bacteria, purify the blood, and so forth.
Right. Eating a variety of foods helps insure an adequate diet. This may help resist infections, but immunity to pathogens is obtained by immunization. Several body mechanisms help maintain blood composition and the kidneys normally rid the blood of excess waste products.

17. *Myth.* Eating of food grown on depleted soil causes malnutrition. Chemical fertilizers "poison" the crops.
Right. Soil deficiencies stop plant growth; thus, the crop *yield* will be poor. With the exception of iodine, there is little variation in the nutrient value of the food produced. (Using iodized salt provides iodine.) Crops grown on chemically fertilized soil are not nutritionally inferior. Nutritive value is influenced more by variety than by soil fertility.

18. *Myth.* Cooking and processing of foods destroy nutritive value.
Right. Some methods of cooking may reduce nutrient value. Research has developed commercial food-processing methods designed to preserve nutrient value or to restore nutrients to food. Frozen and canned foods are processed at the peak of their nutritional value and some items are enriched or fortified.

19. *Myth.* Physical activity increases the need for meat, eggs, and other protein foods.
Right. Protein needs are based upon age and normal weight. Those growing new body tissue need more protein-rich foods in relation to weight.

20. *Myth.* "Wonder foods" such as yogurt and blackstrap molasses guarantee health.
Right. Yogurt, a fermented milk, has the same nutritive value as the milk from which it is made. It costs more than whole milk.

Figure 2–1 Do you get courage by eating a brave animal? (Courtesy of *The American Weekly.*)

Blackstrap molasses is one of the syrup extractions formed in the process of refining sugar. It does contain a variety of minerals and vitamins, but these are also found in other foods. Molasses is widely used as a food for livestock.

21. *Myth.* The chemicals added to food are detrimental to health.
Right. All food is composed of chemical compounds. (In fact, the body itself is composed of chemicals.) Food purity and food additives are carefully watched by the Food and Drug Administration. Manufacturers must run extensive animal-feeding tests and secure an FDA order permitting additives to be used. Some additives are natural components of food; for example, lecithin, an emulsifier, is found in soybeans and corn; the propionates, which retard bread spoilage, are naturally contained in Swiss cheese.

22. *Myth.* Meat tenderizers cause gastric ulcers and/or cancer.
Right. Most meat tenderizers are made from papain, an enzyme found in papaya, and do soften tough meat tissues. Cooking inactivates the enzyme.

23. *Myth.* To be well nourished one must take vitamin concentrates.
Right. The foods in an adequate diet provide the best source of vitamins. A diet not including the basic-four but supplemented with vitamin concentrates may be lacking in protein, minerals, or other nutrients. Concentrates cannot take the place of food. If a deficiency exists, the supplementation should be prescribed by the physician to insure that the vitamin needed is obtained in the correct amount. Emphasis on nutritive requirements and the specific function of each nutrient leads many people to think that nutrient concentrates and food supplements are essential to health. The variety of nutrients found in grocery store foods contribute more toward maintaining a healthy body than the single nutrient or limited combinations found in concentrates. In 1963 the United States Department of Agriculture published a survey that had been made of the diets of older people living in one city; over one third were using a vitamin-mineral formula supplement. Approximately half of those using the supplement

were consuming diets which already contained the recommended allowances, thus did not need a supplement; the remaining half were divided approximately as follows:

One fourth were using supplements containing none of the nutrients which were inadequate in their diets.

Half were using supplements that provided some but not all the nutrients that were inadequate.

One fourth were using supplements which did provide the nutrients needed to supplement the food intake.

In other words, only 12 of every 100 families were spending their supplement money wisely. This again emphasizes the necessity of purchasing diet supplements only when prescribed by a physician.

24. *Myth.* Food cannot be stored in the can after it is opened.

Right. It is safe to leave food in its original container. The can was sterilized during processing and thus may be more sanitary than another container. The acid foods may dissolve a little metal from the can, which may change flavor but is not dangerous to health.

25. *Myth.* Athletes should have different diets from the general population.

Right. The type of athletic activity determines the caloric need. Playing volleyball uses up about 2.5 calories per minute, cross-country running, about 10.6. Variations in protein intake do not seem to influence performance, provided growth and maintenance needs in the young athlete are met. The use of alcohol is avoided because of its deleterious effects on coordination. Caffeine-containing beverages may decrease awareness of fatigue, so that large amounts are not recommended. Sodium intake may be increased if unusually warm conditions prevail. Except for calories, the nutritional needs of the athlete and the non-athlete are comparable (72).

26. *Myth.* Many members of my family are overweight; therefore, I inherited my tendency to be fat.

Right. An overweight person eats food containing more calories than he uses. Heredity may be one of the factors related to weight control, but probably the family eating habits are a greater factor. If it is customary to have second servings, eat the spoonful of whipped cream "so it won't go to waste," or celebrate family occasions with large meals, several members of the family may be overweight. Actually both underweight and overweight persons usually have normal metabolic rates.

27. *Myth.* You should feed a cold but starve a fever.

Right. A fever increases the metabolic rate, and more calories are needed. Additional fruit juice or water may be recommended for a cold.

28. *Myth.* Lack of pep, fatigue, or a "worn-out feeling" is due to mineral or vitamin deficiencies in the diet.

Right. It is normal for a healthy, active person to occasionally experience fatigue and lack of pep. If the feeling persists, one should seek medical advice and find the *real cause.*

29. *Myth.* Drinking water with your meals causes weight gain.

    Right. Edema (abnormal water retention in body tissues) increases the number of pounds recorded on the scale (water weighs about one half pound per cup), but with medical treatment the excess water can be removed from the tissue and the weight of the water is no longer recorded on the scales.

30. *Myth.* Fasting should be practiced periodically by everyone.

    Right. Fasting is not the way to reduce the total amount of food taken. It disturbs body functions and can result in serious complications, especially if done for a prolonged time. Fasting or eating only one meal a day is not conducive to developing good food habits that are necessary if *weight control* is to be achieved.

31. *Myth.* Any food craving indicates the body needs the nutrients in that food.

    Right. Many people are overweight, so we know that appetite is not always a reliable guide to food needs. Appetites reflect those foods to which we are accustomed. "Craving" often is tied to the association a person has with that food.

32. *Myth.* A diet of protein and fatty foods but little or no carbohydrates; a diet containing grapefruit at every meal; or one of certain food combinations such as skimmed milk and bananas or only lamb chops and pineapple, would be a good way to lose weight.

    Right. To lose weight, calorie intake must be less than calories used and should be planned to provide the nutrients necessary to protect general health. No food burns more calories than it provides for the body. Fad diets usually deprive the body of necessary nutrients while attempting to bring down weight. The so-called Mayo Diet does not come from the Mayo Clinic in Rochester, Minnesota.

    The bizarre weight reduction diets are a radical departure from the normal diet. A successful weight control diet has calorie reduction but is enjoyable to eat. It is based on foods normally consumed and is related to your own way of living. This develops the eating patterns which you will follow the rest of your life to help you maintain your desired weight.

    The 1200 calorie diet shown in Appendix 3 contains the foods found in the basic-four food pattern (changing the 2 glasses of whole milk to non-fat milk would make the number of calories approximately 1000). Remember that the diet which contains a variety of common foods in moderate amounts helps you change your food habits so that you will not regain the lost weight by returning to your previous habits of food consumption.

33. *Myth.* The overweight person is a well-nourished person.

    Right. The overweight person has been eating too many calories: He is overnourished in calories. Many times the high-calorie foods contain few other nutrients; therefore many overweight people are malnourished. These people should learn to choose calories by the company they keep.

34. *Myth.* Organically grown food and natural vitamins are more nutritious than the food found in supermarkets.

    Right. There is no legal definition of organic or natural food; thus the terms can mean different things to different people. "Organically grown" can mean the use of manure and plant wastes instead of commercially produced fertilizers and/or avoidance of weed killers and pesticides. Without a legal definition any fresh produce can be labeled "organically grown." The price will be higher, but the produce is not nutritionally superior. Microorganisms in the soil must break the "organic matter" into its chemical components before the roots of the plant can utilize them, e.g., the plant must have inorganic nitrogen and other elements to synthesize its protein content. The molecular structure of a laboratory-produced vitamin has exactly the same arrangement of atoms as the vitamin which is produced by a microorganism, a plant, or an animal.

The faddist and quack exploit fear and pain. They are sure that if they tell the big lie often enough people will begin to believe it. They employ enough scientific jargon to make quackery seem feasible. Since faddism is expensive the middle class is the usual target. Larrick of the FDA reported a swindle involving selling ocean water at prices up to $15 per gallon. Sea water does contain trace elements, but with the possible exception of iodine these same elements are present in common foods and supplied by the ordinary diet (39:18).

As a result of current research many of our present theories about food may be changed. For example, a joint committee of the American Medical Association and the American Dietetic Association reports:

"Gas-Producing Foods." Probably one of the most established of all popular convictions is that certain foods are "gas producers." Investigations on this matter have, nevertheless, been singularly unsuccessful in substantiating these beliefs. In one study, rectal gas was less when the subject was placed on a high vegetable diet. In another, cabbage, which appears to enjoy an even greater reputation as a gas former than baked beans, produced no more rectal flatus by actual measurement than did many other foods; only the combination of a high-fat intake and vegetables seemed to enhance gas output to some extent. In the third study, a diet of soybeans and fat increased the volume of rectal flatus from 0.6 to 2.9 liters per day in one subject, but the results were inconsistent, and the authors commented: "Although not markedly reflected in the daily egestion of gas, the soybean diet caused subjectively at least a great deal more flatulence."

As this comment suggests, measurements of rectal gas expelled does not necessarily correspond to intestinal gas formation, since unknown amounts of gas may be absorbed. In addition, accurate collection of rectal gas is technically difficult. Finally, if the quality and quantity of rectal gas appear changed the responsible mechanism may not merely be fermentative, but the food may have influenced the amount of air swallowed, or of gases diffusing between blood and bowel, two factors generally believed of major importance in accounting for intestinal gas. Because of our gross lack of knowledge, and because so many factors may influence intestinal gas, *classification of foods according to their gas-forming properties has very little basis* (italics mine) (65:429).

The following sources can give reliable information concerning quackery:

1. The American Dietetic Association
   430 North Michigan Avenue
   Chicago, Illinois 60611
2. U.S. Department of Agriculture
   Washington, D.C. 20250
3. The Council on Foods and Nutrition of the American Medical Association
   535 North Dearborn Street
   Chicago, Illinois 60610
4. The Extension Service and Home Economics Department of the state colleges and universities.
5. The Food and Drug Administration
   Department of Health, Education, and Welfare
   Washington, D.C. 20204
6. The Federal Trade Commission
   Bureau of Deceptive Practices
   Washington, D.C. 20580
   (concerning false or misleading information pertaining to foods, drugs, and cosmetics sold in interstate commerce)
7. The Food and Nutrition Board of the National Research Council
   2101 Constitution Avenue
   Washington, D.C. 20037
8. The individual state dietetic associations.
9. The Nutrition Foundation
   99 Park Avenue
   New York, New York 10017
10. National Better Business Bureau
    230 Park Avenue
    New York, New York 10017
11. National Health Council
    1740 Broadway
    New York, New York 10019
12. American Cancer Society, Inc.
    219 East 42nd Street
    New York, New York 10017
13. The Arthritis Foundation
    1212 Avenue of the Americas
    New York, New York 10036

SUGGESTED READING

American Dietetic Association: *Food Facts Talk Back.*
American Medical Association:
   Facts on Quacks—What You Should Know About Health Quackery, 1967.
Arthritis Foundation: *Arthritis Quackery—A $300,000,000 Racket.*
Bogert, L. Jean, et al.: *Nutrition and Physical Fitness,* 1973.
Carson, Gerald: *One for a Man, Two for a Horse—A Pictorial History Grave and Comic of Patent Medicines,* 1961.
Consumer Reports: *The Medicine Show,* 1975.
Coon, J. M.: "Natural Toxicants in Foods," *Journal of American Dietetic Association,* 67:213, 1975.
Darden, Ellington: "Sense and Nonsense About Health Foods," *Journal of Home Economics,* December, 1972.
Deutsch, Ronald M.: *The Nuts Among the Berries.*
   The Family Guide to Better Food and Better Health, 1971.
DHEW Publications
   No. 74–6011: *Antibiotics and the Foods You Eat,* 1974.

No. 74–2053: *Myths of Vitamins*, 1974.
No. 74–1017: *Quackery*, 1974.
No. 74–2019: *The Food Fad Boom*, 1974.
Edwards, Cecile Hoover, et al.: "Odd Dietary Practices of Women," *J. Am. Dietet. A., 30*:976–981, 1954.
Kaplan, Doris: "Food and Faddists: A Guide to Popular Books on Cooking and Diets,"*Choice*, September, 1974.
Margolis, Sidney:
   The Great American Food Hoax, 1971.
   Public Affairs Pamphlet: *Health Foods*, 1973.
   Health Foods, Facts and Fakes, 1973.
Mayer, Jean: "Pills, Potions, and Promises—The Cruel Hoax of Food Fads," *Family Health*, June, 1974.
Rice, William: "A Surgeon's Magic Touch That's Too Good to be True," *Today's Health*, June, 1974.
Schaller, W. E., and Carroll, C. R.: *Health Quackery and the Consumer.* Philadelphia, W. B. Saunders Company, 1976.
Schanche, Don A.: "Diet Books that Poison Your Mind...And Harm Your Body," *Today's Health*, April, 1974.
Seaver, Jacqueline: *Fads, Myths, Quacks—And Your Health.* Public Affairs Pamphlet No. 415, 1968.
Smith, Ralph Lee:
   "The Bunk About Health Foods," *Today's Health*, October, 1965.
   "Health Books—Reader Beware," *Today's Health*, April, 1969.
   "Mail Order Doctoring—Still a Menace," *Today's Health*, June, 1967.
   "Strange Tales of Medical Imposters," *Today's Health*, October, 1968.
Stare, Fredrick J.:
   "Food Fads and Frauds," *Today's Health*, March, 1969.
   "Good Nutrition from Food Not Pills," *Am. J. of Nursing*, February, 1965.
Stare, Frederick J., and McWilliams, Margaret: *Living Nutrition*, 1973.
Today's Health: "Facts on Quacks," February, 1968, p. 57.
Ward, Donovan F.: "The Four Horsemen of Quackery: Fear, Gullibility, Deceit, and Deadliness," *Today's Health*, January, 1965.
Whelan, Elizabeth M., and Stare, Fredrick J.: *Panic in the Pantry: Food Facts, Fads, and Fallacies*, 1975.

EXERCISES

1. From additional reading, list 10 myths about food values and give the scientific facts disproving each myth.
2. Check food composition tables and decide how you would classify an advertisement showing a can of pork and beans and the statement that beans contain 23 per cent protein. (See Table A–1, p. 327.)
3. Bring to class advertisements which depict appeals to emotions, testimonials, longing for equality, or misinformation.
4. How would you classify a "commercial" which suggests that you need vitamin concentrates because processed food (canned or frozen) is poor in nutrient value? Refer to Figure 9–12.
5. People often state that they don't eat a "starchy food" because the food is too high in calories. Compare the calorie content of the following (Use Table A–1, p. 327.):
   2 slices crisp bacon
   3 ounces regular hamburger
   3 ounces roast pork
   1 cup cooked lima beans
   1 cup cooked macaroni
   1 cup spaghetti in tomato sauce with cheese
6. Be able to list three sources from which you could obtain reliable nutrition information.

CHAPTER **3**

Carbohydrates

TERMS TO UNDERSTAND

Absorb	Detoxification	Impacting
Acidosis	Enzyme	Oxidation
Alimentary canal	Fecal	Plaque
Cellulose	Fermentation	Soluble
Dental caries	Gram	Synthesis
Deplete	Hepatic	

A carbohydrate is a chemical compound of carbon, hydrogen, and oxygen. Plants use water (H_2O) from the soil, carbon dioxide (CO_2) from the air, and with the aid of chlorophyll (the coloring matter of leaves) make carbohydrates. Starches and sugars are carbohydrates. They are the most economical and the most readily digested source of energy for the body. In America, about one half of our calories comes from carbohydrates. The trend in the well-developed countries is to use less starch-containing food and more refined sugar.

Kinds of Carbohydrates

Carbohydrates are classified as follows:

	Examples	*Obtained from*
1. *Monosaccharides* (simple sugars which contain a single unit)	1. Glucose (dextrose)	Corn syrup, fruits, vegetables, honey
	2. Fructose (levulose)	Honey, fruit, vegetables
	3. Galactose	The digestion of lactose
2. *Disaccharides* (double sugars which contain two units)	1. Sucrose = 1 glucose + 1 fructose	Cane, beet, maple sugars and syrups; fruits, vegetables
	2. Lactose = 1 galactose + 1 glucose	Milk
	3. Maltose = 2 glucose	Starch in sprouting grains and digestion of starch

3. *Polysaccharides*
(complex compounds which contain many units)

Digestible:
1. Starch = many units of glucose — Grain products, legumes, root vegetables
2. Dextrin — Result of first chemical change in digestion of starch
3. Glycogen — Animal body converts glucose into glycogen which can readily be converted back into glucose

Indigestible:
1. Cellulose — Structural parts of fruits, vegetables, whole grain cereals, seeds, and nuts

2. Hemicellulose
   a. Pectin — Fruits
   b. Agar-agar — A gelatinous product made from seaweed

Glucose (dextrose, also called grape sugar) is the form of carbohydrate which is in the blood. All other sugars are converted to glucose before they are used by the body tissues. Nerve tissue can use only glucose as its source of energy; thus, a low blood sugar level can result in mental confusion. Given by mouth or intravenously, glucose is ready for immediate body utilization. Glucose tastes about three fifths as sweet as sucrose; therefore, almost two tablespoons of it can be added to a glass of fruit juice and the taste will be no sweeter than if one tablespoon of granulated sugar had been added. Glucose crystals do not go into solution as easily as

Figure 3–1 "He's either the world's worst flyer or his blood sugar is low."

sucrose so they must be very thoroughly stirred or they will settle to the bottom of the glass. Glucose is found in many plants. Corn syrup contains glucose which has been made from corn starch by treating the corn starch with acid and heat.

Fructose (levulose or fruit sugar) is a very sweet sugar (almost twice as sweet as sucrose). It is found in honey and plants, particularly fruits. Some people think that honey can be used as a substitute for sugar in a diabetic or low calorie diet, but this should not be done because honey is approximately 80 per cent carbohydrate.

Cane, maple, and beet sugars are sucrose. Granulated sugar is 99.5 per cent carbohydrate, tastes sweet, crystallizes, and is very soluble in water. If candy, desserts, or other sweets are eaten before a meal, the appetite may be "spoiled," other foods may not be eaten, and the body does not get all of the nutrients needed. Large amounts of concentrated sucrose can cause fermentation in or irritate the lining of the alimentary canal. Digestion converts sucrose into glucose and fructose.

Maltose (malt sugar) is found in sprouting grains and is an intermediate product of starch digestion. It is soluble, does not readily ferment in the digestive tract, and the normal body can use it very easily. A combination of maltose and dextrin is often used in infant formulas. Digestion converts maltose into glucose.

Lactose is the carbohydrate found in milk. It is less soluble, less sweet, and more slowly digested than the other sugars, thereby remaining in the intestines longer and encouraging the growth of bacteria which are useful to the body. Its presence in the small intestine helps with the absorption of calcium, but too much in the intestine can cause diarrhea, so maltose or glucose are the sugars which are frequently added to infant and invalid formulas. Digestion converts lactose into glucose and galactose.

Mannose, sorbitol, and mannitol are carbohydrates. Labels show that one or more of them are added to many foods. The so called "sugarless" chewing gums are sucrose-free but not carbohydrate-free. Each stick has about five calories from one or more of these carbohydrates; regular chewing gum has about eight calories from sucrose and/or corn syrup.

Plants store their carbohydrates in the form of starch which usually is inside a touch cellulose wall. When we chew food, the cellulose wall is crushed and digestive juices can get to the starch. Starch is insoluble in water. In hot water the cell walls of the starch grains are broken open, water is absorbed, and the mixture thickens. The end product of starch digestion is glucose.

Cellulose is a carbohydrate, but it is the insoluble, indigestible framework of plants that gives the plants shape just as bones give an animal shape. Both cellulose and hemicellulose absorb water to provide the "bulk" or "roughage" in our diet. The bulk stimulates peristalsis. Cellulose is found in fruits, vegetables, nuts, and whole grain products.

Chapter 6 has additional information on cellulose.

How the Body Uses Carbohydrates

The body is like the engine of a car which burns gasoline and produces energy to make the car move. When carbohydrate is oxidized (burned) by the body tissues, energy is produced for movement or work and heat is released to maintain body temperature. Carbohydrate must be present for the normal oxidation of fats; otherwise the fats burn incompletely and acidosis results. Adequate carbohydrate will decrease the oxidation of protein for energy purposes.

When starchy foods are cooked or thoroughly chewed, the starch granule walls are broken and the digestive enzymes can get to the starch. An enzyme is a substance made by a living cell which acts upon another substance to bring about a chemical change, but the enzyme itself is not changed. This chemical action can be compared with shooting a gun. The trigger causes the shell to be exploded so that a bullet leaves the gun. The shell (substance) has been changed but the trigger (enzyme) hasn't. Digestion of cooked starch starts in the mouth and is finished in the small intestine. Raw starch and other sugars are changed by enzymes in the small intestine.

The only carbohydrates which can pass through the intestinal wall are glucose, fructose, and galactose. This movement through the intestinal walls into the blood is called absorption. The blood stream takes the carbohydrates to the liver after which glucose goes on to all parts of the body and is used by the tissues. A supply of carbohydrate which would give the moderately active person body fuel for about 12 to 14 hours and the inactive person fuel for about 24 hours is stored in the liver in the form of glycogen. This is changed into glucose and is released into the blood stream if needed. The liver detoxifies more efficiently when the amount of glycogen in storage is not too low. Skipping a meal depletes the liver glycogen.

Regardless of their flavor or how sweet they taste, starches and sugars produce four kilocalories per gram.* There are approximately 30 (28.34) grams in 1 ounce. A teaspoon holds about 5 grams.

Refined sugar, alcohol, soft drinks, some cooking fats, and some refined cereals contain only calories. These foods, which contribute little or nothing except calories, may be called "empty" or "lone-wolf" calorie

---

*Food energy is measured by a unit called the kilocalorie—the amount of heat necessary to raise 1 kg. of water one degree Centigrade. The calorie listing in some food tables represents the direct calorimetric content of the food as obtained by a "bomb" calorimeter using pure oxygen. These determinations vary slightly from the commonly accepted practice of using 4 kilocalories per gram of carbohydrate, 9 kilocalories per gram of fat, and 4 of protein. Alcohol (ethanol) has 7 kilocalories per gram. This does not affect the accuracy of common calculations of calories very much, because the individual's ability to oxidize the nutrients varies much more than "rounding" the figures. The accepted international unit of energy is the joule. Kilocalories $\times$ 4.2 = kilojoules.

foods. Energy foods which contribute other necessary nutrients could be called "armored" calorie foods.

Today in the United States the per capita consumption of sugar is approximately 2 pounds (3492 calories) per week (18:402). These are "empty" calories, yet potatoes and milk are often omitted from the diet because they are thought to be "fattening." Potatoes provide iron and vitamin C; milk is a good source of protein, calcium, and riboflavin. Both, therefore, are "armored" calorie foods.

If a person eats more carbohydrate than the body needs for oxidation or to maintain his emergency supply in the liver, the extra is stored as fatty tissue and he gains weight. Unless he is very active physically, he usually cannot indulge in "empty" calories without gaining weight. Nations which have highly mechanized societies have few adult citizens who can be classified as physically active.

The functions of carbohydrate in the body are as follows:

1. Provides an economical and quick source of calories.

2. Spares protein so protein can be used for its more important function, to build and repair tissues.

3. Lactose encourages the growth of favorable intestinal bacteria, has laxative properties, and enhances the absorption of calcium.

4. Cellulose provides fecal bulk which facilitates good elimination.

5. Aids in efficient and complete oxidation of fats; otherwise ketones are formed.

6. Glucose is the source of energy for the central nervous system.

7. Hepatic glycogen storage enhances normal liver detoxification.

CONVERSION OF STARCH TO GLUCOSE

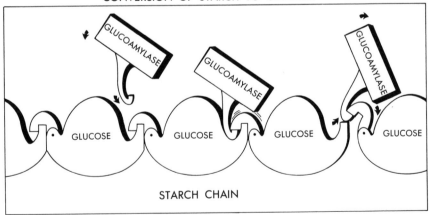

Figure 3-2 Starch digestion. Figuratively speaking, a digestive enzyme "unlocks" one of the glucose links making up the starch chain. In true catalytic fashion the enzyme can trigger the unlocking of the glucose links on down the chain. (Adapted from Association of Home Appliance Manufacturers: *Frontiers and Fundamentals — A Short Course In Appliance Homemaking*, 1968.)

In 1968 the National Research Council stated:

adaptation to diets very low in carbohydrate is possible. But in individuals accustomed to normal diets, at least 100 grams of carbohydrate per day appear to be needed to avoid ketosis, excessive protein breakdown, and other undesirable metabolic responses.(53:10)

Excess carbohydrate in the diet, particularly the sugar, sucrose, may

1. Increase the incidence of dental caries. Microorganisms living in the dental plaque convert the sugar into acids which attack the tooth enamel.

2. Cause obesity because more calories are ingested than expended.

3. Irritate the gastrointestinal mucosa. Large quantities of jelly are not used on toast for the gastric ulcer patient.

4. Depress the appetite. If empty calories instead of basic-four foods are consumed, malnutrition could result.

5. Increase the blood triglyceride level.

Yudkin believes that "sugar is a more likely culprit in producing atherosclerosis than is animal fat . . . that dietary sucrose is involved in the causation of atherosclerosis in general and coronary heart disease in particular." He fed animals, experimentally, starch, sucrose, or mixtures of the two. The animals eating sucrose showed "impaired growth, reduced efficiency of food utilization, decreased longevity, high levels of cholesterol and triglyceride in the blood, changes in the amount of fat in the liver and adipose tissue, and increased levels of several enzymes in the tissue. . . . Sucrose can produce an increase in the stickiness of the blood platelets—an early stage of blood clotting—and an increase in the level of circulating insulin." He suggests that "a high level of insulin may be an early stage, if not the earliest stage, in the development of coronary disease." (98)

An American Dental Association pamphlet* states:

Eating excessive amounts of fermentable carbohydrates, especially sugar, is a direct invitation to tooth decay. These carbohydrates are especially harmful if they are eaten in sticky forms that adhere to the tooth surfaces.

Bacteria in your mouth quickly turn sugar into acids that attack tooth enamel. Each time you eat a sugar-rich confection, your teeth are attacked by acids. Therefore, the less frequently you eat sweet foods the less tooth decay you will have. Several studies have indicated that the amount of tooth decay is related to the frequency of between-meal eating, especially of sticky, sugary foods. . . .

Ordinarily, your mouth is cleansed to some extent by the chewing of fibrous foods. Foods that require thorough chewing, during which they are forced over the teeth and soft tissues, cleaning them, are called *detergent* foods. Examples are firm fresh fruits and raw vegetables. Everyone should make a special effort to ensure that his daily diet contains ample amounts of these foods.

Foods that require little chewing and that tend to cling to the teeth and pack into the fissures and grooves are called *impacting* foods. Examples are cookies, crackers and many candies.

Diet and Dental Health, copyrighted 1963 by the American Dental Association, Chicago.

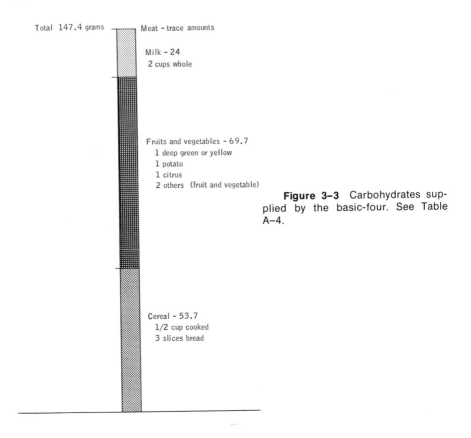

Total 147.4 grams ── Meat - trace amounts

Milk - 24
2 cups whole

Fruits and vegetables - 69.7
1 deep green or yellow
1 potato
1 citrus
2 others (fruit and vegetable)

Figure 3–3 Carbohydrates supplied by the basic-four. See Table
A–4.

Cereal - 53.7
1/2 cup cooked
3 slices bread

Unfortunately, modern man tends to eat too many impacting and too few detergent foods. For this reason it is important to use a tooth brush regularly and carefully, immediately after eating, to remove sticky food residues from the teeth. If you cannot brush your teeth immediately after eating, you should rinse your mouth thoroughly with plain water.

Recipes for confections and desserts nearly always list sugar. A piece of pie may contain from 10 to 14 teaspoons of sugar; a piece of candy from 1 to 7 teaspoons; ½ cup of ice cream, 5 or 6 teaspoons; 6 ounces of carbonated beverage, 3 or 4 teaspoons; ¼ cup of raisins, 4 teaspoons; 1 medium prune, 1 teaspoon; and a stick of gum, ½ teaspoon.*

100 grams sugar = 25 teaspoons = ½ cup = 3½ ounces = 400 calories.

Nizel and Shulman state:

Caries might be better controlled if: (a) we can reduce the intake of sucrose (foods rich in starch, such as bread or potato, are not in themselves a very potent cariogenic factor); (b) we can increase the detergency of the diet and reduce the between-meal frequency of eating re-

---

*Diet and Dental Health, copyrighted 1963 by the American Dental Association, Chicago.

tentive sweets; (c) we can increase the resistance of the tooth by ingesting optimal amounts of fluoride and foods rich in phosphates and proteins, particularly in the tooth development and maturation. (56:472)

Food Sources of Carbohydrate

The following foods contain carbohydrates: Sugar, starch, bread, syrup, molasses, candy, honey, cakes, puddings, pastries, jams, jellies, cereals, flour, Italian pastas, rice, vegetables, fruits, and milk.

SUGGESTED READING

Cole, William: "Hypoglycemia: Shortage of Body Fuel," *Today's Health,* November, 1968.
Lamont-Havers, Ronald W., M.D.: "Surprising Findings About Diabetes," *Today's Health,* April, 1968.
Nizel, Abraham E.: *Nutrition in Preventive Dentistry: Science and Practice.* Philadelphia, W. B. Saunders Co., 1972.
Nizel, Abraham E., and Shulman, Judith S.: "Interaction of Dietetics and Nutrition In Dentistry," *J. Am. Dietet. Assoc.,* November, 1969.

EXERCISES

1. List the foods containing carbohydrate which you ate today. Were the carbohydrates in the form of sugar, starch, or cellulose?
2. List three functions of carbohydrate in the body.
3. If ½ cup cooked rice contains 22 grams of starch, how many calories will the starch provide?
4. List four disadvantages which could result from using large quantities of foods which contain "lone-wolf" calories.
5. What is an "armored" calorie food? Name six that you have eaten in the last week.
6. Why might your dentist object to your mixing honey or jelly with peanut butter for a sandwich?
7. Why might your dentist object to your eating raisins as a mid-afternoon snack?

CHAPTER 4

Fats

TERMS TO UNDERSTAND

Arteriosclerosis   Emulsify   Obesity
Atherosclerosis   Hypercholesteremia   Precursor
Cholesterol   Insulation   Rancid
Decompose   Lipid   Satiety
Disperse   Membrane   Secrete
                    Mucous

Fat is a combination of fatty acids and glycerol containing the elements carbon, hydrogen, and oxygen, but the elements are not in the same proportion as they are found in carbohydrates. In fat, there are more carbon and hydrogen and less oxygen. The taste and texture of fat (liquid, semi-solid, or solid) depend upon the predominating fatty acid present. Each gram of fat burned in the body yields nine calories, which makes fat the body's most concentrated source of energy. In America approximately 40 per cent of our calories come from fats. Many countries with a lower fat intake have a lower incidence of coronary heart disease, which causes some authorities to recommend that fats should provide about 25 per cent of the diet calories. Other authorities state that the lower blood lipid levels could be due to more physical activity, less smoking, less obesity, and so forth. Approximately two thirds of our diet fat is of animal origin and one third is of plant origin.

In the United States the average white, 50-year-old male is about 25 per cent fat—approximately 40 pounds if he weighs 155 pounds; the average 55-year-old female is about 38 per cent fat—50 pounds if she weighs 132 pounds. With increasing age both male and female show an increase in proportion of body fat.

Kinds of Fats

Fat molecules contain glycerol and varying amounts of saturated, monounsaturated, and polyunsaturated fatty acids. Fats are classified according to the type of fatty acids which predominates; for example, if more than half of the fatty acids are polyunsaturated, then that fat is called a polyunsaturated fat. See Table A–13 for the fatty acid composition of some of the common food fats. There are about 20 fatty acids commonly found in food and body fat.

Fats which come from plants and animals may be hard, soft, or oily. Plant oils such as olive, corn, cottonseed, and peanut can have hydrogen added to them and they then become a solid fat. This process is known as hydrogenation and it is the way margarine and many of our common shortenings are prepared. Fortified margarine is comparable to butter in nutritive value and digestibility.

Fats become rancid when exposed to light, heat, and the oxygen in air. Rancid fat has an unpleasant odor and taste and any amount of fat-soluble vitamin it might have contained has been reduced. Hydrogenated fats do not become rancid as rapidly as other fats, such as lard and butter.

The diet contains visible and invisible fats. Butterfat, oil, and fat around the edge of meat are visible, but the fat in chocolate, egg yolk, avocado, fish, whole milk, cheese, and baked products is invisible. Visible fats probably furnish about one third of our fat calories.

As the following terms are defined, refer to Figure 4–1, which is a chemical picture of a fat called triglyceride:

1. A *fatty acid* contains oxygen and a chain of carbon atoms with attached hydrogen atoms.

2. A *saturated fatty acid* has all carbon atoms loaded with hydrogen. There are no double bonds. Animal fats, coconut oil, and the fat in chocolate contain a higher percentage of saturated fatty acids and are called saturated fats. Most of them are solid at room temperature.

3. The *unsaturated fatty acid* has one or more places (double bonds) where hydrogen can be added. Liquid vegetable oils and the fat of fish are relatively higher in unsaturated fatty acids. The *monounsaturated fatty acid* has one double bond, the *polyunsaturated* has two or more double bonds where hydrogen can be added.

4. *Linoleic acid.* The body cannot synthesize the polyunsaturated linoleic acid; it is called an essential fatty acid and must be obtained from food. Linoleic acid is widely distributed in foods; dairy fat, as well as corn or safflower oil, contains it. Briggs suggests 2 to 4 grams of linoleic acid for daily human intake. The amount of linoleic acid is decreased when a fat is hydrogenated.

5. *Hydrogenated fat.* Plant oils such as olive, cottonseed, corn, and soybean can have hydrogen added; they then become solid fat, and they have fewer double bonds. As shown below, the hydrogenated margarines

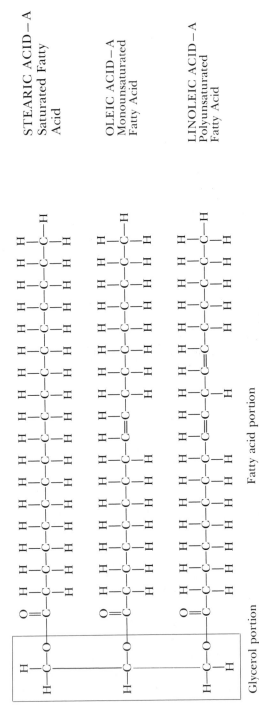

Glycerol portion   Fatty acid portion

STEARIC ACID – A Saturated Fatty Acid

OLEIC ACID – A Monounsaturated Fatty Acid

LINOLEIC ACID – A Polyunsaturated Fatty Acid

Figure 4–1 Diagram of the chemical structure of a fat called a triglyceride. It shows the three kinds of fatty acids attached to glycerol.

and shortenings vary according to the ingredients used and the method of processing.

	Polyunsaturated	*Monounsaturated*	*Saturated*
100 grams special shortening*	22–48	27–55	20–33
100 grams regular shortening	6–15	45–75	22–50

Cholesterol

A condition characterized by deposits on the inside wall of the blood vessel which interfere with the flow of blood is called atherosclerosis (one kind of arteriosclerosis). The deposits contain a waxy substance known as cholesterol. Cholesterol is a normal component of the blood, is found in

---

*The "special" or soft margarines are made by mixing additional vegetable oils with the artificially hardened fat. They are higher in polyunsaturated fatty acids.

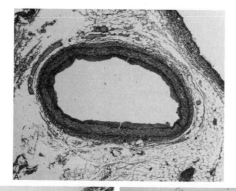

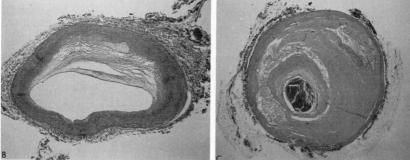

Figure 4–2 Gradual development of atherosclerosis in a coronary artery leading to a heart attack. *A*, Normal artery. *B*, Deposits formed in inner lining. *C*, The narrowed channel is blocked by a blood clot that deprives the heart muscle of blood, resulting in a heart attack. (From The American Heart Association.)

all body cells, especially brain and nerve tissue, and is a precursor of vitamin D and the adrenal and sex (gonadal) hormones. (A precursor is a substance which the body can make into another substance.)

The average diet provides about 300 to 600 milliliters of cholesterol daily, but the greater part of the body cholesterol comes from body synthesis of 1000 milligrams or more per day. Under normal circumstances the body's production of cholesterol decreases as you increase the intake of cholesterol from food, but if the food cholesterol intake is excessive the balance is not maintained. Research indicates that the level of dietary cholesterol may have an effect on serum-cholesterol levels. In 1966 Stare noted "an increase of 100 mg. in dietary cholesterol causes a rise of 5 mg. cholesterol/100 ml. serum" (35). Cholesterol is found in animal fats; the chief food sources are egg yolk, liver, brain, kidney, meat, and shellfish. The cholesterol concentration in blood plasma is highly variable and there is not universal agreement on the normal range. Many doctors hope to keep the level below 200 milligrams per 100 milliliters. In healthy individuals the body controls plasma cholesterol levels by adjustment of synthesis, degradation, and excretion of cholesterol. Cholesterol is excreted from the body via bile and sterols in the feces.

There probably is no one single cause of atherosclerosis. The etiology is probably a combination of factors which include the following:

1. Obesity. Excess calories from carbohydrate or protein as well as from fat increase the content of blood lipids and cause overweight.

2. Physical activity. Exercise may reduce cholesterol levels faster than a change of diet.

3. Sex. To date, the incidence of heart disease has been lower in women, at least until menopause.

4. Inherited predisposition. Ancestry determines the type of blood vessel in the family.

5. Stress. Emotional stress is associated with those people who are aggressive, deadline-oriented, or hard-driving. Classification of individuals according to individual type cannot be precise; neither, therefore, can any relationship between behavioral pattern and the risk of atherosclerosis be exactly defined. Excess epinephrine (adrenalin) and cortisone can increase cholesterol-bearing lipoproteins in the blood. Emotional and physical stresses can increase these adrenal gland secretions, which suggests that tension may be related to hypercholesteremia.

6. Diet.

   a. Type and quantity of dietary fat. At present there are conflicting reports about saturated fats; some think that they are the major factor in coronary disease, others disagree. Some individuals with low serum-cholesterol values do have cardiovascular disturbances, whereas some individuals with hypercholesteremia do not develop them.

   b. Type and quantity of dietary carbohydrate. The blood sugar

Figure 4-3 Nine risk factors of coronary heart disease. (From Blakeslee, A.: The condensed edition of *Your Heart Has Nine Lives*, 1966.)

level and triglyceride level are now suspected to be involved. Diets which have a higher proportion of carbohydrate in the form of starch may help promote normal fat metabolism. There have been recommendations that we obtain more of our carbohydrates from starch than from sucrose.

7. Age. The incidence of atherosclerosis is greater in older people.

8. Hypertension. Elevated pressure may indicate heart conditions in later life. The relation between high sodium intake for many years and hypertension is being questioned.

9. Excessive smoking.

10. Diabetes.

Reports of the American Heart Association emphasize that there is no final proof that heart attacks or strokes can be prevented by dietary changes. But publications of the Association state that atherosclerosis underlies most heart attacks and some kinds of strokes, and that foods high in saturated fats and cholesterol tend to cause hypercholesteremia. The Association recommends that the general public reduces the risk of heart attacks and strokes by observing the following measures:

1. Diet changes

  a. Reduce the saturated fat and cholesterol* content of the diet by substituting polyunsaturated fats. *Note the word is substitute, not add* (my emphasis). You can't eliminate saturated fats entirely because all fats are mixtures of the three types of fatty acids. The monounsaturated fats neither raise nor lower blood cholesterol.

  b. Use fish, veal, and poultry frequently.

  c. Limit beef, lamb, pork, and ham to five moderate size por-

---

*See Table A-2 for cholesterol content of foods.

tions per week, and when serving them, use the lean parts and trim off the visible fat.

    d. Use more liquid vegetable oils and the margarines higher in polyunsaturated fats for cooking. Avoid deep-fat frying.

    e. Drink and cook with non-fat milk and use skim milk cheeses.

    f. Eat no more than 3 egg yolks per week.

    g. Limit shellfish, organ meats, sausage, salami, and other luncheon meats.

    h. Reduce the amount of chocolate, palm oil, and coconut oil used. Palm oil is used in some commercially prepared baked products. Many of the highly advertised non-dairy cream substitutes are made from coconut fat, which is higher in saturated fats than the dairy products. Homemakers could make their own cream substitutes by blending corn oil, powdered non-fat milk, and water.

    2. Do not become overweight. Middle-age men who are 30 per cent overweight have twice the risk of heart attack. Food habits are formed in childhood; overweight children often grow into overweight adults.

    3. Have regular medical check-ups and follow the doctor's instructions. Today everyone is exposed to diet "fads, ads, and fables" which are "popular one year and forgotten the next."

    4. Control hypertension by appropriate medical treatment.

    5. Don't smoke. For heavy cigarette smoking males the heart attack rate is 50 to 200 per cent higher than for non-smokers. Those who quit smoking return to a rate comparable to that of those who never smoked.

    6. Get regular moderate exercise advised by the doctor for your age and physical condition.

The diet recommendations above should be followed only under the guidance of a physician. It should be noted that recommended intake of foods which are good sources of iron (egg yolk, liver, red meats, and such) is limited. Many Americans, especially children and women of childbearing age, are anemic because they are not consuming adequate iron.

All foods containing fat have a place in the diet. Reduction in volume ingested may be advisable, but no type of food should be entirely omitted. *Avoid all dietary extremes; eat all foods in moderation; you can harm yourself by omitting basic-four food groups. Do not make major changes in the diet without medical advice.*

Experimentation has developed many new recipes in which the liquid oils can successfully replace solid fats. These recipes are available from the manufacturers of salad oils and the American Heart Association and could help change the percentage of unsaturated fatty acids in the diet of one advised to do so by a physician.

How the Body Uses Fats

The body needs essential fatty acids (which are unsaturated). They are called essential because they are needed for normal cells and metabo-

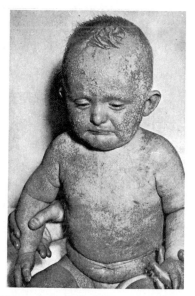 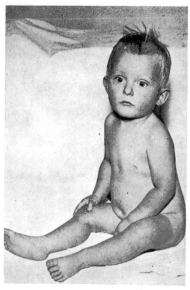

Figure 4-4 *Left,* Child with essential fatty acid deficiency. *Right,* Same child six months later. (Courtesy of Dr. A. E. Hansen.)

lism. They cannot be synthesized by the body; therefore, they must be supplied in the diet. (See Figure 4-4.) Fortunately they are found in salad oils and to a lesser extent in many commonly used foods (egg yolk, butter, meat). The hydrogenation process reduces the amount of essential fatty acids in a fat.

Fats must be emulsified before they can be acted upon by digestive secretions. When finely divided particles of fat are suspended in a liquid we have a temporary emulsion. On standing, the oil, which is lighter, rises to the top (for example, French dressing). When an emulsifying agent such as protein is present, the emulsion becomes permanent (for example, mayonnaise). This is possible because the protein envelops the fat particles. Bile, a liver secretion, is the body's fat-emulsifying agent.

Finely emulsified fats, such as those found in egg yolk, butter, and mayonnaise, start to digest in the stomach. Fats which must be emulsified by bile are digested by a pancreatic enzyme in the small intestine. Digestion breaks fat into fatty acids and glycerol which are absorbed through the intestinal wall. Fats which have a low melting point, such as butter, which melts at 75° F, are more completely absorbed than a hard fat, such as suet, which melts at 95° to 105° F. From 93 to 98 per cent of the commonly used fats are digested and absorbed by the average person. Contrary to what many people think, fried foods are digested; but they do digest more slowly than carbohydrates and proteins. Fat digestion may be less efficient in the infant and the elderly person. Overheated (smoking) fat not only gives the food a burned flavor but also decomposes into products which irritate the mucous membranes of the stomach and intestines. Excessive irritation can cause diarrhea.

Mineral oil comes from petroleum and is often used as a laxative. It is completely indigestible and interferes with the absorption of fat-soluble vitamins so it should not be taken near mealtime. Mineral oil should not be used in cooking or in making salad dressings.

The functions of fat in the body are as follows:

1. Fat supplies heat. One gram gives nine calories. Tissues, except those of the central nervous system, can utilize fat as a source of energy.

2. Subcutaneous fat acts as an insulation of body heat.

3. Fat provides padding around vital organs. It holds them in place and helps absorb the shock of physical blows. However, excessive fat around vital organs interferes with proper functioning of the organs.

4. Fat is the carrier of the fat-soluble vitamins A, D, E, and K.

5. The essential fatty acids are needed for maintenance of body functions. (See Figure 4-4.)

6. Fats have a sparing action on vitamin B_1; that is, if fat consumption is adequate, not as much B_1 is needed.

7. Fat slows up the secretion of hydrochloric acid, muscle contractions, and the rate of digestion. A fatty meal, therefore, stays a longer time in the stomach and the small intestine. When food remains in the stomach and the small intestine, it prevents the quick return of the feeling of hunger. This prevention of hunger is called satiety value.

8. Fats add flavor to many foods. Non-fat (skim) milk does not taste like whole milk.

9. The calories in fat will spare protein from being burned for energy.

10. Cholesterol is needed for the synthesis of sex and adrenal hormones.

11. Substituting a fat high in polyunsaturated fatty acids for a fat high in saturated fatty acids will, in the majority of individuals, decrease the blood cholesterol levels.

Excess fat in the diet may

1. Cause obesity because more calories are consumed than are needed.

2. Abnormally slow the digestion and absorption of food products.

3. Interfere with the absorption of calcium by combining with the calcium to form an insoluble calcium soap. The soap will not diffuse through the intestinal wall.

4. Cause ketosis unless adequate carbohydrate is present to complete the oxidation of fat. The person who is losing weight is losing his own fat tissue to provide calories needed by his body. Metabolizing either dietary or body fat necessitates the concurrent metabolism of carbohydrate to prevent ketosis.

Fat not immediately used by the body is stored as adipose tissue which

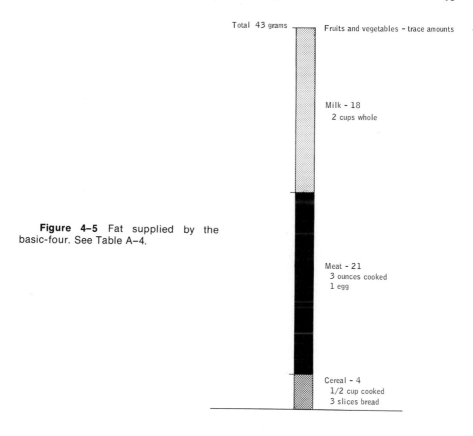

Total 43 grams — Fruits and vegetables – trace amounts

Milk - 18
2 cups whole

Figure 4-5 Fat supplied by the basic-four. See Table A-4.

Meat - 21
3 ounces cooked
1 egg

Cereal - 4
1/2 cup cooked
3 slices bread

in an emergency is used by the body as a supply of energy. However, excess fatty tissue results in overweight. This condition is called obesity. Patients who are obese are more prone to cerebral damage, heart disease, diabetes mellitus, and kidney failure; the life span may be shortened and, in patients needing surgery, risk is increased. Circulatory disease is a principal cause of death in adults over 30 in both Canada and the United States.

Food Sources of Fat

Common food sources of fat are cream, butter or margarine, whole milk, cream and whole milk cheeses, avocado, olives, egg yolk, fish, poultry, nuts, lard and other shortenings, oils, coconut, chocolate, and meats.

Foods which contain predominantly saturated fatty acids (palmitic, stearic) are

Whole milk, cream, ice cream, cheese, butter,
Meat, except poultry, fish, pork,
Coconut and coconut oil,
Chocolate.

Foods which contain predominantly monounsaturated fatty acids (oleic) are

Avocado, olives, olive oil, peanut butter, peanut oil,

Lard, regular margarine, vegetable shortening,

Pork, poultry, eggs,

Cashews.

Foods which contain predominantly polyunsaturated fatty acids (linoleic, linolenic) are

Corn, cottonseed, safflower, soybean, and sunflower oils,

Walnuts,

Special margarines,

Mayonnaise and French dressing, if made with the above oils,

Fish.

SUGGESTED READING

American Heart Association:
  The Way To A Man's Heart—A Fat-Controlled, Low Cholesterol Meal Plan to Reduce the Risk of Heart Attack, 1972.
  Cookbook, 1973.
  Eat Well but Wisely to Reduce Your Risk of Heart Attack, 1969.
  How To Stop Smoking, 1973.
  Physical Activity and Your Heart.
  The Heart and Blood Vessels, 1973.
  Recipes for Fat-Controlled, Low Cholesterol Meals, 1972.
  What We Know About Diet and Heart Disease.
  Why Risk Heart Attack? Six Ways to Guard Your Heart.
DHEW Publication No. 72-251: *Hardening of the Arteries,* 1974.
Harkins, Robert W., and Sarett, Herbert P.: "Medium Chain Triglycerides," *J.A.M.A., 209:* 4:64, January 22, 1968.
Freidman, Glen M., et al.: "Alternate Approach to Low Fat, Low Saturated Fat, Low Cholesterol Diet," *J. of Nutrition Education,* 6:1, 1974.
Irwin, Theodore: *Watch Your Blood Pressure,* Public Affairs Pamphlet No. 483, 1974.
Leverton, Ruth: *Fats in Food and Diet,* Agriculture Information Bulletin No. 361, 1974.
Mayer, Jean: "Keep Your Child's Heart Healthy," *Family Health,* July, 1974.
President's Council on Physical Fitness: *Adult Physical Fitness,* 1973.

EXERCISES

1. List eight functions of fat.
2. List the foods containing fat which you ate today. Were they visible or invisible fats? (Table A-1 can help you determine if the foods contained fat.)
3. If a piece of fudge contains 3 grams of fat and 23 grams of carbohydrate, how many calories does it contain?
4. Why should you keep your shortening or oil in a covered container and in a cool, dark place?
5. Your physician has ordered a diet lower in saturated fats. Name five foods which you will use in smaller quantities.

CHAPTER 5

Proteins

TERMS TO UNDERSTAND

Amino acid	Dynamic equilibrium	Protein
Essential	Edema	*Complete*
Nonessential	Hormone	*Incomplete*
Antibody	Hyperthyroidism	Regeneration
Coagulate	Molecule	Supplementation
	Pancreas	

Proteins are very complex organic compounds containing carbon, hydrogen, oxygen, nitrogen, usually sulfur, and sometimes iron, phosphorus, iodine, and copper. Amino acids are the chemical compounds which make up proteins. A particular protein always has the same number of amino acids in the same sequence.* A change either in the number of amino acids present or in their placement would make the compound a different protein. The protein insulin is pictured in Figure 5–1. The amino acids are often called building stones because no body tissue can be built without them. Those which the body cannot synthesize are called essential amino acids and must be supplied by food. They should be supplied in each meal, preferably divided about equally among the three meals.

Protein allowances are based on age and desirable body weight, not on muscular activity. People doing heavy work often prefer higher protein diets. The extra meat and eggs may fill a "psychological need" even though there is no physical need. In the table inside the front cover, you will note that the recommended allowance decreases from 1.8 grams per

---

*The molecular structure of proteins can be compared to the structure of words. Think of the letters of the alphabet as representing the amino acids. Just as a certain sequence of letters produces a particular word, a certain sequence of amino acids produces a particular protein. Any change in the sequence or the number of amino acids produces a different protein.

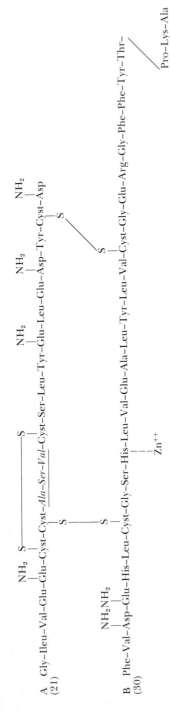

A Gly–Ileu–Val–Glu–Glu–Cyst–Cyst–*Ala–Ser–Val*–Cyst–Ser–Leu–Tyr–Glu–Leu–Glu–Asp–Tyr–Cyst–Asp
(21)

B Phe–Val–Asp–Glu–His–Leu–Cyst–Gly–Ser–His–Leu–Val–Glu–Ala–Leu–Tyr–Leu–Val–Cyst–Gly–Glu–Arg–Gly–Phe–Phe–Tyr–Thr–Pro–Lys–Ala
(30)

Beef — Ala–Ser–Val
Horse — Thr–Gly–Ileu
Swine — Thr–Ser–Leu
Sheep — Ala–Gly–Val
Human — Thr–Ser–Ileu

Molecular weight: 6000.

Figure 5–1   Sequence of amino acids in the insulin molecule. The names of the more common amino acids are as follows:

Essential		*Nonessential*	
Arginine*	Methionine	Alanine	Hydroxyproline
Histidine*	Phenylalanine	Aspartic acid	Norleucine
Isoleucine	Threonine	Cystine	Proline
Leucine	Tryptophan	Glutamic acid	Serine
Lysine	Valine	Glycine	Tyrosine

(From Sanger, F., *in* Pike, R. L., and Brown, M. L.: *Nutrition: An Integrated Approach*, 1967.)

---

*Arginine and histidine are necessary during growth, but not for the adult. They may be called "semiessential."

kilogram of body weight for the 1- to 3-year-old to approximately 1.2 grams per kilogram for the 7- to 10-year-old, is approximately 1.0 gram per kilogram in adolescence, and is 0.8 gram for adults. A kilogram equals 2.2 pounds.

Kinds of Protein

Complete proteins contain the essential amino acids and will build and repair tissues. Animal proteins are complete proteins and for this reason milk, meat, poultry, fish, or eggs should be eaten. It is recommended that an adult receive one third or more of his protein from complete protein foods, and a child from one half to two thirds of his protein from the animal sources.

The incomplete proteins do not contain all of the essential amino acids. These proteins, with the exception of gelatin, are found in plant life. Although gelatin is an animal protein, it too is incomplete. If gelatin were the only protein in the diet, life would not continue.

The expression "biological value" means how serviceable the nutrient is to the body for maintenance or growth. A protein of high biological value would be one which supplies the essential amino acids necessary for building tissues. The incomplete plant proteins have lower biological value. Proteins which do not contain all the essential building stones can be supplemented by another protein which provides the missing amino acids; the mixture of the two will have high biological value. Meats and milk supplement grains very well. The value of the protein in breakfast cereal is increased when it is served with milk because the milk proteins supplement the cereal proteins. *To be effective the protein supplementation should occur during the same meal.*

In the areas of the world where meat, eggs, and milk are not in abun-

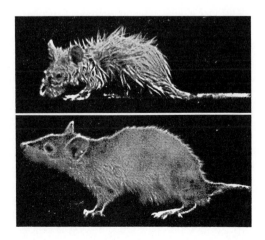

Figure 5–2 Effects of lack of one of the essential amino acids. The upper photograph shows a rat on the twenty-eighth day of valine deprivation. The lower photograph shows the same animal after valine had been administered for 25 days. (Courtesy of Rose and Eppstein and the *Journal of Biological Chemistry.*)

dant supply nor readily available, blends of low cost legumes and cereals which are *carefully chosen to supplement each other* can supply the protein needs. For example, Incaparina is a flour containing corn, cottonseed, sorghum grain, calcium carbonate, vitamin A, and yeast. If prepared according to directions, a glass of Incaparina has as much protein and as many calories as a glass of milk, more vitamin A, iron, thiamin, and niacin, half as much calcium, and one third as much riboflavin. Its ingredients are produced in Latin American countries, where it is being used.

How the Body Uses Protein

All cells need protein to grow and to be repaired. This applies not only to muscle cells but to bone, tooth, and nerve tissue as well. For example, protein is an essential ingredient of the osteoid matrix. Cheraskin's data show that in lower animals protein deprivation has caused alveolar bone loss. In humans a low serum albumin, a clinical test for determining protein level, is related to alveolar bone loss. Conversely, protein supplementation exerted a beneficial effect upon gingiva of dental students. (23a) Another area being studied is protein deprivation in relation to mental development. The human brain has grown to its full size by the time a child reaches the age of five. There is a possibility that protein deprivation in early life would retard mental development or cause permanent change in the intellectual potential. Barnes emphasizes that intellectual development is not just a product of physical development, but is also related to environmental and sensory stimulations from parents and peers. He states:

One of the problems in relating mental development and malnutrition is that during the critical period when an infant or a young child is being malnourished, it is in a state of apathy; it cannot react well with its environment and it cannot absorb those sensory stimuli to which it may be exposed. Furthermore, these stimuli are probably minimal. For these reasons the malnutrition could very well have an effect upon the mental development of the child. This is quite different, however, from the concept that the lack of nutrients at an early period in the development of the brain may have an effect on brain development itself, resulting in retardation in intellectual development. These are two different concepts. (16:673)

Some protein is partially digested in the stomach, but most protein digestion occurs in the small intestine by enzymes of the pancreatic juice and the intestinal juice. Both cooked and uncooked protein is digested and absorbed. All proteins are broken down into amino acids before they can go through the intestinal wall and be taken by the blood to the liver. The liver acts as a distribution and disposal center.

The body uses protein to
1. Build new tissue and repair tissue.
2. Give heat (1 gram yields 4 calories); but protein is an expensive

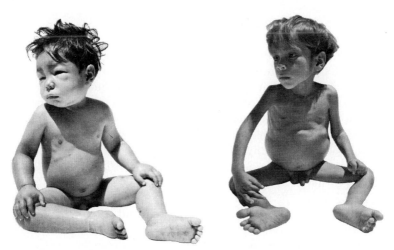

Figure 5-3 Kwashiorkor: three-year, ten-month-old boy (*left*) with severe edema. Five weeks later (*right*) showing underlying malnutrition when the edema had disappeared following high protein feeding. (Courtesy of Instituto de Nutrición de Centro América y Panamá, Guatemala, C. A. [INCAP].)

source of heat. Sufficient carbohydrate and fat in the diet allow the protein to be used for tissue growth instead of being deaminized and then used for energy.

3. Maintain water balance (if there is not enough protein in the blood, fluid will accumulate in the tissues; this is called nutritional edema).

4. Help form antibodies (resist disease).

5. Help make body secretions (enzymes, hormones, milk). Excess dietary protein is converted into body fat instead of being stored as protein.

Larger amounts of protein should be used in the diet during

1. Growth—the child needs more in relation to his weight than the adult does.

2. Pregnancy—especially during the later months.

3. Lactation.

4. Convalescence—such as after surgery or a "wasting" disease.

5. Fevers and infections.

6. Burns.

7. Hyperthyroidism.

Signs of a protein deficiency include weight loss, reduced resistance to infection, impaired healing of wounds, hepatic insufficiency, nutritional edema, easy fatigue, and muscular weakness. Laboratory tests may show abnormally low concentrations of blood proteins when no other clinical signs are present.

Protein is not stored as protein in the body; excess protein in the diet is converted to fat. In the so-called "wasting" diseases, protein is not consumed in sufficient quantity and body cells are used to supply the protein for essential tissue regeneration.

Food Sources of Protein

Fruits and vegetables are poor sources of protein both in quantity and quality. Legumes, nuts, and cereals are fair sources. Meat, eggs, fish, and poultry are good sources in both quantity and quality. Milk does not have a high concentration of protein, but the protein is of such excellent quality that milk is a very valuable source. The foods high in protein usually contain considerable amounts of water and fat and, with the exception of legumes little, if any, carbohydrate. The fat will contribute many calories. For example, 8 ounces of whole milk has 160 calories; 8 ounces of non-fat (skim) milk has 90 calories.

Heat coagulates protein (for example, in the cooking of an egg), and high temperature and overcooking toughen and shrink protein. Room temperature causes foods high in moist protein to decompose; thus eggs, milk, and meat should be refrigerated.

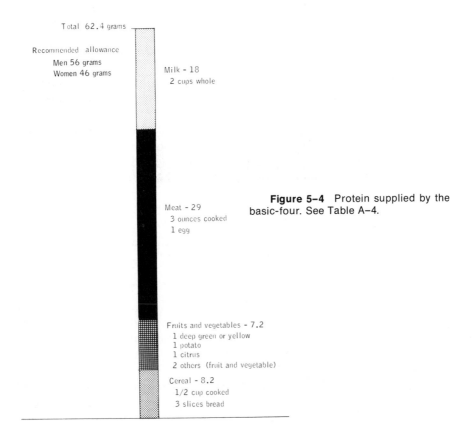

Total 62.4 grams

Recommended allowance
Men 56 grams
Women 46 grams

Milk - 18
2 cups whole

Meat - 29
3 ounces cooked
1 egg

Fruits and vegetables - 7.2
1 deep green or yellow
1 potato
1 citrus
2 others (fruit and vegetable)

Cereal - 8.2
1/2 cup cooked
3 slices bread

Figure 5–4 Protein supplied by the basic-four. See Table A–4.

Daily Recommendations

	Grams		Grams
CHILDREN		FEMALES	
1 to 3	23	15 to 18	48
7 to 10	36	Over 18	46
		Pregnant	+30
MALES		Lactating	+20
15 to 22	54		
Over 22	56		

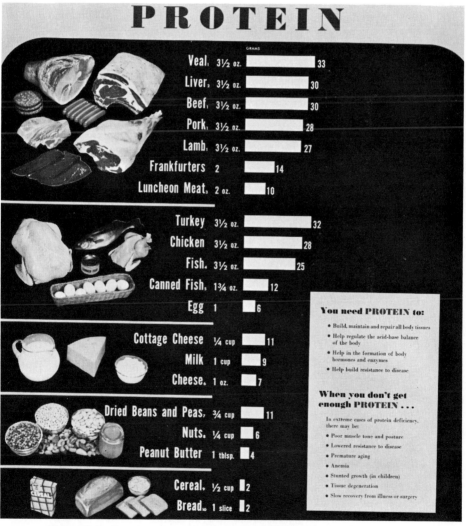

Figure 5–5 Protein sources. (From National Live Stock and Meat Board.)

SUGGESTED READING

Breeling, James L.: "Marketing Protein for the World's Poor," *Today's Health,* February, 1969.

California Dietetic Association: *A Guide to Protein Controlled Diets,* 1973.

Cooley, Donald, G.: "What's So Important About Proteins?" *Today's Health,* October, 1965.

"Foods that Give the Most Protein for Your Money," *Good Housekeeping,* November, 1974.

Grotta-Kursha, Daniel: "Before You Say Baloney — Here's What You Should Know About Vegetarianism," *Today's Health,* October, 1974.

Mayer, Jean: "Protein — The Master Builder," *Family Health,* August, 1974.

Stoia, Rose Greer: *If You Don't Eat Meat What Do You Eat?* Seventh Day Adventist Dietetic Association, 1973.

EXERCISES

1. Make a chart showing the functions, food sources (good, fair, poor), and characteristics (cooking, storage, etc.) of protein.
2. Do you base your protein allowance on actual weight or desirable weight (Table 15–3)? How many grams of protein should you eat every day? Write a menu containing the basic-four. Check with Table A-1 and determine if that menu meets your recommended protein allowance.
3. Why would the one-year-old child need about twice as much protein per unit of weight as the adult?
4. Why would the protein allowance for two men normally weighing 150 pounds be the same even though one is a bookkeeper and the other a brick layer?
5. How many calories are in a glass of milk containing 9 grams of protein, 10 grams of fat, and 12 grams of carbohydrate? If it were skim milk how many calories would it contain?
6. List several ways in which a change in this menu would result in increasing the protein biological value. Why should a change be made?
   Baked potato
   Candied squash
   Asparagus spears
   Boston brown bread
   Butter
   Canned pears
   Oatmeal cookies
   Coffee

CHAPTER 6

Water and Cellulose

TERMS TO UNDERSTAND

Constipation	Exudate	Ischemia
Dehydration	Feces	Peristalsis
Epidemiology	Interstitial	Stagnate
Extracellular	Intracellular	Thrombosis

Oxygen is the body's first need and water its second. A person can live for days or even weeks without food but only a few days without water. A 10 per cent loss of body water causes very serious symptoms; a 20 per cent loss often results in death.

A 160-pound man has a body composition of about 100 pounds water, 29 pounds protein, 25 pounds fat, five pounds minerals, one pound carbohydrate, and one quarter ounce vitamins. (83:255).

Water is found in the blood, in the cells (as intracellular fluid) and also around and between the cells (as extracellular fluid, such as lymph and the fluid which bathes the tissues). About 50 to 65 per cent of the adult body weight is water, and the adult should consume a volume of water equivalent to 3/4 ounce per pound of body weight daily. The infant's body is 70 to 75 per cent water; his need for water is even greater than the adult's. His liquid intake should equal 2 1/4 ounces per pound daily or an amount equivalent to 10 to 15 per cent of his body weight. A cup of water weighs about 1/2 pound. If a 10-pound baby with diarrhea loses 4 cups of water, he has lost 2 pounds, or 20 per cent of his weight, and is very seriously dehydrated.

The body has three sources of water:
1. The water contained in food.
2. Ingested fluids such as water, soups, and beverages.
3. The water formed by the metabolism of food in the body.

Foods vary in the amount of water which they contain. Fruits and vegetables are as much as 95 per cent water. Flour, crackers, and breads are from 5 to 35 per cent. Meats are from 40 to 75 per cent water and milk is 87 per cent water.

To insure adequate fluid intake, a minimum of 5 or 6, and preferably 6 to 8, glasses of water or other beverage should be taken daily. During infections and a fever the fluid intake should be increased.

Water, about 2 to 3 quarts daily, is lost from the body through the skin as perspiration, through the kidneys as urine, through the bowels as feces, and through the expired air of the lungs. Abnormal losses of water occur in vomiting, diarrhea, hemorrhaging, excessive perspiration, and from exudating burns, uncontrolled diabetes mellitus, fever, strenuous exercise, and hot weather. Sodium is lost when fluid is lost from the body, and it too should be replaced. Symptoms of dehydration include fatigue, headache, sullenness, and in extreme cases collapse.

In addition to being part of the body cells and fluids, water is used in the body in many ways. It acts as a solvent during all stages of digestion. It keeps nutrients in solution so that they may be absorbed through the intestinal walls. The water in the blood transports the nutrients to the body cells. Waste products are excreted with water through the bowels and the kidneys. It is a lubricant preventing friction between moving parts. Water regulates body temperature through evaporation from the lungs and the skin.

A moderate amount of water may be drunk with meals, but it should not be used to wash down poorly masticated food.

Cellulose is a fibrous material found in plants, and it is not digested. The chief function of cellulose is to provide bulk, which stimulates peri-

Table 6–1 *The Water Balance of an Average Individual*

	Milliliters	Cups [1]
Water Intake		
Liquid food (water, coffee, milk, soup, etc.)	1100	4¾
Solid food (moisture)	500–900	2 – 3¾
Water of oxidation	400	1¾
	2000–2400	8½ – 10¼
Water Output		
Vaporization (400 ml. expired as moist air from the lung, 600 ml. from the skin as sweat)	920–1000	4 – 4¼
Feces	80– 100	¼ – ½
Urine	1000–1300	4¼ – 5½
	2000–2400	8½ – 10¼

[1] To the nearest ¼ cup

(Adapted from Wohl, M. G., and Goodhart, R. S.: *Modern Nutrition in Health and Disease,* 1968, p. 407.)

stalsis. Peristalsis is the contraction of successive portions of the muscular fibers of the walls of the alimentary tract, which creates a wavelike movement and thus moves the contents of the alimentary tract onward. Peristalsis keeps the mass moving down the intestinal tract, preventing a stagnation of material in the colon, and providing good elimination (see Figure 19–2). Agar-agar from seaweed and pectin from fruit are hemicelluloses and, like cellulose, can absorb a quantity of water, thus increasing intestinal bulk. Pectin (scraped apple) is sometimes used in the treatment of diarrhea. Its therapeutic value may be due to its ability to absorb irritants.

Fruits and vegetables (except peeled potatoes) provide approximately 1 gram of cellulose per serving; whole grain cereals and nuts supply ½ to 1½ grams. The 5 to 7 grams recommended for daily intake is supplied by the basic-four, especially if some whole grain cereals are used.

Fiber has traditionally been considered in relation to the elimination process, but there is clinical and experimental evidence to support the statement that it does have other metabolic effects. Epidemiological data are being assessed to see if the amount of dietary fiber does play a part in

1. Alimentary tract diseases — diverticulosis, hiatus hernia, gallbladder disease, appendicitis, polyps, and colon cancer.

2. Cardiovascular conditions — ischemic heart disease, occlusive vascular disease, varicose veins, hemorrhoids, and deep vein thrombosis.

3. Other metabolic conditions — obesity and diabetes.*

Clinically, increased dietary fiber is being used in the management of colon diverticular disease and atonic constipation. Should the data indicate that too little cellulose is in the average U.S. diet, it is possible that future basic food patterns may stipulate the use of only whole grain cereals.

See Chapter 19 for discussion of constipation.

SUGGESTED READING

Hook, Charles, W.: "Laxatives, $148 Million Fraud?" *Today's Health,* October, 1960.
Lederer, Muriel: "Perspiration — Everybody's Problem," *Today's Health,* August, 1967.
Mayer, Jean: "Water — You Can't Live Without It," *Family Health,* September, 1974.
"Roughage in the Diet," *Medical World News,* September 6, 1974.

EXERCISES

1. List the functions of water.
2. How many grams of cellulose would the basic-four provide? Is this amount adequate?
3. How would you increase the cellulose content of the diet for atonic constipation?
4. Has the amount of cellulose been reduced in pureed food? Why or why not?
5. How does the preparation of pureed food differ from food that has been osterized?

---

*"Roughage in the Diet," *Medical World News, September 6, 1974.*

CHAPTER 7

Digestion, Absorption, and Metabolism

TERMS TO UNDERSTAND

Anabolism	Digestibility	Metabolism
Anus	Eject	Osmosis
Catabolism	Extractive	Pylorus
Chyme	Gastrectomy	Sac
Conducive	Ingest	Semifluid
Diffuse	Masticate	

Digestion

The alimentary canal is a tube extending from the mouth to the rectum. It is about 30 feet long, wide in some parts and narrow in others. Most nutrients have to be changed by the chemical process known as digestion before they can be absorbed through the intestinal wall. If digestion and absorption do not occur, the nutrients are excreted in the feces. If a person has very faulty digestion and absorption, he can eat quantities of food and yet be malnourished; nutrients have not entered the body until they have gone through the walls of the intestine.

When food is taken into the mouth it should be well masticated. Saliva moistens and softens the food. The digestive enzymes can reach only the outside of the pieces of food, so if the pieces are small the enzymes have more opportunity to come in contact with the nutrients. Enzymes have the following characteristics:

1. Each is specific as to the substance which it changes.

2. Each is destroyed by heat but inactivated by cold.

3. Each works most efficiently in a narrow temperature range (optimal temperature is normal body temperature).

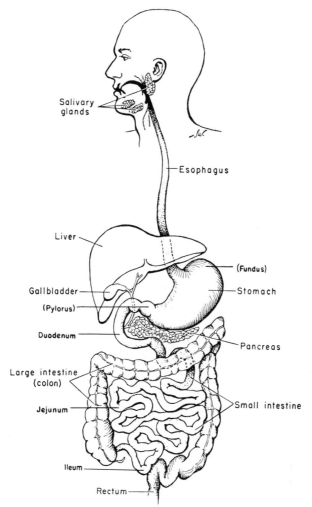

Figure 7-1 The digestive system. (Modified from Brooks: *Basic Facts of General Chemistry.*)

4. Each works most efficiently in its own pH range—either acid or alkali.

The flow of digestive juices is stimulated by
1. The presence of dilute acids (fruit and fruit juice).
2. The presence of meat extractive (broth and gravy).
3. The presence of food and water.
4. A pleasant memory, sight, smell, or taste of food.

The stomach acts as a storage place for food. Since most digestion and absorption occurs in the small intestine, an individual may have a gastrectomy and not become malnourished. The stomach usually empties in two to six hours. Small contractions of the stomach walls mix the food with the gastric juices, making it a semi-fluid mass known as chyme. The chyme passes through the pylorus into the small intestine, which is about 20 feet long. Chyme stays in the small intestine from two to eight hours. The first section of the small intestine is called the duodenum. The pancreatic juice secreted by the pancreas and the bile secreted by the liver are poured into the duodenum. The gallbladder is a storage sac for bile. Cells in the walls of the small intestine secrete intestinal juice. The digestive juices act upon the nutrients in the chyme while the chyme is in the small intestine.

Absorption

With the exception of water, which is also absorbed from the large intestine, almost all nutrient absorption takes place from the small intestine, which is made up of the duodenum, jejunum, and ileum. The intestinal wall is velvety, with many finger-like projections called villi. The villi increase the absorbing surface of the small intestine. Osmosis occurs when two liquids are separated by a membrane. One liquid has more dissolved material than the other and will diffuse (transfer) to the other side of the membrane until the concentrations of the two liquids are equalized. The liquid in the small intestine contains the food nutrients and they diffuse through the villi walls into the blood of lymph capillaries. The amino acids of protein digestion and the simple sugars of carbohydrate digestion are carried by the blood to the liver. Most of the fatty acids and glycerol of the fat digestion are carried by the lymph system to the thoracic duct, where they slowly enter the blood circulation in the left subclavian vein.

The normal person digests and absorbs from 90 to 98 per cent of the food he eats, but any undigested food passes through the ileocecal valve into the large intestine. The large intestine fills slowly. Water is absorbed from the mass before it is ejected from the body as feces. Feces contain cellulose, undigested food, bacteria, mucus, digestive juices, and cellular debris. In liver and pancreatic disease, the deficient flow of bile and pancreatic juice impairs digestion of fat and protein; therefore, larger than normal quantities of undigested fat and protein appear in the stool. Digestibility refers to the completeness of digestion and should not be confused with rate of digestion.

It usually takes from 12 to 48 hours for the food to travel from mouth to the anus. Foods high in carbohydrate are digested most rapidly, proteins next, and fat requires a longer time; but a mixture of the three nutrients requires the longest. Liquid foods are more readily digested and more quickly absorbed than solid ones. For this reason the very sick person is often served gruels, purees, soups, or formula.

Good digestion is helped by thorough mastication, regular mealtimes, relaxed environment, and a pleasant memory, sight, or smell of food. Meat extractives in broth or gravy or mild acid in fruit juices stimulate the secretion of digestive juices. Anger, excitement, fatigue, fear, worry, anxi-

Table 7-1 Summary of Digestion

Mouth — breaks food into smaller pieces
  Chewing breaks food into smaller pieces for mixing with digestive juices.
  Ptyalin in saliva + cooked starch starts breakdown to maltose, a minor part of the digestive process.

Stomach — provides temporary storage of food
  Rennin in gastric juice + casein of milk → coagulation of milk protein and prepares it for action of pepsin.
  Pepsin in gastric juice + protein → proteoses and peptones.
  Lipase in gastric juice + emulsified fats° → fatty acids and glycerol, a very limited amount of action.
  Hydrochloric acid (not an enzyme) activates pepsinogen, very limited destruction of bacteria.
  Temporary storage of food in the fundus.
  Muscular contractions mix food with gastric juice → chyme (semi-liquid state).
  Stomach usually empties in 2 to 6 hours, depending upon the volume and the type of food eaten.

Small intestine (duodenum, jejunum, ileum) — concerned with digestion and absorption of food
  Trypsin, chymotrypsin, and carboxypolypeptidase in pancreatic juice + protein → peptides and amino acids.
  Steapsin in pancreatic juice + fats → fatty acids and glycerol.
  Amylopsin in pancreatic juice + cooked or raw starch → dextrin and maltose.
  Bile from the liver emulsifies fats, thus aiding in their digestion.
  Erepsin in intestinal juice + peptides → amino acids.
  Maltase in intestinal juice + maltose → glucose.
  Sucrase in intestinal juice + sucrose → glucose and fructose.
  Lactase in intestinal juice + lactose → glucose and galactose.
  Digestion and absorption of food (90 to 98%) are completed before the colon is reached.
  Food in the intestine is moved by peristaltic waves.

Large intestine (cecum, colon, rectum) — absorption of water results in formation of feces
  There are no digestive enzymes secreted into the large intestine.
  Water is absorbed, thus feces are formed.
  Peristaltic waves move residue so waste will be eliminated.

°Emulsified when ingested.

ety, and excess fat in the diet retard digestion by slowing down the flow of digestive juices. Food should be attractively served, eaten in pleasant surroundings, and well chewed.

Metabolism

Metabolism is the chemical process of making food into body tissue, the breaking down of body tissue, and the producing of energy. Metabolism is the sum of chemical changes which go on in the body; it is divided into two parts, anabolism and catabolism. Building, maintaining, and repairing tissue are called anabolism. Breaking down tissue into simple substances for excretion and energy production is called catabolism. Anabolism and catabolism result from the process of oxidation in the body. A "basal metabolic test" measures how much oxygen is needed by the body when it is physically and mentally relaxed and when no food has been taken for several hours. Even when the body is at rest many active life processes continue, including respiration, heart beat and blood circulation, peristalsis, and oxidation in every living cell.

Factors which affect the basal metabolic rate (B.M.R.) are

1. Internal secretions: Secretions of the thyroid and adrenal glands affect B.M.R. Generally speaking, hyperthyroidism causes a high basal rate and hypothyroidism causes a subnormal rate. An emotional state that stimulates secretions of the ductless glands could increase the rate of body processes and give an incorrect reading in the traditional B.M.R. test.

2. Age: The child has a higher B.M.R. than the adult. In old age there is a marked decrease.

3. Body shape: A tall, thin person has a higher B.M.R. than a short, fat person.

4. Sex: Women have a lower B.M.R. than men.

When food is metabolized it produces calories. One gram of protein or one gram of carbohydrate yields four calories, and one gram of fat gives nine calories. More calories are needed whenever the body is not at complete rest. The total number of calories needed every day is the sum of

1. Those needed for basal metabolism.

2. Those needed for muscular activity. The greater the physical activity, the greater the caloric need. The calories needed for an hour's mental work can be supplied by half a peanut. If one fidgets or has muscle tension doing mental work, the energy for this increased activity is supplied by very few additional calories. See Tables 15–1 and 15–2 for calories needed for different physical activities.

3. Those needed to digest, absorb, and metabolize the food we eat. (This caloric cost of assimilating food is called specific dynamic action. Metabolism of the large protein molecule utilizes more chemical steps than that of carbohydrates and fats, so proteins have the highest specific dynamic action.) For specific dynamic action, a mixed diet uses from six to ten calories for each 100 calories consumed. No food uses more calories than it contains; therefore it is a fallacy to say that any food will burn body fat and produce weight loss.

To calculate roughly a peron's caloric needs, his ideal weight must be known. Ideal weight is not necessarily the person's actual weight, but the amount which he should weigh for his height. (See Table 15–3 for desirable adults weights.)

For adults, allow 15 to 25 calories for every pound of ideal weight. Those doing light exercise should use about 15 calories per pound, moderate exercise about 19 calories per pound, and heavy exercise about 25. (Nursing is classified as light exercise.) During the first year of life, 50 calories are allowed for each pound of expected growth (51:72); this gradually declines, until the 7- to 10-year-old receives about 36 calories per pound; in the late teens a boy's allowance is about 23 and the girl's allowance is about 18 calories per pound.

The homemaker who has labor-saving devices such as an automatic washer, vacuum cleaner, and electric mixer will not need as many calories per day as the homemaker who does not have this equipment.

After carbohydrates and fats have been used by the tissues (metabolized), the end products are carbon dioxide, which is excreted through the lungs; water, which is excreted by the kidneys and the skin; and calories. The nitrogen part of the amino acid is used for building or repairing tissue; the waste products of proteins are urea, ammonia, carbon dioxide, water, and calories. The urea and ammonia are excreted by the kidney. (See Chapter 15 for information on weight control.)

SUGGESTED READING

American Medical Association:
  Today's Health Guide.
  The Wonderful Human Machine.
Bugg, Ralph: "Your Body's Silent Partners," *Today's Health*, January, 1969.
Ratcliff, J. D.:
  "Enzymes: Your Body's Amazing Chemists," *Today's Health*, September, 1960.
  "I Am Joe's Liver," *Reader's Digest*, September, 1969.
  "I Am Joe's Lung," *Reader's Digest*, March, 1969.
  "I Am Joe's Stomach," *Readers Digest*, May, 1968.
  Your Body and How It Works, 1975.
  "Your Liver's Chemical Magic," *Today's Health*, December, 1963.

EXERCISES

1. Calculate your approximate calorie needs. Use Table 15–3 to find your ideal weight.
2. List the foods you have eaten in the last 24 hours. From Table A–1 calculate the total calories. How does this compare with your approximate needs? Did your diet include the basic-four? Which three foods were highest in calorie content? Which three lowest?
3. Compare the calorie content of the foods listed in the menus following Chapter 15.
4. During weight reduction, is there more anabolism or catabolism?
5. How could a high fever affect digestion?
6. How could taking baking soda for "indigestion" retard digestion?
7. Why is it a good custom to use foods such as soup, fruit cocktail, and fruit juice as the first course of a meal?

CHAPTER 8

Mineral Elements

TERMS TO UNDERSTAND

Acid-base balance	Endemic	Lochia
Alkaline	Etiology	Matrix
Anorexia	Exophthalmic	pH
Ascites	Gingiva	Renal
Assimilate	Goiter	Spasm
Calculus	Hypogeusia	Toxic
Congenital	Immobilize	Uteral
Electrolyte	Languor	

Over three per cent of the body weight is made up of mineral elements. Minerals serve many functions in the body. They are in bones, teeth, soft-tissue, muscles, blood, and nerve cells. They aid in regulating the activity of nerves and muscles, maintaining the acid-base equilibrium, controlling the water balance in the body by means of osmotic pressure, and utilizing foodstuffs. Minerals should be supplied daily because they are excreted every day by the kidney, the bowel, and the skin.

To build new tissue the mineral intake should be increased; therefore more mineral-rich food should be eaten during growth, pregnancy, and lactation. To increase the amount of mineral in the diet one should think not only of how much the food contains but also of how much of that food is used in the diet. For example, molasses is a good source of iron, but so little molasses is used in our menus that we cannot rely upon it as a source of iron. Some foods contain a great deal of mineral, but it is in a form that will not be absorbed through the intestinal wall. Most minerals have been removed from refined cereals.

Calcium and iron are the minerals most often deficient in the American diet, but iodine occasionally is low. If the foods in the diet are supplying these three minerals in adequate amounts, there probably will be enough of all the other minerals which the body needs with the possible exception of fluorine.

68

Calcium

Bone is composed of a protein framework made of cells and an organic matrix, mostly collagen. The mineral compounds which contain calcium, phosphorus, magnesium, sodium, potassium, copper, zinc, strontium, iron, silicon, vanadium, and aluminum are deposited in the protein framework, making it a hard tissue. The skeleton constantly rebuilds itself.

About 99 per cent of the calcium in the body is found in the bones and teeth and gives them rigidity and strength. In children, poor bone formation due to the lack of calcium, phosphorus, and vitamin D is called rickets (see Figure 9–5); in adults, softening of the bones due to a shortage of calcium and phosphorus is called osteomalacia (deossification). Osteomalacia is not common in the United States, but it is often confused with a more common disease of older people called osteoporosis. Osteoporosis is increased porosity of the bone (demineralization). Its etiology may include many years of a deficiency in calcium absorption, the hormonal decline of old age, lack of exercise, or immobilization such as

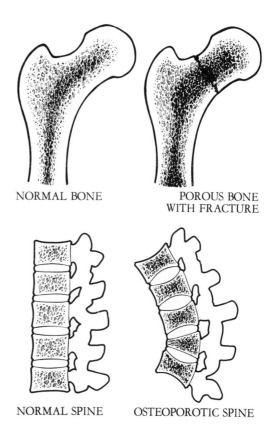

NORMAL BONE

POROUS BONE
WITH FRACTURE

Figure 8–1 Osteoporosis. (U.S. Department of Health, Education and Welfare.)

NORMAL SPINE

OSTEOPOROTIC SPINE

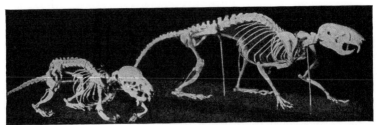

Figure 8–2 *Right,* Skeleton with adequate calcium. *Left,* Inadequate. (Courtesy of Sherman and MacLeod and the *Journal of Biological Chemistry.*)

experienced by fracture patients. The incidence of osteoporosis is higher in females than in males and apparently is higher in whites than in blacks.

Calcium is not the only factor in bone formation. Vitamin D and phosphorus must be adequate, and protein and vitamins A and C are essential for proper bone formation. The hormone of the parathyroid gland helps regulate the calcium metabolism in the body.

The other 1 per cent of the body calcium has many duties. These functions include the following:

1. In the tissue fluids calcium is involved in muscle contraction and relaxation. (This is the tissue fluid which regulates the heart beat.)

2. In blood coagulation.

3. In the normal response of nerve fibers and nerve centers to nerve transmission. (Refer to Chapter 21 for discussion of tetany.)

4. In the cell wall permeability.

5. In activating certain enzymes.

6. In maintaining acid-base balance.

7. In the efficient utilization of iron.

Hypercalcemia can occur with excessive intake of vitamin D, or with the prolonged intake of the milk and alkali regimen of ulcer therapy.

In Canada and the United States, the recommended daily calcium intake is based upon age and, for women, state of pregnancy or lactation.

A liberal amount of calcium in the diet may reduce the amount of radioactive strontium-90 deposited in the body. Milk has received the most publicity, in regard to radioactive contamination, but any food can be contaminated. The higher the calcium-to-strontium ratio in the diet, the less strontium-90 absorbed and deposited. Because the human body discriminates against strontium in favor of calcium, the high calcium content of milk may make milk one of the best protective foods. A process to remove strontium-90 from milk has been developed.

Lactic acid is produced by fermentation of lactose in milk, and this acid medium favors the calcium absorption from the small intestine. Adequate protein and vitamins D and C are also important for calcium absorption. Not all calcium in food may be available to the body. Excess use of fat and fiber interferes with the absorption of calcium. Lutwak found calcium absorption to be somewhat impaired when 40 per cent of the dietary calories, a normal figure for American diets, were provided by fat. (45) Calcium oxalate is insoluble and not used by the body. The calcium in some foods is in the form of calcium oxalate. This explains why greens such as broccoli and mustard are listed as sources of calcium but spinach and beet greens are omitted. Chocolate, cocoa, and rhubarb also contain oxalic acid. The phytates found in cereals can slightly decrease calcium absorption. Neither oxalates nor phytates are a problem if the diet contains a variety of foods.

Food sources of calcium are milk, cheese, milk products except butter, and green leafy vegetables except spinach, beet greens, and chard. In the United States dairy products provide 75 to 85 per cent of the calcium. (53:83) It takes about 11 eggs or 15 or more servings of fruit and vegetables to provide the same amount of calcium as one cup of milk. (See Figure 8–8.)

For normal development of teeth, adequate supplies of nutrients must be furnished while the teeth are developing in the jaws. The four main sections of a tooth are the enamel or the outer covering, dentin, cementum which covers the dentin below the gum surface, and pulp. The

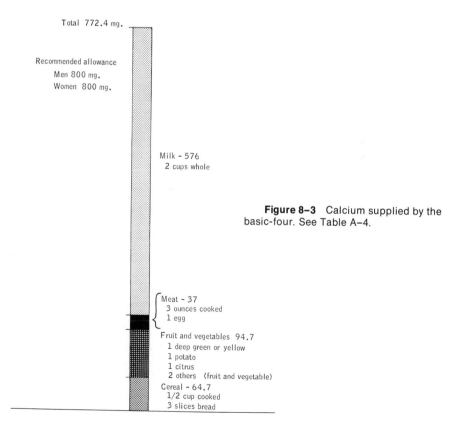

Total 772.4 mg.

Recommended allowance
Men 800 mg.
Women 800 mg.

Milk - 576
2 cups whole

Figure 8–3 Calcium supplied by the basic-four. See Table A–4.

Meat - 37
3 ounces cooked
1 egg

Fruit and vegetables 94.7
1 deep green or yellow
1 potato
1 citrus
2 others (fruit and vegetable)
Cereal - 64.7
1/2 cup cooked
3 slices bread

DECIDUOUS DENTITION

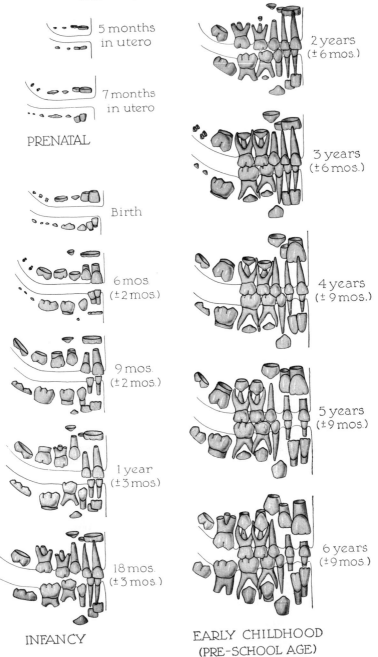

5 months in utero

7 months in utero

PRENATAL

Birth

6 mos. (±2 mos.)

9 mos. (±2 mos.)

1 year (±3 mos.)

18 mos. (±3 mos.)

INFANCY

2 years (±6 mos.)

3 years (±6 mos.)

4 years (±9 mos.)

5 years (±9 mos.)

6 years (±9 mos.)

EARLY CHILDHOOD
(PRE-SCHOOL AGE)

Figure 8–4 Development of the human dentition. Deciduous teeth are shown in darker tone. (Courtesy of I. Schour and M. Massler, University of Illinois College of Dentistry.)

Illustration continued on opposite page.

MIXED DENTITION   PERMANENT DENTITION

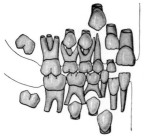
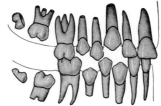

7 years (±9 mos.)

11 years (±9 mos.)

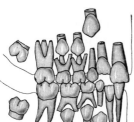
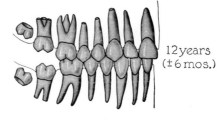

8 years (±9 mos.)

12 years (±6 mos.)

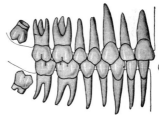

9 years (±9 mos.)

15 years (±6 mos.)

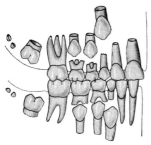
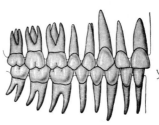

21 years

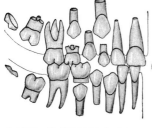

10 years (±9 mos.)

35 years

LATE CHILDHOOD   ADOLESCENCE
(SCHOOL AGE)   and ADULTHOOD

Figure 8–4 *Continued*

enamel and dentin do not contain blood vessels; therefore, after the tooth has erupted, calcium is no longer acquired by the enamel and dentin. The greatest loss of teeth during middle age is caused by diseases of the gum (gingiva) and the bones supporting the teeth. At all ages the basic-four diet is related to maintaining healthy gums and the supporting bones.

Figure 8–4 shows that tooth formation starts very early in uteral life and lasts through adolescence. Unless the woman has been exceptionally well nourished before the onset of pregnancy, an increased intake of calcium may need to be started earlier than the last half of pregnancy. For this reason the consumption of an additional one cup of milk, which would supply calcium, phosphorus, vitamins A and B complex, and protein, is often recommended as soon as pregnancy is known.

If there is poor chest bone development, there may be limited space for lung expansion, which might increase the possibility of tuberculosis or pneumonia. (See Figure 8–2.) Childbirth might be more difficult with a small pelvis. Fever may lower gastric acidity, thereby lowering calcium absorption.

Phosphorus

About 90 per cent of the body's phosphorus is found in the bones and teeth. It is in the nucleus of every body cell and it helps maintain the normal acid-base balance of the body, helps in the transport of fatty acids, helps provide the quick release of energy for muscle contraction, and is a constituent of enzymes that metabolize carbohydrates and fats.

Human milk has twice as much calcium as phosphorus (ratio=2:1). The ratio in cow's milk is 1.2:1. If the infant contracts hypocalcemic tetany (milk tetany) during his first week of life, it is probably due to the heavy load of phosphate. This is a temporary condition soon brought under control by the parathyroid gland.

Phosphorus is found in a greater variety of foods than is calcium. Diets containing enough protein and calcium will be adequate in phosphorus. Good sources of phosphorus are milk and milk products, egg yolk, whole grain cereals, fish, meat, nuts, poultry, and legumes. In general, the seeds and flowers of plant life contain more phosphorus and the leaves contain more calcium.

Iron

The amount of iron found in the body is about as much as the weight of a penny. Iron's primary function in the body is to become part of the hemoglobin, which carries oxygen from the lungs to the tissues and carbon dioxide from the tissues to the lungs. If oxygen does not reach the tissues in adequate amounts, languor and exhaustion are felt. This iron deficiency makes the anemic person feel tired. (See also Chapter 23.) About 90 per cent of the iron in hemoglobin is reused in making new blood cells. Iron is stored chiefly in the liver, bone marrow, and spleen. Iron is lost by any loss of blood such as occurs in surgery, hemorrhage, menstrual flow, blood donation, and tooth extraction.

Iron is poorly absorbed but it is relatively more soluble in an acid medium; therefore ample gastric hydrochloric acid enhances absorption through the duodenum. The healthy adult probably absorbs about one tenth of his dietary iron; children and pregnant women have increased iron needs and absorb a larger percentage. An anemic person may absorb as high as 64 per cent of his dietary iron; the greater the need, the greater the rate of absorption. Phosphate, oxalate, and phytate inhibit iron absorption, but if there is adequate calcium in the diet to combine with them more iron will be absorbed.

Hypogastric acidity, taking alkalies (baking soda), and diarrhea lower iron absorption. A patient with iron deficiency anemia does not obtain enough iron from food sources and therefore is given supplementary iron.

The table inside the front cover shows that the recommended daily allowance of iron (in milligrams) varies with age. (The head of a common pin weighs approximately one milligram.) Iron is frequently inadequate in the diet of

1. The infant. If the baby does not receive iron-bearing foods before he is six months old, he will be anemic before he is a year old.

2. The menstruating woman. Inadequate intake keeps her from accumulating adequate iron stores.

3. The pregnant woman. If she has had inadequate iron storage before conception, she and her fetus may be borderline nutritional anemia patients.

The iron needs of pregnancy change with the red cell volume in the fourth month of gestation and continuously increase until parturition, when iron is lost as blood and lochia. During the last half of pregnancy, iron is transferred to the growing fetus. In order to have iron stored in the fetal liver, it is very important that the mother have ample dietary iron during the last half of her pregnancy. If the baby does not have a three to six months' reserve supply in his liver, the infant will develop iron deficiency (nutritional or hypochromic) anemia. (Milk is a very poor source of iron.) The newborn's iron needs are relatively high. His blood volume is increasing and he needs the iron for hemoglobin to form his new red blood cells. However, a baby who swallows adult iron pills should be rushed to the doctor. He can develop fatal diarrhea.

Iron preparations are often sugar coated and may contain 300 mg. of ferrous sulfate. Six or seven of these tablets are equivalent to 400 mg. of elemental iron, which is potentially fatal to a young child. Iron is added to many pediatric vitamin preparations. Parents should be advised to keep iron dietary supplements out of the reach of small children because inges-

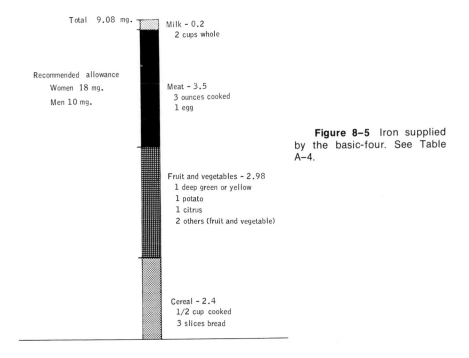

Total 9.08 mg.

Recommended allowance
Women 18 mg.
Men 10 mg.

Milk - 0.2
2 cups whole

Meat - 3.5
3 ounces cooked
1 egg

Fruit and vegetables - 2.98
1 deep green or yellow
1 potato
1 citrus
2 others (fruit and vegetable)

Cereal - 2.4
1/2 cup cooked
3 slices bread

Figure 8–5 Iron supplied by the basic-four. See Table A–4.

tion of iron-containing preparations is the fourth most common cause of poisoning in children under five years of age.*

The usual mixed American diet provides five to six milligrams of iron per 1000 calories; thus children and women consuming the recommended 2000 or less calories per day would have an intake of less than 12 milligrams of iron daily. Greater iron enrichment of grain products would probably be the most practical means of increasing dietary iron. If cereal enrichment becomes the means of increasing iron intake, it is imperative that education in the necessity of using cereals be better. Often the two groups, teenagers and menstruating women, who are in need of more iron, omit cereals because they wrongly believe them to be high in calories. (See Figure 8–5.) Food cooked in iron pans, such as grandmother's cast iron skillet or Dutch oven, will contribute more iron to the diet.

Food sources of iron are organ meats, especially liver, lean red meats, egg yolks, legumes, green and yellow vegetables, yellow fruits, whole grain and enriched cereals, potatoes, and tomatoes. Molasses, nuts, and raisins are good sources of iron but are used infrequently in many menus. Milk is a very poor source of iron, but the very small amount which is there is readily absorbed and assimilated. In general, to cut food into small pieces before cooking and to use excess cooking water increases iron

---

*J.A.M.A., *229*:324, 1974.

loss. Using the fruit pulp in the juices (orange, tomato, apricot), the meat drippings for gravy, and cooking potatoes without peeling will increase the iron content of the diet.

Iodine

Iodine is necessary for the thyroid gland to synthesize thyroxin. Thyroxin is one of the important regulators of energy metabolism.

The water supply and the vegetables grown in the Great Lakes region and in the Pacific Northwest lack iodine. People living in these areas, called "goiter belts," may have enlarged thyroid glands if they use only locally grown food and no iodized salt. The enlarged thyroid gland is called common, simple, or endemic goiter.

If the pregnant woman's thyroid is not adequately supplied with iodine, her child may be a cretin. At birth the infant's thyroid gland is enlarged, his appetite is poor, mental development is slow, the basal metabolic rate is low, and if the condition is not corrected the child will not grow properly. Myxedema is a condition due to deficient thyroid secretion or removal of the gland. It is not congenital.

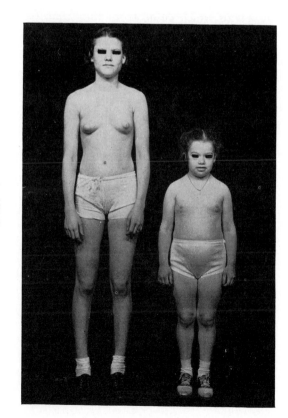

Figure 8–6 Iodine deficiency — normal girl and cretin. (Courtesy of Department of Pediatrics, University of Iowa Hospitals.)

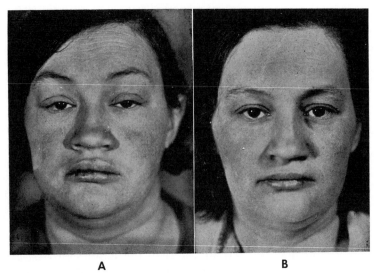

A   **B**

Figure 8–7 Iodine deficiency. *A,* Before treatment. *B,* After treatment. (Cecil and Loeb: *Textbook of Medicine.*)

Foods which come from the ocean (sea foods) contain iodine. The other reliable source is iodized salt; its use is especially important during pregnancy and adolescence. In Switzerland and Canada iodization of salt is compulsory.

Sodium

Sodium is readily absorbed from the small intestine. The average adult uses about 10 grams (two teaspoons) of table salt daily. This is at least twice as much as needed for sodium balance. The excess is excreted in the urine. If the sodium intake is reduced, the amount of sodium in the urine very quickly diminishes. Sodium is found mainly in the extracellular body fluids. If the concentration of sodium in the fluid rises, extra water will be retained in the body to dilute the sodium content of the fluid. The amount of dietary sodium is restricted in edema caused by abnormal sodium retention, ascites, and some types of cardiovascular and kidney diseases. Reducing the concentration of sodium in the extracellular fluid by using unsalted food (no salt added during cooking or at the table) and by omitting relishes and pickles, cured meats and fish, olives, salted nuts, and crackers will result in the excretion of the excess water in the urine. Diets with a sodium restriction below 1000 milligrams have such small servings of some foods that they may be deficient in other nutrients. They are monotonous and unappetizing because they are quite restricted in the variety of foods allowed. A 200 milligram sodium diet is so restricted in animal protein that its prolonged use may cause nutritional edema. Mayer has suggested that a high intake of table salt over a prolonged time may be correlated with greater risk of hypertension. (48:206)

Sodium helps regulate acid-base equilibrium and cell permeability, and maintain normal nerve irritability (transmits the impulses which result in normal muscle contraction), water balance, and osmotic pressure. Most foods contain some sodium. Good sources are table salt, baking soda, baking powder, milk, cheese, egg white, meat, and some vegetables, particularly carrots, spinach, beets, and celery. One gram of table salt contains 393 milligrams of sodium. The drinking water in some communities is high in sodium.

Additional sodium may be needed following extensive loss of blood, profuse sweating, recurrent vomiting, protracted diarrhea, burns, adrenal cortical insufficiency, chronic renal disease, and a prolonged use of diuretics. Sodium depletion symptoms include nausea, headache, anorexia, lassitude, muscle weakness (which may progress to painful spasms), and in severe cases, mental confusion.

Fluorine

Many communities add one part of fluorine to one million parts of their drinking water. This is a safe, inexpensive, and effective way to provide the necessary amount of fluorine. Larger quantities (one and one half parts or more per million) cause slight mottling of the tooth enamel.

Children who consume fluorine while their teeth are forming in the gum will decrease tooth decay by at least 50 per cent; some communities have reported decreases of over 60 per cent. Tooth enamel which contains fluorine is more resistant to the organic acids formed by mouth bacteria reacting with carbohydrates, particularly granulated sugar. Diefenbach reports that children who drink water containing the optimal fluoride level have teeth of better color and appearance than those who live where the water supply has either a deficiency or an excess of fluoride (29a). Recent research indicates that fluoride also favors the deposition of calcium, thereby strengthening bones. Fluoride makes the adult bone more resistant to fracture, and if a fracture does occur the bone heals more quickly.

Potassium

Like sodium, potassium is a vital mineral in the body fluids, but it is found mainly in the fluids within the cells. Its excretion pathway is primarily the urine and, as with sodium, if its intake is decreased the blood supply is conserved. The basic-four food groups supply ample potassium to the healthy person.

Potassium is used for body water balance, for maintaining acid-base balance, for carbohydrate metabolism, for the conduction of nerve impulses, and for contraction of muscle fibers. This is particularly true of the heart muscle: a small variation in potassium concentration will show electrocardiographic changes.

Potassium deficiencies are not seen under normal conditions. They do occur in diabetic acidosis, adrenal gland tumors, extensive tissue destruction as in severe burns; diarrhea, vomiting, gastric suction, prolonged intravenous feedings, and the continued use of diuretics also may produce a potassium deficiency. Diuretics should be taken only under the supervision of a doctor. Symptoms of hypokalemia include apathy, muscular weakness (which can progress to paralysis), loss of gastrointestinal tone (which leads to abdominal distention), respiratory muscle failure, and heart beat abnormalities (which can lead to tachycardia and cardiac arrest). Adrenal cortical deficiency (Addison's disease) and renal failure result in hyperkalemia. Its symptoms are severe dehydration, shock, poor respiration due to the weakening of the respiratory muscles, and dilation of heart muscles resulting in weakened contraction, which shows the heart rate.

Most foods contain potassium and will furnish an ample intake except in the above-noted disease conditions. Whole grains, meat, legumes, and some fruits and vegetables* are considered the better sources. See Table A–2 for the potassium content of some common foods.

Chromium†

Chromium is involved in glucose metabolism, and in a few cases of maturity-onset diabetes there was improvement when a supplement of 150 to 1000 micrograms of chromium chloride was given for several months. Human tissue levels of chromium decrease with age and a common finding among aging Americans is abnormal glucose tolerance tests. Sources of chromium include the germ and bran layers of cereals, beer, meat, green beans, carrots, and spinach. The phytate content of whole-grain cereals may interfere with the absorption of chromium.

---

*These foods, in the listed quantities, supply approximately 0.5 gram (500 milligrams) potassium:

Apricots, fresh–6	Figs–4	Prune juice–1 cup
Banana–1 medium	Lentils–⅓ cup	Prunes–7 large
Brussels sprouts,	Orange juice–½ cup	Squash, winter–¾ cup
cooked–10	Orange-grapefruit juice–	Raisins, dark–½ cup
Cantaloup–½	1¼ cups	Sweet potato–1 large
Dates–7 or 8	Potato, white–1 large	Tangerine juice–1¼ cups

(*J. Am. Dietetic Association,* April, 1970, p. 298.)

†From Address on *Trace Elements* to the Food Editors in Dallas, Texas, October 16, 1974, by Ann L. Burroughs, Ph.D., Associate Director, Biochemistry and Nutrition, Del Monte Corporation Research Center, Walnut Creek, California.

Zinc*

Zinc is required by humans. (A deficiency frequently causes hypogeusia—decreased sharpness of sense of taste—in both adults and children.) It is necessary for

1. The synthesis of insulin—refer to Figure 5–1.
2. Normal growth—17- to 21-year-old young Egyptian men and women had the appearance of 8- to 11-year-old-children: the girls did not ovulate and the boys did not produce spermatozoa.
3. Normal wound healing.

The recommended zinc allowance is 15 milligrams per day and the typical U.S. adult diet provides 12 to 15 milligrams; thus U.S. diets are providing marginal amounts of zinc.

The amount of zinc in a human's hair seems to be a good indication of zinc nutrition. Some patients with myocardial infarctions and atherosclerosis show subnormal hair zinc levels. Sources of zinc include oysters and shellfish, wheat germ, legumes, nuts, eggs, fish, meat, leafy vegetables, and milk. A food's high fiber content may interfere with zinc absorption. (*Never* use a zinc-coated (galvanized) container for mixing or storing acid foods, as toxic quantities of zinc go into solution.)

Other Minerals

Chlorine, sulfur, and magnesium are necessary for human life, but they are found in so many foods that they are supplied by most diets. Sulfur is found in the body cells, saliva, bile, and insulin. Protein foods are good sources of sulfur.

Traces of other elements such as copper, cobalt, manganese, molybdenum, arsenic, selenium, silicon, bromine, aluminum, and nickel are found in the body. Copper acts as a catalyst when iron becomes part of the hemoglobin.

Trace elements often are measured in parts per million† or parts per billion and may be obtained by eating a variety of foods. Supplementation with any mineral or vitamin will show improvement only if the individual has a deficiency of that particular mineral or vitamin. After intake is adequate, increasing amounts will not give further improvement and in some cases may produce toxic effects.

---

*From Address on *Trace Elements* to the Food Editors in Dallas, Texas, October 16, 1974, by Ann L. Burroughs, Ph.D., Associate Director, Biochemistry and Nutrition, Del Monte Corporation Research Center, Walnut Creek, California.

†Dr. Burroughs illustrates the ppm ratio by comparing 1 inch to 15.78 miles.

Acid-Base Balance

The symbol pH followed by a number shows the degree of acidity or alkalinity of a solution. A neutral solution has a pH of 7. A solution with a pH below 7 is acid. The blood is normally slightly alkaline, having a pH of 7.35 to 7.45. The pH of the stomach ranges from 1.8 to 4.5, that of the urine from 4.8 to 8.0. Fruits have a pH range of 3 to 6, so they normally would not influence stomach acidity.

The kidneys, which filter chemicals from the blood stream, are a major factor in maintaining normal body pH. Eating mostly acid ash or alkaline ash foods can change the pH of urine. The mineral content of the food determines its ash. The body readily makes the pH adjustments. Therefore, the reaction of the diet has no practical significance in health. Those who are greatly concerned about food acidity or alkalinity have been misinformed either by the food quack or by misleading advertising.

The sour taste of fruit is due to its organic acids, which are completely oxidized in the body to carbon dioxide and water. An alkaline ash remains after metabolism; therefore the taste of a food is not an indication of whether the body will use it to produce an alkaline or an acid residue. From Table 8–1, note that meat, eggs, and cereals, which do not have an acid taste, produce an acid ash. This is due to the kinds of minerals found in these foods.

Foods containing a preponderance of sulfur, phosphorus, and chlorine produce acid residue; those containing more sodium, potassium, calcium, and magnesium produce alkaline residue. Eating a variety of foods helps maintain the body's acid-base balance.

Table 8–1   *Reaction of Foods*

Acid Forming	Alkaline Forming	Neutral
Bread	Fruits	Butter
Cereals	All except prunes,	Coffee
Cheese	cranberries,	Cooking fats
Corn	and plums	Cream
Eggs	Milk	Starch
Fish	Molasses	Sugars
Fruits	Nuts	Syrup
Cranberries	Almond	Tapioca
Plums	Chestnut	Tea
Prunes	Coconut	
Lentils	Olives	
Mayonnaise	Vegetables	
Meat	Except corn	
Nuts		
Brazil		
Peanuts		
Walnuts		
Poultry		

SUGGESTED READING

Berland, Theodore: "Periodontal Disease: Hidden Threat to Grown-up's Teeth," *Today's Health*, August, 1969.

Committee on Iron Deficiency, Council on Foods and Nutrition: "Iron Deficiency in the United States," *J.A.M.A.*, February 5, 1968.

Crosby, William H., M.D.: "Intestinal Response to the Body's Requirement for Iron," *J.A.M.A.*, April 14, 1969.

Goulding, Peter C.: "Why Doctors Vote Yes to Fluoridation," *Today's Health*, October, 1965.

Lane, Mary Margaret: "The Origin and Prevention of Osteoporosis," *Nursing Homes*, 1968.

Maddox, Gaynor: "Iron-Rich Answers to Tired Food," *Today's Health*, April, 1970.

Stahl, S. Sigmund, D.D.S.: "Nutritional Influences on Periodontal Disease," *Food and Nutrition News*, National Livestock and Meat Board, February, 1969.

Swanson, Pearl: *Calcium in Nutrition*. National Dairy Council.

U.S. Department of Health, Education, and Welfare:
Facts About Osteoporosis. Public Health Service Publication No. 405, 1966.
Healthy Teeth. Public Health Service Publication No. 1217, 1965.

White, Philip L. and Hilda S.: "The Critical Question of Dietary Iron," *Food and Nutrition News*, National Livestock and Meat Board, April, 1968.

EXERCISES

1. Write a menu containing the basic-four except milk, cheese, and any food containing them. From Table A–1 determine if this menu gives the 0.8 gram of calcium recommended for an adult. Add two glasses of milk. Compare this calcium total with the recommended allowance.
2. Why might calcium be given to a patient before surgery?
3. As public health measures, what two minerals are added to widely used products?
4. In general, the darker the color of the food, the more _____ (which mineral?) it will contain.
5. Why might a doctor prescribe the daily use of a glass or more of milk for an adult complaining of leg cramps?
6. Why would it be incorrect to say, "I don't eat grapefruit because it makes my body acid"?
7. Why do carbohydrates and fats have a neutral pH?

Table 8-2   *Minerals*

	Function	Deficiency Symptoms	Sources
Calcium	Development of strong bones and teeth Help muscles contract and relax normally Utilization of iron Normal blood clotting Maintenance of body neutrality Normal action of heart muscle	Rickets Porous bones Bowed legs Stunted growth Slow clotting of blood Poor tooth formation Tetany	Milk, cheese Mustard, turnip greens Clams, oysters Broccoli, cauliflower, cabbage Molasses Small amount in egg, carrot, celery, orange, grapefruit, figs, and bread made with milk
Phosphorus	Development of bones and teeth Multiplication of cells Activation of some enzymes and vitamins Maintenance of body neutrality Participates in carbohydrate metabolism	Rickets Porous bones Bowed legs Stunted growth Poor tooth formation	Milk Cheese Meat Egg yolk Fish Nuts Whole grain cereals Legumes
Iron	Constituent of hemoglobin, which carries oxygen to the tissues	Nutritional anemia Pallor Weight loss Fatigue Weakness Retarded growth	Red meats, especially liver Green vegetables Yellow fruits Prunes Raisins Legumes Whole grain and enriched cereals Molasses Egg yolk Potatoes
Iodine	Constituent of thyroxin, which is a regulator of metabolism	Enlarged thyroid gland Low metabolic rate Stunted growth Retarded mental growth	Iodized salt Sea foods Foods grown in nongoiterous regions
Sodium	Constituent of extracellular fluid Maintenance of body neutrality Osmotic pressure Muscle and nerve irritability	Muscle cramps Weakness Headache Nausea Anorexia Vascular collapse	Sodium chloride (table salt) Sodium bicarbonate (baking powder, baking soda) Monosodium glutamate (Accent) Milk, cheese Meat, egg white
Fluorine	Resistance to dental caries Deposition of bone calcium		Water supply containing 1 p.p.m. Small amount in many foods
Potassium	Acid-base balance Carbohydrate metabolism Conduction of nerve impulses Contraction of muscle fibers	Apathy Muscular weakness Poor gastrointestinal tone Respiratory muscle failure Tachycardia Cardiac arrest	Whole grains Meat Legumes Some fruit and vegetables (See footnote page 80.)

Daily Recommendations

	Milligrams			Milligrams
CHILDREN			FEMALES	
1 to 3	800		15 to 18	1200
7 to 10	800		Over 18	800
MALES			Pregnant	1200
15 to 18	1200		Lactating	1200
Over 18	800			

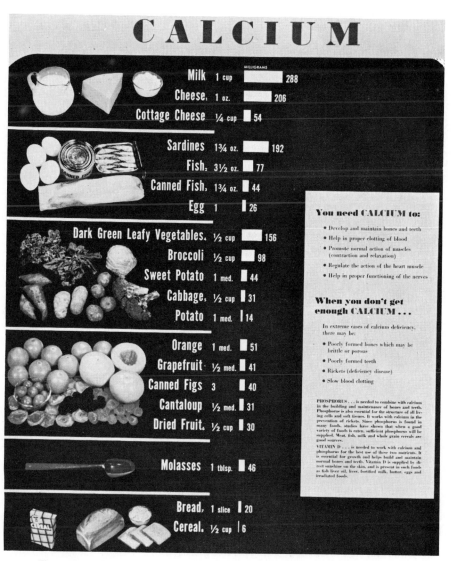

Figure 8–8 Calcium sources. (From National Live Stock and Meat Board.)

Daily Recommendations

	Milligrams		*Miligrams*
CHILDREN		FEMALES	
1 to 3	15	15 to 18	18
7 to 10	10	Over 18	18
MALES		Over 50	10
15 to 18	18	Pregnant	18+
Over 18	10	Lactating	18

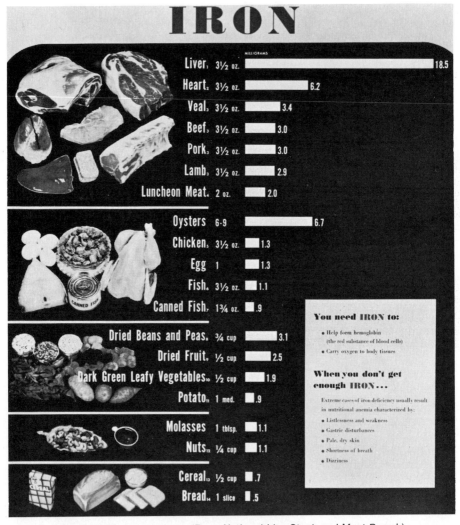

Figure 8–9   Iron sources. (From National Live Stock and Meat Board.)

CHAPTER 9

Vitamins

TERMS TO UNDERSTAND

Adverse	Dermatitis	Medication
Alopecia	Erythrocyte	Microbe
Ameloblast	Flora	Oral
Anorexia	Hemolysis	Peroxidation
Atrophy	Hepatomegaly	Provitamin
Azotemia	Hydrocephaly	Synthesis
Bilirubinemia	Hyperostosis	Tetany
Catalyst	Hypothesis	Toxic
Collagen	Kernicterus	
Concentrate		

The vitamins are chemical substances needed in very small quantities for growth and good health. They function in the absorption and utilization of the nutrients in food. This includes cell formation, blood clotting, wound healing, the integrity of the epithelial cells, to name a few. Foods which provide for the recommended allowance of vitamins A, B_1, B_2, C, and for children, D, will nearly always provide the other vitamins. The adult's body contains about one fourth ounce of vitamin compounds. Food is the natural source of vitamins. With modern food processing, the vitamin loss in the preparation of food is minimal. Vitamins can be lost when food is improperly stored or cooked and when food is refined.

There are two groups of vitamins—the fat-soluble vitamins A, D, E, and K and the water-soluble vitamins C and the B complex. The functions, deficiency symptoms, and the important food sources of the well-known vitamins are shown in Tables 9–1 and 9–2.

Avitaminosis is the deficiency disease due to lack of a vitamin. Avitaminosis is very seldom seen in the United States or Canada; however, there are a few people who have deficiency symptoms because they are not getting as much of the vitamins as they need.

In general, the fat-soluble vitamins

1. Are not destroyed by ordinary cooking methods.

87

Figure 9–1 "I've worked on vitamins for years and I've discovered that the three most important elements necessary to life are breakfast, lunch and dinner!" (Courtesy of George Lichty and the Chicago Sun-Times Syndicate.)

2. Are stored in the body.

3. Are destroyed by rancidity.

4. Are not absorbed if mineral oil is present in the intestine.

The water-soluble vitamins

1. May be affected by cooking methods.

2. Have little or no body storage.

3. Can be lost in varying quantities by discarding the water in which the food was cooked or soaked.

A few of the vitamins are synthesized in the intestine. Oral administration of some drugs, such as the sulfonamides or antibiotics, may interfere with the activity of the intestinal bacteria, thus reducing the synthesis.

Vitamin concentrates should be used only when a doctor prescribes them. They cannot take the place of food which contains other nutrients as well as vitamins. Vitamins are catalysts (like enzymes, which help with a reaction without becoming part of it). To get normal chemical reactions the other nutrients have to be present, too, as co-workers. If a vitamin is lacking or not present in sufficient quantities, the cell does not get the correct nutrition from the food. For example, the skin cells show dermatitis when niacin is lacking, and the capillaries of the circulatory system do not receive enough cementing substance when vitamin C is lacking and are therefore fragile and will allow hemorrhaging. Excess vitamins can upset metabolism. In some diseases and during drug therapy the concentrates are very useful medications, but when the emergency is over they should be discontinued as any other medication would be. It is possible that all of the vitamins have not been discovered so that a concentrate may not contain them.

The American Medical Association recommends that if a vitamin concentrate is taken daily no vitamin in it should be more concentrated than the amount listed in the table of recommended daily allowances in the table inside the front cover. A therapeutic vitamin preparation contains three to five times the recommended daily allowance and is used for treating specific vitamin deficiencies which can occur in some chronic diseases. "The decision to employ vitamin preparations in therapeutic amounts clearly rests with the physician. For example, the cause of an anemia is determined by the use of clinical and laboratory procedures; then the specific vitamin or therapeutic agent is prescribed. There is no reason to use preparations which contain most or all of the anti-anemic factors which include B_{12}, vitamin C, folic acid, iron, and copper. . . . The use of vitamin mixtures in the self-treatment of suspected disease is a dangerous procedure. An individual 'who always feels tired' should contact his physician rather than employ remedies glowingly advertised to the public."(12)

Fat-Soluble Vitamins

Vitamin A (Retinol)

True vitamin A is almost colorless (pale yellow) and is found in animal products such as fish liver oils, liver, milk fat, and egg yolk. It is

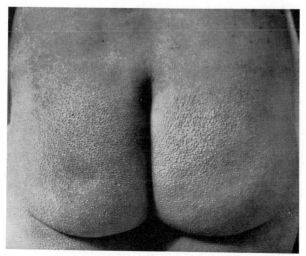

Figure 9–2. Vitamin A deficiency—follicular hyperkeratosis. (Reproduced by courtesy of Section of Dermatology and Syphilology, Mayo Clinic.)

added to fortified margarine. Its provitamin, or precursor, which is called carotene, is yellow, is insoluble in water, and is not absorbed so readily as vitamin A. (A provitamin, or precursor, is a substance the body can make into a vitamin.) Their carotene content would make green vegetables yellow if the dark green chlorophyll color did not predominate. Animal fats can contain varying amounts of the precursor as well as vitamin A. The precursor could make some milk more yellow than others but not necessarily higher in the total possible value of vitamin A.

Functions of vitamin A are as follows:

1. To assist in the synthesis of mucous secretions which keep the epithelial tissues from shrinking, hardening, and degenerating. The epithelial tissues are found in the outer surface of the skin, in the lining of the internal cavities of the nose, mouth, and respiratory and digestive tracts, and in the organs. Although healthy membranes resist microbe invasion, the addition of vitamin A to the diet will not cure an infection already present in the body.

2. To maintain normal vision in dim light. Visual purple (rhodopsin) in the retina of the eye is decomposed in bright light and restored with the help of vitamin A. Difficulty in adjusting to dim light or the glare of an automobile headlight is due to the slow regeneration of visual purple. This condition is called night blindness, or nyctalopia. (See Figure 9–3.)

A

Figure 9–3   Vitamin A deficiency—night blindness. Both the normal individual and the vitamin A-deficient subject see the headlights of an approaching car as shown in *A*. After the car has passed the normal individual sees a wide stretch of road, as it appears in *B*.

Illustration continued on opposite page

B

C

Figure 9–3 *Continued.* The vitamin A-deficient subject, whose view of the road is shown in *C*, can barely see a few feet ahead and cannot see the road sign at all. (Courtesy of The Upjohn Company: *Vitamin Manual,* 1961.)

3. To produce normally functioning ameloblasts. These enamel-producing epithelial cells do not yield a sound tooth structure unless vitamin A is present.

4. To promote normal growth. The synthesis of protein is adversely affected by a deficiency of vitamin A.

Vitamin A is stored in the liver. Excessive intake causes toxicity in both children and adults. "Regular ingestion of more than 2000 retinal equivalents (6700 I.U.*) of preformed vitamin A above that already in the diet should be carefully monitored by a physician. Excessive intake of carotenes is not harmful but may result in a yellow coloration of the skin that disappears when the carotenoid intake is reduced." (53:54) Deficiency and toxicity symptoms of vitamin A are listed in Table 9–1.

Vitamin D (Calciferol, 7-Dehydrocholesterol)

The adult vitamin D requirement can be met by skin irradiation. Therefore the need for ingested vitamin D is influenced by the amount of skin exposure to ultraviolet light.

Functions of vitamin D are the following:

1. To aid in normal skeletal development. Without vitamin D bones do not calcify properly. For good bone and tooth development calcium, phosphorus, and protein as well as vitamins A, C, and D must be present in the diet. In the child, ·poor bone calcification is called rickets; in the adult, osteomalacia. Osteomalacia is often seen in women who have frequent pregnancies and poor diets. A deficiency in vitamin D may result in teeth which are more susceptible to caries.

2. To facilitate the absorption of calcium and phosphorus. Insufficient calcium in the body results in tetany and affects skeletal development.

In general, natural foods contain insignificant amounts of vitamin D. Vitamin D has two precursors, ergosterol, found in plant life, and cholesterol, found in animal tissues. These substances are converted into vitamin D by action of ultraviolet rays. Viosterol is irradiated ergosterol in oil. Crystalline D is called calciferol. Ultraviolet rays of the sun or of lamps react with the skin cholesterol to give the body vitamin D. Clothing, fog, smoke, and window glass filter our ultraviolet rays. There is no recommended allowance of vitamin D for adults. For children and pregnant and nursing women, the allowance is 400 I.U., which is the amount in one quart of "fortified," or vitamin D, milk. "Excessive intakes of vitamin D are dangerous and should be avoided. Amounts of vitamin D above 2000

---

*International Units. A potency measurement of the ability to promote growth or to cure a deficiency when test doses are fed to animals. The result of this "bioassay" is expressed in units.

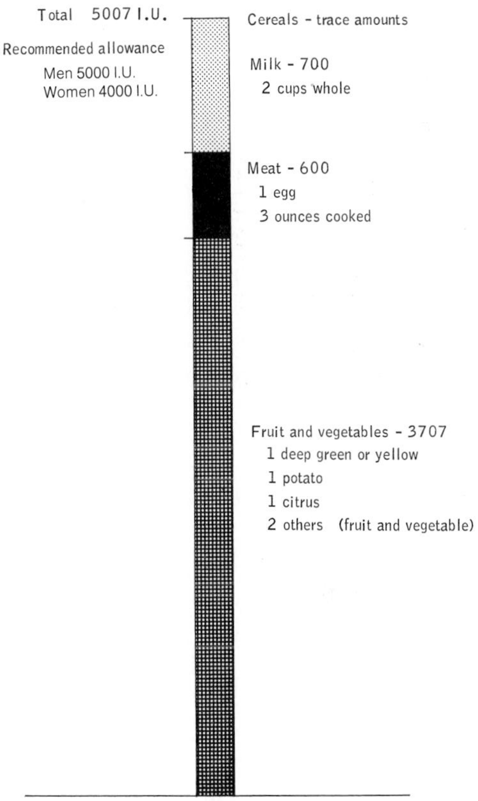

Total 5007 I.U.

Recommended allowance
Men 5000 I.U.
Women 4000 I.U.

Cereals – trace amounts

Milk – 700
2 cups whole

Meat – 600
1 egg
3 ounces cooked

Fruit and vegetables – 3707
1 deep green or yellow
1 potato
1 citrus
2 others   (fruit and vegetable)

Figure 9–4   Vitamin A supplied by the basic-four. See
Table A-4.

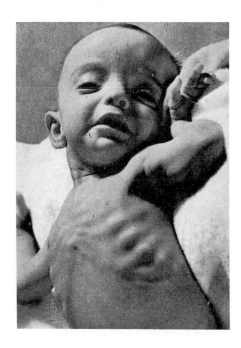

Figure 9–5   Child with vitamin
D deficiency—rachitic rosary. (Lyon,
R. A., and Wallinger, E. M.: *Mitchell's
Pediatrics and Pediatric Nursing,* 4th
Ed.)

Table 9-1 *Fat-Soluble Vitamins*

	Deficiency Symptoms	Toxicity Symptoms	Important Sources	Characteristics
Vitamin A (retinol) (carotene-precursor)	Night & glare blindness; Inflammation of the eye; Rough, scaly skin; Dry mucous membranes, causing a general lowered resistance to microbe invasion; Poor tooth formation	Anorexia; Fatigue; Weight loss; Irritability; Skin lesions; Joint and bone pains; Spleen and liver enlargement; Loss of hair; Increased intracranial pressure	Liver and liver sausage; Butter, cream, whole milk; Egg yolks; Green & yellow vegetables; Yellow fruits; Ripe tomatoes; Fortified margarine; Fish liver oils	Mineral oil interferes with absorption; Stable to acid and alkali; Destroyed by wilting; Destroyed by rancidity; Stable to heat by the usual cooking methods but slowly destroyed by exposure to air, heat, drying; Stored in the liver; Bile is necessary for absorption
Vitamin D (calciferol)	Soft bones; Bowed legs; Poor teeth; Lowered amount of calcium & phosphorus in the blood; Poor posture	Anorexia; Fatigue; Weight loss; Nausea and vomiting; Diarrhea and polyuria; Weakness; Headache; Renal damage; Calcification in the soft tissues of the heart, blood vessels, lungs, stomach, renal tubules	Vitamin D milk; Small amounts in butter, egg yolk, liver, salt water fish; Fish liver oils	Stable to heat and oxidation; Destroyed by rancidity; Skin synthesis by activity of ultraviolet light on cholesterol; Stored in the liver; Enhances absorption of calcium and phosphorus
Vitamin E (tocopherol)			Vegetable oils; Green leafy vegetables; Margarine; Egg yolk; Milk fat; Nuts; Wheat germ oil	Stable to light and heat, except deep fat frying; Destroyed by rancidity; Destroyed by ultraviolet irradiation; Is a strong antioxidant; Synthesis in the intestine
Vitamin K (menadione)	Prolonged clotting time of the blood; Hemorrhagic disease in newborn	Hyperbilirubinemia; In infants: Jaundice; Kernicterus; Mild hemolytic anemia	Green leafy vegetables; Liver; Cauliflower; Cabbage	Easily destroyed by light, alkali; Fairly stable to heat, oxygen; Synthesis in the intestine; Mineral oil interferes with absorption

I.U. per day (5 times the child's recommended daily allowance) for prolonged periods have produced hypercalcemia in infants and nephrocalcinosis in infants and adults. It should be emphasized that ingestion of vitamin D in excess of recommended amounts provides no benefit and that large excesses are potentially harmful." (53:56)

Vitamin E (Tocopherols)

The exact way in which vitamin E functions in the body is unknown, but it appears to be needed to insure the stability and integrity of membranes. There is little transfer of vitamin E through the placenta, so newborn infants have little tissue concentration. Human milk meets the infant's needs for tocopherol but cow's milk, which has a relatively low content, is not adequate. Liver disease and pancreatic insufficiency affect the body's ability to absorb vitamin E. Likewise, ingestion of mineral oil reduces the amount of vitamin E absorbed.

The tocopherol in fat tends to reduce oxidation and thus retard rancidity; commercially, vitamin E is often added to food to help stabilize nutrients. This strong antioxidant property may account for its usefulness to the animal body. To date, the role of vitamin E in human metabolism has not been demonstrated, but there are several possibilities.

1. Vitamin E may protect the erythrocytes from hemolysis. Malnourished infants with macrocytic anemia have responded to vitamin E therapy. (61:86)

2. Vitamin E may protect vitamin A from oxidation in the intestine and thus could be said to spare vitamin A.

3. When the diet is high in polyunsaturated fats, particularly linoleic acid, more vitamin E is needed.

4. Vitamin E may have a role in the aging of cells. Tappel states this hypothesis:

At a time when our hopes are rising that we have found, in the polyunsaturated fats, dietary means of combating atherosclerosis, evidence has also been discovered that these same beneficial fats may well be a primary source of radicals within the cell that cause it to age. For example, when radiant energy, which can penetrate throughout the body entering every cell, strikes a polyunsaturated lipid that is present as a nutrient, one of two things happen. If enough vitamin E is present, the radiation will have little effect. If, however, there is an intracellular deficiency of vitamin E, the energetic rays will strike a lipid molecule and knock loose a hydrogen atom. This would typically initiate the peroxidation of polyunsaturated lipid. Peroxidation involves the direct reaction of oxygen and lipid to form free radical intermediates. The free radical flies about within the cell under terrific force and without any pattern to its movement until it strikes another molecule and causes all sorts of damage. Lipid peroxidation is, therefore, widely regarded as the main spring in the aging process.

Free radical damage isn't just an isolated incident; it is occurring all the time in the body. Perhaps the reason that some people look older than their years is that they have been more vulnerable to this damage than those who don't show their age. In any event, when enough cells are affected, the host looks old and soon succumbs to disease.

These events all take place at the most fundamental level of cellular physiology because they begin with molecular reactions involving vital cell constituents. As the process continues and becomes more widespread, structural damage to parts of the cell increases. This is followed by malfunction of the chemical mechanisms in the cell that controls its normal physiology and that disposes of its damaged parts. When this sequence is completed, the cell is old and decrepit. It either is unable to function properly or dies, and the man, woman or child is one cell older. (75:2–3)

Vitamin E is related to the reproductive cycle in rats, but it has not been demonstrated to be related to human reproduction.

Vitamin E is so widely distributed in foods that there is little chance of a deficiency in a normal human diet. Good food sources include vegetable oils, leafy green vegetables, milk, eggs, meat, fish, and cereals. In the United States, 64 per cent of the vitamin E is supplied by the intake of salad oil, shortening, and margarine; 11 per cent by fruits and vegetables; and 7 per cent by grain products.* The oils which are a good source of polyunsaturates are usually also a good source of tocopherol.

Vitamin K (Menadione, Phylloquinone)

Like vitamin E, vitamin K is so widely distributed in nature that it would almost be impossible for one not to eat adequate amounts. Vitamin K helps in the production of prothrombin, a substance necessary for the coagulation of blood. If hemorrhage occurs in the patient who has been

---

*NRC: Publication No. 1694, 1968.

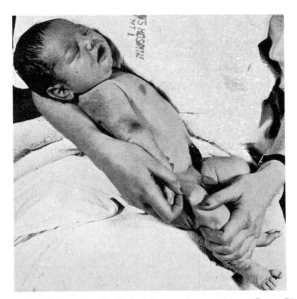

Figure 9–6 Child with vitamin K deficiency—hemorrhage. (From Bicknell, F., and Prescott, F.: *The Vitamins in Medicine.* London, William Heinemann Medical Books, Ltd.)

given an anticoagulant, vitamin K may be among the medications used. The anticoagulant property of dicoumarol is due to its ability to block the action of vitamin K.

Vitamin K is synthesized by intestinal bacteria. The newborn infant has a sterile intestine so his supply of vitamin K may be inadequate until the normal intestinal flora are established. K is often administered particularly to the premature infant, immediately after birth. The practice of giving K to the mother in labor has been discontinued, since too much K may lead to hemolytic anemia in the infant. The use of oral antibiotics and sulfa drugs interferes with intestinal synthesis.

Menadione, synthetic vitamin K, has water-soluble derivatives. All forms of vitamin K should be kept in dark bottles because the vitamin is sensitive to light and radiation. Food sources include green, leafy vegetables, cabbage, liver, cauliflower, with smaller amounts in tomatoes, egg yolk, and whole milk products.

Since bile salts aid in the absorption of A, D, E, and K, liver disease may affect the amounts of these vitamins absorbed from the intestine.

Water-Soluble Vitamins

The water-soluble vitamins are affected by cooking methods. A portion of these vitamins is dissolved in the cooking or soaking water. The larger the piece of food cooked, the less the loss into the cooking water. Overcooking of meat and vegetables also results in some loss.

The functions of the B complex (group) vitamins are closely related, and each works with the other members of the B complex. A deficient or excessive intake of any one of the group may impair the utilization of the others in the group. The members of the B group tend to be found in the same foods. Therefore, if deficiency symptoms are observed, they will usually be the result of deficiency in several vitamins rather than one. As a group they help provide the ability to obtain energy from food. Some are involved in the metabolism of a specific nutrient; for example, B_1 is involved in the metabolism of carbohydrates.

If there are adequate thiamin, riboflavin, and niacin in the diet, there probably will be adequate B complex intake.

Whole grain cereals are a good source of the B complex vitamins. The center part of the grain is mostly starch; the bran layer contains cellulose, B vitamins, minerals, especially iron and phosphorus, and some incomplete protein; the germ contains B vitamins, incomplete protein, fat, vitamin E, and iron. When a cereal is refined, the bran layer and germ are removed, which means that the refined cereals keep better (no fat to become rancid), but the nutrient value is greatly reduced.

Much of the flour and cereal on the market has been enriched. To enrich a cereal, thiamine, or B_1, riboflavin, or B_2, niacin, and iron are added to the refined cereal. (See Figure 32–2.) "Restored" is a term referring to the replacement of some nutrients removed during refining. The cereal label usually states what nutrient and how much has been restored. The term "fortified" refers to the addition of one or more nutrients not originally found in the food, such as vitamin D (fortified) milk.

Surveys made in the United States and Newfoundland indicate that eating enriched cereals contributes to better health. This enrichment program, which was started during World War II, is an excellent one because it has helped improve the health of the population of these two areas.

Thiamine (B_1)

People who severely restrict their thiamine, or vitamin B_1, intake (for example, people who, to lose weight, omit milk, cereals, and meat from their diets) may suffer mental depression, become moody, quarrelsome, and uncooperative; however, the addition of thiamine to the diet does not cure mental disorders.

Other than depression, symptoms of thiamine deficiency are the following:
1. Fatigue.
2. Irritability.
3. Lack of appetite.
4. Atonic constipation.
5. Muscle cramps.
6. Nerve pains. The central nervous system gets its energy from glucose. Without thiamine for normal cabohydrate metabolism, neural activity diminishes, resulting in apathy, fatigue, and degeneration of myelin nerve sheaths, which results in nerve pain and prickly sensations.
7. Weakness and a feeling of heaviness in the legs. This is followed by calf muscle cramps and loss of ankle and knee jerk reflexes. In beriberi walking becomes progressively more difficult, leg muscles atrophy, and finally there is paralysis of the legs. With laboratory animals the paralysis has been reversed within a few hours after feedings foods high in thiamine.

Body thiamine needs are calculated in relation to calorie intake, particularly carbohydrate intake. Thiamine is often given concurrently with glucose intravenous solutions.

Thiamine loss during cooking varies widely, but it is increased with high temperatures, prolonged cooking or overcooking, discarding of water in which the food was cooked, and presence in the food of an alkali such as baking soda. Good food sources are listed in Table 9–2.

Riboflavin (B_2)

Riboflavin is destroyed on exposure to light. If a milk bottle is left standing on the doorstep for two hours more than two thirds of the

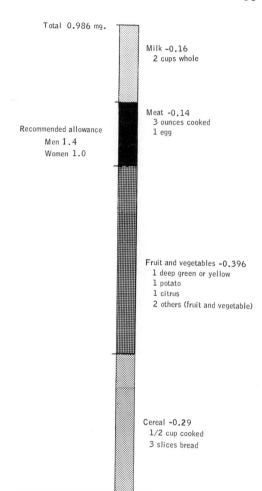

Figure 9-7 Thiamine supplied by the basic-four. See Table A-4.

riboflavin can be destroyed; the use of cardboard cartons and colored bottles reduces riboflavin losses. One report indicates that, under ordinary store conditions, enriched white bread wrapped in clear cellophane paper loses 30 to 60 per cent more vitamin B_2 than that wrapped in opaque waxed paper. (37:793)

The need for B_2 is related to body size, rate of growth, and metabolic rate because riboflavin is needed for cell respiration of carbohydrate, protein, and fat. Riboflavin deficiencies usually occur in conjunction with protein and other B complex vitamin deficiencies.

Ariboflavinosis is marked by tissue breakdown, and the symptoms include the following:

1. The mouth has cracks at the corners that are symptoms of a condition called cheilosis.

2. The eyes are sensitive to light and are easily fatigued; they itch

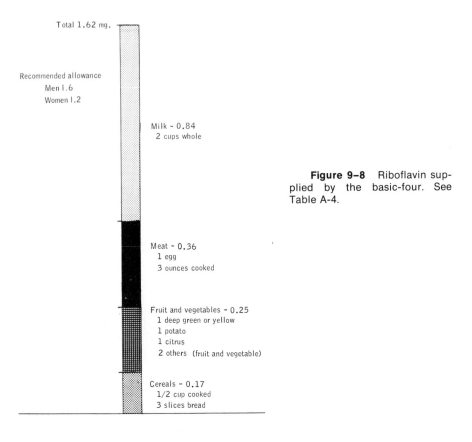

Total 1.62 mg.

Recommended allowance
Men 1.6
Women 1.2

Milk - 0.84
2 cups whole

Figure 9–8 Riboflavin supplied by the basic-four. See Table A-4.

Meat - 0.36
1 egg
3 ounces cooked

Fruit and vegetables - 0.25
1 deep green or yellow
1 potato
1 citrus
2 others (fruit and vegetable)

Cereals - 0.17
1/2 cup cooked
3 slices bread

and water, and vision is blurred. The bloodshot appearance is due to increased corneal capillary degeneration.

3. The lips and tongue are swollen and have a shiny, purplish-red appearance as a result of glossitis.

4. The skin has greasy eruptions which occur especially in the skin folds and around the nose.

Common cooking procedures do not greatly affect riboflavin retention but using baking soda is deleterious, as is exposure of foods to light. Food sources are listed in Table 9–2.

Niacin (Nicotinamide)

Niacin deficiency symptoms occur chiefly in the skin, gastrointestinal tract, and nervous system:

1. Early signs include fatigue, listlessness, anorexia, weight loss, headache, and backache.

2. The tongue and lips become abnormally red; the mouth and tongue are so sore it is difficult to eat.

3. There is diarrhea which results in dehydration.

Table 9–2 *Water-Soluble Vitamins*

	Deficiency Symptoms	Important Sources	Characteristics
Vitamin C (ascorbic acid)	Sore mouth Stiff, aching joints Weak-walled capillaries (hemorrhages in joints, muscles, subcutaneous tissue, gums) Lassitude Impaired wound healing Improper bone and cartilage development	Fresh fruits, especially citrus, strawberries, cantaloup Canned fruit juices Tomatoes, fresh or canned Raw vegetables, especially greens, cabbage, broccoli, peppers Potatoes Ascorbic acid tablets	Very soluble in water Most easily destroyed vitamin Destroyed by heat, alkali, aging, drying, oxidation Acid inhibits destruction Copper accelerates destruction Very little lost in commercial canning and quick freezing Very little stored in body
Vitamin B_1 (thiamine)	Anorexia Fatigue Constipation, atonic Depression Irritability Tenderness of the leg calf with some loss of muscular coordination Abnormal carbohydrate metabolism	Meat, especially pork Whole grain & enriched cereals Organs, especially liver Nuts and peanut butter Legumes, especially soy beans Milk, dairy foods Eggs Brewer's yeast & wheat germ	Stable in the dry form Quickly destroyed by heat in neutral & alkaline solutions Destroyed by sulfites & alkali Limited intestinal synthesis Very little stored in body
Vitamin B_2 (riboflavin)	Burning & itching eyes Blurred & dim vision Eyes sensitive to light Inflammation of the lips and the tongue Lesions in the angles of the mouth Digestive disturbances Greasy, scaly skin	Milk, dairy foods Organs, especially liver Meat, legumes Eggs Enriched & whole grain cereals Green leafy vegetables Brewer's yeast, liver concentrates	Destroyed by light, alkali Stable to heat, acids Very limited body storage
Niacin (tryptophan – precursor)	Fatigue Dermatitis Sore mouth, especially the tongue Gastrointestinal disturbances (diarrhea and vomiting) Nervous disturbances Mental depression Weakness Anorexia	Meat, especially liver Fish Poultry Whole grain & enriched cereals Nuts Legumes, peanuts Brewer's yeast, liver concentrates	Stable to heat, light, acids, alkali Very limited body storage Body synthesis 60 mg. tryptophan equivalent to 1 mg. niacin

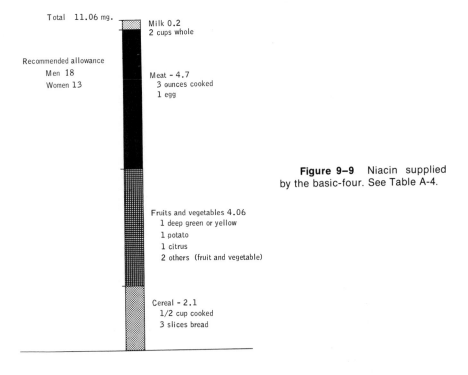

Total 11.06 mg.

Milk 0.2
2 cups whole

Recommended allowance
Men 18
Women 13

Meat - 4.7
3 ounces cooked
1 egg

Figure 9–9   Niacin supplied
by the basic-four. See Table A-4.

Fruits and vegetables 4.06
1 deep green or yellow
1 potato
1 citrus
2 others (fruit and vegetable)

Cereal - 2.1
1/2 cup cooked
3 slices bread

4. There is a characteristic dermatitis, especially of those body areas exposed to light. At first the skin is tender, swollen, and red; if niacin does not become available, the skin becomes rough, cracked, scaly, and ulcerated. Sunshine aggravates the dermatitis.

5. Neurological symptoms appear: mental confusion, dizziness, irritability, hallucinations, and delusions of persecution.

6. Anemia may accompany niacin deficiency.

Severe niacin deficiency leads to pellagra, or the "3-D disease" (depression or dementia, dermatitis, particularly on skin exposed to light, and diarrhea). The enrichment of cereals and greater diversification of the diet have helped lower the incidence of pellagra. People who subsist primarily on corn products may show pellagra symptoms because corn is low in niacin and also in the proteins which contain tryptophan. The "3-M diet" (meat, in the form of salt pork, which is mostly fat, molasses, and maize) may lead to pellagra.

Niacin is the water-soluble vitamin for which toxicity symptoms have been recorded. Because of its vasodilating properties, niacin in large doses causes skin flushing, dizziness, and head throbbing. Other side effects which have been observed are dryness of the skin, brown pigmentation, decreased glucose tolerance, and a tendency for serum uric acid levels to rise slightly. (32:171)

Unless the cooking water is discarded niacin is retained in the food;

the amino acid, tryptophan, is a precursor of niacin. Good food sources are listed in Table 9-2.

Pantothenic Acid

In humans, the function of pantothenic acid is related to carbohydrate, protein, and fat metabolism, synthesis of cholesterol and steroid hormones, and the functioning of the adrenal cortex. It is found in both plant and animal foods.

Pantothenic acid sources are meat, especially organ meats, fish, egg yolk, peanuts and peanut butter, broccoli, cauliflower, sweet potatoes, peas, cabbage, potatoes, and whole grain cereals.

It does not correct the graying of hair in humans even though the graying of rats' and dogs' hair is often reversed when pantothenic acid is restored to their diet.

Biotin

Biotin participates in the metabolism of carbohydrates, fatty acids, and amino acids. Intestinal synthesis probably forms enough biotin for our needs. It is widely distributed in foods, especially egg yolk, milk, molasses, organs, and tomatoes. A deficiency of biotin can be caused by adding to the diet large quantities of raw egg white. A deficiency does not occur except under highly abnormal conditions and then is characterized by dermatitis, nausea, vomiting, depression, and loss of appetite.

Pyridoxine (B_6, Pyridoxal, Pyridoxamine)

Pyridoxine is a catalyst in carbohydrate, protein, and fat metabolism (a high-protein diet increases the need for vitamin B_6), in the conversion of tryptophan to niacin, and in the conversion of linoleic acid to arachidonic acid. Infants fed formulas low in B_6 were irritable, had muscle twitching, and developed convulsive seizures. The ordinary mixed diet provides the recommended allowance; however, when deficiencies are experimentally produced, the symptoms are anemia, dizziness, irritability, confusion, kidney stones, convulsions, and anorexia.

The use of oral steroid contraceptives results in increased urinary excretion of tryptophan metabolites. The diet does not provide enough B_6 to prevent or correct these changes in women taking steroid contraceptives. (53:76)

Pyridoxine is heat stable but sensitive to light and alkalies. Isoniazid is an antagonist of B_6; therefore, pyridoxine is given to tuberculosis patients receiving this chemotherapy.

Food sources are whole grain cereals, especially wheat, corn, and

brown rice; meat, especially organ meats; and soy beans, peanuts, tomatoes. Small amounts are found in milk, eggs, and vegetables.

Folacin (Folic Acid, Pteroylmonoglutamic Acid)

Folacin deficiency results in glossitis, diarrhea, and megaloblastic anemia. The megaloblasts, young red blood cells, fail to mature during folic
acid deficiency. Currently, non-prescription multivitamin preparations
cannot contain more than 0.1 milligram of folacin per daily dose. Higher
dosage might prevent the diagnosis of pernicious anemia; blood cell regeneration occurs, but the degenerative neurological damage of pernicious anemia continues. Protein malnutrition may impair the utilization
and function of folacin.

Folic acid requirements are increased during pregnancy. To prevent
any fetal damage, the intake is doubled. Both human milk and cow's milk
provide the infant with ample folic acid, but if goat's milk is used, folic
acid supplementation should be given. (53)

Folacin is used in the treatment of megaloblastic anemia and is used
in conjunction with B_{12} in the treatment of sprue.

Many foods contain folic acid, but glandular meats, green leafy vegetables, and yeast are particularly good sources. It is synthesized in the intestine, but not in sufficient quantities to meet body needs.

Cobalamin (B_{12})

Vitamin B_{12} controls both the blood-forming defect and the neurological involvement of pernicious anemia. B_{12} is involved with carbohydrate, protein, and fat metabolism, nucleic and folic acid metabolism, and
the normal functioning of all cells—particularly those in the bone marrow, the nervous system, and the gastrointestinal tract. Persons living
exclusively on vegetables "may develop sore tongue, paresthesis, amenor-
rhea, low serum vitamin B_{12} levels, and signs of degeneration of the spinal
cord as a result of the low intake of B_{12}, but anemia is uncommon in this
group." (53)

The intrinsic factor in the gastric secretions must be available if B_{12},
the extrinsic factor, is to be absorbed through the ileum. Persons with a
total gastrectomy are given B_{12} shots. The ability to absorb B_{12} seems to
decrease with age. This vitamin is stored in the body.

B_{12} comes from foods of animal origin. Organ meats, especially liver,
lean meat, eggs, and dairy products are the best sources. The vitamin is
quite stable to cooking, but severe heating of meat may cause degradation.

Ascorbic Acid (C)

Many animals can synthesize ascorbic acid, but humans cannot and therefore require it in their diet. Men and boys often do not eat as many foods high in vitamin C as women and girls. Elderly people may omit the citrus fruits because they incorrectly believe the fruit will make their body too acid.

Scurvy, the vitamin C deficiency disease, can be prevented by the minimal daily intake of 10 milligrams. (An orange three inches in diameter will supply about 70 milligrams.)

Other functions of ascorbic acid include

1. Production of collagen (intercellular cement compound), which holds cells in their proper relation to each other. The development and maintenance of capillary walls, tooth dentine, cartilage, bones, and connective tissues depend upon the formation of collagen. Proper wound healing is also dependent upon collagen.

2. Reduction of ferric iron to ferrous iron in the gastrointestinal tract so that the iron is more readily absorbed.

3. Formation of red blood cells in bone marrow.

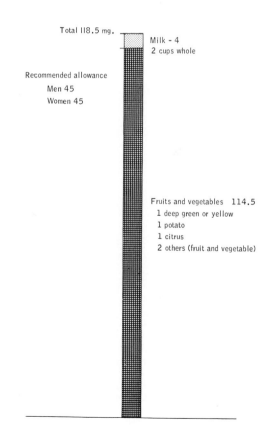

Total 118.5 mg.

Milk – 4
2 cups whole

Recommended allowance
Men 45
Women 45

Fruits and vegetables 114.5
1 deep green or yellow
1 potato
1 citrus
2 others (fruit and vegetable)

Figure 9–10   Ascorbic acid supplied by the basic-four. See Table A-4.

4. Metabolism of the amino acids phenylalanine and tyrosine. It may be involved in the synthesis of steroid hormones from cholesterol.

Some research has associated large doses of vitamin C with severe di-

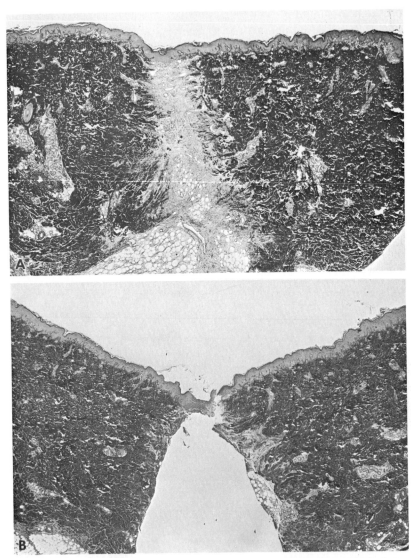

Figure 9–11 Impaired wound healing. The first satisfactorily controlled experiment in human scurvy was conducted when J. H. Crandon placed himself on an ascorbic acid–free diet, supplemented by all other known vitamins, for six months. After he was on the diet for three months, when the ascorbic acid level in the blood had been zero for 44 days, a wound was made in the midback region. *A,* Biopsy 10 days after this wound shows healing that clinically and pathologically appeared normal, but comparison with *C* indicates that it was probably suboptimal. After six months of the scorbutic diet another wound was made. *B,* Biopsy 10 days after second wound shows no healing except of the epithelium (gap in tissues was filled with a blood clot).

Illustration continued on opposite page

Figure 9–11 *Continued.* *C,* After 10 days of ascorbic acid treatment another biopsy of the second wound shows healing with abundant collagen formation—considerably more than occurred in the first wound. (From The Upjohn Company: *Vitamin Manual,* 1961.)

arrhea, oxalate renal stones, and false indications of sugar levels when testing the diabetic's urine. (73)

Vitamin C is the most easily destroyed vitamin but is less quickly destroyed in acid foods. For maximum retention of vitamin C in food the following should be observed (if these practices can conserve an easily destroyed nutrient, they will help retain other nutrients, too):

1. Refrigerate or store food in a cool, dark place. Cover to reduce oxidation.

2. If possible cook vegetables without peeling and in large pieces. The greater the cut surface, the greater the loss of water-soluble nutrients.

3. Cook in as little water as possible. Use the cooking water and juice in canned foods that contain water-soluble nutrients.

4. Cook vegetables in the shortest time possible and serve immediately. Cooking time is shorter if vegetables are started in boiling water. Long cooking, reheating, and stirring cause greater loss of any nutrient which oxidizes.

5. Do not use baking soda when cooking vegetables. Alkalies destroy some nutrients.

6. The metals copper and iron tend to increase the loss of vitamin C. Use plastic, glass, stainless steel, or aluminum utensils when preparing and cooking foods containing appreciable amounts of ascorbic acid.

Very little C is lost if food is processed properly. Figure 9–12 shows that there is very little difference in the amount of ascorbic acid in fresh,

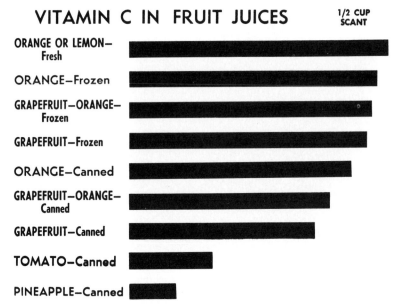

Figure 9–12   Vitamin C in fruit juices. (From Health Education Division, The Fife-Hamill Memorial Health Center, Philadelphia.)

frozen, and canned orange juice. Storing frozen juice above 0° F or leaving a can open, or leaving fresh juice unrefrigerated and uncovered, does cause loss.

The citrus fruits and their substitutes are good sources of vitamin C. (See Table 9–2.)

Vitamin research is continuing, and at the present time researchers are studying the functions of several substances.

Although vitamin concentrates are taken by some people in the belief that they help prevent or will cure a cold, "The truth is that supplementary vitamins—in or out of cold remedies—can neither keep you from getting a cold nor help you once you have it." (17:87) The cold is highly contagious. On the average, an American contracts two or three colds a year. Illness resulting from colds causes an estimated billion dollar annual loss to business. Sound precautions to reduce the number and severity of colds include avoiding close contact with those who have colds and keeping in good physical condition. Infections occur more frequently when body resistance is low. Adequate sleep, exercise, and a nourishing diet (the inclusion of the basic-four food groups) provide good insurance against colds.

Foods which contribute only empty calories should not be fortified—for example adding vitamin C to soft drinks or thiamine and niacin to alcohol because we see cases of scurvy, alcoholic beriberi, and alcoholic pellagra. If we ate a greater variety of foods, further enrichment and fortification programs probably would be unnecessary; food variety should provide an intake of those nutrients for which we do not know the amount needed.

Antivitamins (Vitamin Antagonists)

Antivitamins are substances which inactivate vitamins, interfere with their absorption or their synthesis. Excess raw egg white contains avidin, a compound which combines with biotin and prevents its absorption. Oral antibiotics destroy normal bacterial intestinal flora, thus inhibiting synthesis of vitamin K and some of the B vitamins. More research is needed in this area.

SUGGESTED READING

American Medical Association:
  Council on Foods and Nutrition: "Vitamin Preparations as Dietary Supplements and Therapeutic Agents," *J.A.M.A.*, *169*:41, January 3, 1959.
  Vitamin Supplements and Their Correct Use.
Bogert, L. Jean, et al.: *Nutrition and Physical Fitness*, 1973.
Cooley, Donald G.: "What is a Vitamin?" *Today's Health*, January, 1963.
DHEW Publications:
  No. 73–3021: *The Pill*, 1974.
  No. 74–2004: *Vitamin E – Miracle or Myth*, 1974.
  No. 73–7018: *Vitamins, Minerals, and FDA*, 1974.
National Dairy Council: *The Great Vitamin Mystery.*
U.S. Department of Agriculture: *Food for Us All: The Yearbook of Agriculture*, 1969, pp. 254–259.

EXERCISES

1. What vitamin is usually added in the manufacture of margarine? To milk?
2. Which vitamins would be reduced under the following conditions?
    (a) cabbage shredded several hours before serving
    (b) rancid cod liver oil
    (c) adding baking soda to cream of tomato soup
    (d) uncovered, non-refrigerated glass of orange juice
    (e) discarding meat drippings
3. Why is it misleading to say that vitamin A is an anti-infection vitamin?

See figures on the following pages

Daily Recommendations
International Units

CHILDREN		FEMALES	
1 to 3	2000	Over 11	4000
7 to 10	3300	Pregnant	5000
MALES		Lactating	6000
Over 11	5000		

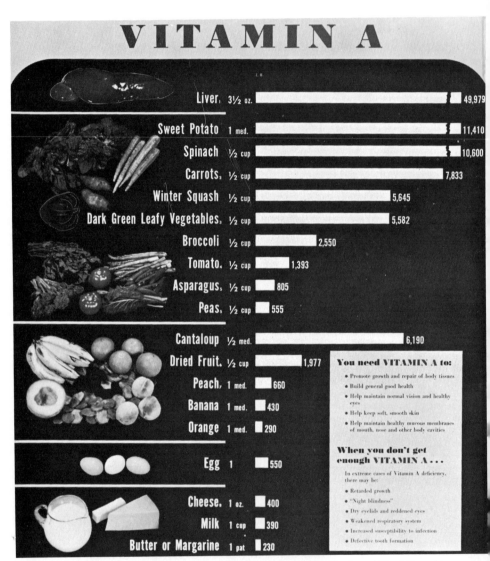

Figure 9–13 Vitamin A sources. (From National Live Stock and Meat Board.)

Daily Recommendations

CHILDREN	Milligrams	FEMALES	Milligrams
1 to 3	0.7	15 to 18	1.1
7 to 10	1.2	Over 23	1.0
MALES		Pregnant	+0.3
15 to 18	1.5	Lactating	+0.3
Over 23	1.4		

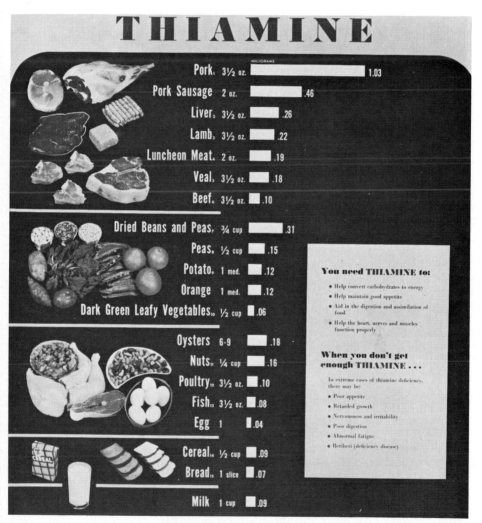

Figure 9–14   Vitamin B₁ sources. (From National Live Stock and Meat Board.)

Daily Recommendations

	Milligrams			*Milligrams*
CHILDREN			FEMALES	
1 to 3	0.8		15 to 18	1.4
7 to 10	1.2		Over 23	1.2
MALES			Pregnant	+0.3
15 to 18	1.8		Lactating	+0.5
Over 23	1.6			
Over 51	1.5			

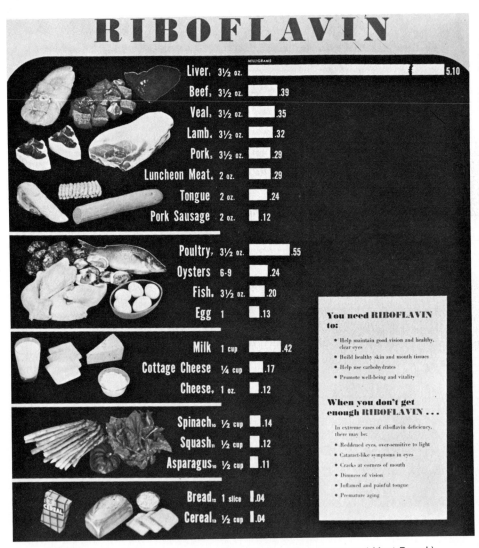

RIBOFLAVIN

MILLIGRAMS

Liver, 3½ oz.	5.10
Beef, 3½ oz.	.39
Veal, 3½ oz.	.35
Lamb, 3½ oz.	.32
Pork, 3½ oz.	.29
Luncheon Meat, 2 oz.	.29
Tongue 2 oz.	.24
Pork Sausage 2 oz.	.12
Poultry, 3½ oz.	.55
Oysters 6-9	.24
Fish, 3½ oz.	.20
Egg 1	.13
Milk 1 cup	.42
Cottage Cheese ¼ cup	.17
Cheese, 1 oz.	.12
Spinach, ½ cup	.14
Squash, ½ cup	.12
Asparagus, ½ cup	.11
Bread, 1 slice	.04
Cereal, ½ cup	.04

You need RIBOFLAVIN to:

- Help maintain good vision and healthy, clear eyes
- Build healthy skin and mouth tissues
- Help use carbohydrates
- Promote well-being and vitality

When you don't get enough RIBOFLAVIN ...

In extreme cases of riboflavin deficiency, there may be:

- Reddened eyes, over-sensitive to light
- Cataract-like symptoms in eyes
- Cracks at corners of mouth
- Dimness of vision
- Inflamed and painful tongue
- Premature aging

Figure 9–15   Vitamin B$_2$ sources. (From National Live Stock and Meat Board.)

Daily Recommendations

	Milligrams			*Milligrams*
CHILDREN		FEMALES		
1 to 3	9	15 to 18		14
7 to 10	16	Over 23		13
MALES		Pregnant		+2
15 to 18	20	Lactating		+4
Over 23	18			

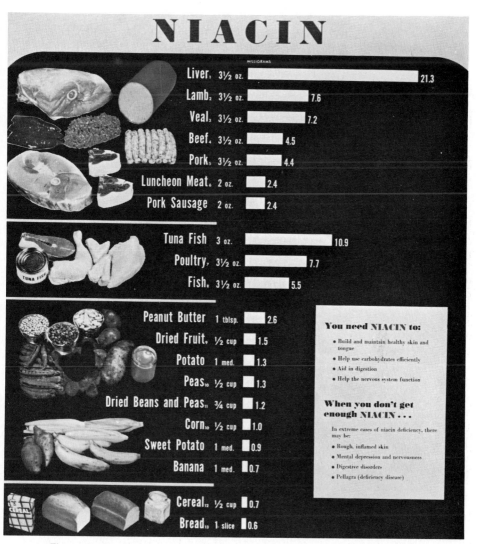

NIACIN

MILLIGRAMS

Liver, 3½ oz.	21.3
Lamb, 3½ oz.	7.6
Veal, 3½ oz.	7.2
Beef, 3½ oz.	4.5
Pork, 3½ oz.	4.4
Luncheon Meat, 2 oz.	2.4
Pork Sausage 2 oz.	2.4
Tuna Fish 3 oz.	10.9
Poultry, 3½ oz.	7.7
Fish, 3½ oz.	5.5
Peanut Butter 1 tblsp.	2.6
Dried Fruit, ½ cup	1.5
Potato 1 med.	1.3
Peas, ½ cup	1.3
Dried Beans and Peas, ¾ cup	1.2
Corn, ½ cup	1.0
Sweet Potato 1 med.	0.9
Banana 1 med.	0.7
Cereal, ½ cup	0.7
Bread, 1 slice	0.6

You need NIACIN to:

• Build and maintain healthy skin and tongue
• Help use carbohydrates efficiently
• Aid in digestion
• Help the nervous system function

When you don't get enough NIACIN . . .

In extreme cases of niacin deficiency, there may be:

• Rough, inflamed skin
• Mental depression and nervousness
• Digestive disorders
• Pellagra (deficiency disease)

Figure 9–16 Niacin sources. (From National Live Stock and Meat Board.)

Daily Recommendations

	Milligrams		Milligrams
CHILDREN		FEMALES	
1 to 3	40	Over 11	45
7 to 10	40	Pregnant	60
MALES		Lactating	80
Over 11	45		

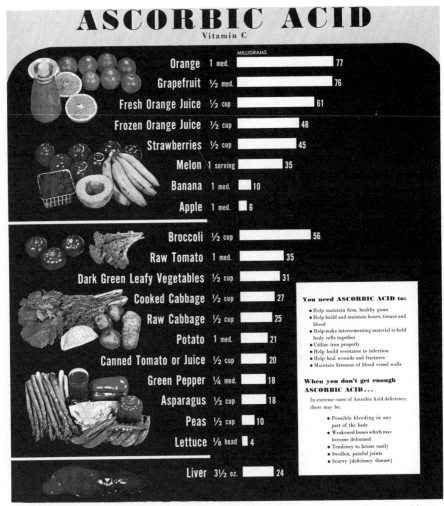

Figure 9–17   Vitamin C sources. (From National Live Stock and Meat Board.)

CHAPTER 10

Menu Planning

Gristle   Food inspection
Fluctuate   Meal pattern
Food grade   Menu
                            Staple

Meals should be planned to include foods which will supply the basic nutrients and also appeal to the appetite. The following factors should be considered:

1. **Include all of the food groups in the basic-four every day.**

2. **Each meal should have**
   Three of the basic-four groups.
   A good source of protein. (A serving from the meat or milk group or both.)

3. **Variety:**
   Color: Avoid a menu of all white or neutral colored foods and choose color combinations which appeal to the eye.
   Texture: Palatability is increased by contrasting textures. Do not use all soft or all crisp foods. Overcooking makes foods so soft they have an undesirable texture.
   Flavor: Balance bland and highly flavored foods. Relishes and seasoning add flavor to foods.
   Shape: Foods should not be all round, flat, whole, shredded, or diced.
   Satiety value: Fat and protein foods have higher satiety value than carbohydrates.
   Overemphasis on one type of food: Roast veal, macaroni and cheese, and custard should not be used for one meal because they are all

115

high in proteins. Spanish rice, potatoes, and cake are high carbohydrate foods and they, too, are a poor combination in a menu.

4. **Sociologic and Personal Preferences:**
   Family: The older person without teeth usually will not eat carrot and celery sticks, the two-year-old should not have pastries, and the overweight person may wish to omit the concentrated fat and carbohydrate foods; but menus should be planned to give all of them the needed nutrients.

   Religious and national customs: Substitutes in each food group of the basic-four should be made to meet religious and national customs.

5. **Time and energy:**
   Efficient organization saves time and steps. Elaborate meals may leave the homemaker so tired that she does not eat properly or so irritable that meals are an unpleasant experience for the family.

6. **Appearance:**
   Attractive food on a clean plate and placed on a well-arranged table is much more appetizing than, for example, greasy food with gravy spilled over the edge of a plate placed on a cluttered, unclean table.

7. **Economical use of fuel:**
   An all-oven meal can save fuel. For example, a child's baked apple can be prepared at the same time that an apple pie is cooking.

8. **Food costs:**
   A specific amount of money per person or the percentage of the total income which should be spent for food cannot be definitely stated because
   (a) Homemakers vary in shopping ability, cooking skills, and knowledge of ways to use foods.
   (b) Entertaining done in the home may increase food costs.
   (c) Prices vary with the season and the geographical region.
   (d) The purchasing power of the dollar fluctuates, but at any time meat, bacon and eggs are relatively high priced, while the cost of unsweetened cereals is relatively low.
   (e) The amount of food needed varies with family size, with the age, and with the physical activity of the members. For example, the family with two adults and three young children probably will use more milk than will the family of five adults.

(f) Food habits and modified diets affect selection and cost of food.

(g) The opportunity to produce, freeze, or can a portion of the food supply decreases the amount which has to be purchased.

(h) If storage space is available, food on special sale can be purchased in quantity.

A budget plan which has been suggested as a guide and which can be modified to fit the family's need is to divide the food dollar as follows:

25¢ Meat, eggs, fish, cheese, and dried beans
20¢ Milk
20¢ Fruits and vegetables
20¢ Bread and cereals
15¢ Fats and sweets   (58:2)

Table 10-1   *Typical Meal Patterns*

Breakfast

Light	Moderately Light	Moderately Heavy
Fruit	Fruit	Fruit
Breadstuff	Cereal or breadstuff	Cereal
Hot beverage	Hot food	Hot food (1 or 2)
	Hot beverage	Breadstuff
		Hot beverage

Luncheon or Supper

Light	Moderately Light	Heavier
Soup	Soup	Soup
Salad	Salad	Main dish with vegetables
Beverage	Dessert	Salad or dessert
or	Beverage	Beverage
Salad	*or*	
Dessert	Hot dish with vegetable	
Beverage	Salad	
	Dessert	
	Beverage	

Dinner

Light	Moderately Light	Heavier
Meat course	Soup	Appetizer
Salad	Meat course	Soup
Dessert	Salad	Meat course
Beverage	Dessert	Salad
	Beverage	Dessert
		Beverage

(Adapted from Bogert, L. Jean: *Nutrition and Physical Fitness*, 8th ed., 1966, pp. 493–495.)

Table 10-2 Family Food Plan at Low Cost*

Weekly Quantities of Food for Each Member of the Family

Family members	Leafy green, yellow vegetables	Citrus fruit, tomatoes	Potatoes, sweet potatoes	Other vegetables and fruit	Milk (a)	Meat, poultry, fish	Eggs	Dry beans and peas, nuts	Flour, cereals (b)	Fats and oils (c)	Sugar, sirups, preserves
	Lb. Oz.	Lb. Oz.	Lb. Oz.	Lb. Oz.	Qt.	Lb. Oz.	No.	Lb. Oz.	Lb. Oz.	Lb. Oz.	Lb. Oz.
Children under 12 years											
9-12 months	1 - 8	1 - 12	0 - 8	1 - 0	6	0 - 4	5	0 - 1	0 - 10	0 - 1	0 - 1
1-3 years	1 - 12	1 - 12	1 - 0	1 - 0	5½	(d)0 - 8	5	0 - 1	0 - 12	0 - 2	0 - 2
4-6 years	1 - 12	1 - 12	1 - 8	1 - 4	5½	1 - 8	5	0 - 2	1 - 12	0 - 6	0 - 6
7-9 years	2 - 0	2 - 0	2 - 8	1 - 8	5½	1 - 8	5	0 - 4	2 - 4	0 - 8	0 - 10
10-12 years	2 - 4	2 - 4	3 - 0	1 - 12	6	1 - 12	5	0 - 4	3 - 4	0 - 12	0 - 12
Girls:											
13-15 years	2 - 4	2 - 4	3 - 4	1 - 12	6½	(d)2 - 0	5	0 - 4	3 - 8	0 - 12	0 - 12
16-20 years	2 - 4	2 - 4	3 - 0	1 - 12	5	(d)2 - 0	5	0 - 4	3 - 4	0 - 12	0 - 10
Boys:											
13-15 years	2 - 8	2 - 8	4 - 0	2 - 4	6½	2 - 0	5	0 - 8	4 - 8	1 - 0	0 - 14
16-20 years	2 - 12	2 - 8	5 - 0	2 - 8	6½	2 - 0	5	0 - 8	5 - 12	1 - 6	1 - 0
Women:											
Sedentary	2 - 4	2 - 0	2 - 4	1 - 12	5	2 - 0	5	0 - 4	2 - 0	0 - 10	0 - 10
Moderately active	2 - 4	2 - 0	3 - 0	1 - 12	5	2 - 0	5	0 - 4	3 - 4	0 - 12	0 - 12
Very active	2 - 8	2 - 8	4 - 0	2 - 0	5	2 - 0	5	0 - 6	4 - 4	1 - 0	1 - 0
Pregnant	3 - 0	2 - 8	2 - 8	2 - 4	7½	(d)2 - 4	7	0 - 4	2 - 12	0 - 10	0 - 8
Nursing	3 - 8	3 - 12	4 - 0	2 - 4	10½	(d)2 - 8	7	0 - 4	3 - 0	0 - 10	0 - 8
60 years or over (e)	2 - 8	2 - 4	2 - 8	1 - 12	5	(d)2 - 0	4	0 - 2	2 - 4	0 - 8	0 - 8
Men:											
Sedentary	2 - 4	2 - 0	3 - 0	1 - 12	5	2 - 0	5	0 - 4	3 - 4	0 - 12	0 - 12
Physically active	2 - 8	2 - 8	4 - 0	2 - 0	5	2 - 0	5	0 - 6	4 - 4	1 - 0	1 - 0
With heavy work	2 - 8	2 - 8	6 - 0	2 - 8	5	2 - 0	5	0 - 10	7 - 12	1 - 14	1 - 0
60 years or over (e)	2 - 8	2 - 4	3 - 4	1 - 12	5	2 - 0	4	0 - 2	3 - 4	0 - 10	0 - 10

*From Church, Charles F., and Church, Helen N.: Bowes and Church's Food Values of Portions Commonly Used, 12th ed. Philadelphia J. B. Lippincott, Publisher, 1975, p. 184.

(a) Or its equivalent in cheese, evaporated milk, or dry milk.

(b) Count 1½ pounds of bread as 1 pound of flour. Use as much as possible in the form of whole grain, enriched or restored products.

(c) For small children and pregnant and nursing women, cod liver oil or some other source of vitamin D is also needed. For elderly persons and for persons who have no opportunity for exposure to clear sunshine a small amount of vitamin D is also desirable.

(d) To meet iron allowance, one large or two small servings of liver or other organ meats should be served each week.

(e) The nutritive contents of the weekly food quantities for a man and woman 60 years or over were based on the National Research Council's recommended daily allowances for the sedentary man and woman.

Table 10–3 Family Food Plan at Moderate Cost*

Weekly Quantities of Food for Each Member of the Family

Family members	Leafy, green, yellow vegetables Lb. Oz.	Citrus fruit, tomatoes Lb. Oz.	Potatoes, sweet potatoes Lb. Oz.	Other vegetables and fruit Lb. Oz.	Milk (a) Qt.	Meat, poultry, fish Lb. Oz.	Eggs No.	Dry beans and peas, nuts Lb. Oz.	Flour, cereals (b) Lb. Oz.	Fats and oils (c) Lb. Oz.	Sugar, sirups, preserves Lb. Oz.
Children under 12 years:											
9-12 months	1 - 8	1 - 12	0 - 8	1 - 0	6	0 - 4	5	0 - 1	0 - 10	0 - 1	0 - 1
1-3 years	2 - 0	2 - 0	0 - 8	1 - 12	6	(d)0 - 12	6	0 - 1	1 - 4	0 - 2	0 - 2
4-6 years	2 - 4	2 - 4	1 - 0	2 - 4	6	1 - 4	7	0 - 1	1 - 8	0 - 6	0 - 8
7-9 years	2 - 8	2 - 8	1 - 12	2 - 8	6½	1 - 12	7	0 - 2	2 - 0	0 - 8	0 - 12
10-12 years	3 - 0	2 - 12	2 - 4	2 - 8	7	2 - 4	7	0 - 2	2 - 12	0 - 12	0 - 14
Girls:											
13-15 years	3 - 8	2 - 12	2 - 8	3 - 8	7	(d)2 - 12	7	0 - 2	2 - 12	0 - 14	0 - 14
16-20 years	3 - 8	2 - 12	2 - 8	3 - 8	6	(d)2 - 12	7	0 - 2	2 - 8	0 - 12	0 - 14
Boys:											
13-15 years	3 - 8	3 - 0	3 - 8	3 - 8	7	3 - 0	7	0 - 4	4 - 0	1 - 2	1 - 2
16-20 years	4 - 0	3 - 8	4 - 8	3 - 8	7	3 - 4	7	0 - 6	5 - 4	1 - 6	1 - 4
Women:											
Sedentary	3 - 4	2 - 8	1 - 12	3 - 4	5	2 - 8	7	0 - 1	1 - 12	0 - 10	0 - 12
Moderately active	3 - 8	2 - 8	2 - 8	3 - 8	5	2 - 12	7	0 - 2	2 - 8	0 - 14	0 - 14
Very active	3 - 12	3 - 0	3 - 4	4 - 0	5	3 - 0	7	0 - 4	3 - 12	1 - 2	1 - 2
Pregnant	4 - 0	4 - 8	2 - 4	3 - 0	7½	(d)3 - 0	7	0 - 2	2 - 4	0 - 10	0 - 10
Nursing	4 - 0	4 - 8	3 - 0	3 - 8	10½	(d)3 - 0	7	0 - 2	2 - 8	0 - 12	0 - 12
60 years or over (e)	3 - 8	2 - 12	2 - 0	3 - 0	5½	2 - 8	6	0 - 1	1 - 12	0 - 8	0 - 10
Men:											
Sedentary	3 - 8	2 - 8	2 - 8	3 - 8	5	2 - 12	7	0 - 2	2 - 8	0 - 14	0 - 14
Physically active	3 - 12	3 - 0	3 - 4	4 - 0	5	3 - 0	7	0 - 4	3 - 12	1 - 2	1 - 2
With heavy work	4 - 0	3 - 8	5 - 0	4 - 4	5	3 - 8	7	0 - 6	7 - 0	2 - 0	1 - 4
60 years or over (e)	3 - 8	2 - 12	2 - 12	3 - 0	5½	2 - 12	6	0 - 2	2 - 8	0 - 12	0 - 12

*From Church, Charles F., and Church, Helen N.: *Bowes and Church's Food Values of Portions Commonly Used*, 12th ed. Philadelphia, J. B. Lippincott, Publisher, 1975, p. 184.

(a) Or its equivalent in cheese, evaporated milk, or dry milk.

(b) Count 1½ pounds of bread as 1 pound of flour. Use as much as possible in the form of whole grain, enriched or restored products.

(c) For small children and pregnant and nursing women, cod liver oil or some other source of vitamin D is also needed. For elderly persons and for persons who have no opportunity for exposure to clear sunshine a small amount of vitamin D is also desirable.

(d) To meet iron allowance, one large or two small servings of liver or other organ meats should be served each week.

(e) The nutritive contents of the weekly food quantities for a man and woman 60 years or over were based on the National Research Council's recommended daily allowances for the sedentary man and woman.

American diets can be improved by using more milk, vegetables, and fruits. When the food money is limited, the need for an adequate milk supply is very great.

Two factors which can influence the pattern by which we plan our meals are

1. Activity: The sedentary person usually eats a lighter breakfast. The physically active person usually eats a larger luncheon than the person who spends the afternoon doing sedentary work.

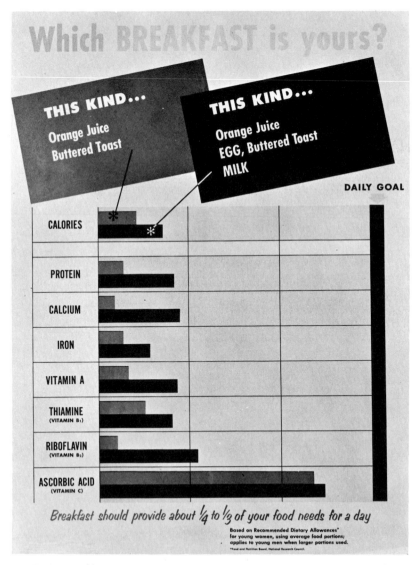

Figure 10–1   Nutrients in a good and a poor breakfast. (From National Dairy Council.)

2. Habits: If the dinner is a large meal, the other two meals usually tend to be lighter. If the lunch-hour time is limited, the luncheon tends to be smaller.

In many homes breakfast is a starchy meal, but if a protein food is included there is greater satiety value, which reduces the tendency to eat snacks or a large lunch. Some industries are encouraging their employees to eat more adequate breakfasts, feeling that the employees may be less fatigued, the accident rate may be decreased, and efficiency may be

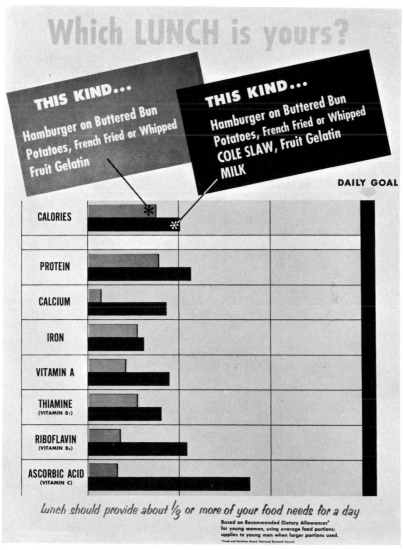

Figure 10–2 Nutrients in a good and a poor lunch. (From National Dairy Council.)

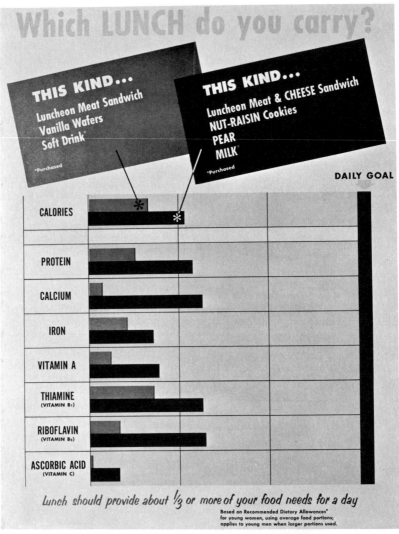

Figure 10–3 Nutrients in a good and a poor carried lunch. (From National Dairy Council.)

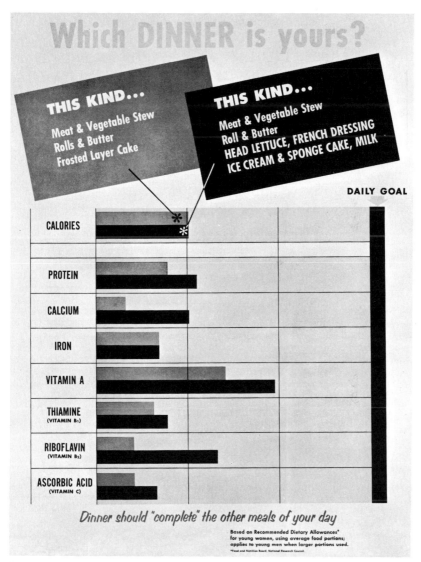

Figure 10–4   Nutrients in a good and a poor dinner. (From National Dairy Council.)

increased. In general it is well to distribute the food intake so that from one quarter to one third of the daily food intake is eaten at breakfast as well as the other two meals. *Using food from three of the basic-four groups in each meal will help do this.*

SUGGESTED READING

Metropolitan Life Insurance Company: *The Case for Better Breakfasts.*
National Dairy Council:
   Comparison Cards (shows nutrient values of various foods).
   Lower Cost Meals That Please in Our Senior Years, 1971.
   Make Lunch Count (Poster).
   School Lunch.
   Your Guide to Good Eating and How to Use It.
Society for Nutrition Education: *Vegetarians and Vegetarian Diets,* 1974. A resource list of educational materials on vegetarian diets.
U.S. Department of Agriculture:
   Conserving the Nutritive Values in Foods. Home and Garden Bulletin No. 90.
   Consumers All, The Yearbook of Agriculture, 1965.
   Eat a Good Breakfast to Start a Good Day. Leaflet No. 268, 1971.
   Family Fare: Food Management and Recipes. Home and Garden Bulletin No. 1, 1973.
   Family Food Budgeting for Good Meals and Good Nutrition, 1969.
University of California Extension Service: *Balance Food Values and Cents,* 1973.

EXERCISES

1. Plan a week's menu for your family. Using Table 10–3, make up a weekly market order. I suggest using headings to make each list. For example: vegetables, fruits, dairy products, meat or substitute, cereals, fats, eggs, miscellaneous (sugar, salt, etc.).
2. Why is the light breakfast in Table 10–1 inadequate?
3. How many of the basic food groups are provided by a hamburger sandwich? (A leaf of lettuce or a slice of tomato is not a ½ cup serving, so would not count as a vegetable serving.) What could be served with the hamburger to provide an adequate meal?
4. Would the following groups of foods provide three of the basic-four groups?

(a) Orange, medium size	(b) Wiener, 2 oz.	(c) Meat loaf, 2 oz.
Oatmeal, ¾ cup	Hot dog roll, 2 oz.	cooked ground
Milk, 1 glass	Coke	meat
		Cabbage salad, ¾
		cup
		Milk, 1 glass

5. Study Figures 10–1 to 10–4. Do your eating habits compare with the good or poor meals?

CHAPTER 11

Cultural and Religious Food Habits

TERMS TO UNDERSTAND

Diversity	Predominate
Kosher	Stature
Orthodox	Vegetarian
Pasta	

In the United States there are so many ways of transporting food that all types of food can be found in any area. Nevertheless, we do find regional food patterns. For example, the South uses many hot breads, salt pork, chicken, and canned milk, and prefers sweet potatoes to white potatoes. The West uses large quantities of meat, especially beef, fresh fruits, fresh milk, and more canned and frozen fruits and vegetables than are used in other sections of the country.

People living in other countries often have adequate diets even though their food habits are different from ours. The Eskimo gets a very limited amount of sunlight but he eats the organs and blood of slaughtered animals and thus gets his vitamin D.

Many immigrants to the United States have come from rural areas where a part of their food was home grown. In the United States immigrants tend to gather in large cities. Milk, fruits, and vegetables seem expensive to them. Because they cannot grow their own food, many immigrants tend to eat poorly planned meals, which are inadequate because they are predominantly starch.

The Mexicans use little milk or cheese in their diets but large quantities of corn. In Mexico whole kernel corn is soaked as needed in a lime solution and ground while wet. The ground corn supplies calcium because of the limewater soaking. Mexicans eat the whole grain product containing the germ of the corn, which is different in food value from the refined corn meal purchased in this country. Although they may not eat much fruit they use many tomatoes, which are a good source of vitamins A and C. Chili peppers and many different varieties of beans are used in large amounts. Beef and chicken are used more than pork, lamb, or fish. Butter and eggs are rarely used. Mexicans living in the United States should be encouraged to use more milk, eggs, vegetables, and whole grain cereals.

Chinese tend to have vegetarian habits because in China space for raising livestock is very limited. In South China rice is the chief carbohydrate food, but in North China wheat is more popular. Cereals provide about 80 per cent of the calories in the Chinese diets. Soybeans and soybean products are high in good quality protein. In the coastal area, fish is used. Chicken, pork, and eggs are eaten when there is money to buy them. Orientals wisely do not overcook vegetables. Oriental children raised in the United States and consuming more meat and milk usually have greater stature than other Orientals. (Incidentally, chop suey is not a Chinese dish. It originated in America and seldom is eaten by Chinese.)

The Slavic people get from 60 to 70 per cent of their calories from grains and potatoes. The central European area produces such grains as rye and barley and more root than green vegetables, which accounts for the predominance of these foods in their diets. Spices and sour cream are used for seasoning the foods. Pork, fish, and cottage cheese provide most of the animal proteins. Cabbage, especially in the form of sauerkraut, is used extensively. Slavic families should be encouraged to use more milk, fruit, and raw vegetables.

Armenian, Greek, and Turkish people use a great deal of sour or fermented milk. In Armenia sour milk is called matzoon and in Turkey it is called yogurt. They eat few potatoes; cracked wheat and rice furnish most of their carbohydrate. Lamb is the only meat used extensively. Olive oil is used for cooking and is mixed with vinegar for salad dressings. Desserts usually are fruits and nuts.

In Italy the people use large amounts of goat's milk and cheese, which are quite cheap. They do not like our domestic cheese and the imported cheese is so expensive that little is used. Green leafy vegetables and fruits, especially grapes and oranges, are plentiful in Italy. In northern Italy, a little meat is included in the diet. Since fishing is one of the chief occupations of southern Italy much fish is eaten in this section. Macaroni, spaghetti, legumes, or polenta made from corn meal are used for the main dish of many meals. Olive oil, garlic, green peppers, and wine are used abundantly. Italian immigrants should be urged to continue using green vegetables, fruits, and pastas and to supplement them with milk, whole grain cereals, potatoes, and root vegetables.

The Puerto Rican family uses small amounts of beef or pork to flavor stews and vegetable combinations. Fresh, dried, and salted fish are used, but legumes furnish most of the protein in the diet. Rice is the cereal most often used. The tropical fruits—plantain, bananas, oranges, pineapple—are favorites. When finances permit, dairy products are used. Vinegar, onion, and garlic are the favorite seasonings. Coffee is the beverage of choice.

Soul food is a unique type of American cooking first developed by the Southern Negro. He used the low cost simple foods to develop tasty "soul-satisfying" or gourmet dishes. Currently, these early recipes and basic Southern cooking recipes constitute that group of foods referred to as soul foods. Favorites include sweet potato pie, ham hocks and collard greens, hush puppies, black-eyed peas, fried green tomatoes, fried pies, cornbread with molasses or buttermilk, hot biscuits, tomato conserve, dumplings in various combinations, hominy grits, fried cabbage, cracklin' bread, ox tails, and hog chitlins.

Other ethnic groups are beginning to publicize, with justified pride, their cultural recipes. The addition of the soul foods, the Mexican American, and the American Indian foods will add variety, flavor, and interest to the now well-known Italian, Spanish, Scandinavian, Basque, German, Slavic, and Oriental foods found in our restaurants. Many cookbooks today include recipes for foods which are native to these cultural groups.

Religion influences the diet pattern of many people. Catholics have some days on which no meat is consumed. Mormons do not use tea, coffee, or alcoholic beverages. The Jewish food laws place many restrictions upon meals. In caring for a Jewish patient, much more detailed information should be secured because only a few food customs are listed here.

Jews who observe the dietary laws use meat only from those animals that chew a cud and have a divided hoof. Absolutely no pork is used. The animals are killed in a prescribed manner and processed to remove as much blood as possible. Meat prepared in this manner is known as kosher meat. Only fish that have fins and scales are eaten. This eliminates lobster, shrimp, oyster, and eel. Many Jewish homes prepare a delicacy called gefüllte fish. An egg yolk with a drop of blood is forbidden. Dairy products and meat are not served in the same meal; consequently, butter sauces and white sauces are not served if meat is served. In the Orthodox Jewish home separate sets of cooking utensils are used for cooking milk and meat dishes. Cereals, fruits, vegetables, and a bread which contains neither milk nor animal fat are neutral foods and may be eaten at any meal. Jewish people use many pastries, cakes, preserves, pickles, and stewed fruits. In the most orthodox homes absolutely no cooking is done on the Sabbath, which extends from sundown on Friday to sundown on Saturday. Chicken is the traditional dish to serve for the Sabbath evening meal. Yom Kippur is a day of fasting.

SUGGESTED READING

Krause, Marie V., and Hunscher, Martha A.: *Food, Nutrition and Diet Therapy,* 1972. Ch. 13.

EXERCISES

1. Discuss in class other known native food habits and social customs.

CHAPTER 12

Acquiring Food Acceptance

TERMS TO UNDERSTAND

Allergy	Consecutive	Hunger
Appetite	Cultural	Potential
Aversion	Gustatory	Status

Factors Influencing Food Choices

Our willingness to accept different foods is a product of our personal experiences, customs, attitudes, ideas, likes, and dislikes in regard to food, which in turn are products of our cultural, social, and economic environment. We are not born with food likes and dislikes, but we can and do develop preferences. *Since we are physically what we eat, our food habits can be very important to general health.* Willingness to eat a variety of foods rather than to limit ourselves to favorites indicates that our food habits are good and that we have set the stage for optimum nutrition. If our eating habits are built on indifference, whim, prejudice, complacency, or ignorance we may not develop to our full physical, social, and emotional potential.

Food has social and ceremonial implications. Holidays and religious and social festivities are often celebrated by serving traditional foods; for example, the multi-tiered wedding cake, the Thanksgiving turkey, and the German Christmas breakfast bread, stöllen. The texture or content of a food may make it objectionable to us—we may feel that purees and milk are baby foods, that salads are feminine or suitable only for low-calorie diets, and social status may dictate some of our choices. Meat stews, meat loaf, and cornstarch puddings usually are not considered "company" foods even though they are nutritious. Caviar, champagne, eel, avocado, imported delicacies, or out-of-season fresh fruits may be used because

129

they imply social prestige or show that the family can afford to purchase "exotic" foods. History records gustatory excesses being used as a form of "conspicuous consumption." This was true in the Roman Empire and is still true in many countries. In some areas of the world, obesity indicates the means to purchase ample food. In other societies, the term "matronly" is not flattering because it connotes both plumpness and age.

Attitudes and associations affect food acceptance. Foods which have become associated with happy experiences usually are well accepted; on the other hand, if one is forced to eat or if food is withheld in punishment, eating becomes an unpleasant experience and a dislike or disinterest in food may develop. Foods given during a period of stress, such as in a severe illness, famine, or war, often are disliked or omitted forever after from the diet. Over-ripe or under-ripe fruits, casseroles made from leftovers which were not properly stored, or other foods which made us ill often become unacceptable thereafter.

If the nutrition instructor has never used or has an aversion to using a certain food (for example, powdered milk or the organ meats), her teaching will not be so effective as the teaching of someone who has eaten and who likes the food she recommends in her classes. A person from a farm may consider corn and non-fat milk as food for live stock and therefore unacceptable. Odor, color, and texture may have pleasant or unpleasant associations and thus become standards for judging the palatability of foods.

The person who has an allergic reaction to a food each time he eats it will omit it from his diet. For example, if he experiences the discomfort of hives each time he eats strawberries, he will omit strawberries and may be quite emphatic in his rejection if urged to eat them.

Food customs are influenced by geographical locations. Persons living near the seacoast are apt to consume more varieties of salt water fish than those living inland; in the temperate zones, the starch eaten is often wheat, but in the subtropics rice is used. The French consider snails a delicacy and the Ifugao of the Philippines use crickets and beetles for food.

Advertising and fads influence food choices. Many radio and television commercials are directed toward particular groups or to developing product and brand loyalty.

People who wish to appear emotionally mature may regard food rejection as childish or as an indication of narrow social experience.

Correct information concerning the needs of our body is an important factor in food selection. Much progress is being made in nutrition education, but in all nations of the world much remains to be done.

Developing Food Habits

Environment plays an important part in determining what people are. Food, which is part of everyone's environment, influences social and emotional growth as well as chemical and physical growth.

Hunger is the physical need for food. In the infant a natural sequence of hunger, ingestion, satisfaction, and physical well-being occurs. Appetite, or desire for food, reflects pleasant experiences with food and can be suppressed by unpleasant memories in regard to food or by other unpleasant food associations. Unless emotional upsets, illness, distraction, overstimulation, or fatigue is present, a child's appetite determines the *volume* of food he takes. The emotions of worry, anxiety, or discontent interfere with eating. Food can act as a symbol (for example, of security and comfort); thus a child can overeat to compensate for something missing in his life.

Human beings acquire food habits by imitating those around them. If parents eat a large variety of food, do not express dislikes of foods, and are casual in their attitude that a child will eat, the child usually does. The child is inclined to eat everything unless it is suggested that he has a choice of liking, disliking, accepting, or rejecting food. If most vegetables, fruits, cereals, and meats are introduced to him when he is young (in the first year of life, approximately), he develops a wide taste range. Introducing a new food to a child is a learning experience for him. The texture, flavor, and temperature are different from those of his milk. Offer the new food in very small portions. If the food is not accepted the first time, repetition of the experience usually results in acceptance, especially if the food is offered with the attitude that it will be eaten. The nurse's, nursery school teacher's, or parent's attitude or statements about food may influence the child's reaction toward the food. For example, emphasizing that vegetables are "good for you" may make the child feel guilty if he omits them occasionally—or using desserts as a reward for "cleaning his plate" can put too much emphasis on desserts or make them the only desirable part of the meal. If the dessert is composed of foods found in the basic-four (for example, custard or fruit), does it matter too much if the child occasionally ignores the adult habit of eating dessert at the end of the meal? (This assumes, of course, that the dessert is nutritious). The adolescent may be showing his freedom of parental domination when he indulges in many "wrong" foods and few "right" foods.

The infant is born with the sucking-swallowing reflex. Food put into the front of the mouth will be expelled, not because he doesn't like it but because he can't move it to the back of his mouth so that it can be swallowed. The child usually develops this tongue movement between three and five months of age. Babies do not develop at the same rate, but they do follow a general pattern.

It should not be surprising that a child seems to develop an early appetite for sweets. Sugar is added to his formula, to his cereals, and to his pureed fruit. We teach him to like the flavor of sugar and then wonder why he has a "sweet tooth." Taste discrimination is present at birth. The child has many taste buds (they will decrease in number until teen age), and thus food which tastes slightly scorched to an adult may taste quite burned to the infant. Sight, smell, and texture also affect the child's reactions to food. Permitting a child to help prepare food may stimulate his interest in eating that food. If he is allowed to be in the kitchen while food is being prepared, he will become accustomed to food odors.

Foods high in fat and bulk may remain in a child's gastrointestinal tract an extended period of time, thus reducing the physical signs of hunger, which in turn affect his desire for food. Small children should not eat fried and highly seasoned foods, hot breads (they are not thoroughly chewed), desserts high in fat and sugar, stimulating beverages, and tough, fibrous, high-roughage foods.

A small child has a short attention span and cannot sit quietly for a long time. To reduce his restlessness, allow the child to serve himself, take his dishes to the sink, or pick up dessert from the serving area. The child learns gradually to handle a cup, knife, and fork. By two years he has a reasonable amount of skill, but at three years he will still be spilling food. The five-year-old may have difficulty cutting even tender food. If he eats quietly, habitually uses his silver (occasionally resorting to fingers), and seldom upsets his milk, he is making normal progress. Occasionally he remembers to say please and thank you. He should have eating utensils small enough to fit his grasp, a chair and table of suitable size and height, attractive food and dishes, and an atmosphere free of emotional tension.

As a child grows older he eats less in proportion to his size because he is growing more slowly. To coax, beg, bribe, or force him to eat may produce a scene which gives him the center of the stage, with its attending excitement and satisfaction. Casual praise for eating well is more effective than attention for poor eating.

For the preschool child, make the serving size of each solid food approximately one level tablespoonful for each year of age. If the child wishes seconds he will ask for them. To give a two-year-old an adult-size serving is comparable to serving the adult from three to five complete meals at one sitting, a quantity of food that would probably discourage an adult from eating. *Think in terms of a well-planned adequate daily diet, not in terms of one meal. The inclusion of the basic-four over a period of time rather than the acceptance or rejection of a meal is the important factor. The healthy child will not become malnourished if he misses a few consecutive meals.*

Leverton reminds us that self-demand and self-selection in child feeding do not mean self-indulgence or self-destruction. If a child is to be allowed to choose his foods, the adult must be responsible for offering him choices which will furnish his needed nutrients as well as help him develop good habits in choosing a variety of foods. *A child's appetite cannot be relied upon to help him make his food selection in relation to his nutrient needs.*

In summary, the following are conducive to developing a favorable attitude in a child toward eating:

1. Adults should set a good example.
2. Casually assume that the child is going to eat the offered food.
3. Use a variety of foods to develop a wide taste range. Offer foods with pleasing colors and with a variety of textures and flavors.
4. Do not use food to reward or to bribe. Do not withhold food to punish.

5. Use small servings and give seconds if requested.

6. Expect the child to know when his appetite has been satisfied.

7. Know that appetite varies from meal to meal and from day to day.

8. Remove food in a casual, friendly manner when the child begins to dawdle.

9. Realize a child eats less for his size as his growth slows.

10. Give assistance when a small child has become too tired to finish feeding himself.

11. Recognize when he is too tired to eat well.

12. Give love and attention to the child throughout the day.

13. Do not use meal time as discipline time.

14. Have regular meal hours preceded by a quiet, restful period.

15. Make sure that the size of the chair, table, and utensils is right for the child.

16. Expect the child to spill food and be messy until he has developed the muscular coordination necessary for the mechanics of eating.

17. Do not mix unpleasant tasting medications with food.

When feeding a child, the same general principles should be observed as those for feeding a helpless patient:

1. Before bringing the food, prepare the individual by washing his hands, giving any indicated mouth care, and protecting him with a bib or a napkin.

2. Be congenial but not overtalkative. Remember that the patient may resent his inability to feed himself. The infant may wish to start learning to feed himself.

3. If possible, be seated. This tends to reflect a more relaxed and unhurried atmosphere.

4. Place the tray so the food may be seen and smelled.

5. Feed small quantities very slowly.

6. Have the hot foods and liquids hot. Remember that the helpless patient can be burned by a scalding temperature and will be dissatisfied if foods that should be hot are served lukewarm or cold.

Changing Established Habits

Adults as well as children do not change their habits unless they sincerely desire to change the habit. Patient and understanding guidance is of help to anyone, but it is particularly necessary when the adult is trying to help the child change an undesirable habit.

To stimulate interest in good food habits we can appeal to the teenager's desire for attractiveness, physical superiority, and the charm which is associated with good health; to the pregnant woman's desire for the best possible physical condition of her unborn child; to the obese child's desire for greater participation in physical activities; to the adventurous person's desire to try something new. And the person of any age should respond to the idea that good nutrition extends the vitality of the "prime of life" into the years of retirement.

To establish communications with a patient or student, the health educator must understand that food is more than calories or material for tissue repair. Food carries "not only the feelings of security, protection, love, and developing strength, but also the sense of pain, rejection, deprivation, and the potential terror of starvation." (15a:546)

To help an individual to change his habits we must understand how discovering the answers to one or more of the following questions may help the individual in his attempt to change:

1. Can new foods be associated with old foods by the manner of serving?

2. Can a highly valued or traditional dish be included in the diet and thus remove objections to the other changes in the diet?

3. Are some foods "company foods" due to regional variations?

4. Is the serving size varied with the individual's size?

5. Is mealtime often a distressing experience?

6. Is dessert a reward, making other food courses less acceptable?

7. Is food so associated with home that unfamiliar food produces unhappiness and homesickness?

8. Do slogans such as "A well nourished nation is a contented nation" or "Man does not live by bread alone" transform a biological hunger into a culturally patterned appetite?

9. Do beliefs about elimination affect food choices?

10. Do faddists or people with self-diagnosed gastrointestinal or other disorders place a strong reliance on particular foods?

11. Is the difference between acceptance or rejection of foods due to traditional table setting or containers? How or by whom the food is served?

To understand food problems requires tolerance. The old Quaker saying "Everyone is queer but thee and me, and sometimes me thinks thee is a little queer" applies to our food habits as well as to other phases of social relationships.

SUGGESTED READING

Babcock, Charlotte G.: "Attitudes and the Use of Foods," *J. Am. Dietet. A.,* June, 1961.

Breckenridge, Marian E., and Murphy, Margaret Nesbitt: *Growth and Development of the Young Child,* 1969.

Breckenridge, Marian E., and Vincent, Elizabeth: *Child Development,* 1965.

Brozek, Josef (Ed.): "Nutrition and Behavior, A Symposium," *Am. J. Clin. Nutrition,* March–April, 1957.

Lee, Dorothy: "Cultural Factors in Dietary Choice," *Am. J. Clin. Nutrition,* March–April, 1957.

Richter, Carl P.: "Hunger and Appetite," *Am. J. Clin. Nutrition,* March–April, 1957.

U.S. Department of Agriculture: *Consumers All: The Yearbook of Agriculture,* 1965.

CHAPTER 13

Nutrition During the Life Span

TERMS TO UNDERSTAND

Abortion	Fetus	Neonatal
Albumin	Geriatric	Placenta
Amniotic	Gingivitis	Proprietary
Bizarre	Incidence	Toxemia
Conception	Lactation	Trimester
Contaminate	Motility	Uterus
Eclampsia		

Before Conception

It is particularly important that future parents be aware that an individual's current nutritional status reflects his nutrient intake from his own time of conception. Before conception is the time for the prospective mother to improve diet habits, to eliminate previous pregnancy or lactation depletions, and to attain normal weight.

Considerable recent interest has centered on nutritional implications of oral contraceptives. Biochemical evidence suggesting possible increased needs of a number of nutrients, including folic acid, vitamins B_2, B_6, B_{12}, and C, and certain trace metals, has been reported. While the clinical significance of these observations is unclear at present, patients taking oral contraceptives should be observed carefully for evidence of deficiencies of these types. In view of the frequent increase in menstrual blood loss associated with an intrauterine contraceptive device, IUD users should have particular attention paid to iron status.*

---

*American College of Obstetricians and Gynecologists: *Nutrition in Maternal Health Care,* 1974.

Pregnancy and Lactation Diets

Nutritional life begins with conception. Eating for two doesn't mean eating twice as much, but it does mean the health of two people is dependent upon what the pregnant woman puts into her stomach. If she eats the proper foods she protects her own health, and her baby is more likely to be born in good physical condition.

During childhood the skeleton is built and the functional capacity of tissues and organs is determined. Therefore, nutrition during childhood may have some influence on reproductive capacities in the adult. If the mother is well nourished *prior* to her child's conception, there are fewer complications during pregnancy, the chance of premature birth is decreased, and the baby will be healthier.

Teen-agers, who have the least satisfactory diet of any age group, account for one quarter or more of all first pregnancies. The teen-age girl often views any weight gain with alarm. She may omit from her diet enriched flours and cereals and may avoid meat and eggs—all good sources of iron. This poor dietary intake of iron, combined with iron lost during menstruation, may result in a deficient iron storage for the teen-age girl. If she becomes pregnant, she may develop a moderate to severe iron deficiency anemia and her child may also be anemic. With rare exception the pregnant woman should receive 30 to 60 mg. of elemental iron during pregnancy and for two to three months post partum. Since dietary sources of folic acid may not meet pregnancy needs, some doctors are routinely using a 0.4 to 0.8 mg. supplementation daily.* Routine use of other vitamins and mineral concentrates is not necessary.

Excellent diets *during* pregnancy result in fewer complications of pregnancy and less difficult labor and delivery. With poor diets there is a higher incidence of abortions, stillbirths, premature births, and neonatal deaths. A low intake of vitamin C may result in a higher rate of gingivitis; low protein may result in an increased incidence of abortion; low iodine, goiter in the mother or baby; low calcium, poor development of skeletal tissues; and low iron, anemia. The mother must take in more iron to allow for iron storage in the fetal liver. Since milk is low in iron, the infant draws upon his stored supply until iron-bearing foods are added to his diet.

Calorie needs are greater in the last two trimesters. The pattern of weight gain is often one to two kilograms (2 to 4½ pounds) in the first trimester and then averages 0.4 kilogram (slightly less than one pound) per week during the last six months. The pattern of gain is more important than the total gain, which may vary from 10 to 16 kilograms (20 to 35 pounds). It is necessary to differentiate between actual tissue gain and

*Ibid.

pounds due to fluid retention.* If a woman is obese or has too rapid a weight gain, there may be a *moderate* restriction in calories, but, to insure adequate nutrient intake, it is unwise to attempt weight reduction unless the diet is watched very closely.

A diet of less than 1800 calories usually does not provide the needed nutrients. A caloric intake that does not meet the needs of a pregnant woman may result in protein being used for energy needs instead of for tissue building. Vitamin and mineral supplements do not furnish protein; calcium tablets do not supply the protein and vitamins found in milk.

The increased need for nutrients in the prenatal diet makes necessary an increased intake of foods in the basic-four group to provide the extra calories, protein, vitamins, and minerals. "Empty" calorie foods probably will have to be curtailed or eliminated. Foods containing iron should be emphasized. (See Table A–1.) Adding coffee or chocolate flavor, an extract, or spices, such as cinnamon or nutmeg, may make milk acceptable to the woman who dislikes plain milk. An increase to three cups of milk daily (five for the teen-ager) may be advisable as soon as the woman knows she is pregnant. Fetal organs are being formed during the first eight weeks of pregnancy and skeletal tissues are being laid down. About two thirds of the total fetal weight gain occurs during the last half of pregnancy; thus, intake of the rest of the basic-four foods is increased at that time.

Doctors do not agree on the cause of toxemia of pregnancy, and some say the etiology is unknown. Its symptoms are edema in the hands and legs, headache, albumin in the urine, and elevated blood pressure. In the eclamptic stage, convulsions and coma may develop. Evidence indicates that the incidence of toxemia is lower among women who have adequate protein in their diets. Incidence of toxemia seems increased among women who are underweight or overweight.

The NRC reports that the use of low sodium diets during pregnancy is potentially dangerous. Restricting sodium will decrease the amount of meat, milk, and eggs which can be used, resulting in decreased protein intake. The use of diuretics in conjunction with low sodium diets is common, but no drug, even aspirin, should be used during pregnancy without the advice of the obstetrician. (54)

---

*Williams lists the average weight of products of a normal pregnancy:

	Pounds	
Fetus	7.5	
Placenta	1	
Amniotic fluid	2	
Uterus (weight increase)	2.5	
Breast tissue (weight increase)	3	
Blood volume (weight increase)	4	(1500 ml.)
Maternal stores	4 to 8	
	24 to 28	(94:371)

Table 13–1 *Dietary Allowances for Women
National Research Council, Eighth Edition 1974**

	Nonpregnant Females				Pregnancy	Lactation
	11–14 yr[a]	15–18 yr[b]	19–22 yr[c]	23–50 yr[c]		
Energy (kcal)	2,400	2,100	2,100	2,000	+300	+500
Protein (g)	44	48	46	46	+30	+20
Vitamin A (IU)	4,000	4,000	4,000	4,000	5,000	6,000
Vitamin D (IU)	400	400	400		400	400
Vitamin E (IU)	12	12	12	12	15	15
Ascorbic acid (mg)	45	45	45	45	60	80
Folacin (mcg)	400	400	400	400	800	600
Niacin (mg)	16	14	14	13	+2	+4
Riboflavin (mg)	1.3	1.4	1.4	1.2	+0.3	+0.5
Thiamin (mg)	1.2	1.1	1.1	1.0	+0.3	+0.3
Vitamin B$_6$ (mg)	1.6	2.0	2.0	2.0	2.5	2.5
Vitamin B$_{12}$ (mcg)	3	3	3	3	4	4
Calcium (mg)	1,200	1,200	800	800	1,200	1,200
Phosphorous (mg)	1,200	1,200	800	800	1,200	1,200
Iodine (mcg)	115	115	100	100	125	150
Iron (mg)	18	18	18	18	†	18
Magnesium (mg)	300	300	300	300	450	450
Zinc (mg)	15	15	15	15	20	25

*From *Nutrition in Maternal Health Care,* American College of Obstetricians and Gynecologists, 1974.

[a]Weight 44 kg (97 lb), Height 155 cm (62 in)
[b]Weight 54 kg (119 lb), Height 162 cm (65 in)
[c]Weight 58 kg (128 lb), Height 162 cm (65 in)
†The increased requirements of pregnancy cannot usually be met by ordinary diets; therefore, the use of supplemental iron is recommended.

Many women have nausea during the first three months of pregnancy. If vomiting is extensive and continues over a prolonged length of time, malnutrition and dehydration can develop. Often, small frequent feedings of dry, low fat foods are retained. If so, then small amounts of liquids are added. Other patients may be helped by consuming fluids between meals rather than at mealtime, by having smaller and more frequent meals, or by eating dry toast or crackers before arising.

Constipation may result from decreased physical activity or hindrance of normal motility of the intestine by growth of the fetus. Ample intake of fluids, as well as fruits and vegetables (especially raw vegetables), and whole grain cereals lessens this problem for most women.

Food cravings developed by some women during pregnancy are not an indication of nutritional need. Restlessness, a desire to follow the pattern of relatives or friends, or a need for more attention may be factors in the development of the craving. Unless the cravings are unreasonable or interfere with good food habits, they may be humored (42:118).

The stomach empties very slowly during labor. Food and drink may be withheld to decrease the danger of vomiting and aspiration during general anesthesia.

During lactation additional amounts of nutrients and fluids should be consumed. The lactating mother may need to have between-meal feed-

Table 13-2   *Changes in Basic-Four During Pregnancy and Lactation*

	Nonpregnant	Pregnant (2nd half)	Lactating
Milk			
Adult	2 or more cups	3 or more cups	4 or more cups
Adolescent	4 or more cups	5 or more cups	5 or more cups
Vegetable-fruit			
Citrus or substitute	1 serving	2 servings	2-3 servings
Dark green or deep yellow vegetable	1 serving at least every other day	1 serving daily	1-2 servings daily
Other fruits or vegetables, including potatoes	2 servings	2 servings	2 servings
Meat or alternate	2 or more servings	3 or more servings (6 oz. cooked) Include liver or heart every week.	
Cereal-bread	4 or more servings	4 or more servings	4 or more servings
		If fortified milk is not used, obtain physician's instructions for vitamin D supplementation. Use iodized salt. Use water or other beverages — at least 6 to 8 cups daily.	

Additional servings of these or any other food may be added as needed to provide the necessary calories and palatability.

ings. When lactation is terminated, calorie intake must be reduced to normal needs. Otherwise, weight gain follows.

In the preceding paragraphs it has been noted that more of all the nutrients are needed during pregnancy and lactation. Table 13-1 shows the recommended normal nutritional allowances for a woman and what her allowances would be during pregnancy and lactation. Table 13-2 suggests how to change the basic-four to meet these increases.

Children's Diets

"Certainly from a nutritional point of view — the advertisers of all proprietary infant foods notwithstanding — breast milk is biologically adequate, species-specific food which is preferable." If the mother has the desire and capacity to breast feed, the infant benefits by being picked up, fondled, and cuddled. Rigid scheduling has largely been replaced by allowing the infant to self-regulate his feeding pattern. Usually within the first few weeks of life he develops a schedule of approximately two to four hours. "Whether an individual baby's feeding interval is shorter or longer has no bearing on his ultimate developmental progress," but if forced to conform with a rigidly imposed schedule it may influence the "baby's emotional reactions to his parents and ultimately to other adults and his environment" (66:656–659). Breast milk tends to stimulate rapid development of a favorable microflora in the infant's intestinal tract. It is safer than formula if the mother has little understanding of cleanliness or if she has limited ability to mix ingredients.

Breast feeding not only is the ideal form of infant feeding, but in low income areas prolonged breast feeding often is the key to the baby's survival. With urbanization come new social values and in some developing countries the bottle-fed baby has become a status symbol. These countries should be concerned about the economic loss due to the decline in breast feeding. Berg* states that in Chile in 1970 the milk of 32,000 cows would be required to compensate for the loss of mother's milk, in "Kenya the estimated $11.5 million annual loss in breast milk is equivalent to two-thirds of the national health budget. . . . A laborer in Uganda may need to spend 33 per cent of his daily wage for baby's milk; in Chile, 20 per cent; in Tanzania 50 per cent."

With low income, mother's milk is often replaced with water thickened with starch (barley, rice, corn, wheat, etc.); any available milk is often mixed with contaminated water and poured into a dirty bottle topped with a crusty nipple. Poor sanitation increases the incidence of diarrhea, and as costs increase the formula becomes more diluted; thus the infant's chances for survival decrease. The use of formula feeding among the lower income, particularly urban, families is a world wide and increasing problem.

The pediatrician will specify the ingredients of the formula for the baby who is not breast-fed. Cow's milk is the common base for the formula. It is diluted with water to reduce the protein concentration, and carbohydrate (often Karo) is added to make up the calorie and carbohydrate deficit. Evaporated milk diluted with an equal amount of water can be used in place of whole milk. The advantages of evaporated milk are uniformity, availability, sterility, long shelf life, decreased curd tension which allows faster digestion, easy portability without refrigeration, and lower cost. Since milk is deficient in iron and ascorbic acid, prolonged feeding of only milk results in symptoms of anemia and scurvy. Unless vitamin D milk is used, rickets can develop. From Figure 9–12 note that if tomato juice is the source of vitamin C, twice as much should be used. (See Table 13–3 for milk composition.)

---

*Berg, Alan: "The Economics of Breast Feeding," *Saturday Review of the Sciences,* May, 1973.

Table 13-3 *Composition of Milk (100 Grams)*

	Cow's, fluid, whole	Goat's, fluid	Human
Water, per cent	87.2	87.5	85.2
Calories	66	67	77
Protein, grams	3.5	3.2	1.1
Fat, grams*	3.7	4.0	4.0
Carbohydrate, grams	4.9	4.6	9.5
Ash, grams	0.7	0.7	0.2
Calcium, milligrams	117	129	33
Phosphorus, milligrams	92	106	14
Iron, milligrams	Trace	0.1	0.1
Sodium, milligrams	50	34	16
Potassium, milligrams	140	180	51
Vitamin A value, I.U.	150	160	240
Thiamine, milligrams	0.03	0.04	0.01
Riboflavin, milligrams	0.17	0.11	0.04
Niacin, milligrams	0.1	0.3	0.2
Ascorbic acid, milligrams	1	1	5
Vitamin D, I.U.+	0.3-4.0		0.4-10.0

*See Table A-13 for fatty acid composition.
†From Burton, Benjamin T.: *The Heinz Handbook of Nutrition*, 1965, p. 173.
From U.S. Department of Agriculture, Handbook No. 8: *Composition of Foods*, 1963.

Terminal heating is recommended for making formulas. (See Figure 13-1.) Steps in terminal heating are

1. Wash and rinse all equipment (do not sterilize at this step).

2. Carefully measure and mix all ingredients, bottle, and cap. (Divide ingredients equally among the number of bottles needed for 24 hours. Add nipple and nipple cap. Do not screw covers tightly—during sterilization caps may be blown off.)

3. Heat bottles in a *covered* kettle (water half way up the bottles should be kept at a fast boil for 25 minutes).

4. Cool bottles in *covered* kettle (to retard scum formation).

5. Remove bottles, tighten covers, and refrigerate until needed.

In the aseptic method, the heated formula is poured into sterile bottles, and the sterile nipples and covering added. There is more danger of formula contamination with this method.

At birth the infant's stomach will hold about two tablespoons (one ounce) and at 12 months about one cup of food. As indicated on page 408, it will be years before his serving size will be comparable to an adult's (the adult's stomach holds approximately two quarts). The pediatrician will supplement the milk feedings with other liquids, cereals, and purees. The time for supplementing solid foods varies with the infant because it is influenced by his maturity and appetite. In general, a source of vitamins C and D is given when he is about two weeks of age; cereal, vegetable and

A *Cleaning inside of bottles and nipples*

B *Mix milk, water, and sugar in a pan*

C *Pour mixture into nursing bottles*

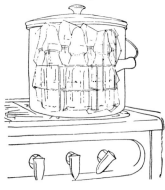

D *Set bottles on kettle rack to boil*

Figure 13–1 Basic steps in terminal sterilization method of making baby's formula. (From U.S. Department of Health, Education and Welfare, Children's Bureau Publication No. 8: *Infant Care.*)

E *Store capped bottles in refrigerator*

fruit puree from two to six months; egg yolk from four to six months; and pureed meat from two to six months. Chopped food is usually added before the end of the first year. Weaning the breast-fed baby is usually started when he is six to nine months of age; the bottle-fed, at about one year.

Typical feeding schedules are found in Appendix 3 with children's diets.

Infants usually double their birth weight in four to five months and triple it by the end of the first year. Height and weight increases are slower as age increases. A consistent gain in weight and height is one indication of good dietary habits. *Children have periods of rapid and slow growth. When growth is slower, a smaller volume of food is consumed.*

Normally, 90 per cent of the development of the brain and its integration into functional units occurs within the first four years of life. If there is moderate or prolonged undernutrition during these years, the child may become mentally retarded and may be unable to realize his adult potential.

It is not unusual for a baby to spit out his first taste of solid food. It feels different and is being served in a different manner from the liquid to which he is accustomed. A dislike for a certain food may develop because it is served too hot and the child's mouth is burned, because the food has a poor flavor due to spoilage or scorching, because the serving size is too large, *or because the child sees another person refuse a food or hears another person express a dislike for a food.* Children learn their customs and mannerisms by imitating others. (See Chapter 12, section on developing food habits.)

A child may not feel hungry because he is consuming too many fatty or fried foods, which leave the stomach more slowly than high carbohydrate and protein foods. Dr. Scull* says that it is not unusual for him to have "appetite lags and food jags." Under these conditions a good slogan for the mother is "Don't nag, don't nag." A normal healthy infant or child will ordinarily consume food without urging.

Table 13–4 is Dr. Scull's outline of normal behavior patterns in small children. Adults frequently associate some of these "behavior patterns" with "behavior problems."

In studying the table remember that each child's pattern of development is as uniquely his own as is his personality; therefore, his actions may not coincide with the outlined age. For example, one child may walk when he is nine months old and another not until he is fifteen months old, yet both can be normal children.

A "good eater" is not necessarily a "big eater." Babies soon learn that not eating is an almost foolproof way of getting more attention.

It is natural for a child to develop finicky food habits when he is two to three years old. His growth is slowing down, his appetite is decreasing, and he is beginning to assert his independence, and refusing food is one way of expressing his individuality. By age five he often prefers to see the meat, potatoes, and vegetables as separate servings rather than eat a stew or a casserole dish. The first and second grader can become so excited

---

*Alvis Joe Scull, M.D., Formerly Assistant Professor of Pediatrics, Stanford University School of Medicine; Staff, Child Guidance Clinic, California State Health Department.

Table 13-4 Normal Behavior Patterns of Children Which Appear as or Precipitate Problems for Parents

Developmental Areas	Age 1-3 Months	3-6 Months	6-9 Months	9-12 Months	12-15 Months	15-18 Months	18-21 Months	21-24 Months
Motor			Sitting, creeps.	Crawls, pulls up, walks alone.				Runs well; goes up and down stairs alone.
Language							Into everything (investigating and learning)[1]	Uses pronouns: I, you, me. Stuttering common, not significant.
Social	Smiles with stimulation.	Interested in attention from others; spontaneous smiles; recognizes desertion—cries if left. Thumbsucking.	Shy—recognizes and fears strangers; responds to familiar people; responds to play.	Anger—Breath holding first appears.	Jealousy appears. Hyperactive—into everything. "Bites" frequently.	Sensitive – avoid shaming and punishment as yet; parents prone to expect too much conforming to adult standards.	Tendency to run around nude too often shame used as corrective measure. Negativism; learning to control people. Frequent temper tantrums appear. Frequent waking. demands.	Negativism increased; accept with out retaliation; temper tantrums persist. Shy of strangers, but adjusts quickly if not pressed. Strong fear of desertion. Good to sing or rock to sleep. Sitter troubles – avoid trips away unless baby along.
Feeding	Nursing—? breast or bottle. Spitting up, colic.	Starting solid foods; may fight spoon. (Go easy.)	Holds bottle alone; usually big appetite. Often refuses solids, however. (Negativism.)	Messy eater, finger-feeds self; long retention of food; refuses bottle often. 11-month abrupt decrease in appetite.	Grabs at dishes, cups; messy eater.	Wants to feed self; spills; must eat when hungry, can't wait at all. Changes food likes, dislikes. Peak of thumbsucking (as tension outlets?).	Good appetite; if easily distracted – feed before others. Strong food preferences.	Finicky about foods; color, taste, or consistency.
Sleep	Irregular patterns.	Teething.	Rhythm movements; good to rock to sleep.	Sleep resistant (10 mo.).	Wakeful at night – 1-2 hours often.		Frequent waking at nights, not fear. Numerous demands. Pleasure of using words.	
Toilet Habits		Bowel irregularities.	Attempt to toilet train may be premature, unwise.		If regular – try training; starting sphincter control; fear of toilet noises if undiapered or loosens diapers. Urge use of potty chair.	May resist if just starting toilet training.	Smearing of stools especially after naps. Girls beginning to stay dry – not boys. Boys often demand to be fully undressed before will try bowel movement.	Strong fear of bed wetting; never punish – reassure. Usually toilet trained by now.
Sexual				Genital play if undiapered. (Self-discovery.)				
School								Only if unavoidable; needs good introduction with mother along. Short attendance periods – avoid overstimulation; don't expect participating play.

Developmental Areas	Age 2½ (30 Months)	The 3rd Year	The 4th Year	The 5th Year	The 6th Year—An Age of Tension—Lots of Tension—Time of Many Problems
Sleep	Rigid ritual of bedtime; resists naps — climbs out of bed. Keep bedroom window secured.	A.M. waking problem; wants to get into parents' bed. Likely very upset if wakens and parents not quickly at hand.	Dreams evident. (Animals OK.) Good time to change to junior bed.	Frightening dreams. Select bedtime reading and shows carefully.	
Toilet Habits	Boys usually dry now also.		If still having accidents, wonder why?	Cares for self at toilet.	Probably occasional "accidents" again, bowel and bladder—usually afternoons (mostly tension outlet).
Sexual	Confusion and concern over own sex. Needs reassurance and chance to discuss perceptions of sex differences.	Frequent use of bathroom language. Sex questions begin—satisfy; don't evade. Interest in each other's bodies (not naughty).		Very interested in babies (pets), where they come from (don't evade). Awareness and interest in sexual characteristics in others. Modest about self exposure. Both boys and girls express desire to "have babies" themselves.	Very interested in marriage and sexual roles; but as to responsibilities, not intercourse. Interested in babies; reenact baby roles, i.e. wetting, crawling, putting on diapers, cuddling. Exhibitionistic drives (don't shame). Boys—show and compare genitalia. Girls—more apt to pull panties off younger children. Frequently play doctor; taking temperature (rectal or vaginal). (After 4-5, good to use oral thermometer in hospital, office.)
School		3½ good time to start school. Accepts suggestion readily.		Hates "have to rest" naps; otherwise enjoys routine. Adjusts well to school or kindergarten.	Likes school—yet apprehensive and unsure of self; frequently ill till too late to go but recovers quickly. (100% attendance not important.) Embarrassed to ask teacher to go to rest rooms; unable to go to toilet frequently, and fear of accidents leads to fear of going to school. Many children control selves nicely in school then release controls and are "hard to handle" when home (again—help parents understand this as needed outlet if they are to conform at school). High incidence of nail biting, thumbsucking, chewing on objects as school starts. School discipline often conflicts with permissiveness at home—"hard to take"—child must suppress tension. Marked interest in making and being friends; difficult to maintain as each wants own way in association. (Reassure.) Very "tattle-tale."

Table continued on following page

Table 13-4   Normal Behavior Patterns of Children Which Appear as or Precipitate Problems for Parents (Continued)

Developmental Areas	Age 2½ (30 Months)	The 3rd Year	The 4th Year	The 5th Year	The 6th Year—An Age of Tension—Lots of Tension—Time of Many Problems
Motor		Can now dress alone with easy garments; not self-sufficient.	Dress and undress self; not tie shoes yet.	Ties shoes alone; definite handedness; fastens buttons.	Constantly in motion, but tires easily. Headstrong; clumsy—prone to falls.
Language	Constant talking.	Stuttering again. (Go easy.)	Lots of silly language.		Giggly—frequent use of bathroom terms in calling "names."
Parent-Child Relation					Beginning to achieve feeling of independence (good). Is at worst and best behavior with mother (ambivalence). Difficult to punish; "take out" on mother (threatens to get another). Begins to realize parents not omnipotent.
Social	Definite preference for mother or father. Avoid moving homes if can; do not rearrange furniture; prefers environment static. Everything has its place (go along with it).	Peak of imaginative life. Can tolerate mother's being away — understands she will always return, if so assured. (Day nursery if mother works.)	Temper tantrums and negativism subsiding. Boasts and shows off. Tendency to visit about neighborhood but is not running away. (Good. Let them go.)	Poised. Strong sense of pride in possession. Dogmatic re: own ideas. Self-assertion — even if different from parents. Lies — if frequently, probably "pressured." If angry — stubborn, resistant; whines and pouts — but easily placated with fairness and tact.	Scuffling, wrestling and roughhousing. Easily distracted in dressing—dawdles. Is center of universe; must be first; must win. "poor loser"—will cheat to win. Lacks self-confidence; apprehensive; needs reassurance and uncritical or patient relationship with parent and teacher. Very sensitive, highly emotional. Marked increase in auditory and spatial phobias (acrophobia, claustrophobia, firewagons, fireworks, etc.)
Feeding	Beginning to snack between meals. Excessive candy demands.	Prone to wander around at meals. Eats better alone—dawdles.	Few problems. May talk so much interferes with eating (be tolerant).	Wiggles lots. Tends to monopolize conversation. Nail biting, nose picking are tension outlets.	Overeats, stuffs self; loses all manners. Is clumsy—grabs, knocks food over and spills · kicks table, tips chair back, etc. Prone to likes and dislikes, but rational about it.

when telling his family about school experiences that he may find it difficult to eat. By seven or eight he has a big appetite and strong food preferences even though he will accept small servings of disliked foods. Around nine or ten he often becomes very interested in food and likes to "help" mother in the kitchen. The school child too often omits breakfast; if he does, by mid-morning he will feel tired and listless, scholastic achievement decreases, and he may be irritable, sarcastic, and emotionally unstable. An adequate breakfast provides at least one fourth of the day's nutrients (and should include a food which is high in protein); it is almost impossible to supply the entire day's nutrients unless three meals are eaten.

Candy, pickles, preserves, pastries, fat meats, gravies, stimulants, and fried foods should be omitted or given sparingly during early years to avoid crowding out the basic-four, which provide the body-building nutrients.

*Advice to Parents from Pre-Schoolers**

1. Please don't walk so fast when we go places together—my legs are short and I can't keep up with your long legs. Besides, there are many things I need to see and investigate along the way.

2. My attention span is short—lots of things last too long—like shopping and visiting and sometimes even the games you play with me.

3. When I'm frightened of a big dog or something, please pick me up and hold me; that helps more than telling me you won't let anything hurt me.

4. Sometimes it would be nice if you would talk to me and explain why we have to do things, or tell me what is going to happen ahead of time when it is something new to me—then I'll know what to do. Sometimes, you might even just have a conversation with me about anything; it would make me feel that I belong to this family, too.

5. Sometimes big people get in such a hurry they tell me about six things all at the same time. I get confused when people say things like—"this afternoon we're going to grandmother's, get your coat, finish your lunch, choose what toy you want to take, wash your hands and what shoes do you have on?"

6. I have trouble sitting still in the car even when you keep telling me to, 'cause it's not very interesting to look at the back of the seat or that dashboard thing—I'm too little to see what's outside and sit down like you want me to. While we're on the subject, sometimes my neck hurts trying to see what's on the dining room table or looking at big people's faces. Please put me on a chair or you bend down to me.

7. Would you please fix it so you know whether or not I understand what you want me to do before you get mad at me for not doing something you expected me to do.

8. Please give me time to do things for myself. I'm slow and haven't learned how to put my clothes on yet, much less do it fast. What's all the hurry about, anyway?

9. Please remember that I am in the room as a person and not a piece of the furni-

---

*Dr. Ruby Harris, of the Staff of the University of California Extension Service, Berkeley, California.

ture when you tell secrets or private things to other big people. How do I know what should not be repeated?

10. When you or daddy won't eat certain foods, talk about being afraid of the water, not liking school, are afraid of dentists and hospitals and doctors, why do you then expect me to like them or not be afraid?

11. Sometimes I wish you'd explain to me why you get in arguments with me. I know I lost, but it is sometimes fun to get you riled up, but why do you let yourself get involved? *You* know better!

12. I may be small and don't know about lots of things yet, but I'm not stupid! Please don't treat me as if I can't understand anything that is going on.

Teen-Age Diets

There is need for improvement in diets of many teen-agers, but not all teen-agers are poorly fed. Because their bodies mature rapidly, teen-agers need more nutrients if they are to enter adulthood with healthy bodies.

Teen-agers assert themselves as individuals and move toward freedom of choice and new responsibilities. Food intake may be one means by which independence is asserted. Fads and bizarre eating habits may shock the parents and adult counselors, but to conform with the activities, routines, and interests of his own age group is more important to the teen-ager than adult approval.

No two teen-agers have the same food needs, but the following general statements may be made.

1. Food and calorie needs are great. With the exception of infancy, the growth rate of the adolescent is greater than at any other time during his life span. Increased nutrients are needed to provide for the growth in height, in size and strength of muscles, in bone density, and in the developing endocrine system. Girls tend to grow most rapidly between 12 and 14 and boys between 14 and 16, but growth continues at a slower rate for another 4 or 5 years. The growth spurt may be as great as 3 to 5 inches and a weight gain of 10 to 15 pounds annually. Only during pregnancy and lactation does a woman need more nutrients than she does as a teen-ager.

2. Protein is needed in larger amounts for the building of cells. One half to two thirds of it should be derived from animal foods, but the biological value of plant proteins increases if animal protein is included at the same time. Protein is necessary to synthesize antibodies which help control infections. (It is well to remember that adolescent girls have a higher incidence of tuberculosis than do other age groups.)

3. If enough calcium, iodine, and iron are provided in food, these same foods will provide enough of the other minerals. Girls need more iron at the onset of menses. A hormone imbalance, excitement, or a

previously poor diet affects the ability of the body to use calcium efficiently. A poor childhood diet may result in a need for eight cups of milk daily for about six months before the body can efficiently use the calcium from the recommended allowance of four cups (92:7).

4. Intake of vitamin C and the B complex vitamins should be watched. Because of his large appetite a boy often makes a better food selection than a girl does, but he is inclined to omit foods containing vitamin C. The girl may get her vitamin C by eating salads and fruit, but have a low intake of iron and protein.

5. Girls need almost as much protein, minerals, and vitamins as do boys, but only two thirds to three quarters as many calories; therefore, girls should select foods more carefully. Eating fewer fried foods, gravies, dressings, cakes, pies, soft drinks, and candy reduces caloric intake. Girls have a greater tendency to be overweight than do boys; lack of exercise may be one factor in the weight gain. Another factor may be that the teen-ager is misinformed and therefore thinks milk and cereals are "fattening" foods. Reread Myths 7, 15, 26, 32, 33, and 34 in Chapter 2.

6. Snacks are a social custom and a part of the adolescent's diet habits. Snacks often contribute calories but not many nutrients. Fruit, nuts, ice cream, hamburgers, hot dogs, pizza, and milk, instead of the sticky, sweet foods help meet nutrient allowances and help prevent dental caries. Four fifths of 18-year-old boys and girls have one or more decayed teeth; almost one third of 18-year-old girls have five or more decayed teeth, and the proportion of boys with five or more teeth needing attention is even greater (93:87).

7. The pregnant teen-ager is developing her body as well as the fetus; therefore, her needs are greater than those of other adolescents.

8. Eating a variety of foods gives the teen-ager a better diet than if he eats a restricted number of foods. Eating breakfast, improving snack food habits, and adding more milk, fruits, and vegetables high in vitamin C content and more green and yellow vegetables improve the adolescent's diet.

9. Education regarding good food habits should be given in early childhood, for adult counseling probably has little effect on the adolescent. Have nutritious snacks available for his social gatherings. Furnish him with the extra nutrients, calories, and social contacts needed at this time in his life span.

Adult Diets

The nutrients needed by the young or older adult are the same as at any other time during the adult life span and will be provided by using a large variety of foods from the basic four groups.

In the developed countries, weight control and dental diseases are common problems. Increased use of whole grain cereals, milk, vegetables, and fruit could give more minerals and vitamins (and cellulose if constipation is a problem). Reducing the consumption of sweets (e.g., candy and sweet rolls), alcoholic beverages, high fat foods (e.g., doughnuts, corn and potato chips, dips made from mayonnaise and sour cream, and gravy), and empty calorie snacks, and increasing the amount of physical exercise should benefit adults.

Anyone responsible for feeding others welcomes suggestions and ideas for variety in food combinations and new methods of food preparation. Visits to grocery stores, thumbing through cookbooks, current newspapers and magazines, U.S. government publications, and advice from the Home Economists in Business should add "spice" to menu planning. Also see Chapters 10, 11, and 30.

Geriatric Diets

As mentioned before, what we eat throughout our life span affects how and when we start to age. Some of the illness of later years may be the delayed effects of poor nutrition. Many factors influence dietary planning for the aged. Older persons may have rigidly established eating habits. They may believe that an obese person is a healthy person or that certain foods are "baby" foods. Their income may be lower and therefore familiar foods cannot be purchased.* Their physical incapacities may interfere with meal preparation. Their marketing and storage problems may require that the eating of fresh foods be curtailed. Loneliness, grief, and other emotional problems can affect the older person's desire to eat. He needs to feel that he is loved and needed by someone, that he is a useful member of society. Eating often improves when the food is served in a social setting. Physical changes—need for dentures, reduction of calorie requirements, decrease in the volume of digestive juices—may also necessitate diet changes, but his need for nutritious foods is the same as that of the younger adult. *As at any other time during life, the nutrients can be obtained from foods in the grocery store.* The concentrates and the specially prepared, high-priced foods usually do not provide so balanced an intake of nutrients as do milk, cereals, eggs, meat, vegetables, and fruit. (Calcium, iron, protein, and vitamin A and C deficiencies appear with some regularity in older people because part of the basic-four is omitted.) If food intake is restricted, the physician should be the one to order any supplement. Reread Myth number 23, Chapter 2.

As mentioned above, calorie needs are decreased because of a lower

*Over one third of all Americans over 65 have incomes below the poverty level. Rising food prices have increased their nutrition problems.

basal metabolic rate and less physical activity. The 20-year-old male who uses about 3000 calories per day will need only 2700 by age 25, and by 50 the need decreases to 2400; the 20-year-old female needs 2100 calories, but this need decreases to 2000 by 25 and to 1800 by 50.

With the slowdown of body processes, the volume of digestive juices is reduced, and efficient absorption may be decreased. Thus nutrient intake will need to be increased even though calories are decreased. Careful selection of foods to eliminate "empty calorie" foods becomes more important. Previously tolerated fats may now cause discomfort. The doctor may recommend that the fats used be low in saturated fatty acids. Either protein or iron deficiency results in fatigue, and protein deficiency may cause edema and increase susceptibility to infections owing to inadequate antibody synthesis.

Adequate fluid intake aids digestion and kidney function. Adding bulk and more liquid to the diet helps control the constipation which frequently afflicts the elderly. To increase cellulose intake, two tablespoons of wheat bran may be added to the morning cereal and, for those who have a mastication problem, salads such as raw vegetable carrot-raisin or cabbage-pineapple may be put into a blender. The appearance of a blenderized salad is not optimal, but it does add variety and flavor to the diet. If bulk is increased, the liquid intake must be increased to reduce the possibility of impaction. Addition of cellulose and liquid decreases the need for laxatives and stool softeners. Strained (pureed) food contains less bulk. Using adequate milk provides liquid, as well as many necessary nutrients. In relation to its cost, powdered milk provides many nutrients.

If two or more people have to be fed, group them in one place, and give one and then another a small bite of food. The interval between bites will provide for the elderly patient time for leisurely mastication which in turn allows easier swallowing. This can save the nurse time and effort.

The older person may prefer his "basic-four" in four or five small, easy-to-eat feedings rather than in three large meals. Frequently the older person who lives alone does not cook a real meal for himself. The older woman eats many meals of tea and toast, while the older man, who probably does not know how to cook, will open one can per meal. Malnutrition often results.

The operator of a nursing or boarding home soon recognizes that "feeding people is far more than serving groceries." The transition from the family home to the institution can be made easier by doing the following things:

1. Change diet gradually. By forcing unfamiliar foods, she may substitute emotional problems for nutritional ones. Not every older person needs soft or bland foods; tasting and chewing familiar foods may be one of the few pleasures he can still enjoy. The family bringing in a favorite food will provide a stimulus for eating.

2. Concentrate nutrients into a few bites. Adding an extra cup of

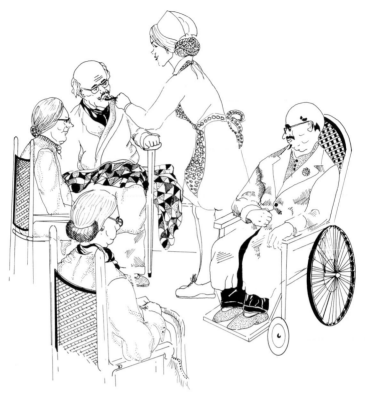

Figure 13-2   Elderly slow eaters may increase food intake if fed in a social situation. Offering food alternately to the group gives the elderly time for chewing, savoring flavors, and swallowing; the nurse also utilizes her time more efficiently.

powdered milk to a pudding or additional eggs or ground liver to the meat loaf, or cooking cereal in milk instead of water increases nutrient intake.

3. Arrange food attractively and in small portions. Appealing, tasty meals can assure the elderly person that someone still cares about him. Soup served in a cup may be easier to handle.

4. Give adequate liquids. If water is not well accepted offer other beverages often, as liquid intake is important.

5. Encourage companionship during meal hours. The individual who is able to get out of bed and join others has a better appetite. (25)

Dentures can cause difficulties for all who wear them. The wearer may have too much pride to tell the family why he no longer eats ham, cookies with nuts, caramel candy, or other previously enjoyed foods. The nurse should realize that tactful discussion can help the individual to accept the necessity for rinsing dentures in mid-meal, cutting meat into tiny pieces, and returning to the dentist for refitting of dentures. She should know about the new products that make dentures more comfortable to wear.

SUGGESTED READING

Pregnancy, Lactation, Infancy
American College of Obstetricians and Gynecologists: *Nutrition in Maternal Health Care,* 1974.
American Medical Association: *Growing Pains,* 1969.
Bauer, Charles: "Taking the Danger Out of Diarrhea," *Family Health,* June, 1974.
Brewer, Thomas H.: "Good Prenatal Nutrition Prevents Toxemia of Late Pregnancy," *Post-graduate Medicine,* February, 1966.
Brown, Roy E.: "Breast Feeding In Modern Times," *American Journal of Clinical Nutrition,* May, 1973.
Dairy Council Digest: *Nutritional Needs During Pregnancy,* July-August, 1974.
"Health and Your Child," *Family Health,* October, 1974.
Gerber Products Company: *Current Practices in Infant Feeding.*
Krupp, George R., M.D.: "Why Some Mothers Fatten Their Children," *Today's Health,* November, 1967.
Linde, Shirley Motter: "Common Problems of Pregnancy and What to Do About Them," *Today's Health,* April, 1968.
National Foundation – March of Dimes:
  Be Good to Your Baby Before It Is Born.
  Unprescribed Drugs – Birth Defects Prevention.
Seifrit, Emma: "Changes in Beliefs and Food Practices in Pregnancy," *J. Am. Dietet. A.,* November, 1961.
Smith, Beverly Bush: "Breast Feeding: Facts and Fallacies," *Today's Health,* February, 1966.
Today's Health: "Protecting the Infant – A Special Section," January, 1968.
Turtle, William John: *Dr. Turtle's Babies,* 1973.
U.S. Department of Health, Education, and Welfare, Children's Bureau:
  Food For Your Baby's First Year, 1969.
  Infant Care, 1973.
  Prenatal Care, 1973.
  When Your Baby Is on the Way, 1968.
  Your Baby's First Year, 1968.
  Your Premature Baby.
Wessel, Morris A.: "Calming the Colicky Baby," *Family Health,* February, 1975.

Children
Breckenridge, Marian E., and Murphy, Margaret: *Growth and Development of the Young Child,* 1969.
Breckenridge, Marian E., and Vincent, Elizabeth L.: *Child Development.*
Hatfield, Antoinette, and Stanton, Peggy: *Help! My Child Won't Eat Right,* 1973.
Lynch, Harold D.: *Your Child Is What He Eats,* 1958.
National Dairy Council:
  Feeding Little People.
  Food Before Six, 1968.
  Source Book on Food Practices with Emphasis on Children and Adolescents, 1968.
  Your Health – How Can You Help?
U.S. Department of Agriculture: *Food for the Family with Young Children.* Home and Garden Bulletin No. 5, 1969.
U.S. Department of Health, Education, and Welfare, Children's Bureau:
  A Creative Life for Your Children. (By Margaret Mead.)
  A Healthy Personality for Your Child.
  Feeding the Child with a Handicap.
  Foods for the Preschool Child.
  Your Child from One to Six.
  Your Child from One to Three.
  Your Child from Six to Twelve.
  Your Child from Three to Four.
University of California Agricultural Extension Service: *Happiness Is Fun at the Table – Eating for Children Three to Four,* 1967.

Teen-age
American Dietetic Association: *Give Yourself a Break.*

Contra Costa County Health Dept. (Calif.): *Healthy Snacks for Teens,* 1974.
General Mills Nutrition Service: *Feeding the Teen Machine.*
Metropolitan Life Insurance Company: *To Parents About Drugs,* 1970.
National Dairy Countil:
  A Boy and His Physique, 1971. (By Walter H. Gregg.)
  A Girl and Her Figure.
  Grin? or Grouch. (By W. W. Bauer.)
  Meals and Snacks to Match Your Mood.
  The Teens and the Teeth. (By Barbara Abel.)
  Your Food — Chance or Choice.
  Your Snacks — Chance or Choice. (Poster.)
Today's Health: "School Athletics — Food Facts and Myths," September, 1966, Pp. 85, 86.
U.S. Department of Agriculture: *Improving Teen Age Nutrition.*
U.S. Department of Health, Education, and Welfare, Children's Bureau: *The Adolescent in Your Family.*

Geriatric
American Dietetic Association:
  Eating Is Fun — For Older People Too.
  Forget Birthdays — Enjoy Good Eating.
American Medical Association: *Your Age and Your Diet,* 1967.
Butler, Jean: "False Teeth: The Problem May be More Mental Than Dental," *Today's Health,* August, 1974.
"Diets of the Elderly, Nutrition Labeling, and Nutrition Education," *Journal of Nutrition Education,* July-September, 1974.
General Mills, Inc.:
  After the Kids Have Gone.
  Meal Planning for the Golden Years, 1972.
Irwin, Theodore: How to Handle Problems of Aging," *Today's Health,* July, 1969.
King, Charles Glen, and Britt, George: *Food Hints for Mature People.* Public Affairs Pamphlet No. 336.
Thompson, Prescott W.: "Let's Take A Good Look at the Aging," *Am. J. Nursing,* March, 1961.
U.S. Department of Agriculture:
  Home and Garden Bulletin No. 17: *Food Guide for Older Folks,* 1973.
  Home and Garden Bulletin No. 194: *A Guide to Budgeting for The Retired Couple,* 1973.
U.S. Department of Health, Education, and Welfare:
  Planning for the Later Years, 1969.
  The Fitness Challenge . . . in The Later Years, 1973.

EXERCISES

1. List several ways in which the pregnant woman who doesn't wish to drink more than two glasses of milk daily can incorporate the recommended allowance in her diet.
2. Plan a day's feedings on a two-hour schedule for a patient with pernicious vomiting of pregnancy.
3. Measure two level tablespoons of vegetable and compare this serving for a 1- to 2-year-old with the 1/2 to 2/3 cup serving for an adult.
4. Plan three days' menus for an elderly person who will not wear his dentures, but who refuses to eat "baby food" (purees).

DIET THERAPY

INTRODUCTORY STATEMENT

Diet therapy, which is the use of food in the treatment of disease, is accomplished by modifying the normal diet to meet the doctor's orders. He may wish it changed in nutrient content, making it, for example, a low fat, high carbodydrate, or high bulk diet; in consistency, directing that, for example, all foods be liquid or puréed; or restricted in amount, to, for example, 1 gram of sodium, 1200 calories, or the quantity to be given at a feeding. Keep in mind that the adjectives high or low mean more or less; for example, high protein means modifying the basic-four with more or larger servings of foods which are a good source of protein, and low protein means fewer or smaller servings per day.

Whenever the success of the diet is based upon nutrient quantities the diet order should be very specifically written: a low-salt diet does not indicate how much the sodium is to be restricted, but there can be no doubt about an order which reads 800 milligrams sodium.

Controlled research which establishes the merit of a particular modified diet is often non-existent. Because the human body is very adaptable, different modified diets for the same diagnosis often seem to work equally well.

The modified diet is given on order just as a medication is given on order. If the nurse does not know exactly what the diet involves, she should seek further advice from the physician or a dietitian. It is customary to contact the dietitian of the hospital where the attending physician is on the staff. The dietitian will ask for the signed diet order just as the pharmacist asks for a prescription order. A dietitian gives detailed information regarding foods to use or to omit. For example, some frozen foods are slightly brined before packaging and could not be used on a 500-milligram sodium diet.

155

In feeding any person, one should remember that there are many factors with which one has to be concerned. For example,

1. The patient's response to a disease is dependent to a large extent on his state of nutrition.

2. Food may be symbolic of cultural patterns—some people consider snails a delicacy, others refuse to taste them; ancestral superstitions may make some foods taboo.

3. Food may denote status—dark bread has been thought of as peasant food, and it's a step up the social ladder when one can afford refined sugar and flour; we serve expensive meat cuts to guests although a meat loaf would provide comparable nutrient value.

4. Food may be used to express love—when an absent member of the family returns home or if a member of the family is experiencing stress, both the family and he like to have his favorite dishes served.

5. Food habits may reflect living habits—one family may regularly have a substantial breakfast, another who views the late evening television shows is apt to sleep later and eat a "skimpy" breakfast.

In addition to these factors the sick person's attitudes or degree of co-operation may be influenced by

1. Financial worry about the mounting bills.

2. Resentment due to the physical confinement or the therapy which is being given.

3. Misunderstanding about the relation of the new food pattern to convalescence.

4. Medications which may influence the taste of food.

5. Inability to purchase the prescribed diet—for example, a high pro-tein diet is more expensive; diet instruction should include advice on how to purchase and use the inexpensive cuts of meats, how to use the cheaper types of milk, and making sure that the patient understands that the lower grade foods are as nutritious even though the quality is not as great.

6. Dislike of food cooked in large quantity because it does not con-form to the favorite recipe or the individualized seasoning used in the pa-tient's home.

There are many modified diets, a few of which are discussed in this section. The diet prescribed for a patient may be further modified, owing to additional pathologic conditions, to psychologic aspects, to religious concepts, or to environment, such as lack of, or refusal to wear, dentures. In many diseases of metabolism which have a genetic pattern (the reces-sive traits are transmitted by genes from parent to offspring), a modified diet is prescribed by the physician. (See illustration of pattern of genetic inheritance on page 199.)

A limited number of specific diet patterns are given in the appendices following the last chapter.

Remember that the modified diet should be prescribed by a doctor. As research continues the application of the principles of nutrition will change. Members of the medical team should constantly review and incorporate the new findings.

SUGGESTED READING

Morris, Ena: "How Does a Nurse Teach Nutrition to Patients?" *Am. J. Nursing,* January, 1960.

CHAPTER **14**

Hospital House Diets

TERMS TO UNDERSTAND

Convalescence   Gristle
Distention   Gruel
                                            Tolerance

In the hospital a modified diet is a variation of the liquid, soft, light, or general diet tray. All, except the liquid diets, are written to try to include the principles of the basic-four. The modified diet served in a home could be similar to the family's meal. For example, if buttered carrots are on the menu for the family, the carrots could be cooked and then a serving removed and mashed for the patient with ulcerated gums.

Legumes, melons, and strongly flavored vegetables, such as cabbage and cauliflower, have often been spoken of as foods which may cause flatulence, heartburn, or distention. Because clinical evidence shows that *tolerance to specific foods varies widely from person to person,* the patient's experience rather than generalized rules should be observed when writing the diet.

Foods allowed on trays will vary with each hospital. Currently the trend is to be more liberal in the variety of foods served. In general this pattern will be followed.

Liquid Diets

It will help the dietitian to know why the patient is on a liquid diet. A surgery patient gets a different type of liquid diet from the patient who has a broken jaw and cannot chew any solid food.

Clear (surgical) liquid—tea or coffee without cream or milk, fat-free broth and Jello. Carbonated beverages, strained vegetable or fruit juice, and gruel may be allowed. Except for providing liquid it is nutritionally unimportant; often used pre- and post-operatively for one or two days.

Full liquid—any food liquid at body or room temperature usually in six or more feedings daily. Foods allowed include milk, cream, ice cream, gruel, vegetable and fruit juices, eggnog, plain gelatin desserts, Junket (milk rennet pudding), sugar, butter or margarine, strained soups, strained meat in broth, tea, coffee, carbonated beverages. It is used for patients who are acutely ill or are unable to chew or swallow solid food. The iron intake is often inadequate.

Soft Diets

The soft diet usually is used between the full liquid and general diets for the patient who needs easily chewed foods. It may be prescribed for those convalescing from surgery, gastrointestinal disturbances, and acute infections. It can be planned to be nutritionally adequate.

Foods allowed:

Soups—broth, cream, strained vegetable.

Eggs—except fried.

Milk and milk products—all. Cheddar cheese may be used in cooking.

Vegetables—cooked. Some hospitals omit strongly flavored ones such as broccoli, cabbage, onions, and cauliflower, and fibrous ones such as corn.

Fruit—cooked and bananas.

Cereals—cooked enriched, or finely ground, Italian pastas and rice. Some hospitals allow ready-to-eat cereals but may restrict those high in cellulose, such as All-Bran.

Meats—ground or minced, baked, boiled, broiled, and creamed. Sweetbreads, liver, poultry, and fish are used.

Desserts—ice cream, sherbet, plain cakes and cookies, and simple puddings such as custard, tapioca, and blanc mange.

Beverages—all.

Omit: Fried foods, nuts, coarse cereals, fibrous vegetables, meat tough with gristle, salads, pastries, pickles.

A mechanically soft or dental soft diet requires little or no chewing.

Foods allowed:

Soups—all.

Eggs—all.

Milk products—all.

Vegetables—all. Some patients may need them puréed, chopped, or diced. Others can use corn cut from the cob, finely chopped lettuce in a sandwich, raw tomatoes, fried onion rings, and such.

Fruit — all. Hard fruits such as raw pineapple may need to be omitted, skins may need to be removed from apples, and so on.

Meats, fish, poultry — ground or finely chopped and served with gravy or broth to assure easy swallowing.

Desserts — all, including pastries.

Beverages — all.

Any general diet food can be blenderized. Roast beef, steaks, and such, prepared this way, do add variety in flavor.

The puréed vegetables and fruits in a mechanically soft diet are not well accepted by most adults; therefore, the nutrient intake may be very low. Evidence is lacking that the fiber in a general diet is as irritating as once thought; for example, for many years puréed foods have been used for diverticulosis patients, but recently the normal diet, which stimulates more peristalsis, has been used successfully and, in many cases, may even be better.

Light Diets

Many hospitals omit either the soft or light diet classification because they are so similar.

Foods allowed:

All on the soft diet plus simple salads such as fruit and cottage cheese or sliced tomato.

Omit: Fried foods, pastries, fibrous vegetables, nuts.

General, Full, House, Normal, or Regular Diets

This diet usually has from 2000 to 2500 calories, and provides 70 to 90 grams of protein, 80 to 100 grams of fat, and 200 to 300 grams of carbohydrate daily. Foods allowed:

All — some hospitals may restrict the amount of pastries, fried foods, strongly flavored vegetables, and highly seasoned food. If fried foods are used the cooking fat should be watched very carefully so that it does not become overheated.

CHAPTER 15

Weight Control

TERMS TO UNDERSTAND

Actuarial	Calipers	Kilogram
Adipose	Diaphragm	Obesity
Amphetamine	Fluctuation	Overweight
Anorexigenic	Hypertension	Protoplasm

Overweight

In the United States 25 to 36 per cent of all adults are 10 per cent or more overweight, and the incidence is increasing. Fifteen to 20 per cent of teen-agers (at least 10 million) are over their recommended weight. Even though overnourished in calories, overweight persons often are malnourished, owing to an insufficient intake of one or more nutrients. Cardiovascular disease mortality is 40 per cent higher among the moderately overweight and 65 per cent higher among the markedly overweight. (95:VII and 5) The desire for a better appearance combined with the knowledge of a possible health hazard makes overweight people prone to be the victims of every newly proposed "magic way" to weight loss. Diet books form a lucrative part of the $10 billion "pounds off" industry.* "One single company grossed eight million in ten months on one single worthless 'drug'; the net was two million. Most of the sales cost was consumed by advertising, two million dollars on TV spots alone, with some of the best known shows selected." (48:4)

If any of the fad diets were a satisfactory remedy for weight reduction, why would there be new ones being proposed every few months? It seems that the more bizarre the diet, the more apt it is to be published

---

*Today's Health, April, 1974, p. 56.

and to be tried by the public, who wish a fast, convenient means of losing weight without changing accustomed food habits. Six months or a year later the same people spend additional money on the latest highly touted "new idea" diet. The best that can be said for fad diets is that people seldom remain on them long enough to induce malnutrition.

The overweight person weighs 10 to 20 per cent above the average for his sex, age, and height; the obese person weighs more than 20 per cent above the average.

Fat deposition results when caloric intake exceeds caloric output. To gain one pound of weight, approximately 3500 calories above metabolic needs have to be consumed; to lose that pound, 3500 calories less than metabolic needs have to be omitted. One hundred calories a day (33 per meal), which actually is less than 5 per cent of the recommended adult caloric intake, is enough to deposit 10 pounds of fat a year in the body. Men usually lose weight on diets of 1500 to 2000 calories per day; women on diets of 1000 to 1500 calories daily.

It is not uncommon to see an advertisement which claims that, if you will use this drug, device, or diet, you can lose seven pounds in seven days or 20 to 25 pounds the first month. Remember that to lose one pound of fat you have to expend 3500 calories more than you consume. This applies to both male and female. The recommended daily caloric intake for the average 30-year-old woman is 2000 and for the average 30-year-old man is 2700. Multiplying these by seven would give a recommended weekly caloric intake of 14,000 for women and 18,900 for men. To lose seven pounds of fat you would have to omit seven times 3500, or 24,500 calories. You can readily see that omitting all food would not cut your calories enough. If the scales show a loss of seven pounds in a week, there has been dehydration and/or minimum calorie intake combined with very vigorous exercise.

The amount of exercise needed to use up calories is much greater than most people realize. In Table 15–1 you will note that it takes 34 minutes of swimming to use the 377 calories in a piece of apple pie—this is 34 swimming minutes, not swimming 14 minutes and suntanning 20 minutes. Walking a mile uses up about 92 calories; thus one must walk about 38 miles to use up 3500 calories. Nevertheless, a daily walk lasting 1 hour and 25 minutes, at the rate of approximately four miles per hour, will provide a calorie deficit of 500. This walk or equivalent exercise, when taken daily, will cause weight loss of one pound per week; a 1.3-mile hike per day could result in a loss of 12 pounds per year. *Consistent moderate exercise does contribute to weight loss.*

Formerly, overweight was often considered a moral problem, but in reality it is a medical problem requiring much patience and understanding. Modern living conditions contribute to the obesity problem because of several factors:

1. We use less energy, owing to mechanized equipment (lawn mowers and ditch diggers as well as washing machines and vacuum cleaners).

2. Our income is often large enough to buy the attractively packaged, well advertised, perhaps non-basic-four, but high caloric, food products.

3. Our cultural habits are conducive to "snacks" during television programs, club meetings, and entertaining guests.

4. We may respond to the tension of modern life by eating because we lack a physical outlet, such as chopping wood.

5. We tend to watch rather than participate in sports.

6. We use mechanized transportation instead of walking or bicycling.

Those who have deeply set emotional problems need to have the emotional problem treated before reducing is started. Regular exercise adapted to the patient's physical ability is often helpful. The person who was obese since childhood is less likely to be successful in his reducing regimen. Eating habits are acquired, and the older the person, the more difficult it is for him to change them.

Weight taken off and then regained is not real weight loss. To avoid regaining the weight the diet pattern should (1) be adequate in nutrients (the need for protein, minerals, and vitamins is constant), and (2) provide a "pattern of living" which changes eating habits and trains the appetite. This change of habits, which is to become the life-long pattern, is not considered by the faddist. He may

pay lip service to the laws of energy intake and expenditure, but many advertise that, with the aid of their preparations, no dieting is necessary. Many of these diet aids are simply vitamin- and mineral-supplemented candy, sweetened skim milk powder concentrates, or inert bulk-producing compounds. Even granulated sugar has recently been advertised as an aid to dieting on the basis that blood-sugar level is the major determinant of food intake in man. These claims, of course, are unfounded and merely remind us that both experimental and clinical studies support the hypothesis that high-protein, moderate-fat intakes are more conducive to comfortable weight reduction than a high-carbohydrate regimen of the same caloric value. (59:779)

The basic-four is seldom maintained on fad diets, and without the basic-four malnourishment usually results. McLester and Darby state:

For reasons of health, as well as of looks, the person whose body weight exceeds the normal by 20 per cent or more should endeavor to reduce. This does not of necessity apply to persons who are only slightly (10 to 15 per cent) above the ideal, unless they are handicapped also by heart disease or a tendency, latent or manifest, to such metabolic disorders as gout or diabetes. Persons of the last-mentioned group should endeavor to remain always a few pounds underweight. The reasons for advising weight reduction in the average case are many: (1) Life expectancy, as shown by actuarial tables as well as by clinical experience, is greater if with advancing years the person remains thin. (2) The dangers of disease, notably the hazards of acquiring diabetes or of succumbing to an operative procedure, are distinctly less in a thin person. (3) A condition of overweight in the presence of transient tachycardia increases enormously the hazard of subsequent sustained hypertension. (4) Advanced arteriosclerosis is more common in obese persons than in those whose weight is normal. (5) Too much fat interferes materially with physical activity and reduces muscular efficiency. (6) Obesity handicaps the heart by increasing the load to be carried, while at the same time, because of the collection of fat in and around this organ, it interferes with the efficiency of its contractions. (7) Deposits of fat in the abdominal cavity interfere with the movement of the diaphragm and abdominal muscles. (8) Extensive deposits of fat in the skin impair its function of regulating heat loss and maintaining body temperature. These influences place a great handicap upon the obese person, and it is chiefly for their relief that his weight should be reduced. (50:334)

Table 15-1 *Energy Equivalents of Food Calories Expressed in Minutes of Activity*

Food	Calories	Walking* min.	Riding bicycle+ min.	Swimming‡ min.	Running§ min.	Reclining# min.
Apple, large	101	19	12	9	5	78
Bacon, 2 strips	96	18	12	9	5	74
Banana, small	88	17	11	8	4	68
Beans, green, 1 c.	27	5	3	2	1	21
Beer, 1 glass	114	22	14	10	6	88
Bread and butter, 1 slice	78	15	10	7	4	60
Cake, 1/12, 2-layer	356	68	43	32	18	274
Carbonated beverage, 1 glass	106	20	13	9	5	82
Carrot, raw	42	8	5	4	2	32
Cereal, dry, 1/2 c., w/milk and sugar	200	38	24	18	10	154
Cheese, cottage, 1 tbsp.	27	5	3	2	1	21
Cheese, cheddar, 1 oz.	111	21	14	10	6	85
Chicken, fried, 1/2 breast	232	45	28	21	12	178
Cookie, plain, 148/lb.	15	3	2	1	1	12
Doughnut	151	29	18	13	8	116
Egg, boiled	77	15	9	7	4	59

	Calories	Walking*	Riding bicycle+	Swimming#	Running§	Reclining#
French dressing, 1 tbsp.	59	11	7	5	3	45
Halibut steak, 1/4 lb.	205	39	25	18	11	158
Ham, 2 slices	167	32	20	15	9	128
Ice cream, 1/6 qt.	193	37	24	17	10	148
Mayonnaise, 1 tbsp.	92	18	11	8	5	71
Milk, 1 glass	166	32	20	15	9	128
Milk, skim, 1 glass	81	16	10	7	4	62
Orange, medium	68	13	8	6	4	52
Pancake with syrup	124	24	15	11	6	95
Peach, medium	46	9	6	4	2	35
Peas, green, 1/2 c.	56	11	7	5	3	43
Pie, apple, 1/6	377	73	46	34	19	290
Pizza, cheese, 1/8	180	35	22	16	9	138
Pork chop, loin	314	60	38	28	16	242
Steak, T-bone	235	45	29	21	12	181

*Energy cost of walking for 70-kg. individual = 5.2 calories per minute at 3.5 m.p.h.
+Energy cost of riding bicycle = 8.2 calories per minute.
#Energy cost of swimming = 11.2 calories per minute.
§Energy cost of running = 19.4 calories per minute.
#Energy cost of reclining = 1.3 calories per minute.

From Konishi, F.: "Food Energy Equivalents of Various Activities," *J. Am. Dietet. A.*, March 1965.

Table 15–2 *Energy Expenditure by a 150 Pound Person in Various Activities**

Activity	Gross Energy Cost—Cal. per hr.
A. Rest and Light Activity	**50–200 per hr.**
Lying down or sleeping	80
Sitting	100
Driving an automobile	120
Standing	140
Domestic work	180
B. Moderate Activity	**200–350 per hr.**
Bicycling (5½ mph)	210
Walking (2½ mph)	210
Gardening	220
Canoeing (2½ mph)	230
Golf	250
Lawn mowing (power mower)	250
Bowling	270
Lawn mowing (hand mower)	270
Fencing	300
Rowboating (2½ mph)	300
Swimming (¼ mph)	300
Walking (3¾ mph)	300
Badminton	350
Horseback riding (trotting)	350
Square dancing	350
Volleyball	350
Roller skating	350
C. Vigorous Activity	**over 350 per hr.**
Table tennis	360
Ditch digging (hand shovel)	400
Ice skating (10 mph)	400
Wood chopping or sawing	400
Tennis	420
Water skiing	480
Hill climbing (100 ft. per hr.)	490
Skiing (10 mph)	600
Squash and handball	600
Cycling (13 mph)	660
Scull rowing (race)	840
Running (10 mph)	900

*The standards represent a compromise between those proposed by the British Medical Association (1950), Christensen (1953) and Wells, Balke, and Van Fossan (1956). Where available, actual measured values have been used; for other values a "best guess" was made.

Prepared by Robert E. Johnson, M.D., Ph.D., and colleagues, Department of Physiology and Biophysics, University of Illinois, August, 1967.

(From *Exercise and Weight Control*, Committee on Exercise and Physical Fitness of the American Medical Association and the President's Council on Physical Fitness in cooperation with the Lifetime Sports Foundation.)

The daily diet is usually 500 to 1000 calories below metabolic needs and contains from 1 to 1.5 grams of protein per kilogram of body weight (the closer to 1.5, the greater the appetite control); about 40 grams of fat will be acceptable to the patient, but often he feels more satisfied if it is

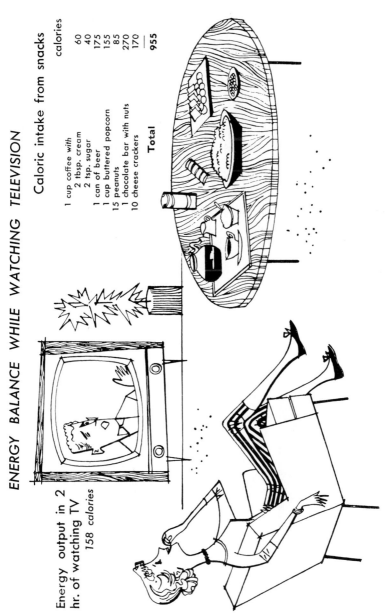

ENERGY BALANCE WHILE WATCHING TELEVISION

Caloric intake from snacks

	calories
1 cup coffee with	60
2 tbsp. cream	40
2 tsp. sugar	175
1 can of beer	155
1 cup buttered popcorn	85
15 peanuts	270
1 chocolate bar with nuts	170
10 cheese crackers	
Total	**955**

Energy output in 2
hr. of watching TV
158 calories

Figure 15–1 Energy balance while watching television. (From *J. Am. Dietet. A.*, September, 1956, p. 806.)

higher (up to 80 or 90 grams), with the remainder of the calories in foods low in carbohydrate content. (This allows more volume than the greater concentrated carbohydrate foods would and so reduces the feeling of hunger. A chronically hungry person can develop a food obsession.) The food intake is divided into three or more meals approximately equal in caloric value. Foods to avoid include cream, high percentage fruits and vegetables, Italian pastas, salad dressings, gravy, poultry stuffing, alcohol, fried foods, popcorn, nuts, soft drinks, sugar, concentrated sweets, pastries, and foods high in fat, such as avocado and olives. *Foods high in calories are usually greasy-crisp, oily, sweet, or sticky, thick or concentrated, or alcoholic. Foods low in calories tend to be watery-crisp, clear, dilute or thin, or raw.* The diabetic exchange lists have been successfully used to restrict calories and give variety to the diet. Refer to the restricted calorie and diabetic diets in the appendices.

The 1200 calories in the basic-four could be reduced to approximately 1000 by using 2 eight-ounce cups skim milk, which provide 180 calories. Any of the following would increase the calories by approximately 200: a ginger-ale highball; 2 ounces candy; 2 tablespoons mayonnaise, margarine, or butter; 1/6 quart of vanilla ice cream; 1 cup chocolate-

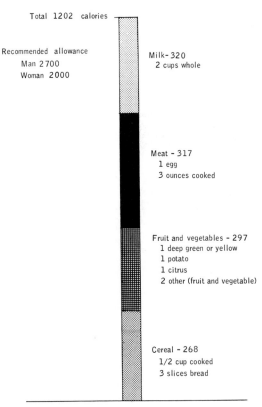

Total 1202 calories

Recommended allowance
    Man 2700
    Woman 2000

Milk- 320
2 cups whole

Meat - 317
    1 egg
    3 ounces cooked

Fruit and vegetables - 297
    1 deep green or yellow
    1 potato
    1 citrus
    2 other (fruit and vegetable)

Cereal - 268
    1/2 cup cooked
    3 slices bread

Figure 15-2 Calories supplied by the basic-four food groups. Note that the cereal group contributes fewer calories than the vegetable-fruit group.

Figure 15–3 "I'll have a banana split with chopped nuts and lots of whipped cream...and a diet soda, please."

flavored milk; 2 large cookies; or 3 tablespoons jelly, jam or sugar. The total intake then would be almost 1400 calories. The Food and Nutrition Board reports that for some persons who drink alcoholic beverages, the alcohol provides five to ten per cent of the energy intake and can go as high as 1800 calories daily. (53:33) A handful of nuts and a couple of cocktails may yield 1000 calories; therefore at a cocktail party it is easy to consume several hundred calories before eating anything substantial. The extra calories consumed in this way aggravate the problem of overweight: they replace essential nutrients in the diet and thus account to some extent for the metabolic ailments seen with chronic alcoholism.

Losing weight is a slow process. The patient should realize that the first two or three weeks on a well-planned low-calorie diet may bring no weight loss (often there is a small gain due to water retention as fat is being catabolized) and that there may be future periods when there is little or no loss (it is then that the patient is apt to become discouraged and want to discontinue). The ideal weight loss is from one to three pounds per week. Weight may vary two or three pounds during the day, depending upon the elapsed time between water intake and output and the last meal. It is often recommended that one weigh himself before dressing in the morning. Many Americans eat a skimpy breakfast and lunch, and a large dinner. Experiments in animals suggest that a more equal distribution of calories into three meals, or even calorie-controlled nibbling, is better for health and weight control. Recent studies have been made to determine how the number of feedings per day, type of food included, or omission of food for specific periods of time would affect appetite as well as weight. Both success and failure have been reported, and much more study needs to be done. *One should not attempt to lose weight by omitting all food, unless hospitalized and under constant medical supervision.*

The future should include education programs on prevention of obesity because the easiest pound to lose is the pound which was never gained.

Weight control is highly individualized. In addition to calorie control and consistent exercise, the factors which help the individual control his weight vary because of his emotional reactions and past experiences. Random ideas follow to help the nurse understand the patient's reactions and to assist the patient in understanding what is happening.

Obesity is most apt to develop in infancy, the age of starting to school, puberty, and, for females, pregnancy and menopause. Once childhood obesity has occurred, treatment is difficult because the fat cells have increased in number. Hirsch suggests that the potential number of fat cells in an individual is established during adolescence or early adult life. Once this potential is reached weight changes vary the cell size, not the number of cells; thus, weight reduction may be most effectively prevented or treated before establishment of the total possible fat cells. In weight loss, adipose cells are reduced in size, not in number. (36) Peckham has demonstrated that it is easy for animals that have been obese to regain weight: there are a large number of adipose cells waiting to be refilled with fat. (63)

The use of calipers to measure skinfolds* is a practical method of determining the overall fatness of the body, because about 50 per cent of the total fat in the body is situated immediately under the skin. However, even the active individual, as he ages, has fat infiltration into the muscle tissue. In those individuals who remain physically active muscle replacement by fat proceeds very, very slowly.

There is no food which renders other food calories unavailable or which burns body fat.

Do obese people, particularly children, really overeat? Do they eat the wrong snack-foods? Or do they get their surplus calories from under-exercising? Huenemann found that both boys and girls classified as obese ate fewer calories than other groups studied and were quite inactive but described themselves as being physically active. (95:59 and 65) Mayer found, when studying the activity of obese adolescents, that many of the overweight are quite unaware of their lack of activity. Motion pictures

---

*Skinfold tests are described in Mayer, Jean: *Overweight*, 1968, Chapter 2.

taken while they were playing volleyball, swimming, or playing tennis showed that overweight girls were almost motionless when compared to girls of normal weight. (48:126).

A decrease in weight as small as 20 pounds may considerably increase one's ability to move around and adds to the enjoyment one gets from life. "The work of breathing is increased if considerable additional weight is carried on the chest wall. Excessive adipose tissue also adds to the problem of keeping the whole body oxygenated. Obese people have, accordingly, a diminished exercise tolerance, and they show greater difficulty in normal breathing, particularly in the presence of any—even mild—respiratory infection." (48:155)

Excessive perspiration is common among the obese because there is a restriction of normal heat loss from the body. Rashes, inflammation, and boils tend to form where there is constant friction between the moist areas of skinfolds.

Mild restriction of table salt is a much safer measure to prevent excessive water retention during weight reduction than the use of diuretics.

Most parents are very proud of the baby who is showing very rapid growth and weight gain. Overfeeding an infant can establish the pattern of overeating which results in a life span of overweight. Eighty-six per cent of overweight boys and 80 per cent of overweight girls become overweight adults. (95:5)

There probably is a genetic tendency to overweight; if one parent is overweight there is a 50 per cent chance the child will be overweight; if both parents are overweight, the probability increases to 80 per cent. (95:3) *The diet and exercise patterns of the family should also be considered as potential causes of overweight.*

Some people like to have their calorie allotment divided into several (perhaps six) equal sized meals; others would be repulsed by the small size of the servings. (Using a smaller serving plate will make the portions look larger.) The liquid or powder formula diets provide a rigid control of calorie intake and may be useful when starting a reducing regime, but they do not reeducate the person to good eating habits. Formula diets can be useful in the weight maintenance program by using them to replace one meal a day. Some people, when told there are foods which should be omitted, such as pie, develop an obsession for those foods. These people may be able to reduce their calories by using their customary foods but cutting all servings in half (a 3000 calorie intake becomes 1500). Others, if they have one bite of a restricted food, are unable to forego eating a quantity of it.

The amphetamines and related compounds are anorexigenic agents (appetite depressants). They can be useful for those who recently became overweight, for those who are just starting a weight reduction regimen, or for those who have had repeated failures in losing weight. Adults who were obese as youngsters are likely to have failed repeatedly to control their weight in the past; the amphetamines may give them the opportunity to experience a successful weight loss. These drugs may cause side-effects of dry mouth, insomnia, restlessness, irritability, and sometimes constipation. The effectiveness of the depressants ordinarily lasts about four to six weeks while weight is slowly but consistently lost and the patient is educated to the use of a lower-calorie diet. (48:163)

Using a "crash diet" does not make a fundamental change in eating habits; therefore the relapse rate for regaining weight is extremely high. Mayer contends that a diet containing

no less than 14 percent of protein, no more than 30 percent of fat (with saturated fats cut down), and the rest carbohydrates (with sucrose—ordinary sugar—cut down to a low level), is still the best diet. It contains all the nutrients needed for life-long nutrition; it does not, through excessively low carbohydrate content, introduce an additional cause of fatigue and irritability; it does not, through excessively high fat content, promote high cholesterol. At the same time, the protein and fat content are still high enough to promote long-term satiety (while the carbohydrates in the diet promote short-term satiety as well). A varied diet staying within this range is infinitely preferable to any of the fad diets . . . the grapefruit diet, the banana diet, the hard boiled egg diet, and many others. (48:160)

In his book, *Overweight,* Jean Mayer, M.D., states that the following questions are often asked him concerning weight control.

1. Is it true that the body has no need for carbohydrates? And his reply——The brain must be supplied with glucose or blood sugar; if carbohydrates are not available from the diet then the body breaks down its own protein; in other words, muscle tissue is used to make carbohydrate for the brain. Concentrated sources of table sugar should be avoided but starches, particularly in the form of cereals and potatoes, are acceptable components of a reducing diet.

2. What type of milk or cheese should be used by an adult? He answers——Non-fat milk, buttermilk, and cottage cheese (particularly the low-fat cottage cheese) are lower in fat and therefore lower in calories than whole milk. Dairy fat does contain saturated fats too, and these may be involved in the development of atherosclerosis. When counting calories it is probably desirable to use non-fat or low-fat dairy products rather than those made with whole milk.

3. Should one eat slowly?——It takes time to develop the feeling of satiety, and probably those individuals who tend to overeat when they eat rapidly would use less food if they ate more slowly; those mechanisms that are involved in metering the food ingested would have time to be used, and the individual would therefore feel more satisfied.

4. Other than one's general appearance, are there really any benefits in reducing?——Those individuals who develop diabetes, during middle age, usually are those who are overweight. Hypertension usually responds to weight reduction. An obese arthritic patient can often be made more mobile by weight reduction.

5. Are there any specific necessary foods?——Other than milk for small babies, no special food is necessary, only the nutrients that food contains. Even milk is not a complete food. It is low in copper, iron, and vi-

tamin C. Small children who drink only milk may become obese, usually are anemic, and may show some signs of scurvy. For older children and adults good nutrition is obtained from a varied diet in sufficient but not excessive amounts. When any one of the basic-four food groups is eliminated, there is a chance the person will be deficient in some nutrient, unless he knows a great deal about nutrition and knows exactly what other foods must be used in larger quantities to provide the nutrients that would have been provided by the eliminated food group.

6. How can one take off fat in a particular part of the body? —— When on a low calorie diet the calories do not come from the fat located in just one portion of the body. However, exercise, through developing muscle tone, is instrumental in remolding the shape of the body.

7. What factors are involved in the particular spot where fat accumulates in the body? —— (a) The sex of the person; (b) the individual's inherited skeletal type, which influences his body build; (c) muscular activity; and (d) endocrine secretion (for example, steroid hormones would promote the development of a lot of fat around the belt and in the back of the neck).

8. Isn't most excess weight due to salty water in the body? —— The excess weight in the obese person is due to fat. Adipose tissue is over 80 per cent fat, but there is some water and protoplasm found in fatty tissue. When losing weight there is very often water retained in the body in that space freed by the disappearance of fat. In some cases it may be several days or even a few weeks before that water gets excreted and the scales show an actual weight loss. This phenomenon is more common in inactive older women than in other age groups who are losing weight.

9. Does alcohol stimulate the appetite? —— Generally, no. However, if someone is very tense and he drinks a moderate amount of alcohol to relax then he may regain his appetite. Alcohol does contain 7 calories per gram, which is about 100 calories per ounce, and these calories do count. They have to be added in when totaling caloric intake.

10. Are the home exercising machines of any value in weight reduction? —— If they are used enough and with sufficient energy, they certainly can be the exercise that is involved in weight control. Frequently the machines are costly and not used enough to warrant their purchase. Exercise of short duration but of high intensity, leading to pulse rates of 120 or higher, does have a useful effect on the cardiovascular system. Exercising vigorously on a bicycle ergometer or rowing machine for no less than fifteen minutes at least three times a week or walking moderately fast for three quarters of an hour or more every day is of great value.

11. Does protein rapidly decrease the appetite? —— No. Sugars have the most immediate effect on hunger contractions, but proteins and fats have a more lasting effect. When granulated sugar is consumed in large amounts it may stimulate excessive insulin production which in turn accelerates fat synthesis and then the reappearance of hunger. A small meal

containing carbohydrate, fat, and protein is probably the best way to take care of immediate and long-term satiety.

12. Is smoking an appetite curb?——Often someone who has stopped smoking will rapidly gain 5 to 7 pounds and then lose it very slowly. A few will gain a greater amount when they stop smoking. However, heavy cigarette smoking is much more injurious to health than marked obesity. "Depending on the age, a pack of cigarettes a day may have statistically the same deleterious effect as 50 to 100 pounds of excess weight." (48:203)

13. Should one cut the number of meals to only one or two per day while trying to reduce?——Dividing the allowed number of calories among a large number of small meals or small meals and nutritious snacks is a more effective method of reducing. Usually when one has left out one meal he then feels entitled to eat a very large meal, which often contains more calories than two smaller meals.

14. Have the millions of dollars worth of low-calorie foods which are being sold and consumed made a material contribution to weight reduction? Have they helped people to consume fewer calories?——The answer can be yes, but three things should be remembered about these so-called low-calorie foods. (a) A number of them represent only a very small decrease in the total number of calories;* (b) many people who use a serving of a low-calorie food often assume it to be a calorie-free food; therefore they feel free to use a second dessert or a larger serving and thus end up consuming more calories; (c) do not confuse something that is marked low calorie to mean low carbohydrate. This is not necessarily true. A low or carbohydrate free diet is often a high fat diet and undesirable because it may promote higher blood cholesterol.

15. Does eating table salt or excessive table salt cause obesity?——People in the United States tend to salt their food more than people from other nations. There is no known relationship between salt intake and obesity. If weight is lost rapidly, fluid can accumulate. The fluid retention is less likely if the intake of salt is reduced. There is some indication that using a large amount of salt may be associated with a greater risk of hypertension. Reducing the consumption of table salt may be a useful health measure; the body quickly adjusts both to the reduction of the sodium content of the diet and the difference in taste.

---

*Learn to read food labels. Agricultural Handbook No. 8 shows that 100 grams of ice cream contain 20.8 grams of carbohydrate, 4.6 grams of protein, 10.6 grams of fat, and 193 calories. The label on a package of ice cream labeled "diabetic" shows that 100 grams contain 16.84 grams of carbohydrate, 4.29 grams of protein, 10.2 grams of fat, and 176.3 calories.

Contents on the label of a highly advertised (supposedly nutritious) space food read: Sucrose, corn syrup, partially hydrogenated vegetable oil, sodium caseinate, caramel flavor, synthetic glycerin, modified food starch, salt, vegetable monoglycerides, citric acid, artificial flavoring, artificial coloring, and (listed last) vitamin and mineral components. This product is obviously expensive candy fortified with traces of vitamins and minerals.

By law, ingredients are listed in order of decreasing predominance.

16. Is it true that one gets a higher percentage of nourishment from the food if he eats a small amount of food? —— No. Approximately the same percentage of the nutrient content is absorbed and metabolized no matter what volume of food you eat.

17. Is the water content of an obese person higher? —— No. The proportion of body weight in water in an overweight person is actually lower than in the non-obese individual because adipose tissue contains very little water as compared to muscle and organ tissue.

18. Are steam baths useful in weight reduction programs? —— There is dehydration due to loss of water by sweating. When the individual quenches his thirst, water replaces that lost and the weight is regained.

19. Are fasts useful in reducing programs? —— Long fasts do cause weight loss but should be conducted only in a hospital under constant supervision because of the serious medical and psychological risks. Some doctors do use a two or three day fast at the start of a reducing regimen. Mayer's "impression is that such fasts are not, in fact, necessary in the majority of cases, although, I would agree that a few days of dieting, at a very low caloric level (e.g., 600 or 800 calories per day) can often be useful at the start of a reducing regimen, the level being brought afterwards to 1000, 1200 or whatever number of calories the physician thinks adequate for the longer pull." (48:193)

20. "Has it been proved that repeated fluctuations in weight, resulting from temporary successes of weight reduction attempts followed by failures, may be more harmful than a continuing condition of being moderately obese? We have evidence that in at least one strain of obese and diabetic mice, the repeated practice of weight gain and weight loss (which I have called elsewhere the "rhythm method of girth control") leads to shorter life expectancy than maintenance of an obese weight. On the other hand, reducing them and keeping them reduced does significantly increase their life span." (48:108)

The way to lose weight is to eat less and exercise more.

Underweight

Underweight (more than 15 per cent below the recommended weight) should not be ignored because it can predispose to or be a symptom of another disease. Also, work efficiency and resistance to disease may be lowered.

To gain weight the patient should build body tissue, not increase pounds by increasing the amount of body fat; therefore the diet should contain extra protein and calories. Mid-morning and mid-afternoon feedings are given if they do not interfere with the amount eaten at regular meals. It is much better to eat three well-planned meals and a bed-time feeding than to have between-meal nourishment and then eat very little at

Table 15-3 *Weights of Persons 20 to 30 Years Old*

Height (without shoes)	Weight (without clothing)		
	low	average	high
Men	Pounds	Pounds	Pounds
5 feet 3 inches	118	129	141
5 feet 4 inches	122	133	145
5 feet 5 inches	126	137	149
5 feet 6 inches	130	142	155
5 feet 7 inches	134	147	161
5 feet 8 inches	139	151	166
5 feet 9 inches	143	155	170
5 feet 10 inches	147	159	174
5 feet 11 inches	150	163	178
6 feet	154	167	183
6 feet 1 inch	158	171	188
6 feet 2 inches	162	175	192
6 feet 3 inches	165	178	195
Women			
5 feet	100	109	118
5 feet 1 inch	104	112	121
5 feet 2 inches	107	115	125
5 feet 3 inches	110	118	128
5 feet 4 inches	113	122	132
5 feet 5 inches	116	125	135
5 feet 6 inches	120	129	139
5 feet 7 inches	123	132	142
5 feet 8 inches	126	136	146
5 feet 9 inches	130	140	151
5 feet 10 inches	133	144	156
5 feet 11 inches	137	148	161
6 feet	141	152	166

If you have a small skeletal frame, your weight probably should not be greater than the amount shown in the average column; if you have a large frame, your desirable weight range is between the average and high columns. Your desirable mid-twenties weight is considered the best weight for the remainder of your life span.

Very general criteria are: A man has a small frame if he wears a hat smaller than size 7, a medium frame if size 7 to 7½, large if over 7½. A woman has a small frame if her glove size is below 6, medium if 6 to 7, large if over 7.

From: U.S. Department of Agriculture, Home and Garden Bulletin No. 74: *Food and Your Weight.*

the noon and evening meals. The underweight person should rest regularly, as it helps conserve energy.

After the basic-four is met, emphasis can be placed on high caloric foods, larger servings, candy at the end of meals, cream added to milk, and so on. The formula diets (e.g., those which contain 300 calories per cup) can be used as the beverage. This would add a concentrated source of calories. If normal weight is reached and the high calorie diet is continued, obesity could result.

SUGGESTED READING

American Dietetic Association: *Step Lively and Control Weight.* (This leaflet is especially valuable for its substitution lists.)

American Medical Association Council on Foods and Nutrition:
Can Food Make the Difference?
Fit for Fun.
"Formula Diets and Weight Control," *J.A.M.A., 176:*439.
The Healthy Way to Weigh Less.

Bradfield, Robert B.: "The Relative Importance of Physical Activity," *Nutrition News.* National Dairy Council, December, 1968.

California Dietetic Association, Los Angeles District: *A Dozen Diets For Better or For Worse,* 1974.

Conniff, James C. G.: "Can You Stay Slim After Dieting?" *Reader's Digest,* February, 1969.

Hicks, Clifford B.: "Eat! Says Fat Little Johnny's Mother," *Today's Health,* February, 1970.

Irwin, Michael H. K.: *Overweight—A Problem for Millions.* Public Affairs Pamphlet No. 364.

Krupp, George R.: "Why Some Mothers Fatten Their Children," *Today's Health,* November, 1967.

Mademoiselle: "Are You Really Too Fat?" October, 1974.

Metropolitan Life Insurance Company:
Four Steps to Weight Control, 1974.
Stress.

National Dairy Council:
Choose Your Calories By the Company They Keep.
The Food Way to Weight Reduction.
Personalized Weight Control.
Weight Control Source Book.

Pascoe, Jean: "How Weight Watchers Lose Weight," *Reader's Digest,* July, 1969.

President's Council on Physical Fitness:
Adult Physical Fitness.
The Fitness Challenge, An Exercise Program for Older Americans.
Vigor: A Complete Exercise Plan for Boys 12 to 18.
Vim: A Complete Exercise Plan for Girls 12 to 18.

Royal Canadian Air Force: *Exercise Plans for Physical Fitness.*

Schanche, Donald A.: "Diet Books That Poison Your Mind . . . and Harm Your Body," *Today's Health,* April, 1974.

Shipman, W. G.: "Predicting Results for Obese Dieters," *Nutrition News.* National Dairy Council, April, 1968.

U.S. Department of Agriculture:
Calories and Weight Control, The U.S.D.A. Pocket Guide. Home and Garden Bulletin No. 153. (This pamphlet is particularly good for its actual-size drawings of servings of meat. It is 3½" × 5" × ³/₁₆" so can easily fit into one's pocket.)
Food and Your Weight, 1973.

U.S. Department of Health, Education, and Welfare:
Alcohol and Alcoholism.
Drugs of Abuse.
How Safe Are Our Drugs? 1968.
Publication No. 73–3024: *New Restrictions on Diet Pills,* 1974.
The Up and Down Drugs: Amphetamines and Barbiturates, 1969.

University of California Agriculture Extension Service, HXT-89: *Calorie Control.*

EXERCISES

1. Many people do not know the caloric value of food. From the table of nutritive values found in the appendix, make lists of foods which have about 500, 300, 200, 100, and 50 calories per serving.
2. If you eat 500 extra calories every day for a week, how much weight would you gain during the week?

3. Assuming that you do not increase your caloric intake but walk for an hour each day and expend 200 calories during that hour, how many days would it take you to lose 1 pound of weight?
4. (a) Evaluate the following adult menus. Do both contain the basic-four?
   (b) At the end of Menu 1 fill in either the Canadian or U.S. recommended allowances to use as a basis for making comparisons.
   (c) Learn to use the nutrient table in the appendix by filling in the blank spaces for the foods at the end of Menu 2. (1 cup = 16 tbsp.; 1 tbsp. = 3 tsp.)
   (d) List the foods which are high in calories.
   (e) Which foods are "lone-wolf" calorie foods?
   (f) Would the lower-calorie menu contain the previously discussed protein allowances for a 128-pound (58-kilogram) woman?
   (g) What percentage of the calories came from fat?
   (h) What is the basis for the statement—"It isn't the potato or bread (etc.) that is high in calories; it is what you put on it"?
   (i) Compare the calories in the cereal servings, the fruit and vegetable servings, the meats, and the dairy products. Is protein, fat, or carbohydrate the greatest source of calories in each group?
   (j) Is the intensity of the green or yellow color related to the amount of vitamin A and iron in fruits and vegetables?
   (k) Compare the amount of iron in the meats.
   (l) Are cereals just "empty calorie" foods? Compare the amount of nutrients in four servings with the recommended allowances.
   (m) Does Menu 1 contain the recommended allowance for iron? List three suggestions for improving the iron intake.
   (n) List five low-calorie, nutritious snacks which could have been used in Menu 2.
   (o) Is margarine less nutritious or lower in calories than butter?
   (p) Is Jello a low-calorie food? Sponge cake?
   (q) True or false?—Sour cream has a very low calorie content as compared to sweet cream.

Adult Menu 1

	Grams	Calories	Protein	Fat	CHO	Calcium	Iron	Vitamin A	Thiamine	Riboflavin	Niacin	Ascorbic Acid
Breakfast:												
1 orange, 3" diameter	210	75	1	Trace	19	67	.3	310	.16	.06	.6	70
1 c cooked oatmeal, with	236	130	5	2	23	21	1.4	0	.19	.05	.3	0
¼ c whole milk	61	40	2	2	3	72	Trace	88	.02	.10	.03	.5
2 poached eggs	100	160	12	12	Trace	54	2.2	1180	.10	.30	Trace	Trace
1 slice whole wheat toast, 20 slices per loaf	23	55	2	1	11	23	.5	Trace	.06	.03	.7	Trace
1 tbsp. butter	14	100	Trace	11	Trace	3	0	460	0	0	0	0
1 c skim milk	246	90	9	Trace	13	298	.1	10	.10	.44	.2	2
1 c black coffee	5	5	Trace	Trace	.8	5	.2	0	Trace	Trace	.9	0
TOTAL		655	31	28	69.8	543	4.7	2048	.63	.98	2.73	72.5
Luncheon:												
1 c canned consomme	240	30	5	0	3	Trace	.5	Trace	Trace	.02	1.2	0
Salad												
1 raw tomato 2" × 2½"	150	35	2	Trace	7	20	.8	1350	.10	.06	1.0	34
1 c uncreamed cottage cheese	225	195	38	1	6	202	.9	20	.07	.63	.2	0
1 leaf lettuce	25	5	Trace	Trace	1	17	.3	475	.01	.02	.1	4
1 slice raisin bread, 20 slices per loaf	23	60	2	1	12	16	.3	Trace	.01	.02	.2	Trace
1 tbsp. butter	14	100	Trace	11	Trace	3	0	460	0	0	0	0
2 halves canned pears with 2 tbsp. medium syrup	117	90	Trace	Trace	23	6	.2	Trace	.01	.02	.2	2
1 c skim milk	246	90	9	Trace	13	298	.1	10	.10	.44	.2	2
1 c tea	2	5	Trace	0	.4	5	.2	0	0	.04	.1	1
TOTAL		607	56	13	65.4	567	3.3	2315	.30	1.25	3.2	43

Adult Menu 1 Continued on following page

Adult Menu 1 (Continued)

	Grams	Calories	Pro-tein	Fat	CHO	Calcium	Iron	Vitamin A	Thiamine	Ribo-flavin	Niacin	Ascorbic Acid
Dinner:												
3½ oz. lean roast leg of lamb	100	266	26	18	0	11	1.8	—	.15	.27	5.6	0
3½ oz. baked, in skin, potato with	100	93	3	Trace	21	9	.7	Trace	.10	.04	1.7	20
¼ c (4T) light sour cream	60	120	Trace	12	4	60	Trace	520	Trace	.08	Trace	Trace
1 c green snap beans	125	30	2	Trace	7	62	.8	680	.08	.11	.6	16
2 large outer celery stalks	80	10	Trace	Trace	4	32	.2	200	.02	.02	.2	8
2 wafers 1⅞" × 3½" Rye Krisp	13	45	2	Trace	10	7	.5	0	.04	.03	.2	0
½ cantaloupe, 5" diameter	385	60	1	Trace	14	27	.8	6540	.08	.06	1.2	63
1 c black coffee	5	5	Trace	Trace	.8	5	.2	0	Trace	Trace	.9	0
TOTAL		629	34	30	60.8	213	5.0	7940	.47	.61	10.4	107
DAY'S TOTAL		1891	121	71	196	1323	13.0	12303	14.0	2.84	16.33	222.5

Select one U.S. or Canadian standard to use from the Recommended Allowances. See inside of front or back cover.

U.S.		Canadian	
Child,	1–3	Child,	1–3
Male,	11–14	Male,	10–12
	19–22		16–18
	23–50		36–50
	51+		51+
Female,	11–14	Female,	10–12
	19–22		16–18
	23–50		36–50
	51+		51+

(Nutrient Sources = Church and Church:*Food Values of Portions Commonly Used.*
U.S.D.A. Agricultural Handbook No. 8: *Composition of Foods.*
U.S.D.A. Home and Garden Bulletin No. 72: *Nutritive Value of Foods.*)

Adult Menu 2

	Grams	Calories	Protein	Fat	CHO	Calcium	Iron	Vitamin A	Thiamine	Riboflavin	Niacin	Ascorbic Acid
Breakfast:												
1 c raw grapefruit sections with	194	75	1	Trace	20	31	.8	20	.07	.03	.3	75
1 tbsp. brown sugar	14	50	0	0	13	12	.5	0	Trace	Trace	Trace	0
1 oz. plain corn flakes with	28	110	2	Trace	24	5	.4	0	.12	.02	.6	0
¼ c (4T) light cream	60	120	Trace	12	4	60	Trace	520	Trace	.08	Trace	Trace
2 fried eggs in 2 tsp. margarine	104	220	12	18	.6	54	2.2	1404	.08	.26	Trace	0
2 strips fried bacon	16	100	5	8	1	2	.5	0	.08	.05	.8	0
1 slice white toast, 20 slices per loaf, 3 to 4% non-fat dry milk	23	60	2	1	12	19	.6	Trace	.06	.05	.6	Trace
1 tbsp. margarine	14	100	Trace	11	Trace	3	0	460	0	0	0	0
1 tbsp. jam	20	55	Trace	Trace	14	4	.2	Trace	Trace	.01	Trace	Trace
1 c coffee with		5	Trace	Trace	.8	5	.2	0	Trace	Trace	.9	0
1 tbsp. light cream	15	30	Trace	3	1	15	Trace	130	Trace	.02	Trace	Trace
1 tbsp. white sugar	12	45	0	0	12	0	Trace	0	0	0	0	0
TOTAL		970	22	53	102.4	210	5.4	2534	.41	.52	3.2	75
Coffee Break:												
1 cinnamon bun with raisins	60	183	3	5	33	35	1.2	210	.1	.01	.9	0
1 tbsp. butter	14	100	Trace	11	Trace	3	0	460	0	0	0	0
1 c coffee with		5	Trace	Trace	.8	5	.2	0	Trace	Trace	.9	0
1 tbsp. light cream	15	30	Trace	3	1	15	Trace	130	Trace	.02	Trace	Trace
1 tbsp. sugar	12	45	0	0	12	0	Trace	0	0	0	0	0
TOTAL		363	3	19	46.8	58	1.4	800	.1	.03	1.8	0

Adult Menu 2 Continued on the following page

Adult Menu 2 (Continued)

	Grams	Calories	Protein	Fat	CHO	Calcium	Iron	Vitamin A	Thiamine	Riboflavin	Niacin	Ascorbic Acid
Luncheon:												
1 c canned beef noodle soup	250	70	4	3	7	8	1.0	50	.05	.06	1.1	Trace
2 soda crackers, 2½″ square	11	50	1	1	8	2	.2	0	Trace	Trace	.1	0
1 tuna salad sandwich	105	278	11	14	26	48	1.2	231	.1	.1	4	1
1 sweet pickle, 2¾ by ¾″	20	30	Trace	Trace	7	2	.2	20	Trace	Trace	Trace	1
10 potato chips, 2″ diameter	20	115	1	8	10	8	.4	Trace	.04	.01	1.0	3
1-4″ sector apple pie	135	345	3	15	51	11	.4	40	.03	.02	.5	1
1 c chocolate-flavored milk drink, made with skim milk	250	190	8	6	27	270	.4	210	.09	.41	.2	2
1 c tea with		2	Trace	0	.4	5	.2	0	0	.04	.1	1
1 tbsp. light cream	15	30	Trace	3	1	15	Trace	130	Trace	.02	Trace	Trace
1 tbsp. sugar	12	45	0	0	12	0	Trace	0	0	0	0	0
TOTAL		1155	28	50	149.4	369	4.0	681	3.1	6.6	7.0	9
Mid Afternoon:												
2½ oz. candy bar, chocolate covered		336	6	16	43	62	2	0	.03	.1	4.0	0
TOTAL												
Dinner:												
3½ oz. baked ham, medium fat	100	289	21	22	0	9	2.6	—	.47	.18	3.6	0
3½ oz. boiled potato, peeled before cooking with ¼ c (4T) gravy	100	65 / 164	2	Trace	15	6	.5	Trace	.09	.03	1.2	16
1 c beets, diced	165	50	2	Trace	12	23	.8	40	.04	.07	.5	11
Salad:												
1 c pineapple, raw	140	75	1	Trace	19	24	.7	100	.12	.04	.3	24
1 oz. cream cheese	28	105	2	11	1	18	.1	440	Trace	.07	Trace	0
1 tbsp. mayonnaise	15	110	Trace	12	Trace	3	.1	40	Trace	.01	Trace	0

Food												
1 muffin, 2¾″ diameter with	48	140	4	5	20	50	.8	50	.08	.11	.7	Trace
1 tbsp. margarine	14	100	Trace	11	Trace	3	0	460	0	0	0	0
1 c plain, ready to eat gelatin dessert	239	140	4	0	34	0	0	0	0	0	0	0
1 angel food cake, 2″ sector	40	110	3	Trace	24	4	.1	0	Trace	.06	.1	0
1 c coffee with	15	5	Trace	Trace	.8	5	.2	0	Trace	Trace	.9	0
1 tbsp. light cream	12	30	Trace	3	1	15	Trace	130	Trace	.02	Trace	Trace
1 tbsp. sugar		45	0	0	12	0	Trace	0	0	0	0	0
TOTAL		1428	39	64	138.8	160	5.9	1260	.8	.59	7.3	51
Evening Snack:												
1 cake-type doughnut	32	125	1	6	16	13	.4	30	.05	.05	.4	Trace
1 c cola-type beverage	240	95	0	0	24	0	0	0	0	0	0	0
TOTAL		220	1	6	40	13	.4	30	.05	.05	.4	0
DAY'S TOTAL		4472	99	208	520.4	872	19.1	5205	.98	1.95	23.7	135

12 oz. beer
1 tbsp. peanut butter
2 oz. liver, beef, fried
3 oz. heart, beef, lean, braised
3 oz. salmon, pink, canned
3 oz. chicken flesh, broiled
1 c prunes, unsweetened with ⅓ c liquid
1 tbsp. French dressing
1 c kale, cooked, leaves and stems
1 sweet potato, candied, 3½″ × 2¼″
1 c yogurt, partially skimmed milk
1 tbsp. cream, whipping, heavy
1-1″ cube, Cheddar cheese

(Nutrient Sources = Church and Church: *Food Values of Portions Commonly Used.*
U.S.D.A. Agricultural Handbook No. 8: *Composition of Foods.*
U.S.D.A. Home and Garden Bulletin No. 72: *Nutritive Value of Foods.*)

CHAPTER 16

Nutrient Deficiencies

TERMS TO UNDERSTAND

Achlorhydria
Debilitate
Dermatosis
Electrolyte

Emaciation
Exudate
Flora, bacterial
Hydrolysate

Subclinical nutrient deficiencies occur more often than do the nutrient diseases. In this deficiency the tissues are not adequately supplied with one or more nutrients. This inadequacy may be due to

1. Poor food habits and consequent inadequate intake.

2. Consumption of food which is nutrient deficient because of refining or poor storage.

3. Anorexia, a condition which accompanies some diseases.

4. Diarrhea, which causes food to be moved along the intestinal tract too rapidly for digestion and absorption to be completed.

5. Alcoholism, with its frequent lowered food intake and impaired function of vital organs.

6. Faulty therapeutic diets, which result in inadequate intake.

7. Poor use of ingested food as in, for example, achlorhydria, which impairs iron absorption; hepatic insufficiency, resulting in poor fat and fat-soluble vitamin absorption; as in the use of mineral oil, which interferes with fat-soluble vitamin absorption.

8. Reduced vitamin synthesis in the intestinal tract due to oral antibiotic therapy, which modifies or reduces the normal bacterial flora.

9. Ignorance of food values and body needs due to lack of education, poor habits, emotional problems, or indifference.

For a discussion of the mineral and vitamin deficiency diseases and symptoms, review Chapters 8 and 9.

184

Nutritional (Starvation) Edema

Protein deficiency, from lack of food containing protein, is quite widespread throughout the world. Laboratory tests will show low blood serum protein before the clinical symptoms are noticed. Water retention is usually noted first in the legs and then it spreads to other body areas.

Protein deficiency may also occur with
1. Hepatic injury which prevents normal synthesis of protein.
2. Excessive protein metabolism during fever.
3. Hyperthyroidism.
4. Poor wound healing following surgery.
5. Burn healing.
6. Diabetic acidosis.
7. Above normal body loss as in hemorrhage, burn or wound exudates, and nephrosis.

Treatment is a slow process and seems to be more successful with dietary protein than vith protein hydrolysates. The latter are expensive and not very palatable. The diet usually ordered is 1.5 to 2 or more grams of protein per kilogram of body weight.

Protein-Calorie Malnutrition

Kwashiorkor is a disease found among the one to four year olds mainly in the tropics and subtropics; it is a disease associated with low protein intake, but the calorie intake may be adequate. (See Figure 5–3.) Symptoms include edema, which masks the muscular wasting; mental apathy; scaly, flaking, depigmented skin; depigmented hair; body retention of sodium; marked reduction of cellular potassium and magnesium; severe vitamin A deficiency which can result in blindness; and reversible fat infiltration of the liver. Treatment includes correction of the electrolytic balance, particularly potassium; protein in the form of non-fat milk (dried is very satisfactory); and a good diet.

In marasmus both calories and protein are deficient. It is most common among children under two years of age where there is parental rejection of the child, no medical care for dysentery, parasites, or such, or in any country having socioeconomic deprivation. Emaciation is not masked by edema; therefore, the child appears to be a living skeleton; diarrhea is common, but there is little or no depigmentation or dermatosis. The infant sleeps restlessly and is apathetic, and he may have a subnormal temperature due to the lack of subcutaneous fat. Treatment includes correction of the electrolytic balance and gradually increasing the servings of a mixed-food intake; and, if there has been social rejection, tender loving care (TLC) is an important factor in treatment.

CHAPTER 17

Preoperative and Postoperative Diets

Preoperative

Surgery represents a period of stress to the body; a person who is planning or who has undergone surgery may need more than the usual amounts of nutrients. The convalescent period is shorter for those who have been on good diets before surgery.

Although not more than a 12- to 24-hour supply of glucose can normally be stored in the body, a liver containing its optimal storage of carbohydrates suffers less damage from the anesthetic. Protein provides the amino acids for wound healing and the building of antibodies to resist infection, reduces the possibility of edema which would retard wound healing, helps counteract the negative nitrogen balance due to the increased protein catabolism of immobilization, and may help prevent postoperative shock. Ascorbic acid deficiency predisposes to poor wound healing and vitamin K and calcium deficiency impairs blood clotting. Obesity is a surgical hazard.

For a week or two before planned surgery, more and more physicians are prescribing a daily intake of protein to 100 grams, increased carbohydrate, and perhaps vitamin concentrates. Liberal use is made of milk which has been fortified with whole egg, egg whites, or non-fat dry milk, or both, fruit juices with added carbohydrates, liberal amounts of jam or jelly on bread or crackers, hard candies, and vegetables that have been

186

flavored with margarine or butter. If nausea should develop, the sugars and fats may have to be decreased.

Hemorrhage, diarrhea, and vomiting cause loss of fluids and nutrients; dehydration increases the danger of acidosis.

Before surgery is started, the stomach should be empty to reduce vomiting and aspiration of vomitus. In planned surgery, food and liquid are withheld 6 to 8 hours; in an emergency, gastric lavage may be used to empty the stomach. In intestinal surgery the diet may be low in bulk two or three days preceding the operation, and an enema is often given to free the intestine of residue and reduce postoperative distention. Any dehydration may be eliminated, if necessary, by intravenous feeding.

Postoperative

During immobilization following surgery, loss of nutrients, particularly protein and calcium, is accelerated. This loss is not so great if protein, calcium, and calories can be fed in abundance. Disease and tissue damage increase nitrogen loss, which can lead to malnutrition if not compensated by a higher protein intake. Oral feedings are started when peristalsis and gastrointestinal secretions are resumed. Most patients prefer solid foods to liquids and therefore small feedings should be resumed as soon as possible. Most of the gas in the gastrointestinal tract is due to air which is swallowed; it is important to stress that food should be eaten slowly and in small bites in order that as little air as possible is swallowed.

The danger of shock is increased when protein deficiency exists because the loss of plasma proteins, the decrease in circulating red cell volume, and a reduction in the blood volume contribute to the development of shock.

The National Research Council, in its pamphlet *Therapeutic Nutrition,* discusses vitamin intake for the post-surgical patient in the following manner:

1. A healthy person with no previous history of malnutrition who is ambulatory and eating well has no need to take vitamin concentrates.

2. The patient who does not meet the above qualifications needs only one to two times the normal recommended daily allowance.

3. The patient who is receiving an intravenous diet should receive from one to two times the minimum requirement for parenteral injection with additional amounts of vitamin C.

4. The patient with a severe burn, serious illness, or severe trauma should be given five to ten times the usual recommended allowance for the first few days; thereafter only two to three times the basic allowance until recovery is complete.

Tube feedings are used for the patient who has undergone radical neck or facial surgery, who is comatose, or who is severely debilitated. Samples of tube feedings appear in the appendix.

Postoperative dietary treatment is related to the type of surgery. If vomiting occurs, oral feedings may be omitted for the first 24 to 48 hours. When oral feedings are not tolerated, blood transfusions and intravenous feedings containing glucose, minerals, fatty acids, vitamins, and/or protein hydrolysates may be used. Following abdominal surgery, such as a hysterectomy, the following oral routine might be used:

Second or third postoperative day—restricted fluids such as tea, broth, and Jello.

Third or fourth day—full liquid.

Fourth or fifth day—soft high protein, high vitamin, high calorie.

Fifth or sixth day—general high protein, high vitamin, high calorie.

Tonsillectomy patients may be given milk, ice cream, bland fruit juices, and iced beverages, adding strained soups, finely ground meat, purées, and soft puddings on the third or fourth day. Following tooth extraction, liquid and soft foods are used. Mouth and esophagus surgery may require tube feeding.

A high percentage of patients with burns have to undergo surgery. These patients lose large amounts of protein, minerals, and fluid both before and after the operation. A very high-protein (perhaps as much as 300 grams), high-calorie (3500 to 5000), and high-vitamin diet may be used. Whole blood transfusions or transfusions of red blood cells seem to combat the anemia better than dietary iron does.

The fracture patient has increased metabolism of protein which may be accompanied by loss of phosphorus, potassium, and sulfur. Fever and infection may increase these losses. The patient may need a diet containing as much as 150 grams of protein, which supplies the nitrogen, phosphorus, potassium, and sulfur that are being lost in such large quantity. The liberal protein intake should help develop the matrix of the bone so that calcium can be deposited. A high-calorie intake will permit the maximum utilization of the protein for synthesis of cells. Complete immobilization may necessitate calcium restriction to lessen the danger of renal calculi; otherwise, calcium-bearing foods are used.

Feeding after rectal surgery usually starts within 24 hours. Some surgeons order a low residue (cellulose) diet to discourage early bowel movement; others give a general diet. See appendix for modified cellulose (residue) diets.

CHAPTER 18

Fevers and Infection

Extensive, rapid, worldwide travel of many citizens increases the possibility of diseases appearing in all geographical areas. Fever and infection are often accompanied by intolerance of food and loss of appetite.

In fevers the metabolic rate increases about 7 per cent for every Fahrenheit degree of fever (13 per cent for every degree Centigrade). If extra calories are not given in the diet, body tissue is used for this energy. Extra fluids, three or more quarts, are given to help the kidneys in their work of disposing of the metabolic waste products and to avoid dehydration. If there is considerable sweating, extra salt is added. Usually the patient welcomes fruit juices, lemonade, milk, carbonated beverages, and water because they are cool. Dextrose or other carbohydrates may be added to the liquids, but very sweet-tasting liquids are often refused. Fat-free clear broth has no food value, except that it provides water and can be used as a medium for adding salt to the diet. Broth does contain meat extractives which give it flavor, and these extractives do stimulate appetite, peristalsis, and digestive secretions.

An acute fever is one which is relatively severe but has a short duration. During the high fever, liquids are given freely, and the calorie and protein content of the diet is increased as soon as possible (1 to 2 grams protein per kilogram; 3000 to 4000 calories). The protein is needed to replace body tissue and for the formation of antibodies. Chronic fevers may last for months and sometimes even years. The diet needs to be adequate in protein and calories to maintain normal weight. Malaria is an example of a recurrent infection. In general, the fever diet may be described as high protein, high calorie, high vitamin, starting with the liquid consistency and progressing to soft or light, and regular.

Fever accompanies many diseases. When studying these chapters on diet therapy, you should keep in mind that if there is a combination of diseases, the diets will be further modified.

In the comparatively few areas of the world where it still exists, the fever of poliomyelitis is of short duration. There is a great deal of body tissue destruction which causes an increased loss of potassium from the body, requiring that foods high in potassium be included. Orange juice is usually very well accepted. The polio patient may have difficulty in swallowing, and under these conditions a plastic tube is passed through the nose into the stomach and feedings which contain glucose, fat emulsion, protein hydrolysates, vitamins, and electrolyte solutions are given. As soon as the ability to swallow returns, liquid feedings by mouth are started. The few patients who are permanently immobilized lose nitrogen and calcium from their tissues very rapidly. The loss of calcium from the bones leads to increased urinary excretion of calcium and the possible formation of renal calculi.

Asiatic cholera is caused by an intestinal bacterial infection which causes a sudden massive diarrhea, resulting in the loss of electrolytes, especially sodium, and massive dehydration. In the acute stage, rehydration is accomplished by intravenous feeding. As soon as possible there is an oral administration of electrolytes, glucose, and antibiotics. The death rate in Asiatic cholera has always been very high, but it is hoped that the control of dehydration and the quick replacement of electrolytes will lead to a much greater percentage of recovery for these patients.

In typhoid fever the intestinal tract becomes ulcerated and the diet should be low in roughage. Protein and calories are increased. Large quantities of milk, soft cooked eggs, and custards are given. In the acute stage the diet is restricted to liquids, and solid foods are added very gradually.

In tuberculosis the patient usually has little appetite, so it is important that the foods be appetizing and be attractively served. Calories may not have to be increased as much as for fever in other conditions because metabolism may not be increased as much. There should be a liberal protein, high calcium (1 quart or more of milk a day), and a high vitamin intake, especially vitamins A and C. Increase iron if there has been hemorrhaging. Because isoniazid, a drug used to treat tuberculosis, is an antagonist of vitamin B_6, pyridoxine may be given as a vitamin supplement.

In malaria there may be liver impairment; therefore, the diet is moderate or low in fat, high in protein, and high in carbohydrate.

Scarlet fever patients may follow the typical fever diet, or the protein may be restricted because of the tendency to develop nephritis. See appendix for increased or restricted protein diets.

Patients with colds and influenza are usually given the typical fever diet regimen, and fluids are forced. In pneumonia the frequent distention seems to be related to the disease itself, not to the food intake.

SUGGESTED READING

American Lung Association:
  Air Pollution, the Facts.
  Asthma, the Facts.
  Chronic Bronchitis, the Facts.
  Cigarette Smoking, the Facts.
  Common Cold, the Facts.
  Emphysema, the Facts.
  Pneumonia, the Facts.
  TB, the Facts.
American Medical Association: *Old King Cold.*
Farber, Seymour M.: "Coughing: Bad or Beneficial," *Today's Health,* April, 1966.
Irwin, Theodore: "Fever: How to Play It Cool," *Today's Health,* December, 1968.
Katz, Sol: "Evaluating the Cold Remedies," *Today's Health,* February, 1974.
Ratcliff, J. D.: "I Am Joe's Lung." *Reader's Digest,* March 1969.
Scott, Byron: "Asthma—The Demon That Thrives on Myths," *Today's Health,* June, 1970.
U.S. Department of Health, Education, and Welfare:
  About Syphilis and Gonorrhea.
  Asthma.
  The Common Cold.
  Sinus Infection.

EXERCISE

1. What is fallacious about the old saying, "Feed a cold and starve a fever"?

CHAPTER 19

Gastrointestinal Disorders

TERMS TO UNDERSTAND

Adhesion	Diverticula	Impaction
Antisecretory	Dyspepsia	Intermediate
Buffer	Electrolyte	Mucosa
Colostomy	Ferment	Mucus
Congenital	Flatulence	Occult
Constipation	Gastritis	Sphincter
Defecate	Gruel	Varicose

Indigestion

Indigestion (dyspepsia) "is an indefinite term frequently used to describe any discomfort occurring from a disorder of the digestive tract." The trouble may originate in the stomach itself or be a symptom of other organic disorders, such as diseases of the colon, chronic appendicitis, gallbladder disease, diabetes, or renal calculus. Emotional disturbance as well as poor mastication, rapid eating, poor diet, overindulgence in high fat food, concentrated sweets, or incorrectly cooked foods can cause dyspepsia. The cause, mental or physical, will usually be determined by the doctor before any dietary prescription is given. For simple indigestion, good eating habits combined with an adequate diet may be sufficient corrective measures. If a modified diet is used, it frequently is a bland type progressing to the regular.

Peptic Ulcers

The cause of gastric ulcers and the more common duodenal ulcers is unknown, but it has been suggested that one or more of the following may be predisposing factors: poor diet habits, emotional conflict, nervous

Figure 19–1   Gastric ulcer. (From Bockus, H. L.: *Gastroenterology.* Vol. 1.)

strain, anxiety, inadequate rest, gastric juice erosion, poor circulation near the site of the lesion, excessive smoking or alcohol consumption, or a focus of infection, such as diseased tonsils, teeth, or sinuses. If the ulcer has perforated, there will be occult blood in the stools due to hemorrhage. Treatment includes diet, physical and mental rest, and usually alkaline or antisecretory drugs. The diet may consist of small, frequent feedings of chemically, thermally, and mechanically non-irritating foods,* foods which do not stimulate gastric secretion, with gradual progression to an adequate diet. Protein is used because of its ability to combine with the hydrochloric acid and thus free the ulcerated area from irritation, and because of its ability to build cells which heal the ulcer; fat (but not fried foods) is used because it inhibits the secretion of juices and reduces motility. Recently, the use of a diet high in milk fat had been questioned because of the relationship of saturated fatty acids to the level of serum cholesterol and the development of atherosclerosis. Skim milk to which vegetable oil has been added has been found to have a buffering capacity equal to the mixture of half milk and half cream. Healing usually is completed in about 40 days but may vary from 14 to 100.

---

*Opinions vary, but traditionally these would be defined as follows: Chemical irritants = meat extractives, concentrated sweets, tea, coffee, alcohol, and the spices: black pepper, chili pepper, cloves, mustard seed, and possibly nutmeg. Mechanical irritants = those which might be abrasive to the ulcerated area, such as raw foods and foods high in cellulose. Thermal irritants = very hot or very cold foods which irritate the lesion by the thermal effect on the surface blood vessels and which may stimulate flow of gastric secretion or motility.

Doctors order various regimens; the current trend is toward a more liberal diet, similar to the usual soft or light hospital diet, but involving frequent, small feedings. *Frequent feedings are more important than the type of food used. Good mastication and slow eating are more important than low fiber diets.* Restriction of all spices is not necessary; however, black pepper, chili pepper, alcohol, and caffeine* seem to be gastric irritants. Some diet orders restrict saturated fats and dictate the use of skim milk and vegetable oils instead of milk and cream. When properly cooked, the strongly flavored vegetables are tolerated by many people.

Dumping Syndrome (Jejunal Hyperosmolic Syndrome)

The dumping syndrome occurs in some patients who have been subjected to a total or subtotal gastrectomy. It is characterized by pallor, weakness, sweating, rapid pulse, nausea, and epigastric discomfort. Dumping occurs when the stomach is no longer storing food normally (food is moving rapidly into the small intestine). Fluid is drawn from the bloodstream into the intestinal tract, resulting in a blood pressure drop and signs of cardiac insufficiency. About two hours later symptoms of hypoglycemia occur, because the concentration of rapidly digested and absorbed carbohydrates causes a rise in the blood glucose which stimulates an overproduction of insulin. This, in turn, leads to the hypoglycemia. Ingestion of carbohydrates, particularly sugar, and liquids tends to precipitate the syndrome. Treatment consists of six to eight small feedings which are high in protein (115 to 150 grams) and low in carbohydrate (100 to 125 grams), and in which the fat content is usually between 170 and 225 grams. Lean meat is well tolerated. Fluids are given between meals. In the absence of adequate gastric hydrochloric acid and the intrinsic factor, the physician must watch the postgastrectomy patient for subsequent anemia development (impaired iron and vitamin B_{12} absorption).

Hyperchlorhydria

Hyperchlorhydria, or hyperacidity, is excess hydrochloric acid in the stomach which irritates the gastric mucosa, causing discomfort. Fats are included to retard gastric secretion. Sometimes the use of a low fiber diet

---

*Cola drinks, including diet brands, contain about 52 milligrams of caffeine per 12 ounces. The average amount of caffeine in a cup of coffee is about 83 milligrams and about 42 mg. for a cup of tea. *Family Health*, p. 7, July, 1974.

is adequate for control. This condition is not nearly as prevalent as one would think from reading or listening to advertisements.

Hypochlorhydria

With less hydrochloric acid in the stomach carbohydrates ferment readily, protein digestion is retarded, and bacterial action is increased. Digestive disturbances, including diarrhea, may occur. Fruit juice and broth are used freely. Fats, concentrated sweets, fried foods, and cold foods are restricted. Starch, which ferments less readily, is preferred over sugar. Cultured milks (see p. 265) may be tolerated better than sweet milk. If diarrhea is present, fiber is restricted.

Flatulence

Flatulence, which is distention of the stomach or intestines with air or gas, is usually caused by swallowing air or by bacterial fermentation of undigested food; it may occur following abdominal surgery or may be a symptom of another disease. If it is due to bacterial action, the diet may be lowered in fat, fiber, and/or carbohydrate content.

Opinions differ as to whether certain foods are flatulence producing. Those who believe foods are involved often list navy, lima, and kidney beans, banana, broccoli, Brussels sprouts, cabbage, cantaloup, candy, carbonated beverages, cauliflower, condiments, corn, cucumbers, fermented cheese, garlic, honeydew melon, kohlrabi, leeks, lentils, nuts, onions, peas, peppers (both red and green), pimiento, radishes, raisins, raw apple, rutabaga, sauerkraut, scallions, shallots, soybeans, turnips, watermelon, and extremely hot or cold foods. It should be remembered that individuals vary in their reactions to foods. (See quoted statement on "Gas-Producing Foods" at end of Chapter 2.)

Gastritis

Gastritis is an inflammation of the gastric mucosa usually caused by dietary excesses, by ingesting foods to which the patient is sensitive, or by ingesting toxic substances, such as strong acids or alkalies, some drugs, or alcohol. In treatment the stomach is usually emptied by lavage or vomiting and the colon may be emptied too. Food is withheld for 24 to 48 hours (liquid may be given intravenously or rectally), and then very small amounts of bland food may be used. Often a regimen similar to the progressive peptic ulcer diet is used (see appendix).

Carcinoma

Gastric cancer onset is usually very gradual. In any continued abdominal distress, anorexia, weight loss, vomiting, or loss of strength (especially in middle age), a doctor should be consulted. If the cancer is accompanied by either hypo- or hyperchlorhydria the previously outlined diets are often used. If it is inoperable, the patient is permitted, if possible, to eat anything he wishes. Attractive, appetizing food is essential because anorexia is nearly always present.

If a colostomy has been performed, liquids and a low fiber diet are given in the postoperative period, followed as soon as possible by a general diet.

Constipation

Abnormally long retention of the feces in the colon, causing them to become hard and dry, is known as constipation. (But a *daily* bowel movement is not essential to the health and comfort of everyone.) Causes of constipation include poor diet habits, missed meals, fatigue, tension, anxiety, excitement, limited fluid intake, poor personal hygiene (not responding to the defecation urge or irregular defecation habits), lack of exercise, and excessive use of enemas, laxatives, cathartics, and bran. High bran and low liquid intake, especially in the elderly, may cause an impaction.

In atonic constipation food is not moved down the intestinal tract at the normal rate because the intestinal muscles lack tone and produce weak peristaltic waves. Atonic constipation is most frequently found among older persons, among obese persons, during pregnancy, and among those who habitually take laxatives. Increased intake of cellulose, which absorbs water, is necessary so that the bulk will stimulate peristalsis and regular defecation. The cellulose content of a normal diet is about 5 to 7 grams daily. For atonic constipation this should be increased to 10 to 12 grams. This is done by using the basic-four with increased amounts of fruits, vegetables, and only whole grain cereals. The diet is called high residue, high bulk, or high fiber diet. A vitamin B complex supplement may be ordered to help restore intestinal muscle tone. It is important to increase water intake to at least eight to ten glasses daily.

Spastic constipation is the opposite of atonic. The muscle tone is heightened, causing irregular contractions of the bowel. Food residue irritates the walls of the intestine and causes greater spasm; therefore, a nonresidue or a low-residue diet is used. This low fiber diet is composed of strained soup, meat, eggs, milk, cheese, starches, and enriched cereals. As improvement is noted, puréed fruits and vegetables are added. Omit nuts, fried and highly seasoned foods, jam and alcohol. The person suffering from spastic constipation is often malnourished because he has eaten poorly to avoid pain.

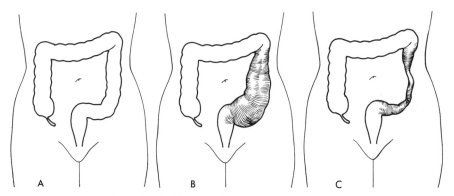

Figure 19–2   Colon. *A*, Ideal; *B*, atonic; *C*, spastic.

In obstructive constipation the residue passage is hindered by an abnormality such as cancer, tumor, adhesions, or impaction of the bowel. Surgery may be necessary. The diet is usually a low fiber one as in spastic constipation. Refer to appendix for residue (cellulose) modified diets.

Diverticulitis

Diverticula, which are small pouches in the wall of the intestines and appear most frequently in the colon, become filled with fecal matter. Infection, ulceration, or perforation sometimes results. If surgery is not indicated, the patient fasts for 24 to 48 hours; he may then be given a bland liquid diet, which is gradually increased to a low fiber diet. Adequate water (8 to 10 glasses) is advised. Recently the general or high residue diet has been tried in place of the low fiber diet, with good results reported. A high residue diet should be accompanied by increased fluid intake.

Hemorrhoids

Varicose veins in the area of the anal sphincter are called hemorrhoids. They may result from childbearing, constipation, hepatic cirrhosis, or from prolonged use of enemas and cathartics. The diet provides comfort, not treatment. A low fiber diet is prescribed. Eight to 10 glasses of liquid should be drunk daily to keep the stools soft and so reduce irritation. Severe cases may require surgery.

Diarrhea

The rapid passage of food along the digestive tract prevents complete digestion and absorption. Dehydration and loss of electrolytes, especially sodium, are very great. This fluid and electrolyte loss is very critical, especially in infants and children. Intravenous fluids may be ordered to repair the fluid and electrolyte loss.

If the diarrhea is the simple type, such as that caused by food poisoning, dietary excesses, use of cathartics, fermentation of carbohydrate or putrefaction of protein, nervous irritability, stress, or fright, a fast of one or two days is often prescribed. Tea, broth, gruel, and toast are given first, followed by foods low in fiber, and then by a general diet.

If the diarrhea is of the organic type caused by ulcerative colitis, amebic dysentery, external poison, or bacterial invasion, the low fiber, high calorie, high protein, high vitamin, bland foods may have to be used over an extended period of time.

Pectin found in apples tends to help in the treatment of mild diarrhea.

Some doctors are reporting good results by using a high residue diet for diarrhea. Fluid intake should be increased when a high cellulose diet is used.

Colitis

The etiology of colitis is unknown, but it occurs more frequently in the overtired, meticulous, neurotic, or emotional person. Deficiency of protein and B complex vitamins, infections, and allergy may be other factors. The patient frequently is malnourished and underweight and may be anemic, owing to loss of blood. In mucous colitis there is secretion of abnormal amounts of mucus. In simple colitis constipation may alternate with diarrhea.

In ulcerative colitis the mucosa of the large intestine is inflamed and ulcerated. Blood, pus, and mucus appear in the frequent stools. For all types relief of tension and fear must accompany the high protein, high calorie, high vitamin, low fiber diet which is given in frequent small feedings. If the etiology is a food allergen, this must be eliminated from the diet.

Steatorrhea

Excess fat in the stool is a symptom, not a disease. The underlying cause (such as pancreatitis or sprue) must be determined and treated.

Amebiasis and Amebic Dysentery

Inflammation of the intestines, particularly the colon, is caused chiefly by ingestion of contaminated food and drink. The disease is more common in the tropics than in the temperate zones. During the acute stage broth, tea, coffee, fruit juice, and gruel are given. Milk is added when tolerated, and as symptoms subside a low fiber diet is used.

Malabsorption Syndromes Due to Inborn Errors of Metabolism

The intestinal malabsorption syndrome includes the disaccharidase deficiencies, defective monosaccharide absorption, tropical sprue, cystic fibrosis, celiac disease, and idiopathic steatorrhea. The syndromes occur because there is a lack of a specific enzyme or group of enzymes in the body.

The disaccharidase deficiencies and defective absorption of monosaccharides syndrome have been recognized only recently.

Some people cannot synthesize, owing to a genetic defect, the digestive enzyme necessary to break the disaccharide into its two parts. Because the sugar is not broken into its component parts, it cannot be absorbed. This inborn error of metabolism is called a disaccharidase deficiency. In people with this syndrome, the consumption of food containing the particular disaccharide is followed by diarrhea and abdominal pain. (See section on kinds of carbohydrates, Chapter 3, for food disaccharide sources.) The diagnosis is confirmed by laboratory findings of the undigested disaccharide in the stool.

Lactose intolerance, the most prevalent of the disaccharidase defi-

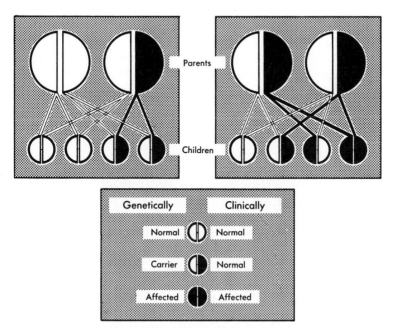

Figure 19–3 Pattern of genetic disease. Transmission of recessive traits follows Mendel's law. If two carriers marry, one child will be normal, one child will manifest the trait, and two children will be carriers. (From Williams: *Nutrition and Diet Therapy*, 1973.)

ciencies, is due to a deficiency of the enzyme lactase. Infant lactose intolerance seems to be a congenital deficiency. The severe and immediate symptoms occur when the infant ingests milk, no matter whether it is breast milk or formula.

The milk-substitute formula may consist of Nutramigen or Sobee, which are distributed by Mead Johnson and Company; Mul-soy, distributed by the Borden Company; or a meat base formula, distributed by the Gerber Products Company. As the child grows older the soybean milks can be used to replace all milk and may be used in recipes for ice cream, chocolate milk, cream soup, or any other cream dish. (See Chapter 26, section on milk-free diet, for the other foods which contain milk.) All medication containing lactose must also be omitted.

Lactose intolerance which doesn't occur until adulthood is probably an acquired intolerance such as that seen in some subtotal gastrectomy patients. The intolerance may be intermittent with mild or severe symptoms which are of a recent origin or have persisted for years. If the adult can tolerate very small amounts of milk, consumption of the small amount should be encouraged. But if he cannot, a calcium supplement must be given. The adult who has not drunk milk for several years may have a lactose intolerance; he may be able to develop a tolerance by gradually increasing his daily intake of milk as a beverage or in cooked foods.

Lactose intolerance has been reported as a symptom found in kwashiorkor, celiac disease, cystic fibrosis, tropical sprue, ileitis, and colitis.

Sucrose intolerance is treated by omitting granulated sugar, brown sugar, molasses, syrups, and foods containing any of them. Apricots, bananas, dates, pineapples, peas, melons, and oranges have to be omitted because of their sucrose content.

Invertase-isomaltase deficiency requires omitting sucrose and the starch of wheat and potato. Isomaltase is one of the intermediate products of starch digestion. Corn and rice starches yield very little isomaltase; therefore, some corn and rice starches may be tolerated by these patients.

Defective Monosaccharide Absorption

Glucose-galactose malabsorption is another very rare disorder. It is most unusual for the intestinal wall not to permit absorption of monosaccharides. To be completely free of symptoms, all carbohydrates, with the exception of fructose, are omitted. Such a diet would be very difficult to plan.

Sprue

Tropical sprue responds to an adequate diet supplemented with folic acid or vitamin B_{12} or both.

Non-tropical sprue (celiac disease), with its symptoms of steatorrhea, sore mouth, anemia, tetany, and osteomalacia, is treated with a diet high in protein (6 or more grams per kilogram of body weight), especially rich in liver and lean meat; fat, low to moderate; carbohydrate in the form of sugar and the sugars in fruits and vegetables; and calories, increased 20 per cent or more. This diet is supplemented with liver extract, folic acid, vitamin B_{12}, calcium, and iron. In celiac disease the digestion of starch is inhibited and the absorption of the digested fat is poor; this in turn interferes with the absorption of iron, calcium, and fat-soluble vitamins. Diet orders exclude grains which contain gluten; therefore rice, corn, and soyflour are used. Gluten is found in wheat, rye, barley, and oats.

Cystic fibrosis is essentially a disease of infants and children, and a discussion of it will be found in Chapter 27, Childhood Illness.

Idiopathic Steatorrhea

Fat in the ordinary diet consists mainly of the long chain fatty acids, and is digested and absorbed by a very complicated process involving bile salts and the digestive enzyme, lipase. In several of the malabsorption syndromes the long chain fatty acids are not absorbed and therefore appear in the stool. For these patients a synthesized product containing almost entirely 8- and 10-carbon fatty acids is substituted for the regular fat in the diet. The synthesis of the fat containing only short or medium chain fatty acids is accomplished by obtaining the fatty acids from coconut oil or butter and then combining them with glycerol to form a fat. This product is called medium chain triglyceride or MCT. It can be incorporated into recipes in the same fashion as vegetable oil. MCT has been shown to be of value in treating tropical sprue, cystic fibrosis, pancreatitis, biliary atresia, subtotal gastrectomy, the massive resection of the small intestine, chyluria, and chylothorax.

SUGGESTED READINGS

American Cancer Society: *The Hopeful Side of Cancer.*
Mead Johnson Laboratories:
  Physician's Handbook, Portagen and MCT Oil.
  Recipes Using MCT Oil and Portagen.
Metropolitan Life Insurance Company: *Facts about Cancer.*
Peltz, Edith M.: "Bland Diets Need Not Be Dull," *Today's Health,* July, 1969.
Ratcliff, J. D.: "I Am Joe's Stomach," *Reader's Digest,* May, 1968.
Today's Health: "How to Eat Well on a Gluten-Free Diet," October, 1965.
Wood, Marion N.: "Eating Well on a Wheat-Free Diet," *Today's Health,* February, 1970. (Has gluten-free recipes.)

EXERCISES

1. Write a day's menu which would contain 10 to 12 grams of cellulose.
2. Write a day's menu for a convalescent ulcer patient.
3. Write a day's menu which would contain 100 grams of protein.
4. List 10 foods which might be emphasized on a high vitamin diet.
5. Write a day's menu which is low in mechanical irritants. How would this be changed if it also has to be low in chemical and thermal stimulants? What is the common name for this latter diet?

CHAPTER 20

Liver, Gallbladder, and Pancreatic Disturbances

TERMS TO UNDERSTAND

Ascites
Cholecystectomy
Cholecystitis

Cholelithiasis
Cirrhosis
Granulation

Liver

The liver is the largest glandular organ and has many functions, including the following:

1. Converting glucose to glycogen and storing the glycogen.
2. Storing iron, copper, and vitamins.
3. Converting carotene to vitamin A and storing it.
4. Assisting in the breakdown and synthesis of amino and fatty acids.
5. Detoxifying substances which come from drugs, bacterial action, or parasitic infections.
6. Manufacturing bile, cholesterol, and phospholipids.

A diseased liver, if given adequate treatment, has a great capacity for repair and regeneration.

From $\frac{1}{2}$ to $1\frac{1}{2}$ quarts of bile are produced daily. Bile is stored in the gallbladder, where it becomes concentrated. When fat enters the duodenum, a hormone is secreted and carried by the blood to the gallbladder, which contracts, and the concentrated bile is poured into the intestine, where it emulsifies fat.

Jaundice is a symptom of a diseased biliary tract. In jaundice there is an abnormal amount of bile pigments in the blood, giving the tissues a yellowish color. It may arise from poisons, virus infections, flow obstruction, as in stone formation or tumor, from toxemia of pregnancy, or from an abnormal destruction of the red blood cells.

202

"Biliousness" may be related to a diseased liver but it is more apt to result from overeating, overdrinking, poor food choice, or constipation. During the acute stage low fat foods are given and gradually a normal diet is resumed.

Infectious hepatitis is inflammation of the liver caused by bacterial or virus infection. Jaundice often appears. Consumption of alcohol or a low protein diet leads to complications and a prolonged convalescence. Serum hepatitis caused by transfusions of contaminated blood or contaminated instruments requires the same dietary treatment.

Cirrhosis is progressive destruction of the liver cells. It may be accompanied by hardening and granulation of tissue and an increase of connective tissue. Its etiology may be chronic infections, including hepatitis; malnutrition, including that caused by chronic alcoholism; cholecystitis; and cholelithiasis. Acute thiamine deficiency often occurs in alcoholism. Fat metabolism is impaired.

The dietary treatments for the aforementioned liver diseases follow a similar pattern: increased protein, 1.5 to 2 grams per kilogram (75 to 150 grams) from milk, eggs, meat, fish, and poultry; high carbohydrate (300 to 500 grams); moderate fat (100 to 150 grams), mainly from milk, butter, salad oils, and eggs; high vitamin and iron. The diet is often supplemented with vitamin concentrates and liver extracts. Fluid may be increased to 3000 to 3500 milliliters. Omit fried foods, nuts, highly seasoned foods, alcohol, pastries, strongly flavored vegetables, and high fat meats such as pork, duck, and goose.

In acute hepatitis or advanced cirrhosis (where the liver cells are severely damaged), ammonia intoxication occurs. The brain tissue is very sensitive to ammonia, and drowsiness, lethargy, disorientation, and then coma result. This condition is known as hepatic coma. The diet of those with acute hepatitis or cirrhosis should be low enough in protein (20 to 50 grams) to prevent the above symptoms. If gastrointestinal hemorrhaging occurs, the blood provides protein, and thus the protein content of the diet may need to be further reduced.

If varicose veins (esophageal varices) develop in the esophagus of the cirrhotic patient, fiber may have to be reduced or eliminated. Fluids and sodium (as low as 500 milligrams) may have to be restricted if ascites is present. Salt substitutes containing ammonia should never be used.

Refer to protein and sodium modified diets in the appendix.

Gallbladder

The gallbladder's function is to concentrate and store the bile until needed in the digestive tract. Inflammation, stones, obesity, constipation, or pregnancy may cause malfunctioning. With fat present in the intestine, the gallbladder is stimulated to contract; and if the bile is prevented from flowing to the intestine, pain results. The diet is controlled fat (40 to 60 grams) and provided by the foods in the basic-four. Gallstones often contain a high percentage of cholesterol, but the evidence is conflicting as to whether or not a low cholesterol diet is beneficial. It has been customary to omit the strongly flavored vegetables (often labeled gas-forming), but studies show that patients with gastrointestinal disease have no more food intolerances than patients without gastrointestinal disease. Obese persons usually are encouraged to reduce. Following a cholecystectomy the controlled fat diet is continued for several weeks while the inflammation subsides and then is gradually increased to the normal fat content.

Pancreas

Food and hydrochloric acid in the duodenum stimulate pancreatic juice secretion, and fat in the duodenum stimulates bile secretion. When a patient has pancreatitis he is given a diet to depress these mechanisms. In acute pancreatitis nothing is given orally. In milder attacks a low fiber, controlled fat (25 grams or less) diet is used. Some patients do better when the medium chain triglycerides (MCT) are substituted for the regular fat in the diet. Alcohol, which irritates the duodenum, is prohibited. Six small meals seem to be better tolerated than the usual three.

SUGGESTED READINGS

Carper, Jean: "Cirrhosis: A Growing Threat to Life," *Today's Health*, February, 1970.
Irwin, Theodore: "Attacking Alcoholism as a Disease," *Today's Health*, September, 1968.
Ratcliff, J. D.: "I Am Joe's Liver," *Reader's Digest*, September, 1969.
U.S. Department of Health, Education, and Welfare, Public Health Service Publication No. 164: *Alcohol and Alcoholism.*

CHAPTER 21

Metabolic Disturbances

TERMS TO UNDERSTAND

Acetone	Hyperglycemia	Polydipsia
Exophthalmos	Hypoglycemia	Polyphagia
Glycosuria	Ketones	Polyuria

Diabetes Mellitus

Diabetes mellitus is a complex disease in which the cell partially or completely loses its capacity to metabolize sugar. Because the cell cannot get its energy needs from carbohydrate, the metabolism of protein and fat is affected. The unused sugar accumulates in the blood (see Figure 21–1) and is excreted in the urine.

Treatment is largely by diet, with or without insulin administration or an oral hypoglycemic agent. Because the body can use 58 per cent of the protein molecule and 10 per cent of the fat molecule as carbohydrate, the "prescribed diet" states the number of grams of carbohydrate, protein, and fat which the patient is to have and how the carbohydrate is to be divided among the meals. Sometimes the doctor wishes the protein to be divided in the same pattern. The dietitian writes the meal pattern according to the doctor's orders. The diabetic often is allowed a "free diet"; he eats as desired as long as he maintains normal weight and regulates his insulin so that there are no ketone bodies in the urine. He often has mild glycosuria.

Purchase of a special diabetic food is expensive and usually unnecessary.* The patient should eat a variety of foods as do other family members, the only omission being sugar and foods prepared with sugar, such as candy, carbonated beverages, fruits canned with sugar, and

---

*See footnote on page 174.

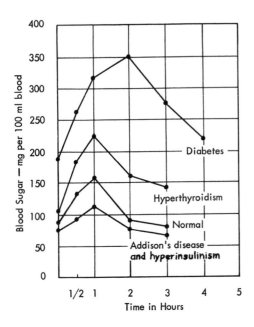

Figure 21–1 Glucose tolerance curves. (From Wayler, T. J., and Klein, R. S.: *Applied Nutrition*, The Macmillan Company, 1965.)

some bakery goods. Fat-free, clear broth, vinegar, spices and saccharin are used as desired unless prohibited by the doctor. Food given to the diabetic patient may be measured or weighed.

Many adult diabetics are overweight. The doctor usually prescribes a diet which will cause the patient to lose weight and then one which will keep him slightly underweight. The diabetic is quite susceptible to infections. The doctor should always be notified if the diabetic has a fever or an infection because the diet may have to be changed for the duration of the infection. Moderate, consistent exercise is of great value to all diabetics.

Two types of diabetes are recognized—the juvenile, where the onset is prior to the age of 20, and the maturity onset or adult diabetes. The juvenile form develops rapidly and is more severe and unstable, the child is usually underweight, acidosis is common, and insulin is used in its control. The adult type occurs usually after the age of 30 with a high incidence in the 50's and 60's. Eight out of ten adult onset diabetics are or have been 5 per cent or more overweight. Adult diabetes often can be controlled by diet alone or by diet plus one of the oral hypoglycemic agents; acidosis is infrequent.

Symptoms of diabetes include polyuria, polydipsia, polyphagia, dehydration (due to the excessive urinary output), blurred vision, drowsiness, general weakness, acetone (fruity) breath odor, loss of weight, and skin infections (boils and so forth). The feet are particularly susceptible to infections. There are hyperglycemia, glycosuria, and ketosis or acidosis, which is the abnormal accumulation of ketones in the blood (coma occurs when

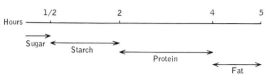

Figure 21–2   Availability of carbohydrate from the nutrient groups. Within 20 minutes sugar is in the bloodstream. Most of the carbohydrate from starch, protein, and fat becomes available within the periods indicated.

too much sugar and acetone collect in the blood). Degenerative tissue changes include retinitis, peripheral neuritis, atherosclerosis, and vascular changes in the kidneys. These degenerative changes are particularly prevalent in poorly controlled diabetics.

Committees of the American Diabetes Association, Inc., and The American Dietetic Association in cooperation with the Chronic Disease Program, Public Health Service, have prepared a simplified method of calculating a diabetic diet. These nine meal plans contain from 1200 to 3500 calories with 40 per cent of the calories coming from carbohydrate. All use the exchange lists. The exchange lists and meal plans are found in the appendix. Look at these diabetic exchange lists very carefully. Note that bacon is considered a fat, not a meat, that some hot breads are included in the bread exchange, that regular ice cream and sponge cake can be part of the diabetic's food intake. The diabetic child can have his birthday party with cake and ice cream. The tendency to diabetes mellitus can be inherited. See Figure 19–3 for the pattern of genetic disease.

Hyperinsulinism
(Spontaneous Hypoglycemia)

Hyperinsulinism causes a low level of blood sugar. Symptoms include hunger, trembling, weakness, anxiety, irritability, headache, vision changes (e.g. double vision), and sweating. If hyperinsulinism occurs in the presence of a tumor of the pancreas, surgery is the preferred treatment. Carbohydrates stimulate insulin secretion; therefore, the correct diet is low carbohydrate (50 to 100 grams), high protein (125 to 150 grams), and fat, to maintain the caloric needs of the individual. The food intake is divided into at least five or six feedings.

Levine states, "Hypoglycemia has taken the place of the 'psychosomatic' illness of 15 to 20 years ago as a medical fad." The condition is quite rare and seldom is the cause of the above listed symptoms.*

---

*"Hypoglycemia," *J.A.M.A.*, October 21, 1974.

Addison's Disease
(Adrenocortical Insufficiency)

Addison's disease, involving the malfunctioning of the adrenal cortex, is rare. Drugs have decreased the necessity of using a low potassium diet in this condition. In a mild case use of salt tablets may maintain electrolytic balance; in a slightly more severe case cortisone may be needed in addition. With the introduction of hormone therapy the diet for severe cases has been changed to include frequent feedings of high protein, low carbohydrate, high sodium foods and high fluid intake. Occasionally foods high in potassium are restricted. (See Table A–12.) Vitamin concentrates may be used. If diarrhea is present, the fiber content is lowered.

Tetany

Abnormal calcium metabolism which results in muscle spasms or convulsions is called tetany. The low blood calcium may result from a diet too

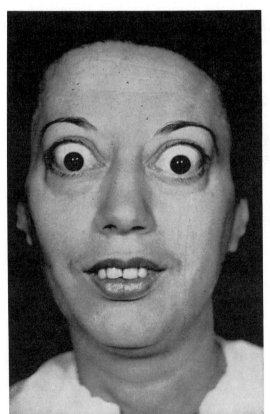

Figure 21–3 Exophthalmic goiter. (From Robbins, S . L.: *Textbook of Pathology,* 3rd Ed., 1967.)

low in calcium, from poor calcium absorption or utilization (parathyroid hypofunction), or from alkalosis which may follow prolonged vomiting or excessive intake of alkaline compounds such as baking soda. The diet is increased in milk and vitamin D; usually, calcium salts and vitamin D concentrates are given. Tetany resulting from alkalosis is treated by giving hydrochloric acid or an acid-producing salt.

Hypo- and Hyperthyroidism

For hypothyroidism (myxedema, cretinism) see the section on iodine in Chapter 8. Thyroid extract is administered and a low calorie diet to reduce weight is used.

In hyperthyroidism there is increased production of thyroxin, which increases the metabolic rate. Exophthalmos may be a symptom in this disease. The diet usually is liberal in protein (up to 100 grams), high in calorie (4000 to 6000), and often supplemented with mineral, especially calcium, and vitamin concentrates. Often milk is used in large quantities, but the stimulating beverages — coffee, tea, and alcohol — are omitted or limited.

SUGGESTED READING

Borden's Review of Nutrition Research: *Nutritional Aspects of Diabetes Mellitus, 29*:15, 1968.

Cole, William: "Hypoglycemia: Shortage of Body Fuel," *Today's Health,* November, 1968.

Kory, Mitchell: *Insulin: Its Source and Action,* 1964. Eli Lilly and Company, Indianapolis, Indiana.

Lamont-Havers, Ronald W.: "Surprising Findings About Diabetes," *Today's Health,* April, 1968.

Ratcliff, J.D.: "I Am Joe's Hypothalamus," *Reader's Digest,* March, 1970.

Rosenthal, Alan: "Learning to Lead Not-So-Normal Lives," *Today's Health,* April, 1970.

U.S. Department of Health, Education, and Welfare:

   Diabetes. Health Information Series No. 70.

   Diabetes and You. Public Health Service Publication No. 567.

   Diabetes — Guide for Nurses. Public Health Service Publication No. 861.

CHAPTER 22

Cardiovascular System

Cardiac Disease

Over half of the deaths in the United States are due to cardiovascular diseases.

Distention in the stomach or intestine, infections, obesity, hypertension, or constipation complicate and make the treatment of heart disease more difficult. If the cardiac patient is overweight, it is essential that he lose weight because this reduces the work of the heart. Fluids, including coffee and tea, are usually allowed ad lib. But alcoholic beverages are used only when allowed by the physician.

In cardiac disease the valves of the heart, blood vessels in the heart, the outer covering (pericardium), the lining membrane (endocardium), the heart muscle (myocardium), or all five may be affected. If the heart is beating faster and has enlarged to maintain normal circulation, the condition is called compensation. In this condition the diet is normal except that five or six small meals may be used instead of three large meals, and the fibrous foods are omitted or restricted so that the stomach does not become distended and cause pressure on the heart. The calorie content is adjusted to keep the patient approximately 10 per cent below normal weight.

When the heart can no longer maintain normal circulation, the condition is called decompensation. In severe cases, such as coronary occlusion, the diet is very restricted, and in the acute stage of heart failure the doctor often specifies the exact foods and liquids which he wishes the patient to eat. It may be the Karrell diet, which consists of 800 cubic centimeters of milk in four equal feedings. When the acute phase is passed, the diet is gradually liberalized. If edema is present, sodium is restricted to the amount ordered by the doctor. Protein is kept at or close to the 1 gram per kilogram of normal body weight, but milk, eggs, and meat are relatively high in sodium; therefore, their intake must be controlled. A low-sodium or dialyzed milk is available in many areas. Carbohydrates are the chief source of calories because fats tend to remain in the stomach longer.

Foods contain varying amounts of sodium. Table 22–1 lists the sodium content of the foods found in the basic diet pattern. It is estimated that the average resident of the United States has a daily intake of 6,000 to 18,000 milligrams of sodium. Salt is 40 per cent sodium. (One teaspoon salt = 2400 milligrams sodium.) Using a variety of food to which no salt has been added yields approximately 2000 milligrams of sodium daily.

The American Heart Association has published three booklets describing exchange lists for different levels of sodium restriction:

1. *Your Mild Sodium-Restricted Diet.* Light salting of food, such as is

Table 22–1 *Sodium Content of Basic-Four Foods*

Food	Amount	Sodium (milligrams)
Milk, whole	1 pint	244 (low sodium 9-25)
Meat, poultry, or fish	5 ounces before cooking	104
Egg	1 medium	70
Citrus fruit	1 serving	1
Other fruit	2 servings	5
Potato, white	1 medium	4
Leafy, green, or yellow vegetable	1 serving	9
Other vegetable	1 serving	4
Whole grain or enriched bread	3 slices	414 (without added sodium 2-10)
Whole grain or enriched cereal	1 small serving	1
Butter or margarine	2 tablespoons	280 (unsalted 3)

Mild sodium restriction (1500 to 3000 mg.)—Reduce the amount of salt in cooking, add none at the table. Avoid: salt preserved foods as bacon, dried beef, sauerkraut, olives, anchovies; bouillon cubes; highly salted foods as crackers, potato chips, salted nuts; relishes as pickles, catsup, prepared mustard; garlic, onion, and celery salt; cheese and peanut butter unless prepared without salt.

Medium sodium restriction (500 to 1500 mg.)—Avoid: salt in cooking; canned fish, meat, vegetables, and soup; frozen fish fillets, lima beans, and peas; shellfish except oysters; and fruits preserved with benzoate of soda.

Severe sodium restriction (less than 500 mg.)—Avoid: salted fats as butter, margarine, and bacon fat; ordinary bread and milk; kale, beet greens, chard, spinach, beets, celery, white turnips, carrots; any product prepared with baking powder or soda; prepared flours and mixes; instant coffee, tea, and Postum; Dutch process cocoa, malted milk, Ovaltine; quick cooking and ready-to-eat cereals.

(Data from Bowes, Anna dePlanter, and Church, Charles F.: *Food Values of Portions Commonly Used.*)

done in canning, is permitted. Omit brined foods and those prepared with monosodium glutamate. The patient adjusts quite readily because the diet is palatable. Refer to notes at bottom of Table 22–1.

2. *Your 1000-Milligram Sodium Diet, Moderate Sodium Restriction.* (43 mEq.) The quantity of meat and milk is restricted. Some vegetables are omitted.

3. *Your 500-Milligram Sodium Diet, Strict Sodium Restriction.* (22 mEq.) Many foods are too high in natural sodium to be allowed on this diet. It often is not accepted well by the patient. The strict sodium restriction is used for congestive heart failure and occasionally in sclerosis with ascites or renal disease with edema.

The patient on a restricted sodium diet should be instructed to watch all food labels for such words as self-rising, cured or brined, sodium bicarbonate, monosodium glutamate, baking powder or soda, sodium benzoate, sodium propionate, sodium alginate, sodium citrate, and sodium acetate. He should know that some dentifrices and drugs* are high in sodium, and that the local water supply, especially if it has been softened, may be high in sodium. Mayonnaise, dehydrated soups, gravies, catsup, chili sauce, frozen peas and lima beans, and most canned foods and convenience foods (frozen dinners, frozen waffles, packaged mixes, and such) have had sodium added. Vegetables canned without added salt can be purchased; sodium is not added to canned fruits. Many foods have had sodium added during processing. Examples: disodium phosphate to the quick-cooking cereals; sodium benzoate, a preservative, is used in relishes, salad dressings, jams, jellies, and catsup; monosodium glutamate (Accent or MSG) is added to many foods to enhance flavor; sodium alginate often is added to chocolate milk and ice cream to give a smooth texture; sodium hydroxide softens the skin of hominy and olives; sodium propionate added to cheese and bread inhibits the growth of mold; and sodium sulfite will bleach fruits. Kosher meat and fowl have been treated with salt to extract as much blood as possible.

Salt substitutes should not be used without the physician's permission. Some of them contain sodium, others contain potassium, which is harmful if there is the complication of kidney insufficiency, and still others may contain ammonium, which is harmful to the patient with liver disease.

The patient and his family should also be instructed to watch for these symptoms and report them to the doctor, because they may indicate that the sodium has been so restricted that there now is a sodium deficiency; abdominal cramps, weakness, lethargy, nausea, anorexia, muscle spasms, headache, and in severe cases mental confusion.

To some people, food without salt is unpalatable. The National

---

*Such as sodium salicylate and sodium penicillin. Many laxatives, antacids, headache remedies, sedatives, and cathartics contain sodium.

Research Council in its Publication No. 325, *Sodium Restricted Diets,* suggests using these flavorings rather than salt:

Allspice	Horseradish	Peppermint extract
Almond extract	(not prepared)	Pimiento
Anise	Leeks	Poppyseed
Basil	Lemon juice or extract	Poultry seasoning
Bay leaf	Mace	Rosemary
Caraway	Maple extract	Saccharin
Cardamom	Marjoram	Saffron
Chives	Mint	Sage
Cinnamon	Mustard, dry	Savory
Cloves	Nutmeg	Sesame
Cocoa (not	Onion juice	Sucaryl calcium
Dutch Process)	Orange extract	Sugar, brown (in
Coriander	Orange peel	small amounts)
Curry	Oregano	Sugar, white
Dill	Paprika	Tarragon
Fennel	Parsley	Thyme
Garlic	Pepper—black,	Turmeric
Ginger	red, or white	Wine

Some flavor combinations for cooked meats and vegetables are suggested in the following list:

Beef—dry mustard, marjoram, nutmeg, onion, sage, thyme, pepper, bay leaf, grape jelly.
Pork—onion, garlic, sage; with applesauce, spiced apples.
Lamb—mint, garlic, rosemary, curry; with broiled pineapple rings.
Veal—bay leaf, ginger, marjoram, curry, currant jelly, spiced apricots.
Chicken—paprika, mushroom, thyme, sage, parsley, cranberry sauce.
Fish—dry mustard, paprika, curry, bay leaf, lemon juice, mushrooms.
Eggs—pepper, green pepper, mushroom, dry mustard, paprika, curry, jelly or pineapple omelet.
Asparagus—lemon juice.
Beans, green—marjoram, lemon juice, nutmeg, unsalted French dressing, dill seed.
Broccoli—lemon juice.
Cabbage—mustard dressing, dill seed, unsalted butter with lemon and sugar.
Carrots—parsley, unsalted butter, mint, nutmeg; glazed with butter and sugar.
Cauliflower—nutmeg.
Corn—green pepper, tomatoes.
Peas—mint, mushroom, parsley, onion.
Potatoes—parsley, unsalted butter, mace, chopped green pepper, onion; baked, French fried.
Squash—ginger, mace.
Sweet potatoes—candied or glazed with cinnamon or nutmeg; escalloped with apples, sugar.
Tomatoes—basil.

Cooked cereals gain in appeal when they are served with honey or a fresh fruit topping. Fried mush with jelly or marmalade provides variety.

Some vegetables are highly acceptable as constituents of raw vegetable salads and lemon or tomato aspic salads, and may be included liberally except where restriction of the fiber content of the diet is necessary. Such salads may be eaten with sodium-restricted mayonnaise or French dressing as desired.

A small amount of sugar added to vegetables during the cooking period helps to bring out the natural flavor of the food. (41)

The local heart association and members of the American Dietetic Association can usually provide low sodium recipes which would incorporate locally grown food.

See the appendix for fat- and sodium-controlled diet patterns.

Vascular Disease

Hypertension may occur as a separate entity or in combination with arteriosclerosis, some types of cardiac and renal disease, goiter, and sometimes during pregnancy. Its etiology is unknown. Hypertension in the younger person is usually more serious than in the older age group, where the incidence is higher. There is a difference of opinion as to dietary treatment; however, if the patient is obese, calories are reduced until weight is normal or slightly below normal. Sodium, highly seasoned foods, and stimulants may be restricted. The Kempner rice diet has been used. It consists of approximately 2000 calories, 200 milligrams of sodium, 20 grams of protein, 5 grams of fat, 460 grams of carbohydrate from rice, sugar, and fruit, and 700 to 1000 cubic centimeters of fruit juice. Iron and vitamin supplements are given.

The use of the rice diet has been almost completely abandoned because most people do not stay on it over a prolonged period of time; therefore, the previously discussed sodium restricted diets of 500 to 2000 milligrams are more often used. Improvement of the hypertension may not be noticed until the controlled sodium diet has been used for four to six weeks. No salt substitute should be used without the approval of the physician because those containing potassium should not be used if there is an accompanying kidney disease. It has been suggested that a prolonged high intake of sodium is related to the incidence of hypertension. For this reason salt and monosodium glutamate have been removed from many baby foods. The babies accept the unsalted food even though the mothers do not like the taste as well.

Arteriosclerosis is a thickening of the arterial walls. As the deposits which contain cholesterol thicken, the walls become less elastic and the heart has to work harder to pump the blood supply. Heart attack or coronary occlusion occurs when a blood clot forms and catches in the coronary artery which has been narrowed by atherosclerosis. Whenever arterial blood vessels in the body are occluded, the surrounding tissue is deprived of the blood supplying its nutrients and oxygen. In coronary vascular disease one cannot say that diet alone is the cause; undoubtedly there are other major factors which play a part, such as hypertension, diabetes, obesity, sedentary living, cigarette smoking, sex, and age. As in hypertension, disagreement exists as to diet. Some use a controlled fat—low cholesterol diet, which means omitting or restricting whole milk, butter, and eggs; others control total fat; others restrict animal fats (see Chapter 4); others order a definite P:S ratio;* and others use a normal diet with ca-

---

*Serum cholesterol tends to increase when the predominant fat in the diet is saturated. On the other hand, it tends to decrease if the diet fats are primarily polyunsaturated. A P:S ratio defines the amount of polyunsaturated fat in ratio to the amount of saturated fat in the diet.

loric content sufficient to maintain normal weight. If there is renal impairment, protein may be reduced; if cardiac impairment, sodium may be restricted.

A vascular brain lesion caused by hemorrhage, embolism, or thrombosis is called a cerebral accident. It may be followed by speech impairment, motor impairment, or mental confusion. In paralysis, tube feeding may be necessary until the patient can swallow. The consistency of the diet is very soft so that the patient will have to do little or no chewing. As the patient recovers, the diet can be returned to normal unless calories or sodium are restricted by the doctor. The patient should be encouraged to consume his food without feeling hurried.

SUGGESTED READING

Alexander, James K.: "Cardiovascular Complications of Obesity," *Cardio Vascular Nursing,* 5:5:19, September-October, 1969.
American Heart Association:
  Anticoagulants—Your Physician and You.
  Cookbook, 1973.
  Diet and Heart Disease, 1968.
  Eat Well But Wisely to Reduce Your Risk of Heart Attack.
  Facts About Congestive Heart Failure.
  Heart Disease in Children, 1966.
  Hypertension.
  If You Have Angina, 1968.
  Physical Activity and Your Heart.
  The Way to a Man's Heart. A Fat-Controlled, Low Cholesterol Meal Plan to Reduce The Risk of Heart Attack.
  What We Know About Diet and Heart Disease.
  Why Risk Heart Attack? 1967.
Bugg, Ralph: "They're Mending Hearts With Exercise," *Today's Health,* October, 1967.
California Heart Association: *For Your Heart—The Fat-Controlled Diet—A Family Guide for Daily Eating.*
Dawber, Thomas R., and Thomas, H. Emerson: "Risk Factors in Coronary Heart Disease," *Cardio Vascular Nursing,* 6:1:20, January-February, 1970.
Deutsch, Patricia and Ron: "The Heart Attack You Didn't Know You Had," *"Today's Health,* July, 1969.
Earles, Virginia: "Fluids, Electrolytes, and Circulation," *Cardio Vascular Nursing,* 6:2:35, March-April, 1970.
Freidman, Glenn, M., et al.: "Alternate Approach to Low Fat, Low Saturated Fat, Low Cholesterol Diet," *J. Nutrition Education,* January, 1974.
Freidman, Glenn, and Goldberg, Stanley J.: "Normal Serum Cholesterol Values." *J. American Medical Association,* 225:6, August 6, 1973.
Liebowitz, Daniel, Brown, W. Gann, and Olness, Marlene R. D.: *Cook To Your Heart's Content On a Low-Fat, Low-Salt Diet,* 1969. (An excellent gourmet recipe book for these diets, published by Pacific Coast Publishers, Menlo Park, California.)
Mayer, Jean: "Keep Your Child's Heart Healthy," *Family Health,* July, 1974.
Metropolitan Life: *New Metropolitan Cook Book,* 1973.
New York City Department of Health: *How to Follow The Prudent Diet,* 1969.
Payne, Alma Smith, and Callahan, Dorothy: *The Low Sodium Cook Book.*
Ratcliff, J. D.:
  "How to Avoid Harmful Stress," *Today's Health,* July, 1970.
  "I Am Joe's Heart," *Reader's Digest,* April, 1967.

San Francisco Heart Association:
 Sodium in Medicinals.
 Sodium in Soft Drinks.
Soffer, Alfred: "What You Should Know About Strokes," *Today's Health*, August, 1968.
Standard Brands, Inc.:
 Dietary Control of Cholesterol, 1969.
 Low Sodium Diets Can Be Delicious, 1969.
U.S. Department of Health, Education, and Welfare:
 Blood Pressure As It Relates to Physique, Blood Glucose, and Serum Cholesterol. Public Health Service Publication No. 1000.
 Strike Back At Stroke. Public Health Service Publication No. 596.
 Varicose Veins. Public Health Service Publication No. 154.
University of Iowa: *A Low Cholesterol Diet Manual.*

CHAPTER 23

Blood Diseases

Achlorhydria   Erythrocyte
Anemia   Leukocyte
  Hemolytic
  Hypochromic
  Macrocytic
  Microcytic

Anemia

Blood has three functions: to carry nutrients to the cells, to carry oxygen to the cells, and to carry waste products from the cells. Anemia exists if there are too few red blood cells (erythrocytes), if they are not of normal size, or if they do not contain a normal amount of hemoglobin. General malnutrition may be found in the anemic patient.

The anemias are found worldwide. General health and working capacities are decreased or impaired and therefore the underdeveloped countries which have a high incidence of anemia may expect a delay in their economic progress.

The life span of the red blood cell is not more than 120 days. A man has about 5,000,000 erythrocytes per cubic millimeter; a woman about 4,500,000 per cubic millimeter. Two vitamins, folic acid and B_{12}, are necessary for the formation of the red blood cells, just as iron is essential for the formation of hemoglobin. If either of the vitamins is deficient, the number of red blood cells in the blood is reduced. They are large and are filled with hemoglobin; thus these anemias are called hyperchromic, macrocytic anemias.

The iron deficiency (hypochromic or low color) anemias may be caused by

1. Blood loss, as in accidental hemorrhage.

2. Hemorrhaging associated with a chronic disease or large menstrual loss.

3. Poor iron intake or absorption (diarrhea and achlorhydria interfere with absorption).

4. Poor intake of other needed nutrients such as protein and copper.

5. Growth in blood volume as during infancy, adolescence, and pregnancy.

The diet emphasizes foods high in iron content such as meat, especially liver and the other organs, egg yolk, enriched and whole grain cereal products, potatoes, green vegetables, legumes, molasses, raisins, figs, prunes, and apricots. With emphasis on meat the protein would be increased. In hypochromic anemia the diet cannot supply enough iron for absorption, so a ferrous iron supplement is prescribed until the hemoglobin content of the red blood cells has returned to normal. Since vitamin C facilitates absorption of iron, two servings daily of foods high in ascorbic acid are desirable.

In pernicious anemia there are fewer but larger than normal red cells. These cells have been released by the bone marrow before becoming mature. The diet should be increased in protein (perhaps as much as 1.5 grams per kilogram of normal weight), iron, and vitamins. Liver extract or vitamin B_{12} is used as medication. In untreated cases there are neurologic lesions which are helped by B_{12} but not by folic acid. Multivitamin capsules which contain folic acid may mask the development of the neurologic manifestations of pernicious anemia; therefore, by law, only prescription vitamin preparations can contain more than 0.1 milligram of folic acid.

The macrocytic anemia due to folic acid deficiency also can occur in tropical sprue, in pregnancy, in infants born to mothers with a deficient folic acid intake during pregnancy, and in alcoholic cirrhosis. The diet is increased in protein, iron, and vitamins. If macrocytic anemia develops within two to five years after a gastrectomy, vitamin B_{12} is given. This anemia develops as a result of the absence of the gastric juice with its intrinsic factor, which facilitates the absorption of vitamin B_{12}.

Hemolytic anemia is a condition in which the rapid destruction of the red blood cells causes the release of excess iron into the blood serum. Favism is a severe form of hemolytic anemia found in sensitive individuals who have eaten the fava bean or inhaled its pollen. When such an individual eats the bean, his red blood cells are unable to complete the oxidation of glucose to carbon dioxide and water with the concurrent release of energy. Hydrogen peroxide accumulates in the red blood cell and destroys it. Some people living in the Eastern Mediterranean and in Africa and as many as 10 per cent of Americans, whose forebears lived there, exhibit this genetic trait. Susceptible individuals will show the favian reaction when treated with the malaria drug, primaquine, or the analgesic, phenacetin.

Leukemia

In leukemia there is an abnormally high white cell (leukocyte) count. Often the patient's mouth becomes very sore, making it necessary to eat food with a soft consistency and to omit tart, spicy, and very hot foods. If edema develops as a result of the hormone therapy, sodium is decreased.

Polycythemia

Polycythemia is an excess number of red blood cells which have a high concentration of hemoglobin. An excess of cobalt may lead to polycythemia. Cobalt is essential for the synthesis of vitamin B_{12}, an essential factor in erythrocyte formation.

Blood Donors

The habitual blood donor needs a well-planned diet which emphasizes protein and iron to promote rapid regeneration of blood constituents.

SUGGESTED READING

Maddox, Gaynor: "Iron-Rich Answers to Tired Food," *Today's Health*, April, 1970.
U.S. Department of Health, Education, and Welfare, Public Health Service Publication No. 790: *Blood and the Rh Factor.*

CHAPTER 24

Urinary System

TERMS TO UNDERSTAND

Albumin   Dialysis
Calculi   Glomerulonephritis

Kidneys filter waste products from the blood stream, maintain the acid-base and water balances in the body, and help maintain the normal composition of the blood. The filtering unit in the kidney is the nephron. Waste matter is sent to the bladder, where it accumulates until eliminated as urine, which is 95 per cent water and 5 per cent waste.

Nephritis, or Bright's disease, may follow an infection such as streptococcal sore throat or scarlet fever. In acute glomerulonephritis an attempt is often made to rest the kidneys for a few days. Fluid intake should equal output; therefore, it may be restricted to 1000 cubic centimeters or less. Sodium is restricted if hypertension or edema appears. For the first few days intake may be restricted to fruit juice, cooked fruit, cereals, toast, and milk. There is controversy as to whether protein should be restricted: some doctors do restrict it for two or three weeks and then gradually return the protein to normal; other doctors use the normal amount of protein from the beginning. In chronic glomerulonephritis a low protein diet (40 to 50 grams) may be used, but more frequently the patient is given maintenance protein plus the equivalent of the amount of albumin which is excreted in the urine. These diets may contain 100 to 125 grams of protein: sodium is restricted if edema or hypertension is present; water usually is not restricted. Salt substitutes containing potassium should not be used.

Nephrosclerosis, hardening of the renal arteries, is often associated with hypertension in the elderly. The diet has a low (40 to 50 grams) to normal protein content depending upon the blood urea nitrogen level. Sodium is restricted if there is hypertension. (See Chapter 22 for flavorings which can be used.) Unless there is scanty urine output liberal amounts of fluids are given. It is desirable that weight be kept within the normal range.

In nephrosis there is degeneration in the kidney tissues with edema and albuminuria. The diet tries to replace urinary protein losses and sodium is restricted. Many lay people think that red meat should be restricted, but there is no scientific evidence to substantiate this idea. In fact the iron it contains may help the anemia frequently present.

Patients with uremia show an abnormally high blood content of urea nitrogen and suppression of urinary output. If the patient can eat and retain food, the diet is low in protein (20 to 40 grams), fluids are adjusted so that intake equals output, carbohydrate is 300 to 400 grams, and fat is 70 to 90 grams. Sodium and potassium may be restricted.

Patients undergoing intermittent dialysis must have rigid dietary control to prevent excessive accumulation of metabolic waste products. In the 1960's the low protein–essential amino acid diet, which is a modified Giordano-Giovannetti regimen, was tried by many clinics in the United States. This essentially is a 2000 to 3000 calorie diet, with 20 or less grams of food protein with the essential amino acid supplementation, about 350 grams of carbohydrate, and 80 to 90 grams of fat. The protein comes from one egg, six and one-half ounces of milk, low protein cereals such as corn and rice, and low protein vegetables; the carbohydrates from fruits, bread made from a low protein wheat starch, and sugar; and the fats are unsalted. The egg protein was selected because it has the highest biological value of any of the high protein foods. Under this diet, blood urea concentration was decreased, nitrogen balance became positive or reached equilibrium, and the clinical symptoms disappeared or were improved. These diet plans are difficult to follow. The protein, sodium, and potassium food exchange lists, the recipes, and the food preparation have to be carefully explained to the homemaker and to the patient. There must be a great deal of follow-up and support to carry out the plan.

Refer to the appendix for protein and sodium restricted diets.

Urinary calculi (stones) are found in the kidneys and bladder. In most cases the etiology of the stones is unknown. Factors in prevention include a high intake of fluids to produce a dilute urine and controlling the pH of the urine by means of drugs or an acid- or alkaline-ash diet (see Chapter 8 for the foods involved); for example, some calcium salt stones precipitate in an alkaline media and therefore tend to stay in solution if the urine has a low pH.

Laboratory analysis can determine the exact composition, but about 95 per cent of the kidney stones contain calcium. With calcium phosphate and calcium carbonate stones, milk may be restricted to the equivalent of one or two cups daily, all food fortified with vitamin D is excluded, and the patient may be given an acid-ash diet which would emphasize meat, eggs, fish, poultry, and cereals. Cranberry juice seems to have a strong effect on lowering the urinary pH so is frequently used as a dietary supplement. With calcium oxalate stones, milk may be restricted to the equivalent of one or two cups daily and the urine is kept alkaline; therefore, vegetables and fruits are emphasized.

About four per cent of the stones consist of uric acid. Uric acid results from the metabolism of purines. Diet may not have much, if any, effect, but low purine diets have been used, in which case the intake of meat (especially organs), legumes, and whole grain cereals is decreased. Fluid is increased to produce not less than 3 liters of urine daily, and an alkaline-ash diet supplemented with alkaline medications to keep the pH of the urine as high as possible is used.

Cystine stones, about one per cent of the total, will be precipitated when the renal tube is not normally reabsorbing the non-essential amino acid cystine. The protein content of the diet seems to have no effect on the cystinuria. A large fluid intake and alkaline therapy are used.

None of these diets remove formed stones, but may be helpful in preventing recurrence of stones.

In prolonged immobilization (paralytic polio, pelvic fractures) there is increased calcium excretion, which may result in urinary calculi. Acid-ash diets may be recommended.

Medication has almost replaced dietary treatment of renal infections (cystitis, pyelitis, pyelonephritis), but acid- or alkaline-ash diet may be used concurrently with the medication.

SUGGESTED READING

Bugg, Ralph: "Your Body's Silent Partners," *Today's Health*, January, 1969.
Ratcliff, J.D.: "I Am Joe's Kidney," *Reader's Digest*, May, 1970.
Today's Health: "Are Kidney Stones Really Stones?" August, 1969. Pp. 67, 68.

CHAPTER 25

Musculoskeletal and Nervous Systems

TERMS TO UNDERSTAND

Gonadal
Matrix
Muscle, striated

Ossification
Porous
Remission

Arthritis

Arthritis is inflammation of a joint. Its cause is often unknown. Various diets, such as the low calorie, high vitamin D, or low carbohydrate diets, have been tried but have had no effect. The most common rheumatic diseases are rheumatoid arthritis, ankylosing spondylitis, osteoarthritis, rheumatic fever, and gout.

Rheumatoid arthritis is most crippling and most painful. The chronic inflammation affects connective tissue in the entire body, including the organs, but is most often found in the joints and their surrounding tissue. There is damage to the bones, cartilage, and all joint tissues; nodules often appear. There may be fever, muscular weakness, fatigue, anemia, or weight loss due to anorexia. Remissions are common with this disease. This, as well as the fact that there is no specific cure for arthritis, is probably why quackery has been able to get such a firm foothold. The annual cost of "worthless or harmful treatments, cures, and devices" is more than $310 million. (15:18) Treatment includes rest, exercise, and heat, and the use of aspirin is common. The diet should consist of the basic-four with enough calories to maintain normal weight or slight underweight, and emphasis should be placed on protein and high iron foods.

Ankylosing spondylitis affects the spine. There is progressive stiffening of the back associated with pain. The cause is unknown. It affects more men than women. Exercise, heat application, and a diet which includes the basic-four with calories to maintain normal weight are the treatment used.

Osteoarthritis, the most common form of arthritis, occurs primarily in elderly people. The cause is unknown, but heredity is probably a factor. The joint cartilage and other joint tissues break down so that the joints are stiff and painful and motion is limited. The finger joints, especially in women, develop bony enlargements. There is no cure for osteoarthritis, but symptoms can be alleviated and joint function can be improved. Aspirin is widely used but the choice of medication is made by the physician; overweight is common so again a lower calorie, basic-four diet emphasizing calcium-containing foods is used. To obtain calcium non-fat milk, lower in calories than whole milk, may be used.

Gout is a disease which affects the joints and the kidneys. Caused by overproduction of uric acid from purine (a constituent of nucleoproteins found in all cells) and by not excreting uric acid rapidly enough through the urine, the condition is hereditary. Crystals of sodium urate are deposited in the joints, especially those of the toe and hand, and there is a tendency to develop kidney stones. If the patient is obese, calories are reduced until normal weight, or ten per cent below normal, is attained. Drugs are replacing the use of a low purine diet. If the diet is restricted, most of the protein comes from egg, cheese, and milk. The intake of alcohol and fatty foods is decreased. During the acute stage the doctor may give orders to omit all meat, especially organ meats, gravy, broth, fish, poultry, condiments, alcohol and beer, asparagus, mushrooms, spinach, and legumes. During the chronic stage, a small serving of fish, poultry, or meat, except the organ meats, may be used daily, and an occasional serving of the other restricted foods is permissible. (See Table A–3 for purine content of food.)

Rheumatic fever is mentioned with arthritis because its most dramatic symptoms also involve very painful joints. The arthritis which accompanies rheumatic fever is very painful but seldom cripples. A person of any age may develop rheumatic fever, but it is most frequently found in the ages of five to 15. The main target of rheumatic fever is the heart. Streptococcus infection nearly always precedes rheumatic fever. One who has had it once frequently contracts it again. However, by the proper use of antibiotics to prevent the streptococcus infection, recurrent attacks of rheumatic fever can nearly always be prevented. The treatment of rheumatic fever consists of rest, anti-inflammatory drugs such as aspirin, and sometimes the administering of cortisone compounds. The diet is normal, with a possible increase in protein and vitamin C and a decrease in sodium if edema results from the use of the cortisone drug. Red meats do not have to be restricted.

Osteoporosis

The etiology and treatment of osteoporosis are poorly understood. Any bone in the body may be affected. The following factors are probably involved in its development:

1. Endocrine disorders such as hyperthyroidism, hyperparathyroidism, hyperadrenocorticism
2. Immobilization
3. Rheumatoid arthritis
4. Sickle-cell anemia
5. Nutritional deficiencies, such as calcium, protein, ascorbic acid, vitamin D.

The disease is frequently found with a low protein intake which decreases the amount of bone matrix; there is also a correlation of mineralization of the bone which would be influenced by a low intake of calcium and vitamin D. Osteoporosis is most often found among women who have had frequent pregnancies and occurs four times as frequently in post-menopausal women as in middle-aged men. Symptoms of osteoporosis are severe low back pain, frequent vertebral or hip fractures, stooped posture, a reduction in height, and a bone mass loss as great as 30 per cent. (See Figure 8-1.) This is due to a reduction in the number of cells, which increases the porosity of the bone. The chemical composition of the remaining bone and its structure are not changed. Treatment includes gonadal hormone therapy. The diet includes the basic-four, with at least a quart of milk per day and liberal amounts of protein foods. Calcium supplements, vitamin D, and fluorine may help increase ossification.

In the older person fluoride helps maintain normal calcification of the bone; prescribing fluoride for older persons in an area without fluoridated water may prevent senile osteoporosis and frequent fractures. Shambaugh and Petronic reported: "The incidence of calcification of the aorta [is] twice as frequent especially among men in the low-fluoride areas as in the high-fluoride communities. Thus an 'adequate' intake of fluoride appears to become increasingly necessary with advancing age to keep calcium where it belongs—in the bones, rather than in the arteries." (70:111)

Muscular Dystrophy

In muscular dystrophy there is a progressive wasting and weakness of the striated muscles. It is difficult for the patient to feed himself, but continued use of the muscle tends to prevent atrophy. The normal diet, perhaps slightly raised in protein, is used. The use of selenium or vitamin E has not altered the course of the disease in humans.

Dental Caries

An adequate diet for the pregnant mother and for the child from infancy through adolescence seems to reduce the incidence of dental caries. Minute amounts of fluorine taken by the child during the period when dentine and enamel are being formed may reduce the incidence of caries about 65 per cent. (See Figure 8–4.) Sticky, sweet foods which adhere to the teeth seem to increase the possibility of decay more than does sugar in solution. The bacteria in the dental plaque rapidly attack the adhesive carbohydrates, forming an acid which erodes the tooth enamel. The more often sugar is introduced into the mouth, the greater the incidence of caries. Brushing the teeth or rinsing the mouth immediately after meals removes food particles and reduces reactions. The caries-prone individual is encouraged to omit from his diet candy, sugar, jam, jelly, sweet desserts, sugared beverages, and soft drinks.

Lead Poisoning

Lead may enter the body when lead dust is inhaled, when food or drink is contaminated with lead, or when cosmetics and hair dye containing lead are used; if children eat flakes of lead-based paint or if they consume acid food which was stored in improperly glazed dishes. The lead content in glaze gives the smooth, lustrous finish. Some of the cheaper imported pieces and those done by amateurs whose hobby is ceramics may have a poor job of glazing. The acid in fruit, pickles, and other acid foods will etch into the surface of that glaze and release lead. (34:20)

If the lead is stored in the bones there are no toxic symptoms, but if the blood contains more than a minute amount of lead, the patient may develop constipation, weakness, anemia, colic, vomiting, and joint pains. During the acute stage a high calcium diet often is used. This favors deposition of lead in the bones. Some doctors keep the patient on a relatively high calcium diet indefinitely and others gradually lower the calcium content to withdraw the lead slowly from the bones so it can be excreted by the kidneys.

Epilepsy

Epilepsy is a disease affecting the nervous system; it is usually treated with drug therapy. With the good control achieved by most patients under modern drug therapy, the epileptic can and should be encouraged to lead a normal socially and economically productive life. Avoiding a large intake of food or liquid at any one meal is recommended. Formerly the unpalatable ketogenic diet was extensively used. It restricts fluids and salt, is very high in fat, very low in carbohydrate (50 to 60 grams), and moderate to low in protein.

Migraine

The severe headache may be accompanied by nausea and vomiting. Research seems to indicate a possible relationship to heredity, allergy, and emotion, but the exact cause is unknown. If there is a food allergy, that food should be omitted; otherwise a normal diet usually is used.

Multiple Sclerosis

In multiple sclerosis hardening of some of the tissues of the brain and spinal cord occurs. The cause is unknown. Although the quack or faddist may promise a cure, in general, the prognosis is poor. An adequate diet is used. As muscle atrophy increases and coordination decreases, food may have to be liquefied to facilitate swallowing.

Ménière's Syndrome

Ménière's syndrome is associated with changes in the organ of equilibrium of the inner ear. If there is localized edema, sodium is restricted.

SUGGESTED READING

American Dental Association: *Your Guide to Oral Health.*
American Heart Association: *What You Should Know About Rheumatic Fever.*
American Medical Association: *Arthritis.*
Arthritis and Rheumatism Foundation: *Arthritis, Symptoms and Treatment.*
Arthritis Foundation:
   Arthritis and Modern Woman.
   Arthritis Quackery, A $300,000,000 Racket.
   Diet and Arthritis, 1968.
   Gout—A Handbook for Patients.
   Osteoarthritis—A Handbook for Patients.
   Rheumatoid Arthritis—A Handbook for Patients.
   Today's Facts About Arthritis.
   You and Arthritis.
Berland, Theodore, and Seyler, Alfred E.: "Teeth Care for Teen-Agers," *Today's Health,* March, 1968.
Bugg, Ralph: "Fighting the Masked Crippler: Rheumatic Fever," *Today's Health,* March, 1968.
Cole, William: "New Insight Into the Brain's Defenses," *Today's Health,* March, 1970.
DiOrio, L. P., and Madsen, K. O.: "A Personalized Approach: Discussing Food in Prevention of Dental Disease," *Nutrition News.* National Dairy Council, February, 1970.
DuVries, Henri L.: "Five Myths About Your Feet," *Today's Health,* August, 1967.
Epilepsy Foundation of America:
   Epilepsy: Answers to Some of the Most Frequently Asked Questions About Epilepsy.

Ishmael, William K.: "Primary Osteoarthritis, Migraine Headaches, and Motion Sickness," *J.A.M.A., 201*:103–105, July 10, 1967.

National Dairy Council: *For Good Dental Health — Start Early.*

Nizel, Abraham, E.:

"The Contribution of the Science and Practice of Nutrition to Prevention and Control of Dental Caries," *Food and Nutrition News.* National Livestock and Meat Board, January and February, 1970.

"Food Habits and Their Modification for Caries Control," *Nutrition News.* National Dairy Council, February, 1969.

Randal, Judith, E.: "A Pill That Lets Shaking Palsy Patients Eat Jello," *Today's Health,* January, 1970.

U.S. Department of Health, Education, and Welfare:

Arthritis and Rheumatism.

Diet and Arthritis. Public Health Service Publication No. 1857, 1969.

Facts About Osteoporosis. Public Health Service Publication No. 1217.

Gout.

Headache, Hope Through Research. Public Health Service Publication No. 905.

Healthy Teeth. Public Health Service Publication No. 405.

Multiple Sclerosis.

Pyorrhea and Other Gum Diseases. Public Health Service Publication No. 1482.

CHAPTER 26

Allergy and Skin Disorders

TERMS TO UNDERSTAND

Papule
Pollen

Allergy

Allergy is a sensitivity to such substances as pollens, dust, cosmetics, drugs, vaccine and serum injections, insect and snake bites, and food. Heredity probably has a role in allergy, so a careful medical history is important. One does not inherit sensitivity to a specific substance nor the particular manifestations which will occur. Allergy symptoms include digestive upsets, hives (urticaria), edema, hay fever, asthma, rash, migraine, eczema, dermatitis, and acne. The symptoms are more apt to appear or be more serious during an emotional upset or fatigue.

Any food may produce an allergy, but foods which most frequently cause allergies include milk, eggs, chocolate, wheat, fish, tomatoes, and strawberries.

As skin tests often do not accurately indicate food sensitivities, an elimination diet may be used.

If a person is on an elimination diet, only a few foods are given until the symptoms disappear, then one food at a time is added until those causing the sensitivity are found. If there is a moderate sensitivity, small amounts of food can be eaten occasionally. For example, the person may be able to eat one egg a week but not an egg every day. If there is a high sensitivity, the food must be completely eliminated.

A fruit-free diet leaves out all fruits and such things as Jello because Jello contains fruit flavors.

If corn is to be eliminated, commercial baking powders are not used because many of them contain cornstarch. Products such as Mazola, which is corn oil, may not be used.

An egg-free diet excludes eggs as such and also cake, cookies, crackers, mayonnaise, muffins, pies, macaroni, spaghetti, noodles, custard, French toast, hollandaise sauce, meringue, Ovaltine, ice cream, Cocomalt, almond cakes, almond paste, sherbet, waffles, prepared cake and pancake flours, and baking powders. Nearly all commercial bread contains powdered eggs. The virus vaccines developed from chick embryos, such as influenza vaccine, must be avoided.

A wheat-free diet will exclude most bakery bread, cakes, cookies, pies, noodles, graham bread, gluten and gluten bread, soups containing noodles or spaghetti, puddings, cake flours, malted milk, sausage, Cream of Wheat, Wheatena, farina, Ralston, puffed wheat, Pep, Grapenuts, crackers, macaroni, spaghetti, Nestlés' food, Postum, pancake flour, and many so-called "health breads" supposedly wheat-free. Salad dressing may contain wheat as a binder.

A milk-free diet will exclude milk and all dairy products, margarine, cake, chocolate, Cocomalt, Ovaltine, sherbets, Zwieback, cookies, pastries, ice cream, malted milk, custards, ordinary bread, macaroni, spaghetti, noodles, cheese and many other foods. No recipe containing butter or margarine can be used. "Soybean milk" is a milk substitute containing protein of good biological value and is fortified with minerals.

Manufacturers of foods entering interstate commerce are required to list on the packages the ingredients of their products unless they have standards of identity. (See Chapter 29, Food Legislation.) These lists of ingredients should be noted carefully when certain kinds of foods are to be avoided. If the listing contains a general term such as "spices" or "shortening" the food product may have to be avoided. For example, shortening may be any one or a combination of the animal or vegetable fats.

Acne

In acne vulgaris, pink papules, often with blackheads, appear. The sebaceous glands are inflamed due to retained secretions. The incidence of acne seems to increase during adolescence when hormone activity is greatest; and it seems to be more prevalent in those persons with oily skin. Various diets have been tried, but one which contains ample meat, cereals, vegetables, fruits, eggs, and milk, and thus provides adequate nutrients, seems most satisfactory. Acne is not primarily a dietary disease. Occasionally fats and fried foods, chocolate, candy, or condiments are restricted; but recent studies have shown that adolescents who ate chocolate had no higher incidence of acne than those who ate none. Regular meal hours, adequate fluids, good elimination, rest, good health habits, and thorough and frequent skin cleansing seem to help.

The dermatitis due to essential fatty acid or vitamin deficiencies has been discussed in previous chapters.

SUGGESTED READING

Allergy Foundation of America: *Allergy in Children.*

American Dietetic Association: *Allergy Recipes.*

American Medical Association: *The Look You Like,* 1974. (See section on skin care.)

Fisher, Alexander A.: "Tracking the Mystery Rash," *Today's Health,* January, 1969.

Fulton, James E., et al.: "Effect of Chocolate on Acne Vulgaris," *J.A.M.A., 210:*2071-2075, December15, 1969. This is an excellent discussion showing that diet has little, if any, effect on the incidence of acne.

National Tuberculosis Association: *Hay Fever, the Facts.*

Quaker Oats Company: *Wheat, Milk, and Egg Free Recipes.*

Rowe, Albert H.: *The Elimination Diets.* (Booklet available from Sather Gate Book Shop, 2335 Telegraph Avenue, Berkeley, California 94704.)

Smith, Lendon: "What Parents Can Do About Food Allergies," *Today's Health,* July, 1969.

U.S. Department of Agriculture, Home and Garden Bulletin No. 147: *Baking for People With Food Allergies.*

U.S. Department of Health, Education, and Welfare: Health Information Series No. 75, *Cancer of the Skin.*

Wood, Marion N.: "Eating Well on a Wheat-Free Diet," *Today's Health,* February, 1970.

CHAPTER 27

Childhood Illness

TERMS TO UNDERSTAND

Colic
Phenylalanine
Regress

The sick child in a hospital is in a strange environment, among strange people, and may come in contact with equipment which frightens him. Under these conditions it should not be surprising that he may refuse food entirely or regress to former behavior patterns. For example, he may wish to eat only the very familiar foods, such as milk and bread, or he may wish the security of having an adult feed him.

The sick child confined to bed in his own home can be cared for more easily if there is a bed table which can be used as a play table between meals. (A board placed across two chairs, one on either side of the bed, makes a satisfactory table.) If used in moderation, gay dime-store dishes, a chop frill, a cellophane straw, a flower in a bud vase, or bread cut in an animal shape may add enough interest to stimulate some food consumption.

Few people enjoy eating alone; therefore, if a member of the family is present, more food may be consumed.

A few points to remember in caring for an ill child are

1. Be cheerful—a smile can be very encouraging.

2. Be aware that he may not have the strength or desire to chew food.

3. Consider the food requirements for the specific age when planning the menu.

4. Do not try to introduce new foods at this time.

5. Use small servings.

6. Give small bites and allow him time to chew and swallow before offering the next bite.

232

7. Use foods at moderate temperatures rather than at extremes of hot and cold.

8. Include a variety of foods—not just his favorites.

9. Do not try to force him to eat—appetite usually returns in a few days.

10. Try to avoid accumulating medicine bottles, wash bowls, and stacks of toys or books which would make his area appear cluttered.

11. Use simple but nourishing foods when his appetite returns. Elaborate foods as, for example, an eggnog fortified with cream, malted milk, sugar and/or ice cream may cause vomiting. The high fat content may decrease the appetite.

12. Be honest about an unpleasant tasting medication and *don't combine it with food.*

13. Don't awaken him for a feeding except on doctor's order.

14. Realize that he may not understand the necessity for remaining in bed during his convalescence.

The infant may have abdominal pain (often called colic). The distention may be caused by swallowing air as he nurses, by gas formed due to bacterial action on the food, perhaps by ingesting cold food, and by excitement or fatigue. If the colic is due to gas formation, the sugar in the formula may be reduced or changed to a less fermentable type or acidified milk may be used. Colic usually disappears when the child is three or four months old.

Infant diarrhea can be caused by a contaminated formula, a formula too high in fat or carbohydrate, and allergy. The formula may be changed to skim or acidified milk, the sugar may be omitted, or the formula changed to incorporate a milk substitute. Sometimes powdered or scraped fresh apple is given. For small children dehydration and electrolyte imbalance can develop rapidly; if untreated, death may result.

Fevers, ulcers, constipation, anemia, abnormal weight, diabetes, rickets, scurvy, renal diseases, epilepsy, and lead poisoning occur in childhood, too. The principles of the diets prescribed in these diseases have been listed in the preceding chapters.

Cystic Fibrosis

Cystic fibrosis is a congenital disease of the pancreas which results in a deficiency or absence of pancreatic enzymes. In this disease, pancreatic enzymes are given to the child with each feeding to aid digestion. The diet is high calorie (as much as 50 per cent above normal; sugar is digested better than starches), protein is increased, fat is decreased, and vitamin supplements are given. Extra salt is given if there is excessive perspiration.

Celiac Disease

The child who has celiac disease usually is under 5 years of age. Symptoms include protruding abdomen, retarded growth, and stools containing unabsorbed fat. A restricted-starch, high-protein, low-fat diet is used occasionally; more often a diet free of the cereal protein, gluten, is ordered. Corn, rice, and soy flour are allowed but no wheat, rye, oats, or barley is used. Bananas are well tolerated and can be used to provide many calories.

Inborn Errors of Metabolism
(Molecular Disease)

A few children are born without the ability to produce an enzyme needed for a metabolic process (see Figure 19–3). Phenylketonuria (PKU) and galactosemia are examples. In phenylketonuria, the infant does not metabolize the amino acid, phenylalanine, which accumulates in the blood, causing mental and physical deterioration. Early diagnosis and treatment are necessary to prevent brain damage. Few proteins are devoid of phenylalanine; therefore the diet is extremely low in natural protein and supplemented with commercially prepared synthetic protein products (Ketonil, Lofenalac, Enal), which contain no phenylalanine. Fruit, fruit juice, cereals and vegetables, except legumes, are gradually introduced into the infant's diet. An exchange list which groups foods of approximately the same phenylalanine content can be found in the Children's Bureau Publication No. 388, *Phenylketonuria*. The length of time for administering this diet is unknown. However, it is probable that at least until adolescence and perhaps throughout life therapy is needed. The diaper test is probably more widely known by the general public but those states having laws concerning PKU screening use the more sensitive blood tests.

In galactosemia, the body does not utilize the carbohydrate galactose. The infant develops jaundice, anorexia, enlarged liver and spleen, physical and mental retardation, ascites, and caratacts. When milk and milk products are removed from the diet, the symptoms, except brain damage and possibly cataracts, regress. The casein hydrolysate preparations, such as Nutramigen, or a meat base formula is used. The foods listed under milk allergy, Chapter 26, should be avoided, as should peas, beets, lima beans, liver, brains, sweetbreads, cocoa and chocolate, soybeans, cottonseed, and flaxseed. The oils of soybeans, cottonseed, and flaxseed may be used, as they are galactose-free.

Maple sugar urine disease results from inability to use the amino acids—leucine, isoleucine, and valine. The name describes the characteristic odor of the urine. The disease is usually fatal.

Diabetes and the disaccharidase deficiencies, discussed in previous chapters, are also inborn errors of metabolism.

Handicapped Children

Children with cerebral palsy or cleft palate and lip may have difficulty swallowing. Volume is kept to a minimum by using foods as concentrated as possible in protein and calories. Vitamin and mineral supplements are usually given. If the palsied child has constant movement, he needs extra calories. Inactivity of the child with spastic palsy may lead to overweight.

Babies with cleft palate cannot suck like other infants. They may have to be fed with an eyedropper or a syringe. They must be burped often as they tend to swallow air. If the use of tart and spicy foods irritates the mouth, those foods have to be omitted. Creamed foods, peanut butter, leafy vegetables, nuts, cooked cheese dishes, and peelings of raw fruit may stick to the roof of the mouth. Others with cleft palates may have no difficulty swallowing any food. Following surgery, a liquid or puréed diet is given until healing is complete.

The mentally retarded child usually goes through the same physical development sequence as any other child. Neglect, overfeeding, or lack of discipline may affect his nutritional status. He may suck his hand, vomit, be very messy, or eat very slowly. Patience, ingenuity, and loving attention are very important for the mentally retarded child.

Unless extra time and patience are given to feeding the handicapped, malnutrition usually occurs. Frequent small meals may be better than three larger meals. Though a messy eater, the child should be permitted to feed himself if possible. Physical and occupational therapists have developed many instruments and techniques that can be very helpful in feeding any handicapped person and in helping him to feed himself.

SUGGESTED READING

American Cancer Society: *Cancer In Children.*
Children's Bureau:
   Accidents and Children.
   The Child with Cerebral Palsy.
   The Child with a Cleft Palate.
   The Child with Epilepsy.
   The Child Who Is Hard of Hearing.
   The Child with a Missing Arm or Leg.
   The Child with Rheumatic Fever.
   Growing Pains.
   The Mongoloid Baby.
   Phenylketonuria—Detection in the Newborn Infant as a Routine Hospital Procedure.
   The Preschool Child Who Is Blind.
   Your Premature Baby.

California State Department of Public Health: *PKU. A Diet Guide for Parents of Children with Phenylketonuria.*

di Sant'Agnese, Paul A.: "Unmasking the Great Impersonator—Cystic Fibrosis," *Today's Health,* February, 1969.

Hansen, R. G.: "Hereditary Galactosemia," *J.A.M.A., 208*:43, June, 1969.

Kempler, Walter: "Uncovering Your Child's Masked Messages," *Today's Health,* April, 1970.

Krebs, Marguerite and Robert: "Are You Raising A Perfectionist?" *Today's Health,* August, 1970.

Linde, Shirley Motter: "What We Know About Children's Convulsions," *Today's Health,* October, 1967.

Mead Johnson Laboratories: *Phenylketonuria—Low Phenylalanine Dietary Management with Lofenalac.*

Metropolitan Life Insurance Company: *ABC's of Childhood Disease.*

Morrison, C. V. and Dorothy N.: "Help Found: Team Care for Disturbed Children," *Today's Health,* April, 1970.

Rabasca, Iris M.: "Predictable Hazards of Childhood," *Today's Health,* January, 1970.

Stimson, Cyrus W.: "Understanding the Mongoloid Child," *Today's Health,* November, 1968.

U.S. Department of Health, Education, and Welfare:
Chickenpox.
Diphtheria.
Mental and Emotional Illness in the Young Child. Public Health Service Publication No. 1877.
Mumps.
Smallpox.
Whooping Cough.

CHAPTER 28

Mental Illness

The prevention and treatment of mental illness has been brought increasingly to public attention during the past few years as people have come to realize that the stress of modern living may cause more people to have problems of emotional adjustment or to become mentally ill. In 1969 there were approximately 1,650,000 hospital beds in the United States. Psychiatric patients occupied 570,550 of these beds. (101:473) The majority of these patients were in state or county hospitals; the balance were cared for in private hospitals, general hospitals, or in private homes.

Dr. E. H. Crawfis has said, "Food is one of our most important social instruments, and mental illness is a disorder involving difficulties in social adjustments." (26) The underlying purpose of all treatments for the mentally ill is to re-establish social contact, and since meals are one of the most common forms of socialization, food service plays a most important part in the rehabilitation of the mentally ill. It is not only essential to provide meals which supply all the required nutrients but also to furnish an environmental setting to encourage the patient to eat. Since most of the mentally ill are able to eat in dining rooms, they should be as attractive as possible in order to stimulate the patient's appetite if necessary, induce socialization with others, and generally provide an atmosphere conducive to good eating. In institutions food may be served cafeteria-style, with patients carrying their trays or family style at the tables, or waitress service may be given. Regardless of the serving method, the above principles should be used. If patients require hospital tray service, the tray should be attractively arranged and delivered to the patient with hot foods hot and cold foods cold.

Dining rooms should be quiet, free from disturbances, and pleasantly decorated; floral decorations should be used if possible, dishes and silver should be spotlessly clean and pleasing in appearance; servers should be neatly and cleanly dressed, and service should be unrushed and leisurely.

In general, feeding the mentally ill follows the same pattern as feeding any other group of people, since the nutrient requirements are similar. The emotional disturbances of each patient may present an individual feeding problem. An overactive patient may require more food because of energy expenditure; a patient may have the delusion that he is being poisoned; he may feel that he is not "good enough to deserve to eat" or that he is depriving others of food; he may hear voices which command him not to eat—and he may reject food to the point of starvation or subnutrition. It may be necessary to "coax" the patient to eat; in some cases he may have to be spoonfed, or it may be necessary to provide foods in an easily recognizable form (a whole banana rather than a diced banana in a pudding). (6) Modifications in the diet should not be made unless prescribed by the doctor to meet dietary or physical needs (as in the case of a patient who may have difficulty swallowing or chewing).

Sometimes as part of the rehabilitation therapy program, a patient may be assigned to assist in the preparation or in the service of food as a means of helping to solve the patient's conflicts and frustrations, build up self-confidence and self-esteem, develop steady work habits, and prepare him for useful work on leaving the hospital. (52)

A home-type cooking class in which the patient may actually plan, prepare, and serve food of a party nature for groups of fellow patients or visitors has also proved to be effective therapy which gives the patients an opportunity to be creative. (67)

The attitude of the employee, friend, or relative working with the mentally ill patient is very important. He must have patience, understanding, and respect for the individuality of the person, since often some unkind word or deed may undo in a moment what has taken months to accomplish. The emotionally depressed patient may be helped more by kind firmness than by the solicitous person who "just can't do enough."

The mentally ill, like all other patients, should receive good food, served attractively in pleasant surroundings. "Food is one therapy in a mental hospital that is available to all patients three times a day. As such it becomes an important instrument for the treatment and rehabilitation of the mentally ill." (60) This statement also applies to a patient living at home.

During the past several years 75 to 80 per cent of persons admitted to mental hospitals have been discharged and returned to community life. The present trend is to treat some patients with mental illness in out-patient clinics and allow them to live in their homes. More progressive treatment programs have been used, more money is being spent on research, more general interest is being expressed, and community programs have been educating the public to recognize and seek help with their problems.

SUGGESTED READING

Manfreda, Marguerite Lucy: *Psychiatric Nursing.*

Mark, Norman: "Calm Down at Your Own Risk—A Comprehensive Evaluation of Over-the-Counter Tranquilizers," *Today's Health,* March, 1974.

Owens, Lavern and White, Jean Sando: "Observations on Food Acceptance During Mental Illness." *J. Am. Dietet. A., 30*:1110–1114.

Rakstis, Ted J.: "Sensitivity Training: Fad, Fraud, or New Frontier?" *Today's Health,* January, 1970.

U.S. Department of Health, Education, and Welfare:
  The Child Who Is Mentally Retarded.
  Facts About the Mental Health of Children: Publication No. 74–70, 1974.

SELECTION AND CARE OF FOOD

INTRODUCTORY STATEMENT

The meals which are planned and prepared by employing the science and art of cookery help insure good health and vitality. One may purchase nutritious food items but through improper storage or improper cooking destroy a portion of the nutrients.

In many homes in the United States the purchase of food takes between 15 and 20 per cent of the disposable income. If the family income is low, the percentage spent for food will be higher than the percentage spent by a family with a larger income; therefore food selection is a greater problem for the lower income family.

The following chapters discuss the means of obtaining the most nutrients for the least money and conserving the nutrients by means of proper storage and proper cooking procedures.

Since there are excellent, moderately priced cook books, no recipes are included in this manual. In many cook books (for example, *Betty Crocker's Picture Cook Book)*, cooking equipment and measuring techniques are well explained or illustrated.

A glossary of cooking terms may be found in Kansas State College, Department of Foods and Nutrition: *Practical Cookery and the Etiquette and Service of the Table*, or in Dodd: *America's Cook Book.*

Many food products show a United States Department of Agriculture inspection stamp. This means that the food and its processing plant were inspected for sanitation.

Grade is an indication of quality determined by general appearance, palatability, size, and maturity. *It is related to product acceptance, not to nutrient value.* In the United States food grading is voluntary; in other words, it is not required by law. If grading is requested the food processors and

U.S. Department of Agriculture grade and inspection marks. *A*, Inspection mark only. *B*, Combined inspection and grade mark. *C*, Combined grade and size mark for eggs. *D*, Grade label for meat.

packers pay a fee for the grading service. The government grader examines the food and certifies that it measures up to the standard of quality for that product. Foods most often graded are beef, lamb, butter, and eggs. The grade mark is often shield-shaped. Don't confuse this with the federal government inspection mark which is round in shape. All meat and poultry which cross state lines must be federally inspected. Remember, grading is for quality and is voluntary; inspection is for wholesomeness and is mandatory. You will note in the following chapters that grade terminology varies with different food products.

In Canada, as in the United States, inspection means wholesomeness and grade means quality. If shipped in interprovince trade, most fresh fruits and vegetables, all butter, honey, and processed fruits and vegetables prepared in plants registered with the Canadian Department of Agriculture must be graded. Only graded poultry is sold in many communities; beef is extensively graded.

The factors determining Canadian and United States grades are similar, but terminology differs. Examples of Canadian grade terms are:

Beef
Canada Choice (Red Brand)
Canada Good (Blue Brand)
Canada Standard (Brown Brand)
Canada Commercial

Butter
Canada First Grade
Canada Second Grade
Canada Third Grade
Below Canada Third Grade

Eggs
Canada Grade A1
Canada Grade A
Canada Grade B
Canada Grade C

Poultry
Canada Grade Special (Purple)
Canada Grade A (Red)
Canada Grade B (Blue)
Canada Grade Utility (Blue)
Canada Grade C (Yellow)

Canned Fruits and Vegetables
Canada Fancy
Canada Choice
Canada Standard
Sub-standard

Honey
No. 1
No. 2
No. 3
Sub-standard

When dehydrated, frozen, or canned fruits and vegetables are imported, they must comply with Canadian grading regulations, but the label does not have to carry the word "Canada."

According to the Nationwide Household Food Consumption Survey in the spring of 1965, the U.S. food dollar was divided as follows: meat 38¢; vegetable-fruit 20¢; milk 13¢; cereals 12¢; other food 17¢ (baking products, sugar, beverages, fat, oils, and so forth).

For those families who wish or need to reduce their food bills, the chapters in this section should be of help. Undoubtedly the greatest sav-

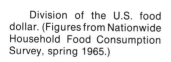

Division of the U.S. food dollar. (Figures from Nationwide Household Food Consumption Survey, spring 1965.)

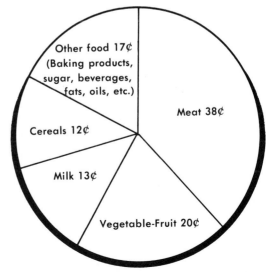

ing can be made in purchasing the cheaper cuts of meat. These cuts take a lower cooking temperature, more time to cook, and more knowledge to be able to use them successfully, but their nutrient value is as great as any other cut and their flavor is equal to or better than the more expensive cut. The more exercise a muscle gets during the animal's life, the more flavor the flesh has; therefore, the beef round has more flavor than the loin. Chapter 31 has tables on meat cuts, the method to use when cooking them, and how to calculate the cost per serving.

Properly stored food reduces waste and thus reduces food bills. (See Chapter 30.) The calendar of the best food buys shows when foods are in their peak season and, therefore, should be least expensive. The table of bargains shows the basic-four foods which are usually less expensive and, therefore, have more food value for the money.

SUGGESTED READING

Canadian Department of Agriculture, Publication No. 1048: *Buy by Grade — Consumer's Guide to Buying Graded Foods.*

Maddox, Gaynor: "The Wise Snack — No Nutritional Joke," *Today's Health,* March, 1970.

U.S. Department of Agriculture:
Federal Food Standards, 1974.
How to Use USDA Grades In Buying Food. Consumer and Marketing Service.
USDA Grade Names. Agricultural Handbook No. 342.
What Makes Food Prices? Economic Research Service ERS-308.

CHAPTER 29

Food Legislation

TERMS TO UNDERSTAND

Adulterate	Gel	Sprout
Antimycotic	Humecant	Stabilize
Buffer	Myriad	Turbidity
Emulsify	Sequestrant	Unit pricing

Legislation

In 1938 the Federal Food, Drug, and Cosmetic Act supplanted the original 1906 law. Its objectives are to assure consumers that foods are pure, safe, wholesome, and processed under sanitary conditions; that therapeutic devices, drugs, and cosmetics are effective and safe; and that these products have labels which are truthful and informative. Labels for foods to be used on modified diets must give specific information: for example, the amount of sodium contained in a 100-gram serving of the food. The law applies to imports as well as to goods shipped across state boundaries. It prohibits the movement in interstate commerce of misbranded or adulterated food. *The federal law considers a food misbranded if*

1. The label makes false claims.
2. The size of the container is misleading.
3. The statement of weight, measure, or count is incorrect.
4. The label does not list the manufacturer, packer, or distributor.
5. Artificial coloring or flavoring is not listed, except in dairy products.
6. Preservatives are not listed.

The federal law considers a food adulterated if

1. Diseased animals are used.
2. Poisons or any other health-damaging products are used.
3. Spoiled or dirty products are used.

243

4. Packaging is done under unsanitary conditions.
5. The container is made of substances which would impair health.
6. Substances are added to conceal a poor-quality product.
7. It contains unsafe coal-tar colors, additives, or pesticide residues.

The food and drug law also provides for the following standards (most fresh and dried fruits and vegetables are exempt):

Standards of Identity. These standards tell the minimum and maximum amounts of ingredients in a product when asked for by its common name; for example, jellies and fruit preserves must have 45 parts by weight of fruit to every 55 parts of sugar. Regardless of the process, the specific ingredients and amounts are the same.

The label of a food for which a standard has been established does not have to state the ingredients (the standards of identity set up what is in it and how much), but optional ingredients and preservatives are listed. If there is any deviation in the kind or amount of ingredients, the label then must list all the ingredients used. Over 300 products have food standards. Examples for which standards have been established are: chocolate and cocoa products, macaroni and noodle products, fruit butters, and mayonnaise. Non-standardized food labels list the common names of ingredients in their order of predominance by weight.

Standards of Quality. These standards establish specifications for color, tenderness, and freedom from defects. A food below the established standard is labeled "Below Standard in Quality" and followed by a statement listing how—for example, "excessive peel" or "excessively broken." These foods are not lower in nutritional value and therefore can be used if the original appearance or texture of the product is not important to the purchaser.

Standards of Fill of Container. These standards tell how full the container must be. They are useful for products which settle or shake down after packaging and which have a number of pieces packed in liquid—for example, fruit cocktail.

Standards for Enriched Products. These standards list specifications to assure uniformity of enrichment. They prevent claims of enrichment in special or superior ways and insure that traces of nutrients are not added just for the purpose of advertising.

In 1958 the Food, Drug, and Cosmetic Act was amended to require industry to provide evidence of the safety of chemicals used in the processing of foods and of the pesticides used on crops.

The Food and Drug Administration does not have jurisdiction over advertising. It does enforce the Caustic Poison Act, which requires that the label of caustic or corrosive household chemicals state that the contents are poisonous and that it list the antidote.

The Meat Inspection Act, passed in 1906, and its amendments provide for inspection of all exported or imported meat and all meat for interstate commerce. The courts have ruled that any extensively advertised product is intended for interstate commerce. The law requires

1. That all animals for slaughter be inspected.
2. That carcasses and all meat products be inspected. Any which are not fit for consumption are destroyed.
3. That all sanitary regulations be observed.
4. That no harmful preservatives be used.

Federally inspected meat always carries an inspection stamp. Animals which are killed and sold within one state do not have to be federally inspected. Such meat comes under state and local regulations, if any.

The Fair Packaging and Labeling Act, passed in 1966, requires that the food's identity, the name and address of the manufacturer, packer, or distributor, and the net contents in standard measure be prominently displayed on the label. No qualifying terms such as "giant quart" or "jumbo pound" may appear. Many people hoped that there would be a reduction in the number of package sizes and that packaging of amounts such as 1.24 ounces would disappear. The elimination of odd sizes would enable the purchaser to do unit pricing.

The decade of the 1960's saw the beginning of the consumer movement, and the 1970's will probably see more laws intended for the protection of the consumer. Laws can give protection, but they also can restrict or be so protective that freedom of choice of both the seller and purchaser can be unduly limited.

Consumer education could give the purchaser the ability to make good choices among the myriad of available products, to know why some food groups are necessary for health and others could be optional purchases. The consumer should be able to recognize misinformation, to question the qualifications of people presenting statements, and to know where to obtain reliable information.

Food labeling. Nutrients of minor or no dietary value, e.g., bioflavinoids, cannot be mentioned on the package. The picture panel must accurately reflect the appearance of the food within the package. The nutrition information panel, if any, must list the information in a standard format. Ingredient listing must show the ingredients by weight in decreasing order. Serving size is legally defined as the amount usually eaten by an adult male engaged in light physical activity. Additives must be listed. Artificial colorings and flavorings have to be declared either individually or collectively.

Full nutritional labeling is voluntary except under these two conditions which make the labeling mandatory:

1. If a nutrition or health claim is made for the food, either on a label or in an advertisement — vitamins added, highest in proteins, etc.
2. If nutrients have been added to the product. There are a few legal exceptions, e.g., iodine and salt. Many food companies are voluntarily putting the nutrition information panel on their products.

Food Additives

However one views the use of food additives, it is a fact that without additives many food products now found in the stores would not be available. Whenever a chemical is added to food, the choice must be made between the possible risk to the consumer and the increase in quantity produced or the extension of its shelf life. The National Research Council defines a food additive as "A substance or mixture of substances other than a basic foodstuff, which is present in food as a result of any aspect of production, processing, storage, or packaging." The additives can be classified as follows:

1. Intentional additives which perform a specific function:
   (a) To improve nutritional value by adding amino acids, vitamins, and minerals, for example, iodine to salt.
   (b) To improve sensory appeal by adding color, aroma, texture, and flavoring agents; gelling and bodying agents; glazes, waxes, and bleaches.
   (c) To preserve food beyond harvest and processing time by adding antioxidants to retard, for example, fat rancidity or fruit discoloration; by adding antimycotic agents which inhibit mold and bacterial growth; by adding humecants to keep food moist; and by adding anticaking agents.
   (d) To facilitate processing by adding emulsifiers, stabilizers, thickeners, buffers, maturing, and antifoaming agents; by adding sequestrants which combine with trace substances, thus inactivating them, so they do not interfere with the processing (for example, sequestrants react with minerals in the water so there is no turbidity after processing of soft drinks); and by adding acids or alkali which affect color, flavor, or texture of a cooked product.

Some common intentional food additives are shown in Table 29–1. Their use is carefully controlled by the Food and Drug Administration.

2. Small amounts of incidental additives which are still present and have already performed a function:
   (a) To protect crops before and after harvest, pesticides, fungicides, herbicides, rodenticides, nematocides, and defoliants are used. If the use of these were forbidden United States agriculture probably could not produce ample food for our population, much less enough for shipments to developing countries. The Food and Drug Act establishes procedures for setting tolerances (safe limits of residue permitted on the crops). There is more chance of residue on fresh food than in processed food. Research should continue in an attempt to find biological controls to replace the chemicals presently used.
   (b) To regulate growth of animals and plants by using antibiotics,

Table 29–1   *Some Examples of Intentional Food Additives*

Function	Chemical compound	Common food uses
Acids, alkalis, buffers	Sodium bicarbonate	Baking powder
	Tartaric acid	Fruit sherbets
		Cheese spreads
Antibiotics	Chlortetracycline	Dip for dressed poultry
Anticaking agents	Aluminum calcium silicate	Table salt
Antimycotics	Calcium propionate	Bread
	Sodium propionate	Bread
	Sorbic acid	Cheese
Antioxidants	Butylated hydroxyanisole (BHA)	Fats
	Butylated hydroxytoluene (BHT)	Fats
Bleaching agents	Benzoyl peroxide	Wheat flour
	Chlorine dioxide	
	Oxides of nitrogen	
Color preservative	Sodium benzoate	Green peas
		Maraschino cherries
Coloring agents	Annatto	Butter, margarine
	Carotene	
Emulsifiers	Lecithin	Bakery goods
	Mono- and diglycerides	Dairy products
	Propylene glycol alginate	Confections
Flavoring agents	Amyl acetate	Soft drinks
	Benzaldehyde	Bakery goods
	Methyl salicylate	Candy; ice cream
	Essential oils; natural extractives	
	Monosodium glutamate	Canned meats
Non-nutritive sweeteners	Saccharin	Diet packed canned fruit
		Low calorie soft drinks
Nutrient supplements	Potassium iodide	Iodized salt
	Vitamin C	Fruit juices
	Vitamin D	Milk
	Vitamin A	Margarine
	B vitamins, iron	Bread and cereals
Sequestrants	Sodium citrate	Dairy products
	Calcium pyrophosphoric acid	
Stabilizers and thickeners	Pectin	Jellies
	Vegetable gums (carob bean, carrageenin, guar)	Dairy desserts and chocolate milk
	Gelatin	Confections
	Agar-agar	"Low calorie" salad dressings
Yeast foods and dough conditioners	Ammonium chloride	Bread, rolls
	Calcium sulfate	
	Calcium phosphate	

(From Williams, S. R.: *Nutrition and Diet Therapy,* 1973, p. 234.)

hormones, tranquilizers, sprouting inhibitors, inhibitors of rotting until seeds sprout, root promoters, fruit setters, and agents which stop premature drop of fruit.

As this book goes to press, The Food and Drug Administration and the Federal Trade Commission are proposing regulations which will affect many phases of the food industry. Implementation is a time-consuming process; hearings are held on the proposals, and often the validity of the proposals as well as the law is tested in court.

SUGGESTED READING

"Food Labeling: Phase IV," *Journal of Nutrition Education*, July–September, 1974.
General Mills. *A Guide to the Side of the Box—Food Labeling Explained.*
U.S. Department of Agriculture:
  Consumers All—Yearbook of Agriculture, 1965.
  Food For Us All—Yearbook of Agriculture, 1969.
  Pesticide Safety in Your Home, 1970.
  That We May Eat—Yearbook of Agriculture, 1975.
U.S. Department of Health, Education, and Welfare:
  The Federal Hazardous Substances Labeling Act, 1966.
  Keys to Quality—Food Buying Guides from U.S.D.A., 1974.
  Publication No. 74-2058: *Food Labeling Revolution*, 1974.
  Publication No. 74-2002: *Primer on Food Additives*, 1974.

CHAPTER 30

Food Hygiene

TERMS TO UNDERSTAND

Algae	Pasteurize	Ptomaine
Blanch (*preparation of vegetables*)	Pathogen	Vacuum
Encyst	Perishable	Vermin

Food Preservation

Food preservation checks the decay of food which is caused by
1. Harmful bacteria, yeast, mold, or algae.
2. Internal changes due to the disintegration of the food itself. Enzymes in food can cause deterioration, discoloration, and rancidity.

There are four common ways of preserving foods. They are
1. Removing moisture.
2. Using a high temperature and sealing.
3. Using a low temperature.
4. Using a preservative.

Research is under way in another process, irradiation, which will kill microorganisms. However, many foods lose their flavor when exposed to this atomic treatment.

Reducing the water content of the food so that microorganisms do not grow is known as dehydration or drying. Food dried slowly (without artificial heat or a vacuum) may be discolored. In drying fruit, sulfur may be used to minimize color changes. Dried foods containing fat must be handled with great care to keep the fat from turning rancid. During the drying process, ascorbic acid, thiamine, and carotene may be lost. When food is dried, the flavor usually is changed. The most common dried foods are milk, eggs, fruit, some vegetables, and the long list of instant foods—potatoes, tea, coffee, cream substitutes, soups, and sauces.

Preserving food in air-tight containers at high temperatures is called canning. Foods may be canned by the cold-pack method or by steam pressure, but in both cases the food and utensils must be sterilized and air must be excluded from the can. Any canned food which appears spoiled or has an "off odor" should be discarded *without tasting.* If a can of food shows bulging, gas has been formed, which is a sign of spoilage. Foods most commonly canned are milk, fruits, vegetables, and meat. If proper canning procedures are followed, there is little or no nutrient loss.

Pasteurization is the other method of preserving food by heating. Pasteurizing milk involves heating it until all pathogenic organisms have been killed. Cheese and ice cream made of unpasteurized milk can carry disease-bearing organisms.

Refrigeration, or cold storage, is a means of keeping for a limited time perishable meats, eggs, milk, fruits, and vegetables. The low temperature slows down the action of the natural food enzymes, thus retarding the ripening process. Cold storage also inhibits the action of molds and bacteria. Since humidity is an important factor in food preservation, commercial cold storage plants regulate humidity as well as temperature.

Many kinds of frozen foods can be purchased. Blanching destroys the natural enzymes, thus stopping the metabolic plant processes. Quick freezing (about $-35°$ F. or, if liquid nitrogen is used, $-320°$ F.) produces smaller ice crystals; therefore less damage is done to the cells, and when the food is thawed the texture is closer to that of the original fresh food. Frozen foods are perishable and should be stored at $0°$ F. or lower, should be kept frozen until ready for use, and should not be refrozen. Freezing does not kill all bacteria or mold spores.

Dehydro-freezing is a new process combining the best features of freezing and drying. Drying removes 50 per cent of the original volume and weight of the fruit or vegetable, and freezing then preserves it. The quality of the product is comparable to that of other frozen food but is lighter in weight and bulk; therefore there is less to package, store, and ship.

Food preservation by means of freeze-drying enables food to be stored for long periods of time on the shelf instead of in the refrigerator or freezer. The food is first quick-frozen and then placed in a vacuum chamber. Heat is applied and the ice crystals, without returning to the liquid stage, turn to a vapor which is immediately drawn off by a vacuum pump. The process is comparable to drying clothes on a sunny winter day. The wet clothes freeze, become stiff, and later are soft and dry, although the temperature never rose above freezing. The advantages of freeze-drying are that the food retains a better flavor, color, and nutritive value. The cellular structure is retained so that the freeze-dried product is very similar to the fresh product. The food rehydrates very easily because the spaces remain where the water can re-enter. The foods are light in weight and keep well for long periods with very little change in quality. Astronauts take some freeze-dried foods with them on their space flights.

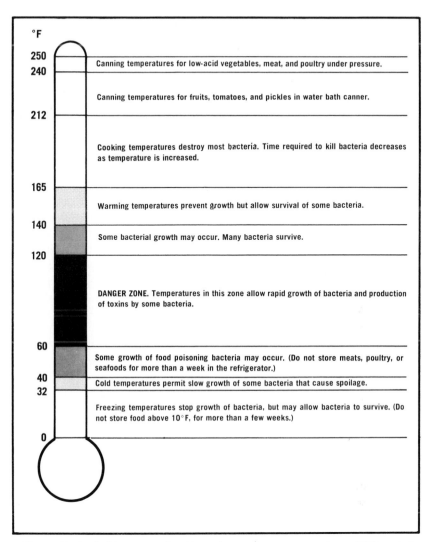

Figure 30–1 Refrigerators should not have a temperature above 40°F. and steam tables should not be less than 140°F. (From *Keeping Food Safe to Eat.* U.S.D.A. Home and Garden Bulletin No. 162, 1971.)

The process is considerably more expensive than most other preservation methods, and foods have to be specially packed because the products crumple or crush easily. New freeze-dried products in grocery stores include coffee, mushrooms, chives, dried soup mixes, and those foods which are purchased by the sportsman to be included in packs when he is hiking.

Poultry may have its freshness extended by the use of antibiotics during processing. Sugar, vinegar, spices, salt, and other chemicals added to

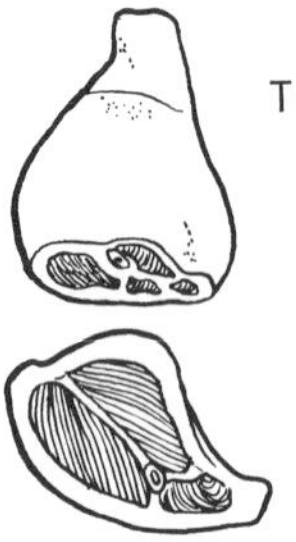

Temperature	24 Hours	96 Hours
55° F	32	390,130
40° F	3	224
35° F	- -	8

Figure 30–2 Bacterial growth in meats (total count). (Adapted from a Kodachrome slide. California Department of Public Health, Bureau of Adult Education, 2151 Berkeley Way, Berkeley, California.)

food tend to preserve the food. Concentrated sugar keeps jams, jellies, and marmalades from spoiling. Mold will grow unless air is excluded, but bacteria and yeast do not grow in concentrated sugar mixtures. Salt is used for preserving meats and vegetables, for example, ham, bacon, and sauerkraut. The spices in sausage tend to retard spoilage. The creosote of burning wood closes the pores of the meat, excluding the air, and so aids in keeping smoked meat. Insects avoid the creosote covering. Pickles keep because they are in a vinegar solution. Other chemicals are allowed by law to be used as food preservatives, but the amount which can be used is limited and the labels on the food must show that the chemical has been added.

Ultraviolet light kills bacteria on directly exposed surfaces.

Care of Food

Food is perishable and therefore must be handled with care. These general rules apply to any kitchen—home, institution, or restaurant.

1. All food handlers should be free from all types of infection. Periodic physical examinations are important.

2. Always wash the hands with soap *in running water* before handling food. Jewelry such as rings should not be worn in the kitchen. (Rings and long fingernails can collect dirt and food particles.)

3. Never smoke, use a handkerchief, or go to the toilet without washing the hands before again handling food. Disease and food poisoning microorganisms can easily travel the fecal-oral route.

4. Keep hands away from the mouth, nose, and hair.

5. Use forks, spoons, wax paper, and such for handling food. Pick up utensils by the handles. The worker might as well put his hands into the food as to put his hand on the bowl of the spoon which is then put into food.

6. Have screens on all doors and windows.

7. Use only clean utensils for food preparation.

8. Use hand towels for hands and dish towels for dishes.

9. Never taste from the mixing spoon. Use a clean spoon which is not dipped into food after having come in contact with the mouth.

10. No animals should be allowed in the dining room or kitchen.

11. Keep garbage in covered containers and dispose of it regularly. Thoroughly wash and scald the garbage can before reusing.

12. When washing dishes, wash glasses first, then silver, then china, and the cooking utensils last. Rinse with water that is not less than 180° F.

13. Do not use galvanized iron containers for cooking or storing foods. Acid foods can dissolve large quantities of the zinc, which would make the food unsafe to eat.

14. Be cautious in using metal food containers. If cadmium or lead contaminates either food or water, a serious metallic poisoning can occur.

15. All fruits and vegetables should be carefully washed before cooking or serving raw.

16. Creamy mixtures such as custards, cream puffs, gravies, pie fillings, or chocolate eclairs should be refrigerated until served. They should be used the same day that they are made. During the hot weather many areas prohibit the sale of bakery products which have a cream filling because there is so much danger of staphylococcal or other food poisoning.

17. Food served to an individual but not eaten should be discarded.

18. Bulk staples should be stored in a clean, dry, well-ventilated place which is free from all vermin.

19. Semi-perishables should be refrigerated.

20. Left-over food should not stand at room temperature. Cover, refrigerate, and use within 48 hours. Use shallow pans for storage to insure temperature of 40° F. or below in the middle of the food.

21. Do not stuff poultry or fish until it is ready to be put into the oven. The center of the stuffing should reach 165° F. or more during the roasting.

22. Wash the hands after touching raw meat, poultry, or eggs.

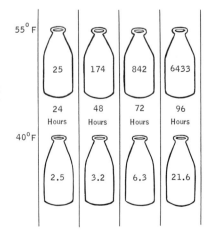

Figure 30–3 Bacterial growth in milk (colony count). (Adapted from a Kodachrome slide. California Department of Public Health, Bureau of Adult Education, 2151 Berkeley Way, Berkeley, California.)

23. Thoroughly wash dishes and work surfaces after each use. Can openers, meat grinders, cutting boards, and blenders particularly need washing with soap and water or rinsing with water containing chlorine laundry bleach in the proportion recommended on the chlorine container.

Anyone with a cold or skin infection, including pustules, should not handle food. Handle food as little as possible and only with clean hands or utensils. Contaminated food kept at room temperature for more than an hour can cause food poisoning. Contaminated foods may show no signs of spoilage, so don't rely on taste, odor, or appearance to insure food safety.

The best way to keep picnic food is to use an insulated box with a lot of ice. Be sure the ice that you use is made from a source of drinking water. If the temperature rises to 40° F. get more ice, dry ice, or reusable ice packs. Dry ice should be placed on the top of the food because the chilling gas is heavier than air and therefore the cold goes down. Cans of frozen juice would help to keep food cold and could be made into beverages at the picnic site. Put the picnic food inside the car and out of the direct rays of the sun instead of in the trunk where the temperature gets considerably higher.

Wrap sandwiches needing refrigeration snugly in waxed paper or aluminum foil and then pack them into the chilled, insulated box immediately before leaving home; or keep the chicken, tuna, egg, or meat salad mixtures under refrigeration and make the sandwiches at the picnic site. If there are no facilities for keeping food at the proper temperature, then plan picnic menus around such items as canned or preserved food or fresh fruits and vegetables. Do not serve scalloped or creamed dishes, especially those using eggs, milk, flour, or starch, unless they are made at the picnic site and kept hot until served. The cookout picnic foods (hot dogs, baked potatoes, corn on the cob, and so forth) are the safest. They should be eaten as soon as they are cooked, because there is no chance for food poisoning to develop or for the foods to become contaminated by contact with insects.

Never use insect spray when food is being served or when food is uncovered. The indiscriminate use of sprays around foods, cooking utensils, barbecues, and grills can cause illness.

Do not eat (or give to your pet) meat or meat-containing dishes, eggs, fish, poultry, salads with mayonnaise, creamed foods, gravy, custard, or any other protein foods if they have been unrefrigerated for a few hours.

The delivery of prepared meals to shut-ins, "meals-on-wheels," requires the same careful handling and transportation as picnic food.

Food Poisoning

There are three ways in which illness can be caused by food.
1. By chemical poisons present in the food:

Poisonous mushrooms can cause death; the green leaves (not stems) of rhubarb can cause illness; Pacific Coast mussels should not be eaten from May first through October because they produce a heat-resistant poison which can cause gastrointestinal upsets; green parts of white potatoes can cause illness.

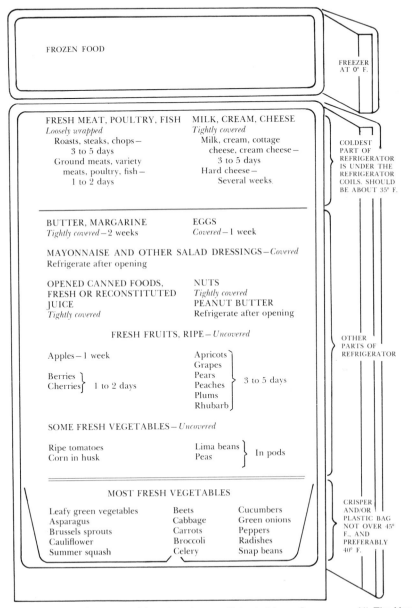

Figure 30–4 Guide to refrigerator storage. (Adapted from *Consumers All,* The Yearbook of Agriculture, 1965, p. 433.)

Table 30–1 *Bacterial Foodborne Illness: Causes, Symptoms, and Control*

Name of illness	*What causes it*	*Symptoms*
Salmonellosis	Salmonellae. Bacteria widespread in nature, live and grow in intestinal tracts of human beings and animals. About 1,200 species are known; 1 species causes typhoid fever. Bacteria grow and multiply at temperatures between 44° and 115° F.	Severe headache, followed by vomiting, diarrhea, abdominal cramps, and fever. Infants, elderly, and persons with low resistance are most susceptible. Severe infections cause high fever and may even cause death.
Perfringens poisoning	*Clostridium perfringens.* Spore-forming bacteria that grow in the absence of oxygen. Spores can withstand temperatures usually reached in cooking most foods. Surviving bacteria continue to grow in cooked meats, gravies, and meat dishes held without proper refrigeration.	Nausea without vomiting, diarrhea, acute inflammation of stomach and intestines.
Staphylococcal poisoning (frequently called staph. Probably the most common foodborne disease in the U.S.)	*Staphylococcus aureus.* Bacteria fairly resistant to heat. Bacteria growing in food produce a toxin that is extremely resistant to heat. Bacteria grow profusely with production of toxin at temperatures between 44° and 115° F.	Vomiting, diarrhea, prostration, abdominal cramps. Generally mild and often attributed to other causes.
Botulism	*Clostridium botulinum.* Spore-forming organisms that grow and produce toxin in the absence of oxygen, such as in a sealed container. The bacteria can produce a toxin in low-acid foods that have been held in the refrigerator for 2 weeks or longer. Spores are extremely heat resistant. Spores are harmless, but the toxin is a deadly poison.	Double vision, inability to swallow, speech difficulty, progressive respiratory paralysis. Fatality rate is high, in the United States about 65 per cent.

Characteristics of illness	*Control measures*
Transmitted by eating contaminated food, or by contact with infected persons or carriers of the infection. Also transmitted by insects, rodents, and pets. Onset: Usually within 12 to 36 hours. Duration: 2 to 7 days.	Salmonellae in food are destroyed by heating the food to a temperature of 140° F. and holding for 10 minutes or to higher temperatures for less time. Refrigeration at 45° F. inhibits the increase of Salmonellae, but they remain alive in the refrigerator or freezer, and even in dried foods.
Transmitted by eating food contaminated with abnormally large numbers of the bacteria. Onset: Usually within 8 to 20 hours. Duration: May persist for 24 hours.	To control growth of surviving bacteria on cooked meats that are to be eaten later, cool meats rapidly and refrigerate promptly at 40° F. or below.
Transmitted by food handlers who carry the bacteria and by eating food containing the toxin. Onset: Usually within 3 to 8 hours. Duration: 1 or 2 days.	Growth of bacteria that produce toxin is inhibited by keeping hot foods above 140° F. and cold foods at or below 40° F. Toxin is destroyed by boiling for several hours or heating the food in pressure cooker at 240° F. for 30 minutes.
Transmitted by eating food containing the toxin. Onset: Usually within 12 to 36 hours or longer. Duration: 3 to 6 days.	Bacterial spores in food are destroyed by high temperatures obtained only in the pressure canner.[1] More than 6 hours is needed to kill the spores at boiling temperature (212° F.). The toxin is destroyed by boiling for 10 or 20 minutes; time required depends on kind of food.

(From U.S. Department of Agriculture, Home and Garden Bulletin No. 162: *Keeping Food Safe to Eat—A Guide for Homemakers.*)

[1]For processing times in home canning, see Home and Garden Bulletin 8, *Home Canning of Fruits and Vegetables,* and Bulletin 106, *Home Canning of Meat and Poultry.*

2. By chemicals added to foods:

Lead arsenic used for insect spray on growing fruits or vegetables, some insecticides used for pest and insect control, silver polishes which contain cyanide, and vermin poisons can cause illness.

3. By disease-producing organisms in the food:

It is known that the following diseases can be transmitted through foods: tuberculosis, diphtheria, scarlet fever, septic sore throat (strep-tococcal), dysentery, typhoid fever, tularemia, staphylococcal food poison-ing, brucellosis (undulant fever), foot-and-mouth disease, botulism, tape worm, pinworm, and trichinosis. Handling infected rabbits with bare hands may result in tularemia. Milk pasteurization and meat inspection have nearly eliminated bovine tuberculosis.

The foods which are most commonly involved in food poisoning are ham, poultry, custard- or cream-filled baked products, eggs, and vegeta-bles. The vinegar in mayonnaise does inhibit the growth of common orga-nisms, but when mayonnaise is added to salads or other foods the vinegar is not concentrated enough to provide protection against the growth of food poisoning organisms. Food poisoning bacteria may contaminate ready-to-serve food if it is kept longer than one hour at room tempera-ture.

Streptococcus infections from food occur occasionally. The foods most often involved are meat, poultry dressing, and milk. The incubation period ranges from two to 18 hours. The organism is slightly heat resis-tant; pasteurization does not suffice to destroy it but thorough cooking of food will. Adequate refrigeration prevents growth of streptococcus.

Trichinosis is caused by a nematode worm, *Trichinella spiralis*. Human trichinosis usually results from the consuming of raw or incompletely cooked pork containing the encysted larvae. The worm goes through its life cycle in hogs, mice, rats, cats, dogs, and bears, as well as in man. Thor-ough cooking of pork ensures the destruction of any trichinae that may have been present.

SUGGESTED READING

Sanitation
California State Department of Public Health:
   Beware of Botulism. (leaflet)
   Is Potluck Lucky? (leaflet)
Freese, Arthur S.: "Salmonella: Food Poison Plus," *Today's Health,* April, 1969.
Frobisher, Martin, and Fuerst, Robert: *Microbiology In Health and Disease,* 1973.
Martin, Robert: "What You Don't See Can Hurt You," *Today's Health,* November, 1965.
U.S Department of Agriculture:
   Brown Bag Lunches—Questions and Answers, 1973.
   Facts About Food Poisoning, 1974.
   Keeping Food Safe to Eat—A Guide for Homemakers, 1971.
   Summertime Foods, Questions and Answers, 1973.
U.S. Department of Health, Education and Welfare:
   Publication No. 74–2052: *Can Your Kitchen Pass the Food Storage Test?,* 1974.
Valentry, Duane: "The Fantastic Fly," *Today's Health,* August, 1969.

Food Preservation
Earl, Howard G.: "Food Poisoning: The Sneaky Attacker," *Today's Health,* October, 1965.
U.S. Department of Agriculture:
    Conserving the Nutritive Values in Foods.
    Home Canning of Fruits and Vegetables.
    Home Care of Purchased Frozen Foods.
    Home Freezing of Fruits and Vegetables.
    Storing Perishable Foods in the Home.
    What to Do When Your Home Freezer Stops.
University of California Agricultural Extension Service, Circular 500: *Freezing Foods At Home.*

EXERCISES

1. Check local ordinances for regulations pertaining to food service establishments in your area.
2. Why would refrigerated cooked fruit deteriorate more slowly than refrigerated fresh fruit?
3. In what part of the refrigerator should you store meat, milk, and eggs? Why?

CHAPTER 31

Groceries, Nutrition, and Dollars

TERMS TO UNDERSTAND

Blintzes
Culture
Dahl
Homogenize

Lentil
Modify
Pasteurize
Reconstitute

In the United States, weekly food purchases per person average 10 pounds of fruit and vegetables, 4½ quarts of milk or its equivalent in cheese or ice cream, 4 pounds of meat, 7 eggs, 1 pound of fat, 2 pounds of sugar, and 3 pounds of cereal products. This is about 1500 pounds of food per person per year. The farmer receives about 40 per cent of each food dollar and the rest goes to the marketing services—handling, transporting, processing, packaging, refrigerating, distributing, etc.*

Either cost per retail unit or cost per serving can be used to compare food prices. If the packages are the same size, e.g., pound or two pound packages of coffee or cheese, then unit cost can determine which is the better buy. For meat, fruits, and vegetables, cost per serving is a better comparison, e.g., will a pound of peas in the pod yield the same number of servings as the package of frozen peas of equal cost? Often there is a difference in cost between fresh, canned, and frozen foods, but nutrient value will be comparable if they have been correctly stored. Sometimes the fresh food is cheaper, sometimes the canned or frozen. Often canned poultry or meat is more expensive than fresh, whereas canned fish is usually cheaper. In general, a larger package costs less per ounce, but not

---

*Cooperative Extension, University of California: *Balance Food Values and Cents*, 1973.

260

always; therefore, divide the package cost by the volume to check the better portion buy, e.g., the cost of an ounce of serving of cereal from a family size box vs. the individual serving box.

The store without charge accounts usually is the most economical market. See Tables 31–10 and 31–11 for food bargains.

General Shopping Hints

1. Buy the less expensive forms of food. Bread is more economical than sweet rolls, and day-old bread costs less than fresh. Store brands may be comparable to brand names in quality and they usually cost less.

2. Fancy packaging, canisters, etc., increase the purchase price. Convenience (ready-to-eat or ready-to-heat) and highly processed foods often cost more per serving because you have to pay for the "maid-service" done for you. There are some exceptions—e.g., out-of-season fresh produce and frozen orange juice concentrate, a serving of which usually costs about half as much as home squeezed juice. Some convenience foods do cost less because they have less waste and there was no cost in shipping and storing that waste.

3. Bakery and delicatessen products—salads, pastries, puddings, meat dishes, etc.—cost more than the same products prepared at home. Bacon, pies, cakes, cream, pickles, relishes, jam and jelly, French fries, potato chips, pretzels, candy, and carbonated beverages give you very few nutrients when compared to their cost and number of calories.

4. Buy foods which are in season and in good supply. Store them properly to avoid spoilage and loss of nutrients.

5. Buy staples when they are on sale. Advertisements list weekly specials.

6. Buy in quantity if adequate storage space is available and if the food will be used before spoiling. A box of apples will cost less per pound than apples purchased in small lots.

7. Buy bulk foods if they are sold under sanitary conditions. Packaging adds materially to the cost of products.

8. Buy those foods which your family will eat and enjoy. No food is a bargain if it ends up as garbage. A new food is more apt to be accepted if it is served with a family favorite. Use left-over foods.

9. Know what is a good buy. Bananas at half price but so overripe that many must be discarded are a poor purchase. Cheaper cuts of meat have good nutrient value but can be very expensive if they are mostly bone and gristle. If the store has unit pricing, use it to compare various brands and package sizes of the same product.

10. Avoid impulse buying. Shopping when hungry seems to increase impulse buying. It has been estimated that with preplanning and thoughtfulness family food costs could be reduced by 25 per cent. (62:96)

Table 31–1   *One Menu at Two Cost Levels for Family of Four*
(Father and Mother 33 Years of Age, Girl 8, Boy 11)[*]

Meal	Menu 1 (more costly)	Menu 2 (less costly)
Breakfast	Grapefruit juice (frozen) Ready-to-eat cereal (oat) Poached eggs (large) Enriched English muffins Butter Black coffee (name brand) Milk for two (fluid, whole)	Grapefruit juice (canned) Oatmeal Poached eggs (medium size) Whole wheat toast Margarine Black coffee (store brand) Milk for two (reconstituted non-fat dry)
Lunch	Onion soup (canned) Tuna salad sandwiches (chunk style tuna) Cabbage slaw (ready-made) Peaches (heavy syrup) Milk for all (fluid, whole)	Onion soup (dehydrated) Tuna salad sandwiches (grated style tuna) Cabbage slaw (homemade) Peaches (light syrup) Milk for all (non-fat dry)
Dinner	Cubed steaks Frozen baked potatoes, au gratin Frozen carrots in butter sauce Tossed green salad with French dressing (commercial) Whole wheat brown-and-serve rolls Butter Frozen apple pie (commercial) Milk for all (fluid, whole) Black coffee for adults (name brand)	Meat loaf Baked potatoes Fresh carrots, seasoned Romaine salad with vinegar and oil dressing (homemade) Whole wheat bread slices Margarine Baked apples Milk for all (non-fat dry) Black coffee for adults (store brand)
Total cost†	$8.89	$4.85

Savings:
One day	$4.04
One week	$28.28
One month (30 days)	$121.20
One year	$1474.60

[*]Adapted from Groppe, C., and Ferree, M.: *Balance Food Values and Cents*, 1973. University of California Agricultural Extension Service, Pub. HXT-42, pp. 8-9.
†Prices based on foods purchased in the San Francisco area on February 10, 1975.

11. Plan menus or partial menus in advance. This allows for economical buying and cooking. The supply of prunes cooked for breakfast can be large enough to make a prune whip later in the week.

12. Buy those things for which you have the time and skill for preparation—homemakers usually have to budget time. Recipes may require too many ingredients or contain too many servings to be economical for small families.

Table 31–2   *Cost of Cereals (5 Servings)*

To-be-cooked	5 ounces	$0.12–$0.26
Ready-to-eat	5 ounces	$0.20–$0.66
Sugared	5 ounces	$0.36–$0.50
Individual packages	5 packages	$0.37–$0.58
Bread	5 slices	$0.12–$0.18
Rolls	5 rolls	$0.37–$0.72
Rice, enriched and brown	5 ounces	$0.13–$0.26
Rice, seasoned	5 ounces	$0.38–$0.75
Pasta	5 ounces	$0.12–$0.20

Prices obtained from super market chain in San Francisco Bay Area, February 10, 1975.

Buying The Basic-Four Food Groups

Cereals

Cereals are a bargain in nutrition. (See Figure 32–1.) The processed cereals are usually enriched. Ready-to-eat breakfast cereals, especially if instant, sweetened, or containing fruit, nuts, etc., almost without exception will cost more than the to-be-cooked cereals. Sealed and packaged breakfast cereals, cornmeal, rice, pasta, and flour have almost eliminated insect infestation.

Sweetened or frosted rolls are more expensive than plain rolls, which in turn cost more than loaf bread. The aroma and flavor of freshly baked homemade bread will delight family members and it is not as much work as many homemakers fear.

Whole wheat, white, and raisin bread have identity standards, so the basic ingredients do not have to be listed on the label. Day-old bread and

Table 31–3   *Buying Guide for Cereal and Cereal Products*

	Size of Serving[1]	Servings per Pound
Flaked corn cereals	1 cup	18-24
Other flaked cereals	¾ cup	21
Puffed cereals	1 cup	32-38
Cornmeal	½ cup	22
Wheat cereals		
Coarse	½ cup	16
Fine	½ cup	20-27
Oatmeal	½ cup	16
Hominy grits	½ cup	20
Macaroni and noodles	½ cup	17
Rice	½ cup	16
Spaghetti	½ cup	18

[1]Serving size is for the cooked product, except for the ready-to-eat kinds.

(From U.S. Department of Agriculture, Home and Garden Bulletin No. 1: *Family Fare: Food Management and Recipes,* 1960. p. 20.)

bakery items at reduced rates can be frozen up to three months and used as desired.

Cake flour is more costly than all-purpose flour.

Milk Group

Most of the milk sold in the United States is cow's milk. Goat's milk, a specialty product, is sold canned or fresh. Multiquart containers usually cost less per quart and home delivered milk will be more. Carefully measured reconstituted concentrated or dried milk prepared a few hours before it is drunk will taste like the milk from which it was made (non-fat milk does not have the flavor of whole milk). For economy, buy dried milk in as large a package as you can store – the individual packages, measured to make one quart, are the most expensive form.

Mixing equal quantities of reconstituted non-fat dry milk and fluid milk makes a beverage with good flavor and is cheaper than fluid milk alone. Yogurt is always more expensive than the milk from which it was made. It takes two cups of ice cream to approximate the calcium in one cup of milk and the two cups of ice cream will cost three or more times as much as one cup of milk.

When buying milk and cream, the purchaser has many types from which to choose. Depending upon bacterial count, the milk and cream may be graded A, B, or C.

1. *Fresh milk.* In some areas fresh milk can be bought as raw, certified, or pasteurized. Many health departments recommend that only pasteurized milk be used for drinking. If any harmful bacteria are present, they are destroyed by pasteurization; but pasteurization does not affect the major nutrients in milk – the calcium, the protein, the vitamin A, and the riboflavin.

2. *Modified fresh milk.* Modified fresh milk includes skim or non-fat, low-fat, homogenized, fortified, concentrated, and cultured. Skim milk has no fat or vitamin A (unless vitamins A and D are added) but otherwise contains the carbohydrates, proteins, minerals, and vitamins found in whole milk. Homogenized milk is whole milk which has been mechanically treated to make the fat particles so small and dispersed that the cream does not rise to the top. Fortified milk has had vitamin D and perhaps minerals added. Much of the milk on the market is fortified with vitamin D. Low-fat milk (2 per cent fat) has had some milk fat removed. It is comparable to whole milk in nutrient value but lower in calories (135 per cup). Concentrated milk is whole milk which has had two thirds of its water content removed by a low temperature under vacuum conditions and can be reconstituted by adding 2 quarts of water to 1 quart of concentrated milk. This provides the same nutrient value that is found in 3 quarts of whole milk, and it has the same flavor.

3. *Cultured milk.* The cultured milks include buttermilk, yogurt, and acidophilus. Specially prepared bacterial cultures are used to produce the desired acidity, body, flavor, and aroma in all cultured milks. Most of the cultured buttermilk sold in the United States is made from fresh fluid skim milk; however, fresh fluid whole milk, concentrated fluid milk, or reconstituted non-fat dry milk can be used. If the buttermilk has yellow flecks, these are pieces of butter which have been added to give the cultured buttermilk additional flavor and eye appeal. The tart flavor of cultured milks is due to the changing of lactose to lactic acid by the bacterial culture. Yogurt has the same nutrient value as the milk from which it was made—whole, low-fat, or non-fat. In some markets another cultured milk, known as acidophilus milk, is available. It is made from skim milk, and is used mainly in modified diets because it has a softer and more finely divided curd than the other milks. Like yogurt, the other cultured milks have the same nutrient value as the milk from which they were made.

4. *Canned milks.* Evaporated milk has had 60 per cent of its water content removed by means of evaporation. The temperature used is above boiling; this high temperature caramelizes the lactose, giving the typical evaporated milk flavor. Sweetened condensed milk has had water removed but sugar has been added until the carbohydrate content is about 40 per cent. Never use condensed milk for baby formulas because it is too high in sugar and too low in calcium and milk vitamins.

5. *Powdered or dry whole, low-fat, and non-fat milk.* Non-fat dry milk is the least expensive form of milk on the market. Adding water to the dry milk gives it the food value of the milk from which it was made.

6. *Cream.* Half-and-half is approximately 12 per cent fat, coffee or table cream from 18 to 20 per cent, light whipping or all-purpose 30 to 36 per cent, and pastry or whipping cream is not less than 36 per cent fat. Sour cream usually is made from table cream, about 20 per cent fat.

7. *Filled and imitation milks.*

In many of the major marketing areas, certain products, packaged in the same type of carton as fresh fluid milk, ostensibly serving as replacements for whole fresh milk, have appeared in the dairy cases in grocery stores. One of the chief selling points of these products is that they cost less than fluid milk. Composition and terminology are highly variable. In this discussion the following terminology, based on the interpretation of the Federal Filled Milk Act, is used:

Filled Milk. Filled milk is a product made by combining fats or oils other than milk fat with milk solids, and the resulting product is in semblance of milk. The type of milk solids specified in the Federal Filled Milk Act is "any milk, cream, or skimmed milk, whether or not condensed, evaporated, concentrated, powdered, dried, or desiccated . . . ."

Imitation Milk. Imitation milk purports to be or resembles milk, but contains no milk products as defined above.

There are now two types of filled milk being sold. One is a combination of fluid skim milk with or without skim milk solids and a vegetable fat made in semblance of milk. A second type basically contains water, nonfat dry milk, vegetable fat, and an additional source of protein such as soy protein or sodium caseinate. Products classified as imitation milks under the above definition contain such ingredients as water, corn syrup solids, sugar, a vegetable fat, and a source of protein such as sodium caseinate or soy protein. The primary and, in most instances, the sole fat used in both filled and imitation milks is coconut oil. Sometimes manufacturers add extra vitamins, especially vitamins A and/or D, and various additives, such as sodium citrate, salt, stabilizers, or mono- or di-glycerides to improve flavor or functional characteristics. Both filled milks and imitation milks are subject to variable state regulations, but generally they are not governed by the rigid regulations on sanitation and composition of Grade A pasteurized milk or milk products in general. In contrast to the filled milks, imitation milks do not fall under provisions of the Federal Filled Milk Act and can be shipped in interstate commerce. For information on state regulations regarding composition, sanitation, or labeling of these products in a specific state, it would be wise to contact the state health department or other appropriate state agency. (28:4)

Coconut oil is the fat of choice in these products because it has practically no flavor and is cheaper, but remember that it is a fat high in saturated fatty acids and low in the essential fatty acids. In fact, coconut oil is higher in the saturated fatty acids than the original dairy fat would have been.

There are over 400 varieties of cheese, but those commonly found in the retail market include:

Hard:
Without air holes—Cheddar, Edam, Gouda, Cheshire or Chester, Romano, Provolone, Sapsago, Colby, Nokkelost, Kumminost
With air holes—Parmesan, Swiss, Gruyère

Semi-hard:
Mold—blue, Gorgonzola, Roquefort, Stilton
Bacteria—brick, Muenster, Bel Paese, Jack, Port du Salut, Tilsit

Soft:
Unripened—cottage, cream, Neufchatel, Mozzarella, Ricotta, Teleme
Mold—Brie, Camembert
Bacteria—Liederkranz, Limburger
Processed—Cheeses blended with an emulsifying agent and pasteurized.

Cheddar cheese, also called American, may be graded AA, A, or B. Cheese food and cheese spread contain more moisture than processed cheeses and cost more per ounce. Imported, aged, and sharp cheeses are expensive. Cheese bought in bulk oftens keeps better and is cheaper than grated or individually wrapped slices.

Fruit and Vegetable Group

News media often carry the U.S.D.A. listing of food products, especially fruits and vegetables, which are currently in plentiful supply and are therefore comparatively good buys. The time of year determines which is the best buy, but in general canned fruits and vegetables tend to be cheaper. Medium size fresh produce is usually the best buy.

A family of four will use approximately 100 servings of fruit and vegetables per week. Saving only three cents per serving would save $3.00 per week or over $150 per year. Fresh fruits and vegetables are of the best quality and flavor and lowest in price when they are in peak season. When appearance is not important, blemished produce is less expensive; skin blemishes do not affect eating quality or nutrient value. Pinching fresh produce causes spoilage, and food lost by careless handling has to be paid for by charging higher prices for the food that is sold. By the time a dozen people have pressed on the stem end of a cantaloup it will be soft, but no riper than before it was bruised. Fresh citrus which is heavy for its size will have more pulp and juice. Less than perfectly ripened and poorly shaped fruit makes good jam, sauces, or juice. Fruit and vegetables which appear wilted or shrivelled are not fresh and are a poor buy if affected by decay.

Head vegetables, such as lettuce or cabbage, should be heavy for their size, free of worm holes, discoloration, and soft rot. Stalk vegetables, such as asparagus, should be tender and firm. Tight flower clusters are an indication of the best heads of broccoli and cauliflower. Root vegetables should be smooth and firm; they may be cheaper per serving than other fresh vegetables. Oversize carrots, turnips, beets, and parsnips may be tough or woody. Avoid deep-eyed potatoes, which are wasteful when peeled, and the green-skinned potatoes, which have a bitter taste. Well-filled but not bulging pods that are not dry, spotted, or yellow contain the best peas and lima beans.

Buying a one ounce package of potato chips at 19 cents makes potatoes cost $3.04 per pound.

Read the label on canned food. Heavy and extra heavy syrup on canned fruits is more expensive than light syrup. A label marked juice is juice; a "juice drink" may have added water, sugar, and flavorings. The canned fruit which has broken pieces of fruit is cheaper and is suitable for use in puddings, pastries, diced fruit salads, etc. A well-known brand may be no better than the less highly advertised product. Avoid cans that bulge at the ends or show leakage. These are indications of spoilage.

In the United States, canners are not required to grade label. Most canned produce is sold by brand name rather than grade; therefore the homemaker must learn to judge the quality of each brand. Should the label list the grade, then the following uses are suggested:

Grade A or Fancy stands for "excellent." Use this for special occasions.

Grade B, Choice, or Extra Standard is for "good." Use it for everyday.

Grade C or Standard is for "fair." Use this grade for thrift. (77:251)

Grade D or Substandard can be used for pies, sauces, stews, casseroles, and puddings.

If the label lists the serving size as one-half cup, this is approximately 100 grams.

Dried fruit and vegetables should be firm and bright in color.

There is no waste when frozen fruits and vegetables are purchased. Choose packages that are hard frozen. Packages which are limp, wet, sweating, or stained by the contents are either defrosted or in the process

Table 31–4   *Servings of Fruit in a Market Unit*

	Servings per market unit [1]
FRESH FRUIT	
Apples	
Bananas	
Peaches	3 or 4 per pound
Pears	
Plums	
Apricots	
Cherries, sweet	5 or 6 per pound
Grapes, seedless	
Blueberries	4 or 5 per pint
Raspberries	
Strawberries	8 or 9 per quart

[1] As purchased.

	Servings per package (*10 or 12 oz.*)
FROZEN FRUIT	
Blueberries	3 or 4
Peaches	2 or 3
Raspberries	2 or 3
Strawberries	2 or 3

	Servings per can (*1 lb.*)
CANNED FRUIT	
Served with liquid	4
Drained	2 or 3

	Servings per package (*8 oz.*)
DRIED FRUIT	
Apples	8
Apricots	6
Mixed fruits	6
Peaches	7
Pears	4
Prunes	4 or 5

(88:18)

Table 31-5 *Servings of Vegetable in a Market Unit*

	Servings per pound [1]		Servings per package (9 or 10 oz.)
FRESH VEGETABLES		**FROZEN VEGETABLES**	
Asparagus	3 or 4	Asparagus	2 or 3
Beans, lima [2]	2	Beans, lima	3 or 4
Beans, snap	5 or 6	Beans, snap	3 or 4
Beets, diced [3]	3 or 4	Broccoli	3
Broccoli	3 or 4	Brussels sprouts	3
Brussels sprouts	4 or 5	Cauliflower	3
Cabbage:		Corn, whole kernel	3
Raw, shredded	9 or 10	Kale	2 or 3
Cooked	4 or 5	Peas	3
Carrots:		Spinach	2 or 3
Raw, diced or shredded [3]	5 or 6		
Cooked [3]	4		Servings per can (1 lb.)
Cauliflower	3	**CANNED VEGETABLES**	
Celery:		Most vegetables	3 or 4
Raw, chopped or diced	5 or 6	Greens, such as kale	
Cooked	4	or spinach	2 or 3
Kale [4]	5 or 6		
Okra	4 or 5		
Onions, cooked	3 or 4		Servings per pound
Parsnips [3]	4	**DRY VEGETABLES**	
Peas [2]	2	Dry beans	11
Potatoes	4	Dry peas, lentils	10 or 11
Spinach [5]	4		
Squash, summer	3 or 4		
Squash, winter	2 or 3		
Sweetpotatoes	3 or 4		
Tomatoes, raw, diced or sliced	4		

[1] As purchased.
[2] Bought in pod.
[3] Bought without tops.
[4] Bought untrimmed.
[5] Bought prepackaged.

(88:17–18)

of defrosting. Poorer texture, flavor, and color result if the contents are refrozen. Frozen vegetables which have butter, sauces, and seasonings added or have boil-in-the-bag packaging are more expensive than plain frozen vegetables. Frozen vegetables packed in large plastic bags usually cost less per serving and allow measuring out the amount needed for one meal, thus eliminating left-overs. Maintaining a storage temperature of 0° F or lower and moisture-proof packaging add to the cost of frozen produce.

Meat Group

Approximately thirty-five cents of every food dollar is spent for foods in the meat group. Legumes, eggs, nuts, and fish are cheaper protein sources than beef, pork, and lamb. The leaner beef (if graded, the lower grades) is less expensive, lower in saturated fat, and if cooked properly can be tender and flavorful. Most United States citizens could eat less meat without having any danger of protein shortage. Except shellfish, fish is usually a good buy and has little waste. Pink salmon and flaked or grated tuna cost less than red salmon and solid pack tuna. Turbot and ocean perch can replace the more costly sole and flounder. Calves liver is more expensive but not more nutritious than beef, lamb, or pork liver.

Nuts with clean, bright shells are likely to have good kernels; cracked, stained, dull, or dirty shells are more apt to have defective kernels. The heavier the nut in relation to its size, the greater the proportion of kernel. To compare prices—one pound of nuts in the shell gives approximately the following: walnuts, 7 ounces; almonds, 6½ ounces; Brazil nuts, 8 ounces; filberts, 7 ounces; pecans, 6¾ ounces; and black walnuts, 3½ ounces. Broken kernels are less expensive than whole or half kernels. A yellowish, oily appearance usually indicates stale flavor and possibly rancidity.*

Dried legumes are excellent buys. When a soybean product is mixed with ground meat, the resulting meat loaves, hamburgers, meatballs, etc. are cheaper but are good sources of protein.

Since it is difficult to judge the quality of meat, the homemaker can be more sure of obtaining the type she wishes if she buys United States Department of Agriculture grades, which are uniform throughout the entire nation. The U.S. Department of Agriculture never uses letters such as AA or A as meat grades but rather the terms prime, choice, good, standard, commercial, utility, cutter, and canner. The round stamp indicates that the meat has been inspected and passed as wholesome food. Grading is voluntary and done only when requested by the wholesaler, retailer, or packer. Although pork is seldom graded, beef, veal, lamb, and mutton are graded. Over 75 per cent of the meat sold in the United States carries the U.S. Department of Agriculture round inspection label and it must do so if the meat enters interstate commerce.

Beef of the higher grades has a high proportion of meat to bone. The lean is firm, fine-textured, and bright red in color. It is well marbled with fat. The bones are red and porous. Fine texture and velvety appearance are associated with tenderness. Beef that is well marbled tastes juicy and rich. Meat from younger animals is likely to be tender; red, porous bones indicate that the meat is from a young animal and are therefore associated with tender cuts.

How To Get The Most For Your Food Dollar, Award Books, 1970.

Beef which has been aged or ripened is beef which has been held under controlled humidity and temperature. Aged beef costs more because of the cost of refrigeration, shrinkage, and trimming due to the fact that the outside of the lean meat has turned a dark color during aging. However, aging does develop a characteristic flavor and makes the meat more tender and juicy.

The "tender" steaks and roasts come from the rib and loin cuts, which are less than 30 per cent of the carcass. Figure 31–1 indicates that these cuts are more expensive owing to greater demand but limited supply. Price is not an indication for nutritive value.

Veal is the meat of the calf. The flesh is a gray-pink color and has a fine texture but little or no marbling. The porous bones have a red tinge, and the small amount of subcutaneous fat is clear and hard.

Pork is the meat of the pig and has a pinkish white color. The flesh is firm and well marbled with fat and the bones have a slightly reddish tinge.

Lamb is the meat of immature sheep. The flesh is light pink with firm, white fat and porous, moist, slightly red bones.

Poultry may be bought alive, dressed, or ready-to-cook. Dressed poultry has the feet, head, and internal organs in place but it has been bled and picked. Eviscerated or ready-to-cook birds have had the internal organs, oil sac, head, feet, and pin feathers removed. Both the inside and the outside of the eviscerated bird have been cleaned.

Well-fleshed, large birds usually have more meat in proportion to bone. For broiling or frying, a plump young chicken which has a flexible breastbone, tender meat, and a smooth, tender skin should be chosen. Capons and roasting chickens should be young birds but larger than fryers. The older bird with coarse skin and a firm breastbone is used for stewing and braising and in casseroles and salads.

In preparing poultry for market, it is permissible to add a small

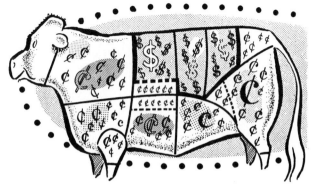

Figure 31–1 Beef chart—expensive and inexpensive cuts. (From Hilda Faust: *Use Economy Cuts of Beef*. University of California, Agricultural Extension Service.)

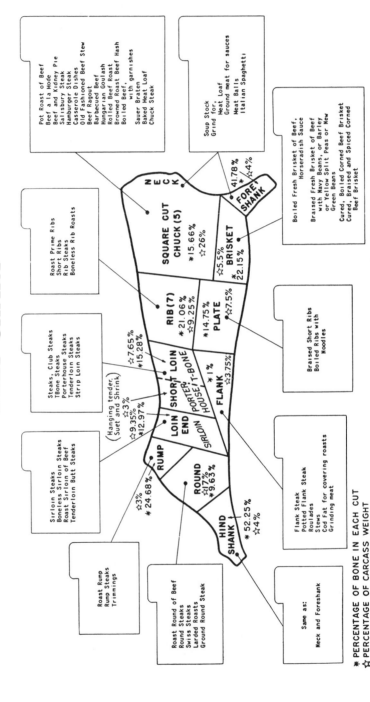

Figure 31–2   Beef chart—wholesale cuts. (Courtesy of Armour and Co.)

BONES IDENTIFY SEVEN GROUPS OF RETAIL CUTS

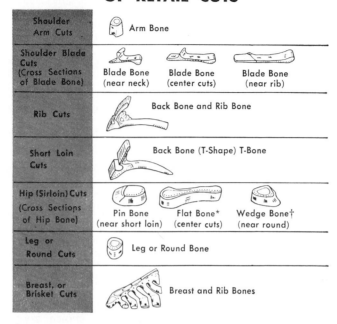

Shoulder Arm Cuts	Arm Bone		
Shoulder Blade Cuts (Cross Sections of Blade Bone)	Blade Bone (near neck)	Blade Bone (center cuts)	Blade Bone (near rib)
Rib Cuts	Back Bone and Rib Bone		
Short Loin Cuts	Back Bone (T-Shape) T-Bone		
Hip (Sirloin) Cuts (Cross Sections of Hip Bone)	Pin Bone (near short loin)	Flat Bone* (center cuts)	Wedge Bone† (near round)
Leg or Round Cuts	Leg or Round Bone		
Breast, or Brisket Cuts	Breast and Rib Bones		

*Formerly part of "double bone" but today the back bone is usually removed leaving only the "flat bone" (sometimes called "pin bone") in the sirloin steak.

†On one side of sirloin steak, this bone may be wedge shaped while on the other side the same bone may be round.

Figure 31–3 (From National Live Stock and Meat Board: *Lessons on Meat*, 1965.)

amount of an antibiotic to the ice water in the chilling tanks. This delays bacterial growth, thus increasing the refrigerated shelf life of the poultry. The antibiotic is destroyed during the cooking process.

Fish is sold fresh, frozen, or canned. Drawn fish has had the internal organs and scales removed. The organs, scales, head, tail, and fins are removed for pan-dressed fish. Steaks are cross-section slices from a large fish. Cutting the fleshy sides of the fish so that they are practically boneless produces fillets. A whole fish is marketed just as it comes from the water. Following are signs of freshness in a whole fish:

Eyes—bright, clear, and bulging.

Gills—reddish-pink, free from slime.

Scales—tight to the skin, bright and shiny.

Flesh—firm and elastic, springing back when pressed and not separating from the bones.

Odor—fresh.

Beef grades are listed in Table 31–6. Pork grades are choice, medi-

Table 31-6   *Grades of Beef*

Prime[1]	Prime is the highest grade. The lean is firm, bright red, fine textured, and has pronounced marbling. The fat is smooth and heavy on the outside. These characteristics are associated with good flavor, tenderness, and juiciness. Prime meat is seldom found in the average retail market.
Choice	Choice is the highest grade which usually is found in a market. There is extensive marbling and the fat is smooth and moderately thick.
Good	Good is the most popular grade of meat. It has a higher ratio of lean to fat than the above two grades, but it is not quite as juicy or as tender.
Standard	This grade includes the young animals formerly in the commercial grade. The cuts are moderately tender.
Commercial	Commercial grades come from older animals. The fat covering is thin and there is practically no marbling.
Utility	Utility is usually from the older animals. The fat covering is very thin and rarely shows marbling, and the cuts lack tenderness and juiciness.
Cutter and Canner	Cutter and canner are the lowest two grades. They seldom appear in the retail markets. They are used for canning, sausage, and dried beef.

[1]This nomenclature is based on tenderness, juiciness, and flavor.

um, and cull. Veal, lamb, and mutton grades are choice, good, commercial, utility, and cull. Poultry grades for chicken, ducks, and turkeys are A, B, and C. A poultry label may also show names such as mature turkey, stewing hens, young broiler, or fryer.

Purchasing Eggs

To get high-quality eggs, purchase eggs which are in cartons and which are kept under refrigeration. The label should show the grade, which refers to the interior quality and the appearance and condition of the shell; the size, which refers to the weight per dozen; and the date of grading. The weight per dozen of the four sizes commonly found on the market is

Extra large—at least 27 ounces
Large—at least 24 ounces
Medium—at least 21 ounces
Small—at least 18 ounces

Grades AA and A are top-quality eggs. When eggs of these grades are broken open, a firm, round, high yolk stands on top of a thick white. They are good for all desired uses, but are especially good when appearance is important (poaching, frying, or cooking in the shell) or when whites are to be whipped separately. For general cooking and baking, grade B eggs are satisfactory and are cheaper. Grade B eggs do not have so delicate a flavor; the white is thin and spreads out on a flat surface.

They do not have a good appearance when poached or fried, but are satisfactory for custards, scrambling, and baked dishes. The person grading an egg determines the grade by the soundness and the cleanliness of the shell, the size of the air cell, and the condition of the yolk and white. The condition of the yolk and white and the size of the air cell are determined by candling. Grade (quality) and size are entirely different. Large eggs may be any of the three grades; and the three grades may be any of the six sizes. The size and the grade of an egg have no relation to nutrient value.

If small eggs cost one fourth less than large eggs, they are as economical as large eggs; medium-sized eggs, to be equally economical, should be one eighth cheaper than large eggs. In general if there is less than seven cents per dozen difference between one size egg and the next smaller size in the same grade, you get more for your money by buying the larger size. Large eggs when selling for 60 cents per dozen are equivalent to 40 cents per pound for high-quality protein food.

The color of the egg shell is determined by heredity and the color of the yolk is determined by diet, but the lightness or darkness of either the yolk or the shell does not determine the flavor, the nutritive value, or the cooking performance.

Agricultural Handbook No. 75, *Egg Grading Manual,* lists the following as abnormalities in eggs:

1. Double-yolked eggs result when two yolks are released about the same time or when one yolk is lost into the body cavity for a day and is picked up by the funnel when the next day's yolk is released.
2. Blood spots are caused by a rupture of one or more small blood vessels in the yolk follicle at the time of ovulation.
3. Meat spots have been demonstrated to be either blood spots which have changed in color, due to chemical action, or tissue sloughed off from the reproductive organs of the hen.
4. Soft-shelled eggs generally occur when an egg is prematurely laid, and insufficient time in the uterus prevents the deposit of the shell.
5. Thin-shelled eggs may be caused by dietary deficiencies, heredity, or disease.
6. Glassy- and chalky-shelled eggs are caused by malfunction of the uterus of the laying bird. Glassy eggs are less porous and will not hatch but may retain their quality.
7. Off-colored yolks are due to substances in feed that cause off-color.
8. Off-flavored eggs may be due to disease or certain feed flavors.

Since meat is the most expensive food group, many homemakers wish to find lower cost entrees. Recipe books include many non-meat, main-dish ideas—look for sections labeled brunch, luncheon, supper, cereals and pasta, or meat substitutes. Specialty cookbooks—mushroom, ground meat, casserole, egg, poultry, pasta, vegetarian, or foreign cookery—have many less expensive recipes. Indexes list recipes which could include soufflés, croquettes, fritters, stews, enchiladas, fondues, blintzes, legumes, chow mein, egg foo young, curries, dahl, deviled eggs, lasagna, pizzas; omelets with mushroom, ham, Spanish sauce, cheese, vegetables, sour cream, or onion fillings, lentil loaves, French toast or waffles, and casseroles (e.g., eggplant, cheese, and tomato mix). Food companies often distribute recipe pamphlets with suggestions for using their products.

Table 31–7 *Shoppers' Dictionary for Meat Cuts*

Meat cut names may vary among cities and among markets within a city. Following are some of these variations and their location in the carcass. This can help in choosing correct preparation method. When in doubt about a meat cut, ask the meat-cutter.

Location and Common Name	Other Names Used
LOIN	
Club Steak	Delmonico Steak, Rib Steak
Rib Eye Steak	Market Steak, "Spencer Steak," Delmonico Steak
T-Bone	Divided into NY Steak and Filet Mignon
Tenderloin	Filet Mignon, Tenderloin Tips, Chateaubriand
Sirloin	Sirloin Tip Roast, Tip Steak
PLATE	
Skirt Steak	Skirt Steak, Skirt Steak Fillets
Chuck	Shoulder Roast, Boneless Chuck, Cross Rib, Rolled Cross Rib, Arm Roast, Round Bone Roast, Blade Cut Chuck Roast, 7-Bone Roast, Boston Cut, Boneless English Cut, Triangle Roast, Flatiron Roast, Scotch Tender, Jewish Tender, Kosher Fillet, Top Eye Pot Roast, Jewish Fillet, Barbecue Steak
BRISKET	Boneless Brisket, Fresh Brisket, Corned Beef
MECHANICALLY TENDERIZED STEAKS	"Cubed," "Chicken," Minute, Quick Steaks, Sandwich Steaks
BONELESS STEAKS From:	
Chuck	Breakfast Steak, Luncheon Steak
Round	Breakfast Steak
Top of Rib	Rib Lifter Steak

(98:6)

(From University of California Extension Service, HXT-75: *Shopping for Meat, Fish, Poultry and Eggs.*)

SUGGESTED READINGS

Avon Books: *How to Get the Most for Your Food Dollar,* 1970.
Better Homes and Gardens: "New Look in Meat Labels," June, 1974.
McGill, Marion: "Nutrition Labeling," *Family Health,* November, 1974.
National Dairy Council:
   Can We Eat Well for Less?
   Food News—Consumer Topics.
   Food News—Metrics/Labeling.
   Today's Dairy Foods.
U.S. Department of Agriculture:
   Cheese Buying Guide for Consumers. Marketing Bulletin No. 17.
   Cheese Varieties. Handbook No. 54.

Table 31–8   *Servings of Meat, Poultry, and Fish in a Market Unit*

	Servings per pound[1]
MEAT	
Much bone or gristle	1 or 2
Medium amounts of bone	2 or 3
Little or no bone	3 or 4
POULTRY (READY-TO-COOK)	
Chicken	2 or 3
Turkey	2 or 3
Duck and goose	2
FISH	
Whole	1 or 2
Dressed or pan-dressed	2 or 3
Portions or steaks	3
Fillets	3 or 4

[1]Three ounces of cooked lean meat, poultry, or fish per serving.

(88:17)

Facts About the Hot Dog Label, 1974.
Hamburger — Questions and Answers, 1973.
Home & Garden Bulletin No. 43: *Money Saving Main Dishes.*
Home & Garden Bulletin No. 183: *Your Money's Worth in Foods, 1974.*
How to Buy Butter.
How to Buy Canned and Frozen Vegetables, 1969.
How to Buy Cheddar Cheese.
How to Buy Dried Beans, Peas, and Lentils.
How to Buy Eggs.
How to Buy Instant Non-fat Milk.
How to Buy Meat for Your Freezer.
Know the Eggs You Buy (chart).
Know the Poultry You Buy (chart).
Packet for the Bride — Titles include: *How to Buy Fresh Fruits, How to Buy Fresh Vegetables, How to Buy Beef Steaks, How to Buy Beef Roasts, How to Use U.S.D.A. Grades in Buying Food, Vegetables in Family Meals, Beef and Veal in Family Meals, Food for the Young Couple, A Guide to Budgeting for the Young Couple, Family Fare — A Guide to Good Nutrition,* 1973.
University of California Cooperative Extension Service:
HXT-42: *Balance Food Values and Cents,* 1973.
HXT-77: *Shopping for Milk and Dairy Products.*
HXT-75: *Shopping for Meat, Fish, Poultry and Eggs.*
HXT-76: *Shopping for Fruits and Vegetables.*

EXERCISES

1. Are grade B eggs of such low quality that they are unfit for human consumption?
2. Why should a homemaker who is buying eggs look for the grading date?
3. Compare the cost per ounce of different size packages of one kind of cereal.
4. What is the service charge for home delivery of dairy products in your community?
5. List the meat dishes you plan to serve in your home next week. Also list the amount and cut you plan to buy and calculate its cost. How should you plan to cook it and how long will it take to cook? Refer to Chapter 35 for cooking meats, and Table 31–9 for costs.

Table 31-9 *Calculating Amounts to Buy and Comparing Costs of the Meat Group Foods*

How to use this table:

(a) To determine the amount to buy, multiply the factor (sixth column) by the number of people to be served. This equals the amount in the size of the market unit (second column).
Example: For a family of five buying fresh cubed steak

$$0.25 \text{ (factor)} \times 5 = 1.25 \text{ or } 1\frac{1}{4} \text{ pounds}$$

(b) To make cost comparisons, multiply current price per market unit by factor (sixth column). This equals the cost per serving.
Example:

Round steak @ \$ .99/lb.   \$ .99 × 0.31 = \$.306 per serving
Cubed steak @ 1.59/lb.   1.59 × 0.25 = .397 per serving
T-Bone steak @ 1.69/lb.   1.69 × 0.50 = .845 per serving

Description of food as purchased	Size of market unit	Description of food as prepared after purchase	Servings or measures per market unit	Size of serving or measure	Amount-to-buy factor
Beans:					
Dry, all varieties	16 ounces	Uncooked	$2\frac{1}{2}$	1 cup	.42
		Cooked, drained	11	$\frac{1}{2}$ cup	.09
Dry, canned:					
With franks in sauce.	12 ounces	Heated	$2\frac{1}{2}$	$\frac{1}{2}$ cup	0.39
With pork	16 ounces	Heated	$3\frac{1}{2}$	$\frac{1}{2}$ cup	.29
Kidney:					
Canned	16 ounces	Heated	$3\frac{1}{2}$	$\frac{1}{2}$ cup	.28
Lima:					
Fresh, in pod	Pound	Shelled, cooked, drained.	$2\frac{1}{4}$	$\frac{1}{2}$ cup	.47
Canned	16 ounces	Heated, drained	$3\frac{3}{4}$	$\frac{1}{2}$ cup	.27
Frozen	10 ounces	Cooked, drained	$3\frac{1}{4}$	$\frac{1}{2}$ cup	.30
Bean Sprouts:					
Canned	16 ounces	Heated, drained	$3\frac{1}{2}$	$\frac{1}{2}$ cup	.30

Beef:					
Fresh:					
Brisket:					
With bone	Pound	Simmered	2	3 ounces without bone.	0.50
Without bone	Pound	Simmered	3	3 ounces	.33
Ground	Pound	Cooked	4	3 ounces	.25
Roasts:					
Chuck:					
With bone	Pound	Cooked	2½	3 ounces without bone.	.40
Without bone	Pound	Cooked	3¼	3 ounces	.31
Rib:					
With bone	Pound	Cooked	2½	3 ounces without bone.	.40
Without bone	Pound	Cooked	3	3 ounces	.33
Round, without bone.	Pound	Cooked	3½	3 ounces	.29
Rump:					
With bone	Pound	Cooked	2½	3 ounces without bone.	.40
Without bone	Pound	Cooked	3½	3 ounces	.29
Short ribs, with bone.	Pound	Cooked	1½	3 ounces without bone.	0.67
Steaks:					
Club, with bone	Pound	Cooked	2	3 ounces without bone.	.50
Cubed (minute)	Pound	Cooked	4	3 ounces	.25
Flank, without bone.	Pound	Cooked	3½	3 ounces	.29
Porterhouse, with bone.	Pound	Cooked	2¼	3 ounces without bone.	.44
Round:					
With bone	Pound	Cooked	3¼	3 ounces without bone.	.31
Without bone	Pound	Cooked	3¾	3 ounces	.27
T-bone, with bone.	Pound	Cooked	2	3 ounces without bone.	.50
Stew meat, without bone.	Pound	Cooked	3½	3 ounces	.29
Variety meats:					
Heart	Pound	Cooked	2	3 ounces	.50
Kidney	Pound	Cooked	2	3 ounces	.50
Liver	Pound	Cooked	3¾	3 ounces	.27
Oxtail	Pound	Trimmed, cooked	1½	3 ounces without bone.	0.67
Tongue	Pound	Cooked	3	3 ounces	.33

(Table continues on next page.)

Table 31-9   *Calculating Amounts to Buy and Comparing Costs of the Meat Group Foods* (Continued)

Description of food as purchased	Size of market unit	Description of food as prepared after purchase	Servings or measures per market unit	Size of serving or measure	Amount-to-buy factor
Cured:					
Corned beef brisket,					
without bone.	Pound	Simmered	3	3 ounces	.33
Tongue, smoked	Pound	Cooked	2½	3 ounces	.40
Canned:					
Corned	12 ounces	Heated	4	3 ounces	.25
Dried:					
Chipped	4 ounces	As purchased	1¼	3 ounces	.60
Beef products:					
Canned:					
With barbecue sauce.	12 ounces	Heated	3½	2 ounces meat plus sauce.	.29
Patties in gravy	11 ounces	Heated	3¾	2 ounces meat plus gravy.	.31
Stew	24 ounces	Heated	2¾	1 cup	.36
Frozen:					
Barbecued in bun	8 ounces	Thawed	2	1 sandwich	0.50
Patties in gravy	8 ounces	Cooked	2	2 ounces	.48
Pie	1 5-inch pie	Cooked	1	1 pie	1.00
Blackeye peas (cowpeas):					
Fresh	Pound	Cooked, drained	4¾	½ cup	.21
Canned	14½ ounces	Heated, drained	3	½ cup	.33
Frozen	10 ounces	Cooked, drained	3½	½ cup	.28
Chicken, ready-to-cook:					
Fresh or frozen:					
Fryers:					
Whole or cut-up	Pound	Cooked	2¼	3 ounces	0.43

Parts:					
Breasts (about 9½ ounces each).	Pound	Cooked	3¼	½ breast (about 2½ ounces without bone).	.30
Drumsticks (about 3 ounces each).	Pound	Cooked	2¾	2 drumsticks (about 2¾ ounces without bone).	.37
Thighs (about 3¼ ounces each).	Pound	Cooked	2½	2 thighs (about 3¼ ounces without bone).	.40
Wings (about 2½ ounces each).	Pound	Cooked	1½	4 wings (about 3¼ ounces without bone).	.63
Stewing chicken	Pound	Stewed	2½	3 ounces without bone.	.40
Canned:					
Whole, in broth	52 ounces	Heated, drained	6½	3 ounces without bone.	0.16
Boneless, in broth	5 ounces	Heated, drained	1	3 ounces	.93
Chicken products:					
Canned:					
Chow mein	16 ounces	Heated	1¾	1 cup	.54
Fricassee	14 ounces	Heated	1½	1 cup	.63
Frozen:					
Chow mein	16 ounces	Heated	2¼	1 cup	.43
Pie	8 ounces	Heated	1	1 pie	1.00
Clams:					
Fresh, shucked	Pound	Cooked	2½	3 ounces	0.40
Canned, minced	7½ ounces	Heated	2½	3 ounces	.40
Clam chowder:					
Canned:					
Condensed	10½ ounces	Reconstituted, heated.	2½	1 cup	.40
Ready-to-serve	8 ounces	Heated	1	1 cup	1.00
Clam juice:					
Canned	8 fluid ounces	As purchased	2	½ cup	.50

(Table continues on next page.)

Table 31-9   *Calculating Amounts to Buy and Comparing Costs of the Meat Group Foods* (Continued)

Description of food as purchased	Size of market unit	Description of food as prepared after purchase	Servings or measures per market unit	Size of serving or measure	Amount-to-buy factor
Crabs:					
Fresh:					
Cooked in shell:					
Blue	Pound	Cooked, shelled	³/₄	3 ounces	1.33
Dungeness	Pound	Cooked, shelled	1¹/₄	3 ounces	.80
Crabmeat:					
Fresh, cooked	16 ounces	As purchased	5	3 ounces	.20
Canned	6¹/₂ ounces	Drained	1³/₄	3 ounces	.57
Crab products:					
Frozen:					
Crab cakes, fried	6 ounces	Heated	2	1 cake	0.50
Deviled crab	6 ounces	Heated	2	1 portion	.50
Eggs:					
In shell	Dozen (any size)	Shelled	12	1 egg	.08
Fish:					
Fresh or frozen:					
Dressed	Pound	Cooked	2¹/₂	3 ounces	.40
Fillets	Pound	Cooked	3¹/₂	3 ounces	.29
Steaks, with back bone.	Pound	Cooked	3	3 ounces without bone.	.33
Frozen portions or sticks:					
Breaded, fried	8 ounces	Heated	2¹/₂	3 ounces	.40
Fish flakes:					
Canned	7 ounces	Drained	2	3 ounces	.50
Frankfurters:					
8 per pound	Pound	Heated	4	2	.25
10 per pound	Pound	Heated	5	2	.20

Gefilte fish:					
Canned	16 ounces	Drained	3	3 ounces	.33
Lamb:					
Fresh:					
Chops:					
Loin, with bone	Pound	Cooked	2½	3 ounces without bone.	.40
Rib, with bone	Pound	Cooked	2	3 ounces without bone.	.50
Ground	Pound	Cooked	3½	3 ounces	.29
Roasts:					
Leg:					
With bone	Pound	Roasted	2¾	3 ounces without bone.	0.36
Without bone	Pound	Roasted	3½	3 ounces	.29
Shoulder:					
With bone	Pound	Roasted	3	3 ounces without bone.	.67
Without bone	Pound	Roasted	3¼	3 ounces	.33
Lobster:					
Fresh:					
Cooked in shell	1 lobster (about 1 pound).	As purchased	1	1 lobster	1.00
Cooked meat	Pound	Drained	4¾	3 ounces	.21
Frozen:					
Cooked meat	Pound	Thawed, drained	4¾	3 ounces	.21
Spiny tails	Pound	Cooked	2½	3 ounces	.40
Luncheon meats	Pound	As purchased	8	2 ounces	0.12
Oysters:					
Fresh, shucked	Pound	Cooked, drained	2¼	3 ounces	0.44
Canned	5 ounces (net weight)	Drained	1¾	3 ounces	.57
Frozen:					
Breaded, uncooked	7 ounces	Cooked	2¼	3 ounces	.44

(Table continues on next page.)

Table 31-9 Calculating Amounts to Buy and Comparing Costs of the Meat Group Foods (Continued)

Description of food as purchased	Size of market unit	Description of food as prepared after purchase	Servings or measures per market unit	Size of serving or measure	Amount-to-buy factor
Oyster stew:					
Canned:					
Ready-to-serve	10½ ounces	Heated	1¼	1 cup	.80
	8 ounces	Heated	1	1 cup	1.00
Peanuts:					
Roasted in shell	Pound	Shelled	2¼	1 cup	.45
Shelled	Pound	As purchased	3¾	1 cup	0.31
Peanut butter	10 ounces	As purchased	8¾	2 tablespoons	.11
	12 ounces	As purchased	10½	2 tablespoons	.09
Pork:					
Fresh:					
Chops:					
Loin, with bone	Pound	Cooked	2½	3 ounces without bone.	.40
Rib, with bone	Pound	Cooked	2¼	3 ounces without bone.	0.44
Roasts:					
Ham:					
With bone	Pound	Cooked	2½	3 ounces without bone.	.40
Without bone	Pound	Cooked	3	3 ounces	.33
Loin:					
With bone	Pound	Cooked	2¼	3 ounces without bone.	.44
Without bone	Pound	Cooked	3¼	3 ounces	.31
Shoulder:					
Boston butt:					
With bone	Pound	Cooked	3	3 ounces without bone.	.33
Without bone	Pound	Cooked	3½	3 ounces	.29
Picnic:					
With bone	Pound	Cooked	2	3 ounces without bone.	.50
Without bone	Pound	Cooked	3	3 ounces	.33

Food	Unit of purchase	Form	Servings per unit	Size of serving	Cost per serving
Sausage:					
Bulk	Pound	Cooked	2½	3 ounces	0.40
Link	Pound	Cooked	2½	3 ounces	.40
Spareribs	Pound	Cooked	1¾	3 ounces without bone.	.57
Variety meats:					
Heart	Pound	Cooked	2¼	3 ounces	.44
Liver	Pound	Cooked	3	3 ounces	.33
Cured (mild):					
Ham:					
Canned, boneless	Pound	Sliced, cold	4½	3 ounces	.22
		Heated, sliced	4	3 ounces	.25
Cook-before-eating:					
With bone	Pound	Baked	3½	3 ounces without bone.	.29
Without bone	Pound	Baked	4	3 ounces	.25
Fully cooked:					
With bone	Pound	Heated	3½	3 ounces without bone.	.29
Without bone	Pound	Heated	4	3 ounces	.25
Shoulder:					
Boston butt:					
With bone	Pound	Cooked	3	3 ounces without bone.	0.33
Without bone	Pound	Cooked	3½	3 ounces	.29
Picnic:					
With bone	Pound	Cooked	2½	3 ounces without bone.	.40
Without bone	Pound	Cooked	3¼	3 ounces	.31
Pork products:					
Canned:					
Luncheon meat with natural juices.	12 ounces	Drained	3½	3 ounces	.28
Sausage links	9 ounces	Drained, heated	2	2 ounces	.49
Frozen:					
Sausage, precooked	8 ounces	Heated	3¼	2 ounces	.31

(Table continues on next page.)

Table 31-9   *Calculating Amounts to Buy and Comparing Costs of the Meat Group Foods* (Continued)

Description of food as purchased	Size of market unit	Description of food as prepared after purchase	Servings or measures per market unit	Size of serving or measure	Amount-to-buy factor
Salmon:					
Fresh or frozen:					
Steaks	Pound	Cooked	3	3 ounces	.33
Canned	16 ounces	Drained	4¼	3 ounces	.24
Sardines:					
Canned:					
Maine	4 ounces	Drained	1¼	3 ounces	.80
Pacific, in sauce	15 ounces	Drained	3¾	3 ounces	.27
Scallops:					
Fresh, shucked	Pound	Cooked	3¼	3 ounces	0.31
Frozen, breaded, fried	7 ounces	Heated	2¼	3 ounces	.44
Shrimp:					
Fresh or frozen:					
Uncooked, in shell	Pound	Cooked, peeled, cleaned.	2¾	3 ounces	.36
Canned	4½ ounces	Drained	1½	3 ounces	.67
Frozen:					
Uncooked, peeled, cleaned.	7 ounces	Cooked	1½	3 ounces	.67
Breaded:					
Uncooked	16 ounces	Cooked	4½	3 ounces	.22
Fried	6 ounces	Heated	1¾	3 ounces	.57
Turkey, ready-to-cook:					
Fresh or frozen:					
Whole, with giblets	Pound	Cooked	2¼	3 ounces without bone.	0.43
Parts:					
Breast	Pound	Cooked	2½	3 ounces without bone.	.38
Leg	Pound	Cooked	2½	3 ounces without bone.	.42

Canned:					
Boneless, in broth	5 ounces	Drained	1	3 ounces	.93
Frozen:					
Roasts, boneless	Pound	Cooked	$3\frac{1}{4}$	3 ounces	.31
Rolls, precooked	Pound	Heated	5	3 ounces	.20
Veal:					
Fresh:					
Chops:					
Loin, with bone	Pound	Cooked	$2\frac{3}{4}$	3 ounces without bone	.36
Rib, with bone	Pound	Cooked	$2\frac{1}{2}$	3 ounces without bone	.40
Cutlet:					
With bone	Pound	Cooked	$3\frac{1}{2}$	3 ounces without bone	.29
Without bone	Pound	Cooked	4	3 ounces	.25
Roasts:					
Breast:					
With bone	Pound	Cooked	2	3 ounces without bone	.50
Without bone	Pound	Cooked	3	3 ounces	.33
Leg:					
With bone	Pound	Cooked	$2\frac{1}{2}$	3 ounces without bone	0.40
Without bone	Pound	Cooked	$3\frac{1}{2}$	3 ounces	.29
Loin:					
With bone	Pound	Cooked	$2\frac{1}{2}$	3 ounces without bone	.40
Without bone	Pound	Cooked	$3\frac{1}{2}$	3 ounces	.29
Rib:					
With bone	Pound	Cooked	$2\frac{1}{4}$	3 ounces without bone	.44
Without bone	Pound	Cooked	$3\frac{1}{2}$	3 ounces	.29
Shoulder:					
With bone	Pound	Cooked	$2\frac{1}{2}$	3 ounces without bone	.40
Without bone	Pound	Cooked	$3\frac{1}{2}$	3 ounces	.29
Variety meats:					
Heart	Pound	Cooked	$1\frac{3}{4}$	3 ounces	.57
Liver	Pound	Cooked	3	3 ounces	.33

(From U.S. Department of Agriculture, Home Economics Research Report No. 37: *Family Food Buying*, 1969.)

Table 31–10 *Bargains in the Basic-Four Food Groups*

Food group	Usually less expensive, more food value for the money	Usually more expensive, less food value for the money
Milk products	Concentrated, fluid and dry nonfat milk, buttermilk, evaporated	Fluid whole milk, chocolate drink, condensed milk, sweet or sour cream
	Mild cheddar, Swiss, cottage cheese	Sharp cheddar, Roquefort or blue, grated or sliced cheese, cream cheese, yogurt
	Ice milk, imitation ice milk, imitation ice cream	Ice cream, sherbet
Meats		
Meat	Good and standard grades	Prime and choice grades
	Less tender cuts	Tender cuts
	Home-cooked meats	Canned meats, sliced luncheon meats
	Pork or beef liver, heart, kidney, tongue	Calf liver
Poultry	Stewing chickens, whole broiler-fryers, large turkeys	Poultry parts, specialty products, canned poultry, small turkeys
Fish	Rock cod, butterfish, other fresh fish in season, frozen fillets, steaks, and sticks	Salmon, crab, lobster, prawns, shrimp, oysters
Eggs	Grade A	Grade AA
Beans, peas, and lentils	Dried beans, peas, lentils	Canned baked beans, soups
Nuts	Peanut butter, walnuts, other nuts in shell	Pecans, cashews, shelled nuts, prepared nuts
Vegetables, fruits	Local vegetables and fruits season	Out-of-season vegetables and fruits, unusual vegetables and fruits, those in short supply
Vitamin A rich	Carrots, collards, sweet potatoes, green leafy vegetables, spinach, pumpkin, winter squash, broccoli, and in	Tomatoes, Brussels sprouts, asparagus, peaches, watermelon, papaya, banana, tangerine

Table 31–10   *Bargains in the Basic-Four Food Groups* (Continued)

Food group	Usually less expensive, more food value for the money	Usually more expensive, less food value for the money
Vitamin C rich	season cantaloup, apricots, persimmons Oranges, grapefruit and their juice, cabbage, greens, green pepper, cantaloup, strawberries, tomatoes, broccoli in season	Tangerines, apples, bananas, peaches, pears
Others	Medium-sized potatoes, non-baking types	Baking potatoes, new potatoes, canned or frozen potatoes, potato chips
	Romaine, leaf lettuce	Iceberg lettuce, frozen specialty packs of vegetables
Breads, cereals	Whole wheat and enriched flour	Stone-ground, unenriched, and cake flour
	Whole grain and enriched breads	French, Vienna, other specialty breads, hard rolls
	Homemade rolls and coffee cake	Ready-made rolls and coffee cakes, frozen or partially baked products
	Whole grain or restored uncooked cereals	Ready-to-eat cereals, puffed, sugar-coated
	Graham crackers, whole grain wafers	Zwiebach, specialty crackers and wafers
	Enriched uncooked macaroni, spaghetti, noodles	Unenriched, canned, or frozen macaroni, spaghetti, noodles
	Brown rice, converted rice	Quick-cooking, seasoned, or canned rice

(From Cook, F., and Groppe, C.: *Balance Food Values and Cents*, 1973, University of California Agricultural Extension Service HXT-42.)

Table 31-11 *Calendar of the Best Food Buys*

Month	Meat, Fish, etc.	Dairy Products	Vegetables	Fruit	Miscellaneous
January	Chicken (broilers & fryers), pork and pork products, eggs		Potatoes, cabbage, onions, lettuce	Oranges, apples, tangerines, grapefruit	Tree nuts, raisins, honey
February	Eggs, better-grade beef		Lettuce, celery, potatoes, cabbage	Oranges, grapefruit	Tree nuts, raisins, honey
March	Chicken (broilers & fryers), frozen fish, eggs		Dried beans, potatoes	Canned & frozen citrus fruit, juices	Raisins, prunes
April	Chicken (broilers & fryers), pork and pork products, eggs	Cottage cheese	Cabbage, carrots, potatoes, spring greens, celery	Apples, oranges	Raisins, prunes
May	Chicken (broilers & fryers), eggs	Butter, milk, cheese, cottage cheese	Asparagus, onions, lettuce, cabbage, spring greens	Strawberries	
June	Chicken (broilers & fryers), fresh fish	Butter, milk, cheese, ice cream	Potatoes, onions, lettuce, snap beans	Berries, cantaloup	

Chapter 31 • Groceries, Nutrition, and Dollars — 291

Month					
July	Chicken (broilers & fryers), turkey (fryers & roasters)	Cheese, ice cream, cottage cheese	Cabbage, tomatoes, potatoes, local vegetables	Lemons, peaches, watermelons, cantaloup, limes, plums, apricots	
August	Fresh fish	Ice cream	Local vegetables	Grapes, pears, watermelons, peaches, plums	Rice
September	Stewing chicken, lamb	Cottage cheese	Onions, carrots, cabbages, tomatoes, corn	Grapes, pears	Rice
October	Stewing chicken, turkey, lamb, pork	Cheese	Potatoes, onions, sweet potatoes, cauliflower, dried beans, pumpkins, cabbage	Apples, pears	Honey
November	Turkey, pork and pork products		Potatoes, onions, sweet potatoes, cauliflower, cabbage, pumpkins	Cranberries, apples	Tree nuts, raisins, honey
December	Turkey, pork		Onions, sweet potatoes, potatoes	Grapefruit, cranberries, oranges, dried fruit	Honey, tree nuts

(From Troelstrup, A. W.: *The Consumer in American Society: Personal and Family Finance*, 1970, pp. 208–209.)

CHAPTER 32

Cereals

Composition of Cereals

Cereals provide about one quarter of the calories in the average American diet. The average-sized serving of cooked or dry cereal has 10 to 25 grams of carbohydrate and 2 to 4 grams of protein. The vitamin and mineral content of grains is found in the outer layers. Whole grain products have the nutrient value of the original grain regardless of the grinding process. The extra cost of stone-ground whole wheat flour brings you flavor and texture, not nutrient value. Refined cereals lose a great deal of their food value during milling. Enriched cereals have specific amounts of thiamine, riboflavin, niacin, and iron added; the amounts are set by the Federal Food and Drug Administration. Restored cereals may be restored in several nutrients or in only one or two; there is no standard for restored cereals. Therefore, the manufacturer determines the nutrients to be restored and the amount to be added. Review the material on B complex vitamins in Chapter 9 and Figure 32–2. When buying rice one also sees the term *converted*. This refers to white rice processed by a method which forced much of the B-vitamin content into the grain before the bran was removed.

Storage of Cereals

Store cereals in a dry, cool place which is free of insects and vermin. Dry cereals which have absorbed moisture from the air can be crisped by thinly spreading the cereal in a pan and placing in the oven for a few minutes. Bread keeps its freshness at room temperature, but in hot, humid weather refrigeration retards mold growth.

Cooking Cereals

The three purposes of cooking cereal are the following:
1. To soften and rupture the cellulose walls.

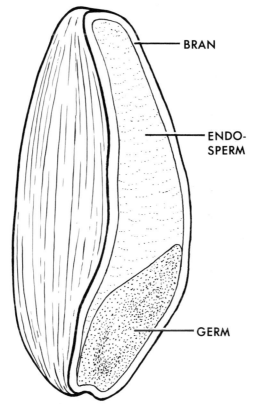

- BRAN
- ENDO-
SPERM
- GERM

Figure 32–1 A kernel of wheat. (Wheat Flour Institute, Chicago, Illinois.)
Endosperm—about 83% of the kernel and the source of white flour.
    Contains: nearly all the starch
                small amount of incomplete protein
                traces of minerals and vitamins.
Bran—about 14$\frac{1}{2}$% of the kernel.
    Contains: nearly all the cellulose
                small amount of incomplete protein
                some minerals and B complex vitamins.
Germ—about 2$\frac{1}{2}$% of the kernel.
    Contains: nearly all the fat and vitamin E
                small amount of incomplete protein
                some B complex vitamins.

2. To improve the flavor.

3. To cook the starch, which helps prepare it for digestion.

Ready-to-eat cereals have been completely cooked at the processing plants. Most of the other cereals have been partially cooked by the manufacturer, and the length of pre-cooking varies according to each manufacturing process. The amount of cooking needed for each type is shown on the label of the package. To cook longer than directed causes vitamin (especially thiamine) loss, and to undercook leaves the product with a raw-starch flavor.

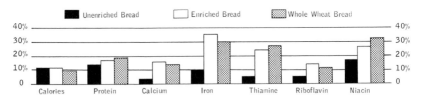

Figure 32–2 Most Americans consume 5 to 6 slices of bread a day. This chart compares the nutrient contribution of 6 slices of enriched, unenriched, and whole-wheat bread to the recommended dietary allowance for the normal man. (Adapted from Sebrell, W. H., Jr.: "Preventive Medicine at Work: The Story of Enriched Bread," *Today's Health,* September, 1961, p. 59.)

SUGGESTED READINGS

Davis, Thomas R., and Sebrell, William H., Jr.: *The Dietary Role of Cereals in the United States,* Cereal Institute, Inc.

Kansas Wheat Commission: *Wheat—Field to Market.*

U.S. Department of Agriculture, Home and Garden Bulletin No. 150: *Cereals and Pasta in Family Meals, A Guide for Consumers.*

University of California Agricultural Extension Service: HXT-71, *Bread Belongs in Every Meal.*

EXERCISES

1. List the individual nutrients found in whole grain, enriched, restored, and refined cereals.
2. Does "steel-cut" oatmeal have more nutrient value than other oatmeal?
3. Does home-ground wheat flour contain more nutrients than whole wheat (graham flour) does?
4. Both whole grain and enriched cereals are in the basic-four food groups. Does whole grain contain a greater variety of nutrients than enriched?

CHAPTER 33

Dairy Products

Curdle
Disperse
Homogenize

Pasteurize
Precipitate
Reconstitute

Milk

Composition of Milk

Every 100 grams of milk contain approximately 3½ grams of protein, which has all of the essential amino acids, 4 grams of emulsified fat, 5 grams of carbohydrate in the form of lactose, and 87 grams of water. The minerals supplied are calcium (milk is the best dietary source), phosphorus, potassium, magnesium, and a very minute amount of iron of the highest biological quality. The vitamins are A, B_1, riboflavin, a small amount of niacin, and B_{12}. Since the presence of milk in the intestinal tract favors niacin synthesis, drinking milk does add to the body's supply of niacin. Natural milk is considered a poor source of vitamins C, D, and niacin, and of the mineral, iron; but it is difficult to substitute for milk in the basic-four because milk contains more nutrients in better proportions than other foods do.

Storage of Milk

In storing all dairy foods, follow the rule of the three C's: Keep them cold, keep them clean, and keep them covered.

Milk should be stored in the coldest part of the refrigerator (under 40° F) and kept away from strongly flavored foods, since milk readily absorbs flavors and odors. For the best flavor, use milk within five days. Milk is packaged in sterile containers and there is less chance of contamination if the milk is stored in its original container. Milk is an excellent medium for the growth of microorganisms, and unless it is stored below 40° F the number of bacteria will increase very rapidly. This is illustrated in Figure 30–3. A clear glass quart bottle of milk can lose 20 to 40 per cent of its riboflavin if exposed to sunlight for one hour. Store all dry milk in a tightly closed container. Non-fat dry milk can be stored at room temperature but after the seal on a can of powdered whole milk is broken, the milk will become rancid if it is not kept under refrigeration. After canned milk is opened, it too should be refrigerated. Freezing does not alter milk's nutrient content.

Cooking Milk

If a double boiler is used for cooking milk or milk products instead of applying heat directly to the pan containing the milk, the temperature does not reach as high a point and there is little danger of scorching. Placing a pan of custard in a pan of water while baking utilizes the principle of the double boiler in oven cookery. The coating on the sides and bottom of the pan is due to precipitation of protein. If the scum which forms on the top of heated milk is discarded, nutrients are lost. The scum is very easily broken up into tiny particles by using an egg beater. Scum does not form if milk is covered during the heating process. If milk is heated to the boiling point or above, the size of the curd formed in the stomach is smaller. Prolonged heating of an acid and milk mixture, such as tomato soup, encourages curdling. The chances for curdling are reduced if the acid is slowly added to slightly thickened milk which is being stirred.

Milk has many uses in the menu. As a beverage it may be served plain, in chocolate milk, or in cocoa. It is used in cream soups, white sauces for creaming vegetables or meats, soufflés, escalloped potatoes and other baked dishes, as well as in desserts such as Junket, custard, pudding, ice cream, or sherbet.

If powdered milk is added to liquid milk or incorporated in recipes (sandwich fillings, meat loaf, puddings, cake mixes), the nutrient value of the food is increased.

Ice Cream and Similar Frozen Foods

Composition of Frozen Desserts

Ice cream is highest of frozen desserts in milk fat and milk solids. (See Table 33–1 for the percentage composition of these frozen foods.) If fruit, nuts, candy, and so forth are added, the milk fat and milk solid content is lowered slightly but the same basic mix is used.

Table 33–1　*Common Ingredients of Frozen Food Desserts*

	% Milk Fat	% Total Milk Solids	% Sweetener	% Acid Ingredients	% Egg Yolk Solids	% Vegetable and Animal Fats
Plain Ice Cream	10–14	20	15–16	–	–	–
Bulky Flavored Ice Cream	8	16	15–16	–	–	–
Frozen Custard, French Ice Cream, French Custard Ice Cream	10–16	20	15–16	–	1.4	–
Ice Milk	2–7	11–15	17–19	–	–	–
Fruit Sherbet	1–2	2–5	25–35	0.35–0.5	–	–
Water Ices	–	–	25–35	0.35–0.5	–	–
Mellorine	–	20	15–16	–	–	8–10

(From National Dairy Council: *Ice Cream and Similarly Frozen Foods. Information Sheet*, 1969, p. 3.)

Frozen custard, French ice cream, and French custard ice cream have a higher content of egg yolk solids than other similarly frozen foods.

Ice milk usually has more sugar than ice cream, fewer milk solids, and less milk fat. It is made in the same manner as ice cream. Soft ice milk or ice cream has the same formula as its corresponding ice milk or ice cream. They are soft and are ready to eat when drawn from the freezer. Most of the soft frozen desserts sold are ice milks.

Fruit sherbet is a low-fat, low-milk-solid frozen food, and it has more sugar than ice cream. Its tart flavor comes from added fruit and fruit acid.

Water ices contain no dairy products. From 15 to 20 per cent of their weight is fruit juice, 70 to 75 per cent is water, the sugar content is high, and they have a tart flavor.

Mellorine is very similar to ice cream, the only appreciable difference being that the milk fat is replaced by a vegetable or other animal fat. The fat used usually is soy bean or cottonseed oil, but coconut oil, corn oil, peanut oil, and meat fat can be used. There are some states in which mellorine cannot legally be sold.

In some states, products called imitation ice milk or imitation ice cream are sold. Their fat content is a vegetable fat instead of dairy fat. Since they usually have the same recipes as ice cream or ice milk, they are equal in calories to their counterparts.

Storage of Frozen Desserts

Ice cream and similar products can be stored in the freezing compartment of the refrigerator for two to three weeks. Once the carton has been opened, cover the exposed surface with a piece of foil or transparent plastic wrap. This prevents the ice cream from absorbing refrigerator odors. Ice cream can be stored in a home freezer at 0° F or below up to two months. The carton will need to be moved into the food storage compartment of the refrigerator for about 30 minutes so that it will be soft enough to serve. Upon returning the carton to the freezer, cover the exposed surface. Ice cream should not be allowed to partially melt and then refreeze. This causes the ice crystals to increase in size, resulting in a coarse, icy product.

Cheese

Composition of Cheese

The nutrient value of cheese varies according to the type of milk used, for example, cow's milk, goat's milk, whole or skim milk. Cheese curd is formed either by acid which results from bacterial growth or by adding rennet to the milk. The whey left after the formation of the curd does contain some protein, lactose, and water-soluble vitamins and minerals. If cottage cheese is made from skim milk, it is about 1 per cent fat and 19 per cent protein and will be higher in calcium value if the cheese has been made by the rennet method rather than by using a bacterial culture. Cheddar, often called American cheese, is approximately 25 per cent protein, 32 to 35 per cent fat, and 35 per cent water. It takes about five quarts of milk to make one pound of cheddar.

Sapsago, a lower-fat cheese, varies from 5 to 10 per cent in fat.

Storage of Cheese

Soft cheese needs to be stored tightly covered at 35° to 40° F, in the refrigerator. Use cottage cheese within five days, the others within two weeks. Wrap hard cheese tightly and refrigerate. It will keep for several weeks.

Freezing damages the texture of most cheeses. The exceptions are Brick, Cheddar, Edam, Gouda, Muenster, Port du Salut, Swiss, Provolone, Mozzarella, and small pieces of Camembert. Blue, Gorgonzola, and Roquefort crumble when frozen, but they can still be used after freezing, in salads or salad dressings. As with any other frozen food, frozen cheese should be stored at 0° F or lower for not longer than six months.

Cooking Cheese

Since cheese is a high-protein food, it must be cooked at low temperatures for as short a time as possible, or a tough, stringy product results and the fat separates out.

Table 33–2   *Calories in Milk Products*

The list below shows the approximate number of calories in 1 cup (8 fluid ounces) of selected milk and other dairy products:

MILK

Buttermilk, made from skim milk	90
Chocolate milk, made from whole milk and chocolate	210
Chocolate-flavored drink, made from lowfat milk and cocoa	190

Dry:

Nonfat, reconstituted (3.2 ounces per quart)	85
Nonfat, reconstituted (3.75 ounces per quart)	95
Whole, reconstituted (4 ounces per quart)	140
Whole, reconstituted (4.5 ounces per quart)	165

Evaporated (diluted with equal volume of water):

Skim	90
Whole	170

Fresh skimmed:

Lowfat (1 percent milkfat)	110
Skim	90
2 percent	130
2 percent (added nonfat solids)	145

Fresh whole:

Cream-line	160
Homogenized	160
Sweetened condensed, undiluted	980
Yogurt, made from partially skimmed milk	120

HALF-AND-HALF

Half-and-half (11 percent milkfat)	325
Sour half-and-half (11 percent milkfat)	325

CREAM

Sour (18 percent milkfat)	505
Table or coffee (18 percent milkfat)	505

Whipping (unwhipped):

Heavy (36 percent milkfat)	840
Light (30 percent milkfat)	715

FROZEN DESSERTS

Frozen custard (10 percent milkfat)	290
Ice cream, plain (10 percent milkfat)	290
Ice milk (5 percent milkfat)	220
Ice milk, soft serve (5 percent milkfat)	255
Sherbet, fruit (1.2 percent milkfat)	260

NOTE: The number of calories in frozen desserts varies with the amount of milkfat in the mix and the volume of air incorporated into the product during processing.

For milk products frequently used in small amounts, the approximate number of calories in 1 tablespoon is listed below:

MILK

Dry:

Nonfat, instant (powder)	15
Whole, instant (powder)	25
Evaporated, whole, undiluted	20
Fresh skim	5
Fresh whole	10
Sweetened condensed, undiluted	60
Yogurt, made from partially skimmed milk	10

HALF-AND-HALF

Half-and-half (11 percent milkfat)	20
Sour half-and-half (11 percent milkfat)	20

CREAM

Sour (18 percent milkfat)	30
Table or coffee (18 percent milkfat)	30

Whipping (unwhipped):

Heavy (36 percent milkfat)	55
Light (30 percent milkfat)	45

(From U.S. Department of Agriculture, Home and Garden Bulletin No. 127: *Milk In Family Meals, A Guide for Consumers,* 1967.)

SUGGESTED READING

American Dry Milk Institute, Bulletin No. 522: *Instant Nonfat Dry Milk in Family Meals.*
American Medical Association Council on Foods and Nutrition: "Substitutes for Whole Milk," *J.A.M.A.*, 208:9:58, June 2, 1969.
National Dairy Council:
  Cheese (Information Sheet).
  Cottage Cheese (Information Sheet).
  Milk Information Sheet.
  Milk — It's Food Value.
  Newer Knowledge of Cheese.
  Newer Knowledge of Milk.
"Relative Value of Filled and Imitation Milks," *Dairy Council Digest*, March-April, 1968.
U.S. Department of Agriculture:
  Cheese in Family Meals, A Guide for Consumers. Home and Garden Bulletin No. 112.
  Milk in Family Meals, A Guide for Consumers. Home and Garden Bulletin No. 127.
University of California Agriculture Extension Service: HXT-72, *Serve Milk and Other Dairy Foods Often.*

EXERCISES

1. Which is the correct procedure for making tomato soup?
   (a) Pouring hot milk into the hot tomato sauce.
   (b) Mixing cold tomatoes with cold milk and then heating.
   (c) Pouring hot tomato sauce into the hot milk.
   (d) Thickening (with a starch) either the cooked tomatoes or hot milk and pouring the hot tomato sauce into the hot milk.
2. What is the daily milk allowance for
   (a) An 8-year-old boy?
   (b) A 60-year-old man?
   (c) A 30-year-old pregnant woman?
   (d) A 16-year-old girl?
3. Why is cottage cheese used in place of Cheddar cheese in a low-calorie diet?
4. What is the rule for cooking protein food? Why?
5. Should soda be added to cream of tomato soup to prevent curdling? Why or why not?
6. Are these statements true or false?
   Milk and cheese are gas-forming.
   Milk and cheese are constipating.

CHAPTER 34

Eggs

TERMS TO UNDERSTAND

Clarify
Coagulate

Leaven
Penetrate

Composition of Eggs

Eggs are 12 per cent fat, 13 per cent protein of the complete type, and 74 per cent water. Egg protein is at the top of the list for biological value. An average size egg weighs about 50 grams; therefore it contains about 6 grams of fat and 6 grams of protein. The protein content of nine eggs is equivalent to three quarters of a pound of lean meat or two quarts of milk. Iron, phosphorus, and vitamins A, D. B_1, and B_2 are found in the egg yolk. The fat content of the egg is in the yolk; therefore the use of whole eggs is limited on a low fat diet. Sulfur is found in egg white; it is this sulfur which combines with silver and makes the tableware turn dark. Eggs are low in calcium, niacin, and ascorbic acid.

Storage of Eggs

Eggs should be stored in a covered pan at a temperature below 40° F and away from strongly flavored food. For best flavor and cooking quality, use eggs within a week after purchase. Washing an egg before storing removes the natural protective coating and results in easier bacterial penetration of the shell. Left-over egg whites may be stored up to 10 days in the refrigerator in a tightly covered jar. Egg yolks do not keep as well but they can be stored for two or three days if covered by water. After the container is opened, dried eggs should be refrigerated.

A grade A egg (with its shell protected and packed in a clean case) will remain at grade A quality for 6 months or longer if stored at 29° to

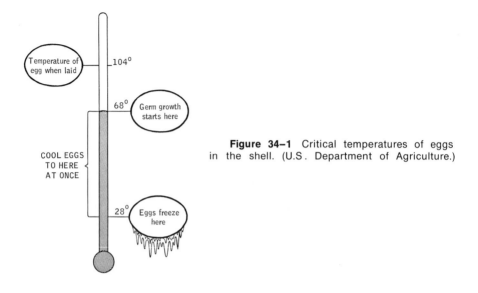

Figure 34–1 Critical temperatures of eggs in the shell. (U.S. Department of Agriculture.)

31° F. The following shows the time necessary for infertile grade AA eggs to become grade C:

     3 days at 98.6° F
     8 days at 77.0° F
     23 days at 60.8° F
     65 days at 44.6° F
     100 days at 37.4° F

The above listing shows that if eggs are not refrigerated one may be paying for a high-grade egg but actually receiving a lower-grade egg.

Cooking Eggs

If a recipe calls for a cupful of eggs, from four extra large to seven small eggs will be needed. It takes six extra large and ten small whites or 12 to 18 yolks to fill one cup.

In the preparation of foods, the Poultry and Egg National Board suggests using the versatile egg to

   1. Bind, as in meat loaves or croquettes.
   2. Clarify, as in the preparation of consommé.
   3. Coat, as in breaded meats.
   4. Emulsify, as in salad dressings and cream puffs.
   5. Garnish, as in salads, canapés, and soups.
   6. Hinder crystallization, as in frosting or candy making. (Always slowly pour the hot mixture into the beaten egg while stirring.)
   7. Leaven by beating to incorporate air, as in cakes. (An egg yolk will separate from the egg white more quickly and better if the egg is about

60° F. Egg whites beat to a greater volume if they are around 70° F (room temperature) and are beaten until stiff but not dry.)

8. Thicken, as in custard and puddings.

Always soak or rinse egg dishes in cold water. Hot water coagulates and cooks the egg on the dish, making dish washing more difficult.

Eggs should be cooked or baked at low temperatures to prevent discoloration, curdling, and toughness. Overcooking toughens and shrinks the protein. Simmering water (185° F) is used to cook poached eggs. To soft-cook an egg, lower it into boiling water, removed from direct heat, and let stand eight to 10 minutes, or put eggs in a pan and completely cover with cold water. Heat the water slowly to simmering, cover the pan, remove it from the heat and let it stand three to five minutes. The longer time is necessary for a larger number of eggs or for a firmer consistency. For hard-cooked eggs use the same process, but when the water gets to simmering, allow the eggs to stand in it for 20 to 25 minutes. Do not let the water boil. The green discoloration which sometimes appears between the yolk and the white of a hard-cooked egg is the result of a chemical reaction between the sulfur in the white and the iron in the yolk. The discoloration is unattractive, but perfectly harmless. It can be prevented or at least reduced in amount by cooking the egg at the low or simmering temperature, by avoiding overcooking, and by cooling promptly. Rapid cooling facilitates removing the shell from a hard-cooked egg. To avoid curdling when combining eggs with a hot liquid, slowly pour a small amount of the hot mixture into the beaten eggs, stirring all the while. Add more mixture while continuing to stir, then thoroughly blend the egg combination into the rest of the hot mixture. The object here is to heat the eggs gradually and thus prevent curdling. In sauces or puddings which have a starchy thickening agent, cook the starch mixture thoroughly before adding the eggs because the starch needs longer cooking than the eggs do. Baked egg dishes should be cooked in a slow or moderate oven and usually are placed in a pan of water. The double boiler can be used for making soft custards and scrambled eggs.

SUGGESTED READING

U.S. Department of Agriculture: *Eggs in Family Meals, A Guide for Consumers.* Home and Garden Bulletin No. 103.

EXERCISES

1. Why is a low temperature used for cooking eggs?
2. Why is it recommended that eggs be purchased in stores which refrigerate them?
3. Are eggs comparable in their fat and protein content?

CHAPTER 35

Meats, Fish, and Poultry

Capon   Meat
Eviscerate   *Dressed*
                                                         Marbled

---

Composition of Meat, Fish, and Poultry

The proteins of meat, fish, and poultry are complete and of a high biological value. The amount of protein in a cut of meat depends upon the proportion of the muscle to the fat; the greater the amount of fat, the lower the amount of protein. Most meats average from 15 to 25 per cent protein. The lean of the meat is a source of the minerals phosphorus, sulfur, potassium, iron, and the B vitamins. Pork is high in thiamine and red meats are high in iron. Salt water fish is an excellent source of iodine.

The organ meats, such as liver, kidney, and heart, are especially rich in the B vitamins and iron. Liver is an excellent source of vitamin A.

Storage of Meat, Fish, and Poultry

Fresh poultry, meat, and fish should be refrigerated uncovered or loosely covered. Cooked meat, fish, or poultry should be covered, kept in the refrigerator, and used within a few days. The variety meats, which include kidney, liver, heart, tongue, sweetbreads, brains, tripe, and oxtail, are even more perishable. Smoked meats and smoked and unsmoked sausage may be wrapped during storage. They will keep longer than the unsmoked and non-spiced meats. Frozen meat, poultry, or fish should be kept in a moisture-proof wrapping at a temperature of 0° F or lower. The recommended maximum freezer storage for fat fish is one to three months, for lean fish, four to six months, and for shellfish, one to four months.

Cooking Meats, Fish, and Poultry

Regardless of cut, properly cooked meat will be tender. (See cooking guides at end of chapter.)

Medium or low temperatures should always be used for meat cookery. The low temperatures will produce more palatable meat because it is more tender and juicy. High temperatures produce as much as 30 per cent shrinkage, which gives fewer servings per pound. Low temperatures keep the shrinkage to approximately 10 per cent. For example, a 24-pound, 4-ounce rib roast cooked at constant low oven temperature of 250° F to an internal doneness of 137° F will lose 2 pounds, 6 ounces in weight, which is a 9.8 per cent loss; but a 24-pound, 4-ounce rib roast cooked at a constant high oven temperature of 450° to a 137° internal temperature will lose 7 pounds, 1 ounce—a shrinkage of 29.1 per cent. (55:7)

Searing does not hold in the juices. Experiments show that constant low oven temperature gradually browns the meat and that constant low temperature produces less shrinkage than if the meat had been seared. Also the low temperature uses less fuel. A beef roast which is cooked well done will shrink more than a roast which is medium or rare.

For dry heat cookery (broiling, pan frying, and roasting), the choice or good grades give more palatable meat. For moist heat cookery (braising, pot roasting, and stewing), standard or commercial grade is suitable. Ground meat from commercial or utility beef is more economical and just as satisfactory as the good or choice.

The color of cooked meat and poultry is not always a sign of how well done it is. To most of us pink meat means rare, but turkey, fresh pork, and veal occasionally remain pink when thoroughly cooked. Often the meat of young birds or animals shows a pink-colored rim extending about one half inch into the cooked meat, because the meat lacked the shield of fat which prevents a chemical reaction. Pinkness occurs when the meat or poultry is exposed to certain gases (such as carbon monoxide or nitric oxide) which are formed in gas and electric ovens. These gases combine with the hemoglobin in the meat tissue to form a heat-stable pink color. If your meat thermometer indicates that the meat is cooked, and yet it is pink, you may assume that these chemical changes have taken place; stop the cooking and consume the meat before it is overdone.

Discolored meat around the bones of young frozen poultry is due to the leaking of blood from the porous bones of the young poultry. The blood goes from the bone into the surrounding soft tissues and you observe a red or brownish discolored area in the cooked meat. The wholesomeness of the meat is not affected.

Rainbow-like, iridescent color, which is sometimes observed on sliced ham, is caused by the refraction of light on the ends of muscle fibers of the meat. The meat is safe.

Frozen meats may be cooked without thawing. For lamb roasts allow 10 minutes per pound extra, for pork 20 minutes extra, and for beef 25 minutes extra. To cook chops and steaks without thawing, allow from 2 to 15 minutes longer, depending upon the thickness. A general rule is that it takes one third to one half longer to cook the cut than it would take if it were not frozen. If frozen meats are thawed, they should be used promptly and not be refrozen.

Beef may be cooked well done, medium, or rare. Veal and especially pork should always be well done, but lamb is cooked either well done or medium.

Roasts may be salted when put into the oven, but broiled and fried meat should not be salted until after it is browned and turned. Salt penetrates about one half inch into the flesh and tends to remove juices and extractives.

When broiling or frying meat, turn the meat only once. Do not use a cover when roasting meat; a cover is used in pot roasting, which is mois⁺ cookery.

SUGGESTED READING

National Livestock and Meat Board: *Lessons on Meat.*
Swift and Company: *Martha Logan's Meat Handi-book.*
U.S. Department of Agriculture:
   Freezing Meat and Fish in the Home. Home and Garden Bulletin No. 93, 1968.
   Lamb in Family Meals, A Guide for Consumers. Home and Garden Bulletin No. 124.
   Meat and Poultry, Care Tips for You. Home and Garden Bulletin No. 174, 1970.
   Meat and Poultry, Standards for You. Home and Garden Bulletin No. 171, 1969.
   Money Saving Main Dishes. Home and Garden Bulletin No. 43, 1969.
   Nuts in Family Meals, A Guide for Consumers. Home and Garden Bulletin No. 176.
   Pork in Family Meals, A Guide for Consumers. Home and Garden Bulletin No. 160.
   Poultry in Family Meals, A Guide for Consumers. Home and Garden Bulletin No. 110.
University of California Agricultural Extension Service: *Use Meat in Your Meals.*

EXERCISE

1. In what part of the refrigerator should you store these higher protein foods? See Figure 30–4.

Table 35–1   *Storing Chart for Meat and Poultry*

Product	Storage Period (To maintain its quality)	
	Refrigerator 35° to 40° F. *Days*	Freezer 0° F. *Months*
Fresh meats		
Roasts (Beef and Lamb)	3 to 5	8 to 12
Roasts (Pork and Veal)	3 to 5	4 to 8
Steaks (Beef)	3 to 5	8 to 12
Chops (Lamb and Pork)	3 to 5	3 to 4
Ground and Stew Meats	1 to 2	2 to 3
Variety Meats	1 to 2	3 to 4
Sausage (Pork)	1 to 2	1 to 2
Processed meats		
Bacon	7	1
Frankfurters	7	$\frac{1}{2}$
Ham (Whole)	7	1 to 2
Ham (Half)	3 to 5	1 to 2
Ham (Slices)	3	1 to 2
Luncheon Meats	3 to 5	Freezing
Sausage (Smoked)	7	not recom-
Sausages (Dry and Semi-Dry)	14 to 21	mended
Cooked meats		
Cooked Meats and Meat Dishes	1 to 2	2 to 3
Gravy and Meat Broth	1 to 2	2 to 3
Fresh poultry		
Chicken and Turkey	1 to 2	12
Duck and Goose	1 to 2	6
Giblets	1 to 2	3
Cooked poultry		
Pieces (Covered with Broth)	1 to 2	6
Pieces (Not Covered)	1 to 2	1
Cooked Poultry Dishes	1 to 2	6
Fried Chicken	1 to 2	4

(89:7)

Table 35–2   *Meat Cooking Guide*

Beef	Veal	Lamb	Pork
		ROASTING	
Chuck or shoulder	Loin	Leg	Fresh and cured ham
Rib	Leg	Loin	Fresh and cured
Round	Shoulder	Rib	shoulder
Rump		Shoulder	Loin
Sirloin			Spareribs
Sirloin tip			
Tenderloin			
		BROILING	
Patties (ground)	Liver	Chops	Bacon
Thick steaks:		Liver	Canadian bacon
Chuck		Patties (ground)	Chops
Club			Cured ham slices
Porterhouse			
Rib			
Top round			
Sirloin			
T-bone			
		PAN-BROILING, PAN-FRYING	
Liver	Cube steaks	Chops	Bacon
Patties (ground)	Liver	Liver	Canadian bacon
Thin steaks:	Patties (ground)	Patties (ground)	Cured ham slices
Club	Cutlets or round		Liver
Cube steaks	steak		Thin chops
Porterhouse	Loin and rib chops		Thin steaks
Rib			
Round			
Sirloin			
T-bone			
		BRAISING, POT-ROASTING	
Chuck or shoulder	Cutlets	Breast	Chops
Flank	Loin and rib chops	Neck slices	Ham slices
Liver	Roasts:	Shanks	Liver
Round	Round	Shortribs	Shanks
Rump	Rump	Shoulder cuts	Spareribs
Shortribs	Shoulder		Steaks
Sirloin tip			Tenderloin
		SIMMERING, STEWING	
Brisket	Breast	Breast	Cured ham
Corned beef	Riblets	Neck slices	Cured shoulder
Heel of round	Shanks	Shanks	Hocks
Neck			Shanks
Shanks			Spareribs
Shortribs			(88:29)

Table 35-3 *Poultry Roasting Guide*

Kind of poultry	Ready-to-cook weight [1]	Approximate roasting time at 325° F. for stuffed poultry [2]	Internal temperature of poultry when done
	Pounds	*Hours*	° F.
Chickens_____ (Broilers, fryers, or roasters)	1½ to 2½___ 2½ to 4½___	1 to 2_____ 2 to 3½_____	
Ducks_____	4 to 6_____	2 to 3_____	
Geese_____	6 to 8_____ 8 to 12____	3 to 3½_____ 3½ to 4½_____	
Turkeys_____	6 to 8_____ 8 to 12____ 12 to 16____ 16 to 20____ 20 to 24____	3 to 3½_____ 3½ to 4½_____ 4½ to 5½_____ 5½ to 6½_____ 6½ to 7_____	180 to 185 in center of inner thigh muscle.

[1] Weight of giblets and neck included.
[2] Unstuffed poultry may take slightly less time than stuffed poultry. Cooking time is based on chilled poultry or poultry that has just been thawed—temperature not above 40° F. Frozen unstuffed poultry will take longer. Do not use this roasting guide for frozen commercially stuffed poultry; follow package directions.

(88:38)

Table 35–4   Timetable for Cooking Fish

Cooking method and market form	Approximate ready-to-cook weight or thickness	Cooking temperature	Approximate cooking time in minutes
BAKING			
Dressed	3 pounds	350° F.	45 to 60
Pan-dressed	3 pounds	350° F.	25 to 30
Fillets or steaks	2 pounds	350° F.	20 to 25
Portions	2 pounds	400° F.	15 to 20
Sticks	2¼ pounds	400° F.	15 to 20
BROILING			
Pan-dressed	3 pounds		10 to 16 [1]
Fillets or steaks	½ to 1 inch		10 to 15
Portions	⅜ to ½ inch		10 to 15
Sticks	⅜ to ½ inch		10 to 15
CHARCOAL BROILING			
Pan-dressed	3 pounds	Moderate	10 to 16 [1]
Fillets or steaks	½ to 1 inch	Moderate	10 to 16 [1]
Portions	⅜ to ½ inch	Moderate	8 to 10 [1]
Sticks	⅜ to ½ inch	Moderate	8 to 10 [1]
DEEP-FAT FRYING			
Pan-dressed	3 pounds	350° F.	3 to 5
Fillets or steaks	½ to 1 inch	350° F.	3 to 5
Portions	⅜ to ½ inch	350° F.	3 to 5
Sticks	⅜ to ½ inch	350° F.	3 to 5
OVEN-FRYING			
Pan-dressed	3 pounds	500° F.	15 to 20
Fillets or steaks	½ to 1 inch	500° F.	10 to 15
PAN-FRYING			
Pan-dressed	3 pounds	Moderate	8 to 10 [1]
Fillets or steaks	½ to 1 inch	Moderate	8 to 10 [1]
Portions	⅜ to ½ inch	Moderate	8 to 10 [1]
Sticks	⅜ to ½ inch	Moderate	8 to 10 [1]
POACHING			
Fillets or steaks	2 pounds	Simmer	5 to 10
STEAMING			
Fillets or steaks	2 pounds	Boil	5 to 10

[1] Turn once.

(88:43)

Table 35-5   *Timetable for Roasting Meats*

Kind and cut of meat	Ready-to-cook weight	Approximate roasting time at 325° F.	Internal temperature of meat when done
BEEF	*Pounds*	*Hours*	°*F.*
Standing ribs:			
Rare_____	6 to 8	2½ to 3	140
Medium_____	6 to 8	3 to 3½	160
Well done_____	6 to 8	3⅔ to 5	170
Rolled rump:			
Rare_____	5	2¼	140
Medium_____	5	3	160
Well done_____	5	3¼	170
Sirloin tip:			
Rare_____	3	1½	140
Medium_____	3	2	160
Well done_____	3	2¼	170
VEAL			
Leg_____	5 to 8	2½ to 3½	170
Loin_____	5	3	170
Shoulder_____	6	3½	170
LAMB			
Leg (whole)_____	6 to 7	3¼ to 4	180
Shoulder_____	3 to 6	2¼ to 3¼	180
Rolled shoulder_____	3 to 5	2½ to 3	180
PORK, FRESH			
Loin_____	3 to 5	2 to 4	170
Shoulder_____	5 to 8	3½ to 5	185
Ham, whole_____	10 to 14	5½ to 6	185
Ham, half_____	6	4	185
Spareribs_____	3	2	185
PORK, CURED			
Cook-before-eating:			
Ham, whole_____	12 to 16	3½ to 4¼	160
Ham, half_____	6	2½	160
Picnic shoulder_____	6	3½	170
Fully cooked: [1]			
Ham, whole_____	12 to 16	3 to 3¾	130
Ham, half_____	6	1½ to 2	130

[1] Can also be served without heating, if desired.   (88:30)

Table 35–6　　*Timetable for Broiling Meats*

Kind and cut of meat	Approximate thickness	Degree of doneness	Approximate total cooking time [1]
	Inches		*Minutes*
Beef steaks_____	1	Rare_____	10 to 15
(Club, porterhouse, rib, sirloin,	1	Medium_____	15 to 20
T-bone, tenderloin)	1	Well done_____	20 to 30
	1½	Rare_____	15 to 20
	1½	Medium_____	20 to 25
	1½	Well done_____	25 to 40
	2	Rare_____	25 to 35
	2	Medium_____	35 to 45
	2	Well done_____	45 to 55
Hamburgers_____	¾	Rare_____	8
	¾	Medium_____	12
	¾	Well done_____	14
Lamb chops_____	1	Medium_____	12
(Loin, rib, shoulder)	1	Well done_____	14
	1½	Medium_____	18
	1½	Well done_____	22
Cured ham slices_____	¾	Well done_____	13 to 14
(Cook-before-eating)	1	Well done_____	18 to 20

[1] Meat at refrigerator temperature at start of broiling.　　　　　(88:31)

Table 35–7　　*Timetable for Braising Meats*

Kind and cut of meat	Approximate ready-to-cook weight or thickness	Approximate total cooking time
BEEF		*Hours*
Pot roast, such as chuck or round_____	3 to 5 pounds_____	3 to 4
Steak, such as chuck or round_____	1 to 1½ inches_____	2 to 2½
Short ribs_____	2 to 2½ pounds_____	2 to 2½
VEAL		
Chops_____	½ to ¾ inch_____	¾
Shoulder, rolled_____	3 to 5 pounds_____	2 to 2½
LAMB		
Chops_____	½ to ¾ inch_____	½ to ¾
Shanks_____	1 pound each_____	1½ to 2
Shoulder, rolled_____	3 to 5 pounds_____	2 to 2½
PORK		
Chops_____	½ to 1 inch_____	¾ to 1
Spareribs_____	2 to 3 pounds_____	1½ to 2½

(88:32)

CHAPTER 36

Fruits

Composition of Fruits

Most fruits vary in carbohydrate content from 3 to 25 per cent, but dried fruits such as prunes and raisins are over 70 per cent carbohydrate. Fresh fruits are from 80 to 95 per cent water, and even dried fruits are about 25 per cent water. The protein and fat content of fruits, with the exception of the fat which is found in avocado and olives, is negligible. Peristalsis is stimulated by the organic acids and the bulk provided by the cellulose.

New methods of handling, processing, shipping, and storing keep nutrient losses to a minimum; canned or frozen fruits and vegetables are comparable in nutrient value to fresh fruits and vegetables.

Storage of Fruits

Slightly underripe avocados, peaches, pears, plums, and similar fruits will ripen at room temperature. Cantaloup does not improve in flavor but will soften at room temperature. Watermelons, cantaloups, and Persian and honeydew melons should be cut from the vine at maturity. Casabas, honeyballs, and cranshaws are usually ripened off the vine.

The following is a list of fresh fruits that may be stored in the refrigerator and the time they can be held for high quality:

Apples, eating ripe — 1 week   Grapes — 3 to 5 days
Apricots — 3 to 5 days   Nectarines — 3 to 5 days
Avocados — 3 to 5 days   Peaches — 3 to 5 days
Blackberries — 1 or 2 days   Pears — 3 to 5 days
Blueberries — 3 to 5 days   Plums — 3 to 5 days
Cherries — 1 or 2 days   Raspberries — 1 to 2 days
Cranberries — 1 week   Rhubarb — 3 to 5 days
Figs — 1 or 2 days   Strawberries — 1 or 2 days
     Watermelon — 3 to 5 days   (90:5)

If refrigerated, bananas will turn a dull brown. Fully ripe bananas will keep one or two days and the green-tip bananas for three to five days in a room at 60° to 70° F. Bananas ripen at room temperature and seem to keep better if kept in a paper bag with a moist cloth. Leaving the caps on strawberries and the stems on cherries, not washing them, and placing them loosely in a shallow container will retard molding, thereby extending their refrigerator life. Citrus fruits will keep a few days in a room at 60° to 70° F, but will keep longer if refrigerated; however, cold temperatures may cause the skin to pit and the flesh to discolor. Pineapples should be used promptly after purchasing but can be refrigerated for a day or two. Keep underripe melons at room temperature, but refrigerate ripe melons and use in a few days.

Canned fruits should be stored in a dry place at room temperature not above 70° F. Frozen fruit can be stored in the freezing unit of a refrigerator up to one week. For longer storage, keep in a freezer at 0° F or lower until ready to use and do not refreeze. Dried fruit may be stored in tightly closed containers at room temperature, preferably not above 70° F.

Cooking Fruits

Cooking fruits softens the cellulose walls, adds variety to the menu, and improves the keeping qualities. Unless the fruits are to be canned, the cooking should be at a simmering temperature because the higher temperatures toughen the fruit. Cooking fruits only until tender retains color, flavor, and nutrients. To help fruit keep its shape, drop it into a sugar syrup. Adding the sugar at the beginning makes the fruit less able to absorb moisture and it will hold its shape better. Very firm fruits or fruits to be puréed can be cooked in water, adding sugar during the last few minutes so that they will be softer. Dried fruits are soaked in water before cooking and then cooked in that water.

Fruits which turn color (because of oxidation) when they are peeled may have the original color preserved by dropping the fruit into a weak salt or acid solution or by putting it into fruit juice. Fresh pineapple juice contains an enzyme which not only keeps the white fruits, such as pears, bananas, and apples, from turning dark, but also bleaches them so that they become even whiter. Fresh and frozen pineapple keeps gelatin mixes from solidifying; canned pineapple can be used because its enzymes have been destroyed during the canning process.

SUGGESTED READING

U.S. Department of Agriculture: *Fruits in Family Meals, A Guide for Consumers.* Home and Garden Bulletin No. 125.
University of California Agricultural Extension Service:
  HXT-80, *Drying Fruits at Home.*
  HXT-14, *Fruits and Vegetables for Vitamin C.*
  HXT-32, *Home Canning of Fruits.*

CHAPTER 37

Vegetables

Composition of Vegetables

Most vegetables are from 2 to 25 per cent carbohydrate, but dried vegetables such as dried peas go as high as 60 per cent. Dried vegetables are from 10 to 15 per cent water and fresh vegetables from 80 to 95 per cent. With the exception of legumes, the protein content is poor and little or no fat is found in vegetables. Legumes vary from the 6 per cent protein found in green peas to 14 per cent in fresh soybeans. Vegetable cellulose is a source of bulk in the diet. Table 1–2 lists the nutrients found in each group of vegetables.

Storage of Vegetables

Tomatoes will ripen during storage at room temperature. Unhusked corn stays fresh longer than husked corn. Removing the tops of carrots and beets lessens wilt.

Frozen vegetables should be stored at 0° F or lower and should not be refrozen. Keep canned vegetables in a dry place, preferably not above 70° F. Dried vegetables may be placed in a covered can or jar and kept at room temperature. As the product is used, it is a good practice to transfer the remaining dried food to a smaller jar. Unless the container is kept filled with food, oxidation occurs, with the resulting slight decrease in nutrients.

If vegetables are not used fresh from the garden, the following may be used as a guide for the time they can be held for high quality:

Refrigerated, covered or in a plastic bag
   Asparagus—1 or 2 days
   Beans, snap or wax—3 to 5 days
   Beets, tops removed—1 or 2 weeks
   Broccoli, Brussels sprouts—1 or 2 days
   Cabbage—1 or 2 weeks
   Carrots, tops removed—1 or 2 weeks
   Cauliflower—3 to 5 days

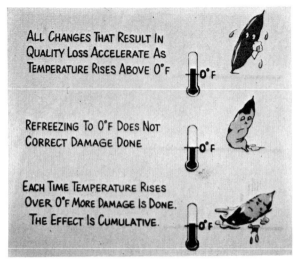

ALL CHANGES THAT RESULT IN
QUALITY LOSS ACCELERATE AS
TEMPERATURE RISES ABOVE 0°F

0°F

REFREEZING TO 0°F DOES NOT
CORRECT DAMAGE DONE

0°F

EACH TIME TEMPERATURE RISES
OVER 0°F MORE DAMAGE IS DONE.
THE EFFECT IS CUMULATIVE.

0°F

Figure 37–1   Frozen vegetable storage. (From Ebbs, J. C.: "New Horizons for Food," *J. Am. Dietet. A.,* Vol. 39, p. 102.)

Celery – 3 to 5 days
Cucumbers – 3 to 5 days
Greens – spinach, kale, collards
    chard, beet, turnip, mustard – 1 or 2 days
Lettuce and other salad greens – 1 or 2 days
Mushrooms – 1 or 2 days
Okra – 3 to 5 days
Onions, green – 1 or 2 days
Parsnips – 1 or 2 weeks
Peppers, green – 3 to 5 days
Radishes, tops removed – 1 or 2 weeks
Squash, summer – 3 to 5 days
Refrigerated, uncovered
Beans, lima, in pods – 1 or 2 days   Peas, in pod – 1 or 2 days
Corn, in husks – 1 or 2 days   Tomatoes – several days

Cool room temperature (60° F or below)
Eggplant – 1 or 2 days
Onions, dry – several weeks in a
    ventilated, open mesh container
Potatoes – several weeks in a dark, dry, ventilated area
Rutabagas – several weeks
Squash, hard-rind winter – several months
Sweet potatoes – several weeks

(91:6)

Many people say they dislike vegetables, especially cooked. An over-cooked vegetable is a tasteless, unattractive thing. Orientals excel in vegetable cookery; the vegetables are never overcooked and they are served immediately.

Vegetables are more colorful and more palatable, and will retain more nutrients, if these rules are followed:

1. *Cooking Time.* All vegetables should be cooked as short a time as possible, but the time varies with the kind of vegetable and its maturity (see Tables 37–1 and 37–2). An overcooked vegetable is not as attractive, colorful, crisp, palatable, or nutritious as the one which is cooked until tender (pierces easily) but has not lost its original shape. Serve immediately. Flavor and nutritive value may be lost if the vegetables are allowed to stand after they become tender. Extended exposure to heat and air reduces vitamin C content.

2. *Amount of Water.* Always drop the uncooked vegetable into boiling water. As soon as boiling resumes, turn the heat down so that evaporation is lessened and scorching avoided. Using a heavy cooking kettle also reduces danger of scorching. Cook mildly flavored vegetables in water one quarter to one half inch deep. Root and strongly flavored vegetables need more water, but tender greens need no water; they can be cooked in the water which adheres to the leaves as they are washed. The liquid from cooked or canned vegetables should be saved because it contains vitamin C, the B complex vitamins, and iron. Use this left over liquid in soup, cream sauce, or gravy.

Water is boiling when the center section rolls toward the edge of the pan. At sea level boiling temperature is 212° F; the temperature is the same if the water rolls gently or very rapidly. It takes the same length of time to cook a vegetable in rapidly or gently boiling water, but in a rapid boil the pieces of vegetable have more tendency to mash or lose their shape.

3. *Size of Pieces.* There is considerable nutrient loss if vegetables are cut and then allowed to stand before being cooked. Cutting vegetables into small pieces increases the amount of surface which is exposed to the cooking water, and thus allows more nutrients to be dissolved. Since vitamins and minerals occur in greatest concentrations near the skin, an unpeeled vegetable will contain more nutrients than a peeled vegetable. The dark green outer leaves of vegetables such as broccoli, cabbage, head lettuce, and romaine are higher in calcium, iron and vitamins; therefore trim them sparingly.

4. *Color Retention.* The chlorophyll in green vegetables turns an olive green color in the presence of acid. Plants contain enough natural vegetable acid to produce color change. Since the volatile vegetable acids are given off during the first few minutes of cooking, a greener color is retained if the utensil is uncovered during the first 1 to 4 minutes of boiling. Adding baking soda retains the color but destroys the vitamins C, K, B_1, and B_2, if present, and ruins the texture of the vegetable. Overcooking turns a bright green vegetable bronze green.

The steps, then, in cooking a green vegetable are the following:

1. Drop the green vegetable into as small an amount as possible of boiling water.

2. Cover until the water comes to a boil.

Table 37–1   *Boiling Guide for Fresh Vegetables*

Vegetable	Cooking time after water returns to boil	Approximate amount as purchased for six servings (about ½ cup each)
	Minutes	*Pounds*
Asparagus	10 to 20 (whole spears)	2½ for spears.
	5 to 15 (cuts and tips)	1¾ to 2 for cuts and tips.
Beans, lima	25 to 30	2¾ in pods.
Beans, snap	12 to 16 (1-inch pieces)	1.
Beets	30 to 45 (young, whole)	2½ with tops or 1½ without tops.
	45 to 90 (older, whole)	
	15 to 25 (sliced or diced)	
Broccoli	10 to 15 (heavy stalks split)	1¾.
Brussels sprouts	15 to 20	1¼.
Cabbage	3 to 10 (shredded)	1¼.
	10 to 15 (wedges)	1½.
Carrots	15 to 20 (young, whole)	1½ without tops.
	20 to 30 (older, whole)	
	10 to 20 (sliced or diced)	
Cauliflower	8 to 15 (separated)	2.
	15 to 25 (whole)	
Celery	15 to 18 (cut up)	1½.
Corn	5 to 15 (on cob)	3 in husks.
Kale	10 to 15	1¼ untrimmed.
Okra	10 to 15	1¼.
Onions, mature	15 to 30	1¾.
Parsnips	20 to 40 (whole)	1½.
	8 to 15 (quartered)	
Peas	12 to 16	3 in pods.
Potatoes	25 to 40 (whole, medium)	1½.
	20 to 25 (quartered)	
	10 to 15 (diced)	
Spinach	3 to 10	2 untrimmed or 1½ prepackaged.
Squash, summer	8 to 15 (sliced)	1½.
Squash, winter	15 to 20 (cut up)	3.
Sweetpotatoes	35 to 55 (whole)	1½.
Tomatoes	7 to 15 (cut up)	1¼.
Turnip greens	10 to 30	2¾ untrimmed.
Turnips	20 to 30 (whole)	1¾ without tops.
	10 to 20 (cut up)	

(91:9)

3. Uncover for one to four minutes depending upon how much vegetable is in the pan.

4. Re-cover and cook until just done.

No vegetable except the green needs to have the vegetable acid volatilized. The other vegetables will retain their color better if the cover remains on the pan throughout the entire cooking period.

The anthocyanin pigment of red vegetables is stable in acid but in alkali will turn blue, yellow, or green, depending upon the degree of alkalinity. Cooking with a cover and adding a few drops of vinegar or lemon juice when ready to serve help retain red color. The red pigment will turn bluish-red or violet when in contact with iron or tin; therefore red fruits and vegetables are canned in lacquered tin cans.

The white pigments are stable in acid but turn yellow in alkali. White vegetables become a yellowish-gray if they are overcooked. This color change also occurs if the water is very hard. Adding a pinch of cream of tartar to the cooking water reduces the color change.

Neither acid nor alkali affects the yellow pigments but the vegetables will darken if excessively overcooked.

Commercially canned vegetables are completely cooked. For serving bring the liquid from the can to a boil, add the vegetable, heat to the boiling point and serve. The nutritive values of commercially canned vegetables are well retained. Water soluble nutrients are distributed evenly in

Table 37-2 *Boiling Guide for Frozen Vegetables*

Vegetable	Cooking time after water returns to boil	Approximate amount as purchased for six servings (½ cup each)
	Minutes	*Ounces*
Asparagus, whole	5 to 10	24
Beans, lima	10 to 18	16
Beans, snap, cut	12 to 20	16
Broccoli spears	8 to 15	20
Brussels sprouts	10 to 15	16
Carrots, sliced or diced	5 to 10	16
Cauliflower	5 to 8	20
Corn:		
Whole kernel	3 to 6	20
On cob	3 to 5	32
Kale	8 to 12	24
Peas	3 to 5	20
Potatoes, small, whole	10 to 12	21
Spinach	5 to 14	24
Squash, summer, sliced	10 to 12	24
Turnip greens	15 to 20	28

(91:14)

Table 37–3 *Boiling Guide for Dry Beans, Peas, and Lentils*[1]

Vegetable (1 cup)	Amount of water	Boiling time	Yield
	Cups	Hours	Cups
Black beans	3	About 2	2
Blackeye beans (blackeye peas, cowpeas)	2½	½	2½
Cranberry beans	3	About 2	2
Great Northern beans	2½	1 to 1½	2½
Kidney beans	3	About 2	2¾
Lentils	[2]2½	½	2½
Lima beans, large	2½	1	2½
Lima beans, small	2½	About ¾	2
Pea (navy) beans	3	1½ to 2	2½
Peas, whole	2½	1	2½
Pinto beans	3	About 2	2½
Split Peas	2¼	⅓	2½

(91:16)

[1]Soak dry beans and whole peas overnight or boil for 2 minutes, remove from heat, soak 1 hour, and then cook.
[2]Add this amount of water; no soaking required.

Table 37–4 *Guide for Cooking Panned Vegetables**
6 servings (½ cup each)

Vegetable	Amount of—				Cooking time
	Vegetable	Fat	Salt	Water	
	Quarts	Tablespoons	Teaspoons	Tablespoons	Minutes
Beans, snap, sliced in 1-inch pieces_____	1	1½	½	10 (½ cup plus 2 table-spoons).	20 to 25.
Cabbage, finely shredded___	1½	1½	¾	3_____	6 to 8.
Carrots, thinly sliced_____	1	2	½	3_____	10.
Corn, cut_____	1	1½	½	6 (¼ cup plus 2 table-spoons).	15 to 18.
Spinach, finely shredded____	3	2	½	_____	6 to 8.
Summer squash, thinly sliced_____	1	1½	½	3_____	12 to 15.

*Panning vegetables
1. Shred or slice vegetable
2. Heat butter, margarine, or drippings in heavy frypan over moderate heat.
3. Add vegetable and spinkle with salt.
4. Add water and cover pan to hold in steam.
5. Cook over low heat until vegetable is tender; stir occasionally to prevent sticking.

(91:13)

Table 37–5 *Give Vegetables a Gourmet Touch With Spices and Herbs*

Vegetable	Spice or herb
Asparagus	Mustard seed, sesame seed, or tarragon.
Lima beans	Marjoram, oregano, sage, savory, tarragon, or thyme.
Snap beans	Basil, dill, marjoram, mint, mustard seed, oregano, savory, tarragon, or thyme.
Beets	Allspice, bay leaves, caraway seed, cloves, dill, ginger, mustard seed, savory, or thyme.
Broccoli	Caraway seed, dill, mustard seed, or tarragon.
Brussels sprouts	Basil, caraway seed, dill, mustard seed, sage, or thyme.
Cabbage	Caraway seed, celery seed, dill, mint, mustard seed, nutmeg, savory, or tarragon.
Carrots	Allspice, bay leaves, caraway seed, dill, fennel, ginger, mace, marjoram, mint, nutmeg, or thyme.
Cauliflower	Caraway seed, celery salt, dill, mace, or tarragon.
Cucumbers	Basil, dill, mint, or tarragon.
Eggplant	Marjoram or oregano.
Onions	Caraway seed, mustard seed, nutmeg, oregano, sage, or thyme.
Peas	Basil, dill, marjoram, mint, oregano, poppy seed, rosemary, sage, or savory.
Potatoes	Basil, bay leaves, caraway seed, celery seed, dill, chives, mustard seed, oregano, poppy seed, or thyme.
Spinach	Basil, mace, marjoram, nutmeg, or oregano.
Squash	Allspice, basil, cinnamon, cloves, fennel, ginger, mustard seed, nutmeg, or rosemary.
Sweetpotatoes	Allspice, cardamom, cinnamon, cloves, or nutmeg.
Tomatoes	Basil, bay leaves, celery seed, oregano, sage, sesame seed, tarragon, or thyme.
Green salads	Basil, chives, dill, or tarragon.

Pepper and parsley may be added to any of the above vegetables. Curry powder is good with creamed vegetables. (91:18)

the solids and liquids. Usually the contents of the can are about one third liquid. If this liquid is discarded, one third of the water soluble nutrients is lost. With the exception of spinach and corn, all home-canned vegetables should be brought to a rolling boil and boiled 15 minutes. It is safer to boil corn and spinach for 20 minutes.

Carefully follow directions for cooking vegetables in the pressure cooker because overcooking occurs in a matter of seconds and will lower quality and nutritive value. Pressure cooking takes less time because steam under pressure has a higher temperature than boiling water. At sea level 5 pounds of pressure has a temperature of 228° F; 10 pounds, 240° F and 15 pounds, 250° F.

Cook frozen vegetables according to the directions on the package. The vegetables should not be thawed before they are added to the boiling water.

Soaking dehydrated or dried vegetables will return the water to the product, but the flavor and texture of dried vegetables are not always as good as those of the fresh vegetables.

SUGGESTED READING

Kraft, Ken and Pat: "Victory Gardens for Vegetable-Hating Kids," *Today's Health*, May, 1970.
Smith, Beverly Bush: "More Winning Ways with Vegetables," *Today's Health*, May, 1970.
U.S. Department of Agriculture: *Vegetables in Family Meals, A Guide for Consumers.*
University of California Agricultural Extension Service: HXT-54, *Home Canning of Vegetables.*

CHAPTER 38

Salads

A salad appeals to the appetite if top quality fruits and vegetables have been used, if the ingredients are simply but attractively arranged and are cold and crisp. Wilting and sogginess are prevented by draining the canned or cooked foods, by drying the greens, and by using just enough salad dressing to moisten. A raw vegetable salad should have its dressing added just before serving.

Salads have many menu uses:

1. The main dish salads will provide the protein of the meal. They may be made of meats, eggs, cheese, fish, poultry, or beans with a cooked or mayonnaise dressing.

2. The salad which accompanies another dish is usually a combination of vegetables or fruits. Tart French dressing, mayonnaise, and cooked dressings are used.

3. Relishes, which often include raw vegetables, may be served without a dressing. Examples of this type are celery stalks stuffed with a cheese mixture or carrot sticks.

4. The dessert salad nearly always is fruit. It may be frozen or a combination of fruits, nuts, cream cheese, marshmallows, or whipped cream. Clear, sweet French dressings, as well as mayonnaise which has been thinned with cream or fruit juice, are used for fruit salads.

French and mayonnaise dressings contain oil and therefore are high in calories. To prevent rancidity, they should be covered and kept in a cool place. The common types of oil used for making these salad dressings are olive, corn, and cottonseed. If cooked dressings are thinned with cream, they too are high in calories.

French dressing is a temporary emulsion of oil and acid. Mayonnaise has the oil held in an emulsified form by egg. Cooked dressings are thickened by egg or starch.

Salads add minerals, vitamins, and bulk to the diet. They often can be used as a nutrient supplement. For example, the protein content of the diet is increased by serving a peach and cottage cheese, a tomato stuffed with tuna, or a pear and grated American cheese salad with a menu which has a meat course.

The four types of lettuce found in many markets are the crisp head, the butterhead, leaf, and romaine. Other leafy vegetables which can be used as greens include Australian lettuce, beet tops, broccoli, chard, chicory, collards, dandelions, endive, escarole, kale, mustard, sorrel, spinach, turnip tops, and watercress.

CHAPTER 39

Simple Desserts

Most people derive satisfaction from having a sweet at the end of a meal. But pastries and puddings which have a high fat content digest slowly and may cause distress to the bed patient; therefore they are either omitted or served in limited quantity.

If extra protein is needed, desserts containing milk and eggs supply it. Powdered milk, concentrated milk, or an extra egg may be added to the recipe. Calories can be increased by using ice cream, ices, frappés, sherbets, fruits canned in sugar syrup, cakes, cookies, and bread, rice, or tapioca puddings. Fresh fruits served as dessert in low calorie meals provide bulk, minerals, and vitamins. The growing child or geriatric patient may benefit if more fruit is used.

Many retail stores stock water-pack canned fruits and gelatin and pudding mixes which contain no sugar but usually have an artificial sweetener.

Desserts may be garnished with sliced or crushed fruit, custard or fruit sauce, whipped evaporated milk or whipped cream, or decorative icings.

As with any other food, the dessert should be attractive; small servings will be more acceptable to the person with a poor appetite.

Cold desserts should be served cold in chilled dishes and hot desserts hot in warmed dishes.

Tables

Table A-1 *Nutritive Value of the Edible Part of Foods*

[Dashes in the columns for nutrients show that no suitable value could be found although there is reason to believe that a measurable amount of the nutrient may be present]

Food, approximate measure, and weight (in grams)	Water	Food energy	Protein	Fat	Fatty acids Saturated (total)	Fatty acids Unsaturated Oleic	Fatty acids Unsaturated Linoleic	Carbohydrate	Calcium	Iron	Vitamin A value	Thiamin	Riboflavin	Niacin	Ascorbic acid
	Per cent	Calories	Grams	Grams	Grams	Grams	Grams	Grams	Milligrams	Milligrams	International units	Milligrams	Milligrams	Milligrams	Milligrams
MILK, CHEESE, CREAM, IMITATION CREAM; RELATED PRODUCTS															
Milk:															
Fluid:															
1 Whole, 3.5% fat ____ 1 cup _____ 244	87	160	9	9	5	3	Trace	12	288	0.1	350	0.07	0.41	0.2	2
2 Nonfat (skim) ____ 1 cup _____ 245	90	90	9	Trace				12	296	.1	10	.09	.44	.2	2
3 Partly skimmed, 2% nonfat milk solids added ____ 1 cup _____ 246	87	145	10	5	3	2	Trace	15	352	.1	200	.10	.52	.2	2
Canned, concentrated, undiluted:															
4 Evaporated, unsweetened ____ 1 cup _____ 252	74	345	18	20	11	7	1	24	635	.3	810	.10	.86	.5	3
5 Condensed, sweetened ____ 1 cup _____ 306	27	980	25	27	15	9	1	166	802	.3	1,100	.24	1.16	.6	3
Dry, nonfat instant:															
6 Low-density (1⅔ cups needed for reconstitution to 1 qt.) ____ 1 cup _____ 68	4	245	24	Trace				35	879	.4	[1]20	.24	1.21	.6	5
7 High-density (⅞ cup needed for reconstitution to 1 qt.) ____ 1 cup _____ 104	4	375	37	1				54	1,345	.6	[1]30	.36	1.85	.9	7
Buttermilk:															
8 Fluid, cultured, made from skim milk. ____ 1 cup _____ 245	90	90	9	Trace				12	296	.1	10	.10	.44	.2	2
9 Dried, packaged ____ 1 cup _____ 120	3	465	41	6	3	2	Trace	60	1,498	.7	260	.31	2.06	1.1	
Cheese:															
Natural:															
Blue or Roquefort type:															
10 Ounce ____ 1 oz. _____ 28	40	105	6	9	5	3	Trace	1	89	.1	350	.01	.17	.3	0
11 Cubic inch ____ 1 cu. in. _____ 17	40	65	4	5	3	2	Trace	Trace	54	.1	210	.01	.11	.2	0

[1] Value applies to unfortified product; value for fortified low-density product would be 1500 I.U. and the fortified high-density product would be 2290 I.U.

Taken from "Nutritive Value of Foods," U.S. Department of Agriculture Home and Garden Bulletin No. 72.

Table A-1 Nutritive Value of the Edible Part of Foods (Continued)

[Dashes in the columns for nutrients show that no suitable value could be found although there is reason to believe that a measurable amount of the nutrient may be present]

	Food, approximate measure, and weight (in grams)	Water	Food energy	Protein	Fat	Fatty acids Saturated (total)	Unsaturated Oleic	Unsaturated Linoleic	Carbohydrate	Calcium	Iron	Vitamin A value	Thiamin	Riboflavin	Niacin	Ascorbic acid
		Percent	Calories	Grams	Grams	Grams	Grams	Grams	Grams	Milligrams	Milligrams	International units	Milligrams	Milligrams	Milligrams	Milligrams
	MILK, CHEESE, CREAM, IMITATION CREAM; RELATED PRODUCTS—Con. Cheese—Continued Natural—Continued															
12	Camembert, packaged in 4-oz. pkg. with 3 wedges per pkg. 1 wedge, 38	52	115	7	9	5	3	Trace	1	40	0.2	380	0.02	0.29	0.3	0
	Cheddar:															
13	Ounce, 1 oz., 28	37	115	7	9	5	3	Trace	1	213	.3	370	.01	.13	Trace	0
14	Cubic inch, 1 cu. in., 17	37	70	4	6	3	2	Trace	Trace	129	.2	230	.01	.08	Trace	0
	Cottage, large or small curd: Creamed:															
15	Package of 12-oz. net wt. 1 pkg., 340	78	360	46	14	8	5	Trace	10	320	1.0	580	.10	.85	.3	0
16	Cup, curd pressed down. 1 cup, 245	78	260	33	10	6	3	Trace	7	230	.7	420	.07	.61	.2	0
	Uncreamed:															
17	Package of 12-oz. net wt. 1 pkg., 340	79	290	58	1	1	Trace	Trace	9	306	1.4	30	.10	.95	.3	0
18	Cup, curd pressed down. 1 cup, 200	79	170	34	1	Trace	Trace	Trace	5	180	.8	20	.06	.56	.2	0
	Cream:															
19	Package of 8-oz. net wt. 1 pkg., 227	51	850	18	86	48	28	3	5	141	.5	3,500	.05	.54	.2	0
20	Package of 3-oz. net wt. 1 pkg., 85	51	320	7	32	18	11	1	2	53	.2	1,310	.02	.20	.1	0
21	Cubic inch, 1 cu. in., 16	51	60	1	6	3	2	Trace	Trace	10	Trace	250	Trace	.04	Trace	0
	Parmesan, grated:															
22	Cup, pressed down. 1 cup, 140	17	655	60	43	24	14	1	5	1,893	.7	1,760	.03	1.22	.3	0
23	Tablespoon. 1 tbsp., 5	17	25	2	2	1	Trace	Trace	Trace	68	Trace	60	Trace	.04	Trace	0
24	Ounce, 1 oz., 28	17	130	12	9	5	3	Trace	1	383	.1	360	.01	.25	.1	0
	Swiss:															
25	Ounce, 1 oz., 28	39	105	8	8	4	3	Trace	1	262	.3	320	Trace	.11	Trace	0
26	Cubic inch, 1 cu. in., 15	39	55	4	4	2	1	Trace	Trace	139	.1	170	Trace	.06	Trace	0

No.	Food	Measure	Grams	Water	Cal.	Protein	Fat	Sat.	Oleic	Lino.	Carb.	Calcium	Iron	Vit. A	Thiamine	Riboflavin	Niacin	Ascorbic
27	Pasteurized processed cheese: American: Ounce	1 oz.	28	40	105	7	9	5	3	Trace	1	198	.3	350	.01	.12	Trace	0
28	Cubic inch	1 cu. in.	18	40	65	4	5	3	2	Trace	Trace	122	.2	210	Trace	.07	Trace	0
29	Swiss: Ounce	1 oz.	28	40	100	8	8	4	3	Trace	Trace	251	.3	310	Trace	.11	Trace	0
30	Cubic inch	1 cu. in.	18	40	65	5	5	3	2	Trace	Trace	159	.2	200	Trace	.07	Trace	0
31	Pasteurized process cheese food, American: Tablespoon	1 tbsp.	14	43	45	3	3	2	1	Trace	1	80	.1	140	Trace	.08	Trace	0
32	Cubic inch	1 cu. in.	18	43	60	4	4	2	1	Trace	1	100	.1	170	Trace	.10	Trace	0
33	Pasteurized process cheese spread, American.	1 oz.	28	49	80	5	6	3	2	Trace	2	160	.2	250	Trace	.15	Trace	0
34	Cream: Half-and-half (cream and milk).	1 cup	242	80	325	8	28	15	9	1	11	261	.1	1,160	.07	.39	.1	2
35		1 tbsp.	15	80	20	1	2	1	1	Trace	1	16	Trace	70	Trace	.02	Trace	Trace
36	Light, coffee or table..	1 cup	240	72	505	7	49	27	16	1	10	245	.1	2,020	.07	.36	.1	2
37		1 tbsp.	15	72	30	1	3	1	1	Trace	1	15	Trace	130	Trace	.02	Trace	Trace
38	Sour	1 cup	230	72	485	7	47	26	16	1	10	235	.1	1,930	.07	.35	.1	2
39		1 tbsp.	12	72	25	Trace	2	1	1	Trace	1	12	Trace	100	Trace	.02	Trace	Trace
40	Whipped topping (pressurized).	1 cup	60	62	155	2	14	8	5	Trace	6	67	Trace	570	Trace	.04		Trace
41		1 tbsp.	3	62	10	Trace	1	Trace	Trace	Trace	Trace	3		30		Trace		
42	Whipping, unwhipped (volume about double when whipped): Light	1 cup	239	62	715	6	75	41	25	2	9	203	.1	3,060	.05	.29	.1	2
43		1 tbsp.	15	62	45	Trace	5	3	2	Trace	1	13	Trace	190	Trace	.02	Trace	Trace
44	Heavy	1 cup	238	57	840	5	90	50	30	3	7	179	.1	3,670	.05	.26	.1	2
45		1 tbsp.	15	57	55	Trace	6	3	2	Trace	1	11	Trace	230	Trace	.02	Trace	Trace
46	Imitation cream products (made with vegetable fat): Creamers: Powdered	1 cup	94	2	505	4	33	31	1	0	52	21	.6	[2]200	0	Trace		
47		1 tsp.	2	2	10	Trace	Trace	Trace	Trace	0	1	1	Trace	Trace	0			
48	Liquid (frozen)	1 cup	245	77	345	3	27	25	1	0	25	29	Trace	[2]100	0			
49		1 tbsp.	15	77	20	Trace	2	1	Trace	0	2	2		[2]10	0			
50	Sour dressing (imitation sour cream) made with nonfat dry milk.	1 cup	235	72	440	9	38	35	1	Trace	17	277	.1	10	.07	.38	.2	1
51		1 tbsp.	12	72	20	Trace	2	2	Trace	Trace	1	14	Trace	Trace	Trace	Trace	Trace	Trace
52	Whipped topping: Pressurized	1 cup	70	61	190	1	17	15	1	0	9	5		[2]340	0	Trace	Trace	Trace
53		1 tbsp.	4	61	10	Trace	1	1	Trace	0	Trace	Trace		[2]20	0			

[2] Contributed largely from beta-carotene used for coloring.

Table continued on following page

Table A-1   Nutritive Value of the Edible Part of Foods (Continued)

[Dashes in the columns for nutrients show that no suitable value could be found although there is reason to believe that a measurable amount of the nutrient may be present]

	Food, approximate measure, and weight (in grams)	Water	Food energy	Protein	Fat	Fatty acids — Saturated (total)	Fatty acids — Unsaturated Oleic	Fatty acids — Unsaturated Linoleic	Carbohydrate	Calcium	Iron	Vitamin A value	Thiamin	Riboflavin	Niacin	Ascorbic acid
		Percent	Calories	Grams	Grams	Grams	Grams	Grams	Grams	Milligrams	Milligrams	International units	Milligrams	Milligrams	Milligrams	Milligrams
	MILK, CHEESE, CREAM, IMITATION CREAM; RELATED PRODUCTS—Con.															
	Whipped topping—Continued															
54	Frozen .... 1 cup 75	52	230	1	20	18	Trace	0	15	5	---	²560	---	0	---	0
55	1 tbsp. 4	52	10	Trace	1	1	Trace	0	1	Trace	---	²30	---	0	---	0
56	Powdered, made with whole milk. 1 cup 75	58	175	3	12	10	1	Trace	15	62	Trace	²330	.02	.08	.1	Trace
57	1 tbsp. 4	58	10	Trace	1	1	Trace	Trace	1	3	Trace	²20	Trace	Trace	Trace	Trace
	Milk beverages:															
58	Cocoa, homemade ... 1 cup 250	79	245	10	12	7	4	Trace	27	295	1.0	400	.10	.45	.5	3
59	Chocolate-flavored drink made with skim milk and 2% added butterfat. 1 cup 250	83	190	8	6	3	2	Trace	27	270	.5	210	.10	.40	.3	3
	Malted milk:															
60	Dry powder, approx. 3 heaping teaspoons per ounce. 1 oz. 28	3	115	4	2	---	---	---	20	82	.6	290	.09	.15	.1	0
61	Beverage .... 1 cup 235	78	245	11	10	---	---	---	28	317	.7	590	.14	.49	.2	2
	Milk desserts:															
62	Custard, baked ..... 1 cup 265	77	305	14	15	7	5	1	29	297	1.1	930	.11	.50	.3	1
	Ice cream:															
63	Regular (approx. 10% fat). ½ gal. 1,064	63	2,055	48	113	62	37	3	221	1,553	.5	4,680	.43	2.23	1.1	11
64	1 cup 133	63	255	6	14	8	5	Trace	28	194	.1	590	.05	.28	.1	1
65	3 fl. oz. cup ... 50	63	95	2	5	3	2	Trace	10	73	Trace	220	.02	.11	.1	1
66	Rich (approx. 16% fat). ½ gal. 1,188	63	2,635	31	191	105	63	6	214	927	.2	7,840	.24	1.31	1.2	12
67	1 cup 148	63	330	4	24	13	8	1	27	115	Trace	980	.03	.16	.1	1
	Ice milk:															
68	Hardened .... ½ gal. 1,048	67	1,595	50	53	29	17	2	235	1,635	1.0	2,200	.52	2.31	1.0	10
69	1 cup 131	67	200	6	7	4	2	Trace	29	204	.1	280	.07	.29	.1	1
70	Soft-serve .... 1 cup 175	67	265	8	9	5	3	Trace	39	273	.2	370	.09	.39	.2	2

No.	Food	Measure	Grams	Water (%)	Food energy (cal.)	Protein (g)	Fat (g)	Saturated fatty acids (g)	Oleic (g)	Linoleic (g)	Carbohydrate (g)	Calcium (mg)	Iron (mg)	Vitamin A (I.U.)	Thiamine (mg)	Riboflavin (mg)	Niacin (mg)	Ascorbic acid (mg)
	Yoghurt:																	
71	Made from partially skimmed milk.	1 cup	245	89	125	8	4	2	1	Trace	13	294	.1	170	.10	.44	.2	2
72	Made from whole milk	1 cup	245	88	150	7	8	5	3	Trace	12	272	.1	340	.07	.39	.2	2
	EGGS																	
	Eggs, large, 24 ounces per dozen:																	
	Raw or cooked in shell or with nothing added:																	
73	Whole, without shell	1 egg	50	74	80	6	6	2	3	Trace	Trace	27	1.1	590	.05	.15	Trace	0
74	White of egg	1 white	33	88	15	4	Trace	—	—	—	Trace	3	Trace	0	Trace	.09	Trace	0
75	Yolk of egg	1 yolk	17	51	60	3	5	2	2	Trace	Trace	24	.9	580	.04	.07	Trace	0
76	Scrambled with milk and fat.	1 egg	64	72	110	7	8	3	3	Trace	1	51	1.1	690	.05	.18	Trace	0
	MEAT, POULTRY, FISH, SHELLFISH; RELATED PRODUCTS																	
77	Bacon, (20 slices per lb. raw), broiled or fried, crisp.	2 slices	15	8	90	5	8	3	4	1	1	2	.5	0	.08	.05	.8	—
	Beef,³ cooked:																	
	Cuts braised, simmered, or pot-roasted:																	
78	Lean and fat	3 ounces	85	53	245	23	16	8	7	Trace	0	10	2.9	30	.04	.18	3.5	—
79	Lean only	2.5 ounces	72	62	140	22	5	2	2	Trace	0	10	2.7	10	.04	.16	3.3	—
	Hamburger (ground beef), broiled:																	
80	Lean	3 ounces	85	60	185	23	10	5	4	Trace	0	10	3.0	20	.08	.20	5.1	—
81	Regular	3 ounces	85	54	245	21	17	8	8	Trace	0	9	2.7	30	.07	.18	4.6	—
	Roast, oven-cooked, no liquid added:																	
	Relatively fat, such as rib:																	
82	Lean and fat	3 ounces	85	40	375	17	34	16	15	1	0	8	2.2	70	.05	.13	3.1	—
83	Lean only	1.8 ounces	51	57	125	14	7	3	3	Trace	0	6	1.8	10	.04	.11	2.6	—
	Relatively lean, such as heel of round:																	
84	Lean and fat	3 ounces	85	62	165	25	7	3	3	Trace	0	11	3.2	10	.06	.19	4.5	—
85	Lean only	2.7 ounces	78	65	125	24	3	1	1	Trace	0	10	3.0	Trace	.06	.18	4.3	—
	Steak, broiled:																	
	Relatively fat, such as sirloin:																	
86	Lean and fat	3 ounces	85	44	330	20	27	13	12	1	0	9	2.5	50	.05	.16	4.0	—
87	Lean only	2.0 ounces	56	59	115	18	4	2	2	Trace	0	7	2.2	10	.05	.14	3.6	—
	Relatively lean, such as round:																	
88	Lean and fat	3 ounces	85	55	220	24	13	6	6	Trace	0	10	3.0	20	.07	.19	4.8	—
89	Lean only	2.4 ounces	68	61	130	21	4	2	2	Trace	0	9	2.5	10	.06	.16	4.1	—
	Beef, canned:																	
90	Corned beef	3 ounces	85	59	185	22	10	5	4	Trace	0	17	3.7	20	.01	.20	2.9	—
91	Corned beef hash	3 ounces	85	67	155	19	10	5	4	Trace	9	11	1.7	—	.01	.08	1.8	—
92	Beef, dried or chipped	2 ounces	57	48	115	15	4	2	2	Trace	0	11	2.9	—	.04	.18	2.2	—
93	Beef and vegetable stew	1 cup	235	82	210	15	10	5	4	Trace	15	28	2.8	2,310	.13	.17	4.4	15

² Contributed largely from beta-carotene used for coloring.

³ Outer layer of fat on the cut was removed to within approximately ½-inch of the lean. Deposits of fat within the cut were not removed.

Table continued on following page

Table A-1   Nutritive Value of the Edible Part of Foods (Continued)

[Dashes in the columns for nutrients show that no suitable value could be found although there is reason to believe that a measurable amount of the nutrient may be present]

	Food, approximate measure, and weight (in grams)	Water	Food energy	Pro-tein	Fat	Fatty acids — Satu-rated (total)	Fatty acids — Unsaturated Oleic	Fatty acids — Unsaturated Lin-oleic	Carbo-hy-drate	Cal-cium	Iron	Vita-min A value	Thia-min	Ribo-flavin	Niacin	Ascor-bic acid
		Per-cent	Calo-ries	Grams	Grams	Grams	Grams	Grams	Grams	Milli-grams	Milli-grams	Inter-national units	Milli-grams	Milli-grams	Milli-grams	Milli-grams
	MEAT, POULTRY, FISH, SHELLFISH; RELATED PRODUCTS—Continued															
94	Beef potpie, baked, 4¼-inch diam., weight before baking about 8 ounces. 1 pie — 227 g	55	560	23	33	9	20	2	43	32	4.1	1,860	0.25	0.27	4.5	7
	Chicken, cooked:															
95	Flesh only, broiled — 3 ounces — 85	71	115	20	3	1	1	1	0	8	1.4	80	.05	.16	7.4	---
	Breast, fried, ½ breast:															
96	With bone — 3.3 ounces — 94	58	155	25	5	1	2	1	1	9	1.3	70	.04	.17	11.2	---
97	Flesh and skin only — 2.7 ounces — 76	58	155	25	5	1	2	1	1	9	1.3	70	.04	.17	11.2	---
	Drumstick, fried:															
98	With bone — 2.1 ounces — 59	55	90	12	4	1	2	1	Trace	6	.9	50	.03	.15	2.7	---
99	Flesh and skin only — 1.3 ounces — 38	55	90	12	4	1	2	1	Trace	6	.9	50	.03	.15	2.7	---
100	Chicken, canned, boneless 3 ounces — 85	65	170	18	10	3	4	2	0	18	1.3	200	.03	.11	3.7	3
101	Chicken potpie, baked 4¼-inch diam., weight before baking about 8 ounces. 1 pie — 227	57	535	23	31	10	15	3	42	68	3.0	3,020	.25	.26	4.1	5
	Chili con carne, canned:															
102	With beans — 1 cup — 250	72	335	19	15	7	7	Trace	30	80	4.2	150	.08	.18	3.2	---
103	Without beans — 1 cup — 255	67	510	26	38	18	17	1	15	97	3.6	380	.05	.31	5.6	---
104	Heart, beef, lean, braised 3 ounces — 85	61	160	27	5	---	---	---	1	5	5.0	20	.21	1.04	6.5	1
	Lamb,³ cooked:															
105	Chop, thick, with bone, 1 chop, 4.8 ounces. broiled. 1 chop — 137	47	400	25	33	18	12	1	0	10	1.5	---	.14	.25	5.6	---
106	Lean and fat — 4.0 ounces — 112	47	400	25	33	18	12	1	0	10	1.5	---	.14	.25	5.6	---
107	Lean only — 2.6 ounces — 74	62	140	21	6	3	2	Trace	0	9	1.5	---	.11	.20	4.5	---
	Leg, roasted:															
108	Lean and fat — 3 ounces — 85	54	235	22	16	9	6	Trace	0	9	1.4	---	.13	.23	4.7	---
109	Lean only — 2.5 ounces — 71	62	130	20	5	3	2	Trace	0	9	1.4	---	.12	.21	4.4	---
	Shoulder, roasted:															
110	Lean and fat — 3 ounces — 85	50	285	18	23	13	8	1	0	9	1.0	---	.11	.20	4.0	---
111	Lean only — 2.3 ounces — 64	61	130	17	6	3	2	Trace	0	8	1.0	---	.10	.18	3.7	---

No.	Food and description	Approximate measure	Weight (g)	Water (%)	Food energy (cal)	Protein (g)	Fat (g)	Saturated fatty acids (g)	Oleic (g)	Linoleic (g)	Carbohydrate (g)	Calcium (mg)	Iron (mg)	Vitamin A (IU)	Thiamine (mg)	Riboflavin (mg)	Niacin (mg)	Ascorbic acid (mg)
112	Liver, beef, fried	2 ounces	57	57	130	15	6	---	---	---	3	6	5.0	30,280	.15	2.37	9.4	15
	Pork, cured, cooked:																	
113	Ham, light cure, lean and fat, roasted	3 ounces	85	54	245	18	19	7	8	2	0	8	2.2	0	.40	.16	3.1	---
	Luncheon meat:																	
114	Boiled ham, sliced	2 ounces	57	59	135	11	10	4	4	1	0	6	1.6	0	.25	.09	1.5	---
115	Canned, spiced or unspiced	2 ounces	57	55	165	8	14	5	6	1	1	5	1.2	0	.18	.12	1.6	---
	Pork, fresh,³ cooked:																	
116	Chop, thick, with bone	1 chop, 3.5 ounces	98	42	260	16	21	8	9	2	0	8	2.2	0	.63	.18	3.8	---
117	Lean and fat	2.3 ounces	66	42	260	16	21	8	9	2	0	8	2.2	0	.63	.18	3.8	---
118	Lean only	1.7 ounces	48	53	130	15	7	2	3	1	0	7	1.9	0	.54	.16	3.3	---
	Roast, oven-cooked, no liquid added:																	
119	Lean and fat	3 ounces	85	46	310	21	24	9	10	2	0	9	2.7	0	.78	.22	4.7	---
120	Lean only	2.4 ounces	68	55	175	20	10	3	4	1	0	9	2.6	0	.73	.21	4.4	---
	Cuts, simmered:																	
121	Lean and fat	3 ounces	85	46	320	20	26	9	11	2	0	8	2.5	0	.46	.21	4.1	---
122	Lean only	2.2 ounces	63	60	135	18	6	2	3	1	0	8	2.3	0	.42	.19	3.7	---
	Sausage:																	
123	Bologna, slice, 3-in. diam. by ⅛ inch	2 slices	26	56	80	3	7				Trace	2	.5	---	.04	.06	.7	---
124	Braunschweiger, slice 2-in. diam. by ¼ inch	2 slices	20	53	65	3	5			Trace	Trace	2	1.2	1,310	.03	.29	1.6	---
125	Deviled ham, canned	1 tbsp.	13	51	45	2	4	2	2	Trace	0	1	.3	---	.02	.01	.2	---
126	Frankfurter, heated (8 per lb. purchased pkg.)	1 frank	56	57	170	7	15			1	1	3	.8	---	.08	.11	1.4	---
127	Pork links, cooked (16 links per lb. raw)	2 links	26	35	125	5	11	4	5	1	Trace	2	.6	0	.21	.09	1.0	---
128	Salami, dry type	1 oz.	28	30	130	7	11				Trace	4	1.0	---	.10	.07	1.5	---
129	Salami, cooked	1 oz.	28	51	90	5	7				Trace	3	.7	---	.07	.07	1.2	---
130	Vienna, canned (7 sausages per 5-oz. can)	1 sausage	16	63	40	2	3				Trace	1	.3	---	.01	.02	.4	---
	Veal, medium fat, cooked, bone removed:																	
131	Cutlet	3 oz.	85	60	185	23	9	5	4	Trace	0	9	2.7	---	.06	.21	4.6	---
132	Roast	3 oz.	85	55	230	23	14	7	6	Trace	0	10	2.9	---	.11	.26	6.6	---
	Fish and shellfish:																	
133	Bluefish, baked with table fat	3 oz.	85	68	135	22	4				0	25	.6	40	.09	.08	1.6	---
	Clams:																	
134	Raw, meat only	3 oz.	85	82	65	11	1				2	59	5.2	90	.08	.15	1.1	8
135	Canned, solids and liquid	3 oz.	85	86	45	7	1				2	47	3.5	---	.01	.09	.9	---
136	Crabmeat, canned	3 oz.	85	77	85	15	2				1	38	.7	---	.07	.07	1.6	---

³ Outer layer of fat on the cut was removed to within approximately ½-inch of the lean. Deposits of fat within the cut were not removed.

Table continued on following page

Table A-1   Nutritive Value of the Edible Part of Foods (Continued)

[Dashes in the columns for nutrients show that no suitable value could be found although there is reason to believe that a measurable amount of the nutrient may be present]

	Food, approximate measure, and weight (in grams)	Water	Food energy	Protein	Fat	Fatty acids Saturated (total)	Fatty acids Unsaturated Oleic	Fatty acids Unsaturated Linoleic	Carbohydrate	Calcium	Iron	Vitamin A value	Thiamin	Riboflavin	Niacin	Ascorbic acid
		Per cent	Calories	Grams	Grams	Grams	Grams	Grams	Grams	Milligrams	Milligrams	International units	Milligrams	Milligrams	Milligrams	Milligrams
	MEAT, POULTRY, FISH, SHELLFISH; RELATED PRODUCTS—Continued															
	Fish and shellfish—Continued															
137	Fish sticks, breaded, cooked, frozen; stick 3¾ by 1 by ½ inch. 10 sticks or 8 oz. pkg. Grams 227	66	400	38	20	5	4	10	15	25	0.9	----	0.09	0.16	3.6	----
138	Haddock, breaded, fried 3 oz. 85	66	140	17	5	1	3	Trace	5	34	1.0	----	.03	.06	2.7	2
139	Ocean perch, breaded, fried 3 oz. 85	59	195	16	11	----	----	----	6	28	1.1	----	.08	.09	1.5	----
140	Oysters, raw, meat only (13–19 med. selects). 1 cup 240	85	160	20	4	----			8	226	13.2	740	.33	.43	6.0	----
141	Salmon, pink, canned 3 oz. 85	71	120	17	5	1	1	Trace	0	⁴167	.7	60	.03	.16	6.8	----
142	Sardines, Atlantic, canned in oil, drained solids. 3 oz. 85	62	175	20	9	----			0	372	2.5	190	.02	.17	4.6	----
143	Shad, baked with table fat and bacon. 3 oz. 85	64	170	20	10	----			0	20	.5	20	.11	.22	7.3	----
144	Shrimp, canned, meat 3 oz. 85	70	100	21	1	----			1	98	2.6	50	.01	.03	1.5	----
145	Swordfish, broiled with butter or margarine. 3 oz. 85	65	150	24	5	----			0	23	1.1	1,750	.03	.04	9.3	----
146	Tuna, canned in oil, drained solids. 3 oz. 85	61	170	24	7	2	1	1	0	7	1.6	70	.04	.10	10.1	----
	MATURE DRY BEANS AND PEAS, NUTS, PEANUTS; RELATED PRODUCTS															
147	Almonds, shelled, whole kernels. 1 cup 142	5	850	26	77	6	52	15	28	332	6.7	0	.34	1.31	5.0	Trace
	Beans, dry: Common varieties as Great Northern, navy, and others: Cooked, drained:															
148	Great Northern 1 cup 180	69	210	14	1	----			38	90	4.9	0	.25	.13	1.3	0

No.	Food, approximate measure	Measure	g	%	cal	prot	fat	sat	oleic	lin	carb	Ca	Fe	vit A	thia	ribo	niac	asc
149	Navy (pea)	1 cup	190	69	225	15	1	—	—	—	40	95	5.1	0	.27	.13	1.3	0
	Canned, solids and liquid: White with—																	
150	Frankfurters (sliced)	1 cup	255	71	365	19	18	—	—	—	32	94	4.8	330	.18	.15	3.3	Trace
151	Pork and tomato sauce	1 cup	255	71	310	16	7	2	3	1	49	138	4.6	330	.20	.08	1.5	5
152	Pork and sweet sauce	1 cup	255	66	385	16	12	4	5	1	54	161	5.9	—	.15	.10	1.3	—
153	Red kidney	1 cup	255	76	230	15	1	—	—	—	42	74	4.6	10	.13	.10	1.5	—
154	Lima, cooked, drained	1 cup	190	64	260	16	1	—	—	—	49	55	5.9	—	.25	.11	1.3	—
155	Cashew nuts, roasted	1 cup	140	5	785	24	64	11	45	4	41	53	5.3	140	.60	.35	2.5	—
	Coconut, fresh, meat only:																	
156	Pieces, approx. 2 by 2 by 1/2 inch	1 piece	45	51	155	2	16	14	1	Trace	4	6	.8	0	.02	.01	.2	1
157	Shredded or grated, firmly packed	1 cup	130	51	450	5	46	39	3	Trace	12	17	2.2	0	.07	.03	.7	4
158	Cowpeas or blackeye peas, dry, cooked	1 cup	248	80	190	13	1	—	—	—	34	42	3.2	20	.41	.11	1.1	Trace
159	Peanuts, roasted, salted, halves	1 cup	144	2	840	37	72	16	31	21	27	107	3.0	—	.46	.19	24.7	0
160	Peanut butter	1 tbsp	16	2	95	4	8	2	4	2	3	9	.3	—	.02	.02	2.4	0
161	Peas, split, dry, cooked	1 cup	250	70	290	20	1	—	—	—	52	28	4.2	100	.37	.22	2.2	—
162	Pecans, halves	1 cup	108	3	740	10	77	5	48	15	16	79	2.6	140	.93	.14	1.0	2
163	Walnuts, black or native, chopped	1 cup	126	3	790	26	75	4	26	36	19	Trace	7.6	380	.28	.14	.9	—
	VEGETABLES AND VEGETABLE PRODUCTS																	
	Asparagus, green: Cooked, drained:																	
164	Spears, 1/2-in. diam. at base	4 spears	60	94	10	1	Trace				2	13	.4	540	.10	.11	.8	16
165	Pieces, 1 1/2 to 2-in. lengths	1 cup	145	94	30	3	Trace				5	30	.9	1,310	.23	.26	2.0	38
166	Canned, solids and liquid	1 cup	244	94	45	5	1				7	44	4.1	1,240	.15	.22	2.0	37
	Beans:																	
167	Lima, immature seeds, cooked, drained	1 cup	170	71	190	13	1				34	80	4.3	480	.31	.17	2.2	29
	Snap: Green:																	
168	Cooked, drained	1 cup	125	92	30	2	Trace				7	63	.8	680	.09	.11	.6	15
169	Canned, solids and liquid	1 cup	239	94	45	2	Trace				10	81	2.9	690	.07	.10	.7	10

⁴ If bones are discarded, value will be greatly reduced.

Table continued on following page

Table A–1   Nutritive Value of the Edible Part of Foods *(Continued)*

[Dashes in the columns for nutrients show that no suitable value could be found although there is reason to believe that a measurable amount of the nutrient may be present]

Food, approximate measure, and weight (in grams)			Water	Food energy	Protein	Fat	Fatty acids			Carbohydrate	Calcium	Iron	Vitamin A value	Thiamin	Riboflavin	Niacin	Ascorbic acid
							Saturated (total)	Unsaturated									
								Oleic	Linoleic								
		Grams	Per cent	Calories	Grams	Grams	Grams	Grams	Grams	Grams	Milligrams	Milligrams	International units	Milligrams	Milligrams	Milligrams	Milligrams
VEGETABLES AND VEGETABLE PRODUCTS—Continued																	
Beans—Continued																	
Snap—Continued																	
Yellow or wax:																	
170 Cooked, drained	1 cup	125	93	30	2	Trace				6	63	0.8	290	0.09	0.11	0.6	16
171 Canned, solids and liquid.	1 cup	239	94	45	2	1				10	81	2.9	140	.07	.10	.7	12
172 Sprouted mung beans, cooked, drained.	1 cup	125	91	35	4	Trace				7	21	1.1	30	.11	.13	.9	8
Beets:																	
173 Cooked, drained, peeled: Whole beets, 2-in. diam.	2 beets	100	91	30	1	Trace				7	14	.5	20	.03	.04	.3	6
174 Diced or sliced	1 cup	170	91	55	2	Trace				12	24	.9	30	.05	.07	.5	10
175 Canned, solids and liquid.	1 cup	246	90	85	2	Trace				19	34	1.5	20	.02	.05	.2	7
176 Beet greens, leaves and stems, cooked, drained.	1 cup	145	94	25	3	Trace				5	144	2.8	7,400	.10	.22	.4	22
Blackeye peas. See Cowpeas.																	
Broccoli, cooked, drained:																	
177 Whole stalks, medium size.	1 stalk	180	91	45	6	1				8	158	1.4	4,500	.16	.36	1.4	162
178 Stalks cut into ½-in. pieces.	1 cup	155	91	40	5	1				7	136	1.2	3,880	.14	.31	1.2	140
179 Chopped, yield from 10-oz. frozen pkg.	1⅔ cups	250	92	65	7	1				12	135	1.8	6,500	.15	.30	1.3	143
180 Brussels sprouts, 7-8 sprouts (1¼ to 1½ in. diam.) per cup, cooked.	1 cup	155	88	55	7	1				10	50	1.7	810	.12	.22	1.2	135
Cabbage: Common varieties:																	

No.	Food	Measure	Grams	Water (%)	Food energy	Protein (g)	Fat (g)	Saturated	Oleic	Linoleic	Carbohydrate (g)	Calcium (mg)	Iron (mg)	Vitamin A (I.U.)	Thiamine (mg)	Riboflavin (mg)	Niacin (mg)	Ascorbic acid (mg)
181	Cabbage: Raw: Coarsely shredded or sliced.	1 cup	70	92	15	1	Trace	---	---	---	4	34	.3	90	.04	.04	.2	33
182	Finely shredded or chopped.	1 cup	90	92	20	1	Trace	---	---	---	5	44	.4	120	.05	.05	.3	42
183	Cooked.	1 cup	145	94	30	2	Trace	---	---	---	6	64	.4	190	.06	.06	.4	48
184	Red, raw, coarsely shredded.	1 cup	70	90	20	1	Trace	---	---	---	5	29	.6	30	.06	.04	.3	43
185	Savoy, raw, coarsely shredded.	1 cup	70	92	15	2	Trace	---	---	---	3	47	.6	140	.04	.06	.2	39
186	Cabbage, celery or Chinese, raw, cut in 1-in. pieces.	1 cup	75	95	10	1	Trace	---	---	---	2	32	.5	110	.03	.03	.5	19
187	Cabbage, spoon (or pakchoy), cooked.	1 cup	170	95	25	2	Trace	---	---	---	4	252	1.0	5,270	.07	.14	1.2	26
188	Carrots: Raw: Whole, 5½ by 1 inch, (25 thin strips).	1 carrot	50	88	20	1	Trace	---	---	---	5	18	.4	5,500	.03	.03	.3	4
189	Grated.	1 cup	110	88	45	1	Trace	---	---	---	11	41	.8	12,100	.06	.06	.7	9
190	Cooked, diced.	1 cup	145	91	45	1	Trace	---	---	---	10	48	.9	15,220	.08	.07	.7	9
191	Canned, strained or chopped (baby food).	1 ounce	28	92	10	Trace	Trace	---	---	---	2	7	.1	3,690	.01	.01	.1	1
192	Cauliflower, cooked, flowerbuds.	1 cup	120	93	25	3	Trace	---	---	---	5	25	.8	70	.11	.10	.7	66
193	Celery, raw: Stalk, large outer, 8 by about 1½ inches, at root end.	1 stalk	40	94	5	Trace	Trace	---	---	---	2	16	.1	100	.01	.01	.1	4
194	Pieces, diced.	1 cup	100	94	15	1	Trace	---	---	---	4	39	.3	240	.03	.03	.3	9
195	Collards, cooked.	1 cup	190	91	55	5	1	---	---	---	9	289	1.1	10,260	.27	.37	2.4	87
196	Corn, sweet: Cooked, ear 5 by 1¾ inches[5].	1 ear	140	74	70	3	1	---	---	---	16	2	.5	[6]310	.09	.08	1.0	7
197	Canned, solids and liquid.	1 cup	256	81	170	5	2	---	---	---	40	10	1.0	[6]690	.07	.12	2.3	13
198	Cowpeas, cooked, immature seeds.	1 cup	160	72	175	13	1	---	---	---	29	38	3.4	560	.49	.18	2.3	28
199	Cucumbers, 10-ounce; 7½ by about 2 inches: Raw, pared.	1 cucumber	207	96	30	1	Trace	---	---	---	7	35	.6	Trace	.07	.09	.4	23
200	Raw, pared, center slice ⅛-inch thick.	6 slices	50	96	5	Trace	Trace	---	---	---	2	8	.2	Trace	.02	.02	.1	6
201	Dandelion greens, cooked.	1 cup	180	90	60	4	1	---	---	---	12	252	3.2	21,060	.24	.29	---	32

[5] Measure and weight apply to entire vegetable or fruit including parts not usually eaten.

[6] Based on yellow varieties; white varieties contain only a trace of cryptoxanthin and carotenes, the pigments in corn that have biological activity.

Table continued on following page

Table A-1 *Nutritive Value of the Edible Part of Foods (Continued)*

[Dashes in the columns for nutrients show that no suitable value could be found although there is reason to believe that a measurable amount of the nutrient may be present]

	Food, approximate measure, and weight (in grams)	Water	Food energy	Pro-tein	Fat	Fatty acids Satu-rated (total)	Unsaturated Oleic	Unsaturated Lin-oleic	Carbo-hy-drate	Cal-cium	Iron	Vita-min A value	Thia-min	Ribo-flavin	Niacin	Ascor-bic acid
		Per-cent	*Calo-ries*	*Grams*	*Grams*	*Grams*	*Grams*	*Grams*	*Grams*	*Milli-grams*	*Milli-grams*	*Inter-national units*	*Milli-grams*	*Milli-grams*	*Milli-grams*	*Milli-grams*
	VEGETABLES AND VEGETABLE PRODUCTS—Continued															
202	Endive, curly (including escarole). 2 ounces ... 57 *Grams*	93	10	1	Trace				2	46	1.0	1,870	0.04	0.08	0.3	6
203	Kale, leaves including stems, cooked. 1 cup ... 110	91	30	4	1				4	147	1.3	8,140				68
	Lettuce, raw:															
204	Butterhead, as Boston types; head, 4-inch diameter. 1 head ... 220	95	30	3	Trace				6	77	4.4	2,130	.14	.13	.6	18
205	Crisphead, as Iceberg; head, 4¾-inch diameter. 1 head ... 454	96	60	4	Trace				13	91	2.3	1,500	.29	.27	1.3	29
206	Looseleaf, or bunching varieties, leaves. 2 large ... 50	94	10	1	Trace				2	34	.7	950	.03	.04	.2	9
207	Mushrooms, canned, solids and liquid. 1 cup ... 244	93	40	5	Trace				6	15	1.2	Trace	.04	.60	4.8	4
208	Mustard greens, cooked. 1 cup ... 140	93	35	3	1				6	193	2.5	8,120	.11	.19	.9	68
209	Okra, cooked, pod 3 by ⅜ inch. 8 pods ... 85	91	25	2	Trace				5	78	.4	420	.11	.15	.8	17
	Onions: Mature:															
210	Raw, onion 2½-inch diameter. 1 onion ... 110	89	40	2	Trace				10	30	.6	40	.04	.04	.2	11
211	Cooked. 1 cup ... 210	92	60	3	Trace				14	50	.8	80	.06	.06	.4	14
212	Young green, small, without tops. 6 onions ... 50	88	20	1	Trace				5	20	.3	Trace	.02	.02	.2	12
213	Parsley, raw, chopped. 1 tablespoon ... 4	85	Trace	Trace	Trace				Trace	8	.2	340	Trace	.01	Trace	7
214	Parsnips, cooked. 1 cup ... 155	82	100	2	1				23	70	.9	50	.11	.12	.2	16
	Peas, green:															
215	Cooked. 1 cup ... 160	82	115	9	1				19	37	2.9	860	.44	.17	3.7	33
216	Canned, solids and liquid. 1 cup ... 249	83	165	9	1				31	50	4.2	1,120	.23	.13	2.2	22

No.	Food, approximate measure	Measure	Grams	Water (%)	Food energy (Cal.)	Protein (g)	Fat (g)	Saturated fat (g)	Oleic (g)	Linoleic (g)	Carbohydrate (g)	Calcium (mg)	Iron (mg)	Vitamin A (I.U.)	Thiamine (mg)	Riboflavin (mg)	Niacin (mg)	Ascorbic acid (mg)
217	Canned, strained (baby food)	1 ounce	28	86	15	1	Trace				3	3	.4	140	.02	.02	.4	3
218	Peppers, hot, red, without seeds, dried (ground chili powder, added seasonings)	1 tablespoon	15	8	50	2	2				8	40	2.3	9,750	.03	.17	1.3	2
	Peppers, sweet: Raw, about 5 per pound:																	
219	Green pod without stem and seeds	1 pod	74	93	15	1	Trace				4	7	.5	310	.06	.06	.4	94
220	Cooked, boiled, drained 1 pod	1 pod	73	95	15	1	Trace				3	7	.4	310	.05	.05	.4	70
	Potatoes, medium (about 3 per pound raw):																	
221	Baked, peeled after baking	1 potato	99	75	90	3	Trace				21	9	.7	Trace	.10	.04	1.7	20
	Boiled:																	
222	Peeled after boiling	1 potato	136	80	105	3	Trace				23	10	.8	Trace	.13	.05	2.0	22
223	Peeled before boiling	1 potato	122	83	80	2	Trace				18	7	.6	Trace	.11	.04	1.4	20
	French-fried, piece 2 by ½ by ½ inch:																	
224	Cooked in deep fat	10 pieces	57	45	155	2	7	2	2	4	20	9	.7	Trace	.07	.04	1.8	12
225	Frozen, heated	10 pieces	57	53	125	2	5	1	1	2	19	5	1.0	Trace	.08	.01	1.5	12
	Mashed:																	
226	Milk added	1 cup	195	83	125	4	1				25	47	.8	50	.16	.10	2.0	19
227	Milk and butter added	1 cup	195	80	185	4	8	4	3	Trace	24	47	.8	330	.16	.10	1.9	18
228	Potato chips, medium, 2-inch diameter	10 chips	20	2	115	1	8	2	2	4	10	8	.4	Trace	.04	.01	1.0	3
229	Pumpkin, canned	1 cup	228	90	75	2	1				18	57	.9	14,590	.07	.12	1.3	12
230	Radishes, raw, small, without tops	4 radishes	40	94	5	Trace	Trace				1	12	.4	Trace	.01	.01	.1	10
231	Sauerkraut, canned, solids and liquid	1 cup	235	93	45	2	Trace				9	85	1.2	120	.07	.09	.4	33
	Spinach:																	
232	Cooked	1 cup	180	92	40	5	1				6	167	4.0	14,580	.13	.25	1.0	50
233	Canned, drained solids	1 cup	180	91	45	5	1				6	212	4.7	14,400	.03	.21	.6	24
	Squash: Cooked:																	
234	Summer, diced	1 cup	210	96	30	2	Trace				7	52	.8	820	.10	.16	1.6	21
235	Winter, baked, mashed	1 cup	205	81	130	4	1				32	57	1.6	8,610	.10	.27	1.4	27
	Sweetpotatoes: Cooked, medium, 5 by 2 inches, weight raw about 6 ounces:																	
236	Baked, peeled after baking	1 sweetpotato	110	64	155	2	1				36	44	1.0	8,910	.10	.07	.7	24
237	Boiled, peeled after boiling	1 sweetpotato	147	71	170	2	1				39	47	1.0	11,610	.13	.09	.9	25

Table continued on following page

Table A-1   Nutritive Value of the Edible Part of Foods (Continued)

[Dashes in the columns for nutrients show that no suitable value could be found although there is reason to believe that a measurable amount of the nutrient may be present]

	Food, approximate measure, and weight (in grams)		Water	Food energy	Protein	Fat	Fatty acids			Carbohydrate	Calcium	Iron	Vitamin A value	Thiamin	Riboflavin	Niacin	Ascorbic acid
							Saturated (total)	Unsaturated									
								Oleic	Linoleic								
		Grams	Percent	Calories	Grams	Grams	Grams	Grams	Grams	Grams	Milligrams	Milligrams	International units	Milligrams	Milligrams	Milligrams	Milligrams
	VEGETABLES AND VEGETABLE PRODUCTS—Continued																
	Sweetpotatoes—Continued																
238	Candied, 3½ by 2¼ inches.	1 sweetpotato. 175	60	295	2	6	2	3	1	60	65	1.6	11,030	0.10	0.08	0.8	17
239	Canned, vacuum or solid pack.	1 cup 218	72	235	4	Trace	------	------	------	54	54	1.7	17,000	.10	.10	1.4	30
	Tomatoes:																
240	Raw, approx. 3-in. diam. 2⅛ in. high; wt., 7 oz.	1 tomato 200	94	40	2	Trace	------	------	------	9	24	.9	1,640	.11	.07	1.3	[7]42
241	Canned, solids and liquid.	1 cup 241	94	50	2	1	------	------	------	10	14	1.2	2,170	.12	.07	1.7	41
	Tomato catsup:																
242	Cup	1 cup 273	69	290	6	1	------	------	------	69	60	2.2	3,820	.25	.19	4.4	41
243	Tablespoon	1 tbsp. 15	69	15	Trace	Trace	------	------	------	4	3	.1	210	.01	.01	.2	2
	Tomato juice, canned:																
244	Cup	1 cup 243	94	45	2	Trace	------	------	------	10	17	2.2	1,940	.12	.07	1.9	39
245	Glass (6 fl. oz.)	1 glass 182	94	35	2	Trace	------	------	------	8	13	1.6	1,460	.09	.05	1.5	29
246	Turnips, cooked, diced	1 cup 155	94	35	1	Trace	------	------	------	8	54	.6	Trace	.06	.08	.5	34
247	Turnip greens, cooked	1 cup 145	94	30	3	Trace	------	------	------	5	252	1.5	8,270	.15	.33	.7	68
	FRUITS AND FRUIT PRODUCTS																
248	Apples, raw (about 3 per lb.),[5]	1 apple 150	85	70	Trace	Trace	------	------	------	18	8	.4	50	.04	.02	.1	3
249	Apple juice, bottled or canned.	1 cup 248	88	120	Trace	Trace	------	------	------	30	15	1.5	------	.02	.05	.2	2
	Applesauce, canned:																
250	Sweetened	1 cup 255	76	230	1	Trace	------	------	------	61	10	1.3	100	.05	.03	.1	[8]3
251	Unsweetened or artificially sweetened.	1 cup 244	88	100	1	Trace	------	------	------	26	10	1.2	100	.05	.02	.1	[8]2

No.	Food	Measure	Weight (g)	Water (%)	Food energy (cal.)	Protein (g)	Fat (g)	Saturated fatty acids (g)	Oleic (g)	Linoleic (g)	Carbohydrate (g)	Calcium (mg)	Iron (mg)	Vitamin A (I.U.)	Thiamine (mg)	Riboflavin (mg)	Niacin (mg)	Ascorbic acid (mg)
	Apricots:																	
252	Raw (about 12 per lb.)[6]	3 apricots	114	85	55	1	Trace	---	---	---	14	18	.5	2,890	.03	.04	.7	10
253	Canned in heavy sirup	1 cup	259	77	220	2	Trace	---	---	---	57	28	.8	4,510	.05	.06	.9	10
254	Dried, uncooked (40 halves per cup)	1 cup	150	25	390	8	1	---	---	---	100	100	8.2	16,350	.02	.23	4.9	19
255	Cooked, unsweetened, fruit and liquid	1 cup	285	76	240	5	1	---	---	---	62	63	5.1	8,550	.01	.13	2.8	8
256	Apricot nectar, canned	1 cup	251	85	140	1	Trace	---	---	---	37	23	.5	2,380	.03	.03	.5	[8] 8
	Avocados, whole fruit, raw:[5]																	
257	California (mid- and late-winter; diam. 3⅛ in.)	1 avocado	284	74	370	5	37	7	17	5	13	22	1.3	630	.24	.43	3.5	30
258	Florida (late summer, fall; diam. 3⅝ in.)	1 avocado	454	78	390	4	33	7	15	4	27	30	1.8	880	.33	.61	4.9	43
259	Bananas, raw, medium size.[5]	1 banana	175	76	100	1	Trace	---	---	---	26	10	.8	230	.06	.07	.8	12
260	Banana flakes	1 cup	100	3	340	4	1	---	---	---	89	32	2.8	760	.18	.24	2.8	7
261	Blackberries, raw	1 cup	144	84	85	2	1	---	---	---	19	46	1.3	290	.05	.06	.5	30
262	Blueberries, raw	1 cup	140	83	85	1	1	---	---	---	21	21	1.4	140	.04	.08	.6	20
263	Cantaloups, raw; medium, 5-inch diameter about 1⅔ pounds.[5]	½ melon	385	91	60	1	Trace	---	---	---	14	27	.8	[9] 6,540	.08	.06	1.2	63
264	Cherries, canned, red, sour, pitted, water pack	1 cup	244	88	105	2	Trace	---	---	---	26	37	.7	1,660	.07	.05	.5	12
265	Cranberry juice cocktail, canned	1 cup	250	83	165	Trace	Trace	---	---	---	42	13	.8	Trace	.03	.03	.1	[10] 40
266	Cranberry sauce, sweetened, canned, strained	1 cup	277	62	330	Trace	1	---	---	---	85	14	.5	50	.02	.02	.1	5
267	Dates, pitted, cut	1 cup	178	22	490	4	1	---	---	---	130	105	5.3	90	.16	.17	3.9	0
268	Figs, dried, large, 2 by 1 in.	1 fig	21	23	60	1	Trace	---	---	---	15	26	.6	20	.02	.02	.1	0
269	Fruit cocktail, canned, in heavy sirup	1 cup	256	80	195	1	Trace	---	---	---	50	23	1.0	360	.05	.03	1.3	5

[5] Measure and weight apply to entire vegetable or fruit including parts not usually eaten.

[7] Year-round average. Samples marketed from November through May, average 20 milligrams per 200-gram tomato; from June through October, around 52 milligrams.

[8] This is the amount from the fruit. Additional ascorbic acid may be added by the manufacturer. Refer to the label for this information.

[9] Value for varieties with orange-colored flesh; value for varieties with green flesh would be about 540 I.U.

[10] Value listed is based on products with label stating 30 milligrams per 6 fl. oz. serving.

Table continued on following page

Table A-1   *Nutritive Value of the Edible Part of Foods (Continued)*

[Dashes in the columns for nutrients show that no suitable value could be found although there is reason to believe that a measurable amount of the nutrient may be present]

	Food, approximate measure, and weight (in grams)	Water	Food energy	Protein	Fat	Fatty acids Saturated (total)	Fatty acids Unsaturated Oleic	Fatty acids Unsaturated Linoleic	Carbohydrate	Calcium	Iron	Vitamin A value	Thiamin	Riboflavin	Niacin	Ascorbic acid
		Grams / Percent	Calories	Grams	Grams	Grams	Grams	Grams	Grams	Milligrams	Milligrams	International units	Milligrams	Milligrams	Milligrams	Milligrams
	FRUITS AND FRUIT PRODUCTS—Con.															
	Grapefruit:															
	Raw, medium, 3¾-in. diam.⁵															
270	White ½ grapefruit	241 / 89	45	1	Trace	----	----	----	12	19	0.5	10	0.05	0.02	0.2	44
271	Pink or red ½ grapefruit	241 / 89	50	1	Trace	----	----	----	13	20	0.5	540	0.05	0.02	0.2	44
272	Canned, sirup pack 1 cup	254 / 81	180	2	Trace	----	----	----	45	33	.8	30	.08	.05	.5	76
	Grapefruit juice:															
273	Fresh 1 cup	246 / 90	95	1	Trace	----	----	----	23	22	.5	(¹¹)	.09	.04	.4	92
	Canned, white:															
274	Unsweetened 1 cup	247 / 89	100	1	Trace	----	----	----	24	20	1.0	20	.07	.04	.4	84
275	Sweetened 1 cup	250 / 86	130	1	Trace	----	----	----	32	20	1.0	20	.07	.04	.4	78
	Frozen concentrate, unsweetened:															
276	Undiluted, can, 6 fluid ounces	207 / 62	300	4	1	----	----	----	72	70	.8	60	.29	.12	1.4	286
277	Diluted with 3 parts water, by volume 1 can	247 / 89	100	1	Trace	----	----	----	24	25	.2	20	.10	.04	.5	96
278	Dehydrated crystals 4 oz	113 / 1	410	6	1	----	----	----	102	100	1.2	80	.40	.20	2.0	396
279	Prepared with water (1 pound yields about 1 gallon) 1 cup	247 / 90	100	1	Trace	----	----	----	24	22	.2	20	.10	.05	.5	91
	Grapes, raw:⁵															
280	American type (slip skin) 1 cup	153 / 82	65	1	1	----	----	----	15	15	.4	100	.05	.03	.2	3
281	European type (adherent skin) 1 cup	160 / 81	95	1	Trace	----	----	----	25	17	.6	140	.07	.04	.4	6
	Grapejuice:															
282	Canned or bottled 1 cup	253 / 83	165	1	Trace	----	----	----	42	28	.8	----	.10	.05	.5	Trace
	Frozen concentrate, sweetened:															
283	Undiluted, can, 6 fluid ounces 1 can	216 / 53	395	1	Trace	----	----	----	100	22	.9	40	.13	.22	1.5	(¹²)

No.	Food, approximate measure, and weight (grams)			Water (%)	Food energy	Protein	Fat	Saturated	Oleic	Linoleic	Carbohydrate	Calcium	Iron	Vitamin A	Thiamine	Riboflavin	Niacin	Ascorbic acid
284	Diluted with 3 parts water, by volume	1 cup	250	86	135	1	Trace	—	—	—	33	8	.3	10	.05	.08	.5	(12)
285	Grapejuice drink, canned	1 cup	250	86	135	Trace	—	—	—	—	35	8	.3	—	.03	.03	.3	(12)
286	Lemons, raw, 2⅛-in. diam., size 165.⁵ Used for juice	1 lemon	110	90	20	1	Trace	—	—	—	6	19	.4	10	.03	.01	.1	39
287	Lemon juice, raw	1 cup	244	91	60	1	Trace	—	—	—	20	17	.5	50	.07	.02	.2	112
288	Lemonade concentrate: Frozen, 6 fl. oz. per can	1 can	219	48	430	Trace	Trace	—	—	—	112	9	.4	40	.04	.07	.7	66
289	Diluted with 4⅓ parts water, by volume	1 cup	248	88	110	Trace	Trace	—	—	—	28	2	Trace	Trace	Trace	.02	.2	17
290	Lime juice: Fresh	1 cup	246	90	65	1	Trace	—	—	—	22	22	.5	20	.05	.02	.2	79
291	Canned, unsweetened	1 cup	246	90	65	1	Trace	—	—	—	22	22	.5	20	.05	.02	.2	52
292	Limeade concentrate, frozen: Undiluted, can, 6 fluid ounces	1 can	218	50	410	Trace	Trace	—	—	—	108	11	.2	Trace	.02	.02	.2	26
293	Diluted with 4⅓ parts water, by volume	1 cup	247	90	100	Trace	Trace	—	—	—	27	2	Trace	Trace	Trace	Trace	Trace	5
294	Oranges, raw, 2⅝-in. diam., all commercial, varieties⁵	1 orange	180	86	65	1	Trace	—	—	—	16	54	.5	260	.13	.05	.5	66
295	Orange juice, fresh, all varieties	1 cup	248	88	110	2	1	—	—	—	26	27	.5	500	.22	.07	1.0	124
296	Canned, unsweetened	1 cup	249	87	120	2	Trace	—	—	—	28	25	1.0	500	.17	.05	.7	100
297	Frozen concentrate: Undiluted, can, 6 fluid ounces	1 can	213	55	360	5	Trace	—	—	—	87	75	.9	1,620	.68	.11	2.8	360
298	Diluted with 3 parts water, by volume	1 cup	249	87	120	2	Trace	—	—	—	29	25	.2	550	.22	.02	1.0	120
299	Dehydrated crystals	4 oz.	113	1	430	6	2	—	—	—	100	95	1.9	1,900	.76	.24	3.3	408
300	Prepared with water (1 pound yields about 1 gallon)	1 cup	248	88	115	2	1	—	—	—	27	25	.5	500	.20	.07	1.0	109
301	Orange-apricot juice drink	1 cup	249	87	125	1	Trace	—	—	—	32	12	.2	1,440	.05	.02	.5	¹⁰40

⁵ Measure and weight apply to entire vegetable or fruit including parts not usually eaten.

¹⁰ Value listed is based on product with label stating 30 milligrams per 6 fl. oz. serving.

¹¹ For white-fleshed varieties value is about 20 I.U. per cup; for red-fleshed varieties, 1,080 I.U. per cup.

¹² Present only if added by the manufacturer. Refer to the label for this information.

Table continued on following page

Table A-1 Nutritive Value of the Edible Part of Foods (Continued)

[Dashes in the columns for nutrients show that no suitable value could be found although there is reason to believe that a measurable amount of the nutrient may be present]

Food, approximate measure, and weight (in grams)	Water	Food energy	Protein	Fat	Fatty acids Saturated (total)	Fatty acids Unsaturated Oleic	Fatty acids Unsaturated Linoleic	Carbohydrate	Calcium	Iron	Vitamin A value	Thiamin	Riboflavin	Niacin	Ascorbic acid
	Percent	Calories	Grams	Grams	Grams	Grams	Grams	Grams	Milligrams	Milligrams	International units	Milligrams	Milligrams	Milligrams	Milligrams
FRUITS AND FRUIT PRODUCTS—Con.															
Orange and grapefruit juice:															
Frozen concentrate:															
302 Undiluted, can, 6 fluid ounces. 1 can 210	59	330	4	1	---	---	---	78	61	0.8	800	0.48	0.06	2.3	302
303 Diluted with 3 parts water, by volume. 1 cup 248	88	110	1	Trace	---	---	---	26	20	.2	270	.16	.02	.8	102
304 Papayas, raw, ½-inch cubes. 1 cup 182	89	70	1	Trace	---	---	---	18	36	.5	3,190	.07	.08	.5	102
Peaches:															
Raw:															
305 Whole, medium, 2-inch diameter, about 4 per pound.⁶ 1 peach 114	89	35	1	Trace	---	---	---	10	9	.5	[13]1,320	.02	.05	1.0	7
306 Sliced. 1 cup 168	89	65	1	Trace	---	---	---	16	15	.8	[13]2,230	.03	.08	1.6	12
Canned, yellow-fleshed, solids and liquid:															
Sirup pack, heavy:															
307 Halves or slices. 1 cup 257	79	200	1	Trace	---	---	---	52	10	.8	1,100	.02	.06	1.4	7
308 Water pack. 1 cup 245	91	75	1	Trace	---	---	---	20	10	.7	1,100	.02	.06	1.4	7
309 Dried, uncooked. 1 cup 160	25	420	5	1	---	---	---	109	77	9.6	6,240	.02	.31	8.5	28
310 Cooked, unsweetened, 10–12 halves and juice. 1 cup 270	77	220	3	1	---	---	---	58	41	5.1	3,290	.01	.15	4.2	6
Frozen:															
311 Carton, 12 ounces, not thawed. 1 carton 340	76	300	1	Trace	---	---	---	77	14	1.7	2,210	.03	.14	2.4	[14]135
Pears:															
312 Raw, 3 by 2½-inch diameter.⁵ 1 pear 182	83	100	1	1	---	---	---	25	13	.5	30	.04	.07	.2	7
Canned, solids and liquid:															
Sirup pack, heavy:															
313 Halves or slices. 1 cup 255	80	195	1	1	---	---	---	50	13	.5	Trace	.03	.05	.3	4

	Food	Measure	Weight (g)	Water (%)	Food energy	Protein	Fat	(fatty acids)			Carb.	Calcium	Iron	Vit. A	Thiamine	Riboflavin	Niacin	Ascorbic acid
	Pineapple:																	
314	Raw, diced	1 cup	140	85	75	1	Trace	---	---	---	19	24	.7	100	.12	.04	.3	24
	Canned, heavy sirup pack, solids and liquid:																	
315	Crushed	1 cup	260	80	195	1	Trace	---	---	---	50	29	.8	120	.20	.06	.5	17
316	Sliced, slices and juice.	2 small or 1 large.	122	80	90	Trace	Trace	---	---	---	24	13	.4	50	.09	.03	.2	8
317	Pineapple juice, canned	1 cup	249	86	135	1	Trace	---	---	---	34	37	.7	120	.12	.04	.5	[8]22
	Plums, all except prunes:																	
318	Raw, 2-inch diameter, about 2 ounces.[5]	1 plum	60	87	25	Trace	Trace	---	---	---	7	7	.3	140	.02	.02	.3	3
	Canned, sirup pack (Italian prunes):																	
319	Plums (with pits) and juice.[5]	1 cup	256	77	205	1	Trace	---	---	---	53	22	2.2	2,970	.05	.05	.9	4
	Prunes, dried, "softenized", medium:																	
320	Uncooked[5]	4 prunes	32	28	70	1	Trace	---	---	---	18	14	1.1	440	.02	.04	.4	1
321	Cooked, unsweetened, 17–18 prunes and ½ cup liquid.[5]	1 cup	270	66	295	2	1	---	---	---	78	60	4.5	1,860	.08	.18	1.7	2
322	Prune juice, canned or bottled.	1 cup	256	80	200	1	Trace	---	---	---	49	36	10.5	-----	.03	.03	1.0	[8]5
	Raisins, seedless:																	
323	Packaged, ½ oz. or 1½ tbsp. per pkg.	1 pkg.	14	18	40	Trace	Trace	---	---	---	11	9	.5	Trace	.02	.01	.1	Trace
324	Cup, pressed down	1 cup	165	18	480	4	Trace	---	---	---	128	102	5.8	30	.18	.13	.8	2
	Raspberries, red:																	
325	Raw	1 cup	123	84	70	1	1	---	---	---	17	27	1.1	160	.04	.11	1.1	31
326	Frozen, 10-ounce carton, not thawed.	1 carton	284	74	275	2	1	---	---	---	70	37	1.7	200	.06	.17	1.7	59
327	Rhubarb, cooked, sugar added.	1 cup	272	63	385	1	Trace	---	---	---	98	212	1.6	220	.06	.15	.7	17
	Strawberries:																	
328	Raw, capped	1 cup	149	90	55	1	1	---	---	---	13	31	1.5	90	.04	.10	1.0	88
329	Frozen, 10-ounce carton, not thawed.	1 carton	284	71	310	1	1	---	---	---	79	40	2.0	90	.06	.17	1.5	150
330	Tangerines, raw, medium, 2⅜-in. diam., size 176.[3]	1 tangerine	116	87	40	1	Trace	---	---	---	10	34	.3	360	.05	.02	.1	27
331	Tangerine juice, canned, sweetened.	1 cup	249	87	125	1	1	---	---	---	30	45	.5	1,050	.15	.05	.2	55
332	Watermelon, raw, wedge, 4 by 8 inches (¹⁄₁₆ of 10 by 16-inch melon, about 2 pounds with rind).[5]	1 wedge	925	93	115	2	1	---	---	---	27	30	2.1	2,510	.13	.13	.7	30

[5] Measure and weight apply to entire vegetable or fruit including parts not usually eaten.

[8] This is the amount from the fruit. Additional ascorbic acid may be added by the manufacturer. Refer to the label for this information.

[13] Based on yellow-fleshed varieties; for white-fleshed varieties value is about 50 I.U. per 114-gram peach and 80 I.U. per cup of sliced peaches.

[14] This value includes ascorbic acid added by manufacturer.

Table continued on following page

Table A–1　Nutritive Value of the Edible Part of Foods (Continued)

[Dashes in the columns for nutrients show that no suitable value could be found although there is reason to believe that a measurable amount of the nutrient may be present]

	Food, approximate measure, and weight (in grams)	Water	Food energy	Protein	Fat	Fatty acids — Saturated (total)	Fatty acids — Unsaturated Oleic	Fatty acids — Unsaturated Linoleic	Carbohydrate	Calcium	Iron	Vitamin A value	Thiamin	Riboflavin	Niacin	Ascorbic acid
		Percent	Calories	Grams	Grams	Grams	Grams	Grams	Grams	Milligrams	Milligrams	International units	Milligrams	Milligrams	Milligrams	Milligrams
	GRAIN PRODUCTS															
	Bagel, 3-in. diam.:															
333	Egg — 1 bagel	55														
		32	165	6	2				28	9	1.2	30	0.14	0.10	1.2	0
334	Water — 1 bagel — 55	29	165	6	2				30	8	1.2	0	.15	.11	1.4	0
335	Barley, pearled, light, uncooked — 1 cup — 200	11	700	16	2	Trace	1	1	158	32	4.0	0	.24	.10	6.2	0
336	Biscuits, baking powder from home recipe with enriched flour, 2-in. diam. — 1 biscuit — 28	27	105	2	5	1	2	1	13	34	.4	Trace	.06	.06	.1	Trace
337	Biscuits, baking powder from mix, 2-in. diam. — 1 biscuit — 28	28	90	2	3	1	1	1	15	19	.6	Trace	.08	.07	.6	Trace
338	Bran flakes (40% bran), added thiamin and iron. — 1 cup — 35	3	105	4	1				28	25	12.3	0	.14	.06	2.2	0
339	Bran flakes with raisins, added thiamin and iron. — 1 cup — 50	7	145	4	1				40	28	13.5	Trace	.16	.07	2.7	0
	Breads:															
340	Boston brown bread, slice 3 by ¾ in. — 1 slice — 48	45	100	3	1				22	43	.9	0	.05	.03	.6	0
	Cracked-wheat bread:															
341	Loaf, 1 lb. — 1 loaf — 454	35	1,190	40	10	2	5	2	236	399	5.0	Trace	.53	.41	5.9	Trace
342	Slice, 18 slices per loaf. — 1 slice — 25	35	65	2	1				13	22	.3	Trace	.03	.02	.3	Trace
	French or vienna bread:															
343	Enriched, 1 lb. loaf — 1 loaf — 454	31	1,315	41	14	3	8	2	251	195	10.0	Trace	1.27	1.00	11.3	Trace
344	Unenriched, 1 lb. loaf — 1 loaf — 454	31	1,315	41	14	3	8	2	251	195	3.2	Trace	.36	.36	3.6	Trace
	Italian bread:															
345	Enriched, 1 lb. loaf — 1 loaf — 454	32	1,250	41	4	Trace	1	2	256	77	10.0	0	1.32	.91	11.8	0
346	Unenriched, 1 lb. loaf — 1 loaf — 454	32	1,250	41	4	Trace	1	2	256	77	3.2	0	.41	.27	3.6	0
	Raisin bread:															
347	Loaf, 1 lb. — 1 loaf — 454	35	1,190	30	13	3	8	2	243	322	5.9	Trace	.23	.41	3.2	Trace

No.	Food	Measure	Weight (g)															
348	Slice, 18 slices per loaf	1 slice	25	35	65	2	1	—	—	—	13	18	.3	Trace	.01	.02	.2	Trace
	Rye bread:																	
	American, light (⅓ rye, ⅔ wheat):																	
349	Loaf, 1 lb	1 loaf	454	36	1,100	41	5	—	3	8	236	340	7.3	0	.82	.32	6.4	0
350	Slice, 18 slices per loaf	1 slice	25	36	60	2	Trace	—	—	—	13	19	.4	0	.05	.02	.4	0
351	Pumpernickel, loaf, 1 lb	1 loaf	454	34	1,115	41	5	—	—	—	241	381	10.9	0	1.04	.64	5.4	0
	White bread, enriched: [15]																	
	Soft-crumb type:																	
352	Loaf, 1 lb	1 loaf	454	36	1,225	39	15	—	3	8	229	381	11.3	Trace	1.13	.95	10.9	Trace
353	Slice, 18 slices per loaf	1 slice	25	36	70	2	1	—	—	—	13	21	.6	Trace	.06	.05	.6	Trace
354	Slice, toasted	1 slice	22	25	70	2	1	—	—	—	13	21	.6	Trace	.06	.05	.6	Trace
355	Slice, 22 slices per loaf	1 slice	20	36	55	2	1	—	—	—	10	17	.5	Trace	.05	.04	.5	Trace
356	Slice, toasted	1 slice	17	25	55	2	1	—	—	—	10	17	.5	Trace	.05	.04	.5	Trace
357	Loaf, 1½ lbs	1 loaf	680	36	1,835	59	22	—	5	12	343	571	17.0	Trace	1.70	1.43	16.3	Trace
358	Slice, 24 slices per loaf	1 slice	28	36	75	2	1	—	—	—	14	24	.7	Trace	.07	.06	.7	Trace
359	Slice, toasted	1 slice	24	25	75	2	1	—	—	—	14	24	.7	Trace	.07	.06	.7	Trace
360	Slice, 28 slices per loaf	1 slice	24	36	65	2	1	—	—	—	12	20	.6	Trace	.06	.05	.6	Trace
361	Slice, toasted	1 slice	21	25	65	2	1	—	—	—	12	20	.6	Trace	.06	.05	.6	Trace
	Firm-crumb type:																	
362	Loaf, 1 lb	1 loaf	454	35	1,245	41	17	—	4	10	228	435	11.3	Trace	1.22	.91	10.9	Trace
363	Slice, 20 slices per loaf	1 slice	23	35	65	2	1	—	—	—	12	22	.6	Trace	.06	.05	.6	Trace
364	Slice, toasted	1 slice	20	24	65	2	1	—	—	—	12	22	.6	Trace	.06	.05	.6	Trace
365	Loaf, 2 lbs	1 loaf	907	35	2,495	82	34	—	8	20	455	871	22.7	Trace	2.45	1.81	21.8	Trace
366	Slice, 34 slices per loaf	1 slice	27	35	75	2	1	—	—	—	14	26	.7	Trace	.07	.05	.6	Trace
367	Slice, toasted	1 slice	23	35	75	2	1	—	—	—	14	26	.7	Trace	.07	.05	.6	Trace
	Whole-wheat bread, soft-crumb type:																	
368	Loaf, 1 lb	1 loaf	454	36	1,095	41	12	—	2	6	224	381	13.6	Trace	1.36	.45	12.7	Trace
369	Slice, 16 slices per loaf	1 slice	28	36	65	3	1	—	—	—	14	24	.8	Trace	.09	.03	.8	Trace
370	Slice, toasted	1 slice	24	24	65	3	1	—	—	—	14	24	.8	Trace	.09	.03	.8	Trace

[15] Values for iron, thiamin, riboflavin, and niacin per pound of unenriched white bread would be as follows:

	Iron *Milligrams*	Thiamin *Milligrams*	Riboflavin *Milligrams*	Niacin *Milligrams*
Soft crumb	3.2	.31	.39	5.0
Firm crumb	3.2	.32	.59	4.1

Table continued on following page

Table A-1 Nutritive Value of the Edible Part of Foods (Continued)

[Dashes in the columns for nutrients show that no suitable value could be found although there is reason to believe that a measurable amount of the nutrient may be present]

	Food, approximate measure, and weight (in grams)		Water	Food energy	Protein	Fat	Fatty acids Saturated (total)	Unsaturated Oleic	Unsaturated Linoleic	Carbohydrate	Calcium	Iron	Vitamin A value	Thiamin	Riboflavin	Niacin	Ascorbic acid
		Grams	Percent	Calories	Grams	Grams	Grams	Grams	Grams	Grams	Milligrams	Milligrams	International units	Milligrams	Milligrams	Milligrams	Milligrams
	GRAIN PRODUCTS—Continued																
	Bread—Continued																
	Whole-wheat bread, firm-crumb type:																
371	Loaf, 1 lb ____ 1 loaf____	454	36	1,100	48	14	3	6	3	216	449	13.6	Trace	1.18	0.54	12.7	Trace
372	Slice, 18 slices per loaf. 1 slice____	25	36	60	3	1				12	25	.8	Trace	.06	.03	.7	Trace
373	Slice, toasted_____ 1 slice____	21	24	60	3	1				12	25	.8	Trace	.06	.03	.7	Trace
374	Breadcrumbs, dry, grated. 1 cup____	100	6	390	13	5	1	2	1	73	122	3.6	Trace	.22	.30	3.5	Trace
375	Buckwheat flour, light, sifted. 1 cup____	98	12	340	6	1				78	11	1.0	0	.08	.04	.4	0
376	Bulgur, canned, seasoned. 1 cup____	135	56	245	8	4				44	27	1.9	0	.08	.05	4.1	0
	Cakes made from cake mixes:																
	Angelfood:																
377	Whole cake_____ 1 cake____	635	34	1,645	36	1				377	603	1.9	0	.03	.70	.6	0
378	Piece, 1/12 of 10-in. diam. cake. 1 piece____	53	34	135	3	Trace				32	50	.2	0	Trace	.06	.1	0
	Cupcakes, small, 2½ in. diam.:																
379	Without icing____ 1 cupcake__	25	26	90	1	3	1	1		14	40	.1	40	.01	.03	.1	Trace
380	With chocolate icing. 1 cupcake__	36	22	130	2	5	2	2	1	21	47	.3	60	.01	.04	.1	Trace
	Devil's food, 2-layer, with chocolate icing:																
381	Whole cake_____1 cake____	1,107	24	3,755	49	136	54	58	16	645	653	8.9	1,660	.33	.89	3.3	1
382	Piece, 1/16 of 9-in. diam. cake. 1 piece____	69	24	235	3	9	3	4	1	40	41	.6	100	.02	.06	.2	Trace
383	Cupcake, small, 2½ in. diam. 1 cupcake__	35	24	120	2	4	1	2	Trace	20	21	.3	50	.01	.03	.1	Trace
	Gingerbread:																
384	Whole cake_____ 1 cake____	570	37	1,575	18	39	10	19	9	291	513	9.1	Trace	.17	.51	4.6	2
385	Piece, 1/9 of 8-in. square cake. 1 piece____	63	37	175	2	4	1	2	1	32	57	1.0	Trace	.02	.06	.5	Trace
	White, 2-layer, with chocolate icing:																
386	Whole cake_____1 cake____	1,140	21	4,000	45	122	45	54	17	716	1,129	5.7	680	.23	.91	2.3	2

No.	Food, description	Measure																
387	Piece, 1/16 of 9-in. diam. cake.	1 piece	71	21	250	3	8	3	3	1	45	70	.4	40	.01	.06	.1	Trace
388	Cakes made from home recipes:¹⁶ Boston cream pie; piece ½ of 8-in. diam.	1 piece	69	35	210	4	6	2	2	1	34	46	.3	140	.02	.08	.1	Trace
	Fruitcake, dark, made with enriched flour:																	
389	Loaf, 1-lb.	1 loaf	454	18	1,720	22	69	15	37	13	271	327	11.8	540	.59	.64	3.6	2
390	Slice, 1/30 of 8-in. loaf.	1 slice	15	18	55	1	2	Trace	1	Trace	9	11	.4	20	.02	.02	.1	Trace
	Plain sheet cake: Without icing:																	
391	Whole cake.	1 cake	777	25	2,830	35	108	30	52	21	434	497	3.1	1,320	.16	.70	1.6	2
392	Piece, 1/9 of 9-in. square cake.	1 piece	86	25	315	4	12	3	6	2	48	55	.3	150	.02	.08	.2	Trace
393	With boiled white icing, piece, 1/9 of 9-in. square cake.	1 piece	114	23	400	4	12	3	6	2	71	56	.3	150	.02	.08	.2	Trace
	Pound:																	
394	Loaf, 8½ by 3½ by 3 in.	1 loaf	514	17	2,430	29	152	34	68	17	242	108	4.1	1,440	.15	.46	1.0	0
395	Slice, ½-in. thick.	1 slice	30	17	140	2	9	2	4	1	14	6	.2	80	.01	.03	.1	0
	Sponge:																	
396	Whole cake.	1 cake	790	32	2,345	60	45	14	20	4	427	237	9.5	3,560	.40	1.11	1.6	Trace
397	Piece, 1/12 of 10-in. diam. cake.	1 piece	66	32	195	5	4	1	2	Trace	36	20	.8	300	.03	.09	.1	Trace
	Yellow, 2-layer, without icing:																	
398	Whole cake.	1 cake	870	24	3,160	39	111	31	53	22	506	618	3.5	1,310	.17	.70	1.7	2
399	Piece, 1/16 of 9-in. diam. cake.	1 piece	54	24	200	2	7	2	3	1	32	39	.2	80	.01	.04	.1	Trace
	Yellow, 2-layer, with chocolate icing:																	
400	Whole cake.	1 cake	1,203	21	4,390	51	156	55	69	23	727	818	7.2	1,920	.24	.96	2.4	Trace
401	Piece, 1/16 of 9-in. diam. cake.	1 piece	75	21	275	3	10	3	4	1	45	51	.5	120	.02	.06	.2	Trace
	Cake icings. See Sugars, Sweets.																	
	Cookies: Brownies with nuts:																	
402	Made from home recipe with enriched flour.	1 brownie	20	10	95	1	6	1	3	1	10	8	.4	40	.04	.02	.1	Trace
403	Made from mix.	1 brownie	20	11	85	1	4	1	2	1	13	9	.4	20	.03	.02	.1	Trace

¹⁶ Unenriched cake flour used unless otherwise specified.

Table continued on following page

Table A–1   Nutritive Value of the Edible Part of Foods (Continued)

[Dashes in the columns for nutrients show that no suitable value could be found although there is reason to believe that a measurable amount of the nutrient may be present]

| | Food, approximate measure, and weight (in grams) | | Water | Food energy | Protein | Fat | Fatty acids | | | Carbohydrate | Calcium | Iron | Vitamin A value | Thiamin | Riboflavin | Niacin | Ascorbic acid |
| | | | | | | | Saturated (total) | Unsaturated Oleic | Unsaturated Linoleic | | | | | | | | |
		Grams	Percent	Calories	Grams	Grams	Grams	Grams	Grams	Grams	Milligrams	Milligrams	International units	Milligrams	Milligrams	Milligrams	Milligrams
	GRAIN PRODUCTS—Continued																
	Cookies—Continued																
	Chocolate chip:																
404	Made from home recipe with enriched flour. 1 cookie	10	3	50	1	3	1	1	1	6	4	0.2	10	0.01	0.01	0.1	Trace
405	Commercial 1 cookie	10	3	50	1	2	1	1	Trace	7	4	.2	10	Trace	Trace	Trace	Trace
406	Fig bars, commercial 1 cookie	14	14	50	1	1	—	—	—	11	11	.2	20	Trace	.01	.1	Trace
407	Sandwich, chocolate or vanilla, commercial. 1 cookie	10	2	50	1	2	1	1	Trace	7	2	.1	0	Trace	Trace	.1	0
	Corn flakes, added nutrients:																
408	Plain 1 cup	25	4	100	2	Trace	—	—	—	21	4	.4	0	.11	.02	.5	0
409	Sugar-covered 1 cup	40	2	155	2	Trace	—	—	—	36	5	.4	0	.16	.02	.8	0
	Corn (hominy) grits, degermed, cooked:																
410	Enriched 1 cup	245	87	125	3	Trace	—	—	—	27	2	.7	17 150	.10	.07	1.0	0
411	Unenriched 1 cup	245	87	125	3	Trace	—	—	—	27	2	.2	17 150	.05	.02	.5	0
	Cornmeal:																
412	Whole-ground, unbolted, dry. 1 cup	122	12	435	11	5	1	2	2	90	24	2.9	17 620	.46	.13	2.4	0
413	Bolted (nearly whole-grain) dry. 1 cup	122	12	440	11	4	Trace	1	2	91	21	2.2	17 590	.37	.10	2.3	0
	Degermed, enriched:																
414	Dry form 1 cup	138	12	500	11	2	—	—	—	108	8	4.0	17 610	.61	.36	4.8	0
415	Cooked 1 cup	240	88	120	3	1	—	—	—	26	2	1.0	17 140	.14	.10	1.2	0
	Degermed, unenriched:																
416	Dry form 1 cup	138	12	500	11	2	—	—	—	108	8	1.5	17 610	.19	.07	1.4	0
417	Cooked 1 cup	240	88	120	3	1	—	—	—	26	2	.5	17 140	.05	.02	.2	0
418	Corn muffins, made with enriched degermed cornmeal and enriched flour; muffin 2⅜-in. diam. 1 muffin	40	33	125	3	4	2	2	Trace	19	42	.7	17 120	.08	.09	.6	Trace

No.	Food, approximate measure	Measure	Grams	Water (%)	Food energy (cal.)	Protein (g)	Fat (g)	Saturated fat (g)	Oleic (g)	Linoleic (g)	Carbohydrate (g)	Calcium (mg)	Iron (mg)	Vitamin A (I.U.)	Thiamin (mg)	Riboflavin (mg)	Niacin (mg)	Ascorbic acid (mg)
419	Corn muffins, made with mix, egg, and milk; muffin 2⅜-in. diam.	1 muffin	40	30	130	3	4	1	2	1	20	96	.6	100	.07	.08	.6	Trace
420	Corn, puffed, presweetened, added nutrients.	1 cup	30	2	115	1	Trace	—	—	—	27	3	.5	0	.13	.05	.6	0
421	Corn, shredded, added nutrients.	1 cup	25	3	100	2	Trace	—	—	—	22	1	.6	0	.11	.05	.5	0
	Crackers:																	
422	Graham, 2½-in. square.	4 crackers	28	6	110	2	3	—	1	—	21	11	.4	0	.01	.06	.4	0
423	Saltines.	4 crackers	11	4	50	1	1	—	1	—	8	2	.1	0	Trace	Trace	.1	0
	Danish pastry, plain (without fruit or nuts):																	
424	Packaged ring, 12 ounces.	1 ring	340	22	1,435	25	80	24	37	15	155	170	3.1	1,050	.24	.51	2.7	Trace
425	Round piece, approx. 4¼-in. diam. by 1 in.	1 pastry	65	22	275	5	15	5	7	3	30	33	.6	200	.05	.10	.5	Trace
426	Ounce.	1 oz.	28	22	120	2	7	2	3	1	13	14	.3	90	.02	.04	.2	Trace
427	Doughnuts, cake type.	1 doughnut	32	24	125	1	6	1	4	Trace	16	13	[18].4	30	[18].05	[18].05	[18].4	Trace
428	Farina, quick-cooking, enriched, cooked.	1 cup	245	89	105	3	Trace	—	—	—	22	147	[19].7	0	[19].12	[19].07	[19]1.0	0
	Macaroni, cooked: Enriched:																	
429	Cooked, firm stage (undergoes additional cooking in a food mixture).	1 cup	130	64	190	6	1	—	—	—	39	14	[19]1.4	0	[19].23	[19].14	[19]1.8	0
430	Cooked until tender.	1 cup	140	72	155	5	1	—	—	—	32	8	[19]1.3	0	[19].20	[19].11	[19]1.5	0
	Unenriched:																	
431	Cooked, firm stage (undergoes additional cooking in a food mixture).	1 cup	130	64	190	6	1	—	—	—	39	14	.7	0	.03	.03	.5	0
432	Cooked until tender.	1 cup	140	72	155	5	1	—	—	—	32	11	.6	0	.01	.01	.4	0
433	Macaroni (enriched) and cheese, baked.	1 cup	200	58	430	17	22	10	9	2	40	362	1.8	860	.20	.40	1.8	Trace
434	Canned.	1 cup	240	80	230	9	10	4	3	1	26	199	1.0	260	.12	.24	1.0	Trace
435	Muffins, with enriched white flour; muffin, 3-inch diam.	1 muffin	40	38	120	3	4	1	2	1	17	42	.6	40	.07	.09	.6	Trace
	Noodles (egg noodles), cooked:																	
436	Enriched.	1 cup	160	70	200	7	2	1	1	Trace	37	16	[19]1.4	110	[19].22	[19].13	[19]1.9	0
437	Unenriched.	1 cup	160	70	200	7	2	1	1	Trace	37	16	1.0	110	.05	.03	[19].6	0

[17] This value is based on product made from yellow varieties of corn; white varieties contain only a trace.

[18] Based on product made with enriched flour. With unenriched flour, approximate values per doughnut are: Iron, 0.2 milligram; thiamin, 0.01 milligram; riboflavin, 0.03 milligram; niacin, 0.2 milligram.

[19] Iron, thiamin, riboflavin, and niacin are based on the minimum levels of enrichment specified in standards of identity promulgated under the Federal Food, Drug, and Cosmetic Act.

Table continued on following page

Table A–1   Nutritive Value of the Edible Part of Foods (Continued)

[Dashes in the columns for nutrients show that no suitable value could be found although there is reason to believe that a measurable amount of the nutrient may be present]

	Food, approximate measure, and weight (in grams)	Water	Food energy	Protein	Fat	Fatty acids Saturated (total)	Fatty acids Unsaturated Oleic	Fatty acids Unsaturated Linoleic	Carbohydrate	Calcium	Iron	Vitamin A value	Thiamin	Riboflavin	Niacin	Ascorbic acid
		Percent	Calories	Grams	Grams	Grams	Grams	Grams	Grams	Milligrams	Milligrams	International units	Milligrams	Milligrams	Milligrams	Milligrams
	GRAIN PRODUCTS—Continued															
438	Oats (with or without corn) puffed, added nutrients. 1 cup —— *Grams* 25	3	100	3	1	---	---	---	19	44	1.2	0	0.24	0.04	0.5	0
439	Oatmeal or rolled oats, cooked. 1 cup —— 240	87	130	5	2	---	---	1	23	22	1.4	0	.19	.05	.2	0
	Pancakes, 4-inch diam.:															
440	Wheat, enriched flour (home recipe). 1 cake —— 27	50	60	2	2	Trace	1	Trace	9	27	.4	30	.05	.06	.4	Trace
441	Buckwheat (made from mix with egg and milk). 1 cake —— 27	58	55	2	2	1	1	Trace	6	59	.4	60	.03	.04	.2	Trace
442	Plain or buttermilk (made from mix with egg and milk). 1 cake —— 27	51	60	2	2	1	1	Trace	9	58	.3	70	.04	.06	.2	Trace
	Pie (piecrust made with unenriched flour): Sector, 4-in., ⅐ of 9-in. diam. pie:															
443	Apple (2-crust) 1 sector —— 135	48	350	3	15	4	7	3	51	11	.4	40	.03	.03	.5	1
444	Butterscotch (1-crust) 1 sector —— 130	45	350	6	14	5	6	2	50	98	1.2	340	.04	.13	.3	Trace
445	Cherry (2-crust) 1 sector —— 135	47	350	4	15	4	7	3	52	19	.4	590	.03	.03	.7	Trace
446	Custard (1-crust) 1 sector —— 130	58	285	8	14	5	6	2	30	125	.8	300	.07	.21	.4	0
447	Lemon meringue (1-crust). 1 sector —— 120	47	305	4	12	4	6	2	45	17	.6	200	.04	.10	.2	4
448	Mince (2-crust) 1 sector —— 135	43	365	3	16	4	8	3	56	38	1.4	Trace	.09	.05	.5	1
449	Pecan (1-crust) 1 sector —— 118	20	490	6	27	4	16	5	60	55	3.3	190	.19	.08	.4	Trace
450	Pineapple chiffon (1-crust). 1 sector —— 93	41	265	6	11	3	5	2	36	22	.8	320	.04	.08	.4	1
451	Pumpkin (1-crust) 1 sector —— 130	59	275	5	15	5	6	2	32	66	.7	3,210	.04	.13	.7	Trace
	Piecrust, baked shell for pie made with:															
452	Enriched flour 1 shell —— 180	15	900	11	60	16	28	12	79	25	3.1	0	.36	.25	3.2	0
453	Unenriched flour 1 shell —— 180	15	900	11	60	16	28	12	79	25	.9	0	.05	.05	.9	0

No.	Food	Measure	Grams	Water (%)	Food energy	Protein	Fat	Saturated	Oleic	Linoleic	Carbohydrate	Calcium	Iron	Vitamin A	Thiamin	Riboflavin	Niacin	Ascorbic acid
	Piecrust mix including stick form:																	
454	Package, 10-oz., for double crust.	1 pkg.	284	9	1,480	20	93	23	46	21	141	131	1.4	0	.11	.11	2.0	0
455	Pizza (cheese) 5½-in. sector; ⅛ of 14-in. diam. pie.	1 sector	75	45	185	7	6	2	3	Trace	27	107	.7	290	.04	.12	.7	4
	Popcorn, popped:																	
456	Plain, large kernel	1 cup	6	4	25	1	Trace	—	—	—	5	1	.2	—	—	.01	.1	0
457	With oil and salt	1 cup	9	3	40	1	2	1	Trace	Trace	5	1	.2	—	—	.01	.2	0
458	Sugar coated	1 cup	35	4	135	2	1	—	—	—	30	2	.5	—	—	.02	.4	0
	Pretzels:																	
459	Dutch, twisted	1 pretzel	16	5	60	2	1	—	—	—	12	4	.2	0	Trace	Trace	.1	0
460	Thin, twisted	1 pretzel	6	5	25	1	Trace	—	—	—	5	1	.1	0	Trace	Trace	Trace	0
461	Stick, small, 2¼ inches	10 sticks	3	5	10	Trace	Trace	—	—	—	2	1	Trace	0	Trace	Trace	Trace	0
462	Stick, regular, 3⅛ inches	5 sticks	3	5	10	Trace	Trace	—	—	—	2	1	Trace	0	Trace	Trace	Trace	0
	Rice, white: Enriched:																	
463	Raw	1 cup	185	12	670	12	1	—	—	—	149	44	[20]5.4	0	[20].81	[20].06	[20]6.5	0
464	Cooked	1 cup	205	73	225	4	Trace	—	—	—	50	21	[20]1.8	0	[20].23	[20].02	[20]2.1	0
465	Instant, ready-to-serve.	1 cup	165	73	180	4	Trace	—	—	—	40	5	[20]1.3	0	[20].21	[20]—	[20]1.7	0
466	Unenriched, cooked	1 cup	205	73	225	4	Trace	—	—	—	50	21	.4	0	.04	.02	.8	0
467	Parboiled, cooked	1 cup	175	73	185	4	Trace	—	—	—	41	33	[20]1.4	0	[20].19	[20]—	[20]2.1	0
468	Rice, puffed, added nutrients.	1 cup	15	4	60	1	Trace	—	—	—	13	3	.3	0	.07	.01	.7	0
	Rolls, enriched: Cloverleaf or pan:																	
469	Home recipe	1 roll	35	26	120	3	3	1	1	1	20	16	.7	30	.09	.09	.8	Trace
470	Commercial	1 roll	28	31	85	2	2	Trace	1	Trace	15	21	.5	Trace	.08	.05	.6	Trace
471	Frankfurter or hamburger.	1 roll	40	31	120	3	2	1	1	1	21	30	.8	Trace	.11	.07	.9	Trace
472	Hard, round or rectangular.	1 roll	50	25	155	5	2	Trace	1	Trace	30	24	1.2	Trace	.13	.12	1.4	Trace
473	Rye wafers, whole-grain, 1⅞ by 3½ inches.	2 wafers	13	6	45	2	Trace	—	—	—	10	7	.5	0	.04	.03	.2	0
474	Spaghetti, cooked, tender stage, enriched.	1 cup	140	72	155	5	1	—	—	—	32	11	[19]1.3	0	[19].20	[19].11	[19]1.5	0

[19] Iron, thiamin, riboflavin, and niacin are based on the minimum levels of enrichment specified in standards of identity promulgated under the Federal Food, Drug, and Cosmetic Act.

[20] Iron, thiamin, and niacin are based on the minimum levels of enrichment specified in standards of identity promulgated under the Federal Food, Drug, and Cosmetic Act. Riboflavin is based on unenriched rice. When the minimum level of enrichment for riboflavin specified in the standards of identity becomes effective the value will be 0.12 milligram per cup of parboiled rice and of white rice.

Table continued on following page

Table A-1   Nutritive Value of the Edible Part of Foods (Continued)

[Dashes show that no basis could be found for imputing a value although there was some reason to believe that a measurable amount of the constituent might be present]

Food, approximate measure, and weight (in grams)	Water	Food energy	Protein	Fat	Fatty acids Saturated (total)	Fatty acids Unsaturated Oleic	Fatty acids Unsaturated Linoleic	Carbohydrate	Calcium	Iron	Vitamin A value	Thiamin	Riboflavin	Niacin	Ascorbic acid
	Percent	*Calories*	*Grams*	*Grams*	*Grams*	*Grams*	*Grams*	*Grams*	*Milligrams*	*Milligrams*	*International units*	*Milligrams*	*Milligrams*	*Milligrams*	*Milligrams*
GRAIN PRODUCTS—Continued															
Spaghetti with meat balls, and tomato sauce:															
475 Home recipe ____ 1 cup ____ 248 *Grams*	70	330	19	12	4	6	1	39	124	3.7	1,590	0.25	0.30	4.0	22
476 Canned ____ 1 cup ____ 250	78	260	12	10	2	3	4	28	53	3.3	1,000	.15	.18	2.3	5
Spaghetti in tomato sauce with cheese:															
477 Home recipe ____ 1 cup ____ 250	77	260	9	9	2	5	1	37	80	2.3	1,080	.25	.18	2.3	13
478 Canned ____ 1 cup ____ 250	80	190	6	2	1	1	1	38	40	2.8	930	.35	.28	4.5	10
479 Waffles, with enriched flour, 7-in. diam. 1 waffle ____ 75	41	210	7	7	2	4	1	28	85	1.3	250	.13	.19	1.0	Trace
480 Waffles, made from mix, enriched, egg and milk added, 7-in. diam. 1 waffle ____ 75	42	205	7	8	3	3	1	27	179	1.0	170	.11	.17	.7	Trace
481 Wheat, puffed, added nutrients. 1 cup ____ 15	3	55	2	Trace	------	------	------	12	4	.6	0	.08	.03	1.2	0
482 Wheat, shredded, plain_ 1 biscuit_ 25	7	90	2	1	------	------	------	20	11	.9	0	.06	.03	1.1	0
483 Wheat flakes, added nutrients. 1 cup ____ 30	4	105	3	Trace	------	------	------	24	12	1.3	0	.19	.04	1.5	0
Wheat flours:															
484 Whole-wheat, from hard wheats, stirred. 1 cup ____ 120	12	400	16	2	Trace	1	1	85	49	4.0	0	.66	.14	5.2	0
All-purpose or family flour, enriched:															
485 Sifted ____ 1 cup ____ 115	12	420	12	1				88	18	¹⁹3.3	0	¹⁹.51	¹⁹.30	¹⁹4.0	0
486 Unsifted ____ 1 cup ____ 125	12	455	13	1				95	20	¹⁹3.6	0	¹⁹.55	¹⁹.33	¹⁹4.4	0
487 Self-rising, enriched_ 1 cup ____ 125	12	440	12	1				93	331	¹⁹3.6	0	¹⁹.55	¹⁹.33	¹⁹4.4	0
488 Cake or pastry flour, sifted. 1 cup ____ 96	12	350	7	1				76	16	.5	0	.03	.03	.7	0
FATS, OILS															
Butter:															
Regular, 4 sticks per pound:															
489 Stick ____ ½ cup ____ 113	16	810	1	92	51	30	3	1	23	0	²³3,750	------	------	------	0

No.	Food, approximate measure	Measure	Grams	Water (%)	Food energy (cal.)	Protein (g)	Fat (g)	Saturated (g)	Oleic (g)	Linoleic (g)	Carbohydrate (g)	Calcium (mg)	Iron (mg)	Vitamin A (I.U.)	Thiamin (mg)	Riboflavin (mg)	Niacin (mg)	Ascorbic acid (mg)
490	Tablespoon (approx. ⅛ stick).	1 tbsp	14	16	100	Trace	12	6	4	Trace	Trace	3	—	470[21]	—	—	—	0
491	Pat (1-in. sq. ⅓-in. high; 90 per lb.).	1 pat	5	16	35	Trace	4	2	1	Trace	Trace	1	—	170[21]	—	—	—	0
	Whipped, 6 sticks or 2, 8-oz. containers per pound:																	
492	Stick.	½ cup	76	16	540	1	61	34	20	2	Trace	15	—	2,500[21]	—	—	—	0
493	Tablespoon (approx. ⅛ stick).	1 tbsp	9	16	65	Trace	8	4	3	Trace	Trace	2	—	310[21]	—	—	—	0
494	Pat (1¼-in. sq. ⅓-in. high; 120 per lb.).	1 pat	4	16	25	Trace	3	2	1	Trace	Trace	1	—	130[21]	—	—	—	0
	Fats, cooking:																	
495	Lard.	1 cup	205	0	1,850	0	205	78	94	20	0	0	0	0	0	0	0	0
496		1 tbsp	13	0	115	0	13	5	6	1	0	0	0	0	0	0	0	0
497	Vegetable fats.	1 cup	200	0	1,770	0	200	50	100	44	0	0	0	0	0	0	0	0
498		1 tbsp	13	0	110	0	13	3	6	3	0	0	0	0	0	0	0	0
	Margarine:																	
	Regular, 4 sticks per pound:																	
499	Stick.	½ cup	113	16	815	1	92	17	46	25	1	23	—	3,750[22]	—	—	—	0
500	Tablespoon (approx. ⅛ stick).	1 tbsp	14	16	100	Trace	12	2	6	3	Trace	3	—	470[22]	—	—	—	0
501	Pat (1-in. sq. ⅓-in. high; 90 per lb.).	1 pat	5	16	35	Trace	4	1	2	1	Trace	1	—	170[22]	—	—	—	0
	Whipped, 6 sticks per pound:																	
502	Stick.	½ cup	76	16	545	1	61	11	31	17	1	15	—	2,500[22]	—	—	—	0
	Soft, 2 8-oz. tubs per pound:																	
503	Tub.	1 tub	227	16	1,635	1	184	34	68	68	1	45	—	7,500[22]	—	—	—	0
504	Tablespoon.	1 tbsp	14	16	100	Trace	11	2	4	4	Trace	3	—	470[22]	—	—	—	0
	Oils, salad or cooking:																	
505	Corn.	1 cup	220	0	1,945	0	220	22	62	117	0	0	0	0	0	0	0	0
506		1 tbsp	14	0	125	0	14	1	4	7	0	0	0	0	0	0	0	0
507	Cottonseed.	1 cup	220	0	1,945	0	220	55	46	110	0	0	0	0	0	0	0	0
508		1 tbsp	14	0	125	0	14	4	3	7	0	0	0	0	0	0	0	0
509	Olive.	1 cup	220	0	1,945	0	220	24	167	15	0	0	0	0	0	0	0	0
510		1 tbsp	14	0	125	0	14	2	11	1	0	0	0	0	0	0	0	0
511	Peanut.	1 cup	220	0	1,945	0	220	40	103	64	0	0	0	0	0	0	0	0
512		1 tbsp	14	0	125	0	14	3	7	4	0	0	0	0	0	0	0	0
513	Safflower.	1 cup	220	0	1,945	0	220	18	37	165	0	0	0	0	0	0	0	0
514		1 tbsp	14	0	125	0	14	1	2	10	0	0	0	0	0	0	0	0
515	Soybean.	1 cup	220	0	1,945	0	220	33	44	114	0	0	0	0	0	0	0	0
516		1 tbsp	14	0	125	0	14	4	4	7	0	0	0	0	0	0	0	0

[19] Iron, thiamin, riboflavin, and niacin are based on the minimum levels of enrichment specified in standards of identity promulgated under the Federal Food, Drug, and Cosmetic Act.

[21] Year-round average.

[22] Based on the average vitamin A content of fortified margarine. Federal specifications for fortified margarine require a minimum of 15,000 I.U. of vitamin A per pound.

Table continued on following page

Table A–1　　*Nutritive Value of the Edible Part of Foods (Continued)*

[Dashes in the columns for nutrients show that no suitable value could be found although there is reason to believe that a measurable amount of the nutrient may be present]

Food, approximate measure, and weight (in grams)	Water	Food energy	Protein	Fat	Fatty acids			Carbohydrate	Calcium	Iron	Vitamin A value	Thiamin	Riboflavin	Niacin	Ascorbic acid
					Saturated (total)	Unsaturated Oleic	Linoleic								
	Percent	*Calories*	*Grams*	*Grams*	*Grams*	*Grams*	*Grams*	*Grams*	*Milligrams*	*Milligrams*	*International units*	*Milligrams*	*Milligrams*	*Milligrams*	*Milligrams*

(Weight in Grams column precedes each food entry)

FATS, OILS—Continued

Salad dressings:

No.	Food	Weight (g)	Water %	Food energy	Protein	Fat	Saturated	Oleic	Linoleic	Carbohydrate	Calcium	Iron	Vitamin A	Thiamin	Riboflavin	Niacin	Ascorbic acid
517	Blue cheese ___ 1 tbsp.	15	32	75	1	8	2	2	4	1	12	Trace	30	Trace	0.02	Trace	Trace
	Commercial, mayonnaise type:																
518	Regular ___ 1 tbsp.	15	41	65	Trace	6	1	1	3	2	2	Trace	30	Trace	Trace	Trace	------
519	Special dietary, low-calorie. ___ 1 tbsp.	16	81	20	Trace	2	Trace	Trace	1	1	3	Trace	40	Trace	Trace	Trace	------
	French:																
520	Regular ___ 1 tbsp.	16	39	65	Trace	6	1	1	3	3	2	.1	------	------	------	------	------
521	Special dietary, low-fat with artificial sweeteners. ___ 1 tbsp.	15	95	Trace	Trace	Trace	------	------	------	Trace	2	.1	------	------	------	------	------
522	Home cooked, boiled ___ 1 tbsp.	16	68	25	1	2	1	1	Trace	2	14	.1	80	.01	.03	Trace	Trace
523	Mayonnaise ___ 1 tbsp.	14	15	100	Trace	11	2	2	6	Trace	3	.1	40	Trace	.01	Trace	------
524	Thousand Island ___ 1 tbsp.	16	32	80	Trace	8	1	2	4	3	2	.1	50	Trace	Trace	Trace	Trace

SUGARS, SWEETS

Cake icings:

No.	Food	Weight (g)	Water %	Food energy	Protein	Fat	Saturated	Oleic	Linoleic	Carbohydrate	Calcium	Iron	Vitamin A	Thiamin	Riboflavin	Niacin	Ascorbic acid
525	Chocolate made with milk and table fat. ___ 1 cup	275	14	1,035	9	38	21	14	1	185	165	3.3	580	.06	.28	.6	1
526	Coconut (with boiled icing). ___ 1 cup	166	15	605	3	13	11	1	Trace	124	10	.8	0	.02	.07	.3	0
527	Creamy fudge from mix with water only. ___ 1 cup	245	15	830	7	16	5	8	3	183	96	2.7	Trace	.05	.20	.7	Trace
528	White, boiled. ___ 1 cup	94	18	300	1	0	------	------	------	76	2	Trace	0	Trace	.03	Trace	0
	Candy:																
529	Caramels, plain or chocolate. ___ 1 oz	28	8	115	1	3	2	1	Trace	22	42	.4	Trace	.01	.05	.1	Trace
530	Chocolate, milk, plain. ___ 1 oz	28	1	145	2	9	5	3	Trace	16	65	.3	80	.02	.10	.1	Trace
531	Chocolate-coated peanuts. ___ 1 oz	28	1	160	5	12	3	6	2	11	33	.4	Trace	.10	.05	2.1	Trace

Item No.	Food, approximate measure	Measure	Grams	Water (%)	Food energy (cal.)	Protein (g)	Fat (g)	Saturated (g)	Oleic (g)	Linoleic (g)	Carbohydrate (g)	Calcium (mg)	Iron (mg)	Vitamin A (I.U.)	Thiamin (mg)	Riboflavin (mg)	Niacin (mg)	Ascorbic acid (mg)
532	Fondant; mints, uncoated; candy corn.	1 oz.	28	8	105	Trace	1				25	4	.3	0	Trace	Trace	Trace	0
533	Fudge, plain.	1 oz.	28	8	115	1	3	2	1	Trace	21	22	.3	Trace	.01	.03	.1	Trace
534	Gum drops.	1 oz.	28	12	100	Trace	Trace				25	2	.1	0	0	0	Trace	0
535	Hard.	1 oz.	28	1	110	0	Trace				28	6	.5	0	0	0	0	0
536	Marshmallows.	1 oz.	28	17	90	1	Trace				23	5	.5	0	0	0	Trace	0
	Chocolate-flavored sirup or topping:																	
537	Thin type.	1 fl. oz.	38	32	90	1	1	Trace	Trace	Trace	24	6	.6	Trace	.01	.03	.2	0
538	Fudge type.	1 fl. oz.	38	25	125	2	5	3	2	Trace	20	48	.5	60	.02	.08	.2	Trace
	Chocolate-flavored beverage powder (approx. 4 heaping teaspoons per oz.):																	
539	With nonfat dry milk.	1 oz.	28	2	100	5	1	Trace	Trace	Trace	20	167	.5	10	.04	.21	.2	1
540	Without nonfat dry milk.	1 oz.	28	1	100	1	1	Trace	Trace	Trace	25	9	.6		.01	.03	.1	0
541	Honey, strained or extracted.	1 tbsp.	21	17	65	Trace	0				17	1	.1	0	Trace	.01	.1	Trace
542	Jams and preserves.	1 tbsp.	20	29	55	Trace	Trace				14	4	.2	Trace	Trace	.01	Trace	Trace
543	Jellies.	1 tbsp.	18	29	50	Trace	Trace				13	4	.3	Trace	Trace	.01	Trace	1
	Molasses, cane:																	
544	Light (first extraction).	1 tbsp.	20	24	50	—	—				13	33	.9	—	.01	.01	Trace	—
545	Blackstrap (third extraction).	1 tbsp.	20	24	45	—	—				11	137	3.2	—	.02	.04	.4	—
	Sirups:																	
546	Sorghum.	1 tbsp.	21	23	55	—	—				14	35	2.6	—	—	.02	—	—
547	Table blends, chiefly corn, light and dark.	1 tbsp.	21	24	60	0	0				15	9	.8	0	0	0	0	0
	Sugars:																	
548	Brown, firm packed.	1 cup.	220	2	820	0	0				212	187	7.5	0	.02	.07	.4	0
	White:																	
549	Granulated.	1 cup.	200	Trace	770	0	0				199	0	.2	0	0	0	0	0
550		1 tbsp.	11	Trace	40	0	0				11	0	Trace	0	0	0	0	0
551	Powdered, stirred before measuring.	1 cup.	120	Trace	460	0	0				119	0	.1	0	0	0	0	0
	MISCELLANEOUS ITEMS																	
552	Barbecue sauce.	1 cup.	250	81	230	4	17	2	5	9	20	53	2.0	900	.03	.03	.8	13
	Beverages, alcoholic:																	
553	Beer.	12 fl. oz.	360	92	150	1	0				14	18	Trace		.01	.11	2.2	—
	Gin, rum, vodka, whiskey:																	
554	80-proof.	1½ fl. oz. jigger.	42	67	100	—	—				Trace	—	—	—	—	—	—	—
555	86-proof.	1½ fl. oz. jigger.	42	64	105	—	—				Trace	—	—	—	—	—	—	—
556	90-proof.	1½ fl. oz. jigger.	42	62	110	—	—				Trace	—	—	—	—	—	—	—

Table continued on following page

Table A-1 Nutritive Value of the Edible Part of Foods (Continued)

[Dashes in the columns for nutrients show that no suitable value could be found although there is reason to believe that a measurable amount of the nutrient may be present]

	Food, approximate measure, and weight (in grams)	Water	Food energy	Protein	Fat	Fatty acids Saturated (total)	Fatty acids Unsaturated Oleic	Fatty acids Unsaturated Linoleic	Carbohydrate	Calcium	Iron	Vitamin A value	Thiamin	Riboflavin	Niacin	Ascorbic acid
		Percent	*Calories*	*Grams*	*Grams*	*Grams*	*Grams*	*Grams*	*Grams*	*Milligrams*	*Milligrams*	*International units*	*Milligrams*	*Milligrams*	*Milligrams*	*Milligrams*
	MISCELLANEOUS ITEMS—Continued															
	Beverages, alcoholic—Continued															
	Gin, rum, vodka, whiskey—Con.															
557	94-proof ____ 1½ fl. oz. jigger. *Grams* 42	60	115						Trace							
558	100-proof ____ 1½ fl. oz. jigger. 42	58	125						Trace							
	Wines:															
559	Dessert ____ 3½ fl. oz. glass. 103	77	140	Trace	0				8	8			.01	.02	.2	
560	Table ____ 3½ fl. oz. glass. 102	86	85	Trace	0				4	9	.4		Trace	.01	.1	
	Beverages, carbonated, sweetened, nonalcoholic:															
561	Carbonated water ____ 12 fl. oz. 366	92	115	0	0				29			0	0	0	0	0
562	Cola type ____ 12 fl. oz. 369	90	145	0	0				37			0	0	0	0	0
563	Fruit-flavored sodas and Tom Collins mixes. 12 fl. oz. 372	88	170	0	0				45			0	0	0	0	0
564	Ginger ale ____ 12 fl. oz. 366	92	115	0	0				29			0	0	0	0	0
565	Root beer ____ 12 fl. oz. 370	90	150	0	0				39			0	0	0	0	0
566	Bouillon cubes, approx. ½ in. 1 cube 4	4	5	1	Trace				Trace							
	Chocolate:															
567	Bitter or baking ____ 1 oz. 28	2	145	3	15	8	6	Trace	8	22	1.9	20	.01	.07	.4	0
568	Semi-sweet, small pieces. 1 cup 170	1	860	7	61	34	22	1	97	51	4.4	30	.02	.14	.9	0
	Gelatin:															
569	Plain, dry powder in envelope. 1 envelope 7	13	25	6	Trace				0							
570	Dessert powder, 3-oz. package. 1 pkg 85	2	315	8	0				75							
571	Gelatin dessert, prepared with water. 1 cup 240	84	140	4	0				34							

Item No.	Food, approximate measure	Grams	Water (%)	Food energy (cal.)	Protein (g)	Fat (g)	Sat. fatty acids, total (g)	Oleic (g)	Linoleic (g)	Carbohydrate (g)	Calcium (mg)	Iron (mg)	Vit. A (I.U.)	Thiamin (mg)	Riboflavin (mg)	Niacin (mg)	Ascorbic acid (mg)
	Olives, pickled:																
572	Green — 4 medium or 3 extra large or 2 giant.	16	78	15	Trace	2	Trace	2	Trace	Trace	8	.2	40	—	—	—	—
573	Ripe: Mission — 3 small or 2 large.	10	73	15	Trace	2	Trace	2	Trace	Trace	9	.1	10	Trace	Trace	—	—
	Pickles, cucumber:																
574	Dill, medium, whole, 3¾ in. long, 1¼ in. diam. — 1 pickle	65	93	10	1	Trace	—	—	—	1	17	.7	70	Trace	.01	Trace	4
575	Fresh, sliced, 1½ in. diam., ¼ in. thick. — 2 slices	15	79	10	Trace	Trace	—	—	—	3	5	.3	20	Trace	Trace	—	1
576	Sweet, gherkin, small, whole, approx. 2½ in. long, ¾ in. diam. — 1 pickle	15	61	20	Trace	Trace	—	—	—	6	2	.2	10	Trace	Trace	—	1
577	Relish, finely chopped, sweet. — 1 tbsp.	15	63	20	Trace	Trace	—	—	—	5	3	.1	—	Trace	Trace	—	—
	Popcorn. See Grain Products.																
578	Popsicle, 3 fl. oz. size — 1 popsicle.	95	80	70	0	0	0	0	0	18	0	Trace	0	0	0	0	0
	Pudding, home recipe with starch base:																
579	Chocolate — 1 cup	260	66	385	8	12	7	4	Trace	67	250	1.3	390	.05	.36	.3	1
580	Vanilla (blanc mange) — 1 cup	255	76	285	9	10	5	3	Trace	41	298	Trace	410	.08	.41	.3	2
581	Pudding mix, dry form, 4-oz. package — 1 pkg.	113	2	410	3	2	1	1	Trace	103	23	1.8	Trace	.02	.08	.5	0
582	Sherbet — 1 cup	193	67	260	2	2	—	—	—	59	31	Trace	120	.02	.06	Trace	4
	Soups:																
	Canned, condensed, ready-to-serve:																
	Prepared with an equal volume of milk:																
583	Cream of chicken — 1 cup	245	85	180	7	10	3	3	3	15	172	.5	610	.05	.27	.7	2
584	Cream of mushroom — 1 cup	245	83	215	7	14	4	4	5	16	191	.5	250	.05	.34	.7	1
585	Tomato — 1 cup	250	84	175	7	7	3	2	1	23	168	.8	1,200	.10	.25	1.3	15
	Prepared with an equal volume of water:																
586	Bean with pork — 1 cup	250	84	170	8	6	1	2	1	22	63	2.3	650	.13	.08	1.0	3
587	Beef broth, bouillon consomme — 1 cup	240	96	30	5	0	—	—	—	3	Trace	.5	Trace	Trace	.02	1.2	—
588	Beef noodle — 1 cup	240	93	70	4	3	1	1	1	7	7	1.0	50	.05	.07	1.0	Trace
589	Clam chowder, Manhattan type (with tomatoes, without milk). — 1 cup	245	92	80	2	3	—	—	—	12	34	1.0	880	.02	.02	1.0	—
590	Cream of chicken — 1 cup	240	92	95	3	6	2	3	1	8	24	.5	410	.02	.05	.5	Trace
591	Cream of mushroom — 1 cup	240	90	135	2	10	3	3	5	10	41	.5	70	.02	.12	.7	Trace
592	Minestrone — 1 cup	245	90	105	5	3	—	—	—	14	37	1.0	2,350	.07	.05	1.0	—

Table continued on following page

Table A-1　Nutritive Value of the Edible Part of Foods (Continued)

[Dashes in the columns for nutrients show that no suitable value could be found although there is reason to believe that a measurable amount of the nutrient may be present]

	Food, approximate measure, and weight (in grams)		Water	Food energy	Pro-tein	Fat	Fatty acids			Carbo-hy-drate	Cal-cium	Iron	Vita-min A value	Thia-min	Ribo-flavin	Niacin	Ascor-bic acid
							Satu-rated (total)	Unsaturated									
								Oleic	Lin-oleic								
			Per-cent	*Calo-ries*	*Grams*	*Grams*	*Grams*	*Grams*	*Grams*	*Grams*	*Milli-grams*	*Milli-grams*	*Inter-national units*	*Milli-grams*	*Milli-grams*	*Milli-grams*	*Milli-grams*

MISCELLANEOUS ITEMS—Continued
Soups—Continued
Canned, condensed, ready-to-serve—Con.
Prepared with an equal volume of water—Con.

	Food, approximate measure, and weight	Grams	Water	Food energy	Pro-tein	Fat	Satu-rated (total)	Oleic	Lin-oleic	Carbo-hy-drate	Cal-cium	Iron	Vita-min A value	Thia-min	Ribo-flavin	Niacin	Ascor-bic acid
593	Split pea ——— 1 cup ———	245	85	145	9	3	1	2	Trace	21	29	1.5	440	0.25	0.15	1.5	1
594	Tomato ——— 1 cup ———	245	90	90	2	3	Trace	1	1	16	15	.7	1,000	.05	.05	1.2	12
595	Vegetable beef ——— 1 cup ———	245	92	80	5	2	---	---	---	10	12	.7	2,700	.05	.05	1.0	---
596	Vegetarian ——— 1 cup ———	245	92	80	2	2	---	---	---	13	20	1.0	2,940	.05	.05	1.0	---
	Dehydrated, dry form:																
597	Chicken noodle (2-oz. package). 1 pkg———	57	6	220	8	6	2	3	1	33	34	1.4	190	.30	.15	2.4	3
598	Onion mix (1½-oz. package). 1 pkg———	43	3	150	6	5	1	2	1	23	42	.6	30	.05	.03	.3	6
599	Tomato vegetable with noodles (2½-oz. pkg.). 1 pkg———	71	4	245	6	6	2	3	1	45	33	1.4	1,700	.21	.13	1.8	18
	Frozen, condensed: Clam chowder, New England type (with milk, without tomatoes):																
600	Prepared with equal volume of milk. 1 cup———	245	83	210	9	12	---			16	240	1.0	250	.07	.29	.5	Trace
601	Prepared with equal volume of water. 1 cup———	240	89	130	4	8	---			11	91	1.0	50	.05	.10	.5	---
	Cream of potato:																
602	Prepared with equal volume of milk. 1 cup———	245	83	185	8	10	5	3	Trace	18	208	1.0	590	.10	.27	.5	Trace
603	Prepared with equal volume of water. 1 cup———	240	90	105	3	5	3	2	Trace	12	58	1.0	410	.05	.05	.5	---

No.	Food, approximate measure, and weight	Measure	Weight (g)	Water (%)	Food energy	Protein	Fat	Saturated	Oleic	Linoleic	Carbohydrate	Calcium	Iron	Vitamin A	Thiamine	Riboflavin	Niacin	Ascorbic acid
604	Cream of shrimp: Prepared with equal volume of milk.	1 cup	245	82	245	9	16	---	---	---	15	189	.5	290	.07	.27	.5	Trace
605	Prepared with equal volume of water.	1 cup	240	88	160	5	12	---	---	---	8	38	.5	120	.05	.05	.5	---
606	Oyster stew: Prepared with equal volume of milk.	1 cup	240	83	200	10	12	---	---	---	14	305	1.4	410	.12	.41	.5	Trace
607	Prepared with equal volume of water.	1 cup	240	90	120	6	8	---	---	---	8	158	1.4	240	.07	.19	.5	---
608	Tapioca, dry, quick-cooking.	1 cup	152	13	535	1	Trace	---	---	---	131	15	.6	0	0	0	0	0
609	Tapioca desserts: Apple.	1 cup	250	70	295	1	Trace	---	---	---	74	8	.5	30	Trace	Trace	Trace	Trace
610	Cream pudding.	1 cup	165	72	220	8	8	4	3	Trace	28	173	.7	480	.07	.30	.2	2
611	Tartar sauce.	1 tbsp	14	34	75	Trace	8	1	1	4	1	3	.1	30	Trace	Trace	Trace	Trace
612	Vinegar.	1 tbsp	15	94	Trace	Trace	0	---	---	---	1	1	.1	---	---	---	---	---
613	White sauce, medium.	1 cup	250	73	405	10	31	16	10	1	22	288	.5	1,150	.10	.43	.5	2
614	Yeast: Baker's, dry, active.	1 pkg.	7	5	20	3	Trace	---	---	---	3	3	1.1	Trace	.16	.38	2.6	Trace
615	Brewer's, dry.	1 tbsp	8	5	25	3	Trace	---	---	---	3	17	1.4	Trace	1.25	.34	3.0	Trace

Yoghurt. See Milk, Cheese, Cream, Imitation Cream.

Table A–2   Cholesterol Content of Foods

Food	Mg. per 100 gm.	Food	Mg. per 100 gm.
Beef, heart	140	cod	46
kidney	350	crab	125
liver	250	haddock	64
roast, chuck	55	halibut	33
rump	58	herring	75
round steak	68	lobster	200
tallow	56	mackerel	80
tripe	150	oysters	161
Brain, calf	1810	perch	63
Caviar	290	pike	71
Cheese, American process	87	salmon	55
Bleu	157	sardine	70
Cheddar	98	scallops	166
Cream	140	shrimp	161
Cottage cheese		sole	20
creamed	15	trout	57
dry	1	tuna	57
Emmentaler	130	Lamb, chops	66
Gouda	33	Lard	95
Limburger	92	Pork, chops	55
Mozzarella		ham	42
(part skim)	61	tenderloin and	
		Canadian bacon	57
Parmesan	74		
Roquefort	73	Sweetbreads (thymus)	280
Swiss	91	Turkey, dark	96
Chicken, dark	76	light	61
light	54	Veal, brains	1810
Duck	70	flesh	71
Fish, carp	490	kidney	350
clams	118	liver	350

Food	Mg. per serving	Food	Mg. per serving
Butter, 1 tsp.	10	Mayonnaise, 1 tbsp.	15
Cereal	0	Milk, 1 cup whole	35
Cream, 1 tbsp.	18	1 cup skim	1
Egg, 1 yolk	240	1 cup fortified	
1 white	0	skim (less than	
		0.5% butterfat)	6
Fruits	0		
Ice Cream, ½ cup	30–45	Peanut butter	0
Ice Milk, ½ cup	17	Sherbet, ½ cup	3
Margarine, vegetable fat	0	Vegetables	0
65% animal fat	70	Vegetable oils	0

(From Keyes, Ancel and Margaret: *Eat Well and Stay Well*, 1963; Turner, Dorothea: *Handbook of Diet Therapy*, 1965; and University of Iowa Medical Center: *Recent Advances in Therapeutic Diets*, 1970.)

Table A–3   *Purine Content of Foods*

Group A: (Foods containing a high purine concentration, 150 to 1000 mg. per 100 gm.)

Liver
Sweetbreads
Brains
Fish roes
Beer
Kidney
Sardines
Gravies
Mussels
Wine
Anchovies
Meat extracts, consomme
Heart
Herring

Group B: (Foods containing moderate amounts of purines, 50 to 150 mg. per 100 gm., which the physician usually limits to one serving each day.)

Meats
Peas
Cauliflower
Lentils
Yeast
Beans
Asparagus
Mushrooms
Spinach
Whole grain cereals
Fowl
Fish (except as noted above)
Other sea foods

Group C: (Foods containing negligible amounts of purines, which are not subject to limitation.)

Vegetables (except as noted above)
Fruits
Milk
Cheese
Eggs
Spices and condiments, including salt and vinegar
Refined cereals and cereal products
Butter and fats (in moderation)
Sugars and sweets
Vegetable soups (clear)
Nuts

(From U.S. Department of Health, Education, and Welfare, National Institutes of Health: *Gout,* 1968.)

Table A-4　Evaluation of the Foundation of an Adequate Diet for an Adult

FOOD	AVERAGE SERVING Household Measure	AVERAGE SERVING Weight Gm.	CALORIES	PROTEIN GM.	FAT GM.	CARBO-HYDRATE GM.	MINERALS Calcium Mg.	MINERALS Iron Mg.	VITAMINS A. (I.U.)	VITAMINS Ascorbic Acid Mg.	VITAMINS Thiamine Mg.	VITAMINS Riboflavin Mg.	VITAMINS Niacin Mg.
Milk, whole (or equivalent)	1 pt.	488	320	18.0	18	24	576	.2	700	4	.16	.84	.2
Meat group													
Eggs	1	50	80	6.0	6	tr.	27	1.1	590	—	.05	.15	tr.
Meat, poultry, fish[1]	3 oz. (cooked)	85	237	23.0	15	0	10	2.4	10	—	.09	.21	4.7
Vegetable–fruit group													
Vegetables:													
Deep green or yellow[2]	1 salad or cooked	50 raw or 75 cooked	27	1.4	tr.	6	36.7	.6	3016	20.5	.046	.08	.4
Other, cooked[3]	½ cup	80	41	2.5	tr.	7.7	15	.93	225	11	.12	.06	1.5
Potato, peeled, boiled	1 medium	122	80	2.0	tr.	18	7	.6	tr.	20	.11	.04	1.4
Fruits:													
Citrus[4]	1 serving	125	57	.8	tr.	14	28	.35	302	58	.09	.03	.36
Other (fresh and canned)[5]	1 serving	150	92	.5	tr.	24	8	.5	164	5	.03	.04	.4
Bread–cereal group													
Cereal (whole grain and enriched)[6]	½ cup cooked	28 (dry)	88	2.2	1	17.7	7.7	.6	—	—	.11	.02	.3
Bread (whole grain and enriched)	3 slices	69	180	6.0	3	36	57	1.8	tr.	tr.	.18	.15	1.8
Totals[7]			1202	62.4	43	147.4	772.4	9.1[8]	5007[8]	118.5	.986[9]	1.62	11.6[10]
Recommended Daily Dietary Allowances*													
Man (Age, 35–55; wt., 70 kg., ht., 173 cm.)			2700	56			800	10	5000	45	1.4	1.6	18[11]
Woman (Age, 35–55; wt., 58 kg.; ht., 160 cm.)			2000	46			800	18	4000	45	1.0	1.2	13[11]

[1] Evaluation based on figures for cooked (lean and fat) beef, lamb, and veal.
[2] Evaluation based on lettuce, cooked carrots, green beans, winter squash and broccoli.
[3] Evaluation based on average for cooked peas and beets.
[4] Evaluation based on Florida orange and white and pink grapefruit; whole and juice.
[5] Evaluation based on canned peaches, applesauce, raw pears, apples and bananas.
[6] Evaluation based on oatmeal and cornflakes.
[7] With the addition of more of the same foods, or other foods, to meet calorie requirement, the totals will be increased.

[8] With the use of liver this figure will be markedly increased.
[9] With the use of pork, legumes and liver this figure will be markedly increased.
[10] The average diet in the United States, which contains a generous amount of protein, provides enough tryptophan to increase the niacin value by about a third.
[11] These figures are expressed as niacin equivalents, which includes dietary sources of the preformed vitamin and the precursor, tryptophan.
* Recommended Dietary Allowances. Washington, D. C., National Research Council, 1974.

Table A–5 *Height-Weight-Age Table for Boys of School Age*

(Weight is expressed in pounds)

HT. INS.	5 YRS.	6 YRS.	7 YRS.	8 YRS.	9 YRS.	10 YRS.	11 YRS.	12 YRS.	13 YRS.	14 YRS.	15 YRS.	16 YRS.	17 YRS.	18 YRS.	19 YRS.	HT. INS.
38	34	34														38
39	35	35														39
40	36	36														40
41	38	38	38													41
42	39	39	39	39												42
43	41	41	41	41												43
44	44	44	44	44	44											44
45	46	46	46	46	46											45
46	47	48	48	48	48											46
47	49	50	50	50	50	50										47
48		52	53	53	53	53										48
49		55	55	55	55	55	55									49
50		57	58	58	58	58	58	58								50
51			61	61	61	61	61	61								51
52			63	64	64	64	64	64	64							52
53			66	67	67	67	67	68	68							53
54				70	70	70	70	71	71	72						54
55				72	72	73	73	74	74	74						55
56				75	76	77	77	78	78	78	80					56
57						79	80	81	82	83	83					57
58						83	84	84	85	85	86	87				58
59						87	88	89	89	90	90	90				59
60						91	92	92	93	94	95	96				60
61							95	96	97	99	100	103	106			61
62							100	101	102	103	104	107	111	116		62
63							105	106	107	108	110	113	118	123	127	63
64								109	111	113	115	117	121	126	130	64
65								114	117	118	120	122	127	131	134	65
66									119	122	125	128	132	136	139	66
67									124	128	130	134	136	139	142	67
68										134	134	137	141	143	147	68
69										137	139	143	146	149	152	69
70										143	144	145	148	151	155	70
71										148	150	151	152	154	159	71
72											153	155	156	158	163	72
73											157	160	162	164	167	73
74											160	164	168	170	171	74

The following percentages of net weight have been added for clothing (shoes and sweaters not included): 35 to 64 pounds: 3.5 per cent; 64 pounds and over: 2.0 per cent.

[1]From material prepared by Bird T. Baldwin, Ph.D., Iowa Child Welfare Research Station, State University of Iowa, and Thomas D. Wood, M.D., Columbia University, New York.

Appendix 1

Table A–6 *Height-Weight-Age Table for Girls of School Age*
(Weight is expressed in pounds)

HT. INS.	5 YRS.	6 YRS.	7 YRS.	8 YRS.	9 YRS.	10 YRS.	11 YRS.	12 YRS.	13 YRS.	14 YRS.	15 YRS.	16 YRS.	17 YRS.	18 YRS.	HT. INS.
38	33	33													38
39	34	34													39
40	36	36	36												40
41	37	37	37												41
42	39	39	39												42
43	41	41	41	41											43
44	42	42	42	42											44
45	45	45	45	45	45	45									45
46	47	47	47	48	48										46
47	49	50	50	50	50	50									47
48		52	52	52	52	53									48
49		54	54	54	55	55	56	56							49
50		56	56	57	58	59	61	62							50
51			59	60	61	61	63	65							51
52			63	64	64	64	65	67							52
53			66	67	67	68	68	69	71						53
54				69	70	70	71	71	73						54
55				72	74	74	74	75	77	78					55
56					76	78	78	79	81	83					56
57					80	82	82	82	84	88	92				57
58						84	86	86	88	93	96	101			58
59						87	90	90	92	96	100	103	104		59
60						91	95	95	97	101	105	108	109	111	60
61							99	100	101	105	108	112	113	116	61
62							104	105	106	109	113	115	117	118	62
63								110	110	112	116	117	119	120	63
64								114	115	117	119	120	122	123	64
65								118	120	121	122	123	125	126	65
66									124	124	125	128	129	130	66
67									128	130	131	133	133	135	67
68									131	133	135	136	138	138	68
69										135	137	138	140	142	69
70										136	138	140	142	144	70
71										138	140	142	144	145	71

The following percentages of net weight have been added for clothing (shoes and sweaters not included): 35 to 65 pounds: 3.0 per cent; 66 to 82 pounds: 2.5 per cent; 83 pounds and over: 2 per cent.

[1]From material prepared by Bird T. Baldwin, Ph.D., Iowa Child Welfare Research Station, State University of Iowa, and Thomas D. Wood, M.D., Columbia University, New York.

Table A-7   *Cooking Temperatures*

Simmering water	185-210° F
Boiling water (sea level)	212° F
Soft-ball stage (candies)	234-240° F
Jellying state	220-222° F
Very slow oven	250-275° F
Slow oven	300-325° F
Moderate oven	350-375° F
Hot oven	400-425° F
Very hot oven	450-475° F
Extremely hot oven	500-525° F

Table A-8   *Abbreviations*

Capacity
  t. or tsp. = teaspoon
  T. , Tb. , or Tbsp. = tablespoon
  c. = cup
  pt. = pint
  qt. = quart
  gal. = gallon
  bu. = bushel
  pk. = peck
  cc. = cubic centimeter
  l. = liter
  ml. = milliliter

Temperature
  °C = degrees Centigrade
  °F = degrees Fahrenheit

Weight
  oz. = ounce
  lb. = pound
  mcg. = microgram
  mg. = milligram
  g. , gm. = gram
  kg. = kilogram

Length
  in. = inch
  ft. = foot
  yd. = yard
  mm. = millimeter
  cm. = centimeter
  m. = meter

Table A-9   *Food Yields and Measures*

Cereal products

All-purpose flour	1 pound = 4 cups sifted
Cake flour	1 pound = 4 3/4 cups sifted
Whole wheat flour	1 pound = 3 3/4 cups stirred
Macaroni and spaghetti	1/4 pound (1 cup) = 2 1/4 cups cooked
Noodles	1/4 pound (1 cup) = 1 1/2 cups cooked
Rice, milled white	1 cup = 3 cups cooked
Rice, quick cooking brown	1 cup = 3 cups cooked
Bread, fresh	1 5/8 inch slice = 1 cup soft bread cubes or crumbs
Bread, dry	1 5/8 inch slice = 1/3 cup dry bread crumbs
Cereal flakes	3 cups approx. = 1 1/3 cups fine crumbs
Graham crackers	15 = 1 cup fine crumbs
Soda crackers	22 = 1 cup fine crumbs
Thickening agents	1 tablespoon flour = 1/2 tablespoon corn, rice, potato, or arrowroot starch = 2 teaspoons quick-cooking tapioca

Dairy products

Butter or margarine	1 pound = 4 sticks = 2 cups
Cheddar (American) cheese	1/4 pound = 1 cup grated
Cottage cheese	1 pound = 1 pint = 2 cups
Nonfat dry milk:	
Powder	1 pound = 4 cups = 5 quarts milk
Crystals	1 pound = 5 2/3 cups = 4 1/4 quarts milk
Whipping cream	1 cup = 1/2 pint = 2 cups whipped

Substitutions:
  1 cup butter = 1 cup margarine = 7/8 cup lard + 1/2 teaspoon salt = 7/8 to
    1 cup hydrogenated fat + 1/2 teaspoon salt unless recipe uses melted fat,
    then use equivalent oil
  1 cup milk = 1/3 cup concentrated milk + 2/3 cup water = 1 cup skim milk +
    2 teaspoons butter = 1/2 cup evaporated milk + 1/2 cup water
  1 cup sour milk or buttermilk = 1 tablespoon vinegar or lemon juice +
    sweet milk to fill the cup
  1 cup coffee cream (thin or 20%) = 7/8 cup milk + 3 tablespoons butter or
    margarine

Eggs

Egg whites	1 cup = 8 to 10
Egg yolks	1 cup = 12 to 14

Legumes

Kidney beans	1 cup = 2 3/4 cup cooked

Table A-9 Food Yields and Measures (Continued)

Lima beans	1 cup = 2 to 2 1/2 cups cooked (smaller size bean = fewer cups)
Navy beans	1 cup = 2 1/2 cups cooked
Split peas	1 cup = 1/2 pound = 2 1/2 cups cooked

Nuts

Almonds in shell	1 pound = 1 1/2 cup kernels
Pecans in shell	1 pound = 2 1/4 cup halves = 2 cups chopped
Walnuts in shell	1 pound = 1 1/2 to 2 cups kernels = 1 1/4 cups chopped approximately

Sugars

Brown	1 pound = 2 1/4 cups firmly packed
Confectioner's	1 pound = 3 1/2 cups sifted
Granulated	1 pound = 2 cups
Superfine granulated	1 pound = 2 1/3 cups

Substitutions:
  1 cup granulated sugar = 1 cup firmly packed brown sugar = 1 cup honey
    with liquid reduced 1/4 to 1/3 cup
  1 cup honey = 1 1/4 cups sugar plus 1/4 cup liquid

Miscellaneous

Chocolate	1 ounce = 1 square = 3 tablespoons grated
Chocolate chips, morsels	1 cup = 6 ounces
Coconut, flaked	3 1/2 ounces = 1 1/3 cups approximately
Coconut, grated	7 ounces = 2 cups
Coffee, ground	1 pound (5 cups) = 40 to 50 cups
Coffee, instant	2 ounces (1 cup) = 25 to 30 cups
Fat	1 pound = 2 cups
Marshmallows	1/4 pound = 16 regular size
Onion	1 medium = 2/3 to 1 cup chopped
Peanut butter	1 pound = 2 cups
Salt, table	1 pound = 1 1/2 cups
Tea	1 pound (6 to 8 cups) = 300 cups

Substitutions:
  1 teaspoon baking powder = 1/4 teaspoon baking soda + 1/2 teaspoon cream
    of tartar = 1/4 teaspoon baking soda + 1/2 cup sour milk or buttermilk =
    1/4 teaspoon baking soda + 1/4 to 1/2 cup molasses
  1 square (1 ounce) chocolate = 3 tablespoons cocoa + 1 tablespoon fat
  1 cup grated coconut = 1 1/3 cups flaked coconut
  1 chopped small onion = 1 tablespoon instant minced onion
  2 tablespoons minced fresh parsley = 1 tablespoon dried parsley flakes

Taken from: University of California Agricultural Extension Service: *Food Yields and Measures.*

Table A–10   Measure and Weight Equivalents

1 bushel = 4 pecks = 8 gallons = 2150.42 cubic inches

1 peck = 8 quarts = 2 gallons

1 gallon = 4 quarts = 231 cubic inches

1 quart = 2 pints = 4 cups = approximately 1000 cubic centimeters
  = 946.4 milliliters = 32 fluid ounces = 960 grams = 57 3/4 cubic inches

1 cup = 16 tablespoons = 8 fluid ounces = 2 gills = 237 milliliters = 1/2
  pint = 1/2 pound = 240 cubic centimeters (approximately) = 240 grams

1 tablespoon = 3 teaspoons = 1/2 fluid ounce = 15 cubic centimeters
  = 15 grams

1 teaspoon = approximately 5 cubic centimeters = 5 milliliters = 1/6 ounce
  = 60 drops

1 liter = 1000 milliliters = 1.06 quarts = 1000 cubic centimeters = 61.02
  cubic inches

1 inch = 2.54 centimeters = 25.399 millimeters

1 foot = 12 inches = 1/3 yard = 30.48 centimeters

1 centimeter = one hundredth meter = 0.3937 (approximately 2/5) inch
  = 0.0328 feet

1 meter = 39.37 inches = 3.28 feet

1 millimeter = one thousandth meter = 0.03937 (approximately 1/25) inch
  = 1000 microns

1 micron (μ) = 1/2500 inch = 0.001 millimeter

1 gram = one thousandth kilogram = 1 cubic centimeter = 1 milliliter

$$= 15.43 \text{ grains} \left.\begin{array}{l} \\ 0.563 \text{ drams} \\ 0.035 \text{ ounces} \\ 0.0022 \text{ pound} \end{array}\right\} \text{Avoir.} \qquad \begin{array}{l} = 0.257 \text{ dram} \\ 0.032 \text{ ounce} \\ 0.0027 \text{ pound} \end{array}\left.\begin{array}{l} \\ \\ \end{array}\right\} \text{Apoth.}$$

1 kilogram = 2.2045 (2.2) pounds = 35.27 ounces

1 ounce = 28.35 grams (approximately 30) = 28.35 cubic centimeters
  = 16 drams = 437.5 grains

3 1/2 ounces = approximately 100 grams

1 pound = 16 ounces = 453.6 grams = 7000 grains = 27.7 cubic inches
  = 1.215 pounds Troy

1 grain = 0.065 (approximately 3/50) gram

1 dram = 1.77 (approximately 1 3/4) grams

1 milliequivalent = 1 thousandth equivalent

1 microgram = 1 thousandth milligram

1 milligram = 1 thousandth gram

kilogram = $\dfrac{\text{pounds}}{2.2}$ or pounds x 0.45

centimeters = inches x 2.54

milliequivalents = $\dfrac{\text{milligrams}}{\text{atomic weight}}$ x valence

Element	Atomic Weight	Valence
Calcium	40.08	2
Chlorine	35.46	±1,5,7
Phosphorus	30.98	± 3,5
Potassium	39.10	1
Sodium	23.00	1

Table A–11   *Equivalents of Centigrade and Fahrenheit Thermometric Scales**

CENT.	FAHR.	CENT.	FAHR.	CENT.	FAHR.
Deg.	Deg.	Deg.	Deg.	Deg.	Deg.
−40	−40.0	9	48.2	57	134.6
−39	−38.2	10	50.0	58	136.4
−38	−36.4	11	51.8	59	138.2
−37	−34.6	12	53.6	60	140.0
−36	−32.8	13	55.4	61	141.8
−35	−31.0	14	57.2	62	143.6
−34	−29.2	15	59.0	63	145.4
−33	−27.4	16	60.8	64	147.2
−32	−25.6	17	62.6	65	149.0
−31	−23.8	18	64.4	66	150.8
−30	−22.0	19	66.2	67	152.6
−29	−20.2	20	68.0	68	154.4
−28	−18.4	21	69.8	69	156.2
−27	−16.6	22	71.6	70	158.0
−26	−14.8	23	73.4	71	159.8
−25	−13.0	24	75.2	72	161.6
−24	−11.2	25	77.0	73	163.4
−23	−9.4	26	78.8	74	165.2
−22	−7.6	27	80.6	75	167.0
−21	−5.8	28	82.4	76	168.8
−20	−4.0	29	84.2	77	170.6
−19	−2.2	30	86.0	78	172.4
−18	−0.4	31	87.8	79	174.2
−17	+1.4	32	89.6	80	176.0
−16	3.2	33	91.4	81	177.8
−15	5.0	34	93.2	82	179.6
−14	6.8	35	95.0	83	181.4
−13	8.6	36	96.8	84	183.2
−12	10.4	37	98.6	85	185.0
−11	12.2	38	100.4	86	186.8
−10	14.0	39	102.2	87	188.6
−9	15.8	40	104.0	88	190.4
−8	17.6	41	105.8	89	192.2
−7	19.4	42	107.6	90	194.0
−6	21.2	43	109.4	91	195.8
−5	23.0	44	111.2	92	197.6
−4	24.8	45	113.0	93	199.4
−3	26.6	46	114.8	94	201.2
−2	28.4	47	116.6	95	203.0
−1	30.2	48	118.4	96	204.8
0	32.0	49	120.2	97	206.6
+1	33.8	50	122.0	98	208.4
2	35.6	51	123.8	99	210.2
3	37.4	52	125.6	100	212.0
4	39.2	53	127.4	101	213.8
5	41.0	54	129.2	102	215.6
6	42.8	55	131.0	103	217.4
7	44.6	56	132.8	104	219.2
8	46.4				

*Temperature conversion formulae:

$°C. = 5/9 \ (°F. - 32)$

$°F. = 9/5 \ °C. + 32$

Table A–12 Sodium and Potassium Content of Foods

FOOD	SODIUM	POTASSIUM
	mg./100 gm.	mg./100 gm.
All-Bran cereal	1400	1200
Allspice	62	680
Almond		
Raw	3	690
Roasted in oil, salted	160	710
Anchovy paste	9800	200
Apples		
Juice (sweet cider), bottled	4	100
June, less skin and core	0.1	71
Mackintosh, less skin and core	0.2	90
Red Delicious, less skin and core	0.3	76
Sauce, canned	0.3	55
Apricot		
Canned in sirup	2	65
Dried	11	1700
Raw, with skin	0.6	440
Artichoke, globe	43	430
Asparagus		
Spears, canned	410	130
Tips, fresh	2	240
Tips, frozen	3	320
Avocado	3	340
Bacon		
Fried crisp	2400	390
Raw	680	110
Baking powder		
Alum type	10,000	150
Phosphate type	9000	170
Tartrate type	7300	5000
Banana	0.5	420
Barley, pearled	3	160
Beans		
Baked, Heinz, Navy		
With pork and tomato sauce, canned	480	210
With tomato sauce, canned	400	140
Dry, Navy	1	1300
Green, in pods		
Canned	410	120
Fresh	0.9	300
Frozen	2	110
Lima		
Canned	310	210
Fresh	1	680
Frozen	310	580
Beef		
Corned	1300	60
Dried	4300	200
Lean, koshered, raw	1600	290
Lean, raw	51	360
Beer	8	46
Beets		
Canned	36	120
Greens, fresh	130	570
Raw	110	350

FOOD	SODIUM	POTASSIUM
	mg./100 gm.	mg./100 gm.
Blackberry	0.2	150
Blueberry	0.6	89
Bouillon cube	24,000	100
Brain, pig	150	340
Bran, wheat, crude	15	980
Brandy	3	4
Brazil nuts		
Raw	1	670
Roasted in oil, salted	190	730
Bread		
Boston brown, with raisins	280	360
Low-sodium—4 laboratory samples	3	94
Low-sodium cinnamon roll—		
laboratory sample	2	120
Low-sodium—14 commercial "salt-free" breads:		
Maximum	76	200
Minimum	4	72
Average	28	120
Passover—See matzoth		
Rye and wheat	590	160
White, enriched	640	180
Whole wheat	930	230
Whole wheat and white	620	250
Breakfast cereals—See individual cereal		
Broccoli		
Fresh	16	400
Frozen	13	250
Brussels sprouts		
Fresh	11	450
Frozen	9	300
Butter		
Theoretical sodium value based on		
U. S. average salt content of 2.5%	980	
4 Indiana samples	880	23
Unsalted	5	4
Buttermilk, cultured	130	140
Cabbage	5	230
Candy		
Bar, Baby Ruth	170	300
Bar, Milky Way	220	150
Bar, Oh Henry	76	420
Gum drop	41	18
Marshmallow	41	6
Milk chocolate	86	420
Necco Wafers	5	2
Peppermint patty, Schrafft's	10	110
Sweet chocolate	35	230
Cantaloupe	12	230
Caraway seed	17	1400
Carbonated drinks—See individual drinks		
Carrots		
Canned	280	110
Scraped and trimmed	31	410
Casein		
Acid-washed	0.4	2
Low-ash commercial	13	39
Vitamin-free	160	900

*Courtesy of C. E. Bills, et al., and the *J. Am. Dietet. A.*, 25:304–314. In Krause: *Food, Nutrition and Diet Therapy*, 1966, p. 664.

Table A–12 *Sodium and Potassium Content of Foods (Continued)*

FOOD	SODIUM mg./100 gm.	POTASSIUM m.g./100 gm.
Cashew nuts		
Raw	14	560
Roasted in oil, salted	200	560
Catchup, tomato	1300	800
Catfish (fiddler), Ohio River	60	330
Cauliflower		
Buds	24	400
Buds, frozen	22	290
Caviar, salmon, canned	2200	180
Celery		
Salt	28,000	380
Seed	140	1400
Stalks, less leaves	110	300
Cereals, dry		
Bran		
All-Bran	1400	1200
Crude, unsalted	15	980
Corn flakes	660	160
Farina		
Cream of Wheat, plain	2	86
Cream of Wheat, quick-cooking, enriched	90	84
Grape-Nuts	660	230
Pabena	640	340
Pablum	620	380
Rolled oats	2	340
Ry-Krisp	1500	600
Wheat		
Flakes	1300	320
Germ, malt-flavored, Zing	9	780
Instant Ralston	1	360
Maltex	4	250
Muffets	4	300
Pettijohn's	2	380
Puffed	4	340
Shredded	2	330
Wheatena	2	380
Certo (pectin solution)	15	110
Chard		
Large leaves	210	720
Small leaves	84	380
Cheese		
American Swiss	710	100
Cheddar	700	92
Cottage	290	72
Cream, Philadelphia	250	74
Process	1500	80
Whey, Velveeta	1600	270
Cherries		
Sour, frozen in sirup	2	78
Sweet		
Dark		
Raw	1	260
Canned in sirup	0.8	77
Frozen in sirup	1	280
Light, canned in sirup	3	55
Chestnut	2	410
Chicken, raw		
Breast meat	78	320
Leg meat	110	250

FOOD	SODIUM mg./100 gm.	POTASSIUM mg./100 gm.
Chocolate—See also individual candy		
Syrup, Hershey	60	130
Unsweetened	4	830
Cider, sweet (apple juice), bottled	4	100
Cinnamon	8	200
Citron, candied	290	120
Clam	180	240
Clove	210	1000
Coca-Cola	1	52
Cocoa		
Dutch process	57	3200
Plain, Hershey	5	1400
Coconut		
Dry, shredded	16	770
Meat	29	320
Milk	53	190
Cod		
Raw	60	360
Frozen fillets	400	400
-liver oil	0.1	0
Salted, dried	8100	160
Coffee		
Instant, Nescafé, dry	84	3100
Roasted		
Decaffeinated, Sanka, dry	6	2000
Regular, dry	2	1600
Cookie, salt-free, Betty Bakerite	12	240
Corn		
Flakes	660	160
Meal, yellow, enriched, degerminated	0.7	120
Oil	0.2	0.1
Popcorn, popped and oiled	3	240
Popcorn, popped, oiled, and salted	2000	240
Starch	4	4
Sweet		
White		
Canned	200	200
Milk stage	0.3	240
Yellow		
Canned	210	200
Frozen	9	190
Milk stage	0.4	370
Yellow field, dry—5 varieties	0.6	290
Cowpeas, fresh, shelled	2	560
Crab, canned	1000	110
Crackers		
Graham	710	330
Rye, Ry-Krisp	1500	600
Soda	1100	120
Unsalted, Jewish—See matzoth		
Cranberry		
Raw	1	65
Sauce, canned	1	17
Cream of tartar—theoretical value for pure $KHC_4H_4O_6$	0	20,776
Cream, whipping, 32% fat	40	56
Crisco (vegetable shortening)	4	0
Cucumber, less parings	0.9	230
Currants		
Red	2	160
Zante, dried (Zante raisins)	22	730

Table continued on following page

Table A-12   Sodium and Potassium Content of Foods (Continued)

FOOD	SODIUM	POTASSIUM	FOOD	SODIUM	POTASSIUM
	mg./100 gm.	mg./100 gm.		mg./100 gm.	mg./100 gm.
Curry powder	45	1300	Grapes, continued		
Dandelion greens	76	430	Juice, Concord, sweetened, bottled	1	120
Date, semi-dry, California	1	790	Thompson Seedless, with skin	4	180
Dextri-Maltose			Tokay, less seeds, with skin	0.7	160
No. 1	840	160	Grapefruit		
No. 2	46	160	Fresh	0.5	200
No. 3	46	1300	Juice, sweetened, canned	0.4	150
B	52	360	Sections, sweetened, frozen	5	60
Dextrin	14	14	Grape-Nuts cereal	660	230
Dextrose	1	0.4	Gravy flavoring, Kitchen Bouquet	86	280
Dill, seed	13	1000	Gum, chewing, spearmint	22	27
Duck, domesticated, raw			Halibut		
Breast meat	68	360	Raw	56	540
Leg meat	96	210	Steak, frozen	460	500
Egg			Ham, raw	1100	340
Whites only	110	100	Hash, corned beef, canned	540	200
Whole	81	100	Hazelnuts—See filberts		
Yolks only	26	100	Heart		
Eggplant, less skin	0.9	190	Beef	90	160
Endive greens	18	400	Turkey	69	240
Farina			Hominy, canned	250	22
Cream of Wheat, plain, dry	2	86	Honey	7	10
Cream of Wheat, quick-cooking, en-			Horse-radish, prepared	96	290
riched, dry	90	84	Ice cream	100	90
Figs			Jam, grape	7	78
Canned in sirup	1	105	Kale, leaves and midribs	110	410
Dried	34	780	Kidney, beef	210	310
Raw	2	190	Kumquat, pulp and rind, less seeds	7	230
Filberts (hazelnut)	1	560	Lactalbumin	47	69
Flour			Lactose, U.S.P.	2	0
Bleached			Lamb		
Enriched, Gold Medal	1	86	Chop, lean, raw	98	340
Enriched, phosphated	13	78	Leg, lean, raw	78	380
Buckwheat	1	680	Lard	0.3	0.2
Gluten	2	24	Lemon-lime soda	7	33
Rye, dark	1	860	Lemons		
Self-rising	1500	90	Peel		
Untreated, high-extraction	1	120	Candied	50	12
Whole wheat (Graham)	2	290	Fresh	9	360
Fruit cocktail, canned in sirup	9	160	Pulp and juice	0.7	130
Garlic, less skin	6	510	Lentils, dry	3	1200
Gelatin			Lettuce		
Dessert, flavored, Jell-O	330	210	Head	12	140
Plain	36	22	Leaf	7	230
Gin	0.7	0.3	Lime, pulp and juice	1	100
Ginger	29	1100	Litchi, dried	3	1100
Ginger ale	8	0.6	Liver, raw		
Gizzard, turkey	58	170	Calf	110	380
Gluten flour	2	24	Goose	140	230
Goose, raw			Pig	77	350
Breast meat	76	420	Turkey	51	160
Leg meat	96	420	Lobster, boiled in tap water	210	180
Gooseberry			Lonalac, dry	13	1300
Frozen	2	150	Macaroni, plain, dry	1	160
Raw	0.7	87	Mace	45	180
Grapes			Maize—See corn		
Concord, less seeds and skin	3	84	Maltex cereal, dry	4	250
Emperor, less seeds, with skin	4	180	Maple sirup	14	130
Jam	7	78	Marmalade, orange	13	19

Table A-12 Sodium and Potassium Content of Foods (Continued)

FOOD	SODIUM	POTASSIUM	FOOD	SODIUM	POTASSIUM
Matzoth	*mg./100 gm.*	*mg./100 gm.*		*mg./100 gm.*	*mg./100 gm.*
American style (salted)	470	120			
Egg	16	160	Parsley, fresh	28	880
Farfel (dough balls)	28	130	Parsnip, scraped and trimmed, fresh	7	740
Meal	4	130	Peaches		
Passover (Passover bread)	1	140	Canned in sirup	5	31
Plain	1	160	Dried	12	1100
Poppy seed	350	110	Frozen in sirup	3	120
Thin tea	2	130	Raw, less skin	0.5	160
Whole wheat	280	420	Peanuts		
Mayonnaise	590	25	Butter	120	820
Meat extract, flavored	11,000	6000	Oil	0.2	0.1
Milk			Raw, with skin	2	720
Cow's			Roasted		
Buttermilk, cultured	130	140	Dry, with skin	2	740
Condensed, sweetened	140	340	In oil and salted,		
Evaporated	100	270	with skin	460	700
Fat	0.4	0.3	Pears		
Skim	52	150	Bartlett		
Whole			Canned in sirup	8	52
Dry	410	1100	Raw, less skin and core	2	100
Liquid	50	140	Peas		
Goat's	34	180	Canned, less liquor	270	96
Human			Dry, split	42	880
From 10 mothers, 3 to 10 days post-			Fresh	1	370
partum	37	68	Frozen	100	160
From 4 mothers, 49 to 77 days post-			Pecan, raw	0.3	420
partum	11	51	Pectin solution, Certo	15	110
Low-sodium—See Lonalac			Pepper (spice)		
Malted, dry	440	720	Black	16	880
Molasses, cane	80	1500	Red	46	2400
Muffets cereal	4	300	White	5	48
Mulberry	0.7	200	Peppermint extract	0.3	5
Mushrooms			Peppers, green, empty pods	0.6	170
Canned	400	150	Pepsi-Cola	15	3
Raw	5	520	Persimmon, wild	0.6	310
Mustard			Pettijohn's cereal, dry	2	380
Greens	48	450	Pickle, dill	1400	200
Powder	3	840	Pilchard—See sardine		
Prepared paste	1300	130	Pineapple		
Nectarine, less skin	2	320	Canned in sirup	1	120
Nutmeg	14	160	Frozen in sirup	1	38
Oats, rolled (oatmeal), dry	2	340	Juice, unsweetened, canned	0.5	140
Okra, fresh	1	220	Raw	0.3	210
Oleomargarine	1100	58	Plums		
Olives			Canned in sirup	18	110
Green, pickled	2400	55	Raw	0.6	170
Oil	0.2	0.2	Polyvitamin dispersion, Mead's, dry	6	10
Ripe, pickled	980	23	Pomegranate, pulp and juice	0.3	200
Stuffed, pickled	2800	55	Popcorn		
Onion, less tops and dry skins	1	130	Popped		
Orange Crush	2	100	Oiled	3	240
Oranges			Oiled and salted	2000	240
Juice, unsweetened, canned	0.5	190	Pork		
Pulp and juice	0.3	170	Lean, raw	58	260
Temple, pulp and juice	3	220	Salt	1800	27
Oyster, raw	73	110	Postum		
Pabena cereal, dry	640	340	Cereal beverage, dry	36	1300
Pablum cereal, dry	620	380	Instant, dry	71	2200
Pancreas, pig, raw	57	240	Potatoes		
Paprika	82	2300	Chips	340	880

Table continued on following page

Table A–12   *Sodium and Potassium Content of Foods (Continued)*

FOOD	SODIUM	POTASSIUM	FOOD	SODIUM	POTASSIUM
	mg./100 gm.	mg./100 gm.		mg./100 gm.	mg./100 gm.
Potatoes, continued			Sauerkraut, canned	630	140
Sweet			Sausage		
Canned	48	200	Bologna	1300	230
Raw, less skin	4	530	Frankfurt	1100	220
White			Pork	740	140
Canned	350	240	Scallop, frozen	150	420
Raw, less skin	0.8	410	Shortening, vegetable		
Poultry seasoning	26	840	Crisco	4	0
Pretzel	1700	130	Spry	0.4	0.2
Protenum, dry	360	1100	Shrimp, raw	140	220
Prunes			Sirup		
Canned in sirup	3	220	Chocolate, Hershey	60	130
Dried	6	600	Maple	14	130
Juice, unsweetened, bottled	2	260	Sorghum	21	600
Raw, with skin	0.7	210	Table, corn-and-cane, Karo Crystal		
Pumpkin			White	68	4
Canned	2	240	Soda, baking—theoretical value for		
Raw, less rind and seeds	0.6	480	pure NaHCO₃	27,373	0
Quail, raw			Soft drinks		
Breast meat	35	160	Carbonated water		
Leg meat	44	190	Canada Dry	18	0.6
Quince, less skin and core, raw	0.7	290	Made with Sparklet carbon dioxide		
Rabbit, domesticated, raw			capsule and distilled water	0	0
Foreleg	47	370	White Rock	1	0.6
Loin	34	400	Coca-Cola	1	52
Radish, with skin	9	260	Ginger ale	8	0.6
Raisin			Lemon-lime soda	7	33
Seedless	21	720	Orange Crush	2	100
Zante	22	730	Pepsi-Cola	15	3
Ralston cereal, Instant, dry	1	360	Royal Crown Cola	5	2
Raspberries			Root beer	8	0.5
Black	0.3	190	Sorghum sirup	21	600
Oriental (wineberry)	0.9	170	Soup		
Red	0.5	130	Beef, canned, diluted as served	410	100
Rennet tablets, Junket	38,000	36	Tomato, canned, diluted as served	380	110
Rhubarb			Vegetable, canned, diluted as served	380	120
Frozen in sirup	2	160	Soybeans		
Raw	1	70	Dry	4	1900
Rice, dry			Flour, solvent-extracted	1	1700
Brown	9	150	Spaghetti—See macaroni		
Flakes	720	180	Spinach		
Polished and coated	2	130	Canned	320	260
Puffed	0.9	100	Frozen	60	380
Vitaminized	4	170	Raw	82	780
Wild (*Zizania*)	7	220	Spry (vegetable shortening)	0.4	0.2
Root beer	8	0.5	Squash, raw		
Royal Crown Cola	5	2	Acorn, less rind and seeds	0.4	260
Rum	2	3	Hubbard, less rind and seeds	0.3	240
Rutabaga (yellow turnip), less skin and			White summer, less rind, with seeds	0.2	150
tops, raw	5	260	Yellow summer, less rind, with seeds	0.6	200
Ry-Krisp	1500	600	Squash, cooked, frozen	6	120
Sage	20	670	Starch, corn	4	4
Salmon			Strawberries		
Canned	540	300	Frozen, sweetened	2	180
Raw	48	410	Raw	0.8	180
Salt—theoretical value for pure NaCl	39,342	0	Sugar		
Sardines			Light brown	24	230
Herring, canned in oil	510	560	White	0.3	0.5
Pilchard					
Canned in natural sauce	760	260			
Canned in tomato sauce	400	320			

Table A-12   *Sodium and Potassium Content of Foods (Continued)*

FOOD	SODIUM	POTASSIUM
	mg./100 gm.	mg./100 gm.
Sweetbreads—See pancreas and thymus		
Tangerines		
Juice, sweetened, canned	0.6	170
Pulp and juice	2	110
Tapioca, dry	5	19
Tea, India-Ceylon-Java blend, dry	4	1800
Thyme	38	500
Thymus, beef, raw	96	360
Tobacco, chewing, Spark Plug	1600	1800
Tomatoes		
Canned	18	130
Catchup	1300	800
Juice, canned	230	230
Raw, with skin	3	230
Tongue, beef, raw	100	260
Tripe, pickled	46	19
Tuna, canned	800	240
Turkey, raw		
Breast meat	40	320
Leg meat	92	310
Turmeric	22	2700
Turnips, raw		
Leaves	10	440
White, less skin and tops	37	230
Yellow (rutabaga), less skin and tops	5	260
Vanilla extract	1	74
Veal, lean, raw	48	330
Vinegar		
Cider	1	100
Distilled	0.6	15
Walnuts, raw		
Black	3	460
English	2	450
Water, carbonated—See soft drinks		
Watermelon, pink part of fruit	0.3	110
Wheat		
Beeswing (outermost coats)	4	360
Bran, crude	15	980
Flakes cereal	1300	320
Germ		
Crude	2	780
Malt-flavored, Zing	9	780
Gluten	2	24
Puffed	4	340
Scourings (dirt and fragments)	8	470
Shredded	2	330
Winter, scoured—4 samples	2	370
Wheatena cereal, dry	2	380
Whiskey		
Blended	0.3	1
Bonded	0.1	0.6
Wild rice (*Zizania*), dry	7	220
Wine		
Port	4	75
Sauterne	10	87
Wineberry (oriental raspberry)	0.9	170
Worcestershire sauce	2100	480
Yeast		
Compressed	4	360

FOOD	SODIUM	POTASSIUM
	mg./100 gm.	mg./100 gm
Yeast, continued		
Debittered brewers', dry	150	1700
Primary cultured, dry—19 samples		
Maximum	320	2200
Minimum	9	1700
Average	115	1860
Zwieback	250	150

Table A–13 *Fatty Acid Composition of Food Fats*

Values below are estimated average values; different samples may show considerable variation. Mono-enes and poly-enes produced by hydrogenation tend to resemble saturated fatty acids in affecting the cholesterol level.

	Per Cent Saturated	Per Cent Mono-ene*		Per Cent Poly-ene*	
		Oleic	Other	Linoleic	Other
Animal fats – fish, turtles					
Eel	18	45		–	37
Haddock	19	30		–	51
Halibut	20	39		–	41
Herring	19	23		–	58
Pike	19	37		–	44
Pilchard	27	20		–	53
Salmon	15	32		–	53
Trout	27	38		–	35
Tuna	25	30		–	45
Turtle, green	46	32		–	22
Turtle, sea	46	31		–	23
Animal fats – mammals					
Beef, heart	48	37	3	6	6
Beef, liver	52	25	3	10	12
Beef, flesh	49	45	3	2	1
Butterfat, cow	58	36	2	3	1
Butterfat, goat	62	30	2	5	1
Butterfat, human	46	44	2	7	1
Goat, flesh	58	35	4	2	1
Lamb, flesh	52	39	4	3	2
Pork, flesh	40	47	3	9	1
Pork, liver	45	29	3	14	9
Rabbit, domestic, flesh	42	29	4	15	10
Seal blubber†	18	31		–	51
Veal, flesh	48	42	2	7	1
Venison, flesh	66	25	3	3	3
Whale blubber†	33	30		–	37
Animal fats – poultry					
Chicken, body fat	30	40	4	20	6
Chicken, egg‡	33	46	9	7	5
Duckling, body fat	34	47	6	12	1
Turkey, body fat	28	44	4	21	3

*Ene = unsaturated.
†Note the similarity to fish.
‡Quickly variable according to feed of the hen; poly-ene may surpass 20% if hen is on special feed.
(From Keys, Ancel and Margaret: *Eat Well and Stay Well,* 1963, pp. 351–354.)

Table A–13 *Fatty Acid Composition of Food Fats (Continued)*

	Per Cent Saturated	Per Cent Mono-ene*		Per Cent Poly-ene*	
		Oleic	Other	Linoleic	Other
Nut fats					
Almond	8	71	2	20	–
Brazil	20	51	3	26	–
Cashew	16	72	2	10	–
Filbert (hazelnut)	5	69	6	17	3
Macadamia	16	60	21	3	–
Peanut	18	56	–	26	–
Pecan	7	72	1	20	–
Pistachio	10	69	1	20	–
Walnut, black	6	37	–	50	7
Walnut, English	7	17	4	64	8
Oils and fats – vegetable					
Cacao butter, chocolate	57	39	2	2	–
Coconut	92	6	–	2	–
Corn	15	25	3	56	1
Cottonseed	26	23	–	51	–
Olive	10	82	–	8	–
Peanut	18	56	–	26	–
Safflower	10	12	–	78	–
Sesame	14	44	–	42	–
Soybean	15	25	1	52	7
Sunflower	12	20	–	68	–
Seeds and grain fats					
Barley	13	32	2	50	3
Chick peas	9	52	1	38	–
Corn, kernel	15	25	3	51	1
Corn meal, white	12	38	4	45	1
Millet	32	22	3	37	6
Oatmeal, rolled oats	22	34	2	40	2
Oats	12	43	3	40	2
Pumpkin seed	17	39	1	42	1
Rice	17	44	1	37	1
Rye	16	13	1	62	8
Watermelon seed	16	33	1	49	1
Wheat, flour	15	32	2	47	4
Wheat, germ	16	23	2	52	7

*Ene = unsaturated.

Glossary

acetone (ăs'ĕ-tōn).   A fragrant, volatile, liquid ketone found in small quantities in normal urine and in large quantities in the urine of a diabetic. The odor is suggestive of nail polish remover.

acid (ăs'ĭd).   A chemical substance that contains hydrogen atoms and usually tastes sour. There is hydrochloric acid in your stomach and acetic acid on your kitchen shelf, called vinegar. Acids turn blue litmus paper red and unite with bases to form salts.

acidosis (ăs"ĭ-dō'sĭs).   A pathological condition due to reduced alkalinity of the blood and of the body tissues. The pH is below 7.0.

acute (ah-kūt').   Sharp; attended with severe symptoms and coming speedily to a crisis.

adipose (ăd'ĭ-pōs).   Of a fatty nature; the fat stored in the fat cells distributed through an animal's body.

adulterate (ah-dul'tĕr-āt).   To add a cheap or unnecessary ingredient to cheapen or falsify a preparation.

albumin (ăl-bū'mĭn).   A protein found in the serum of the blood and in milk, muscle, egg, and in many vegetable tissues and fluids. It is high in sulfur, has a complex molecular structure, is soluble in water, and is coagulable by heat.

algae (ăl'jē).   A plant group which does not produce flowers or seeds; the body is unicellular. It includes the seaweeds, allied fresh-water plants, pond scums, stoneworts, and so forth.

alimentary canal (ăl-ĕ-mĕn'tar-ē).   The tubular food-carrying passage extending from the mouth to the anus.

alkali (ăl'kah-lī).   A chemical substance that will neutralize an acid to form a salt. Has an acrid taste. The stronger alkalies are caustic. Ammonia and baking soda are examples. Also called base.

alopecia(ăl"ŏ-pē'she-ah).   Baldness; absence of hair from skin areas where it is normally present.

alveolar (ăl-vē'ŏ-lĕr).   A small saclike dilatation. In anatomy it pertains to the part of the jaws where the sockets of the teeth are situated or to the air cells of the lungs.

ambivalence (am-biv'ah-lĕns). Simultaneous attraction toward and repulsion from the same object.

ambulatory (ăm'bŭ-lah-to"rē). Walking or able to walk; not confined to bed.

amino acid (ă-mē'nō-ăs'ĭd). The component parts of the protein molecule. Often called the building blocks.

amphetamine (am-fet'ah-mĭn). A synthetic drug used to stimulate the central nervous system, increase blood pressure, reduce appetite, and reduce nasal congestion.

anabolism (ăn-ăb'ō-lĭzm). That phase of metabolism which synthesizes new molecules, especially protoplasm; any constructive process by which living cells convert simple substances into complex compounds.

anemia (ah-nē'mē-ah). A reduction below normal in the number of erythrocytes or the quality of hemoglobin; disturbance of the equilibrium between blood loss and blood production.

> *hemolytic* (he'mō-lit'ik). The life span of the erythrocytes is shortened and the bone marrow is unable to compensate for their decreased life span; abnormal destruction of the red blood cells.
>
> *hypochromic* (hī'pō-krō'mĭk). A reduction in the red cell hemoglobin. Often the red cells are also reduced in size.
>
> *macrocytic* (măk'rō-sit-ik). Larger than normal red blood cells.
>
> *microcytic* (mī'krō-sit-ik). The majority of the erythrocytes are smaller than normal.

anorexia (an"o-rĕk'-sē-ah). Lack or loss of appetite for food.

anorexigenic (an"o-rek"sĭ-jen'ik). Diminishing the appetite.

antibody (an'tĭ-bŏd"ē). Any of the various substances in the tissues or fluids, as blood or serum, which act in antagonism to specific foreign bodies, as toxins or microorganisms producing the toxins.

antimycotic (an"tĭ-mī-kot'ĭk). Counteracting the growth of fungi.

anus (ā'nŭs). The distal or terminal orifice of the alimentary canal; the posterior opening of the alimentary canal.

aphasia (a-fā'-zhia). The interference with the comprehension and use of language—the condition may follow injury to or disease of the brain centers.

appetite (ăp'ĕ-tīt). A pleasant sensation—the desire for food. Emotions strongly affect appetite.

arteriosclerosis (är-tī'rē-ō-sklĕ-rō'sĭs). A thickening and hardening of the walls of the arteries and capillaries. This is a generic term that includes a variety of conditions which cause the artery walls to become thick and hard and to lose elasticity.

ascites (ah-sī'tēz). Accumulation of fluid in the peritoneal cavity.

aseptic (ah-sĕp'tĭk). Free or freed from pathogenic organisms.

aspiration (as"pĭ-rā-shun). The act of breathing or drawing in. The removal of fluids or gases from a cavity by means of an aspirator.

assimilation (ah-sim"ĭ-lā-shŭn). The transformation of food into living tissue; constructive metabolism; absorption.

atherosclerosis (ath"er-o"skle-rō'sis). A form of arteriosclerosis. Fatty degeneration of the connective tissue of the arterial walls. The passageway through the arteries is roughened and narrowed by plaques and as a result the blood cannot flow freely. These deposits project above the surface of the inner layer of the artery, decreasing its diameter. Coronary atherosclerosis is a condition in which there are plaques in the arteries that supply the heart muscles with blood. It underlies most heart attacks.

atom (ăt'ŭm). The smallest particle of an element that can exist and still retain the chemical properties of the element.

aversion (ah-vûr'zhŭn). The act of turning away; dislike; repugnance.

base (bās). Also called alkali. A chemical substance that will neutralize an acid to form a salt. Ammonia and baking soda are examples.

blintze (blĭnts). Thin pancake rolled around a filling, e.g., chopped meat, fruit, cream cheese, etc.

buffer (buf'er). Any substance in a fluid which lessens the change in hydrogen ion concentration (pH reaction), which otherwise would be produced by adding either acid or alkali; a substance that resists change in acidity or alkalinity.

bulgur (bŭl'gâr). Parboiled wheat. Whole wheat that is cooked and dried, from which part of the bran is removed before being cracked into coarse pieces. The nutritive value is similar to that of whole wheat.

calculus (kal'ku-lus), pl. calculi. A stone; an abnormal concentration occurring within the animal body and usually composed of mineral salts.

calorie (kăl'-ŏ-rē). A measurement of heat (just as an inch is a measurement of length). The calorie used in human nutrition is the kilocalorie (formerly called the large calorie and capitalized). It is the amount of heat necessary to raise the temperature of one kilogram of water 1° centigrade. This is approximately the amount of heat needed to raise the temperature of four pounds of water 1° Fahrenheit. Synonyms: heat, energy.

capillary (kap'il-lăr"ē). A minute, thin-walled vessel. Especially, those that connect the arterioles and venules, forming a network in all parts of the body. The walls are composed of a single layer of cells through which nutrients and oxygen pass out to the tissues and waste products and carbon dioxide pass from the tissues into the blood stream.

catabolism (kah-tăb'ō-lĭzm). That part of metabolism in which complex substances are converted by living cells into simpler compounds, with the release of energy; destructive metabolism.

catalyst (kat'ah-list). The substance which accelerates a reaction and may be recovered practically unchanged at the end of the reaction. Enzymes are organic catalysts produced by living cells.

cell (sĕl). The smallest structural and functional unit of a plant or animal. It usually is a microscopic mass of protoplasm, generally including a nucleus and surrounded by a semipermeable membrane. The cell is the basis for life. Proper cellular functioning is necessary to maintain the organism's living status; this is variously called metabolism, cellular physiology, and biochemistry.

cereals (sēr'ē-ăl). The seeds of the grass family (wheat, corn, oats, rice, millet, barley, rye) and the foodstuffs prepared from the grain (bread, Italian pastas, and so forth).

> *enriched.* Specific amounts of iron, thiamine, riboflavin and niacin are added to the milled grain. The amounts to add are set by the Federal Food and Drug Administration.

> *refined.* Processing removes the outer layers of the kernel where the minerals and vitamins are found. Refined cereal is the leftover, primarily starch, portion of the kernel.

> *restored.* A partial restoration of some of the milling losses. The selection of the nutrients and their amounts are determined by the manufacturers. There is no legal standard for restored cereals.

> *whole grain.* The entire kernel is present.

cheilosis (ki-lo'sĭs). A condition marked by dry scaling on the surface of the lips and cracks at the angles of the mouth. It is characteristic of riboflavin deficiency.

chlorophyll (klō'rŏ-fĭl). The green coloring matter of plants by which photosynthesis is accomplished. It is essential in the formation of carbohydrate by plants.

cholecystitis (kŏ"lĕ-sĭs-tī'tĭs). Inflammation of the gallbladder.

cholelithiasis (kŏ"lĕ-lĭ-thī'ah-sĭs). The presence or formation of gallstones.

cholesterol (kō-lĕs'tĕr-ōl). A fatlike substance found in all animal fats, bile, skin, blood, and brain tissue. It is a precursor of vitamin D and is related to several body hormones. The most frequently occurring type of gallstone has large quantities of cholesterol; it is also found in the atheroma of the arteries.

cirrhosis, hepatic (sir-rō′sis). A degeneration of liver cells and replacement with fibrous connective or scar tissue; in alcoholics, due to an inadequate diet.

citrus (sit′rus). Pertaining to the rutaceous trees and shrubs, often thorny, bearing large fruits such as citrons, lemons, limes, oranges, grapefruits, and tangerines.

coagulate (kō-ag′ū-lāt). To curdle, clot, congeal, solidify; to become clotted.

colic (kŏl′ĭk). Pertaining to the colon; acute abdominal pain due to spasm, obstruction, or distention.

collagen (kol′ah-jen). The supportive constituent of connective tissue, skin, tendon, bone, and cartilage. It is converted into gelatin by boiling.

colloid (kŏl′oid). A substance such as albumin, gelatin, or starch seemingly soluble in a liquid; any substance containing tiny, solid, evenly dispersed particles which are not dissolved in the medium but which will not settle out.

colostomy (ko-los′to-me). The surgical creation of a new opening of the colon on the surface of the body.

compound (kŏm′-pownd). A distinct substance formed by the union of two or more parts or ingredients. A synthetic compound is identical to the natural compound; chemically manufactured products are identical with the products of biosynthesis. (The ascorbic acid in a pill is identical to the ascorbic acid in an orange.)

congenital (kon-jen′ĭ-tal). Existing at and usually before birth; referring to conditions that are present at birth regardless of their causation.

constipation (kon″stĭ-pā′shun). Abnormally long retention of the feces in the colon causing them to become hard and dry; difficult evacuation of the feces.

convalescence (kon″vah-lĕs′-ĕns). Gradual restoration to health following surgery, an attack of disease, or accidental injury.

cretin (krē′tin). A person affected by the congenital lack of thyroid secretion. There is arrested physical and mental development with dystrophy of the bones and lowered basal metabolism. Myxedema is the adult or acquired form of this deficiency.

culture (kŭl′tūr). Characteristic features of a stage of civilization. *Biol.* Cultivation of microorganisms or tissues in a media conducive to their growth, or a product of such cultivation.

curdle (kûr′d′l). Coagulate, thicken.

dahl (däl). 1. East Indian dish of lentils, rice, onions, and seasonings. 2. Pigeon peas. (Sometimes spelled dhal.)

dawdle (dô′d′l). To waste time; to trifle; to toy; to fidget.

debilitate (dĕ-bĭl′ĭ-tāt). To weaken, enfeeble; to lose strength, to waste.

decompose (dē″com-pōz′). The separation of compound bodies; disintegration, decay, rot. The decomposition of proteins is called putrefaction and that of carbohydrates is called fermentation; fats are said to rancidify.

defecation (def″ĕ-kā′shun). The removal of impurities; the evacuation of fecal material from the rectum.

dehydration (dē′hī-drā′shŭn). A condition resulting from undue loss of water; removal of water from tissue or food.

dermatosis (der″mah-tō′sĭs). Any skin disease.

dialysis (di-al′ĭ-sĭs). Separation; the separation of crystalloids and colloids in solution by means of their rates of diffusion through a semipermeable membrane; removing waste products from the blood by means of a kidney machine.

diaphragm (dī′ah-frăm). The musculomembranous partition separating the abdominal and thoracic cavities.

diffuse (dif-fūz′). To pass through, or to spread widely through a tissue.

digestible (dī-jest′ĭ-bel). Capable of being broken down chemically by the action of secretions containing enzymes. The food is changed into a form the body can absorb.

disperse (dĭs-pûrs′). To scatter, to spread or distribute; to break apart and cause to go in different ways.

distend (dĭs-tĕnd′). To extend; to stretch; to enlarge; to swell.

diuretic (dī″ŭ-rĕt′ĭk). Increasing the secretion of urine; an agent that promotes the secretion of urine.

diverticulitis (dī″ver-tĭk-ū-lī′tis). Inflammation of tiny sacs (diverticula), causing abdominal pain and often fever. Treatment may include rest, antibiotics, and change in the roughage content of the diet.

diverticulosis (dī″ver-tĭk″ū-lō′sis). The presence of tiny sacs which develop in weak spots of the intestinal wall, especially the colon.

dynamic equilibrium (dī-năm′ĭk). Constant cellular replacement.

edema (ĕ-dē′mah). The presence of abnormally large amounts of fluid in the intercellular tissue space of the body; often applied to demonstrable accumulation of excess fluid in the subcutaneous tissues.

electrolyte (ē-lek′trō-līt). The ionized form of an element. The 10 per cent of the body's minerals distributed mainly in the fluids and soft tissues. Common electrolytes in the body are sodium, potassium, chloride, calcium, magnesium, phosphate, bicarbonate, and sulfate.

emaciation (ē-mā″sē-ā′shŭn). Excessive leanness; a wasted condition of the body.

embolism (em′bō-lizm). The sudden blocking of an artery or vein by a clot or an obstruction which was brought to the place via circulating blood.

emulsion (ĕ-mŭl′shŭn). A mixture consisting of one liquid

distributed in small globules throughout the body of a second liquid; an oily mass in suspension in a watery liquid, such as oil suspended in vinegar in French dressing when it has been vigorously shaken.

encysted (en-sist′ed). Enclosed in a sac, bladder, or capsule.

endemic (ĕn-dĕm′ik). Peculiar to a district, or class of persons; present in a community all the time, but occurring in only small numbers of cases; a disease of low morbidity that is constantly present in a human community.

endogenous (ĕn-dŏj′ĕ-nŭs). That which originates from within the cells or tissues of the body. Endogenous cholesterol is synthesized by the body as contrasted with exogenous cholesterol, which refers to cholesterol obtained from food.

endotoxin (en″dō-tok′sin). A heat stable poisonous agent present in the bacterial cell. A fever producing agent of bacterial origin.

enriched. Describes foods in which nutrients that were diminished or lost in processing have been replaced. Enriched bread has had thiamine, riboflavin, niacin, and iron replaced.

entity (ĕn′tĭ-tĕ). Independent existence. A disease entity has reality and distinctness.

epidemiology (ep″i-de″me-ol′ō-jē). Dealing with the relationships of factors which determine the frequency and distribution of a disease in a human community.

epithelial (ep″ĭ-the′le-al). Pertaining to or composed of the internal and external surfaces of the body, including the lining of vessels and other small cavities. The lining consists of cells joined by small amounts of cementing substances.

erythrocyte (e-rith′ro-sīt). Red blood corpuscle (RBC).

etiology (ē-tē-ol′ō-jē). The study or theory of the causation of any disease; the sum of knowledge regarding causes of a disease.

exophthalmos (ek″sof-thal′mos). Abnormal protrusion of the eyeball.

extracellular (eks″trah-sel′ū-lar). Outside of a cell or cells.

extrinsic (ĕks-trĭn′sĭk). Coming from or originating outside; derived from things outside.

exudate (ĕks′ŭ-dāt). Material, such as fluid, cells, or cellular debris, which has escaped from blood vessels and has been deposited in tissues or on tissue surfaces, usually as a result of inflammation.

fat. The term covers both the solid and liquid (oil) plant or animal products. Fatty acids, the basic units (building blocks), are combined with glycerol (glycerin) to form glycerides. Common fats are mixtures primarily of triglycerides.

feces (fē′sēz). The excrement discharged from the intestines, consisting of bacteria, mucus, cells exfoliated from the intestine, secretions, and food residue, chiefly cellulose.

ferment (fûr′měnt). To undergo a chemical change with effervescence (bubble, hiss, and foam) as that produced by yeast. The term is applied to decomposition of carbohydrates.

fetus (fē′tŭs). The developing young in the human uterus after the end of the second month. Before 8 weeks it is called an embryo; it becomes an infant when it is completely outside the body of the mother, even before the cord is cut.

finicky (fĭn′ĭ-kē). Unduly particular; overprecise.

fissure (fĭsh′er). Any cleft or groove, normal or otherwise; a narrow opening made by the parting of any substance; a cleft.

flatulence (flăt′u-lens). Distention of the stomach or intestines by air or gas. Most flatulence is caused by swallowing air.

flora (flo′rah). The life present in or characteristic of a special location. The intestinal flora is the bacteria normally residing within the lumen of the intestine.

fluctuate (flŭk′tŭ-āt). To be constantly changing; waver; vary.

food (food). A substance that the body uses to yield energy, to build or repair tissues, and/or to regulate body processes.

food grade. A designation based on appearance. It does not indicate nutritional value.

food inspection. Evaluation of food for wholesomeness.

food poisoning (poi′z′n). Bacterial food poisoning can be divided into two types: *food infection* due to excessive quantities of bacteria which cause the symptoms; *food intoxication* due to bacteria which grow in the food and produce a toxin (poison). The toxin causes the symptoms. Symptoms from either can include mild to severe abdominal pain, vomiting, diarrhea, chills, and fever.

fortified (for′tĭ-fīd). Adding nutrients above the level of the food in its natural state or adding nutrients not normally found in the food. Margarine is fortified with vitamin A, milk with vitamin D.

fracture. The breaking of a part, especially a bone.

> *compound.* An open wound is produced through which the bone often protrudes.
>
> *compression.* A break produced due to being pressed or squeezed together, such as in a vertebra.
>
> *simple* or *closed.* The skin remains unbroken.
>
> *simple complex.* A closed fracture in which there is considerable injury to adjacent soft tissues.

gel (jĕl). A jelly-like material formed by the coagulation of a colloidal liquid. Agar and pectin make soft gels; gelatin and gum arabic make hard gels.

gingiva (jin′jĭ-vah).   The gums of the mouth.

gavage (gah-vahzh′).   Feeding through a tube passed into the stomach.

glomerulonephritis (glō-mer″u-lō-nĕ-frī′tis).   Inflammation of the capillary loops in the glomeruli of the kidney. It occurs in acute, subacute, and chronic forms and is usually secondary to an infection, especially with hemolytic streptococcus.

glycogen (glī′kō-jĕn).   A polysaccharide, which is the chief carbohydrate storage material in animals. It is formed by and largely stored in the liver and, as needed, converted back to glucose. There is some storage in muscle tissue.

glycosuria (glī″kō-su′rē-ah).   The presence of an abnormal amount of glucose in the urine.

goiter (goi′ter).   An enlargement of the thyroid gland causing a swelling in the front part of the neck.

gonadal (gŏn′ăd-ăl).   Pertaining to an ovary or testis.

gram (grăm).   A metric measurement of weight. There are approximately 30 (28.34) grams in an ounce and 15.432 grains in a gram. Abbreviated g. or gm.

granulation (grăn′ū-lā-shun).   To be formed, crystallized, or collected into grains, as sugar; the formation in wounds of small, rounded, fleshy masses or the mass so formed.

gristle (grĭs′l).   Cartilage; a specialized, fibrous connective tissue; the tissue providing the model in which most of the bones develop and constituting an important part of the growth mechanism of the organism.

gruel (groo′el).   A thin paste or porridge made of cereal grain.

hemoglobin (hē-mō-glō′-bĭn).   The oxygen-carrying pigment of the erythrocytes.

hepatomegaly (hep″ah-to-meg′ah-le).   Enlargement of the liver.

homogenize (hō-mŏ′jĕn-īz).   A mechanical process which breaks the fat in liquids into such small particles that the fat stays in suspension rather than rising to the top. Usually applied to dispersing milk fat into such fine particles that the cream will not rise to the top.

homonyms (hŏm′ŏ-nĭm).   Words that sound alike and are readily confused but have different meaning. For example: ileum, the distal portion of the small intestine, and ilium, the flank bone.

hormone (hôr′mōn).   A chemical substance produced in the body, transported in the body fluid and producing a specific effect on the activity of cells remote from its source. Also known as endocrines.

humectant (hu′mek′tant).   Moistening; a moistening or diluent substance; a substance that absorbs moisture and is used to maintain the water content of materials.

hunger (hŭng′ger).   An uncomfortable sensation – the physical need for food. Food relieves the discomfort caused by the empty stomach's wavelike muscular contractions.

hydrocephalus (hī-drō-sef'ah-lus). Abnormal accumulation of fluid in the cranial vault, accompanied by enlargement of the head, prominence of the forehead, atrophy of the brain, mental weakness, and convulsions.

hydrolysate (hī-drŏl'ĭ-zāt). A compound produced by hydrolysis. Often applied to protein hydrolysate, which is a mixture of amino acids, a result of splitting the protein molecule when the elements of water are added.

hydrolysis (hī-drŏl'ĭ-sĭs). The splitting of a complex molecule into the smaller units of which it is composed by the addition of the elements of water. Carbohydrates, fats, and proteins undergo hydrolysis during digestion.

hyperglycemia (hī"per-glī-sē'me-ah). Abnormally increased content of sugar in the blood.

hyperostosis (hī"per-os-tō'-sis). Enlargement or overgrowth of bone; exostosis.

hypertension (hī"per-ten'shun). High blood pressure. A persistent elevation of blood pressure may lead to increased heart size and kidney damage.

hyperthyroidism (hī"per-thī'roid-izm). Excessive functional activity of the thyroid gland, characterized by increased basal metabolism and resulting in an increased rate of heart beat.

hypervitaminosis (hī"per-vī"tah-min-ō'sis). Toxicity due to the excess of one or more vitamins.

hypochromia (hī"pō-krō'me-ah). Decrease in color; abnormal decrease in the hemoglobin content of the erythrocytes.

hypogeusia (hī"po-gu'ze-ah). Abnormally diminished acuteness of the sense of taste.

hypoglycemia (hī"pō-glī-sē'me-ah). An abnormally diminished content of glucose in the blood. Sweets stimulate the production of insulin which further decreases the glucose content.

ileocecal (ĭl-ē-ō-sē'kăl). Pertaining to the ileum and cecum.

ileum (ĭl'ē-um). The distal portion of the small intestine; the part between the jejunum and the large intestine.

ilium (ĭl'ĭ-ŭm). The expansive superior portion of the hip bone.

immobilize (ĭm-mō'bĭ-līz). To render incapable of being moved.

impaction (im-pak'shun). The condition of being firmly lodged or wedged.

ingest (ĭn-jĕst'). To take food and drink into the stomach.

interstitial (ĭn-ter-stĭsh'ăl). Pertaining to the space between tissues or cells.

intracellular (in"trah-sĕl'ū-lar). Situated or occurring within a cell or cells.

invert sugar (ĭn-vûrt'). The mixture of dextrose and levulose obtained by hydrolyzing sucrose.

ion (ī'on).   An atom or a group of atoms having a charge of positive (cation) or negative (anion) electricity.

ischemia (is-ke'me-ah).   Deficiency of blood in a part, due to functional constriction or obstruction of a blood vessel.

ketone bodies (kē'tōn).   Acetone, acetoacetic acid, and beta-hydroxybutyric acid, intermediate products of fat metabolism. When carbohydrate is inadequate or unavailable, the ketones accumulate and produce acidosis, also called ketosis.

ketosis (kē-tō'sis).   The condition due to accumulation of ketone bodies in the body as a result of incomplete oxidation of the fatty acids.

kilocalorie (kĭl'ŏ; kē'lō-kăl'ŏ-rĭ).   The amount of heat required to raise the temperature of one kilogram of water 1° centigrade (or approximately four pounds of water 1° Fahrenheit).

kilogram (kĭl'ŏ-grăm).   A metric unit of mass and weight, being equal to 1000 grams or 2.2046 pounds avoirdupois. Abbreviated kg.

kosher (kō'shĕr).   Sanctioned by Jewish law; especially, designating food that may be eaten as ritually clean.

languor (lăng'or).   Lassitude; dullness; sluggishness; lack of vigor; stagnation.

lavage (lah-vahzh').   The washing out of an organ, such as the stomach.

leavening agent (lĕv'ĕn-ĭng).   The substance which causes a dough or batter to rise to a light, open texture. Examples are yeast, baking powder, baking soda, the air trapped in beaten egg whites.

legume (lĕg'ūm; lē-gūm').   The fruit or seed of a pod bearing plant — peas, beans, lentils, peanuts.

lentil (lĕn'tĭl).   Small, flat, edible seeds of the lentil plant (pea family). Often used in soups.

leukocyte (lū'kō-sīt).   Any colorless, ameboid cell mass; white blood corpuscle.

lipid (lĭp'ĭd).   A fat.

lochia (lō'kĭ-ah).   The vaginal discharge that takes place during the first week or two after childbirth.

lumen (lū'men).   The space within a tube, vein, artery, or intestine.

lymph (lĭmf).   A transparent, nearly colorless, coagulable fluid contained in the lymphatic vessels. It consists chiefly of blood plasma and colorless corpuscles. It can be opalescent from particles of fat.

malocclusion (mal-ŏ-kloo'zhun).   Condition in which the teeth do not meet properly for correct biting, tearing, or grinding.

masticate (măs'tĭ-kāt).   To chew food until it is broken into fine particles and mix it with saliva.

matrix (mā'trĭks).   The intercellular substance of a tissue; the groundwork on which anything is cast or the basic material from which a thing develops.

meal pattern. A guide or model to be used when deciding upon specific foods. (See Appendix 3 for diabetic meal patterns.)

meat. The flesh of animals used as food.

    extractive. The water soluble substance present in meat which gives flavor; the drippings which result when meat is cooked and are used in the gravy.

    grade. Indicator of quality which is determined by appearance, age, degree of marbling. Not required by federal law in the United States.

    inspection. Check for wholesomeness to see that food is free of observable disease and packed in a sanitary plant; is mandatory for food shipped in interstate commerce.

    marbling. The network of fat extending throughout the muscle.

membrane (mem'brān). A thin layer of tissue which covers a surface or divides a space or an organ.

menses (měn'sēz). The monthly flow of blood from the genital tract of women.

menu (měn'ū). The details of the meal; the specific foods to be served. The terminology used may indicate seasonings or sauces used, shape of food, cooking techniques, and so forth.

metabolism (mě-tab'ō-lĭzm). The chemical changes in living cells by which energy is provided for vital processes and activities and new material is assimilated to repair the waste; the sum of the chemical processes in the body; the speed with which energy is used.

metastasis (mě-tăs'tah-sĭs). The transfer of disease from one organ or part to another (not directly connected to it) with development of the characteristic lesion in the new location, as in cancer.

misconception (mĭs'kŏn-sĕp'shŭn). A belief commonly held as true but not in accord with scientific evidence to date. Can include fallacies, fads, half-truths, and folklore.

modified starch. Starch which has been treated to change its thickening characteristics.

molecule (mŏl'ě-kūl; mō'lě-kūl). A chemical combination of two or more atoms which form a specific chemical substance. To break the molecule into its constituent atoms changes its character. The number of atoms in a molecule varies with the compound.

mucosa (mū-kō'sah). Mucous membrane lining passages and cavities, as in the gastrointestinal tract.

mucus (mū'kus). The secretion of the mucous membranes, composed of secretions of the glands along with various inorganic salts, desquamated cells, and leukocytes.

myxedema (mĭks-ĕ-dē′mă). A condition characterized by a dry, waxy type of swelling, with abnormal deposits of mucin in the skin, and associated with hypothyroidism. The edema is of the non-pitting type, and the facial changes are distinctive, with swollen lips and a thickened nose.

neonatal (nē″ō-na′tal). Pertaining to the first four weeks after birth.

nephritis (nĕ-frī′tĭs). Inflammation of a kidney.

nephrosclerosis (nĕf″rō-skle-rō′sĭs). Sclerosis or hardening of the kidney; the condition of the kidney seen in renal hypertension (cardiovascular-renal disease).

nocturia (nŏk-tu′rē-ah). Excessive urination at night.

nutrient (nū′trē-ĕnt). A chemical in food which provides the body with energy, helps regulate the body's metabolism, and/or builds and repairs tissues.

obesity (ō-bēs′ĭ-tē). Excessive deposits and storage of fat in the body.

occlusion (ŏ-kloo′zhun). The act of closure or the state of being closed; to obstruct.

    dental. To close with the cusps fitting together, as upper and lower teeth.

occult (ŏ-kult′). Obscure; concealed from observation; difficult to be understood.

orthodox (ŏr′thŏ-doks). Conforming to a standardized doctrine.

ossification (ŏs″ĭ-fĭ-kā′shun). The formation of bone or of a bony structure; the conversion of cartilage into bone or a bony substance.

oxidation (ŏk″sĭ-dā′shun). A chemical process by which a substance combines with oxygen.

papule (păp′ūl). A small, circumscribed, solid elevation of the skin; a pimple.

parenteral (pâr-ĕn′tĕr-al). Administered by route other than alimentary canal – subcutaneous, intravenous, or intramuscular.

pasta (pas′tah). (pl. paste). The general name for macaroni products including egg noodles, spaghetti, and macaroni. The dough or paste from which these products are made.

pasteurization (păs″ter-ĭ-zā′shŭn). Heating a liquid for a specific time at a specific temperature to destroy harmful microorganisms.

pathogen (păth-ō-jen′). A disease-producing microorganism or material.

periodontal (per″ē-ō-don′tal). Situated or occurring around a tooth.

periosteum (per″e-os′tē-um). A specialized connective tissue covering all bones of the body.

phenylalanine (fen″il-al′ah-nīn). An essential amino acid.

phlegmatic (flĕg-măt′ik). Heavy, dull, apathetic.

pica (pi′kah). Perverted appetite; for example, eating clay, paper, and so forth.

polydipsia (pol"ē-dip'sē-ah). Excessive thirst persisting for long periods of time.

polyphagia (pol"ē-fā'je-ah). Excessive or voracious eating.

polyuria (pol"e-u're-ah). The passage of a large volume of urine in a given period.

porous (po'rus). Penetrated by pores and open spaces.

precipitate (prē-sip'ĭ-tāt). To cause a substance in solution to settle down in solid particles.

precursor (prĕ-kûr'sĕr). A substance which the body can change into another substance.

prime of life (prīm). A phrase which describes the adult years of greatest health. Slight malnutrition during early and middle life may reduce the number of healthy years and extend the number of years of less than optimal living and increase years of semi-invalidism and senility.

proliferate (prō-lĭf'er-āt). To grow by the reproduction of similar cells.

proprietary (prŏ-prī'ē-tĕr-ē). A proprietary medicine is one protected against free competition as to name, product, composition, or process of manufacture by secrecy, patent, trade mark, copyright, and so on.

protoplasm (prō'tō-plazm). The essential living matter in a cell. It is composed mainly of proteins, lipids, carbohydrates, and inorganic salts.

provitamin (prō-vi'tah-min). The forerunner of a vitamin. A precursor of a vitamin.

pruritus (proo-rī'tus). Itching.

ptomaines (toe'mānz). A large class of nitrogenous substances, some highly poisonous, which are produced during the putrefaction of animal or plant protein. They have a very obnoxious odor and would not be ingested. The word ptomaine is a misnomer when applied to food infections or poisonings, but is often incorrectly used.

puree (pūr'ray). Food which has been strained to remove as much cellulose (fiber) as possible. Using an electrical blender liquefies but does not puree the food.

rancid (răn'sĭd). Having a musty, rank taste or smell; applied to fats that have undergone decomposition, with the liberation of fatty acids.

reconstitute (rē"kŏn-stĭ-tūt'). Restoration to the original form of the substance previously altered for preservation or storage.

regimen (rej'ĭ-men). A strictly regulated scheme of diet, exercise, or other activity designed to achieve certain ends.

regression (rē-grĕsh'ŭn). A return to a former or earlier state; return to infantile objects of attachment.

regurgitate (rē-gûr'jĭ-tāt). The casting up of incompletely digested food; the backward flow of blood to the heart.

remission (rē-mish'ŭn). A diminution or abatement of the

symptoms of a disease; the period during which the diminution occurs.

renal (rē'nal).   Pertaining to the kidney. The renal threshold is that concentration of a substance in the blood above which the excess will be eliminated in the urine. Often applied to glucose.

restored.   Nutrients that were diminished or lost in processing are put back in the food.

sac (sak).   A pouch; a baglike organ or structure.

satiety (sa'tī'ĕ-tē).   The state of being satisfied. The satiety value of a food is its capacity to contribute to the feeling of satisfaction, the sense of comfort, and the retardation of hunger.

sclerosis (skle-rō'sĭs).   Hardening; a chronic thickening of a part due to inflammation and disease; accumulation of fibrous tissue.

sebaceous (se-bā'shus).   Secreting a greasy lubricant; sebaceous glands that are in the skin secrete a greasy substance.

secrete (sē-krēt').   A discharge by a cell, especially by the epithelial cells of glands, as saliva from the salivary glands. Do not confuse the medical term with that term which means "to hide".

sequestrum (sē-kwĕs'trŭm).   A portion of dead tissue, especially bone, which becomes separated from the living portion of tissue.

skeleton (skel'ĕ-ton).   The hard framework of the animal body which supports soft tissues and protects the internal organs.

spasm (spăzm).   A sudden, violent, involuntary, and unnatural contraction of a muscle or a group of muscles, attended by pain and interference with function, producing involuntary movement and distortion. It may be transitory.

spastic (spăs'tik).   Hypertonic, so that the muscles are stiff and the movements awkward; characterized by spasms or convulsions.

specific dynamic action.   The caloric cost of ingesting food. The calories needed to utilize the food average less than 10 per cent of the calories in the food. It is impossible for a food to burn the calories of other foods, or the calories in the fat deposited in the body.

specific gravity (grav'ĭ-tē).   The ratio of the weight of a given volume of a substance to an equal volume of water.

sphincter (sfingk'ter).   A ringlike muscle which closes a natural opening.

stature (stat'ūr).   The height or tallness of a person standing.

sterile (ster'il).   Free from microorganisms; not fertile.

subcutaneous (sub"kū-tā'nē-us).   Situated or occurring beneath the skin.

supplement (sup'plĕ-ment).   To add something. The incomplete protein in a cereal can be supplemented by the complete protein in an animal product (milk, meat), resulting in higher biological value for the cereal protein.

synthesis (sĭn'thĕ-sĭs). The process of combining two or more chemical substances into a new material. The body can use nutrients to synthesize most of its needs.

syndrome (sin'drōm). A set of symptoms which occur together.

tachycardia (tak-e-kar'de-ah). Abnormally fast heart rate. Generally, anything over 100 beats per minute is considered tachycardia.

therapeutics (thĕr″a-pū'tiks). The science and art of healing.

thrombosis (throm-bō'sĭs). The formation or presence of a blood clot (thrombus) inside a blood vessel or cavity of the heart.

tolerance (tol'er-ans). The ability to endure without ill effect, such as ability to endure the continued or increasing use of a drug.

toxic (tok'sik). Pertaining to poison. Any substance may be harmful when ingested in excessive amounts, but individuals vary in the amount they can tolerate. Ingesting inconsequential amounts produces no harm to the body, but any amount above the individual's threshold tolerance will produce injury to the body. In this case it is said that the substance is toxic to the body.

trimester (trī-mĕs'ter). A period of three months.

tryptophan (trip'to-fān). One of the essential amino acids.

turbidity (tur-bid'ĭ-tē). Cloudiness; disturbance of solids (sediments) in a solution, so that it is not clear.

turgor (tûr'gor). State of being swollen and congested.

unit pricing. Listing the price in such a manner that it is easy to compare the cost per pound or per ounce; pricing each individual can or package. Unit pricing eliminates price listings such as "4 for 39¢".

uterus (ū'tĕr-us). The hollow muscular organ in female animals which is the abode and place of nourishment of the embryo and fetus.

vacuum (vak'ū-um). A space devoid of air or other gas; a space from which air has been exhausted.

varicose (var'ĭ-kōs). Unnaturally swollen; an enlarged vein, artery, or lymph vessel.

vasodilation (vas″o-dī-lā'-shun). Enlargement of the vessel; especially dilation of arterioles leading to increased blood supply.

vegetarian (vej″ĕ-târ'ē-an). One whose food is of vegetable origin; in the United States many vegetarians omit meat but will use dairy and egg products.

vertigo (ver'tē-go; ver-tĭ'go). The sensation of revolving in space; dizziness.

volatile (vol'ah-til). Tending to evaporate rapidly.

Medical Prefixes and Suffixes

A nutrition textbook uses medical terms to inform the reader of the varying demands placed upon the human body in health and disease and of the resources available to meet these demands. This section is provided to assist the person not previously trained in any paramedical field. The lists included here have been selected for the student of nutrition and are by no means complete.

Long ago, the Greeks "had a word for it," and medicine is one field where those words are still used. One medical term may frequently be substituted for several commonly used words to convey a complex meaning. For example, gastroenteritis (*gastro* + *enter* + *itis*) means inflammation of the stomach and intestine. It helps to know the component parts of these words so they may be analyzed and understood more easily. Certain stems, prefixes, and suffixes should be memorized to form a basis for a medical vocabulary. A medical dictionary must be available for use and a good textbook in medical terminology is desirable. One further caution: when using medical terminology, beware of words which sound alike but have different meanings, and other terms which may be confusing. Examples are *ileum,* the distal portion of the small intestine, and *ilium,* the flank bone.

Prefixes

Prefix	Meaning	Example
A, AN	without, lack of	
A used before consonants		aseptic
AN used before vowels		anemia
AB	away from	abnormal
AD	toward, to, at	adhesive
ADEN, ADENO	relating to a gland	adenoid
ANA	again, back, building up	anabolism
ANTE, ANTERO	before, in front of	antenatal, anterior
ANTI	against, opposed to	antigen
ARTHRO	pertaining to joints	arthritis
AUTO	self	autovaccine
BIO	pertaining to life	biochemistry
BLAST, BLASTO	cell, germ	blastema
CARDIO	pertaining to the heart	cardiovascular
CHOLE	pertaining to bile	cholelithiasis
CIRCUM	around, about	circumcision
CO, COM, CON	with, together	complication
CONTRA	against, opposite	contraindicate
CYSTO	pertaining to urinary bladder	cystitis
CYTO	pertaining to a cell	cytology
DE	down, away from	deglutition
DERM, DERMATO	pertaining to the skin	dermatology
DI	two, twice, double	diplopia

Prefixes

Prefix	Meaning	Example
DIA	through	dialysis
DIS	reversal, separation	discharge
DYS	difficult, painful	dyspepsia
E, EC, ECTO, EX, EXO	out, outside, away from	extract
EM, EN	in	emphysema
ENDO	within	endoscopy
ENTERO	relation to the intestine	enterocele
EPI	upon, above	epidermis
EXTRA	outside of, beyond, in addition	extracellular
GLYCO	sweetness (sugar)	glycogen
HEM, HEMO, HÆMO	some relation to the blood	hemoglobin
HEMI	half	hemiplegia
HETERO	other, other than, different from	heterogeneous
HISTO	some relation to tissues	histogenesis
HOMEO	similarity	homeostatis
HYDRO	relation to water or hydrogen	hydrolysis
HYPER	above, over, excessive	hyperactive
HYPO	lack, deficiency	hypoglycemia
INFRA	below	inframandibular
INTER	between	interalveolar
INTRA, INTRO	within	intracellular
LAC, LACTO	pertaining to milk	lactose
LEUCO, LEUKO	pertaining to anything white	leukocyte
MACRO	pertaining to anything large	macrocytic
MEGA, MEGALO	pertaining to anything great	megaloblast
META	between, after, beyond— indicates change, transformation into a succeeding stage, exchange	metamorphosis
MICRO	pertaining to anything small	microscopic
NEO	new, recent, young	neonatal
NEPHRO	pertaining to kidneys	nephrosis
NEURO	pertaining to nerves	neuralgia
ODONTO	some relation to teeth	odontocele
OSSEO, OSSI, OSTEO	pertaining to bone	osteoporosis
PARA	beside, beyond, accessory to	paramedical
PATHO	pertaining to disease	pathogen
PERI	around	peristalsis
PHLEB, PHLEBO	pertaining to a vein	phlebitis
PHOTO	pertaining to light	photosynthesis
POLY	many	polyphasia
POST	after, behind	postprandial
PRE	before	predigest
PYO	pertaining to pus	pyogenic
SEMI	half	semiliquid
SEPTI	pertaining to poison	septicemia
SUB	under, almost	subacute
SUPRA	above, over	suprapelvic
SUPER	above, excessive	supersaturate
SYN	union	synthesize
THERMO	relating to heat	thermometer
TOX, TOXI, TOXICO	relating to poison	toxicity
TRANS	across, through	transplant
UNI	one	uniform
VASO	pertaining to vessel	vasodilation

Suffixes

Suffix	Meaning	Example
-AC	pertaining to	hemophiliac
-ÆMIA, -EMIA	denoting a condition of the blood	leukemia
-ALGIA, -ALGY	a painful condition	arthralgia
-ASE	enzyme	sucrase
-BLAST	germ, cell	myeloblast
-CENTESIS	puncture	paracentesis
-COCCUS	round bacterium	streptococcus
-CYTE	hollow vessel, used to denote a cell	lymphocyte
-ECTOMY	excision of	appendectomy
-ITIS	inflammation	tonsillitis
-LOGY, -OLOGY	the science of	bacteriology
-LYSIS	a loosening, a dissolving	hemolysis
-OMA	morbid condition, especially a tumor	adenoma
-OREXIA	appetite, desire	anorexia
-OSCOPY, -SCOPY	inspection, a viewing of	bronchoscopy
-OSE	carbohydrate	glucose
-OSIS	a condition or process, particularly a disease condition or morbid process	carcinomatosis
-OSTOMY, -STOMY	the making of a mouth	colostomy
-OTOMY, -TOMY	a cutting, an incision	hysterotomy
-OUS	full of, having, possessing	fibrous
-PHAGIA	eating	polyphagia
-PHASIA	speech	aphasia
-RRHAGIA	excessive flow	metrorrhagia
-URIA	urine	polyuria

Modified Diet Patterns

Allergy Diets

Allergens gain access to the body through direct contact, injection, inhalation, or ingestion. One may develop an allergy or lose his sensitivity at any age. Protein is probably the most common food allergen.

Elimination test diets such as the Rowe lists will contain foods which rarely produce sensitivity in humans. Protein from either animal or vegetable sources may be eliminated as in the following animal and vegetable protein test diets. The physician usually eliminates beer, coffee, chewing gum, and all medications, including vitamin pills, aspirin, and so forth during the test period. The test period is usually of short duration so one need not be concerned about the nutritive adequacy.

(Tables follow.)

Rowe Elimination Diets*

Diet 1	Diet 2	Diet 3	Diet 4
Rice	Corn	Tapioca	Milk ‡
Tapioca	Rye	White potato	Tapioca
Rice biscuit	Corn pone	Breads made of any combina-	Cane sugar
Rice bread	Corn-rye muffins	tion of soy, lima bean, and	
	Rye bread	potato starch and tapioca	
	Ry-Krisp	flours	
Lettuce	Beets	Tomato	
Chard	Squash	Carrot	
Spinach	Asparagus	Lima beans	
Carrot	Artichoke	String beans	
Sweet potato or yam		Peas	
Lamb	Chicken (no hens)	Beef	
	Bacon	Bacon	
Lemon	Pineapple	Lemon	
Grapefruit	Peach	Grapefruit	
Pears	Apricot	Peach	
	Prune	Apricot	
Cane sugar	Cane or beet sugar	Cane sugar	
Sesame oil	Mazola	Sesame oil	
Olive oil †	Sesame oil	Soybean oil	
Salt	Salt	Salt	
Gelatin, plain or flavored with	Gelatin, plain or flavored with	Gelatin, plain or flavored with	
lime or lemon	pineapple	lime or lemon	
Maple syrup or syrup made	Karo corn syrup	Maple syrup or syrup made	
with cane sugar flavored with	White vinegar	with cane sugar flavored with	
maple	Royal baking powder	maple	
Royal baking powder	Baking soda	Royal baking powder	
Baking soda	Cream of tartar	Baking soda	
Cream of tartar	Vanilla extract	Cream of tartar	
Vanilla extract		Vanilla extract	
Lemon extract		Lemon extract	

Sample Menus for Rowe Elimination Diets

Diet 1	Diet 2	Diet 3
BREAKFAST	BREAKFAST	BREAKFAST
Grapefruit half	Stewed prunes	Grapefruit half
Cooked rice with maple syrup	Corn flakes	Soybean biscuit with peach
Sautéed lamb liver (using oil	Bacon	marmalade
allowed)	Rye toast with apricot jam	Bacon
LUNCHEON OR SUPPER	LUNCHEON OR SUPPER	LUNCHEON OR SUPPER
Lamb patties	Cold sliced chicken	Beef liver and bacon
Carrots	Asparagus tips vinaigrette	Lima beans
Spinach with lemon slices	(made with allowed oil and	Sliced tomatoes
Rice bread with grapefruit mar-	vinegar)	Potato flour biscuit with apricot
malade	Corn-rye muffin with apricot	jam
Lime gelatin	jam	Lime gelatin with sliced peaches
Lemonade	Fresh peach slices	Lemonade
	Apricot juice	
DINNER	DINNER	DINNER
Roast leg of lamb	Chicken roasted with prunes	Boiled beef with carrots, potato
Baked sweet potato	Baked squash	and peas
Head lettuce with allowed oil	Pickled beets and artichoke	Grapefruit sections with allowed
and lemon juice	hearts	oil and lemon juice
Rice biscuit with grapefruit	Ry-Krisp with apricot jam	Apricot tapioca
marmalade	Pineapple gelatin	
Baked pear	Apricot juice	
Grapefruit juice		

* Rowe, A. H.: Elimination Diets and the Patient's Allergies. 2nd ed. Philadelphia, Lea & Febiger, 1944.

† Allergy to it may occur with or without allergy to olive pollen. Mazola may be used if corn allergy is not present.

‡ Milk should be taken, up to 2 or 3 quarts a day. Plain cottage cheese and cream may be used. Tapioca cooked with milk and milk sugar may be taken.

ANIMAL PROTEIN TEST DIET*
The diet is inadequate in iron, thiamine, and ascorbic acid.

	Foods Allowed	Foods to Avoid
Beverages	Tea, milk, cream	Fruit juice, coffee
Breads	Arrowroot cookies	All others
Cereals	Arrowroot starch only	All others
Desserts	Arrowroot pudding (caramel), Junket (vanilla, caramel), baked or stirred custard (butterscotch, caramel, or vanilla), gelatins without added fruits or fruit juice	All others
Eggs	Baked, soft or hard cooked, poached, fried in animal fats only	
Fats	Lard, bacon fat, chicken fat, any meat fat	No vegetable fat or oils
Fruits and Fruit Juices	None	All
Meat, Fish, Poultry, or Cheese	All plain meats, fish, and poultry; unprocessed cheese	Breadings or batters, meats containing cereal products, processed cheese containing vegetable gums
Potatoes or Substitutes	None	All
Sugar and Sweets	Refined sugar	All others
Soups	Meat soups thickened only with arrowroot	Any vegetable or cereal additions
Vegetables and Vegetable Juices	None	All
Miscellaneous	Salt, small amount of pepper	Nuts, peanut butter, chili sauce, catsup, spices, herbs

Suggested Menu Pattern

Breakfast	Dinner	Supper
1 egg, soft cooked	3 oz. roast beef sirloin, U.S. Choice	3 oz. plain chicken in
3 bacon strips	½ cup beef broth	¼ cup warm whole milk
4 arrowroot cookies	4 arrowroot cookies	½ cup cottage cheese
1 tsp. butter	1 tsp. butter	4 arrowroot cookies
1 cup whole milk	1 cup flavored gelatin cubes with ¼ cup custard sauce	1 tsp. butter
Cream and sugar, if desired	1 cup whole milk	1 cup Junket
Tea	Cream and sugar, if desired	1 cup whole milk
	Tea	Cream and sugar, if desired
		Tea

*From University of Iowa Medical Center: *Recent Advances in Therapeutic Diets*, 1970, pp. 95 and 96.

Vegetable Protein Test Diet*

The diet is inadequate in calcium, riboflavin, and vitamin D.

	Foods Allowed	Foods to Avoid
Beverages	Tea, coffee (1 cup only per day), fruit juices, soybean milk	Milk and milk drinks
Breads	All breads, crackers, and hot breads which do not contain milk, eggs, or animal fat	All others containing milk, eggs, or animal fats
Cereals	All that do not contain animal protein	Dry cereals containing dried milk
Desserts	Fruit, puddings made with fruit and thickened with cornstarch or tapioca, fruit pies and baked goods made with vegetable shortening, fruit ices (no gelatin or egg white)	Those which contain cream, eggs, animal fats, milk, or gelatin
Eggs	None	All
Fats	Vegetable fats and oils, margarine free of animal fat or protein	Butter, mixed margarine, any meat fat, mayonnaise containing egg
Fruits and Fruit Juices	All fresh, frozen, canned, and dried fruit	None
Meat, Fish, Poultry, or Cheese	Soybean foods	All others
Potatoes or Substitutes	Baked, broiled, fried, and steamed potatoes	Noodles; all foods prepared with or containing milk, cheese, or animal fat
Sugar and Sweets	Sugar, jam, jellies, marmalade, honey, syrup	Those containing butter, gelatin, and egg
Soups	Vegetable soup made without meat stock	Meat, cream, or noodle soups
Vegetables and Vegetable Juices	All fresh, frozen, canned, and dried	None
Miscellaneous	Peanut butter, nuts, salt, pepper, spices, herbs	Seasoned sauces containing animal products

Certain additives which have been included in food products may cause allergic reactions. Vegetable gums (gum acacia, carob bean gum, guar gum, gum karaya, and gum tragacanth), sodium benzoate, benzoid acid, soybean seed, and cottonseed (but not cottonseed oil) may be eliminated from the diet by carefully reading the labels and avoiding these products. Products which may contain these additives are listed below.

Vegetable Gum	Sodium Benzoate	Soybean Seed	Cottonseed
Prepared mustard	Margarine	Margarine	Dog food
Processed cheese	Preserves	Soybean milks:	Pan-greasing
Cold pack cheese foods	Jam	Mull-soy	compounds
Cream cheese	Jellies	So-Bee	Brown cookies
Neufchatel cheese	Dried fruits	Soylac	Fig bars
Cheese spreads	Dried vegetables	Soy nuts	Fried cakes
Ice cream	Concentrated orange	Joy Anne ice cream	
Ice milk mixes	drink and juice	K-biscuits or	
Commercial frozen desserts		crackers	
Salad dressing		La Choy sauce	
Prepared salads		Heinz Worcestershire	
Cake icing mixtures		sauce	
Commercial whipped toppings		Cellu-soy flakes	
Certain brands of		Pork links	
chewing gum		Sausage	
Certain brands of		Frankfurters	
cake mixes		Luncheon meats	
Toothpaste		Candies containing	
Soft candy fillings		lecithin	

Suggested Menu Pattern

Breakfast	Dinner	Supper
½ cup frozen orange juice	1 cup pineapple-grapefruit juice	1 cup tomato juice
½ cup Cream of Wheat cereal	1 baked potato with	½ cup green beans (no butter)
1 slice toast, milk-free	1 tsp. vegetable shortening	½ cup cabbage salad
2 tsp. peanut butter	½ cup cooked carrots (no butter)	1 Tbsp. French dressing
2 tsp. grape jelly	½ cup spinach (no butter)	2 slices bread, white milk-free
1 tsp. sugar	¾ cup tossed lettuce salad	2 Tbsp. honey
Coffee	French dressing	Peach cobbler made with
	1 slice bread, white milk-free	vegetable shortening
	1 Tbsp. grape jelly	Sugar, if desired
	½ cup apricot tapioca	Tea
	Sugar, if desired	
	Tea	*Evening nourishment*
		½ cup stewed prunes
		2 graham crackers

°From University of Iowa Medical Center: *Recent Advances in Therapeutic Diets*, pp. 96 and 98.

Calorie Restricted Diets

Exercise as well as caloric intake should be used to control weight. Reduction diets for men range from 1400 to 1800 calories, for women usually from 1000 to 1400 calories, and during pregnancy about 1800. A diet of less than 1000 calories probably would be nutritionally inadequate. Review Chapter 15.

SAMPLE DIET PLANS*

Use the diabetic exchange lists under "Diabetic Diet."

	1000 Cal. 60 gm.Pro.	1200 Cal. 65 gm.Pro.	1500 Cal. 70 gm.Pro.	1800 Cal. 95 gm.Pro.
Breakfast				
Fruit alternate	1	1	1	1
Meat alternate (Egg)	1	1	1	1
Bread alternate	1	1	2	2
Butter alternate	1	1	1	2
Milk alternate	..	..	..	1 (whole)
Coffee or tea				
Lunch				
Meat alternate	2	2	2	3
Vegetable A	As desired	As desired	As desired	As desired
Bread alternate	1	2	2	1
Butter alternate	1	1	1	1
Fruit alternate	1	1	1	1
Milk alternate	1 (skim)	1 (skim)	1 (whole)	1 (whole)
Coffee or tea				
Dinner				
Meat alternate	2	2	3	3
Vegetable A	As desired	As desired	As desired	As desired
Vegetable B	1	1	1	1
Bread alternate	1	2	2	2
Butter alternate	1	1	1	1
Fruit alternate	1	2	1	1
Milk alternate	1 (skim)	1 (skim)	1 (whole)	1 (whole)
Coffee or tea				
Supplementary feeding				
Milk alternate				1 (whole)

*From University Hospital, University of Michigan: *Diet Manual,* 1963, pp. 25–26.

*1200 CALORIE DIET PATTERN**

This pattern, which may be more acceptable in our society, contains about 1200 calories. Most women will lose about one pound per week; men, about two pounds (if the loss is greater, 1500 calories would be preferable). Food consumption can be interchanged, e.g., milk at breakfast and the fruit carried to work for the morning snack.

Breakfast
> Fruit — 1 medium serving, fresh or unsweetened canned
> Egg — 1, poached or soft cooked
> Toast — 1 slice with 1 teaspoon butter or margarine, or cereal — ½ cup with ¼ cup milk, no sugar
> Coffee or tea — no cream or sugar

11 A.M. (or about one hour before lunch)
> Non-fat milk or buttermilk — 1 glass

Luncheon
> Meat (or substitute for meat) — one 3-ounce portion. Use lean beef, lamb, veal, chicken, fish, plain cottage cheese, cheddar cheese.
> Vegetable — 1 medium serving; may be raw, as a salad such as lettuce and tomato, or cooked. Use lemon or vinegar for seasoning rather than butter or salad dressing.
> Fruit — 1 medium serving, fresh or unsweetened canned
> Bread — 1 slice
> Butter or margarine — 1 teaspoon or 1 pat
> Tea or coffee — no cream or sugar

Mid-afternoon
> Iced tea, lemonade, soft drink, non-fat milk, or buttermilk

Dinner
> Bouillon or consommé or vegetable-juice cocktail — 1 serving
> Meat — one 3-ounce portion (see Luncheon)
> Potato (or a substitute for potato) — 1 small serving of mashed or baked potato, steamed rice, corn, lima beans, or macaroni; or 1 slice bread
> Vegetable — 1 serving, raw, as a salad, or cooked. (Note: one vegetable a day should be green or yellow)
> Butter or margarine — 1 teaspoon for potato, or ½ tablespoon French dressing for salad
> Fruit — 1 medium serving, fresh or unsweetened canned
> Tea or coffee — no cream or sugar

Evening or bedtime
> Non-fat milk, buttermilk, soft drink, or glass of beer
> Saltines or pretzels — 2

Watch your bathroom scales. If you are losing too fast (more than one and one-half pounds a week), add a little of this pattern.

---

*From Stare, Frederick J.: *Eating for Good Health,* 1964, pp. 119–121.

Whole milk in place of non-fat milk	165 Calories
1 cocktail	150 "
1 serving ice cream	150 "
1 piece angel or sponge cake, not iced	150 "
1 ounce cooked meat or 1 egg	80 "
1 serving of cream soup	150 "
10 potato chips	110 "
1 slice bread	60 "
1 pat butter	50 "

If you don't seem to lose, be patient. It may take you a couple of weeks to adjust to the new routine. Don't eat any less. If you have been faithful for about two weeks and nothing happens, think over your activities. Maybe you are not only cutting down on your calories but also on your exercise. Take a short walk twice a day, fifteen minutes or so at a time.*

Children's Diets

BIRTH TO ONE YEAR

A typical cow's milk formula is:
>   1½ to 2 fluid oz. of whole milk per pound of body weight
>   1 oz. sugar (syrup or dextrin equivalents) for each 10 oz. milk
>   Add water to give 2½ oz. of fluid for each pound of body weight

Basic infant feeding requirements include:

1. Calories—at birth, 50 to 55 calories per pound (120 per kg.) at one year, 45 calories per pound (100 per kg.). (From one to three years of age this will decrease annually about 10 calories per kg.)

2. Protein—breast fed infants at birth, 1 gram per pound (2 to 2.5 gm. per kg.).
   Formula fed infants at birth, 1.5 to 2 grams per pound (3 to 4 gm. per kg.); from six months to a year, 1 to 1.5 grams per pound (2 to 3 grams per kg.).

3. Fat—both breast milk and cow's milk provide the essential fatty acids. Larger quantities of fat are not well tolerated.

4. Carbohydrate is added to meet caloric needs; usually not more than 40 to 45 per cent of the formula calories are from carbohydrate. Extra carbohydrate will satiate the infant before other basic nutritional needs are met. Karo provides 60 calories per tablespoon, 1 oz. of whole milk has 20 calories, 1 oz. of evaporated milk has 40 calories.

5. Water—an infant's fluid needs are relatively high; dehydration can occur rapidly. Use 2 to 3 oz. per pound (130 to 200 cc. per kg.) in a temperate climate. In a hot climate or during the summer months this may need to be increased.

6. Calcium—either cow's or breast milk gives adequate skeletal mineralization.

---

*From Stare, Frederick J.: *Eating for Good Health*, 1964, pp. 119–121.

7. Iron—this is not met by either cow's or breast milk. An adequate prenatal diet provides fetal iron storage to last about three months, after which time dietary iron is added in the form of special infant cereals, egg yolk, meat, or green vegetables.
8. Vitamin A—both human and cow's milk fluctuate in vitamin A content, but the recommended 1500 I.U. is usually supplied by either. Most vitamin D supplements contain vitamin A. The allowance of vitamin A is met when strained green or yellow vegetables are added.
9. Vitamin D—neither breast nor cow's milk, unless fortified, contains adequate vitamin D. Since the young baby does not consume a quart of fortified milk daily, a supplement to total 400 I.U. is prescribed by the second or third week of life.
10. Vitamin C—mother's milk will vary depending upon the adequacy of her diet. Cow's milk is deficient. The use of orange juice or other source of vitamin C is recommended by the second or third week.
11. Phosphorus, thiamine, riboflavin, niacin, and the other nutrients ordinarily are met by the milk plus the solid foods which are added between two and four months of age.

Between the fifth month and one year the feeding pattern may be:*

6 to 7 A.M.	Bottle
10 to 11 A.M.	Cereal with egg yolk
	Bottle
2 to 3 P.M.	Pureed fruit
	Cottage or cream cheese
	Bottle
6 to 7 P.M.	Pureed meat
	Pureed vegetable
	Bottle
9 to 11 P.M.	Bottle, if desired

Desserts (ice cream, sweet puddings, etc.) may encourage the child to develop poor eating habits.

OVER ONE YEAR

Shortly after the first year, feeding difficulties may appear. The child gained about 15 pounds during his first year and now the annual gain is closer to five. The slower growth makes him less receptive to food.

The toddler and preschool child will eat only if he feels hungry. He has not yet acquired the cultural custom of our three meal routine and therefore often refuses a meal. He will eat if he is permitted to get hungry. If milk is used in greater amounts than two to three cups per day, he probably will not eat as many solid foods as shown in the meal pattern.†

---

*Lynch, Harold D.: *Your Child Is What He Eats*, Chap. 4.
†Lynch, Harold D.: *Your Child Is What He Eats*, Chap. 8.

Morning: Fruit or juice
         Egg or meat
         Toast or cereal
         Milk

Noon and evening: Cheese, egg, meat, fish, or fowl
         Fruit and/or vegetable
         Bread or crackers with butter or margarine
         Milk

*Recommended Intake for Good Nutrition According to Food Groups and the Average Size of Servings at Different Age Levels**

FOOD GROUP	SERVINGS PER DAY	AVERAGE SIZE OF SERVINGS					
		1 year	2-3 years	4-5 years	6-9 years	10-12 years	13-15 years
Milk and cheese (1.5 oz. cheese = 1 C milk) (C = 1 cup − 8 oz. or 240 gm.)	4	½ C	½-¾ C	¾ C	¾-1 C	1 C	1 C
Meat group (protein foods)	3 or more						
Egg		1	1	1	1	1	1 or more
Lean meat, fish, poultry (liver once a week)		2 Tbsp.	2 Tbsp.	4 Tbsp.	2-3 oz. (4-6 Tbsp.)	3-4 oz.	4 oz. or more
Peanut butter			1 Tbsp.	2 Tbsp.	2-3 Tbsp.	3 Tbsp.	3 Tbsp.
Fruits and vegetables Vitamin C source (citrus fruits, berries, tomato, cabbage, cantaloupe)	At least 4, including: 1 or more (twice as much tomato as citrus)	⅓ C citrus	½ C	½ C	1 medium orange	1 medium orange	1 medium orange
Vitamin A source (green or yellow fruits and vegetables)	1 or more	2 Tbsp.	3 Tbsp.	4 Tbsp. (¼ C)	¼ C	⅓ C	½ C
Other vegetables (potato and legumes, etc.) *or*	2	2 Tbsp.	3 Tbsp.	4 Tbsp. (¼ C)	⅓ C	½ C	¾ C
Other fruits (apple, banana, etc.)		¼ C	⅓ C	½ C	1 medium	1 medium	1 medium
Cereals (whole-grain or enriched) Bread	At least 4	½ slice	1 slice	1½ slices	1-2 slices	2 slices	2 slices
Ready-to-eat cereals		½ oz.	¾ oz.	1 oz.	1 oz.	1 oz.	1 oz.
Cooked cereal (including macaroni, spaghetti, rice, etc.)		¼ C	⅓ C	½ C	½ C	¾ C	1 C or more
Fats and carbohydrates	To meet caloric needs						
Butter, margarine, mayonnaise, oils: 1 Tbsp. = 100 calories		1 Tbsp.	1 Tbsp.	1 Tbsp.	2 Tbsp.	2 Tbsp.	2-4 Tbsp.
Desserts and sweets: 100-calorie portions as follows: ⅓ C pudding or ice cream 2-3″ cookies, 1 oz. cake, 1⅓ oz. pie, 2 tbsp. jelly, jam, honey, sugar		1 portion	1½ portions	1½ portions	3 portions	3 portions	3-6 portions

*From Nelson, Vaughan, and McKay: *Textbook of Pediatrics*, 1975, p. 159. Prepared in collaboration with Mildred J. Bennett, Ph.D., Univ. of California, Berkeley, from "Four Groups of the Daily Food Guide," Institute of Home Economics, U.S.D.A., and Publication No. 30, Children's Bureau of the U.S. Department of Health, Education and Welfare.

One tablespoon means a level tablespoon. One rounded tablespoon is equal to two level tablespoons.

Diabetic Diet

The diabetic diet is prescribed for each individual, taking into account the severity of his disease, the amount of exercise he performs, the type of insulin therapy he receives, and the calorie content which will maintain the desired weight.

Nine meal plans using exchange lists were developed by the American Dietetic Association, the American Diabetes Association, and the U.S. Public Health Service.

A. D. A. SAMPLE MEAL PLANS

Diet	CHO Gm.	Pro. Gm.	Fat Gm.	Calories	Carbohydrate Distribution Breakfast	Lunch	Dinner	Bedtime
1	125	60	50	1200	25	37	32	27
2	150	70	70	1500	25	52	47	27
3	180	80	80	1800	40	52	47	42
4	220	90	100	2200	40	67	72	42
5*	180	80	80	1800	37	52	59	27
6*	250	100	130	2600	52	77	74	42
7*	370	140	165	3500	82	122	ˎ114	52
8	250	115	130	2600	55	82	72	42
9	300	120	145	3000	70	82	102	42

Total Day's Food in Sample Meal Plans

Diet	Milk	Veg. A	Veg. B	Fruits	Bread Ex.	Meat Ex.	Fat Ex.
1	1 pt.	As desired	1	3	4	5	1
2	1 pt.	As desired	1	3	6	6	4
3	1 pt.	As desired	1	3	8	7	5
4	1 pt.	As desired	1	4	10	8	8
5*	1 qt.	As desired	1	3	6	5	3
6*	1 qt.	As desired	1	4	10	7	11
7*	1 qt.	As desired	1	6	17	10	15
8	1 pt.	As desired	1	4	12	10	12
9	1 pt.	As desired	1	4	15	10	15

Composition of Food Exchanges

List	Food	Measures	Gm.	CHO	Pro.	Fat	Cal.
1	Milk exchanges	1/2 pint	240	12	8	10	170
2a	Vegetable exchanges	as desired	....				
2b	Vegetable exchanges	1/2 cup	100	7	2	..	36
3	Fruit exchanges	varies	..	10	..	..	40
4	Bread exchanges	varies	..	15	2	..	68
5	Meat exchanges	1 oz.	30	..	7	5	73
6	Fat exchanges	1 tsp.	5	..	..	5	45

*These diets contain more milk and are especially suitable for children.

To illustrate this method, the 1800 calorie meal plan 5 follows.

A.D.A. Meal Plan No. 5

For _____

Use only as your doctor prescribes.

Carbohydrate 180 grams, Protein 80 grams, Fat 80 grams: Calories 1800

This meal has been prepared to use with the Meal Planning Booklet.

YOUR FOOD FOR THE DAY

Amount	Kind of Food	Choose From
1 quart	milk	List 1
Any amount	vegetable exchanges A	List 2A
1	vegetable exchanges B	List 2B
3	fruit exchanges B	List 3
6	bread exchanges	List 4
5	meat exchanges	List 5
3	fat exchanges	List 6

Divide this food as follows:

YOUR MEAL PLAN

Breakfast

1 fruit exchange from List 3
1 meat exchange from List 5
1 bread exchange from List 4
1 fat exchange from List 6
1 cup milk from List 1

Lunch or Supper

1 meat exchange from List 5
2 bread exchanges from List 4
vegetable from List 2A (any amount)
1 fruit exchange from List 3
1 fat exchange from List 6
1 cup milk from List 1

Dinner or Main Meal

3 meat exchanges from List 5
2 bread exchanges from List 4
vegetable from List 2A (any amount)
1 vegetable exchange from List 2B
1 fruit exchange from List 3
1 fat exchange from List 6
1 cup milk from List 1

Bedtime Meal

1 cup milk from List 1
1 bread exchange from List 4

List 1. *Milk Exchanges*
Carbohydrate–12 gm., Protein–8 gm., Fat–10 gm., Calories–170

	Meas.	Gm.
[1] Milk	1 cup	240
Milk, evaporated	½ cup	120
[1] Milk, powdered	¼ cup	35
[1] Buttermilk	1 cup	240

[1] Add two fat exchanges if fat free.

LIST 2. *Vegetable Exchanges*

A.—These vegetables may be used as desired in ordinary amounts. Carbohydrates and calories negligible.

Asparagus	Eggplant	Lettuce
Broccoli	Beet greens	Mushrooms
Brussels sprouts	Chard	Okra
Cabbage	Collard	Pepper
Cauliflower	Dandelion greens	Radishes
Celery	Kale	Rhubarb
Chicory	Mustard greens	Sauerkraut
Cucumbers	Spinach	String beans, young
Escarole	Turnip greens	Summer squash
		Tomatoes

B.—Vegetables: 1 Serving equals ½ cup equals 100 grams. Carb.—7 gm., Protein— 2 gm., Calories—36.

Beets	Peas, green	Squash, winter
Carrots	Pumpkin	Turnips
Onions	Rutabaga	

LIST 3. *Fruit Exchanges*

Carbohyrate—10 gm., Calories—40

	Meas.	Gm.
Apple	1 sm. (2″ diam.)	80
Applesauce	½ cup	100
Apricots, fresh	2 medium	100
Apricots, dried	4 halves	20
Bananas	½ small	50
Berries: straw., rasp., black	1 cup	150
Blueberries	⅔ cup	100
Cantaloup	¼ (6″ diam.)	200
Cherries	10 large	75
Dates	2	15
Figs, fresh	2 large	50
Figs, dried	1 small	15
Grapefruit	½ small	125
Grapefruit juice	½ cup	100
Grapes	12	75
Grape juice	¼ cup	60
Honeydew melon	⅛ (7″ diam.)	150
Mango	½ small	70
Orange	1 small	125
Orange juice	½ cup	100
Papaya	⅓ medium	100
Peach	1 medium	100
Pear	1 small	100
Pineapple	½ cup	80
Pineapple juice	⅓ cup	80
Plums	2 medium	100
Prunes, dried	2 medium	25
Raisins	2 tbsp.	15
Tangerine	1 large	100
Watermelon	1 cup	175

LIST 4. *Bread Exchanges*

Carbohydrate—15 gm., Protein—2 gm., Calories—68

	Meas.	*Gm.*
Bread	1 slice	25
Biscuit, roll	1 (2″ diam.)	35
Muffin	1 (2″ diam.)	35
Cornbread	1 (1½″ cube)	35
Flour	2½ tbsp.	20
Cereal, cooked	½ cup	100
Cereal, dry (flake & puffed)	¾ cup	20
Rice, grits, cooked	½ cup	100
Spaghetti, noodles, etc., cooked	½ cup	100
Crackers, graham (2½″ sq.)	2	20
Oyster	20 (½ cup)	20
Saltines (2″ sq.)	5	20
Soda (2½″ sq.)	3	20
Round, thin (1½″ diam.)	6-8	20
Vegetables		
Beans & peas, dried, cooked	½ cup	90
(lima, navy, split peas, cowpeas, etc.)		
Baked beans, no pork	¼ cup	50
Corn	⅓ cup	80
Parsnips	⅔ cup	125
Potatoes, white, baked, boiled	1 (2″ diam.)	100
Potatoes, white, mashed	½ cup	100
Potatoes, sweet, or yams	¼ cup	50
Sponge cake, plain	1 (1½″ cube)	25
Ice cream (omit 2 fat exchanges)	½ cup	70

LIST 5. *Meat Exchanges*

Protein—7 gm., Fat—5 gm., Calories—73

	Meas.	*Gm.*
Meat & poultry (med. fat)	1 oz.	30
(beef, lamb, pork, liver, chicken, etc.)		
Cold cuts (4½″ sq., ⅛″ thick)	1 slice	45
Frankfurter	1 (8-9/lb.)	50
Fish: cod, mackerel, etc.	1 oz.	30
Salmon, tuna, crab	¼ cup	30
Oysters, shrimp, clams	5 small	45
Sardines	3 medium	30
Cheese, cheddar, American	1 oz.	30
Cottage	¼ cup	45
Egg	1	50
Peanut butter[1]	2 tbsp.	30

[1]Limit use or adjust carbohydrate.

List 6. *Fat Exchanges*

Fat—5 gm., Calories—45

	Meas.	*Gm.*
Butter or margarine	1 tsp.	5
Bacon, crisp	1 slice	10
Cream, light, 20%	2 tbsp.	30
Cream, heavy, 40%	1 tbsp.	15
Cream cheese	1 tbsp.	15
French dressing	1 tbsp.	15
Mayonnaise	1 tsp.	5
Oil or cooking fat	1 tsp.	5
Nuts	6 small	10
Olives	5 small	50
Avocado	⅛ (4″ diam.)	25

The following seasonings may be used freely, if desired:

Chopped parsley	Pepper and other spices	Nutmeg
Garlic	Lemon	Cinnamon
Celery	Mint	Saccharin
Mustard	Onion	Vinegar

These foods may be used as desired:

Coffee	Bouillon (without fat)	Pickles, sour
Tea	Gelatin, unsweetened	Pickles, unsweetened dill
Clear Broth	Rennet tablets	Cranberries

Fat-restricted Diets

The first diet restricts the fat content to 50 grams. The 1800 calorie and the 1200 calorie diets obtain about 35 per cent of their calories from fat, with as much as possible from polyunsaturated sources. Meat and eggs contain saturated fats. The meat and eggs are restricted in amounts, not eliminated, because they are valuable sources of protein, vitamins, and minerals. All four diets are nutritionally adequate.

50 GRAM FAT DIET*

Foods allowed

Beverages—buttermilk, skim milk, fruit juice, coffee, tea, carbonated

*From University Hospital, University of Michigan: *Diet Manual.*

Bread and cereals—any kind

Desserts—angel food cake, plain cookies, fruit whip made with egg white, gelatin, puddings made with skim milk, fruit ices

Fats—3 teaspoons (1 tablespoon) daily of any kind

Fruits and vegetables—any kind, except avocado and olives

Meat or substitute—1 egg; 5 to 6 ounces of lean beef, fish, lamb, liver, poultry, or veal; 1/4 cup cottage cheese can be used for 1 ounce of meat

Seasonings—any kind

Sweets—jams; jellies; preserves; candy, except chocolate

Foods omitted

All pork products and cold cuts, whole milk, cream, most cheese, ice cream, gravy, shortening and oil except the three teaspoons allowed, nuts, potato chips, chocolate, fried foods, pie, cake, pastry, dough-nuts.

Sample Menu Pattern for 50 Gram Fat Diet

Breakfast	*Lunch and Dinner*
Citrus fruit	Appetizer
Cereal	Meat, lean
Egg	Potato
Toast, 1 teaspoon butter	Vegetable
Beverage	Salad, fat-free dressing
	Bread, 1 teaspoon butter
	Dessert
	Beverage

FAT CONTROLLED 1200 AND 1800 CALORIE DIETS*

	1200	1800	Foods to be Used
Milk	1 pint	1 pint	Skim, buttermilk, or reconstituted non-fat dry.
Vegetables	3 or more servings	4 or more servings	1 serving per day should be dark yellow or deep green. If corn, potato, or dried peas and beans are used count them as a cereal serving.
Fruit	3 servings	3 servings	1 serving should be citrus or substitute. Any fresh or canned unsweetened fruit or juice except avocado and olives.
Bread and cereals—one serving from the sugars and sweets list may be substituted for not more than 1 serving of cereal	4 servings	7 servings	Do not use biscuits, muffins, cornbread, or griddle cakes unless they are made at home using the fats allowed.
Meat, fish, or poultry	6 ounces cooked	6 ounces cooked	Only three times a week for dinner or lunch can very lean beef, leg of lamb, lean pork loin, or lean ham be used. For the other 11 meals use turkey or chicken without skin, fish, veal, uncreamed cottage cheese, low-fat yogurt, dried peas or beans, peanut butter, or nuts (especially walnuts).
Eggs	3 or less per week	3 or less per week	Use plain or in cooking. Two rounded tablespoons cottage cheese or 1½ tablespoons peanut butter may be used as a substitute.
Fat	1⅔ level tablespoons (5 tsp.) plus 1 level tsp. special margarine.	3 level tablespoons (9 tsp.) plus 1 level tbsp. special margarine.	Use only corn, cottonseed, safflower, sesame, soybean, or sunflower oil. If made with allowed oils 1 tsp. mayonnaise = 1 tsp. oil; 1½ tsp. French dressing = 1 tsp. oil. Special margarines or shortenings should contain at least 25 per cent linoleic acid and not more than 25 per cent saturated fatty acids.

Table continued on following page.

FAT CONTROLLED 1200 AND 1800 CALORIE DIETS* *(Continued)*

	1200	1800	Foods to be Used
Sugars and sweets	None	2 servings	1 serving is 1 tablespoon white, brown, or maple sugar; corn or maple syrup; honey, molasses, jam, jelly, marmalade. Or 1/4 cup tapioca or cornstarch pudding made with fruit juice or skim milk; 1/4 cup fruit whip; 1/3 cup gelatin; 1/4 cup water ice; 6 ounces sweetened carbonated beverage; 2/3 cup cocoa made from skim milk allowance; 3 medium gum-drops or marshmallows.

*From American Heart Association pamphlets.

Other dessert recipes are available from American Heart Association. These may be used as desired: coffee and its substitutes, tea, unsweetened carbonated beverages, lemons and lemon juice, unsweetened gelatin, artificial sweeteners, fat-free broth or bouillon, pickles, relishes, vinegar, mustard, catsup, and seasonings. Foods to be avoided are on the next page.

*Foods to Avoid**

These are the foods that are not allowed on your diet, because they contain either too much fat or the wrong kind of fat.

MEATS

Beef except very lean cuts
Lamb except leg
Pork except lean loin and well-trimmed ham
Bacon, salt pork, spareribs

Frankfurters, sausage, cold cuts
Canned meats
Organ meats such as kidney, brain, sweetbread, liver
Any visible fat from meat

POULTRY AND FISH

Skin of chicken or turkey
Duck and goose

Fish canned in olive oil

DAIRY FOODS

Whole milk, homogenized milk, canned milk
Sweet cream, powdered cream
Ice cream unless home-made with nonfat dry milk powder

Sour cream
Whole milk buttermilk and whole-milk yogurt
Butter
Cheese made from whole milk

FATS AND OILS

Butter
Ordinary margarines
Ordinary solid shortenings
Lard

Salt pork
Chicken fat
Coconut oil
Olive oil
Chocolate

BREADS AND BAKERY GOODS

Commercial biscuits, muffins, cornbreads, griddlecakes, cookies, crackers
Mixes for biscuits, muffins, and cakes

Coffee cakes, cakes (except angel food), pies, sweet rolls, doughnuts, and pastries

DESSERTS

Puddings, custards, and ice creams unless home-made with skim milk or nonfat dry milk powder

Whipped cream desserts
Cookies unless home-made with allowed fat or oil

MISCELLANEOUS

Sauces and gravies unless made with allowed fat or oil or made from skimmed stock
Commercially fried foods such as potato chips, French fried potatoes, fried fish
Cream soups and other creamed dishes
Frozen or packaged dinners
Olives

Avocado
Chocolate
Candies made with chocolate, butter, cream, or coconut
Foods made with egg yolk unless counted as part of your allowance
Fudge, chocolate
Commercial popcorn

*From American Heart Association pamphlets.

Fat Controlled 1200 Calorie Sample Menu

Breakfast	*Lunch*	*Dinner*
Chilled half grapefruit	Tomato stuffed with chicken	Baked fish fillet (3 ounces)
¾ cup dry cereal	(use 1 tomato; ½ cup diced	with 1 teaspoon oil
1 cup skim milk	chicken; 2 teaspoons mayon-	Broccoli with 1½ teaspoons
1 soft-cooked egg	naise; capers; parsley; celery;	Hollandaise sauce
1 slice toast	lettuce)	Scalloped tomatoes (use ½ cup
1 teaspoon special margarine	1 small hard roll	canned tomatoes; 1 slice diced
Coffee or tea	1 cup skim milk	bread; 1 teaspoon oil; salt;
	1 small banana, sliced	pepper; basil)
	Coffee or tea	1 fresh or canned pear
		(unsweetened)
		Coffee or tea

Fat Controlled 1800 Calorie Sample Menu

Breakfast	*Lunch*	*Dinner*
Chilled half grapefruit	Tomato stuffed with chicken	Baked fish fillet (4 ounces)
¾ cup dry cereal	(use 1 tomato; ½ cup	(use 1 teaspoon oil and
1 cup skim milk	diced chicken; 1 tablespoon	¼ cup bread crumbs)
1 soft-cooked egg	mayonnaise; capers;	Broccoli with 1½ teaspoons
1 slice toast	parsley; celery; lettuce)	Hollandaise sauce
1 teaspoon special margarine	1 large or 2 small hard rolls	Scalloped tomatoes (use ½ cup
1 tablespoon marmalade	2 teaspoons special margarine	canned tomatoes; 1 slice diced
1 tablespoon sugar for cereal,	1 cup skim milk	bread; 1 teaspoon oil; salt;
fruit, or beverage	1 small banana, sliced	pepper; basil)
Coffee or tea	Coffee or tea	1 canned pear, sweetened, with
		syrup
		Coffee or tea

The Fat-Controlled Diet – A Family Guide for Daily Eating†

	Use Regularly	Avoid	To Know
*Milk Group	Non-fat (skim) milk Choc-Drink Non-fat dry milk powder Buttermilk made from skim milk Low-fat yogurt (made from skim milk) Cheeses: Cottage cheese (preferably uncreamed) Hoop cheese, Sapsago Ices (in place of ice cream or sherbet)	Whole (regular) milk Canned milk (evaporated or condensed) All creams including sour, half & half, whipped Whole milk yogurt Ice cream Butter All other cheeses Non-dairy cream and milk substitutes	Recommended Daily: Non Fat Milk – 1 pint or more per day Low Fat milk and ice milk are only partially de-fatted, having about ½ the butterfat of whole milk. Sherbet is made with milk. Substitutes for coffee cream usually contain coconut oil and therefore should not be used – use non fat dry milk
*Meats	Chicken, turkey, veal, fish, in most of your meals for the week. Beef, lamb, pork, ham, in 3 or 4 meals per week. Remove all visible fat before cooking. Broil, roast, or bake.	Duck, goose Meats heavily marbled with fat: Spareribs, mutton, frankfurters, sausage, hamburger, bacon, luncheon meats, liver and other variety meats	Recommended Daily: One or more servings from the meat group Fish, chicken, turkey and veal are low in saturated fat, but certain cuts of veal are high. Poultry skin is high in saturated fat, therefore not to be eaten. Lean beef and other lean meats are limited to one serving per day to further limit the saturated fat intake. Broil, roast or bake so that the fat which cooks out of the meat can be discarded. Avoid pan frying or deep fat frying, as the fat does not drip out. Shellfish are low in fat but high in cholesterol. Liver, kidney, brain, sweetbreads are very high in cholesterol. Shellfish (such as crab, lobster, shrimp, clams) may be substituted for egg yolk: 2 oz. = 1 egg yolk.
*Fats and Oils	Oils and margarines high in polyunsaturates Safflower, corn, soybean, sunflower seed, sesame seed, or cottonseed oil. (These are "allowed oils.") Salad dressings: Mayonnaise and liquid salad dressing made of allowed oils. Special soft (tub) margarine in cooking and as spread for bread, etc.	Butter Regular margarine (stick-type) Lard Solid fats & shortening Salt pork fat, chicken fat, meat fats Coconut oil Roquefort or cream dressings	Recommended Daily: 4 or more tablespoons fats & oils daily, ¼ of which may come from the margarine group. French dressings are o.k., but it is preferable that they be made with allowable oils. Olive oil and peanut oil are neutral oils and have no cholesterol lowering effect. The special soft margarines and shortenings contain large amounts of polyunsaturated liquid vegetable oil.

Table continued on following page

THE FAT-CONTROLLED DIET—A FAMILY GUIDE FOR DAILY EATING† (Continued)

	Use Regularly	Avoid	To Know
Eggs	Egg whites as desired. Egg yolk—limit to 3 per week including those used in cooking	Egg yolk except as limited under "Use Regularly" column. Foods containing egg yolk, such as certain cakes, batters, sauces, souffles, etc.	Yolks are extremely high in cholesterol and saturated fat, therefore must be limited. Most prepared cake mixes contain egg yolks.
*Vegetables and Fruits	Unrestricted: Vegetables, fruits, juices. Dried beans, peas, or lentils (1 cup cooked) may be substituted for meat serving if wished, for equivalent protein intake.	Vegetables cooked in or with fats from the above "Avoid" list	Recommended Daily: At least 1 yellow or leafy green vegetable and 1 citrus fruit or juice. (Total recommended 4 or more servings—at least ½ cup per serving.) Restrict the use of olives & avocados, as these are high in total fat calories and low in polyunsaturated fat.
*Bread Cereal Group	Hot or cold cereal, rice, macaroni, melba toast, matzo, pretzels, flour. Breads, including white enriched, oatmeal, raisin and wholewheat bread, French, Italian and English bread, English muffins, rye, pumpernickel, bagels, and breads made with allowable oils. Biscuits, muffins and griddlecakes made at home using an allowed liquid oil as shortening.	Butter rolls, commercial biscuits, muffins, donuts, sweet rolls, crackers. Commercial mixes containing dried eggs and whole milk.	Recommended Daily: 4 or more servings—select preferably whole grain or enriched products. Commercial biscuits, muffins, cornbread and griddlecakes contain more fat than other bread products. Do not eat them unless they are made at home with polyunsaturated oil. Most crackers and mixes for biscuits and muffins also have considerable saturated fat.

Desserts
Beverages
Snacks
Condiments

LOW OR NO CALORIE
Water ices
Gelatin, fruit whip, and puddings made with nonfat milk
Cocoa powder
Artificial sweeteners
Tea, coffee (no cream)
Low calorie drinks
Vinegar, mustard, ketchup, herbs, spices

HIGH IN CALORIES
Imitation ice cream made with safflower oil
Cakes, pies, cookies, pastries, puddings, made with oil in place of solid shortening
Angel food cake
Nuts, especially walnuts
Peanut butter (non-hydrogenated)
Bottled drinks, fruit drinks
Wine, beer, whiskey
Jelly, jam, marmalade, honey, pure sugar candy such as gum drops, hard candy.

Coconut
Commercial cakes, pies, and cookies
Commercially fried foods, sauces, gravies
Frozen packaged meals (as most contain some foods or substances in the above "Avoid" list)
Whole milk puddings
Substitutes for coffee cream
Chocolate and bon bons

In frozen packaged meals there is no way of knowing how much fat or what kind of fat they contain.
Substitutes for coffee cream usually contain coconut oil and therefore should not be used.
Chocolate and bon bons are high in total fat and should be avoided.
Cocoa powder is fat free and can be used.

NOTE: If overweight, cut down calories by taking less total fat, sugar, alcohol.
*Basic Food Groups—Select from each daily.
†From California Heart Association: *The Fat Controlled Diet*, 1968.

Fiber (Residue) Modified Diets

Fiber (cellulose which is the nondigestible carbohydrate in fruits, vegetables, and whole grain cereals) produces bulk in the intestinal tract and thus is a stimulant to defecation.

All foods have some residue. Milk increases stool bulk even though it has no fiber content; thus milk is classified as a moderate residue food. A diet can be low in fiber without being low in residue.

HIGH FIBER (HIGH RESIDUE, HIGH BULK) DIET

Emphasis is placed on whole grain cereals, fruits, and vegetables. Often 3 servings (1 tablespoon per serving) of 100% Bran, All-Bran, Bran Flakes, etc. are added daily. The diet is nutritionally adequate.
DRINK EXTRA LIQUIDS WITH THE HIGH RESIDUE DIET.

High Fiber Sample Menu

		SERVINGS	
		Weight	*Household*
MEAL PLAN	SAMPLE MENU	*Grams*	*Measure*
BREAKFAST			
Fruit juice	Orange juice	248	1 glass (8 oz.)
Fruit	Stewed prunes	135	½ cup
Cereal, whole grain	Cooked oatmeal with 1 T. Bran	118	½ cup
Egg	Poached egg	50	1
Bread, whole grain	Toasted whole wheat bread	23	1 slice
Butter or margarine	Butter or margarine	7	1 pat
Milk	Milk	122	½ glass (4 oz.)
Coffee	Coffee	200	1 pot
Cream	Cream	60	2 ounces
Sugar	Sugar	15	3 teaspoons
LUNCHEON			
Soup	Vegetable soup with 1 T. Bran	125	½ cup
Protein dish/meat	Macaroni and cheese	110	½ cup
Vegetable	Cooked green beans	63	½ cup
Salad	Sliced tomato salad	100	1 medium
Bread	Whole wheat bread	23	1 slice
Butter or margarine	Butter or margarine	7	1 pat
Milk	Milk	244	1 glass (8 oz.)
Fruit	Mixed fruit cup	128	½ cup
DINNER			
Meat, fish, poultry	Roast beef	85	3 ounces
Potato	Mashed potato	98	½ cup
Vegetable/large serving	Cooked spinach	135	¾ cup
Salad	Head lettuce salad	50	⅙ head
Bread, whole grain	Whole wheat bread	23	1 slice
Butter or margarine	Butter or margarine	7	1 pat
Milk	Milk	244	1 glass (8 oz.)
Fruit	Fresh pear	182	1 medium

LOW FIBER (Low Residue, Low Bulk, Soft) DIET

The low fiber diet is nutritionally adequate.

Foods allowed:

Beverages—coffee, tea, cocoa, Postum, carbonated, 1 pint milk

Cereals—enriched, ready-to-eat, enriched white bread and crackers, rice, pasta

Desserts—puddings—cream, bread, rice, tapioca, junket, custard
Gelatin with allowed fruits
Cake, no nuts
Ice cream, no nuts or fruit with seeds

Fats—any kind

Fruits—any juice or puree. Also
Fresh—banana, avocado
Cooked or canned—apples, apricots, cherries, peaches, pears, plums without skins

Meat or substitute—ground or tender beef, veal, lamb, pork, organs. Poultry, fish, cheese, eggs. Gravy may be used.

Vegetables—any vegetable juice or puree. Also the following, cooked: Asparagus tips, beans green or yellow, beets, carrots, eggplant, mushrooms, peas, potatoes white or sweet, pimiento, pumpkin, spinach or other greens, squash, tomatoes, preferably juice or puree.

Seasoning—any kind in moderation

Sweets—sugar, honey, jelly, marshmallow, hard candy

Foods omitted:

Nuts, raisins, fruits with seeds
Bran cereals
Raw fruits or vegetables, except those listed

Low Fiber Sample Menu

Breakfast	*Lunch*	*Dinner*
Orange juice	Peach-cottage cheese salad, one lettuce leaf	Roast beef
Cornflakes, milk		Buttered noodles
Poached egg	Asparagus tips	Carrots seasoned with thyme
Enriched white toast, butter, jelly	Enriched white bread, margarine	Melba toast
Beverage	Chocolate ice cream	Applesauce
	Beverage	Sugar cookie
		Beverage

Formulas for Use in Tube Feeding

	GRAMS	CALORIES PER FLUID OZ.
I*		
Water	1000	45
Sustagen (Mead Johnson Co.)	500	
Pour the required amount of warm water (120°F.) into a pan of suitable size. Add the required amount of Sustagen to the surface of the water. Allow the powder to absorb the water. Mix until blended and smooth. Strain.		
II*		
Whole milk	1000	30
Meritene (Dietene Co.)	150	
Pour milk into a covered jar, mixer or beater. Add Meritene and shake, mix or beat until smooth.		
III*		
Whole milk	1000	48
Egg yolks	4 yolks	
Heavy cream, 40 per cent	240	
Karo syrup	100	
Yeast: 2 cakes dissolved in 200 ml. hot water. Mix all together and cook in a double boiler. Cool, strain and add orange juice	200	
Cod liver oil	16	
IV*		
Water	1000	38
Skim milk powder	225	
Whole milk powder	200	
The water in this formula is used to reconstitute the skim milk.		
Low Sodium†		
Water	670	45
Lonalac, dry (Mead Johnson Co.)	150	
Casec, dry (Mead Johnson Co.)	25	
Eggs (two)	100	
Dextrose	120	
Vitamin supplement (ml.)	.5	
This formula contains 155 mg. sodium and 1,400 mg. potassium.		
Blended Formula†		
Water	250	30
Strained meat (beef)	100	
Strained vegetable (peas)	100	
Strained fruit (pears)	100	
Evaporated milk	410	
Eggs (two)	100	
Dextrose	25	
Vitamin supplement (ml.)	0.5	

Approximate Analysis

	Cal- ories	Pro- tein Gm.	Fat Gm.	Cho. Gm.	Ca. Gm.	Fe. Mg.	Vit. A I.U.	Ascor- bic Acid Mg.	Thia- mine Mg.	Ribo- flavin Mg.	Nia- cin Mg.
Formula I°	2035	118	18	323	3.5	8	2778	167	5.5	5.5	56.0
Formula II°	1205	84	40	131	2.6	22	9550	136	3.8	8.1	34.0
Formula III°	2321	54	158	183	1.5	7	7270	110	0.9	2.9	10.2
Formula IV°	1798	132	56	193	4.8	3	2890	28	1.4	7.3	3.9
Low Sodium†	1495	75	55	175	1.7	2.6	7260	50	2.09	2.66	24.6
Blended†	1005	60	45	90	1.0	6	8310	57	1.97	2.45	25.6
Recommended	2800	65			0.8	10	5000	60	1.4	1.7	18.0

Recommended allowances for a 70 kg. (154 lbs.), 25 year old man, moderately active, are used for comparison. For some patients it may be advisable to give certain vitamins and iron by medication to prevent deficiencies.

*Adapted from Wohl, G. W., and Goodhart, R. S.: Modern Nutrition in Health and Disease. 2nd ed. Philadelphia, Lea & Febiger, 1960, p. 608.

†Clinical Center Diet Manual, Nutrition Dept., The Clinical Center, National Institutes of Health, U.S. Dept. of Health, Education and Welfare, Public Health Service Pub. No. 989, 1963.

Formulas for Use in Tube Feeding (Continued)

The following formula is easily prepared from household food supplies.*

	Weight, Gm.	Approximate Household Measure
Whole milk	1000	4 cups
Egg yolks	100	5 yolks
Dried skim milk	150	5⅓ oz.
Cream, 20%	200	1 cup
Sugar	125	4⅓ oz.
Orange juice	200	7 fl. oz.
Dried brewer's yeast	50	3½ tbsp.
Salt	5	1 tsp.

This formula, which is homogenized in a food blender, contains 2700 calories, 129 gm. protein, 113 gm. fat, 300 gm. carbohydrate, 3520 mg. calcium, 18.5 mg. iron, 6700 I.U. vitamin A, 6.35 mg. thiamine, 8.0 mg. riboflavin, 21.1 mg. niacin, and 102 mg. ascorbic acid. Use 150 to 200 cc. per feeding.

Gluten Restricted Diet†

Omit wheat, rye, oats, barley, buckwheat, and any product containing them. Corn, rice, wheat starch, potato flour, soybean flour, and tapioca may be used. Maximum calories, protein, vitamins, and minerals should be used because many gluten-induced enteropathy patients have poor absorption of nutrients.

Read all food labels carefully because many processed foods contain wheat, rye, oats, and barley. This diet is adequate even if there is an additional restriction of fat or fiber.

	Foods Allowed	Foods to Avoid
Beverages	Milk, carbonated beverages, coffee, tea, decaffeinated coffee, fruit-flavored beverages	Cereal beverages, malted milk, beverage products containing restricted cereals, ale and beer
Breads	Breads or quick breads made from cornmeal, gluten-free wheat starch, and corn, potato, rice, soybean, or tapioca flours	All bread and crackers containing wheat, rye, oats, barley or buckwheat
Cereals	Cornmeal, rice, precooked rice cereal, dry cereals containing only rice or corn	All cooked and prepared cereals containing wheat, rye, oats, barley, buckwheat, or malt

*From *Heinz Handbook of Nutrition*, 1965, pp. 243–245.

†From: University of Iowa Medical Center: *Recent Advances in Therapeutic Diets*, 1970, pp. 100–101.

	Foods Allowed	*Foods to Avoid*
Desserts	Custard; gelatin desserts; fruit ice; pudding made with cornstarch, gluten-free wheat starch, rice, or tapioca; ice cream or sherbet; cake or cookies and other desserts made with allowed flours	Cakes, cookies, or pastries and commercial pudding mixes containing foods to avoid; ice cream cones; fruit sauces thickened with wheat flour; commercial ice cream or sherbet containing stabilizer which is a wheat product
Eggs	Baked, poached, soft or hard cooked, scrambled, fried	Creamed eggs, souffle, or fondue unless made with allowed flours
Fats	Butter, margarine, cream, vegetable oil and shortening, lard, bacon, salad dressings thickened with allowed flours	Excessive amounts of fried foods, commercially prepared salad dressings and gravies unless prepared with allowed flours
Fruits and Fruit Juices	All fresh, frozen, canned and dried	None unless unable to tolerate roughage
Meat, Fish, Poultry and Cheese	Baked, broiled, roasted, or steamed beef, lamb, liver, pork, veal; chicken, turkey, duck, fish; cottage, cream, or nonprocessed cheese	Meat, fish, or poultry and commercial products containing cereals not allowed. The following foods frequently contain gluten: meat loaves, meat patties, breaded meat, fish, or poultry, canned meat products, cold cuts unless guaranteed all meat, cheese spreads
Potatoes or Substitutes	White or sweet potatoes, hominy, potato chips	Creamed or escalloped potatoes unless made with allowed flours, macaroni, noodles, spaghetti
Soups	Broth-base or cream soups made from foods allowed	Soups containing wheat, rye, oats, barley, or products made from them; commercial soups thickened with wheat flour
Sugar and Sweets	Sugar, syrup, honey, jelly, jam, molasses, candy, chocolate in moderation, chewing gum	Commercial candies containing cereal products not allowed
Vegetables and Vegetable Juices	All fresh, frozen, canned	None unless unable to tolerate roughage
Miscellaneous	Salt (iodized), flavorings, spices in moderation, vinegar, peanut butter, coconut, popcorn, olives, pickles, catsup, mustard, chocolate, pure cocoa, gravy or cream sauce if thickened with allowed flours	Pretzels

Suggested Menu Pattern

Breakfast
½ cup frozen orange juice
1 cup puffed rice cereal
1 egg, soft cooked
1 rice muffin
1 tsp. butter
2 tsp. grape jelly
1 cup whole milk
2 tsp. sugar
Coffee

Dinner
3 oz. roast beef sirloin, U.S. Choice
½ cup cubed white potatoes
½ cup carrots
¾ cup tossed lettuce salad
1 Tbsp. French dressing
1 cornmeal muffin
2 tsp. butter
½ cup vanilla ice cream
1 cup whole milk
1 tsp. sugar
Coffee

Supper
2 oz. broiled chicken
½ cup green beans
1 leaf lettuce and ½ tomato
1 Tbsp. mayonnaise
½ cup canned peaches, sliced, with heavy syrup
1 corn stick
1 cup whole milk
1 tsp. sugar
Coffee

Protein Modified Diets

Exchange*	Grams Protein per Exchange	Number of Exchanges					
Milk	8	½	1	2	3	4	5
Vegetable B	2	2	2	1	2	2	2
Bread	2	6	4	4	4	4	4
Meat	7	—	3	5	6	8	10
Total grams of protein		20	41	61	78	100	122

*Use exchange list under "Diabetic Diet" for foods allowed.

40 GRAM PROTEIN DIET

This diet lacks calcium, iron, riboflavin, and niacin. See the above listing for food exchanges. Sugar, fats (limit cream to 2 tablespoons light or 4 tablespoons heavy per day), and fruits may be used as desired. Omit peas, lima beans, and dried legumes.

Sample Menu Pattern for 40 Gram Protein Diet

Breakfast	Lunch	Dinner
Fruit	Cheese, 1 ounce	Meat, 2 ounces
Cereal	Vegetable B	Potato, butter
Bread, 1 slice	Salad, dressing	Vegetable B
Butter	Bread, 1 slice	Salad, dressing
Milk, 1 cup	Butter	Bread, 1 slice
Beverage	Fruit	Butter
Sugar	Beverage	Fruit
	Sugar	Beverage
		Sugar

100 GRAM PROTEIN DIET

This diet is nutritionally adequate. See the above listing for food exchanges. Sugars, fats, and fruits may be used as desired. Fluid intake should be increased when protein intake is increased.

Sample Menu Pattern for 100 Gram Protein Diet

Breakfast	Lunch	Dinner
Fruit	Sandwich, 2 ounces meat	Meat, 4 ounces
Cereal	Vegetable B	Vegetable B
Eggs, 2	Salad, dressing	Salad, dressing
Bread, 1 slice	Custard	Fruit
Butter	Beverage	Beverage
Beverage	Sugar	Milk
Milk		Sugar
Sugar		

Bedtime — milk

SELECTED PROTEIN DIET (MODIFIED GIOVANNETTI DIET)*

This diet supplies 18 to 20 grams of protein, meeting the minimal daily requirements of the essential amino acids. All foods are processed and cooked without salt, and all fluid is drained from the food when served. This diet contains less than 1200 mg. sodium and approximately 1000 mg. potassium.

This diet is low in iron, calcium, thiamine, riboflavin, and ascorbic acid.

	Foods Allowed	*Foods to Avoid*
Beverages	¾ cup whole milk, ¾ cup tea or coffee, 1 cup cranberry juice or cranberry sauce, unsweetened Kool-Aid, ginger ale, carbonated water, gin, rum, and whiskey in any quantity	All others
Breads	Low protein bread (11 slices)	All others
Cereals	½ cup Cream of Rice or Cream of Wheat	All others
Desserts	(One ½-cup serving daily). Special low protein cakes, cookies, and pies; fruit tapioca pudding; fruit pudding thickened with low protein flour; fruit crisp, fruit ices (no milk or egg) if prepared from fruit allowance	All others
Eggs	One daily (unsalted)	
Fats	Unsalted butter, margarine, and oil in any quantity	All others
Fruits and Fruit Juices	(Four ½-cup servings per day, one as a fruit crisp or pudding). Applesauce, frozen apples, apple juice, raw or frozen blackberries, canned sour red cherries, canned grape juice, canned peaches, pear nectar (1 cup = 1 serving), canned pears, canned pineapple, green gage plums, frozen strawberries, frozen red raspberries, watermelon. (Use the fruit or fruit juice in the form indicated; i.e., if canned is indicated, use only canned.)	All others
Meat, Fish, Poultry, and Cheese	None	All
Potatoes or Substitutes	½ cup cooked rice, instant rice, or noodles; 3 to 6 Tbsp. wheat starch, tapioca, or cornstarch used in cooking in addition to the fruit pudding and bread	All others
Soups	Broth (low sodium)	All others
Sugar and Sweets	Granulated sugar, 3 Tbsp. honey, gum drops, hard candy, jelly beans	Brown sugar, jams
Vegetables and Vegetable Juices	(Two servings daily, no salt added) ⅓ cup canned asparagus, ½ cup canned green or wax beans, ¼ cup canned beets, ¼ cup cooked cauliflower, ¼ cup cooked or canned carrots, ½ cup canned corn, ½ cup cooked eggplant, ½ head iceberg lettuce, ¼ cup frozen okra, 3 green onions, ½ cup cooked mature onion, ½ cup canned peas, 1 small green pepper, ⅓ cup cooked summer squash, ½ cup canned sweet potatoes, ⅓ cup cooked turnips. (Use the vegetable or vegetable juice in the form indicated; i.e., if canned is indicated, use only canned.)	All others
Miscellaneous	Distilled vinegar, curry, pepper	Nuts, popcorn, pretzels, sauces unless thickened with protein-free flour

*From University of Iowa Medical Center: *Recent Advances in Therapeutic Diets*, 1970, pp. 69–71.

Suggested Menu Pattern

Breakfast	*Dinner*	*Supper*
½ cup cranberry juice	1 egg, scrambled	Pineapple slice and
½ cup Cream of Wheat cereal	½ cup rice	peach half on
2 slices bread, low protein	½ cup cooked carrots	lettuce
2 tsp. butter	6 slices cucumber on	2 slices bread, low protein
2 tsp. honey	1 leaf lettuce	½ cup green beans
¼ cup whole milk	2 slices bread, low protein	2 tsp. butter
2 tsp. sugar	2 tsp. butter	1 low-protein cookie
¾ cup coffee	½ cup sweetened canned pears	1 high-fat, low-protein popsicle
	1 tsp. sugar	1 tsp. sugar
	1 cup Kool-Aid	½ cup whole milk

Purine Restricted Diet*

Foods containing purines are restricted, as are fats, which possibly may interfere with the excretion of uric acid from the kidneys. This diet is nutritionally adequate, but if all meat, fish, and poultry were eliminated, the diet would be low in iron, thiamine, and niacin.

	Foods Allowed	*Foods to Avoid*
Beverages	Skim milk, coffee, tea, decaffeinated drinks, cocoa, carbonated beverages	Alcohol, whole milk, cream
Breads	White refined bread, cornbread	Rye bread or crackers, whole wheat bread, whole grain products
Cereals	All refined cereals, macaroni, rice, noodles, spaghetti	Oatmeal, whole grain products
Desserts	Plain cookies, angel food cake, custards, gelatin desserts, low-fat puddings, ice milk	Rich desserts, ice cream, rice cake and cookies, desserts made with mincemeat
Eggs	Soft or hard cooked, poached	Fried
Fats	All (limit to 3 tsp. per day)	Gravy (avoid excessive amounts)
Fruits and Fruit Juices	All	None
Meat, Fish, Poultry, and Cheese	Lean beef, veal, lamb, chicken, turkey, fish, washed cottage cheese, skim milk cheese	Organ meats, meat extracts, anchovies, sardines, ham, pork, pork sausage, goose; creamed cottage cheese, cheeses made from whole milk
Potatoes	All potatoes	Fried potatoes, potato chips
Soups	Soups made with skim milk and allowed vegetables	Bouillon, broth, consomme, meat extract soup
Vegetables and Vegetable Juices	All except those to avoid	Asparagus, beans (except string), cauliflower, peas, lentils, spinach, mushrooms
Miscellaneous	Salt, herbs, nuts, pickles, popcorn, vinegar	Yeast

*From University of Iowa Medical Center: *Recent Advances in Therapeutic Diets,* 1970, p. 103.

Suggested Menu Pattern

Breakfast	*Dinner*	*Supper*
½ cup frozen orange juice	2 oz. roast beef sirloin	2 oz. washed cottage cheese
½ cup cooked farina	½ cup cubed white potatoes	½ cup rice
1 slice toast, white enriched	½ cup cooked carrots	½ cup green beans
1 tsp. butter	¾ cup tossed lettuce salad	½ tomato on lettuce
1 cup skim milk	1 slice bread, white enriched	1 slice bread, white enriched
2 tsp. sugar	1 tsp. butter	1 tsp. butter
Coffee or tea	1 cup skim milk	1 cup skim milk
	½ cup orange sherbet	½ cup canned peaches, sliced,
	1 tsp. sugar	with heavy syrup
	Coffee, if desired	1 tsp. sugar
		Coffee, if desired

Sodium Modified Diets

Salt substitutes contain potassium or ammonium ions and should be used only when ordered by the physician.

Ideally, the diet order should specify the total milligrams of sodium desired. As restriction is increased foods have to be chosen with more care. Bakery products, precooked foods, frozen foods with added sodium, meat, eggs, cheese, fish, and milk have to be restricted. Some natural water supplies, as well as softened water, may be high in sodium. When milk is dialyzed, potassium is exchanged for sodium (approximately 200 mg. of potassium per 100 ml.) and the riboflavin is decreased by approximately half. Medications, toothpaste, etc., should be checked for sodium content.

NO ADDED SALT DIETS

These diets contain 2 to 4 grams (87 to 174 mEq.) sodium. No salt is added as food is prepared. Foods avoided include: gravy, most sauces, broth, meat tenderizers, salted meats, cold cuts, frankfurters, cheese, salted nuts, salted crackers, potato chips; onion, celery and garlic salt; relishes, catsup, olives, pickles, peanut butter, and canned tomato juice. The diet is nutritionally adequate.

Condiments for Low Sodium Diets: Where to Use Herbs*

	Basil	Bay Leaf	Cayenne	Celery Seed	Ginger	Marjoram	Sage	Thyme	Oregano	Rosemary	Tarragon	Savory
APPETIZERS	tomato juice	tomato juice						tomato juice	guaca-mole	fruit cup	fruit cup	
SOUP	tomato spinach	stock			cold tomato	spinach onion	cream	borscht vegetable	tomato	pea spinach chicken	consomme chicken mushroom tomato	
MEAT	lamb	roast stew fricassee	beef veal lamb			pot roast lamb veal		meatloaf veal	meatloaf pork lamb	lamb stews	veal	veal
FISH	all			all		broiled baked creamed		all		salmon	broiled	broiled baked
GAME FOWL	duck						poultry game stuffing	poultry	stuffing	stuffing	poultry	chicken
EGGS DAIRY	scramb. eggs	all	eggs			cottage cheese omelet scramb.	scramb. eggs cottage cheese	cottage cheese	boiled or poached eggs		all eggs	scramb. eggs
SAUCES GRAVIES	tomato					cream	chicken gravy	tomato	spaghetti sauce spanish		vinegar	
VEGETABLES	tomato peas squash beans	boiled potato carrots tomato		tomato potato	squash	carrots zucchini peas spinach	eggplant tomato	onions carrots beets	tomato	peas spinach	baked potato	rice
SALADS	tomato greens					greens		tomato			greens	greens green-beans

The following items *should NOT be* used for seasoning on a 1000 mg. Sodium Diet:

Salt
Seasoned Salts
Catsup
Chili Sauce
Worcestershire Sauce and other steak sauces
Pickles
Relish
Olives
Salt Pork
Ham Hocks
Soy Sauce
Accent (monosodium glutamate)
Bouillon Cubes or Granules
Cheeses

The following items *may be used* for seasoning on a 1000 mg. Sodium Diet:

Tabasco Sauce
Garlic Powder
Vinegar
Pepper and all other dry spices such as curry, paprika, cinnamon, etc.
All herbs listed on this page
Special dietetic Low Sodium Catsup and Chili Sauce. Low Sodium Mustard
Special dietetic Low Sodium Bouillon Cubes
Salt Substitutes
Dry Mustard

*From Wadsworth Hospital Dietetic Service, Veterans Administration Center, Los Angeles: *Cooking for the 1000 mg. Low Sodium Diet*, 1968.

Sodium is moderately restricted. The diet is nutritionally adequate.

	Foods Allowed	*Foods Omitted*
Beverages	Milk, 3 cups whole or skim; dialyzed (low sodium) milk as desired; tea, coffee, Coca Cola, cocoa (made with plain cocoa).	Commercial milk drinks, instant cocoa powders, carbonated beverages unless sodium content is less than 3 mg. per 8 oz., softened water, buttermilk unless it is unsalted
Cereals	Low sodium white or whole wheat yeast bread; hot breads made with sodium-free baking powder; whole grain or enriched cereals, cooked without added salt; puffed wheat; puffed rice; shredded wheat; low sodium cornflakes; pasta and rice cooked without added salt	Salted crackers; quick cooking cereals; all commercial bread, rolls, biscuit and bread mixes; self-rising flours; ready-to-eat cereals except those listed
Cheese	Low sodium cheddar, unsalted cottage cheese (large curd cottage cheese can be rinsed in running water)	All others
Desserts	Baked desserts if made with sodium-free baking powder and unsalted shortening; fruit pie, unsalted crust; fruit whips; gelatin; ½ cup ice cream, sherbet, or milk pudding (if an additional dessert is made with milk, deduct ½ cup milk unless it is made with low sodium milk)	Desserts made with salt, baking powder, or baking soda; all commercial pies, pastries, and bakery products; all commercial cake, cookie, and pudding mixes; regular flavored gelatin desserts
Eggs	1 per day without added salt	
Fats	1 teaspoon salted butter; unsalted (sweet) butter and margarine as desired; unsalted salad dressings, salad oils; heavy or light cream; hydrogenated shortenings; lard, sour cream	Salted butter, margarine and salad dressing; all commercial salad dressings and salad dressing mixes; bacon and ham drippings
Fruits and Fruit Juices	All canned, cooked, fresh, or frozen	Dried fruits containing sodium preservatives; glazed fruit; maraschino cherries
Meat, fish, poultry	6 oz. meat, fish, or poultry broiled, roasted, or fried without added salt or Accent (MSG); unsalted canned tuna or salmon	Salted, smoked, canned, cured, or brined meat, fish or poultry; all glandular meats except liver and heart; shellfish except fresh oysters; frankfurters; TV dinners; luncheon meats (cold cuts); frozen fish fillets usually have had salt added.
Soups	Sodium-free broth or soup made with allowed milk and vegetables	No commercial soups except those labeled low sodium; bouillon cubes; consomme
Sugar and sweets	Granulated sugar, jam, jelly, marmalade, maple syrup, unsalted candy, honey	Brown sugar; molasses; sweets with added salt or sodium
Vegetables	Fresh or canned sweet or white potato without added salt; frozen French fries; all fresh, or canned vegetables or juice without added salt or sodium; frozen vegetables (see exceptions)	Regular canned vegetables; potato chips; frozen prepared potato products; hominy; frozen peas and lima beans and the mixed vegetables containing them; celery; sauerkraut; vegetables and juices canned with added salt; tomato juice
Miscellaneous	Spices, herbs, seasonings (see preceding list); vinegar; unsalted popcorn and nuts; unsalted peanut butter; plain cocoa; tabasco sauce; low sodium catsup, Worcestershire and chili sauce; sodium-free baking powder; extracts, cream of tartar, yeast, potassium bicarbonate	Prepared sauces and gravies, saccharine, olives, party spreads and dips, pickles, relishes, soy sauce, meat tenderizers, seasoned salts, Accent (MSG), regular baking powder, baking soda; horseradish; prepared mustard, catsup, rennet tablets

Sample Menu Pattern for 1000 Milligram Sodium Diet

Breakfast	*Lunch and Dinner*
Fruit	Meat, 2 to 3 ounces
Cereal, unsalted	Vegetables, 2 servings, unsalted
Egg, 1	Salad, unsalted, dressing
Muffin, made with sodium free baking powder	Bread, unsalted
Butter, unsalted as desired	Butter, unsalted as desired
Jelly, sugar	Fruit or baked dessert
Beverage	Beverage
Milk	Milk

500 MILLIGRAM (21.7 mEq.) SODIUM DIET

Foods allowed as in the 1000 mg. diet, except:

Beverages — Restrict milk to 2 cups (2 cups of dialyzed [low sodium] may be substituted for 1 cup whole milk). Omit chocolate milk, condensed milk, milk shakes, malted milk, milk mixes, fountain drinks.

Desserts — All milk in a dessert should be subtracted from the milk allowance.

Fats — No salted butter or margarine; restrict cream to 2 tablespoons.

Meat — Restrict to 4 ounces.

Vegetables — Also omit beets, beet greens, carrots, artichokes, Swiss chard, mustard greens, kale, spinach, dandelion greens, turnips.

Sample Menu Pattern for 500 Milligram Sodium Diet

Breakfast	*Lunch and Dinner*
Fruit	Meat, 2 ounces, unsalted
Cereal, unsalted	Vegetables, 2 servings, unsalted
Egg, 1	Salad, salad dressing, unsalted
Bread, butter, unsalted	Bread, butter, unsalted
Jelly	Jelly, sugar
Cream, 2 tablespoons	Fruit
Beverage	Beverage
Sugar	Milk

Ulcer Diet Patterns

Frequently ulcer diets are inadequate in vitamin C and iron. Using milk or skim milk in place of cream will reduce the fat intake.

The current tendency is to use a liberal diet in the treatment of peptic ulcer. The patient is allowed the foods customarily excluded. He often is happier. The relaxed, pleasant conditions promote healing. Frequent feedings seem to be more important than the type of food used. Allspice, cinnamon, mace, paprika, thyme, sage, and caraway seed in food do not seem to hinder ulcer healing. Black and chili pepper, mustard seed, cloves, and possibly nutmeg may be gastric irritants.

Review Chapter 19.

TYPICAL REGIMEN FOR DIETARY MANAGEMENT OF PEPTIC ULCER*

		8 A.M.	10 A.M.	12 NOON	3 P.M.	6 P.M.	8 P.M.
First Stage: 3 to 4 oz. milk or milk and cream (half and half) are served every 1 to 2 hours on the hour, 7 A.M. through 9 P.M. and during the night if necessary							
Second Stage Supplementary feedings added as tolerated (6 to 8 oz.)	1 feeding	Farina with cream and sugar					
	2 feedings	Boiled rice with cream and sugar					
	3 feedings	Farina with cream and sugar		Milk toast		Baked custard	
	4 feedings	Oatmeal with cream and sugar	Poached egg on toast	Strained cream soup with white crackers		Gelatin and cream / Vanilla ice cream with sugar cookies	
	5 feedings	Cream of wheat with cream and sugar	Soft cooked egg with 1 slice toast	Boiled rice with cream and sugar	Bread pudding with cream	Cream soup with croutons	
Third Stage (Six feedings) (10 to 12 oz.)	As long as indicated	Strained and diluted orange juice (end of meal) / Farina with cream and sugar / Milk and cream (6 oz.)	Poached egg on toast / Milk (8 oz.)	Strained creamed pea soup / Crackers / Cottage cheese / Baked potato (no skin) / Enriched white bread and butter / Strawberry gelatin	Milk-rennet pudding / Milk (8 oz.)	Strained diluted tomato juice / Broiled beef patty / Buttered noodles / Enriched white bread and butter / Baked custard / Milk and cream (4 oz.)	Eggnog with cinnamon / Soda crackers
Fourth Stage	Low-fiber diet for Ambulatory patient	Strained orange juice (end of meal) / Cream of wheat with cream and sugar / Soft cooked egg / Buttered enriched white toast / Milk (8 oz.) / Decaffeinated coffee with cream and sugar	Milk (8 oz.)	Cream of spinach soup / Crackers / Cottage cheese / Baked potato (no skin) / Asparagus tips / Enriched white bread and butter / Canned peaches / Milk (8 oz.)	Milk (8 oz.)	Tender roast beef / Boiled rice / Cooked beets / Enriched white bread and butter / Vanilla ice cream / Milk (8 oz.)	Milk (8 oz.)

*From Krause, Marie V. and Hunscher, Martha A.: *Food, Nutrition, and Diet Therapy,* 1972, p. 343.

SIX-FEEDING DIET FOR PEPTIC ULCER PATIENT*

MEAL PLAN	SAMPLE MENU	Weight Grams	SERVINGS Household Measure
	BREAKFAST		
Fruit	Strained, diluted orange juice (taken at end of meal)	124	½ cup
Cereal	Cooked farina	119	½ cup
Milk and cream	Milk and cream	181	1 glass (6 oz.)
Cream	Cream (for cereal)	60	2 ounces
Sugar	Sugar (for cereal)	10	2 teaspoons
	10:00 A.M.		
Egg	Poached egg	50	1
Bread	Toasted enriched white bread	46	2 slices
Butter	Butter or margarine	7	1 pat
Milk	Milk	244	1 cup
	LUNCHEON		
Soup	Strained cream of pea soup	128	½ cup
Crackers	Soda crackers	11	2
Cheese	Cottage cheese	56	2 ounces
Vegetables	Baked potato	99	1 medium
Bread	Enriched white bread	23	1 slice
Butter	Butter or margarine	14	2 pats
Dessert	Strawberry gelatin	120	1½ cup
	3:00 P.M.		
Dessert	Milk-rennet dessert	100	½ cup
Milk	Milk	244	1 cup
	DINNER		
Vegetable	Strained, diluted tomato juice (taken in middle of meal)	120	½ cup
Meat	Broiled beef patty	57	2 ounces
Cereal product	Noodles, buttered	80	½ cup
Bread	Enriched white bread	23	1 slice
Butter	Butter or margarine	7	1 pat
Dessert	Baked custard	124	½ cup
Milk and cream	Milk and cream	121	½ cup
	8:00 P.M.		
Crackers	Soda crackers	11	2
Milk beverage	Eggnog	244	1 cup

*From Krause, Marie B. and Hunscher, Martha A.: *Food, Nutrition, and Diet Therapy,* 1972, p. 341.

BIBLIOGRAPHY

1. Abersold, Paul C.: Radioisotopes—New Keys to Knowledge, Washington, D.C., *Annual Report of the Board of Regents of the Smithsonian Institution, 1953.*
2. Allen, P. C., and Lee, H. A.: *A Clinical Guide to Intravenous Nutrition.* Oxford, Blackwell Scientific Publications, 1969.
3. American Heart Association: *American Heart Association Cookbook.* New York, David McKay Company, 1973.
4. ——— *Diet and Heart Disease.*
5. American Home Economics Association: *Handbook of Food Preparation.* Washington, American Home Economics Association.
6. *Am. J. Clin. Nutrition:* "Symposium on Nutrition and Behavior," 5:103–236, March-April, 1957.
7. American Medical Association: *The Wonderful Human Machine.*
8. ——— *Today's Health Guide.*
9. ——— *Facts On Quacks—What You Should Know About Health Quackery,* 1967.
10. ——— *Let's Talk About Food.*
11. ——— *The Look You Like.*
12. ——— *Vitamin Supplements and Their Correct Use.*
13. American Medical Association and American Academy of Pediatrics: *Growing Pains.* Chicago, American Medical Association, 1969.
14. American Medical Association Council on Foods and Nutrition: "Vitamin Preparations as Dietary Supplements and as Therapeutic Agents," *J.A.M.A., 169*:41–45, January 3, 1959.
15. Arthritis Foundation: *Rheumatoid Arthritis—A Handbook for Patients.*
15a. Babcock, Charlotte G.: "Attitudes and the Use of Food," J. Am. Dietet. A., *38*:546–551, June, 1961.
16. Barnes, Richard H.: "Effects of Malnutrition on Mental Development—Truths and Half-Truths," *Journal of Home Economics, 61*:671–676, November, 1969.
17. Berland, Theodore: "Do Cold Cures Really Work?" *Today's Health,* January, 1961.
18. Bogert, L. Jean, et al.: *Nutrition and Physical Fitness.* Philadelphia, W. B. Saunders Company, 1973.
19. Breckenridge, Marian E., and Murphy, Margaret Nesbitt: *Growth and Development of the Young Child.* Philadelphia, W. B. Saunders Company, 1969.
20. Breckenridge, Marian E., and Vincent, E. Lee: *Child Development—From Age 6 Through Adolescence.* Philadelphia, W. B. Saunders Company, 1965.
21. Brown, Lester R., and Finsterbusch, Gail W.: *Man and his Environment: Food.* New York, Harper and Row, 1972.
22. Carey, Ruth Little, et al.: *Commonsense Nutrition.* Mountain View, Calif., Pacific Press Publishing Assoc., 1971 (by school of Nutrition and Dietetics, Loma Linda University).
23. Carson, Gerald: *One for a Man, Two for a Horse—A Pictorial History Grave and Comic of Patent Medicines,* Doubleday and Company, Inc., 1961.
23a. Chersakin, E.: "Protein and Oral Health," *Food and Nutrition News,* National Livestock and Meat Board, February, 1967.
24. Church, E. C., and Church, H. M.: *Bowes and Church's Food Values of Portions Commonly Used.* Philadelphia, J. B. Lippincott Company, 1975.
25. Contra Costa County Health Department: *Food and Nutrition Notes for Nursing and Boarding Homes,* December, 1965.
26. Crawfis, E. H.: "The Dietitian in the Mental Hospital," *J. Am. Dietet. A., 30*:464–465, May, 1954.
27. Dahl, Crete: *Food and Menu Dictionary.* Boston, Institutions/Volume Feeding Magazine, 1972.

28. *Dairy Council Digest:* "Relative Nutritional Value of Filled and Imitation Milks," *39:*2:7, March-April, 1968.
29. Deutsch, Ronald M.: *The Family Guide to Better Food and Better Health.* Des Moines, Creative Home Library, 1971.
29a. Diefenbach, V. L., et al.: "Fluoridation and the Appearance of Teeth," *J. Am. Dental Assoc.,* November, 1965.
29b. Foman, S. J.: *Infant Nutrition.* Philadelphia, W. B. Saunders Company, 1974.
30. Frobisher, Martin, et al.: *Microbiology in Health and Disease.* Philadelphia, W. B. Saunders Company, 1974.
31. Ganong, William F.: *Review of Medical Physiology.* Los Altos, Lange Medical Publications, 1973.
32. Goldsmith, Grace A.: "Niacin: Antipellagra Factor, Hypocholesterolemic Agent," *J.A.M.A., 194:*167, October 11, 1965.
33. Goodhart, Robert S. and Shils, Maurice E.: *Modern Nutrition in Health and Disease.* Philadelphia, Lea & Febiger, 1973.
34. Guitar, Mary Anne: "R$_x$ for Philip," *Good Housekeeping,* May, 1970.
35. Harper, Harold A.: *Review of Physiological Chemistry.* Los Altos, Lange Medical Publications, 1973.
36. Hirsch, J., et al.: "Cell Lipid Content and Cell Number in Obese and Nonobese Human Adipose Tissue," *J. Clin. Invest., 45:*1023, 1966.
37. *J. Am. Dietet. A.:* August, 1955, p. 793.
38. —— "Foods Suitable for Potassium Supplementation," *56:*298, April, 1970.
39. *J.A.M.A.:* "Larrick Outlines FDA Activities," *176:*17–18, May 27, 1961.
40. —— "Special Shortenings," *187:*766, March 7, 1964.
41. Krause, Marie V., and Hunscher, Martha A.: *Food, Nutrition, and Diet Therapy.* Philadelphia, W. B. Saunders Company, 1972.
41a. Lagua, Rosalinde, et al.: *Nutrition and Diet Therapy Reference Dictionary.* St. Louis, The C. V. Mosby Co., 1974.
41b. Lappe, Frances Moore: *Diet for a Small Planet.* Friends of the Earth/Ballantine Books, 1971.
42. Leverton, Ruth M.: *Food Becomes You.* Lincoln, University of Iowa Press, 1965.
43. —— "Nutritional Well-Being in the U.S.A.," *Nutrition Reviews, 22:*321, November, 1964.
44. Liebowitz, Daniel, et al.: *Cook To Your Heart's Content on a Low-Fat, Low-Salt Diet.* Menlo Park, Pacific Coast Publishers, 1969 (many gourmet recipes).
45. Lutwak, Leo: "Interrelationships of Calcium and Fat Metabolism," *Nutrition News,* National Dairy Council, April, 1969.
46. Margolius, Sidney: *The Great American Food Hoax.* New York, Walker and Company, 1971.
47. ——: *Health Foods Facts and Fakes.* New York, Walker and Company, 1973.
48. Mayer, Jean: *Overweight, Causes, Cost, and Control.* Englewood Cliffs, N.J., Prentice-Hall, Inc., 1968.
49. —— (Ed.): *U.S. Nutrition Policies in the Seventies.* San Francisco, W. H. Freeman and Company, 1973.
50. McLester, James S., and Darby, William J.: *Nutrition and Diet in Health and Disease,* 6th ed. Philadelphia, W. B. Saunders Company, 1952.
51. Meyer, Herman Frederic: *Infant Foods and Feeding Practice.* Springfield, Ill., Charles C Thomas, 1960.
51a. Miller, Benjamin F., and Keane, Claire Brackman: *Encyclopedia and Dictionary of Medicine and Nursing.* Philadelphia, W. B. Saunders Company, 1972.
52. Miller, Verdi: "Role of the Dietetic Service in a Neuropsychiatric Hospital," *J. Am. Dietet. A., 30:*465–469, May, 1954.
53. National Academy of Sciences: *Recommended Dietary Allowances.* Washington, National Research Council, 1974.
54. —— *Maternal Nutrition and the Course of Human Pregnancy.* Washington, D.C., 1970.
55. National Livestock and Meat Board: *Cooking Meat in Quantity,* 2nd ed. Chicago, National Livestock and Meat Board, Department of Home Economics, 1946.
56. Nizel, Abraham E., and Shulman, Judith S.: "Interaction of Dietetics and Nutrition with Dentistry," *J. Am. Dietet. A., 55:*470–475, November, 1969.
57. ——: *Nutrition in Preventive Dentistry—Science and Practice.* Philadelphia, W. B. Saunders Company, 1972.

58. Ohio Department of Health: *Budget-Wise Family Meals . . . Nutritious, Too,* 1958.
59. Olson, Robert E.: "Research, Fads, and Practical Dietetics," *J. Am. Dietet. A., 31*:777–782, August, 1955.
60. Owens, Lavern, and White, Gene Sando: "Observations on Food Acceptance During Mental Illness," *J. Am. Dietet. A., 30*:1110–1114, November, 1954.
61. Oski, F. A., and Barnes, L. A.: "Vitamin E Deficiency: A Previously Unrecognized Cause of Hemolytic Anemia in the Premature Infant," *J. Pediatr., 70*:211, 1967.
62. Packard, Vance: *The Hidden Persuaders.* New York, David McKay Company, Inc., 1957.
63. Peckham, S. C., et al.: "The Influence of a Hypercaloric Diet on Gross Body and Adipose Tissue Composition in the Rat," *J. Nutrition, 77*:187, 1962.
64. Readings from *Scientific American: Food.* San Francisco, W. H. Freeman and Company, 1973.
65. Report of the Joint Committee of the American Dietetic Association and the American Medical Association: "Diet as Related to Gastrointestinal Function," *J. Am. Dietet. A., 38*:425–432, May, 1961.
66. Richmond, Julius B., and Pollack, George H.: "Psychologic Aspects of Infant Feeding," *J. Am. Dietet. A., 29*:656–659, July, 1953.
67. Rosenmeir, Margaret R.: "Cooking—A Therapy for the Mentally Ill Patient," *J. Am. Dietet. A., 30*:470–474, May, 1954.
68. Seaver, Jacqueline: *Fads, Myths, Quacks—And Your Health.* Public Affairs Pamphlet No. 415, 1968.
69. Sebrell, William H., and Haggerty, James J.: *Food and Nutrition.* New York, Time-Life Books, 1971.
70. Shambaugh, George E., and Petrovic, Alexandre: "Effect of Sodium Fluoride on Bone," *J.A.M.A., 204*:11:111, June 10, 1968.
70a. Society for Nutrition Education: *Nutrition Information Resources for Professionals.*
70b. ———: *Nutrition Information Resources for the Whole Family,* 1975.
70c. ———: *Vegetarians and Vegetarians Diets.* Resource Series No. 8, 1974.
71. Solomon, Neil: *The Truth About Weight Control.* New York, Stein and Day, 1971.
72. Stare, Fredrick J.: "Diet for Athletes," *J. Am. Dietet. Assoc., 37*:371, October, 1960.
73. ——— and McWilliams, Margaret: *Living Nutrition.* New York, John Wiley and Sons, 1973.
74. Sternberg, Thomas H.: *More Than Skin Deep.* Garden City, Doubleday, 1970.
75. Tappel, A. L.: "Where Old Age Begins," *Nutrition Today, 2*:4:2–7, December, 1967.
76. Time-Life Books: *The Healthy Life—How Diet and Exercise Affect Your Heart and Vigor.*
77. Troelstrup, Arch W.: *The Consumer in the American Society.* New York, McGraw-Hill Book Company, Inc., 1974.
78. Turner, Dorothea: *Handbook of Diet Therapy,* University of Chicago Press, 1970.
79. Turtle, William John: *Dr. Turtle's Babies.* Philadelphia, W. B. Saunders Company, 1973.
80. U.S. Department of Agriculture, Handbook No. 8: *Composition of Foods—Raw, Processed, Prepared.*
81. ——— *Consumers All—The Yearbook of Agriculture,* 1965.
82. ——— *Food—The Yearbook of Agriculture,* 1959.
83. ——— *Food For Us All, Agricultural Yearbook,* 1969.
84. ——— *Protecting Our Food, Agricultural Yearbook,* 1966.
85. ——— *Handbook for the Home,* Agricultural Yearbook, 1973.
86. ——— *Shopper's Guide,* Agricultural Yearbook, 1974.
87. U.S. Department of Agriculture, Home and Garden Bulletin No. 72: *Nutritive Value of Foods,* 1971.
88. ——— Home and Garden Bulletin No. 1: *Family Fare: A Guide to Good Nutrition,* 1973.
89. ——— Home and Garden Bulletin No. 174: *Meat and Poultry Care Tips for You,* 1970.
90. ——— Home and Garden Bulletin No. 125: *Fruits in Family Meals, A Guide for Consumers,* 1968.
91. ——— Home and Garden Bulletin No. 105: *Vegetables in Family Meals, A Guide for Consumers,* 1969.
92. University of California Extension Service: *Food Facts for Teens,* 1958.
93. U.S. Department of Health, Education, and Welfare, Children's Bureau Publication No. 347: *The Adolescent in Your Family.*
94. Williams, Sue Rodwell: *Nutrition and Diet Therapy.* Saint Louis, The C. V. Mosby Company, 1973.

95. Wilson, Nancy L. (Ed.): *Obesity.* Philadelphia, F. A. Davis Company, 1969.
96. Winick, Myron (Ed.): *Nutrition and Development.* New York, John Wiley and Sons, 1972.
97. Young, James Harvey: *The Medical Messiahs,* Princeton, Princeton University Press, 1967.
98. Yudkin, John: "Dietary Sugar and Coronary Heart Disease," *Nutrition News,* National Dairy Council, October, 1969.
99. ———: *Sweet and Dangerous.* Bantam, 1973.
100. ——— and McKenzie, J. C.: *Changing Food Habits,* London, MacGibbon and Kee, Ltd.
101. *Hospitals, J.A.H.A.*: Guide Issue, August, 1970.
102. Huffman, Edna K.: *Manual for Medical Record Librarians.* Berwyn, Physicians' Record Company, 1960.

INDEX

Page numbers in *italics* indicate illustrations and tables.

STUDIES IN
AMERICAN SOCIOLOGY
UNDER
THE GENERAL EDITORSHIP OF
STANFORD M. LYMAN

VOLUME II

CIVILIZATION

Contents, Discontents, Malcontents, and Other Essays in Social Theory

Stanford M. Lyman

The University of Arkansas Press

Fayetteville   1990   London

HM
22
.U5
L95
1990

Designer: Chang-hee H. Russell
Typeface: Linotron 202 Bembo
Typesetter: G & S Typesetters, Inc.
Printer: Braun-Brumfield Inc.
Binder: Braun-Brumfield Inc.

The paper used in this publication meets the minimum requirements of the
American National Standard for Permanence of Paper for Printed Library
Materials z39.48-1984. ∞

Library of Congress Cataloging-in-Publication Data

Lyman, Stanford M.
  Civilization : contents, discontents, malcontents, and other essays in social
theory / Stanford M. Lyman.
    p.   cm. — (Studies in American sociology : v. 2)
  Includes Index.
  ISBN 1-55728-136-x (alk. paper)
    1. Sociology—United States.   2. United States—Civilization.   3. United
States—Race relations.   4. Social change.   5. Symbolic interactionism.
I. Title. II. Series.
HM22.U5L95   1990
306'.0973—dc20   89-20221
                                                                        CIP

Dedicated to
Kenneth E. Bock—
Mentor and Scholar

CONTENTS

The Existential Self: Language and Silence in the
Formation of Human Identity

ACKNOWLEDGMENTS

CIVILIZATION: CONTENTS, DISCONTENTS, MALCONTENTS first appeared in *Contemporary Sociology, An International Journal of Reviews* (a review essay of Erving Goffman, *Relations in Public: Microstudies of the Public Order*), Vol. 2, No. 4 (July 1973), published by The American Sociological Association.

TWO NEGLECTED PIONEERS OF CIVILIZATION ANALYSIS: THE CULTURAL PERSPECTIVES OF R. STEWART CULIN AND FRANK HAMILTON CUSHING first appeared in *Social Research,* Vol. 49, No. 3 (Autumn 1982). This paper owes its origins to my studies with Kenneth E. Bock at the University of California in Berkeley from 1951 to 1960 and also to the researches on the Chinese in America that culminated in my doctoral dissertation, *The Structure of Chinese Society in 19th-Century America,* in 1961. While doing researches on the latter work, I first came across the writings of Stewart Culin. Hunting down his entire corpus has since become a continuing aspect of my research. By happenstance the curators of the Brooklyn Museum made it possible for me to locate an entire cache of Culin's work that had remained hidden from view for almost fifty years. My most recent investigations of this subject have been aided immeasurably by student assistants: Ying-jen Chang, James Cleland, Cecil Greek, Brian Hamilton, Gary Kriss, Reuben Norman, Steven Seidman, and Richard Stillman. I am indebted to the critical advice of Randall Collins, Guy Oakes, Marvin B. Scott, and Arthur Vidich. The final draft of this paper would not have been possible without the editorial assistance of the late Ms. Daria Cverna Martin.

The civilizational analytic developed by Professor Benjamin Nelson provided me with a new perspective for study and acted as a stimulus to my own investigations. Fortunately I was able to serve as a colleague of Professor Nelson from 1972 until his untimely death in 1977. Our close association in the Department of Sociology at the Graduate Faculty of Political and Social Science, New School for Social Research, as well as our many informal discussions, proved to be a catalyst for this paper and many other lines of research. Professor Nelson will be sorely missed by his colleagues and students at the New School. This paper is dedicated to his memory.

ASIAN AMERICAN CONTACTS BEFORE COLUMBUS: ALTERNATIVE UNDERSTANDINGS FOR CIVILIZATION, ACCULTURATION, AND ETHNIC MINORITY STATUS IN THE UNITED STATES first appeared in *Japanese Americans: IJU Kara Jiritsu Eno Ayumi,* ed. Togami Sohken (Kyoto: Mineruva Shobo, 1985), Mineruva Shobo Publishers.

THE SCIENCE OF HISTORY AND THE THEORY OF SOCIAL CHANGE first appeared in *Max Weber's Political Sociology: A Pessimistic Vision of a Rationalized World,* ed. Ronald M. Glassman and Vatro Murvar (Westport, Ct.: Greenwood Press, 1984). Copyright © 1984 by Ronald M. Glassman and Vatro Murvar. Reprinted with permission. I am indebted to Guy Oakes, Marvin B. Scott, and Arthur J. Vidich for criticism and advice on this essay and to Ronald Glassman for the invitation to present it at the Fourth Annual Max Weber Colloquium, October 31, 1980.

THE ACCEPTANCE, REJECTION, AND RECONSTRUCTION OF HISTORIES: ON SOME CONTROVERSIES IN THE STUDY OF SOCIAL AND CULTURAL CHANGE, ed. Richard H. Brown and Stanford M. Lyman, first appeared in *Structure, Consciousness, and History* (New York: Cambridge University Press, 1978), published by the Syndics of the Press of Cambridge University. Publication of this essay affords the author a long overdue opportunity to acknowledge and thank certain persons instrumental in the formation of his ideas. Most significant is Kenneth E. Bock, whose years of patient research and quiet but forceful teaching have carried forward the project originated by F. J. Teggart in the Department of Social Institutions at the University of California at Berkeley. My own reservations about certain aspects of that project are not a rejection but rather a reaffirmation of its significance.

While preparing this paper I incurred debts of gratitude to several scholars and students working in related areas. Richard H. Brown has been a resource, critic, and colleague in this endeavor. Marvin B. Scott read and criticized early drafts of the paper. Arthur J. Vidich gave me the benefit of his always perceptive critical judgment. George V. Zito interpreted technical aspects of Pachter's work. Steven Seidmen, Jerry Gittleman, Gary Kriss, Cecil Greek, James Cleland, and Gary Johnson aided in the gathering of materials.

THE RACE RELATIONS CYCLE OF ROBERT E. PARK first appeared in *Pacific Sociological Review,* Vol. 11, No. 1 (Spring 1968), published by Pacific Sociological Association. It is a revised version of the invitational paper presented at the annual meeting of the Pacific Sociological Association,

Long Beach, California, March 30–31, 1967. The author is indebted to Donald Ball, Horace R. Cayton, Nathan Glazer, William Petersen, and Marvin B. Scott for their criticism and advice at various stages of the paper's development.

INTERACTIONISM AND THE STUDY OF RACE RELATIONS AT THE MACRO-SOCIOLOGICAL LEVEL: THE CONTRIBUTION OF HERBERT BLUMER first appeared in *Symbolic Interaction,* 7:1 (Spring 1984), published by JAI Press, Inc. A revised version of this paper was presented to the World Congress of Sociology, Mexico City, August 1982. The author would like to acknowledge the advice and criticism of Herbert Blumer, Marvin B. Scott, Arthur J. Vidich, John Johnson, and four anonymous reviewers.

CONFLICT AND THE WEB OF GROUP AFFILIATION IN SAN FRANCISCO'S CHINATOWN, *1850–1910* first appeared in *Pacific Historical Review,* The Asian American, Vol. XLIII, No. 4 (November 1974). Copyright © 1974 by The Pacific Coast Branch, American Historical Association.

CHERISHED VALUES AND CIVIL RIGHTS first appeared in *Crisis,* Vol. 71, No. 10 (December 1964), published by the National Association for the Advancement of Colored People.

SYSTEM AND FUNCTION IN ANTEBELLUM SOUTHERN SOCIOLOGY first appeared in *The International Journal of Politics, Culture, and Society,* Vol. 2, No. 1 (Fall 1988), published by Human Sciences Press. A revised version of this paper was presented at the annual meeting of The Southern Sociological Society, Nashville, Tennessee, March 19, 1988. The author wishes to acknowledge the criticism and commentary of John Shelton Reed, Don Doyle, Arthur J. Vidich, and Abby Sher.

LE CONTE, ROYCE, TEGGART, BLUMER: A BERKELEY DIALOGUE ON SOCIOLOGY, SOCIAL CHANGE, AND SYMBOLIC INTERACTION first appeared in *Symbolic Interaction,* Vol. 11, No. 1 (1988), published by JAI Press, Inc. I would like to thank Peter Adler, Patti Adler, Arlie Hochschild, Virginia Olesen, Jacqueline P. Wiseman, Arthur J. Vidich, Gary Alan Fine, and two anonymous reviewers for their comments on an earlier version of this paper, originally presented as part of the symposium "A California School of Interactionism?" at the annual meeting of the Society for the Study of Symbolic Interaction, New York City, September 1986.

LEGITIMACY AND CONSENSUS IN LIPSET'S AMERICA: FROM WASHINGTON TO WATERGATE first appeared in *Social Research,* Vol. 42, No. 4 (Winter 1975). The author gratefully acknowledges the critical advice of Charles

R. Freeman, Marvin B. Scott, and Arthur J. Vidich during the preparation of this paper.

SYMBOLIC INTERACTIONISM AND MACROSOCIOLOGY first appeared in *Sociological Forum,* Vol. III, No. 2 (Spring 1988), published by Eastern Sociological Society.

THE EXISTENTIAL SELF: LANGUAGE AND SILENCE IN THE FORMATION OF HUMAN IDENTITY was presented in the Session on qualitative sociology, New York State Sociological Association Annual Meeting, Potsdam, New York, October 28–29, 1983.

Preparation of the book manuscript has been aided immeasurably by Joan Schilling, who typed portions of the current version, maintained relevant records, diskettes, and correspondence, and buoyed the author's spirits with coffee and good cheer. A fine index was prepared by Dr. Paul Cantrell. The staff and editorial board of the University of Arkansas Press once again proved to be the best of their profession.

CIVILIZATION

Introduction

A recent and critical discussion of sociological thought asserts that "Sociological theory attempts to make sense of the social world."[1] Although the author of this statement has leveled a sharp assault based on her findings—viz., that "Sociology inherited a sex-dichotomized scientific approach as well as the nineteenth-century cultural ideal of the dichotomized relationship between the sexes as appropriate to their 'natural' talents"[2]—she has not challenged or reconsidered the alleged aim of the discipline itself. In the essays that follow this introduction, I hold to an alternate view of what our discipline is, or ought to be, about. The sensibleness of the world, I hold, is a problem for the social actor. Insofar as the sociologist produces a sensible understanding, he or she is behaving like one or a group of the social actors under study, but, in the event, claiming a privileged position over, or a greater knowledge than that of, the social actor.

My own position has been developed in a series of monographs co-authored with Marvin B. Scott—*A Sociology of the Absurd*,[3] *The Revolt of the Students*,[4] and *The Drama of Social Reality*[5]—and in my own study, *The Seven Deadly Sins: Society and Evil*,[6] and need not be detailed here. Suffice it to say that my position on the nature of sociology is the spirit that gives *elan vital* to the present work. The essays that follow constitute studies that have foreshadowed, elaborated, or flowed from my perspective. They also, more significantly, constitute sociological and metasociological studies in their own right, independent works that illuminate the range of concerns that have stimulated me in my scholarly efforts.

Much of sociological theory in the 1980s has been focused on shoring up the fractured bridge that connects, or is supposed to connect, micro- to macrosociological investigations. In part this issue has arisen out of the crisis[7] in sociological theorizing said to have occurred when its reigning paradigm, a synthesis of behavioristic positivism and structural-functionalism, reached marginal utility in the mid-1970s.[8] As positivists and functionalists have sought to defend their position against the rising tides of sociobiologism, phenomenologism, neo-Marxism, and post-structuralism (as well as the curious syntheses, coalitions, and alliances that have been formed between and among these contending schools of thought), the supposed division between approaches to small group phenomena and large-scale activity have seemed once again significant—the strategic research site wherein paradigmatic dilemmas might be confronted and epistemological problems resolved. Thus, to take a pertinent example, in a recent study, Arne L. Kallenberg writes, "The failure of industrial sociology to develop a theory linking macro to micro levels was largely responsible for its demise in the 1960s as a field on the forefront of the study of important changes in the correlates and consequences of work."[9] Like many who have entered into this debate, Kallenberg draws an arbitrary line to divide the arenas that constitute the appropriately micro and macro research sites—viz., the micro world of the sociology of work is concerned with "managerial leadership, workplace relations, and worker morale and productivity," whereas the macro situs addresses "problems related to economic growth, international competition, and worldwide inflation."[10] Others imagine the line to distinguish two- from multi-person encounters, intra- from intergroup relations, intra- from interstate or cultural contacts, and so forth.[11]

The absence of a clear micro-macro division in the worlds of human conduct addressed by sociologists has led most of those concerned with this issue to relocate the problem to a place within the divisions of the discipline itself. Thus, Jeffrey C. Alexander writes, "Exchange, interactionism, and ethnomethodology have usually been characterized as 'micro' traditions because they are concerned with the microscopic focus on small, or individual, units. Conflict theories, Marxism, and functionalism, by contrast, are conceived of as 'macro' because they are concerned with units of larger size, like institutions or whole societies."[12] Given this claim of established subdisciplinary situs distinctiveness, and the worry that this division is symptomatic of a crisis, it is no wonder that a rush to build linkages has been begun by both micro and macro theorists, each seeking to institute the grounds, path, or chain that would lead, direct, or bind the one to the other. George Ritzer, a leading figure in this aspect of metatheory reconstruction, regards the recent theoretical efforts of Hechter, Collins, Coleman, Boudon, Kurzweil, Smelser, Schegloff, Emerson, and Knorr-Cetina and Cicourel to be moves from a micro to a macro linkage; while, at the same time, he believes that the works of Habermas, Alexander, Münch, Luhmann and Burt indicate that macro theorists have been moving toward a convergence with micro orientations to which they had not been previously attached. Moreover, again according to Ritzer, Giddens's "structuration theory," Bourdieu's focus on "habitus," Hindess's attempt to forge a middle way between the extremes of "theoretical humanism" and "structuralism," Fararo's and Skvoretz's integration of "network" and socio-psychological "expectation states" theory, and his own "integrated sociological paradigm" are each "overtly integrative works without [the authors] . . . apparent prior commitment to the macro or micro end of the continuum."[13] The architectonic of theory construction in the present era seems to be focused on fostering a convergence in micro and macro paradigms.

However, in the essays that follow, a micro-macro linkage is taken to be an already established feature of sociology, one that does not require (not that it would necessarily oppose) an instauration of a new epistemology of sociological knowledge. The essays, primarily inspired by my own attempts to synthesize the ideas of Erving Goffman, Frederick J. Teggart and his school, Émile Durkheim and Marcel Mauss, Max Weber, Georg Simmel, Alfred Schutz, and Herbert Blumer, and reflecting my abiding interest in the structures and processes attending race relations, minority communities, and the constitution of the social self, move, quite naturally and reflexively, within micro and macro arenas and issues. Precisely because I had never supposed that there is a fundamental micro-macro dichotomy, it never occurred to me to need to justify my studies by constructing a new paradigm. Now that the issue has been joined, it seems best if I declare explicitly the position that, upon reinspection, I discover to be implicit in the essays contained in this book.

Randall Collins has developed, in his own way, a position that is close to my own. Collins describes a synthesis of three sociological traditions—the conflict perspective, which Collins associates with Marx and Weber and their respective epigoni, but from which I derive most of my own inspiration in the writings of Simmel; the Durkheimian school, especially with respect to its emphasis on rituals and sentiments; and, finally, what he calls "the micro-interactionist tradition" and associates with the works of Charles Horton Cooley, George Herbert Mead, Herbert Blumer, Erving Goffman, and the ethnomethodologists. Linking the three traditions, Collins proposes the following picture of a society:

> The entire society can be visualized as a long chain of interaction rituals, with people moving from one encounter to another. There need be

nothing rigid about this structure. Any combination of people might come together in a face-to-face encounter. But once they are there, they are faced with negotiating some kind of relationship, some ritual conversation. How they do this depends on the cultural capital, the symbolically charged ideas they bring to the encounter. Various outcomes are possible, depending on how each person's cultural capital matches up with the other person's cultural capital.[14]

Collins's societal picture resonates strongly with the one that Marvin Scott and I have designated appropriate to our "sociology of the absurd." As we have seen the matter, the world makes no ultimate ontological sense. Such a philosophical position is, however, untenable to the natural actor; for him or her, the world always—or almost always—makes perfect sense, having defined rules, roles, and relationships. In the process of acting on this belief, the natural actor fosters, creates, and sustains a definition of the situation that he or she already believes to predate the action undertaken. What Collins calls "cultural capital" is, in Lyman's and Scott's perspective, the sense of the past, of the normative, and of the predictable that each actor brings to bear on the situation. What macrosociologists call "social forces" or "social factors" exist as intersubjective mental constructs that each actor employs in working out the encounter. The macro and micro are linked by the actors. Hence—to use an instance from one of the essays in the present volume—when I point out (in "Asian American Contacts before Columbus," *infra*) that a California Supreme Court Chief Justice declared "Chinese" residents of that state to be "Indians" and, therefore, ineligible to testify in court cases involving white people, I show that he was not only legitimating a definition of an inchoate situation but also, in the process, bringing to bear on a particular court matter his own resolution of a world-historical issue: the 362-year-old debate over the geo-cultural origins of the American Indians. This microecological encounter in a courtroom is explained in macro (indeed, in civilizational) terms.

In many of the following essays I provide a critique of a major figure in sociology or anthropology. The critiques are a necessary step in clearing away the intellectual obstacles that stand in the way of recognizing the micro–macro synthesis that already exists. In order to open sociology to the recognition of a social world of contingencies and of an obdurate but protean reality that changes shape as humans define and elaborate upon it, I have sought to reintroduce the concept of "civilization"—associated with such classical figures as Durkheim, Mauss, and Cushing and, more recently, with the late Benjamin Nelson—and to employ it as both an intellectual resource and a proper topic for sociological investigations.

The civilizational perspective permits me, in the title essay of the present collection, to challenge the claim that Erving Goffman's work is strictly microecological and to enlarge on the situs of his studies, showing them to be instituted within the larger contexts of the sociology of law and of religion and to encompass the international culture of the Occident. A closely related civilizational analysis also informed the kind of anthropology developed by the all-too-neglected Frank Hamilton Cushing and Robert Stewart Culin, and, as I point out in the essay on this subject, their analyses antedated as well as adumbrated the epistemological basis and methodological ways of ethnomethodology. The question to which Cushing and Culin provided a heterodoxical answer—the origin of American Indian civilization—was itself fundamental to the theories of knowledge, the several political and juridical praxes, and the common understandings of social scientists and ordinary people. In exploring this debate, my researches on Asian American contacts before Columbus open up new questions and challenge hitherto unchallenged verities in the fields of race relations and minorities, as well as the long-held division of the sociocultural world between anthropology and sociology.

Of all the issues affecting civilizational studies, sociocultural investigations, and macro as well as micro empirical works, none is more significant than the quest for a sound theory of social change and a grounded social science of history. In two essays critically appraising the contributions of Frederick J. Teggart and Max Weber, I have attempted to resolve the unanswered questions raised by their respective works by offering a synthesis of the phenomenological ideas to be found in the works of Kenneth Burke, Georg Simmel, Alfred Schutz, and Erving Goffman. Taken separately or together, these essays form and inform my understanding of the civilizational concept, its resource usages as well as its topicality, and, further, stand as a substantive affirmation of the pre-established reality of a micro-macro sociology.

American sociological thought has been haunted by the spectre of race and its problems. Of all the issues taken up for the kind of sociological investigation that promised a scientifically grounded solution, none has received greater attention and less amelioration than the many-sided "race problem."[15] Two of my essays on the subject presented in the volume take sociological approaches themselves to be problematic. Robert Park's well-known theory and model of a race relations cycle is shown to be symptomatic of the ahistorical processual approach characteristic of much of sociological thought since Comte introduced his "comparative method"; yet, reconceived as a body of sensitizing conceptualizations, it might still serve valuably in an historically-informed and phenomenologically based science of race relations. Herbert Blumer's contributions to the study of race prejudice and discrimination, although originally guided by Park's formulations, transcended them, and provide a basis for just the kind of approach suggested in my critique of Park.[16] By the same token, in elaborating on and employing Goffman's concept of total institution to sensitize and inform the study of the ethno-economic and political-social forms of minority policy undertaken by local, state, and national governments, I have carried out an original analysis of the significance of Asians in American history, and, applying Simmel's conceptualizations of "conflict" and of "the web of group affiliation," provided an historical sociology of San Francisco's Chinatown.[17] Civil rights are the rightful demand of minorities seeking justice in American society in accordance with the professed values of that society. Often seen as a macro issue—which it certainly is—the quest for civil rights is enacted on what are too often deemed microecological niches of restricted space. These engender what I call the drama-in-the-routine of everyday life, and, in the process, link a dramaturgical sociology to the fundamental values and normative practices of a whole society.

The critique of functionalism has been as much a cause as a part of the recently enunciated crisis in sociological thought.[18] Usually associated with Talcott Parsons and his school, functionalism has in fact an older and much hidden antecedent in the works of America's first sociologists, the Southern Comteans,[19] who, in the years just before and just after the Civil War, developed an elaborate theory of the social system. That theory was eufunctionally linked to macrosocietal issues: slavery, agricultural seigneurial socialism, and also it addressed the race problem, the woman question, and the political economy most appropriate to a social order dependent on the cooperative participation of farmers, workers, and intellectuals. Moreover, there lurked a latent phenomenology in some of the Southern Comteans' works that in dialogical form and intergenerational debate—true to Whitehead's dictum about forgetting one's founders—provided a basis for the development of symbolic interactionism.

The debates on policy and stance in sociology—from the functionalist critique of the Watergate scandal to the functionalist assault on symbolic interactionism—constitute elements of a larger debate—that which would see the linkages that always existed between supposedly microecological settings and macrosocietal problems. Of these, the study of the self is crucial. The self is taken in the modern era to be both a problem for the social actor's sense of authenticity and an issue in its presentation to others. The recognition of the protean and existential characteristics of the self is taken to be testimony to its central place—in the modern conceptualizations of sociology and of society—as both resource and topic. Yet, it too is linked to the civilizational question of the Occident that has been posed since the writings of the ancient Hebrews. Language and silence, words and the unutterable, form a dialectic that constrains and confounds modern society, that links person to group at the very moment that the self cries out for its unrealized and un-realizable liberation.

In a recent essay on Modernism in theater, Thomas M. Disch points out:

> What is distinctively Modernist is an insistence on dispensing with illu-sion, on making the audience see the work of art from its maker's per-spective. It is not the model that is naked, in Modernist practice, but the artist.[20]

In the sociology that is presented here, it is the social world (or, rather, worlds) of the actor that is a work of art, sometimes sufficiently Mod-ern so as to reveal its all-too-human creator, but usually sufficiently pre-Modern to be unproblematically intelligible to its audience-makers. Such a sociology calls upon us to dispense with the illusion of a fun-damental micro-macro gulf that needs to be bridged; rather, we so-ciologists should approach the world-as-it-is-created with an artistic, architectonic, and dramaturgic eye. Such a sociology requires looking at the subject in a way similar to that which Disch says a naive viewer approaches a painting by Braque: "The naive viewer is apt to approach such paintings by trying to reconstitute the fractured surface into familiar images: a face, a violin, a coffee cup."[21] However, for the sociologist, the mundane world—its commonplace scenes and situations, its well-established verities, its customs, codes, and laws, its crimes, deviancies, and disturbances, its delinquencies and drifts, its bohemians and its bour-geoisie, its centered or decentered selves—must each be seen as if it were a painting by Braque. Only in such a sociology is every person a Braque and every social situation threatening to become as impenetrable as those of this Modernist master. The canvas might be large or small, the brush narrow or wide, the colors bright or dull, the number of artists one or many, the audience a solitary individual or the assembled peoples of the world. The basic problem for the sociologist is not how to link, theoreti-cally or methodologically, the micro to the macro, but rather how every-day people, some powerful, some impotent, move in, between, around, through, and over the various and sundry micro-macro configurations that constitute their *Umwelten*.

PART I

Civilization

Civilization

Contents, Discontents, Malcontents

Do we really understand his* work? According to Gouldner,[1] Goffman has departed from functionalism to build a non-hierarchical sociology of drama and tactfulness that, nevertheless, resonates against the new experiences of the educated middle classes—an aesthetical sociology of appearances. But Collins and Makowsky[2] locate Goffman "squarely in the Durkheimian functionalist tradition, a more empirically oriented Talcott Parsons." However, Messinger, et al.[3] have warned that Goffman's "dramaturgic approach" wavers imprecisely between the analyst's and the subject's view of the world, calling into question, then, the very empiricism on which it is allegedly grounded, while Blumer[4] has charged that it diverts analysis "far from the process which George Herbert Mead has made the keystone of his profound analysis of social interaction." Berger and Luckmann[5] suggest that Goffman's "model" should not be equated with a "dramatic model," since there "have been other dramas, after all, than that of the contemporary organization man bent on 'impression management.'" And finally there is the dispute about Goffman's alleged cynicism. According to Martindale,[6] "at bottom, in Goffman's view, contemporary man is an amoral merchant of morality and a confidence man." Cuzzort[7] seems to accept this view, but allows that "if Goffman is able to penetrate into the most subtle irrationalities of human conduct, he simultaneously is generous in the extent to which his conception of humanity embraces all men."

When we turn to evaluations of his methods, there is an equal amount of confusion. Everyone seems to recognize that Goffman is no

---

*Erving Goffman, *Relations in Public: Microstudies of the Public Order* (New York: Basic Books, Inc., 1971) ix–xvii + 366 pp. Index.

ordinary social scientist. He does not occupy himself with the usual "hard data" analysis that characterizes the studies of most American sociologists. Neither does he do field work in the usual way; for when he reports on his observations, let us say, of gambling in a Las Vegas casino, we are likely to hear less about the actual conduct of bettors than about the universal properties of risk taking. His footnotes reveal primary source reliance on novels (usually English novels of morals and manners), manuals of etiquette, biographies, and private letters of sympathetic sociologists. More recently there is a noticeable interpretive usage of studies in animal ethology.[8] There is an implicit suggestion—never, in fact, carried out—that Goffman might deliver himself wholly into the arms of the pan-zoologists,[9] who, likely as not, would welcome so formidable a scholar as an ally. Cuzzort,[10] who admires Goffman's work, dismisses the debate over whether his work is properly scientific by reminding us that his methods "consist largely of careful observation combined with extensive scholarship" and that they "flow from his general conception of human conduct." Ultimately, Cuzzort concludes, his "conception of humanity forces us to see our conduct as though it were a work of art." Glaser and Strauss,[11] while not unsympathetic to Goffman's approach, are more discerning in their critique of his methodology. First they point to the perhaps unintended effect of his own artful discourse—that it *persuades* the reader far more than it *proves* its point. Second, they note that through an enormous proliferation of illustrations for each introduced category, Goffman is building a theoretical system; however, the system is incomplete. Because his system is integrated at the *logical* rather than the *empirical* level, its validity is ambiguous: "To some degree his theory is grounded but to what degree, and how, is difficult to know." Most recently Goffman has been taken up—unwillingly, I suspect—by at least one of the theorists of radical reconstruction in the 1970s. To this political scientist[12] Goffman's methods seem to be less relevant than his point of view. Goffman, a great student of social life in the 1950s, is credited with being the Kafka of the 1970s. *Relations in Public,* according to this perspective, is grounded "at a distinct point in history; its essays describe the absurdities and horrors of our time." Goffman, we learn, is "glad to see 'the solid buildings of the world' shake." And, hence, for Goffman there is an invitation: "In the last decade, Goffman's work has been a source of power and inspiration, and we will need him even more for the work that lies ahead."

Until the writing of this book Goffman has been more or less aloof to criticism. He gives no map of his place in the debate over functionalism. He says nothing about whether his image of man is over-dramatized (or for that matter, whether Parsons' is oversocialized). He maintains a strict silence as to whether he is a close adherent, a modifier, or an apostate to the tenets of symbolic interactionism. He refuses to speak directly to his humanism, whether to acknowledge a generous view of man or to align himself with the current radical liberals. On methods he adopts a defense: his own have weaknesses but the prevailing scientism has not proved it has much better to offer. Goffman thus remains a man of mystery; his work, in all its possible interpretations, constitutes his testament. About him might accurately be said what Weber said of Simmel:

> In particular, crucial aspects of his methodology are unacceptable. His substantive results must with usual frequency be regarded with reservations, and not seldom they must be rejected outright. In addition his mode of exposition strikes one at times as strange, and often it is at the very least uncongenial. On the other hand one finds oneself absolutely compelled to affirm that his mode of exposition is simply brilliant and, what is more important, attains results that are intrinsic to it and not to be attained by any imitator. Indeed nearly every one of his works abounds in important new theoretical ideas and the most subtle observations. Almost every one of them belongs to those books in which not only the valid findings, but even the false ones, contain a wealth of stimulation for one's own further thought, in comparison with which the majority of even the most estimable accomplishments of other scholars often appears to exude a peculiar odor of scantiness and poverty. The same holds true of his epistemological and methodological foundations and, again, doubly so just where they are perhaps ultimately not tenable. Altogether then . . . even when he is on the wrong path, [he] fully deserves his reputation as one of the foremost thinkers, a first-rate stimulator of academic youth and academic colleagues . . .[13]

In his most recent works Goffman has set out to establish a special domain for his sociological analysis. Although he has employed different terminology in his several studies, here Goffman calls it "the ground rules and the associated orderings of behavior that pertain to public life—to persons commingling and to places and social occasions where this face-to-face contact occurs." Goffman wishes to restore the study of face-to-face encounters to a special place in sociology. At one time these were thought to be the locus of "primary relations"—until Faris[14] demonstrated that not all face-to-face relations had intimate qualities to them and that intimacy could transcend spatial proximity. Once the territorial irrelevance to primary relations had been established, sociologists appear to have abandoned interest in any of the properties of spatially proximate relationships until Goffman and a few others[15] reestablished its importance. However, Goffman modifies this domain ever further—he wishes to study and delineate the properties of face-to-face relationships in "American society," although caution and a bit of admitted conceptual embarrassment cause him to suggest that what generalizations he makes are in fact applicable to the English-speaking world, the Anglo-American community, West European nations, Protestant countries, Christian society, and the West. Goffman considers that the term "civilization" might be adequate to encompass the locus of the practices to be described, but rejects it as too vague. His rejection of the term is too hasty, however, and we shall have to reconsider this possibility shortly.

Goffman appears to hold to at least one of the basic assumptions of the functionalists—namely that "When persons engage in regulated dealings with each other, they come to employ social routines or practices, namely *patterned adaptations* to the rules—including conformances, by-passings, secret deviations, excusable infractions, flagrant violations, and the like. These . . . constitute what might be called a 'social order'." (Emphasis supplied). Admitting that there is a social order is not the same as admitting that one adheres to it, or that it is "natural," or "good," or "functionally necessary"—and Goffman is careful to point this out. Moreover, he recognizes that these rules exist for the most part at a subliminal level, below the level of conscious awareness—until they are violated. (Thus, without using the terms, Goffman harks back to the hoary distinction—now sadly neglected, although it adumbrated the early work of W. I. Thomas[16] and generated an altogether different theory of social change than currently prevails—between *habit and attention*. Habit prevails when social order is secure, when means adduced produce ends desired, and when predictions are likely to come true; attention arises when catastrophe strikes, when the relation between means and ends is suddenly obscure, when the *Lebenswelt* is in crisis). As Goffman puts it: ". . . when an order actually does break down, a great flood of social disturbance can result, the participants then being forced to appreciate all the uses they had made of the prior order and all the dependency they had developed on it." Goffman's functionalism then is not "extreme" but more closely resembles that "moderate" form described by Gellner[17] and which Gellner attributes to Durkheim. Nevertheless it is a functionalist perspective and thus cannot escape certain fundamental difficulties to which we shall have to return.

Goffman justifies his method by first admitting to its weaknesses—unsubstantiated generalizations, the limited truth value of statements which are introduced by qualifiers, and the conceptual vagueness of locating the behaviors to be described in such an amorphous entity as American Society—and then defends himself by charging that the traditional approaches have weaknesses that are equally as bad, or even worse. His commentary on the traditional methods is a candid indictment:

A sort of sympathetic magic seems to be involved, the assumption being that if you go through the motions attributable to science then science will result. But it hasn't. (Five years after publication, many of these efforts remind one of the experiments children perform with Gilbert sets: "Follow instructions and you can be a real chemist, just like the picture on the box.") Fields of naturalistic study have not been uncovered through these methods. Concepts have not emerged that reorder our view of social activity. Frameworks have not been established into which a continuously larger number of facts can be placed. Understanding of ordinary behavior has not accumulated; distance has.

One need not disagree with this charge against the narrow range positivists and the ordinary functionalists to still inquire after the logic, epistemology, and grounding of Goffman's own approach. He suggests that it is more than an idiosyncratic art and couches his aims in behalf of a better, though conventionally conceived, social science, yet he eschews an exhaustive analysis of his own approaches. But if this special domain of social science is to have a lifetime beyond that of its founder, then indeed there is a need to get into just these issues. This is not to say that Goffman himself is required to describe, evaluate, and justify his own methodology; scientists, like lawyers, are often poor defenders of their own cause. Rather, it is for those who subscribe to Goffman's theoretical orientation to provide a precise methodology and a sound justification for it. In the process, they may produce more than they imagined— a whole new idea of social science.

It would be otiose to delineate the contents of *Relations in Public*. It is a brilliant *tour de force* through the mind and imagination of a towering intellect, a perceptive observer, and an iconoclastic critic of American society whose previous works have preeminently established a permanent claim on the discipline. Moreover, Goffman's work defies reproduction since its artfulness is an integral part of its presentation. Like poetry in a foreign language that loses something in translation, Goffman's observations lose much in summary. Perhaps it is better, then, to see his work in terms of a sociology of religion and of law. For Goffman's sociology, without admitting such, seems to turn on the sacred character of the person and the rituals and rules which guard it.

It is precisely in an age in which doctrinal religions lose their force that individuals, thrown back upon themselves, discover the sacredness of their own persons. It is not that the person is necessarily less sacred when the force of organized religion prevails, but rather that the consciousness of his or her own sacredness is beneath the level of awareness, while its expression is usually projected onto the sacred deities. This goes far, perhaps, to explain why Goffman's sociology resonates with a contemporary reading public: it is aware more than ever of its

individual sacred character, but unable to articulate it. And, as a perspective of incongruity would seem to dictate, the language of the mundane (if not the profane) world—the concepts derived from animal ethology—seem to get at this sacred character better than most other
languages. Thus Goffman can describe the leeway that must be given to
an individual by seeing him or her as a "vehicular unit" who must be
obedient to and respected by "traffic patterns"; he can perceive the self
as having no less than eight "territories," claimed by the employment of
"markers" and violated by a variety of transgressions and encroachments. Ultimately Goffman is able to argue that the notion of personal
will and volition, that which sets humans apart from lower animals, is
a quality which must be inserted into human agents so that the reciprocated activities of maintaining respect and establishing regard are
possible.

The sacredness of the individual, recognized in his or her territorial
unity, spatial claims, and volitional agency, is in turn maintained and
reinforced by codes of linguistic behavior. These codes constitute the
juridical support for humankind's sacred personification. They take form
in "supportive interchanges" (including greetings, gestures of recognition, various forms of polite inquiry) and extend beyond intimates to
include even those who are socially distant but physically required
to interact and those whose circumstances are woeful but who must
not be recognized accordingly. Among the supportive interchanges the
greeting-farewell continuum constitutes one of the most delicate of
rituals since preservation of the sacredness of the self must be integrated
with the practicalities and temporalities of contact and with other situational exigencies. The chances for profanation are great, and individuals must be on their guard to prevent embarrassment and humiliation
to self and others. The curiosities and nuances of these matters are
Goffman's specialty and cannot be reproduced here. More important
is Goffman's suggestion that the greeting ritual is so useful to facilitate
relationships among strangers or those long out of touch that its absence constitutes a special case for investigation.

Precisely because social life is so precarious, there are numerous breakdowns, but these in turn are prevented from producing the
Hobbesian pit by the ready evocation of "remedial interchanges" in the
form of those "accounts," "apologies," or "requests" by which individuals exculpate themselves from blame or receive permission to perform otherwise prohibited acts with impunity. Remedial interchanges
perform a dual role with respect to the sacredness of self and society.
They reestablish the self that has been profaned by its culpable acts, and
they reinstate the validity of the norm that has been challenged by the
violation. Thus social order is seen to rest not on a prior social contract

but on a promissory note that fractured sociation will be mended by the giving and receiving of remedial exchanges. Although Goffman's approach here might have led him to an abandonment of all functionalist trappings, his analysis does not reach that extreme. Rather, he seems to be saying that social order drifts somewhere between the inflexibility of a custom-bound social system and the openness suggested in *A Sociology of the Absurd*.[18]

However, the foundations for any social order are not exhausted by the discovery of remedial interchanges. A more positive aspect of pattern maintenance is revealed in Goffman's analysis of "tie-signs," the bits and pieces of information which co-present persons must give to one another to indicate the nature and degree of bondedness in their relationship. Various postures, gestures, and vocal mechanisms are relevant here, and again there lurk both dangers and pleasantries in the operation. Whereas at times Goffman is at pains to show us the fragility of the social order—and in this section that is certainly made plain—he is also insistent on telling us that there is an order that is regularly, though not inevitably, produced by individuals giving and receiving impressions and exculpations, observing territorial imperatives, and scanning and reading the expressions of relationship that make interaction possible.

However, if tie-signs "make it possible for individuals in public to engage in encounters without too much fear that their innocence will be misunderstood and that compromising will occur," these same individuals depend on "normal appearances" to make it so. Normal appearances constitute the orientation that permits on-going routines to continue, including the routinized and situational warinesses that are ordinarily attached to the environment. The *Umwelt* is the sphere around an individual from which the potential destruction of normal appearances can arise, from which alarms can be sounded. Here more than in any other chapter—and his discussion of normal appearances takes up nearly one-fourth of the book—Goffman reveals the socially constructed nature of both normalcy and its absence. The competencies expected of objects, self, and others; the range and extent of "lurk lines," wherein individuals cannot fully protect themselves; the unguarded access points through which the perpetrators of evil may enter; the social net which envelops the individual in public places with persons who just might assault him or her suggest a potentiality for heightened awareness and appropriate action that is usually associated with paranoia. But this is precisely Goffman's point: social order is maintained by the absence, or rather the low frequency, of the alarm-producing phenomena. Thus, in what must be taken as one of his most chilling observations, Goffman characterizes our present condition as one of increasing alarms:

The vulnerability of public life is what we are coming more and more to see, if only because we are becoming more aware of the areas and intricacies of mutual trust presupposed in public places. Certainly circumstances can arise which undermine the ease that individuals have within their Umwelt. Some of these circumstances are currently found in the semi-public places within slum housing developments and slum neighborhoods, and there is no intrinsic reason why some of these sources of alarm (as well as some additional ones) cannot come to be found in the residential community of the respectable classes, causing the fragile character of domestic settings to be evident there, too: certainly the great public forums of our society, the downtown areas of our cities, can come to be uneasy places. Militantly sustained antagonisms between diffusively intermingled major population segments—young and old, male and female, white and black, impoverished and well-off—can cause those in public gatherings to distrust (and to fear they are distrusted by) the persons staying next to them. The forms of civil inattention, of persons circumspectly treating one another with polite and glancing concern while each goes about his own separate business, may be maintained, but behind these normal appearances individuals can come to be at the ready, poised to flee or to fight back if necessary. And in place of unconcern there can be alarm—until, that is, the streets are redefined as naturally precarious places, and a high level of risk becomes routine.

Goffman comes then to his conclusion—appending an essay "The Insanity of Place" to remind us that we come to know ourselves and our everything from the contrast and startle given to us by the "manic" and by "other categories of troublemaker who do not keep their place," and that what we know is "that this everything is not very much." Weber had imagined a possible future in which life was devoid of zest, deadened by routine, in which societies would be increasingly inhabited by socially mortified victims of "mechanized petrifaction, embellished with a sort of convulsive self-importance."[19] Goffman has shown us an even darker side. His concluding quotation from Lévi-Strauss—"and it is because the fundamental attitude towards you is one of prayer, even when you are being robbed, that the situation is so utterly and completely unbearable"—indicates the dialectical inversion of the sacred qualities of the individual by those whose circumstances require shrewd strategies which profane the person in the very act of recognizing his or her deified character. Thus, in the very moment when we may glorify humanity we cease to do so; for the conditions of trust no longer prevail, and each person is thrown back on a frightening aloneness, requiring a kind of psychic self-sufficiency that is in short supply.

But, although we recognize the brilliance of the analysis and shudder at the possibilities that loom so large in the prophecy of doom that Goffman has given us, we can still consider certain fundamental matters, which, although they first appear as criticism of Goffman's perspective, in fact strengthen it, giving it, hopefully, historical and theoretical depth and, perhaps, resolving certain difficulties.

First, let us reexamine the locus of Goffman's perspective. What is in fact the spatio-temporal zone of his observations? Goffman writes:

> . . . I use the phrases "In Western society," "In the American middle classes," and so forth. The issue here is deeper than that of the questionability of using a pat device to guard against ethnocentric overgeneralizations. To say that a particular practice is found in a given place (or a given class of places) leaves a great deal unspecified even when systematically collected data are available. For it is often unclear whether it is claimed that the practice occurs throughout the place or only somewhere in it, and if throughout, whether this is the only place it occurs. Furthermore, the social arrangements and small behaviors considered in this book have the awkward property of pertaining not to a set of individuals that can be bounded nicely, like the citizens of a particular nation state, but to groupings whose boundaries we know very little about. Class, region, ethnic group, and age-grade are involved, and these are familiar enough. But the other reference units cause trouble. There is "epoch," which carries the difficulty that persons in certain parts of the world are more old-fashioned than their age mates in other parts. And the other reference units are not much better. There is the English-speaking world, the Anglo-American community, West European nations, Protestant countries, Christian society, and the West. Such are the units we are led to if we are interested in the full location of the practices to be considered in this volume. In any case, the reference unit, "American society" (which I use throughout), is something of a conceptual scandal, very nearly a contradiction in terms; the social unit "civilization" (whatever that might mean) is as relevant as that of nation state.

The term "civilization," however, despite Goffman's off-handed dismissal, is appropriate to his work. Durkheim and Mauss had introduced it to sociology long ago.[20] Pointing to the often seen but rarely noticed fact that certain phenomena—including tools, aesthetic styles, languages, and institutions—thrive beyond politically determined boundaries and "extend over less easily determined spaces," they note that these phenomena have a life that is "supranational" and yet linked into some kind of interdependence. Furthermore, these phenomena are not isolated by the political borders, which may separate their agents, but rather they form complex reciprocated systems, "which without being limited to a determinate political organism are, however, localizable in time and space." It would appear that the very phenomena that Goffman has described belong to "civilizations," and that the concepts that he has innovated, freed from any national identities, are precisely the ones that might be employed for the socio-historical analysis of civilization and inter-civilization relations.

Second, the employment of the locus "civilization" might facilitate the development of that theory of social change which is so embarrassingly missing in Goffman's analysis. It is not that social change goes totally unrecognized by Goffman. Rather it appears casually and incidentally in descriptive notices which are devoid of theoretical content. Thus Goffman recognizes *en passant* that there are cultural drifts which eliminate or introduce certain practices without much fanfare, such as the decline in hat-tipping; that there are sudden, remarkable crises that force change in the *Umwelt;* that there are cycles of process that have a patterned form or "natural" histories. But, as Herbert Blumer has noted[21] there is no systematic examination of how the norms, and the patterned adaptations and violations of these norms in the public arena, come into being or pass away. One reason for this failure of analysis in general in sociology is the functionalist insistence on the existence of a system, an insistence which seems to lead inevitably to a set of *a priori* assumptions about the nature, rate, direction, and outcome of sociocultural change. Thus, for functionalists, the empirical analysis of social change becomes redundant.[22] It is not clear whether Goffman has adopted this particular view, however, since, except for passing references, he does not analyze change at all.

Goffman's postulated patterns and norms require establishment of a definite time-space in order that the study of their origins and development can begin. Without going into all its ramifications (for these one must turn to the writings of Benjamin Nelson), civilization suggests itself as the referent that might organize time and space to make such analysis possible. Moreover, one of the metatheories of social change that is implicit in Goffman's work suggests itself as a method. Let us assume that all norms and patterned activities have their origins in a usage that is *ab initio* new, idiosyncratic, and without legitimacy. Then, it would seem to follow, the establishment of norms and patterns is part of the *political* process, broadly conceived as containing initial acts, persuasion, adoption, and ultimately general acceptance. It is at least theoretically possible to imagine, then, that the slightest of norms—the nod of the head, the aversion of the eyes—was first of all an innovative gesture that had to struggle and win its recognition in some sociocultural context. The political arena of states is not necessarily the appropriate arena for the analysis of norm and pattern origins and certainly not the circumscription of their diffusion. *Civilization* and with it an attendant recognition of the multiplicity of elites—including sociocultural elites—would seem to provide the proper place of departure for such a study. Moreover, political sociology might be redirected from its present narrow concern with the patterns of politics in national states to turn its attention to the origin of norms in civilizational complexes.

A comparative historical analysis of norms could then begin, in the methodological tradition that Weber had anticipated.[23]

Still another thorny problem arises from the definite need to discover the *point of view* from which Goffman's analysis proceeds. In part this debate over perspective is reminiscent of that between Simmel and Weber, wherein the former treated as belonging together both the subjectively intended and objectively valid meanings of situations while the latter required the psychocultural dimension of social action to stand independently as the domain for sociological investigation.[24] Goffman comes closer to Simmel in this regard, although his analysis of motives —especially in the chapter on remedial interchanges—seems to relocate the whole issue as a problem for the actor rather than one ultimately referable to the sociologist.

Finally, let us abandon the idea of closure in our studies of any social order. It is premature, and one of the most constricting elements of functionalism. Then, together with Goffman, our understanding of the terror in the breakdown of normal appearances would come even closer to that of Merleau-Ponty, who, on discussing similar issues, concluded:

> The human world is an open or unfinished system and the same radical contingency which threatens it with discord also rescues it from the inevitability of discord and prevents us from despairing of it, providing only that one remembers its machineries are actually men and tries to maintain and expand man's relations to man.[25]

Two Neglected Pioneers
of Civilizational Analysis

The Cultural Perspectives of
R. Stewart Culin and Frank Hamilton Cushing

Civilization, once a promising domain of sociological research, has lan-guished for the last half-century. In 1971 Benjamin Nelson reintroduced the subject through his translation of the "Note on the Notion of Civi-lization" by Durkheim and Mauss.[1] Subsequent work by Nelson and his colleagues has done much to advance the conceptual understanding of the term "civilization" and to encourage both historical and compara-tive investigations.[2] However, still worthy of analysis are the civiliza-tional perspectives of those early American social scientists whose work did not become part of the discipline's mainstream. An appraisal of the theoretical, empirical, and methodological perspectives of R. Stewart Culin (1858–1929)[3] and Frank Hamilton Cushing (1857–1900)[4] will in-dicate not only how a concern for uncovering the nature and origins of civilization led to significant breakthroughs in social-scientific research but also how much value their work still has for civilizational analysis in sociology.

Durkheim and Mauss asserted that civilization is an appropriate topic for sociology because there are certain phenomena that "are not strictly attached to a determinate social organism" and that "extend into areas that reach beyond the national territory or . . . develop over peri-ods of time that exceed the history of a single society."[5] They proposed that sociologists study such problems as "the diverse conditions which determine variations in the area of civilizations, why have they stopped here or there, what forms have they taken and what factors determine these forms."[6] Such problems had already animated the ethnological imaginations of R. Stewart Culin and Frank Hamilton Cushing, two American social scientists who in the 1890s became convinced of the divinatory origins of cultural forms and, more daringly, of their spread from prehistoric America to Asia and then around the world. Cushing and Culin did not accept the boundaries of tribes, national states, or empires as barriers to cultural diffusion. Their studies are part of the early development of a civilizational analytic. As such they left not only part of the legacy appropriate to present-day civilizational scholars, but also were innovative conceptual and methodological contributors to a subject still in its embryonic stage of development.

Implicit in the works of these two social scientists is a phenomenological element that promises aid in breaking out of the current conventional bifurcation in social science that confines cognitive and characterological analysis to the microecological arena while allowing only positivist or large-scale structural analysis for macrohistorical and civilizational questions. Culin's and Cushing's employment of the methods of participant-observation and, more significantly, Cushing's discovery of "experimental archaeology" and "manual concepts" as ethnomethods capable of uncovering the character of an entire civilization reveal how social-scientific approaches that are at the present time limited to the analysis of face-to-face encounters have a far wider applicability than has been imagined.

Cushing and Culin are associated with the diffusionist approach in anthropology as well as with the "doctrine of survivals." Both approaches are usually thought to be part of the antievolutionist theme in social science. Yet neither of them renounced evolutionism. Civilizational analysis, especially since Nelson's seminal works, challenges both the teleological ahistoricism of evolutionary functionalism and the nonprocessual concentration on brute facticity in neopositivist historicism. By recalling the phenomenological elements in the works of Culin and Cushing, the present essay invites even further attention to these neglected masters of social science and opposes, by their example, the argument that a science that does not forget its founders is doomed to sterility.

CULIN, CUSHING, AND THE AMERICAN ORIGINS OF ASIATIC CIVILIZATION

In 1902 Stewart Culin put forth an hypothesis on the origin of world civilization that called for a fundamental revision of ideas about its prehistoric origins and its place in ethnological theory.[7] According to

Culin, America had been the "cradle of Asia"—that is, the civilization of China, Japan, Korea, and the Asiatic hinterland had arisen first in Paleolithic North America. Culin went on to proclaim that America was an "old world" and not the "new world" that had been acknowledged since Columbus's voyages. As an "old world," America had been the site wherein an original civilization had emerged, evolved, and changed over the centuries, spread to encapsulate most, if not all, of the aboriginal peoples in North America, and diffused beyond the continental and oceanic barriers across the Pacific and into Asia. Once on the Asiatic continent, moreover, this civilization continued to spread as well as evolve, and, as Culin's subsequent studies argued, it expanded into Europe. Ultimately, Culin asserted, it returned to America embedded in the motifs and games brought to the United States by immigrants from Europe and Asia. Thus Culin proposed that a single civilization had come to be part of almost all world societies, and that America, rather than Eurasia or Africa, had been its place of origin. In a project he had begun with Cushing, Culin hoped to prove that the processes of its development and diffusion had modified the course and evolution of world culture patterns.[8]

The Culin-Cushing project adumbrated the civilizational proposal put forward in *L'Année sociologique* in 1913 by Durkheim and Mauss in six distinct but related ways: one, it perceived civilizational processes operating before the advent of, within, and beyond established state societies; two, it treated civilizations as moral milieux within the framework of what Mauss referred to as categories of the human spirit;[9] three, it evoked the necessity for studying the conditions modifying the forms of civilizational expression; four, it gave an arresting but concrete answer to the question of the origin and diffusion of civilization; five, it presented an historical dimension to the thesis later to be advanced by Durkheim and Mauss in *Primitive Classification;*[10] and six, it represents a social morphological approach,[11] a commitment to an empirical orientation within the idealist tradition, and contains "Durkheimian" concepts and hypotheses still to be applied and tested. Each of these ways deserves further discussion.

(1) PROGRESS, EVOLUTION, CIVILIZATION

Neither Culin nor Cushing adhered to the prevalent idea that civilization necessarily implied "progress" from some pre-civilized state of

savagery or barbarism to some determinate and exalted condition of social enhancement. Although both Culin and Cushing operated generally within the optimistic ethnological theories of their day, they did not
associate "progress" with civilizational expansion nor did they perceive
civilization as the ultimate stage of a trajectory of human development.
Indeed, in virtual though unstated opposition to such views as those expressed by Sir John Lubbock in 1870 that civilization referred exclusively to the contemporary condition of European sociocultural life,[12]
or to Marx's and Engels's argument in 1847 that the modern European
bourgeoisie's need for markets "draws all, even the most barbarian, nations into civilization . . . [and] compels them to introduce what it calls
civilization into their midst, i.e., to become bourgeois themselves,"[13]
Culin and Cushing believed that civilization had begun in the prehistoric period, that it had emerged in North America—that is, *not* in
the Middle East as most thinkers held—among the ancestors of what
are now called Indians—that is, among so-called savages—and that its
territorial base and spread were neither found in nor fettered by political
boundaries or economic needs.

Although Culin's and Cushing's ideas on this subject have not
been accepted—or even subjected to rigorous analytical investigation—
it should be noted how closely they foreshadow and embrace the *concept*
of civilization that Durkheim and Mauss would later enunciate. How
much of Culin's, Cushing's, and, for that matter, Durkheim's and
Mauss's message has been lost is illustrated by the fact that to most contemporary archaeologists—followers for the most part of Morgan's and
Childe's definitions of civilization as a completed condition of European
society—there is no civilization to be found in Paleolithic Europe or
America.[14]

(2) RELIGIOUS ORIGINS OF CIVILIZATION

Culin and more especially Cushing located the origin of civilization in the moral and spiritual expressions of human existence and the
attempts by aboriginal peoples to divine the unknown and predict the
future. Again this complemented the perspective of Durkheim and
Mauss, who separately and jointly affirmed that religion was the most
primitive of all social phenomena and who opposed the materialist conception of institutional origins and historical development that was becoming so pronounced in their own day.[15] For Cushing, the games and

ceremonies of the contemporary Zuni of New Mexico represented a de-
volved survival of an original

> dramaturgic tendency—that tendency to suppose that even the phenom-
> ena of nature can be controlled and made to act more or less by men,
> if symbolically they do first what they wish the elements to do, accord-
> ing to the ways in which, as taught by their mystic lore, they suppose
> these things were done or made to be done by the ancestral gods of crea-
> tion time.[16]

Hence a comparative and protostructuralist analysis of the games played
by children and youths of these contemporary "primitives" would yield
the original divinational form and usage.

Culin, building cautiously on the work of his colleague, concluded
that the aboriginal American games had divinatory origins, basing his
belief "upon Mr. Cushing's suggestion that the gaming implements
which are sacrificed upon the Zuni altar were symbols of the divination
with which the ceremonies were originally connected." As a practical
procedure, Culin suggested, these divination rights

> might be regarded as an experiment in which the dramatization of war,
> the chase, agriculture, the magical rites that secured success over the
> enemy, the reproduction of animals and the fertilization of corn, is per-
> formed in order to discover the probable outcome of human effort, repre-
> senting a desire to secure the guidance of the natural powers by which
> humanity was assumed to be dominated.[17]

In the Culin-Cushing project, it is worth noting, a basic everyday
noneconomic practice, gaming, and the implements associated with it,
constitute the data base and the representative artifacts for a study of
spiritual foundations. That the economic factor is ever-present is not
disputed. Rather, as Durkheim once put it, "[I]t is indisputable that in
the beginning the economic factor is rudimentary while religious life is,
on the contrary, rich and overwhelming."[18] From out of this religious
life, Culin and Cushing observed, there developed divination rites and
rituals, dramaturgic ceremonies, that over the centuries became secularized and diminished in their social importance, surviving as games
and appearing in aesthetic motifs. In these later forms, these elements of
civilization became in effect cultural chattel, transported and diffused
over the face of the earth.

(3) FORM AND VARIATION IN CIVILIZATIONAL EXPRESSION

Civilization might begin in the sacred, symbolic, and transcendent aspects of the social, as Durkheim and Mauss contended, but over the centuries and across the reaches of its expansion it changed and secularized in both its ideal and material directions and usages. Thus Cushing found in the game of *sho-li-we,* played by his Zuni comrades in order to secure rain, a master clue to the foundations of Zuni religion and, ultimately, the basis for the original American civilization.[19] Culin pushed further, looking for what he called "games *par excellence*"—that is, those games that could be shown to be direct descendants of divinatory practices. Such games, he argued, "hold a peculiar position among the world's amusements [because they] frequently retain something of their original character and often survive in two forms, more or less distinct—as a divinatory rite and as a simple amusement."[20] From his discovery of "games *par excellence*" among Koreans, Chinese, and Japanese—identifiable from their common usage of an original American arrow motif—Culin was able to trace the diffusion of the original Paleolithic American civilization to Asia and, later, from his analysis of textile patterns, art styles, and design motifs among Eastern European peasantry, to suggest its expansion into the Occident.[21]

Neither Culin nor Cushing gave a direct answer to Durkheim's and Mauss's basic question about precisely what factors encourage the internationalization and expandability of civilizational phenomena. As the French scholars observed, that question went beyond the disciplinary confines of ethnology and was properly in the domain of sociology. That question remains unexamined, a project for sociologists of today and tomorrow.

(4) CIVILIZATION—MULTICENTRIC OR UNICENTRIC ORIGINS?

Durkheim and Mauss posed an implicit hypothesis in their observation that "If there does not exist one human civilization, there have been and there still are diverse civilizations which dominate and develop the collective life of each people."[22] Few would challenge the thesis that there are several civilizations in various degrees of efflorescence, stasis,

transformation, and decline today, but the question of their origins remains unanswered. Whether the civilizations of today emanated from a
single place of origin or from separate centers of genesis is yet unresolved. Those who share the view of Europocentric civilization see it
as a development from an original ancient center usually said to have
been in the Near East.[23] Similarly, those who insist that the prehistoric
and classical civilizations of Central and South America could not have
arisen independently postulate a diffusion of peoples and cultures, flora
and fauna to the American continent at some unrecorded date and
speculate as to whence and when this migration occurred.[24] The 500-
year debate over the origins of the American Indians and their civilization constitutes one of the most interesting and strategic research sites
for civilizational study.[25] Innovative pioneers in that matter, Culin and
Cushing counted themselves among the advocates of unicentric civilization beginnings. But, unlike almost all other scholars who have
opted for the unicentric position, they proposed North America as the
originating site and Asia and Europe as the receiving and hence dependent areas. Because of the equivocal character of the data upon which
any historical theory of preliterate social phenomena must depend for
evidence, every conclusion is necessarily speculative and rooted in some
form of conjecture. Nevertheless, although the data are inevitably imperfect, the forms of conceptualization, modes of interpretation, employment of sensitizing concepts, and sheer intellectual power required for
such projects are more than sufficient grist for a revitalized civilization-
oriented sociological imagination.

The Culin–Cushing project was neither completed nor recognized
in its own day. The untimely death of Cushing in 1900, combined with
the fact that Culin, a life-long museum curator, had no students, no
successors, and no disciple of eminence, undoubtedly contributed to the
demise of the project. However, as I have suggested elsewhere,[26] the
breadth, scope, vision, and, more to the point, icon-shattering character of the project flew against too many group and creedal interests and
illusions of the age for it to have gathered a following. More significantly, American sociology, then as now all too influenced by the German concept of *Kultur*,[27] has confined its study of sociocultural processes for the most part to settings that are no larger than the national
state and to periods coterminous with present time. Such limitations on
spatial and temporal horizons keep studies that would transcend these
communal, national, intrasocietal, and temporal limits from being
undertaken or even being recognized as part of the discipline. The tendency of the functionalists to concentrate analysis on a "social system,"
to treat the largest social system unit as a territorial state, and to treat a
social system as an "organism" in a state of dynamic equilibrium virtu-

ally forecloses studies that are civilizational or intercivilizational in character and certainly seems to foreclose outlooks that are nonteleological. Thus it is that six decades after Culin's death, his project is in limbo and its unacknowledged contribution to the mission of Durkheim's and Mauss's social anthropology is almost completely unknown. When, in 1973, Benjamin Nelson wrote that "We dare no longer suppose that . . . [sociocultural] processes can effectively be gotten at by confining ourselves to settings which are local, parochial, or instantial in terms of the level of interaction . . . ,"[28] he reopened the door to an intellectually viable classical tradition that indeed should no longer be neglected. It had once been a part of the incipient discipline of ethnology in America. The Culin-Cushing project still holds out promise to those who would take up the challenge of its emphases on the locus of cultural origins, the basis for civilizational diffusion, and the configurational outcomes of civilizational encounter.

(5) BEYOND PRIMITIVE CLASSIFICATION

That civilizations emerge and spread across natural obstacles and man-made barriers was a central thesis of Durkheim and Mauss. Yet they did not set forth precisely the manner whereby this process of civilizational expansion might be charted and documented. Cushing, and more especially Culin, however, employed a method for doing just such an investigation. This method, in effect, makes use of the kind of comparative analysis that was being developed by Durkheim and Mauss in their essay on *Primitive Classification* but carries that mode of analysis one step farther by adding a historico-diffusionist dimension to it. In their seminal work of 1903, Durkheim and Mauss compare the basic schema for classification among the aboriginal Australians, the Zuni, the Sioux, and the Chinese peoples. Their own aim was to arrive at some generalizations about the primal collective mentality that produces the organization of things and its links to a corresponding social organization. However, their work contains so many statements about the similarities between these separate peoples' modes of thinking that a question is raised whether these similarities arose independently or through some ancient encounter. Thus they observe:

> Indeed, though we have no means of establishing an historical link between the Chinese system and the types of classification that we studied earlier, it is impossible not to remark that it is based on the same principles as they are. The classification of things under eight headings, the

eight powers, actually gives a division of the universe into eight families which is comparable, save for the fact that the notion of clan is absent, to the Australian classifications. Also, we have found at the bases of the system, as among the Zuni, a completely analogous division of space into fundamental regions. These regions are likewise connected with the elements, compass points, and the seasons. As among the Zuni, again, each region has its own colour and is placed under the preponderant influence of a certain animal, which symbolizes at once the elements, powers, and moments of time. . . . China is not the only civilized country where we find at least traces of classification recalling those observed in simpler societies.[29]

Even before the French social anthropologists, who drew on Culin's and Cushing's works for their own speculations, Culin had come to the conclusion that the most ancient religious procedure and the one that would produce a variety of rites, rituals, and games was divination. Durkheim and Mauss had asserted that "The Chinese classification was essentially an instrument of divination" and that "a divinatory rite is generally not isolated; it is part of an organized whole." Ultimately, "At the base of a system of divination there is thus, at least implicitly, a system of classification."[30] Eight years before Durkheim and Mauss published their conclusions on the divinatory basis of primitive classification, Culin had put forward a similar hypothesis about the origin of games. Although he allowed that "Modern games have so nearly lost their original meaning that even with the light afforded by history it is practically impossible to trace their origin," Culin believed that a comparative analysis of games would yield their true origins in divination:

> Games, I hold, must be regarded not as conscious inventions, but as survivals from primitive conditions, under which they originated in magical rites, and chiefly as a means of divination.[31]

Whereas Durkheim and Mauss were content to rest their case on *logically* derived generalizations based on ethnographic similarities, Cushing and Culin proposed that the similarities provided a basic piece of evidence for the *historical* connection of peoples and the discovery of the origins of games, rites, and other contemporary civilizational phenomena. It was upon Cushing's suggestion "as to the object and origin of American games" that Culin "recognized a means of removing the study of games from the uncertain domain of so-called Folklore into the realm of true scientific investigation."[32] This method of "true scientific investigation" turned out to be the combined application of the doctrine of survivals and the principle of diffusion to the discovery of geographically distant cultural similarities. As Culin put it in 1902, when he offered his hypothesis of American origins for Asiatic civilization:

. . . [T]here remain to be explained the curious and bewildering similarities between the culture of the two continents. Many of them may be
referred to the universal sameness of man's physical and intellectual necessities; and others, more intricate, may be dismissed by the aid of some
such theory of psychological identity. . . . But there are other parallels
which even the most devoted advocate of the theory of independent origin cannot ignore. . . .

We find upon the Western continent things not only similar to those of
Asia, but precisely identical with them; things not only the same in form
and use, but in source and development as well, and at the same time so
empirical and complex that no theory of their having been produced independently under like conditions, of their being the products of a similar
yet independent creative impulse, seems longer tenable.

If we reject the theory of Asiatic origin, there are two explanations
open to us: First, that at one period of man's history he had certain ideas in
common on both continents; that his customs were fundamentally the
same and knew no geographical boundaries. Second, that these identical
customs originated in America, and were disseminated thence over the
world; that the American culture, no longer to be regarded as sterile and
unproductive, must be given its due place among the influences which
have contributed to the origin and development of our own civilization.[33]

In this pithy statement Culin located the comparative historical
study of civilizations squarely at the center of the perspectival debates
raging in ethnology, anthropology, and sociology: Should the study of
cultural development focus on the products of a humankind that was
everywhere psychically the same and thus limited in its inventions only
by the differential effects of varying environments? Or should similarities in datable cultural phenomena found among geographically distant peoples be the occasion for searching for some as yet undocu-
mented encounter between these peoples, or some third party carrying
the phenomena in question from one people to the other? Culin put
himself unequivocally in the latter camp. However, this did not foreclose the application of certain evolutionary concepts to his investigations. For Culin the discovery of dated or datable similarities evoked the
need to discover the original root that occasioned them and to search
out its historic or prehistoric beginnings. Thus quite different kinds
of artifacts—games, textile motifs, decorative sticks, visiting cards—
might, upon careful inspection, prove to have some basic similarity and
thus a common root. The several forms toward which that root had
proceeded over the centuries were explainable in terms of a multiplicity
of interrelated processes including evolution, survival, intrusion, inherent decay, and external stimulation.

A telling example of Culin's method is found in his analysis of the
I Ching, or *Book of Changes*. This ancient classic of Chinese literature
first penetrated American culture in the 1880s, when it was employed

by Chinese immigrants to guide their conduct and to divine their futures,[34] and it has recently re-entered American popular thought via a renewed interest in exotic Oriental cosmology that emerged in the 1960s.[35] The *I Ching* attracted scholarly interest in Europe after it was translated into English by Legge[36] and German by Wilhelm[37] and was discussed by the great Dutch student of Chinese religion de Groot.[38] Culin was among the first in the Occident to realize the civilizational significance of this work and to perceive in the ritual and implements it employed not merely a game but a survival of ancient Amerindian divination rites. Recent scholarship on the *I Ching*—especially by the late Russian sinologist Shchutskii[39]—has thrown further light on the complex origins of this work, as well as on the limitations of earlier *I Ching* researches, but has ignored altogether the unique contribution of Culin. Culin as well as Durkheim and Mauss selected the *I Ching* as a major piece of evidence in their respective projects. For the French scholars, who relied on de Groot's discussion and Legge's translation of the *I Ching*,[40] it proved to be a principal exemplar of China's system of primitive classification; for Culin, however, it yielded up not only a basic system of classification bearing a remarkable resemblance to that of the Zuni but also a divination ritual that referred back to the arrow sign, a sure indication of American origins.

It is instructive to compare the method and findings of Shchutskii with those of Culin. Both had in common a strong interest in the nature and origins of the *I Ching,* although each pursued this problem in quite different but not wholly unrelated ways. Such a comparison is also desirable because Culin's conclusion postulates an ancient intercivilizational encounter and the penetration of Asiatic culture by Amerindian symbol systems to such an extent that a single civilization emerged therefrom, while Shchutskii is content to rest his case for *I Ching* origins on Asiatic intracivilizational developments. The Russian scholar— whose researches, completed in 1937, eight years after Culin's death, did not come to light until 1960, twenty-three years after this remarkable Soviet sinologist was beaten to death in a Siberian slave labor camp[41]—employed the method of comparative historical linguistics to unearth the origins of the Chinese classic. It is worth noting that in 1895 Culin had called attention to the value of such an approach: "Without the confirmation of linguistic evidence they [i.e., games] are insufficient to establish the connection of races or the transference of culture."[42] Shchutskii, in contrast to European scholars of his day, who supposed the *I Ching* was a dictionary, concluded that the "*Book of Changes* is a document of feudal literature not only in terms of time, but also in terms of the class which used it"; that "[t]hroughout the course of the seventh century B.C. the feudal lords used the *Book of Changes* exclusively as a divinatory text"; and that "[t]hus the basic text of the *Book of Changes* is originally a divinatory and subsequently a philosophical text which took shape from the materials of agricultural folklore in the Chin or Ch'in territories between the eighth and seventh centuries B.C." [43] Employing a different procedure, Culin also claimed divinatory origin for the *I Ching,* but he assigned an earlier and non-Asiatic beginning for it.

Culin's method—reconstructed from his brief but seminal methodological discussions scattered through several major works—proceeded in a manner not unlike that of his contemporaries in the Austro-German *Kulturkreise* school. [44] Like the scholars of the latter school, Culin combined documented "histories" of preliterates with inferences derived from ethnology and archaeology in order to uncover lineages of the living civilizations of his own day. Unlike some evolutionists, however, he did not construct a definite sequence of stages; rather he employed the doctrine of survivals to link extreme antiquity and the artifacts of prehistoric man with the cultures, social organization, and everyday practice and amusements of the peoples of the present. [45] The logic of his method proceeded in four steps: first, the discovery and designation of the nature and emergence of the primordial symbol and artifact that is the root from which springs the multitude of forms, motifs, activities, games, etc. that are found in several contemporary East Asian and Amerindian societies or other social aggregates; second, observation, comparison, and classification of the similarities in numerical categories and philosophical systems among the peoples of Eastern Asia (especially the Chinese and Koreans) and those of preliterate America; third, examination and detailed description of these same symbol systems, or the artifactual derivations from them, found in the *I Ching,* in Chinatown gambling games, in Korean amusements, in Zuni icons and implements, and, for all these peoples, in public notices, visiting cards, and other paraphernalia of ordinary usage; [46] and fourth, designation of the place and, insofar as possible, the period or epoch whence these systems and motifs originated. In fact, the procedure had occurred in a slightly different order. The observation of manifest similarities in seemingly disparate and distant cultural phenomena had led Culin to search for a common but latent characteristic, trait, or form. Once that common element was discovered—by Culin's acceptance of Cushing's hypothesis about the antiquity and divinatory symbolism of the arrow—Culin recognized that this primordial common trait was the missing link that brought together the otherwise seemingly unrelated cultural phenomena of the Asiatics and the Amerindians. He reasoned that these phenomena bore the mark of a "survival" from some antique civilization, and that the mark must at one time have been carried abroad from its geocultural center of origin. The arrow root of these otherwise unrelated cultural phenomena dictated that that center had to have been prehistoric America and, most likely, the Southwest, where the Zuni tribe of his own day was to be found.

Without Cushing's painstaking researches and bold inferences, Culin's project might never have begun. For if Cushing had not investigated the nature and significance of the arrow and its relationship to Indian spiritual and material cultures, or if Culin had not considered and then built his own geohistorical theory upon his colleague's observations, the similarities in East Asiatic and Zuni cultural phenomena might have been linked only by logical inferences. Cushing claimed that the invention of the arrow had preceded that of the bow by a considerable period. Indeed, he observed, "the arrow in its ancestral or embryonic form at least, [is] as old as either the stone axe or the shaped knife of flint, if not older; [is,] in fact, coeval with the knotted clubs and rough stones men picked up at need in the wilds they earliest traversed. . . ."[47] Moreover, Cushing conceived the arrow as a fundamental generative form, illustrative of the process whereby a

> certain few human things and activities have been born . . . have grown . . . and in so doing have sometimes given rise to multitudinous other diverse things and activities, thus profoundly affecting man's psychological as well as racial development, and hence contributing inexorably both good and evil lessons and influences to his culture everywhere and everywhere similarly.[48]

Armed with his knowledge of this pristine root form, Culin approached the *I Ching* and other more common games and aesthetic motifs with a powerful key to their significance and origin. Both the games of divination (e.g., the *I Ching*) and chance played in Chinatown and the amusements of Korean children utilized elements of the classificatory system common to Asiatics and the Amerindians;[49] moreover, both bore marks, signs, and symbols that were representations of or derivations from the arrow design.[50] Close examination of the divinatory rods used by *I Ching* practitioners revealed a set of arrow signs and motifs. As Culin wrote in 1902 about "what is reputed to be the oldest surviving book in Chinese literature, the Yi King or 'Book of Changes,' a work which the Chinese revere as dating from the twelfth century B.C.":

> This curious volume is a treatise on fortune-telling or divination, and consists of sixty-four magical diagrams, under each of which are oracular explanations. The appendices to the work are attributed to Confucius. In the practical employment of the Yi in fortune-telling, fifty slender polished wood or ivory rods are manipulated. . . . Divination with these

splints is widely practised at the present day by the literary class in China, Korea, and Japan. . . .

Now the splints used in Asia find their exact counterpart in America in the gambling-sticks used by many tribes. . . . In Asia we have the custom with its literary traditions, but with no suggestions or explanation as to the origin of the bundle of splints. . . . In America it becomes apparent that the splints are merely other forms of the large gambling-rods, such as are found on the Pacific Coast—rods which with their bands or ribbons of color may be referred to the similarly marked shaftments of arrows, from which they are clearly derived.

In America the arrow seems to have been the chosen symbol of the warrior, of the man. . . . the narrow playing cards (money cards) of China, with their suits of nine cards each, frequently bear the old notches as numeral and suit-marks at the ends, and are clearly the legitimate descendants of the arrow-derived gambling-sticks. . . . A conventionalized arrow is used today in China as the man-representing counter in the game "Chief of the Literati," and as the notice-tablet of the merchant's guild hall. . . .

The games of the Eastern continent—and I speak now not so much of the present day, but from what we know of the remote past—are not only similar to, but practically identical with, those of America, and are not only alike in externals, but, if we may so apply the word, in their morphology as well. And, it may be added, they extend over into Asia from America as expressions of the same underlying cultures. They belong to the *same* culture.[51]

Culin's examination of the *I Ching* and related Asian cultural phenomena not only anticipated Shchutskii's proof of its divinatory foundations and gentry usages but daringly proposed an origin for it extended beyond the Asiatic mainland. Not content merely to notice similarities in seemingly disparate and distant cultural things, and unwilling—unlike Durkheim and Mauss—to reach a purely *logical* deduction as to their common basis, Culin, with the aid of Cushing's seminal insights, proposed the geographical place and epochal time of the origin of civilization itself. By pressing for recognition of American origins Culin was aware that "it premises the same, if not a higher, antiquity for man on the American continent as is revealed by the most remote historical perspective of Egypt or Babylon," and that it required him "to establish the American origin of the particular things to which he refers, their birth and subsequent development in America, and furthermore to demonstrate the probability of their transfer from America to other civilizations."[52] Not only his original essay of 1902 but the bulk of his career for the remaining twenty-seven years of his life was spent in behalf of meeting those requirements.[53] As a civilizational analyst Culin laid both a substantive and a methodological foundation for subsequent

investigations—once the idea of civilization and intercivilization encounters would be recognized as a proper domain for social science.

(6) MICROECOLOGICAL AND
MACROSOCIETAL RESEARCH

At the present time it has become a more or less taken-for-granted
feature of the sociological enterprise to divide investigative labors into
microecological or macrosociological endeavors. The justification for
this division of labor and primitive classification of types of social units
is presumably that either the nature of the phenomena, the character of
the findings, the scope of the findings' impact, the distinctive scientific
methods, or all of these are fundamentally distinct for each type, although such accounts of these distinctions are grounded neither in convincing proofs nor unambiguous reasoning. Indeed, the character and
size of the units located in each of the categories are by no means clearly
established and often overlap. It is something of a conceptual scandal
that this vague classification continues to dictate the dimensions of most
sociological investigations.[54] In this respect it is worth noting that one
recent critic of the state of sociological theory felt compelled to point
out that although much fruitful effort had been expended in recent years
in developing concepts and suggestive propositions about social relationships among different kinds of units, very little had been done to
develop concepts or categories that would describe the nature and differentiate among the kinds of units that are modified by these relationships.[55] Even earlier, Timasheff pointed to the embarrassing fact that the
term "microsociology" was employed to embrace collectivities with
enormous differences in size—from two-person groups to large-scale
collectivities of strangers assembled in a laboratory for the specific purpose of a scientific experiment to naturalistic groupings of persons in
primary or secondary relationships with one another.[56] Perhaps the
foremost investigator of conduct in "microecological" settings, Erving
Goffman,[57] has lately confessed to complete bafflement with respect to
the proper designation for the geocultural domain of his own "microstudies," puzzling inconclusively over whether their locus is spatially
enclosed by such gross glosses as the "English-speaking world, the
Anglo-American community, West European nations, Protestant countries, Christian society, and the West," or conceptually grasped by
terms like "American society" or by the "social unit 'civilization' (what-

ever that might mean)." Despite such ambiguities in conceptualization and classification, sociologists continue to treat the micro-macro distinction as if it were an established dichotomy. Thus, G. Duncan Mitchell informs us that "Macrosociology is the term given to the endeavour to study and compare total societies and cultures, or major aspects of them," but later he uncritically expands the scope of the term to include "civilisations," "high cultures," or "world cultures," buttressing this unanalyzed enlargement of the scope of macrosociology only with a remark that scholars "are agreed that it is reasonable to think about human social life on a large scale in such terms."[58] Don Martindale distinguishes between macro- and microfunctionalists, insisting that the former are the intellectual epigoni of the "positivistic organicists," that they "attempt repeatedly to give an exact definition of 'society,'" and that beginning "with societies as their unitary system, the macrofunctionalists tend to extend analysis downward to include less inclusive systems," hence entering into the realm of the microfunctionalists. But, he goes on, the "microfunctionalists . . . seem to be in the process of working out a general functional theory from the opposite direction"[59] marked by a distinctively different conceptual frame. Such confusion in unit boundaries and over frames of reference clearly indicates that the clarification of the conceptual dimensions of social morphology, a task that Durkheim thought fundamental to the establishment of sociology among the social sciences, has not yet been completed.

From the conceptual and methodological perspective of Cushing and Culin, the micro-macro distinction can be criticized as an instance of the bifurcation of a natural class at an unnatural joint. Both men proceeded with their own investigations without placing any morphological limitation on the scope of the unit or the style of research each would employ. This is relevant because both combined extensive use of the most intensive forms of participant-observation with historical, documentary, and archaeological methods.[60] And both conducted researches that would today be called "microecological" in order to solve problems at the civilizational level. Yet today, microecologists, employing laboratory experiments, ethnographic investigation, or participant observation, tend to restrict the scope of their problems or the meaning of their findings to the size of the unit they investigate. Most believe that the study of any large-scale units requires massive surveys or other nonobservational documentations, such as the introduction of cybernetic models.[61] Culin and Cushing in fact proved that social scientists could carry out the grandest civilizational investigations through the imaginative usage of localized ethnographic methods.

Both Culin and Cushing firmly believed that a researcher must make himself a living analogue of the people or culture he is studying.

Hence Culin carried out his study of Chinese games by moving to Philadelphia's Chinatown, learning the language firsthand, becoming an habitue of gambling dens, secret-society halls, and clan meetings, and getting deeply and even dangerously involved in the personal lives and interassociation conflicts of the denizens of that ghetto.[62] By that means he made himself into a functional or moral equivalent of a Chinese and could report with confidence on the actually experienced meaning of Chinese conduct. Learning Chinatown culture and social organization "from the inside," Culin could then combine his personally acquired knowledge with that obtained from the comparative examination of Chinese and Amerindian artifacts, and then test his hypothesis about civilizational origins and diffusion.

Cushing was an even more intensive ethnographer. Now regarded as the principal pioneer of participation-observation, he was in fact the most full-fledged participant in Zuni life that ethnology ever allowed. He journeyed to the territory of New Mexico, persuaded the Zuni to let him live among them, join their tribe, and share their joys and sorrows. Eventually, he rose to the rank of war chief and became an initiate into their sacred mysteries as well. From the time of his boyhood, spent mostly in the woods of upstate New York, he had discovered what J. W. Powell would later credit as a "new method of research in prehistoric archaeology . . . experimental reproduction,"[63] that is, he had learned to reproduce both the methods and products of aboriginal labor so perfectly that his arrowheads were a match to those made by the aborigines themselves. Through making his exact reproduction of both method and product of aboriginal labor, Cushing believed that he had made himself into a living, thinking, and acting representative of the producers of those artifacts. As he put it about the implications for ethnographic science of his own arrow-making:

> I tell you in detail, then, how, through making many arrows, I have studied the arrow and its development practically: how, by using it unweariedly and consorting with those who used it actually with natural purpose and method, as well as by pondering deeply upon it in the most primitive moods I could muster, I have studied, theoretically, too its meanings and relations; the place it held in men's hearts and minds ere ever they knew of goodlier friend or deadlier foe.[64]

Cushing's scientific intent in learning both the practical and esoteric Zuni ways was to reproduce in himself the civilization and culture of that people so that by recording and reporting on his own conduct, beliefs, fears, and joys, he would be producing on paper a picture—an individualized collective representation—of the original civilization of which he had made himself a wholly integrated part. The charge of "subjectivism" leveled against such endeavors (e.g., when Kroeber says of Cushing: "His observations were of the keenest, but almost impossible to disentangle from his imaginings"[65]) fails on two counts: It treats the researcher's state of mind and conduct, his sociological imagination and praxis, as if it existed in a sociocultural void and had arisen absolutely independent of the rules, roles, and relationships of the society in which the researcher partakes as a participant-observer. It fails to see that the individual's or the collectivity's reflexivity with respect to his, her, or its own understanding of its actions and beliefs may by extension and self-analysis become a researcher's own reflexive understanding of him/herself and, more precisely, of that self that has emerged in the sociocultural milieu in which she/he has been deeply immersed. For Cushing, who took regular inventory of his emerging self in Zuni-land, hence, it would *not* be proper social-scientific procedure to accept the limitations on ethnographic methods recently enunciated by Anthony Giddens:

> To study, say, the practice of sorcery in an unfamiliar culture, an anthropologist has to master the categories of meaning whereby sorcery is organized as an activity in that culture. But it does not follow from this that he has to accept as valid the belief that sickness can be induced in a victim by means of magical ritual.[66]

Indeed, for Cushing—even more than for the much maligned Castaneda[67]—it was quite the other way around. Both men became accomplished sorcerers in order to uncover an aboriginal way of knowledge.[68] As Cushing put it in describing why he had to become a practicing Zuni arrow-maker:

> If I would study any old, lost art, let us say, I must make myself the artisan of it—must, by examining its products, learn both to see and to feel as much as may be the conditions under which they were produced and the needs they supplied or satisfied; then, rigidly adhering to those conditions and constrained by their resources alone, as ignorantly and anxiously strive with my own hands to reproduce, not to imitate, these things as ever strove primitive man to produce them.[69]

And, not only did Cushing believe that the ethnographer had to absorb the religious and practical beliefs and learn the ordinary and extraordinary ways of life of his subjects in order to uncover and master the categories of meaning that inhered therein,[70] he also and more significantly perceived this method of ethnographic acculturation and socialization as precisely the approach that would permit revelation of the macrostructure and processes of the original culture and of civilization itself. Pointing to some basic similarities between himself and an aborigine, Cushing remarked:

I have virtually the same hands he had, the same physique, generally or
fundamentally the same activial and mental functions too, that men had
in ages gone by, no matter how remote. If, then, I dominate myself with
their needs, surround myself with their material conditions, aim to do as
they did, the chances are that I shall restore their acts and their arts, however lost or hidden; shall learn precisely as they learned, rediscovering
what they discovered precisely as they discovered it. Thus may I produce
an art in all its stages; see how it began, grew, developed into and affected
other arts and things—all because, under the circumstances I limit myself
to the like of,—it became and grew and differentiated in other days.[71]

For Cushing, anthropology was coextensive with personal history ("If,
moreover, I am at times seemingly too personal in style of statement,
let it be remembered that well-nigh all anthropology is personal history;
that even the things of past man were personal, like as never they are to
ourselves now"[72]). In his much-criticized "personal" ethnographic reports, Cushing presented not only the substance of whatever culture he
had studied but also put that presentation into the style of its subjects—
that is, into his own newly acquired style since he had become one of
his subjects. Thus his so-called personal imaginings were reproductions
of the values, attitudes, beliefs, and myths of the aborigines, were statements about a civilization produced in an English prose translation
of the manner of that civilization. For example, Cushing wrote his
own understanding of the outlook—an outlook he had absorbed—that
primitive man had on the relationship of the arrow to his world:

I would divine how the men of old felt about their arrows, and what,
therefore, they did to them and with them. They were simple, like little
children, given to looking on their favorite toys, with a vast deal of personal feeling, emphasized in their case, to huge proportions, by the tremendous part these arrows bore in their lives. They had no knowledge of
physics to guide them. Analogy was their explanation of relations, and
the dramatic interpretation of these relations and the phenomena thereof
their only logic, and so behold, the arrow was for ages looked on as a
wand of enchantment to those who made and used and lived by and loved
it; was to them a symbol—a veritable portion and potency of the might-
iest forces and beings that they thought the world and four quarters, the
sky, or the under earth held; was thus transcendent over the skill of their
deftest archer; was a thing of magic, and was willful, as like to obey the
wind-bird with whose feathers they had winged its shaft withal, the god
in whose breath it wavered, as to obey themselves or him who wrought
or loosed it; for itself would decree his luck or his fate, not he who sped
it, else why all so vainly at times, however great his skill or his effort, did
he speed it? Therefore it played as large a part in their theoretical and
mythical as in their practical life, and must be theoretically and imagina-
tively, no less than practically and experimentally, studied.[73]

Cushing thus sought nothing less than to overcome both of the predicaments of reflexivity that have recently been recognized by studies of hermeneutics, phenomenology, and interpretive sociology.[74] On the one hand he sought to reduce the interference of the observer's standpoint on that which was being observed by making the observer into an homunculus of the people and an acculturated member of the group that he investigated. On the other hand, he sought to liberate his observations from their generalizable limits in contemporaneity and geolocal space by grasping the civilizational character of all that he observed and, together with Culin, unearthing the geotemporal and mythopoetical origins of that civilization.

What has survived of Cushing's praxiological foray into the philosophy and methodology of civilizational analysis is, unfortunately, only a selective portion of his original perspective: his mythopoetical structuralism—which has found much greater elaboration in the work of Lévi-Strauss[75]—and, in unacknowledged and constricted form, his discovery of the manual concept—which has been reinvented by the ethnomethodologist David Sudnow.[76] To the contemporary school of French structuralism, the one perspective in which Cushing's name is still honored, his contribution is perceived as the logical—rather than the historical—study of primitive myths and mentalities. Altogether unnoticed is the relationship between his voluntary acculturation as a Zuni and the recovery and reconstruction of civilizational origins and diffusion.[77] Thus, when Lévi-Strauss states that "Frank Hamilton Cushing's insight and sociological imagination entitle him to a seat on Morgan's right, as one of the great fore-runners of social-structure studies," he discounts the allegations of inaccuracies and exaggerations in Cushing's reports in order to praise him for his formal constructions: "Cushing," Lévi-Strauss insists, "was aiming less at giving an actual description of Zuni society than at elaborating a model . . . which would explain most of its processes and structure."[78] Such an interpretation, however, overlooks the fact that Mauss regarded Cushing "as one of the best describers of societies of all time,"[79] that Culin once experimentally verified one of Cushing's hunches about the hidden substructure of primitive artifacts with the aid of Röntgen rays,[80] and that Levy-Bruhl recognized in Cushing's application of the manual concept not an abstract model but rather a new method whereby the actual structure of primitive cultures could be recovered.[81]

The French structuralists are no doubt in part moved to separate the logical from the historical in Cushing's thought because of the assaults offered on the latter's evolutionism and the charges of inaccuracies and exaggerations in his ethnographic research.[82] Thus Cushing's influence on Durkheim's *The Elementary Forms of the Religious Life* has come

under attack in recent years by those who see the beginnings of a conjectural history in the presumed connection between Australian and
American aboriginal cultures,[83] and by those who seize on Kroeber's
and others' subsequent attacks on Cushing's analysis of Zuni primitive
classification as indicative of an important instance wherein Durkheim
relied on faulty evidence.[84] However, these criticisms do not address
Cushing's own application of evolutionary reasoning, in which, together with Culin, he recognized the fundamental significance of historical contact for the dissemination of culture. In his Zuni studies he
concentrated on showing, as Levy-Bruhl correctly observed, "how a
prelogical and mystic mentality of an already exalted type expands into
a magnificent efflorescence of collective representations destined to express, or even to produce, participations which are no longer directly
felt."[85] Rather than proposing a conjectural history, or depicting change
occurring in orderly stages, Cushing's analysis of prelogical and mystical mentalities and the cultures that represented them was meant to account for the *persistence* over long periods of time and vast amounts of
space of the *same culture and social organization*. Cushing's knowledge of
the basic attitude that informed primitive production convinced him
that, precisely because the maker believed that his tools possessed inherent uncanny powers that could be unleashed against himself unless he
reproduced each item in exactly the same way and form as the original,
there was a powerful constraint against technological innovation or
variation—a religiously based insistence, in effect, on doing the minutest
things as they had always been done.[86] Cushing cannot so easily be
charged with the evolutionist fallacy. His cultural predilections were
much closer to the idea and processes of fixity.

Sudnow's recent reflexive analysis of the ethnomethodological
features of learning to type and to play the piano unwittingly calls attention to the importance of Cushing's discovery of "manual concepts"[87]
for the study of civilization. Although Sudnow's analysis and interpretation do not proceed beyond the instant case of his own manual
learning, Cushing's outlook on the same kind of process extends far
beyond the localized setting or any particular usage of manual skills or
their acquisition. Thus, although Cushing employed his "experimental
archaeology" to demonstrate, *inter alia,* that the prehistoric mound
people probably possessed the knowledge and skills of annealing, fus-
ing, and soldering soft metals and, therefore, could have produced
copper implements at a much earlier period than previously had been
suspected,[88] the larger meaning of his manual conception linked productive labor to first a visceral and then a cognitive language. While
Sudnow is content to describe in minutest detail the ways of the hand in
linking the piano's musical or the typewriter's word-and-sentence pro-

duction to his own understanding of that production, Cushing treated practical problems requiring manual dexterity—for example, the making of arrows, the production of copper tools—as master clues to the thought processes of an entire civilization. As Levy-Bruhl summed up this aspect of Cushing's work: "The progress of civilization was brought about by reciprocal influence of mind upon hand and *vice versa.*"[89]

In "manual concepts" Cushing discovered a primary source for the affiliation of language and primitive productive processes.[90] These "two languages," Levy-Bruhl observed, "the signs of which differ so widely as gestures and articulate sounds, will be affiliated by their structure and their method of interpreting objects, actions, conditions."[91] Just as Sudnow learned to play the piano and to type and in the process described how his hands became agents of musical and word production in their own right, so Cushing (here once more described accurately by Levy-Bruhl), within the framework of a civilizational perspective, with "infinite patience . . . revived the primitive function of his own hands, living over again with them experiences of prehistoric days, with the same material and under the same conditions as at that period, *when the hands were so at one with the mind that they really formed part of it.*"[92] Like Sudnow, Cushing believed there was a language of the hands, but Cushing learned that language not merely to report on his own manual-mental processes but to recover the mentality of a lost civilization. Cushing's discovery of what we might call manual ethnolinguistics led Levy-Bruhl to observe that "The primitive who did not speak without his hands did not think without them either."[93] Cushing was even more specific. Levy-Bruhl has grasped that for Cushing a manual metalinguistic process was involved in tool production and was at the heart of primitive man's speech activities as well, thus accounting for the "extreme specializing of verbs, which we have noted everywhere in the languages of primitives." Such speech development was "a natural consequence of the part which the manual movements play in their mental activity."[94] Cushing's approach to manual ethnolinguistics is civilizational in character and leads us away from the constricted, one-sided understanding of the ethnomethodologists and other recent adherents to a new solipsistic sociology.[95] Rather than emphasizing an acultural indexical perspective toward all human actions, Cushing in effect proposed a foundation for a comparative cognitive sociology of prehistorical, historical, and contemporary cultures and civilizations and provided an empirical basis for sociolinguistic studies.[96]

CONCLUSION

The much-neglected works of Culin and Cushing still provide challenging problems, fresh conceptualizations, bold hypotheses, and suggestive methodological procedures for civilizational investigations. Culin's discovery of the religious and divinatory foundation of ancient amusements, his imaginative application of the concept of diffusion to uncover the origin of Asiatic civilization, and his willingness for the sake of social science to become absorbed by both the cultures of China-town and Zuni-land speak to the breadth of research problems that beckon those who can see civilization in the microcosm. Cushing's pioneering employment of acculturated participation in an aboriginal setting and his invention of "experimental archaeology" and discovery of the "manual concept" provide both methods and substance for macro-societal study. What Levy-Bruhl said about Cushing—namely, "The difficulties which the application of the method suggested and employed by Cushing entail are considerable, [perhaps only] he alone, . . . or men endowed with the same universal tendencies and the same patience as he, would be able to put it into practice" [97]—applies to the different but equally taxing methods and procedures of Culin. Without such bold anthropological and sociological imaginations, coupled with a willingness to put out considerable and painstaking effort, we cannot expect advances in the social sciences.

Culin and Cushing, in their joint and respective projects and procedures, burst through the findings that today separate microecological research from its application to macrosocietal problems. Cushing's uncovering of the bases for ancient Zuni civilization through his material and personal ethnographic researches suggests that the methodological limitations presently imposed on the scope of generalizations possible from field work are more likely debilitating self-restraints foreclosing promising avenues of investigation and placing unwarranted restrictions on social-scientific imagination. (As Levy-Bruhl asked, "If Cushing had not obtained the interpretation of their myths from the Zunis themselves, would any modern intellect have ever succeeded in finding a clue to this prehistoric labyrinth?" [98]) Culin's ability to move from the comparative analysis of games to his hypothesis on the origin and diffusion of civilization shows how the seemingly trivial aspects of culture can be used to provide clues to problems of world-historical scope.

The ethnographic approach, combining observation of material and moral features of a culture with full-fledged participation in it, is dangerous as well as difficult. Culin was involved in the "tong wars" that broke out in Philadelphia's Chinatown in the 1880s and understood both the local and international issues that provoked such bloody violence;[99] following Cushing's lead, he also dwelt among the Zunis, sharing the sorrows, joys, and dangers of the frontier.[100] Cushing was once tried as a sorcerer by his adopted Zuni brothers and escaped with his life only by successfully adapting the rhetoric of his defense to the situation and understandings at hand.[101] Moreover, Cushing's activities as a Zuni war chief aroused the ire of a United States senator, and he was eventually forced out of Zuni-land because of political pressures on the Smithsonian Institution that employed him as an ethnologist.[102] Such difficulties were endured and dangers faced by these researchers because they saw them as more than acceptable risks for those who would take up the study of civilization from the point of view of the originating cultures.

The works of Cushing and Culin are worthy of our continued attention. They adumbrate the fundamental question Benjamin Nelson put to social scientists in 1974:

> As we prepare to celebrate the 200th anniversary of the Declaration of Independence does it not behoove us to recognize that our own so-called "first new nation" is unintelligible without being studied against the background of the civilizational structures with which it has been in contact, the civilizational commitments of those who are its citizens and denizens, the relations it has been having with non-Western civilizations, the societies and civilizations of the Far East and Near East, of Eastern Europe, Africa, of Latin America and so on?[103]

Asian American Contacts before Columbus

Alternative Understandings for Civilization, Acculturation, and Ethnic Minority Status in the United States

INTRODUCTION

Asiatics and Asian Americans occupy two separate loci in American studies. During the thousands of years before 1492, peoples from Asia were, arguably, *a* or *the* contributing population that settled the land mass comprising North, Central, and South America, or, even more controversially, the peoples who benefitted culturally, socially, and politically from an infusion of ideas, motifs, customs, religious orientations, and imperial designs emanating *from* paleoamerica. Three and one-half centuries after Columbus reached Santo Domingo, Asians— Chinese, Japanese, and Koreans—began immigrating to the United States, Canada, Mexico, and Peru. Regarded as an alien and sometimes dangerous population—peoples of a different race and bearers of foreign cultures—these peoples became objects of a century-long debate, one that shows no sign of exhaustion, over whether and in what manner they could be included as Americans. The two loci are separated in social and intellectual thought, in the popular mind, and with respect to policy considerations. Pre-Columbian studies belong to the discipline of pre-history, arouse occult interests or fanciful conjectures among ordinary people, and contribute intermittently to whatever policies might be proposed for contemporary primitives. Asian and Amerindian adjustments to the 500 year old state societies in the Americas are topics for the exercise of the historian's craft and the techniques and theories of the political and sociological sciences, arouse suspicions of disloyalty and prejudice about race in popular thought, and become objects of policies seeking assimilation, pluralism, or selected preservation and enhancement of ethnic culture and consciousness. The academic and popular orientations toward these two arenas of investigation are separated by a seemingly unbridgeable gulf. Pre-Columbian cultures do not figure in the discussions and debates over civil societies; neither Asians nor Amerindians are considered fundamental, integral, and inherent elements of the Euroamerican civilization operant within the political states of the modern, i.e., post-Columbian, epoch. This paper shall attempt to locate the origins of this well-established dichotomy in American studies within the imperatives and constraints of 15th-century Christian thought, and to argue that the proto-anthropological paradigm that is presented in Genesis continues to inform and circumscribe modern scientific thought despite the much-vaunted assault on ecclesiolatry during the Age of Enlightenment. Asian American studies, as a branch of American studies, has not yet evoked a body of disciplines ruled by religiously unfettered reason, and, given the embeddedness of secularized variants of ecclesiastical doctrine, does not seem likely to do so in the near future.

RELIGIOUS ORTHODOXY AND THE THEORY OF ASIATIC-AMERINDIAN ORIGINS

Columbus's "discovery" of America in 1492 raised new and vexing questions for all those who subscribed to the biblical story of creation and all humankind's descent from Adam and Eve and, later, the lineages of Noah.[1] Scripture seemed to give no clue or preparation for the existence of another land mass, unconnected to Eurasia and Africa, inhabited by dark-skinned natives speaking unknown languages and living in a manner so different from that of the peoples on the contiguous continents. Moreover, this other land was covered by unusual plants and shrubs and was the habitat of a bewildering variety of fauna. Convinced that the understanding of these new phenomena must be consistent with holy writ, the cosmographers of Columbus's day posed the question, How had this other continent been peopled? Scripture dictated the foundations for their answer: All of humanity had been descended from the original pair. The home of that pair had been situated somewhere in Asia Minor. Therefore, the peoples encountered by Columbus and subsequent explorers must be descendants of the first family, peoples whose ancestors had migrated to the Americas. Once these ground rules for explanation of Amerindian origins had been established, what remained to be discovered were the ethnic background of the people who had emigrated, the route or routes by which that migration had occurred, the date at which it had happened, and the manner in which flora and fauna had been distributed in such profusion and variety into this "new world."

An alternative theory was possible. It might have been the case that the peoples of the Americas had originated there. Such a view was put forward in 1655 in *Pre-Adamitae* by Isaac de La Peyrere (1596–1676), a French Huguenot who may have been a Marrano Jew.[2] According to de La Peyrere, the Old Testament bible was a book of Jewish not world history; Adam was not the first man, but the first Jew, created by God to save the rest of mankind from aimless drift. The history of the Jews was Providential, of gentiles culturological. De La Peyrere offered the suggestion that the world had already been peopled before the creation of Adam; hence, a woman could be found for Cain to marry, an already inhabited city could be postulated for Cain to dwell in, and, most important, the flood that Noah and his children survived was not universal but confined to Palestine. In subsequent works de La Peyrere argued that recent discoveries in Asia, America, and Oceania refuted Archbishop Ussher's dating of every known and yet to be known event, people, and culture from 4004 B.C., the year of Adam's birth. When Hugo Grotius attacked de La Peyrere's views on the historical and ethical specificity of Genesis as an assault on Christianity and asserted that American Indians must be descendants of ancient Norwegian explorers of the Atlantic, de La Peyrere replied by pointing out that the Eskimos could not be reconstituted Scandinavian descendants of Adam or Noah because their settlements antedated those of the Norsemen. Although the Catholic Church exacted a recantation from de La Peyrere, he never gave up his search for proofs for pre–Adamic man, and more generally, for an historicizing and particularizing of the biblical narrative.

De La Peyrere's perspective remained on the margins of scholarship, even after the much-vaunted assault on Christian ecclesiolatry in the nineteenth century had supposedly ejected religious imperatives from anthropological study. Heterodoxical scholars were attracted to its enlargement of scholarship. Spinoza adopted Peyrerean views in his *Tractatus-Theologico Politicus,* but Spinoza's teacher, Rabbi Manasseh ben Israel, advocate of the thesis that the Ecuadorean Indians were descendants of the Lost Ten Tribes of Israel and that the Amerindians in general were progeny of a people or peoples from China, opposed him.[3] Another student of Manasseh, Juan de Prado, was expelled from Amsterdam along with Spinoza for holding to pre-Adamite views probably derived from de La Peyrere. Peyrerean thought was cautiously hinted at by Henry Home, Lord Kames, one of the members of the sociological school known as the Scottish Moralists. Impressed by the great differences exhibited among human groups, Home ventured to wonder whether God might have "created many pairs of the human race, differing from each other both externally and internally," and whether He might have "fitted these pairs for different climates, and placed each pair in its proper climate." Home pointed out that such a theory of multiple creations would do admirably in resolving the question of the origins of the Amerindians. It would end the search for a migratory group that had somehow gotten itself to America in pre-historic times; it would permit long-term isolation and separate evolution to account for the primitive and rude state of the aborigines at the time of the Conquest; and it might explain later cultural innovations in America as products of historically demonstrable contacts with Europeans or Asiatics. However, like other pre–nineteenth-century polygenists, Lord Kames observed that the pious "were not permitted to adopt" such a heterodoxical hypothesis.[4] Although criticism of and disputes over specific points of the ethnographic argument in Genesis did occur, discussions of Indian origins in that period were characterized by what Lee Eldridge Huddleston calls "a curious mixture of observation and obscurantism."[5] Essentially, disputation on the origin of the Indians centered on trying to decide which among several contending nominees was the true predecessor of the American aborigines. Candidates included various peoples from southern and eastern Europe, northern and eastern Africa, central and eastern Asia, the Ten Lost Tribes of Israel, and the inhabitants of Atlantis. What differentiated the debate and the disputants were methodologies and modes of reasoning; the acceptance, rejection, and interpretation of available data; and the degrees of rigor and credulity employed. A Peyrerean tradition did not develop. If it had, the ecclesiastical hold on ethnological theory might have been utterly broken. Peyrerean thought promised to recognize the religious accounts of every people's origins as having value for comparative historical research. It might have placed every people's sacred tradition on an equal footing, each open to the critical investigation of secular historical ethnologists. It might have forestalled the Christian-influenced paradigm that has irrevocably divided American studies into two culturally separable epochs—the pre-Columbian and the post Conquest periods. It might have introduced a complex but unitary history of intersecting civilizations that precluded Eurocentrism or any other ethnocultural bias.

By the beginning of the eighteenth century, however, two bible-based approaches to the Amerindian question had become fixed. One, called Acostan after its founder Joseph de Acosta (who had published his findings in 1579), was characterized by strict construction of data, and by the refusal to accept the speculative fancy or comparative culturological reasoning common to discussions of the issue. Guided by the argument in Genesis, de Acosta insisted on universal descent from the original pair. He rejected all unproved conjectures, including those proclaiming an ancient ark that carried man to the new world, the biblical origins of aboriginal languages, and unproved assertations of prehistoric transoceanic navigational skills. "It seems to me," he wrote, "quite likely that in times past men came to the Indies driven unwillingly by the wind."[6] The peculiar animals and plants found in the Americas led de Acosta to suppose that "the new world we call the Indies is not completely divided and separated from the other World,"[7] and that animals and men might have crossed into America on a land bridge. Unable to determine whether early Americans might have been Atlanteans, Hebrews, or any of the other putative claimants, de Acosta concluded that it was "rash and presumptuous"[8] to specify any particular people as the origin group of the Amerindians. Furthermore, noting that the aborigines encountered by the Spanish explorers had no written traditions, he hypothesized that the original Americans must have been some group of savage hunters driven to America by starvation or overpopulation. Once in America, he supposed, these savages had settled down, divested themselves or forgotten most if not all of their old world culture, and developed new institutions and customs. Because of this separate historical and cultural development, de Acosta reasoned that it was fallacious—and certainly impossible—to trace the origins of the contemporary Amerindians by means of the comparison of their culture traits with those of living or ancient European, Asiatic, or African peoples. Similarities, he believed, could not be used as evidence for common origins. Although de Acosta's argument seemed to promise an end to fantasies about Amerindian origins, its skepticism about the available evidence and its rejection of conjecture left the matter open to those who cared to speculate more boldly.

Precisely because it virtually foreclosed employment of the ethnological imagination, de Acosta's thesis did not overcome the less rigorous proposal of Gregorio Garcia, first published in 1607. Like de Acosta, Garcia remained firmly within the Church dogma of a single creation and a common descent for man. However, in sharp contrast to the earlier theory, Garcia reopened almost all orthodox debates, discussions, and conjectures about American origins by insisting on the possibility—though not necessarily the probability—of no less than eight separate Indian precursors. (As a devout Catholic, Garcia ruled out of consideration the speculations of Avicenna and Cisalpino that humankind might have emerged out of decaying matter, or the blasphemous idea that some humans might have been created by alchemy.)[9] Garcia asserted that the first settlers in the Indies might have come by sea from Ophir, Tarshish, Carthage, or the legendary isles off the English coast known as the Sporades. It was also possible that Amerindian forebears might include the Ten Lost Tribes of Israel, the refugees who fled Atlantis before it was destroyed, the sailors sent out by King Hesperas or Iberia in 1658 B.C. who discovered and settled the mysterious Isles Hesperides, or Chinese, Tartars, Scythians or some other Asiatic people. Garcia set forth the arguments favoring and opposing the choice of each of these candidates, but he neither chose one over the other nor rejected any of them. He adopted an eclectic view that held out a chance not only for each people and each method of travel to America, but even for all of them. As Garcia put it, the Indians

> proceed neither from one Nation or people, nor went to those parts from one [part] of the Old World. Nor did the first settlers all walk or sail by the same road or voyage nor in the same time, nor in the same manner. But actually they proceeded from various Nations, from which some came by Sea, forced and driven by Storms; others by Art of Navigation looking for those Lands, of which they had heard. Some came by land . . . Some came from Carthage . . . some from the Ten Tribes . . . Ophir . . . Atlantis . . . Greeks . . . Phoenicians . . . Chinese . . . Tartars . . . and other Nations.[10]

Garcia's reopening of the search for new world origins set the stage for a profusion of explanations for Amerindian beginnings that has gone on from 1607 to the present. However, it did more than this. It opened the way for ethnologists to account for the varieties of culture, color, and condition among "new peoples" encountered in the imperial expansion of Europe. So long as the biblical account of the creation and the descent from Adam and Noah was regarded as unchallengeable doctrine, the ancestry and culture history of each people had to be traced within the limitations set by sacred cosmography. Establishment of genetic and cultural lineages for non-literate peoples proved almost insuperable until scientists adopted "the comparative method,"[11] wherein physical features or culture traits might be looked over for those similarities that would link a people or culture to its antique or bible-identified predecessor.

In the 295 years that separated the publication of Garcia's views from those of the iconoclastic champion of Amerindian cultural diffusion to Asia, Stewart Culin, the former tradition luxuriated in its profusion of origins theories. The more cautious Acostan tradition found expression among Northern Europeans, who began to settle in North America after 1600 and to ask searching questions about the origins of the Indians they encountered. Essentially, de Acosta's perspective required that any explanation of Indian origins must also be able to account for the peculiar varieties of flora and fauna found in the new world and explain precisely how they got there. Sea voyages were ruled out, because they were unlikely transportation for ancient plants or animals. Ultimately the followers of de Acosta postulated a northern land bridge from Asia, and declared that the Indians had most probably descended from some people who had come through Siberia. Whether Indian culture was Siberiatic was regarded as another question, however; for by the seventeenth century the identification of the Tartars or the Scythians as Indian progenitors was disputed: it was impossible to know whether the prehistoric migrants to America had come from among those peoples or were a separate people driven out of Siberia by them.[12]

THE LIMITED ASSAULT ON ECCLESIOLATRY

The debate over polygenism in American ethnological thought in the nineteenth century[13] seemed to promise a complete break with ecclesiolatry, a possible revival of Peyrerean thought, and scientific consideration of a heretical hypothesis: Amerindian autochthony. If the autochthony of paleo-Indian culture could be established, it might be but a short step to propose the diffusion of that civilization to other lands. Thomas Jefferson's adherence to Enlightenment philosophy and deism permitted him to disregard Christian dogma on Amerindian origins and propose on the basis of Amerindian-Asian language similarities that a "greater number of . . . radical changes of language having taken place among the red men of America, proves them of greater antiquity than those of Asia."[14] Migration, he supposed, probably had proceeded westward to Asia rather than in the reverse as Scriptures seemed to require.[15] In a similar mode of reasoning a half-century later, Count Gobineau asserted Amerindian origins for the Asiatic peoples: "C'est la response de la physiologie comme de la linguistique."[16] However, polygenism did not survive and although theories of polycultural origins became separated from genetic approaches, the two major positions that emerged postulated either Asian or European origins of the Amerindian people, who subsequently were said to have developed an independent culture. The ethnological debates of the late nineteenth century encouraged Lewis Henry Morgan to put forward his own theory of Asiatic origins and Amerindian cultural autochthony and Daniel Garrison Brinton to claim that glacial-epoch Europeans had migrated to America, adapted themselves racially and culturally to the new environment, and formed a culturally independent American race of red men. Despite their claims of freedom from religious dictates, both positions were compatible with the Acostan tradition and with Matthew Hale's earlier theory of Amerindian cultural forgetfulness and degeneration.

LEWIS HENRY MORGAN (1818–1881)

Among the ethnological pioneers whose work has had a lasting effect on world scholarship is Lewis Henry Morgan. As part of his investigations, Morgan found it necessary to determine the origins of the Amerindians. He set forth one of the first modern statements of the theory of Asiatic origins and also pointed to the cultural significance of the bow and arrow—a central artifact of Stewart Culin's later claim for Amerindian cultural priority. According to Morgan, the people called Indians actually belonged to the "Ganowanian" family of man, "the family of the bow and arrow," who had migrated to America from Asia and first settled in the regions watered by the Columbia River and its tributaries. The Columbia River Valley was, according to Morgan, "the nursery of the Ganowanian family, and the source from which both the northern and southern divisions of the continent mediately or immediately were being replenished with inhabitants, down to the epoch of their discovery . . ."[17] Hence, Morgan was able to assert, the seventy Amerindian tribes, whose organization of consanguinity and affinity he had shown to form one comprehensive system, arose from a single group that had originated in Asia, migrated to and settled in the Pacific Northwest, and from there spread out eastward as far as Florida, southward as far as Patagonia.[18]

Morgan's thesis was a secular variant of the idea that had animated de Acosta. "Assuming the unity of origin of mankind," Morgan wrote in 1877, "the occupation of the earth occurred through migrations from an original center. The Asiatic continent must then be regarded as the cradle-land of the species, from the greater number of original types of man it contains in comparison with Europe, Africa, and America. It would also follow that the separation of the Negroes and Australians from the common stem occurred when society was organized on the basis of sex, . . . that the Polynesian migration occurred later, . . . and finally, that the Ganowanian migration to America occurred later still . . ." Morgan was careful to state that "these inferences are put forward simply as suggestions,"[19] but he employed these suggestions to argue in a manner similar to that of de Acosta that the Ganowanians came into possession of the American continent while still in a savage state and that

> Cut off thus early, and losing all further contact with the central stream of human progress, they commenced their career upon a new continent with the humble mental and moral endowment of savages. The independent evolution of the primary ideas they brought with them commenced under conditions insuring a career undisturbed by foreign influences.[20]

Both Morgan and Brinton insisted that though the Indian peoples were extra-continental in origin, Indian *culture* had developed in America *ab initio*. They disagreed over which land mass had been the original habitat of the Amerindians.

DANIEL GARRISON BRINTON (1837–1899)

Two years before Morgan published *Ancient Society,* the historian Hubert Howe Bancroft had completed his five volume report, the *Native Races of America.* He too found it necessary to review the status of the dispute over Amerindian origins. Conflating the Acostan and Garcian traditions, Bancroft summarized the claims put forward for all overseas and overland nominees in Europe, Asia, and Atlantis, and the more recent proposal of autochthony. Although he concluded his discussion by refusing to accept any of the theories—"no one at the present day," he wrote, "can tell the origin of the Americans; they may have come from any one, or from all the hypothetical sources. . . . And here the question must rest until we have more light on the subject."—he allowed that "the theory that America was peopled, or at least partly peopled, from eastern Asia, is certainly more widely advocated than any other, and, in my opinion, is moreover based upon a more reasonable and logical foundation than any other."[21] It was against the growing climate of opinion favoring Asiatic origins that Daniel Garrison Brinton pitted his efforts.

Brinton proposed that the myths, religion, and symbol systems of the American aborigines must have originated in America as independent inventions.[22] Opposing all proposals of cultural diffusion to America, and especially hostile to any proposal of Asiatic origins, Brinton developed a triple line of assault on such approaches: First, he rejected the authority of the Bible or any religious dogma on the discussion of human origins; second, he offered an anti-diffusionist and evolutionary explanation for the similarities in Asiatic and Amerindian cultures; and third, he refuted the specific claims made by adherents of either the Acostan or Garcian schools. Brinton championed the uniqueness of Amerindian cultures.

Brinton's way of accounting for the presence of prehistoric American humans who had a distinctive culture that nonetheless bore resemblances to those of some peoples in Asia began by distinguishing the question of physical from that of cultural origins: he explained cultural similarities as products of universal humanity. According to Brinton, geology, archaeology, and meteorology dictated that man had first crossed into America from western Europe during the close of the last Glacial Epoch, when the shallow bed of the North Atlantic formed a land bridge.[23] These early migrants settled in the area "east of the Rocky Mountains and between the receding wall of the continental ice sheet and the Gulf of Mexico," where they developed their racial characteristics in isolation from other groups of humans. Brinton insisted on the physical uniformity of what he called the "American race," despite its present division into tribes, and assured his readers that this physical type had evolved and become fixed in its somatic features very early in America, not long after the close of the Pleistocene period.

Brinton regarded cultural development as the representation of the mental endowments of the race. "These [mental endowments]," he asserted, "are what decide irrevocably its place in history and its destiny in time." Recognizing that other ethnologists had disagreed sharply over the rank appropriate to the psychic potentialities of the American race, Brinton proposed that assignment be based "on actual accomplished results not on supposed endowments." Basing his judgment on Morgan's work on governmental institutions and domestic architecture, A. F. Bandelier's investigations of property rights and the laws of war, Gustav Bruhl's examination of social conditions among Amerindians of Mexico and Peru, and his own extensive studies of American aboriginal languages, myths, and religions, Brinton concluded that "the American race certainly stands higher than the Australian, the Polynesian or the African, but does not equal the Asian." Because it fell below the latter, it could not have derived from it.

Brinton's comparative analysis of Indian arts and institutions not only sought to locate their precise place on the cultural ladder, but also to assure their lack of dependence on any other culture. This required the demonstration of a cultural unity among all the Indian tribes and rejection of their division into "wild" and "civilized" groups, a hangover from missionary endeavor. The differences among the several Indian tribes are far less than has been supposed, Brinton argued, and he went on to assert that "the Aztecs of Mexico and the Algonkins of the eastern United States were not far apart, if we overlook the objective art of architecture and one or two inventions," and to conclude that "American culture, wherever examined, presents a family likeness which the more careful observers of late years have taken pains to put in a strong light." A common Amerindian culture had developed out of inherent features, Brinton sought to show, and this culture had a political system and an architecture surpassing anything achieved by Africans or Polynesians, and a stone, clay, and wood artistry that "stands next to [that of] the white race." Moreover, Brinton asserted that he knew of "no product of Japanese, Chinese, or Dravidian sculpture . . . which exhibits the human face in greater dignity than the head in basalt figured by Humboldt as an Aztec priestess." Brinton also found evidence of considerable cultural advancement in the fact that "a phonetic system for recording ideas was reached in Mexico" and that there was "ample evidence that the notion of a single incorporeal Ruler of the universe had become familiar both to Tezcucans and Kechuas previous to the conquest." These internal developments gave important testimony for "a good natural capacity" while the common culture "strongly attests

[to] the ethnic unity of the race." But Brinton believed that "the receptivity of the race for a foreign civilization is not great," and he observed, in contradiction to the advocates of Asiatic cultural origins:

> Nowhere do we find any trace of foreign influence or instruction, nowhere any arts or social systems to explain which we must evoke the aid of teachers from the eastern hemisphere. The culture of the American race, in whatever degree they possessed it, was an indigenous growth, wholly self-developed, owing none of its germs to any other race, earmarked with the psychology of the stock.[24]

There still remained what Brinton acidly referred to as the "various supposed relations between the America and Asian races."[25] Composed of diffusionist arguments about physical and cultural similarities, Brinton disposed of most of these in short order. "But," as Brinton pointed out, "the inner stronghold of those who defend the Asiatic origin of Mexico and Central American civilization is, I am well aware, defended by no such feeble outposts as these, but by a triple line of entrenchment, consisting respectively of the Mexican calendar, the game of *patolli*, and the presence of Asiatic jade in America." Brinton's assault on this triple line constituted a fundamental establishment of American cultural autochthony and a defense of independent invention, isolated evolution, and the psychic unity of humankind. Turning to the alleged similarity between the Mexican and Central American calendar and that found among the tribes of Tibet and Tartary, a comparison first noticed by Alexander von Humboldt and supported by Edward B. Tylor in his famous proposal in behalf of Asiatic origins,[26] Brinton observed that "no one who will carefully trace the evolution of the Mexican calendar through the variations it assumed among the Maya tribes, the Nahuas, the Tarascos and the Mixtecas, can harbor any further doubt about it being a wholly indigenous American production." The resemblance between the Mexican game of *patolli* and the Persian and Hindustani game of *pachisi* was the cornerstone of Tylor's argument for the Asiatic origin of American lot-games and by extension Amerindian culture in general. So central was the *patolli* issue that it would remain one of the cardinal artifactual disputes in the trans-Pacific controversy to the present day. Brinton, relying on the careful investigations of Stewart Culin and Frank Hamilton Cushing, concluded that "*patolli* is thoroughly American in origin, no matter how closely it assimilates the East Indian game." The last bastion of the argument, the allegation that the particular kinds of jade found among the Indians indicated ancient commerce with Asia, was disposed of by showing that jade, jadeite, and nephrite are found in many places in the world and, hence, could not be employed as evidence for American intercourse with Asia. There remained the claims of certain philologists that an affinity existed between Asiatic and Amerindian tongues. Summoning up the authority of a lifetime spent in the study of American languages, Brinton proclaimed "unhesitatingly that no such affinities have been shown." [27]

The contacts between Asia and America alleged by interpreting the parallels, similarities, and identities between Asiatic and Amerindian cultures required more than a refutation of each artifact. Brinton adapted the principle of the psychic unity of humankind to resolve the controversy in favor of American autochthony. For Brinton this principle was "the corner stone of true anthropology." [28] Prior to its enunciation the problem posed by the discovery of similarities in cultures widely separated in space had been solved by postulating descent from a common culture or conjecturing about an earlier contact. After adoption of the principle, as Brinton approvingly quoted S. R. Steinmentz, "the concordance of two peoples in custom, etc. should be explained by borrowing or by derivation from a common source only when there are special, known and controlling reasons indicating this; and when they are absent, the explanation should be either because the two peoples are on the same plane of culture, or because their surroundings are similar." [29] So it was with the much-proclaimed Asiatic-Amerindian correspondences. Brinton observed that "the development of the religious sentiment, the gropings of man in the dark, to find out and define to his intelligence the mysterious power which masters the storm, moves the stars, and visits death and life, fate and fortune, on the sons of men, bear in all times and climes an almost fixed relation to the general intellectual development of the individual and the community." [30] Further, this fact explained not only the Asian-American parallelisms in religious tradition, myths, folklore, and familial institutions, but also the widespread development of such symbols as the swastika, cross, circle, serpent, sacred numbers, and many others. To Brinton these widely dispersed similarities merely proved "how man, everywhere different, is yet everywhere the same; and our reflection is that, whatsoever is his history, by whatsoever environment he is surrounded, in his slow progress from the darkness of savagery to the light of civilization he treads the same path, aids himself by the same weak supports, and seeks the same material wrappings in which to swathe the feeble progeny of his intellect and imagination." [31]

On the basis of his combined arguments, Brinton believed he had made his case for American cultural autochthony. As he wrote in 1894:

> I maintain . . . that up to the present time there has not been shown a single dialect, not an art nor an institution, not a myth or religious rite, not a domesticated plant or animal, not a tool, weapon, game or symbol, in use at the time of the discovery, which had been previously imported from Asia, or from any other continent of the Old World. [32]

Brinton's announcement of his proof for Amerindian autochthony was a revolution in Amerindian origins theories. Like Morgan with his Ganowanian theory, he had managed to circumvent the pre-Adamite controversy by declaring that some Pleistocene Europeans had first settled America, but even more than Morgan, Brinton separated the debate over human origins from that of cultural beginnings. The latter, he showed, had developed in isolation in America, untouched by foreign contacts. Whatever similarities existed between Amerindian and Asiatic, European or other cultures were *parallels,* reflecting the common mental faculties of humankind expressed in manners appropriate to cultural evolution and environmental limitations. In light of subsequent hypotheses proposing Amerindian origins for Asian culture, however, Brinton may have proved too much. Such hypotheses depended as much on the comparison of Asiatic and Amerindian culture traits as that of the Asian diffusionists rejected by Brinton. Moreover, Brinton's championship of the psychic unity of humankind could be turned against hypotheses of diffusion from America. The similarities in Asia and America might be deemed products of common human faculties. His mode of establishing the claim of autochthony for Amerindian culture could also foreclose any assertion of its subsequent movement to Asia.

AMERICA THE CRADLE OF ASIA: C. W. BROOKS AND R. STEWART CULIN

In 1876, Charles Wolcott Brooks, Japan's Consul in California and a member of the California Academy of Sciences, offered a complex theory of ancient American cultural autochthony and pre-Columbian Asian-Amerindian relations, differentiating the origin of the Chinese from that of the Japanese.[33] According to Brooks, the ancestors of the "Chinese race" had been migrants from a highly developed original civilization in South America. Unlike other Asian peoples, whose forebears had moved out from Asia Minor, "The Chinese have an immense antiquity," he reported. "They are . . . peculiar . . . very marked in their features . . . and . . . appear as an isolated people . . . [who] have long preserved the peculiar type of a race wholly unlike any other on the continent of Asia."[34] Refusing to entertain a hypothesis of Asian autochthony for any but pre-Sinic aborigines among the Chinese, Brooks proposed—in accordance with the assertedly perpetual trade wind blowing westward across the Pacific from Peru and the additional wind power supplied by complementary breezes from the Northern American hemisphere—that "if a large junk were started from the coast of Peru, near Central America, and kept off before these fair winds, there is a strong possibility that in sixty days she would strike the southern coast of China, about where early Chinese traditions place the origin of their race."[35] Brooks coupled his meteorological hypothesis with another ethnologist's claim that identical features are to be found among the western tribes of Brazil and the Chinese and with his own interpretation of certain pieces of philological and linguistic evidence. Noting that the remarkable engineering and architectural feats of the ancient peoples of Yucatan could not rule out the presence of correlative shipbuilding and navigational arts, he allowed that there was a "possibility . . . that the ancestry of China may have embarked in large vessels, as emigrants, perhaps from the vicinity of the Chincha Islands; or proceeded with a large fleet . . . from the neighborhood of Peru to the country now known to us as China."[36] Indeed, Brooks asserted that "the construction of a Peruvian or Central American fleet of large vessels, in early ages, capable of transferring to China, if not 100,000 people, certainly quite sufficient to establish a colony, would require far less skill or enterprise, than that which raised the pyramids of either Central America or Egypt."[37] Turning to ancient Chinese annals, Brooks pointed to similarities in terms in Amerindian and Chinese speech and to the earliest record of Chinese political organization, dating from 3588 B.C., reporting the deification of a stranger king from overseas, Tai Ko Foki, who had introduced hieroglyphic characters and lunar monthly and solar annual calendars, i.e., culture products and scientific processes associated with the high civilizations of ancient Peru and Mexico. Moreover, Brooks dismissed the possibility that the ancient Americans had come from Siberiatic Asia via the Bering Straits, for no traces of such a people, employing the arts and architecture that produced the kind of pyramids constructed in India, China, Tahiti, and Central and South America, are to be found along that route. "Long before Egypt, the progenitor of Greece and Europe, was settled," he concluded, "the inhabitants of Yucatan appear by their monuments to have been well advanced in general intellectual attainments, and to have led all known nations in art and science. Why may not a branch of this people have emigrated to China and Egypt, and there have become a large and advanced nation?"[38]

Brooks's separation of Japanese-Amerindian relations from the Chinese proceeds as part of his elaborate proof of world oceanic contacts in antiquity[39] and his argument for Peruvian origins of Chinese civilization. Never designating the precise origins of the Japanese people,[40] Brooks accepted the Japanese claim that they had no ethnical connections to the Chinese. He did not conclude that the people called Japanese had been altogether untouched by an admixture of migrating peoples; rather, his entire ethnological project presupposed that "early races have been far more spread and intermixed by early maritime intercourse than the casual observer would suppose, and that, however distinct any type of mankind may appear, all will be found to be more or less composite, excepting, perhaps, some remnants of early aborigines, driven into a forced seclusion among the fastnesses of interior mountain ranges."[41] Whatever the origins of the composite that makes up the Japanese people, Brooks directed his attention to their subsequent contributions to the recomposition of other peoples, especially the Amerindians.

Noting that every "junk found adrift or stranded on the coast of North America, or on the Hawaiian or adjacent islands, has on examination proved to be Japanese, and [that] no single instance of any Chinese vessel has ever been reported, nor is any believed to have existed," Brooks pointed to the course of the *Kuro Shiwo,* the ocean current that "sweeps northeasterly past Japan toward the Kurile and Aleutian Islands, thence curving around and passing south along the coast of Alaska, Oregon, and California."[42] The current, he argued, made it likely that "Small parties of male Japanese have repeatedly reached the American continent by sea, cast upon its shores after floating helplessly for months." Three years before Brooks put forth his hypothesis, Horace Davis had presented to the American Antiquarian Society a lengthy "Record of Japanese Vessels Driven Upon the North-West Coast of America and its Outlying Islands," speculating that "these facts are very interesting to illustrate the possible course of [an earlier] migration," and adding that "any anomalies observed among the northwest coast Indians may possibly receive some light from the likelihood of an infusion of Japanese blood."[43] Brooks recorded an even longer list of wrecked Japanese junks and reinforced the hypothesis of Japanese-Indian admixture with the evidence of linguistics:

> Many shipwrecked Japanese have informed me that they were able to communicate with and understand the natives of Atka and Adakh Islands. Quite an infusion of Japanese words is found among some of the coast tribes of Oregon and California, either pure, *tsche-tsche,* milk, or clipped, as *hiaku,* speed, found reduced to *hyack,* meaning fast, in Indian; or *yaku,* evil genius in Japanese, similarly reduced to *yak,* devil, by the Indians. In almost all words showing such similarity, the Indian word is always an abbreviated word, or shorter word than the Japanese, from which it may be argued that the latter was the original and the former derived.[44]

Brooks pointed out that "shipwrecked Japanese are invariably enabled to communicate understandingly with the coast Indians, although speaking quite a different language." He reasoned that the earlier Japanese castaway seamen, "often illiterate, and separated from their sources of learning, necessarily lost their own language; but in doing so, doubtless contributed many isolated words to the Indian dialects of this coast."[45]

According to Brooks neither the Peruvians who migrated to China nor the Japanese who drifted to America could return to their lands of origin. The Peruvian fleet that, in Brooks's hypothesis, "may have reached China with the first emigration, perhaps bearing a hero-sovereign and an invading army, . . . [would have been] unable to return against those perpetual winds which brought them . . . [and] were compelled to establish themselves in new territory."[46] By the same token, the Japanese cast up on the coasts of the Americas in prehistoric antiquity would have been unable to evade the "Great Circle" of the *Kuro Shiwo* and could only return if they happened to fall into the current blowing westward from Peru. Such currents could also explain the drift of plants and animals across the Pacific and among the islands of that ocean, so that Brooks provided a solution to the perplexing proliferation of flora and fauna in Asia, the Americas, and Hawaii.

Brooks's hypotheses about Chinese origins in Peru and Japanese contributions to coastal Indian languages were not unrelated to his role as a benevolent advocate of America's imperial mission in Asia and the Pacific.[47] The immigration of Chinese laborers to America seemed to him but one more instance of natural law:

> Chinese are coming; the movement is well under way; its progress seems inevitable; natural laws are at work, greater than man's ability to combat. To forcibly attempt its stay is of no avail, for it is thoroughly legal; whether it develops this year or next, is of little moment.[48]

However, Brooks noted, these Chinese, whose ancient ancestors he would later show to have been Peruvian Indians, were being mercilessly exploited by the coolie trade to South America and were opposed altogether by Irish laborers and their spokesmen in California. To each of these contradictory themes, Brooks gave an answer, couching his firm support for the regulation rather than prohibition of immigration from China within the context of a benevolent, universal, scientific cosmology that heralded American ascendancy in the Pacific. "Earth supplies," he noted, are "in appointed time, from hidden reserves, what becomes necessary for the wants of man."[49] The wants of American men in the late nineteenth century were "cheap muscular labor"[50] in search of which America had become a customer in the labor markets of the entire world. Just as early trade and migrations had made first the Phoenicians and then the South Arabians the masters of the ancient seas and the merchant leaders of antiquity,[51] so in the modern era, wresting command of the Pacific commerce in goods and people vouchsafed a glorious golden age for the United States: "We cannot hold too sanguine a conception of the magnificent future of this great ocean when we predict that the day will come when that nation which controls the Pacific will command a trade equal to that of the world today."[52] America, Brooks went on, was the leader of the West, the empire that was destined to encircle the globe; China, on the other hand, had followed its own historically and culturally ineluctable fate, and remained stationary and settled within its own continental domain. Hence, precisely because China was a land ruled by a conservative oligarchy of scholars, gentry, and literati, an empire that cultivated Confucian familistic idealism and enforced the virtual immobility of its vast population of smallholding peasantry attached to local clans, it neither threatened the impending Occidental mercantile hegemony in the Pacific nor encouraged the emigration of more than its landless, unemployed denizens from overpopulated districts.[53] America, thence, and particularly California, its vanguard on the Pacific, should oppose the shortsighted anti-Chinese attitude of the Irish workers in their midst and "become masters of the situation, . . . direct a system furnishing us Asiatic laborers, so as to advance and elevate all of our present white laboring classes who have within them ability to rise."[54] Brooks proposed an immigration policy that would introduce Chinese laborers into America gradually but constantly. After "supplying the large deficit of labor at the South, and furnishing sufficient for the inauguration of new enterprises, it will enable all who are capable to advance—and keep pace with the gradual withdrawal of their competitors—from menial labor to higher positions."[55] At the same time, Brooks continued, American transportation policy should not take as its model that followed by the Portuguese and Peruvian compradors of the coolie trade at Amoy and Macao, "the disreputable manner in which . . . [Chinese] men were 'shanghaed' for slavery at the Chincha Islands."[56] Thus, Brooks's analysis implied that the lineal progeny of the Amerindian founders of the Chinese civilization established by Tai Ko Foki were forcibly returning its Sinic descendants to the land of their ancestry—as degraded slaves! America ought to honor a greater morality, he urged: "People of China and Japan, ever watchful of our example, may learn that Christian practice is too often at variance with Christian profession, if we treat them now as heathen having no rights which Christians are bound to respect."[57] America should regulate its passenger trade so as to ensure safe and healthy passage to Chinese laborers. Moreover, Brooks urged, it was important to recognize the economic possibilities of Chinese mercantile development for capital investment in America: "If Chinese were not promiscuously stoned and outraged in our streets, their capitalists might come to us. . . . Sums thus received would assist materially in relieving the tightness of our money market, without perceptibly depleting the immense monetary eddy, so long chronic in China, and inaugurate a healthy and complete circulation of specie around the world, highly beneficial to all."[58] Thus would America's place as an originator of civilization at last reap the rewards of its millennia-old enterprise. "Our Golden Gate, so long the outlet, will some day become an inlet of wealth and precious metals. . . ."[59] Ultimately the material benefits will induce a Christian spiritual reawakening: "Pagans, who have beheld the glory of a Western Empire, instructed in civilization, return to their native districts, effective missionaries in the cause of enlightenment; ready and eager to combat the absurdities of paganism in every section of Asia, where foreign footsteps are unknown, and thus largely influence for good, the destiny and future welfare of the human race in Oriental empires."[60]

As Brooks saw the matter, China's four thousand years of recorded history "assisted in molding the character of this secluded race."[61] The Chinese, thence, were "heirs, today, of the collected wisdom of many centuries"[62] and had retained "a peculiar individuality, the result of organization, shut out from active participation with the outside world."[63] The Chinese were "national hermits" whose civilization, once initiated by Peruvian Paleo-Indians, had developed in and encouraged Oriental isolation under the philosophical guidance of Confucius, Brahma, and Zoroaster. In contrast, the Occident had "moved westward under Hebrew and Christian precepts."[64] Because "social progress has been in proportion to intellectual development, and the organization of the best intellects is sure to rule the world,"[65] Brooks sought to add the Chinese to the American advancement westward: "As a race, their mental power will render efficient aid in their service to the people of the United States."[66]

Brooks adopted a different attitude toward the Japanese. As a separate people, whose history, language, and ethnology had no connection to China, they were not to be treated as Asiatic hermits unmindful of the farther reaches of humanity. Their junks had proceeded into the Pacific as far as the island chains west of Hawaii,[67] and Japan's coastal traders were often enough blown across the Pacific to cast up seamen on American shores. The 250 years of isolation imposed by the Tokugawa regime had happily been broken by Perry in 1854 and Japan's intercourse with the world had been given domestic support by the new Meiji regime after 1868. Diplomatic developments had promoted Brooks to the position of Japan's consular representative in San Francisco, led to Japan's abrogation of its ban on repatriation of castaway nationals, and facilitated the Bakufu's acceptance of Brooks's nominees, Professors William P. Blake and Raphael Pumpelly, as, respectively, Imperial Mineralogist and Mining Engineer. Brooks praised the "many young Japanese [who] are already attracted to scientific pursuits" and observed with considerable satisfaction that "their valuable technical as well as general results are beginning to claim the attention of naturalists."[68] Far more than the Chinese, it seemed to Brooks, the Japanese were a people of the rising sun in the Far East. It was the Japanese who had drifted or sailed or been castaway in Paleoamerica, not the Chinese whose legendary claims to pre–Columbian-American contact were too fabulous to be believed. Brooks claimed that Japan, not California, was "Fusang," the fabled land of mulberry cultivation, visited in antiquity by a Chinese Buddhist Priest.[69] The Chinese could not have sailed to America, he insisted. Fusang "was probably reached by a coasting voyage along the western coast of Corea, thence along the northern coast of Niphon, where mulberry trees were than cultivated abundantly. . . ."[70] Brooks disposed of the trans-Pacific claims for China's Buddhist priest in short order: "A careful study of the native records seems to indicate that his much mooted Chinese voyage could not possibly have extended to the American coast."[71] It was, thence, Japan that had inspired China's priestly imagination, Japanese sailors who had contributed to Amerindian cultures, and Japan that would lead in the Westernization of Asia.

More than twenty-five years after Brooks put forward his heterodoxical position, Robert Stewart Culin, curator of the Brooklyn Museum, startled the 1902 annual meeting of the section on ethnology of the American Association for the Advancement of Science with the claim that America was the "cradle of Asia."[72] According to Culin, America was the originating place of the oldest divination ceremonies, the precursor of world civilizations. Following in the tradition first enunciated by de La Peyrere, Culin openly repudiated the designation of America as the "New World." The Old World/New World dichotomy was a product of Christian dogma, he insisted; adherence to it in the modern age amounted to ecclesiolatry. If there was an Old World, he pointed out, it was to be found in America, more particularly among the ancestors of the Southwestern Zuni. Culin was a specialist in the crosscultural study of Asiatic, Amerindian, and Occidental games, which he insisted were the artifactual survival form of antique divination rites associated with the mystical significance of the arrow. He carefully studied the structure, process, history, and movement of games, game implements, and game derivatives in American Chinatowns, Zuni tribal areas, Japan, Korea, China, and Oceania. Culin extended his studies to Central Asia, Africa, and Europe, ultimately proposing a circular global diffusion of the original arrow-based divination culture of paleoamerican Zuniland.

Starting out with the hypothesis that America might be the *old* world led Culin to search out the high antiquity of those game forms represented in surviving Amerindian and Asiatic amusements. His strategic entree to this search was through the arrow,[73] an implement that Culin asserted was also a symbol and an icon.*[80] Believing that the arrow was among the earliest expressions and emblems of man, Culin observed its usages in various aesthetic motifs to represent men and clans; moreover, the arrow was associated with the most primeval gods. Arrow forms, shaftments, and bundles are found throughout the Americas, Culin pointed out, and, in their derivative modifications such as appear in canes, bundles of sticks, and primitive dice, they become the basic elements in games of chance and dexterity among the North American Indians.[81] They are also found in Asiatic games, ancient and modern, in Japan, China, and Korea. Culin was sure that divinatory practices, ceremonials, and the religious precursors of games had originated in America. As he put the matter in 1907:

> There is no evidence that any of the games described were imported into America at any time either before or after the Conquest. On the other hand, they appear to be the direct and natural outgrowth of aboriginal institutions in America. They show no modifications due to white influence other than the decay which characterizes all Indian institutions under existing conditions.[82]

*Culin derived his argument for the antiquity of the arrow and its relationship to divination and thence to games from ethnological reports on the Zuni tribe living in New Mexico. The Zuni played a game called *sho-li-we* that had been described by John G. Owens in 1891.[74] A breakthrough in understanding the great importance of this game for his own thesis came through the comprehensive analysis of *sho-li-we* as a divinatory practice by Frank Hamilton Cushing.[75] As Culin saw it, the central importance of Cushing's discussion of the Zuni game of *sho-li-we* was that it permitted him to reformulate his understanding of the interrelation and common origin of Indian games. Culin had begun to suspect that "behind both ceremonies and games there existed some widespread myth from which both derived their impulse.[76] The myth of the divine Twins, contending offspring of the sun, who live in the east and west, rule over night and day, are the morning and evening stars, and whose virgin mother appears as their sister, wife, and grandmother and is the moon, the earth, and the feminine principle in nature, proved to meet all requirements. Cushing had related this myth in 1896,[77] and Culin identified the Twins as "the original patrons of play, and [he asserted that] their games are the games now played by men."[78] More to the point, however, were the weapons carried by these divine twins. They are always spoken of and pictured with "a throwing-club made of heavy wood. . . . bows and cane arrows, . . . bows interchangeable with a lance, and a netted shield." The four-fold divisions of weapons is in turn matched by a four-fold division in their markings and led to similar divisions in gaming. To Culin, "Gaming implements are almost exclusively derived from these symbolic weapons.[79] Thus, stick dice, counting sticks, engraved and painted tubes, and many other game materials are traceable to arrows, arrow shaftments, or bows. Even Indian ball games—although more difficult to derive from the original mythic artifacts—employ rackets whose origin Culin derived from the divine shield. With a divinatory game that could be traced back to the most ancient period, using a basic form—the arrow—that might evolve and devolve into a variety of specific usages, styles, and motifs, and that might be carried abroad by migrants and travelers and introduced into the artistic, religious, military, and recreational life of other cultures, Culin had the first piece in the solution to his geo-cultural puzzle.

Having suggested the strong likelihood for the antiquity and autochthony of the Amerindian culture complex, Culin challenged the applicability of the theory of psychic unity to explain similarities in Asian
and Amerindian artifacts and practices. The apparent similarities between Asiatic and Amerindian artifacts, Culin argued, represented the
diffusion, evolution, and survival of the Amerindian arrow divination
and ceremonial culture; therefore, they indicated the likelihood of American origins. Culin went beyond the claim for *similarities* and put forward the more extreme suggestion of *identity* between the artifacts of
Asia and the Amerindians, "We find," he asserted, "upon the Western
continent things not only similar to those of Asia, but precisely identical with them . . ." These things were "not only the same in form and
use, but in source and development as well . . ." Ultimately, Culin concluded that Brinton's psychic unity thesis could not account for these
identities because they are "at the same time so empirical and complex
that no theory of their having been produced independently under like
conditions, of their being the products of a similar yet independent
creative impulse, seems longer tenable."[83] Culin sought to establish the
temporal priority of prehistoric American culture in relation to that of
Asia, with special attention to modes of Asiatic divination. Selecting
the *Yi King* (i.e., *I Ching*) as the oldest surviving work of Chinese culture, dating from the Twelfth Century B.C., Culin pointed out that it
was a basic treatise on divination and fortune-telling and that it employed fifty slender polished wood or ivory rods as ritual sticks. These
sticks "find their exact counterpart in America in the gambling sticks
used by many [Indian] tribes." The Chinese believed that the divination
splints were originally made from the stalks of a plant—the *Ptarmica si-
berica*—but Culin insisted that their American precursors—such as
those found among Amerindian natives in California's Hupa Valley and
used for guessing games by Amerindian tribes from the Pacific to the
Atlantic coasts—were "gambling rods which with their bands or ribbons of color may be referred to the similarly marked shaftments of arrows, from which they are clearly derived."[84] In the former area, the
arrow, the symbol of warrior and man, is used in conjunction with
totemic animals to fashion gaming materials. Turning then to his Asiatic materials, Culin observes that Korean playing cards appear to be
derived from a similar divinatory source, since their backs are marked
with pictures of a feather, their fronts with totemic animals, and their
game name is called "fighting arrows." Chinese cards are also notched
in a similar manner. "It is clear," Culin concludes, "that the American
sticks serve to explain the derivation of the Korean cards," while the
Chinese cards "are clearly the legitimate descendants of the arrow-
derived gambling-sticks."[85] But Culin goes even further in his argument. The Chinese cards, originating from the arrow divination rites of

the ancient Amerindians, are in turn the source for European playing cards, the latter being but a broader version of the Asiatic motif still represented in mutated fashion on old Spanish packs. America, thence, was not only a cradle for Asia but for Europe as well.

Culin proceeded to argue for arrow origins—or from ancient Zuni ceremonial and divinatory origins—for a whole series of Asiatic culture forms, art and craft motifs, games, and symbols. The *baho,* East Indian prayer sticks, were originally arrows. Visiting cards, common among Asiatics, also had signs of an arrow origin. In contemporary China the fact that a popular game called "Chief of the Literati" was employed as an emblem of man a counter in the form of an arrow was a clear indication of American origins to Culin. Ainu boys in Japan play a game of "hoop and pole," the hoop of which is traceable to the spider web, hence to ceremonies of generation and fertility, and ultimately to the Spider Goddess known to the Zuni as the virgin mother of the divine Twins. Culin daringly suggested that even the ancient Babylonian seal cylinder was a synthetic derivation of two American antiquities— Pacific coast arrow-headed gambling sticks and cylindrical pottery stamps found farther to the south but "not unlikely of kindred origin."[86]

Culin's researches on Korean and Chinese games had provided him with his first evidence of the originating character of American arrow divination myths and implements. In the games which could be shown to descend directly from the divinatory practices could be found what Culin called "games *par excellence*." Such games "hold a peculiar position among the world's amusements," he observed, because they "frequently retain something of their original character and often survive in two forms, more or less distinct—as a divinatory rite and as a simple amusement." Korean games presented these characteristics, and even more to the point, these games and divinatory practices employed the arrow or its representational substitute as the implement of magic, and thus revealed their ancient American origins. Although he analyzed Chinese and Japanese games, the Korean games proved most hospitable to Culin's thesis. Conditions in that land favored the survival of basic cultural forms and the preservation of pristine mythical orientations. These were still to be found in everyday life. Among these, the most important was the system of division and classification according to four cardinal points—east, south, west, north—and the middle.[87] Found among many American tribes, Culin observed, this system had been declared primordial to the mythology of the ancient Zuni. Among the Koreans this classificatory system found expression in early maps of the world,[88] enrollment procedures and designations for students in modern-day Seoul, the pattern of Korean city development, the geographical and administrative organization of provinces, and the rules of popular Korean games. As a fundamental system, the four-cardinal-points-and-the-middle provided a way of organizing all information, Culin asserted. However, as he observed, "things and affairs were encountered which did not in themselves reveal their proper assignment." To resolve such quandaries, primitive peoples had to resort to magic and divination. "The processes," Culin observed, "at first serious and divinatory, afterwards practiced as a means of diversion as children play at the serious business of life, became games."

Culin's study of Asiatic games grew out of his early contacts with and intensive studies of the Chinese immigrants in Philadelphia and other eastern cities of the United States during the decade between 1887 and 1896. Inspired by Frank Hamilton Cushing's suggestion that Asian and Indian games be compared as part of an investigation of civilizational origins, Culin's researches turned again and again to a detailed investigation of the gambling games played in the ghetto basements and dimly lit meeting halls of Chinatown. These researches resulted in seven separate studies on Chinese religious ceremonies, modes of divination and fortune-telling, and games of chance.[89] The arrow motif was discovered to be at the root of each. In the gambling houses, opium dens, and religious temples of the tiny Asiatic community, Culin—fully aware of but refusing to be swayed by the popular prejudices that denigrated the Chinese immigrants—found further evidence of the origin, trans-pacific migration, and survival of ancient Amerindian culture. The very gambling games—and the divinatory practices associated by the Chinese with them—that were grist for the Sinophobe's mill were to Culin proof of ancient civilization and its resilience.

To complete his thesis, Culin turned to that vital piece of evidence that had captured the imagination of recent champions of Asiatic origins, the supposedly strongest fortress of that triple line of entrenchment to which Brinton had referred, the Mexican game of *patolli*. Culin employed Tylor's conception of diffusion, but reversed his argument. *Patolli,* the Amerindian game, was the precursor, *pachisi* the descendant. The cultural movement had been from America to Asia. Culin delivered a telling blow to Tylor's thesis.[90] *Patolli,* Culin argued, belonged to a division of games all of which were played with dice, whose origin and antiquity he had already ascertained as Amerindian. "After a careful examination of all the forms of the American game," he pointed out, "it is apparent to the present writer that we have in the native [American] culture all contributory and formative elements that led to its invention and development." Culin dismissed as inapplicable the anthropological theorem that held that the oldest forms of a thing "are often found surviving at places most remote from their origin" since in *patolli*'s evolution "we have too many evidences of the orderly development of this game in America to regard it as a case in point." As Culin saw the matter, the ancient Amerindian culture complex produced an

unmistakable line of development, begun in the southwest with divination rods and arrow icons and completed in gambling games played
with sticks and dice. *Patolli,* Culin concluded, "is like all the American
games, so clearly the outgrowth of native rituals and ceremonies, so
identified and bound up with them, that we have no reason to believe it
was borrowed directly from Asia . . ." Moreover, Culin went on, separate lines of development had diverged from their common American
source; "the Asiatic forms, of which there are many, all [exist] along
lines representing a development from, rather than toward America."
"If the relation be that of parent and child," he went on, "the parent, it
would seem, is here."[91]

To Culin all these evidences pointed to the "fallacy of looking for
traces of Eastern civilization upon our continents." Migration and evolution had occurred, Culin argued, in quite the opposite temporal and
geographical order: the Far Eastern civilizations of today exhibit traces
of the Amerindian civilization of antiquity. Culin speculated on how it
could be possible that Amerindian survivals are to be found in Asia. His
answer to this fundamental question—the question that had forced the
cautious de Acosta, who was sure of Asiatic forerunners of the Amerindian civilization, to insist on concrete proofs and specified land bridges—
was less specific, lacked force, and failed to fulfill the promise of his earlier statement that man had "evidently wandered far and wide over the
world before history began." These wanderings, it could be inferred,
included movement from America to Asia and the transportation not
only of people but of culture as well. Beyond this vague statement
Culin did not go. But he had an even greater and more profound thesis
to proclaim. Noting that the games of the ancient East and ancient
America were not merely similar but "practically identical," that they
were alike not only "in externals but, if we may so apply the word, in
their morphology as well," Culin concluded that "they extend over into
Asia from America as expressions of the same underlying culture. They
belong to the *same* culture."[92] As parts of the *same* culture their spread
and adaptation seemed to require no further explanation. Asia and
America comprised a single culture area.

THE TRIUMPH OF THE ACOSTAN POSITION

Despite the intellectual efforts of Brooks and Culin, the twentieth
century has witnessed an overwhelming victory by the Acostan position, favoring Asiatic origins for ancient American peoples and Asian
contributions to Amerindian culture and permitting debate over the

Oriental and autochthonous elements of the ancient civilizations of Mexico and Peru.[93] Both the isolated independent invention thesis and the Acostan perspective give license to the conventional disciplinary bifurcation in historical and social scientific approaches to the Americas: a post-Columbian, "Conquest," or Eurocentric period of state formation and Christian cultural penetration, capable of documentary analysis by historians and sociologists; and a pre-Columbian, pagan, Asian-Amerindian, or pre-civil period, open to the ethnological investigations of archaeologists, paleontologists, anthropologists, and, less legitimately, to occultists. The adjustments, adaptations, and problems of Asian-Americans and Amerindians are thereby conceived in contemporary terms, i.e., in the context of the post-Columbian situation. Hence, the debate between advocates of assimilation, proponents of pluralism, and champions of radical, revolutionary, or secessionist alternatives to Asian-American life turns on the analysis of events temporally confined to the period of modern, i.e. nineteenth- and twentieth-century, immigration and to conditions of adjustment within national and largely Christian state-societies. The "New World" has become a root metaphor, an ingredient deeply embedded in the Occidental, perhaps in the global, cake of intellectual custom and in the common understanding. It carries with it a legacy of presuppositions, perspectives, and consequences, originally religious, that have seeped into the conventions of secular law, social science, politics, and everyday life.

Essential to this heritage of assumption is the idea that Christian, European state-society ascendancy on the American continents was epochal. Spanish, Portuguese, French, and English seaborne empires established outposts in the Americas, and though the capitalized term "Conquest" refers to the victory of Spanish imperial rule over Central and South American Amerindians, the word is a synecdoche for the larger idea of triumphant European hegemony. More significant than military success and political domination is the conqueror's self-proclaimed right to rewrite history, re-interpret philosophy, and re-order the priorities of social science to suit imperial purposes. Theological imperatives, religious missions, and practical interests weaved in and out of one another, at first uneasily, at last producing the skein of the Old and New World distinction.[94] Part of the fabric enlarged the cultural solidarity contained in the idea of Europe,[95] while another emphasized the utter separateness of the Indian and his forebears from the American national fragment and the ineluctable decline of the Amerindian cultures.[96] As a cosmological idea, Europe in the sixteenth, seventeenth, and eighteenth centuries embodied Christendom, and with the Conquest and subsequent settlements, "Europe was to achieve a universal, if temporary, dominance in the world which had been denied to Christendom"[97] before that time.

Asia, once conceived by Herodotus to be an integral part of the unitary land mass that he believed had been mistakenly divided into tripartite Europe, Asia, Africa,[98] was firmly cut off from the idea of Europe after the Conquest. Indeed, from the point of view of the expansion of Eurocentric Christendom, Asia became an objective of the continuation of the Conquest, modified, as was the original European foray into the Americas, by the jurisdictional competition for souls between Roman Catholicism, Greek Orthodoxy, and Protestantism.[99] This paradox—for it was in search of a sea route to Asia that Columbus had sailed—is resolved when we remember the explanatory force that ancient Asiatic migrations to the Americas gave to biblical accounts of the origins of man and his movements over the earth. As either precursors of Amerindian civilization, or, in the heterodoxical version of Brooks, as both contributors and beneficiaries of pre-historic American cultures, the Asians and their civilization were reallocated a pre-Columbian importance that would reduce the significance and vitality of their civilization for the peoples and cultures of the post-Conquest era. Hegel set the tone for this new conception in his introductory lectures on the philosophy of world history, asserting "World history travels from East to West; for Europe is the absolute end of History, just as Asia is the beginning." Confronted by the conundrum posed if world history were to travel west of America and reach Asia, Hegel retorted that "World history has an absolute east, although the term itself is wholly relative; for although the earth is a sphere, history does not move in a circle around it, but has a definite eastern extremity, i.e. Asia. It is here that the external and physical sun rises, and it sets in the west."[100]

In the late eighteenth century, the United States of America emerged as the first post-colonial republic in the Americas. Although it severed its political connections from European imperialism, it adapted the idea of Eurocentric cultural and religious dominance to its own national self-understanding. Indeed, in the prophetic words of Alexander Hamilton, the new republic, if only it remained unified, would become not merely the political successor of Europe on the American continent but the remaker of cosmological definitions of Euro-American connections. As Hamilton saw it, Europe had "by her arms and by her negotiations, by force and by fraud, . . . in different degrees extended her dominion over . . . Africa, Asia, and America . . ." Europe's "superiority," he went on, had "tempted her to plume herself as the Mistress of the World, and to consider the rest of mankind as created for her benefit." The people of the thirteen post-colonial American states would have to disabuse the world of those "Facts [that] have too long supported these arrogant pretensions of the Europeans . . . [and] vindicate the honor of the human race . . ." They could do so by "erecting one great American system, superior to the control of all transatlantic force or influence, and able to dictate the terms of connection between the old and the new world!"[101] The American system that Hamilton had proposed took as its cultural and intellectual model the Anglo-Saxon Puritan covenant; hence it was compelled to pose anew the question of who might be admitted and who excluded from its newly constituted, secular, national compact.[102] In developing answers to this question, American thinkers, legislatures, policy-makers, and courts have applied post-Columbian ecclesiastical and secular thought to the problems of citizenship, civil rights, and civil association. The conclusions about ancient transpacific migrations, the formation of Amerindian human groups, and the continuities, discontinuities, and adaptations of pre-Conquest cultures formed a baseline dividing primitive from modern man. From this line, civic qualifications—admission, exclusion, restriction—might be determined. In effect, racial ideas became conflated with biblical thought and Acostan reasoning, rendering first Indians, then blacks and finally Asiatics, as part of the pre-Columbian, i.e., pre-civilized population groups of America. Their admission to the American compact would be determined by their capacity to acquiesce to post-Conquest, Eurocentric, cultural imperatives. And, when these groups asserted an ethnic self-consciousness under their own group determination, they reached back into the pre-Columbian period to assert claims on a prioritized Americanization.

Neither Amerindians nor Asians in America have attained civic benefits from any form of identification with one another. In 1854, in a celebrated court case, Chinese testimony was placed in the same category as that of Indians and excluded from California's courts in all cases involving white people. In rendering his decision, Chief Justice Murray, speaking for a majority of the state's supreme court, took note of the hypothesis "that this continent was first peopled by Asiatics, who crossed Behring's Straits, and from thence found their way down to the more fruitful climates of Mexico and South America"; pointed to the resemblances of the Aleuts to both the peoples of "Asiatic Kamtschatka" and the "Alaskan Esquimaux," who in turn "resemble other tribes of American Indians"; urged American jurisprudence to give legal credence to Columbus's avowed intention to reach Asia; and, while not altogether rejecting the possibility that future scientific investigations might show the American aborigines to be a "distinct type," declared "that the name of Indian . . . has been used to designate not alone the North American but the whole of the Mongolian race."[103] Sixty-eight years later, the Supreme Court of the United States refused to rule in favor of the petition for citizenship of Takao Ozawa—a man born in Japan, emigrated to Hawaii, educated in the American public schools and at the University of California—on the grounds that, being neither a "free white person" nor a person of "African nativity" or "African descent," he fell outside the categories lawfully eligible for naturalization in the United States.[104] In support of the Court's negative decision, the attorney-general of California had filed an *amicus curiae* brief in which was inserted the testimony of Professor Ales Hrdlicka, curator of the division of physical anthropology, Smithsonian National Museum, before the House of Representatives on July 17, 1922. Hrdlicka was the principal advocate of a strict and conservative Acostan theory of Asiatic Amerindian origins and refused to believe that any humans had lived in North America in the Pleistocene epoch or earlier. As to the formation of an American nation, Hrdlicka dated its morphological beginnings from the seventeenth-century English colonial settlements and its culmination in the fixed establishment of a physically distinctive "old American" type. He scoffed at the idea that the racial trend might move in the direction of the Asia-derived Amerindian body type.[105] The pre-Columbian Americas, he insisted, had been first settled by an utterly alien "yellow-brown" people from eastern Asia.[106]

Ozawa's argument—in great part dependent on the claim that the naturalization of Japanese be considered apart from any impediments previously imposed on an assertedly wholly different people, the Chinese, and in accord with either an ethnological recognition that Japanese might be "white," or, foregoing the divided opinions among ethnologists, an acceptance of the term "white" as referring to all persons not Negro—was rebuffed by Hrdlicka's testimony. Asked if the Japanese could be considered white, Hrdlicka observed that "There can hardly be anything in anthropology more positive than the fact that, on the whole, the Japanese are yellow-brown, or Asiatic, or 'Mongoloids' . . ." Although he allowed that "the Japanese, like the Chinese, the Koreans and all other branches of the yellow-brown people, like the larger groups of our own race, contain some foreign admixture," Hrdlicka insisted that the "proportion of white blood . . . of Japan . . . is practically nil." Moreover, the anthropologist noted, the Japanese not only belong to a race physically different from "white people" but "apparently they also differ from them more or less mentally." Asked whether the term "Mongolian" might be applied to all of the yellow-brown people, Hrdlicka answered "yes; except that originally the Malays and the American Indians were kept separate, until they were sufficiently studied and shown to possess the same basic characteristics, and to have come from somewhere in eastern Asia."[107] Thus, in the views expressed by and before the supreme courts of California and the United States, the Acostan tradition, originally designed to link pre-Columbian investigations to acceptance of the biblical insistence on the common descent of all of humankind, had come to bear witness to the civil dissociation of the Asians and Amerindians from the descendants of the post-Conquest European peoples in America. Naturalization would eventually be extended to the Chinese in 1943 and the Japanese in 1952, but the theoretical and ethnological issues remained unresolved.

In the six decades since the Ozawa decision the Acostan perspective has achieved a virtual monopoly over investigations of Amerindian beginnings and Asian-American contacts. What debate there is centers on locating the precise time and exact place of Asiatic origins of Mexican and Peruvian civilizations and the measured degree to which Asiatics contributed to an otherwise isolated and autochthonous civilizational complex. The Garcian tradition survives among occultists, and recently it has been infused by a resurgent ethno-national consciousness among minority groups in America claiming Norse, African, Japanese, and Jewish contacts with or formation of pre-Columbian Americans. The perspectives associated with Brooks and with Culin, and by extension with de La Peyrere, have virtually no advocates. Neither Brooks nor Culin had students, developed a school around their ethnological orientation, or attracted a following.[108]

· The study of post-Columbian societies has largely been in the hands of historians and sociologists who, by relegating the pre-Columbian epoch and its problems to archaeologists, paleontologists, and anthropologists, give tacit recognition to Eurocentric religious ideas and secular social theory. Among students of Asian-American relations, questions turn on the adjustment of Chinese, Japanese, Korean, and more recently, Indo-Chinese immigrants and their offspring to *white,* Anglo-Saxon, Christian America. Assimilation, the ruling concept of American theories and policies of race and ethnic relations for most of the twentieth century, treated Asiatics as culturally dependent and questionably adaptive foreigners, whose moral duty and—for some sociologists[109] and a great many policy-makers[110]—social fate was to become Americanized and Christianized as rapidly and completely as possible. When a revolution in behalf of revitalized ethnic consciousness swept over America in the 1960s, it supplanted the doctrine of assimilation with the ideology of ethnic pluralism. The new "Asian Americans," organized on college and university campuses and making a bid for official recognition, conceive themselves as a confederation of the descendants of overseas Asiatic and Pacific Island nationals, and they seek to carve out an intellectual, cultural, social, and locally separate political space for themselves within the less than nationally integrated United States of America.[111] Secession or migration to some other land is ruled out as impracticable *ab initio.* More significantly, current pluralist attacks on assimilation tacitly acknowledge the political permanence as well as the cultural circumference of the already established and self-proclaimed national states.[112] Ethnic consciousness and its institutions become artifacts of sub-nationalism, proposed as alternative styles of American life under the protection, support, or grudging acquiescence of the administrative state.[113] Civilization, once conceived as elements of culture that transcended political boundaries, is cabinned and cribbed within the confines of the territorialized political organization.[114]

Modern studies of pre-Columbian Asian-American contacts seem permanently fixed in the Acostan tradition.[115] The assault on European Christian ecclesiolatry did not dispatch the biblical theory of human origins from science; rather science adapted its own secularization to the assumptions of the Book of Genesis. As the Acostan tradition secularized, it developed functional autonomy, internal justifications, and a concentration on methods and techniques.[116] Its usefulness to modern thought, especially in its bifurcation of post and pre-Columbian eras and its equation of civilization with national state development, is recognized not only in the Occident but also in Japan, the new Peoples Republics, and among Sinologists in China and America. China's archaeologists are virtually Acostan in the skeptical attitude and methodological exactitude they apply to recent claims of Chinese contacts with paleo-America.[117] Chinese paleontologists and ethnohistorians emphasize the ancient autochthony of their civilization, refuse to believe that their ancestors borrowed customs or artifacts from their neighbors, acknowledge no significant diffusion or migration from America, and are skeptical but interested in the possibilities of proving ancient Asiatic contacts with America.[118] Beginning in the Meiji era, Japanese scholars and diplomats emphasized the country's connections to Europe and its adaptations of and improvements on European civilization;[119] moreover, they reconceptualized the origin of the despised Eta people as racially foreign and culturally alien, a product of ancient aboriginal settlement or migrations to Japan in antiquity.[120]

Recent evidence suggests that the dating of human and animal existence in America be pushed back thousands of years.[121] Culin had noted that his thesis required proofs of a greater antiquity for man and civilization in America than "is revealed by the most remote historical perspective of Egypt or Babylon" and that it might have been the case "that at one period of man's history he had certain ideas in common on both continents; that his customs were fundamentally the same and knew no geographical boundaries."[122] Such heterodoxical views fly against the secularized biblical illusions of our age,[123] just as they excited the theological imagination of the heresiarch de La Peyrere and intrigued, but did not convince, the impious speculations of the Scottish moralists. The emergence of an Enlightenment completely emancipated from the imperatives of sacred doctrine has yet to occur.

The Science of History and the Theory of Social Change

Much confusion is generated when theorists fail to distinguish between a science of history and a theory of social change. Such confusion has been prevalent in recent years in numerous publications. The particular error that occurs involves a synecdoche; thus certain sociologists have supposed that establishing a theory of social change will also perforce establish a science of history. In fact, however, any theory of social change is and must be only a part of any science of history. To equate a theory of social change with the whole of a science of history is to foreshorten the scope of the latter. Moreover, there is another type of error entailed here: equating changes with history, assuming that all of history is change and that history can embrace no topic other than change. History, however, can and does include stasis, the cake of custom, formed and maintained over a long period of time.

Among the great scholars of both history and social change this error of conflation was not committed. Here, I will mention two major figures: Frederick J. Teggart and Max Weber. Both Teggart and Weber developed sciences of history, and each also contributed a theory of social change. In the cases of both Teggart and Weber their distinctive sciences of history are distinguishable from their respective theories of social change. However, in the years that followed their productive periods, a tendency to perceive sciences of history within theories of social change has led to a certain confusion in the understanding of each of these men's works and in the relation of history to social change. The confusion finds its most representative form in the assertion that a theory of social change is of itself a complete science of history. By reviewing both Teggart's and Weber's sciences of history and theories of social

change, I hope to contribute to ending this confusion and also, by elaborating Weber's theory of social change, to provide a basis for a theory of
change appropriate to a sociology of the absurd, i.e., that sociology developed a decade ago by Marvin B. Scott and me in order to elaborate
an existential-phenomenological perspective.

TEGGART'S SCIENCE OF HISTORY

Teggart's science of history may be designated as a variant of
positivism. According to its essential principles history is to be conceived of as a plurality of happenings whose relationship to one another
may be obtained by the processes of hypothesis and "experiment." The
hypothesis for Teggart must always take the form of a statement of
causal or correlational probability that links happenings or sets of happenings to one another in a patterned geo-temporal manner. The "experiment" consists not of a laboratory reproduction of the happenings—which would be impossible in the nature of the case—but rather
of a careful investigation and classification of the occurrences recorded
in the historical record, respecifying these happenings in an array such
that time and space phenomena can be shown to have the hypothesized
relationship to one another, and filling in the explanatory links.[1] Teggart's best-known study employing this method is *Rome and China*.[2]
That work, published in 1939, constituted the single most significant
case of what I have elsewhere designated as neopositivist historicism.[3]

TEGGART'S THEORY OF SOCIAL CHANGE

It is sometimes supposed that Teggart's science of history is the
same as his theory of social change. Such is suggested, for example, in
Robert Nisbet's *Social Change and History*.[4] In fact, however, Teggart's
theory of social change is separated from his science of history and, I
would argue, given the nature of the case would have to be since, as
Teggart himself insisted, history includes long periods of time in which
no social change occurs.[5] For Teggart, then, as for ourselves as well, a
science of history would embrace far more kinds of phenomena and far
more varied periods of duration than would a theory of social change.
A theory of social change is but one aspect of a science of history.

Teggart's theory of social change is built around the central significance of a phenomenological process that he calls release.[6] According to Teggart, what goes on most of the time in most places, past or present, is conduct oriented by habit and tradition. People carry on their daily lives in accordance with customs and ways that are deeply ingrained in their culture and in their consciousness. These customs and ways constitute the taken-for-granted features of their culture—or, in the words of Alfred Schutz, the "recipes for living" that every member of the society and culture knows.[7] Elaborating the tacit phenomenology entailed in Teggart's position, I would like to add that knowledge of these customs and ways resides at the subliminal level of consciousness, finding its expression in conduct rather than cognition. Further, let me suggest that the way to obtain an actor's knowledge of these habits, customs, and deeply ingrained ways of living is to carry out an ethnomethodological experiment wherein the effect of the strange behavior of the experimenter forces the content of that subliminal consciousness to rise to either cognitive or emotional awareness.[8]

Of course Teggart—who died twenty years before Garfinkel enunciated the principles of ethnomethodology—was aware that no direct experiment on the peoples, cultures, societies, and civilizations that historians wished to study could be performed. However, Teggart noticed, history itself provided the kind of occurrences that lead to a general breakdown of the habits and customs of a people and would, thence, give rise to a naturalistic ethnomethodological experience, i.e., a liberation from habitual ways of thinking. Such events in history, Teggart reasoned, were rare and occasional. When they did occur, however, a fundamental social change could be brought about by and through the innovative outlooks that arose to replace the moribund folkways. But, Teggart thought, the character and content of that change could not be predicted in advance. Teggart's nonteleological theory of social change stands in sharp contrast to those that claim to see a definite and unmistakable trajectory of change in history.

For Teggart the principal phenomenon triggering social change was "release" from the slavery of habit. Such a "release" could only occur when a major crisis intruded on the ordinary lives of people. The effect of a major intrusion was to make the "recipes-for-living" that "everyone knew" inoperative or inefficacious. At such moments of terrible intrusion people would be released from their unconscious commitment to these habits, ways, and customs and in this state of liberation placed in a position to engage in innovative conduct, entering into new roles and new relationships with others. For Teggart the most significant example of a major social change was the foundation of the state. The state, as Teggart conceived of it, was a particular kind of or ganization that had been invented several times in the past. Central to the formation of the state was the release of individuals from their commitment to ascriptive solidarities such as families, clans, ethnic groups, and racial aggregations. The state, by embracing peoples in relationships that transcended their ascriptive associations, constituted a fundamental social change, bringing into existence new roles, new role relationships, new sources of authority, and new conditions for status.

Teggart reasoned that the ascriptive solidarities with their powerful commitment based on blood could not be broken down easily. The kinds of conduct, the patterns of everyday life, the developments of economy and polity and other forms of sociality that were occasioned by membership in clans, races, or tribes are buttressed by mystery and tradition.[9] These could only be undermined and broken through by an especially powerful or especially long-term intrusion that would render these awesome associations powerless or ineffective. As Teggart saw it, certain migration patterns led in turn to certain forms of settlements at borderlands and hinterlands. The borderland settlers were placed in the unenviable position of having to defend entrance to the land behind them when it had filled up. The invaders—would-be settlers being held back by the borderland forces—would hammer away for decades or even centuries at the borderland settlements. In turn, the modes of social, political, and economic organization at the borderlands would be battered down by these successive assaults, and their principal mode of association—ascriptive solidarity—would be weakened if not destroyed. Out of this weakening or destruction would emerge the individual released from his identification with and commitment to family clan or race and open to the formation of new commitments, new identities, and new social relations based on something other than principles of birth. New associations formed voluntarily constituted the beginnings of the political state. Conquerors or adventurers who left the borderland society would in turn politicize the interior.

WEBER'S CONTRIBUTION
TO A SCIENCE OF HISTORY

Like Teggart, Weber recognizes that history consists of a concatenation of happenings or events, but unlike Teggart, Weber's approach to history stresses the consequences of one type of happening or event for another. What is significant about Weber's attitude toward history is the emphasis he places on the unintended consequences of happenings or events. Perhaps the best-known effort of Weber in this respect is *The Protestant Ethic and the Spirit of Capitalism,* in which he traced how the unintended consequences of Puritanism led to the development of a capitalist ethos.[10] The matter is so well-known as to require no extensive elaboration here. Suffice it to note that Weber also elaborated his original study of capitalism by carrying out a series of "experiments," that is, comparative studies, each seeking to elucidate the unintended consequences of certain value patterns or religions for economic and social development and institutionalization and vice versa. These studies, taken as a whole, comprise Weber's efforts to present an example of an empirical science of history.[11] At their most general and abstract level these studies indicated the relationship between institutionalized values and socioeconomic formations.

WEBER'S THEORY OF SOCIAL CHANGE

Unlike a science of history, a theory of social change depends on the employment of temporarally neutral concepts to formulate understanding of recurrent social processes. Although Teggart expresses some doubt about a timeless sociology, his theory of social change, centered in the concept of "release," employs such an atemporal conceptualization. The supposition that sociology can provide a single theory of social change is, however, chimerical, although some theories of social change have been incredibly ambitious, for example, Marx's theory of the significance of the economic substructure, whereby all social change is understood in terms of the conflicts which stem from the social relations of production;[12] or Talcott Parsons's theory of structural differentiation, whereby specialized structures emerge as adaptations to tensions in the social system;[13] or Pitirim Sorokin's vast and invisible pendulum that ineluctably swings all civilizations through a grand sweep from "ideational" to "sensate."[14]

A theory of social change properly associated with a sociology of the absurd[15] is modestly adapted from Weber's theory of social change. The absurdist theory of social change begins with recognition of the significance of Weber's discussion of leadership. A principal consequence of charismatic leadership is the emergence of new obligations, new roles, new role relationships, new orientations toward authority, and new outlets for the expression of sentiment and feeling. Just how these new obligations are brought about is a particular contribution of empirical studies in the sociology of the absurd, and these studies would constitute its most important contribution to the elaboration of a theory of social change.

Max Weber is certainly a precursor of the idea of the absurd.[16] For Weber, as for sociologists associated with the idea of the absurd, reality is infinite and can be divided up in an infinity of ways.[17] Following Weber, we, or anyone, may freely construct one-sided exaggerations of reality—that is, ideal types—if these permit us to elevate our understanding.[18] Like Weber, but unlike Marx, Parsons, and other nonabsurdists, we do not believe that there are definite, unambiguous, central structural mechanisms that are necessary for understanding the essential features of the social world. In other words, following in the spirit of Weber, the sociology of the absurd rejects the positivist goal of discovering sets of general laws, and we further reject the claim made by nonabsurdists that certain structures in society or certain mechanisms are always present and always salient to the same degree in every society.

Weber's theory of social change is organized around the phenomenon of charisma and its routinization. Charisma and its routinization are for Weber the two engines of social change.[19] So also for the absurdist theory of change.

Absurdity can be located at two quite distinct levels. At one level—that of the philosopher or of the sociologist about to perform a study—the absurd, with its emphasis on the notion of an essentially meaningless world, is a way of posing the problem of social order. Thus, the sociologist of the absurd, starting with the assumption of an ultimately meaningless world, immediately notes that everywhere the world has meaning. The paradox that is thus made manifest—an essentially meaningless world that is always meaningful—provides the basic problem for which his or her particular sociological investigation is constructed. The sociologist of the absurd seeks to uncover how it is possible for ordinary as well as extraordinary people to convert the meaningless world into one that is meaningful and to do so without a conscious philosophy or elaborated praxis to guide them.

At quite a different level, however, one can discuss absurdity as a category of members' knowledge. This is a somewhat philosophical way of pointing to the occasionally experienced social fact of absurdity. This is to say that absurdity—in the form of irreconcilable contradictions, unresolved paradoxes, and a felt sense of meaninglessness—can be a feature of any person's perception. The meaningless world is, hence, not only a philosophical assumption or an heuristic device; it is also recognized and recognizable as a phenomenon among ordinary people "out there in the world." The experience of absurdity is, however, uncomfortable. Those who find themselves in an absurd situation, that is, a situation characterized by seemingly unresolvable contradiction, absolute meaninglessness, or gnawing anomie, will try to obviate the absurdist elements from it, or, failing that, they might try to remove themselves from the absurd situation. However, even when it is impossible to extricate oneself from a situation whose absurdity has become clear or to modify the situation so as to remove the absurdity, it is usually possible *to imagine* what would be required to end the condition of absurdity. This is the sense that things would be all right, "if only. . . ."

The perception of absurdity, then, is a potential feature of the ordinary world. To be sure it is only *a* feature and it is experienced only by some. Moreover, the perception of absurdity is temporal, that is to say, it occurs occasionally and unpredictably, and therefore it cannot be predicted with the same degree of accuracy as those phenomena that are foreseen by predictive social scientific theories. However, it is sometimes the case that the experience of absurdity, when not allowed to remain merely personal and private, will not only receive a wide hearing but create a following. This is often the case because others are experiencing the same kind of irreconcilable contradictions but are unable to articulate them with the clarity voiced by the original perceiver of the absurd condition. It follows then that the announcement of the existential presence of the absurd is likely to create a kind of excitement and contagion and, following this, to constitute the basis for the emergence of charisma.

Charisma is more than a characteristic attributable to an individual. The person who can give voice to his or her experience of absurdity is filled with a dynamism that permits him or her literally to "charm" the audience. *Charm* here refers both to the magical aspects inherent in that term and to the dramatic expression and effect that Stanislavsky has pointed to in his discussions of charm in acting.[20] A person capable of "charming" an audience is like one who is possessed, and when one who is possessed "charms" an audience, he or she is capable of making it feel possessed as well. Like some remarkable actors and awe-inspiring leaders, charismatic persons may *express* the absurdity felt inarticulately by their audience but not *experience* it in themselves.

Much of the effect of the charismatic figure is derived from non-symbolic communication. The audience—those who listen to the charismatic figure as he or she makes meaningful the meaningless world—feel as if a new force is entering them; they lose their ordinary role vigilance and give up personal control. As an event in group psychology the effect of the charismatic leader on his or her followers may be compared to hypnotism. The charismatic leader uses "charm" to hypnotize the audience. The audience in turn feels itself to be "charmed." A magical force has taken over and entered into them. They are, as it were, in a trance, and in this trance they are in a position to realize new identities, new roles, new role relations, or, indeed, a new world.

"Charm," then, that emerges from this personal and, shall we say, aesthetic confrontation with absurdity, is the basis of the hypnotic power that the charismatic leader exercises over his or her followers. The charismatic leader gives voice first to the experience of meaninglessness and then points out the line of conduct and thought that will reduce the anxiety of that absurdity. Those who have been hypnotized or "charmed" by the charismatic leader may then become "reborn" in terms of that leader's resolute interpretation of the situation. In other words, absurdity as a condition of human existence constitutes a basis for the emergence of the charismatic leader; in turn, "charm" provides the energy and catalyst for the mobilization of a collectivity.

The absurd is a limbo land in which few care to live. When a person's homeland is experienced as this limbo land of absurdity the individual will seek out something to relieve this condition and remove him or her from the land of meaninglessness. The absurd situation, then—a situation of irreconcilable contradiction—may lead *inter alia* to a challenge to authority, especially when the structure of or personnel in authority is believed to be the very source for and maintenance of the absurd situation. The collectivity, aroused by its desire to end existence in absurdity, will then engage in a struggle and, by its actions, hope to remove the source of authority and thereby remove themselves from limbo.

The charismatic aspects of social change and its relation to the reduction of absurdity have been exemplified recently by Bryan Wilson,[21] who points to the peculiar significance of conquest, imperialism, and colonialism for generating a recognition of an absurd condition among the natives. It is, for example, after the imposition of European ways upon the land and life of the Amerindian aborigines that we find emergence of charismatic leaders and fateful confrontations. Moreover, in the very content of their speech these charismatic leaders voice their perception of paradox and give instruction in new and sometimes magical lines of conduct. These noble savages, as Wilson calls them, are charismatic leaders of the first order, and, indeed, they possess and are possessed by "charm." In turn they possess their followers who, believing themselves to be magically protected by their own collective charisma, reorganize their lives, formulate an attack, and move haplessly toward a terrible fate.

The absurdist theory of social change notes then that both actions and character are reconstructed to form new social meanings, and through these actions and these new characters the condition of absurdity is transcended. Contrary to the belief of certain critics of the sociology of the absurd, the theory does provide a generalizable or timeless theory of social change. It is a theory which assumes that absurdity is not only a philosophical orientation or a methodological decision but also and more importantly a realizable and occasionally realized human condition. Once this human condition has been sensed and been given expression and will, there will come not merely the pressure for change but change itself.

The Acceptance, Rejection, and Reconstruction of Histories

On Some Controversies in the Study of Social and Cultural Change

EVOLUTIONISM AND FUNCTIONALISM

Basic Evolutionism

The dominant school of thought in current sociology is evolutionist functionalism. To those familiar with the discussion, the name Talcott Parsons immediately evokes the quintessential statement on the subject. In Parsons' book *The Social System* we may find a most complete presentation of functionalist sociology at the societal level;[1] in his *Societies: Evolutionary and Comparative Perspectives* we discover the linkage to older evolutionary theories of change.[2] At one time the functionalist approach served as a special kind of critique of older developmental theories of change. However, the grounds of both theories are ultimately to be found in the solution proposed by Aristotle to the study of order and change. Since sociology in particular and the social sciences in general were founded to discover the bases for order, the causes and consequences of change, and the nature and possibilities of permanence, the Aristotelian answer and its modern counterpart in evolutionist functionalism stand as one of the most significant proposals ever offered to the original question of the discipline.

Evolutionary approaches to the understanding of social change first of all assert that *change is always going on*. Every unit under study is undergoing a constant shift from one state of being to another. Each state of being, hence, is in a process of becoming. Since the evolutionist never assumes that change is *not* going on, or that it is intermittent, the causes of change are not a matter of investigative concern. Instead, the roots of change are said to reside in the thing changing. Change is immanent. For the evolutionist, the real issue is to discover the direction of change, the rate of change, and the (temporary) impediments to change.

The rate of change is also established through an assumption. Change, according to the evolutionist, is not only continuous, but *slow* and *orderly* as well. The organization of action cannot occur faster than the nature of the thing changing. Most changes occur so slowly that they cannot be noticed except by careful measurement or by the discerning eye of later historians. Closely related to the slowness of change is its *orderliness*. Changes that are sudden, chaotic, and irruptive cannot last; only the orderly processes that resonate with the existing state of being and the quality of immanence in the thing changing can form a part of the social trend. In accordance with Leibniz's famous dictum, *Natura non facit saltum,* social change is regarded as *gradual*. In societies and civilizations, as in nature, argues the evolutionist, there is no discontinuity, gap, leap, or failure of growth; there is only gradual and cumulative development. Thus, every present contains the seeds of its own future while at the same moment it embodies the fruits of its own growth from the past.

The direction of change is contained in the *telos* of the thing changing. Evolutionary theory is deterministic in the sense that it holds that every thing contains its own potential; things become what it is in their nature to become. *Entelechy* is the vital process governing the path that societies, cultures, and civilizations traverse. Thus societies do not move toward chaotic, directionless, and unknowable outcomes. Their destination is contained in their present, rooted in their past, and realized in their future. For the social scientist to discover the telic force at work in any society he must uncover the tap root of that society. Origin is destiny.

Basic to the evolutionist perspective is the conception of development as organic growth. Societies, cultures, and civilizations are treated as if they are organisms. History thus conceived becomes natural history. Growth is defined as the passage through inevitable phases of development until maturity is achieved. In some conceptions, societies, cultures, and civilizations are likened in their natural history to the life cycle of a mortal: They are born, nurtured, and educated in their "early" periods; they then expand, test their musculature and possibilities in an "adolescence"; achieve knowledge, attempt greatness, and then affirm the limits of their condition in a "mature" period; and, finally, weaken and decay in their "old age" until decline and death remove them from the worldly scene. Even when their descriptions of social, cultural, or civilizational development do not approximate the life cycle so boldly, evolutionists nevertheless cling to a general, vague, but powerful sense that growth as measured and conceived by science is organic.

The organic analogy led to the designation of development in stages. Evolutionists depicted the stages of social, cultural, or civilizational growth in terms strikingly close to that of biological organisms. Nonliterate peoples tended to be treated as representatives of "early" stages of development, described as "savages," and, as such, compared to infants with respect to mental capacity.[3] Evolutionary historians identified certain occurrences as either exemplars of the telic force at work or impediments to it. The original argument, developed by Aristotle in *Physics,* was taken over in its entirety, including the doctrine of accidents (or, as we shall see presently, impediments or obstacles) that had accompanied it.

The doctrine of accidents is the single most important element in the evolutionist argument. According to this doctrine not everything that happens is "natural." Mistakes and fortuitous occurrences are not unknown; "chance" produces unusual happenings. What occurs in the world, then, is either "natural" or it is not. As Aristotle conceived of it, there could be no science of unnatural phenomena. Only natural things could be the subjects of science. Two tests might be applied to distinguish the natural from the accidental: Any "thing" that did not contain within itself the principle of immanent and telic change was not natural; any occurrence in the history or experience of a "thing" that could not be associated with its true potential must be regarded as accidental to it.[4]

Armed with knowledge of the "natural" and the "accidental," the evolutionist approached the record of history with confidence. Those occurrences that exemplified the inherent potential of the society, culture, or civilization under study were proper data of a social science; those that were incidental, contingent, or unrelated to that elemental immanence were "accidents." The record of history thus offered no mystery.[5] Once the potential of the specific entity under study had been established, the record of occurrences disclosed itself as a dichotomous paradigm of natural or nonnatural phenomena.

However, following a clue in Aristotle's discussions of the subject, the evolutionist employed the doctrine of accidents as an explanatory device. It was not merely the case that accidents sometimes occurred. When they occurred they might stand in the way of natural development. Accidents, thus, could be impediments, obstacles, or interferences. Once he or she knew the dysfunctional consequences of accidents, the evolutionist could explain how it was that a society, culture, or civilization had failed to become what its potential dictated. A society had not advanced into the next stage of its inevitable developmental sequence because something had interfered. Put another way, the evolutionist could argue the case in the future perfect tense. A society would have taken on the character and institutions associated with the next stage in its natural and inherent development if the designated obstacle had not been encountered. In the hands of a deft evolutionist, the doctrine of accidents could be employed to preserve the developmental hypothesis in the face of overwhelming evidence to the contrary. Rather than disconfirming the hypothesis, the seemingly negative evidence might be regarded as a table of impediments preventing the realization of developments in what otherwise would have been a natural sequence.

It is a commonplace of current anthropological and sociological discussion to assert that the evolutionist position has been abandoned in the face of the criticism leveled against it by Boas and his followers.[6] Yet, whatever the lip service paid to diffusionist and related alternatives to developmental theories, evolutionism has survived in other terms, and a neoevolutionist revival is noticeable in recent sociology and anthropology.[7] Indeed, diffusionist ideas had been absorbed by certain evolutionary theories from the beginning, giving added strength to the latter.[8] More recently, the revival of diffusionist approaches to social change has not occasioned an abandonment of evolutionary orientations but instead evoked a call for a more encompassing theory, recognizing both exogenous happenings as diffusionist elements and endogenous trends as evolutionary facets of an enlarged conception of sociocultural change.[9]

Despite the rejection of the "comparative method," certain anthropologists still employ it without explicit identification as such.[10] A striking example is found in a recent socioanthropological study of Chinese social organization in nineteenth-century Singapore by Maurice Freedman.[11] Taking *contemporary* modes of Chinese social organization in Sarawak as the model for all *early* phases of overseas Chinese community form, Freedman designates *contemporary* modes of Chinese social organization in Singapore as "the model of the most developed form of immigrant Chinese settlement in Southeast Asia." Although there is evidence from Freedman's own investigations of the matter that the actual social organization of the earliest Chinese settlement in Singapore was far more complex than that of contemporary Sarawak, he nevertheless reasons that a simpler and smaller scale organization *must* have preceded that of later Singapore. Thus, in strict conformity to the rules of the "comparative method," Freedman has arranged his depiction of spatially and temporally coexistent Chinese communities in Sarawak and Singapore in the form of a chronological natural history. The belief in a uniform development of social institutions, proceeding from small and simple to large and complex forms, has taken precedence over the facts of history uncovered in the investigation.[12]

Although a common thesis holds that sociological employment of the evolutionist perspective is a product of Darwinism, the fundamental ideas of the perspective predate Darwin's work by thousands of years.[13] As Bock has urged, Darwin ought not be charged with the burdens and difficulties of sociological evolutionary functionalism.[14] One form of developmentalism in American sociology derived from a synthesis of German sociological thought. Robert Park's race relations cycle, which seems to have arisen from his original combination of the formal sociology of Georg Simmel with the historicist ideas of Wilhelm Windelband and other German historical thinkers, provides, perhaps, the paradigmatic example.[15] Taking several social forms—contact, competition, accommodation, assimilation—Park arranged them in a conjectural chronological sequence. Race relations, he argued, proceed from contact to assimilation, passing through two intermediate stages—competition and accommodation. In presenting this theory Park combined the idea of the recurring cycle with that of the inevitable sequence, an intellectual feat that had previously proved difficult for other social thinkers. As a *cycle* of recurring forms, the phases of race relations occurred for every racial group that came in contact with another group at a racial frontier. At any moment in history several racial groups might be at different points on the cycle: Some were assimilating; others lived in a state of accommodation; still others were suffering the difficulties of competition; and there were yet some groups just starting on the long road to inevitable assimilation. Furthermore, implicit in the argument was the possibility that a racial group might not have even begun the cycle since it had not yet made sustained contact with another race. A race relations cycle recurs so long as races continue on the move and encounter one another in different places on the earth. As a *sequence,* however, Park argued that the stages in the cycle moved down a road on which it was impossible to turn back. Once contact had been made the subsequent phases of orderly transition became irrepressible. As Park himself expressed it: "The race relations cycle which takes the form, to state it abstractly, of contacts, competition, accommodation and eventual assimilation, is apparently progressive and irreversible."[16] Thus the sequence is a covering law outlining the origin, way stations, and inevitable dissolution of race relations at the universal level. The recurring cycle describes the discrete experiences of different racial groups as they travel down the common road to their own inevitable extinction.

However, Park's cyclical sequence did not conform to the record of happenings in the actual world, either as experienced by the social actors or as reported by the sociological observers. Particularly vexing was the failure of the final stage—assimilation—to emerge for any significant number of America's immigrants during the lifetime of Park or his disciples. Faced with a bitter disappointment with their predictive hypothesis, and—for some—an even more bitter dejection over a failure of the fulfillment of what they believed to be an ameliorating step in the general process moving humankind toward a raceless and cosmo-politan world, some disciples of Park searched for the inordinately tough and as yet impenetrable obstacles that hindered the march of progress in race relations.[17] Others constructed more elaborate cycles to account for a particular group's variation.[18] And the most embittered re-jected the cycle altogether and with it any possibility of a science of race relations.[19] Those sociologists concerned with the logic of their own sci-ence sometimes sought to rescue the race relations cycle by converting it from a "theory" to a "model." Asked to state just what phenomenon it was a model of, however, they admitted that it was a model of race relations with many exceptions.[20]

By encouraging research that would uncover exceptions, some evolutionary thinkers sought to legitimate the defects in developmental models, such as Park's race relations cycle, thereby converting their em-pirical shortcomings into theoretical virtues. Applied to the race rela-tions cycle, this approach would assert that it is not a strictly universal law that admits of no exceptions. Rather it is a quasi-law that ought to be employed as an aid to uncovering the as yet hidden conditions of its own applicability.[21] As these conditions—interferences with natural processes—are disclosed, the lawlike aspect of the race relations cycle is steadily encumbered with an increasing number of qualifications that enrich its own application to the world of race relations. Viewed in this light, Park's own development of a table of impedimenta—skin color, group temperament, racial prejudice, and the absence of interracial pri-mary relations—constitutes an elaboration of the original cycle and an invitation to enlarge and verify even further his enumeration of limiting conditions.[22]

However, the search for exceptions as a clue to the conditions of applicability of a lawlike proposition does little more than patch a gap-ing hole in the scientific procedure of social evolutionism. In terms fa-miliar to readers of Karl Popper, the principal defect is unfalsifiability.[23] Evolutionary cycles, natural histories, and sequences of inevitable stages are not hypotheses in the narrow and restricted meaning of that term, since no set of procedures can be brought to bear as a reasonable and fair test. Such a test would be possible if the doctrine of accidents could be removed from the argument employed by the evolutionist. Unable to preclassify events as "natural" or "accidental," the social scientist could then search for the evidence that would cause him or her to reject the original hypothesis. Still another approach, only slightly more elabo-rate than the one just mentioned, would be the reelaboration of the hy-pothesis with a fixed and finite set of qualifiers such that a discovery of failure in its predictive capacity could be referred to the limiting factor already enunciated, if that factor could also be shown to be present in the existential world of the object under study. If, however, the doctrine of accidents is attached as a corollary to evolutionist theories, no hypothesis can be tested at all; rather, each datum in what would otherwise be recognized as a body of negative evidence will be classified as an interference, obstacle, or accident to the developmental thesis.[24]

The doctrine of accidents also encourages and legitimates *ad hoc* explanations and procedures. Faced with what appears to be disconfirming evidence of a developmental hypothesis, the researcher might seek about for any kind of element, factor, or occurrence to account for the discrepancy between scientific prediction and recorded performance. The history of the use of the doctrine of accidents by scholars investigating Park's race relations cycle is alarmingly instructive on this point. One researcher, seeking to explain why one Japanese community in California seemed to be living in a state of accommodation rapidly approaching assimilation whereas another only a few hundred miles away was riddled with intracommunity conflict, introduced geographical, civic, and collective psychological factors indiscriminately to account for the differences.[25] Seeking to explain why a Jew who had assimilated rapidly and completely was nevertheless rejected by his gentile peers and business associates, Louis Wirth explained that the man had moved too fast: He had acted as an assimilate in the era of accommodation.[26] And Rose Hum Lee, chagrined to find that the Chinese had not assimilated after more than a century of settlement in the United States, charged them with a vested interest in segregation and a failure of nerve.[27] With the recalcitrance of geography, the rhythms of time, and the rumblings of collective and individual psyches available to the researcher seeking an accident, it is no wonder that chaos prevails in the demonstration of these kinds of scientific propositions. The doctrine of accidents provides an embarrassment of untapped riches for an otherwise impoverished mode of social scientific procedure.

Functionalism

Although functionalists are commonly credited with having provided a major critique of evolutionism and with proposing an alternative to it, in fact their original intent was quite limited and, in the end, their approach to the study of social change has become one basis for a neo-evolutionist revival. The functionalists insisted that before the stages of societal change could be delineated, an adequate picture of the nature and workings of a society would have to be established. Thus the functionalists did not address themselves to the central problem of evolutionist science—the construction of laws of social dynamics—but rather urged that the evolutionist project be postponed until an adequate account of the unit undergoing change had been rendered. Indeed, the functionalists also opposed the "historical" criticism of evolutionism presented by the diffusionist school. By insisting on the prior importance of establishing the nature of societies, and by opposing a historical analysis of different societies with similar traits or institutions in the manner proposed by Boas and his followers, the functionalists shifted attention from the comparative analysis of societies in history to the intensive analysis of the structure and coherence of discrete societies independent of one another.

However, it would be incorrect to suppose that the functionalists eschewed the study of change. In fact their analyses of particulate societies focused on the manner in which order could persevere in the face of change. Functionalists took over the organic metaphor and insisted that societies, like organisms, were composed of interdependent parts. The basic idea was admirably stated by John Stuart Mill:

> The state of every part of the social whole at any time, is intimately connected with the contemporaneous state of all the others. Religious belief, philosophy, science, the fine arts, the industrial arts, commerce, government, are all in close mutual dependence on one another, insomuch that when any considerable change takes place in one, we may know that a parallel change in all the others has preceded or will follow it.[28]

Later functionalists, seeking to open the social system sufficiently to permit voluntaristic action, provided for changes that were spontaneous, disjunctive, and deviant.[29] The functionalists had not abandoned the study of change; they had redirected the effort to study it to the interior of discrete societies conceived as social systems.[30]

Moreover, functionalists did not give up Aristotelian ideas of teleology or determinism. Instead, in the spirit of a more objective and value-free social science, they exorcised the explicit values that inhered in older teleological conceptions. In societies, they argued, there was a strain toward equilibrium. Changes did occur, societies were dynamic, but the direction of change was toward the reestablishment of a balanced interdependence among the parts and a continuous re-creation of consensus and coherence.[31] Some functionalists seized upon the social psychology of George Herbert Mead to elaborate this thesis. Just as the impulsive and creative "I," in Mead's famous formulation, is always being checked, modified, and incorporated into an intersubjective consensus by the "me," so also the larger units of the society might "act" disjunctively but *eventually* be brought into line by the new equilibrium that incorporates innovative activity and by that stroke robs it of its deviant and dysfunctional effect.[32] The functionalist thus introduced a blood-less entelechy that not only resonated with organic imagery but also elevated processes above the happenings of which they are composed.

Finally, the functionalists have also held on to the doctrine of accidents but introduced it in a disguised form. Changes within a system are either immanent or "historical." The former fall into two classes: those that are eufunctional and contribute to system maintenance; and those that are dysfunctional (arising, in the usual explanation, from imperfections in socialization and a less than equal intensity of incorporation of fundamental norms and values among the several strata of the society) and disturb systemic balance. Insofar as the system continues to reconstitute itself in a state of dynamic equilibrium, dysfunctional aspects are only harmful in the short run; in the long run their negative effects are absorbed and a new balance is effected. However, the second class of changes—the "historical" ones—are not deducible from the principles of systemic sociology. Often—but not always—these non-systemic happenings come from "outside" the particular society in the form of invasions, migrations, changes in the world economy, or cataclysmic disasters. In other cases they are unexpected occurrences within the system, such as the sudden mobility of a hitherto stratum-bound group, innovative ideologies, economic depressions, and the like. And in a few perceptive analyses a combination of exogenous and endogenous elements produce a change not anticipated by analysis of immanent elements alone.[33] The "historical" occurrences that are presented to account for the failure of expected changes to occur or to explain changes that do occur but are unexpected by pure systemic analysis are in effect *accidents*. As such they function in precisely the same way as accidents do in evolutionist theories. And just as the doctrine of accidents may encourage particular explanations for exceptions to developmentalist theories, so also it operates in functionalist theories to encourage the *ad hoc* procedure that renders such theories unfalsifiable.

Evolutionist Functionalism

When functionalists seek to explain change at the intersocietal or inter-civilizational level, they resort to a modified form of evolutionism, usually called neoevolutionism. The recent revival of modified Spencerian ideas among those who once scoffed at the Victorian scholar's efforts illustrates how wrong it has been to suppose that functionalism could only contribute to the study of social statics. In fact functionalism and evolutionism are two aspects of the same basic idea, one which might properly be called *Aristotelianism*. Essential to this idea are the organic model, the assumption that change is always going on, the assertion of entelechy, the insistence that historical events are unique, and the doctrine of accidents.[34] When evolutionist functionalists assert that they have surmounted the difficulties of earlier forms of evolutionism by eliminating unilinearity, neutralizing a once-value-laden entelechy, and giving up their belief in irreversibility, they are not addressing the central question raised against the Aristotelian conception of science. The central questions have been addressed by those scholars interested in scientific history and in a scientific sociology of social change.

THE NEOPOSITIVIST POSITION

For more than fifty years there has been a powerful but subterranean stream of criticism against the several aspects of the Aristotelian position in history, anthropology, and sociology. The principal figures in this neopositivist school are Frederick J. Teggart, Margaret T. Hodgen, Kenneth E. Bock, and Robert A. Nisbet. Their works, although directed to different aspects of the Aristotelian heritage, constitute a thorough-going critique of evolutionary developmentalist theories. In addition they offer an approach to the scientific study of history in general and social change in particular that avoids the pitfalls of the developmentalist school. Their neopositivism rejects the original organic analogy that inspired Aristotle's perspective and that has remained central to the developmental approaches. In lieu of the organic analogy they favor a quite different analytical conception of the study of social change that, in Teggart's words "must be founded upon a comparison of the particular histories of all human groups, and must be actuated by the conscious effort to take cognizance of all the available facts."[35]

Central to the neopositivist position is the attention given to the basic unit of study—the *event*. Neopositivists reject both the evolutionists' disposal of happenings as epiphenomena and the narrative historians' treatment of them as grist for the development of a dramatic narrative. As Teggart once put it:

> We have before us, in the form of documents and other memorials, evidences of what has taken place in the past. The historian seizes upon these materials and endeavors to "reconstruct the past." What he does is to create for himself, from the data available, a drama of events, and he does this by selecting what he deems to have been the episodes of cardinal importance, supplementing the record by the imaginative reconstruction of the motives of the participants. It is all human and romantic, and, in the

hands of a master, of absorbing interest; but the story will never be the same in any two "histories," and the propositions of the "accidental" will vary with every treatment.[36]

The proper scientific study of humanity, according to the neopositivists, rejects both romantic reconstructions and the *a priori* division of happenings into the "natural" and the "accidental." Teggart asserts that:

> The scientific investigator, approaching the same materials will, on the other hand, begin with the present, and he will utilize the facts available in regard to what has happened in the past as so much evidence from which to isolate the various processes through which the existing situation or condition has come to be as it is.[37]

Thus, as the neopositivists see it, it is from the analysis of specific temporal and geographical social facts that the social processes may be uncovered. As Margaret Hodgen claimed:

> Guided by precise statements of the temporal and geographical incidence of cultural phenomena, it is not only possible . . . to reconstruct maps of dated distributions of social facts, to arrange dated distributions in their dated order and compare them for the purpose of obtaining insight into time and space similarities or differences, it is also possible to use other dated information for the study of how things worked in past time to produce the results called "distributions," or to deal with the problem of recovering historical processes.[38]

The neopositivist approach to what Teggart called the "humanistic study of change in time"[39] is founded on a fundamental rejection of the evolutionary and Aristotelian paradigm and a revival of the methods associated with David Hume[40] and Anne Robert Jacques Turgot.[41] A true social science must, according to Kenneth Bock, commit itself unequivocally to a comparative study of actual happenings as they occurred in time and space.[42] On behalf of this postulated necessity, Hodgen investigated the distribution of technological innovations in England from 1000 to 1899 and showed that innovations tended to recur in those villages and parishes where a precedent of accepting changes had been established earlier,[43] and, in his most thorough-going study, Teggart uncovered a hitherto unnoticed relationship between the Barbarian invasions of Europe and the wars that were fought on the eastern frontiers of the Roman Imperium and the western regions of the Chinese Empire.[44] Such investigations require, as Bock has suggested, "as a first step toward the formulation of testable statements of social or cultural processes, abandonment of the assumption that historical events are unique and acceptance of the assumption that there are discernible regularities in *all* historical occurrences."[45] Theories of social change thus might arise from the testing of hypotheses formulated around the relation of one class of occurrences to another.[46]

A second aspect of the neopositivist rejection of the Aristotelian paradigm is abandonment of the biological model that has been employed by both evolutionists and functionalists. Bock presents this position most clearly:

> Use of the biological analogy in any form and to any extent is unwarranted and dangerous. Considerations of the possible utility of analogical reasoning for conceptualization notwithstanding, the repeated experiences of Western scholars over more than twenty-five hundred years demonstrates unequivocally that the analogy between society and an organism has worked uniformly to stop inquiry and to produce images of social process plainly contradicted by evidence at hand.[47]

Abandonment of the biological analogy also entails a rejection of its subsidiary concepts and orientations about change. Bock points out that these include "the notions that change has been always from the simple to the complex, from the homogeneous to the heterogeneous, or from the undifferentiated to the differentiated."[48] Ultimately this requires rejection of the Aristotelian picture of motion:

> The belief derived from analogy that society is a process of slow and continuous change generated and directed by potential present within the thing changing from the beginning, has served only to divert attention from the evidence that must be admitted in any candid search for processes—evidence that cannot be dismissed as "secondary" factors of "unnatural" interventions or "anti-evolutionary" forces.[49]

Studies done in the neopositivist tradition have indicated the weaknesses that exist in the more traditional Aristotelian approach. Hodgen's study of technological innovation in England showed, among other things, that "the oft-spoken dictum that man lives in a world of change emerges as only half-true; and the purported naturalness, continuity and universality imputed by social evolutionists to the process of change is not confirmed."[50] Teggart has shown how classifications of discrete historical occurrences in Rome and China may be correlated to upset long-held theories accounting for major intercivilizational encounters.[51] More recently, Lyman has shown how commitment to the Aristotelian paradigm has led three generations of American sociologists to neglect the historical record of blacks in America, stultified the explanation of Chinese immigration and settlement in America, and produced an irremediable muddle in the most prominent paradigm of American political sociology.[52]

Moving from the neopositivist critique of the Aristotelian paradigm to its own constructive formulation we may note four basic postulates: fixity or persistence; crisis and catastrophe; discontinuity and nonuniformity; and open-ended or nonteleological change. Nisbet, in the most recent statement of the neopositivist argument, has presented a discussion of these four basic elements of the approach.[53] With certain emendations and qualifications, we shall follow his line of explication.

To study social change, the neopositivists insist that research begin with at least the heuristic assumption that change is not always going on. The alternative, that of assuming a universal, permanent, and uniform rate of change, begs the very question that the study sets out to investigate—the causes or conditions of social change. Thus Hodgen makes no assumption about the trend of technological innovations in England before beginning her study; rather she lets the sited and dated distribution of the innovative happenings produce a pattern for which an account is then required. Teggart refuses to accept the widely held belief that overpopulation produced the Barbarian invasions; rather he carefully notes the temporal and geographical instances of these irruptions and looks to see if there is an antecedent element common to all cases. Thus, the actual pattern of social change emerges from the collection and array of specific historical findings, and the causal agency from the discovery of a recurrent antecedent event or class of events.

Crisis and catastrophe are held out as likely sources for the breakdown of the cake of custom and the continuity of habit. In calling attention to these two elements the neopositivists evoke the earlier work of W. I. Thomas[54] and anticipate some recent phenomenological ideas of Alfred Schutz.[55] Thomas had developed a nonevolutionary approach to the study of social change, emphasizing the relationship between habit, crisis, and attention. Societies persisted in habitual orientations until some crisis upset familiar modes of thought and encouraged innovative attention to the fore. Social changes occurred in such historical moments. In a more individualistic and psychological vein, Schutz emphasized the crisis in the *Lebenswelt* that occurs when habitual modes of action no longer prove efficacious or when familiar human abilities suddenly become inoperative. Such crises cause humans to perceive the hitherto taken-for-granted but fundamental workings of social life, and, possibly, to discover new ways to persevere.

Standing at midpoint between the psychologistic sociology of Thomas and the phenomenological psychology of Schutz is the Jamesian cognitive phenomenology of Teggart. In Teggart's concept of release there is described the fundamental individual and collective force potential to the triggering of social change. "The hypothesis," Teggart observed, "may now be stated in the form that human advancement follows upon the mental release of the members of a group or of a single individual from the authority of an established system of ideas."[56] Release, Teggart supposed, occurred for the most part as a consequence of the first contacts and subsequent conflicts among culturally or socially distinctive peoples. Thus, he placed great emphasis upon the socio-psychological effects of forced migration and intergroup collision, processes that, whatever calamities they might cause, accomplished "the release of the individual mind from the set forms in which it has been drilled," and gave the persons so liberated "opportunity to build up a system for themselves anew."[57] Hodgen employed this concept to help account for the adoption of technological innovations among the English. Pointing to the basic conservatism of English villagers and their reluctance to embrace the new or different, she emphasized the disruptions of habitual modes of production created by the influx of foreign settlers and the rare but significant willingness of certain villages to take up or initiate new ways.[58] The processes of release are the products of "intrusions," the *event* emphasized by Teggart's approach to the study of social change. However, whereas Teggart laid great emphasis on the function of migrations, invasions, wars, and involuntary movements of masses of peoples in creating such "intrusions," he also pointed to the role of new ideas as intruders on the habitual consciousness and thought processes of people, liberating them from older habits of mind and giving rise to social and cultural changes.[59] The energies of men, Teggart pointed out—borrowing the phrase from William James—are constrained by convention and habit. Excitements, startling ideas, contacts with new peoples constitute the crucial events in history since they disrupt convention, defeat habit, and deliver humankind from its sociocultural prison houses. Human advancement is achieved at the price of whatever social security resides in the old and settled ways, the customs, folkways, and mores of established social organization.

In attacking the evolutionists on their belief in continuity and uniformity the neopositivists strike a blow against one of the more sacred elements of Occidental thought. Social change is real but rare argue the neopositivists. It occurs where the social milieu will permit it, where habit has broken down, where custom no longer prevails. Hence the orderly development seen in evolutionist descriptions is unlikely. Hodgen shows that the bursts of technological innovation in England occurred only in certain places whereas in the other areas during the same period no change occurred.[60] Teggart's investigations of the Barbarian invasions show that they are intermittent in time and discrete in place.[61] Particular changes have particular causes, argue Teggart and his followers, and, although a pattern of change is deducible from the occurrences in history, that pattern is likely to be one of discontinuities and nonuniformities. Max Weber's position on this question is quite close to that of Teggart. While observing that "a genuinely analytic study comparing the stages of development of the ancient *polis* with those of the medieval city would be welcome and productive," Weber urged that "such a comparative study would not aim at finding 'analogies' and 'parallels,' as is done by those engrossed in the currently fashionable enterprise of constructing general schemes of development. The aim should, rather, be precisely the opposite: to identify and define the individuality of each development, the characteristics which made the one conclude in a manner so different from that of the other. "This done," Weber concludes in a manner strikingly similar to that adopted later by Teggart in his study *Rome and China,* "one can then determine the causes which led to these differences."[62]

According to the neopositivists there is no definite direction or trajectory of social change. Change is neither necessary nor irreversible. Neopositivist sociologists have cast considerable doubt on the findings of Aristotelian-inspired studies. To refute Park's assertion that the race relations cycle is both progressive and irreversible,[63] the neopositivists point to the actual evidence concerning the modes of adjustment and adaptation of America's various racial and ethnic groups. Furthermore, they expose and criticize the embarrassing explanations that Park's disciples employ to rescue his theory from disconfirmation.[64]

In explaining how an investigation of social change ought to be carried out, the neopositivists place their greatest emphasis on the collection, classification, and comparison of specific happenings. To the historian who insists on the singularity of each occurrence, the neopositivist emphasizes the nonunique elements that make for the possibilities of classes of occurrences.[65] To the sociologist who doubts the reliability and validity of documentary reports of happenings in earlier eras, the neopositivists emphasize the superior truth value of such documents over conjectural histories,[66] and they point to the absurdity of placing more trust in the social scientific instruments handled by hardly trained students than in the shrewd perceptions of such on-the-scene investigators as Hesiod, Machiavelli, or Voltaire.[67]

How historical occurrences are to be investigated requires further specification. Without using these precise terms, Teggart distinguishes between "exogenous" and "endogenous" events with respect to any system of experience. The former are intrusions and, as such, more likely to upset habitual modes of activity and promote change:

> This identification of "events" as "intrusions" is a matter of some importance. To reach an understanding of "how things work" in the course of time, we may envisage the facts of experience as arranged in a series of concentric circles. Outermost, we would have the stellar universe; within this, the world of organic life; within this, the world of human activities; within this, the local community; and finally, within this, the individual.[68]

Each circle represents a realm of experience. But to Teggart, each ring might produce happenings that have an effect on the next circle within the concentric set. "In such a series," continues Teggart, "it is obvious that change in any outer circle will affect all that lies within it." Interest in establishing the study of social change on a sound scientific basis led Teggart to define events in terms of his conceptualization of concentric circles: "We may, then, define an 'event' as an intrusion, from any wider circle, into any circle or condition which may be the object of present interest."[69] Events then are defined in terms of their function for subsequent happenings in the next lower circle of experience.

Teggart's major investigation, that accounting for the invasions of the Roman Empire between 58 B.C. and 107 A.D., gives a good example of his conceptualization of the event as intrusion. The study focuses on intrusions from the third circle, that of human activities, on to the second, that of the local group or the subnation. More specifically it explains the relationships between wars, interruptions in trade, and Barbarian invasions in Europe. Teggart described his method as:

> first, to recognize the existence of a class of events, and hence of a problem for investigation; second, to examine the theories or explanations heretofore put forward to account for the occurrences; third; when these theories were found to be at variance with the facts, to assemble all data which might be regarded as pertinent to the subject.[70]

Employing his method to provide a scientifically grounded explanation for the Barbarian invasions of the Roman Empire, Teggart set down, in chronological order, all known events, wars, disturbances in each separate kingdom or region of the Eurasian continent for a period of five hundred years. The next step was to compare occurrences in each of the many areas for which it was possible to find evidence either in European or Asiatic sources.[71] As a result of this comparison it was discovered that during one period of a century and a half (58 B.C. – 107 A.D.):

> every uprising on the European borders of the Roman Empire had been preceded by the outbreak of war either on the eastern frontiers of the empire or in the 'Western Regions' of the Chinese. Moreover, the correspondence in events was discovered to be so precise that, whereas wars in the Roman East were followed uniformly and always by disturbances on the lower Danube and the Rhine, wars in the eastern Tien Shan were followed uniformly and always by disturbances on the Danube between Vienna and Budapest.[72]

The paired "uniformities" are credited by Teggart with being a "discovery, for the first time, of correlations in historical events," and furthermore with being a demonstration of "the existence of a type of order of historical facts which has not hitherto received attention." But correlation is not the ultimate aim of Teggart's investigation. He also wishes to find a single cause for this class of events. His causal account takes the form of "an hypothesis, and as such [it] is open to revision." As Teggart puts it, "Without further elaboration, I may say that as the outcome of this long and difficult phase of the investigation I reached the conclusion that the correspondence of wars in the East and invasions in the West had been due to interruptions of trade."[73] Thus, the collection, classification, and comparison of happenings results in the discovery of a *correlation*. The correlation, in turn, evokes interest in the suggestion and elaboration of a *causal* hypothesis. Presumably, although Teggart did not himself carry it out, the hypothesis itself could be tested, refined, and, if necessary, reformulated. It could also be rejected if the evidence did not sustain it.

Central to Teggart's general theory of social change is the claim that a class of occurrences locatable in one circle of human experience has the capacity to act as an intrusive event on another, more specifically, on a settled custom-bound population. In his study of the Barbarian invasions his argument proceeds as follows: The general covering argument is stated directly. "Now, wars at all times break in upon the established routine of orderly existence and interfere with the everyday activities of the peoples in conflict, and more especially they put a stop to usual forms of intercourse between the inhabitants of the opposing countries." This statement is itself unproven and rests upon its own implicit plausibility, its appeal to common sense, and the reader's own experience. Read another way it could be taken as an hypothesis that remains to be demonstrated by appropriate historical investigations. Whatever its scientific status, however, the statement circumscribes the specific train of facts arrayed by Teggart's formulation. "Hence, when China initiated war in Mongolia or against the kingdoms in the Tarim basin, and when Rome invaded Parthia or Armenia, the inception of hostilities automatically interrupted communications, however well established, across the border." The next logical step for Teggart is the application of his theory of intrusion and interruption to the explanation of the Barbarian uprisings:

> It follows, therefore, that the problem of the relationship between wars in the Far or Near East and the barbarian uprisings in Europe calls for the identification of some usual activity of men which would be subject to immediate interruption in the event of war, and which also might be resumed promptly on the return of peace. The activity which at once suggests itself as complying with these requirements or conditions is that of trade or commerce.[74]

Why trade or commerce "at once" suggests itself as the kind of activity meeting theoretical requirements is not made clear. The general run of the argument would suggest a materialist theory of history standing behind this discussion, but no admission or elaboration of it is made. Rather, with the interruption of trade designated as a causal agency, it remains but to suggest that in the instant cases, those of China, Parthia, and Rome, wars interrupted commerce and the cessation of trade led in turn to hostilities all along the trade routes.

Teggart is careful to add that the train of happenings set in motion by the wars was not part of the intentions of the emperors and statesmen who led their people into military affrays. "It is of some importance to note that the statesmen who were responsible for or advocated the resort to war, on each of forty occasions, were entirely unaware of the consequences which this policy entailed."[75] Teggart's study thus corresponds with an idea developed at some length by Robert K. Merton—that of the unanticipated consequences of purposeful action, also known to sociologists as the concept of latent function.[76] However, Teggart's intentions are quite different from those of Merton. Whereas the latter sought to elaborate and extend the idea of function, Teggart's purposes are threefold: to issue a caveat about the relationship between the intentions of statesmen and their decisions; to suggest a specific role for the informed citizen of the modern *polis;* and, most significantly, to indicate the usefulness of scientific history for public affairs. Teggart neither accuses nor blames the leaders of China or Rome for the outbreaks occasioned by their decisions to go to war. Instead, he credits them with judiciousness and wisdom. In the case of the Chinese, he points out that their wars "were initiated only after lengthy discussions at the imperial court by ministers who were well versed in Chinese history, and who reasoned from historical experience no less than from moral principles and from expediency." However, these Chinese statesmen did not know that their decisions would lead to conflicts and devastations in regions of which they had never heard, that is, in Europe. The Romans were equally statesmenlike, and, though not entirely ignorant of the fact that disturbances in the East were followed by irruptions in Europe, they failed to make the causal connection. "So Augustus persisted in his attempts to dominate Armenia, though the actual results on the Danube and the Rhine could have been unerringly predicted."[77]

Precisely because unanticipated consequences of purposive decisions can be predicted by persons informed by a scientific approach to history, Teggart proposes a role in public affairs for the private citizen educated in the method and findings of such a history. The Roman statesmen, according to Teggart, were typical of rulers in every age. Dependent on the state of knowledge available to their own generation, they were also too concerned with the immediate present. In times of crisis they could not take the time necessary for prolonged and painstaking investigation. The private citizen, on the other hand, freed from the cares and demands of immediate problems, is, as Teggart sees it, in a position to give aid to the future statesmen in precisely this neglected area. Although the objective of an applied science of history may appear unattainable at the present time, Teggart argues, hope for the future, for avoiding the misfortunes wreaked by well-intentioned but uninformed leaders, rests on the establishment of new forms of knowledge obtained from the record of human experiences. That record, history, has been manifested thus far in literary narratives and patriotic polemics. However, once liberated from these shibboleths, a truly scientific history could save humankind from repetition of its worst errors.

The possibilities for and benefits from a new type of scientific historical investigation have not yet been recognized.[78] According to Teggart, the nineteenth century produced histories that escalated the tensions among nationalities and peoples.[79] Literary and poetic usages of historical materials, he argues, are either irrelevant or pernicious.[80] But, a return to the original promise and hope elicited by the discovery of the scientific approach could reorganize history not only as a useful science but also as a guide to statecraft.[81] Once statesmen understand the relationships of causes to effects, of intended goals and unintended consequences, they might, Teggart seems to suggest, so arrange their affairs that most harmful effects would be avoided. Scientific history, Teggart offers, could become a boon to mankind.[82]

That neither the scientific nor beneficent possibilities of historical investigation had been realized caused Teggart to continue and indeed to intensify his plea for an end to retrogressive, unscientific, and moribund developmentalist approaches. At the time of his death in 1946 he had just completed a long and mournful essay on the argument of Hesiod's *Works and Days*.[83] In that essay he lamented the fact that the ancient poet's ode to even-handed justice as the basis for human progress had been replaced, first by Thucydides' thesis that cultural advancement would follow a determinate trajectory of growth, if nothing interfered, and later by Plato's argument that the good life would follow from an authoritarian state-enforced division of labor. Neither the scientific history that Teggart had labored for nearly four decades to establish nor the melioristic application of a grounded social science to human affairs had found widespread appreciation or legitimation during his own lifetime.

Teggart's legacy is manifold, but his dream of a scientific history aiding in both the advancement of knowledge and the elimination of "the war-compelling spirit of nationality" has not been realized.[84] The iconoclastic perspective that startled and dismayed his more conventional peers did inspire some daring and innovative approaches by younger scholars. Perhaps the two most important historians who took up aspects of Teggart's approach were Arnold J. Toynbee and Joseph Needham. According to Toynbee, "Professor F. J. Teggart, in his *Theory of History*, Chapter 14, showed me where to find the entry into my subject after I had been groping for it without succeeding in discovering it by my own native lights." Toynbee took three of Teggart's directives "to heart, and . . . followed them from beginning to end" in *A Study of History*. These directives, Toynbee observed, proved to be "a sovereign clue which . . . not only initiated me into my subject but also piloted me through it." The directives were first, that "in the study of Man . . . the first step must be a return to the Present"; second, that "the point of departure must necessarily be observation of the differences which particularize the condition of Humanity in different parts of the world"; and, third, that "the observation of the cultural differences which distinguish human groups leads at once to the recognition of the major problem of the Science of Man," namely "How are these differences to be accounted for?"; "How have the differences which we observe in the cultural activities of men come to be as we find them at the present time?"[85]

Teggart's impact on Toynbee was indeed of the greatest significance, for in *The Theory of History* Teggart had singled out for special notice Toynbee's earlier teleological orientation, criticizing its substitution of analogical reasoning for historical investigation. That Toynbee altered his approach fundamentally after reading Teggart may be instantly recognized if we recall the passage by the former that Teggart selected as typifying a mode of history that instituted "an analogy between the life cycle of the individual and the entire existence of humanity":

> The germ of Western society, says Arnold Toynbee, first developed in the body of Greek society, like a child in the womb. The Roman Empire was the period of pregnancy during which the new life was sheltered and nurtured by the old. The "Dark Age" was the crisis of birth, in which the child broke away from its parent and emerged as a separate, though naked and helpless, individual. The Middle Ages were the period of childhood, in which the new creature, though immature, found itself able to live and grow independently. The fourteenth and fifteenth centuries, with their marked characteristics of transition, may stand for puberty, and the centuries since the year 1500 for our prime.[86]

Toynbee's subsequent adoption of a comparative historical approach in *A Study of History,* though not without its theological biases and religio-ethnic prejudices—especially its anti-Semitism[87]—has been hailed by Kenneth Bock because it "accepts the canons of scientific inquiry so disdainfully rejected by Spengler" and because it is "a tremendous effort . . . to bring large masses of empirical data to bear on explicitly formulated hypotheses." As Bock has observed, Toynbee made

a breakthrough in historiography—the formulation of testable hypotheses and the raising of specific questions: "Toynbee," Bock points out,
"can be refuted, rather than just maligned, by those who would go to
the trouble." [88]

Although Joseph Needham's employment of Teggart's work seems
to be confined to an examination of the war, migration, and invasion
thesis presented in the latter's *Rome and China,* in fact the entire enterprise of his own mammoth research project is within the spirit of Teggart's proposed scientific historical orientation. [89] Needham begins with
the statement of a problem and observes that the only way to solve that
problem is to engage in a careful comparative history of the relevant
cultures and civilizations guided by a specific hypothesis. As Needham
states the question:

> Why, then, did modern science, as opposed to ancient and medieval science
> (with all that modern science implied in terms of political dominance),
> develop only in the Western world? Nothing but a careful analysis, a veri-
> table titration, of the cultures of East and West will eventually answer this
> question. Doubtless many factors of an intellectual or philosophical char-
> acter played their part, but there were certainly also important social and
> economic causes which demand investigation. [90]

That Needham is directing his efforts toward a comparative analysis of sociocultural change, very much like that employed by Hodgen in
her study *Change and History,* is indicated in his own use of the term
"titration," borrowed from chemistry, to designate his methodological
procedure:

> We may say that titration is the determination of the quantity of a given
> chemical compound in a solution by observing that amount of a solution
> of another compound at known strength required to convert the first
> completely into a third, the end-point being ascertained by a change of
> colour or other means . . . Now in my work with my collaborators on
> the history of discovery and invention in Chinese and other cultures we
> are always trying to fix dates—the first canal lock in China in A.D. 984,
> the first irrigation contour canal in Assyria in 690 B.C., the first transport
> contour canal in China in 219 B.C., the first eyeglasses or spectacles in
> Italy in A.D. 1286, and so on. In such a way one can "titrate" the great
> civilizations against one another, to find out and give credit where credit
> is due, and so also, it seems, must one analyse the various constituents,
> social or intellectual, of the great civilizations, to see why one combina-
> tion could far excel in medieval times while another could catch up later
> on and bring modern science itself into existence. [91]

Precisely because Needham presents his work in the form of a specific
problem, a formulated hypothesis, and an empirical investigation of all
the known and relevant facts, his thesis is subject to concrete criticism,

factual refutation, and hypothetical reconsideration. Like the work of Toynbee, then, that of Needham can be treated according to the canons of scientific evaluation, by either raising questions about the nature and approach of the governing hypothesis or by reinvestigating the factual materials.[92]

Hailed as "unquestionably the foremost writer in this country, if not in the world, on the theoretical basis of the new history as a science of social change,"[93] Teggart was nevertheless ignored by most of his peers and colleagues, and except for the notable scholars just mentioned, his influence has been confined to his few students and to those historians and sociologists who borrow portions of his outlook to serve their own intellectual purposes. Carl Becker supposes that, if persistently applied, Teggart's approach would explain the "universal processes of historical change."[94] But as Harry Elmer Barnes observes, "Of all the important writers on the newer methods and attitudes in history, no other suffered more from the discrepancy between his merits and his influence than Professor Teggart." Barnes attributes Teggart's failure to influence large numbers of scholars to "his preference to play a lone hand—denying the significance of what most others have done and refusing to associate himself actively with those who have succeeded in establishing the new history."[95] Leaving aside whatever personality considerations are suggested in this explanation, it is important to see the lacunae in Teggart's own use of resources. Most notable is the neglect of the work of Max Weber, Georg Simmel, Émile Durkheim, and other sociologists in the classical tradition. As Robert Nisbet reports, "Under Teggart I studied essentially—Teggart! . . . I never once heard him refer to Durkheim, Simmel, Weber, Tönnies, Cooley, Thomas, Mead, Tocqueville (Comte, Marx, Spencer, yes, but inevitably critically), or any of the other titans of the sociological tradition."[96] Only a few efforts directed toward uniting the outlook of Teggart with that of Weber and other classical sociologists have been undertaken. Both Bock and Nisbet see Weber's work as falling within the scope of the general orientation proposed by Teggart and, especially, as standing apart from and opposed to the evolutionary tradition represented by Parsons.[97] The recent translations into English of Weber's *Roscher and Knies* and *The Agrarian Sociology of Ancient Civilizations* should reenforce their observations.[98] However, attempts to specify Teggart's relationship to the classical tradition in sociology have proved difficult. At one time Howard Becker argued that Teggart belonged together with that group of scholars—Shotwell, Robinson, Durkheim, and Tönnies—who identified the trend of social development as moving toward greater measures of accessibility, differentiation, integration, and secularization coupled with coordinate trends toward individuation, compartmentalization, and rationality.[99] Furthermore, Becker continued, Teggart's methodological approach was to be distinguished from that of Weber in that the latter insisted on "the methodological precision of culture case study and the ideal-typical method."[100] More recently Boskoff located Teggart with a rather large and disparate aggregate—Weber, MacIver, Mannheim, Sorokin, Redfield, Becker, Pareto, Gluckman, Merton, Toynbee, and Bateson—who, he claims, share an interest in peculiarly *social* theories of social change, ascribing "a critical role to the operation of normally dynamic aspects of social structure—such as systems of stratification, the power structure, institutional role configurations."[101] If Teggart played too much of "a lone hand," his admirers have submerged his original contribution too deeply in a sea of quite different classical and contemporary thinkers. Praised, preserved, and prescribed, Teggart's thought has become more monument than guide.

Among sociologists and anthropologists Teggart has had a small but selective impact. Perhaps most use has been made of his concept of "release," central to the cognitive sociology and sociocultural phenomenology of his theory of social change.[102] Robert E. Park, to take one prominent example, found much theoretical and conceptual value in Teggart's idea of culture, employed Teggart's perspective on the relationships between civilizational change and migration and conquest in his own analysis of race and culture contacts, and made a most fruitful usage of Teggart's idea of "release" to formulate the character of the marginal man. He did not, however, abandon the cyclical schema of his own perspective on race relations.[103] Becker and Barnes, who admired the "sociological orientation of the ablest historical methodologist in the United States, F. J. Teggart," utilized his theory of "release" to explain the passage from sacred to secular modes of social organization,[104] and Becker did much to elaborate Teggart's original insight on the effects of migration on mental mobility, personality development, and social change.[105] However, aside from these pioneering efforts and the work of Hodgen already mentioned,[106] Teggart's approach has been so woefully neglected that in 1957 McKinney felt it necessary to point to the fact that "F. J. Teggart . . . made a major contribution to methodology which has been largely ignored by sociologists,"[107] while a decade later Goldstein paused in his criticism of the revival of ahistorical evolutionary and developmental theories in anthropology to observe how "very much worth reading" Teggart's *Theory of History* remains for understanding "present-day developmentalism" such as that found in Leslie White's *The Evolution of Culture*.[108]

In the four decades since Teggart's death, the debate over social change and historical process has continued without any single viewpoint emerging over all others. A proliferation of only slightly varying evolutionist, neoevolutionist, and functionalist approaches has been predominant,[109] but there has also been a revival of diffusionist theories[110] and a growth in awareness of difficulties in developmentalism. Moreover, Teggart's disciples have continued and enlarged his project. Hodgen has explored the varieties of resistance to a scientific history in medieval and modern anthropological thought.[111] Bock has analyzed the "comparative method," traced the Attic origins of developmentalism, called attention to those classical sociologists who did not succumb to Aristotelian orientations, revealed the connections of functionalism to evolutionism, reiterated the basic objections to the biological analogy, and continued the sociological study and opposition to war and racism.[112] Nisbet has continued the criticism of neoevolutionism by pointing to its effects on functionalist theories of change and its revival in the work of Talcott Parsons, insisted on Teggart's idea that history is plural, showed that sociology as an art form would abhor development of a systems approach, explored the attitude toward history in the writings of Émile Durkheim, analyzed both the French and American revolutions as intrusions, and attested to the significance of Frederick Teggart in the establishment of humane letters and social science at the University of California.[113] The challenge to social theory presented by Teggart, Hodgen, and Bock has recently been taken up by an erstwhile Marxist, Ronald L. Meek. Seeking to rescue Turgot[114] and the Scottish Moralists from charges of ahistoricism, Meek has revived interest in the thesis that economic and social development has proceeded through four stages of subsistence—hunting, pasturage, agriculture, and commerce—and urged that the developmentalist ideas in the works of Adam Smith and Lord Kames are not entirely bereft of historical evidence.[115] Two other recent Marxist writers seem to have taken very seriously the climate of opinion opposed to evolutionary theory. Seeking to revitalize the idea that the passage of legal ideology and institutions moved from a *Gemeinschaft* to a *Gesellschaft* form, Eugene Kamenka and Alice Erh-Soon Tay reject a "simple, straightforward evolutionary schema," recognize "that *Gemeinschaft*, *Gesellschaft* and bureaucratic-administrative strains will coexist in all, or at least most, societies," and suggest that "social relations, even in allegedly 'primitive' societies, are complex" and will display at least incipient representations of all characteristics at each stage of social development.[116] Although still adhering to a stage theory of social change, these writers seem nevertheless to have acknowledged much of the message that Teggart sought to deliver. Yet Richard Beardsley's remarks presented on the recent death of Leslie A. White—the single most important contemporary advocate of the revival of evolutionism—signify how little of Teggart's thought has affected anthropology and related disciplines: "No scholar today is regarded as rash . . . for asserting that human institutions persist and change for systemic reasons rooted in culture; or for formulating ideas or schemes that assert general evolutionary sequences of institutions." [117]

DILEMMAS OF THE NEOPOSITIVIST APPROACH

Although it would be appropriate recognition of an all-too-neglected perspective in social science to halt functionalist investigations, reign in the neoevolutionist revival, and resuscitate the original project enunciated by Teggart and his followers, certain unresolved difficulties require a more critical stance. Most important is a further critique of the concept of "event." Common to all adherents of the neopositivist school is the argument that a properly conducted scientific study of social change requires the comparative analysis of *happenings* and the discovery of a prior intrusive *event* or *class of events* that may be designated as the causal agency. The principal problem of this position, a problem that none of the adherents of neopositivism has addressed directly, is the unanalyzed assumption that both "happenings" and "events" are unambiguously available and clearly identifiable to the researcher. Once the key terms "happenings" and "events" are scrutinized, we discover problematic elements in their recognition as such and a host of difficulties in their usage for comparative historical inquiry.

Central for identifying an "event" or a "happening" is the task of establishing temporal and spatial boundaries. Teggart, of course, recognizes this issue and insists on the classification of occurrences designated specifically in terms of their location in time and space. [118] But this begs the question of what are the peripheries of space and the termini in time that grid happenings? Who establishes these boundaries? Is the establishment of boundaries uniform over time and space so that comparison of like phenomena is possible? Conventional comparative historians have usually treated "happenings" and "events" as if they were uniform in spatio-temporal type and equally available to anyone who cared to take cognizance of the historical record. The historical record, however, like history itself, is a human activity. Hence, as a record, it is subject to the very queries of temporality and parameter, the modifications of crime and custom, the vicissitudes of idiosyncrasy and persecution that are aspects of history itself.

The problem of establishing the spatio-temporal boundaries of "happenings" has been noticed in one of the criticisms of Teggart's study of the Barbarian invasions. C. Martin Wilbur observed, concerning Teggart's claim to have identified no less than forty-nine major disturbances:

> He presents pertinent facts in great detail but fails to indicate clearly which, among the welter of invasions, uprisings, punitive operations, and defensive measures in Europe, were separate occurrences. It is almost impossible to isolate the thirty-one disturbances there and the eighteen in the Roman East theoretically resulting from previous wars in the Near and Far East respectively.[119]

Pitirim Sorokin, in another review of *Rome and China,* goes even further in this line of criticism, suggesting that the temporal boundaries of these supposedly discrete happenings may have been rendered more distinct by Teggart's method than the facts of the case actually warrant:

> Though Professor Teggart claims again and again that the events on the Rumanian Danube, the Rhine, and in the West regularly (he says even "invariably") followed the disturbances in the Chinese West and the Roman East, such uniformity of a temporal sequence is not proved by him. As the beginning and end of each war or uprising is unknown, for this reason only it is hardly possible to contend that the uprisings on the Danube and the Rhine regularly lagged behind the wars or uprisings in the East. As many of these movements went on sporadically in various parts of the Roman Empire, without any clear-cut caesura between them, no convincing evidence is given to support the claim of the uniform sequence . . . This means that there is no possibility to claim which disturbances, those of the Far East or those of the West, led and which lagged in time.[120]

Space and time are indeed the boundaries of "happenings" and the contexts of "events." But to claim that either space or time have fixed and invariable parameters that are universally known, forever beyond custom and culture, and immutable over time or even within the same time period is to accept assumptions about these basic elements that are grounded neither in experience nor experiment.[121] Once we grant that even the members of a given society might disagree over the onset or terminus of anything and the exact length and breadth over which it occurs, we admit ourselves to the world of frame analysis.[122] In such a world the organization of experience is perceived by the social scientist as a problematic feature for those who are experiencing it. Structures of consciousness become important—indeed fundamental—to the understanding of just what is going on, where, and when.

If "happenings" are rendered problematical by the mysteries and variations of time and space, "events"—in the special sense that Teggart used this term—raise even greater questions. Ironically, Teggart's formal and methodical usage of the term—elements in a set of concentric circles representing realms of experience that intrude from one outer circle on to an inner one—suggests a sociocultural system not entirely dissimilar from that "action system" developed by the "Social Relations" School at Harvard University years later.[123] Boundaries are imposed by such a system or more accurately by the system makers, but they exist at the expense of the meanings and relationships that actually prevail among the members of a given society. The imposition of a system *a priori* would seem to divorce the subject matter of a historical sociology from its substance, giving it a chimerical, conjectural, and literary quality quite independent from its actual context. Teggart's original aim was to liberate social science from this quality.

There is a further logical problem presented by Teggart's concept of "event" that is best exhibited in the sole attempt (to my knowledge) to give methodological precision to the term. In a recent essay Pachter has defined "an event E as *the juncture between two situations S' and S"*, separating as well as linking them together, and in the process defining both."[124] More prosaically, Pachter tells us that an event has a function, namely, "that the world was never the same afterward." As examples of events Pachter mentions the Battle of Waterloo, the "Battle of Britain" (the intermittent series of air engagements over Britain for ten months of 1940–41), and, from World War I, Ludendorff's "blind assault all along the Allied lines for over a year." Events are those collections of happenings that, treated as a unit, can be seen to change the course of history. Pachter further allows for "chance" events and for the treatment of the failure of any change to occur when one might be expected.[125]

However, the event, E, is a social or personal construction of the historian, as is the original situation, S', and the subsequent situation, S". History, even when it employs the symbols of science (e.g., E, S', S", and such formulae, suggested by Pachter, as $S_a^n S'$ (E) S"), would appear to be a human rendering of raw reality. It is, thus, *interpretive* and must be. But what are the criteria of that interpretation to be? Shall sociologists accept the historian's prior claims on the ordering of what is "out there," or shall we ponder more empathically over the condition of Fabrizio, in Stendhal's *La Chartreuse de Parme* (an example suggested by Pachter!), when he finds himself a witness to a welter of happenings—hussars galloping past, peasants in flight, burning homes, guns firing all around—and only later discovers that what he had experienced as a violent chaos now has a name—the Battle of Waterloo. Pachter's "scientific" approach to history leads us back to a fundamental question—whose history, those who live it, or those who interpret it?

The neopositivist position holds that explanations in history can take the form of causal "laws." One set of happenings is interpreted or accounted for as having occurred because of an event or set of events. Not only does this raise the question of what an event actually is, but also of what the causal relationship is composed. Neopositivists would appear to be content to rest their claim on the argument that a cause is a recurrent juxtaposition of similar events and happenings, thus admitting Hume's well-known objections without abandoning the search for the uniform sequences he described.

However, most sociologists appear unsatisfied to discover and report statistical correlations. They want also to understand and explain them. Teggart not only claimed to discover a historical correlation but also presented a hypothesized causal explanation. He did not, however, demonstrate that his causal hypothesis had validity beyond the immediate case he had investigated, and, indeed, in that case, it rests on its plausibility alone and the willingness of the readers—not all of whom acquiesced[126]—to suspend disbelief in the assumptions grounding it. It would appear that much of the brilliance of neopositivist social science rests not on its mastery of techniques to render raw reality into statistical arrays and formulated findings, but rather on the ingenious arguments that appear *ad hoc* to give *meaning* to these formulations. Perhaps the classic example is that of Durkheim's *Suicide,* which, as Jack Douglas has shown, smuggles in both a latent phenomenology and a familiar narrative and story line to bolster and indeed provide social substance to its scientific value as explanation.[127]

In general, the connection that sociologists employ to stitch together two sets of happenings, or by which they connect an event, E, to an earlier situation, S', and a later one, S'', is said to be both *logical* and *meaningful.* However, there are problems with each of these aspects of the connection. The logic employed by most social scientists is the formal logic associated with the original work of Aristotle. Over against this logic are the numerous logics-in-use employed by the historical actors on the scene. The rules of understanding that apply in the former situation may not apply at all at the actual scene of social action and among the social actors who actually produce the happening that the scientist seeks to explain.

The problem of establishing both causal and intelligible explanations in a science of history was addressed most forcefully by Max Weber. Defining sociology as "a science which attempts the interpretive understanding of social action in order thereby to arrive at a causal explanation of its course and effects,"[128] Weber objected to those social scientific approaches—such as that of Wilhelm Roscher—that sought to establish general laws. "The logical ideal of such a science would be a system of *formulae* of absolutely general validity." Composed of statements constituting "an abstract representation of the features common to all historical events," Weber observed that such a system would never permit historical reality to be deduced from it. "Causal 'explanation,'" Weber concluded, "would simply amount to the formation of increasingly *general* relational concepts which would have the purpose of reducing, insofar as possible, all cultural phenomena to purely quantitative categories of some sort."[129] Whether these categories contribute to the intelligibility of history would be formally irrelevant to this kind of science, thus robbing the social sciences of their cultural and humanistic content.

A sociologist who takes Weber seriously must recognize that his or her own task has not even begun when she or he collects sets of happenings and finds correlations among them. The sociologist must also ascertain the subjective state of mind and discover the meanings that can be imputed to the intentional actor. Interpretation (*Deuten*) is aimed at the uncovering of meaning (*Sinn*), and meaning in turn refers to the contents of the subjective state of mind or to the symbol systems in use in the minds of the actors.

When faced with asserting a logico-meaningful linkage, a neopositivist all too easily succumbs to the unstated and uncriticized assumption that a common vocabulary of motives obtains among the social or historical actors under study, the social scientist doing the investigation, and the body of scholars and peers who make up the readership of his or her monograph. Of course there has been much reflection by critical philosophers of history on the subject of empathic understanding, meaning and its social construction, and interpretive procedures in historical scholarship. (Perhaps most important is the attempt by Wilhelm Dilthey to demonstrate that historical understanding can never exceed the empathic imagination of the historian.)[130] Yet when neopositivist social scientists employ a logico-meaningful explanation, they rarely account for the apparent contradiction between the causal mode of historical understanding stressing interpretive understanding (*verstehen*) and that causal mode based on the correlated relationship among happenings.

The phrase logico-meaningful thus would appear to arise as a compound of Aristotelian systems of logic and Diltheyan hermeneutics. Seeking to combine these two into a single philosophical perspective, neopositivists have glossed over the contradictions and problems in each and failed to indicate how such a union can be established. Gadamer has recently argued that Dilthey himself failed to resolve all the difficulties of such a position and believes that it awaits the application of Heidegger's and post-Heideggerian historical thought for a solution.[131]

ALTERNATIVES TO NEOPOSITIVISM

In current sociological thought there are a number of approaches and perspectives that grapple with one or another of the problems raised by the debate between the evolutionary functionalists and the neopositivists. Although each of these orientations attempts to resolve at least some of the difficulties, to take a tentative position, and to proceed with the business of basic sociological research, none has found a fully satisfying resolution to all of the problems raised. Among the several innovative suggestions in sociology, we shall deal with three: neofunctionalism, the "mythic" approach, and certain "phenomenological" orientations to history. Finally, we shall suggest that a "phenomenological" approach offers an embracement of all the schools we have considered.

Neofunctionalism

Neofunctionalism here refers to a functionalist orientation that proceeds with a reflexive awareness of the problems of its own methodological foundations. On perhaps less firm ground but yet from a more sophisticated basis, neofunctionalism introduces a number of qualifications and reservations to theorizing and research. First, the *a priori* positing of a given nature to any social system is no longer admissible. Instead, neofunctionalism rejects the closed and determinate systemics of Parsons in favor of the open systems approach associated most prominently with von Bertalanffy and his followers.[132] Second, over against the formal and one-sided functionalism of Parsons, neofunctionalism reverts to that of Evans-Pritchard or Radcliffe-Brown, functionalists who attempted to make themselves analogs of the system that they studied.[133] Finally, neofunctionalism proposes what might be called a "soft" interdependence; rather than assuming the interdependence of parts *a priori,* neofunctionalism seeks to discover the actual interdependencies-in-use among societal members. Thus, the determinacy of the system is, in the spirit of Ernest Gellner's discussion of functionalism, a feature of the actors' own constructions of consensus and order.[134]

In an earlier section of this essay we spoke of the two sides of evolutionary functionalist thought. As an answer to the question of social order the functionalist posits a condition of homeostasis; as an answer to the question of social change, the evolutionist posits dynamic equilibrium within the systems and slow, orderly, continuous, and teleological changes among systems and over long periods of time. Neofunctional-

ists certainly speak of social change or evolution, but unlike their predecessors, they now must do so with the realization that they are engaged
in a conjectural history. Their schema may be presented as a form of
classification for data that otherwise would be too complicated to form
into a coherent unit. This classification system, although uni- or multilinear and evolutionary in nature, is neither accurate with respect to the
dynamic of open systems nor strictly historical in its depiction of sequences. It is not causal, predictive, or a chronicle of what actually happened. It is a heuristic device for ordering data. The justification for the
kind of neofunctionalism is an aesthetic one—that of symmetry.

There remains the question of defining a happening. Neofunc-
tionalists have not proposed an answer to this question directly, but a
suggestion for a definition may be extracted from the writings of Erving Goffman. Although Goffman has never addressed himself directly
to the problems of history, comparative analysis, or social change, it is
nevertheless possible to use portions of his approach as a point of departure for our problem.[135]

In his analysis of games, Goffman raises the question, what is a
game? Employing chess as an example, Goffman observes that although
a vase of flowers might be placed next to the chess board, it has no place
whatsoever in the attempt of the players to gain checkmate. That is, we
know the happenings in chess by resort to the *rules of irrelevance,* those
understandings that distinguish among the items in the environment according to their usage for a particular activity. A happening is known to
us, Goffman seems to be saying, by the process of separating that which
does not count in the particular activity in which the happening is
embedded.[136]

However, the activity in which the happening occurs is part of an
engagement of happenings, the sum total of which may form an event.
If the rules of irrelevance constitute a jurisdictional boundary around the
activity then it follows that the *rules of relevance,* the "juridical" code-in-
use within the activity, describe its positive composition and web of relationships. Only by ascertaining both "juridical" and "jurisdictional"
codes does the sociologist complete his or her embracement of the activity, encapsulate the event, and contextually establish the affiliated
network of happenings.

Although Goffman's approach and our own extension and application of it suggest a possible resolution of the problem of defining
happenings and events, it is self-consciously located in cultural and sub-
cultural specificity. Happenings and events established by this procedure are inextricably connected to the time, place, environment, and
belief systems of which they are an expression. Given their embeddedness, the sociologist interested in comparative analysis and cross-cultural

or intercivilizational research is confronted with the question of whether he or she is dealing with comparable units. The greater the contextual knowledge of happenings and events, the less the items under study appear to be similar.

Of course the question we are raising with regard to Goffman's approach is not unique to it. The same difficulties apply to any contextual model employed, whether it is organic, mechanical, dramaturgic, or gamelike. Every model that requires a specification of the nature of that which it represents establishes a unique configuration and a particularity of boundaries.

Before we accept the narrative historian's conclusion that the enterprise proposed by the neopositivists is impossible, however, it might be well to reconsider what it is we are seeking to compare. Rather than comparing happenings or events, perhaps the proper comparative historical task is to look for the *underlying rules* that permit the embeddedness of happenings and events in contexts. Such an enterprise would seek to understand the codes that permit, shape, and encourage the social constructions of reality. Examining the rules of relevance and irrelevance in the several societies, cultures, and civilizations might lead to generalizations about the fundamental basis of human affiliation.

One recent school of thought that bids fair to accept this challenge is ethnomethodology.[137] Although not addressed to historical sociology and never interesting itself directly in any of the problems posed by that subdiscipline, it nevertheless has something to say about the discovery of the rules lying below contextually embedded conduct. Ethnomethodology burrows behind the accepted facticity of positivist sociology in an attempt to describe precisely how social reality becomes an accomplishment of the actors on the scene. Its developments thus far point toward a full-scale analysis of the common sense understandings that undergird both social reality and social science. Its own emphasis on the reflexivity and indexicality of all social expressions, however, would seem to threaten rather than rethread the social scientific project proposed by the neopositivists.

The "Mythic" Alternative

To be properly understood within the context of the present discussion, the "mythic" approach to historical sociology must be considered in its relation to the original project of Teggart and his followers, especially as it has been developed in the works of Bock and Nisbet. Both Bock and Nisbet have been interested in establishing a firm grounding for the sociological study of *social change*. A presumption of their position—one so basic it was never subjected to critical attention—is that social change has occurred and is still occurring. Although the presumption of social change as an on-going process has rarely been challenged by sociologists, it is a worthy subject for critical philosophical investigation. Implicit in the work of the French structuralist anthropologist, Claude Lévi-Strauss, and dramatically realized in the writings of Kenneth Burke, is an approach that challenges the presumption of social change and that offers an alternative to the study of society and process.

In their own discussions of a theory of social change, Teggart, Hodgen, Bock, and Nisbet object to the evolutionary functionalists' assumption that the forces of social change are *always* at work. In contrast, the neopositivists assert that whether, to what extent, at what rate, and with what effect social change is going on are empirical questions that ought to be investigated without the adumbration of any question-begging assumptions. However, the neopositivists do not consider the possibility that social change has never occurred, that the subject has no locus or objectification in the socio-historical world. That there can never be anything new under the sun is an hypothesis not entertained by neopositivist sociologists.

The conception of a static world in which social change only appears to go on may seem strange, but it can be derived from the writings of the French structuralist Lévi-Strauss's approach to the significance of myth for the study of social structures and from Kenneth Burke's analysis of attitudes toward history.

In the structuralist approach of Lévi-Strauss there is a vision of a formal ahistorical position.[138] According to Lévi-Strauss, the properties of mind are in everywhere and in every time the same: The mind works through the analysis of forms. Forms, furthermore, are always of the same structure, consisting in the creation of paired and balanced opposites. These opposites are built up in various algebraic ways becoming complex structures, which are, of course, capable of decomposition into their fundamental components through structural analysis. In social life, where interaction between persons is basic, there are three basic structures produced: kinship, which structural analysis reformulates as the exchange of women; economy, the exchange of goods and services; and language, the basis of exchange itself.

Lévi-Strauss seems to suggest a role for myth in the construction and the analysis of social history phenomena. Action—in history and in the present and future—occurs as the working out in many diverse ways of a few fundamental myths. The myths in turn are *forms* that can be exposed in their ultimate composition by the same kind of structural analysis that is employed to uncover mental phenomena. Myths, as the *forms* of reality, are understood to be transcendent and permanent, existing above, beyond, and apart (analytically speaking) from the transitory appearances of entities and transformations experienced in history and everyday life. Moreover, all intellectual efforts to find the absolute or fundamental grounding of ontic reality are themselves products of mythological formulations. In Lévi-Strauss's view, Freud's analysis of the Oedipus myth must be treated precisely in the same manner as that of Sophocles. The myth forms are the ultimate reality. The method and approach are Platonic.[139] Like Husserl's presuppositionless philosophy or Chomsky's deep structures of prelinguistic mentation, Lévi-Strauss's formal anthropology of mind and myth seeks to decode or translate its claimed fundamental entity—mind or myth—by looking "behind" the happenings of history and everyday life.

The mythic approach holds, in effect, that there is no history, or rather no history to which the social scientist need attend. Rather, history gives the appearance of change, whereas the ultimate scientific reality is the severality of forms that are behind, beneath, or beyond that appearance. The mythic approach would seem to hold that there is a finite body of ultimate myths that describe the basis for all possible human activities. What historians record are the epiphenomena of these myths. The social scientist must burrow beneath these epiphenomena to find the basic form. Thus, although historical data are epiphenomena they are also representative or indexical, referring back to the basic mythic text of which they are a particular expression. The project for Lévi-Strauss's approach to social science, then, is the uncovering of the basic myths. Presumably, once they have all been discovered and decoded, all human activity—past, present, and future—will be available to us as extrapolations and variations on these pristine and primary forms.

The mythic approach, however, does not presume to possess any epistemic superiority to its own subject matter. The truths of science are not arrayed against the myths of history; rather, science is itself an expression of myth. Structuralism thus belongs self-consciously to that perspective known as symbolic realism, that is, the myth structures are not taken to stand for some reality that can be objectively known, but, instead, they are taken to be the only reality that we can know. To analyze or explain history in terms of structural analysis, then, is to restate the expression of one discipline in the vocabulary of another, to translate the "epiphenomena" of happenings into the semiotic of a new comparative literature.

The methodological underpinnings of structuralism suggest that it is both a literary approach (and thus another variant on that approach to history that Teggart had originally opposed) and also that it employs a functionalist orientation. Lévi-Strauss borrows the dialectical idea from Hegel and Marx to insist that every myth is a complex structure of paired opposites poised in a state of dramatic tension. The form thus embodies both the homeostatic principle of dynamic equilibrium and the eufunctional thesis about the role of immanent conflict in systemic social formations. Finally and not coincidentally, it might be suggested that the work of Talcott Parsons, reconceived as a formulated mythic structure, fits more closely into the project of Lévi-Strauss than either scholar realizes.

Yet another formalistic, mythic approach derives from the work of Kenneth Burke.[140] Just as Plato's *Republic* is a philosophical-political utopia presented as a dramatic dialogue, so Burke suggests that our understanding of history seems to be a recounting of basic dramatic plots. Some of these dramas tell of the return of the prodigal son, the death of the king, sibling rivalry, and so on, but are applied to groups, societies, and nations that are anthropomorphized as persons. Ironically, the study of history as dramatic mode bids fair to become what Plato opposed—a kind of "cookery." Actual histories are the products of "recipes"—combinations, recombinations, remakes, and warmed over scraps of the same basic plots. The dramatistic approach that derives from Burke holds up "cookery" as a process-in-use by historical actors, historians, and historiographers. As a form of structuralism, however, it suggests a comparative structure of basic plots and an ultimate reduction of all histories to a repertory of scenarios that are enacted and reenacted throughout the ages. (It is not the case, however, that a dramatistic sociology must necessarily avoid matters of history. In a recent study in which they amplify and urge adoption of a dramatistic perspective for sociology, Lyman and Scott have carried out case studies of resistance to black slavery and of nineteenth-century social banditry in the American West.[141] Their effort shows that a serious comparative historical sociology can employ an approach that Teggart feared might be too literary and still pay close attention to all the relevant facts.)

The formal approach—Lyman and Scott excepted—resolves the problem of historiography by rejecting history. There are no histories that we must accept. Instead, the welter of happenings, the profusion of events, and the worlds of life are perceived as representations, metaphors, and variations of basic dramas or myths. Once the fundamental structure of these basic scenarios is decoded, the secret of all histories is revealed and neither past, present, nor future can withhold its mystery from the researcher.

A "Phenomenological" Alternative

Phenomenology has only recently been rediscovered with respect to its potential contribution to sociology and the historical sciences. Although its definition and scope are imprecise and much controversy ranges around the term, we shall employ it in a special way to refer to an approach that sees histories as structures of consciousness. At any moment in time these histories have varying degrees of popularity, political sway, and public support.

According to this phenomenological approach, there are two kinds of history.[142] The first kind is found in the schools, official archives, regal courts, or tribal councils. It prevails in those societies in which there is a sense of the relevance of the past and some kind of bureaucracy through which the accepted version of the past is transmitted from generation to generation. The agency of transmission may take the form of repeated and memorized folk tales, history courses in schools, sacred archival ceremonials, or some other mode that ensures intergenerational continuity and uniformity. Such history enjoys the support of the authoritative elements, is endowed with the claim of superior truth, and stands above refutation and revocation by dint of its embeddedness within the fundamental values and beliefs of the society. It is *legitimated* history.

There is, however, a second type of history. It is unofficial and exists only in the consciousness of people, although in what number, to what extent, and with what variations we can rarely know. It prevails in both societies that have no officially enforced sense of the past and in those where the legitimated history is unsatisfactory for the popular purposes for which the unofficial history is employed. Unofficial history finds expression in proverbs, legends and folk tales, hidden and secret stories of the past, uncovered but inauthenticated truths, and popular but unproven hypotheses about the relationship between past and present. In brief, *nonlegitimate* history consists in whatever notions, elements, data, or dimensions of the past ordinary individuals and nonelites bring to bear on their everyday understanding of the present.

No difference between these two types of history resides in them of themselves. In fact, one type might become the other as the vicissitudes of power and authority shift the fortunes of those who hold to one or another view of the past. Official history is that brand that has won acceptance and is backed by authoritative force. Unofficial history, although it has not obtained political recognition and the stamp of public approval, nevertheless operates as a form of populist and folk wisdom among unknown numbers of the population. As nostalgia, fables, anecdotes, traditions, apocryphal stories, fairy tales, suppressed genealogies, ethnic legends, and the like, this unofficial history is typically supposed to reside in the imaginations of children, primitives, the uneducated, unacculturated immigrants, and unsocialized persons in general. Indeed, its delegitimation in the face of official history consists precisely in the argument that it is magical, superstitious, childish, naïve, primitive, or not properly documented.

The two types of history are both the same and yet different. They are the same in the sense that both are forms of contemporary consciousness about the past. More clearly stated, this phenomenological approach regards history as constituted neither of event or deeds in the past, nor of happenings as expressions of consciousness in the past. Rather, in this approach history is both *conscious* and *contemporary*. In the phenomenological view both official and unofficial histories are expressions of contemporary consciousness. However, official and unofficial history differ from one another in two principal ways. First, official history characteristically has an inner logic and is articulated with a precise and formal cogency. It also has a greater chance for permanence because it tends to be transmitted via the printed page, conveyed in official media, or carved in stone. In contrast, unofficial history is characteristically malleable because its expression has not been rationalized and justified in the terms and canons of formal logic and routinized according to approved methodologies. The formal properties of official history—its logic, permanence, and uniformity—lend to it the potential of becoming a state supported ideology, formally organizing seemingly separate realms of data as a basis for mobilizing collective action. It was precisely this potential for becoming ideology in the several national histories that had alarmed Teggart and led him to search for a scientific basis and a truly objective history.

Official history is buttressed by political and economic power, and in modern societies it is institutionalized in bureaucracies. In contrast, unofficial history finds its domain at the interstices of social life, in the little places, corners, crevices, and private arenas where official history either fears to tread or has no right of entry. Unofficial history is a part of the idiosyncratic domain of private life, sustained by personal as opposed to public relations, emotional as opposed to affectively neutral sustenance, and private and folkish rather than literate and correct language. Thus, despite the power that official history may lend to its own version of the past, unofficial history retains a compelling and potentially subversive potency.

Whether official and unofficial history have a patterned relationship is a worthy topic for speculation. It might be the case that the greater the arenas of discourse that are governed by official history, the lesser and more constricted are the arenas of operation for unofficial history, and vice versa. Furthermore, we might speculate that, insofar as unofficial history satisfies a desire for affective sensibility that is not provided by official history, the greater the spread and development of official history, the greater also will be the sense of emotional loss, of deadening ennui, of overrationalized understanding. In such a situation, individuals and groups may redouble their efforts to find release from the iron cage of rationalized official history by resort to ever more fabulous and exotic versions of unofficial history. In a dialectical fashion, then, it may be hypothesized that the very success of the spread of official history means that it will eventually fail, as the forces of unofficial history rise in revolt against their sense of affective deprivation and emotional loss. And, to turn the dialectical screw once more, should unofficial history achieve public dominion, it too will fail, in that it becomes official and loses its subterranean emotive quality.

Although our discussion would seem to suggest that official and unofficial history form a dyadic pair, self-contained in a dialectical structure, in fact the situation is even more complex. Elites vying with one another will have competing versions of official history and aspiring nonelites will cherish and proclaim their versions of the past as well. Indeed, what Herbert Blumer has suggested as the situation in which race prejudice emerges—competing elites struggling for domination in a context of ambiguous and recent race contact[143]—is in fact the general condition for the formation of an official history. Beyond existing elites and up-and-coming near-elites are individuals, groups, and masses of people who, without political aspirations, nevertheless have conceptions of pasts that they can put into use in their everyday lives. Moreover, precisely because it is unofficial—because it tends to pass from person to person by word of mouth, because it is communicated anecdotally or as a brief but definite commentary on the situations in which people find themselves—unofficial history will be much more multifarious and multiform than official history. There will be more unofficial histories than there are official ones.

Although unofficial history is treated as primitive, childish, and magical, its own statements often take the form of lawlike pronouncements. Proverbs are good examples. As aspects of a folk knowledge employed in everyday life, proverbs rest upon the assumption that their truth value is rooted in the accumulated wisdom of the ages. Unlike statements of cause and correlation that arise from the researches of Teggart and Hodgen, proverbial wisdom is not subjected to careful empirical tests. Moreover, in the proverbs, there would appear to be a folk analog to Adam Brateson's principle concerning contradictory laws about the same phenomena—for example, the wave-particle theories of light. In juxtaposing proverbs such as "look before you leap" and "he who hesitates is lost," there is presented the well-known problem that requires a specification of just which conditions must prevail for one or the other prescription to be correct.

The fact that proverbs are not subject to carefully controlled empirical tests makes them more rather than less like official history. For both official history and proverbs are usually pronounced and proclaimed. In the case of folk history a lack of any formal testing procedure derives from the very nonpositivist conditions of its own development, that is, from a lack of formal cogency from which some indication of a test might be derived. In addition there is the "economic" problem of a paucity of resources for mobilizing the necessaries for experiment. Official history, by contrast, need not be subjected to continued empirical verification when it is supported by powerful elites in governmental and educational circles. Such ruling groups may command the resources to make empirical tests possible, but at the same time, out of consideration for the role that official history plays in legitimating their regime, refuse to allocate these resources for that purpose.

Both official and unofficial histories are sediments within structures of consciousness, differing only in terms of their socially constructed and politically supported legitimacy and their institutionalization. From the perspective of a "pure" phenomenology there is no distinction between the two types of history.

A special word must be said about scientific historiography. The history of historiography makes it clear that the modern version of "scientific" historiography had been considered subversive in other times. It too had to struggle for its current place among the officially recognized modes of historical methods. However, at all times, during its nonlegitimate and its legitimate periods, scientific historiography resided in the consciousness of a number of individuals. An investigation of the nature of scientific historiography must examine the structure, contents, and rules of relevance peculiar to this particular form of historical discourse.

CONCLUSION

The final discussion of the phenomenological approach offers an embracement of all the schools thus far examined. By recognizing that histories and historiographies can be neither more nor less than structures of consciousness with varying degrees of support and popularity, a "phenomenological" approach vitiates the claims for paradigmatic domination of all contending schools at the same time that it recognizes the likelihood of one or another school to achieve domination. Our position bears close resemblance to that of Simmel.[144] As the German philosopher sociologist saw it, histories were contents of realized experience expressed in selected established forms. As such they could not re-present happenings as they actually occurred; instead they could order achieved experience according to interests. The elaboration of these interests are many and varied and the forms of history select their contents accordingly.

Although offering no version of history or method of historiography as its own, the "phenomenological" approach puts each perspective in its respective place. At the same time, it offers a truly sociological approach to the study of social change. The study of social change according to a phenomenological perspective becomes a study of present-day structures of consciousness of the past that are brought to bear upon the present or upon some postulated future. According to this view there is only a succession of "presents" and of prevailing notions of the past in relation to them. The particular schools of socio-historical thought—such as the neopositivist school of Teggart, Hodgen, Bock, and Nisbet—become themselves topics of sociological investigation rather than resources for that investigation.

And what of social change itself? At this juncture in the argument we are in a position similar to that of Nicklaus in the epilogue of Offenbach's opera *Tales of Hoffman*. Like Nicklaus we now perceive that all our tales (historiographies) are a part of one larger tale. Evolutionary functionalist historiography indeed tells us stories, but these conjectural histories can no longer claim that they are accounts of what actually happened; mythic history takes accounts of what purportedly has happened and renders them as timeless social forms; neopositivist historical sociology provides us with a correlated and causal explanation of social changes, but its selection of "events" is problematical and the boundaries of experience it describes are ambiguous. A phenomenological approach insists that there is no one, single, absolute history, but rather that there are only structures of historical consciousness—structures that compete with or accommodate to one another and whose contents, processes, and struggles are grist for a historical sociology.

PART II

Race, Culture, and History

The Race Relations Cycle of Robert E. Park

Robert E. Park's well-known race relations cycle[1] constitutes a major contribution to sociological thought, but, despite widespread discussion and criticism, its full potentiality for theory has yet to be tapped. Our concern in this paper is to arouse renewed interest in the cycle and to expose the as yet unexamined possibilities it possesses as a model through a critical examination of its uses as a descriptive theory. Not only sociological theory in race relations will benefit by a revival of interest in Park's cycle, but also a pressing problem of scientific sociology might be brought closer to solution.

The ambiguous generality in which Park couched his cycle of contact, competition, accommodation, and assimilation[2] has been a cause of major concern to those who sought to use it as a generalized law of human relations. It was at once a law of all of humankind's race relations as a whole[3] and a description of California's Oriental "problem" from 1850 to 1930.[4] It was ideology too, for Park supposed that the end of the race relations cycle cleared the social arena in which an inevitable class struggle would take place. Clouded by ideological obfuscations and befogged by its never clarified particularist-universalist ambiguity, Park's cycle appeared less useful for sociology than for politics and social reform.

More serious for its sociological potential was the cycle's apparent commitment to an evolutionist bias which, once the "functionalist" and other anti-evolutionist schools of thought had disposed of the theoretical errors of social evolutionism, made it even more hidebound. In particular Park's use of the doctrine of obstacles seemingly to explain away the empirical contradictions to the cycle's operation and direction made the race cycle, like other cycles of civilization and human emergence, only a museum piece for students of the history of sociology. To restore the cycle's usage to sociological thought as a model, we must first carefully examine the use Park made of the doctrine of obstacles and the criticism of those who followed after him.

THE DOCTRINE OF OBSTACLES

Park did not carry out any full-scale study of ethnic groups to see whether his cycle approximated reality. But he did supervise the ethnic studies of his students, write numerous essays about race relations in general and various ethnic groups in particular, and he proposed a large-scale race relations survey along the Pacific Coast of the United States, especially designed to study the Chinese and Japanese in America. In 1926 a team of researchers, led by Park, made an attempt to carry out this race relations survey. Over and over their reports provided evidence contradicting the direction, and indeed, the operation of the proffered cycle. The two most famous Japanese rural communities were found to be living in a precariously balanced peace with their white neighbors, and one was torn asunder by internal ethnic rivalries.[5] The Chinatown ghetto was complexly differentiated and conflict ridden but showed no signs of political or economic disintegration.[6] The American-born Chinese and Japanese had adopted much of the culture, language, dress, habits, and opinions of conventional American society, and were less frequently the victims of assaults or race riots, but considerable discrimination and social distance still separated them from white America.[7] The evidence Park and his associates collected also suggested that a racial minority's adoption of the larger society's culture did not necessarily guarantee its acceptance into that society.

When evidence suggested that the cycle was not in fact in operation Park and his colleagues disposed of it by introducing, in effect, the age-old Aristotelian doctrine of "obstacles"—the doctrine which held that progress along an hypothesized line was inevitable, except when something interfered with it. For Park, physical traits and the failure to establish interracial friendships were the chief but not the only obstacles to the working out of the cycle. Indeed, accidents of settlement, minority group size and composition, and other interferences were often cited. Thus, the orderly transition from competition to accommodation to assimilation by the Japanese living in Florin, California, in 1926 was impeded, according to Winifred Raushenbush,[8] Park's associate, in part because Florin is located near Sacramento, the seat of anti-Orientalism. But, failure to assimilate was also "due in part to an ignorant tactlessness. It should be the first rule in the book of etiquette on race relations," continued Ms. Raushenbush, "that the foreigner should never become the major element in the population unless he is a slave; in fact unless the foreigner remains a very small element in the population there is inevitable friction and alarm."[9] On the other hand, Ms. Raushenbush considered Livingston, California, to be "really a laboratory experiment in race relations" because the Japanese there, unlike those in Florin, did not constitute a majority of the population, did not monopolize the business interests on Main Street, had not divided into quarreling Christian and Buddhist sects, and had acquiesced quietly to business and residential segregation within a racial ghetto.[10] Characteristically, the analysis did not explain how acceptance of this "accommodated" status by Livingston's Japanese would lead to assimilation, but much evidence was introduced which suggested that it would not. Park, however, in opening the discussion of these findings, was quite sure that deepening interpersonal relations between the races would break down stereotyped thinking and thus insure assimilation. "Personal relations and personal friendships are the great moral solvents. Under their influence all distinctions of class, of caste, and even of race, are dissolved into the general flux which we sometimes call democracy."[11]

Of all the obstacles that Park enumerates—and throughout his writings many appear as *ad hoc* soldiers fighting a losing war against ultimately victorious assimilation—the one to which he always returns is the failure to establish interracial primary relations. "Peoples we know intimately we respect and esteem. In our casual contacts with aliens, however, it is the offensive rather than the pleasing traits that impress us. These impressions accumulate and reinforce natural prejudices."[12] Thus Park's prediction of the inevitable transition from accommodation to assimilation requires the "great moral solvent" of interpersonal intimacy to flow across racial lines. But Park did not worry over the fact that interracial intimacy is a consequence of the nature and frequency of contact. Indeed, he asserted that "we [students of race relations] have not reckoned with the effects of personal intercourse and the friendships that inevitably grow up out of them." These interracial friendships "cut across and eventually undermine all the barriers of racial segregation and caste by which races seek to maintain their integrity."[13] Except for his assertion that slavery had assimilated African Negroes "rapidly and as a matter of course"[14] by providing for extensive intimate contacts between white masters and Negro slaves, Park eschewed analysis of the relationship between social organization and intimacy. Thus he cut off his observations at precisely the point where sociological investigation should have begun.

The doctrine of obstacles implicit in Park's thought permits him to draw a radical distinction between events and processes. Nowhere does he present the history of a single racial group showing that it in fact passed through the hypothesized stages. Instead particular conditions of a variety of racial groups are used to illustrate the several stages, and the cycle is asserted to be true in all stages for each group. Although often regarded as a *theory,* Park's cycle is most fruitful if regarded as a *model.* It fails as a theory because of its built-in unfalsifiability.[15] Park did not regard contradictory data as an indication of the cycle's fruitlessness. Indeed he used disconfirming data to support the cycle's utility. Thus Park wrote, "It does not follow that because the tendencies to the assimilation and eventual amalgamation of races exist, they should not be resisted and, if possible, altogether inhibited. On the other hand, it is vain to underestimate the character and force of the tendencies that are drawing the races and peoples about the Pacific into the ever-narrowing circle of a common life. Rising tides of color and oriental exclusion laws are merely incidental evidences of these diminishing distances."[16] As Lipset has observed concerning the *theoretical* aspects of Park's cycle, "by their very nature, hypotheses about the inevitability of cycles, whether they be cycles of race relations or the rise and fall of civilization, are not testable at all."[17] It has been the fate of Park's cycle to be treated as a theory and, as such, to be regarded as empirically unvalidated and theoretically unsound.

CRITICISM OF THE RACE CYCLE

Since Park's formulation of the cycle, unacknowledged confusion over its nature as a theory or a model has resulted in vitriolic debate over it and bitter disappointment with it. Those who have insisted that it is a universally applicable empirical generalization, a law of human behavior, have been puzzled by widespread disobedience to that law. The works of Louis Wirth[18] and Rose Hum Lee[19] illustrate the problems that arise when one adheres to Park's cycle as an unalterable description and prescription for all ethnic groups in America. Both find in their empirical studies of the Jews and Chinese in America, respectively, that complete assimilation has not in fact occurred. Wirth attributes this in part to the rise of anti–Semitism but more significantly to the presence of congregative sentiments and institutions. However, he appears to regard these as "obstacles" to the working out of the Jews' historical destiny in America. As late as 1945 Wirth seems not to have abandoned his faith in the eventual assimilation of minorities if only they are allowed to fulfill their sociological destiny, for he wrote in that year that although a race relations cycle properly includes a stage in which a minority group seeks "toleration for its cultural differences," assimilation would follow "if sufficient toleration and autonomy is attained" in the "pluralist" stage. Only if frustrated in its drive toward assimilation would a minority resort to "secessionist tendencies" or "the drive to be incorporated into another state."[20]

Rose Hum Lee is disconcerted to find that after more than a century of settlement the Chinese have not completely assimilated into American Society. Despite acculturation Chinese ghettos are still to be found in America's larger cities, and, although the absolute number of Chinatowns has declined, the population and size of the urban Chinese quarters have increased. Lee contrasts this state of affairs among the Chinese with that of the more rapidly assimilating Japanese, and noting that both groups have been victims of prejudice and discrimination, is disappointed with the character of America's Chinese. Since in recent years Sinophobia has nearly disappeared as an active force in Chinese-American relations, she can only conclude that the failure to assimilate is due in part to Chinatown's elites and their vested interests in maintaining an exclusive community, but more significantly to a lack of nerve and will on the part of the mass of Chinese. In the final pages of her study Professor Lee exhorts the Chinese to assimilate as rapidly and completely as possible, thus converting Park's prophecy into a plea.

Other adherents of the cycle as a theory were disappointed when they discovered that assimilation had not yet occurred. Bogardus[21] developed three cycles to describe the several situations which his research had uncovered. Brown asserted that either isolation, subordination, or fusion were final outcomes; assimilation and fusion are "perhaps ultimately inevitable but immediately improbable," he concluded.[22] Masuoka believes three generations are required for the fulfillment of the cycle, but that in the third "A genuine race problem arises in the history of race relations."[23] Both Glick[24] and Lieberson[25] believe that the final outcome of racial cycles is problematical, resulting in integration, nationalist movements, or permanent minority status. Etzioni has gone further than most critics in urging abandonment of Park's racial cycle as theory: "While groups are often forced into contact by the process of technological, economic, and social change, and perhaps this is an unavoidable process, the remaining stages [of Park's race relations cycle] should be seen as alternative situations rather than links in an evolutionary process culminating in assimilation. Groups are either in conflict or accommodation or assimilation."[26]

Among the critics, Brewton Berry stands out for his criticism of Park's and later sociologists' cycles and his resulting pessimism about the possibilities of theory construction in racial relations. "Some scholars," he writes, "therefore question the existence of any universal pattern and incline rather to the belief that so numerous and so various are the components that enter into race relations that each situation is unique and the making of generalizations is a hazardous procedure."[27] He then proceeds to describe race relations in Brazil, Hawaii, and between American Indians and whites and concludes that, although the course of race relations is not identical in any two situations, certain phenomena—conflict, biological mixture, cultural exchange, and domination—are widespread, if not universal and inevitable.

Other analysts have come closer to perceiving the heuristic assets of Park's cycle despite its failure as theory. Shibutani and Kwan point out there are "so many exceptions" to Park's cycle conceived as a "natural history," but they conclude that "Park's race relations cycle is a useful way of ordering data on the manner in which immigrants become incorporated into an already-established society."[28] Frazier, after years of research, gave up the attempt to empirically verify the sequential order of Park's stages and conceded that "the different stages in the race relations cycle may exist simultaneously," but he insisted on retaining the cycle as "logical steps in a systematic sociological analysis of the subject."[29]

Seeking a path out of the profusion of research and confusion of thought arising out of Park's race relations cycle is not easy. Before dismissing what has gone before, sociologists should recognize that Park's race relations essays in general and his race cycle formulation in particular have focused critical attention on a significant aspect of human relations, provided research topics for a generation of scholars, and aided in the amelioration of social conditions. Park's stature as a theorist, empiricist, and meliorist is secure and rightfully so.[30]

PARK'S CYCLE AS A MODEL

The future of Park's cycle is to be realized in its value as a model. Much debate over the meaning of model and theory still goes on in sociology, and this debate cannot be resolved in this paper.[31] Following Weber,[32] however, Park's cycle may be conceived as a developmental model containing four ideal types. The test of its utility lies in its ability to organize a vast body of otherwise discrete data, sensitize sociologists to specific forms of human organization, and generate hypotheses for research. There can be no doubt that Park's cycle has lived up to these desiderata. Moreover, once the cycle is regarded as a model, the questions of verification or falsification no longer are relevant. Rather, the issue is to establish the conditions under which the descriptive conditions of the model are true. In this light then, the speculations of Park and Raushenbush discussed earlier take on a new significance as notes toward hypotheses (rather unrefined, to be sure) designating the conditions under which the postulates are not true. They provide the grounds for conducting case studies testing the validity of the alleged postulate-preventing factor.

However, each of Park's stages is much in need of examination along the lines originally suggested by Weber to see whether the model meets the requirements of an ideal-type. The concentration on "assimilation"[33] has been fruitful for this purpose alone—although even that ideal-type is not unambiguously represented in the contemporary sociological literature—but little more than illustration has yet been done on "contact," "competition," or "accommodation." The specific logico-empirical content of each of these is a worthy enterprise of future sociological research.

Much ambiguity continues to exist in sociological discussions of assimilation. Park himself succumbed to the doubts his colleagues had expressed about the final outcome of race relations and, at the age of 73, reformulated the racial cycle, asserting that it "continues until it terminates in some predestined racial configuration, and one consistent with an established social order of which it is a part."[34] In the spirit of Park's cautious reappraisal, sociologists ought to consider just what the cultural and behavioral content of assimilation is in various societies, and in America in particular. One specific error, committed by friends and foes of Park alike,[35] is to equate assimilation with fusion, or a "melting pot" and to regard the continuing existence of identifiable ethnic groups in America as a sign of non-assimilation. The equation of fusion with assimilation is proper if and only if fusion is a core value of American society.[36] If, however, pluralism, and one of its most specific forms, racial and ethnic endogamy, are elements of the core culture, or if maintenance of ethnic group identity is a culturally permissible alternative, then a people who persist in endogamy and who maintain or establish those ancillary institutions necessary to insure endogamy are not necessarily unassimilated by those practices. Thus, if Jews or blacks, for example, come to share in the dominant values of American society—
e.g., achievement, work, moral orientations, humanitarian mores, efficiency and practicality, progress, material comfort, equality, freedom, conformity, science and secular rationality, national patriotism, democracy, individualism, and ambivalence about the relevance of race and ethnicity[37]—but practice in-marriage and so structure the institutions of

intimate contact between marriageable members of their group that mating is likely to occur within the confines of the group, shall we not say they are indeed assimilated? It would appear that both reason and evidence would support this view of assimilation, and thus we may clear away the obfuscation that endogamy has caused for students of assimilation.

PARK'S CYCLE AS THEORY: UNSOLVED PROBLEMS

Finally, if Park's cycle is to be treated as a theory, then all the dilemmas arising out of this kind of theory in general are applicable to it in particular. These dilemmas have not yet been resolved, but Park's cycle provides a crucial case upon which analytic thought and empirical research might be focused to help in this effort. Briefly stated these dilemmas are:

1.   The debate over whether the forms of theory construction in natural science are to be adopted strictly and uncritically in social science.[38] This debate is too well-known to be commented on further here, but resolution of it is vital for usage of Park's cycle as theory.

2.   The debate over falsification and verification of an hypothesized developmental sequence.[39] Park's cycle takes the form: If P, then Q; if Q, then R; if R, then S. Should empirical research reveal a result contrary to the prediction of the hypothesis, the hypothesis could be abandoned as incorrect, or the principle of *ceteris paribus* introduced to account for the discrepancy. However, no introduction of an unlimited universe of interferences can be allowed unless we wish to be left in the unscientific position of unfalsifiability described earlier. The way out of this dilemma is to verify and construct a definite and finite set of ideal-typical interferences, the presence of any of which would constitute an adequate explanation of the failure of the predictive hypothesis. Park's discussions of what I term "obstacles" provide a suggested beginning to this needed next step, and his work should be carefully studied for clues to and examples of the relevant interferences.

3.   The debate over causal explanations in relation to developmental theories.[40] To present Park's cycle as a theory is not to account for the sequence coming to pass. Park himself, and other sociologists who subscribe to evolutionary theories, have not explicitly designated the causal nexus by which one stage of development succeeds another. Often enough causal explanations are implicit in the descriptive statements about the stages.

Future research must make explicit and empirically validate the independent variables whose form and presence are necessary and sufficient to bring on the successor stage.

Park's racial cycle, thus, is still most fruitful for the sociological enterprise. Not only does it serve as a model useful in the study of race relations in general and assimilation in particular, but it also provides an opportunity for research into the basic problems of sociological theory itself.

Interactionism and the Study of Race Relations at the Macrosociological Level

The Contribution of Herbert Blumer

In 1970 Lewis Killian remarked that "If the average sociologist were asked to list the outstanding students of race relations, it is most unlikely that he would name Herbert Blumer."[1] Despite Killian's attempt to delineate the contrast between Blumer's and others' approaches to the subject and Blumer's own elaboration and modification of his approach in essays written since 1970, there still has been no noticeable recognition of the contribution that symbolic interaction has to make to the macrosociological approach to race and ethnic relations. The present paper intends to set forth Blumer's conceptualization of the sociology of race and ethnic relations and to suggest its relevance for contemporary studies of that topic.

Blumer's approach currently stands in a peripheral and shaded area of the landscape of related theories. There are probably two reasons for this: one, ignorance of his work, and two, misunderstandings of symbolic interaction in relation to the study of race and ethnic relations.

That Blumer's work in this area is almost unknown to most sociologists is indicated in the absence of any discussion of it in recent major works on race and ethnic relations. Peter Rose credits Blumer, together with Robert Park, Louis Wirth, Robert Redfield, and Everett C. Hughes, with initiating the first sociology courses in race and ethnic relations, but he does not discuss any specific theoretical or empirical contribution made by Blumer.[2] In the third edition of Rose's *They and We: Racial and Ethnic Relations in the United States,*[3] there is no mention of Blumer's theory of race prejudice as a sense of group position, no bibliographic citation of any of Blumer's works, and no listing of his name in the index. Hubert M. Blalock's two major works on theory and concept formation in race and ethnic relations[4] include no discussion of Blumer's approach. J. Milton Yinger does not note any contribution by Blumer to recent developments in minority and race relations in his five-year review of writings on those subjects,[5] while the first volume in the annual *Research in Race and Ethnic Relations* cites Blumer as a representative of the "social movement model" of mass behavior, but makes no mention of any of his specific studies on the racial order, race prejudice, or the origins, persistence, and reduction of group tensions.[6] Blumer's name does not appear among the 121 contributors or 173 consultants to the *Harvard Encyclopedia of American Ethnic Groups*.[7] Among such important recent anthologies in intergroup relations and minority problems as those by Yetman and Steele,[8] Rose and Rose,[9] and van den Berghe,[10] there is no representation of Blumer's work. Recent textbooks by Kitano[11] and Davis[12] also fail to mention Blumer's approach to the subject. In singular contrast, Vander Zanden[13] contains a useful summary of Blumer's analysis of the etiology of race prejudice.

When students of race and ethnic relations do take notice of Blumer's contribution, they usually turn to his general conceptualizations of symbolic interaction or mass behavior, or to a specific empirical point without reference to its relation to his theory of race and ethnic relations. Thus, Milton Gordon presents a cogent and well-informed discussion of Blumer's elaboration of George Herbert Mead's social psychology but makes no connection of it to Blumer's work in race and ethnic relations.[14] Michael Banton points to Blumer's discussions of the role of the federal government as a change agent in the South, and of the alignment of industrialization with the racial order, but he does not integrate these points with Blumer's theoretical approach to race relations or suggest that Blumer has developed such.[15] In an important critical study of ideological intrusions upon sociological theories of race and ethnicity, Harry H. Bash[16] employs Blumer's general critiques of concept formation in the social sciences, but he is apparently unaware of the latter's conceptual and empirical studies of minorities, race problems, and racial and ethnic conflict. More recent works do the same: John W. Cell[17] credits Blumer with the insight that neither the city nor the factory determine the form of race and ethnic relations, but he does not relate this to Blumer's larger theoretical perspective. Donald G. Baker[18] employs many insights from Blumer's *Symbolic Interactionism* to aid in his analysis of race, class, and power in the United States, Canada, Australia, New Zealand, South Africa, and Rhodesia, but is apparently unaware of any of Blumer's studies of the same topic in some of these same countries. Even Shibutani's and Kwan's[19] symbolic interactionist analysis of ethnic stratification refers only to Blumer's studies of collective behavior and does not employ his theoretical and field investigations of the topic.

The neglect of Blumer's many works on race and ethnic relations may be attributed in part to the fact that they have never been collated or collected in a single volume and are scattered in various kinds of publications throughout North and South America, the Caribbean, Oceania, and the British Commonwealth.[20] Moreover, Blumer's contributions to the sociology of race relations might have been eclipsed by his better-known debates with behaviorist, positivist, and functionalist theorists and with Iowa-school representatives of symbolic interactionism, many of them published in mainstream journals. Finally, Blumer's long association with the University of California at Berkeley, the last major institution of higher learning in America to establish a department of sociology, might have affected the recognition and reception of his work. According to Edward Shils,[21] the Berkeley department was representative of so many divergent viewpoints that no single perspective could stand out. Whatever weight might be assigned to each of these factors, it is suggested that in the case of Blumer's *oeuvre* on race and ethnic relations, neglect is partly related to a difficulty of access and, perhaps, to Blumer's controversial and marginal status in the profession.

Blumer's approach to race and ethnic relations has not been the subject of any full-scale criticism. Neglect of his works might be related to misunderstandings of his general approach to symbolic interaction rather than criticism of his specific applications of it to the race question. Among these is the controversy over whether Blumer has paid sufficient attention to the stability of social interaction.[22] For Blumer race and ethnic relations are to be studied as aspects of an historical process wherein domination and subordination are established as group positions with appropriately attendant ideologies, rationales, and beliefs. Hence, in Blumer's approach, attention is paid to both the pattern and the process of race relations—with greater attention to the latter. Race relations are subject to codification and legalization, but they are also subject to interactions that arise in the process of taking account of the other. For Blumer race relations are attended by a dynamic that always portends the dissolution of static patterns.

To those theorists who insist on the priority of structural or institutional effects, Blumer's version of symbolic interaction seems useless because it allegedly envisions a society that is "nothing more than a plurality of disembodied selves interacting in structureless situations."[23] Were this an accurate description of Blumer's perspective, race relations, in the literal sense of the topics embraced by that sub-discipline, would not occur. However, Blumer neither denies the existence of bodied selves (a race, according to Blumer, is "a class or group of human beings who are regarded and treated in social life as a distinctive biological group with a common ancestry"[24]) nor of social structure (as a sense of group position, racial prejudice, according to Blumer, "refers to the

position of group to group, not to that of individual to individual"[25]).
Finally, proponents of a structural as opposed to a symbolic interactionist approach accuse Blumer of eschewing the significance of power
in race and ethnic and all other social relations.[26] However, as Banton
among others has noticed, Blumer has paid special attention to the role
played by institutionalized authority in bringing about the reduction of
race prejudice. The value of symbolic interactionism to the sociology of
race and ethnic relations would appear to depend in great part on over-
coming the misunderstandings still extant about that perspective.

Race relations theory in American sociology has not followed the
several historico-dialectical leads that Blumer—and before him, Park
and the Chicago School—had introduced. Rather, disappointed by the
failure of the assimilative process to have absorbed most of America's
minorities, and nonplussed by the apparent insolubility of the "Negro
question," some sociologists withdrew from studying the problem altogether. Others gave the subject up to social psychologists, who narrowed the field to the minuscule analysis of attitudes held by members
of one race toward another. Still others left the field to utopian functionalists or radical materialists who promised to bring an end to race
relations through the allegedly inexorable operation of the social process.

Blumer developed his approach to race and ethnic relations in
critical opposition to various forms of psychological reductionism. Although the attitudinal survey, a one-sided orientation toward the subjective aspect of human relations, had been given impetus early in the
century by W. I. Thomas's distinction between the individual's attitude
and the "objective" value[27]—an approach criticized by Blumer in his
doctoral dissertation in 1928[28]—it did not become the predominant approach in race relations until the 1930s and 1940s.[29] Combining Freudian
concepts with questionnaire surveillance and clinical interviews, the
psychological approach to race prejudice reached its apex in 1950 with
the publication of the mammoth research report *The Authoritarian Personality*[30] by Frankfurt School leader T. W. Adorno and his colleagues.
Blumer had opposed such unilateral approaches since 1939.[31] His voice,
however, could not prevail over the chorus of enthusiasts who thought
they might save the soul of the nation by salvaging the psyches of its
most virulent and pathological racists. Once Allport[32] disclosed that almost everyone was prejudiced, the solution of the race problem appeared to wait upon mass therapeutic intervention.

Blumer's understanding of race relations did not require—indeed,
it abjured—the idea that society was filled with sick people. Race relations were not a peculiar feature of social organization wholly divorced
from all others; rather they were a basic feature of social organization
itself, a social organization based on hierarchy and racial group posi-

tion. As such, the particular relations that prevailed at any one time among the races were not immobile. Any established pattern of race relations indicated the structure of group positions that had been institutionalized in time and space by the concrete acts of men and women in power. Race prejudice was a matter of history and politics, not a function of individual attitudes. Attitudes in turn were merely the lowest form of expression of these historically established positions, and were not irremediably correlative with conduct.

Blumer faced a predicament similar to that presented to the much neglected John Cummings by the bio-sociologists of the 1890s. Cummings had had to contend not with a psychological but an anatomical theory of race relations and social development. Just as Blumer lashed out at the absurd and likely impossible attempt to make the racial world over by restoring the millions of allegedly sick psyches of Americans to a supposedly "normal" state of tolerance, so Cummings disparaged the claim that physical features—head size, eye shape, skin color—had need of reform or reconstruction in order to ameliorate the human condition.[33] "Phrenology, like astrology," Cummings observed, "has had its day; and the sort of racial phrenology with which modern anthropologists are engaged is bound to go to the same limbo. Sociology may then breathe again naturally."[34] Both Cummings and Blumer conceive of race relations *in historical terms*. To them modern racial relations begins with the expansion of Europe in the Sixteenth Century, introducing European peoples, customs, and power into the lives of Africans, Asians, Oceanians, and Amerindians and establishing new hierarchies of racial group position in all the areas of the world where the contacts and collisions of such peoples took place.

Much of the physical determinism that Cummings opposed had been if not banished to limbo at least subordinated and made the object of criticism by the time Blumer first began to write about race relations.[35] But sociology still could not breathe naturally. In place of the shape and color of the body there had emerged a new obstacle: the attitude and its manifestation in racial prejudice. That orientation would continue to dominate sociological thinking on the subject until the middle 1960s so that Blumer, like Cummings before him, found it necessary to engage in a body of critical writing to clear away the accumulated scholastic debris. The sociological outlook during the period in which Blumer chose to attack the subject was well summarized by H. H. Smythe in 1958:

> Following the accumulation of a considerable body of data revealing the impossibility of demonstrating differences on a racial basis . . . emphasis has turned to an analysis of prejudice and its ramifications with students concentrating on stereotypes, the reduction of tension, influence of prejudice on personality and its role in discriminatory segregatory practices.[36]

Against this new illusion of the epoch, Blumer posed the idea that race prejudice is "a sense of group position," not an attitude; that race relations could be studied by carefully charting the movement of the "color line" in various institutional sectors and settings; and that racial conflict and accommodation belonged to an historically informed political and industrial sociology and not to psychology or psycho-analysis.

As a "sense of group position," race prejudice emerges as a form of social hierarchization embracing "four basic types of feeling . . .": one, a feeling of superiority, two, a feeling that the subordinate race is intrinsically different and alien, three, a feeling of proprietary claim to certain areas of privilege and advantage, and four, a fear and suspicion that the subordinate race harbors designs on the prerogatives of the dominant race."[37] The argument of Blumer—the basic elements of which had been made in 1939[38]—was reiterated in the 1950s and elaborated in a recent reformulation in 1980.[39] In great measure it is a response to *The Authoritarian Personality* and other psychologistic and psychoanalytic formulations that had come to dominate social scientific studies of the subject since the 1930s. "The idea that the make up of the 'prejudiced individual' is responsible for racial prejudice," Blumer remarked in 1955, "is the most dominant of the theoretical notions guiding research in the past decade. It reached its climax in the identification of the 'authoritarian personality'. Prejudice, of course," Blumer pointed out, speaking of it as understood by the surveyors of individual attitudes, "is a factor in behaviour; but to treat it as the factor which accounts for behaviour is to go astray." What was wrong with the first decade of postwar studies of racial prejudice, Blumer noted, was that they "just have not treated prejudice in terms of how it enters into and functions in behavior; actually they have treated it as a thing apart, and have been content with the mere presumption that it accounts for racial behaviour."[40] As a result, Blumer concluded, despite "its vastness, research over the past decade has contributed little to solid theoretical knowledge of race relations," nor had "race relations research in the last decade . . . contributed a great deal to policy knowledge."[41]

In America, and especially with black-white relations, Blumer asserted, the sense of group position might be understood in terms of the "color line."[42] The "color line," a term once employed by Ray Stannard Baker[43] in a work that had influenced Park, was in Blumer's formulation the form that the complex race relations of the South had taken. It "comes into play when members of the two races meet each other not on an individual basis but as representatives of their respective groups"; it "is a collective definition of social position and not a mere expression of individual feelings and beliefs"; it "is not appropriately represented by a single, sharply drawn line but appears rather as a series of ramparts, like the 'Maginot Line,' extending from outer breastworks to

inner bastions."[44] Since the end of the Second World War, Blumer
pointed out, the South has been increasingly incorporated into the social, economic, and political life of the nation. One result of this loss of
regional autonomy and sociocultural isolation was increasing pressure
on the various echelons of the color line that are in the public arena.[45]
"The acquisition of civil rights by Negroes in the South," Blumer
wrote in 1965, "will thus have two stages, so to speak—first, being
brought abreast of the general level of enjoyment of such rights as exists
elsewhere in the nation, and then sharing in the further struggle to extend those rights that is occurring on a national basis."[46] However, civil
rights did not constitute in and of themselves the solvent of the color
line. Blumer noted that "Whites are generally disposed, it is true, to
view the matter in this way." But in fact another "band" of the color
line "consists of the barriers confronting the Negro in his efforts to improve his economic lot," and the "future of the color line in this intermediate band remains a highly problematic matter."[47] There also remained what Blumer called "the inner citadel of the color line," the
"intimate and private circles, represented by social sets, cliques, private
clubs, friendship sets, family circles, courtship, and marriage." Although equalization in political and economic status among blacks and
whites might be expected to soften the resistance of interracial intimacy,
Blumer called attention to the fact that this area lay outside of society's
formal controls, and to the possibility that "even in a situation of equal
social status the Negro group would accommodate to exclusion as a
separate racial group—as, indeed, Jews have done in large measure."[48]
Blumer's orientation rejected any inevitable outcome. Thoroughly secular, he offered neither the hope of eschatological theodicy nor the promise of evolutionary sociodicy. Humans make their own history in the
world and in relation to human constraints on freedom; race relations
were part of that history.

Blumer's open-ended orientation toward race relations also includes a devastating critique of conventional views about the impact of
industrialization on them.[49] His analysis, though unacknowledged as
such, is Weberian in character, taking a relative view of the rationalization process characteristic of industrialization, and indicating its differential effects on race relations in various industrializing national and colonial settings. Blumer addresses his criticism to the materialist utopian
view still prevalent in sociological theory that holds that industrialization will bring down any social order not based on values of universality and achievement. Blumer summarizes that position thus:

> In the long run, race vanishes as a factor which structures social relations.
> Workers will compete with one another on the basis of industrial aptitude
> and not on the basis of racial makeup. Correspondingly, members of the

managerial force will be chosen and placed on the basis of managerial competence and not of racial affiliation. Imagination, ingenuity, and energy and not racial membership will determine success in industrial entrepreneurship. Ascent on the social ladder will depend on the possession of necessary skills and ability, wealth or capital; racial makeup becomes extraneous. The premium placed on rational decisions will relegate racial prejudice and discrimination to the periphery. The dominance of contractual relations and the resulting impersonal markets will undermine identification with racial groups. Physical movement from job to job and from one to another entrepreneurial opportunity, social mobility upward and downward in the occupational structure, differential accumulations of wealth and capital, and different directions of specialization in the expanding array of career lines in industry—all these will have the effect of parcelling out and intershuffling racial members among one another in the industrial and social structure.

It is important to recognize that in detailing and then criticizing what he calls the conventional sociological view of the impact of industrialization, Blumer is waging intellectual war against the central thrust and the principal methodological orientation of Occidental sociology. His criticism is probably the most profound assault on the domain assumptions of functionalism, positivism, and behaviorism that has ever been leveled from inside the discipline. Blumer appears to agree with Maitland that, "the fault . . . of the would-be scientific procedure of our sociologists lies in the too-frequent attempt to obtain a set of 'laws' by the study of only one class of phenomena . . ." In the nineteenth century, when Maitland made this statement, this procedure lent itself to the postulation of a determined unilinear series as in the projected sociological history of the ancient family. About that supposedly lawlike sequence Maitland observed: "When this evidence about barbarians gets into the hands of men who have been trained in a severe school of history and who have been taught by experience to look upon all the social phenomena as interdependent, it begins to prove far less than it used to prove. Each case begins to look . . . unique and a law which deduces that 'mother-right' cannot come after 'father-right,' or that 'father-right' cannot come after 'mother-right,' or which would establish any other similar sequence of 'states' begins to look exceedingly improbable."[50] In the twentieth century, Blumer had to contend with the intellectual epigoni of Spencer, sociologists such as Harvard's two great scholars Thomas Nixon Carver and, more recently, Talcott Parsons. The latter's interpretation in 1966 of the social processes entailed in America's value-valenced social system promised full citizenship to the American black according to an orderly timetable and a particular sequence that was inevitable—unless something interfered.[51] Blumer's insistence on rejecting pre-packaged utopias, on adopting a clear-eyed view of what actually occurs in this world, and on formulating a frame of reference that permits comparative differential and historical analysis places his sociology in a subterranean stream close to that developed by Frederick J. Teggart and his school at the University of California—although no one, not even Blumer, seems to have noticed this—and makes it one of the most significant attempts to create an anti-evolutionary, non-positivist, independent perspective.

Blumer pointed out that none of the alleged consequences of industrialization on race relations were proven, and that quite different and varied outcomes seemed—and could be shown to be—just as likely. It was by no means historically the case, he showed, that industrialization inevitably undermines the traditional or established racial order. "In early industrialisation," Blumer pointed out, "the rational or secular perspective, which industrialism admittedly fosters and stresses, may compel an adherence to the racial system rather than a departure from it . . . [The] *rational* operation of industrial enterprises which are introduced into a racially ordered society may call for a deferential respect of the canons and sensitivities of that racial order." And, Blumer insists, "This observation is not a mere *a priori* speculation. It is supported by countless instances of such decisions in the case of industrial enterprises in the Southern region of the United States, in South Africa and in certain colonial areas." Indeed, Blumer concluded on this point, ". . . the rational imperative in industrial operations may function to maintain and reinforce the established racial order."[52]

Blumer goes on to argue that "the intrinsic structural requirements of industrialism need not, contrary to much *a priori* theorizing, force a rearrangement of the relations set by the racial system."[53] Moreover, by the same token, the introduction of rational industrial techniques did not in and of themselves necessarily provoke racial tension. Instead, the "empirical evidence pertaining to this matter presents a very varied picture." The assumption so widespread in industrialization theories—and, incidentally, we may add, in Marxist theories about the effects of capitalism on the formation of social classes, of which Blumer's argument is an implicit critique—that rationalization of production and geographic mobility will "open access in such a society to one another's occupations, lines of industrial endeavour, areas of entrepreneural opportunities, and residential areas is not true." If industrialization occurs together with new racial contacts wherein relationships are at first vague and undefined, "they come to be defined quickly—defined under the overbridging sway of traditional views of the appropriate position of the races." Racial friction in strongly organized racially structured industrial societies is more likely to occur, Blumer argues, "at the points of contact between different subordinate racial groups" because in "the reshuffling which industrialisation induces, such subordinate

groups may be brought into competition at scattered points in the industrial structure with resulting strain and discord." Pointing to such
outbreaks of friction as those between Negroes and Mexicans in the
United States and between Africans, Colored, and Indians in South Africa, and to the varied modes of accommodation that arise between industrial elites and the peoples brought in to work for them, Blumer
concluded that "members of the dominant and subordinate racial groups
are not thrown into the competitive relationship that is presupposed by
a priori theorising." [54] The Marxists' claim of the overriding solidarity of
class over racial consciousness is not demonstrated by the evidence.

Finally, Blumer attacks the thesis that industrialization will oblit-
erate the significance of race in modern societies. This claim about the
effects of rationalization, or about the consequences of introducing a
money economy, or about industrial society's supposed tendency to
hire workers and assign tasks solely on the basis of considerations of the
most economical productivity has been one of the most powerful domain assumptions in sociological theory. It finds various forms of expression in the works of Marx,[55] Simmel,[56] and J. S. Mill.[57] More recently, it has been reasserted by William J. Wilson, who holds that race
is declining in significance in contemporary America,[58] and by Annie
Phizacklea and Robert Miles,[59] who believe that racial identity is less
important than class consciousness in modern multi-racial Britain. According to Blumer, "the view that industrialisation moves ahead naturally to dissolve the racial factor is not borne out by the facts, certainly
not in the case of [such] racially ordered societies . . . [as the] Southern
United States, South Africa, and some of the colonial areas." Blumer
thus rejects the scenario that Marx, Mill, Simmel, John Cummings, and
other more recent materialists have proposed, viz., that economic relations would inevitably subsume race relations. Blumer has on his side
the facts of history that show that "the hiring and assignment of industrial workers from subordinate racial groups did not follow the postulates of industrialism; members of such groups have not found entrance
into managerial ranks; and entrepreneurs from such groups were confronted by high walls barring them from exploiting opportunities lying
in the province of the dominant group." To those who claim that the
"transfer of the lines of racial patterning to the industrial enterprise"
was "merely a temporary stage in which the forces of industrialisation
have not had opportunity to come to natural expression; [and that] with
time, or in the long run, the industrial imperatives would gain ascen-
dency, stripping the racial factor of any importance," Blumer replies,
"We do not know how much time is needed to constitute the 'long-run';
certainly half a century of industrial experience in both South Africa and
the South in the United States brought no appreciable change in the
position of the races in the industrial structure." On this point Blumer

concludes that the "picture presented by industrialisation in a racially ordered society is that industrial imperatives accommodate themselves to the racial mould and continue to operate effectively within it," and not *vice versa*. If there are a set of factors that will necessarily disintegrate a racial order, Blumer asserts, it will have to be found outside of the much vaunted industrial imperatives.[60]

Blumer's approach to race relations incorporates the concepts of Park's race relations cycle, but he separates them from the formal linear sequence into which Park had put them. Thus, Blumer can speak of contacts, competition, accommodation, and assimilation not as an irrevocable pattern of development but rather as forms that might become temporarily constituted in various places and different times, without any preordained sequence, during the historical course of population movements. "We should clearly understand," he observes, ". . . that neither industrialisation nor the body of race relations is uniform or constant."[61] The "explanation of race relations," he asserts, "must be sought in social conditions and historical experience . . ."[62] Blumer lists no less than seven "lines of relation" that form part of the "complex number of factors" affecting racial relations, that intersect with, shape, and are shaped by "happenings and . . . situations," and that make for these relations being "subject to much change, occasionally approaching pronounced transformation": one, formal economic relations; two, formal status relations; three, preferential relations; four, ideological relations; five, attitudinal or feeling relations; six, orderly or discordant overt relations; seven, organized manipulative relations.[63]

Essentially, Blumer insists, racial relations proceed in and as a hierarchical order. That order might be brought into existence by the conquest of one land by the people of another, the dominating group establishing an economic, political, and cultural order that legitimates the relative position and status of the two or more peoples involved; by the importation of one or more peoples into an already established order of life wherein the new arrivals are redefined in terms of rights, privileges, and social prestige; by voluntary or involuntary migration of one or more peoples to an inhabited area wherein they must compete for various valued elements with the older established groups.[64] In effect, racial relations in the United States have arisen out from all three modes—the conquest of the Indians, the forced importation of Africans, the more or less solicited coming of Europeans, Asians, and Latinos.[65] Once the definition of the racial situation has been enunciated—by a political process of discussion, decision-making, and dissemination of opinion in the public arena[66]—it must also find a way to maintain itself against countervailing pressures. Race prejudice as the sense of this group position, hence, "has a history, and the history is collective." To understand it as an incident in a natural history of preordained human relations or as occupying only the arena of individual feeling or individual experience is to be sociologically misdirected.

In his most recent formulation of a theory of race relations, in 1980, Blumer, joined by another Berkeley sociologist, Troy Duster, specifically separates his own approach from the assimilation orientation that had characterized the work of Park and other Chicago sociologists. At the same time, Blumer and Duster reject biological determinism, the prejudice-discrimination argument, the Marxist and structural-functionalist schemes of explanation in which "racial groups become essentially a kind of epiphenomenon," and the colonial exploitation model.[67] It is not within the scope of our argument to discuss Blumer's and Duster's critique of each of these schools of thought. Suffice it to say that they show that each of them fails in one or more ways to satisfy their criteria for a scholarly and creditable theory of race relations:

> Any theory of race relations which seeks to gain scholarly creditability must obviously be able to cover and explain the significant happenings that are to be noted in the empirical world of race relations. This means that the theory must be able to identify races and the relations between races; it must be able to handle whatever may be the diversity of relations existing between races; it must be able to explain the variations and shifts that occur over time between any two racial groups; and it must be able to analyse the interplay of whatever may be racial factors and other factors in actual ongoing group life.[68]

However, Blumer's open rejection of assimilation as the necessary and historically directed final outcome of race relations—his rejection, in effect, of Park's race relations cycle—marks a turning point in Chicago-California theory. In 1972, Stanford M. Lyman—a former student of Blumer—had published a thorough going critique of developmentalist theories of race relations in America, from Ward to Parsons. Included in it was a chapter on Park and the Chicago School that took as its point of departure what Lyman called "a failure of perspective"—the *a priori* organic and system theorizing that appears to justify a non-empirical and ahistorical analysis.[69] In 1980, Blumer and Duster applied a similar criticism to the race relations cycle of Park: "However captivating may be its logic and however neat its fit to the experience of any immigrant groups in the United States, the assimilation theory of Park is now known to be inadequate as an explanation of race relations."[70] The repudiation of assimilation as *the final solution to* and the rejection of the race relations cycle as *the natural history of* the race question mark a thoroughly secular break with the innerworldly sociodicies and profanely transvalued religious utopias that had been derived from Protestant sources.[71] This worldly rejection of religion and its secular surrogates—Park's utopian assimilation, Parsons' promissory "inclusion" thesis, Adorno's tentative hopes for a society cleansed of its prejudiced members—places sociology squarely in the center of history and happenings, forced to look at the actual situation, past or present, as it actually was or is.[72]

Blumer's approach to race relations theory leads sociology out of utopia. But it does not stop at the critical level; it offers a new approach that replaces both the non-empirical functionalist and the psychologically reductionist orientations. Race relations, he argues, partake first and foremost of a social construction of an invidious reality, a classifying process wherein peoples are categorized as belonging to hierarchically perceived racial groups. Membership in these groups, in turn, is given decisive weight in policies, programs, customs, and attitudes that determine a people's status, rights, and life chances. The classifying process is carried out in the public arena by the spokesmen for a variety of prevailing interests. However, the process of defining and maintaining a racial order is not a once-and-for-all-time activity but rather an ongoing affair, buffeted and modified by events and the shifting grounds of interest and the relative strength of interest groups. Hence race relations has a history "that is by no means a simple linear development, arising in response to a fixed cause or a set of such factors . . . preordained to move in ordered sequence to a given destiny."[73] Typically race relations take on an hierarchical character, fixing for a moment one or a cluster of dominant groups over one or more subordinate ones. Subordinated groups are thereby caught in either the push toward moving up and into the dominant group or the call to move or remain out of and independent from their self-proclaimed superiors. The dominant group, for its part, is caught between maintaining the exclusionary tendency that originally justified its arrogation of a superordinate positional monopoly, or originating a gate-opening policy that, by carefully monitoring the conditions of entry, justifies the original ideology of the hierarchy while at the same time helping to open up its once seemingly impenetrable barriers. The "play of these sets of antagonistic forces constitutes the core of happenings in race relations . . . [that] should form the stuff of primary scholarly concern."[74] Sociologists seeking to understand such current race relations conflicts as the struggle to desegregate schools in the cities of the North; the court battles over affirmative action programs in industry and higher education; the surge toward electing non-white, non-Anglo candidates to local, state, and national offices; the search to carve out niches of ethno-cultural identity and aroused consciousness in the arts, politics, pedagogy, and culture; and the seemingly contradictory demands for ethnic pluralism and political-economic integration would do well to begin with the outlook provided by Blumer's seminal essays on the subject.

The Significance of Asians in American Society

Traditionally studies of race relations in America have focused on the regional character of racist practices. Thus, it is a commonplace report that blacks in the South have been victims of a caste order;[1] that Indian troubles are a feature of westward expansion;[2] that Mexican-Americans are the principal object of ethnic intolerance in the southwest;[3] that anti-Semitism is a creature of midwestern populism;[4] and that Sinophobia and anti-Japanese sentiment are peculiar products of conditions on the Pacific Coast.[5] The image of the segmented and geographical character of American racism has facilitated a local view of the phenomenon, concentrating primarily on the origins of prejudice and discrimination in the immediate area and eschewing any analysis of racism as a central value of American society.[6] However, the 1968 report of the National Advisory Commission on Civil Disorders challenged this view when it asserted that

> Race prejudice has shaped our history decisively in the past; it now threatens to do so again. White racism is essentially responsible for the explosive mixture which has been accumulating in our cities since the end of World War II.[7]

The Kerner Report suggested that racism was endemic to America. Recent research has delved even more deeply and discovered that racism arose as a central value in the post-medieval Occident. Winthrop Jordan has shown that racist ideas were intellectual, political, and social products of the encounter between Europeans on the one hand and Africans and Indians on the other in the sixteenth century and thereafter.[8] Africans were reputed to be living representatives of the once mythical savage, descendants of the biblically accursed Ham, and an inferior species of man, while a more refined intellectual tradition failed to resolve the question of Indian origins and laid the basis for the anti-Indian sentiment of a later age.[9] The vicissitudinal moral and political character of European images of dark-skinned peoples has been documented in the works of Henri Baudet,[10] Kathleen George,[11] and Thomas Gossett.[12] Once the idea of white superiority became both accepted and diffuse, it generated a wide variety of racist practices with respect not only to the Africans and Indians, but also to the "colored" inhabitants of Oceania,[13] and the Asian Mainland.[14] The mindless genocide of the native Hawaiian population, which literally decimated it in the century between Captain Cook's "discovery" of the Sandwich Islands and the American annexation of the once proud Hawaiian Kingdom,[15] the murderous destruction of the Tasmanian people by Australian and British colonists,[16] the notorious practices of "blackbirding" carried on throughout the South Pacific,[17] and the imperialist incursions into Indo-China[18] and the Chinese Empire[19] all testify to the merger of a general Occidental racism with political domination and economic advantage.[20]

Despite a new intellectual recognition of racism as part of the central value system of the western world, little research has been done to ascertain the forms in which it asserted itself and the causes for changes in those forms. It is the intent of this essay to present a hypothesis on the characteristic features and etiology of racist institutions in America and to show the pivotal role in the creation of these institutions played by Asians in the west.

AMERICAN RACISM IN TOTAL INSTITUTIONS

America emerged in modern world history as a republic organized to promote the general welfare and provide for the continental domination and collective security of its white Anglo-Saxon denizens. At the outset of its political and social establishment, this new society was faced by three ethnic types which challenged its originating idea: settlers and immigrants from continental Europe who did not bear the Anglo-Saxon stamp of moral and social approval in their character or culture; Africans and their descendents in America, whose dark skins and cultural practices were anathema to a white racial and Anglo-Saxon cultural order; and indigenous Indians whose copper-colored bodies and social and political codes challenged the racial and territorial plans for continental domination by the white, European Occidentals. In responding to the challenges posed by these three orders of humankind,

America forged both the character and institutions of a racist yet still pluralistic society. The central characteristics of this racist pluralism were its rules of inclusion and exclusion with respect to racial types and the mechanisms adduced to enforce these rules.

Essentially the decision was made—but only gradually worked out in piecemeal fashion—that America was to be a white man's country. Eligible for inclusion within the folds of full citizenship were all those Europeans who would renounce their continental cultures in favor of at least outward conformity to the dictates of Anglo-Saxon ways.[21] "Colored" peoples, on the other hand, would be excluded from full citizenship rights, but neither expelled from the American domain nor absorbed into its mainstream by interbreeding. Color castes, created by institutionalizing the ubiquitous relevance of skin pigmentation, establishing barriers against intermarriage, and experimenting with modes of racial isolation and concentration, would control the dark-skinned peoples. Theories of cultural assimilation and doctrines of a racial hierarchy—supported at various times by state, church, and science—would, supposedly, justify the arrangements to all concerned.

The Europeans were co-opted slowly and steadily, with only occasional eruptions and isolated rebellions, into the Anglo-Saxon core group. The fact that English became the *lingua franca* and official dialect of discourse perhaps did more than any other single process to promote Anglo-conformity as a "natural" and "taken-for-granted" process of Americanization.[22] For Europeans, acculturation proceeded naturally and as a matter of course—or so it seemed.[23] In fact, religio-ethnic enclaves managed to preserve themselves—sometimes by a self-enforced cultural and geographical isolation, as among the Amish and the Hutterians;[24] sometimes by securing linguistic, national, or cultural values within the confines of church, private school, or some other secluded institution[25]—and thus created a dual national existence for themselves.

In the one hundred and thirty-seven years that separated the writing of the Constitution from the xenophobic immigration act of 1924—the final and most important victory of American nativism[26]—the Anglo-conformity doctrine triumphed over its pluralistic competitors.[27] The "melting pot" dream of the "American farmer," J. Hector St. John de Crevecoeur, was for Europeans only.[28] It was realized in the almost unnoticed erosion of Germanic culture,[29] the steady diminution and sometimes forcible eradication of Gaelic nationalism,[30] the decline of Greek-American institutions,[31] and the social isolation of steadily diminishing enclaves of other non-Anglo Europeans, including Italians,[32] Russians,[33] Poles,[34] and Jews.[35] Not a few immigrants became disenchanted and returned to their homelands.[36] More ominous was the vicissitudinal occurrence of nativist movements in America,[37] espousing a xenophobic bigotry, promoting the fear that Catholic immigrants were the advance legions of a papal conspiracy,[38] and that Jewish intelligence would subvert both Christianity and capitalism.[39] Liberty Leagues, Know-Nothing parties, and the Ku Klux Klan took care to fan the flames of hatred for foreigners and to instill terror in the hearts of all those restive blacks and as yet unacculturated Europeans.[40] Finally, ordinary newly-arrived Europeans soon learned that there were three ready testaments by which the newcomers could assure their American hosts that they were willing to assume the obligations of citizenship and fully incorporate themselves into the body politic. They could share with the dominant white Americanized natives their profound pride in the fact that they too were white; they could voice their equally profound assurance that they too abhorred the "colored" peoples; they could join together with their fellow *Landsmänner* and with immigrants from other lands in associations that, whatever their social, political, and economic aims, took care to exclude non-whites.[41]

The co-optation of continental Europeans was conducted concomitant with the enclosure of non-whites in total institutions. Africans were enslaved within the first half of the seventeenth century and Negro identity became coterminous with slave status.[42] Plantation slavery not only permanently excluded blacks from the societal mainstream, but also imposed coercive controls which destroyed all but the vestiges of Old World culture.[43] The plantation dominated black life from the cradle to the grave. Denied the right to vote, sue, own property, make contracts, choose his place of abode, marry according to his choice and rear his own children, the male African-American slave was reduced to a pitiful existence combining the "benevolent" despotism of permanent childhood with the desperate terror of the concentration camp.[44] Black women were treated no better and were subjected to wanton rape by their white masters, denial of the full rights of wife- or motherhood, and countless varieties of sexual as well as racial harassment. Despite over two hundred slave insurrections,[45] countless runaways,[46] occasional manumissions,[47] and a small but increasingly vocal free Negro population,[48] the blacks remained in nearly total subjugation until after the Civil War. Denied essential citizenship privileges and basic human rights, they were effectively excluded from the body politic and from the society.

Early attempts at enslavement of the Indians proved to be counterproductive, but the "solution" to the Indian "problem" nevertheless assumed total institutional proportions. Disease introduced by European contact took its toll in countless lives among the Red Men and Women.[49] As the Americans pushed westward against the frontier horizons, massacre and conquest continued their decimation of the Indian nations.[50] The system of relocation, ultimately to be followed by incarceration of the Indians on wastelands unwanted by the mineral- and land-hungry "pioneers," emerged as the most efficacious "final" solution.[51] Although Indian tribes resisted unconditional surrender to white America until well past the opening of the twentieth century, and although a few escaped to Canada, the survivors of the military campaigns were eventually removed from their homelands and imprisoned on reservations.[52] There they fell under the domination of missionaries and bureaucrats who permitted them but the most modest preservation of their own way of life at the same time that they denied them knowledge about and access to the dominant society. Eating, sleeping, working, playing, and mating under the ever-watchful surveillance of the Bureau of Indian Affairs, the Amerindian, like the Negro, could not exercise any meaningful influence on or enter into any productive relationship with white society.[53]

Through the first half of the nineteenth century the Anglo-conformists were largely successful in their drive to insure white racial and Anglo-Saxon cultural domination of the American continent. European immigrants learned to publicly profess their desire to "Americanize" themselves, even as they stepped off the ships;[54] black leaders were divided over whether their people's liberation could be achieved in America or whether an exodus to Africa or to some other new land must precede jubilee day.[55] Indians retreated before the advance of white armies, many dying in proud defiance; others were degraded in the demoralizing confines of white America's fenced and guarded enclosures that were especially created to isolate them and break their spirit.[56] Freed from the aristocratic controls of Europe and almost untouched by its doctrine of *noblesse oblige,* white America subjugated its "colored" peoples. The United States appeared to have found the solution to establishing an economically thriving overseas homeland for English-speaking Caucasians of European extraction.

Then the Asian appeared on the American frontier. In light of America's treatment of "colored" peoples, the single most important fact about the first Chinese in America is that they were neither enslaved nor corralled. Arriving in California at the time of the earliest rumblings of incipient industrialism and the final onslaught on chattel slavery in America, the Chinese challenged the evil genius of this Anglo-Saxon society to wreak its racist havoc on them in some new manner, consistent with its exclusionist doctrines yet attuned to the condition of their peculiar mode of existence.[57]

ASIANS AND THE BEGINNINGS
OF MODERN INSTITUTIONAL RACISM

The arrival of Asians in America preceded by but a few years the rise of industrialization and extensive urban settlement. So long as the United States depended on primary extractive and agricultural pursuits for this economic development, an excluded people—such as blacks or Indians—might be exploited through enclosure in total institutions,[58] plantations, or reservations. But with the advent of large-scale industrial production and extensive settlement in cities, the total institutional approach was not only inefficient but also counterproductive.[59] A docile labor force was needed to work uncomplainingly in the new urban factories. But if such a work force was to be drawn from a people otherwise ineligible to civic, economic, and social equality, methods would have to be found which would simultaneously permit the exploitation of them in a wide variety of settings and yet keep them apart from white society.[60] The Chinese arrived just in time to become what Alexander Saxton has called an "indispensable enemy."[61] In working out its response to the Asian challenge to white Anglo-Saxon dominance, America perfected the institutions of modern racism, institutions which had seen only their unorganized beginnings in the treatment of free Negroes in the slave era.

Unlike the total institutions of plantation slavery and rural reservations, modern racism is characterized by a diffuse, subtle—indeed, sometimes unconscious and invisible—prejudice found in a vast congeries of organizations, associations, and social practices, none of which encompass the totality of the phenomenon, and each of which operates to degrade, demote, demoralize or defame non-white peoples.[62] Instead of finding its principal locus of operation at reservations or plantations, modern racism affects nearly all the institutions of modern industrial America—those in the political, economic, religious, educational, social, and interpersonal spheres of life. Modern racism encompasses America with its rules, roles, and relationships.[63]

When it became clear that Chinese and, later, Japanese might, if left to their own inclinations, ultimately participate at every level of American society and thus sully the white racial and Anglo-Saxon cultural domination which prevailed, each institutional sphere adopted restrictive or exclusionist practices to halt the potential Asian "invasion." Although some of these institutions were so situated that they operated only at a local level (during the first two decades of their American venture the Chinese were largely employed in rural mines, railroad construction, wineries, swamp drainage, and agricultural labor, work in which their total supervision and segregation were assured), two important decisions at the national level gave impetus and legitimacy to even more extensive local and state institutional developments. The first of these was the limitation on family formation imposed by the Immigration Act of 1882; the second was the exclusion from naturalization imposed on Asians by legislation and judicial interpretation.

Like most immigrants to a frontier area, Chinese men had not been accompanied to America by their wives. Chinese custom and the self-acknowledged sojourner status of the first immigrants dictated this move as "natural."[64] However, when Chinese settlements appeared and the likelihood of long-term habitation in America seemed obvious, the federal government excluded the coming of the wives of immigrant Chinese laborers.[65] Not only did this legislative action insure domestic hardship and personal loneliness for the hapless Chinese working man, it also guaranteed that no significant second generation of Chinese would be produced in America. The immigrant generation, excluded from replenishing itself by further migration after 1882, would eventually die out with no effective trace left in America.[66] The Chinese ghetto would be composed of homeless, aging bachelors whose recreational pursuits, domestic arrangements, and social formations would stamp them as morally reprehensible in white American eyes.[67]

A few Chinese had been naturalized in the local communities and several states to which they had migrated before 1882.[68] However, in that year the same statute that barred the further coming of Chinese laborers and their wives also expressly excluded the Chinese from naturalization.[69] Forty years later the Supreme Court interpreted the naturalization laws then in effect to bar Japanese aliens from citizenship as well.[70] To gauge their full effect, the prohibition of the entrance of Chinese wives and the exclusion from citizenship must be read together. Even if aliens are declared to be ineligible to citizenship, their children *born on American soil* are citizens. By barring wives and declaring Chinese alienage to be permanent, the federal statutes effectively denied citizenship to almost all Chinese. Immigrants could no longer apply for naturalization and, without wives, no very significant number of natural-born citizens would arise.[71] The prohibition on acquiring citizenship had one other advantage for exclusionary procedures in a wide variety of situations. It introduced the category "alien ineligible to citizenship," which would be used as a further bar to other rights, privileges, and sanctuaries of white Anglo-Saxon domination. Laws and statutes regulating hunting, fishing,[72] land ownership, and corporate formations[73] introduced restrictions on ineligible aliens in the years that followed. Moreover, jobs, scholarships, and other opportunities were foreclosed to Asians by the bar of citizenship prerequisites.

The federal legislation and judicial interpretations provided greater impetus and legislative justification for further racist practices against Asians, and for the establishment of generalized restrictions which might later be used against emancipated blacks and detribalized Indians. Thus, in education, California's Superintendent of Education successfully complained against the presence of "Africans, Chinese, and Diggers" in 1859 and the offending races were excluded from the public schools in the following year.[74] In the years thereafter separate public schools were established for Chinese children. Even this did not contain the Asian population enough. Japanese students were ordered removed to the "Chinese school" in 1905 in what was to escalate into an international incident of bellicose proportions.[75] Nativists and patriotic organizations aroused deep-seated anxieties about intermarriage in a prolonged demagogic campaign of more than two decades to further segregate schools in the west.[76] Attempts by Chinese to desegregate San Francisco's schools in 1902[77] and those of Mississippi in 1927[78] were unsuccessful. Despite the overturn of *de jure* segregation in public schools in 1954,[79] many school systems, including those with predominant Chinese American minorities, remain segregated on a *de facto* basis. Moreover, the long history of exclusionist and separatist practice has taken its toll not only in inferior and unequal education, but also in the rise of a form of anti-racist ethnic nationalism among some Chinese. Strong feelings thus exist today among Chinese Americans attending San Francisco's almost all-Chinese Jean Parker Elementary School, Francisco Junior High School, and Galileo High School. A movement to implement not desegregation, but some form of pedagogic cultural nationalism expressible in the schools, is now afoot. In public education, as elsewhere, the triumph of white racism and Anglo-conformity has produced a restive and nationalistic counteractive drive for ethnic pluralism.

State legislation controlling freedom of choice in marriage also closed the one loophole in family formation available to the homeless bachelor Chinese after 1882. Rendered ineligible for domesticity by the prohibition on immigrant wives, threatened with denial of readmission to the United States if they made home visits to their long-suffering wives in China,[80] Chinese men might have resolved their personal difficulties through intermarriage with white women as, for example, the homeless Chinese in Indonesia did when they married into the native population there.[81] However, a series of anti-miscegenation laws ultimately passed in forty of the United States barred most Chinese from this possibility for family life.[82] Thus, the very same kind of provisions that kept black slaves from legitimately amalgamating with white masters and Indians from mingling their blood with that of all but the hated "Squaw Man" kept the Chinese from becoming a part of white America. Permitted neither to procreate nor intermarry, the Chinese immigrant was told, in effect, to remigrate or die out—white America would not be touched by his presence.

Jobs and occupations have provided the ladder of success by which European immigrants climbed out of their original poverty and enculturation and on to the plateau of mainstream America. Entering America at a time of great industrial growth and expansion, European laborers charted the course of their own journey into America's cultural heartland by the map laid out by Anglo-Conformist leaders. Significant here is the fact that American labor's rights to organize, bargain collectively, and sit at the table reserved for legitimate associations were won at the price of excluding non-whites from the movement.[83] The first to be *systematically* excluded were the Chinese, although free blacks, as Frederick Douglass's autobiography makes poignantly clear,[84] were often excluded from the workmen's associations that preceded national labor organization. The Sinophobia of Denis Kearney's Irish workers[85] and the vitriotic anti-Chinese sentiments of the Knights of Labor[86] set the stage for the wholesale exclusion of Chinese workers from the American Federation of Labor by Samuel Gompers.[87] And this exclusion of a whole race—a practice that violated Gompers' own strictures against dividing the labor force and establishing the conditions for rival racial unions to organize—in turn created the climate by which other racial and ethnic groups, notably blacks, Indians, and Mexican-Americans, might later be restricted in their labor union association or excluded altogether from the ranks and protection of organized labor.[88] Thus, the Chinese who could not vote or study beside the white man could not work beside him either. And the Chinese example, once begun, would be applied to the other colored peoples, insuring a division between white and colored workers that has lasted to the present day.

Modern racism is symbolized by the presence of the urban ghetto. Typically, the scene is that of a black enclave in the recesses of a northern metropolis, surrounded by the invisible barrier of real estate restrictions and burdened with its own peculiar brands of poverty and subculture.[89] But again the ghetto arose most starkly among the Chinese and was greeted with pleasure and pressure for maintenance by the minions of modern white racist America. Chinatowns are racial ghettos whose origins are to be found in the congregative sentiments and peculiar institutions of a non-Occidental people who, in order to preserve life itself, banded together to control a piece of territory as their own.[90] They are a colonialized people's response to their condition urging, on the constructive side, that the separate culture and special identity of their own kind be preserved in dignity.[91]

But Chinatown is also and at the same time a slum. It is a gilded ghetto whose tinseled streets and brightly lit shops barely camouflage a pocket of poverty in the metropolis.[92] With the closing off of immigration, the refusal to permit amalgamation, the restriction in the public schools, and the denial of membership in the organized labor force of white America, Chinatown's survival as a ghetto was assured. With its establishment by all these institutional forces working separately but in tandem to insure the security and virginity of white Anglo America, the stage was set for similar ghettos to be established when freed blacks tired of the caste restrictions of the Redemptionist South and moved north to find a new freedom, and when detribalized Indians moved or were thrown out of their reservations and also sought the city. The ghetto with its congregational inner spirit and its surrounding segregationist pressure, with its nationalistic fervor and its economic debilitation, with its powerful concentration and its political impotence, is a creature of modern racism whose perfection was first worked out with respect to the Asian challenge to a modern industrial racist society.

CONCLUSION

Until recently the Asian has occupied an insignificant place in the annals of American history and the analyses of American society. Their annals, they were told, constituted only a local and regional story, perhaps of interest to the historical buffs of Pacific Coast lore but of no importance to understanding America. Recent research suggests, however, a very different interpretation.[93] If American racism may be defined as the attempt to impose white Anglo-Saxon culture on the inhabitants of a continent, then two epochs may be distinguished. The first, that of total exclusion for non-whites and imposed acculturation on continental Europeans, may be said to have begun in 1607 and ended in the twentieth century. Characteristic of the exclusionist mechanisms of this first period were total institutionalization of the non-white population on plantations and reservations. The second epoch continues the cultural imposition of Anglo-Saxon norms on Europeans, but substitutes segmented, partial, institutionalized racism in a wide variety of arenas of action for the abandoned and moribund method of total incarceration. The pivotal group for the study of this transition from total to partial institutionalized racism is the Asian and especially the Chinese. Neither an indigenous people to be conquered and incarcerated nor a people forcibly removed from their homeland to build the economy of a racist society, the Asians could not justifiably be enslaved or put away on reservations. In responding to the challenge of their presence, the many and varied institutions of white America segregated the schools on a racial basis, restricted citizenship to include only free whites and native-born free blacks, attempted the slow genocide possible by prohibiting family formation, and enclosed the white working class from contact with its Asian peers. In so doing it insured the survival of a Chinese ghetto and established the ghetto as the urban successor to the plantation and the reservation. In treating with the Asian, white America perfected its plans for a modern, institutional, racist society.

Conflict and the Web of Group Affiliation in San Francisco's Chinatown, 1850–1910

Although the early history of the Chinese in America has been explored by many authorities, most attention has been focused on the anti-Chinese movement. The structure and operations of Chinese associations established in the Asian ghettoes of the West have received scant and stereotyped treatment.[1] The net effect of these analyses has been a perfectly correct but one-sided image of victimization unrelieved by any analytical accounts of the organizational activity or associational creativity of the Asian victims.

Most of the contemporary reports on nineteenth-century Chinatowns that treat the basic types of traditional Chinese organizations—clans, *Landsmannschaften,* and secret societies—betray a Sinophobia deeply embedded in the general racism of that era. It is not surprising that scholars of a later generation, seeking to redress this racist balance, would concentrate on the popular tribunals, prejudicial reports, and painful pejorative heaped upon the hapless Chinese. Moreover, in seeking to overturn the obloquy and slander of a whole people, sympathetic American scholars have tended to engage in a selective perception reflecting their own less venal outlook. Clans became "family associations," *Landsmannschaften* were transformed into "benevolent societies," and the activities of the once feared secret societies were said to be vastly exaggerated, if not wholly fabricated. To these liberal-minded scholars Chinese immigrants were white people with yellow skins.

In fact the first six decades of Chinese settlement in San Francisco were distinguished by Chinese immigrants, beset with a hostile racist movement opposing their very presence in America,[2] building their own special community. This community—Chinatown—was remarkable for its fierce internal conflicts, its lack of solidarity, and its intensive disharmony. Popularly known as "tong wars," the violent battles in Chinatown actually involved clans, *Landsmannschaften,* and secret societies. These fights raged intermittently but frequently for sixty years. Then, in the years closing the first decade of the twentieth century, an era seemed to come to an end. The last major reorganization of the immigrants' perfectual associations—the absorption of the Yan Hoi group into the Sue Hing Association—occurred in 1909. Three years later secret society and merchant leaders—who had been at odds with one another for more than fifty years—formed the Chinese Peace Society in the hope that they could end tong wars in Chinatown. In 1911 the Republican Revolution ended dynastic rule in China and ushered in an era of class and cosmopolitan politics that also found expression in political and radical parties in the overseas Chinese colonies. By 1910 most of the immigrant Chinese laborers had been driven off the farmlands and out of most of the urban jobs in and around San Francisco and forced to work as well as live in Chinatown. An aging population that could not be replenished by immigration—forbidden since 1882—or by procreation—prevented by the enormous imbalance in the sex ratio—seemed in danger of extinction during the next half century.[3] But instead of disappearing, Chinatown in the years following 1910 became an established tourist attraction, dominated by its merchant and association leaders, exploiting the labor of its poorer elements, and hiding its fetid squalor under the show of its pagoda roofs, parades on Chinese New Year, and patriotic drives in behalf of the *Kuomintang.*[4] Yet, beneath the surface, the basic structure that had been established at such fearful cost during its first sixty years remained. It still does.

In this paper, the structure and operation of San Francisco's nineteenth-century Chinatown are presented in a schematic and sociological fashion. The argument can be stated quite succinctly: Nineteenth-century Chinatown was a complex, highly organized community whose associations were not in constant harmony with one another. Most important were the activities of the secret societies, whose competition for control of vice and whose political battles were fierce. As a result of inter-society conflicts and traditional modes of resolving them, violent altercations erupted repeatedly within the ghetto. Since these disputes were intramural, they acted as a further barrier to contacts with the larger society, placed many individuals under cross-pressures of loyalty to the several associations whose membership overlapped, and fastened on the Chinese community a pattern of antagonistic cooperation. Thus intra-community conflict and cooperation acted together to help isolate the Chinese from the metropolis.

Chinese communities in the United States have enjoyed a measure of isolation and communal self-government far exceeding that of other ethnic communities.[5] One reason for the unusual separation of China-

towns from regular public municipal controls was their long period of
electoral irrelevance to American politics. Denied naturalization and the
franchise for nearly a century, the Chinese, unlike European immigrants, were not the objects of any local ward politician's solicitations.
Left to themselves—except during anti-Chinese campaigns—the Chinese organized their own benevolent, protective, and governmental
bodies. In effect, the Chinese community in America is more like a colonial dependency than an immigrant settlement in an open society. The
relationship between the ghetto community and metropolitan authorities bears a close resemblance to that which prevailed in the British,
Dutch, and French colonies in Oceania and Southeast Asia.[6] The "mayor
of Chinatown,"[7] a person whose authority is tacitly acknowledged by
civic officials in the United States, is, in most respects, nothing less than
an American equivalent of the *Kapitan China,* an official who represented
the Chinese inhabitants of the European colonies in Southeast Asia.[8]

Inside a Chinatown like that which developed in San Francisco, a
merchant class soon became the ruling elite.[9] Because commercial success was so closely tied to social acceptance and moral probity in America, this elite enjoyed good relations with public officials. Chinatown
merchants controlled immigrant associations, dispensed jobs and opportunities, settled disputes, and acted as advocates for the Chinese sojourners before white society.[10] The power of these merchants rested on
a traditional foundation. They governed Chinatown through the complex interrelationships of clans and *Landsmannschaften,* or mutual aid societies.[11] Opposition to this system of authority came primarily from
members of secret societies. Eventually secret society leaders infiltrated
the legitimate associations and a mercantile power structure emerged
uniting the purveyors of legal and illegal goods and services.

CLANS

One of the most important of the legitimate associations was the
clan, an organization which traces its origins to the lineage communities of southeastern China.[12] Although descent in the lineage community was usually carefully recorded so as to exclude all except direct
descendants, such meticulousness was impossible to maintain in the
fast-changing social conditions of the overseas colonies. There the surname alone established identity, and clan brothers assumed their blood
relationship on the basis of their common name.[13] Moreover, practical
considerations often superseded loyalty to ideals of lineal purity, producing combinations of clan names and the admission of different sur-

names into the same association.[14] Real or assumed kinship provided the basis for clan solidarity, while "practical reasoning" resolved those questions which tended to engender disunity.[15]

Overseas clans were organized by prominent ghetto merchants who assumed many of the duties and responsibilities that lineage communities had been responsible for in China. In place of the territorially compact village, the overseas clan was organized around a leading merchant's store.[16] The merchant usually exerted leadership in his clan, established a hostelry above the store for his kinsmen, and provided aid, advice, comfort, and shelter. The clan provided the boundary of the incest taboo, and marriage was prohibited among persons bearing the same surname.[17] Clans further served to remind the sojourner of his obligations to village and family in China, and, in the absence of lineage authorities, overseas clan leaders acted *in loco parentis*.[18]

In addition to their assumption of traditional lineage authority, clans afforded an opportunity for commercial monopoly. Just as certain clans in China kept trade secrets confined to their members and restricted the entrance of upstarts,[19] so the overseas clans organized brotherhoods in trade, manufacture, and types of labor. The Dear clan, for example, operated the San Francisco Chinatown's fruit and candy stores; the Yee and Lee clans owned better-class restaurants and supplied most of the cooks in domestic service. Because they varied in location and membership, the clans could (and still can) be classified according to their economic and community dominance.[20] Thus, the Lees are most prominent in Philadelphia; the Toms in New York City; the Loys in Cleveland; the Ongs in Phoenix. In some Chinatowns more than one clan is conspicuous by its size. Thus, the Fongs and Yees both predominate in Sacramento as do the Moys and Chins in Chicago. Small Chinatowns probably sprang up on the basis of a single clan, and in the smaller towns of the Rocky Mountain areas, there have rarely been more than four clans.[21]

HUI KUAN

In addition to clans, immigrant Chinese, during the first decade of their sojourn in America (1851–1862), established five *hui kuan,* organizations which were functionally similar to but structurally different from the clan.[22] The overseas *hui kuan,* similar to its urban counterpart in China,[23] unites all those who speak a common dialect, hail from the same district of origin, or belong to the same ethnic group. In many ways it is similar to those immigrant aid societies (*Landsmannschaften*) formed by Europeans in America; however, the scope of *hui kuan* controls and the diversity of its functions far exceed those of its European counterparts. For example, wherever Chinese groups settled, their local *hui kuan* served as caravansary, credit and loan society, and employment agency.[24] It also acted in a representative capacity, speaking for its members to other *hui kuan* and to white society as well.[25] In addition, it provided arbitration and mediation services for its members, settling disputes and adjudicating issues that might otherwise erupt in open violence, or, among a people who trusted public law more than the Chinese, might have found their way into the municipal courts.[26] As a combined eleemosynary, judicial, representative, and mutual aid society, the *hui kuan* exercised a wide span of control over its members. Precisely because of its multiplicity of functions, the *hui kuan* could command allegiance. To the individual Chinese who refused it fealty, it could withhold financial aid, order social ostracism, render a punitive judgment in a suit brought before its tribunal, and arrange for false charges and incriminating testimony in public courts.[27]

The *hui kuan* confederated in 1858, i.e., during the first decade of Chinese settlement in San Francisco. At first composed of five prominent *Landsmannschaften,*[28] the confederation expanded because of the addition of new speech groups, the disintegration and reformation of already established *hui kuan,* and the admission, after much pressure, of secret societies and other associations.[29] The consolidated federation of *hui kuan* commanded at least the grudging allegiance and obedience of the Chinatown masses during the latter half of the nineteenth century, and it also earned the respect of many urban whites. Popularly called the Chinese Six Companies[30] in San Francisco, the Chinese Consolidated Benevolent Association acted as an unofficial government inside Chinatown and was the most important voice of the Chinese immigrants speaking to American officials.

As a spokesman group the Chinese Consolidated Benevolent Association has frequently protested against the legal impositions and social indignities heaped upon Chinese immigrants in America, and on occasion it has requested judicial extraterritorial rights over those Chinese likely to be accused of crimes. Among its more significant proclamations and protests were the "Letter of the Chinamen to his Excellency Governor Bigler" in 1852; the "Reply to the Message of His Excellency, Governor John Bigler" in 1855; a "Remonstrance from Chinese in California to the Congress of the United States" in 1868; a "Memorial from the Six Chinese Companies: an address to the Senate and House of Representatives of the United States" in 1877; and, in 1916, a protest to the President of the United States over the onerous burden of America's exclusionist immigration practices.[31]

However, despite its growth in status, the Consolidated Benevolent Association did not have much success in preventing the passage of new discriminatory laws or revoking any laws already in existence.[32] Neither did it succeed in establishing exclusive jurisdiction over Chinese criminals or in stopping the mobs that attacked Chinatowns throughout the latter decades of the nineteenth century.[33] For many years the Chinese spokesmen could not overcome the charge—levelled against them by anti-Chinese demagogues—that they held the people they claimed to represent in unlawful serfdom.[34] On the other hand, they were not always able to command complete obedience. For example, in 1893, when they ordered Chinese not to register in accordance with a newly enacted immigration act, and subsequently lost their appeal against the act in the courts, they encountered open resistance in Chinatown.[35] To most Chinese, the consequence of failure to register—deportation—was simply too grave. Eventually, however, after the worst phase of the anti-Chinese movement was over, and with the aid of white apologists who exaggerated its community services and charitable deeds, the confederated *hui kuan* achieved recognition as the sole spokesman for Chinese in America.[36] But recognition by white America was not matched by appreciation from the inhabitants of Chinatown. The latter often grumbled about the exploitative power of the combined *hui kuan* and occasionally revolted, without success, against its excesses.[37]

The community dominance of the Consolidated Benevolent Association was rooted not only in its traditional authority but also in its control over debts, labor, commerce, and disputes.[38] The bulk of Chinese immigrants were debtors, and their obligations were owned or supervised by the *hui kuan* merchants. Moreover, the *hui kuan* acted as a general collection agency and creditor for its more affluent members. In addition, it charged its members entrance and departure fees and insisted that all debts be cleared before an immigrant returned to China. The *hui kuan* also provided the organizational base for a rotating credit system that became the principal source of capital for entrepreneurship and business development in Chinatown. Its power to give or withhold needed money served as a source of anger among those who suffered from its onerous exactions or its outright refusal to make needed loans.[39]

The *hui kuan* appear to have supervised contract labor among the immigrants and also to have provided an organizational basis for craft and commercial guilds.[40] Although apologists for the Chinese denied that the *hui kuan* had anything to do with the labor system that existed among the sojourners, there is evidence that the *hui kuan* operated the "credit-ticket" system (by which Chinese borrowed money to come to America), acted as subcontractors for white labor recruiters, and may have supplied the bosses for Chinese labor gangs deployed in various parts of the country.[41]

The pattern of both labor and business organization in Chinatown reflected the *hui kuan*'s interest. Common laborers, service workers, and skilled operatives were organized according to their dialect or their district of origin in China.[42] Crafts and commercial establishments were similarly organized so that district and linguistic group monopolies over labor and business prevailed in every major Chinatown. Stores and restaurants in Chinatown were allocated space according to a traditional property right system under the control of the *hui kuan*. The property right system protected group monopolies from excessive competition and the entrance of upstarts.[43]

Perhaps the most important power of the consolidated *hui kuan* was juridical in nature.[44] Mention has already been made of the mediation and arbitration service provided in individual clans and *hui kuan*. When an individual felt wronged in his original suit or when disputes arose among associations, an appeal could be lodged with the tribunal of the confederated *hui kuan*. The Benevolent Association was thus the supreme organ for settlement of disputes. So long as the Chinese were either denied the right to testify in public courts or unwilling to employ the American legal system,[45] the merchant elite of Chinatown exercised an awesome authority. Persons who were not in good standing with their clan or *hui kuan* could be refused a hearing. Those who openly revolted against the Chinatown establishment might be stripped of their property, boycotted, ostracized, or, in extreme cases, given even more violent treatment.[46]

SECRET SOCIETIES

Clans and *hui kuan* were traditional and lawful societies in China and in the overseas colonies; secret societies were traditional in China, but they usually became criminal or subversive associations. Nineteenth-century migrants from Kwangtung included not a few members of the Triad Society, China's most famous clandestine association.[47] Active in rebellions and crime for centuries in China, the Triad Society provided the model for the secret societies that sprang up overseas.[48] In some settlements, such as those in rural British Columbia, where clans and *hui kuan* had failed to form, secret societies became the sole community organization.[49] The secret societies enrolled members according to interest, rather than by kin or district ties, and in one recorded instance in 1898 admitted an American journalist.[50] From the beginning of Chinese settlement in America the secret societies, popularly known as *tongs*,[51] have remained a significant part of Chinatown's organizational structure.

The scope of operations of secret societies was wide, but confined for the most part to Chinatown. On the basis of available data, their activities may be classified according to their political, protest, criminal, and benevolent character.

Political Activities

Secret societies in the Chinese community of the United States and other areas of immigrant settlement did not seek to alter, oppose, or subvert the national political structure of their host countries. They did, however, attempt to influence the course of political events in China. For the most part, their political activities failed, but in the establishment of Dr. Sun Yat Sen's republic in 1911 their efforts were significant. Sun found considerable support for his anti-Manchu movement among the overseas Chinese and especially within the secret societies.[52] A founder of two revolutionary societies himself, Sun joined or participated with many others and persuaded them to give money and, on a few occasions, men to the cause.[53] On his trip to the United States in 1904 he worked with the *Chih-kung T'ang*, an overseas branch of the Triad Society, because "there was at the time no other organization which could claim membership all over America."[54] Purposefully vague about the precise nature of his revolutionary aims, Sun did not openly challenge the secret societies' interest in restoring the Ming Dynasty.[55] Ultimately he prevailed over several rival insurrectionist groups by organizing his own revolutionary party and by gaining the support of Christian and non-Christian Chinese, a few prominent whites, and most of the secret societies.[56] So successful was Sun's movement in America—the money for the new republic was printed in San Francisco's Chinatown—that by 1910 he seriously considered transferring his headquarters from Japan to the United States.[57]

Protest

As was the case in China, secret societies provided the organizational base and the muscle for protest against individual or collective oppression. However, the secret societies in the United States did not direct their actions against white racism, Sinophobic legislation, or anti-Chinese mobs. Rather, their attention was concentrated on the power elite of Chinatown. The secret societies provided a check on clan and *hui kuan* exploitation and control over the sojourners.

There is evidence to suggest that the more notorious toughs and thugs employed by the secret societies in the United States were recruited from those who revolted against or were alienated from the merchant elite oligarchy of the *hui kuan*. Elmer Wok Wai, severely disturbed by the way of life in his broken family and bereft of clan protection, ran away from home at fifteen, became a gunman for the *Hop Sing Tong*, and served seventeen years in prison before he went to work as a domestic servant for a white family.[58] Mock Wah, certain that his inability to secure a favorable hearing before the Chinese Six Companies' tribunal stemmed from the fact that he came from a weak clan, established the *Kwong Duck Tong*.[59] Num Sing Bark, a scholar and intellectual from China, founded the *Hip Sing Tong* to take revenge on those powerful Chinatown clans that he blamed for his failure in business.[60]

Business failure because of Chinatown's clan and *hui kuan* monopolies also led Wong du King and Gaut Sing Dock to join secret societies, while an unsuccessful suit before the tribunal of the Chinese Consolidated Benevolent Association caused Yee Low Dai to form the *Suey Sing Tong* and to take by force what he could not obtain by law.[61] Hong Ah Kay, a notorious gunman for the *Suey Sing Tong,* entered the society only after losing both his father and his mistress through clan and *hui kuan* machinations.[62] Two tong leaders were apparently alienated intellectuals. Kung Ah Get of the San Jose Chapter of the *Hip Sing Tong* was a self-educated and literate orator of considerable eloquence, while another *Hip Sing* leader, Ton Back Woo, was an erstwhile military student in China who had passed only the first of his examinations before adverse circumstances forced him to emigrate to New York City.[63] Just as the secret societies of China recruited those Chinese who had fallen or been forced out of the traditional ascriptive associations, so the clandestine lodges among the Chinese in America gathered their members from among those angered by and ostracized from Chinatown's more powerful clans and *hui kuan*.[64] However, unlike the situation in China, where bandit dynasties had occasionally been established, a tong bandit could not hope to utilize his overseas tong connections to become an emperor.[65] He might occasionally participate from afar in China's political upheavals, but usually he spent his days looking after the society's criminal operations and fighting in its many feuds.

Criminal Activities

Provision of illegal goods and services—opium, gambling, and prostitution—became the economic base for secret societies.[66] A few early efforts of the clans and *hui kuan* to subvert tong business operations were successful. However, American authorities refused the merchant leaders' requests for extraterritorial rights over Chinese criminals in

America.[67] Later, after 1882—the precise date is not clear—secret society leaders were admitted to the ruling elite of Chinatown; thereafter, the strong opposition of the secret societies to traditional authorities was gradually replaced by attempts to hide and to regulate vice operations. By 1913, secret society members held positions in the Chinese Peace Society, which had been established to end internecine fights in Chinatown.[68]

The criminal activities of the secret societies were nearly impervious to American agencies of law enforcement. Policemen on the Chinatown detail were easily bribed.[69] Moreover, the widespread police practice of vice control, rather than total abolition, led them into tacit cooperation with the secret societies.[70] In some cases a Chinese tong leader used both the police and the courts to his own advantage. For example, Fong Ching, popularly known as "Little Pete," regularly informed the police about vice operations in San Francisco's Chinatown. After the arrest of the malefactors, he would reopen their establishments under police protection, the reward for being an informer.[71] The municipal courts could also be subverted by tong machinations. Tong gunmen could count on perjured testimony to be presented in their behalf and on the effective bribery of court interpreters as well.[72] Indeed, according to a set of instructions taken from a secret society thug in British Columbia in 1887, the tong promised its "salaried soldiers" protection against conviction in the courts, and, should that fail, the society further guaranteed financial aid for the convicted felon and for his family while he served his prison sentence, and burial and other death benefits should he die while working in behalf of his secret society.[73]

Benevolent Activities

The charitable and fraternal activities of the secret societies were confined to aiding their own members. As the societies prospered they erected elaborate halls in Chinatown which not only reflected their affluence but also were used for fraternal and charitable purposes. For example, when the Chinese Society of Free Masons, a euphemism for the Triad Society,[74] opened a new building in San Francisco in 1907, a local newspaper reported that one of its floors would house destitute widows and orphans because "care will be taken of all those in any way connected with the lodge, who have been overtaken with misfortune."[75] Mutual aid was also a feature of rural lodges of the secret societies, but charity was chastened by a cautious regard for the small treasury available and by the fear that interlopers would presume upon the tong's benevolence. A set of secret society rules from a lodge in the Fraser River area illustrates the conservatism and apprehensions of the small isolated chapters. The society provided a bunkhouse, arbitration and mediation services, and sickness and death benefits, but, perhaps in keeping with the womanless condition of the miners, no funds were provided for expenses related to childbirth, marriage, or funerals.[76] A partial exception to this rule seems to have been made in the case of secret society thugs. There is evidence that at least one such thug was promised a $500 death benefit, free medical care, a subvention of $10 per month, and a flat fee of $250 plus the cost of transportation back to China in case of permanent disability.[77] The rural chapters, beset by local problems and worried about interlopers from San Francisco's Chinatown, took care to protect their jurisdiction from frauds. A British Columbia lodge rule read: "Headmen from San Francisco intending to establish a forum for teaching disciples whether in the town or in the mining areas must hold a license from the *Chih-kung-T'ang.* Anyone without such a license pretending to be a Headman will be prosecuted."[78] Penury and fear seemed to place significant limitations on mutual aid and benevolence within the secret societies.

Conflict and the Web of Group Affiliation in Chinatown

Chinese communities were highly organized, but organizations rested on different and in some cases contradictory foundations. The aims of the clans, *hui kuan,* and secret societies often clashed, and their peaceful competition not infrequently gave way to violence. Chinese immigrants frequently fell out with one another in quarrels over women, money, or politics. Sometimes these disputes escalated into group conflicts. Although the term "tong war" suggests that the violent altercations within America's Chinatowns were confined to the several secret societies, in fact these struggles included all three of the basic types of associations. For many decades the internal conflicts among the Chinese sojourners isolated them from the larger society and bound them together in an antagonistic cooperation.

Violent conflicts in Chinatown arose for the most part out of four major kinds of situations: rival aspirations for control of the illegal commerce in drugs, gambling, and prostitution; transplantation of mainland civil wars or revolutions to the overseas Chinatowns; revolts of the poor against the merchant oligarchy of Chinatown; and rival claims to a woman. The first is illustrated by the unfortunate career of Fong Ching, a secret society leader whose daring plan to take control of vice in San Francisco's Chinese quarter resulted in the formation of a coalition of tongs to oppose his scheme, and, finally, in his assassination in a Chinatown barbershop.[79] An example of the second situation is the

Weaverville War (1854), the California version of China's Hakka-Punti War (1855–68).[80] The third situation is represented by the war between the wealthy Yee clan and the On Yick Tong, a secret society composed largely of underpaid workers.[81] The last situation has countless illustrations. The shortage of women among the overseas Chinese led many of the young male immigrants to resort to prostitutes, most of whom were Chinese girls brought to America under contract as indentured domestic servants and put to work in the brothels that dotted San Francisco's Chinatown.[82]

At the turn of the century, several powerful secret societies fought one another for monopoly of vice operations in Chinatowns throughout the United States.[83] The worst of these fights occurred in San Francisco and New York, although branches and chapters in smaller Chinese settlements also took part. Since stakes in these battles were high, the fighting was fierce. Ultimately the less powerful secret societies were destroyed or co-opted into the larger ones. The outcome of these struggles was the admission of secret society leaders into the councils of the confederated *hui kuan* and a consolidation of crime and vice in Chinatown under the control of a restive secret society oligopoly.

Although secret societies were at first opposed by clan and *hui kuan* leaders, the latter's efforts to stamp them out failed. Buoyed by their success in vice, the secret societies challenged the right of the clan-*hui kuan* elites to dominate Chinatown. In the late 1880s a violent struggle broke out between the Suey Sing Tong and the Wong Clan in San Francisco;[84] a few years later another bloody fight between the Yee Clan and the On Yick Tong ended the armed truce that characterized Chinatown after the Suey Sing-Wong fight had ended.[85] In another bloody fight in 1893 the secret societies sought to end *hui kuan* authority in Chinatown. After a financially exhaustive and abortive attempt by San Francisco's Six Companies to test the constitutionality of the Geary Act, several secret societies combined in a violent and vituperative campaign to persuade the rank and file Chinese to renounce their allegiance to the confederation of *hui kuan*.[86] That effort failed, but secret society leaders were soon established within the power structure of Chinatown.[87]

Not all the fights in Chinatown were related to local matters. Another source of violence in the Chinese communities of San Francisco and elsewhere were the rivalries between lineage communities and ethnic groups in southeastern China that were carried overseas by the emigrants.[88] A local incident might spark the renewal of a feud that had originated in the homeland. Thus, the Hakka-Punti war was fought not only in Kwangtung between 1855 and 1868, but also in Malaya as the Larut War of 1872–1873 and in the United States as the Weaverville War of 1854.[89] In the American phase of this war, the *Sam Yap Hui Kuan,* composed of Cantonese, fell out with the *Yan Wo Hui Kuan,* which represented the Hakka group, at China Camp and at Weaverville, California. In one battle at Kentucky Ranch, some 900 "soldiers' of the Yan Wo met 1200 of the Sam Yap "army" and fought until the latter were victorious.[90] Both groups secured military assistance from local white Californians.

After 1900 not a few of the so-called "tong wars" in America's Chinatowns were among rival factions seeking to overthrow the Manchu dynasty. Although Dr. Sun was able to unite the warring factions in many overseas areas, including the United States, these united fronts did not last long. Disputes among societies supporting different leaders and ideologists broke out before and after the Chinese Revolution of 1911.[91] Because the secret societies were essentially criminal and rebellious rather than political and revolutionary, these fights also coincided with local struggles for power, wealth, and women.

Some of the conflicts in San Francisco's Chinatown were primitive class conflicts. They represented the inarticulate, non-ideological revolts of poor Chinese against a system which they resented and did not control. One example of this pre-modern class struggle is found in the war between the Yee Clan and the On Yick Tong.[92] Ostensibly begun because of an argument over a prostitute, the bloody fight also reflected the resentment of the secret society members toward the Yee clan because of its wealth, status, and power. The clan was composed of many prosperous merchants, and its treasury allegedly contained hundreds of thousands of dollars. In sharp contrast the On Yick group consisted primarily of laborers, cooks, and restaurant workers, who lived in the Chinatowns of Stockton, San Francisco, and Portland. In this "war," as in most such fights, the merchants were eventually victorious.

Still another source of hostility in San Francisco and elsewhere was the extreme imbalance in Chinatown's sex ratio, a situation which helps explain the numerous fights that broke out over women.[93] These quarrels between suitors were often used as a pretext to reopen old feuds, or as justification for a violent seizure of power. Not only did such fights break out between rival suitors but also between love-struck men and the brothel-keepers who held women under contract.[94] Sometimes a young Chinese would offer to buy up a prostitute's contract, and if he was refused he would kidnap her. The brothel-keeper would call on his secret society protectors to recover the woman, and the kidnapper would enlist the aid of his clan or *hui kuan*. The resulting struggle would be short, bloody, and usually fatal for the couple.[95] So long as the shortage of females in Chinatown remained acute, and it remained so until the late 1920s, rivalries and feuds over women continued to generate wars among associations.

This analysis of the first six decades of organizational life inside Chinatown permits a concluding discussion that is both sociological and historical. In the first sixty years of their settlement in San Francisco, Chinese immigrants, hard-pressed by the anti-Chinese movement, still managed to forge a community in the strange and hostile environment of the West. It was a traditional community, transplanting to the urban overseas Chinatown many of the institutions and customs of imperial China. Thus clans, *hui kuan,* and secret societies emerged among the immigrants as the principal organizations promoting, respectively, familial solidarity, mutual aid, and organized crime and rebellion. In the new Chinatowns these traditional associations vied with one another for the allegiance of the immigrants, overall community domination, and, in the case of the *hui kuan,* the jurisdictional right to speak for all the Chinese in the city.

The organizational developments and internecine fights that took place in Chinatown from 1850 to 1910 indicate that forming an overseas Chinese community was not an easy task. Principles of clan solidarity, barriers of language and dialect, allegiance to rebellious secret societies, and their own competitive interest in making enough money to permit retirement in China divided the loyalties of the Chinese immigrants. Yet during the same period the depredations of anti-Chinese mobs, the difficulties and indignities imposed by restrictive immigration legislation, the occupational discrimination created by state and local laws prohibiting or limiting the employment of Chinese, and the active opposition of the American labor movement to the Chinese working man all seemed to call for a community united in the face of its enemies. What emerged out of this condition of pressures from without the ghetto and divisions within was a pattern alternating between order and violence. By 1910 this pattern had assumed a complex but recognizable sociological form: that of the community whose members are bound to one another not only because of external hostility but also because of deadly internal factionalism.[96]

Both community order and inter-association conflict developed patterns and rituals in Chinatown. When order did prevail in the Chinese quarter, it was grounded in the community's institutions of law, arbitration, and conflict resolution. Most of the disputes within and among clans, *hui kuan,* and secret societies were settled by arbitration, and many appeals were amicably resolved by the tribunal of the confederation of *hui kuan.* Of course, some litigants did not accept the judgments of the tribunals. In some cases angry losers to a suit would withdraw from the association, join or found a new *hui kuan* or secret society, or rebel against the established authority in Chinatown.[97] But any system of law and order implies, if it does not generate, resistance and rebellion. Although the desire for order in Chinatown was strong during the nineteenth century, conflict was more in evidence. Even during the peaceful periods, ghetto life more nearly resembled an armed truce than a harmonious community.

If order in Chinatown was governed by traditional law, the violence in the ghetto had a definite ritual to it. In accordance with Chinese custom, no inter-association feud began without a ceremonial exchange of insults and the posting of a *chun hung*, i.e., a declaration of war.[98] Thus, the Weaverville War of 1854 began with the antagonists hurling carefully worded abusive statements at one another followed by a challenge to fight. In another case, that of the abortive attempt to overthrow the president of San Francisco's Consolidated Benevolent Association in 1893, the secret societies posted a properly worded and insulting *chun hung* on the bulletin boards and store windows of Chinatown.[99] The mode of fighting and the designation of those who would be permitted to engage in armed violence were also carefully regulated. The secret societies maintained their own bands of "salaried soldiers," and, although the evidence is not so clear, the clans and *hui kuan* probably did the same.[100] According to the instructions given to one thug by his secret society, he was forbidden to use weapons except in service to the tong.[101] In any fight the number of casualties on each side was carefully enumerated, and a crude version of the *lex talionis* seems to have governed the taking of life. A fight was brought to an end by diplomatic negotiations carried out by representatives of the belligerent parties and, often enough, presided over by a neutral mediator. The end of a "tong war" was solemnized by the signing of a treaty of peace and followed by a ceremonial banquet.[102] These rules, codes, and rituals provided a measure of stability to the wars and even curbed, but did not altogether eliminate, violence.[103]

San Francisco's Chinatown witnessed both a considerable amount of conflict and an increasingly complex web of group affiliation in the years between 1850 and 1910. On the one hand, the intramural struggles for wealth, women, and power certainly did not lend themselves to peaceful relations among the immigrants. On the other hand, the fabric of group affiliation was woven more tightly[104] as wars generated the need for allies and a system of collective security. And throughout this period of intra-community conflict, the *hui kuan* leaders presented themselves to municipal authorities, state legislators, and congressional investigators as the spokesmen for the entire Chinese community.[105]

Viewed from the perspective of a sociology of conflict, Chinatown in the years between 1850 and 1910 appears to be an extremely complex example of the thesis first developed by Georg Simmel and elaborated by Edward Alsworth Ross and Lewis Coser.[106] As Coser states it: "It seems to be generally accepted by sociologists that the distinction between 'ourselves, the we-group, or in-group, and everybody else, or the other-groups, out-groups' is established in and through conflict."[107] The social organization of San Francisco's Chinatown was comprised of a number of we-groups, each one of which looked at the others as an out-group. At times these we-groups were arrayed against one another in deadly combat. Yet, at other times, for example, when the Chinese immigrants as a whole felt threatened by white American racism, these opposed groups would postpone or put aside their differences and appear to form a united front.[108] The oscillation between intramural wars and the semblance of solidarity required in the face of a common enemy must have modified the strength and character of the Chinese associations, although, one must add, the evidence for this statement is not readily available.

The intramural conflicts probably added to the already considerable isolation of the Chinese community from the larger society. Feuds among clans, tong wars, and fights to depose the headmen of the Consolidated Benevolent Association must have seemed incomprehensible to most white Americans, who were not informed about traditional Chinese modes of organization or conflict resolution. These wars did generate a widespread stereotype of Chinatown that included lurid stories about opium dens, sing-song girls, hatchet men, and tong wars.[109] The real Chinese society was difficult to discern behind this kind of romantic illusion.

However, if intramural conflicts isolated Chinatown from the metropolis, they also very probably challenged the complex structures of solidarity inside the ghetto. Although we need much more evidence than we now have, including such documents as the biographies and papers of many ordinary Chinatowners, it is not unreasonable to suppose that feuds and fights among associations were the occasions for discovering and testing group loyalty. Clan, *hui kuan,* and secret society leaders very likely made demands of allegiance, service, and money on their members during times of hostilities in the ghetto. And it seems equally reasonable to suppose that, at different times and in different situations, the ordinary clan, *hui kuan,* or secret society member was variously disposed to regard his own association with warm feelings, fierce patriotism, troublesome annoyance, and even, perhaps, nagging fear. Yet in times of fighting, there was no mass exit of Chinese from Chinatown. At the very least, then, it would appear that the ordinary Chinese immigrant acquiesced in the difficulties imposed by his ghetto situation, and, at the most, some must have joined feverishly in support of their associations.

Simmel pointed to the fact that enmities and reciprocal antagonisms maintain established systems by encouraging a balance among their components.[110] The conflicts in Chinatown seem to bear out his observation in two distinct ways. First, the very fact that fights were confined to the ghetto and limited to matters affecting its Chinese denizens helped to establish and maintain the boundaries of the ghetto community. Chinese clans feuded with one another and not with white American families or Irish or any other ethnic group's clans. The *hui kuan* established its merchant oligopoly in Chinatown and not throughout the city, and the primitive class conflicts against its economic domination took place inside the Chinese quarter. The secret societies organized vice and crime in the ghetto and not elsewhere, and their gang wars were also confined to Chinatown. Moreover, the fights that broke out among the associations were aimed at issues and elements that were physically, socially, and politically located inside Chinatown (or, on occasion, in China). It is true that occasionally outsiders—police, clergy, diplomats, and the representatives of the Chinese government—became involved in the wars in Chinatown. But outsiders served only in an *ad hoc* capacity; their services were employed to balance the power of one or another of the contending factions.

The second sense in which Chinatown conflict provided for balance in the community arises from the fact that it was not directed at the absolute obliteration of opponents.[111] It must be remembered that hardly any struggle in Chinatown ever ended with unconditional surrender or total annihilation. The balance of power among contending parties prevented such an outcome. And this balance established the precarious stability in the community's structure. When peace treaties were signed, each party recognized the rights of the other to exist and to continue in the competition for women, wealth, and power. Chinatown was thus something of a Hobbesian cockpit, except that no fight ever escalated into a war of all against all or ended with a genocidal "final solution." We may speculate that the condition of long-term armed watchfulness probably generated an interest in the conservation of the existing institutions, since any party had an interest in knowing just who was representing any other body of Chinese and how many persons he represented. Thus, community conflict and group maintenance complemented one another. Conflict in Chinatown generated the need for groups to form and cohere; groups found added sources of *esprit de corps* in the conflicts that erupted. Conflict and group affiliation were the warp and woof of the first six decades of the Chinese community.

Cherished Values and Civil Rights

I want to see if I can provide a background for understanding the contemporary scene in the civil rights movement. I think it is fair to say, at the outset, that nearly every American has been surprised at the extent and the intensity of the civil rights movement in the last five to seven years. Not only have everyday people: people who read the newspapers, or people whose job, like the policeman's, brings them in rather regular encounter with the civil rights movement, been surprised by its extent and intensity, but also the academicians and the people who have concerned themselves primarily with understanding and predicting the nature of race relations. We have a definitive statement to this effect at the last convention of the American Sociological Association when the new president of the association utilized his presidential address entitled "Race Relations and Sociological Imagination" to announce publicly that the entire profession, himself included, has been astounded by, and unprepared for, the nature of the movement for civil rights. Therefore, I think that we share in common, academicians and laymen and people with special jobs, a common feeling and experience of surprise, and perhaps a certain amount of apprehension, about this movement.

I think the real reason that the civil rights movement bothers us so much is because this time it's definitely for real. That is to say, this time the Negro, and, to a certain extent, every other minority group that has been thus far living in second-class citizenship in America, is making a meaningful, and effective, claim on the regular, ordinary, everyday institutions of American life to which he or she has, in various ways, been denied. And it is precisely because the things we take for granted are being subjected to attack, or if you prefer the word, to demonstration—

it is precisely because these institutions which we take for granted are being subjected to this extraordinary onslaught—that I think we are surprised by the movement, and that we are troubled by it. Let me show you what I mean perhaps by a brief historical reflection on what most Americans *think* the civil rights movement has amounted to up to now. With the exception of certain Supreme Court cases, which slowly and arduously advanced the cause of civil rights in the last fifty years, most Americans believe that civil rights in America has, for the most part, amounted to pious phrases from well-meaning groups urging on others tolerance, good feeling for their fellowman, and very little else in real and effective activity.

BETTERMENT OF HUMANKIND

I think there can be no doubt that the bulk of the race relations and civil rights movement in America, until 1954, amounted primarily to movements for the betterment of humankind through exhorting a change in the personality of the American people. For a long time many people, Negroes included, were willing to accept this or were unable to do anything else. But things have changed now. There has developed a significant vocal, speaking, writing, and acting Negro leadership, a leadership by no means always united, and this leadership is making demands for something more than a pious phrase, more than a promise of a future Utopia held out in exchange for the present status quo. Negro leadership and masses are demanding more than this. But this is the interesting thing about what some people call the "Negro revolution"; the Negro doesn't seem to be demanding what other revolutionaries have demanded.

Revolutionaries, in the past, have demanded an over-turning of society, have demanded the destruction of the political institutions, have demanded the exchange of the present social order for new political, social, and economic institutions. I find almost none of this in the present civil rights movement. Instead, what is interesting about the present civil rights movement, is the demand for access to, regular access to, institutions of the already existing society. The right to attend, on an integrated basis, the already established schools, and the right to enter, without fear or favor, the already existing hotels, the restaurants, and the public gathering places of our society. There is no revolution here in the sense that there is an attempt to destroy the social structure of America. There is, instead, something quite different going on: The demand that the promise of American society be met by the performance of American people and American institutions, and that this gap between promise and performance—which in many ways is the whole theme of American history—be closed. But this closing of the gap means that certain things that we take for granted can no longer be taken for granted. I want to talk about those things.

We have now to come to re-examine such conventional notions as the home, and the club, and the conditions of group membership. We have to re-examine the notion of what constitutes private business and the so-called rights of owners of business to invite or exclude people from entering their shops. We have to examine the whole idea of qualifications for jobs to see what constitutes a real qualification, and what constitutes an obstacle to ever obtaining a job. We have to examine the whole religious structure of America in terms of seeing how the various denominations of our churches have acted, unwillingly sometimes, and not unwillingly in others, to maintain a segregated influence in their religious life. We have to examine the entire educational process in America, not only in terms of access to and egress from the schools, but also in terms of what constitutes education in America: What do we teach our children in American history, what do we neglect, and what is the vision of America they carry away from our schools?

IRONIC TIME

All this must be examined and yet so many things in American history seem to come at an ironic time. This whole examination comes at a time when there are great changes going on in American society that have nothing directly to do with the civil rights movement and yet will have undoubted monumental effects on that movement and on the structure of American society. I mean, for instance, the fact that we are becoming, more and more, an automated society. We are becoming a society in which work, once held to be the only virtuous activity for men, may no longer suffice to keep people busy. There may not be enough work available for everyone as we continue to make more efficient the production of goods and services and as we continue to remove the human element in the productive process. At the same time that work is losing its virtuous aspect in American society, leisure is coming to take on, or will have to come to take on, a more virtuous view than it has had in the past.

An interesting thing about Americans is that they are a work-oriented people who believe in the virtues of work, considering those not at work to be somehow ill-suited to live in this society; and who believe, deep in their hearts in many ways, that leisure is something that one does not deserve, and that one should not practice, certainly not on a full-time basis—and yet that one should practice with great care on a part-time basis. However, we may very well be coming to that time when we will have to cultivate leisure as an art and a science in the same way that we have, for the last hundred and fifty years, cultivated work. Coming at a time when Negroes are demanding such things as a job, this emphasis and movement (not usually recognized in my opinion) away from work toward leisure is going to have profound and unsettling effects on the civil rights movement, and profound and unsettling effects on the American Negro, and on every other minority group.

Now let's take a look at these specific things that I said we have to look at. Let us talk for a moment about homes and clubs, or the whole constellation of things that constitutes property and membership. Up until now, Americans have largely believed, sometimes contrary to the law as lawyers have recently reminded us, that property is sacrosanct. Now actually the history of common law and statute law, in both Britain and America, will give us a long statement to the contrary. There has always been the right of the lawmaker and of the people to control and regulate property. (Take an example that doesn't arise very much in the civil rights movement: we have a very complicated law on the disposal of property at death, the law of wills, and failure to make out a will properly can constitute failure of the testator to provide for those he wants to provide for; and this the courts have recognized for a long time regardless of how the testator wanted to provide for his relatives or friends.) At any rate, there has been a long history of actual legal control of private property.

Nevertheless, there is the feeling, generated I suspect by the fact that we don't often get into legal situations involved in property or domestic relations, that property is sacrosanct. This idea is now being challenged by the civil rights movement. Putting it bluntly, we have to face up to the fact that there will be members of minority groups living on our blocks, living next door to us or across the street, and that the right to own property will also be matched by the right to acquire it. So we have a test going on in the form of a referendum in California as to whether property owners and sellers may continue to recognize color as a prerequisite for acquiring property. But regardless of the fate of the Rumford Act, it is clear to me that, ultimately, and very shortly, members of minority groups will not be stigmatized because of their color or creed in the ability to attain, own, and use property.

NATURE OF BUSINESS

More difficult to deal with, I think, is the whole nature of business. Business, after all, is something we see quite regularly. One walks to the grocery stores, buys groceries, puts them in the cart, walks up to the counter, pays the clerk, and leaves; and this standard routine practice seems to constitute very little expenditure of emotion. Well, it doesn't constitute a major social act for most of us to buy in a grocery store. We don't pay much attention to this activity as a major kind of thing that we do during the day. Grocery stores are so routine that television programs cannot even make a hero out of the grocery clerk in the same way they can out of the doctor, the lawyer, the policeman, or the fugitive. The grocery clerk constitutes what might be called a dull figure in American society. His activities are routine, neither romantic nor exciting. Yet today we have a challenge in this mundane, routine place, the grocery store. To everyone's surprise, the Negro appears, or the minority group appears, or the civil rights group appears, black or white, and demonstrates that in this dull, mundane, routine place, in its complexity of activities, the drama of racial relations is actually performed.

It comes as a great surprise. We witness the shop-in. We are shocked because the things taken for granted now take on a wholly different meaning; grocery stores, we tell ourselves, should not be subject to the civil rights movement. That movement, many of us in the Bay Area seem to think, is something that takes place in the South, something that takes place outside the community, something that occurs somewhere else to someone else, and in places that are dramatic. A grocery store in San Francisco presents none of these characteristics. Why then grocery stores? It is not that grocery stores themselves represent anything more significant than any other business. Nor is it an outstanding example of business. We take it for granted. What should come to our mind is that the activities that white people carry on, that the activities that they carry on with ease, are not carried on with ease by persons whose skins are darker, by those who are constantly confronted by fear and who cannot predict what will happen to them in an ordinary routine situation. The grocery store has been chosen as the place for a dramatic presentation of the racial confrontation precisely because it is in the routine activities of America that the real conflict between civil rights and human performance takes place. It is in the ordinary things and it is in these ordinary taken-for-granted places that we can expect, in the next ten or twelve years, to find the civil rights confrontation. And it will continue to surprise you, and it will continue to unsettle us. And it will surprise and unsettle us precisely because we are looking for the dramatic and the distant, not realizing that the dramatic exists for our racial groups in the routine.

The same is true for hotels. The Sheraton Palace demonstration recently aroused a great deal of protest from all kinds of people. Some people felt that this palatial hotel, historically significant in San Francisco, should not be subject to a civil rights confrontation. Some people felt that even if it were subject to a civil rights confrontation it should not be subject to this kind of civil rights confrontation. And some people felt that even if it were subject to this kind of civil rights confrontation certain particular activities should not take place. Sometimes these tactical questions blind us to the over-arching situation, which is the fact that the everyday routine, going into a hotel, working in a grocery store, is very meaningful activity for those who have thus far been denied the privilege of enjoying ordinary life because of their color.

UNSETTLING THING

I predict that there will be an even more unsettling thing that will take place. I predict that civil rights leaders will begin to say the whole notion of qualifications for jobs might seriously be re-examined. Qualifications for jobs have become a never-ending gap, with the Negro here, and the job qualification there. I suspect, I predict, that the notion, the "sacred" notion, of job qualification may soon come under criticism. There has been a change in the last thirty years in America—a tremendous professionalization of what were once unprofessional occupations. Take, for example, librarianship. I spoke to a dean of a large school of librarianship the other day. He told me that one of his major problems is that there are librarians working today in libraries who graduated from college forty years ago. They didn't go to librarian's school because there was no such thing; they received a bachelor's degree, and then they spent a semester earning a certificate in librarianship, and then they became a librarian. Now that is no longer possible. Now one enters the School of Librarianship after one gets a B.A., one then gets a Bachelor of Library Science. Tomorrow, to really get ahead in the field of librarianship one is going to have to have a master's degree, and soon, I suspect, one will have to have a Doctor of Library Science. Yet many are doing the same job as the person who had a Certificate of Librarianship. I suspect that what the dean said about librarianship is true of almost every other skilled occupation and that professionalization, the addition of qualifications, is a means of raising that occupation's status in the society.

But what about the man who has always been on the bottom? What about the man who has from the beginning in America accumulated a set of disadvantages so that by the time he reaches high school, he is subjected to an inferior education? By the time he reaches college age, he can't even go to college, or, if he can, he ends up in one of the lesser or less valued colleges, and when he gets out of college, he is unprepared even for the job for which he studied. What about him, what about his claim for a job and the right to earn a living? I suspect he will make a claim for this. And, I suspect, the demand for equity in education and work will be made by women of all races soon. We will have to examine this situation, and it will unsettle us because this notion of qualification, like the sacredness of property, has become an almost untouchable thing. Sacred, cherished, not to be examined.

The other powerful notion, sometimes so powerful in America that it divides liberal-minded people, is that only people who have "earned" their rights deserve them. I was discussing the civil rights movement with a friend recently and he said to me that he had gone along with the civil rights movement for a long time but he just couldn't go along with it anymore. "Now," he said, "Negroes seem to be saying that people ought to just have rights because they are people and not earn them, and yet, look at me! My father came over from Japan, a very poor man, saved his money, said nothing, suffered great discriminations, and sent me to college. I earned a Bachelor's and a Master's degree, and now I enjoy the rights of an American. Seems to me that Negroes are demanding to enjoy the rights of Americans without earning them." The idea expressed here is widespread in American society. One doesn't have rights because one is human; one has rights because one "earns" them. Yet there is no statement in the Constitution to this effect. The whole promise of American society has been the establishment of rights because one is a human being, not because one has gone to college. One doesn't *gradually acquire* rights. Yet this notion of "earned" rights is so powerful today, the notion that one must earn one's rights first and enjoy them second, that it becomes the argumentative line that shears off many people who have been sympathetic to the civil rights movement for a long time. They insist the Negroes must "earn" respect before they can enjoy Constitutional rights.

To be able to speak this way one must always have "good" examples. A friend of mine told me that there was a Negro living on his block, and having said that, he went on to tell me that the Negro living on his block is extremely polite. "Whenever his children see my wife," he proudly reported, "they always say hello." And he went on in some detail about this. I noticed that he didn't speak this way about his other neighbors and so I inquired about his other neighbors. Are they polite? Did they greet his wife? He didn't notice one way or the other, he admitted; some of them did, some of them didn't. I asked him whether he felt it reasonable to ask the neighbors who didn't greet his wife with politeness to move. He was startled and asked what right had he to ask them to move. If this Negro had not been polite, I suggest, if this Negro had not engaged in this American conventionality, many of us would certainly think about asking him to move, or moving ourselves.

There is a curious notion that in order to be accepted a Negro must be, in fact, such a conventional member of the middle class in American society that he will stand out in his caricature of it. For many, moreover, this *has been* a path of success. Many deprived peoples have discovered that the way to convince Americans that one is worthy of esteem is to play the conventional role; some of them played it so well that it became part of their "nature" and they could no longer stop playing the role. We don't require such stereotyped behavior of white people, we really don't. But we require Negroes to "behave" in order that they might enter stores, hold jobs, or live next door. We do require that they demonstrate beyond a reasonable doubt their conventionality. In short, we require our minorities to *earn* their rights. Well, I suspect that this requirement is no longer going to be taken seriously by the civil rights movement. The assumption that because a man is a human being, he has certain rights, is an old one in the Judaeo-Christian tradition. It is an assumption, I think, that is going to have to be readopted in American society, and with great pain for some.

NO HISTORY

We will have to re-examine what we teach our children. I recently had occasion to speak in several places on this subject. I am surprised at what passes for history in our public school books. It is commonplace to say, from what you read in our school books, that the Negro has no history. That's true if the school history books are your only guide, for in them the Negro *has* no history. Having been wiped out of the history books, most people believe that the Negro people have not been in history. I think investigation will show that our books have created a subtle and powerful distortion; our books have laid an ideological claim on our minds in which history is something that only white men possess. Negroes are of concern to other subject matter. They have anthropologies. The Negro has anthropology, the white man a history, and anthropology, of course, is the science of "primitive" society, and therefore the Negro must be a primitive.

But anthropology today is rapidly being priced out of the market insofar as it retains the notion that it is the study of primitive societies; most anthropologists have dropped this notion. Those who retain it are discovering that there are not very many "primitive" societies around to study. Africa, once the hunting ground of the anthropologist, and the place where the historian never ventured, is now the hunting ground of the historian and the political scientist. There now is a whole field called political anthropology, which is in fact political science, where there was no political science before, and there are now African historians. And it is being discovered that, contrary to our state-sponsored history books—e.g., our world history books that start in Ancient Egypt and journey across Central Europe to North America, and tell us that this is "world" history—something happened in Africa and Asia, something that may be, in fact, very important.

NEGRO HISTORY

All this is true in American history as well. After all, what have we learned in American history books about the Negro? I suspect most of us remember, vaguely, that Negroes landed or arrived in 1619 and probably we were mistakenly told that they arrived as slaves. The Negro arrived as an indentured servant with the right to buy and earn his freedom, and as a matter of fact, a few did. The first major legal case involving a runaway slave in America involved a Negro master recovering his escaped white slave from a white master who had sneaked off with him. (This case, by the way, is a landmark in American history for it fastened the yoke of slavery into our legal system, but it was a Negro master recovering a white slave.) After having arrived in 1619, the Negro virtually disappears from our history books. We see him again in 1787 when the history book tells us that the Congress creates him 3/5 of a man. And then he disappears again until 1863 when President Lincoln emancipates him from his condition of slavery, and that finishes his role in American history.

What have we learned of the Negro? If anything, we have learned that he is an object of American history, but never the subject. He has been the object of some people's concern, but never an active participant in it. Looking back at the biographies of the Negro, the separate and special history of the Negro, we would learn that this history-book approach is false. The history of America has excluded the history of the American Negro. I suspect that so powerfully has this error of omission been ingrained in our American people, children and adults, that we cannot believe that Negroes have a history, and therefore we can please ourselves in living-room conversations by saying, "Where is the Negro Thomas Edison?" "Where is the Negro Alexander Graham Bell?" or "Where is the Negro civilization equal to that of Rome?" And so long as we refuse to re-examine history, these complaints of the living room become a self-fulfilling prophecy. The history books will confirm our prejudices. This history will also have to be considered at some great pain to those who re-examine it, and to those who read it.

I think we ought to be clear on the peripheral and the ephemeral elements of the civil rights movement that are so often magnified as to be the major elements of it. Let me take these up. The most pressing problem seems to concern who heads the civil rights movement. And why is that person there? We hear a great deal of talk today about who is in the civil rights movement and a great deal of castigation of those who are in it. After the Sheraton Palace demonstration, for instance, the newspapers, the Mayor of San Francisco, the Governor of California, a Rabbi, a Priest, and a Minister all, in various ways and with certain degrees of qualification, concurred, it seems, that the demonstration was something less than right because most of the demonstrators were white. This was a striking comment to me. The argument was, presumably, that the demonstrators should be black, and if they were not black it meant that the Negro was not interested, and that this movement is unrepresentative. Such an argument, it seems to me, must be met head-on.

AMERICAN RIGHTS

First, it seems to me, the civil rights movement is a movement having to do with rights, not colors. That is to say, guarantees of the American constitution are, in the words of one of the justices of the Supreme Court, color-blind, and therefore those who seek to ensure these rights in America do not have to justify their thinking after the fact by being a certain color. The advancement of rights is the advancement of something that is, on its face, correct and legitimate, and it is not tainted because the persons who advocate it happen to be of a different color than the group most likely to be affected. Again I say, to put it very bluntly, that I was deeply disturbed by the attitude of the mayor, the governor, the rabbi, the priest, and the minister. It is a shocking distortion of the central concept of civil rights to claim that civil rights must be advocated only by black people in order to be enjoyed by them. To argue this distorted position is to assert not a struggle for rights at all, but a struggle for power, and that since it is a struggle for power, it ought to be black people struggling for black power. But as I said in the earlier part of this discussion, this is not a struggle simply for power; it is not a revolution but a movement seeking to enter the Negro into American society as it is. It is not a power struggle in which the blacks are seeking to subvert the whites. Therefore, one should expect that the people who participate in it will not be necessarily black.

Second, many people are concerned by the fact that so many of the participants in the civil rights movements are young. Youth is a curious thing in American society. We usually assign to youth a postponement of responsibility. We claim that young people should, in a certain sense, be tolerated in their strange beliefs, and we even provide institutionalized ways to tolerate them. For instance, it is widely held in America, though by no means in other countries, that colleges are a place where young people may enjoy a form of escape from the responsibilities of life, a place in which they might enjoy a kind of four-year moratorium before they enter into the responsibilities of adulthood. Therefore, within the bounds of reason and law, this argument continues, young people in colleges should not be held seriously accountable for what they do, and second, we adults should not regard what they say as very important: after all, they are just young people. Of course, the argument concludes, we should watch to see that they don't violate any property rights, or commit any crimes, but on a whole, we should tolerate their strangeness and curiosity: they'll grow up.

And so some people are prepared to consign the whole movement of civil rights to the errant activity of a few eighteen-to-twenty year olds who will get over it. But why are so many young people in the civil rights movement? I think the answer is this. American ideology has always contained within it a reservoir of altruism. Contrary to the cynical beliefs that so often seem to prevail today, Americans really are idealistic. They hide it; they deny it; and they take great pains to make sure that no one sees any of them as an individual idealist; as a matter of fact, it is an insult today to call someone an idealist. And yet the interesting thing is that American society today is a society full of people who are idealists. When I say there is a reservoir of idealists, I use that word purposely, because the idealism in American society is like water behind a dam. It can be let loose or it can be stored up. It can be clamped down on. But it makes its appearance felt in different ways. And the epochs of American history are in part the epochs recounting the variations of expression of the American idea.

LEGITIMATION FOR IDEALISM

I think it is probably correct to say that from 1945 to 1960 American idealism had no legitimate basis in American society, that is to say, there was no legitimate public institution in American society that rewarded idealism. And so American idealism went underground, was denied, found its expression in curious forms, or disappeared altogether. But then came 1960 and a whole new era began in Washington, D.C. A rather curious thing about the Kennedy Administration was its frank avowal of and legitimation for idealism.

I suggest to you that the civil rights movement provides another part of this expression. I suggest to you that people born in the years 1944 and 1945 grew up in the period of the postwar; gained their political ideas in an era in which they found that for the most part they and everyone else were cynics. And there was no legitimate institution for the expression of idealism. Then along came the Civil Rights movement. This movement is grounded in the historical record and liberal hope of America, grounded in the great promises of the Constitution and the Declaration of Independence, sanctified in the Supreme Court decisions, and yet it needs activity, and that need for activity tapped the great reservoir of youthful idealism in America. I suspect that this idealism is the explanation for the youthful response to the civil rights movement. The youthful and "white" aspects of the civil rights movement are grounded in this reservoir of altruism. That, I think, is the place to look for its sources.

Let us conclude this way: it seems to me that we face a very severe challenge, and I do not want for one moment to underestimate its seriousness or extent. The challenge has to do with resolving, on the one hand, the discrepancies between the promise of American ideals and the performance of American people with respect to our minorities. That is the immediate challenge, but much more fundamental today is the examination of the entire institutional system to see whether or not its privileges and perquisites, even when enjoyed by all our citizens regardless of race and creed, are enough in fact to create the kind of society in which we all want to live.

PART III

Functionalism and Interactionism

System and Function in
Antebellum Southern Sociology

The conventional imagery of American sociology's paternity tends to designate William Graham Sumner, Lester Frank Ward, Albion Woodbury Small, Franklin Henry Giddings, Charles Horton Cooley, and their *fin de siecle* contemporaries as the discipline's "founding fathers." Moreover, in the writings of some of its practitioners—most recently Lewis Coser and Jeffrey Alexander—the development of sociological thought is depicted as having proceeded from a more simplified study of social problems to a quite complex theory of society as a social system. The latter conception pictures society moving in orderly cadences motored by an inherent process, and always remaining or coming to a steady state, dynamic equilibrium. The name Talcott Parsons is associated with the idea of the social system and with the uncovering of its source and direction of motion. While there can be little doubt that the early post–Civil War masters contributed much to the development of sociology's present paradigms, and that the late Talcott Parsons (1902–79) is the Twentieth Century's pre-eminent structural functionalist, a quartet of antebellum sociologists from the South laid the groundwork for the functionalist paradigm that enjoys considerable commitment from contemporary sociologists. These Southern, slavocratic, Comtean sociologists—Henry Hughes (1829–62), a Mississippi attorney who, as L. L. Bernard once noted, was America's first sociologist,[1] George Fitzhugh (1806–81), George Frederick Holmes (1820–97), and Joseph Le Conte (1823–1901)—have been largely neglected or forgotten altogether by those who seek to reconstruct the historical sociology of American sociology.[2] (Fitzhugh may be the exception, since his sociological writings have recently received the attention of such prominent historians as C. Vann Woodward[3] and Eugene Genovese.[4]) Consideration of their contribution requires a revision of the conventional understanding of how sociology developed in the United States.

The present paper discusses Henry Hughes and George Fitzhugh, two members of this quartet. Elsewhere I have denominated the entire foursome as "the Southern Comteans." In subsequent papers, I hope to delineate the contributions of the remaining two: George Frederick Holmes[5] and Joseph Le Conte.[6]

HENRY HUGHES: SYSTEM AND SLAVERY

Henry Hughes provided the most elaborate picture of a dual and self-contradictory American social system, resting in the North on the principles of a free market in labor and in the South on an ideology he called "warranteeism," the reciprocal obligations of master and servant to work on behalf of each's "warrant" to serve, produce, and promote the social order.[7] Justifying the ownership of labor power (but not, Hughes insisted, the laborer's body or soul) as prerequisite to an ordered relationship of production to distribution and consumption, Hughes also detailed the subsystems of his ideal typification of American society and asserted the rightfulness of its caste-status hierarchy of races and genders.[8] In the process, he provided for a rigid system of stratification embracing an essentially immobile structure of rights, duties, and obligations for whites, blacks, Chinese, Indians, women, men, and children.

Hughes's finely meshed subsystemic "heptarchy" was both ideology and utopia (see Figure 1). It would be presided over by a white male seigneurial elite who administered the warranted reciprocities that constituted the basis for both domestic order and national security. Warranteeism "with the ethnical qualification,"[9] as Hughes phrased it, provided for the care, feeding, and old-age needs of the black "warrantees," i.e., slaves, and also enclosed an interdependent five-fold network of institutional arrangements ("municipalities," in his terminology[10]) assuring "economic association, adaptation, and regulation"; hygienic protection and regulation; "philosophic" educational standards; "the production of societary pleasure"; and "domestic tranquility."[11] Given its unique institutionalization of rights, duties, obligations, and interdependencies, there is little wonder that later analysts of Hughes's theory of the social system found it to be, respectively, an adumbration of Booker T. Washington's program of vocational education and limited opportunity for freedmen and women,[12] a foreshadowing of President

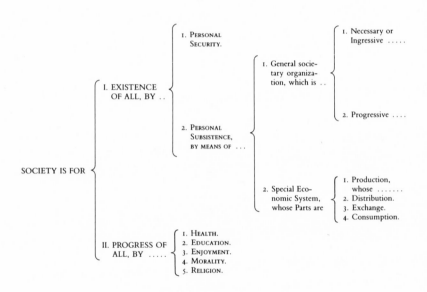

FIGURE 1
Reprinted from Henry Hughes, *A Treatise on Sociology: Theoretical and Practical* (New York: Negro Universities Press, 1968).

The Hughes Heptarchy

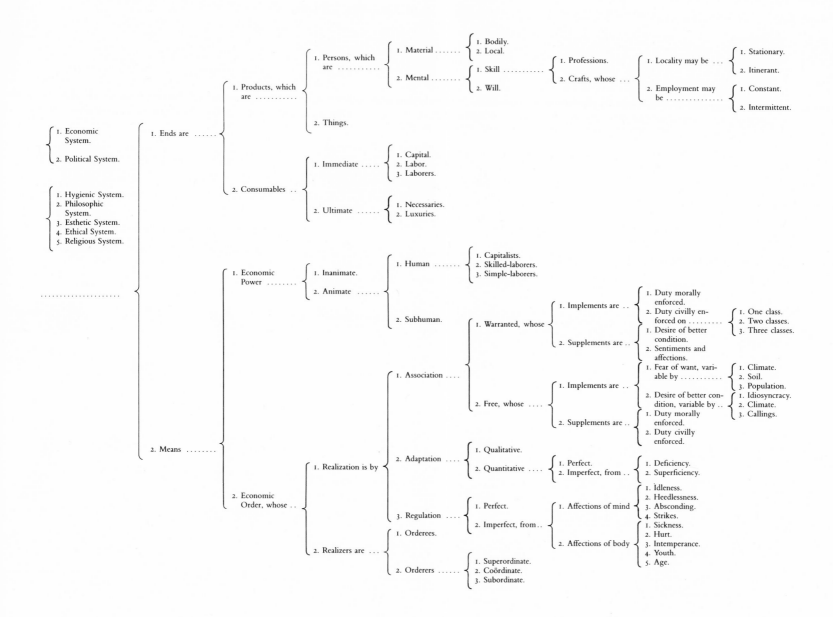

Franklin D. Roosevelt's New Deal policies,[13] an American design for Leninist totalitarianism,[14] or another variant of Marxism for the master class.[15]

The central focus of Hughes's thesis was on slavery in the South. On the one hand he sought to defend that institution against the Northern abolitionists' mounting accusations that it was cruel, immoral, unethical, improvident, and failing in any provision for the human and humane welfare of its subjects. At the same time, Hughes hoped to advance the spread of slavery to encompass Cuba, and Central and South America, to reopen the African slave trade (forbidden, according to Article I, Section 9, of the United States Constitution, after 1808), and to introduce Chinese workers into the ranks of the South's black "warrantees."[16] His theory of the social system was at one and the same time prescriptive and descriptive, repudiating the charges of the Northern abolitionists while requiring the State to enforce a Protestant ethic of arduous endeavor among those who, Hughes insisted, were constitutionally unable to internalize and acquiesce to its imperatives voluntarily. At the same time, it was utopian in its promise of an inspired social order that would prevail once warranteeism had superseded the alternative system of the supposedly free market of capitalist labor:

And when in other generations, this progress, which is now a conception and a hope of all, shall be a memory and a fact; when what is now in the future, shall be in the present or the past; when the budding poetry of the all-hoping sociologist, shall ripen to a fruitful history; that history will be thrice felicitous; for it shall unroll the trophied poem, the rhapsody of a progressive epic in its grandeur; pastoral in its peace; and lyric in its harmony. Such shall be its fulfillments. And then on leagued plantations over the sun-sceptred zone's crop-jeweled length, myriad eyes, both night-faced and morning-cheeked, shall brighten still the patriot's student glance and fondly pore upon the full-grown and fate-favored wonder, of a Federal banner in whose woven sky of ensign orbs, shall be good stars only, in such happy constellations that their bonds and beams, will be sweeter than the sweet influences of the Pleiades, and stronger than the bands of Orion; unbroken constellations—a symbol sky—a heaven which also, shall declare the glory of God, and a firmament which shall show His handiwork. Then, in the plump flush of full-feeding health, the happy warrantees shall banquet in PLANTATION-REFECTORIES; worship in PLANTATION-CHAPELS; learn in PLANTATION-SCHOOLS; or in PLANTATION-SALOONS, at the cool of the evening, or in the green and bloomy gloom of cold catalpas and magnolias, chant old songs, tell tales; or, to the metred rattle of chattering castanets, or flutes, or rumbling tamborines, dance down the moon and evening star; and after slumbers in PLANTATION-DORMITORIES, over whose gates Health and Rest sit smiling at the feet of Wealth and Labor, rise at the music-crowing of the morning-conchs, to begin again welcome days of jocund toil, in reeling fields, where, weak with laughter and her load, Plenty yearly falls, gives up, and splits her o'erstuffed horn, and where behind twin Interest's double throne, Justice stands at reckoning dusk, and rules supreme. When these and more than these, shall be the fulfilment of Warranteeism; then shall this Federation and the World, praise the power, wisdom, and goodness of a system, which may well be deemed divine; then shall Experience aid Philosophy, and VINDICATE THE WAYS OF GOD, TO MAN.[17]

Hughes treated the subsovereign status of blacks and Chinese as an accident of history rather than a mandate of nature. Although he railed against intermarriage as the first step toward political equality,[18] and regarded mulattoes as monstrous products of what he—curiously—called "incest,"[19] he offered neither a brief nor a sustained analysis of the biological basis of race nor any socio-biological theory of racial inferiority. Instead, he treated his system of warranteeism with its ethnical qualification as an established but fortuitous American social fact, one that might be undone by the forces of politics or the accidents of history.[20] Yet he regarded slavery as an institution that should not be undone: its promise of a positive polity and a productive and peaceful social order was too great. At the same time, he supposed that the ethnic basis of America's warranteeism might eventually be obliterated by the processes of evolution or race extinction: "The societary organization of the United States South, is warranteeism, with the ethnical qualification. This qualification is not essential to theoretical or abstract warranteeism. It is accidental. Warranteeism without the ethnical qualification, is that to which every society of one race, must progress."[21]

GEORGE FITZHUGH:
THE FUNCTIONS OF SOCIAL CONFLICT

Although Hughes's conceptions of society and social theory were discarded after the Civil War and not rediscovered until L. L. Bernard made a vain attempt to have him recognized as a founder of the discipline, George Fitzhugh's main works are more readily available, having been reprinted in the last two decades and extensively treated by such scholars as Harvey Wish,[22] and the aforementioned Eugene Genovese and C. Vann Woodward. However, precisely because Fitzhugh's works have been analyzed by historians interested in them primarily as apologies for slavery, their general value *for* and *as* sociology has been neglected.

Fitzhugh does not seem to have employed the term "social system"[23] in any significant or systematic manner, claiming the time was not yet ripe for such an elaboration and concentrating on an analysis of the American political economy.[24] Nevertheless, his writings centered on an idealized imagery of both civilization and slavery. Fitzhugh's analysis of the relationship between civilization and slavery turned on an elaborate critique of laissez-faire liberalism and a contention that slavery was an ancient, if less than honorable, institution that was perfectly suited to both agricultural and industrial societies. Slavery was the natural and proper condition of those who labored, regardless of race, culture, or heritage. Hence, Fitzhugh asserted that the seemingly free market in white labor that prevailed in the North was in fact a disfigured and inefficient slavocracy: "You [he addressed the Northern capitalists], with the command over labor which your capital gives you, are a slave owner—a master, without the obligations of a master. They who work for you, who created your income, are slaves, without the rights of slaves. Slaves without a master! Whilst you were engaged in amassing your capital, in seeking to become independent, you were in the White Slave Trade."[25] Moreover, the "White Slave Trade"— Fitzhugh's designation of labor recruitment in a capitalist political economy that had abjured the formal institutionalization of human chattel— established a stratified order with leisurely white male owners and employers at the top and a mass of largely unprotected white and black laborers supporting them at the bottom. Unlike Hughes, who emphasized the lack of control over and the inconsistent and uneven motivations of the Northern white worker, Fitzhugh held that "The capitalists, in free society, live in ten times the luxury and show that Southern masters do, because the slaves to capital work harder and cost less than negro slaves."[26]

By the same token Fitzhugh alluded to what—in modern social systems theory—might be regarded as a dangerous strain in the capitalist political economy—the absence of state-sponsored or publicly supported welfare institutions and policies. This neglect of the workers, he insisted, arose as a result of the refusal of capitalists and abolitionists to recognize that they, like all other humans, had sought after, and in the case of the former had in fact already obtained, a *property right* in these workers:

> "Property in man" is what all are struggling to obtain. Why should they not be obliged to take care of man, their property, as they do of their horses and their hounds, their cattle and their sheep. Now, under the delusive name of liberty, you work him "from morn to dewy eve"—from infancy to old age—then turn him out to starve. You treat your horses and hounds better. Capital is a cruel master. The free slave trade, the commonest, yet the cruellest of trades.[27]

Implicit in Fitzhugh's thesis and explicit in that of Hughes was the functional necessity of a norm of reciprocity among masters and servants, employers and workers. For Hughes mutuality of obligation was elaborated in the doctrine of *warranteeism* whereby the "subsovereign" class of blacks was formally obliged to labor for the benefit of a production-oriented agricultural economy; in return, its members would receive cradle-to-the-grave subsistence, health, clothing, and other benefits basic to life.[28] The seigneurial state, envisioned as an administrative and adjudicative complex manned by a power elite of white male agriculturalists or their professional representatives (e.g., lawyers and journalists, like Hughes himself),[29] would oversee and enforce this reciprocity of obligations and thus keep the society in a condition of dynamic equilibrium.

To Fitzhugh's way of thinking, the socialist writers of his day had already amply demonstrated the failure of a social system built upon *laissez-faire* and limited government. Their mistake, however, had been to repudiate the idea and doctrine of human chattel in the name of extending the ideology of individual liberty and human freedom. In fact, Fitzhugh believed, slavery had been and would continue to be the best institutional arrangement for securing the welfare, care, and feeding, as well as the productivity, of a naturally stratified society.

Fitzhugh, like Comte and subsequent structural-functionalists, subscribed to and elaborated upon the organic metaphor, likening human societies to those of ants and bees: "An isolated man is almost as helpless and ridiculous as a bee setting up for himself. Man is born a member of society and does not form society. Nature, as in the cases of bees and ants, has it formed for him. He and society are congenital. Society is the being—he one of the members of that being."[30] A properly established society develops like an organism, i.e., it is built up slowly in an orderly manner; moreover, Fitzhugh insisted, it depends for its stability upon the organic association of its parts.

However, Fitzhugh believed that this organic inter-dependence had been fractured in *laissez-faire* societies. Moreover, the "dissociation of labor and disintegration of society, which liberty and free competition occasion, is especially injurious to the poorer class; for besides the labor necessary to support the family, the poor man is burdened with the care of finding a home, and procuring employment, and attending to all domestic wants and concerns."[31] Slavery, on the other hand, relieves the laborer of these cares, and, in Fitzhugh's perspective, "is the very best form of socialism." What is required for a true socialist society is a representative autarchy: "The association of labor properly carried out under a common head or ruler, would render labor more efficient, relieve the laborer of many of the cares of household affairs, and protect and support him in sickness and old age, besides preventing the too great reduction of wages by redundancy of labor and free competition."[32]

Precisely because he regarded slavery to be a universal as well as universally beneficent form of societal organization, Fitzhugh did not confine its domain to that of blacks. Although he justified the South's enslavement of blacks by asserting "The average of negroes [to be] equal in formation, in native intelligence, in prudence, or providence, to well-informed white children of fourteen," the emancipation of whom would be "criminal"[33] in its consequences, Fitzhugh held that "the white race is the true and best slave race" because it alone "is most social, tame, domestic, skilful, educatable, and most readily submits to government in all its usual forms." For the white race, then, compulsory slavery is a non-coercive matter: "The labor which white men and blooded horses submit to so cheerfully is involuntary labor, because agreeable from habit acting on their refined, domestic and civilizable natures. They work for others from necessity, but do not require the stimulant of physical force to make them work."[34] By contrast, Fitzhugh went on, "Mules and negroes . . . can only be *half* tamed, domesticated, civilized, and enslaved . . . The mule and the negro are weighed down by the *'vis inertiae'* of their natures, never hurt themselves by overwork, and require the sight or the infliction of the lash to keep them at work at all." Submission to the social system of slavery thus called for a hierarchy, and a gender-as-well-as-race-based differentiation of sanctions:

> Married women, children, sailors, soldiers, wards, apprentices, &c., are not governed by law, but by the will of superiors, their *persons* are enslaved. Patient submission to their situation, and ready obedience to their superiors, is virtuous conduct on their part, and evinces high and civilized natures. Negroes and Indians do not fulfill the duties arising from these relations with equal patience and fidelity, for hatred of restraint, of the duties, forms, fashions observances and conventionalities of civilized life and the love of unbridled liberty, are the leading traits of savages.[35]

Fitzhugh developed his analysis in a different direction after the Civil War and the Thirteenth Amendment had put an end to the South's "peculiar institution." Although he did not repudiate his original defense of a socialist system of benevolent slavery and in fact took up the thesis of black inferiority with a vengeance, he turned his attention to the issues of conflict in modern societies and its consequences. In so doing he elaborated even further on the analogy of the natural to the social sciences and urged theses not too dissimilar from those later advanced by the Italian engineer and social theorist Vilfredo Pareto (whose methodological position, Charles Camic has recently reminded us, had a profound influence on the systems theory of Talcott Parsons).[36] Fitzhugh, seeking even more than earlier to repudiate the freedom of Reason and the liberty of Enlightenment doctrines, turned to an essentially affective phenomenology: "Rejecting reason as a guide, we will follow the promptings of feeling and instinct, and the diverse and shifting lights of human experience. We shall deal only with *phenomena* (appearances) because we know nothing and can never know anything about *noumena* (realities)."[37] Putting forward a new subdisciplinary paradigm that he called "antinomic pathology," Fitzhugh not only proposed to adapt sociology to a "medical" ministry of society, but also urged that analysis and understanding of the feelings, intuitions, judgments, and common sense of such role-occupants as parents and teachers were "almost infallible guides"[38] to such a ministry. Moreover, he urged a thesis not dissimilar from that which would soon be put forward in Germany by Georg Simmel and in America by E. A. Ross, viz., the positive functions of conflict. Although in 1866 he despaired of the survival of the American Republic:

> The American Republic is near its end. Affairs will, probably, wind up with civil war and military despotism in the North, in which the South will be reluctantly involved; and then for ages to come, the nation will be involved in continual civil war, for we are not prepared for hereditary monarchy, and have no materials out of which to construct an Established Church and a hereditary aristocracy, as props and stays to such a monarchy.[39]

Fitzhugh had developed in embryonic form a hypothesis concerning the eufunctional consequences of conflict. "Peace and war are antinomes," he observed in 1866, "whose due alteration perceives the health and well-being, and promotes the growth, progress and improvement of society."[40] Although he emphasized the shift from peace to war, Fitzhugh clearly believed that harmony and peaceloving community encouraged internal calumny and corruption: "When nations, communities, sects, or individuals, resolve never to fight, and persevere in practicing their resolves, they take to cheating, and become thoroughly contemptible, selfish, and sensual—lose their intellectual and moral natures, assimilate themselves to the lowest order of the brute creation, and grow fat and lazy, like well-fed pigs."[41] War, on the other hand, "draws men closer together, makes them dependent on each other, allays domestic strife and competition, in a great measure equalizes conditions, banishes selfishness, and makes men live, labor and fight for each other; and continually seeing and feeling their mutual inter-dependence, it begets brotherly love."[42]

Fitzhugh came near to combining his thesis on struggle with his views on capitalism, property, and race. Although often accused of inconsistency and hypocrisy, he insisted that there was a common thread of scientific reasoning running through all of his writings. A onetime opponent of capitalism, Fitzhugh came to see its processes as fulfilling his theses about the eufunctional effects of conflict: "The war between Capital and Labor is evidence of a healthy state of society. When it ceases, despotism, ignorance and pauperism will supervene."[43] The "monopoly of property, or capital, by the few, and the consequent subjection of the many to the dominion, taxation and exploitation of these few—is not an evil, as generally esteemed, but the greatest of human blessings, because it is the only means of begetting, sustaining and advancing civilization."[44] However, the blessings of the struggle for and against capital were confined to the members of the white race, in Fitzhugh's estimation: They, he argued, "are ever *discontented,* rivalrous, emulative, rapacious, ambitious, proud, provident, selfish, jealous, aspiring and accumulative." Blacks, on the other hand, having not been socialized as participants in the struggle to obtain property— having, in fact, as slaves, been the object of that struggle—were not properly conditioned for capitalism and its human requirements. Although he allowed for the fact that, "In our neighborhood, for the last two years, a force of negroes diminished by more than a third has produced more than a force a third larger before the war," Fitzhugh argued that in this case the "fear of losing employment is a better stimulant to labor than was the fear of bodily punishment."[45] What was required for the welfare of blacks under competitive capitalism, he believed, was a vast system of regulatory law and paternalistic institutions, shielding them from social and economic integration into the competitive struggle, coercing their labor at menial and unskilled jobs, and providing for their care, feeding, maintenance, and old age. Thus, according to Fitzhugh, did sociology—the sociodicial science of a sick society—refute political economy—the pseudoscience of a *laissez-faire* illusion.

CONCLUSION

Elements of what later would be called "structural-functionalism" and "social systems theory" are to be found in the sociologies of slavery developed by Henry Hughes and George Fitzhugh. The abstract imagery of Hughes's warranteeism employs the organic metaphor, asserts the significance of functional interdependence, designates the complex of interrelated subsystems, describes and prescribes for the processes of stratification and mobility, and presents an intimation of processes effecting dynamic equilibrium. In the less systematic but wider-ranging sociology of George Fitzhugh there is a formulation of American sociology as a variant of socialism—ownership of the human means of production—as well as an early statement of conflict's eufunctional effects on both self and society. Both Hughes and Fitzhugh founded their systems on the questions of slavery and race—and in a larger sense on the necessary limitations of personal freedom conducive to economic security. In so doing they wrestled with the value to be assigned to ascriptive statuses and to individual achievement, the nature and consequences of social orders built on caste and heredity, and the social structures necessary to restrict groups that were deemed "sub-sovereign" to white men, e.g., blacks and women, from arising therein and exercising and displaying their individual and group talents.

Although Talcott Parsons' structural-functionalism is derived from his reordering of the works of Pareto, Marshall, Durkheim, Weber, and Freud, and was indirectly and perhaps unconsciously influenced by the ideas of Harvard's Comtean, Thomas Nixon Carver,[46] it bears a number of striking similarities to that developed by the antebellum Southerners described above. There are differences of course. For Parsons, the problems of legitimacy and order are solved by a seemingly inexorable socialization process that nevertheless produces "strains" and provokes deviancy. For Hughes, who was more reliant on unmediated state power than Parsons, legitimacy and order are constituted in magistracies composed of nature's and history's anointed leadership group and enforced by force. For Parsons, the racial integration of society is achieved by a slow process of orderly advancement, as appropriately qualified groups are admitted, one by one, to "full citizenship" by a liberal and benevolent set of gatekeepers. For Hughes, "warranteeism with the ethnical qualification" rests upon an accident of history and remains status-bound unless events so befall the society that its contingent caste structure is undone.

In 1983, Jeffrey C. Alexander—a strong advocate of Parsonian theory and of the thesis that Parsons' work constitutes, thus far, the ultimate projection of sociological thought developed from that of the classical European masters—nevertheless complained that "Sociology has yet to produce a consistently multidimensional theory, the elements of which have certainly been provided by Marx, Durkheim, Weber, and Parsons." And he went on to proclaim, "To do so must be its most sought after goal."[47] It is to be noted that Alexander appears unaware of the comprehensive theory that might arise from considering a "structure of social action" and a theory of the "social system" that could be culled from the works of Hughes, Fitzhugh, Holmes, and Le Conte. More recently, Richard Münch asserted that the "Parsonian theoretical tradition is undergoing a remarkable renewal,"[48] but he called for a "cross-fertilization between Parsonian theory and competing theoretical approaches . . . [to] allow us to make progress along the road toward a new synthesis." Setting aside for the moment the question of whether progress with or rejection of Parsonian theory would be better for theoretical advance in sociology, the present paper would suggest that theoretical researchers might take time out from their reading of European neo-Marxist, post-Weberian, Critical, and Structurationist theories to examine the all-too-neglected antebellum Comteans who first introduced sociology and structural-functionalism to America.

Finally, the discovery and delineation of antebellum structural functionalism and social systems theory suggests the need to reconsider the perspective on American sociology's development that has been put forward by those who seek to make Parsonian theory its end point. Lewis Coser has written that "the appearance of Talcott Parsons' *The Structure of Social Action* heralded the emergence of a theoretical orientation considerably at variance with that developed at the University of Chicago" and, holding that the previous decades in which Chicago sociology predominated in the discipline were "a period of incubation," believes that with Parsonian sociology in the forefront, "sociology could embark on its mature career."[49] Coser's argument proceeds according to the assumptions of developmentalist theories and suffers from the defects of this type of theorizing.[50] Imagining sociology to develop like an organism, he seeks to chart its "birth," "incubation" period, and steady progress toward "maturity." However, Coser has not carried this metaphor to its organic conclusion—"old age" and the "death of the discipline." Moreover, armed with the knowledge that the idea of the social system was developed first by Henry Hughes and that the "conflict" and "phenomenological" variants of structural-functionalism received an impetus from George Fitzhugh, we might question whether any maturation has taken place in the discipline. The current interest in keeping Parsonianism alive might be an instance of pouring older wine into old bottles.

Le Conte, Royce, Teggart, Blumer

A Berkeley Dialogue on Sociology, Social Change, and Symbolic Interaction

INTRODUCTION

Although a department of sociology was not established at the University of California at Berkeley until 1946, a tradition of sociological discourse had begun at that institution of higher learning from the moment of its founding in 1868. That tradition has been largely neglected in discussions of the history of sociology, the development of American sociological theory, and the several critiques of sociological paradigms. When sociology at Berkeley is mentioned—as in Edward Shils' wide-ranging and critical account of the role that intellectual tradition and departmental ecology played in the advancement and variations of the discipline [1]—it is treated as arising *de novo* from the time of its departmentalization, and at the same time, as derivative. Shils describes the department as comprised of "an aggregation of outstanding and productive sociologists whose works drew the attention of the country and the world," but nevertheless as one that "lacked the coherence which Durkheim, Park, and Parsons gave to their respective circles of colleagues, collaborators, and pupils." [2] Shils' assertion that "the size of the staff of the department and the size of the student body as well as the amplitude of resources all made for centrifugality" and his charge that "Berkeley did not show a capacity to create a *Nachwuchs* which could renew the department while unifying it or to produce a body of graduates who could diffuse its 'line' more widely in the United States" proceed from his assumption that sociology had no home at Berkeley until Herbert Blumer (1900–87) arrived to chair the new department, some five years after it had been established. Like most commentators on the institutional development of sociology in the United States, Shils has failed to take cognizance of the intellectual tradition that preceded departmentalization at Berkeley by 78 years. Moreover, by identifying sociology at Berkeley with perspectives developed earlier at the University of Chicago and Columbia, Shils overlooked the representatives of the autochthonous Berkeley tradition—Margaret Hodgen, Kenneth Bock, and Robert Nisbet—who served at Berkeley before departmentalization, and who were a significant part of the original nucleus of the new department. Together with Herbert Blumer they helped establish the curriculum and research program for sociology at the University of California. In that program there were continuities as well as elaborations and departures from the original Berkeley tradition. But the tradition was not abandoned.

A reading of the sociological thought that developed at Berkeley in the seven decades following the appointment of the university's first sociologist, Joseph Le Conte, reveals a multifaceted discourse and debate—a veritable dialogue across the decades—on the epistemological nature of the sociological enterprise, the causes, conditions, and characteristic processes surrounding social and cultural change, and the relationship between mental states and social action. At the same time—as Vidich and Lyman have discussed elsewhere[3]—there is exhibited an uneven and, in the case of Josiah Royce to be discussed *infra,* a sometimes resisted process of disciplinary secularization: The rhetorics of sociology shift from providing secular theodicies of the Social Question to proposing inner-worldly sociodicies and a basis for a new public philosophy. The sociological discourse at Berkeley and the secularization of the discipline are intimately related. Moreover, that discourse indicates the presence there of the very essence of what Shils regards as the sociological tradition. As he puts it, the tradition "lives in the self-image which links those now calling themselves sociologists with a sequence of famous authors running back into the nineteenth century."[4] At Berkeley, students of Herbert Blumer and subsequent symbolic interactionists could enrich their own comprehension of that perspective by studying and debating the discussions of societal development, social change, and individual and group conduct that were to be found in the works of Frederick Teggart and the teachings of his disciples. In the course of their own investigations they might have been led to the writings of Joseph Le Conte. Le Conte had been the principal mentor of Josiah Royce, and, as readers of George Herbert Mead's essays would discover, Mead had formulated much of his perspective on mind, self, and society as a critique of Royce's Le Contean metaphysic. When Herbert Blumer brought the interactionist position to Berkeley, he was in a sense bringing it to its place of origin.

At the head of Berkeley's sequence of authors reaching back to the nineteenth century is Auguste Comte. However, the virtual dialogue with his social scientific spirit that characterized the discourse on sociology at the University of California ultimately produced what I should like to denominate as a prolegomena to a phenomenological theory of social change. That prolegomena emerges from a joint reading of the works of Teggart and Blumer. As yet undeveloped beyond the formulations of its originators, the incipient theory not only rejects the ahistorical developmentalism of Comte's "comparative method" but also locates in its place the role of "intrusions," "interruptions," and (to use the language of Schutz) "crises-in-the-*Lebenswelt*" in triggering the conditions for social change. Recognition, elaboration, and application of the central concepts of that theory—Teggart's idea of "release," Blumer's of "reverie"—could not only revitalize the sociological enterprise but also place symbolic interactionism at the center of macrosociological studies. The full complement of Blumer's intellectual legacy has neither been distributed nor probated. Part of that task is the mission of this article: an explication of the Berkeley tradition of which he is a part—and to which he contributed.

THE SCIENCE OF HISTORY AND THE THEORY OF SOCIAL CHANGE AT BERKELEY

The teaching of sociological theory at Berkeley began in 1868 with the appointment of that university's first professor, Joseph Le Conte (1823–1901). Designated as a teacher of natural history and geology, Le Conte brought to bear on his lectures and writings a complex synthesis of the central ideas of Comte, Agassiz, and Darwin; he employed this orientation to develop, *inter alia,* an economic sociology of slavery and agricultural labor in America and a multilinear theory of social change. Specifically, Le Conte attempted three projects: to resolve the contradictions between Agassiz's creationist theories and Darwinian evolution; to elaborate upon the South's justification for slavery and provide a new perspective on the political economy of race and labor; and to outline a theory of the normative and pathological trajectories of societal development.

Le Conte's adherence to Comteanism led him to designate sociology as the paramount science and to propose a hierarchy of scientific disciplines. It began with geology at its base and reached to the science of society via a regularized ordering of the several natural and human sciences.[5] Each of the disciplines took change as its central concern. Le Conte held that Darwin's ideas about variation, natural selection, and the survival of the fittest were applicable to all levels of phenomena, but the processes characterizing change increased in complexity as the nature and structure of the kind of phenomena that each discipline described advanced.[6] However, Darwinian evolution only described developments that took place after the original creation; Le Conte's scientism acknowledged God as a first cause and was rooted in a deeply ingrained deism.[7]

Le Conte took as one of his central problems the analysis of the transition from slave to free labor in modern societies. Socio-economic changes in the organization of labor, the value of work, and the conditions affecting workers' motivations were the strategic research sites for his empirical researches and would continue to be topics for investigation at Berkeley. Le Conte regarded black slavery as an inevitable consequence of the operation of the laws of natural evolution. The coercive character of slavery followed from the "survival of the law of force and the right of the strongest inherited by man from the animal kingdom.[8] However, like other institutions that partook of the continuous changes in humankind's social arrangements, slavery would have come to a natural end as other forms of the labor process evolved to supersede it. But, Le Conte insisted, in America natural evolution had been interrupted by artificial action—the Civil War, itself brought about by "the irrational, unscientific, empirical methods of politics."[9] The war had put into operation a revolution in the organization of race and labor and had irrevocably set aside the orderly process that, if left to its own devices, would have guided the South's peculiar institution through an inevitable cycle of growth, maturation, and decline. The idea that changes would occur naturally and teleologically unless artificial interferences blocked their orderly development was derived by Le Conte from Comte's evolutionary schema and applied to showing the probability of trajectory detours down "pathological" roads and toward pseudo-development—unless something could be done to stop the operation of such "unnatural" interferences.[10]

Le Conte's theory of social change supposed that although societies tended to move forward in accordance with an original impetus to reach some inevitable end, accidents and interferences could derail their movement, deter their speed, or detour them down unprogressive side roads.[11] Hence, his evolutionary science of history would describe analytically parallel tracks of development indicating the operation of such processes as natural history, embryonic organicism, "geological" placement, and pathological arrests of development.[12] Nevertheless, Le Conte believed that human action, timed and charted to accord with the original *telos* of the society in which it took place, could aid in restoring the appropriate conditions for progress and the natural development.[13] His social science would help by prescribing the appropriate—i.e., natural and scientific—action.

Much of the social philosophy that Josiah Royce (1855–1916) developed—and that George Herbert Mead later criticized[14]—was derived from his undergraduate studies with Le Conte at Berkeley. Royce acknowledged his debt to Le Conte during his brief instructorship at and on later visits to Berkeley. Le Conte, who had been a prominent slaveowner and a chemist with the Confederate Nitre Bureau during the Civil War, found refuge from possible trial as a war criminal at Berkeley, where he assumed the mantle of a "gentle prophet of evolution."[15] Royce, born amidst what he later recalled as a morally bereft gold-rush California that had all too easily acquiesced to the style, manner, and racial ideas of the Southern cavalier,[16] sought religio-philosophic guidance and scientific grounding for the restoration of an ethical social order from his studies with Le Conte. Appalled by the violent character, corrupt politics, and social disorder that he saw on the Pacific coast and assumed to be widespread in the rest of America, Royce, always more religious than his revered but complacently deistic mentor Le Conte, adapted the latter's evolutionism to an elaborate theory of the social system, harmonizing both mind and society with the will of God.[17] Royce's approach started out with Le Conte's notion that evolution "is under the influence of two opposite forces, or principles—the one progressive and the other conservative, the one tending to changes, the other to stability"—and, together with Le Conte, Royce concluded that all social change is "subject to [the] law of cyclical movement."[18] In Royce's hands, however, this orientation led to an optimistic resolution, "the philosophy of loyalty,"[19] a metaphysical sociology that asserted the positive and progressive functions of social conflict. As with Le Conte, Royce's writings take the Civil War to be the significant historical episode in the development of the United States. But where Le Conte saw the war as an obstacle to the natural development of a racially stratified organization of labor, Royce conceived of it as a conflict that led to a higher sense of national community: The Union and Confederate armies "actually served the one cause of the now united nation. They loyally shed their blood, North and South, that we might be free from their burden of hatred and horror."[20]

Royce's philosophical sociology contributed indirectly but significantly to the development of the discipline at Berkeley. As a devoted student of Le Conte, he carried an interpretation of his Comtean mentor's perspective to Harvard, where he influenced a generation of students among whom was George Herbert Mead, the principal intellectual influence on Herbert Blumer. Royce's period of service at Harvard coincided with the first decades of that of Thomas Nixon Carver, an avowed Comtean who made the latter's "comparative method" the central focus of his own approach to social change and who had some influence on the sociological perspective of Talcott Parsons. Royce and Carver helped set the terms for American sociology's evolutionist-functionalist paradigm, while Royce's student, Mead, turned away from his teacher's metaphysics and sought to locate social science and social philosophy in an empirically grounded phenomenology. Herbert Blumer would later carry Mead's perspective to Berkeley, where it fit into the critiques of Comte and Le Conte that had already developed there under Teggart and his disciples.

Royce's evolutionism conceived of America as a self-enhancing moral community that would achieve its ultimate integration through the dialectical workings of its own philosophy of loyalty. The latter was an ever deepening faith that reached its apex in loyalty to fidelity itself. Racial antipathies—which Le Conte had treated as an unfortunate consequence of premature emancipation that could be remedied by eugenically sound and scientifically controlled interbreeding—had positive functions in Royce's metaphysic. Loyalties to one's own racial group and opposition to others—the ubiquitous process entailed in what William Graham Sumner designated as ethnocentrism[21]—would ultimately move America toward its *telos,* a racially synthetic and ethically higher moral community.[22] In Royce's adaptation of Le Conte's cyclical evolutionism, the dialectic of conflict would always lead—ultimately—to a positive result. In effect, Royce provided a social theodicy for American social philosophy, a theory of process and change that converted virtually all human conflicts into episodes that moved society toward the realization of ideal social harmony.[23]

Royce credited Le Conte with supplying the social scientific underpinnings for his own quest for a respiritualized moral community in America. However, Royce could not accept Le Conte's complacent deism. In its place he put forward St. Paul's designation of a third entity that would have to be added to the "two beings to whom Christian love is owed: God and the neighbor." That third and "corporate entity is the Christian community," Royce asserted. Royce's moral community of love, which would arise out of the eufunctional processes of loyalty conflicts, has as its individual component the Christian neighbor who, as in the Pauline text, "has now become a being who is primarily the fellow-member of the Christian community."[24] In later years, and by means of an epistemology that did not acknowledge the contribution of Royce, Talcott Parsons would formulate a similar sociodicy for the United States. Parsons not only promised eventual and complete inclusion of the Negro but also made his own secular and processual restatement of the Pauline-Puritan communitarian ethos, now calling it dynamic equilibrium. Where Mead would feel the need to rescue social philosophy from the metaphysical unreality of Royce's evolutionism, Blumer, a generation later, would assert the necessity of liberating sociology from the abstract illusions of Parsonian systems theory.

The transition in thought from Royce to Blumer depends on the measured response to the former in the writings of George Herbert Mead. Mead elaborated important aspects of his own social philosophy of mind, self, and society as a critique of Royce's religious and metaphysical evolutionism. Basically, Mead regarded Royce's ideas to be at odds with the realities of self-development, community formation, and societal solidarity in the United States. He criticized Royce's variant of Le Conte's cyclical evolutionism, the infinite series that evolved into a morally sound self-identity, as contrary to actual human experience; and rejected the Protestant-Pauline community metaphysic as "part of [Royce's] . . . escape from the crudity of American life, [but] not an interpretation of it."²⁴ Mead laid one of the foundations for Blumer's development of symbolic interactionism by refashioning Royce's religious and metaphysical arguments into a secular social philosophy. As Vidich and Lyman summarized Mead's work in this regard: "For the Infinite Self he substituted the self-reflective self; for Christian values, the generalized other; for the ultimate community of Pauline believers, the penultimate society of interacting selves."²⁶

At Berkeley, Blumer went even further down the road to grounding sociology in a secular and noneschatological paradigm. Although Mead's conception of a fundamentally civil morality formed within and through the making and sustaining of a civil society provided a background against which Blumer developed his own sociology, Blumer recognized that in the United States both mind and self developed within the context of something quite different from Royce's Christian community—a pluralized and fractionated society. Composed of diverse races, numerous ethnic groups, several religious denominations, incipient sectarian formations, fluid social classes, and shifting lifestyles, American society seemed to defy the grounding of a single uniform generalized other. In 1981, Blumer acknowledged that while "the generalized other is the chief position from which a human participant grasps and understands the social world inside of which he has to develop his conduct, [Mead had given] no aid in tracing how people construct their 'generalized others' [nor any] techniques which would enable people . . . to improve their ability to take group roles." Society, in Blumer's understanding of it, did not move according to the dictates of Royce's sacred eschatology, nor did it unfold in accordance with a secular variant of Le Conte's historical teleology or Parsons's dynamic equilibrium; rather, it developed haphazardly out of the changing definitions of self and of the selves who composed it. Blumer conceived the moral order of society to arise not from an ultimately evolved harmony of opposed interests, but instead from the ceaseless quest for a civil ordering of conflicts. "[S]elf interaction," Blumer pointed out, "has the potential of placing an individual in opposition to his associates and to his society."²⁸ In a society like that of the United States, where there is little shared tradition to bind people into a corporate community of common outlook, where heterodox subcultures, heterogeneous beliefs, and the varieties of religious and irreligious experiences have evoked in some sociologists a call for a spiritualized American civil religion²⁹ and a reaffirmation of the habits of the heart,³⁰ Blumer regards the fundamental empirical question to be the discovery and praxis of a public philosophy suited to the vagaries of politically democratic but socially massified society.³¹

TEGGART'S CRITIQUE OF COMTE AND THE PHENOMENOLOGY OF "RELEASE"

Mead's and Blumer's critiques of Roycean and related social philosophies and social science were paralleled by Berkeley Professor Frederick J. Teggart's critique of Comte and all other teleological social scientists. Teggart (1870–1946), a "new historian" whose wholesale rejection of German Romantic historicism had made him unwelcome in the University of California's history department, in 1919 founded and chaired Berkeley's unique Department of Social Institutions. That department served as the forerunner of the university's Department of Sociology and Social Institutions, established in 1946 after Teggart's death. Although he was aware of Le Conte's adaptation of the ideas of Comte, Agassiz, and Darwin to the development of a theory of evolution and cited his book on the subject in a footnote,³³ Teggart devoted his own critical remarks on the subject to the classical Greek thinkers and to their major modern epigoni, especially Comte. Interested in grounding history in a thoroughly secular science, Teggart felt it necessary to clear away the vast pileup of metaphysical, sacred, and unscientific debris that stood in the way of a rational and positive approach. Despite his commitment to a positive science of society, Comte, Teggart asserted, has set forth an intellectually debilitating paradigm for the recasting of history as such a science.³⁴ It is beyond the scope of the present essay to provide a comprehensive account of Teggart's critique of developmentalism and his own version of neo-positivist historicism.³⁵ Suffice it to say that Teggart adumbrated a portion of the critique that Blumer would later develop against social systems theorists³⁶ and, like Blumer, he also insisted that every science must be empirical within the character of its particular subject matter.

Teggart held that any social science that proceeded by uncritically appropriating the methodological orientation of a natural science, that supposed that it must emulate physics, physiology, or biology, or that assumed *a priori* that societies had the characteristics of living organisms had violated the basic principles of a sound philosophy of science. "[I]t must always be kept in mind," he wrote, "that social and cultural phenomena are 'historical' throughout, that is, they can be identified or set forth explicitly only in terms of time and place."[37] The "failure of humanists to achieve the desired end of a science of man," Teggart wrote in 1926, "might possibly be due to the acceptance (consciously or unconsciously) of assumptions of presuppositions which have had an adverse influence on the conduct of their inquiries."[38] Among these assumptions the most commonly employed was that analogizing a society to a biological organism. It led to a division of thought, describing social stability as a product of homeostasis and social change in terms of gradual stages proceeding in an orderly sequence and terminating in a predetermined end.[39]

Comte, whom Teggart believed to be the "outstanding figure in the effort to create a scientific study of man, or of society, during the nineteenth century," had been the principal figure in sending social science down the wrong road. Comte's *Course de philosophie positive* was "not the product of a firsthand investigation of social phenomena," but rather "a demonstration, carried out by the use of deduction and analogy, of the relation in which such a social science might conceivably stand to existing 'natural sciences'."[40] In setting forth the "natural" and "physiological" terms for social science to develop its own paradigms of social persistence and social change, Comte, Teggart charged, had led sociology as well as anthropology and other newly-forming social sciences away from the humanistic study of change in time and space and toward a largely conjectural approach that would prove—indeed, had already proved—sterile.

It is important to note that Blumer had read Teggart's *Processes of History and Theory of History* while researching his own doctoral dissertation[41] and that with certain qualifications and disagreements he seems to have employed aspects of the critical stance contained therein in his own critique of the approach taken by those scholars seeking to promulgate universal laws of history.[42] For example, Blumer remarks in passing on the "naivete" of E. P. Cheyney's presentation of six laws of universal history (law of continuity, law of impermanence, law of interdependence, law of democracy, law of necessity for free consent, law of moral progress) and states that such formulations "must cause the sociologist to smile."[43] However, Blumer raised questions about the alternative proposed by Teggart, viz., the possibility that a science of human conduct might be developed out of a systematic comparison of an array of historical events or episodes. The result of any such comparative study—actually carried out by Teggart in the 1930s as an experiment complete with guiding hypothesis, classification of discrete types of happenings, and the avowed intention of discovering correlations in historical events affecting Rome and China,[44] and, employing the same approach, by Teggart's principal disciple, colleague, and successor at Berkeley, Margaret Hodgen, in order to discover the factors affecting technological innovation in England from 1000–1899 A.D.[45]—does not," according to Blumer, "indicate the existence of general principles of human association or conduct, but merely implies that a number of things share in what amounts to be a unique situation."[46]

Teggart's comparative historical investigation *Rome and China* was transcultural in scope and sought to uncover correlations in an array of time-and-space happenings that, interpreted in a complex causal manner, could explain the onset of invasions and wars.[47] Blumer, writing several years earlier about this type of study, pointed out that its very fundamental datum—the historical instance, episode, or event—"does not have a self-sufficing intelligibility inherent in itself, . . . it secures this intelligibility always in the eyes of the interpreter." Moreover, varying interpretations are not to be ascribed necessarily to "deceit, conscious bias, or shabby scholarship," but rather to the incontrovertible fact that the several interpreters have "different backgrounds emphasizing different meanings and values."[48]

In contrast to Teggart, who acknowledged and, indeed, advocated an ethical role for the interpreter of historical events—one that would be used to guide statesmen away from making those decisive decisions that had had unfortunate consequences in earlier but similar situations[49]—Blumer confined his caveats about the promise of such a science of history to pointing out its limitations. When, for example, the scientific historian sought to excise the variability of meaning to which a single episode might be subjected by different interpreters, Blumer observed, he tended to strip it down to "bare behavior." But, Blumer says, "this procedure omits the very meaning which one hopes to retain. . . . The classification of such bare events yields, at the best, a very general principle which impresses one as lacking vitality and significance."[50] In effect, Teggart's thirty-year debate with Comte and his epigoni, coupled with his proposal for a neo-positivistic historiography, had hoped to inspire a scientifically grounded American statesmanship that Blumer showed could only be purchased at the price of disavowing the obdurate reality of interpretive variation.

THE PHENOMENOLOGY OF
SOCIAL CHANGE: TEGGART AND BLUMER

Although there is little convergence in the approaches of Teggart and Blumer to a science of history and human conduct, their separate and distinctive orientations to the study of social change show a certain affinity. There is no evidence of direct contact and the sharing of ideas. However, it is worthy of note that Robert E. Park, certainly one of the Chicago sociologists whose ideas influenced Blumer, designated the approach to social change advocated by Teggart as the "catastrophic theory of progress" and defined it as the "notion that society and intellectual life have advanced as a consequence of events that disturbed a pre-existing social equilibrium."[51] Park employed Teggart's phenomenological concept, "release," to highlight his own conception of the marginal man and to account for the onset of social changes in society.[52] Here I wish only to suggest that Teggart's employment of "release" and its effect on social change resembles Blumer's usage of Mead's concept of "reverie" to help account for the reordering of an individual's or a group's scheme of social life. In addition, both concepts—"release" and "reverie"—and their respective and concomitant theories are not dissimilar from conceptualizations employed in W. I. Thomas's formulation of "habit-crisis-attention" as stages in a developing trajectory of social change.[53]

As I have pointed out elsewhere,[54] a science of history is not confined to delineating a theory of social change. In the case of Teggart, his proposed science of history is neo-positivistic and geo-temporal in character, while his theory of social change is derived from William James and is phenomenological. In Blumer's work there is no attempt to put forward a general social science of history, but his approach to the study of social change is squarely in the symbolic interactionist tradition with which he is associated. Moreover, in both Teggart's and Blumer's approaches the direction and outcome of social change is indeterminate and futures are open-ended.

Teggart and the Idea of Release

Teggart developed his theory of social change as part of his critique of Comte and other developmentalist thinkers. Comte and his followers held that change was natural, that it occurred slowly, gradually, continuously, and teleologically, that it was progressive, and that its processes were analogous to those of biological organisms. Against what he regarded as this illusion of the scientific age, Teggart proposed that changes in fact were not natural, that they might occur rapidly, suddenly, and irregularly, and that they were by no means determinatively progressive. "Changes," Teggart observed, "are not the product of any slow, gradual, and continuous evolution, but are disturbances of relatively stabilized conditions occasioned by intrusive influences."[55] Thus, Teggart noted by way of illustration, "the present state of culture in England is not the product of uninterrupted growth, or a 'slow, gradual, and continuous' development, but . . . has been deeply affected by a succession of intrusive influences, marked, in the earlier periods, by a succession of warlike invasions, and, in later times, by a succession of cultural contributions from other areas."[56] An examination of the actual facts of any people's culture history, Teggart insisted, would reveal "that the course of change has not been 'uninterrupted,' that it has not been without 'breaks'."[57] Social changes are neither immanent nor teleological in Teggart's formulation.

As part of his critique of Comteanism Teggart found it necessary to assault those theories of social and cultural change that attributed it to ascriptive factors, natural features, or constitutional characteristics. Among these were those theories of racial superiority that supposed that both human advance and social decline might be attributed to the innate characteristics of a particular gene group. Both Comte and Le Conte had subscribed to such theories. In response to such ideas Teggart cited with approval R. G. Latham's observation of 1859 that civilization or advancement was "a result of the contact of more peoples than one," and he lent his support to Theodor Waitz's contention that (as paraphrased by Teggart) "differences in the culture of peoples depend, in the main, upon change in the general conditions of life, and upon the vicissitudes of history."[58] Comte's Eurocentric and Francophilic theory of human advancement[59] had, as Teggart saw the matter, been refuted both theoretically and empirically by Waitz's careful ethnographic investigations.[60] In distinct contrast to the racially eugenic approach taken by Le Conte, who, it should be recalled, proposed that a melioristic advance in American society could be achieved by breeding the newly emancipated Negroes out of existence, Teggart distinguished the study of social changes, of "how man has come to be as we find him everywhere in the world today," from sciences directed to discover "how man is constituted":

> Inquiry into the physical differences between the 'black,' 'yellow,' and 'white' divisions of the human family can be conducted only by biologists; the question as to whether there are psychological differences in human 'races' can be dealt with only by psychologists. In the present inconclusive state of scientific knowledge on these points . . . the only

course open to humanists is to accept man 'as given,' to assume that human groups everywhere are constituted of much the same human elements.[61]

Because he believed that the "present differences in the activities of human groups cannot be accounted for in terms of . . . 'race' alone,"[62] Teggart proposed that students of social change investigate "the effect of collision and conflict in breaking down an established social order" and pay special attention to the attendant process of "release" that ensues.[63] "Release," he argued, had the effect of "freeing the individual judgment from the inhibitions of conventional modes of thought"[64] and setting in motion the opportunity for creative social and cultural transformations.

Teggart's phenomenological approach to the understanding of social change is built around the process that he called "release."[65] According to Teggart, a social change is triggered by an intrusive event that evokes an individual's or a group's "release" from slavery to habit. As Teggart conceived of the matter, what goes on most of the time, for most people in most places, past or present, is habitual conduct oriented to deeply ingrained customs or well-established traditions. Whatever their value, however, these customs and traditions act as constraints on creative human endeavor. But, unlike those thinkers who postulated a necessarily positive or progressive result arising out of the emancipation of any set of human creatures from their habits, Teggart believed that there was no possibility of predicting with any certainty the character, form, type, or value of the changes in conduct or understanding that the newly released might undertake. Freedom from cultural restraint entailed a recognition by him of its open and utterly possibilist character.

For Teggart, a careful attention to the historical record indicated the kind of occurrences that would lead to a general breakdown of the habits and customs of a people. Such occurrences introduced dilemmas into ordinary affairs by undermining the understandings of knowledge and conduct in everyday life. They are the "intrusions" that puncture the seemingly solid cake of societary custom and produce the kind of situation that W. I. Thomas had earlier characterized as a "crisis" and that later Alfred Schutz would call a "crisis in the *Lebenswelt*."[66] The particular effect of these intrusions is similar to that ensuing from the experimentally-designed interruptions that ethnomethodologists at one time unceremoniously introduced into the everyday lives of ordinary people: They convert the taken-for-granted social resources of everyday life, the recipes-for-living that everyone knows, into topics for reflection, interrogation, and evaluation. In Teggart's words (written, of course, long before the ethnomethodologists appeared on the scene), the rare but world-historically significant events that serve as intrusions break down the "system of ideas" that has formed the *Weltanschauung* of a people. Such a "breakdown of the old and unquestioned system of ideas," Teggart pointed out, "though it might be felt as a public calamity and a personal loss, accomplishes the release of the individual mind from the set forms in which it has been drilled, and leaves men opportunity to build up a system for themselves anew."[67] Although Teggart allowed that the new systems of ideas and institutions that would be built up following upon an effective intrusion would contain elements of the older systems, they would not be the same as the old, "for the consolidated group, confronted with conflicting bodies of knowledge, of observances, and of interpretations, will experience a critical awakening, and open wondering eyes upon a new world."[68]

Although Teggart acknowledged that his own investigations had not "been carried to a point at which they might constitute a hypothesis explanatory of human advancement,"[69] he did suggest conceptual foundations for a phenomenological theory of social change. In support of his thesis, he appealed to the writings of William James, especially "The Energies of Men,"[70] for confirmation of his own formulation of the release process. In that essay, James, as quoted by Teggart, pointed out that "as a rule men habitually use only a small part of the powers which they actually possess and which they might use"; that ordinary men and women were inhibited in the use of their full powers by convention; that "an intellect thus tied down by literality and decorum" is weakened in the same manner as "an able-bodied man would [be should he] habituate himself to do his work with only one of his fingers, locking up the rest of his organism and leaving it unused"; and that humanity might be loosed from the chains of its own conventionality by "[e]xcitements, ideas, and efforts."[71]

Reverie and the Folkways:
Blumer's Formulation of Social Change

Although Blumer has nowhere set down an explicit formulation of a theory of social change, discussions of such inform much of his critical writings. Moreover, specific hypotheses of social change are to be found in his conclusions to his own empirical investigations of the effect of movies on individual conduct and collective behavior and within his presentation of a theory of the onset and dissolution of race prejudice.

A concept and phenomenon that Mead had paid passing attention to—"reverie"—loomed large in one of Blumer's early formulations of social change. Essentially, Blumer's attention to the process of "reverie" and its effects adumbrated his later critique of conventional sociologists. The latter, Blumer asserts, in their eagerness to delineate some factor that plays upon human society in a supposedly particular and undirectional way—e.g., industrialization that, when introduced into a political economy characterized by a racial hierarchy of work and opportunity, will, supposedly, inevitably dissolve the racist elements in an emerging interracial structure of classes[72]—"either ignore the role of the interpretive behavior of acting units in the given instance of change, or else regard the interpretative behavior as coerced by the factor of change."[73] Human beings, Blumer argues, do not merely react to intrusive factors that become features of their environment; they respond to them by interpretation: "[A]ny line of social change, since it involves change in human action, is necessarily mediated by interpretation on the part of the people caught up in the change." And, Blumer went on to say, "[T]he change appears in the form of new situations in which people have to construct new forms of action."[74] Among the situations that provided opportunities for people to formulate new lines of conduct, Blumer paid critical attention to those that afforded, indeed encouraged, the opportunity for free-floating daydreaming, for the complex mental processes to be set free to imagine schemes of life and to rehearse actions hitherto not imagined or raised to critical awareness. The movies, Blumer argued in 1935, provided one such opportunity.

In Blumer's investigations of the effects of films on young people,[75] notice was taken of how movies encouraged a considerable amount of imagistic daydreaming by their young audiences. Mead had earlier alluded to daydreaming and reverie in his writings.[76] He had also spoken of the social functions of dramas and novels as presenting a situation "which lies outside of the immediate purview of the reader in such form that he enters into the attitude of the group in the situation."[77] In movies, however, Mead had supposed that a visual imagery of hitherto unarticulated desires is given to an audience that, by the very nature of its composition—an aggregate of isolates or small clusters—"does not lend itself to shared experience."[78] "[W]hat the average film brings to light is that the hidden unsatisfied longings of the average man and woman are very immediate, rather simple, and fairly primitive."[79] Nevertheless, for all his caveats about movies and their effects on reverie, Mead pointed out that they can provide "a certain release, and relief from restraint . . . which the inner imagination can never offer," and that the reverie and the social constructions which they permit pass "into the universal meanings of common discourse and cooperative effort, and out of it arise the forms of universal beauty, the intuitions of the inventor, the hypotheses of the scientist, and the creations of the artist."[80] As Mead conceived of the process, reverie marked "man's isolation within society," providing "that part of the inner life . . . which cannot be given its implicated meaning because of the incompleteness of social organization."[81]

Blumer adapted Mead's understandings of the process entailed in reverie to his own findings of the effects of film-induced daydreaming on the dreamers. In effect, Blumer treats the movies as an intrusion, in the sense that Teggart used that term, into the local cultures of the American people, one that functions to introduce novel images of a social life and open up opportunities for the creative imagination to reconstruct that social life. Reconstruction takes place first in the imaginative scene played out in a movie-goer's film-inspired reverie, then, perhaps, in external conduct and, possibly, in the adoption of new ways of life or the formation of new social institutions. At the same time, Blumer observes, intrusive films reinforce elementary human qualities while providing newly imagined ways for their expression. Just as Teggart's conception of the effect of intrusions included a certain sustaining of older ideas within the configuration of a new form of social organization, so Blumer asserted that the general influence of movies was "a reaffirmation of basic human values but an undermining of the mores."

Blumer emphasized that movies lent moral support to such verities as "bravery, loyalty, love, affection, frankness, personal justness, cleverness, heroism and friendship," but he pointed out that "the social patterns or schemes of conduct inside of which these primary human qualities are placed are likely to be somewhat new, strange and unfamiliar."[83] Hence "motion pictures operate like all agencies of mass communication to turn the attention of individuals outward from their areas of locally defined life." However, like the intrusive effect that Teggart claimed a lengthy military siege would have on the allegiance to habit among the besieged,[84] so also the impact of the movies on the individual outlook and collective mentality of the audience "is not merely a direction of attention to the outside of local culture; it is an attack upon the local culture."[85] And, as a result, this sustained mass media assault on the folkways, when coupled with a presentation of the manner in which ways of life reaffirming cherished values can be realized in novel social forms, awakens "appetites, impulses, desires, yearnings, and hopes which, even though experienced only momentarily and given expression only in daydreaming, orient the individual in directions different from those prescribed by the tradition and culture."[86]

In effect, Blumer's elaboration of the functions of reverie fills out the infrastructure of the "release" process that Teggart had described earlier. As Blumer put it, "mass reverie not only reflects the spirit and feelings of people but also invigorates and moulds this spirit and these feelings."[87] The "play of reverie," he pointed out, "whether ordered as in the motion picture or free as in individual daydreaming . . . sketches schemes of possible conduct and launches the individual upon vicarious journeying in new social worlds."[88] Hence, Blumer suggested, the "free play of the masses does not represent inevitably an endless period of disintegration and absence of discipline," as many traditionalists had supposed. Rather, it "may be merely transitional and preparatory to a new order of life measuring to a newly developing taste."[89]

Blumer's several discussions of the structure and processes of race prejudice show further affinity between his (and Mead's) approach to the relation of social stability to social change and that of Teggart's ideas about "fixity" and social innovation. Teggart had emphasized how the legitimation and institutionalization of an idea, or an idea complex, provided a telling example of the conservatising and tradition-building tendencies of humankind.[90] For Blumer, race prejudice constituted such an idea—it was, he said, "a sense of group position." Blumer has always insisted that all sociological studies that claim to be empirical in their methods focus on acting units.[91] However, he has never reduced his outlook to an explicit or implicit claim that the actions of each acting unit are of equal effectiveness or that the only acting unit available for sociological observation is a discrete individual. Any theory of race relations, he pointed out, must be "concerned with the establishment and maintenance of hierarchical racial order within a given society."[92] In the United States, South Africa, and other societies that Blumer has studied, the racial hierarchy has arisen and been legitimized as the sense of group position as a result of decisions made in the collective process of group characterization. The significant acts in that process are carried out by social, political, and economic elites. Further, that process, continuously defining and justifying the established racial hierarchy, "operates chiefly through the public media in which individuals who are accepted as the spokesmen of a racial group characterize publicly another racial group."[93] What sociologists call race prejudice, thus, is a cluster of interrelated ideas organized in support of a racial hierarchy. These ideas have been elevated to form part of a public philosophy supporting the society's fundamental structure, everyday operations, and the basic definition of itself and its situation.

Presumably, one type of social change in a society organized around a hierarchy of racial groups would occur if the hierarchy was dismantled altogether and the justifications for its existence refuted, denied, or abandoned. Such a metamorphosis, Blumer reminds us,[94] is not the inevitable or even the likely outcome of the introduction of a new form of economic organization, e.g., industrialization; a new socio-economic policy, e.g., socialism; or a massive psychic reconstruction, e.g., a psychoanalysis of the hearts and minds of its citizenry. In the case of the United States, Blumer observes, race prejudice has built up a solid bastion of support in its various and multifarious institutionalizations of "the color line."[95] Whereas Teggart borrowed Bagehot's imagery of the "cake of custom" that could only with great difficulty be broken down, and that would crumble "when the sudden impact of new thoughts and new examples breaks down the compact despotism of the single consecrated code,"[96] Blumer likens America's color line to a military fortification: "[A]s a metaphor, the color line is not appropriately represented by a single, sharply drawn line but appears rather as a series of ramparts, like the 'Maginot Line,' extending from outer breastworks to inner bastions." Breaking down the cake of hierarchical racial custom will be an arduous and complex task; for "[o]uter portions of it may, so to speak, be given up only to hold steadfast to inner citadels."[97] And just as Teggart focused on the rare but significant agents of social change that appeared historically in the forms of intrusive events, remarkable persons, or new ideas, so Blumer focused on the points of entry into, or the points of vulnerability in, the bastions of racist power. As a sense of group position, he pointed out, race prejudice could decline "[w]hen events touching on relations are not treated as 'big events' and hence do not set crucial issues in the arena of public discussion; or when the elite leaders or spokesmen do not define such big events vehemently or adversely; or where they define them in the direction of social harmony; or when there is a paucity of strong interest groups seeking to build up a strong adverse image for special advantage."[98] The school desegregation process, as a particular line of assault on an intermediate citadel of the racial hierarchy, might proceed more effectively, though not without great difficulty and hardship, Blumer thought, if decisive action was taken to control "the decisions of the main functionaries who carry a given form of racial segregation to actual execution."[99]

In its most general sense, Teggart's theory of fixity pointed to the tendency of customary conduct to continue unchanged until an intrusion of great force and magnitude coerces the discovery of new lines of efficacious behavior and permits innovative strata with leadership abilities to emerge and consolidate the emerging ways of doing things. Blumer's careful evaluation of the strengths and resistances—as well as the weaknesses and vulnerabilities—of America's color line provides a particular specification of the processes entailed in a single instance of the attempt to overturn custom-bound conduct. Subsequent empirical research on the status of the color line in the South since 1954[100] has done much to validate Blumer's observations.

CONCLUSION

Sociology at Berkeley has a much longer history than that of the department bearing its disciplinary name. When Herbert Blumer assumed the chairmanship and took over direction of development of the newly formed Department of Sociology and Social Institutions in 1952, he could build on a tradition of independent and critical scholarship that had begun with the appointment of the University's first professor, the Comtean natural historian Joseph Le Conte. For those who would study the intellectual efforts undertaken at the University of California in the years of curricular development and change, from 1868 to 1958, despite the many theoretical perspectives and the various disciplinary names given to fields of study in the human sciences at that institution, it is possible to discern a thread of dialogical continuity connecting the works of Le Conte and Royce to those of Teggart and Blumer. That thread might be designated a dialogue with the ghost of Comte, the French philosopher who gave sociology its name and, in George Herbert Mead's view, not only sought to build a sociology directly out of biology and without a psychology[101] but also to "fashion a religion of humanity out of . . . love of one's neighbor."[102] Le Conte had abjured Comte's nescient religion of humanity in favor of an evolutionary science of man and society that was compatible with Divine Creation; however, he looked to a socially directed and humanely controlled scientific eugenics program to resolve problems arising from the absence of interracial neighborliness in America. Royce adapted Le Conte's multilinear evolutionism to a metaphysical theory of the dynamic social system, moved by the opposed loyalties of conflicting parties to achieve a higher stage of mutual fidelity and Pauline corporatist communion. At the University of Chicago, Mead did much to deconstruct Royce's philosophy by stripping it of its abstract idealism and unempirical character. In so doing, he inspired Blumer, among others, to make an even greater effort at laying the foundations for a completely secularized science of society. In the same period, at Berkeley, Teggart laid his critical ax to the Greek and medieval predecessors of Comte's brand of positivism. In its place he proposed a new historical science of society and a reconceptualized theory of social change grounded, respectively, on the bedrocks of a comparative study of happenings in the real world and a phenomenological psychology of "intrusion" and "release." When, six years after Teggart's death, Herbert Blumer wrote that

> the likening of human group life to the operation of a mechanical structure, or to the functioning of an organism, or to a system seeking equilibrium, seems to me to face grave difficulties in view of the formative

and explorative character of interaction as the participants judge each other and guide their own acts by that judgment.[103]

he was not only continuing and extending the discourse that had begun with Teggart's critiques of Comte (and, by implication, Le Conte) and Mead's critique of Royce, but also adumbrating a historically grounded and phenomenological sociology that has still to be completed.

Blumer's and Teggart's teachings captivated the sociological imaginations of many of their Berkeley students and encouraged them to contribute their own researches to the continuing discussion. These researches, true to the tradition on which they were formed, took on a character of their own. Closer attention to the facts of the case would, I believe, force a disinterested observer to see in the many studies that have flowed from Berkeley's sociology students since 1952 not a "line," as Shils would have preferred it, but rather the unevenly distributed shares of a legacy like that envisioned by Georg Simmel for those who would come after him: "The estate I leave," Simmel wrote, "is like cash distributed among many heirs, each of whom puts his share to use in some trade that is compatible with *his* nature but which can no longer be recognised as coming from that estate."[104]

Legitimacy and Consensus in Lipset's America

From Washington to Watergate

It has become commonplace to speak of "crisis" as a contemporary characteristic of both society and social science. In recent years a sense of "crisis" has been apprehended in "late" or "advanced" capitalism,[1] Marxism,[2] Western sociology,[3] and in the basis for authority in general.[4] With such a plethora of crises, it is only inevitable that—among the radicals, at any rate—a politics-of-crisis theory[5] would also develop, and that both radical and moderate sociologists would begin to search for the sources and causes of error in their predecessors' and their own work.[6] In fact "crisis" is a complex and ambiguous term, less than adequately suited for conceptual usage in the social sciences.[7] Moreover, the basic sociological ideas of most of the "crisis" theorists are not much different from those of their more conventional opponents. Precisely because of this, it is useful to re-examine the concerns of conventional social science with the structure and dynamics of society and more especially with the political sector. Such a review can throw light on certain persistent problems in conceptualization and theorizing.

There can be little doubt that social science in general and sociology in particular have been dominated by progressively more elaborated versions of the structural-functional orientation. So pervasive has been this approach that, despite effective criticism[8] and a much vaunted premature burial,[9] the fundamental ideas still survive. Indeed, although certain sociologists have insisted that structural-functionalism is peculiarly suited to provide subtle ideological support to the status quo in American society or for capitalism,[10] it has been espoused by East European theorists[11] and for a time was the basis for socioeconomic and political reorganization in societies claiming Marx as their forebear.[12] The near universality of functionalist ideas in sociology led Kingsley Davis to dispute its critics' claim that it is a special variant of the discipline;[13] while Kenneth E. Bock treats its persistence in the face of such extensive criticism as constituting in itself something of a crisis for sociology.[14]

Despite their warnings and alarms, the bulk of the new crisis theorists in sociology are failing to provide any more effective solutions to the problems in sociology or society than those offered by Talcott Parsons, S. M. Lipset and other structural-functionalists. The basic reason for this failure is that crisis theorists adhere to essentially the same paradigm that animated original structural-functionalism. As self-selected heirs of Marx, crisis theorists have adapted the developmentalist, evolutionist, and systemic elements of that theorist's work to an analysis of modern industrial societies and especially of the United States.[15] Thus, critiques of domination, exultation over the coming crises of legitimation in capitalist societies, and the general "critical" theory of society do little more than replace the rhetoric of a Parsonian evolutionist-functionalism with that of neo-Marxian systemic developmentalism. A good example is the recent analysis of the "legitimation crisis" by Jürgen Habermas.[16] Not only do we find the familiar evolutionist stage theory of development resuscitated in the form of preclass, class, and postclass societies (with class societies divided into traditional and modern civilizations, the latter subdivided into capitalist and postcapitalist societies, and the capitalist societies further classified into liberal capitalist and organized or advanced capitalist types), but we also find an unabashed affiliation with the substance of the ideas usually associated with the systemic writings of Parsons. Indeed, the debate with Niklas Luhmann, Germany's leading exponent of Parsonian thought, which closes and in fact epitomizes the current intellectual direction of the "critical" theorists, is a squabble among scholars who share the same basic paradigm but disagree on internal technical elements, points of emphasis, and specification of functional significance. Old wine is poured into older bottles. New labels are attached.

THE UNITED STATES AS THE FIRST NEW NATION

A fine example of a structural-functionalist political sociology—containing its most salient elements and illustrating nearly all of its faults—is that carried out by Seymour Martin Lipset. From his studies of the United States as the "first new nation" through his commentaries on trade unions, intellectuals, nativism, the race question, and the student revolt, and to his most recent commentary on Watergate, Lipset has presented a comprehensive analysis of the structure and processes of what he believes is a social system developing in accordance with its internal dynamic and becoming the progressive democracy destined in its origins.

Combining the functionalist's organic imagery with Max Weber's famous dictum analogizing societal origins to the throwing of loaded dice,[17] Lipset has tried to show that certain values and predispositions established at the outset of any society's history become determinants of the channels and directions of social change. He thus explains how the progressive democratic republicanism of the United States works and why it perseveres on its steady and relatively unturbulent march to the fulfillment of its original promise.[18]

The successful establishment of a viable and operating democracy in the postrevolutionary period in the United States was guaranteed primarily by certain crucial decisions made by the Founding Fathers. Especially significant, according to Lipset, are the Founding Fathers' solutions to the problems of legitimacy and consensus. Washington resolved the problem of national authority by uniting various factions around his own inspiring figure; committing himself and his followers to the principles of constitutional government; exercising paternal guidance over those who operated the machinery of government; remaining in power long enough "to permit the crystallization of factions into embryonic parties"; and setting a precedent for orderly succession to the presidency by voluntarily retiring from office.

National authority was also furthered by systemic operations: the slow development of federal institutions, the balancing off of regional, ethnic, and religious cleavages, the preponderance of common values shared by immigrants from diverse countries in Western Europe, and the channeling of conflicts into two major political parties, which became giant holding companies for the several kinds of interest groups competing for national attention and special favors. In other words, the United States was established normatively as a functioning and dynamic social system. Its basic values, according to Lipset, are achievement and equality.

National unity, according to Lipset, presented a different kind of problem, but, once again, the first new nation resolved it in a masterful fashion. The many and varied European groups settling in America imperiled national consensus. Interested in escaping from the conflicts in but not the whole of their identity with the various mother countries, the European immigrants found Washington's policy of neutrality most palatable. Moreover, neutrality helped to isolate the young republic from the world and permitted the gradual development of an indigenous national consciousness.

The high status of American intellectuals aided in the development of national unity. In the early years of the American republic, intellectuals were found throughout its political, commercial, and agricultural power elite. Jefferson, Madison, Hamilton, Adams, Jay, Franklin, and—for a time—Aaron Burr found positions of authority and prestige in the constitutional democracy. Men of immense learning as well as great influence, they fostered a sense of national unity and high purpose. Although in recent years intellectuals have espoused ideas hostile to consensus in America, Lipset does not consider this later alienation of the intellectuals to be so significant.[19]

Finally, the Puritan tradition helped transform what was once a value of religious universalism into a powerful secular emphasis on achievement. The Puritan commitment to order fostered a respect for education, law, and limited government. And, as Talcott Parsons has suggested, the universalistic doctrines of the Puritans, meshed with egalitarian principles, values of achievement, belief in progress, and a gradualist approach to the solution of social and, especially, racial and ethnic problems, facilitated an assurance that equal rights and equal opportunities would eventually be available to all Americans.[20]

Lipset's insistence on the permanence of equality and achievement as institutionalized values is put forward in opposition to David Riesman's claim that a new character has emerged in America and William F. Whyte's thesis that the organization man has replaced the Puritan achiever.[21] The other-directedness that Riesman claims is new in America is merely the current manifestation of a basic and unchanging egalitarianism built into the institutional structure. Noting that both Riesman and Whyte explain character and values by reference to a special type of economy and its peculiar organization, Lipset points out that British, German, and Swedish societies, with occupational structures roughly equivalent to that of the United States, are not experiencing other-directedness.

Concluding his commentary on the role of persistent values in American society, Lipset points to earlier analysts' tendency to alternate their emphasis on one or the other set of values. In the 1930s social scientists emphasized the decline in equality, the growth of monopoly capitalism, and the calcification of rigid status lines based on inherited wealth. Two decades later social scientists pointed to the excesses of conformist egalitarianism, the rise of monotonous team efforts, and the decline of individual achievement. To Lipset these alternations in pessimistic analyses, pointing now to the decline of achievement and then to the decline of egalitarianism, are signs of the basic tendency of American society to check excesses in its own values. Social equilibrium is accomplished through reciprocal limitations exerted by achievement orientations on the one side and egalitarian strivings on the other.

Turning to the sphere of religious values, Lipset challenges those who argue that religions in America have become more this-worldly and secular.[22] In response Lipset asserts the primacy and priority of original American religious values. The supposedly new tendencies have always been here, argues Lipset, allowing religious institutions to adjust to changes in the size and scope of the nation and to vary in accordance with the alternating emphases in American values.

Lipset points out that the characteristic features in American religious values have been secularism and voluntarism. Secularism is not a recent tendency among American religions. Rather, it is a preëminent feature of higher-status religions, such as Episcopalianism, Congregationalism, and Unitarianism, while orthodoxy and fundamentalism have characterized the religions of low-status groups. What appears to be a trend toward secularization is in fact a specific expression of general upward mobility. On the other hand sectarian developments in American religion are expressions of the presence of economically and socially depressed strata whose theological beliefs deprecate wealth and ostentation. American varieties of religious expression are, thus, further evidence of "the conformist propensity of democratic man."

Religion, observes Lipset, has taken the form of a voluntary association in the United States. The separation of church and state forced religious bodies to compete with other kinds of associations for an individual's allegiance and faith. In turn, the need to capture the interest of congregational followings led to more democracy in the churches and presbyteries and the election of the laity to church-related administrative posts. Finally, Lipset argues that disestablishment encourages a religious and moralistic fervor in American politics. Illustrative of this phenomenon are the movements for restriction of Catholicism, abolition of slavery, temperance, prohibition, and the crusades against Communism. If these movements stem from the "need to assuage a sense of personal responsibility"—one of the basic ideals derivative from Protestantism—the religious support for equality of opportunity and achievement arises from the Arminian[23] emphasis on the personal attainment of grace. In all of this Lipset sees democratic values continuing to affect the development of religious institutions in America.

According to Lipset, achievement and equality also explain the conflicts between labor and capital and the aggravation of crime. Business institutions reflect the achievement orientation, but so does crime. Lipset accepts the view that crime, as Daniel Bell has argued, is "a queer ladder of social mobility," appealing to those individuals and groups who, unable or unwilling to accept the work ethic associated with achievement, nevertheless select a less honorable way to the same goal.[24] If business and crime enshrine the value of achievement for Lipset, trade unionism has institutionalized equality. Lipset makes this statement without any reference to the long history of trade-union hostility to blacks, Chinese, Japanese, and other nonwhite or non-Anglo workers in America.[25] But even in the supposedly democratic labor movement, the paradoxes of the achievement ethic serve to impress a more conservative orientation on union administration, while its aggressive egalitarianism galvanizes militant opposition to status and class differentials. Unions are organized along the same bureaucratic principles as business; yet strikes sometimes escalate into protracted struggles that indicate neither a sense of subordination to management nor a willingness to concede any other form of status inequality. Lipset also suggests that the decentralization of labor-union administration reflects the model of America's federal system. Ultimately he concludes: "Thus in its decentralization, as in its conservative politics and militant strike tactics, the American union may be viewed as an outgrowth of the American social and American value system."

The structural-functional approach, in the hands of an able and perceptive sociologist such as Lipset, promises to explain all variations, changes, and eruptions in American society by reference to the complex dialectical operation of its value system. This system is said to persist through a constant but precarious balancing of contradictory values embedded in a network of interlocking institutions. However, as race inequalities persist, students revolt, and, finally, after Watergate challenged the optimistic vision of progressive development, the structural-functionalists are at greater and greater pains to account for these apparently discrepant events within the framework of systemic stability that should persist in the midst of these changes. If we continue to examine the works of Seymour Martin Lipset we will see that the excess of disturbing changes begins to overflow the theoretical boundaries which are expected to contain it.

THE BLACK AMERICAN IN LIPSET'S POLITICAL SOCIOLOGY[26]

Lipset claims that equality manifests itself in the mutual respect that Americans have for one another. The other-directedness of Americans, flattery, the use of first names among people who hardly know each other or are in a superior-subordinate relation, and the elaborate efforts to avoid hurting the feelings of others reflect the value that all men and women should respect one another. Thus Lipset assigns equality to the arena of interpersonal relationships rather than to economic, political, or social institutions. To Americans, equality implies an emancipation from any system of fixed statuses; it is linked to the value of achievement through the demand for a system of opportunities open to every individual on the basis of talent.

However, the condition of blacks in America appears to confound this sanguine picture. Lipset writes: "American egalitarianism is, of course, for white men only. The treatment of the Negro makes a mockery of this value now as it has in the past." Nevertheless, although Lipset believes the race question is extremely difficult to solve, he is not without hope: "Gunnar Myrdal has convincingly demonstrated in his *An American Dilemma* [that] the American Creed is on the side of the Negro and even men who have strong prejudices against Negroes must assent publicly to their rights."

Hope for the Negro is severely chastened, however, by Lipset's assertions that "the poison of anti-Negro prejudice is a part of American culture, and almost all white Americans have it, to a greater or lesser degree," and that the Negro's problem is more difficult to solve than that of immigrant groups. Writing in 1963 Lipset was less than optimistic. The mere extension of egalitarian practices will not aid blacks. "Perhaps the most important fact to recognize about the current situation of the American Negro," Lipset writes, "is that *equality is not enough to assure his movement into the larger society.*" The legacy of slavery and the less-than-equal treatment of blacks since 1865 have impaired Negroes' capacity to achieve in a suddenly opened market of opportunities or to benefit immediately and significantly from a recently desegregated school system. In order to break the vicious circle of discrimination, deprivation, and demoralization, Lipset argues, "it is necessary to treat the Negro *more than equally,* to spend more money rather than equal amounts for Negro education, to have smaller classes with better teachers in predominantly Negro schools, to enlarge the scope of counseling and recreation facilities available for Negro youth, and the like."

However, Lipset's earlier comments on the balancing of tendencies toward excessive achievement or superfluous egalitarianism would seem to suggest that a move to treat the Negro more than equally would be met by a backlash. Although he does not in fact say so, his subsequent discussion hints at the enormous obstacles to the solution that he has proposed. For the achievement of more-than-equal treatment, Lipset insists, "white Americans today should be prepared to assume responsibility for the educational and economic development of the descendants of those whom earlier white Americans dragooned from Africa to serve them as slaves." But Lipset is only exhortative at this point. Predictions about ultimate equality cannot be made. Instead, a plaintive plea and a peculiarly misplaced observation about the American image abroad follows: "Unless whites are willing to take up their cause in order to force politicians, businessmen, labor organizations, and other relevant groups to support the necessary measures, Negro inequality will remain a blot on the American claim to be democratic and will prevent foreigners from recognizing how real and significant is the national commitment to equalitarianism, as is evidenced in other spheres of American life." While American democracy is stabilized by the shifting balance of achievement and equality, Lipset's solution to the race question requires an *unbalancing* of that system. Although such an imbalance is not impossible, Lipset's *general* systemic analysis would seem to argue that it is not only improbable but also dangerous. Lipset's plea for guilt-directed altruism and his appeal to the sentiments that whites *ought* to feel, while admirable, suggest that the limits of his approach have been passed when he attempts systemic analysis of the race question.

With his recognition that a meritocratic system based on universal education and equality of opportunity is quite likely to produce losers as well as winners in the competition for status advantages, Lipset, writing a decade later, suggests that a demand for equality of result might replace that for equality of opportunity among rising but not yet rewarded minorities.[27] Such a demand is, according to Lipset, not unlike that goal of the old European Communist movement, and thus outside the bounds of balanced values in America. Yet goals which are outside the value boundaries are apparently not outside the demands of American minorities. The value system seems to be vulnerable to nonsystemic elements. Lipset does take considerable comfort from the statistical fact that in 1973 "For the first time the percent of black Americans of college age entering an institution of higher education is identical with the proportion of comparably aged white youth." This certainly does not meet Lipset's earlier requirement of more-than-equal treatment.

Lipset's discussion of the American stratification system in general and the race issue in particular strains his explanatory scheme almost to the breaking point. Despite all of his qualifications and his genuine sympathy with the plight of America's blacks, Lipset wishes to retain his model and image of American society as one that originated in equality and achievement and is dedicated to the ultimate realization of these ideals through the mechanism of its own systemically balanced tendencies. The strategies Lipset employs to keep his model together are most adroit. First, he separates his analysis of the black problem from the central thesis of *The First New Nation* by placing it in an epilogue entitled "Some Personal Views on Equality, Inequality, and

Comparative Analysis." The designation of this excursus as "personal," its compartmentalization away from his general and more sanguine discussion, and the remarkable harshness of his indictment of inequality indicates that he distinguishes the race problem as an exception to the otherwise model democracy he attributes to the United States. Second, the emphasis on the recent educational breakthrough of blacks in his later analysis, together with his careful qualifications about the insufficiencies of education, the threat of older alien norms of equality, and the dysfunctions of meritocratic systems suggests that the "exceptional" nature of the race question is temporary and that it too can be "absorbed" by a dynamically equilibrating social system. By not closing his eyes to the imperfections and inequalities in the system, Lipset has proved to be one of the most perceptive and passionate critics of the social system he champions. By forcing his materials into the systemic mold, however, he unwittingly illustrates not only the weakness of its institutional structures but also, and perhaps in the long run more significantly, the debility of its heuristic value for social science.

THE REVOLT OF THE STUDENTS[28]

Similar problems beset Lipset's analysis of the student revolt.[29] As student revolts began to intensify, Lipset modified his view of American society from one which held out a seemingly unlimited future of pendular shifts between egalitarianism and achievement to one which countenanced a fracture in the social system. His argument reassesses the history of American youth and higher education, and points to the boundary-breaking elements that imperil social systems in general and that of the United States in particular.

There is almost no end of causal explanations for the student revolts of the 1960s.[30] Among the "motivating forces" for student unrest in the sixties, Lipset is able to enumerate no less than nine; while among the "facilitating factors" he finds five. His comprehensive analysis of these fourteen forces and factors, together with his historical analysis, tends to indicate that a severe strain has long existed on the dynamic equilibria and balance of forces in America. Unintentionally, it also reveals inherent weaknesses in the structural-functional model itself. Although Lipset recognizes the significance of the motivating forces and facilitating factors that make up the causal complex for student revolts, he places greater emphasis on those that are more specific and directly related to campus unrest (such as the marginal status of students, the demands of youth culture, the roles of university and faculty) than on those which are so broad and vague as to be incapable of explaining the student revolts (such as rapid rates of social change, a factor which might be used to explain all manner of events). Similarly, when analyzing the five facilitating factors—low commitment of youth; the fact that most college youth are not yet linked to a job, occupation, or career; the fact that most college youth have fewer responsibilities than parents, workers, or their age-peers not enrolled in college; the peculiar opportunity that a campus provides for mobilizing a social movement; and the significance of current events for arousing the interest, consciousness, and conscience of young people—Lipset regards all but the last as permanent features that, alone, cannot explain the sudden explosion in college campuses across the nation.

Historical study, as Lipset shows, reveals that campus unrest and student revolts are not new in the United States. Rather, it would appear that the peaceful period of the 1950s—that very period when some sociologists proclaimed the end of ideology, the rise of other-directed and organization men, and the triumph of liberal elements and middle classes—was a remarkable exception to the general history of university life in the United States. The events of the 1960s, the civil rights movement, the Vietnam War, and the growing sense of helplessness of both people and institutions to advance the former and halt the latter, mobilized college youth to return to positions similar to those held by students in earlier periods of American history.

Lipset's perception of the fragile structure of the American social and political system reveals itself in his predictions about the immediate future. Whatever the resiliency and potency of social systems in general, whatever tensile strength still exists in a system marked at one time by pushes toward equality and at another by pulls toward achievement, the American social system might crack if it cannot find a way to accommodate itself to the demands of radical and liberal student activists. As Lipset put it in 1972: "As in the case of earlier protest and radical movements, the extent to which such groups accommodate to the rules of the game of a democratic political system will depend on how responsive the system seems to be, or as the radicals would put it, how successful it is in coopting protest." The boundaries of systems now seem more like dams holding water under pressure. So long as pressure releases are functioning properly—that is, so long as the system responds effectively to the demands made upon it—the walls will hold. But should the releases break down or function ineffectively, the agitated waters—that is, the restive elements in the population—might push against the walls until they crack or crumble.

By the time the student revolts had run their course, Lipset had

lost more than his faith in the unwavering dynamic progressivism
of American society. The events of a decade had nearly smashed the
model American society he had espoused in 1963. Even more serious,
however, his belief in both the comprehensive and predictive capacities
of the social sciences had been chastened as well: "The brief look presented here into the history of campus-related unrest and protest,"
writes Lipset, "should force us to be humble both about our ability to
understand and to predict waves of discontent." Lipset had at last recognized that students—an inherently unstable and disturbing element—
had to be admitted into the American social system. Apprehensively he
concluded, "But whatever the future of the current wave, this American
record does lend support to those explanations which stress the inherent
potential of students as the most available social base for innovative
forms of cultural behavior and aggressive political action dedicated to
the attainment of 'absolute ends.' It reinforces the conclusion that the
student population is the most volatile and most easily mobilized of all
social strata."

WATERGATE

According to Lipset and his collaborator Earl Raab, the United
States had an "appointment with Watergate."[31] The statement is more
than a mere literary allusion to the "Appointment in Samarra." Just as
death awaits the Oriental servant in the famous tale no matter how he
tries to avoid it, so also Watergate becomes the inevitable outcome of
certain ineluctable processes. Watergate, Lipset and Raab tell us, despite
its own unique aspects, is but the latest episode in a drama that has been
played out regularly in America since 1799. It is one more example of
the apparently perennial paranoid style in American politics.[32] The decade of the 1920s, which, according to Lipset and Raab, "was not only
typical of such episodes in American history but also had a direct relationship to current events," was characterized by the widespread belief
that Catholics and Jews dominated America's cities, displacing rural and
more fundamentalist Protestants. This belief led to a backlash and to
"severe violations of democratic procedure," including a new restrictive
and racist immigration law, the establishment of a General Intelligence
Division in the Attorney General's office, illegal raids and arrests by the
Justice Department, and numerous state and local witch hunts against
suspected radicals, bohemians, prostitutes, and others thought to be
violating moral codes. Noticeably absent in this version of Lipset's
analysis is an argument that the backlash of the 1920s was a rebalancing

of the value emphasis from equality to achievement, and thus part of what might be the expected dynamic of the American social system. Instead, equality and achievement go unmentioned, while provincialism and cosmopolitanism are presented as the paired but opposed elements in the formula that leads to backlash and, ultimately, to Watergate.

According to Lipset and Raab, the provincial-cosmopolitan dichotomy found a locus for joint representation in the public persona of Richard Nixon. As a provincial, he had grown up in the rustic and reactionary backwaters of California, employed the appropriately extremist conspiratorial charges against his earlier political opponents, Jerry Voorhis and Helen Gahagan Douglas, and conspicuously distinguished himself in the anticommunist crusade of the 1950s by a dogged pursuit of Alger Hiss. As a cosmopolitan, on the other hand, Nixon supported internationalism, identified himself with eastern establishment Republicans, orchestrated the Eisenhower administration's suppression of Senator Joseph McCarthy, and opposed far-right orientations for the Republican party. Nixon thus appeared as a complex political ambiguity. By 1968, Nixon, as Lipset and Raab see it, was regarded variously as a perhaps reclaimable member of the communion of backlash ideologues or as a suspect but nevertheless possibly enlightened and re-educated cosmopolitan. To Lipset and Raab—as later and explicitly to Theodore H. White[33]—the cosmopolitan and internationalist Nixon appears as a kind of Dr. Jekyll of dynamic and progressive America, while the provincial ideologue of right-wing backlash is its dysfunctional Mr. Hyde. Watergate was to reveal that the evil and dysfunctional Hyde-Nixon had not been exorcised by several years in the cosmopolitan Senate and two terms in the internationalist vice-presidency.

To Lipset and Raab, Watergate is the extension of the conspiratorial paranoid style of American politics from American backwaters to the White House. They take seriously the statements of Magruder, Dean, Huston, and Mitchell that Nixon and his colleagues acted as they did out of a sincere reaction to "all those activities of the late 1960s ticked off by the Watergate witnesses: disruptive demonstrations, riots, violence, bombings, flag-burnings, civil disobedience." Like the moralists of the 1920s who bitterly resented the looser morals, alcoholic excesses, and revealing clothing of the newly emergent urban cosmopolitans, the Watergate conspirators represented all those who were appalled by the drug, sex, and student revolutions, and resentful of the fact that the United States with all its might could not "defeat a small and underdeveloped Communist enemy in Southeast Asia." In behalf of these beliefs Nixon and his cohorts embarked on a massive attempt to reorganize the security, intelligence, and surveillance apparatuses of the United States and committed a number of illegal, extralegal, and improper acts. Yet Lipset and Raab observe that Watergate was a "pale

and tepid . . . expression of extremist action." The "plumbers" operation "was neither massive nor very efficient"; the burglars were remarkably inept and found nothing; the enemies' lists were used ineffectively
or not at all; the wrong phones were bugged; the use of the IRS to ha-
rass opponents was not impressive; and the general atmosphere created
by the Nixon administration did not "chill" speech or action. Nevertheless, Lipset and Raab assert, the seriousness of Watergate is not mini-
mized by its ineptitude. Most significant, and unlike the backlash demagogues of the 1920s, the Watergate conspirators acted in secret. The
secrecy, and especially the cover-up, are, according to Lipset and Raab,
"a measure of the restraining power of the cosmopolitan climate not
only within the administration but in the nation at large—in, that is, the
growing cosmopolitanization of the American people."

Lipset's and Raab's contention is that secrecy became the mode of
Watergate operations because the emergence of a more cosmopolitan
nation forbade open activities that would have resonated with the more
provincial outlook of Americans a half century ago. In support of their
belief that cosmopolitanization is on the upsurge, Lipset and Raab point
to the fact that American public leaders no longer express themselves in
racist terms, that anti-communist rhetoric no longer arouses uncritical
fervor, and that internationalism and détente have been accepted by
most Americans. However, the linkages of Watergate to backlash politics and Watergate secrecy to growing cosmopolitanism are tenuous.
Certainly Lipset and Raab have not provided what a serious social scientist would accept as evidence of this thesis. Rather, all the characteristic
features of functionalist historicism are pressed into service to show that
Watergate was the inevitable outcome of certain contradictory operations in the American value system. A conjectural history of these
operations is presented, the logic of Nixon's election and its aftermath is
linked to a chain of developments, and, in conclusion, exhortative messages tell us what is necessary to forestall another such debacle. Lipset's
system is now very loosely structured, but, although he will not admit
it, his analysis suggests that America as a social system is coming apart
at the seams.

POLITICAL SOCIOLOGY
IN THE CONTEXT OF AMERICAN SOCIETY

"Begin with an individual, and before you know it you find that
you have created a type; begin with a type, and you find that you have

created—nothing." F. Scott Fitzgerald's perceptive comment provides a pertinent epigraph to a critique of Lipset's sociology. Precisely because it proceeds from a point of view of a formal type, a totally integrated social system, Lipset's analysis of American society cannot contain the irruptive events and innovative institutions that actually mark its history. The essence of systemic dynamics is the absorptive and integrating process. The facts of recent history, however, suggest that absorption and integration are not occurring, that social classes, ethnic groups, and voluntary associations move in a manner not decipherable by a system model, and that supposedly democratic governments proceed in ways not anticipated by societal values or public purposes. In short, the much vaunted homogeneous cosmopolitan American system is a utopia from which sociological theory must be liberated.

Lipset is part of a long tradition in sociology when he suggests that cosmopolitanization will ultimately supersede local, ethnic, and fundamentalist loyalties. Lester Ward pinned his hopes for the good society on the ultimate emergence of a raceless, classless cosmopolis. Robert Park thought he saw the clearing of societal decks for an ultimate class struggle in the workings of his "race relations cycle." And Gunnar Myrdal was sure that the advance of the American creed of democracy and equality would be assured as its "higher" value overcame the parochialism of race prejudice. Yet the virulence of white-backlash eruptions and the rise of ethnic, racial, and other nativistic movements in America in the 1960s should chasten confidence in these evolutionary predictions. Perhaps nativism and ethnic revivalism are not predecessors but successors to economic and social mobility. Such a view, so uncongenial to assimilation-oriented sociologists, was at one time advanced by Gustav Ratzenhofer. Noting that immigrants to America tended at first to abandon their mother tongues in favor of the practical necessities favoring English, Ratzenhofer suggested:

> But the time will come when the population will have become dense. The struggle for existence will have to be more carefully planned. Then the people of America will be forced to stop and reflect. There will be need of attaching themselves to the several political groups into which their individual interests naturally divide them, in order to gain the reinforcement of the group interest for each one's individual interest. When that situation comes about, the memory of racial extraction may at last be reawakened. The different languages may become the rallying centers for the different interests. Thereupon for the first time will America confront decisively the problem of its national unity.[34]

In light of the unmistakable operations of Hansen's Law of "third generation return" among the grandchildren of America's immigrants, the demand for ethnic studies in the curriculum, the recent acquiescence of the Supreme Court to bilingual education in elementary and secondary schools, and the efflorescence of racial, ethnic, and national consciousness among blacks, Asians, Amerindians, and the Aztecas del norte,[35] it would appear that the decisive confrontation that Ratzenhofer predicted is at hand.

Students of American social order have usually been overpessimistic about the effects of rising national, ethnic, and racial solidarity. However, once the homogeneous society is perceived as a particular kind of utopia, sociological attention might be turned to the actual processes and institutional arrangements that prevail in a pluralistic society. Central to such an analysis should be a revival of that concern which Ratzenhofer and Albion W. Small placed at the center of their sociology—*interest*.[36] Interest is not confined to the narrow pecuniary range described by Manchester liberalism; it includes transcendental, national, creedal, class, racial, ethnic, corporate, social, and personal concerns. Interest groups meet in an imperfect marketplace—the *polis*—where they compete, cooperate, coordinate, coerce, or coalesce with one another. As various groups form, reform, dissolve, and fuse, certain interests are emphasized, others neglected, still others forgotten altogether.[37] Moreover, the state, as an expression of a prevailing coalition of powerful interests, is in a position to encourage the development or disregard of interests and the formation or dissolution of interest groups.

The relation of interests to values is quite complex, but it is essentially rhetorical. The values provide accounts—excuses and justifications—that interest-group leaders give to exculpate their actions.[38] However, precisely because acculturation is not complete and certain corporate and social groups adhere to values other than those that enjoy official support, the accounts are not always coordinated or even efficacious. Conflicts arise out of the nonreciprocal "rights" that each group can claim for itself or against the others. Accommodation is possible, but not necessarily likely, because the values permit a wide latitude of interpretation and because rhetorical legerdemain becomes a prized skill among interest-group leaders and intergroup brokers.[39] The Watergate conspirators, to take a pertinent example, appealed to preservationist ethics and what they hoped was a belief in a vague but powerful danger to national security. Such rhetorical flourishes are more than exercises in account structuring. They are the stuff of politics in a plural society.

"The state," wrote Albion W. Small, "is an arrangement of combinations by which mutually repellent forces are brought into some measure of concurrent action."[40] But, one must ask, how is legitimate rule possible? Conventional meritocratic pluralists, as Kingsley Davis has pointed out,[41] have a most utopian answer to this question. Insisting on the positive functions that arise from the preservation of both group-organized ascriptive solidarities and a free and multifaceted sociopolitical marketplace of voluntary associations, they appear to rely on a *genius loci,* nowhere guaranteed by the system, to preserve balance and insure the production of the public good. Lipset's political sociology is a special case in point. To put it in dramaturgical terms, Lipset has peopled America with puppets and presented American history as a puppet show. The ordinary member of a polity is conceived almost exclusively in his capacity as, respectively, a voter, a respondent to public-opinion polls, or a victim of the *voces populi.* The politician in a democratic society is a representative of voters and polled opinions. All are creatures on a string, or rather, on a number of strings, propelled into political participation by pressures. These pressure-strings in turn are moved by the basic mechanisms to which they are attached—class, ethnic, racial, age, and sex groupings. Everywhere there are strings—pulling, pushing, crisscrossing one another in an attempt to move political man in their own way.

Who operates the strings? In Lipset's sociology, there are two distinct but related answers to this question. Quite obviously what order there is must be obtained at the outset from the balance of thrusts and counterthrusts of the several invisible pressures. Hence the Punch and Judy aspect of Lipset's political drama: As Punch goes too far, Judy counterpunches with a frying pan on his head, hard enough to knock him down but not out. Lash and backlash—for example, the pendulum swings of equality (Punch) and achievement (Judy) keep one another in line. But this internal order requires that neither Punch nor Judy will go too far. However, as Lipset shows, each sometimes—in fact, often—does just that. How can order be kept if Punch overwhelms Judy, or Judy hits Punch too hard? Enter Lipset. Like a technical consultant, he advises the actors to reduce the invective and armament that each employs against the other, and warns against future failures to act according to the script. In brief, the puppet-show dramaturgy of structural-functionalism is possible because this kind of sociology permits neither the humanistic individual nor the self-correcting group to be the center or the source of political orientations. Instead, in Lipset's perspective, individuals and the groups to which they belong are creatures of sociological habit. The immediate milieux—represented in age, sex, race, religion, nationality, ethnicity, social class—provide pushes, pressures, and pulls and also give off an illusion of self-control. The concept of society composed of self-correcting and shifting interest groups and formations, however, would suggest that the sociologist look not for a fixed source of legitimacy, consensus, and order but rather for the temporary constellation of coordinate interests that, at any one moment, permits a sense of stability and routine to prevail. An interesting and complex example is that presented by Bensman and Vidich[42] in their examination of the new middle classes in post–New Deal America. Hoisted by the government's largesse to new positions of more than modest status, institutional control, and relative ease and comfort, they form a dense and variegated mesh of common interests. Yet they find it less than easy to countenance the insistent demands, moral imprecations, and loose and exotic lifestyles of their own children. Although they use the language of systemic thinking, Bensman and Vidich portray an America that experiences waves of revolution, revolt, and revaluation, that is dynamically pluralistic in its structure, and that cannot be guaranteed to always promote a neat and proper balance among contending forces.

Everett Hughes once wrote: "Almost every group which has a specialized social function to perform is in some measure a secret society, with a body of rules developed and enforced by the members and with some power to save its members from outside punishment."[43] The presidency and administration of the United States certainly is one such group. The revelations of Watergate have sparked a retrospective review of previous presidencies, with the discovery, embarrassing to those who hoped that Nixonian "exceptionalism" would prove the case for a more general American administrative morality, that so-called good presidents also engaged in or at least contemplated letting their subordinates carry out all manner of dirty work—assassinations, burglaries, hallucinogenic experiments on soldiers and scientists, and interception of the mails. Dirty work would seem to be the stock-in-trade of bureaucracies, whether they are political, economic, educational, or religious. And secrecy is the cloak that covers these evils, that allows public appearances to be believed to represent backstage workings. Lipset and Raab attribute the secrecy surrounding Watergate to a healthy rise in cosmopolitanism. It might better be credited to the routine manner in which bureaucrats usually function. The Watergate conspirators were virtuous, impeccable Christian Scientists recruited from the major advertising agencies and from Disneyland. No better representatives of those who understand how the manipulation of front hides the skulduggery of the back could be found. And the actual doers of the foul deeds—the burglars, would-be bombers, and bagmen—came from among those same elements in society that in another time and another place provided the low level *fonctionnaires* for Hitler's concentration camps. At each level of action interests were served, accounts provided, secrecy almost assured.

If good people and dirty work go together in bureaucratic structures, is Watergate and its aftermath a watershed in American political development? Probably not. Secrecy only appears to be on the decline, the successor president basks in the carefully adorned rays of what seems to be an open administration, and conservatism and its anti-welfare bias are on the upswing. Perhaps a clue to one of the many forms of secrecy that are yet available to any modern administration is the contracting system revealed in previous administrations' dealings with the Mafia. As a loosely structured confederation of gangs holding varying degrees of economic and political power in regions in and outside the United States, the Mafia is in a good position to accept an American presidential administration as one of its clients. Indeed, the decentralization and farming out of nefarious projects may be the newest development in Federal bureaucratic management. Once we understand that politics is the continuation of interest conflicts and crimes by another name, we can begin to imagine the possibilities.

Hughes's suggestion that we examine "the character of the leadership group" leads to some final thoughts on Watergate. The essence of Watergate is the covert criminal practices of a political group that had already achieved power. The actual activities—burglaries, bribery, subornation of perjury, misprision of felony—were carried out by persons who had also at least considered other and more venal crimes. Although at the level of the actual dirty work the motivations of the perpetrators would appear to support elements and strands of the backlash theory offered by Lipset, it is questionable whether these same motivations are also applicable at the level of executive planning and conspiracy. It is doubtful whether we shall ever obtain an accurate statement of the real intentions of Watergate's originators. Nevertheless, their political character is perhaps comprehensible. Nixon's administration did proclaim a hatred of "effete intellectual snobs," war resisters, and counterculture groups. Elected by such a landslide that they could claim a mandate, Nixon and his cohorts utilized that fact to increase their civil and legal distance from the electorate. Developing the power and maximizing the discipline of their own inner circle, Nixon and his fellow planners dissociated themselves from the rules of political conduct expected from men of their station. The Nixon apparatus included circles within circles of conspiratorial actors. The circles struggled with one another for power in the regime. At the center was the corps of planners and executives who plotted what to do and how to cover it up. Believing because of its mandate that it was *the* agency of the state and above and beyond all danger of interference and surveillance, the inner circle almost succeeded in monopolizing control over the investigation of its own malfeasances in office. Secrecy was of the essence—the secret of its real aims, of its methods, of the cover-up of both—and the conspirators attempted to wield the instrumentalities of domestic administration and foreign policy to carry out and cloak their aims with impunity. Government by secrecy is not new, but the recognition that secrecy and dirty work are an inherent part of governments of any kind may be. Recognizing that democratic regimes also burgle, bribe, trespass, and kill without license or right speaks volumes not only to a reconsideration of the philosophy of governance but also toward a revision of the sociology of public administration.

CONCLUSION

Ironically, it is Lipset's own analyses that do so much to expose the weaknesses in "the first new nation" and indicate how precarious is its "stability in the midst of change." The events of recent history that he has so painstakingly researched suggest that American society is far more unstable and much less secure than the society *manqué* described by a model social system. Structural-functional analysis requires the transposition of events into processes—a most difficult task under the best circumstances. The events that Lipset chose to study—racist acts, student revolts, presidential crimes—do not lend themselves to easy translation. As examples of balanced processes, equality and achievement, or provincialism and cosmopolitanism, they seem contrived.

Is there an alternative view? Perhaps. Let us begin with values. Elsewhere I have suggested that racism—the idea that one's membership in an involuntary hereditary aggregate, a "race," is a reasonable criterion to take into account in the political, economic, educational, religious, social, and personal organization of a society—is a value that became embedded in post–sixteenth-century Euro-American social organization.[44] The historical evidence that would support this thesis is being adduced more and more.[45] Of course, racism had to compete with other values that contradicted it—among these, the enlightenment values of equality, achievement, and democracy. And such competition lent itself to the rhetorical and political expression of all value commitments in the social construction of ideologies, utopias, reactions, reforms, and rebellions. Various groups could lay claim to valuable societal resources by couching their appeals in the language of one or another or some combination of these values. Moreover, unscrupulous groups, including the Watergate conspirators, could justify their unlawful acts, and cloak the real reasons they undertook them, by appealing to threats to the value system. A structure of competing and contradictory values has a certain free-floating quality about it. This quality, in turn, lends itself to group efforts to capture, monopolize, and attain mastery over the entire social organization. Totalitarianism is a possible but not necessarily likely outcome of these efforts.

Does a structure of values necessarily imply a social system? I think not. Reflecting upon Watergate, Theodore H. White found it necessary to answer the question of whether there was an American system. Ultimately he concluded that there was no single, coherent, and interlocking system:

> . . . I began to see that there was no such thing as "a system." The central armature of government was the Federal state; and about this state and within it circled many "systems," all of them attempting to sway the state, move it, bend it to their purpose, or wall themselves off from its interference.[46]

White's discovery echoes the recent analysis of American society by Jack Douglas. Douglas rejects the thesis that American society is a social system. Rather, he suggests it is a dense, dynamic, and shifting complex of pluralities better designated a social conglomerate,[47] an organization of units that are to varying degrees integrated within themselves and yet not completely independent of one another.

The idea of America as a social conglomerate is perfectly compatible with an overarching structure of values. The latter serve as dramatic devices, rhetorics of competition, preservation, complaint, and legitimation as social groups struggle for moral and material goods.[48] However, it must not be assumed that groups have internalized these values or that they adhere to them without reservation and qualifications. For the sociologist, acculturation needs to be demonstrated in the face of powerful group pressures against it. Moreover, some groups—indeed, perhaps most—will find ways to enjoy and exploit the "cognitive dissonance" that is supposed to prevail when individuals and groups simultaneously countenance contradictory ideas. Finally, it should be noted that groups will form, dissolve, and re-establish themselves in different form or with different aims and procedures as occasion, chance, opportunity, or desperation demands.[49] The contents of the conglomerate are not stable; its structure is dictated by the relations among units that happen to prevail at any moment.

Lipset's analysis of American society as a social system is both a testimony to the imagination and a signification of the failure of the predominant sociological paradigm. Yet, despite its faults, it has located a number of sensitive issues for discussion, attempted a form of comparative and historical sociology, and displayed a passionate regard for the procedures and problems involved in maintaining a just and rational social democracy. Its ultimate problem is conceptual and rooted at the base of sociological theorizing. Commitment to the structural-functional model foils any attempt to come to grips with the crucial happenings and decisive events that shape and modify society. Since the teleological underpinnings of the model assure a strain toward homeostasis and equilibrium, the actual occurrences must be pressed to produce stability in the midst of change. What happened to Lipset's analysis of America is bound to happen to any analysis—regardless of ideological content—that adopts the structural-functional mode: it is undone by its own data.

Only a fundamental paradigmatic shift will prevent sociologists from remaining mired in the systemic morass. As a first step toward this shift, sociologists should abandon the social-system approach, resist the modern revivals of organic and mechanistic analogies, and eschew the uncritical acceptance of developmentalist orientations toward change. All of this has been said before and with much greater vigor and critical discussion. Unfortunately, "systems," "functions," and "evolution of societies" persist as familiar conceptualizations of both radical and conventional sociology, East and West.

Symbolic Interactionism and Macrosociology

Herbert Blumer died on April 13, 1987. Ten months earlier the University of California Press reissued in cloth and paper editions the work reviewed here.* It had originally been published in 1969 by Prentice-Hall, Inc. The republication constitutes a recognition of the intellectual significance of Blumer's contribution to sociological theory and method. Yet, despite the many honors accorded to Professor Blumer during his long career—culminating in the American Sociological Association's recognition of his lifetime of distinguished scholarly and professional service—his perspective has been misunderstood and maligned. His posthumous status remains what it was during his lifetime—a lone voice crying for sensibility in the wilderness of the ever-enlarging array of sociological factitiousness.

Consider what one leading sociologist has said about Blumer's basic outlook. Lewis Coser wrote in 1976:

> Blumer and his cothinkers wish, in fact, to teach a lesson of humility to the sociological theorist, who is seen as incapable of constructing enduring, objective, theoretical structures, but who must, in their view, be attentive to the subjective interpretations, the definitions of the situations, and the emergent meanings that arise in human interaction and be content with that. Needless to say, though functionalists have availed themselves of many particular insights provided by Mead and his successors in the elucidation of social-psychological processes, they have rejected, as a kind of scientific Luddism, the extreme idiographic and antitheoretical bias inherent in symbolic interactionism. They, as well as other critics, have as-

---

*Herbert Blumer, *Symbolic Interactionism: Perspective and Method* (Berkeley: University of California Press, 1986).

serted that this orientation prevents the understanding of social structures and their constraining characteristics or of patterns of human organization such as class hierarchies or power constellations.[1]

Coser's "extremely negative comments," as Eugene Rochberg-Halton[2] has recently designated them, form a polemical summation of the criticism that has been directed at Blumer in particular and symbolic interactionism in general for the past half-century. It is, of course, the usual last resort of functionalists and positivists to charge their opponents with subjectivism, lack of objectivity, and an antitheoretical bias. But Coser goes further, making of Blumer's many critical sallies against the perspectival positions taken by Parsons, Merton, and Lundberg (who also disagreed with one another on many matters, both theoretical and methodological) a species of mindless destructiveness, "scientific Luddism," aimed at bringing down the entire sociological enterprise. No careful reader of Blumer could come to such a conclusion. What we have in Blumer's *oeuvre* is an alternative philosophy of science for sociology, a proposal that sociology, like every other science, be faithful to the nature of its subject matter. That subject matter is the human actor interacting with and interpreting the meaning of the objects and ideas in his environment. As Blumer puts it in the opening essay of *Symbolic Interactionism:*

> The capacity of the human being to make indications to himself gives a distinctive character to human action. It means that the human individual confronts a world that he must interpret in order to act instead of an environment to which he responds because of his organization.[3]

And Blumer goes on to show how and to what extent this perspective differs from that of the several mainstreams that flow in conventional sociology:

> This view of the human being directing his action by making indications to himself stands sharply in contrast to the view of human action that dominates current psychological and social science. This dominant view . . . ascribes human action to an initiating factor or a combination of such factors. Action is traced back to such matters as motives, attitudes, need-dispositions, unconscious complexes, stimuli configurations, status demands, role requirements, and situational demands. . . . Such an approach ignores and makes no place for the process of self-interaction through which the individual notes and assesses what is presented to him and through which he maps out lines of overt behavior prior to their execution.[4]

However, in this reviewer's opinion, it is unnecessary to defend Blumer's philosophy of science against his positivist, functionalist, and behaviorist critics. During his lifetime, he ably gave answers to these men and women of excessive conventional faith. Whether, since his death, his perspective will persevere will depend on the strength and professional influence of his followers and their opponents. Blumer's orientation, properly conceived, is a conflict approach, and its survival, faithful to its intrinsic character, will be determined by the outcome of conflicts that continue to inspire—as well as plague—the discipline.

It is necessary, however, to respond to another aspect of Coser's aspersions on symbolic interaction. Coser has asserted that symbolic interaction is inimical to "the understanding of social structures, and their constraining characteristics," that it eschews analysis of "patterns of human organization such as class hierarchies or power constellations." Simply put, this statement is utterly false, as anyone who cared to inspect the corpus of Blumer's work would readily find out. However, because Coser has seen fit to reiterate his misrepresentation—minus, to be sure, the epithet "scientific Luddism"—in his popular textbook *Masters of Sociological Thought*,[5] it bids fair to become the conventional sociologist's prevailing understanding, the one given to students and other textbook-dependent teachers and researchers. The danger of institutionalizing Coser's view is all the more imminent because Blumer published his empirical studies of power relations, racial hierarchies, industrial conflicts, and other aspects of social structure in foreign and regional journals and in specialized anthologies devoted to specific areas of academic concern or policy interest, while, in the same period, defending the interactionist perspective against its subdisciplinary enemies in such major journals as the *American Sociological Review*. To those who subscribe solely to the major reviews or who suppose that *Symbolic Interactionism: Perspective and Method* contains all of Blumer's most significant writings, it might come as a surprise to learn that he closely analyzed the power relations that prevail in large-scale industrial disputes, that he investigated the bastion-like structures that make up America's complex color line, that he described the hierarchical structure that defines racial prejudice, that he researched comparatively the types of social, racial, and industrial organizations that prevail in the United States, Brazil, and South Africa, that he examined the structural character and social arrangements that set mass society apart from other types, and that he served as the principal investigator of a study of youthful drug abusers. Many of these studies have been collected and will be reprinted as part of a revisionist perspective that conceives of Blumer as contemporary sociology's most important public philosopher.[6]

Armed with the understanding that symbolic interactionism is neither antitheoretical, purely idiographic, inherently subjective, nor confined to microecological investigations, the sharp-eyed reader of

Symbolic Interaction: Perspective and Method can profitably reinspect what Blumer has to say about the very things that Coser says he neglects or opposes. "From the standpoint of symbolic interactionism," Blumer writes, "human group life is a process in which objects are being created, affirmed, transformed, and cast aside."[7] Blumer calls on those who seek to study human group life to describe and theorize about the process that immerses the human individual in the polity—the latter to be understood in the broadest sense. That process finds its locus in the senses of group position to which the individual and the group must address themselves. The world of objects in which individuals and groups must act includes not only the scenes of everyday private life but also the very items of social structure that Coser denies are part of Blumer's perspective: social, economic, and political hierarchies; races, classes, and their conflicts; and, above all, power and resistance.

Rather than being antitheoretical, as Coser would have us believe, Blumer's approach is specifically aimed at theory. Indeed, as Blumer so eloquently put it, much of conventional sociology has abandoned the discipline's original interest in providing an empirically tested theory of social reality in the name of a reified conception of methodology: "Today 'methodology' in the social sciences is regarded with depressing frequency as synonymous with the study of advanced quantitative procedures. . . . Such conceptions are a travesty on methodology as the logical study of the principles underlying the conduct of scientific inquiry."[8] Central to any social scientific inquiry, Blumer reminds us, are: "The Possession and Use of a Prior Picture or Scheme of the Empirical World under Study . . . The Asking of Questions of the Empirical World and the Conversion of the Questions into Problems . . . Determination of the Data to be Sought and the Means to be Employed in Getting the Data . . . Determination of the Relations Between Data . . . Interpretation of the Findings . . . The Use of Concepts."[9] The full range of methodological issues is properly subsumed under these five elementary forms of the sociological enterprise, Blumer insists, but present-day methodologists have eschewed this problem, preferring to cast studies "in terms of quantifiable variables . . . , the use of sophisticated statistical and mathematical techniques, and . . . elegant logical models conforming to special canons of 'research design'."[10] Such an approach places the cart of social reality before the horse of sociological research, loading the former with preconceived theoretical and abstract constructions and then pushing it along with the bridled head of a constricted and muzzled apparatus. "Reality," Blumer points out, "exists in the empirical world and not in the methods used to study that world. . . . Methods are mere instruments designed to identify and analyze the obdurate character of the empirical world, and as such, their value exists only in their suitability in enabling this task to be done."[11]

The empirical world to which Blumer refers is not the world apprehended by self-styled empirical sociologists, who "collect and analyze various kinds of census data, make social surveys, secure declarations from people through questionnaires, use polls, undertake discriminating clinical examination, employ scales and refined measuring instruments, bring social action into controlled laboratory situations, undertake careful computer simulation of social life, and use crucial empirical data to test hypotheses."[12] That so-called empirical world is in fact a hypostasized construct. Actual social reality, the past or present existent empirical world, embraces the "life of human society, or any segment of it, or any organization in it, or of its participants [and] consists of the action and experience of people as they meet the situations that arise in their respective worlds."[13] And, lest anyone suppose, like Coser, that Blumer's idea of social reality eschews such phenomena as class hierarchies or power constellations, observe what is actually written in *Symbolic Interaction: Perspective and Method:* "This empirical world is evidenced, to take a few examples, by what is happening in the life of a boy's gang, or among the top management of an industrial corporation, or in militant racial groups, or among the police confronted by such groups, or among the young people in a country, or among the Catholic clergy, or in the experience of individuals in their different walks of life."[14]

Finally, let us turn to the claim, made by Coser and some others, that symbolic interaction neglects those macrosociological variables that are best researched in accordance with structural-functionalist or, in critical opposition, the largely Marxist-oriented conflict approaches.[15] The fact of the matter is that Blumer addresses precisely the issues that inspired the questions asked by Marx and Weber. However, unlike their contemporary self-designated heirs and epigoni, he does not mistake the topic under scrutiny for the resource used to undertake that scrutiny. Both functionalists and conflict theorists tend to approach their investigations with preconceived conceptualizations. These seem to be empirically grounded; in fact they are vague and indecisive for ordering perceptions but unwarrantedly determinative in the organization and interpretation of data. Such "sociologists," Blumer points out, "ascribe behavior to such factors as social role, status, cultural prescription, norms, values, reference group affiliation, and mechanisms of societal equilibrium."[16] These approaches, Blumer goes on to say, "grossly ignore the fact that social interaction is a formative process in its own right—that people in interaction are not merely giving expression to such determining factors in forming their respective lines of action but are directing, checking, bending, and transforming their lines of action in the light of what they encounter in the actions of others."[17] When the unit under investigation is some corporate body, the methodological

implications of symbolic interaction ought still to prevail. The collectivity, like the individual, is an actor that forges and directs its lines of
action in the face of powerful opponents and potent resistance. However, "in the case of the social action of a . . . business corporation, a
labor union, an army, a church, a boy's gang, or a nation . . . [the] difference is that the collectivity has a directing group or individual who is
empowered to assess the operating situation, to note different things
that have to be dealt with, and to map out a line of action."[18] Power,
authority, and resistance are essential features of Blumer's vision of collective action; the "acting unit is lifted out of a position of being a neutral medium for the play of determining factors and is given the status
of an organizer of its action."[19]

Symbolic interaction conceives the research problem as one requiring an accurate apprehension of what actually occurs in the world
of collective experience. And, as Blumer points out, this is the case in
precisely those arenas of interest to macrosociologists, arenas wherein
the academic researcher is unlikely to have had firsthand experience and
prone to approach the subject with preconceived system- or conflict-
generated revolutionary conceptualizations—"juvenile delinquency, suicide, revolutionary behavior, the behavior of Negro militants, the behavior of right-wing reactionary groups, or what not."[20] However,
in just such experientially unfamiliar but all-too-relevant places of collective activity the symbolic interactionist position calls for suspension
of the conventionally-held sociological theorem that social action be
seen as product of antecedent etiological forces. In place of that hoary
but problematical position, "the methodological position of symbolic
interaction is that social action must be studied in terms of how it is
formed"; for "its formation is a very different matter from the antecedent
conditions that are taken as the 'causes' of the social action."[21] As a social philosophy, symbolic interaction offers a far more humanistic vision of humankind than that of either functionalism or conflict theory.
While not avoiding the issues of power, inequality, resistance, and defeat,
it constantly reminds us of the essential human activity—constructing,
altering, and resisting the architectonics of social reality and responding
to the constructions of others. What Blumer says about the individual
in this regard is also true of the collectivity: "The human being . . . may
do a poor job in constructing his act, but construct it he must."[22]

Contrary to the nay-sayers who wish to confine symbolic interaction to microecological studies or the functionalist and conflict
theorists who patronize it by availing "themselves of many particular
insights provided by Mead and his successors in the elucidation of
social-psychological processes,"[23] Blumer's vision of symbolic interaction embraces the whole of the sociological enterprise. Central to his

concerns are the situations that plague and plunder the social order. Modern societies are particularly subject to these troubles, and, as Blumer noted in a discussion of social unrest and collective protest, in them there "is absent a politically approved code that would allow officials to tolerate unsanctioned forms of collective protest so as to maintain the adversary process and to ward off intensified polarization."[24] For any social scientist concerned with the issues of caste, race, or class conflict; political and business corruption; stratification of peoples, cultures, and status groups; or the social problems of individuals, families, or nations, this perspective provides a fruitful starting point.

The Existential Self

Language and Silence
in the Formation of Human Identity

A risen spirit is haunting American sociology: the self. I say "risen" rather than "new" because the idea and problematics of self are older than the discipline and have affected its development from the beginning. What has revitalized the reappearance of the self is its emancipation from second-class citizenship as a dependent variable, its recognized autonomy as an independent phenomenon of and topic for investigations into the social construction of human relations. The self is now conceived *existentially,* in terms of its contingent, assembled, changeable, and precarious modalities. Autonomy and emancipation entail a reconceptualization of the relationship of the self to mind and society, a rewriting of the hoary thesis that animated the social psychology of the pragmatists and found its near-iconographic expression in the eponymous book of George Herbert Mead, and in the subsequent writings of Mead's colleagues, interpreters, and critics. The existential self is free-floating, or nearly so, like Mannheim's idealized intellectuals who, having been liberated from ideological constraints and utopian fantasies, might construct and reconstruct the world. What happens to thought and to social institutions is, thus, much less determined by external material forces and far more problematic with respect to the positivists' promise of prediction and control than ever before.

How the existential self appears and assembles itself in society is a topic for a new existential sociology. However, that sociology cannot give a closed, determinate and predictive picture of this process or of its product. To do so would violate the very premises of this perspective. Existential sociology is post-positivist and post-functionalist. It leaps beyond the overthrown paradigms that promised sociological seerdom and social scientific hegemony. It returns sociology to an *unprivileged* position in its relation to human activity. Whereas general social science and, more particularly, conventional sociology have opted for its Baconian elevation above the suspect reasoning capacity of ordinary humans,[1] existential sociology follows the admonition of Pico della Mirandola[2] to place the human studies side by side with their subject, sharing the latter's attributes, deriving their concepts from an acceptance of *humans* for what they are and treating sociology as *their* expressions.

It is thus that, for example, in one recent anthology on the existential self we meet characters that are simultaneously familiar and unorthodox, but never "deviant": victims, ex-nuns, homosexuals, wheelchair runners, organization men and women, and a host of secure, insecure, formed, and forming selves in various states of becoming, persevering, transposing, and dying.[3] Because we are all part of this universe, this is but a small segment of the entire population of existential selves. However, small and unrepresentative as it is, it provides a portraiture and a description of some of the most salient processes, dilemmas, conflicts, and contradictions wherein the self participates and observes its own and others' participation. In the existential world we are all simultaneously ethnographers and subjects of ethnography.

This new sociology takes its departure from the uneasy relationship of experience and meaning. The former has the character of being-in-itself, the truly empirical; the latter of being-once-removed. Yet, experience is in and of itself without meaning; it belongs to the world of the absurd. Meaning is given to experience through language. A sociology of the absurd becomes, then, an existential phenomenology, the discipline that examines how the raw experiences of everyday life are socio-linguistically constituted as parts of the ever reconstructed comprehensible world.[4] The land of the absurd is a labyrinthine limbo where few care to live. Language is the Ariadne's thread that winds each Theseus out from the dangers of Minotauran meaninglessness.

The non-absurd world and the existential self are created within the perimeters of time, place, manner, and power. Although seemingly "out there" for each person, each of these is subject to individual and collective interpretation, reconstruction, counterdefinition, and manipulation. Time retains its Augustinian mystery as *duree,* while its man-made forms appear, *inter alia,* as history, evolution, event, memory, term, hours, minutes, seconds, and the terminable or interminable future. The spaces on the earth are *territorialized* through accomplishment of human dominion over them and exist under such forms as established, contested, or soon-to-be-sovereignized regions, states, provinces, or colonies; as places for public or private activity; as interactional or obstructed trajectories of communication; and as what the philosophers call "extension," i.e. nature's construction of the fleshly limit of the human body. That which is peculiarly human has its pristine character, but such is the distinctiveness of each individual's or group's understanding that personality, group identity, idiosyncracy, inheritance, culture, and situation are said to modify—or mollify—its appearance. And, standing over duration, space, and the mannered self is the protean phenomenon of potency, the capacity to secure compliance in the face of resistance. If we were to look for the sociological concept that expresses the unity of time, place, manner, and power within a singular individual or a collective entity of awesome personification we would find it in *charisma,* acting as form and force, the instrumentality of true social *change* rather than mere historical *passage.*[5]

The existential self has something of the character of Simmel's stranger: It is ever with us but mysterious.[6] For some, e.g., "primitive men," its mystery as well as its existence go unnoticed as self remains an undiscovered and inarticulated aspect of collective humanity. One historian of the individual, Colin Morris, speaks of the emergence of self-referencing in the West in the twelfth century, and surely he is right to point to its intimate connection to the European rediscovery of Latinate humanism.[7] But the existential self has earlier origins in Yahwistic religion, as Max Weber's study *Ancient Judaism* certainly suggests, and later development as a consequence of the Protestant ethic.[8] Yahweh was the self-chosen god of the Hebrews, who were admonished to have no other gods before him and to enter into a contract (covenant) with him for mutual benefit. Yahweh and the Hebrews had constantly to work out, reinterpret, and renegotiate the terms of that contract, and the Hebrews were enjoined to open continuous discussions and debates with Yahweh through their representatives, the prophets. The prophets, as Weber pointed out, were not office holders, bureaucrats, or priests; rather, they were the people who lived on the edges of Hebrew civilization, who would assert their authority as negotiators and spokesmen charismatically, and, by this very process, they suggested an individuation of humankind. Moreover, the covenant with Abraham, especially after its renewal with Moses, was one of laws, and it adumbrated a *politicized state* as the appropriate social organization. The search for a Christian *community* of believers conjoined in faith is a later Pauline development, introducing a respecification of the powers of Yahweh and the weakness of man, and requiring a mystifying obscurantism to replace the no longer negotiable terms of human-god relations.[9] When Calvinism reopened the question of faith and fate once again—this time in relation to a god who was declared to be omniscient, omnipotent, and absolutely prescient—humans were left in a fully determined but absolutely incomprehensible world, granted the free will to choose their path but ever ignorant of their ultimate destiny. The recognition of an absurd condition takes its point of departure from the human condition after the Reformation. The Puritans invited each individual to search out a calling by listening to his or her inner voice. Each person was invited to plunge into the unfathomable void of this world, in the hope of obtaining a sign of his or her place in the next.[10]

The existential self is poised precariously between the two philosophies of absurdity that distinguish in opposed argument the relations between world and meaning. For the first, all that exists meaningfully is language, while the world is a dark cave of shadows and appearances; for the second, the world is an obdurate but solid mystery, possessed of its own intrinsic character, while language is a pale and ephemeral producer of its illusions. For humans, then, the future of an illusion also could mean an illusion of the future. The unarticulated and unwritten word might yet be its most potent element; language consists of "language games," as Wittgenstein reminds us.[11] But we are all in what Nietzsche called the prisonhouse of language and cannot escape to the freedom of existence-in-itself.[12] When the epigoni of the Frankfurt School call for a new emancipation of communicative conduct, they do not call for a liberation *from* it.[13] It would appear that we are all Vladimirs and Estragons,[14] living in a Sartrean world from which there is no exit[15]—we cannot depart from our anxiety-provoking waiting room; we endlessly converse while the time for our appointment with Godot seems always to be postponed.

The existential self is also ambiguously located on two of the dualities that derive from the critique of Cartesianism: embodiment-disembodiment and articulation-ineffability. The self seems to be embodied within the anatomical frame that nature has given it. Moreover, the self is said—or desired—to be just that, i.e., singular. For each human there is, supposedly, but one self. However, contained within a body, this self has organic characteristics. It evolves, develops, grows. And it separates its essence from its appearance. A single body for each human might seem to require a single embodied self, but there are inherent problems arising out of this requirement. The comprehension of the development and the presentation of this self within the same body poses both the difficulty of its empirical discovery and the dilemma of its analytical classification. The self is surely essentially more than and different from its appearances ("roles"), and it is perceived by its possessor at any given moment as fully formed rather than in process, seen as "being" rather than "becoming." Yet its appearances alone are visible and its brute existence and state of motility are not available at all to the observer. These must be inferred. An unbridgeable gulf separates the experience of the self by its possessor from the apprehension of it by its observer.

Moreover, the self is disembodied even as it is supposedly limited by human extension. For the self finds its singularity encompassed within a collectivity that transcends its fleshly limits. Typically we see ourselves as members of historically and socially constituted sodalities. The pronominal "I" defines itself as a member of a plural "we." Asked "who am I" the individual is likely to respond categorically: I am a black, an American, a professor, a homosexual, a cripple, etc. The "I" seems to require a reference *group* that owes its own claim to recognizable existence to the social constitution of collectivities. "I am I" is not an answer that anyone, even I, will respect. Thus we all disembody and socialize the self in the very act of claiming its singular embodiment and individuality. An individual becomes a person, and a person exhibits his or her personification of the social self-referencing group.

Moreover, if disembodiment connects the bodied self to other bodies in space, it also links it to collectivities in time. The disembodied self partakes of history, memory, hope, or dread. To say "I am a Jew" is at the very least potentially to identify with the Yahwist, Elohist, or secularizing conceptions of that people's past, to dredge up to consciousness the recollections of one's own ethnic group life, and/or to connect one's person to the dreams or nightmares of the always problematic future that the cunning of futurity holds out to Jews. The disembodied self can be referred to predecessors, contemporaries, consociates, and successors in a single synthesizing phrase: "I am we." For this apparently inescapable singular plurality the problematics of the "I" are great. Its very "I-ness" is at stake. It struggles against becoming submerged completely in the "we-ness" that gives it its unique identity.

The existential self also seems to depend on language for its own confirmation and for its affirmation of or conflict with the world around it. The conversation of gestures, so basic to symbolic interaction, is vernacular in character: the sign becomes a symbol. The world around us is subdivided into an *umwelt* and all else that is beyond it by the juridical rules of action and the jurisdictional rules that tell us where the action takes place.[16] These rules are articulatable although for most socialized persons they need not be spoken or written down. Hence, a major project of the ethnomethodologists has been to introduce an archaeology into symbolic interaction and to plumb the depths of the juridical and jurisdictional knowledge from which every person's *umwelt* derives.[17] Although much of this work appears to be microecological, it could herald the social scientific reconstruction of civilization itself.[18] Language in its expressed forms and in its deep structures provides the means by which the existential self finds, defines, and re-orders its place in the world.

However, the existential self and its students are also troubled by the limits of language and that which is beyond language—the unutterable. Again we must turn to Yahwistic thought to grasp some clues to this phenomenon. To the ancient Hebrews, and to religiously-minded Jews today, their god's name was unutterable and symbolized by letters that were not pronounced. He was "the lord," "our god," the one "who brought us out of Egypt." Understood through his commandments, contractual arrangements, punishments and rewards, he nevertheless remained ineffable.[19] Identification with him did not permit his name to be spoken. Rather, it was silently understood by all who were members of the covenanted agreement whereby his sacred authority was established. By a dialectical process the very essence of membership in the covenant became itself unutterable so that a constituted sacred peoplehood revealed its awesome roots precisely by being inexplicable to outsiders. The bases for identification with the sacralized we-group became an insoluble mystery to outsiders at the very moment that its unspeakable character formed the ground for an in-group understanding that required—indeed, demanded—no words.[20]

The existential self owes a part of its existence to the supraexistential soul and to the reference groups with which the soul identifies. The soul, it seems, belongs to a soul group. The soul is disembodied at death but remains immortal finding its place in accordance with different eschatologies in transmigration, paradisiacal reward, or hellish torture. The mundane existential self of modern secular humanity has its own intimations of immortality. In its relation to the sacred reference group to which it refers for guidance and self-definition it transcends both embodiment and life. Nowhere is this more revealed than in the selves that find their inspiriting source in ethnicity and its descent, in what Max Weber recognized as the mystery of blood, a primordial irrationality that forms both the taproot of collective ascriptive solidarity and the source for referential individual identification.[21]

The ethnic self constitutes one instance wherein silence confirms identification at the same moment that it confounds comprehension. Ethnicity can conventionally be depicted in terms of color, culture, and condition, but these only act as mediating shibboleths for the unutterable covenant that binds together every member of an ethnic congregation.[22] A most telling example—one that harks back to ancient Hebrew sources and the dialectical desublimation wherein the ineffable character of Yahweh was transformed into the unutterable basis for individual and group identity—is that of "soul" among America's blacks.[23] Although the soul idea among African Americans can be traced back to the transmigratory, disembodiable, and shadow-casting soul-complex of West Africa,[24] its special character in the United States is that of an uncommunicable ineffability that cannot be transmitted to or adopted by outsiders. African American "soul" can be experienced by blacks but not explained to whites. To share in the ethnic legacy of "soul" is also to become a part of the silence which accompanies rightful descent. By contrast, to demand a verbal explanation of "soul" and—worse—to claim the right to partake of it without possessing the appropriate ascriptive credentials are to signal one's fundamental ignorance of the sacred and inexpressible nature of it. The tacit estate of ethnicity is the ineffaceable source of ethnocentrism.

A sociology of the existential self must take as its topic the unremediable marginality of that self. For the existential self is the product of both experience and the language used to render that experience understandable, but it is a member of neither the brute society of experience nor the reconciling community of language. Ethnolinguistics has rightly emphasized the importance of speech communities, but to be faithful to the nature of its subject matter, existential sociology must recognize the representative of humanity as the creature who is never fully realized as a participant in his word and symbol using world. Always there is a striving for that emancipatory self-realization that would translate the self into its irreducible individuality; always there is the agonizing search for recognition and response that, when granted, pulls one back into the collective identity.

Notes
and
Index

NOTES

Introduction

1. R. A. Sydie, *Natural Women, Cultured Men: A Feminist Perspective on Sociological Theory* (New York: New York University Press, 1987) 199.

2. *Ibid.* 206.

3. Stanford M. Lyman and Marvin B. Scott, *A Sociology of the Absurd* (New York: Appleton-Century-Crofts, 1970). A revised and enlarged edition has been published (Dix Hills, New York: General Hall, Inc., 1989).

4. Marvin B. Scott and Stanford M. Lyman, *The Revolt of the Students* (Columbus: Charles Merrill, 1970).

5. Stanford M. Lyman and Marvin B. Scott, *The Drama of Social Reality* (New York: Oxford University Press, 1975).

6. Stanford M. Lyman, *The Seven Deadly Sins: Society and Evil* (New York: St. Martin's Press, 1978). An enlarged edition has been published (Dix Hills, New York: General Hall, 1989).

7. See Alvin W. Gouldner, *The Coming Crisis of Western Sociology* (New York: Basic Books, Inc., 1970).

8. See Stanford M. Lyman, "The Rise and Decline of the Functionalist-Positivist Paradigm: A Chapter in the History of American Sociology," *Hyoron Shakaikagaku* (*Doshisha University Social Science Review*) 20 (March 1982): 4–19.

9. Arne L. Kallenberg, "Linking Macro and Micro Levels: Bringing Workers Back into the Sociology of Work," *Social Forces* LXVII (March 1989): 583.

10. *Ibid.* 582–83.

11. See Randall Collins, "On the Microfoundations of Macrosociology," *American Journal of Sociology* LXXXVI (March 1981): 925–42.

12. Jeffrey C. Alexander, *Twenty Lectures: Sociological Theory Since World War II* (New York: Columbia University Press, 1987) 376.

13. George Ritzer, "Sociology of Work: A Metatheoretical Analysis," *Social Forces* LXVII (March 1989): 597.

14. Collins, *Three Sociological Traditions* (New York: Oxford University Press, 1985) 171.

15. For the present author's earlier critique of this issue, see Stanford M. Lyman, *The Black American in Sociological Thought: A Failure of Perspective* (New York: G. P. Putnam's Sons, 1972).

16. For an elaboration and application of Blumer's orientation to such macro problems as racism, freedom of speech, and industrial conflicts, see Stanford M. Lyman and Arthur J. Vidich, *Social Order and the Public Philosophy: An Analysis and Interpretation of the Work of Herbert Blumer* (Fayetteville: The University of Arkansas Press, 1988).

17. For the present author's other sociological studies of the Chinese in America, see three earlier works: *Chinese Americans* (New York: Random House, 1974); *The Asian in North America* (Santa Barbara: American Bibliographic Center—Clio Press, 1977); *Chinatown and Little Tokyo: Power, Conflict, and Community Among Chinese and Japanese Immigrants in America* (Millwood, New York: Associated Faculty Press, Inc., 1986).

18. For a critical discussion of the development of sociology in the United States, see Arthur J. Vidich and Stanford M. Lyman, *American Sociology: Worldly Rejections of Religion and Their Directions* (New Haven: Yale University Press, 1985).

19. See Stanford M. Lyman, ed., *Selected Writings of Henry Hughes: Antebellum Southerner, Slavocrat, Sociologist* (Jackson: University Press of Mississippi, 1985).

20. Thomas M. Disch, "Theater," *The Nation* CCXLVIII:7 (February 20, 1989): 246.

21. *loc. cit.*

Civilization: Contents, Discontents, Malcontents

1. Alvin Gouldner, *The Coming Crisis of Western Sociology* (New York: Basic Books, 1970) 378–90.

2. Randall Collins and Michael Makowsky, *The Discovery of Society* (New York: Random House, 1972).

3. Sheldon L. Messinger, et al., "Life as Theatre: Some Notes on the Dramaturgic Approach to Social Reality," *Sociometry* XXV (1962): 98–110.

4. Herbert Blumer, "Action vs. Interaction," *Transaction: Social Science and Modern Society* 9:6 (1972): 52.

5. Peter Berger and Thomas Luckmann, *The Social Construction of Reality: A Treatise in the Sociology of Knowledge* (New York: Doubleday, 1966) 189n.

6. Don Martindale, *Institutions, Organizations, and Mass Society* (Boston: Houghton-Mifflin, 1966) 560.

7. R. P. Cuzzort, *Humanity and Modern Sociological Thought* (New York: Holt, Rinehart and Winston, 1969) 192.

8. Hilary Callan, *Ethology and Society* (Oxford: Clarendon Press, 1970).

9. Robert Ardrey, *African Genesis: A Personal Investigation into the Animal Origins and Nature of Man* (New York: Dell, 1961); *The Territorial Imperative: A Personal Inquiry into the Animal Origins of Property and Nations* (New York: Atheneum, 1966); *The Social Contract: A Personal Inquiry into the Evolutionary Source of Order and Disorder* (New York: Dell-Delta, 1970); Desmond Morris, *The Naked Ape: A Zoologist's Study of the Human Animal* (New York: McGraw-Hill, 1967); *The Human Zoo* (New York: McGraw-Hill, 1969); Lionel Tiger, *Men in Groups* (New York: Random House, 1969); Lionel Tiger and Robin Fox, *The Imperial Animal* (New York: Holt, Rinehart and Winston, 1971).

10. Cuzzort 191.

11. Barney G. Glaser and Anselm L. Strauss, *The Discovery of Grounded Theory: Strategies for Qualitative Research* (Chicago: Aldine, 1967) 136–39.

12. Marshall Berman, "Relations in Public: Microstudies in Public Order," review of Erving Goffman, *New York Times* February 27, 1972: 1–2, 10.

13. Max Weber, "Georg Simmel as Sociologist," trans. Donald N. Levine, *Social Research* 39:1 (1972): 158.

14. Ellsworth Faris, *The Nature of Human Nature* (New York: McGraw-Hill, 1937) 36–45.

15. See two works by Robert Sommer, *Personal Space: The Behavioral Basis of Design* (Englewood Cliffs: Prentice-Hall, 1969); and *Tight Spaces: Hard Architecture and How to Humanize It* (Englewood Cliffs: Prentice-Hall, 1974). See also Stanford M. Lyman and Marvin B. Scott, *A Sociology of the Absurd*, 2nd edition (Dix Hills, N.Y.: General Hall, 1989), 22–34.

16. William Isaac Thomas, *Source Book for Social Origins* (Boston: Richard G. Badger, 1909) 16–26.

17. Ernest Gellner, "Concepts and Society," *Rationality,* ed. Bryan Wilson (New York: Harper Torchbooks, 1970) 18–49.

18. Lyman and Scott, *A Sociology of the Absurd,* 2nd edition, 2–20, 182–90, 198–203.

19. Max Weber, *The Protestant Ethic and the Spirit of Capitalism,* trans. Talcott Parsons (New York: Charles Scribner's Sons, 1930) 182.

20. Émile Durkheim and Marcel Mauss, "Note of the Notion of Civilization," trans. Benjamin Nelson, *Social Research* 38:4 (1971): 803–13.

21. Blumer, "Action vs. Interaction," 53.

22. Kenneth E. Bock, "Evolution, Function, and Change," *American Sociological Review* 28:2 (1963): 229–37.

23. Kenneth E. Bock, *The Acceptance of Histories: Toward a Perspective for Social Science* (Berkeley: University of California Press, 1956): 120–21.

24. Weber, "Georg Simmel as Sociologist" 155–63.

25. Maurice Merleau-Ponty, *Humanism and Terror,* trans. John O'Neill (Boston: Beacon Press, 1969) 188.

Two Neglected Pioneers of Civilizational Analysis

1. Émile Durkheim and Marcel Mauss, "Note on the Notion of Civilization," trans. Benjamin Nelson, *Social Research* 38 (Winter 1971): 808–13. Originally published in *L'Année sociologique,* XII (1913): 46–50.

2. See the papers collected from "A Symposium on Civilizational Complexes and Intercivilizational Encounters," *Sociological Inquiry* 35 (Summer 1974): i–ii, 79–142.

3. For biographical information on Robert Stewart Culin, see "Stewart Culin Dies; Noted Ethnologist," *New York Times* April 9, 1929: 31; "Stewart Culin," *Art News* 27 (April 13, 1929): 12; M. D. C. Crawford, "Tribute to Robert Stewart Culin," *Brooklyn Museum Quarterly* 16 (July 1929): 88–89. For a critical analysis of Culin's theory of game diffusion, see Elliott M. Avedon and Brian Sutton-Smith, *The Study of Games* (New York: John Wiley, 1971) 55–62.

4. For biographical information on Frank Hamilton Cushing, in addition to materials cited below, see "In Memoriam: Frank Hamilton Cushing," *American Anthropologist* n.s. 2 (1900): 354–79, 768–811; Ruth Bunzel, "The Bureau of American Ethnology: Areal Research in the Southwest," *The Golden Age of American Anthropology* (New York: George Braziller, 1960) 203–06.

5. Durkheim and Mauss, "Note on the Notion of Civilization" 810–11.

6. *Ibid.* 812.

7. Stewart Culin, "America the Cradle of Asia," address before the section of anthropology, American Association for the Advancement of Science, Washington, D.C., Meeting, December 1902–January 1903, *Proceedings of the Ameri-*

can Association for the Advancement of Science (Washington, D.C.: Gibson Bros., 1903), 52: 493–500. In slightly different form this essay also appeared in *Harper's Monthly Magazine* 106 (March 1903): 534–40.

8. The reports of the development of this project are sketchily presented in Stewart Culin, "Exhibit of Games in the Columbian Exposition," *Journal of American Folk-Lore* 6 (July–September 1893): 215–16; and in the Report of the Secretary, *Annual Report of the Board of Regents of the Smithsonian Institution, Showing the Operations, Expenditures, and Condition of the Institution to July 1894,* House of Representatives, Misc. Doc. 90, Part 1, 53rd Congress, 3rd Session (Washington: Government Printing Office, 1896) 52–53. See also the remarks of Stewart Culin in "In Memoriam: Frank Hamilton Cushing" 376–77.

9. Marcel Mauss, "A Category of the Human Mind: The Notion of Person, the Notion of 'Self'," *Sociology and Psychology: Essays,* trans. Ben Brewster (London: Routledge & Kegan Paul, 1979) 57–94. I have employed the term "spirit" rather than "mind" out of consideration of Benjamin Nelson's translation of a portion of this essay in *Psychoanalytic Review* 55 (1963): 331–62.

10. Émile Durkheim and Marcel Mauss, *Primitive Classification,* trans. and ed. Rodney Needham (Chicago: University of Chicago Press—Phoenix Books, 1967 [1903]).

11. See Émile Durkheim, "Note on Social Morphology," *On Institutional Analysis,* trans. and ed. Mark Traugott (Chicago: University of Chicago Press, 1978) 88–92.

12. Sir John Lubbock, *The Origin of Civilization and the Primitive Condition of Man,* ed. Peter Riviere (Chicago: University of Chicago Press, 1978 [1870]).

13. Karl Marx and Friedrich Engels, "Manifesto of the Communist Party," in Lewis S. Feuer, ed., *Marx and Engels: Basic Writings on Politics and Philosophy* (Garden City: Doubleday-Anchor, 1959) 11.

14. See Ruth Tringham, "The Concept of 'Civilization' in European Archaeology," in Jeremy A. Sabloff and C. C. Lamberg-Karlofsky, eds., *The Rise and Fall of Civilizations: Modern Archaeological Approaches to Ancient Cultures* (Menlo Park: Cummings Publishing Co., 1974) 470–85.

15. See two discussions by Émile Durkheim, "Review of Antonio Labriola, *Essais sur la conception materialiste de l'histoire,*" and "Review of Gaston Richard, *Le socialisme et la science sociale,*" *On Institutional Analysis* 123–38.

16. Frank Hamilton Cushing, "Outlines of Zuni Creation Myths," *Thirteenth Annual Report of the Bureau of American Ethnology, 1891–1892* (Washington, D.C.: United States Smithsonian Institution, 1896) 374. A selection entitled "Form and the Dance-Drama," from which the quotation was taken, is reprinted in Jesse Green, ed., *Zuni: Selected Writings of Frank Hamilton Cushing* (Lincoln: University of Nebraska Press, 1979) 215–18.

17. Stewart Culin, *Games of the North American Indians* (New York: Dover Publications, 1975 [1907]) 34–35.

18. Durkheim, "Review of Antonio Labriola" 129–30.

19. Cushing's account of the game *sho-li-we* is found in Culin, *Games of the North American Indians* 212–17.

20. Stewart Culin, *Games of the Orient: Korea, China, Japan* (Rutland, Vt.: Charles E. Tuttle Co., 1958 [1895]) xix.

21. Representative of Culin's work on the later aspects of the diffusionist project are the following essays and studies: "Christian Relics from Japan," *Brooklyn Museum Quarterly* 5 (July 1918): 141–52; "The Story of the Painted Curtain," *Good Furniture* 11 (September 1918): 133–47; "Japanese Color Prints

Illustrating Samuel Smiles' Self Help," *Brooklyn Museum Quarterly* 6 (April 1919): 111–16; "The Source of Ornamental Design: The Relation of European Peasant Art to the Art of the Orient," *Arts and Decoration* 15 (May 1921): 94–95, 130; "Peasant Art of Central Europe," *Bulletin of the Needle and Bobbin Club* 5 (July 1921): 30–36; "Pistyan," *Brooklyn Museum Quarterly* 9 (April 1922): 81–89; "European Costumes and Keramics," *Brooklyn Museum Quarterly* 10 (April 1923): 61–70; "Illustrations of the Romance of Amir Hamzah," *Brooklyn Museum Quarterly* 11 (October 1924): 139–43.

22. Durkheim and Mauss, "Note on the Notion of Civilization" 812.

23. See, e.g., V. Gordon Childe, *New Light on the Most Ancient East: The Oriental Prelude to European History* (New York: W. W. Norton, 1969).

24. For a representative discussion, see Carroll L. Riley et al., eds., *Man Across the Pacific: Problems of Pre-Columbian Contacts* (Austin: University of Texas Press, 1971).

25. See, e.g., Lee Eldridge Huddleston, *Origin of the American Indians: European Concepts, 1492–1729* (Austin: University of Texas Press, 1967); Paul S. Martin, George I. Quimby, and Donald Collier, *Indians Before Columbus: 20,000 Years of North American History Revealed by Archaeology* (Chicago: University of Chicago Press, 1975 [1947]). For a fine example of seventeenth-century thinking on the subject, see Father Bernabe Cobo, *History of the Inca Empire: An Account of the Indians' Customs and Their Origin Together with a Treatise on Inca Legends, History, and Social Institutions,* trans. Roland Hamilton (Austin: University of Texas Press, 1979 [1653]) 47–93.

26. See Stanford M. Lyman, "Stewart Culin and the Debate over Trans-Pacific Migration," *Journal for the Theory of Social Behaviour* 9 (March 1979): 91–115.

27. See Jurgen Herbst, *The German Historical School in American Scholarship: A Study in the Transfer of Culture* (Port Washington: Kennikat Press, 1972) 99–159.

28. Benjamin Nelson, "Civilizational Complexes and Inter-civilizational Encounters," *Sociological Analysis* 34 (Summer 1973): 79–80.

29. Durkheim and Mauss, *Primitive Classification* 74–75.

30. *Ibid.* 76–77.

31. Culin, *Games of the Orient* xviii.

32. *Ibid.* v.

33. Culin, "America the Cradle of Asia" 494–95.

34. Stewart Culin, "Popular Literature of the Chinese Laborers in the United States," *Oriental Studies: A Selection of Papers Read Before the Oriental Club of Philadelphia, 1888–1894* (Boston: n.p., 1894) 52–62.

35. See Irene Eber, "Introduction," to her translation of Richard Wilhelm, *Lectures on the I Ching: Constancy and Change,* Bollingen Series 19:2 (Princeton: Princeton University Press, 1979) ix–xxiii.

36. *The I Ching: The Book of Changes,* trans. James Legge, 2nd edn. (New York: Dover Publications, 1963 [1899]).

37. The English translation of the German edition, by Cary F. Baynes, is published as *The I Ching, or Book of Changes,* the Richard Wilhelm translation from Chinese into German, rendered into English, 3rd edn., Bollingen Series 19 (Princeton: Princeton University Press, 1967).

38. J. J. M. de Groot, *The Religious System of China, Its Ancient Forms, Evolution, History, and Present Aspect, Manners, Customs, and Social Institutions Connected Therewith* (Taipei: Cheng-wen Publishing Co., 1969 [1892–1910] 3: 991–97.

39. Iulian K. Shchutskii, *Researches on the I Ching,* trans. William L. Mac-Donald, Tsuyoshi Hasegawa, with Hellmut Wilhelm, Bollingen Series 62:2 (Princeton: Princeton University Press, 1979).

40. Durkheim and Mauss, *Primitive Classification* 67–75.

41. See the introductions by Gerald W. Swanton, N. I. Konrad, and N. A. Petrov in Shchutskii, *Researches on the I Ching* vii–lxiv.

42. Culin, *Games of the Orient* xviii.

43. Shchutskii, *Researches on the I Ching* 192–95.

44. See the discussion of the *Kulturkreise* School in Margaret T. Hodgen, *Anthropology, History, and Cultural Change,* Viking Publications in Anthropology, No. 52 (Tucson: University of Arizona Press, 1974) 28–32.

45. See Margaret T. Hodgen, *The Doctrine of Survivals: A Chapter in the History of Scientific Method in the Study of Man* (London: Allenson, 1936).

46. These researches are reported in the following studies by Culin: "Chinese Games with Dice," paper read before the Oriental Club of Philadephia (March 14, 1889) (Philadelphia: Privately printed, 1889): 3–21; "The Gambling Games of the Chinese in America: Fan Tan; The Game of Repeatedly Spreading Out; and Pak Kop Piu or, The Game of White Pigeon Ticket," *Publications of the University of Pennsylvania Series in Philosophy, Literature and Archaeology* 1 (1891): 1–17; "Chinese Games with Dice and Dominoes," *Report of the United States National Museum,* Smithsonian Institute, 1893, 491–537; "Palmistry in China and Japan," *Overland Monthly,* 2nd ser., 23 (May 1894): 476–80; "Tsz' Fa, or 'Word Blossoming': A Lottery Among the Chinese in America," *Overland Monthly,* 2nd ser., 24 (September 1894): 249–55; "Divination and Fortune Telling Among the Chinese in America," *Overland Monthly,* 2nd ser., 25 (February 1895): 165–72; "Dominoes, The National Game of China," *Overland Monthly,* 2nd ser., 26 (November 1895): 559–65; "American Indian Games," *The Journal of American Folk-Lore* 11 (October—December 1898): 245–52; "American Indian Games (1902)," *American Anthropologist* 5 (1903): 58–64; "The Indians of Cuba," *Bulletin of the Free Museum of Science and Art of the University of Pennsylvania* 3 (May 1902): 185–226.

47. Frank Hamilton Cushing, "The Arrow," *American Anthropologist* 8 (October 1895): 307.

48. *Ibid.* 309.

49. Culin, *Games of the Orient.*

50. See the detailed but cautious discussion in Culin, *Chess and Playing Cards,* Annual report of the Board of Regents of the Smithsonian Institution for the year ending June 30, 1896—Report of the U.S. National Museum (New York: Arno Press Reprint, 1976) 807–61 *et passim.*

51. Culin, "America the Cradle of Asia" 495–500.

52. *Ibid.* 495.

53. Representative of Culin's continuing careful pursuit of his proofs are the following essays and studies: "Italian Marionette Theatre in Brooklyn, N.Y.," *Journal of American Folk-Lore* 3 (April—June 1890): 155–57; "Street Games of Boys in Brooklyn, N.Y.," *Journal of American Folklore* 4 (July—September 1891): 221–37; "Mancala, the National Game of Africa," *Report of the United States National Museum, Smithsonian Institution* (June 30, 1894): 595–607; "Hawaiian Games," *American Anthropologist* n.s. 1 (April 1899): 201–47; "Primitive American Art," *University* [of Pennsylvania] *Bulletin* (April 1900): 1–7; "The Origins of Ornament," *Bulletin of the Free Museum of Science and Art, Department of Archaeology and Paleontology, of the University of Pennsylvania* 2 (May 1900):

235–42; "Philippine Games," *American Anthropologist* n.s. 2 (October—December 1900): 643–56; "Christian Relics from Japan," *Brooklyn Museum Quarterly* 5 (July 1918): 141–52; "Chinese Pictures," *Brooklyn Museum Quarterly* 7 (April 1920): 117–21; "Ceremonial Diversions in Japan," *Asia: Journal of the American Asiatic Association* 19 (October 1919): 1026–31; "Japanese Toys and Their Lore," *Asia: Journal of the American Asiatic Association* 20 (April 1920): 295–301; "The Japanese Game of Sugoroku," *Brooklyn Museum Quarterly* 7 (October 1920): 213–33; "The Story of the Japanese Doll," *Asia: The American Magazine on the Orient* 22 (October 1922): 782–85; "Negro Art," *The Arts* 3 (May 1923): 347–50; *Primitive Negro Art—Chiefly from the Belgian Congo* (Brooklyn: Brooklyn Museum Department of Ethnology, 1923); "The Game of Ma-Jong: Its Origin and Significance," *Brooklyn Museum Quarterly* 11 (October 1924): 153–68; "The Japanese Festival Calendar," *Brooklyn Museum Quarterly* 12 (January 1925): 27–49; "The Art of the Chinese," *International Studio* 80 (January 1925): 287–89; "The Magic of Color," *Brooklyn Museum Quarterly* 12 (April 1925): 99–103; "Burri-Burri Gitcho: A Japanese Swinging Bat Game," *Brooklyn Museum Quarterly* 12 (July 1925): 133–39; "The Japanese Game of Battledore and Shuttlecock," *Brooklyn Museum Quarterly* 12 (July 1925): 139–50; "A Korean Map of the World," *Brooklyn Museum Quarterly* 12 (October 1925): 183–93; "Address to the Brooklyn Urban League," July 3, 1926 (typescript); "Voices of the Ages," paper presented at the Art Directors' Luncheon, January 7, 1927 (typescript); "The Road to Beauty," *Brooklyn Museum Quarterly* 14 (April 1927): 41–50.

54. A similar conceptual dilemma in economics has recently been called to the attention of its practitioners by Robert Heilbroner. Noting that "economists conceive of the world in terms that fail to grasp its essential characteristics or that seriously misrepresent them," Heilbroner turns his attention to "the words that economics has imported from physics and made fashionable throughout social science: 'micro' and 'macro.'" These words provide perspectives: "But what is strange is that there is no way of going from one view to the other. . . . Thus macro and micro are not the complementary slides of a stereopticon giving us a single complete picture from two incomplete ones. They are, rather, two quite different pictures that cannot be combined. What, then, is economics?" (Robert Heilbroner, "The New Economics," *New York Review of Books* 27 [February 21, 1980]: 19).

55. See Jonathan H. Turner, *The Structure of Sociological Theory* (Homewood: Dorsey Press, 1974) 299–302.

56. See Nicholas S. Timasheff, *Sociological Theory: Its Nature and Growth,* 3rd edn. (New York: Random House, 1967) 268–69.

57. Erving Goffman, *Relations in Public: Microstudies of the Public Order* (New York: Basic Books, 1971) xiv–xv. On precisely this and related matters, see Stanford M. Lyman, "Civilization: Contents, Discontents, Malcontents," in this volume.

58. G. Duncan Mitchell, *A Hundred Years of Sociology* (Chicago: Aldine, 1968) 234–35.

59. Don Martindale, *The Nature and Types of Sociological Theory* (Boston: Houghton Mifflin, 1960) 501–02.

60. In 1882 Cushing observed that "In order, then, to comprehend the mythology of a people, we must learn their language, acquire their confidence, assimilating ourselves to them by joining in their every-day life, their religious life, even as far as possible in their intellectual life, by remembering with intense

earnestness the reasonings of our own childhood, by constantly striking every possible chord of human sympathy in our own intercourse with those whose inner life we would study.

"I think I have now sufficiently explained why I have entered into relation with the Zuni Indians, and become a participator in their religious practices and, so far as possible, beliefs, to the extent of acquiring membership in their gentile organization as well as in their priesthood; and my attitude toward the audience before me is that of an imperfect exponent of Zuni mythology and belief" (Frank Hamilton Cushing, "The Zuni Social, Mystic, and Religious Systems," *Popular Science Monthly* 21 [June 1882]: 186–87).

Culin in 1924 recalled that "Once in my youth I fell under the spell of a problem which involved a knowledge of the Chinese language. . . . I might have gone to school and taken lessons from a professor. Instead I went to live in one of our Chinese settlements, where in time I came not only to speak the language but, eager and curious, saturated myself with the spirit of these interesting and capable people" (Stewart Culin, "Creation in Art," Lecture, Pratt Institute, New York, February 4, 1924 [Brooklyn: Brooklyn Museum, 1924], unpaginated).

61. See Amitai Etzioni, "Toward a Macrosociology," in John C. McKinney and Edward A. Tiryakian, eds., *Theoretical Sociology: Perspectives and Methods* (New York: Appleton-Century-Crofts, 1970) 69–97.

62. Representative of Culin's ethnographic researches on the Chinese in Philadelphia are the following: "The Religious Ceremonies of the Chinese in the Eastern Cities of the United States," essay read before the Numismatic and Antiquarian Society of Philadelphia, April 1, 1886 (Philadelphia: Privately Printed, 1887) 3–23; "China in America: A Study in the Social Life of the Chinese in the Eastern Cities of the United States," paper read before the American Association for the Advancement of Science (Section on Anthropology), New York, 1887 (Philadelphia: n.p., 1887) 3–16; "The Practice of Medicine by the Chinese in America," *Medical and Surgical Reporter* (March 1887) 355–57; "The I Hing or 'Patriotic Rising,' A Secret Society among the Chinese in America," November 3, 1887, *Report of the Proceedings of the Numismatic and Antiquarian Society of Philadelphia, for the Years 1887–1889* (Philadelphia: Printed for the Society, 1891) 51–58; "Chinese Drug Stores in America," *American Journal of Pharmacy* (December 1887) 593–98; "A Curious People: Sketch of the Chinese Colony in Philadelphia," *Philadelphia Public Ledger* September 22, 1888; "My Friend Herman: A Tale of the Chinese Secret Society of Heaven and Earth," *Philadelphia Press* August 11, 1889; "Chinese Folk-Lore: The Habits and Customs of Our Chinese Neighbors," *Philadelphia Public Ledger* March 1890; "Chinese Secret Societies in the United States," *Journal of American Folk-Lore* 3 (January—March 1890): 39–43; "Customs of the Chinese in America," *Journal of American Folk-Lore* 3 (July—September 1890): 191–200; "T'in Ti Ui: The Chinese Heaven and Earth League," *Philadelphia Public Ledger* August 26, 1890; "I Hing: American Branch of the Heaven and Earth League," *Philadelphia Public Ledger* August 29, 1890; "Opium Smoking: The Habit among the Chinese in Philadelphia," *Philadelphia Public Ledger* August 19, 1891; "Social Organization of the Chinese in America," *American Anthropologist* o.s. 4 (October 1891): 347–52.

63. Remarks by J. W. Powell in "In Memoriam: Frank Hamilton Cushing" 361.

64. Cushing, "The Arrow" 311.

65. Alfred L. Kroeber, "Cushing, Frank Hamilton (1857–1900)," *Encyclo-*

pedia of the Social Sciences, ed. E. R. A. Seligman, 15 vols. (New York: Macmillan, 1930–35) 4: 657.

66. Anthony Giddens, "Hermeneutics, Ethnomethodology, and Interpretive Analysis," *Studies in Social and Political Theory* (New York: Basic Books, 1977) 177.

67. See Carlos Castaneda, *The Teachings of Don Juan: A Yaqui Way of Knowledge* (Berkeley: University of California Press, 1968); *A Separate Reality: Further Conversations with Don Juan* (New York: Simon & Schuster, 1971); *Journey to Ixtlan: The Lessons of Don Juan* (New York: Simon & Schuster, 1972); *Tales of Power* (New York: Simon & Schuster, 1974); *The Second Ring of Power* (New York: Simon & Schuster, 1977). For critical analyses, see Daniel Noel, *Seeing Castaneda: Reactions to the 'Don Juan' Writings of Carlos Castaneda* (New York: Putnam's, 1976); David Silverman, *Reading Castaneda: A Prologue to the Social Sciences* (London: Routledge & Kegan Paul, 1975); Nevil Drury, *Don Juan, Mescalito and Modern Magic* (London: Routledge & Kegan Paul, 1978); and two works by Richard de Mille, *Castaneda's Journey: The Power and the Allegory* (Santa Barbara: Capra Press, 1976) and *The Don Juan Papers: Further Castaneda Controversies* (Santa Barbara: Ross-Erikson, 1980).

68. The criticism leveled against Castaneda—that the isolation and seclusion of his apprenticeship to a Yaqui shaman prohibits verification of his reports—does not apply to Cushing, whose membership in the Zuni sacred, military, and gentile organizations was known to other ethnologists who worked in the area. The Zuni were even aware of Cushing's subterfuge wherein he had a skull from the Smithsonian Institution sent to him to use as his token offering for admission into the sacred mysteries. See the discussion in Stewart Culin, "Zuni Pictures," and "Appendix: Zuni Indians," in Elsie Clews Parsons, ed., *American Indian Life* (Lincoln: University of Nebraska Press, 1967 [1922]) 175–78, 397–98.

69. Cushing, "The Arrow" 310.

70. Levy-Bruhl correctly describes Cushing's method and its consequences for our knowledge of alien cultures: "Cushing had acquired a kind of mental 'naturalization' among the Zunis. Not content with living with, and like, them for many years, he had made their religious rulers adopt him and admit him to their secret societies; in their sacred ceremonies he, like their priests, had his own role, and carried it out. The unfortunately rare works of his which have been published give us, however, the feelings of a form of mental activity with which our own would never exactly correspond. Our habits of thought are too far removed from those of the Zunis. Our language, without which we can conceive nothing, and which is essential to our reasoning, makes use of categories which do not coincide with theirs. Lastly and chiefly, the ambient social reality, of which the collective representations and, to a certain extent, the language, are functions, is with them too far removed from our own case.

"Thus [here Levy-Bruhl might have said, without the aid of Cushing—S.L.] the mentality of inferior peoples, though not so impenetrable as it would be if it were regulated by a logic different from our own, is none the less not wholly comprehensible to us" (Lucien Levy-Bruhl, *How Natives Think,* trans. Lilian A. Clare [London: George Allen & Unwin, 1926] 70–71).

71. Cushing, "The Arrow" 310.

72. *Ibid.* 309.

73. *Ibid.* 310–11.

74. See Garfinkel, *Studies in Ethnomethodology,* esp. 1–34; Alan F. Blum, "The Corpus of Knowledge as a Normative Order," in McKinney and Tiryakian, eds.,

Theoretical Sociology 319–36; Giddens, "Hermeneutics, Ethnomethodology, and Interpretive Analysis" esp. 167–78. For philosophical commentaries on these problems, see, among many others, Hans-Georg Cadamer, *Truth and Method,* trans. and ed. Garrett Barden and John Cumming (New York: Seabury Press, 1975) 153–498; Aaron Gurwitsch, *Phenomenology and the Theory of Science,* ed. Lester Embree (Evanston: Northwestern University Press, 1974) 113–131, 210–68; and the essays by Marvin Farber, Robert Welsh Jordan, and Richard M. Zaner in F. Kersten and R. Zaner, eds., *Phenomenology: Continuation and Criticism—Essays in Memory of Dorion Cairns* (The Hague: Martinus Nijhoff, 1973) 33–61, 105–13, 192–222.

75. See Claude Lévi-Strauss, *Structural Anthropology,* trans. Claire Jacobson and Brooke Grundfest Schoepf (Harmondsworth: Penguin Books, 1963) 218–19, 221, 226–27, 290.

76. See two works by David Sudnow, *Ways of the Hand: The Organization of Improvised Conduct* (Cambridge: Harvard University Press, 1978), and *Talk's Body: A Meditation Between Two Keyboards* (New York: Alfred A. Knopf, 1979).

77. Cushing's contribution to civilizational study and the unfinished Culin-Cushing project are also not mentioned in the intellectual portraits of this neglected figure. See Raymond Stewart Brandes, *Frank Hamilton Cushing: Pioneering Americanist,* diss., University of Arizona, 1965 (Ann Arbor: University Microfilms, 1965); and Joan Mark, "Frank Hamilton Cushing and an American Science of Anthropology," *Perspectives in American History* 10 (1976): 449–86.

78. Lévi-Strauss, *Structural Anthropology* 290.

79. Mauss, "A Category of the Human Mind" 64.

80. Stewart Culin, "An Archaeological Application of the Röntgen Rays," *Bulletin of the Free Museum of Science and Art of the University of Pennsylvania* May 1897: 183.

81. Levy-Bruhl, *How Natives Think* 161, 366–67.

82. Lévi-Strauss, *Structural Anthropology* 218–27.

83. See Émile Durkheim, *The Elementary Forms of the Religious Life,* trans. Joseph Ward Swain (New York: Free Press, 1965) 132–40.

84. See Steven Lukes, *Émile Durkheim: His Life and Work—A Historical and Critical Study* (New York: Harper & Row, 1972) 446–52, 479–80.

85. Levy-Bruhl, *How Natives Think* 366–67.

86. Frank Hamilton Cushing, "Outlines of Zuni Creation Myths," *Thirteenth Annual Report of the Bureau of American Ethnology, 1891–1892* (Washington, D.C.: Smithsonian Institution, 1896) 361–73.

87. Frank Hamilton Cushing, "Manual Concepts: A Study of the Influence of Hand-Usage on Culture Growth," *American Anthropologist* o.s. 5 (October 1892): 289–317.

88. Frank Hamilton Cushing, "Primitive Copper Working," *American Anthropologist* o.s. 7 (January 1894): 93–117.

89. Levy-Bruhl, *How Natives Think* 161.

90. Cushing, "Manual Concepts" 310–11.

91. Levy-Bruhl, *How Natives Think* 162.

92. *Ibid.* 161; emphasis in original.

93. *Ibid.* 162. See also 190–92. Cushing discusses these aspects in "Manual Concepts" 310–11.

94. Levy-Bruhl, *How Natives Think* 162.

95. On this point about solipsism, see Ernest Gellner, "Ethnomethodology: The Re-enchantment Industry or The California Way of Subjectivity," *Spec-*

tacles and Predicaments: Essays in Social Theory, ed. I. C. Jarvie and J. Agassi (Cambridge: Cambridge University Press, 1979) 41–64.

96. Of central importance to Culin's thesis about the American foundation of Asiatic civilization was Cushing's discovery of the primitive American origins of the arrangement of the geographical and cosmological world directional system into quarters around a center (see Cushing, "Manual Concepts" 315–16). When Culin came upon an ancient Korean map similarly arranged, he believed he had one more piece of evidence in support of his hypothesis (see Culin, "A Korean Map of the World" 188–93).

97. Levy-Bruhl, *How Natives Think* 162.

98. *Ibid.* 373.

99. Culin, "Social Organization of the Chinese in America" 348–51.

100. Culin, "The Road to Beauty" 43–45.

101. Cushing, "Tried for Sorcery," *Zuni: Selected Writings of Frank Hamilton Cushing* 157–60.

102. Brandes, *Frank Hamilton Cushing* 96–107. See also Triloki Nath Pandey, "Anthropologists of Zuni," *Proceedings of the American Philosophical Society* 116 (August 1972): 321–26. In 1981 an anthropologist reopened the debate over whether a Paleolithic culture had once existed in North America and spread to Asia. Cushing is credited with constructing a promising but neglected history of the Zuni. However, no mention is made of Culin or of the Culin-Cushing hypothesis and project. See Jeffrey Goodman, *American Genesis: The American Indian and the Origins of Modern Man* (New York: Summit Books, 1981) 198–99.

103. Benjamin Nelson, "De Profundis . . . : Responses to Friends and Critics," in "A Symposium on Civilizational Complexes and Intercivilizational Encounters" 141.

Asian American Contacts before Columbus

1. This debate informs the discussion in Lee Eldridge Huddleston, *Origins of the American Indians: European Concepts, 1492–1729* (Austin: University of Texas Press, 1967).

2. See Richard Popkin, "Bible Criticism and Social Science," *Methodological and Historical Essays in the Natural and Social Sciences,* eds. Robert S. Cohen and Marx W. Wartofsky, *Boston Studies in the Philosophy of Science* XIV (Dordrecht, Holland: D. Reidel Publishing Co., 1974) 339–60.

3. On Manasseh ben Israel see two books by Cecil Roth, *A Life of Menasseh Ben Israel: Rabbi, Printer, Diplomat* (Philadelphia: The Jewish Publication Society of America, 1934) and *A History of the Marranos,* 4th edn. (New York: Schocken Books, 1974) 236–70; Gershom S. Scholem, *Sabbatai Sevi, The Mystical Messiah, 1626–1676,* Bollingen Series xcii (Princeton: Princeton University Press, 1973) 333–45, 518–45; Heinrich Graetz, *History of the Jews* (Philadelphia: The Jewish Publication Society of America, 1967 [1895]) V: 18–50; Ronald Sanders, *Lost Tribes and Promised Lands: The Origins of American Racism* (Boston: Little, Brown and Co., 1978) 365–75; Huddleston, *op. cit.* 128–38; Popkin, *op. cit.* 339–40, 345–48.

4. Henry Home, Lord Kames, *Sketches of the History of Man,* 2nd edn. (Edinburgh: no publisher cited, 1788) I: 3–84. Quoted from George W. Stocking, Jr., *Race, Culture and Evolution: Essays in the History of Anthropology* (New York: The

Free Press, 1968) 38–39. Counting himself among the pious, Home rejected polygenism and proceeded to explain the differences in the cultures and character of mankind by reference to the global scattering occasioned by the catastrophe of the Tower of Babel, and to its consequence that, isolated from one another in different environments, human groups progressed at different rates and in different ways. See Gladys Bryson, *Man and Society: The Scottish Inquiry of the Eighteenth Century* (New York: Augustus M. Kelley, 1968 [1945]) 63–66.

5. Huddleston, *op. cit.* 12.

6. Joseph de Acosta, *Historia natural y moral de las Indias*. (Mexico City: Fondo de Cultura Economica, 1940 [1579]) 72. Trans. and quoted in Huddleston, *op. cit.* 50.

7. Acosta, *op. cit.* 76. Quoted in Huddleston, *op. cit.* 50.

8. Acosta, *op. cit.* 90. Quoted in Huddleston, *op. cit.* 51.

9. For an English translation of Garcia's criticism of Avicenna and Cisalpino, as well as a later emendation to his list of heretical and therefore unacceptable theories made by Andres Gonzales de Barcia Carballido y Zuniga, who included de La Peyrere's pre-Adamite theory among the condemned heterodoxies set forth in 1729, see Hubert Howe Bancroft, *The Native Races: Vol. 5: Primitive History* (San Francisco: The History Co., 1886; New York: Arno Press and McGraw-Hill, n.d.) 4n.

10. Gregorio Garcia, *Origen de los indios de el nuevo mundo, e Indias occidentales . . .*, ed. Andres Gonzales de Barcia Carballido y Zuniga (Madrid: Francisco Martinez Abad, 1729 [1607] 315. Trans. and quoted in Huddleston, *op. cit.* 146.

11. See Kenneth Elliott Bock, *The Comparative Method*, Diss., University of California, Berkeley, 1948, esp. 129–58.

12. The debate over the cultural state of the Amerindians turned on the question of how their customs, habits, and technologies had become so rude if they had originated in the civilizations of East Asia. For those in the Acostan tradition, an answer that adumbrated much of the later thought of anthropologists was supplied by the British historian and ethnographer Sir Matthew Hale in 1677. A strict monogenist and Acostan, Hale supposed that the Americas were settled by migrations across land bridges or by sea voyages taken sometime after the Great Deluge. The Amerindians were in a state of savagery because:

> . . . in the interval of 500 years or thereabouts in all Parts, but in some Parts far greater, there must in all probability happen a great forgetfulness of their Original, a great degeneration from the Primitive Civility, Religion and Customs of those places from whence they were first derived; a ferine and necessitous kind of life, a conversation with those that having been long there were faln into a more barbarous habit of Life and Manners, would easily assimilate at least the next Generation to Barbarism and Ferineness.

Sir Matthew Hale, *The Primitive Origination of Mankind, Considered and Examined According to the Light of Nature* (London: n. p., 1677) 197. Quoted in Bock, *op. cit.* 141.

13. For details of this debate and its effect on racial thought see William Stanton, *The Leopard's Spots: Scientific Attitudes Toward Race in America, 1815–1859* (Chicago: University of Chicago Press, 1960); and John S. Haller, *Outcasts from Evolution: Scientific Attitudes of Race Inferiority* (Urbana: University of Illinois Press, 1971).

14. Thomas Jefferson, *Notes on the State of Virginia* (New York: Harper Torchbooks, 1964) 97.

15. For a discussion of Jefferson's debates with other intellectuals over his

transpacific theories, see Bernard W. Sheehan, *Seeds of Extinction: Jeffersonian Philanthropy and the American Indian* (Chapel Hill: University of North Carolina Press, 1973) 45–65.

16. Quoted in Charles G. Leland, *Fusang, or the Discovery of America by Chinese Buddhist Priests in the Fifth Century* (London: Curzon Books, 1973 [1875]) 176.

17. Lewis Henry Morgan, *Systems of Consanguinity and Affinity of the Human Family*, Vol. XVII of the Smithsonian Contributions to Knowledge (Washington, D.C.: Smithsonian Institution, 1870) 242.

18. Lewis Henry Morgan, *Ancient Society*, ed. Leslie White (Cambridge: Harvard University Press, 1964) 99, 134.

19. *Ibid.* 321.

20. *Ibid.* 393.

21. Bancroft, *op. cit.* 132, 30.

22. See Regna Diebold Darnell, *Daniel Garrison Brinton: An Intellectual Biography*, Master's Thesis, University of Pennsylvania, 1967.

23. Daniel Garrison Brinton, *The American Race: A Linguistic Classification and Ethnographic Description of the Native Tribes of North and South America* (Philadelphia: David McKay, 1901 [1891]).

24. *Ibid.* 17–58 *passim*.

25. Brinton, "On Various Supposed Relations Between the American and Asian Races," *Memoirs of the International Congress of Anthropology, 1893* (Chicago: Schulte Publishing Co., 1894) 145–51.

26. Edward Burnett Tylor, "The History of Games," *Fortnightly Review* XXV (January—June, 1879): 735–47; and "On American Lot-Games as Evidence of Asiatic Intercourse Before the Time of Columbus," *International Archives of Ethnography*, supplement to Vol. IX (1896): 55–67.

27. Brinton, "On Various Supposed Relations . . . ," *op. cit.* 149–50.

28. Brinton, "The Aims of Anthropology," address before the American Association for the Advancement of Science at the Springfield Meeting, August 1895. *Proceedings* XLIV (1895): 4.

29. *Ibid.* 9.

30. Brinton, "On Various Supposed Relations . . . ," *op. cit.* 150.

31. *Ibid.* 150.

32. *Ibid.* 151.

33. Charles Wolcott Brooks, "Origin of the Chinese Race, Philosophy of Their Development, with an Inquiry into the Evidences of their American Origin: Suggesting the Great Antiquity of Races on the American Continent," an address before the California Academy of Sciences, May 3, 1876 (San Francisco: Proceedings of the Academy Reprint, 1876) 3–31.

34. *Ibid.* 20.

35. *Ibid.* 21.

36. *Ibid.* 21–22.

37. *Ibid.* 22.

38. *Ibid.* 30.

39. See Charles Wolcott Brooks, "Arctic Drift and Ocean Currents Illustrated by the Discovery of an Ice-Floe off the Coast of Greenland: Of Relics from the American Arctic Steamer 'Jeanette'" (San Francisco: Geo. Spaulding and Co., 1884) 3–19.

40. At several points in his essays Brooks promises to write a definitive analysis of Japanese origins. I have been unable to locate such a paper and am currently of the opinion that he did not complete his project.

41. Charles Wolcott Brooks, "Early Maritime Intercourse of Ancient Western Nations, Chronologically Arranged, and Ethnologically Considered as Illustrating Facilities for Migration Among Early Types of the Human Race, which Under a Universal Law, May Furnish a Basis to Assist Analogical Researches among Aboriginal Races around the North Pacific Ocean," an address before the California Academy of Sciences, March 15, 1875 (San Francisco: Proceedings of the Academy Reprint, 1876) 13.

42. Charles Wolcott Brooks, "Japanese Wrecks Stranded and Picked Up Adrift in the North Pacific Ocean Ethnologically Considered as Furnishing Evidence of a Constant Infusion of Japanese Blood among the Coast Tribes of Northwestern Indians," Read before the California Academy of Sciences, March 1, 1875 (San Francisco: Printed by the Academy, 1876) 7.

43. Horace Davis, "Record of Japanese Vessels Driven Upon the Northwest Coast of America and its Outlying Islands," Read before the American Antiquarian Society, April 1872 (Worcester, Mass.: Charles Hamilton, 1872) 22.

44. Brooks, "Japanese Wrecks," *op. cit.* 19.

45. *loc. cit.*

46. Brooks, "Origin of the Chinese Race," *op. cit.* 25.

47. Brooks eagerly supported the American takeover of Brooks Island (Midway) in 1867:

We may now welcome Brooks Island as a desirable annexation, remembering that a little stepping-stone may often enable us to cross a stream, which would otherwise bar our progress. How much in this world depends on little things! Although not fully prepared as yet for a permanent coaling station, our China mail-steamers frequently sight this island, and when passing by daylight, exchange signals with the keeper's flag station on the Middle Island.

Brooks predicted that "some persons now living will witness steamers leaving our West Coast daily, for ports in the Orient, and this harbor will benefit the nation which holds it, in time of war as well as in peace." Charles Wolcott Brooks, "Our Furthest Outpost," *Old and New* I (June 1870): 836, 835.

48. Charles Wolcott Brooks, "The Chinese Labor Problem," *Overland Monthly* III (November 1869): 415–16.

49. *Ibid.* 407.

50. *Ibid.* 408.

51. Brooks, "Early Maritime Intercourse," *op. cit.* 5.

52. Brooks, "Chinese Labor Problem," *op. cit.* 407.

53. *Ibid.* 410–17.

54. *Ibid.* 412.

55. *Ibid.* 412.

56. *Ibid.* 416.

57. *Ibid.* 419.

58. *Ibid.* 419.

59. *Ibid.* 419.

60. *Ibid.* 419.

61. *Ibid.* 419.

62. *Ibid.* 419.

63. *Ibid.* 419.

64. *Ibid.* 419.

65. *Ibid.* 419.

66. *Ibid.* 419.

67. Brooks, "Our Furthest Outpost," *op. cit.* 829.
68. Brooks, "Japanese Wrecks" 22.
69. The Fusang legend was first put forth in the West by Pere J. De Guignes in "Les Navigations des Chinois du Cote de l'Amerique it sur plusiers Peuples situes a l'extremite de l'Asie Orientale," *Memoires de l'Academie des Inscriptions et Belles Lettres* XXVIII (1761). Championed by Carl Friedrich Neumann of Munich in 1841 and Colonel Barclay Kennon of the United States Coast Survey in 1874, reinforced with the linguistic interpretation of Hyde Clarke two years earlier, and defended against its detractors by M. Gustave D'Eichtal in 1864 and Charles G. Leland (*op. cit.* 1–187) in 1875, it is the most enduring account of pre-Columbian Chinese (or Afghanistani?) contact with America. Despite continuous refutations by leading scholars in Germany, France, and America, it resurfaces every few years, adding an Oriental religious mystique to the claims of early relations between Asia and America. The definitive English language account claiming America as Fusang is Edward P. Vining, *An Inglorious Columbus, or Evidence that Hwui Shan and a Party of Buddhist Monks from Afghanistan Discovered America in the Fifth Century A.D.* (New York: D. Appleton and Co., 1885). Other champions of Fusang America are Charles G. Leland, *op. cit.*; Frederick J. Masters, "Did a Chinaman Discover America," *Overland Monthly* XXIII (June 1894): 576–88; Douglas S. Watson, "Did the Chinese Discover America?" *California Historical Society Quarterly* XIV (March 1935): 47–58; Robert Larson, "Was America the Wonderful Land of Fusang?" *American Heritage* XVII (1966): 42–45, 106–09; Stan Steiner, *Fusang: The Chinese Who Built America* (New York: Harper and Row, 1979) 3–78; Henriette Mertz, *Pale Ink: Two Ancient Records of Chinese Explorations in America* (Chicago: The Swallow Press, 1953, 1972); Hendon M. Harris, *The Asiatic Fathers of America* (Taipei: Wen Ho Printing Co., n.d.); R. A. Jairazbhoy, *Ancient Egyptians and Chinese in America* (Totowa, N.J.: Rowman and Littlefield, 1974) 100–12. Among the refutations of Fusang America see the reprints of essays by Julius Heinrich von Klaproth and E. Bretschneider in Leland, *op. cit.* 125–87; "Fu-Sang," in Samuel Couling, *The Encyclopedia Sinica* (Shanghai: Kelly and Walsh, 1917) 199; L. Carrington Goodrich, "China's First Knowledge of the Americas," *Geographical Review* XXVIII (July 1938): 400–11. For a recent popular discussion, based on new materials, see David Steinman, "Goodbye Columbus?" *San Diego Magazine* XXXVI (December 1983): 211–14, 233–36, 295–300.
70. Brooks, "Japanese Wrecks," *op. cit.* 21.
71. *loc. cit.*
72. Stewart Culin, "America the Cradle of Asia," address before the section on anthropology, American Association for the Advancement of Science, Washington, D.C., Meeting, December 1902—January 1903. *Proceedings of the American Association for the Advancement of Science* (Washington, D.C.: Gibson Bros., 1903) LII: 493–500.
73. Culin was indebted to Frank Hamilton Cushing, "The Arrow," *American Anthropologist* VIII (October 1895) 307–49. A related idea will be found in Mircea Eliade, "Notes on the Symbolism of the Arrow," in Jacob Neusner, ed., *Religions in Antiquity: Essays in Memory of Erwin Ramsdell Goodenough* (London: E. J. Brill, 1968) 463–75.
74. John G. Owens, "Some Games of the Zuni," *Popular Science Monthly* XXXIX (1891) 41.
75. Cushing's report is published in Culin, *Games of the North American Indians, op. cit.* 212–17.

76. Culin, *Games of the North American Indians, Ibid.* 32.

77. Frank Hamilton Cushing, "Outlines of Zuni Creation Myths," *Thirteenth Annual Report of the Bureau of Ethnology* (1896): 423.

78. Culin, *Games of the North American Indian, op. cit.* 32.

79. *Ibid.* 33. Culin's and Cushing's intriguing theory of the American origin of the arrow was not investigated by Saxton Pope, even after he noticed similarities between Chinese and Yaqui arrows and concluded that "The California Indian makes the best aboriginal arrow of all the specimens examined," while "aboriginal bows are not highly efficient nor well made weapons." Saxton T. Pope, *Bows and Arrows* (Berkeley: University of California Press, 1974 [1923, rev'd., 1930]) 62–63.

80. Stewart Culin, "Games of the North American Indians," *Twenty-Fourth Annual Report of the Bureau of American Ethnology to the Smithsonian Institution, 1902–1903 by W. H. Holmes, Chief* (Washington, D.C.: Government Printing Office, 1907). Citations in the present paper are from the republication of this essay as *Games of the North American Indians* (New York: Dover Publications, 1975).

81. *Ibid.* 32–35.

82. Culin, *Games of North American Indians, op. cit.* 32.

83. Culin, "America the Cradle of Asia," *op. cit.* 500.

84. *Ibid.* 495–96.

85. *Ibid.* 497.

86. *Ibid.* 497.

87. See Stewart Culin, *Games of the Orient: Korea, China, Japan* (Rutledge, Vt., and Tokyo: Charles E. Tuttle, 1968 [1895]).

88. Culin, "A Korean Map of the World," *The Brooklyn Museum Quarterly* XII (October 1925): 183–93.

89. Stewart Culin, "The Religious Ceremonies of the Chinese in the Eastern Cities of the United States," An essay read before the Numismatic and Antiquarian Society of Philadelphia, April 1, 1886 (Philadelphia: privately printed, 1887); "Chinese Games with Dice," Paper read before the Oriental Club of Philadelphia, March 14, 1889 (Philadelphia: Oriental Club, 1889) 5–21; "The Gambling Games of the Chinese in America: Fan T'an; the Game of Repeatedly Spreading Out, and Pak kop Piu; the Game of White Pigeon Ticket," *Publications of the University of Pennsylvania Series in Philology, Literature and Archaeology* I: 4 (Philadelphia: University of Pennsylvania Press, 1891) 1–17; "Chinese Games with Dice and Dominoes," *Report of the United States National Museum, Smithsonian Institution* (Washington, D.C.: Government Printing Office, 1893) 489–537; "Tsz' Fa, or 'Word Blossoming': A Lottery Game Among the Chinese in America," *Overland Monthly,* sec. ser. XXIV (September 1894): 249–54; "Divination and Fortune-Telling Among the Chinese in America," *Overland Monthly,* sec. ser. XXV (February 1895): 165–72; "The Origin of Fan Tan," *Overland Monthly,* sec. ser. XXVII (August 1896): 153–55. Twenty-eight years later Culin published "The Game of Ma-Jong. Its Origin and Significance," *Brooklyn Museum Quarterly* XI (October 1924): 153–68.

90. Edward Burnett Tylor, "On the Game of Patolli in Ancient Mexico and Its probable Asiatic Origin," *Royal Anthropological Institute Journal* VIII (1879): 116–29; and "Backgammon Among the Aztecs," *Popular Science Monthly* XIV (February 1879): 491–501; "On American Lot-Games as Evidence of Asiatic Intercourse Before the Time of Columbus," *op. cit.*

91. Culin, "America the Cradle of Asia" 498–99.

92. *Ibid.* 500.

93. See among hundreds of studies, Carroll L. Riley, J. Charles Kelley, Cambell W. Pennington, and Robert L. Rands, eds., *Man Across the Sea: Problems of Pre-Columbian Contacts* (Austin: University of Texas Press, 1971); and Paul Tolstoy, "Transoceanic Diffusion and Nuclear America," in Shirley Gorenstein, editorial supervisor, *Pre-hispanic America* (New York: St. Martin's Press, 1974) 124–44. The position favoring ancient migration from the Asiatic mainland is developed in a series of papers by Robert Heine-Geldern, "Chinese Influence in the Pottery of Mexico, Central America, and Colombia," *Acts, 334d International Congress of Americanists* I (1959): 207–10; "Representations of the Asiatic Tiger in the Art of the Chavin Culture: A Proof of Early Contacts Between China and Peru," *Ibid.* 321–26; "Chinese Influences in Mexico and Central America: The Tajin Style of Mexico and the Marble Vases from Honduras," *Ibid.* 195–206; "Theoretical Considerations Concerning the Problem of Pre-Columbian Contacts Between the Old World and the New," *Selected Papers, 5th International Congress of Anthropological and Ethnological Scientists,* ed. A. Wallance (Philadelphia, 1960) 277–81; "Traces of Indian and Southeast Asiatic Hindu-Buddhist Influences in Mesoamerica," *Acts, 356th International Congress of Americanists* I (1964): 47–54; "A Note on the Relations Between the Art Styles of the Maori and of Ancient China," *Wiener Beitrage Zur Kulturgeschichte und Linguistik* Band XV (Vienna: Verlag Ferdinand Berger and Söhne Oho, 1966) 45–86; "A Roman Find from Pre-Columbian Mexico," *Anthropological Journal of Canada* V (1967): 20–22; Robert Heine-Geldern and Gordon F. Ekholm, "Significant Parallels in the Symbolic Arts of Southern Asia and Middle America," *The Civilization of Ancient America: Selected Papers, 29th International Congress of Americanists,* ed. Sol Tax (Chicago: University of Chicago Press, 1951) 299–309; and Gordon F. Ekholm, "Wheeled Toys in Mexico," *American Antiquity XI* (April 1946): 222–28; "Is American Indian Culture Asiatic?" *Natural History* LIX (October 1950): 344–51, 382; "The New Orientation Toward Problems of Asiatic-American Relationships," *New Interpretations of Aboriginal American Culture History* Vol. 75 (Washington, D.C.: Anthropology Society of Washington, 1955) 95–109; "The Possible Chinese Origin of Teotihuacan Cylindrical Tripod Pottery and Certain Related Traits," *Proceedings of the 35th International Congress of Americanists* (1962): 39–45. See also G. Elliot-Smith, "The Origin of Pre-Columbian Civilization in America," *Science* n.s. XLIX (August 11, 1916): 190–95; Kamer Aga-Oglu, "Late Ming and Early Ch'ing Porcelain Fragments from Archaeological Sites in Florida," *Florida Anthropologist* VIII (1955): 91–110; Hale G. Smith, "Archaeological Significance of Oriental Porcelain in Florida Sites," *Florida Anthropologist* VIII (1955): 111–16; Gordon R. Willey, "The Prehistoric Civilizations of Nuclear America," *American Anthropologist* LVII (June 1955): 571–93; W. C. McKern, "An Hypothesis for the Asiatic Origin of the Woodland Culture Pattern," *American Antiquity* III (October 1937): 138–43; William Duncan Strong, "Cultural Resemblances in Nuclear America: Parallelism or Diffusion?" *The Civilizations of Ancient America: Selected Papers of the 29th International Congress of Americanists,* ed. Sol Tax (Chicago: University of Chicago Press, 1951) 271–79; F. Ridley, "Transatlantic Contacts of Primitive Man," *Pennsylvania Anthropologist* XXX (1960): 46–57; George F. Carter, "Plant Evidence for Early Contacts with America," *Southwestern Journal of Anthropology* VI (Summer 1960): 161–82; David H. Kelley, "Linguistics and Problems of Trans-Pacific Contacts," *Acts, 35th International Congress of Americanists* I (1964): 17–19; Verla Birrell, "Transpacific Contacts and Peru," *Ibid.* 31–38; Alfonso Caso, "Relations Between the Old and New

Worlds," *Ibid.* 55–71; Philip Phillips, "The Role of Transpacific Contacts in the Development of New World Pre-Columbian Civilizations," *Archaeological Frontiers and External Connections,* ed. Gordon F. Ekholm and Gordon R. Willey (Austin: University of Texas Press, 1966) 296–315; Mino Bradner, "The Protruding Tongue and Related Motifs in the Art Styles of the American Northwest Coast, New Zealand, and China," *Wiener Beitrage Zur Kulturgeschichte und Linguistik* Band XV (Vienna: Verlag Ferdinand Berger and Söhne Ohg, 1966) 5–44. On early Japanese contacts with South America see B. J. Meggers, C. Evans, and E. Estrada, *Early Formative Period of Coastal Ecuador: The Valdivia and Machalilla Phases,* Smithsonian Contributions to Anthropology Vol. I (Washington, D.C.: Smithsonian Institution, 1965); B. J. Meggers and Clifford Evans, "A Transpacific Contact in 3000 B. C.," *Scientific American* CCXIV (January 1966): 28–35; Clifford Evans and Betty J. Meggers, "Transpacific Origin of Valdivia Phase Pottery on Coastal Ecuador," *Acts, 36th International Congress of Americanists* (1966): 63–67. On Shang-Olmec connections see B. Meggers, "Transpacific Origin of Mesoamerican Civilization: A Preliminary Review of the Evidence and its Theoretical Implications," *American Anthropologist* LXXVII (March 1975): 1–27; John B. Carlson, "Lodestone Compass: Chinese or Olmec Primacy," *Science* CLXXXIX (September 1975): 753–60.

94. See J. H. Elliott, *The Old World and the New, 1492–1650* (Cambridge: Cambridge University Press, 1970). For a thoughtful meditation on this theme see Tzvetan Todorov, *The Conquest of America,* trans. Richard Howard (New York: Harper and Row, 1984).

95. See Denys Hay, *Europe: The Emergence of an Idea* (New York: Harper Torchbooks, 1966).

96. The best treatment of this theme is to be found in Louis Hartz, *The Founding of New Societies: Studies in the History of the United States, Latin America, South Africa, Canada, and Australia* (New York: Harcourt, Brace and World, 1964) 11–23, 94–102.

97. Hay, *op. cit.* 125.

98. *Ibid.* 2n.

99. See for China, Jonathan Spence, *To Change China: Western Advisers in China, 1620–1960* (Boston: Little Brown, 1969); and Nigel Cameron, *Barbarians and Mandarins: Thirteen Centuries of Western Travelers in China* (New York and Tokyo: Walker and Weatherhill, 1970) 149–420; Thomas A. Breslin, *China, American Catholicism and the Missionary* (University Park: Pennsylvania State University Press, 1980); Paul A. Varg, *Missionaries, Chinese, and Diplomats: The American Protestant Missionary Movement in China, 1890–1952* (Princeton: Princeton University Press, 1958). For Japan the definitive work is the revealingly partisan study by Otis Cary, D.D., *A History of Christianity in Japan: Roman Catholic, Greek Orthodox, and Protestant Missions* (New York: Fleming H. Revell Co., 1909; Rutland, Vt., and Tokyo: Charles E. Tuttle Co., 1976) II: 355, that concludes: "It may be that at times the Kingdom of God will seem to be losing ground; but those who have faith in God cannot doubt its final establishment in Japan, and they rejoice in the thought of how much this will mean for the regeneration of Asia, and for the hastening of the time when the whole world shall know and serve the living God."

100. Georg Wilhelm Friedrich Hegel, *Lectures on the Philosophy of World History. Introduction: Reason in History,* trans. H. B. Nisbet (Cambridge: Cambridge University Press, 1975) 197.

101. "Publius" [pseud. for Alexander Hamilton], "The Federalist No. 11"

in Alexander Hamilton, James Madison, and John Jay, *The Federalist Papers,* ed. Clinton Rossiter (New York: Mentor–New American Library, 1961) 90–91.

102. For a comprehensive and critical discussion of the impact of Protestant thought on American social science, see Arthur J. Vidich and Stanford M. Lyman, *American Sociology: Worldly Rejections of Religion and their Directions* (New Haven, Yale University Press, 1985).

103. *People vs. Hall,* 4 Cal. 399, 403–04 (1854). Chief Justice Murray's speculation about a distinct type has been given some intellectual backing by Chester S. Chard's postulation of an "Eskimoid" type that was overrun by paleo-Asiatics after it had settled from Kamchatka to Bering Strait. "There was no direct contact or diffusion between the Indians and the Siberians—only participation in the common tradition of their Eskimoid predecessors on the shores of the North Pacific." Chester S. Chard, "Northwest Coast—Northeast Coast Asiatic Similarities: A New Hypothesis," *Selected Papers, 5th International Congress of Anthropological and Ethnological Scientists,* ed. A. Wallace (1966) 235–40.

104. "Ozawa Case," in the Consulate-General of Japan, ed., *Documental History of Law Cases Affecting Japanese in the United States, 1916–1924* (New York: Arno Press, 1978) I: 1–121.

105. Ales Hrdlicka, *The Old Americans* (Baltimore: The Williams and Wilkins Co., 1925) 1–7.

106. See Edwin N. Wilmsen, "An Outline of Early Man Studies in the United States," *American Antiquity* XXXI (October 1965): 179–80.

107. "Ozawa Case" 83–88.

108. For Norse claims, see William S. Godfrey, "Vikings in America: Theories and Evidence," *American Anthropologist* LVII (February 1955): 35–43; Arlington H. Mallery, "The Pre-Columbian Discovery of America: A Reply to W. S. Godfrey," *Ibid.* LX (February 1958): 141–52; O. G. Landsverk, *Runic Records of the Norsemen in America* (Rushford, Minn.: Erik J. Friis, 1974). For recent African claims see Ivan van Sertima, *They Came Before Columbus* (New York: Random House, 1976); Legrand H. Clegg II, "Who Were the First Americans?" *Black Scholar* VII (September 1975): 33–41; Michael Bradley, *The Black Discovery of America* (Toronto: Personal Library-Wiley, 1981), all derivative of Leo Wiener, *Africa and the Discovery of America* (Philadelphia: Innes and Sons, 1920; New York: Krauss Reprint, 1971), 3 vols. For Japanese claims, see "Who Really 'Discovered' America: Norsemen, Italians, or Japanese?" *The Pacific Citizen* LXII (February 11, 1966): 3. For Jewish claims see the vast literature on the Lost Ten Tribes and their possible migration to America. For the fate of Culin's thesis, see three essays by Stanford M. Lyman, "Stewart Culin and the Debate Over Trans-Pacific Migration," *Journal of the Theory of Social Behaviour* IX (March 1979): 91–115, esp. 96–97 and 111–12; "Stewart Culin: The Earliest American Chinatown Studies and a Hypothesis about Pre-Columbian Migration," *Annual Bulletin of Research Institute for Social Science, Ryukoku University* 12 (March 1982): 142–60; "Two Neglected Pioneers of Civilizational Analysis: The Cultural Perspectives of R. Stewart Culin and Frank Hamilton Cushing," in this volume.

109. See, e.g., two works by Emory Bogardus, *Immigration and Race Attitudes* (Boston: D. C. Heath, 1928) 96–102, 133, 212–13; and *Essentials of Americanization* (Los Angeles: University of Southern California Press, 1920) 295–96.

110. In the course of the Congressional hearings on national defense migration in 1942, numerous questions were raised about the relation of Christianity to American patriotism and of Buddhism and other Japanese religions to abject

loyalty to and even worship of the Japanese emperor. An attempt was made by white Christian missionaries and Japanese American Protestants to emphasize the patriotism of Christian Japanese and to downplay or disregard the claims of pro-Japan fealty among adherents of Buddhism. The equation of Christianity with Americanism and both with assimilation was paramount throughout the hearings. Nevertheless, the national-ethnic factor triumphed over the religious: all persons of Japanese descent residing along the American West Coast were imprisoned in specially constructed concentration camps from 1942 to 1945. See *National Defense Migration: Hearings Before the Select Committee Investigating National Defense Migration,* House of Representatives, Seventy-Seventh Congress, 2nd session, parts 29, 30, 31, 1942 (New York: Arno Press, 1978): 11144–46, 11151, 11154, 11195–214, 11355, 11569, 11772, 11808–09. For the problems that Japanese Buddhists faced in America, see Tetsuden Kashima, *Buddhism in America: The Social Organization of an Ethnic Religious Institution* (Westport: Greenwood Press, 1977) esp. 113–224.

111. See, e.g., Amy Tachiki, Eddie Wong, Franklin Odo, and Buck Wong, eds., *Roots: An Asian American Reader* (Los Angeles: UCLA Asian American Studies Center, 1971); Emma Gee, ed., *Counterpoint: Perspectives on Asian America* (Los Angeles: UCLA Asian American Studies Center, 1976); George Kagiwada, "Assimilating Nisei in Los Angeles," rev'd., in Hilary Conroy and T. Scott Miyakawa, eds., *East Across the Pacific: Historical and Sociological Studies of Japanese Immigration and Assimilation* (Santa Barbara: ABC-Clio Press, 1972) 268–78; Shigeo H. Kanda, "Recovering Cultural Symbols: A Case for Buddhism in the Japanese American Communities," *Journal of the American Academy of Religion* XLIV Supplement A (December 1978): 445–75.

112. See the Introduction to Stanford M. Lyman, *Chinatown and Little Tokyo: Power, Conflict, and Community Among Chinese and Japanese Immigrants to America* (Millwood, N.Y.: Associated Faculty Press, 1986).

113. William Petersen, *Japanese Americans* (New York: Random House, 1971) 214–36.

114. Émile Durkheim and Marcel Mauss, "Note on the Notion of Civilization," trans. by Benjamin Nelson, *Social Research* XXXVIII (Winter 1971): 808–13.

115. See, e.g., Taryo Obayashi, "Divination from Entrails Among the Ancient Inca and its Relation to Practices in Southeast Asia," *Acts, 33rd International Congress of Americanists* I (1959): 327–32; Paul Kirchhoff, "The Diffusion of a Great Religious System India to Mexico," *Acts, 36th International Congress of Americanists* I (1964): 73–100; Dennis Lou, "The Mesoamerican 'Mushroom Stones' and the Chinese Ancestor Tablets," summary, *Acts, 36th International Congress of Americanists* I (1966): 91; Paul Shao, *Asiatic Influences on Pre-Columbian Art.* (Ames: Iowa State University Press, 1976).

116. See the symposium, "The Problems of the Unity or Plurality and the Probable Place of Origin of the American Aborigines," *American Anthropologist* XIV (January—March 1912): 159–217; Julian Steward, "Diffusion and Independent Invention: A Critique of Logic," *American Anthropologist* XXXI (July—September, 1929): 491–95; A. L. Kroeber, "Historical Construction of Culture Growths and Organic Evolution," *American Anthropologist* XXXIII (April—June 1931): 149–56; Charles John Erasmus, "Patolli, Pachisi, and the Limitation of Possibilities," *Southwestern Journal of Anthropology* VI (Winter 1950): 369–87; Morris Swadesh, "Diffusional Cumulation and Archaic Residue as Historical Explanations," *Southwestern Journal of Anthropology* VII (Spring

1951): 1–21; Douglas Fraser, "Theoretical Issues in the Transpacific Diffusion Controversy," *Social Research* XXXII (Winter 1965): 452–77; S. A. Arutiunov, "Problems of the Historical-Cultural Connections of the Pacific Basin," *Sovetskais etnografia* V (Summer 1966): 26–31; Harold K. Schneider, "Prehistoric Transpacific Contact and the Theory of Culture Change," *American Anthropologist* LXXIX (March 1977): 9–25.

117. Fang Zhongpu, "Did Chinese Buddhists Reach America 1,000 years Before Columbus?" *China Reconstructs* XXIX (August 1980): 65–66; Gai Pei, "New Research on Chinese Origins of the First Americans," *China Reconstructs* XXXII (January 1983): 38–40; Christy G. Turner, II, "More on the Chinese Origins of the First Americans: Teeth as a Clue," *China Reconstructs* XXXII (July 1983): 44–45.

118. See three works by Kwang-chih Chang, *Early Chinese Civilization: Anthropological Perspectives* (Cambridge: Harvard University Press, 1976); *The Archaeology of Ancient China,* 3rd edn. (New Haven: Yale University Press, 1977); *Shang Civilization* (New Haven: Yale University Press, 1980). See also Ping-ti Ho, *The Cradle of the East: An Inquiry into the Indigenous Origins of Techniques and Ideas of Neolithic and Early Historic China, 5000—1000 B.C.* (Chicago: University of Chicago Press, 1975).

119. See Matsuyama Makoto, "Japan and the Western Powers," *North American Review* CXXVII (November—December 1878): 406–26; S. Kurino, "The Future of Japan," *North American Review* CLX (May 1895): 621–31; Y. Ozaki, "Misunderstood Japan," *North American Review* CLXXI (October 1900): 566–76; and three essays by Baron Kaneko Kentaro, "The Yellow Peril is the Golden Opportunity for Japan," *North American Review* DLXXVI (November 1904): 641–48; "Japan and the United States—Partners," *North American Review* CLXXXIV (March 15, 1907): 631–35; "For a Better Understanding Between the East and the West," *The Independent* LXIII (August 1907): 249–52.

120. Shigeaki Ninomiya, "An Inquiry Concerning the Origin, Development, and Present Situation of the *Eta* in Relation to the History of Social Classes in Japan," *Transactions of the Asiatic Society of Japan* X (December 1933): 49–154.

121. See two essays by Louis B. Leakey, Ruth de Ette Simpson, and Thomas Clements, "Archaeological Excavations in the Calico Mountains, California: Preliminary Report," *Science* CLX (May 31, 1968): 1022–23; and "Man in America: The Calico Mountains Excavations," *Britannica Yearbook of Science and the Future* (Chicago: Encyclopedia Britannica, Inc., 1970) 64–79; Michele Burgess, "Probing Man's Past," *Sky* XII (April 1983): 112–14; Leo J. Hickey, Robert M. West, Mary R. Dawson, Duck K. Choi, "Arctic Terrestrial Biota: Paleomagnetic Evidence of Age Disparity with Mid-Northern Latitudes During the Late Cretaceous and Early Tertiary," *Science* CCXXI (September 1983): 1153–56; Walter Sullivan, "Arctic Theory of Animal Origins Advanced," *New York Times* September 17, 1983: 22; B. O. K. Reeves, "Six Milleniums of Buffalo Kills," *Scientific American* CCXLIX (October 1983): 120–35.

122. Culin, "America the Cradle of Asia," *op. cit.* 495.

123. When in 1947 Gilbert N. Lewis proposed that the paleo-Indians of South America were the pioneers of both American and Asiatic civilization, his hypothesis was greeted as "unorthodox" and was promptly forgotten. Gilbert N. Lewis, "The Beginning of Civilization in America," *American Anthropologist* XLIX (January—March 1947): 1–24. The hypothesis that the races or types of humankind have separate origins has led some paleoanthropologists

to conclude that "there must have been, not one, but several centers where man has developed" and that because of encounters and crossings in the earliest periods "any search for stable archetypes, whether of Negroes, Mongolians, or any of the white racial groups will be condemned to failure." Franz Weidenreich, *Apes, Giants and Man* (Chicago: University of Chicago Press, 1946, 1970) 82–83. More recently, W. W. Howells has expressed reservations about Weidenreich's and Carletoon Coon's postulation of the Peking Man as the exclusive ancestor of the Mongoloids, preferring to see Homo Erectus as a precursor of all of modern humankind's yet-to-be-discovered common ancestor. Howells further supposes that "Mongoloid populations, in history and prehistory, seem to have moved outward rather than to have suffered important incursions of non-Mongoloids; [and that] this is reflected in the original populating of the Americas . . ." W. W. Howells, "Origins of the Chinese People: Interpretations of the Recent Evidence," in David N. Keightley, ed., *The Origin of Chinese Civilization* (Berkeley: University of California Press, 1983) 298.

The Science of History and the Theory of Social Change

1. See Frederick J. Teggart, "World History," *Scientia* 69 (January 1941): 30–35.

2. Frederick J. Teggart, *Rome and China: A Study of Correlations in Historical Events* (Berkeley: University of California Press, 1939).

3. See Stanford M. Lyman, "The Acceptance, Rejection, and Reconstruction of Histories: On Some Controversies in the Study of Social and Cultural Change," in this volume.

4. Robert A. Nisbet, *Social Change and History: Aspects of the Western Theory of Development* (New York: Oxford University Press, 1969).

5. Frederick J. Teggart, *Theory and Processes of History* (Berkeley: University of California Press, 1941) 191–92.

6. *Ibid.* 149–50, 196–97, 272–96, 307–12.

7. See Alfred Schutz, *Collected Papers II: Studies in Social Theory,* ed. Arvid Brodersen (The Hague: Martinus Nijhoff, 1964) 73–78, 95–101, 122–23, 251; and Alfred Schutz and Thomas Luckmann, *The Structures of the Life-World,* trans. Richard M. Zaner and H. Tristram Engelhardt, Jr. (Evanston: Northwestern University Press, 1973) 15, 107–10, 136, 225–26, 271, 284, 311–12.

8. See Harold Garfinkel, *Studies in Ethnomethodology* (Englewood Cliffs: Prentice-Hall, 1967). Garfinkel and his colleagues have emphasized micro-ecological studies of public order and eschewed the issues of history and social change. However, a neglected intellectual ancestor of the perspective that Garfinkel claims to have originated, Frank Hamilton Cushing (1857–1900), employed a variant of ethnomethods—"reproductive archaeology" and "manual concepts"—to discover the bases of civilization and its development. See Stanford M. Lyman, "Two Neglected Pioneers of Civilizational Analysis: R. Stewart Culin and Frank Hamilton Cushing," in this volume.

9. Weber, too, emphasized the elements of irrational mystery that formed the primordial base of any system giving priority to the significance of race, ethnicity, blood, etc. See Max Weber, "Ethnic Groups," *Economy and Society: An Outline of Interpretive Sociology,* ed. Guenther Roth and Claus Wittich (New York: Bedminster Press, 1968) I: 385–98.

10. Max Weber, *The Protestant Ethic and the Spirit of Capitalism*, trans. Talcott Parsons (New York: Charles Scribner's Sons, 1930).

11. See four works by Max Weber, *Ancient Judaism*, trans. and ed. Hans H. Gerth and Don Martindale (Glencoe: The Free Press, 1952); *The Religion of China: Confucianism and Taoism*, trans. and ed. Hans H. Gerth (Glencoe: The Free Press, 1951); *The Religion of India: The Sociology of Hinduism and Buddhism*, trans. and ed. Hans H. Gerth and Don Martindale (Glencoe: The Free Press, 1958); *The Sociology of Religion*, trans. Ephraim Fischoff (Boston: Beacon Press, 1963).

12. Karl Marx and Friedrich Engels, *Basic Writings on Politics and Philosophy*, ed. Lewis S. Feuer (Garden City: Doubleday Anchor, 1959) 246–61.

13. Talcott Parsons, *The Social System* (Glencoe: The Free Press, 1951) 480–535.

14. Pitirim Sorokin, *Social and Cultural Dynamics: A Study of Change in Major Systems of Art, Truth, Ethics, Law and Social Relationships*, rev., abr. edn. (Boston: Porter Sargent, 1957).

15. Stanford M. Lyman and Marvin B. Scott, *A Sociology of the Absurd* (New York: Appleton-Century-Crofts, 1970; 2nd edition, New York: General Hall, 1989).

16. On this point see Marvin B. Scott and Stanford M. Lyman, *The Revolt of the Students* (Columbus: Charles Merrill, 1970) 128–32; and Stanford M. Lyman and Marvin B. Scott, *The Drama of Social Reality* (New York: Oxford University Press, 1975) 13, 55–56, 98–99, 159–61.

17. See Max Weber, *The Methodology of the Social Sciences*, trans. and ed. Edward A. Shils and Henry A. Finch (New York: Free Press, 1949) 80–81.

18. *Ibid.* 72–112.

19. See Weber, *Economy and Society* III: 1111–211, 1375–80.

20. See Constantin Stanislavski, *An Actor's Handbook*, ed. and trans. Elizabeth Reynolds Hapgood (New York: Theatre Arts Books, 1963) 34–35.

21. Bryan Wilson, *The Noble Savages: The Primitive Origins of Charisma and Its Contemporary Survival* (Berkeley: University of California Press, 1975).

The Acceptance, Rejection, and Reconstruction of Histories

1. Talcott Parsons, *The Social System* (Glencoe, Ill.: The Free Press, 1951).

2. Parsons, *Societies: Evolutionary and Comparative Perspectives* (Englewood Cliffs, N.J.: Prentice-Hall, 1966).

3. See, e.g., Joseph-Marie Degerando, *The Observation of Savage Peoples*, F. G. T. Moore, ed. (London: Routledge & Kegan Paul, 1969; orig. pub. 1800).

4. Kenneth E. Bock, "The Comparative Method," Diss., University of California at Berkeley, 1948; "The Comparative Method of Anthropology," *Comparative Studies in Society and History* 8 (1966): 269–80.

5. See, however, William H. McNeil, *A World History* (New York: Oxford University Press, 1967).

6. Franz Boas, *Race, Language and Culture* (New York: The Free Press, 1940) 243–311, 344–55, 626–47.

7. See, e.g., Gerhard Lenski, "Social Structure in Evolutionary Perspective," in *Approaches to the Study of Social Structure*, ed. Peter Blau (New York: The Free Press, 1975) 135–53; "History and Social Change," *American Journal of Sociology* 82 (1976): 548–64.

8. See Paul Honigsheim, "The Problem of Diffusion and Parallel Evolution with Special Reference to American Indians," *Papers of the Michigan Academy of Science, Arts, and Letters* 27 (1941): 515–24.

9. See Anthony Smith, "Social Change and Diffusionist Theories," *Philosophy of Social Science* 5 (1975): 273–87.

10. Kenneth E. Bock, "Evolution and Historical Process," *American Anthropologist* 54 (1952): 486–96; "Comparative Method of Anthropology."

11. Maurice Freedman, "Immigrants and Associations: Chinese in Nineteenth-Century Singapore," *Comparative Studies in Society and History* 3 (1960): 25–48.

12. See Stanford M. Lyman, "Chinese Secret Societies in the Occident: Notes and Suggestions for Research in the Sociology of Secrecy," *The Canadian Review of Sociology and Anthropology* 1 (1964): 101–02.

13. See Thomas Cole, *Democritus and the Sources of Greek Anthropology* (Cleveland: Western Reserve University Press, 1967).

14. See Kenneth E. Bock, "Darwin and Social Theory," *Philosophy of Science* 22 (1955): 123–34.

15. Robert E. Park, "Our Racial Frontier on the Pacific," *Survey Graphic* 9 (1926): 192–96.

16. *Ibid.* 196.

17. See W. O. Brown, "Culture Contact and Race Conflict," in *Race and Culture Contacts,* ed. E. B. Reuter (New York: McGraw-Hill, 1934) 34–47.

18. Emory W. Bogardus, "A Race Relations Cycle," *American Journal of Sociology* 35 (1930): 612–17; "Current Problems of Japanese Americans," *Sociology and Social Research* 25 (1940): 63–66. See also Robert H. Ross and Emory S. Bogardus, "The Second Generation Race Relations Cycle: A Study in Issei-Nisei Relationships," *Sociology and Social Research* 24 (1940): 357–63.

19. Brewton Berry, *Race and Ethnic Relations,* 3rd edn. (Boston: Houghton Mifflin, 1965) 135.

20. Tamotsu Shibutani and Kian Moon Kwan, *Ethnic Stratification: A Comparative Approach* (New York: Macmillan, 1965) 116–35.

21. See Nicholas Rescher, "On the Epistemology of the Inexact Sciences," Appendix II in his *Scientific Explanation* (New York: The Free Press, 1970) 163–208.

22. See the two discussions by Stanford M. Lyman, "The Race Relations Cycle of Robert E. Park," *Pacific Sociological Review* 11 (1968): 16–22; *The Black American in Sociological Thought: A Failure of Perspective* (New York: G. P. Putnam's Sons, 1972) 27–70.

23. Karl Popper, *The Logic of Scientific Discovery* (New York: Harper & Row, Harper Torchbooks, 1965) 78–92.

24. See Lyman, *Black American* 27–35.

25. Winifred Raushenbush, "Their Place in the Sun," *Survey Graphic* 56 (1926): 141–45, 203.

26. Louis Wirth, *The Ghetto* (Chicago: University of Chicago Press, Phoenix Books, 1956; orig. pub. 1928). See also Amitai Etzioni, "The Ghetto—A Re-evaluation," *Social Forces* 37 (1959): 255–62.

27. Rose Hum Lee, *The Chinese in the United States of America* (Hong Kong: Hong Kong University Press, 1960). For a critical discussion, see Stanford M. Lyman, "Overseas Chinese in America and Indonesia," *Pacific Affairs* 34 (1961–62): 380–89.

28. John Stuart Mill, *Auguste Comte and Positivism* (Ann Arbor: University of Michigan Press, 1965) 87.

29. Parsons, *Social System* 249–325.

30. See Robert A. Nisbet, "Social Structure and Social Change," *Research Studies of Washington State College* 20 (1952): 70–76.

31. Talcott Parsons, *The System of Modern Societies* (Englewood Cliffs, N.J.: Prentice-Hall, 1971) 4–28.

32. See S. Kirson Weinberg, "Social-Action Systems and Social Problems," in *Human Nature and Social Process,* ed. Arnold Rose (Boston: Houghton Mifflin, 1962) 401–14.

33. A fine example will be found in Talcott Parsons, "Social Strains in America" (1955) and "Social Strains in America: A Postscript" (1962), both in *The Radical Right,* ed. Daniel Bell (Garden City, N.Y.: Doubleday, 1963) 175–200.

34. See Kenneth E. Bock, "Some Basic Assumptions About Change," *Et Al.* 2 (1970): 44–48.

35. Frederick J. Teggart, *Theory and Processes of History* (Berkeley: University of California Press, 1941) 244.

36. Teggart, "The Approach to the Study of Man," *Journal of Philosophy* 16 (1919): 155.

37. *Ibid.*

38. Margaret T. Hodgen, *Change and History: A Study of the Dated Distributions of Technological Innovations in England,* Viking Fund Publications in Anthropology, no. 18 (New York: Wenner-Gren Foundation for Anthropological Research, 1952) 122.

39. Frederick J. Teggart, "The Humanistic Study of Change in Time," *Journal of Philosophy* 23 (1926): 309–15.

40. Teggart, *Theory and Processes,* 180–87.

41. Frederick J. Teggart, "Turgot's Approach to the Study of Man," *University of California Chronicle* 28 (1926): 129–42.

42. Kenneth E. Bock, *The Acceptance of Histories: Toward a Perspective for Social Science,* University of California Publications in Sociology and Social Institutions 3, no. 1 (Berkeley: University of California Press, 1956) 108–22.

43. Hodgen, *Change and History* 48–72.

44. Frederick J. Teggart, *Rome and China: A Study of Correlations in Historical Events* (Berkeley: University of California Press, 1939).

45. Bock, *Acceptance of Histories* 112.

46. Frederick J. Teggart, "Causation in Historical Events," *Journal of the History of Ideas* 3 (1942): 3–11.

47. Bock, *Acceptance of Histories* 114–15.

48. *Ibid.* 115.

49. *Ibid.*

50. Hodgen, *Change and History* 66.

51. Teggart, *Rome and China* 225–45.

52. See Lyman, *Black American* 171–84; *The Asian in the West,* Social Science and Humanities Publication no. 4, Western Studies Center (Reno: Desert Research Institute, University of Nevada System, 1970); *Chinese Americans* (New York: Random House, 1974) 186–91; "Legitimacy and Consensus in Lipset's America: From Washington to Watergate," in this volume.

53. Robert A. Nisbet, *Social Change and History: Aspects of the Western Theory of Development* (New York: Oxford University Press, 1969) 267–304.

54. W. I. Thomas, "Introductory," *Source Book for Social Origins* (Boston: Richard G. Badger, 1909) 3–28.

55. Alfred Schutz, "Some Structures of the Life-World," *Collected Papers*

III: Studies in Phenomenological Philosophy, ed. I. Schutz (The Hague: Martinus Nijhoff, 1966) 116–32.

56. Teggart, *Theory and Processes of History* 308.

57. *Ibid.* 307.

58. Hodgen, *Change and History* 73–96.

59. Teggart, *Theory and Processes of History* 311.

60. Hodgen, *Change and History* 48–72.

61. Teggart, *Rome and China.*

62. Max Weber, *The Agrarian Sociology of Ancient Civilizations,* trans. R. I. Frank (London: New Left Books, 1976) 385.

63. Park, "Our Racial Frontier" 196.

64. Lyman, *Black American* 27–70.

65. Teggart, *Theory and Processes of History* 51–66.

66. Frederick J. Teggart, "The Capture of St. Joseph, Michigan, by the Spaniards in 1781," *Missouri Historical Review* 5 (1911): 214–28.

67. See Frederick J. Teggart, "The Argument of Hesiod's *Works and Days,*" *Journal of the History of Ideas* 8 (1947): 45–77; Bock, *Acceptance of Histories* 123.

68. Teggart, *Theory and Processes* 151.

69. *Ibid.*

70. Teggart, "Causation in Historical Events" 8.

71. *Ibid.*

72. *Ibid.* 8–9.

73. *Ibid.* 9.

74. Teggart, *Rome and China* 240.

75. *Ibid.* 241.

76. Robert K. Merton, *Social Theory and Social Structure,* rev. and enlarged edn. (Glencoe, Ill.: The Free Press, 1957) 19–84.

77. Teggart, *Rome and China* 241–42.

78. See the appeals by Frederick J. Teggart, "Human Geography, An Opportunity for the University," *The Journal of Geography* 17 (1918): 247–67; "Geography as an Aid to Statecraft: An Appreciation of Mackinder's 'Democratic Ideals and Reality'," *Geographical Review* 8 (1919): 227–42.

79. Familiar as he was with German historians of the period, Teggart may have had in mind the inflammatory writings of Heinrich von Treitschke (1834–96). A passage typical of von Treitschke's style illustrates the kind of argument Teggart found so reprehensible:

Thus manifold have been the conflicting influences of the various living forces of history in national questions. When we examine these complicated conditions more closely we find first of all a great antagonism of races among human kind. . . . [B]ut the historian need only concern himself with the broad divisions of white, black, red, and yellow. The yellow race has never achieved political liberty, for their States have always been despotic and unfree. In the same way the artistic faculty has always been denied to the Mongols, in spite of that sense of comfort which we may admire among the Chinese, if we are soft and effeminate enough to wish to. The black races have always been servants, and looked down upon by all the others, nor has any Negro State ever raised itself to a level of real civilization. Physical strength and endurance are such marked characteristics in the Negro that he is employed inevitably to serve the ends of a will and intelligence higher than his own. The red race of North America, although now fallen into decay, once possessed a remarkable talent for State building. . . . The red and yellow races spring from a common stock. Opposed to them stands the white race, which falls into two classes, the Aryan and the Semitic peoples. (*Politics,* trans. Blanche Dugdale and Torben de Bille, ed. Hans Kohn [New York: Harcourt, Brace & World, 1963] 125.)

80. Teggart, *Rome and China* 242–43.

81. Frederick J. Teggart, "The Obligation of Peace," *The Public: A Journal of Democracy* 22 (August 30, 1919): 928–29; "Education for Life," *The Public: A Journal of Democracy* 22 (1919): 1010–11; "The Responsibilities for Leadership," *The Dial* 67 (1919): 237–39.

82. Teggart, "War and Civilization in the Future," *American Journal of Sociology* 46 (1941): 582–90.

83. Teggart, "Argument of Hesiod's *Works and Days.*"

84. Teggart, *Prolegomena to History: The Relation of History to Literature, Philosophy, and Science,* University of California Publications in History 4 (Berkeley: University of California Press, 1916) 277.

85. Arnold J. Toynbee, *A Study of History* (New York: Oxford University Press, 1954) X: 232.

86. Teggart, *Theory and Processes of History* 49.

87. See Oscar K. Rabinowicz, *Arnold Toynbee on Judaism and Zionism: A Critique* (London: W. H. Allen, 1974).

88. Bock, *Acceptance of Histories* 120.

89. Joseph Needham, *Science and Civilization in China* (Cambridge: Cambridge University Press, 1954) I: 183–87.

90. Needham, *The Grand Titration: Science and Society in East and West* (London: George Allen & Unwin, 1969) 11.

91. *Ibid.* 12.

92. See Benjamin Nelson, "Sciences and Civilizations, 'East' and 'West': Joseph Needham and Max Weber," in *Philosophical Foundations of Science,* ed. R. J. Seeger and R. S. Cohen (Dordrecht: D. Reidel, 1974) 445–93; "Copernicus and the Quest for Certitude: 'East' and 'West,'" in *Copernicus Yesterday and Today,* Proceedings of the Commemorative Conference in Honor of Nicolaus Copernicus, Washington, D.C., 1972, ed. Arthur Beer and K. A. Strand (New York: Pergamon Press, 1975) 39–46; "The Quest for Certitude and the Books of Scripture, Nature, and Science," in *The Nature of Scientific Discovery,* ed. Owen Gingerich (Washington, D.C.: Smithsonian Institution Press, 1975) 355–72.

93. Harry Elmer Barnes, *A History of Historical Writing,* 2nd rev. edn. (New York: Dover Publications, 1962) 378.

94. Quoted in Burleigh Taylor Wilkins, *Carl Becker: The Development of an American Historian* (Cambridge: M.I.T. Press, 1967) 188.

95. Barnes, *History of Historical Writing* 378.

96. Robert A. Nisbet, "Sociology as an Idea System," in *Sociological Self-Images: A Collective Portrait,* ed. Irving Louis Horowitz (Beverly Hills: Sage Publications, 1969) 200.

97. Bock, *Acceptance of Histories* 120–21; Nisbet, *Social Change and History* 276–77.

98. Max Weber, *Roscher and Knies: The Logical Problems of Historical Economics,* trans. Guy Oakes (New York: The Free Press, 1975); *Agrarian Sociology of Ancient Civilizations.*

99. Howard Becker, "Culture Case Study and Ideal-Typical Method: With Special Reference to Max Weber," *Social Forces* 12 (1933): 399–405.

100. Becker, "The Field and Problems of Historical Sociology," in *The Fields and Methods of Sociology,* ed. L. L. Bernard (New York: Ray Long & Richard L. Smith, 1934) 24.

101. Alvin Boskoff, "Social Change: Major Problems in the Emergence of Theoretical and Research Foci," in *Modern Sociological Theory in Continuity and Change,* ed. Howard Becker and Alvin Boskoff (New York: Holt, Rinehart & Winston, 1957) 288.

102. Teggart, *Theory and Processes of History* 149–50, 196–97, 307–12.

103. Robert E. Park, *Race and Culture: The Collected Papers of Robert E. Park* 1, ed. Everett Cherrington Hughes, Charles S. Johnson, Jitsuichi Masuoka, Robert Redfield, and Louis Wirth (Glencoe, Ill.: The Free Press, 1950) 7, 18, 97n, 345, 350–51.

104. Howard Becker and Harry Elmer Barnes, *Social Thought from Lore to Science,* 3rd edn. (New York: Dover Publications, 1951) I: 264–65; III: 990.

105. Howard Becker, "Forms of Population Movement: Prolegomena to a Study of Mental Mobility," pt. 1, *Social Forces* 9 (1930): 147–60; pt. 2, 9 (1931): 351–61; "Processes of Secularization: An Ideal-Typical Analysis with Special Reference to Personality Change as Affected by Population Movement," pt. 1, *Sociological Review* 24 (1932): 138–54; pt. 2, 24 (1932): 266–87.

106. In addition to those cited, the following works by Margaret T. Hodgen were published during Teggart's lifetime: "The Fitness of British Labor to Rule," *Forum* 69 (1923): 1108–19; *Workers' Education in England and the United States* (London: Kegan Paul, Trench, Trubner & Co., 1925); "The Doctrine of Survivals: The History of an Idea," *American Anthropologist* n.s., 33 (1931): 307–24; "Survivals and Social Origins: The Pioneers," *American Journal of Sociology* 38 (1933): 583–94; "The Negro in the Anthropology of John Wesley," *Journal of Negro History* 19 (1934): 308–23; *The Doctrine of Survivals: A Chapter in the History of Scientific Method in the Study of Man* (London: Allenson, 1936); "Domesday Walter Mills," *Antiquity* 13 (1939): 261–79; "Geographical Diffusion as a Criterion of Age," *American Anthropologist* 44 (1942): 340–68; "Fairs of Elizabethan England," *Economic Geography* 18 (1942): 389–400; "Sir Matthew Hale and the Method of Invention," *Isis* 34 (1943): 313–18; "Glass and Paper: An Historical Study of Acculturation," *Southwestern Journal of Anthropology* 1 (1945): 466–97.

107. John C. McKinney, "Methodology, Procedures, and Techniques in Sociology," in *Modern Sociological Theory in Continuity and Change,* ed. Howard Becker and Alvin Boskoff (New York: Holt, Rinehart and Winston, 1957) 230–31.

108. Leon J. Goldstein, "Theory in Anthropology: Developmental or Causal?" in *Sociological Theory: Inquiries and Paradigms,* ed. Llewellyn Gross (New York: Harper & Row, 1967) 172n.

109. See, e.g., Ernest Gellner, "Concepts and Society," in *Rationality,* ed. Bryan R. Wilson (New York: Harper & Row, Harper Torchbooks, 1970) 18–49; Jack Goody, "Evolution and Communication: The Domestication of the Savage Mind," *British Journal of Sociology* 24 (1973): 1–12; Keith Dixon, *Sociological Theory: Pretence and Possibility* (London: Routledge & Kegan Paul, 1973).

110. See Anthony Smith, *The Concept of Social Change: A Critique of the Functionalist Theory of Social Change* (London: Routledge & Kegan Paul, 1973); "Social Change and Diffusionist Theories."

111. See Margaret T. Hodgen, "Similarities and Dated Distributions,"

American Anthropologist 52 *(1950):* 445–65; *"Karl Marx and the Social Scientists,"* *Scientific Monthly* 72 (1951): 252–58; "Anthropology, History and Science," *Scientia* 87 (1952): 282–97; "Johann Boemus (Fl. 1500): An Early Anthropologist," *American Anthropologist* 55 (1953): 284–94; "Sebastian Muenster (1489–1552): A Sixteenth-Century Ethnographer," *Osiris* 11 (1954): 504–29; *Early Anthropology in the Sixteenth and Seventeenth Centuries* (Philadelphia: University of Pennsylvania Press, 1964); "Ethnology in 1500: Polydore Vergil's Collection of Customs," *Isis* 57 (1966): 315–24; "Frederick John Teggart," in *International Encyclopedia of the Social Sciences,* ed. David Sills (New York: Macmillan, 1968) XV: 598–99; *Anthropology, History, and Cultural Change,* Viking Fund Publications in Anthropology no. 52 (Tucson: The University of Arizona Press, The Wenner-Gren Foundation for Anthropological Research, 1974).

112. See Kenneth E. Bock, "History and the Science of Man: An Appreciation of George Cornewall Lewis," *Journal of the History of Ideas* 12 (1951): 599–608; "Discussion," *American Sociological Review* 17 (1952): 164–66; "Evolution and Historical Process"; "Darwin and Social Theory"; "The Study of War in American Sociology," *Sociologus* 5 (1955): 104–13; "Cultural Difference and Race: The History of a Problem," *Commentary* 24 (1957): 86–88; "Evolution, Function, and Change," *American Sociological Review* 28 (1963): 229–37; "Theories of Progress and Evolution," in *Sociology and History: Theory and Research,* ed. Werner J. Cahnman and Alvin Boskoff (London: The Free Press of Glencoe, Collier-Macmillan, 1964) 21–41; "The Comparative Method of Anthropology"; "Some Basic Assumptions About Change"; "Comparison of Histories: The Contribution of Henry Maine," *Comparative Studies in Society and History* 16 (1974): 232–62.

113. See Robert A. Nisbet, "The French Revolution and the Rise of Sociology in France," *American Journal of Sociology* 49 (1943): 156–64; "Bonald and the Concept of the Social Group," *Journal of the History of Ideas* 5 (1944): 315–31; "Social Structure and Social Change," in *Research Studies of Washington State College* 20 (1952): 70–76; *The Quest for Community: A Study in the Ethics of Order and Freedom* (New York: Oxford University Press, 1953); "Sociology as an Art Form," *Pacific Sociological Review* 5 (1962): 64–74; *The Sociological Tradition* (New York: Basic Books, 1966); *Tradition and Revolt: Historical and Sociological Essays* (New York: Random House, 1968); *Social Change and History;* "Sociology as an Idea System"; "Developmentalism: A Critical Analysis," in *Theoretical Sociology: Perspectives and Developments,* ed. John C. McKinney and Edward A. Tiryakian (New York: Appleton-Century-Crofts, 1970) 167–204; *The Sociology of Emile Durkheim* (New York: Oxford University Press, 1974); *Sociology as an Art Form* (New York: Oxford University Press, 1976): "The Social Impact of the Revolution," *The Wilson Quarterly* 1 (1976): 93–107; "An Eruption of Genius: F.J. Teggart at Berkeley," *The California Monthly* 87 (1976): 3, 6–7; "Vico and the Idea of Progress," *Social Research* 43 (1976): 625–36.

114. Meek seems to be unaware of Teggart's essay praising Turgot for being opposed to the organic analogy in the study of cultural change. See Teggart, "Turgot's Approach to the Study of Man."

115. See Ronald L. Meek, ed. and trans., "Smith, Turgot and the 'Four Stages' Theory," *History of Political Economy* 3 (1971): 9–27; *Turgot on Progress, Sociology and Economics* (Cambridge: Cambridge University Press, 1976).

116. Eugene Kamenka and Alice Erh-Soon Tay, "Beyond Bourgeois Individualism: The Contemporary Crisis in Law and Legal Ideology," *Feudalism,*

Capitalism and Beyond, ed. Eugene Kamenka and R. S. Neale (London: Edward Arnold, 1975) 126–44.

117. Richard Beardsley, "An Appraisal of Leslie A. White's Scholarly Influence," *American Anthropologist* 77 (1976): 619–20.

118. See Frederick J. Teggart, "The Circumstance or the Substance of History," *American Historical Review* 15 (1910): 709–19; "Anthropology and History," *Journal of Philosophy* 16 (1919): 691–96; "Clio," *University of California Chronicle* 24 (1922): 347–60; "The Humanistic Study of Change in Time"; "Notes on 'Timeless' Sociology: A Discussion," *Social Forces* 7 (1929): 362–66; *Two Essays on History* (Berkeley: Privately printed, 1930); "A Problem in the History of Ideas," *Journal of the History of Ideas* 1 (1940): 494–503; "World History," *Scientia* 69 (1941): 30–35.

119. C. Martin Wilbur, "Review of *Rome and China: A Study of Correlations in Historical Events,*" *American Historical Review* 46 (1940): 93.

120. Pitirim A. Sorokin, "Review of *Rome and China: A Study of Correlations in Historical Events,*" *American Journal of Sociology* 46 (1940): 388–89.

121. See Stanford M. Lyman and Marvin B. Scott, *A Sociology of the Absurd,* 2nd edition (Dix Hills, N.Y.: General Hall, 1989) 35–50.

122. See Erving Goffman, *Frame Analysis: An Essay on the Organization of Experience* (Cambridge, Mass.: Harvard University Press, 1974).

123. See Talcott Parsons, et al., "Some Fundamental Categories of the Theory of Action: A General Statement," *Toward a General Theory of Action,* ed. T. Parsons and Edward A. Shils (New York: Harper & Row, Harper Torchbooks, 1951) 3–29.

124. Henry S. Pachter, "Defining an Event: Prolegomena to Any Future Philosophy of History," *Social Research* 41 (1974): 443–44.

125. *Ibid.* 448–50.

126. See Sorokin, "Review of *Rome and China*" 389–90; George H. Hildebrand, Jr., "Review of *Rome and China: A Study of Correlations in Historical Events,*" *American Sociological Review* 5 (1940): 822–25.

127. Jack D. Douglas, *The Social Meanings of Suicide* (Princeton, N.J.: Princeton University Press, 1967) 3–78; "The Rhetoric of Science and the Origins of Statistical Social Thought: The Case of Durkheim's *Suicide,*" *The Phenomenon of Sociology,* ed. Edward Tiryakian (New York: Appleton-Century-Crofts, 1971) 44–57.

128. Max Weber, *The Theory of Social and Economic Organization,* ed. Talcott Parsons, trans. A. M. Henderson and Talcott Parsons (Glencoe, Ill.: The Free Press, The Falcon's Wing Press, 1947) 88.

129. Weber, *Roscher and Knies* 64.

130. Wilhelm Dilthey, *Pattern and Meaning in History: Thoughts on History and Society,* ed. H. P. Rickman (New York: Harper & Row, Harper Torchbooks, 1962) 64–168.

131. Hans-Georg Gadamer, *Truth and Method,* ed. and trans. Garett Barden and John Cumming (New York: The Seabury Press, 1975) 192–344.

132. Ludwig von Bertalanffy, *General Systems Theory: Foundations, Development, Applications,* rev. edn. (New York: George Braziller, 1968) 139–54; Ervin Lazlo, ed., *The Relevance of General Systems Theory: Papers Presented to Ludwig von Bertalanffy on his Seventieth Birthday* (New York: George Braziller, 1972).

133. See E. E. Evans-Pritchard, *Social Anthropology and Other Essays* (New York: The Free Press, 1962) 21–63, 172–91; A. R. Radcliffe-Brown, *Structure and Function in Primitive Society* (Glencoe, Ill.: The Free Press, 1952) 178–204.

134. Gellner, "Concepts and Society" 18–49.

135. See Stanford M. Lyman, "Civilization: Contents, Discontents, Malcontents," in this volume.

136. Erving Goffman, *Encounters: Two Studies in the Sociology of Interaction* (Indianapolis: Bobbs-Merrill, 1961) 19–26.

137. Harold Garfinkel, *Studies in Ethnomethodology* (Englewood Cliffs, N.J.: Prentice-Hall, 1967).

138. Claude Lévi-Strauss, *Structural Anthropology,* trans. Claire Jacobson and Brooke Grundfest Schoepf (Harmondsworth: Penguin, 1972).

139. See Mary Douglas, "The Meaning of Myth, with Special Reference to 'La Geste d'Asdiwal'," in *The Structural Study of Myth and Totemism,* ed. Edmund Leach (London: Tavistock, 1969) 49–70.

140. See Kenneth Burke, *Attitudes Toward History* 3rd edition (Berkeley: University of California Press, 1984): 417–34.

141. Stanford M. Lyman and Marvin B. Scott, *The Drama of Social Reality* (New York: Oxford University Press, 1975) 128–46.

142. See Maurice Natanson, "History as a Finite Province of Meaning," in his *Literature, Philosophy and the Social Sciences: Essays in Existentialism and Phenomenology* (The Hague: Martinus Nijhoff, 1962) 172–78.

143. See Herbert Blumer, "Race Prejudice as a Sense of Group Position," *Pacific Sociological Review* 1 (1958): 3–7.

144. See Rudolph H. Weingartner, *Experience and Culture: The Philosophy of Georg Simmel* (Middletown, Conn.: Wesleyan University Press, 1962) 85–139.

The Race Relations Cycle of Robert E. Park

1. The bulk of Park's work on race relations is to be found in Robert Ezra Park, *Race and Culture* (Glencoe: The Free Press, 1950). This book of essays written over the long span of Park's life was published posthumously. The date of each essay will be noted in the footnotes to follow. *Race and Culture* will be designated *RC*.

2. "Our Racial Frontier on the Pacific," *RC* 150 (May 1926).

3. "The Nature of Race Relations," *RC* 116, (1939).

4. "Our Racial Frontier on the Pacific," *RC* 150–51; "Behind Our Masks," *RC* 250–51. (May 1926).

5. Winifred Raushenbush, "Their Place in the Sun," *Survey Graphic* LVI (May 1926): 141–45.

6. Winifred Raushenbush, "The Great Wall of Chinatown," *Survey Graphic* LVI (May 1926): 154–59.

7. Elliot Grinnel Mears, "The Land, the Crops, and the Oriental," *Survey Graphic* LVI (May 1926): 146–50; R. D. McKenzie, "The Oriental Finds a Job," *Ibid.* 151–53; Kazuo Kawai, "Three Roads, and None Easy," *Ibid.* 164–66; William C. Smith, "Born American, But—," *Ibid.* 167–68.

8. "Their Place in the Sun," *op. cit.* 144.

9. *loc. cit.*

10. *loc. cit.*

11. "Behind Our Masks," *RC* 254.

12. "Racial Assimilation in Secondary Groups with Particular Reference to the Negro," *RC* 209. See also "The Bases of Race Prejudice," *Ibid.* 230–43.

13. "Our Racial Frontier on the Pacific," *RC* 150.

14. "Racial Assimilation in Secondary Groups with Particular Reference to the Negro," *RC* 209.

15. For a discussion of unfalsifiability in developmental theories see Kenneth E. Bock, *The Acceptance of Histories: Toward a Perspective for Social Science* (Berkeley: University of California Publications in Sociology and Social Institutions, 1956) III, 49–53 et passim.

16. "Our Racial Frontier on the Pacific," *RC* 151.

17. Seymour Martin Lipset, "Changing Social Status and Prejudice: The Race Theories of a Pioneering American Sociologist," *Commentary* 9 (May 1950): 479.

18. Louis Wirth, *The Ghetto* (Chicago: University of Chicago Press—Phoenix Books, 1956).

19. Rose Hum Lee, *The Chinese in the United States of America* (Hong Kong: Hong Kong University Press, 1960). For further discussion of this work see Stanford M. Lyman, "Overseas Chinese in America and Indonesia," *Pacific Affairs* XXXIV (Winter 1961–62): 380–89.

20. Louis Wirth, "The Problem of Minority Groups," in Ralph Linton, ed., *The Science of Man in the World Crisis* (New York: Columbia University Press, 1945) 347–72, esp. 364.

21. E. S. Bogardus, "A Race Relations Cycle," *American Journal of Sociology* 35 (January 1930): 612–17; Robert H. Ross and E. S. Bogardus, "The Second Generation Race Relations Cycle: A Study in Issei-Nisei Relationships," *Sociology and Social Research* 24 (March 1940): 357–63. See also E. S. Bogardus, "Current Problems of Japanese Americans," *Sociology and Social Research* 25 (July 1941): 562–71; and Robert H. Ross and Emory S. Bogardus, "Four Types of Nisei Marriage Patterns," *Sociology and Social Research* 25 (September 1940): 63–66.

22. W. O. Brown, "Culture Contact and Race Conflict," in E. B. Reuter, ed., *Race and Culture Contacts* (New York: McGraw-Hill, 1934) 34–37.

23. Jitsuichi Masuoka, "Race Relations and Nisei Problems," *Sociology and Social Research* 30 (July 1946): 452–59, at p. 459.

24. Clarence E. Glick, "Social Roles and Types in Race Relations," in A. W. Lind, ed., *Race Relations in World Perspective* (Honolulu: University of Hawaii Press, 1955) 239ff.

25. Stanley Lieberson, "A Societal Theory of Race and Ethnic Relations," *American Sociological Review* 26 (December 1961): 902–10.

26. Amitai Etzioni, "The Ghetto—a Re-Evaluation," *Social Forces* 37 (March 1959): 255–62.

27. Brewton Berry, *Race and Ethnic Relations,* 3rd edn. (Boston: Houghton-Mifflin Co., 1965) 135. In his later work on certain groups of racial hybrids in America, *Almost White* (New York: Macmillan, 1963), Berry avoids theoretical issues entirely and, instead, concentrates on pleading for understanding and compassion. See Stanford M. Lyman, "The Spectrum of Color," *Social Research* 31 (Autumn 1964): 364–73.

28. Tamotsu Shibutani and Kian Moon Kwan, *Ethnic Stratification, a Comparative Approach* (New York: Macmillan, 1965) 116–35 at p. 135.

29. E. Franklin Frazier, "Racial Problems in World Society," in Jitsuichi Masuoka and Preston Valien, eds., *Race Relations, Problems and Theory: Essays in Honor of Robert E. Park* (Chapel Hill: University of North Carolina Press, 1961) 40. See also Frazier, *Race and Culture Contacts in the Modern World* (New York: Alfred A. Knopf, 1957) 31–38.

30. See Jean Burnet, "Robert E. Park and the Chicago School of Sociology: A Centennial Tribute," *Canadian Review of Sociology and Anthropology* 1 (August 1964): 156–69. See also the interesting exchange on Park between Ralph Ellison and Morris Janowitz in Ralph Ellison, "An American Dilemma: A Review," *Shadow and Act* (New York: Random House, 1964) 304–08 and Morris Janowitz, "Review of Shadow and Act," *American Journal of Sociology* LXX (May 1965): 732–34.

31. See Carl G. Hempel, "Typological Methods in the Social Sciences," in Maurice Natanson, ed., *Philosophy of the Social Sciences* (New York: Random House, 1963) 210–30; Don Martindale, "Sociological Theory and the Ideal Type," in Llewellyn Gross, ed., *Symposium on Sociological Theory* (Evanston: Row, Peterson, & Co., 1959) 57–91; May Brodbeck, "Models, Meaning, and Theories," *Ibid.* 373–406; Howard Becker and Harry Elmer Barnes, *Social Thought from Lore to Science* (New York: Dover Publications, 1961) II: 777–87.

32. Max Weber, *The Methodology of the Social Sciences,* trans. and ed. Edward A. Shils and Henry A. Finch (Glencoe: The Free Press, 1949) 89–112.

33. See Milton M. Gordon, *Assimilation in American Life: The Role of Race, Religion, and National Origins* (New York: Oxford University Press, 1964).

34. "The Race Relations Cycle in Hawaii," *RC* 194 (1937).

35. Thus both Louis Wirth and Amitai Etzioni, who strongly disagree with one another on the applicability of Park's cycle to the study of Jews in America, equate assimilation with intermarriage. See Wirth, *The Ghetto, op. cit.* 68, 112–13, 125–26, 145; and Etzioni, *op. cit.* 259–61.

36. See Robin Williams, *American Society: A Sociological Interpretation* (New York: Alfred A. Knopf, 1960) 80–82, 397–470.

37. *Ibid.* 415–68.

38. In addition to the articles cited in footnote 31 *supra,* see Robert O. Brown, *Explanation in Social Science* (Chicago: Aldine Press, 1963); Richard S. Rudner, *Philosophy of Social Science* (Englewood Cliffs: Prentice-Hall, 1966); and the articles by Lundberg, Natanson, Schutz, and Nagel in Natanson, *op. cit.*

39. Hempel, *op. cit.* 223–26.

40. See George A. Theodorson, "The Uses of Causation in Sociology," in Llewellyn Gross, ed., *Sociological Theory: Inquiries and Paradigms* (New York: Harper & Row, 1967) 131–52 and Leon J. Goldstein, "Theory in Anthropology: Developmental or Causal?" *Ibid.* 153–80.

Interactionism and the Study of Race Relations at the Macro-sociological Level

1. Lewis M. Killian, "Herbert Blumer's Contributions to Race Relations," *Human Nature and Collective Behavior: Papers in Honor of Herbert Blumer,* ed. Tamotsu Shibutani (Englewood Cliffs, N.J.: Prentice-Hall, 1970) 179.

2. Peter I. Rose, *The Subject Is Race: Traditional Ideologies and the Teaching of Race Relations* (New York: Oxford University Press, 1968) 3, 75.

3. Rose, *They and We: Racial and Ethnic Relations in the United States,* 3rd edn. (New York: Random House, 1981).

4. Hubert M. Blalock, Jr., *Toward a Theory of Minority Group Relations* (New York: Capricorn Books, 1967); and *Race and Ethnic Relations* (Englewood Cliffs, N.J.: Prentice-Hall, 1982).

5. J. Milton Yinger, "Recent Developments in Minority and Race Rela-

tions," *Annals of the American Academy of Political and Social Science* 378 (July 1968): 130–45.

6. Marguerite Bryan, "The Social Psychology of Riot Participation"; and Cheryl B. Leggon, "Theoretical Perspectives on Race and Ethnic Relations: A Socio-Historical Approach," in Cora Bagley Marrett and Cheryl Leggon, eds., *Research in Race and Ethnic Relations: A Research Annual* (Greenwich, Conn.: JAI Press, 1979) 172, 173, 1–16.

7. Stephan Thernstrom, ed., *Harvard Encyclopedia of American Ethnic Groups* (Cambridge: The Belknap Press of Harvard University Press, 1980).

8. Norman R. Yetman and C. Hoy Steele, *Majority and Minority: The Dynamics of Racial and Ethnic Relations* (Boston: Allen and Bacon, 1971).

9. Arnold M. Rose and Caroline B. Rose, *Minority Problems*, 2nd edn. (New York: Harper and Row, 1965).

10. Pierre van den Berghe, ed., *Intergroup Relations: Sociological Perspectives* (New York: Basic Books, 1972).

11. Harry H. L. Kitano, *Race Relations* (Englewood Cliffs, N.J.: Prentice-Hall, 1974).

12. F. James Davis, *Minority-Dominant Relations: A Sociological Analysis* (Arlington Heights, Ill.: AHM Publishing, 1978).

13. James W. Vander Zanden, *American Minority Relations,* 3rd edn. (New York: Ronald Press, 1972) 90–91.

14. Milton M. Gordon, *Human Nature, Class, and Ethnicity* (New York: Oxford University Press, 1978) 18–20.

15. Michael Banton, *Race Relations* (New York: Basic Books, 1967) 152, 235, 255–56.

16. Harry H. Bash, *Sociology, Race and Ethnicity: A Critique of American Ideological Intrusions upon Sociological Theory* (New York: Gordon and Breach, 1979) 55, 82, 97–99, 135.

17. John W. Cell, *The Highest Stage of White Supremacy: The Origins of Segregation in South Africa and the American South* (Cambridge: Cambridge University Press, 1982) 143.

18. Donald G. Baker, *Race, Ethnicity and Power: A Comparative Study* (London: Routledge and Kegan Paul, 1983) 11, 14, 28, 35, 89, 115, 175, 202. See also Herbert Blumer, *Symbolic Interaction: Perspective and Method* (Englewood-Cliffs: Prentice-Hall, 1969).

19. Tamotsu Shibutani and Kian Moon Kwan, *Ethnic Stratification: A Comparative Approach* (New York: Macmillan, 1965) 96, 308, 365, 395, 406.

20. Such a collection is now available. See Stanford M. Lyman and Arthur J. Vidich, *Social Order and the Public Philosophy: An Analysis and Interpretation of the work of Herbert Blumer* (Fayetteville: University of Arkansas Press, 1988).

21. Edward Shils, *The Calling of Sociology and Other Essays on the Pursuit of Learning* (Chicago: University of Chicago Press, 1980) 225–26.

22. Robert H. Lauer and Warren H. Handel, *Social Psychology: the Theory and Application of Symbolic Interaction* (Boston: Houghton-Mifflin, 1977) 319.

23. Irving Zeitlin, *Rethinking Sociology: A Critique of Contemporary Theory* (New York: Appleton-Century-Crofts, 1973) 217.

24. Herbert G. Blumer, "Reflections on Theory of Race Relations," *Race Relations in World Perspective: Papers Read at the Conference on Race Relations in World Perspective,* ed. Andrew W. Lind (Honolulu: University of Hawaii Press, 1954; Westport, Conn.: Greenwood Press, 1973) 5.

25. Herbert Blumer, "Race Prejudice as a Sense of Group Position," *Pacific*

Sociological Review 1 (Spring 1958): 5; also in *Race Relations,* ed. Jitsuichi Masuoka and Preston Valien (Chapel Hill: University of North Carolina Press, 1961) 215–27.

26. Lauer and Handel 320–21.

27. W. I. Thomas, "The Province of Social Psychology" [1904], *Congress of Arts and Science: Selected Papers* (New York: Arno Press, 1974) 860–78.

28. Herbert Blumer, "Method in Social Psychology," Diss., University of Chicago, 1928, 77–87.

29. George Eaton Simpson and J. Milton Yinger, "The Sociology of Race and Ethnic Relations," *Sociology Today: Problems and Prospects,* ed. Robert K. Merton, Leonard Broom, and Leonard S. Cottrell, Jr. (New York: Basic Books, 1959) 376–79.

30. T. W. Adorno, Else Frenkel-Brunswick, Daniel J. Levinson, and R. Nevitt Sanford, *The Authoritarian Personality* (New York: Harper and Row, 1950).

31. Herbert Blumer, "The Nature of Race Prejudice," *Social Processes in Hawaii* 5 (June 1939): 11–20.

32. Gordon W. Allport, "Prejudice and the Individual," *The American Negro Reference Book,* ed. John P. Davis (Englewood Cliffs, N.J.: Prentice-Hall, 1966) 707.

33. John Cummings, "Ethnic Factors and the Movement of Population," *Quarterly Journal of Economics* 14 (February 1900) 171–211.

34. *Ibid.* 211.

35. Blumer, "The Nature of Race Prejudice."

36. H. H. Smythe, "Race and Intergroup Relations," *Contemporary Sociology,* ed. Joseph S. Roucek (New York: Philosophical Library, 1958) 185.

37. Blumer, "Race Prejudice as a Sense of Group Position" 3–7.

38. Blumer, "The Nature of Race Prejudice" 11–20.

39. Herbert G. Blumer and Troy Duster, "Theories of Race and Social Action," *Sociological Theories: Race and Colonialism* (Paris: United Nations Educational, Scientific, and Cultural Organization, 1980) 211–38.

40. Herbert Blumer, "Research on Race Relations: United States of America," *International Social Science Bulletin* 10: 434.

41. *Ibid.* 433, 432.

42. Herbert Blumer, "The Future of the Color Line," *The South in Continuity and Change,* ed. John C. McKinney and Edgar T. Thompson (Durham: Duke University Press, 1965) 322–36.

43. Ray Stannard Baker, *Following the Color Line: American Negro Citizenship in the Progressive Era* [1908] (New York: Harper Torchbooks, 1964).

44. Blumer, "The Future of the Color Line" 323.

45. Herbert Blumer, "Social Science and the Desegregation Process," *Annals of the American Academy of Political and Social Science* 304 (March 1956): 137–43.

46. Blumer, "The Future of the Color Line" 329.

47. *Ibid.* 329, 335.

48. *Ibid.* 335–36.

49. Herbert Blumer, "Industrialisation and Race Relations," *Industrialisation and Race Relations: A Symposium,* ed. Guy Hunter (London: Oxford University Press, 1965) 220–53.

50. Frederic William Maitland, "The Body Politic," *Maitland: Selected Essays,* ed. H. D. Hazeltine, G. Lapsley, and P. H. Winfield (Cambridge: The University Press, 1936) 288, 249.

51. Talcott Parsons, "Full Citizenship for the Negro American? A Socio-logical Problem," *The Negro American*, ed. Talcott Parsons and Kenneth B. Clark (Boston: Houghton-Mifflin, 1966) 709–54.

52. Blumer, "Industrialisation and Race Relations" 231–33.

53. *Ibid*. 234.

54. *Ibid*. 235–45.

55. Karl Marx, *Early Texts*, trans. and ed. David Mclellan (Oxford: Basil Blackwell, 1972) 178–83.

56. Georg Simmel, "A Chapter in the Philosophy of Value," trans. Albion W. Small, *American Journal of Sociology* 5 (March 1900): 577–78; and *The Philosophy of Money*, trans. Tom Bottomore and David Frisby (London: Routledge and Kegan Paul, 1978) 131–203, 343–54, 409–28.

57. John Stuart Mill, *A Logical Critique of Sociology*, ed. Ronald Fletcher (London: Michael Joseph, 1971) 215–96.

58. William J. Wilson, *The Declining Significance of Race* (Chicago: University of Chicago Press, 1978).

59. Annie Phizacklea and Robert Miles, *Labour and Racism* (London: Routledge and Kegan Paul, 1980) 127–232.

60. Blumer, "Industrialisation and Race Relations" 235–39.

61. *Ibid*. 239.

62. Blumer, "Reflections on Theory of Race Relations" 9.

63. *Ibid*.

64. *Ibid*. 13.

65. Stanford M. Lyman, *The Asian in North America* (Santa Barbara: Clio Press, 1977) 25–37.

66. Blumer, "Race Prejudice as a Sense of Group Position" 3–7.

67. Blumer and Duster 211–21.

68. *Ibid*. 221.

69. Lyman, *The Black American in Sociological Thought: A Failure of Perspective* (New York: G. P. Putnam's Sons, 1972) 27–70.

70. Blumer and Duster, 217.

71. Arthur J. Vidich and Stanford M. Lyman, *American Sociology: Worldly Rejections of Religion and Their Directions* (New Haven: Yale University Press, 1985).

72. Stanford M. Lyman, *The Seven Deadly Sins: Society and Evil* (New York: St. Martin's Press, 1978) 269–76.

73. Blumer and Duster, 236.

74. *Ibid*.

The Significance of Asians in American Society

1. The classic statements of this position are found in John Dollard, *Caste and Class in a Southern Town,* 3rd edn. (Garden City: Doubleday Anchor, 1957); Allison Davis, Burleigh B. Gardner, and Mary R. Gardner, *Deep South: A Social Anthropological Study of Caste and Class* (Chicago: University of Chicago Press-Phoenix Books, 1965); Hortense Powdermaker, *After Freedom: A Cultural Study in the Deep South* (New York: Atheneum, 1968).

2. First of all the historic peoples to acquire California were the Indians. It is therefore pertinent to ask why it is that California is no longer an Indian

country in any sense of the term. The answer . . . [is] that the Indian could not hope to compete with civilized races, though he might have rendered their occupation of California more difficult than in fact he did.
Charles E. Chapman, *A History of California: The Spanish Period* (New York: The Macmillan Co., 1921) 9. For a contrasting and non-ethnocentric view, see Jack D. Forbes, *Native Americans of California and Nevada* (Healdsburg, Calif.: Naturegraph Publishers, 1969).

3. See Leonard Pitt, *The Decline of the California: A Social History of the Spanish-Speaking Californians, 1846–1890* (Berkeley: University of California Press, 1966); Nancie L. Gonzalez, *The Spanish-Americans of New Mexico: A Heritage of Pride* (Albuquerque: University of New Mexico Press, 1969); John H. Burma, *Spanish-Speaking Groups in the United States* (Durham: Duke University Press, 1954) 3–155; William Madsen, *The Mexican-Americans of South Texas* (New York: Holt, Rinehart, and Winston, 1964); Celia S. Heller, *Mexican American Youth: Forgotten Youth at the Crossroads* (New York: Random House, 1966); Julian Samora, *La Raza: Forgotten Americans* (Notre Dame: University of Notre Dame Press, 1966).

4. The populist roots of anti-Semitism were debated by major social scientists during the 1950s. For a discussion and bibliography, see John Higham, "American Anti-Semitism Historically Reconsidered," in *Jews in the Mind of America,* ed. Charles Herbert Stember, et al. (New York: Basic Books, 1966) 237–58. See also John Higham, "Social Discrimination Against Jews in America, 1830–1930," *Publications of the American Jewish Historical Society* XLVII (September 1957): 1–31. Of course, anti-Semitism has its original roots in Christian-Jewish divisions. In this respect, see Jules Isaac, *The Teaching of Contempt: Christian Roots of Anti-Semitism,* trans. Helen Weaver (New York: Holt, Rinehart, and Winston, 1964). For a sociological view, see J. Milton Yinger, *Anti-Semitism: A Case Study in Prejudice and Discrimination* (New York: Freedom Books, 1964).

5. This is the position taken in the two definitive works on the anti-Chinese movement. See Mary Coolidge, *Chinese Immigration* (New York: Henry Holt, 1909); and Elmer C. Sandmeyer, *The Anti-Chinese Movement in California* (Urbana: University of Illinois Press, 1939). For the view that anti-Chinese sentiment existed in the East prior to the coming of the Chinese, see Stuart Creighton Miller, *The Unwelcome Immigrant: The American Image of the Chinese, 1785–1882* (Berkeley: University of California Press, 1969).

6. For a critique of this and related positions with special reference to the African American, see Stanford M. Lyman, *The Black American in Sociological Thought: a Failure of Perspective* (New York: G. P. Putnam's Sons, 1972).

7. *Report of the National Advisory Commission on Civil Disorders,* Otto Kerner, Chairman (New York: Bantam Books, 1968) 203.

8. Winthrop Jordan, *White Over Black: American Attitudes Toward the Negro, 1550–1812* (Chapel Hill: University of North Carolina Press, 1968) 3–269. The Greco-Roman attitude toward blacks was for the most part not marred by racial prejudice. See Frank M. Snowden, Jr., *Blacks in Antiquity: Ethiopians in the Greco-Roman Experience* (Cambridge: The Belknap Press of Harvard University Press, 1970); Racism in antiquity is presenting a topic of renewed interest. See Lloyd A. Thompson, *Romans and Blacks* (Norman: University of Oklahoma Press, 1989).

9. See Lee Eldridge Huddleston, *Origins of the American Indians: European Concepts, 1492–1792* (Austin: University of Texas Press, 1967).

10. Henri Baudet, *Paradise on Earth: Some Thoughts on European Images of Non-European Man,* trans. Elizabeth Wentholt (New Haven: Yale University Press, 1965).

11. Kathleen George, "The Civilized West Looks at Primitive Africa: 1400–1800: A Study in Ethnocentrism," *Isis* XLIX, Part I (March 1958): 62–72.

12. Thomas Gossett, *Race: The History of an Idea in America* (Dallas: Southern Methodist University Press, 1963).

13. See D. G. Cochrane, "Racialism in the Pacific: A Descriptive Analysis," *Oceania* XL: 1 (September 1969): 1–12.

14. See G. F. Hudson, *Europe and China: A Survey of Their Relations, from the Earliest Times to 1800* (Boston: Beacon Press, 1961); Harold R. Isaacs, *Images of Asia: American Views of China and India* (New York: Capricorn Books, 1962); and Harold R. Isaacs, *No Peace for Asia* (Cambridge: The M. I. T. Press, 1967) 7–36, 213–42.

15. The most thorough history of this period is R. S. Kuykendall, *The Hawaiian Kingdom* (Honolulu: University of Hawaii Press, 1953, 1957, 1967). Three volumes. See also Lawrence H. Fuchs, *Hawaii Pono: A Social History* (New York: Harcourt, Brace, and World, 1961) 3–39; and Andrew W. Lind, *Hawaii's People* (Honolulu: University of Hawaii Press, 1967) 15–19.

16. See James Bonwick, *The Last of the Tasmanians; or, The Black War of Van Diemen's Land* (London: Sampson, Low, Son, and Marston, 1870. Australiana Facsimile Editions No. 87. Adelaide: Libraries Board of South Australia, 1969); and Clive Turnbull, *Black War: The Extermination of the Tasmanian Aborigines* (Melbourne: Cheshire-Lansdowne, 1966).

17. Douglas Oliver, *The Pacific Islands,* rev. edn. (Garden City: Doubleday Anchor, 1961) 83–154.

18. See Marvin E. Gettleman, ed., *Viet Nam: History, Documents, and Opinions on a Major World Crisis* (New York: Fawcett Publications, 1965) 9–32; C. P. Fitzgerald, *A Concise History of East Asia* (New York: Frederick A. Praeger, 1966) 218–93; Norton Ginsburg, "Indochina: The Two Viet, Cambodia, and Laos," in *The Pattern of Asia,* ed. Norton Ginsburg (Englewood Cliffs: Prentice-Hall, 1958) 410–39.

19. The infamous imposition of opium on the Chinese is placed in perspective by Wen-Tsao Wu, *The Chinese Opium Question in British Opinion and Action* (New York: The Academy Press, 1928); and Arthur Waley, *The Opium War Through Chinese Eyes* (Stanford: Stanford University Press, 1968). For the American involvement in the Pacific and China, see Foster Rhea Dulles, *America in the Pacific: A Century of Expansion* (Boston: Houghton Mifflin Co., 1932); Tyler Dennett, *Americans in Eastern Asia: a Critical Study of United States' Policy in the Far East in the Nineteenth Century* (New York: Barnes and Noble, 1963); Paul Hibbert Clyde, *United States Policy Toward China: Diplomatic and Public Documents, 1839–1939* (New York: Russell and Russell, 1964); Thomas J. McCormick, *China Market: America's Quest for Informal Empire, 1893–1901* (Chicago: Quadrangle, 1967). Perhaps still the best general account of the early period of European encroachments in China is John King Fairbank, *Trade and Diplomacy on the China Coast: The Opening of the Treaty Ports, 1842–1854* (Cambridge: Harvard University Press, 1964). See also W. C. Hunter, *The 'Fan Kwae' at Canton Before Treaty Days, 1825–1844* (Taipei: Ch'eng-wen Publishing Co., 1965). For the Chinese response, see Earl Swisher, *China's Management of the American Barbarians: A Study of Sino-American Relations, 1841–1861* (New Haven: Far Eastern Publications, 1951); and Franz Schurmann and Orville

Schell, eds., *Imperial China: The Decline of the Last Dynasty and the Origins of Modern China: The 18th and 19th Centuries,* The China Reader, Volume I (New York: Random House, 1967).

20. For the Portuguese colonial empire that in many ways provided an early model of European racism in Asia and the tropics, see three works by Charles R. Boxer, *Race Relations in the Portuguese Colonial Empire, 1415–1825* (Oxford: Clarendon Press, 1963); *Portuguese Society in the Tropics: The Municipal Councils of Goa, Macao, Bahia, and Luanda, 1510–1800* (Madison, The University of Milwaukee Press, 1965); *The Dutch Seaborne Empire: 1600–1800* (New York: Alfred A. Knopf, 1965) 215–41.

21. This, it seems to me, is the inescapable conclusion to be drawn from Oscar Handlin, *The Americans: A New History of the People of the United States* (Boston: Little, Brown and Co., 1963) 148–62.

22. Joshua A. Fishman, *Language Loyalty in the United States: The Maintenance and Perpetuation of Non-English Mother Tongues by American Religious and Ethnic Groups* (The Hague: Mouton and Co., 1966) 29–31. For studies of the struggle over English language hegemony in the United States see Joshua A. Fishman, et al., *The Rise and Fall of the Ethnic Revival: Perspectives on Language of Inequality,* ed. Nessa Wolfson and Joan Manes (Berlin: Mouton, 1985) 3–20, 41–74, 255–72, 311–24.

23. Perhaps the best illustration of this point is the fact that groups with ambiguous racial ancestry in America strive to become "white" and to stave off the label "Negro." See Brewton Berry, *Almost White* (New York: Macmillan, 1963). For a comment, see Stanford M. Lyman, "The Spectrum of Color," *Social Research* 31 (Autumn 1964): 364–73.

24. See John A. Hostettler, *Amish Society,* rev. edn. (Baltimore: Johns Hopkins Press, 1968); and John W. Bennett, *Hutterian Brethren: The Agricultural Economy and Social Organization of a Communal People* (Stanford: Stanford University Press, 1967).

25. See Nathan Glazer, "Ethnic Groups in America: From National Culture to Ideology," in Morroe Berger, et al., eds., *Freedom and Control in Modern Society* (New York: D. Van Nostrand Co., 1954) 158–76. For the political consequences of this development, see Louis L. Gerson, *The Hyphenate in Recent American Politics and Diplomacy* (Lawrence: The University of Kansas Press, 1964).

26. See John Higham, *Strangers in the Land: Patterns of American Nativism, 1860–1925* (New York: Atheneum, 1963) 300–30. For the xenophobic sources of the Immigrant Act of 1924, see William Petersen, *Population* (New York: The Macmillan Co., 1961) 86–113.

27. See Barbara Miller Solomon, *Ancestors and Immigrants: A Changing New England Tradition* (New York: Science Editions, John Wiley and Sons, 1956).

28. What then is the American, this new man? He is either an European, or the descendant of an European, hence that strange mixture of blood, which you will find in no other country. I could point out to you a family whose grandfather was an Englishman, whose wife was Dutch, whose son married a French woman, and whose present four sons now have four wives of different nations. *He* is an American, who, leaving behind him all his ancient prejudices and manners, receives new ones from the new mode of life he has embraced, the new government he obeys, and the new rank he holds. He becomes an American by being received in the broad lap of our great *Alma Mater.* Here individuals of all nations are melted into a new race of men,

whose labours and posterity will one day cause great changes in the world. Americans are the western pilgrims, who are carrying along with them that great mass of arts, sciences, vigour, and industry which began long since in the east. They will finish the great circle. The Americans were once scattered all over Europe; here they are incorporated into one of the finest systems of population which has ever appeared, and which will hereafter become distinct by the power of the different climates they inhabit. The American ought therefore to love this country much better than that wherein either he or his forefathers were born.

J. Hector St. John de Crevecoeur, *Letters from an American Farmer* (New York: E. P. Dutton & Co., 1957. First published in 1782) 39–40.

29. Thus, Carl Schurz admonished his fellow Germans in America:

. . . we as Germans are not called upon here to form a separate nationality, but rather to contribute to the American nationality the strongest there is in us, and in place of our weakness to substitute the strength wherein our fellow-Americans excel us, and blend it with our wisdom. We should never forget that in the political life of this republic, we as Germans have no peculiar interests, but that the universal well-being is ours also.

Quoted in Carl Wittke, *We Who Built America: The Saga of the Immigrant* (Cleveland: The Press of Case Western Reserve University, 1967) 245.

30. See Oscar Handlin, *Boston's Immigrants, 1790–1800: A Study in Acculturation*, rev. ed. (New York: Atheneum, 1968); Thomas N. Brown, *Irish-American Nationalism 1870–1890* (Philadelphia: J. B. Lippincott Co., 1966); William V. Shannon, *The American Irish: A Political and Social Portrait* (New York: The Macmillan Co., 1963).

31. Theodore Saloutos, *The Greeks in the United States* (Cambridge: Harvard University Press, 1964) 138–59, 232–57.

32. See Herbert J. Gans, *The Urban Villagers: Group and Class in the Life of Italian-Americans* (New York: The Free Press, 1965); and Leonard Covello, *The Social Background of the Italo-American School Child: A Study of the Southern Italian Family Mores and Their Effect on the School Situation in Italy and America* (Leiden: E. J. Brill, 1967).

33. Alex Simirenko, *Pilgrims, Colonists, and Frontiersmen: Generation-to-Generation Changes in a Russian Ethnic Community in America* (London: The Free Press of Glencoe, 1964).

34. W. I. Thomas and Florian Znaniecki, *The Polish Peasant in Europe and America* (New York: Dover Publications, 1968) II: 1511–1646.

35. See Louis Wirth, *The Ghetto* (Chicago: University of Chicago Press-Phoenix Books, 1956); Nathan Glazer, *American Judaism* (Chicago: University of Chicago Press, 1957); Albert I. Gordon, *Jews in Suburbia* (Boston: Beacon Press, 1959); Judith R. Kramer and Seymour Leventman, *Children of the Gilded Ghetto: Conflict Resolution of Three Generations of American Jews* (New Haven: Yale University Press, 1961); Marshall Sklare and Joseph Greenblum, *Jewish Identity on the Suburban Frontier: A Study of Group Survival in the Open Society*, The Lakeville Studies, Vol. I (New York: Basic Books, 1967); Benjamin B. Ringer, *The Edge of Friendliness: A Study of Jewish-Gentile Relations*, The Lakeville Studies, Vol. II (New York: Basic Books, 1967).

36. See Theodore Saloutos, *They Remember America: The Story of the Repatriated Greek-Americans* (Berkeley: University of California Press, 1956); and Wilbur S. Shepperson, *Emigration and Disenchantment: Portraits of Englishmen Repatriated from the United States* (Norman: University of Oklahoma Press, 1965).

37. Higham, *Strangers in the Land, op. cit.*

38. Gustavus Myers, *History of Bigotry in the United States,* ed. and rev. Henry M. Christman (New York: Capricorn Books, 1960) 3–276.

39. Myers, *op. cit.* 277–447; Richard Hofstadter, *The Age of Reform: From Bryan to F. D. R.* (New York: Vintage Books, 1960) 77–93; Higham, *Strangers in the Land, op. cit.* 13, 26–27, 66–67, 92–94, 160–61, *et passim.*

40. Solomon, *op. cit.* 82–175; Myers, *op. cit.* 92–191, 211–57; Higham, *op. cit.* 186–299. On the Ku Klux Klan and nativism, see David M. Chalmers, *Hooded Americanism: The First Century of the Ku Klux Klan, 1865 to the Present* (Garden City: Doubleday and Co., 1965); John Moffatt Mecklin, *The Ku Klux Klan: A Study of the American Mind* (New York: Russell and Russell, 1963); William Peirce Randel, *The Ku Klux Klan: A Century of Infamy* (New York: Chilton Books, 1965); Charles C. Alexander, *The Ku Klux Klan in the Southwest* (Lexington: University of Kentucky Press, 1965); Kenneth J. Jackson, *The Ku Klux Klan in the City, 1915–1930* (New York: Oxford University Press, 1967).

41. Cf. Oscar Handlin, *Boston's Immigrants, op. cit.* 133, 215–16; Wyn Craig Wade, *The Fiery Cross: The Ku Klux Klan in America* (New York: Simon and Schuster, 1987).

42. The relation of slavery to racism has recently been debated by major students of the subject. See Oscar and Mary Handlin, "The Origins of the Southern Labor System," *William and Mary Quarterly* VII (April 1950): 199–222; Carl N. Degler, "Slavery and the Genesis of American Race Prejudice," *Comparative Studies in Society and History* II (October 1959): 49–66; Arnold A. Sio, "Interpretations of Slavery: The Slave Status in the Americas," *Comparative Studies in Society and History* VII (April 1965): 289–308; Herbert S. Klein, "Anglicanism, Catholicism, and the Negro Slave," *Comparative Studies in Society and History* VIII (April 1966): 295–327; Winthrop D. Jordan, "Modern Tensions and the Origins of American Slavery," *Journal of Southern History* XXVIII (February 1962): 18–30; David Brion Davis, *The Problem of Slavery in Western Culture* (Ithaca: Cornell University Press, 1966) 3–61, 125–64, 223–90; Joseph Boskin, "Race Relations in Seventeenth Century America: The Problem of the Origins of Negro Slavery," *Sociology and Social Research* 49 (July 1965): 446–55; Eugene Genovese, *The Political Economy of Slavery: Studies in the Economy and Society of the Slave South* (New York: Pantheon, 1965); and Eugene Genovese, *The World the Slaveholders Made: Two Essays in Interpretation* (New York: Pantheon, 1969). See also Edgar T. Thompson, "The Natural History of Agricultural Labor in the South," *American Studies in Honor of W. K. Boyd,* ed. David K. Jackson (Durham: Duke University Press, 1940) 127–45.

43. The terms for the debates over African survivals among American Negroes have been set by Melville Herskovitz, *The Myth of the Negro Past* (Boston: Beacon Press, 1958); *The New World Negro: Selected Papers in Afroamerican Studies,* ed. Frances S. Herskovitz (Bloomington: Indiana University Press, 1966) 1–12, 43–61, 83–101, 122–34, 168–73; E. Franklin Frazier, *The Negro Family in the United States,* rev. and abr. edn. (Chicago: University of Chicago Press-Phoenix Books, 1966) 3–208; and *The Negro in the United States,* rev. edn. (New York: Macmillan, 1957) 3–22. See also Charles Keil, *Urban Blues* (Chicago: University of Chicago Press, 1966) 1–68.

44. See Stanley M. Elkins, *Slavery: A Problem in American Institutional and Intellectual Life* (Chicago: University of Chicago Press, 1959) 81–139.

45. Herbert Aptheker, *American Negro Slave Revolts* (New York: International Publishers, 1963); Eugene Genovese, *From Rebellion to Revolution: Afro-*

American Slave Revolts in the Making of the Modern World (Baton Rouge: Louisiana State University Press, 1979).

46. See Henrietta Buckmaster, *Let My People Go: The Story of the Underground Railroad and the Growth of the Abolition Movement* (Boston: Beacon Press, 1959); Horatio J. Strother, *The Underground Railroad in Connecticut* (Middletown: Wesleyan University Press, 1962); Kenneth M. Stampp, *The Peculiar Institution: Slavery in the Ante-Bellum South* (New York: Alfred A. Knopf, 1963) 109–32.

47. Ulrich Bonnell Phillips, *American Negro Slavery: A Survey of the Supply, Employment and Control of Negro Labor as Determined by the Plantation Regime* (Gloucester: Peter Smith, 1959) 425–31.

48. Leon Litwack, *North of Slavery: The Negro in the Free States, 1790–1860* (Chicago: University of Chicago Press-Phoenix Books, 1965). Benjamin Quarles, *Black Abolitionists* (New York: Oxford University Press, 1969).

49. See e.g., Ralph K. Andrist, *The Long Death: The Last Days of the Plains Indians* (New York: Macmillan, 1964) 14–15; Wendell H. Oswalt, *This Land Was Theirs: A Study of the North American Indian* (New York: John Wiley, 1966) 245–47; Dale Van Every, *Disinherited: The Lost Birthright of the American Indian* (New York: William Morsow, 1966) 70, 251; Clark Wissler, *Indians of the United States,* rev. edn., prepared by Lucy Wales Kluckhohn (Garden City: Doubleday and Co., 1966) 85–86, 107–09, 148, 169, 186; William T. Hagan, *American Indians* (Chicago: University of Chicago Press, 1961) 7, 12, 25, 94.

50. Roy Harvey Pearce, *Savagism and Civilization: A Study of the Indian and the American Mind* (Baltimore: The Johns Hopkins Press, 1967) 1–238; Helen Hunt Jackson, *A Century of Dishonor: The Early Crusade for Indian Reform,* ed. Andrew F. Rolle (New York: Harper Torchbooks, 1965. Originally published in 1881) 298–335.

51. Hagan, *op. cit.* 53–91.

52. Hagan, *op. cit.* 92–120; Pearce, *op. cit.* 239.

53. The Indian is never alone. The life he leads is not his to control. That is not permitted. Every aspect of his being is affected and defined by his relationship to the Federal Government—and primarily to one agency of the Federal Government: the Bureau of Indian Affairs.

From birth to death his home, his land, his reservation, his schools, his jobs, the stores where he shops, the tribal council that governs him, the opportunities available to him, the way in which he spends his money, disposes of his property, and even the way in which he provides for his heirs after death—are all determined by the Bureau of Indian Affairs acting as the agent of the United States Government.

Edgar S. Cahn, ed., *Our Brother's Keeper: The Indian in White America* (New York: Community Press Book, World Publishing Co., 1969) 5.

54. See Marcus Lee Hansen, *The Immigrant in American History,* ed. Arthur M. Schlesinger (New York: Harper Torchbooks, 1964) 77–80.

55. At midcentury the champion of integration in America was Frederick Douglass. See *The Life and Writings of Frederick Douglass,* ed. Philip S. Foner (New York: International Publishers, 1950) II: 168–69, 172–73, 251–54, 387–88, 441–46. Among the leading figures in favor of exodus was Martin R. Delaney, who explored portions of West Africa in the hope of finding a hospitable area for Negroes to settle. See Martin R. Delany, "Official Report of the Niger Valley Exploring Party," in M. R. Delany and Robert Campbell, *Search for a Place: Black Separatism and Africa, 1860* (Ann Arbor: The University of Michigan Press, 1969) 23–148.

56. For a balanced appraisal of the role of reservations in California, whose conclusions might well apply to other areas of Indian incarceration, see Sherburne F. Cook, "The California Indian and Anglo-American Culture," in *Ethnic Conflict in California,* ed. Charles Wollenberg (Los Angeles: Tinnon-Brown, 1970) 25–42.

57. See Stanford M. Lyman, "Strangers in the Cities: The Chinese on the Urban Frontier," in Wollenberg, *op. cit.* 61–100.

58. The term "total institution" is adapted from Erving Goffman, "On the Characteristics of Total Institutions," *Asylums: Essays on the Social Situation of Mental Patients and Other Inmates* (Garden City: Doubleday Anchor, 1961) 1–124. Goffman observes (p. 4):

> When we review the different institutions in our Western society, we find some that are encompassing to a degree discontinuously greater than the ones next in line. Their encompassing or total character is symbolized by the barrier to social intercourse that is often built right into the physical plant, such as locked doors, high walls, barbed wire, cliffs, water, forests, or moors. These establishments I am calling *total institutions.*

59. Thus, as Richard Wade has pointed out, slavery in the cities was a halfway house to freedom. See his *Slavery in the Cities: The South, 1820–1860* (New York: Oxford University Press, 1964).

60. In a recent study of a poverty-stricken white community, David Harvey has suggested that industrialism requires surplus populations of degraded and exploitable people. He writes:

> The industrial system like the school operates with a peculiar and contradictory irony. If it is to survive and maintain its career objectives intact, it must help perpetuate a "careerless" segment of the work force. If the consumer-oriented economy is to survive, it can only do so by generating a group whose consumption ability is severely restricted. . . . But why are these people stigmatized and degraded? Is this really necessary? I believe so! It is one thing to create an industrial reserve army. It is another thing to control them. How does one handle a group of people who *must* remain marginal to society if that society's institutions require them for continued existence. The answer is to render them *passive.* The most efficient way to do this is to attribute to them traits which place them outside of the category of "reputable human." In this way they lie beyond the concern of moral men. At the same time if the stigmatized accept the legitimacy of their own label, they can be taught that they have little right to expect more than they are presently receiving. Finally, those most stigmatized in our society are the least powerful. This includes the lower class.

"Neighborhood Learning Centers as an Agent of Change in Lower Class Communities," Paper presented at the 1970 annual convention of the Council on Exceptional Children, Chicago, April 25, 1970.

61. Alexander Saxton, "The Indispensable Enemy: A Study of the Anti-Chinese Movement in California," diss., University of California, Berkeley, 1967 (Ann Arbor: University Microfilms, 1970).

62. Cf. Louis L. Knowles and Kenneth Prewitt, eds., *Institutional Racism in America* (Englewood Cliffs: Prentice-Hall, 1969) 4–14.

63. See Roger Daniels and Harry H. L. Kitano, *American Racism: Exploration of the Nature of Prejudice* (Englewood Cliffs: Prentice-Hall, 1970) 5–28.

64. See Stanford M. Lyman, "Marriage and the Family Among Chinese Immigrants to America, 1850–1960," *Phylon Quarterly* 29 (Winter 1968): 321–30.

65. The point was litigated in the federal courts. See *Case of the Chinese Wife* 21 Fed. 785 (1884).

66. Thus Robert E. Park, writing in 1926, was moved to observe, "The Chinese population is slowly declining in the United States, but San Francisco, at any rate, will miss its Chinese quarter when it goes." "Our Racial Frontier on the Pacific," *Survey Graphic* LVI (May 1926): 196.

67. See the sympathetic account of Jacob A. Riis, *How the Other Half Lives: Studies Among the Tenements of New York* (New York: Sagamore Press, Inc., 1957. First published in 1890) 67–76.

68. Maurice R. Davie, *World Immigration: With Special Reference to the United States* (New York: Macmillan, 1949) 328.

69. Milton R. Knovitz, *The Alien and Asiatic in American Law* (Ithaca: Cornell University Press, 1946) 10, 79–96.

70. *Ozawa vs United States,* 260 U.S. 178 (1922). For the full particulars of the case, see *Documented History of Law Cases Affecting Japanese in the United States, Vol. I: Naturalization Cases and Cases Affecting Constitutional and Treaty Rights* (San Francisco: Consulate-General of Japan, 1925) 1–121.

71. See Roderick D. McKenzie, *Oriental Exclusion: The Effect of American Immigration Laws, Regulations and Judicial Decisions Upon the Chinese and Japanese on the American Pacific Coast* (Chicago: University of Chicago Press, 1928) 79–97.

72. Milton R. Knovitz, *op. cit.* 161–69, 185–86.

73. Thus California stripped Chinese aliens of their fishing licenses in 1864, Japanese and other ineligible aliens of their fishing licenses in 1943, and all aliens ineligible to citizenship of the right to own land or form corporations in 1913.

74. William Warren Ferrier, *Ninety Years of Education in California, 1846–1936* (Berkeley: Sather Gate Book Shop, 1937) 98.

75. T. A. Bailey, *Theodore Roosevelt and the Japanese-American Crises: An Account of the International Complications Arising from the Race Problem on the Pacific Coast* (Gloucester: Peter Smith, 1964).

76. Yamato Ichihashi, *Japanese in the United States: A Critical Study of the Problems of the Japanese Immigrants and Their Children* (New York: Arno Press and the New York Times, 1969) 228–82; and Jacobus ten Broek, Edward N. Barnhart, and Floyd Matson, *Prejudice, War, and the Constitution,* Vol. III of *Japanese American Evacuation and Resettlement* (Berkeley: University of California Press, 1954) 11–67.

77. *Wong Hin vs Callahan,* 119 Fed. 381 (1902).

78. *Gong Lum vs Rice,* 275 U.S. 78 (1927).

79. *Brown vs. Board of Education,* 348 U.S. 483 (1954).

80. Cf. *Chew Heong vs United States,* 112 U.S. 536 (1884); *United States vs Jung Ah Lung,* 124 U.S. 621 (1887); *The Chinese Exclusion Case,* 130 U.S. 581 (1889).

81. See Donald Earl Willmott, *The Chinese of Semarang: A Changing Minority Community in Indonesia* (Ithaca: Cornell University Press, 1960) 103–16.

82. In fourteen of these laws there was a specific prohibition on marriage between Chinese, or "Mongolians," and whites. California's anti-miscegenation statute was originally enacted in 1872 to bar marriages between Negroes and whites. In 1906 it was amended to prohibit marriages between whites and "Mongolians." In 1948 it was declared unconstitutional. See Huang Tsenming, *The Legal Status of the Chinese Abroad* (Taipei: China Cultural Service, 1954) 260–62. See also Fowler V. Harper and Jerome Skolnick, *Problems of the*

Family (Indianapolis: Bobbs-Merrill, 1962) 96–99. For the California case invalidating the miscegenation statute, see *Perez vs Sharp*, 32 Cal. 711, 2nd Ser. (1948).

83. See Herbert Hill, "The Racial Practices of Organized Labor—the Age of Gompers and After," in *Employment, Race, and Poverty: A Critical Study of the Disadvantaged Status of Negro Workers from 1865 to 1965*, ed. Arthur M. Ross and Herbert Hill (New York: Harcourt, Brace, and World, 1967) 365–402.

84. See Frederick Douglass, *Narrative of the Life of Frederick Douglass, an American Slave* (Garden City: Doubleday Dolphin, 1963, originally published in 1845) 113–14.

85. See James Bryce, "Kearneyism in California," *The American Commonwealth* (New York: Macmillan, 1901) II: 425–88. See also Doyce B. Nunis, Jr., "The Demagogue and the Demographer: Correspondence of Denis Kearney and Lord Bryce," *Pacific Historical Review* 36 (August 1967) 269–88.

86. See W. W. Stone, "The Knights of Labor on the Chinese Question," *Overland Monthly*, 2nd Ser., VII (March 1886): 225–30.

87. See Samuel Gompers, *Seventy Years of Life and Labor: An Autobiography* (New York: E. P. Dutton, 1925) I: 216–17, 304–05; II: 162–69.

88. The definitive studies of occupational discrimination against African Americans have been done by Herbert Hill. A partial bibliography of his works on the subject would include: *No Harvest for the Reaper: The Story of the Migratory Agricultural Worker in the United States* (New York: N.A.A.C.P., n.d.); "A Record of Negro Disfranchisement," *Midstream* (Autumn 1957): 3–12; "Labor Unions and the Negro," *Commentary* (December 1959): n.p.; "Racial Inequality in Employment: The Patterns of Discrimination," *Annals of the American Academy of Political and Social Science* CCCLVII (January 1965): 30–47; "Planning the End of the American Ghetto: A Program of Economic Development for Equal Rights," *Poverty and Human Resources Abstracts* II (March–April 1967): 23–36; "No End of Pledges: Continuing Discrimination in the Construction Unions," *Commonweal* LXXXVII (March 15, 1968): 709–12; "Sewing Machines and Union Machines," *The Nation* (July 3, 1967): n.p.; "The Racial Practices of Organized Labor: The Contemporary Record," in *The Negro and the American Labor Movement*, ed. Julius Jacobson (Garden City: Doubleday Anchor, 1968) 286–357; "Employment, Manpower Training and the Black Worker," *Journal of Negro Education* (Summer 1969): 204–17; "Black Protest and the Struggle for Union Democracy," *Issues in Industrial Society* I (1969): 19–29, 48; "Black Labor in The American Economy," *In Black America, 1968: The Year of Awakening*, ed. Pat Romero (Washington, D.C.: United Publishing Corp., 1969) 179–216.

For discrimination against Mexican-Americans, see Ernesto Galarza, *Merchants of Labor: The Mexican Bracero Story* (San Jose: The Rosicrucian Press, 1964); Truman E. Moore, *The Slaves We Rent* (New York: Random House, 1965); Eugene Nelson, *Huelga: The First Hundred Days of the Great Delano Grape Strike* (Delano, Calif.: Farm Worker Press, 1966); Peter Matthiessen, *Sal Si Puedes: Cesar Chavez and the New American Revolution* (New York: Random House, 1969); Stan Steiner, *La Raza: The Mexican Americans* (New York: Harper and Row, 1969); Charles Wollenberg, "Conflict in the Fields: Mexican Workers in California Agri-business," in Wollenberg, *op. cit.* 135–52.

For discrimination against and response among Indians, see Edmund Wilson, *Apologies to the Iroquois* (New York: Vintage Books, 1966); Cahn, *op. cit.;* Alan L. Sorkin, "American Indians Industrialize to Combat Poverty," *Monthly Labor*

Review (March 1969): 19–25; Stan Steiner, *The New Indians* (New York: Harper and Row, 1968); Vine Deloria, Jr., *Custer Died for Your Sins: an Indian Manifesto* (New York: Macmillan, 1969).

89. See among many studies, Kenneth B. Clark, *Dark Ghetto: Dilemmas of Social Power* (New York: Harper and Row, 1965). For a recent penetrating analysis of black subculture in America, see Ulf Hannerz, *Soulside: Inquiries into Ghetto Community and Culture* (New York: Columbia University Press, 1969).

90. See D. Y. Yuan, "Voluntary Segregation: a Study of New York Chinatown," *Phylon Quarterly* (Fall 1963): 255–65. For the concept of territoriality and its application to Chinatown, see Stanford M. Lyman and Marvin B. Scott, "Territoriality: A Neglected Sociological Dimension," *Social Problems* 15 (Fall 1967): 236–49.

91. Cf. Robert Blauner, "Internal Colonialism and Ghetto Revolt," *Social Problems* XVI (Spring 1969): 393–408.

92. See, e.g., Stuart H. Cattell, *Health, Welfare, and Social Organization in Chinatown* (New York: Community Service Society, 1962); and Stanford M. Lyman, "Red Guard on Grant Avenue," *Trans-action* 7 (April 1970): 21–34.

93. The closing of mainland China to Occidental study since 1949 has, understandably, increased the academic attention paid to overseas Chinese communities. Until recently this new interest was largely confined to Southeast Asia. See Maurice Freedman, "A Chinese Phase in Social Anthropology," *British Journal of Sociology* XIV (March 1963): 1–19. In the last few years, however, an interest in Chinese communities within Occidental settings has arisen. Although none of the works has developed the thesis presented in this paper, they are of substantial interest for just such possibilities. For reviews of the early phase of this renewed interest, see Maurice Freedman and William Willmott, "Southeast Asia, with Special Reference to the Chinese," *International Social Science Journal* 13:2 (1961): 245–70; Stanford M. Lyman, "Overseas Chinese in Indonesia and America," *Pacific Affairs* XXXIV (Winter 1961–62); Stanford M. Lyman, "Up From the 'Hatchet Man'," *Pacific Affairs* XXXVI (Summer 1963): 160–71.

Reports and monographs are now appearing on the Chinese in Canada and Mexico. For the former, see three essays by William Willmott, "Chinese Clan Associations in Vancouver," *Man* LXIV (March–April 1965): 33–37; "Some Aspects of Chinese Communities in British Columbia Towns," *B.C. Studies* I (Winter 1968–69): 27–36; "Approaches to the Study of the Chinese in British Columbia," *B.C. Studies* 4 (Spring 1970): 38–52. See also Stanford M. Lyman, W. E. Willmott, and Berching Ho, "Rules of a Chinese Secret Society in British Columbia," *Bulletin of the School of Oriental and African Studies* 27:3 (1964): 530–39. David Chuenyan Lai, *Chinatowns: Towns within Cities in Canada* (Vancouver: University of British Columbia Press, 1988); and Paul Yee, *Saltwater City: An Illustrated History of the Chinese of Vancouver* (Toronto: Douglas and McIntyre, 1988).

For Mexico, see Charles C. Cumberland, "The Sonora Chinese and the Mexican Revolution," *Hispanic American Historical Review* XL (May 1960): 191–211.

Conflict and the Web of Group Affiliation in San Francisco's Chinatown, 1850–1910

1. See, e.g., George F. Seward, *Chinese Immigration, in Its Social and Economical Aspects* (New York, 1881) 223–42, 261–91; Mary Coolidge, *Chinese Immigration* (New York, 1909) 401–22; Carl Glick, *Shake Hands with the Dragon* (New York, 1941) 34–44, 81–92, 244–45; S. W. Kung, *Chinese in American Life: Some Aspects of their History, Status, Problems, and Contributions* (Seattle, 1962) 76–78, 197–227; Calvin Lee, *Chinatown, U.S.A.* (Garden City, 1965) 28–37, 82–128; Betty Lee Sung, *Mountain of Gold: The Story of the Chinese in America* (New York, 1967) 130–86; Roger Daniels, "Westerners from the East: Oriental Immigrants Reappraised," *Pacific Historical Review* XXXV (1966): 378–84.

2. See Seward, *Chinese Immigration* 292–310; Coolidge, *Chinese Immigration* 26–336; Elmer C. Sandmeyer, *The Anti-Chinese Movement in California* (Urbana, 1939) 25–111.

3. Victor G. Nee and Brett de Bary Nee, *Longtime Californ': A Documentary Study of an American Chinatown* (New York, 1972) 272–73; Richard Dillon, *The Hatchet Men: The Story of the Tong Wars in San Francisco's Chinatown* (New York, 1962) 361; H. Mark Lai, "A Historical Survey of Organizations of the Left among the Chinese in America," *Bulletin of Concerned Asian Scholars* IV (Fall 1972): 10–19; Samuel Gompers, *Seventy Years of Life and Labor* (New York, 1925) I: 216–17, 304–05; II: 160–69; Herbert Hill, "The Racial Practices of Organized Labor—The Age of Gompers and After," in *Employment, Race and Poverty: A Critical Study of the Disadvantaged Status of Negro Workers from 1865 to 1965,* ed. Arthur M. Ross and Herbert Hill (New York, 1967) 365–402; Hill, "Anti-Oriental Agitation and the Rise of Working-Class Racism," *Society* X (Jan.—Feb. 1973): 43–54; Carey McWilliams, *Factories in the Fields: The Story of Migratory Farm Labor in California* (Boston, 1939) 66–88; Lyman, *The Asian in the West* (Reno: Desert Research Institute, 1970) 9–26, 65–80.

4. Stanford M. Lyman, *Chinese Americans* (New York, 1974); Ivan Light, "From Vice District to Tourist Attraction: The Moral Career of American Chinatowns, 1880–1940," *Pacific Historical Review* XLIII (1974): 367–94; Victor Nee, "The Kuomintang in Chinatown," *Bridge Magazine* I (May—June 1972): 20–24.

5. Thus, there has never been a "mayor of Little Tokyo" in the United States, nor have European immigrant *Landsmannschaften* ever secured such a broad span of power over their communities as that of the Chinese *hui kuan.* See Stanford M. Lyman, "The Structure of Chinese Society in Nineteenth Century America," diss., University of California, Berkeley, 1961, 272–76.

6. See C. S. Wong, *A Gallery of Chinese Kapitans* (Singapore, 1964).

7. Stewart Culin, "Customs of the Chinese in America," *Journal of American Folk-Lore* III (July—Sept. 1890): 193.

8. According to the system of colonial administration developed in the British, Dutch, and French colonies in Southeast Asia, a *Kapitan China* was the representative of the Chinese inhabitants. He served on the various advisory councils and usually represented the interests of the dominant clan, speech, or secret societies within the Chinese community. Usually he was elected by the Chinese societies and approved for appointment by the European colonial administration, but the method of securing this office varied. See, for example, J. M. Gullick, *The Story of Kuala Lumpur* (Singapore, 1956) 16–25, 64–79; W. E.

Willmott, *The Political Structure of the Chinese Community in Cambodia* (New York, 1970) 111–26, 141–60.

9. For early evidence, see "Letter of the Chinamen to his Excellency Gov. Bigler," dated San Francisco, April 29, 1852, in *Littel's Living Age* XXIV (July 3, 1852): 32–34.

10. See "New Rules of the Yeung Wo Ui Kun" and "Sze Yap Company," reprinted in William Speer, "Democracy of the Chinese," *Harper's Monthly* XXXVII (Nov. 1868): 836–48; A. W. Loomis, "The Six Chinese Companies," *Overland Monthly* I (Sept. 1868): 221–27; "Address of the Chinese Six Companies to the American Public," April 5, 1876, in "Report of the Joint Special Committee to Investigate Chinese Immigration," 44 Cong., 2 sess., *S. Rept. 689* (Feb. 27, 1877): 39; Pun Chi, "A Remonstrance from the Chinese in California to the Congress of the United States," 1855, in William Speer, *The Oldest and Newest Empire: China and the United States* (Hartford, 1870) 575–81.

11. *Landsmannschaften* is perhaps the only appropriate term to describe the several kinds of mutual aid societies established by Chinese in America. These societies originated in China as select groups founded by rural Chinese who had migrated to China's cities. See Ping-ti Ho, *Chung-Kuo hui kuan shih-lun* (Taipei, 1966).

12. See Maurice Freedman, *Lineage Organization in Southeastern China* (London, 1958).

13. Herbert A. Giles, "The Family Names," *Journal of the Royal Asiatic Society, North China Branch* XXI (Aug. 1886): 255–88; Leong Gor Yun, *Chinatown Inside Out* (New York, 1936) 54–66.

14. Leong Gor Yun, *Chinatown Inside Out* 59; W. E. Wilmott, "Chinese Clan Associations in Vancouver," *Man* LXIV (1964): 33–37.

15. For example, in the United States and Canada there are two distinct clans using the surname "Wong." The characters forming the surname of the two clans are quite distinguishable in written script, but their Anglicization is the same, that is, the English term "Wong." There are members of both clans in each clan organization.

16. Stewart Culin, *China in America: A Study of the Social Life of the Chinese in Eastern Cities of the United States* (Philadelphia, 1887) 10.

17. Sir George Thomas Staunton, trans., *Ta Tsing Leu Lee; Being the Fundamental Laws, and a Selection from the Supplementary Statutes of the Penal Code of China; Originally Printed and Published in Pekin in Various Successive Editions . . .* (London, 1810) 114.

18. See the letters from a mother in China to her son in California and to his clan brothers, in A. W. Loomis, "The Old East in the New West," *Overland Monthly* I (Oct. 1868): 362.

19. Max Weber, *The Religion of China: Confucianism and Taoism,* trans. Hans H. Gerth (Glencoe, 1951) 86–91.

20. Chinese Chamber of Commerce, *San Francisco's Chinatown: History, Function and Importance of Social Organization* (San Francisco, 1953) 3.

21. Leong Gor Yun, *Chinatown Inside Out* 54–66; Chinese Chamber of Commerce, *San Francisco's Chinatown* 3; Mary Chapman, "Notes on the Chinese in Boston," *Journal of American Folk-Lore* V (Oct.—Dec. 1892): 324; Rose Hum Lee, "The Decline of Chinatowns in the United States," *American Journal of Sociology* LIV (1949): 422–32.

22. Cf. Maurice Freedman, "Immigrants and Associations: Chinese in Nineteenth-Century Singapore," *Comparative Studies in Society and History* III (1960): 25–48.

23. Ping-ti Ho, "Salient Aspects of China's Heritage," in *China in Crisis,* ed. Ping-ti Ho and Tang Tsou (Chicago, 1968) Vol. I, Book I, 32–33.

24. Otis Gibson, *The Chinese in America* (Cincinnati, 1879) 49–51; "Report of the Joint Special Committee to Investigate Chinese Immigration" 24; Lyman, "The Structure of Chinese Society" 283–308.

25. Lyman, "The Structure of Chinese Society" 314.

26. Fong Kum Ngon [Walter N. Fong], "The Chinese Six Companies," *Overland Monthly* XXIII (May 1894): 524–25; Speer, "The Oldest and Newest Empire" 836–48.

27. Loomis, "The Six Chinese Companies" 221–27; Gibson, *The Chinese in America* 339–43; Leong Gor Yun, *Chinatown Inside Out* 49–50; "Report of the Joint Special Committee to Investigate Chinese Immigration" 95.

28. *Hui kuan* formed, dissolved, and reconstituted themselves throughout the first sixty years of Chinese settlement. The Canton Association, formed in 1851, reconstituted itself as the Sam Yup Association in the same year; the Sze Yup Association, formed in 1851, dissolved over internal disputes into the Hop Wo Association (also incorporating the entire Yee clan, which had withdrawn from the Ning Yung Association) in 1862 and the Kong Chow Association in 1867; the Young Wo Association formed in 1852; the Sun On Association, formed in 1851, reconstituted itself as the Yan Wo Association in 1854; the Ning Yung Association, formed in 1853, suffered the loss of the Yee clan in 1862 but continued to represent immigrants from Toishan; the Sue Hing Association was formed during the years 1879–82 by dissidents from the Hop Wo Association, while the Yan Hoi Association was founded in 1898, again by Hop Wo defectors; the Look Yup Association was established in 1901 by a coalition of groups from the Sam Yup Association and the Kong Chow Association; in 1909 the Yan Hoi Association was absorbed by the Sue Hing Association. The structure remained stable thereafter for forty-two years; in 1951 the Fa Yuan Association formed as a splinter from the Sam Yup Association. See the historical chart made by Him Mark Lai in Nee and Nee, *Longtime Californ'* 272–73.

29. William Hoy, *The Chinese Six Companies* (San Francisco, 1942) 5, 28, 59–62; Chinese Chamber of Commerce, *San Francisco's Chinatown* 5; Leong Gor Yun, *Chinatown Inside Out* 6–9; Culin, *China in America* 28.

30. Although the number of *hui kuan* increased beyond six, that number has been stereotypically associated with the confederation in San Francisco.

31. See footnotes 9 and 10 *supra;* see also Speer, *The Oldest and Newest Empire* 578–81; Gibson, *The Chinese in America* 315–23; J. S. Tow, *The Real Chinese in America* (New York, 1923) 118–19.

32. The legislation is summarized in Lucille Eaves, *A History of Labor Legislation in California* (Berkeley, 1909) 105–95; Ira B. Cross, *A History of the Labor Movement in California* (Berkeley, 1935) 73–130; Coolidge, *Chinese Immigration* 55–82; Sandmeyer, *The Anti-Chinese Movement in California* 40–77; Lyman, "The Structure of Chinese Society" 383–86; Lyman, *The Asian in the West* 23–24; Robert F. Heizer and Alan F. Almquist, *The Other Californians: Prejudice and Discrimination under Spain, Mexico, and the United States* (Berkeley, 1971) 154–77.

33. For Chinese merchant elites' abortive attempts to obtain extraterritorial rights over Chinese immigrant criminals, see Speer, *The Oldest and Newest Empire* 579–80, 600–01; Gibson, *The Chinese in America* 315–23. For unchecked mob actions in Chinatown, see Lyman, *The Asian in the West* 12–16, 19–23.

34. See, for example, Richard Hay Drayton, "The Chinese Six Companies," *The Californian Illustrated Magazine* IV (Aug. 1893): 472–79.

35. *Fong Yue Ting v. U.S.*, 149 U.S. 698 (1893). It was this decision, sustaining the Geary Act and requiring all Chinese in the United States to register with the collector of internal revenue, that sparked a rebellion against Chun Ti Chu, the Six Companies' president. Chun had provoked the case by ordering Chinese to refuse to register. Thousands of Chinese might have been deported had not Congress, under pressure from the employers of Chinese, hastily enacted the McCreary Amendment, extending the deadline for registration another six months. See Drayton, "The Chinese Six Companies" 472–93; Fong, "The Chinese Six Companies" 525–26; Coolidge, *Chinese Immigration* 209–33.

36. Coolidge, *Chinese Immigration* 409–11; Nee and Nee, *Longtime Californ'* 228–49; James T. Lee, "The Story of the New York Chinese Consolidated Benevolent Association," *Bridge Magazine* I (May—June 1972): 15–18; James T. Lee, "The Chinese Benevolent Association: An Assessment," *ibid.* (July—Aug. 1972): 15–16, 41, 43, 46–47.

37. See Loomis, "The Six Chinese Companies" 222–23; Gibson, *The Chinese in America* 341–43.

38. For a complete discussion, see Lyman, "The Structure of Chinese Society" 288–328.

39. Gibson, *The Chinese in America* 339–41; "Report of the Joint Special Committee to Investigate Chinese Immigration" 24; Hoy, *The Chinese Six Companies* 23; Ivan Light, *Ethnic Enterprise in America: Business and Welfare among Chinese, Japanese, and Blacks* (Berkeley, 1972) 81–100.

40. "Chinese Immigration: Its Social, Moral and Political Effects," *Report to the California State Senate of Its Special Committee on Chinese Immigration* (Sacramento, 1878) 70; *Proceedings of the Numismatic and Antiquarian Society of Philadelphia,* Nov. 7, 1895 (Philadelphia, 1899) 99–100; Fong, "The Chinese Six Companies" 523–24; H. C. Bennett, "The Chinese in California, Their Numbers and Influence," *Sacramento Daily Union* Nov. 17, 1869: 8; Chinese Chamber of Commerce, *San Francisco's Chinatown* 5; Loomis, "The Six Chinese Companies" 226; Coolidge, *Chinese Immigration* 406–07; Rose Hum Lee, *The Chinese in the United States of America* (Hong Kong, 1960) 146, 385–86.

41. Seward, *Chinese Immigration* 136–58; Coolidge, *Chinese Immigration* 48–51. Cf., for example, the "Agreement Between the English Merchant and Chinaman" (1849), a contract for transporting Chinese to California. Subsequent translations have pointed out that the "English" merchant was in fact an American. The contract will be found in the Wells Fargo Bank Historical Collection, San Francisco; see also "Letter of the Chinamen" 32–33; Persia Crawford Campbell, *Chinese Coolie Emigration to Countries within the British Empire* (London, 1923) 27–36, 150–51; Rhoda Hoff, *America's Immigrants: Adventures in Eyewitness History* (New York, 1967) 74–75; "Chinese Immigration: Its Social, Moral, and Political Effects" 70; Fong, "The Chinese Six Companies" 523–24; "Japanese and Other Immigrant Races in the Pacific Coast and Rocky Mountain States," 61 Cong., 2 sess., *S. Doc. 633* (1911) 391–99; Thomas W. Chinn, ed., *A History of the Chinese in America: A Syllabus* (San Francisco, 1969) 11–21; Albert Rhodes, "The Chinese at Beaver Falls," *Lippincott's Magazine* XIX (June 1877): 708–14.

42. Chinese Chamber of Commerce, *San Francisco's Chinatown* 5; Thomas W. Chinn, *A History of the Chinese in America* 47–54.

43. Rose Hum Lee, *The Chinese in the United States* 385–86; Leong Gor Yun, *Chinatown Inside Out* 36–39.

44. Loomis, "The Six Chinese Companies" 223; Fong, "The Chinese Six

Companies," 524–25; Culin, "Customs of the Chinese in America" 193; Speer, "Democracy of the Chinese" 836–48.

45. In 1854 the statute prohibiting Negroes and Indians from testifying for or against Caucasians was extended by the California Supreme Court to ban Chinese testimony as well. *People v. Hall,* 4 Cal. 399 (1854). See also *Speer v. See Yup,* 13 Cal. 73 (1855); *People v. Elyea,* 14 Cal. 144 (1859). The statute was revised to admit the testimony of Negroes in 1863, but Mongolians, Chinese, and Indians remained under the ban until January 1, 1873, when the revised California statutes admitted witnesses to the courts regardless of color or nationality. See Chinn, *A History of Chinese in California* 24; Heizer and Almquist, *The Other Californians* 47, 129–30, 229–34; Coolidge, *Chinese Immigration* 75–76. However, during this period Chinese mounted numerous civil rights cases in the courts where testimony against whites was not a factor. The traditional Chinese opposition to employing public courts predates the coming of Chinese to America. See Sybille van der Sprenkel, *Legal Institutions in Manchu China* (London, 1962) 80–111.

46. "Report of Special Committee to the Honorable, the Board of Supervisors of the City and County of San Francisco," in Willard B. Farwell, *The Chinese at Home and Abroad* (San Francisco, 1885) 51–58.

47. For nineteenth-century reports on the Triad Society, see Jean Chesneaux, *Secret Societies in China in the Nineteenth and Twentieth Centuries,* trans. Gillian Nettle (Ann Arbor, 1971) 1–135; Chesneaux, ed., *Popular Movements and Secret Societies in China, 1840–1950* (Stanford, 1972) 1–144; Gustave Schlegel, *Thian Ti Hwui: The Hung-League or Heaven-Earth-League—A Secret Society with the Chinese in China and India* (Batavia, 1866); William Stanton, *The Triad Society or Heaven and Earth Association* (Shanghai, 1900); J. S. M. Ward and W. G. Stirling, *The Hung Society or the Society of Heaven and Earth,* 3 vols. (London, 1925); Mervyn Llewelyn Wynne, *Triad and Tabut: A Survey of the Origin and Diffusion of Chinese and Mohammedan Secret Societies in the Malay Peninsula, A.D. 1800–1935* (Singapore, 1941) 1–151, 202–352; Leon Comber, *An Introduction to Chinese Secret Societies in Malaya* (Singapore, 1957); Comber, *Chinese Secret Societies in Malaya: A Survey of the Triad Society from 1800 to 1900* (Locust Valley, 1959); Wilfred Blythe, *The Impact of Chinese Secret Societies in Malaya: A Historical Study* (London, 1969); W. P. Morgan, *Triad Societies in Hong Kong* (Hong Kong, 1960).

48. Stewart Culin, "Chinese Secret Societies in the United States," *Journal of American Folk-Lore* III (Jan.—Mar. 1890): 39–43; Culin, "The I Hing or 'Patriotic Rising,' a Secret Society among the Chinese in America," *Proceedings of the Numismatic and Antiquarian Society of Philadelphia for the Years 1887–1889* III (Nov. 1887): 51–57.

49. Stanford M. Lyman, William Willmott, and Berching Ho, "Rules of a Chinese Secret Society in British Columbia," *Bulletin of the School of Oriental and African Studies* XXVII (1964): 530–39.

50. *San Francisco Call,* Jan. 9, 1898.

51. See Stanford M. Lyman, "Chinese Secret Societies in the Occident: Notes and Suggestions for Research on the Sociology of Secrecy," *Canadian Review of Sociology and Anthropology* I (May 1964): 79–102.

52. Sun Yat Sen, *Memoirs of a Chinese Revolutionary* (London, n.d.) 190–93.

53. A romanticized account of the recruitment and training of Chinese youths for service in the revolution will be found in Carl Glick, *Double Ten: Captain O'Banion's Story of the Chinese Revolution* (New York, 1945). See also

Ta-Ling Lee, *Foundations of the Chinese Revolution, 1905–1912* (New York, 1970) 104–09; Carl Glick and Hong Sheng-Hwa, *Swords of Silence: Chinese Secret-Societies—Past and Present* (New York, 1947) 94–235; Harold Z. Schiffrin, *Sun Yat-Sen and the Origins of the Chinese Revolution* (Berkeley, 1968) 243–44, 334–38; Philip P. Choy, "Gold Mountain of Lead: The Chinese Experience in California," *California Historical Quarterly* I (1971): 271.

54. Ta-Ling Lee, *Foundations of the Chinese Revolution* 106.

55. James Cantlie and Sheridan Jones, *Sun Yat-Sen and the Awakening of China* (New York, 1912) 132–34.

56. Schiffrin, *Sun Yat-Sen and the Origins of the Chinese Revolution*, 331–34.

57. For a discussion and a photograph of the money printed in San Francisco, see Alexander McLeod, *Pigtails and Gold Dust* (Caldwell, 1947) 148–50. On the proposed move of Sun's headquarters from Tokyo to San Francisco, see K. S. Liew, *Struggle for Democracy: Sung Chiao-jen and the 1911 Chinese Revolution* (Berkeley, 1968) 79–80.

58. Veta Griggs, *Chinaman's Chance: The Life Story of Elmer Wok Wai* (New York, 1969).

59. St. Clair McKelway, *True Tales from the Annals of Crime and Rascality* (New York, 1951) 153–69; Eng Ying Gong and Bruce Grant, *Tong War!* (New York, 1930) 27–30.

60. Gong and Grant, *Tong War* 30–31.

61. *Ibid.* 31–33, 112–30.

62. *Ibid.* 39–54.

63. *Ibid.* 122–30, 161–62.

64. Lyman, "The Structure of Chinese Society" 246–51.

65. According to Wolfram Eberhard, the founders of the Han Dynasty (206 B.C.–220 A.D.), the Later Liang Dynasty (907–922 A.D.), and the Ming Dynasty (1368–1644) were secret society bandit leaders. Eberhard, *Conquerors and Rulers: Social Forces in Medieval China* (Leiden, 1956) 89–106.

66. "Chinese and Japanese Labor in the Mountain and Pacific States," *Reports of the United States Industrial Commission on Immigration* XV, Part 4 (Washington, D.C., 1901) 773–92; Stewart Culin, "The Gambling Games of the Chinese in America," *Publications of the University of Pennsylvania Series in Philology, Literature, and Archaeology* I (1891): 1–17.

67. Speer, *The Oldest and Newest Empire* 603–04.

68. Hoy, *The Chinese Six Companies* 11, 22–23; Lee, *The Chinese in the United States of America* 156–60; Gong and Grant, *Tong War* 211; C. N. Reynolds, "The Chinese Tongs," *American Journal of Sociology* XL (1935): 623; Dillon, *The Hatchet Men* 361.

69. "Chinese and Japanese Labor in the Mountain and Pacific States" 777; Reynolds, "The Chinese Tongs" 622.

70. Gong and Grant, *Tong War* 59–65.

71. Richard H. Dillon, "Little Pete, King of Chinatown," *California Monthly* LXXIX (Dec. 1968): 42–58.

72. A set of instructions to a "salaried soldier" of a secret society, captured in Victoria, B.C., Canada in 1899, indicates that perjured testimony would be made available for any secret society thug who was charged with a crime committed as part of his societal duties. "Chinese and Japanese Labor in the Mountain and Pacific States" 771; a case of such perjury is reported in Oscar T. Shuck, "Seniors of the Collected Bar—Frank M. Stone," *History of the Bench and Bar of California* (Los Angeles, 1901) 938–42.

73. "Chinese and Japanese Labor in the Mountain and Pacific States" 771; see also Dillon, *The Hatchet Men* 167–205.

74. See Lyman, *The Asian in the West* 34–38.

75. "Fine New Home for Chinese Free Masons," *San Francisco Examiner* Oct. 6, 1907.

76. Lyman, Willmott, and Ho, "Rules of a Chinese Secret Society in British Columbia" 535.

77. "Chinese and Japanese Labor in the Mountain and Pacific States" 771.

78. Lyman, Willmott, and Ho, "Rules of a Chinese Secret Society in British Columbia" 536.

79. Dillon, "Little Pete, King of Chinatown" 52–55.

80. Jake Jackson, "A Chinese War in America"; and H. H. Noonan, "Another Version of the Weaverville War," in *Trinity 1957: Yearbook of the Trinity County Historical Society* (Weaverville, 1957) 5–12.

81. Gong and Grant, *Tong War* 194–202.

82. Lyman, *The Asian in the West* 29–31.

83. Gong and Grant, *Tong War* 50; Drayton, "The Chinese Six Companies" 427–77; Dillon, *The Hatchet Men* 241–340.

84. Gong and Grant, *Tong War* 50–54.

85. *San Francisco Chronicle* Nov. 11, 1909; Feb. 7, 1910.

86. Drayton, "The Chinese Six Companies" 475–76.

87. Hoy, *The Chinese Six Companies* 23–26.

88. Wynne, *Triad and Tabut* 7–15, 49–113, 202–351.

89. E. J. Eitel, "Outline History of the Hakkas," *The China Review* II (1873–74): 160–64; Wynne, *Triad and Tabut* 59–61, 260–80.

90. In addition to the sources cited in footnote 80, *supra,* see McLeod, *Pigtails and Gold Dust* 53–56; Joseph Henry Jackson, *Anybody's Gold: The Story of California's Mining Towns* (San Francisco, 1970) 210–23.

91. Stewart Culin, "The I Hing or 'Patriotic Rising'" 51–57; Liew, *Struggle for Democracy* 68–103, 172–90; Glick and Hong, *Swords of Silence* 160–90, 255–62.

92. Gong and Grant, *Tong War* 194–202; *San Francisco Chronicle* Nov. 11, 1909; Feb. 7, 1910.

93. Lyman, *The Asian in the West* 27–31; John E. Bennett, "The Chinese Tong Wars in San Francisco," *Harper's Weekly* XLIV (Aug. 11, 1900): 746–747.

94. H. H. Bancroft, "Mongolianism in America," *Essays and Miscellany* (San Francisco, 1890) 356; Gibson, *The Chinese in America* 139–40; Farwell, *The Chinese at Home and Abroad* 8–14.

95. *San Francisco Chronicle* Nov. 11, 1909; Feb. 7, 1910; Dillon, *The Hatchet Men* 227.

96. For the formal theory upon which this section of the paper is based, see the two essays by Georg Simmel, *Conflict and the Web of Group Affiliations,* trans. Kurt H. Wolff and Reinhard Bendix (Glencoe, 1955) 11–195.

97. Lyman, "Structures of Chinese Society" 364–77.

98. Examples of these declarations of war will be found in McLeod, *Pigtails and Gold Dust* 53–54.

99. Drayton, "The Chinese Six Companies" 475.

100. Dillon, *The Hatchet Men* 167–206; McLeod, *Pigtails and Gold Dust* 238–52.

101. "Chinese and Japanese Labor in the Mountain and Pacific States" 771.

102. Lyman, "The Structure of Chinese Society" 352–54.

103. The last major tong war appears to have been fought in 1933. Glick, *Shake Hands with the Dragon* 265. Twenty-five years later a dispute between the Hop Sing Tong and the Bing Kung Tong threatened to erupt in violence, but after months of negotiations the matter was settled peacefully. *San Francisco Examiner* Jan. 3, 1958; May 3, 5, 7, and 9, 1958; *San Francisco Chronicle* Jan. 3 and 4, 1958.

104. The number of secret societies in San Francisco rose and fell as wars continued in the period between 1880 and 1910. See Dillon, *The Hatchet Men* 243–367. The *hui kuan* experienced a great number of factional disputes resulting in group defections, establishment of new *Landsmannschaften,* and finally a grudging recognition of the rights of secret societies. Nee and Nee, *Longtime Californ'* 13–124, 228–52.

105. Lyman, "The Structure of Chinese Society" 204–21.

106. Simmel, *Conflict and the Web of Group Affiliations* 11–195; Lewis Coser, *The Functions of Social Conflict* (Glencoe, 1956); Edward A. Ross, *Principles of Sociology* (New York, 1920) 162.

107. Coser, *The Functions of Social Conflict* 35; Ross, *Principles of Sociology* 162.

108. One of the finest examples of this solidarity was shown when hundreds of Chinese, under the direction of the Consolidated Benevolent Association, went to jail to protest San Francisco's lodging house ordinance. See *Ho Ah Kow v. Matthew Nunan,* 5 Sawyer 552 (1879); McLeod, *Pigtails and Gold Dust* 199–212.

109. See William Purviance Fenn, *Ah Sin and his Brethren in American Literature* (Peking, 1933) 1–131; Dorothy B. Jones, *The Image of China and India on the American Screen, 1896–1955* (Cambridge, 1955) 13–42; Colin Watson, *Snobbery with Violence: Crime Stories and Their Audience* (New York, 1971) 109–29.

110. Simmel, *Conflict and the Web of Group Affiliation* 17–28.

111. Cf. *ibid.* 25–26.

System & Function in Antebellum Southern Sociology

1. L. L. Bernard, "Henry Hughes, First American Sociologist," *Social Forces* XV (December 1936): 154–74. See also Stanford M. Lyman, ed., *Selected Papers of Henry Hughes: Southerner, Slavocrat, Sociologist* (Jackson: University Press of Mississippi, 1985).

2. An exception to his statement will be found in Arthur J. Vidich and Stanford M. Lyman, *American Sociology: Worldly Rejections of Religion and Their Directions* (New Haven: Yale University Press, 1985) 9–19, 242–56.

3. C. Vann Woodward, "George Fitzhugh, *Sui Generis,*" introduction to his edition of George Fitzhugh, *Cannibals All! or, Slaves Without Masters* (Cambridge: The Belknap Press of Harvard University Press, 1960, 1973) vii–xxxix.

4. Eugene Genovese, "The Logical Outcome of the Slaveholders' Philosophy: An Exposition, Interpretation, and Critique of the Social Thought of George Fitzhugh of Port Royal, Virginia," in *The World the Slaveholders Made: Two Essays in Interpretation* (New York: Pantheon Books, 1969) 118–244.

5. On Holmes see three essays by Harvey Wish, "George Frederick Holmes and the Genesis of American Sociology," *American Journal of Sociology* XLVI (March 1941): 698–707; "George Frederick Holmes and Southern Periodical Literature of the Mid-Nineteenth Century," *Journal of Southern History* VII (Au-

gust 1941): 343–56; "Aristotle, Plato, and the Mason-Dixon Line," *Journal of the History of Ideas* X (April 1949): 254–66; Leonidas Betts, "George Frederick Holmes: Nineteenth Century Virginia Educator," *Virginia Magazine of History and Biography* LXXVI (October 1968): 472–84; Frederick E. Salzillo, Jr., "The Development of Sociology at the University of Virginia: The First One-Hundred Years, 1873–1973," *Southeastern Review: A Journal of Sociology* III:1 (Winter 1976): 11–25; Joseph Dorfman, *The Economic Mind in American Civilization, 1606–1865* (New York: Viking Press, 1946) II: 920–28; Tipton R. Snavely, *The Department of Economics at the University of Virginia, 1825–1956,* (Charlottesville: The University Press of Virginia, 1967) 66–96; Richmond Laurin Hawkins, *Auguste Comte and the United States, 1816–1853* (Cambridge: Harvard University Press, 1936; New York: Kraus Reprint, 1966) 63–142; Neal C. Gillespie, *The Collapse of Orthodoxy: The Intellectual Ordeal of George Frederick Holmes* (Charlottesville: The University Press of Virginia, 1972).

6. On Le Conte see Vidich and Lyman, *American Sociology* 242–56; Theodore Dwight Bozemen, "Joseph Le Conte: Organic Science and a 'Sociology of the South'," *Journal of Southern History* XXXIX (November 1973): 565–82; Lester D. Stephens, *Joseph Le Conte: Gentle Prophet of Evolution* (Baton Rouge: Louisiana State University Press, 1982); Stanford Lyman, "Le Conte, Royce, Teggart, Blumer: Dialogues on Sociology, Social Change, and Symbolic Interaction at Berkeley," in this volume.

7. Henry Hughes, *A Treatise on Sociology, Theoretical and Practical* (Philadelphia: Lippincott and Grambo, 1854; New York: Negro Universities Press, 1968).

8. Hughes, *Treatise* . . . 227–60.

9. *Ibid.* 237–40, 291.

10. *Ibid.* 64–69.

11. *loc. cit.*

12. Ronald T. Takaki, *Iron Cages: Race and Culture in Nineteenth Century America* (New York: Alfred A. Knopf, 1979) 199.

13. H. G. and Winnie Leach Duncan, "Henry Hughes, Sociologist of the Old South," *Sociology and Social Research* XXI (January—February 1937): 251, 258.

14. Ulrich Bonnell Phillips, *The Course of the South to Secession: An Interpretation* (New York: Hill and Wang, 1964 [1939]) 122.

15. Takaki, *Iron Cages* 128, 134–36.

16. Cf. Stanford M. Lyman, "Henry Hughes and the Southern Foundations of American Sociology," in Lyman, ed., *Selected Writings* 1–72.

17. Hughes, *Treatise* . . . 291–92.

18. *Ibid.* 241.

19. *Ibid.* 239–40.

20. *Ibid.* 207.

21. *Ibid.* 207.

22. Harvey Wish, *George Fitzhugh: Propagandist of the Old South* (Gloucester, Mass.: Peter Smith, 1962).

23. The term "social system" appears first to have been used by Henry Augustine Washington, a biographer of Thomas Jefferson, in his essay "The Social System of Virginia," *Southern Literary Messenger* XIV (February 1848): 65–81.

24. Cf. H. G. and Winnie Leach Duncan, "The Development of Sociology in the Old South," *American Journal of Sociology* XXXIX (March 1934): 655.

25. George Fitzhugh, *Cannibals All!* 17–18.

26. *Ibid.* 18.

27. *Ibid.* 20.

28. Hughes, *Treatise* . . . 207–09, 227–92.

29. *Ibid.* 210–26.

30. Fitzhugh, "Sociology for the South," in Harvey Wish, ed., *Antebellum: Writings of George Fitzhugh and Hinton Rowan Helper on Slavery* (New York: Capricorn Books, 1960) 57.

31. *Ibid.* 58–59.

32. *Ibid.* 59.

33. *Ibid.* 91.

34. George Fitzhugh, "Origin of Civilization—What is Property?—Which is the Best Slave Race?" *DeBow's Review* XXV (December 1858): 663.

35. *loc. cit.*

36. Charles Camic, "The Making of a Method: A Historical Reinterpretation of the Early Parsons," *American Sociological Review* LII (August 1987): 421–39, esp. 432–39.

37. George Fitzhugh, "Antinomic Pathology," *Southern Literary Messenger* XXXVII (1863): 415–19.

38. *loc. cit.*

39. George Fitzhugh, "The Impending Fate of the Country," *De Bow's Review* (1866): 569.

40. George Fitzhugh, "The Uses of Morality in War and Peace," *De Bow's Review* (1866) 75–77.

41. *loc. cit.*

42. *loc. cit.*

43. Quoted in Wish, *George Fitzhugh: Propagandist of the Old South, op. cit.* 338.

44. George Fitzhugh, "Land Monopoly," *Lippincott's Magazine* IV (1869): 286–91.

45. George Fitzhugh, "The Freedman and His Future," *Lippincott's Magazine* IV (1869): 436–39.

46. Cf. Vidich and Lyman, *American Sociology* 82–85.

47. Jeffrey C. Alexander, *The Modern Reconstruction of Classical Thought: Talcott Parsons,* vol. IV of *Theoretical Logic in Sociology* (Berkeley: University of California Press, 1983) 288.

48. Richard Münch, "Parsonian Theory Today: In Search of a New Synthesis," in Anthony Giddens and Jonathan Turner, eds., *Social Theory Today* (Stanford: Stanford University Press, 1987) 116, 149–50.

49. Lewis Coser, "American Trends," in Tom Bottomore and Robert Nisbet, eds., *A History of Sociological Analysis* (New York: Basic Books, 1978) 318.

50. For a fine critique, see Robert Nisbet, "Developmentalism: A Critical Analysis," *The Making of Modern Society* (New York: New York University Press, 1986) 33–69.

Le Conte, Royce, Teggart, Blumer

1. Edward Shils, "Tradition, Ecology, and Institution in the History of Sociology," *The Calling of Sociology and Other Essays on the Pursuit of Learning* (Chicago: University of Chicago Press, 1980) 165–258.

2. *Ibid.* 226.

3. Arthur J. Vidich and Stanford M. Lyman, *American Sociology: Worldly Rejections of Religion and Their Directions* (New Haven, CT: Yale University Press, 1985) 235–80; and Stanford M. Lyman and Arthur J. Vidich, *Social Order and the Public Philosophy: An Analysis and Interpretation of the Work of Herbert Blumer* (Fayetteville: The University of Arkansas Press, 1988).

4. Shils, *op. cit.* 165.

5. Joseph Le Conte, "Lecture on Coal," *Annual Report of the Board of Regents of the Smithsonian Institution* (Washington, DC: Smithsonian Institution, 1857–1858).

6. Le Conte, "The Relation of Organic Science to Sociology," *Southern Presbyterian Review* XIII (April 1860): 39–77.

7. Le Conte, *Evolution: Its Nature, Its Evidences, and Its Relation to Religious Thought* (New York: D. Appleton and Co., 1897) 297, 300, 326, 332, 344, 351.

8. Le Conte, *The Race Problem in the South* (New York: D. Appleton and Co., 1892) 354.

9. *Ibid.* 357.

10. Vidich and Lyman, *op. cit.* 252.

11. Kenneth E. Bock, "The Acceptance of Histories: Toward a Perspective for Social Science," *University of California Publications in Sociology and Social Institutions* III (Berkeley: University of California Press, 1956) 51–53.

12. Vidich and Lyman, *op. cit.* 252.

13. Le Conte, *The Race Problem in the South, op. cit.* 382.

14. George H. Mead, *Selected Writings,* Andrew J. Reck, ed., (Indianapolis: Bobbs-Merrill, 1964) 371–91.

15. Lester D. Stephens, *Joseph Le Conte: Gentle Prophet of Evolution* (Baton Rouge: Louisiana State University Press, 1982).

16. Josiah Royce, *California: From the Conquest in 1846 to the Second Vigilance Committee in San Francisco—A Study of American Character* (New York: Alfred A. Knopf, 1948) 179–82.

17. Royce, *The Problem of Christianity* (Chicago: University of Chicago Press, 1968) 75–98, 229–50.

18. Le Conte, "Critical Periods in the History of the Earth," *Bulletin of the Department of Geology of the University of California* I (1895): 315–16.

19. Royce, *The Philosophy of Loyalty* (New York: Macmillan, 1916).

20. *Ibid.* 193.

21. William G. Sumner, *Folkways: A Study of the Sociological Importance of Usages, Manners, Customs, Mores, and Morals* (Boston: Ginn and Co., 1940) 13–15.

22. Royce, "Race Questions and Prejudices," *Race Questions, Provincialism, and Other American Problems* (New York: Macmillan, 1908) 1–54.

23. Arthur J. Vidich and Stanford M. Lyman, "State, Ethics and Public Morality in American Sociological Thought," *Sociological Theory in Transition,* Mark L. Wardell and Stephen P. Turner, eds. (Boston: Allen and Unwin, 1986) 46.

24. Royce, *The Problem of Christianity, op. cit.* 93–94.

25. Mead, *Selected Writings, op. cit.* 382.

26. Vidich and Lyman, "State, Ethics and Public Morality in American Sociological Thought," *op. cit.* 48.

27. Herbert G. Blumer, "George Herbert Mead," *The Future of the Sociological Classics,* Buford Rhea, ed. (Boston: Allen and Unwin, 1981) 167.

28. *Ibid.* 152.

29. Robert N. Bellah, *Beyond Belief: Essays on Religion in a Post-Traditional World* (New York: Harper & Row, 1970) 168–92.

30. Robert N. Bellah, R. Madsen, W. M. Sullivan, A. Swidler, and S. M. Tipton, *Habits of the Heart: Individualism and Commitment in American Life* (Berkeley: University of California Press, 1985).

31. Herbert Blumer, "Uber das Konzept der Massengesellschaft," *Militanter Humanismus: Von den Aufgaben der Modernen Soziologie,* Alphons Silbermann, ed., (Frankfurt am Main: S. Fischer Verlag, 1966) 19–37; trans. into English in Lyman and Vidich, *op. cit.* 337–52.

32. Frederick J. Teggart, *Prolegomena to History: The Relation of History to Literature, Philosophy, and Science* (Berkeley: University of California Press, 1916).

33. Frederick J. Teggart, *Theory of History* (New Haven, CT: Yale University Press, 1925) 165n.

34. *Ibid.* 94–123.

35. Stanford M. Lyman, "The Acceptance, Rejection, and Reconstruction of Histories: On Some Controversies in the Study of Social and Cultural Change," in this volume.

36. Herbert Blumer, "Symbolic Interaction and the Idea of Social System," *Revue Internationale de Sociologie* XI (1975): 3–12.

37. Grace Dangberg, *A Guide to the Life and Works of Frederick J. Teggart* (Reno: Grace Dangberg Foundation, Inc., 1983) 370.

38. Frederick J. Teggart, "The Humanistic Study of Change in Time," *Journal of Philosophy* XXIII (June 1926): 315.

39. Teggart, *Theory of History, op. cit.* 79–86.

40. *Ibid.* 94, 96–97.

41. Herbert Blumer, "Method in Social Psychology," Diss., University of Chicago, 1928, 434.

42. *Ibid.* 350–60.

43. *Ibid.* 358n.

44. Frederick J. Teggart, *Rome and China: A Study of Correlations in Historical Events* (Berkeley: University of California Press, 1939).

45. Margaret T. Hodgen, *Change and History: A Study of the Dated Distributions of Technological Innovations in England* (New York: Wenner-Gren Foundation for Anthropological Research, 1952).

46. Blumer, "Method in Social Psychology," *op. cit.* 359.

47. Frederick J. Teggart, "Causation in Historical Events," *Journal of the History of Ideas* III (1942): 3–11.

48. Blumer, "Method in Social Psychology," *op. cit.* 352n.

49. Teggart, "Causation in Historical Events," *op. cit.;* and "The Argument of Hesiod's *Works and Days,*" *Journal of the History of Ideas* VIII (1947): 45–77.

50. Blumer, "Method in Social Psychology," *op. cit.* 354.

51. Robert E. Park, *Society: Collective Behavior, News and Opinion, Sociology and Modern Society,* Volume 3, *The Collected Papers of Robert Ezra Park,* Everett Cherrington Hughes, et al., eds. (Glencoe, IL: The Free Press, 1955) 302n.

52. Robert E. Park, *Race and Culture,* Volume 1, *The Collected Papers of Robert Ezra Park,* Everett Cherrington Hughes, et al., eds. (Glencoe, IL: The Free Press, 1950) p. 351.

53. William I. Thomas, "Introductory," *Source Book for Social Origins,* William I. Thomas, ed. (Boston: Richard G. Badger, 1909) 3–28.

54. Stanford M. Lyman, "The Science of History and the Theory of Social Change," in this volume.

55. Dangberg, *A Guide to the Life and Works of Frederick J. Teggart, op. cit.* 397.

56. *Ibid.* 351.

57. *loc. cit.*

58. Teggart, *Theory of History, op. cit.* 107.

59. Auguste Comte, *The Positive Philosophy of Auguste Comte,* trans. and ed. Harriet Martineau, 2nd edn., (London: Trubner, 1875) 151–54.

60. Teggart, *Theory of History, op. cit.* 184.

61. *Ibid.* 176.

62. *Ibid.* 177.

63. *Ibid.* 196.

64. *loc. cit.*

65. Frederick J. Teggart, *The Theory and Processes of History* (Berkeley: University of California Press, 1941) 149–50, 196–97, 272–96, 307–12.

66. Alfred Schutz, *Collected Papers II: Studies in Social Theory,* Arvid Broderson, ed. (The Hague: Martinus Nijhoff, 1964) 73–78, 95–101, 122–23, 251; and Alfred Schutz and Thomas Luckmann, *The Structures of the Life World,* trans. Richard M. Zaner and H. Tristram Englehardt, Jr. (Evanston: Northwestern University Press, 1973) 15, 107–10, 136, 225–26, 271, 284, 311–12.

67. Teggart, *The Theory and Processes of History, op. cit.* 307.

68. *loc. cit.*

69. *loc. cit.*

70. William James, *The Writings of William James,* John J. McDermott, ed. (New York: Random House, 1967) 671–83.

71. Teggart, *The Theory and Processes of History, op. cit.* 311–12.

72. Herbert Blumer, "Industrialisation and Race Relations," *Industrialisation and Race Relations: A Symposium,* Guy Hunter, ed. (London: Oxford University Press, 1965) 220–53.

73. Herbert Blumer, *Symbolic Interactionism: Perspective and Method* (Englewood Cliffs, NJ: Prentice-Hall, 1969) 89.

74. *loc. cit.*

75. Herbert Blumer, *Movies and Conduct* (New York: Macmillan, 1933); and Herbert G. Blumer and Philip M. Hauser, *Movies, Delinquency, and Crime* (New York: Macmillan, 1933).

76. George Herbert Mead, *The Philosophy of the Act,* Charles W. Morris, et al., eds. (Chicago: University of Chicago Press, 1938) 75.

77. George Herbert Mead, *Mind, Self, and Society,* Charles W. Morris, ed. (Chicago: University of Chicago Press, 1934) 257.

78. Mead, *Selected Writings, op. cit.* 303.

79. *loc. cit.*

80. *Ibid.* 304–05.

81. *Ibid.* 305.

82. Herbert Blumer, "Moulding of Mass Behavior through the Motion Picture," *Human Side of Social Planning: Selected Papers from the Proceedings of The American Sociological Society,* Ernest W. Burgess and Herbert Blumer, eds. (Chicago: American Sociological Society, 1935) 124.

83. *loc. cit.*

84. Teggart, *The Theory and Processes of History, op. cit.* 271–310.

85. Blumer, "Moulding of Mass Behavior through the Motion Picture," *op. cit.* 124.

86. *Ibid.* 125.

87. *Ibid.* 126.

88. *loc. cit.*

89. *Ibid.* 127.

90. Teggart, *The Theory and Processes of History, op. cit.* 280–92, 300–12.

91. Blumer, *Symbolic Interactionism: Perspective and Method, op. cit.* 88–89.

92. Herbert Blumer, "Reflections on Theory of Race Relations," *Race Relations in World Perspective,* Andrew W. Lind, ed. (Honolulu: University of Hawaii Press, 1955) 14.

93. Herbert Blumer, "Race Prejudice as a Sense of Group Position," *Pacific Sociological Review* I (Spring 1958): 3.

94. *Ibid.* 3–7; and four essays by Herbert Blumer, "The Study of Urbanization and Industrialization: Methodological Deficiencies," *Boletim de Centro Latino Americano de Pesquisas em Ciencias Sociais* 2 (May 1959): 17–34; "Early Industrialization and the Laboring Class," *Sociological Quarterly* I (1960): 5–14; "Industrialization and the Traditional Order," *Sociology and Social Research* XLVIII (January 1964): 129–38; and "Industrialisation and Race Relations," *op. cit.* 220–53.

95. Herbert Blumer, "The Future of the Color Line," *The South in Continuity and Change,* J. McKinney and E. Thompson, eds. (Durham: Duke University Press, 1965) 322–36.

96. Teggart, *The Theory and Processes of History, op. cit.* 194.

97. Blumer, "The Future of the Color Line," *op. cit.* 323.

98. Blumer, "Race Prejudice as a Sense of Group Position," *op. cit.* 7.

99. Herbert Blumer, "Social Science and the Desegregation Process," *The Annals of the American Academy of Political and Social Science* XXXIV (March 1956): 139.

100. Earl Black and Merle Black, *Politics and Society in the South* (Cambridge: Harvard University Press, 1987).

101. Mead, *Selected Writings, op. cit.* 96n.

102. *Ibid.* 362.

103. Herbert G. Blumer, "Psychological Import of the Human Group," *Group Relations at the Crossroads,* Muzafer Sherif and M. O. Wilson, eds. (New York: Harper and Brothers, 1953) 199.

104. David Frisby, *Georg Simmel* (London: Tavistock, 1984) 150.

Legitimacy and Consensus in Lipset's America

1. Claus Offe employs the term *Spätkapitalismus;* Habermas prefers the term "advanced." See Jurgen Habermas, *Legitimation Crisis,* trans. Thomas McCarthy (Boston: Beacon Press, 1975).

2. Norman Birnbaum, "The Crisis in Marxist Society," *Social Research* XXXV (Summer 1968): 348–80.

3. Alvin W. Gouldner, *The Coming Crisis of Western Sociology* (New York: Basic Books, 1970).

4. Claus Mueller, *The Politics of Communication: A Study in the Political Sociology of Language, Socialization, and Legitimation* (New York: Oxford University Press, 1973) 127–77; Richard Barnet, "The Twilight of the Nation State: A Crisis of Legitimacy," in Robert Paul Wolff, ed., *The Rule of Law* (New York: Simon and Schuster, 1971) 221–42.

5. Russell Jacoby, "The Politics of the Crisis Theory: Toward the Critique of Automatic Marxism II," *Telos* XXIII (Spring 1975): 3–52.

6. Among the radicals in America perhaps the most extreme statement—one that indicts virtually all of American sociology as a species of a supposedly unacceptable "liberal" ideology—is Herman and Julia Schwendinger, *The Sociologists of the Chair: A Radical Analysis of the Formative Years of North American Sociology, 1883–1922* (New York: Basic Books, 1974). Among the moderates, see Robert W. Friedrichs, *A Sociology of Sociology* (New York: The Free Press, 1970); and Paul Halmos, ed., "The Sociology of Sociology," *The Sociological Review*, Monograph 16 (September 1970).

7. For some earlier and more fruitful usages, see W. I. Thomas, "Introductory," *Source Book for Social Origins*, 6th edn. (Boston: Richard G. Badger, 1909) 13–26; Edmund Husserl, *The Crisis of European Sciences and Transcendental Phenomenology: An Introduction to Phenomenological Philosophy*, trans. David Carr (Evanston: Northwestern University Press, 1970) 3–20.

8. For a summary bibliography of the most significant criticisms of the last two decades see footnote 2 in Pierre L. van den Berghe, "Dialectic and Functionalism: Toward a Theoretical Synthesis," *American Sociological Review* XXVIII (October 1963) 695–96.

9. For example, Robert Bierstedt wrote in 1969: "The organic analogy gradually disappeared from the literature of social science during the second and third decades of the twentieth century, and it would now be difficult to find a sociologist who takes it seriously . . ." (*Power and Progress: Essays on Sociological Theory* [New York: McGraw-Hill, 1975] 108). And, more recently, Herminio Martins complains that the "demise of functionalism has not brought about a substantial increment in the degree of temporalism and historism in the theoretical constructs of general sociology . . ." ("Time and Theory in Sociology," in John Rex, ed., *Approaches to Sociology: An Introduction to Major Trends in British Sociology* [London: Routledge and Kegan Paul, 1974] 249).

10. Tom Bottomore, "Out of This World: The Sociological Theory of Talcott Parsons," *Sociology as Social Criticism* (New York: Pantheon Books, 1974) 29–43; Andrew Hacker, "Sociology and Ideology," in Max Black, ed., *The Social Theories of Talcott Parsons* (Englewood Cliffs: Prentice-Hall, 1961) 289–310.

11. Piotr Sztompka, *System and Function: Toward a Theory of Society* (New York: Academic Press, 1974).

12. Peter C. Ludz, "Marxism and Systems Theory in a Bureaucratic Society," *Social Research* XLII (Winter 1975), 661–74.

13. Kingsley Davis, "The Myth of Functional Analysis as a Special Method in Sociology and Anthropology, *American Sociological Review* XXIV (December 1959): 757–72.

14. Kenneth E. Bock, "Evolution, Function, and Change," *American Sociological Review* XXVIII (April 1963): 229–37.

15. That Parsonian functionalism and Marxian analysis have much in common as perspectives but differ on emphasis is indicated by Neil Smelser when he writes: "A major difference between Marx and the functional theorists is that Marx gives primacy to the economic function—the others being subordinated in various ways to it—whereas the functional theorists regard the various functional exigencies as more nearly cognate" ("Introduction," in Neil Smelser, ed., *Karl Marx on Society and Social Change* [Chicago: University of Chicago Press, 1973] xix).

16. Jürgen Habermas, *Legitimation Crisis;* see also Habermas, "Towards a Reconstruction of Historical Materialism," *Theory and Society* II (Fall 1975): 287–300.

17. Max Weber, *The Methodology of the Social Sciences,* trans. and ed. Edward A. Shils and Henry A. Finch (New York: The Free Press, 1959) 181–86.

18. Seymour Martin Lipset, *The First New Nation: The United States in Historical and Comparative Perspective* (New York: Basic Books, 1963).

19. See, for example, Seymour Martin Lipset, *Political Man: The Social Bases of Politics* (Garden City: Doubleday and Co., 1960) 310–42, 403–17.

20. Talcott Parsons, "Full Citizenship for the Negro? A Sociological Problem," in Talcott Parsons and Kenneth B. Clark, eds., *The Negro American* (Boston: Houghton Mifflin, 1966) 709–54.

21. David Riesman, Nathan Glazer, and Reuel Denney, *The Lonely Crowd: A Study of the Changing American Character* (Garden City: Doubleday Anchor, 1950); William H. Whyte, Jr., *The Organization Man* (Garden City: Doubleday Anchor, 1956).

22. Robin Williams, *American Society* (New York: Alfred A. Knopf, 1957) 344–45; Will Herberg, *Protestant-Catholic-Jew: An Essay in American Religious Sociology* (Garden City: Doubleday Anchor, 1955).

23. Arminianism, the theological doctrine that Christ died for all men and not for the elect only, derives its name from Jacobus Arminius (1560–1609), a Dutch Protestant theologian.

24. Daniel Bell, "Crime as an American Way of Life: A Queer Ladder of Social Mobility," *The End of Ideology: On the Exhaustion of Political Ideas in the Fifties* (New York: Collier Books, 1961) 127–50.

25. See, for example, Herbert Hill, "The Racial Practices of Organized Labor—The Age of Gompers and After," in Arthur M. Ross and Herbert Hill, eds., *Employment, Race, and Poverty: Critical Study of the Disadvantaged Status of Negro Workers from 1865 to 1965* (New York: Harcourt, Brace and World, 1967) 365–402; Hill, "Anti-Oriental Agitation and the Rise of Working Class Racism," *Society* X (January—February 1973): 43–54; Paul Jacobs, *The State of the Unions* (New York: Atheneum, 1963) 154–71, 284–89.

26. See Stanford M. Lyman, *The Black American in Sociological Thought: A Failure of Perspective* (New York: G. P. Putnam's Sons, 1972) 145–70.

27. Seymour Martin Lipset, "Education and Equality: Israel and the United States Compared," *Society* XI (March—April 1974): 56–66. In his introduction to the 1979 edition of *The First New Nation* (New York: W. W. Norton, 1979) xxxv, Lipset writes:

My guess is that if significant further progress toward equality of results is to occur, it will take the form of what the British sociologist T. H. Marshall called the expansion of the idea of citizenship to include social rights—that every citizen can claim the right to a share in the prevailing material and cultural standards of the society; in other words, no one, even the runner who finished far back in the pack, will be condemned to a life of suffering and deprivation.

Lipset does not say how this will come about.

28. Understandably, perhaps, the bulk of criticism of Lipset's studies of the student revolt has been politically motivated and ideological in character. Since Lipset has never claimed neutrality of objectivity in his work, and since he has been both participant and observer in many scenes of campus rebellion, his work has excited and in some cases inflamed opinion on all sides. And, as Lipset has pointed out, his stance has aroused the enmity of both radicals and reactionaries, and even turned some moderates against him as well. The passion invoked over this situation makes it a natural and inviting arena for sociological

investigation. My analysis, however, hopes to bypass the rage and rhetoric of the debate between Lipset and his critics and to locate his study within the context of his general analysis of American society as a functioning social system.

29. Seymour Martin Lipset and Sheldon Wolin, eds., *The Berkeley Student Revolt* (Garden City: Doubleday Anchor, 1965); Lipset, ed., *Student Politics* (New York: Basic Books, 1967); Lipset and Philip G. Altbach, *Students in Revolt* (Boston: Houghton-Mifflin, 1969); Lipset and Gerald M. Schaflander, *Passions and Politics: Student Activism in America* (Boston: Little, Brown & Co., 1971); and Lipset, *Rebellion in the University* (Boston: Little, Brown & Co., 1972). Writing in 1989 ("Why Youth Revolt," *New York Times,* May 24, 1989, 27) Lipset attempted to press the revolt of China's students on to a functionalist thesis, noting that conditions for such "a massive outbreak of student activism such as occurred in . . . China today . . . obviously lie with crises in the larger political scene that stimulate opposition." But Lipset insists that this does not explain student activism. He then harks back to Aristotle, to reductionist psychology, and to sociological ideas about student marginality in order to account for the students' role in protest. Lipset claims "students remain adolescents or juveniles sociologically, and they're often explicitly or implicitly treated as such legally, particularly when they violate the law. In many societies, such as China's, a large number of the students involved in politically or otherwise motivated infractions are literally the children of the elite, a fact that serves to reduce the will to punish them." Within ten days of the publication of this essay, the Chinese regime massacred the students in Tienanmen Square and conducted a witch-hunt to find, arrest, and punish the "ringleaders." Such returns to "equilibrium" suggest how sociological concepts obscure the bloody realities of political life.

30. For my own analysis of this situation, see Marvin B. Scott and Stanford M. Lyman, *The Revolt of the Students* (Columbus: Charles Merrill, 1970).

31. Seymour Martin Lipset and Earl Raab, "An Appointment with Watergate" *Commentary* LVI (September 1973): 35–43.

32. Richard Hofstadter, *The Paranoid Style in American Politics and Other Essays* (New York: Alfred A. Knopf, 1965).

33. Theodore H. White, *Breach of Faith: The Fall of Richard Nixon* (New York: Atheneum, 1975) 57–79, 162–63, 193–94.

34. Gustav Ratzenhofer, quoted in Albion W. Small, *General Sociology: An Exposition of the Main Development in Sociological Theory from Spencer to Ratzenhofer* (Chicago: University of Chicago Press, 1905) 256.

35. See, for example, Stanford M. Lyman, *Chinese Americans* (New York: Random House, 1974) 158–81, 186–91; and Jack D. Forbes, *Aztecas del Norte: The Chicanos of Aztlan* (Greenwich: Fawcett, 1973).

36. Small, *General Sociology* 183–324.

37. For two empirical analyses of elements of this process see Stanford M. Lyman, "Generation and Character: The Case of the Japanese Americans," *Asian in the West* (Reno: Desert Research Institute, 1970) 81–98; and Lyman, "Conflict and the Web of Group Affiliation in San Francisco's Chinatown, 1850–1910," in this volume.

38. See Stanford M. Lyman and Marvin B. Scott, *A Sociology of the Absurd* (Pacific Palisades: Goodyear Publishing Co., 1970) 111–44.

39. See Marvin B. Scott and Stanford M. Lyman, "Accounts, Deviance, and Social Order," in Jack D. Douglas, ed., *Deviance and Respectability: The Social Construction of Moral Meanings* (New York: Basic Books, 1970) 89–119.

40. Small, *General Sociology* 253.

41. Kingsley Davis, "American Society: Its Group Structure," *Contemporary Civilization* 2 (Chicago: Scott, Foresman) 171–86.

42. Joseph Bensman and Arthur J. Vidich, *The New American Society: The Revolution of the Middle Class* (Chicago: Quadrangle, 1971).

43. Everett C. Hughes, "Good People and Dirty Work," *The Sociological Eye: Selected Papers on Institutions and Race* (Chicago: Aldine Publishers, 1971) 97.

44. Lyman, *The Black American* 96–97.

45. See, for example, Margaret T. Hodgen, *Early Anthropology in the Sixteenth and Seventeenth Century* (Philadelphia: University of Pennsylvania Press, 1964) 354–432; Winthrop D. Jordan, *White Over Black: American Attitudes Toward the Negro, 1550–1812* (Chapel Hill: University of North Carolina Press, 1968).

46. White, *Breach of Faith* 222.

47. Jack D. Douglas, *American Social Order: Social Rules in a Pluralistic Society* (New York: The Free Press, 1971) 275.

48. See Stanford M. Lyman and Marvin B. Scott, *The Drama of Social Reality* (New York: Oxford University Press, 1975) 111–46.

49. See Stanford M. Lyman and William A. Douglass, "Ethnicity: Strategies and Tactics of Collective and Individual Impression Management," *Social Research* XL (Summer 1973) 344–65.

Symbolic Interactionism and Macrosociology

1. Lewis A. Coser, "Sociological Theory from the Chicago Dominance to 1965," *Annual Review of Sociology* XI (1976): 156–57.

2. Eugene Rochberg-Halton, *Meaning and Modernity: Social Theory in the Pragmatic Attitude,* (Chicago: University of Chicago Press, 1986) 44.

3. Herbert Blumer, *Symbolic Interactionism: Perspective and Method* (Berkeley: University of California Press, 1986) 15.

4. *loc. cit.*

5. Lewis A. Coser, *Masters of Sociological Thought: Ideas in Historical and Social Context,* 2nd Edn. (New York: Harcourt Brace Jovanovich, 1977) 575.

6. Stanford M. Lyman and Arthur J. Vidich, *Social Order and the Public Philosophy: An Analysis and Interpretation of the Work of Herbert Blumer* (Fayetteville: The University of Arkansas Press, 1988).

7. Herbert Blumer, *op. cit.* 12.

8. *Ibid.* 24.

9. *Ibid.* 24–26.

10. *Ibid.* 24.

11. *Ibid.* 27.

12. *Ibid.* 34.

13. *Ibid.* 35.

14. *loc. cit.*

15. Coser, *Masters of Sociological Thought: Ideas in Historical and Social Context, op. cit.* 579–81.

16. Blumer, *op. cit.* 53.

17. *loc. cit.*

18. *Ibid.* 55–56.

19. *Ibid.* 56.

20. *loc. cit.*

21. *Ibid.* 57.

22. *Ibid.* 55.

23. Coser, *Masters of Sociological Thought: Ideas in Historical and Social Context, op. cit.* 575.

24. Herbert Blumer, "Social Unrest and Collective Protest," in Norman K. Denzin, ed., *Studies in Symbolic Interaction: An Annual Compilation of Research* (Greenwich, CT: JAI Press, 1978) I: 53.

The Existential Self

1. See Reinhard Bendix, *Social Science and the Distrust of Reason,* University of California Publications in Sociology and Social Institutions, Vol. I, No. 1 (Berkeley: University of California Press, 1951) 3–6.

2. Pico della Mirandola, *On the Dignity of Man,* trans. Charles Glenn Wallis, The Library of Liberal Arts (Indianapolis: Bobbs-Merrill Co., Inc., 1940) 1–34.

3. Joseph Kotarba and Andrea Fontana, eds., *The Existential Self* (Chicago: University of Chicago Press, 1984, 1987).

4. Stanford M. Lyman and Marvin B. Scott, *A Sociology of the Absurd,* 2nd edition (Dix Hills, N.Y.: General Hall, 1989).

5. See Stanford M. Lyman, "The Science of History and the Theory of Social Change," in Ronald Glassman and Vatro Murvar, eds., *Max Weber's Political Sociology: A Pessimistic View of a Rationalized World* (Westport: Greenwood Press, 1984) 189–200.

6. Georg Simmel, "The Stranger," in *The Sociology of Georg Simmel,* trans. and ed. Kurt H. Wolff (Glencoe: The Free Press, 1950) 402–08.

7. Colin Morris, *The Discovery of the Individual: 1050–1200* (New York: Harper Torchbooks, 1972).

8. Max Weber, *Ancient Judaism,* trans. and ed. Hans H. Gerth and Don Martindale (Glencoe: The Free Press, 1952) 78.

9. See Josiah Royce, *The Problem of Christianity* (Chicago: University of Chicago Press, 1968 [1918]) 94 *et passim.*

10. See Max Weber, *The Protestant Ethic and the Spirit of Capitalism,* trans. Talcott Parsons (London: Allen and Unwin, 1930).

11. Ludwig Wittgenstein, *Philosophical Investigations,* third edn. trans. G. E. M. Anscombe (New York: The Macmillan Co., 1968) 39ᵉ.

12. See the discussion in Fredric Jameson, *The Prison-House of Language: A Critical Account of Structuralism and Russian Formalism* (Princeton: Princeton University Press, 1972).

13. Jürgen Habermas, *Communication and the Evolution of Society,* trans. Thomas McCarthy (Boston: Beacon Press, 1979).

14. The reference is to the principals in Samuel Beckett's drama *Waiting for Godot.* See the excellent discussions in Martin Esslin, *The Theatre of the Absurd,* rev. edn. (Garden City: Doubleday-Anchor, 1969) *passim.*

15. The reference is to the drama by Jean-Paul Sartre *No Exit.* See his discussion in Jean-Paul Sartre, *Sartre on Theatre.* Documents assembled, ed., introduced, and annotated by Michel Contat and Michel Rybalka. Trans. Frank Jellinek (New York: Pantheon Books, 1976) 198–201.

16. See Aron Gurwitsch, "The Last Work of Edmund Husserl," in his *Stud-*

ies in Phenomenology and Psychology (Evanston: Northwestern University Press, 1966) esp. 403–06.

17. See Aaron V. Cicourel, *Cognitive Sociology: Language and Meaning in Social Interaction* (New York: The Free Press, 1974).

18. See Stanford M. Lyman, "Two Neglected Pioneers of Civilizational Analysis: The Cultural Perspectives of R. Stewart Culin and Frank Hamilton Cushing," in this volume.

19. Weber, *Ancient Judaism* 121–22, 221–22.

20. See Stanford M. Lyman and William A. Douglass, "Ethnicity: Strategies of Collective and Individual Impression Management," *Social Research* XL (Summer 1973): 344–65.

21. Max Weber, "Ethnic Groups," *Economy and Society: An Outline of Interpretive Sociology,* ed. Guenther Roth and Claus Wittich (New York: Bedminster Press, 1968) I: 385–97.

22. Lyman and Douglass, "Ethnicity" 345–46.

23. See Ulf Hannerz, "The Significance of Soul," in Lee Rainwater, ed., *Black Experience: Soul* (N.C.L.: Trans-Action Books, 1970) 15–30.

24. Albert J. Raboteau, *Slave Religion: The "Invisible Institution" in the Antebellum South* (New York: Oxford University Press, 1978) 32–33.

INDEX

Founding Fathers: on legitimacy and consensus, 224
Frankfurt School: and communicative
conduct, 253
Frazier, E. Franklin: and race relations, 132
Freedman, Maurice: study of Chinese society, 88
French social anthropology, Culin's influence on, 29–30
French structuralism: and civilizational
analysis, 41; and Cushing's work, 41;
of Lévi-Strauss, 117–19
Freudianism: in Adorno's work, 139
Functionalism: Goffman's relationship
with, 12–16; and theories of social
change, 91–93
Fusang: legend of, 64, 273n.69

Gadamer, Hans-Georg: criticism of
Dilthey, 113
Games: in Cushing's work, 27; in Culin's
work, 30; in Culin's theory of origins,
64–69; Goffman's analysis of, 115
Ganowanian theory: of Morgan, 53
Garcia, Gregorio: on Amerindian origins,
50–51
Garfinkel, Harold: and Cushing, 280n.8
Geary Act: and Fong Yue Ting decision,
308n.35
George, Kathleen: on images of dark
skinned peoples, 150
Ghetto: significance of, 157
Giddens, Anthony: on ethnographic
methods, 39
Glaser, Barney G.: on Goffman's analy-
sis, 12
Glick, Clarence E.: criticism of Park, 131
Goffman, Erving: sociological theory of,
5, 36–37; dramaturgical approach of,
11–21; and neofunctionalism, 115–16;
quoted on total institutions, 301n.58
Goldstein, Leon J.: on Teggart's work, 107
Gordon, Milton: on Blumer's social psychology, 137
Gossett, Thomas: on images of dark
skinned peoples, 150

Habermas, Jürgen: and legitimation cri-
sis, 223
Hakka-Punti War: and the Weaverville
War, 171
Hale, Matthew: on Amerindian origins,
270n.12
Hamilton, Alexander: and the American
republic, 71–72
Hansen's law: on American immigrants,
235–36

Happenings: characteristics of, 109–16;
and histories, 119. See also Event
Harvey, David: on poverty among whites,
301n.60
Hechter, Michael: as a micro-macro theo-
rist, 2
Hegel, Georg Wilhelm Friedrich: on
American history, 71
Heptarchy: in Hughes' work, 192–94
Hermeneutics: Cushing and, 41
Hesiod: Teggart on, 103
Historical sociology: and ethnomethod-
ology, 116
Historicism: and civilizational analysis, 23
History: science of, 79–80, 103; Teggart's
science of, 77
Hodgen, Margaret T.: as a neopositivist,
94–98; theory of social change, 117
Home, Henry (Lord Kames): on Amer-
indian origins, 48–49, 269–70n.4
Hrdlicka, Ales: and Acostan theory, 73
Hughes, Everett C.: courses in race rela-
tions, 136; on groups as secret so-
cieties, 238–39
Hughes, Henry: sociology of, 192–94; as-
sessment of, 199–201
Hui kuan: among American Chinese,
163–66; and clans, 166, 167, 168–69;
clash with clans, 170–72; in the new
Chinatowns, 173–74; oligopoly of,
175; changes in, 307n.28

I: qualities of, 254
I Ching: in civilizational analysis, 31–36;
in Culin's theory of origins, 66
Idealism: American, 188
Industrialization: in Blumer's theory,
142–46, 218
Interpretive sociology: and Cushing's
work, 41

James, William: and Teggart, 215
Japan: in Brooks' origin theory, 64
Japanese: and the Ozawa decision, 73–74;
origins of, 75; court decisions on, 156;
Congressional hearings on, 277–
78n.110
Jefferson, Thomas: and Amerindian ori-
gins, 52
Jews: and assimilation, 130, 133; and anti-
Semitism, 151–52
Jordan, Winthrop: on racism, 149

Kallenberg, Arne L.: on industrial sociology, 2
Kamenka, Eugene: on evolutionary
theory, 108